THE OPERATIONS RESEARCH PROBLEM SOLVER®

REGISTERED TRADEMARK

Staff of Research and Education Association,
Dr. M. Fogiel, Director

Research and Education Association
505 Eighth Avenue
New York, N. Y. 10018

THE OPERATIONS RESEARCH PROBLEM SOLVER ®

Printed in the United States of America

Library of Congress Catalog Card Number 83-62276

International Standard Book Number 0-87891-548-6

WHAT THIS BOOK IS FOR

Students have generally found operations research a difficult subject to understand and learn because of the broad scope of the subject and the large number of complex interrelationships in operations research practices. Despite the publication of hundreds of textbooks in this field, each one intended to provide an improvement over previous textbooks, students continue to remain perplexed as a result of the numerous conditions that must often be remembered and correlated in solving a problem. Various possible interpretations of terms used in operations research have also contributed to much of the difficulties experienced by students.

In a study of the problem, REA found the following basic reasons underlying students' difficulties with operations research taught in schools:

(a) No systematic rules of analysis have been developed which students may follow in a step-by-step manner to solve the usual problems encountered. This results from the fact that the numerous different conditions and principles which may be involved in a problem, lead to many possible different methods of solution. To prescribe a set of rules to be followed for each of the possible variations, would involve an enormous number of rules and steps to be searched through by students, and this task would perhaps be more burdensome than solving the problem directly with some accompanying trial and error to find the correct solution route.

(b) Textbooks currently available will usually explain a given principle in a few pages written by a professional who has an insight in the subject matter that is not shared by students. The explanations are often written in an abstract manner which leaves the students confused as to the application of the principle. The explanations given are not sufficiently detailed and extensive to make the student aware of the wide range of applications and different aspects of the principle being studied. The numerous possible variations of principles and their applications are usually not discussed, and it is left for the students to discover these for themselves while doing exercises. Accordingly, the average student is expected to rediscover that which has been long known and practiced, but not published or explained extensively.

(c) The examples usually following the explanation of a topic are too few in number and too simple to enable the student to obtain a thorough grasp of the principles involved. The explanations do not provide suffient basis to enable a student to solve problems that may be subsequently assigned for homework or given on examinations.

The examples are presented in abbreviated form which leaves out much material between steps, and requires that students derive the omitted material themselves. As a result, students find the examples difficult to understand--contrary to the purpose of the examples.

Examples are, furthermore, often worded in a confusing manner. They do not state the problem and then present the solution. Instead, they pass through a general discussion, never revealing what is to be solved for.

Examples, also, do not always include diagrams/graphs, wherever appropriate, and students do not obtain the training to draw diagrams or graphs to simplify and organize their thinking.

(d) Students can learn the subject only by doing the exercises themselves and reviewing them in class, to obtain experience in applying the principles with their different ramifications.

In doing the exercises by themselves, students find that they are required to devote considerably more time to operations research than to other subjects of comparable credits, because they are uncertain with regard to the selection and application of the theorems and principles involved. It is also often necessary for students to discover those "tricks" not revealed in their texts (or review books), that make it possible to solve problems easily. Students must usually resort to methods of trial-and-error to discover these "tricks", and as a result they find that they may sometimes spend several hours to solve a single problem.

(e) When reviewing the exercises in classrooms, instructors usually request students to take turns in writing solutions on the board and explaining them to the class. Students often find it difficult to explain in a manner that holds the interest of the class, and enables the remaining students to follow the material written on the boards. The remaining students seated in the class are, furthermore, too occupied with copying the material from the boards, to listen to the oral explanations and concentrate on the methods of solution.

This book is intended to aid students in operations research to overcome the difficulties described, by supplying detailed illustrations of the solution methods which are usually not apparent to students. The solution methods are illustrated by problems selected from those that are most often assigned for class work and given on examinations. The problems are arranged in order of complexity to enable students to learn and understand a particular topic by reviewing the problems in sequence. The problems are illustrated with detailed step-by-step explanations, to save the students the large amount of time that is often needed to fill in the gaps that are usually found between steps of illustrations in textbooks or review/outline books.

The staff of REA considers operations research a subject that is best learned by allowing students to view the methods of analysis and solution techniques themselves. This approach to learning the subject matter is similar to that practiced in various scientific laboratories, particularly in the medical fields.

In using this book, students may review and study the illustrated problems at their own pace; they are not limited to the time allowed for explaining problem on the board in class.

When students want to look up a particular type of problem and solution, they can readily locate it in the book by referring to the index which has been extensively prepared. It is also possible to locate a particular type of problem by glancing at just the material within the boxed portions. To facilitate rapid scanning of the problems, each problem has a heavy border around it. Furthermore, each problem is idenitified with a number immediately above the problem at the right- hand margin.

To obtain maximum benefit from the book, students should familiarize themselves with the section, "How To Use This Book," located in the front pages.

To meet the objectives of this book, staff members of REA have selected problems usually encountered in assignments and examinations, and have solved each problem meticulously to illustrate the steps which are usually difficult for students to comprehend. Special gratitude is expressed to them for their efforts in this area, as well as to the numerous contributors who devoted brief periods of time to this work.

Gratitude is also expressed to many persons involved in the difficult task of typing the manuscript with its endless changes, and to the REA art staff who prepared the numerous detailed illustrations together with the layout and physical features of the book.

The difficult task of coordinating the efforts of all persons was carried out by Carl Fuchs. His conscientious work deserves much appreciation. He also trained and supervised art and production personnel in the preparation of the book for printing.

Finally, special thanks are due to Helen Kaufmann for her unique talents to render those difficult border-line decisions and constructive suggestions related to the design and organization of the book.

Max Fogiel, Ph. D.
Program Director

HOW TO USE THIS BOOK

This book can be an invaluable aid to students in operations research as a supplement to their textbooks. The book is subdivided into 13 chapters, each dealing with a separate topic. The subject matter is developed beginning with linear, non-linear, integer and dynamic programming and extending through network analysis, quadratic and separable programming, inventory control and probabilistic methods. Also included are topics in transportation problems, scheduling, production planning, queuing theory, game theory and Markov chains. An extensive number of applications have been included, since these appear to be most troublesome to students.

TO LEARN AND UNDERSTAND A TOPIC THOROUGHLY

1. Refer to your class text and read the section pertaining to the topic. You should become acquainted with the principles discussed there. These principles, however, may not be clear to you at that time.

2. Then locate the topic you are looking for by referring to the "Table of Contents" in front of this book, "The Operations Research Problem Solver."

3. Turn to the page where the topic begins and review the problems under each topic, in the order given. For each topic, the problems are arranged in order of complexity, from the simplest to the more difficult. Some problems may appear similar to others, but each problem has been selected to illustrate a different point or solution method.

To learn and understand a topic thoroughly and retain its contents, it will be generally necessary for students to review the problems several times. Repeated review is essential in order to gain experience in recognizing the principles that should be applied, and to select the best solution technique.

TO FIND A PARTICULAR PROBLEM

To locate one or more problems related to a particular subject matter, refer to the index. In using the index, be certain to note that the numbers given there refer to problem numbers, not to page numbers. This arrangement of the index is intended to facilitate finding a problem more rapidly, since two or more problems may appear on a page.

If a particular type of problem cannot be found readily, it is recommended that the student refer to the "Table of Contents" in the front pages, and then turn to the chapter which is applicable to the problem being sought. By scanning or glancing at the material that is boxed, it will generally be possible to find problems related to the one being sought, without consuming considerable time. After the problems have been located, the solutions can be reviewed and studied in detail. For this purpose of locating problems rapidly, students should acquaint themselves with the organization of the book as found in the "Table of Contents."

In preparing for an exam, it is useful to find the topics to be covered in the exam from the "Table of Contents," and then review the problems under those topics several times. This should equip the student with what might be needed for the exam.

CONTENTS

Chapter No. **Page No.**

5 THE TRANSPORTATION AND ASSIGNMENT PROBLEM 374

6 INTEGER PROGRAMMING 478

7 DYNAMIC PROGRAMMING 580

8 NETWORK ANALYSIS AND SCHEDULING 643

9 NONLINEAR PROGRAMMING - UNCONSTRAINED OPTIMIZATION 727

CHAPTER 1

GRAPHICAL SOLUTIONS TO LINEAR OPERATIONS RESEARCH PROBLEMS

• PROBLEM 1-1

Assume you want to decide between alternate ways of spending an eight-hour day, that is, you want to allocate your resource time. Assume you find it five times more fun to play ping-pong in the lounge than to work, but you also feel that you should work at least three times as many hours as you play ping-pong. Now the decision problem is how many hours to play and how many to work in order to maximize your objective: "fun."

Let

X number of hours spent working, and
Y number of hours spent playing.

You want to maximize your fun, F, where

$$F = X + 5Y. \tag{1}$$

Your total time per day is limited to eight hours:

$$X + Y \leq 8. \tag{2}$$

And, finally, you should work at least three times as long as you play:

$$3Y \leq X. \tag{3}$$

You cannot spend a negative number of hours, hence

$$X \geq 0, \; Y \geq 0. \tag{4}$$

Solution: Graph the "objective function," Equation 1, and the "restrictions," Equations 2, 3, 4, on a coordinate plane. The results appear in Fig. 1.

The shaded area is the "infeasible region" that results from the restrictions, Equations 2 through 4. The question is to find the "best" solution to the problem:

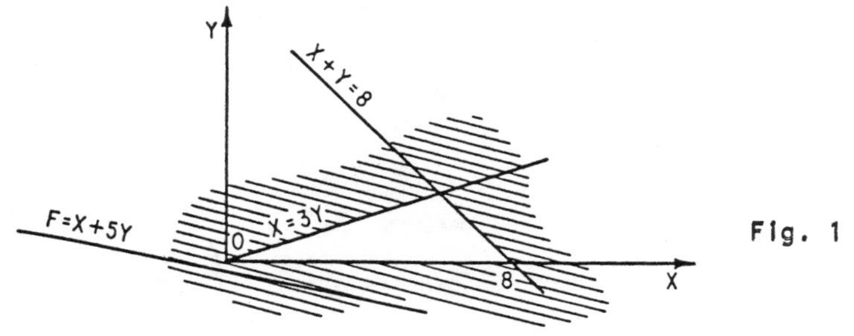

Fig. 1

Maximize F = X + 5Y.

For X = Y = 0, F = 0, which means that you neither play nor work, but do nothing. The solution F = 0 is shown graphically in Fig. 2.

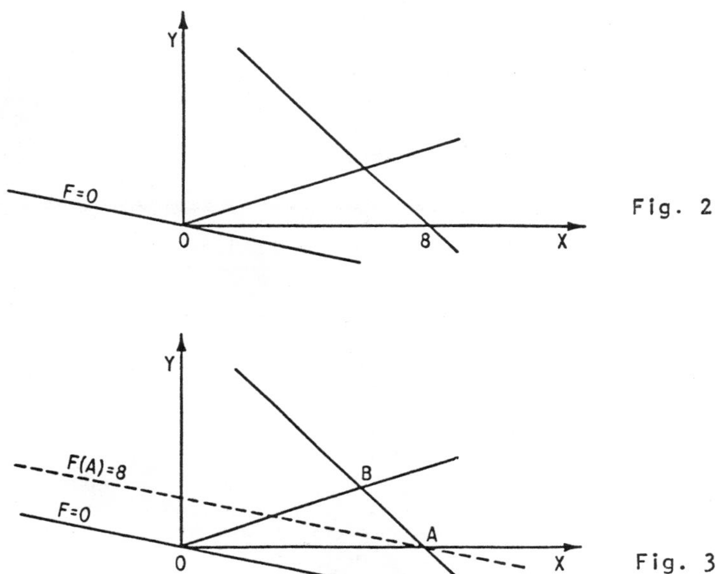

Fig. 2

Fig. 3

Since you want to do some work, increase X, which finds its limit at 8 (Point A), namely, the total number of hours at your disposal. Hence, F(A) = X + 5Y = 8 + 0. (See Fig. 3.)

Fig. 4 demonstrates that raising the value of F from zero to eight corresponds to a parallel translation of the line F. Also, F can be shifted farther in the same direction, always passing through some point of the feasible area, up to Point B.

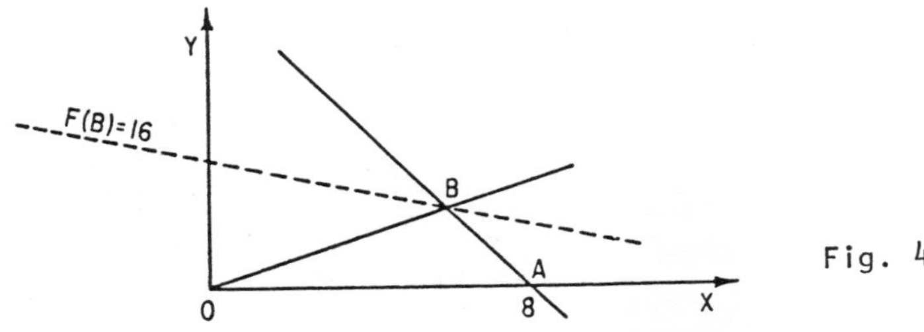

Fig. 4

Now, B is the intersection of lines

$$X + Y = 8$$

and

$$-X + 3Y = 0.$$

That is,

$$B = \{X = 6,\ Y = 2\},$$

so that the objective has assumed its maximum value at B:

$$F(B) = 6 + 5 \times 2 = 16.$$

• PROBLEM 1-2

A small plant makes two types of automobile parts. It buys castings that are machined, bored, and polished. The data shown in Table 1 are given.

Castings for Part A cost \$2 each; for Part B they cost \$3 each. They sell for \$5 and \$6, respectively. The three machines have running costs of \$20, \$14, and \$17.50 per hour. Assuming that any combination of Parts A and B can be sold, what product mix maximizes profit?

TABLE 1

	Part *A*	Part *B*
Machining capacity	25 per hour	40 per hour
Boring capacity	28 per hour	35 per hour
Polishing capacity	35 per hour	25 per hour

<u>Solution</u>: The first step is to calculate the profit per part. This is done in Table 2. From the results shown, if on the average x of Part A and y of Part B per hour is made, the net profit is

$$Z = 1.20x + 1.40y. \tag{1}$$

Because there is no meaning for negative x and y,

$$x \geq 0, \qquad y \geq 0. \tag{2}$$

TABLE 2

	Part *A*	Part *B*
Machining	20/25 = 0.80	20/40 = 0.50
Boring	14/28 = 0.50	14/35 = 0.40
Polishing	17.50/35 = 0.50	17.50/25 = 0.70
Purchase	2.00	3.00
Total cost	3.80	4.60
Sales price	5.00	6.00
Profit	1.20	1.40

x and y cannot be chosen freely, because the capacity limits have to be taken into account. These yield the following results:

Machining	$\frac{x}{25} + \frac{y}{40} \leq 1$
Boring	$\frac{x}{28} + \frac{y}{35} \leq 1$
Polishing	$\frac{x}{35} + \frac{y}{25} \leq 1$

Multiply through to clear fractions and obtain:

Machining	$40x + 25y \leq 1000$	
Boring	$35x + 28y \leq 980$	(3)
Polishing	$25x + 35y \leq 875$	

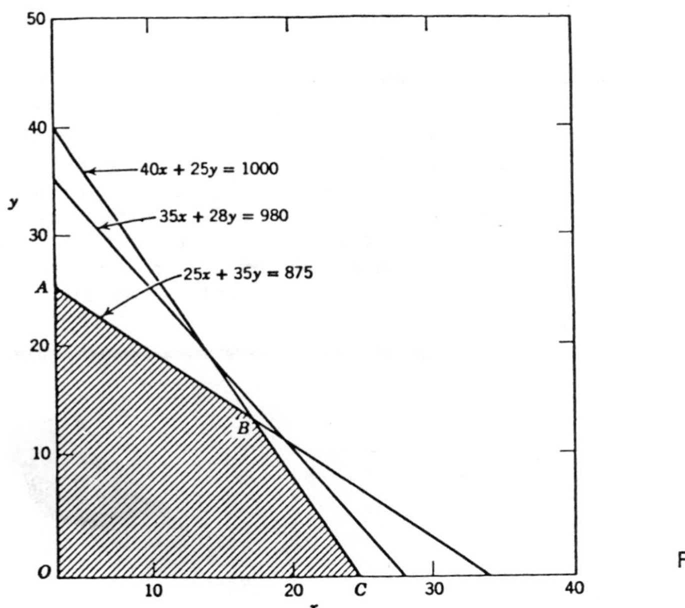

Fig. 1

When the equation 40x + 25y = 1000 is plotted, a line that divides the plane into two regions is obtained (Figure 1). In the region that includes the origin $40x + 25y < 1000$; in the other region $40x + 25y > 1000$. The other two inequalities in (3) divide the plane in a similar fashion. Thus if one regards the decision about the values of x and y as selecting a point in a plane, one sees that the point must lie within or on the boundaries of the region OABC. Because the line 35x + 28y = 980 lies outside this region, the boring constraint is redundant. In other words, any combination of x and y that satisfy the machining and polishing constraints will automatically be within the boring capacity.

The point (x,y) for which profits attain their maximum must lie at one of the corners of OABC. The possible maximizing values are O(0,0), A(0,25), B(16.93,12.90), and C(25,0). The corresponding profits are $Z_0 = 0$, $Z_A = 35$, $Z_B = 38.39$, and $Z_C = 30$, so that the best production plan is 16.93 of A per hour and 12.90 of B per hour. It is not hard to see why the maximizing point (x,y) must lie at a corner. Consider the geometric interpretation of equation 1. If Z is kept fixed (say Z = 20), then as x and y vary, (1) must be represented by a line of equal profit. If one chooses another value of Z (say Z = 25), one shall obtain a parallel line further away from the origin O. As one increases Z, one obtains a family of parallel lines. Clearly, Z is maximized by finding the line of the family furthest from the origin which has at least one point within or on the boundary of OABC. Such a line passes through B. Thus, no matter what boundary figure one draws, the maximizing line must pass through a corner.

• PROBLEM 1-3

A man operates a pushcart. He sells hotdogs and sodas. His cart can support 210 lbs. A hotdog weighs 2 ounces; a soda weighs 8 ounces. He knows from experience that he must have at least 60 sodas and at least 80 hotdogs. He also knows that for every two hotdogs he sells, he needs at least one soda. Given he makes 8¢ profit on a hotdog and 4¢ profit on a soda, find how many sodas and hotdogs he must have in order to maximize profits.

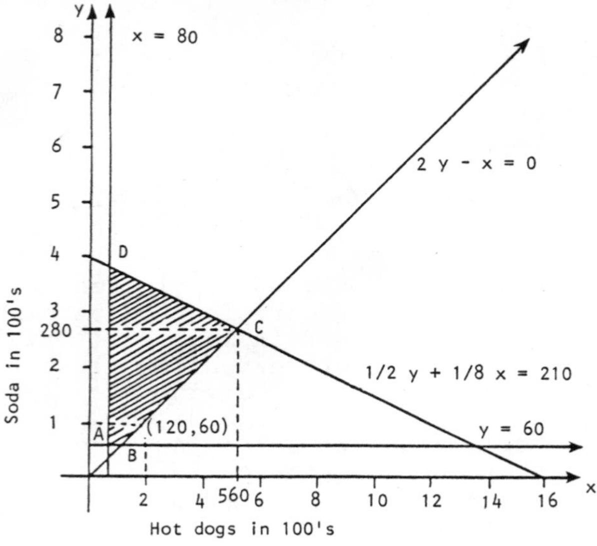

Solution: This is a linear programming problem. To solve, make a graph of hotdogs versus soda and find the point that gives the maximum profit.

The formula for profit is

$$\$.08 \cdot X + \$.04 \cdot Y = \text{profit},$$

where X is the number of hotdogs and Y is the number of sodas sold.

Profits are maximized under the following constraints:

(1) $1/2 \cdot Y + 1/8 \cdot X \le 210$

(2) $Y \ge 60$

(3) $X \ge 80$

(4) $2Y - X \ge 0$

The meaning of the constraints is:

(1) A soda weighs 1/2 of a pound, and a hotdog weighs 1/8 of a pound and the maximum weight the cart can support is 210 pounds.

(2) He must have at least 60 sodas.

(3) He must have at least 80 hotdogs.

(4) He must have at most twice as many hotdogs as sodas (or in other terms at least half as many sodas as hotdogs).

Now put the restraints into a graph, and, according to the theory of linear programming the maximum profit can be found on a corner of the region determined by the constraints.

The shaded region on the above graph is the region which is determined by the constraints. The corners of the region are:

A) $X = 80$ $Y = 60$

B) $X = 120$ $Y = 60$

C) $X = 560$ $Y = 280$

D) $X = 80$ $Y = 420$

Now find the maximum profit by substituting the points into the profit formula.

A) $\$.08 \cdot 80 + \$.04 \cdot 60 = \$8.80$

B) $\$.08 \cdot 120 + \$.04 \cdot 60 = \$12.00$

C) $\$.08 \cdot 560 + \$.04 \cdot 280 = \$56.00$

D) $\$.08 \cdot 80 + \$.04 \cdot 420 = \$18.40$

The maximum profit is obtained at point C. He will take 560 hotdogs and 280 sodas to make the maximum profit of $56.00.

• PROBLEM 1-4

An automobile manufacturer makes automobiles and trucks in a factory that is divided into two shops. Shop 1, which performs the basic assembly operation, must work 5 man-days on each truck but only 2 man-days on each automobile. Shop 2, which performs finishing operations, must work 3 man-days on each automobile or truck that it produces. Because of men and machine limitations Shop 1 has 180 man-days per week available while Shop 2 has 135 man-days per week. If the manufacturer makes a profit of $300 on each truck and $200 on each automobile, how many of each should he produce to maximize his profit?

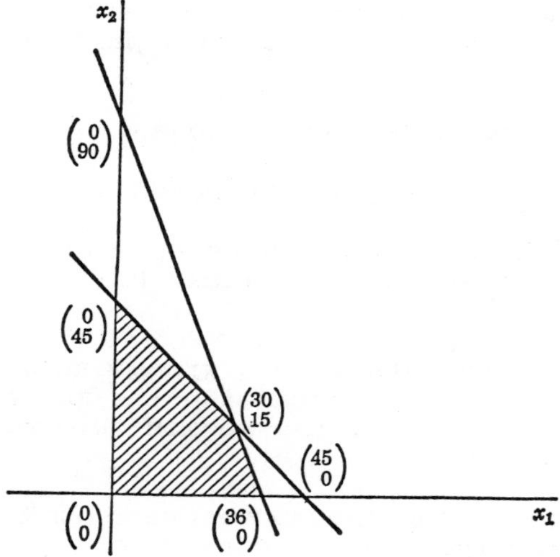

Solution: Let x_1 be the number of trucks and x_2 the umber of automobiles to be produced per week. Thus:

$$5x_1 + 2x_2 \leq 180$$

$$3x_1 + 3x_2 \leq 135.$$

bjective is to maximize the linear function $300x_1$ x_2 where $x_1 \geq 0$ and $x_2 \geq 0$.

the quantities

$$\begin{pmatrix} 5 & 2 \\ 3 & 3 \end{pmatrix}, \quad b = \begin{pmatrix} 180 \\ 135 \end{pmatrix} \text{ and } c = (300,200).$$

linear programming problem can be stated

Maximum problem: Determine the vector x so that the weekly profit, given by the quantity cx, is a maximum subject to the inequality constraints $Ax \leq b$ and $x \geq 0$. The inequality constraints insure that the weekly number of available man-hours is not exceeded and that nonnegative quantities of automobiles and trucks are produced.

The graph of the convex set of possible x vectors is pictured in Figure 1.

The extreme points of the convex set C are

$$T_1 = \begin{pmatrix} 0 \\ 0 \end{pmatrix}, \quad T_2 = \begin{pmatrix} 36 \\ 0 \end{pmatrix}, \quad T_3 = \begin{pmatrix} 0 \\ 45 \end{pmatrix} \text{ and } T_4 = \begin{pmatrix} 30 \\ 15 \end{pmatrix}.$$

Test the function $cx = 300x_1 + 200x_2$ at each of these extreme points. The values taken on are 0, 10800, 9000, and 12000. Thus the maximum weekly profit is $12,000 and is achieved by producing 30 trucks and 15 automobiles per week.

• PROBLEM 1-5

> A company makes desk organizers. The standard model requires 2 hours of the cutter's and one hour of the finisher's time. The deluxe model requires 1 hour of the cutter's time and 2 hours of the finisher's time. The cutter has 104 hours of time available for this work per month, while the finisher has 76 hours of time available for work. The standard model brings a profit of $6 per unit, while the deluxe one brings a profit of $11 per unit. The company, of course, wishes to make the most profit. Assuming they can sell whatever is made, how much of each model should be made in each month?

Solution: The company wishes to make the most profit within the given constraints. Graph the constraints and within the defined region pick the point with the most profit. The profit is found by the formula:

$$\text{Profit} = \$6\ X + \$11\ Y$$

where X stands for the number of standard desk organizers and Y stands for the number of deluxe ones.

The constraints for this problem are:

(1) $X \geq 0$; there cannot be a negative number of standard units.

(2) $Y \geq 0$; there cannot be a negative number of deluxe units.

(3) The finisher has only 76 hours of time available. Since a standard model takes one hour of the finisher's

time, and a deluxe model takes 2 hours of the finisher's time, the constraint is:

$$X + 2Y \leq 76.$$

(4) The cutter has only 104 hours of time available. A standard unit takes two hours of the cutter's time, and a deluxe unit takes one hour of the cutter's time, thus, the constraint is:

$$2X + Y \leq 104.$$

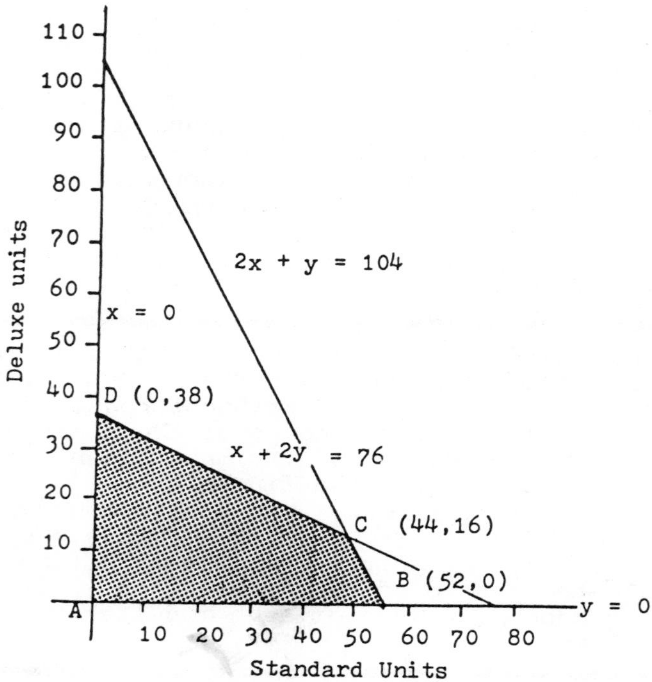

Now these constraints can be graphed to get the region in which the point of maximum profit can be chosen.

The shaded area of the graph is the area which conforms o the constraints. Within this region the point with e maximum profit must be picked. A theorem of linear ogramming states that the point of maximum profit oc-s at a corner of the region. Thus, one needs only to k the corners and take the point with the most it.

),0) Profit = \$6 (0) + \$11 (0) = \$0

,0) Profit = \$6 (52) + \$11 (0) = \$312

16) Profit = \$6 (44) + \$11 (16) = \$440

) Profit = \$6 (0) + \$11 (38) = \$418.

he point with the largest profit is (44,16) Thus, for the company to make the maximum profit of \$440, it must produce 44 standard units and 16 deluxe ones.

• PROBLEM 1-6

A company wishes to bottle 2 different drinks. It takes 2 hours to can one gross of drink A, and it takes 1 hour to label the cans. It takes 3 hours to bottle one gross of drink B, and it takes 4 hours to label the cans. The company makes a \$10 profit on one gross of drink A and a \$20 profit on one gross of drink B. Given that the bottling department has 20 hours available, and the labelling department has 15 hours available, find out how many gross of drink A and drink B must be packaged in order to maximize the profit.

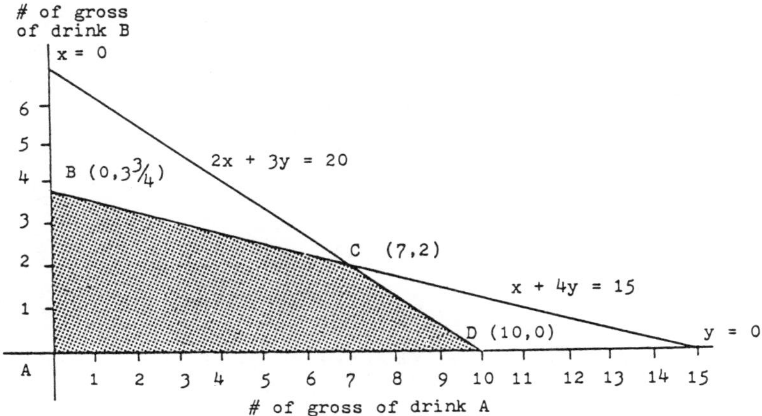

Solution: The company wishes to use their time remaining for the most profit. To do this graph the constraints and get the area of points one of which will yield the maximum profit. If X is the number of gross of drink A and Y is the number of gross of drink B, then the profit can be found via the formula:

$$\text{Profit} = \$10 \cdot X + \$20 \cdot Y.$$

The constraints in the problem are:

(1) $X \geq 0$

(2) $Y \geq 0$

because there cannot be a negative number of gross of a drink.

(3) The canning department also poses a constraint. Because each gross of drink A takes 2 hours to can and each gross of drink B takes 3 hours to can, the number of hours is $2X + 3Y$. But, they only can work 20 hours or less, thus the constraint is:

$$2X + 3Y \leq 20.$$

(4) There is another constraint due to the labelling department. Since they have only 15 hours, and one gross of drink A takes 1 hour to label and one gross of drink B takes 4 hours to label, we get the constraint

$$X + 4Y \leq 15.$$

Now place these constraints on a graph, and the region defined by them is the region in which the number of gross of drinks A and B meet the constraints. Then find the point in that region which yields the maximum profit.

In the graph, the shaded area is the region described by the four constraints. According to a theorem of linear programming, the point of maximum profit must occur at a corner of the region. It is also true that the minimum profit will be found on a corner. This is understandable, since the corners represent the places with the most or least number of gross of drinks that are produced. Thus, to find the point with the maximum profit, check the four corner points and take the corner with the most profit.

A) (0,0) Profit = \$10(0) + \$20(0) = \$0

B) (0,3 3/4) Profit = \$10(0) + \$20(3 3/4) = \$75

C) (7,2) Profit = \$10(7) + \$20(2) = \$110

D) (10,0) Profit = \$10(10) + \$20(0) = \$100.

Thus, the point with the most profit is (7,2). The company must package 7 gross of drink A and 2 gross of drink B yielding a profit of \$110.

• PROBLEM 1-7

'onsider the arbitrage transactions. In exchange mar-
ets such as commodity or stock exchange markets it is
'ten possible to take advantage of an imbalance in the
-ket prices through arbitrage transactions. For
tance, exchanging commodity A for commodity B, B in
for C, and finally exchanging C for A at a net
t. Assume that an arbitrageur faces two possible
actions in three different market commodities.
ction I involves an exchange of commodity C_1 into
ities C_2 and C_3. In particular, for every unit
e can obtain .3 units of C_2 and 1.5 units of C_3.
ion II, on the other hand, allows him to obtain
of C_1 in exchange for .1 units of C_2 plus 1
3. The only constraints imposed on these
ns are those ensuring that the arbitrageur is
on any commodity. This means that he cannot
e of any commodity than he procures. With
tion there is a net cash flow associated,
h inflow or a cash outflow. For every unit
ransaction I, there is a net cash outflow

of \$5, whereas for every unit activity of transaction II, there is a net cash inflow of \$10. Assume that the arbitrageur's objective is to maximize the net cash inflow. Construct a model to depict the phenomenon and solve graphically to get an optimal solution. Give reasons as to why this problem is not realistic.

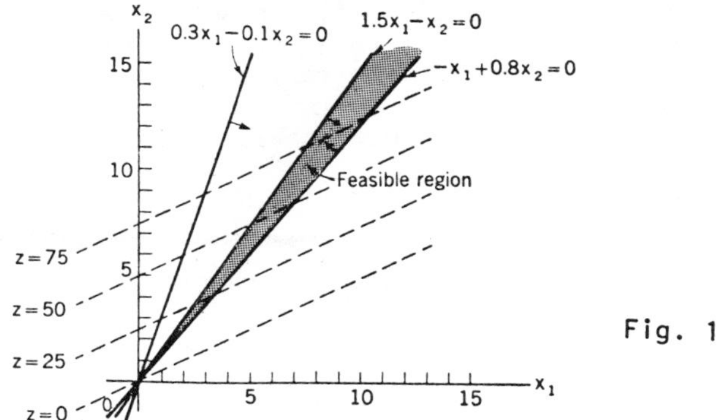

Fig. 1

Solution: Let x_1 be the activity level (in units) of transaction I, and x_2 be the activity level (in units) of transaction II. Then the objective function reads:

$$\max z = -5x_1 + 10x_2.$$

For each commodity the total amount delivered cannot exceed the total amount procured. Take commodity C_1. Every unit activity of transaction I involves an outflow of 1 unit of C_1, whereas every unit activity of transaction II provides an inflow of .8 units of C_1. Hence $.8x_2$ has to be at least equal to or larger than $1x_1$. This yields the following constraint:

$$-x_1 + .8x_2 \geq 0.$$

Similarly, for commodity C_2 and C_3 we get

$$.3x_1 - .1x_2 \geq 0$$

$$1.5x_1 - x_2 \geq 0.$$

Furthermore, the activity levels of both transactions cannot be negative, i.e., $x_1 \geq 0$ and $x_2 \geq 0$. Figure 1 depicts this LP in graphic form. Note that the feasible region is given by the wedge-shaped area that starts at the origin and extends to infinity in the positive quadrant. The objective function for various values of z is given by the dashed lines. Note that as z increases this line moves upwards. Since it never hits an extreme point, z can be increased beyond any bound. Therefore, the solution is unbounded.

This arbitrage problem is obviously an idealization of reality, and LP can hardly be used in any practical arbitrage problem for a variety of reasons, not the least important being that any market imbalances have to be exploited immediately and would not permit for even a minimum turnaround time to formulate the LP mathematically and have it solved on an electronic computer.

In the actual situation, the arbitrage transaction will, by itself, tend to eliminate the imbalance present in the market. Hence, the objective function coefficients used in the problem are valid only for activity levels within a limited range. In fact, for activity levels above a certain amount, the objective function will not behave in a linear fashion any more. Hence, the condition of proportionality will not hold any more.

• PROBLEM 1-8

Solve the following linear programming problem:

$$\text{Maximize} \quad 6L_1 + 11L_2 \tag{1}$$

subject to:

$$2L_1 + L_2 \le 104$$

$$L_1 + 2L_2 \le 76 \tag{2}$$

and $L_1 \ge 0$, $L_2 \ge 0$.

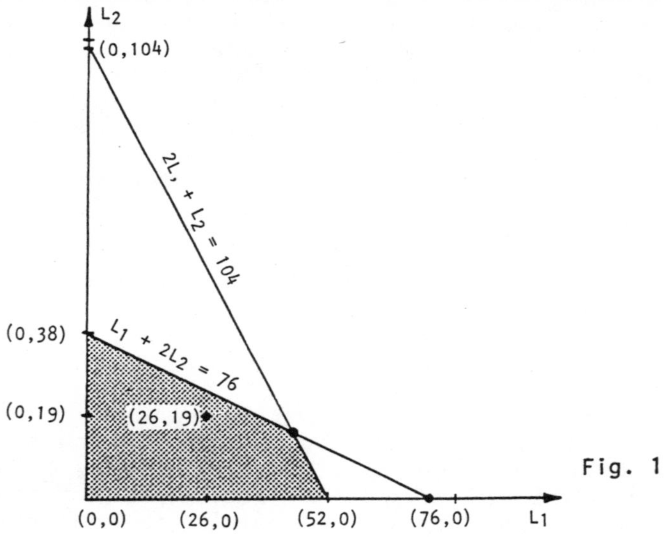

Fig. 1

ion: Since there are only two variables (L_1 and
he above problem can be portrayed geometrically.

constraints, $L_1 \ge 0$ and $L_2 \ge 0$, generate the
adrant of the Euclidean plane. The lines,
d $L_2 = 0$, form the boundaries of this region.

considering the inequalities directly, we
the boundaries of the constraint region.
ivalent to graphing the two lines $2L_1 + L_2$
$+ 2L_2 = 76$.

The feasible region is the area that simultaneously satisfies all four constraints. In Fig. 1, it is the darkened region. The feasible region represents possible solutions to the maximization problem. For example, (26,19) is a feasible solution, and when substituted into the objective function yields a value of

$$6(26) + 11(19) = 365.$$

Yet, a better solution is the point (0,38) on the boundary of the feasible region which yields a value of:

$$6(0) + 11(38) = 418.$$

What is required is a method that will reduce the infinite set of feasible points to a finite number of points. Any point not on the boundary of the feasible region is non-optimal, since (1) can increase by increasing one variable while keeping the other constant and still satisfy the constraints.

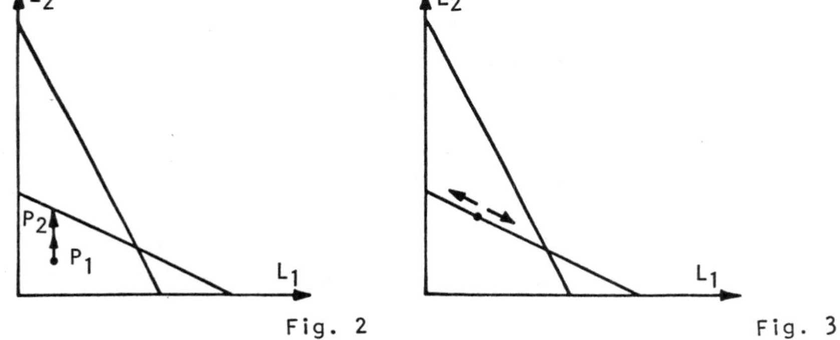

Fig. 2 Fig. 3

Continue to do this until a constraint line is met as in Fig. 2. Thus, the set of optimal points consists of points on the boundary of the feasible region. Now consider a point on the boundary. If movement along the boundary in one direction increases (1), then movement in the opposite direction decreases (1). Now keep on moving in the direction of increasing (1) until another constraint is met. Thus, the points at which (1) is locally maximized occur at the intersection of two or more constraints. Since the number of constraints is finite the set of such points is finite.

The method for solving the problem is: to first find the intersection points of pairs of constraints, then check which points are feasible, and from these basic feasible points find that point which maximizes the objective function.

The four constraints are:

$$L_1 = 0 \qquad (3)$$

$$L_2 = 0 \qquad (4)$$

$$2L_1 + L_2 = 104 \qquad (5)$$

$$L_1 + 2L_2 = 76 \qquad (6)$$

Taking these four equations two at a time there are $\binom{4}{2}$ or 6 points. For example, the solution to (3) and (4) is the point (0,0). The solution to (4) and (6) is (76,0). The point (0,0) is feasible but the point (76,0) is not. In this way we obtain the following table:

System of equations	(L_1, L_2)	Feasible Points
(3) and (4)	(0,0)	yes
(3) and (5)	(0,104)	no
(3) and (6)	(0,38)	yes
(4) and (5)	(52,0)	yes
(4) and (6)	(76,0)	no
(5) and (6)	(44,16)	yes

Next compute the value of (1) for each of the above feasible points.

Feasible points	$f(L_1, L_2) = 6L_1 + 11L_2$
(0,0)	0
(0,38)	418
(52,0)	312
(44,16)	440

Thus, the objective function is maximized when $L_1 = 44$ and $L_2 = 16$. The value of the objective function is then 440.

• PROBLEM 1-9

In a manufacturing process, the final product has a requirement that it must weigh exactly 150 pounds. The two raw materials used are A, with a cost of \$4 per unit and B, with a cost of \$8 per unit. At least 14 units of B and no more than 20 units of A must be used. Each unit of A weighs 5 pounds; each unit of B weighs 10 pounds.

How much of each type of raw material should be used for each unit of final product to minimize cost?

Solution: The objective function is:

$$C = 4x_1 + 8x_2. \qquad (1)$$

The constraints are:

$$5x_1 + 10x_2 = 150$$

$$x_1 \qquad \leq 20$$

$$x_2 \geq 14 \quad (2)$$

$$x_1 \geq 0.$$

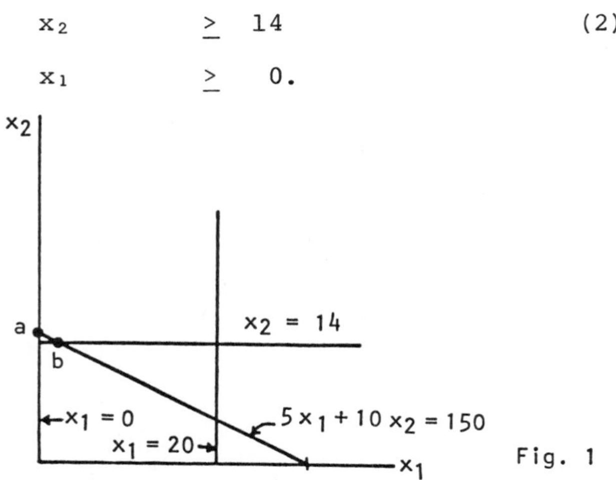

Fig. 1

Take the graphical approach to this linear programming problem. The constraints, (2) are graphed in the figure.

Since the pertinent region lies within $0 \leq x_1 \leq 20$, $x_2 \geq 14$, and on $5x_1 + 10x_2 = 150$, two solutions can be immediately found, points a and b where a = (0,15) and b = (2,14).

	Solution 1	Solution 2
Raw material A, (x_1)	0	2
Raw material B, (x_2)	15	14
Total cost, $4x_1 + 8x_2$	120	120

This is an example of a problem having multiple solutions. In such problems, two or more corner points have the same optimum value.

• PROBLEM 1-10

A publisher is printing a new book. This book may be either a hard cover book or a paperback. There is a \$4 profit on each hard cover and \$3 profit on each paperback. It takes 3 minutes to bind a hard covered book and 2 minutes to bind a paperback. The total available time for binding is 800 hours. Through experience the publisher knows that he needs at least 10,000 hard covered editions and not more than 6,000 paperbacks. Find the number of paperbacks and hard covered editions that must be printed in order to yield the maximum profit.

Solution: Make a graph of the constraints, and from the region thus defined take the point yielding the maximum profit. If X = number of hard covered books and Y = the number of paperbacks, the formula to find the profit is:

Profit = \$4X + \$3Y.

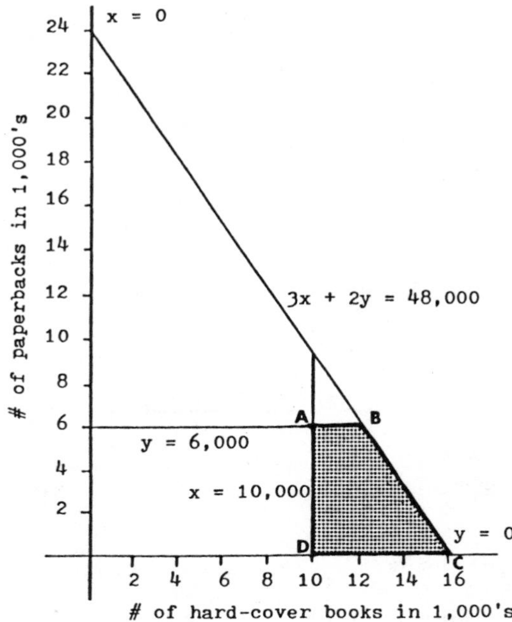

To maximize the profits given the following constraints:

(1) The number of minutes to bind a hard cover book is 3 and the minutes to bind a paperback is 2; since the total number of minutes available is 48,000; (800 hours × 60 min/hr), we have the constraint:

$$3X + 2Y \leq 48,000.$$

(2) The minimum number of hard covered editions is 10,000, thus the constraint:

$$X \geq 10,000.$$

(3) The maximum number of paperbacks is 6,000, thus we get the constraint:

$$Y \leq 6,000.$$

(4) The last constraint is:

$$Y \geq 0$$

because a negative number of books cannot be published.

Now draw the graph of these constraints, and the region defined by these constraints is the region from which the publisher must choose a point in order to publish the books by his specifications. From this region find the point which yields the maximum profit.

The shaded area ABCD in the graph denotes the feasible region. According to a theorem of Linear Programming the points which yield the maximum and minimum profits are on the corners of the feasible region. This seems likely because the corners represent the points in which the minimum and maximum number of the books of each type are produced, meeting the constraints.

A) (10000,6000) Profit = \$4(10,000) + \$3(6,000)
= \$58,000

B) (12000,6000) Profit = \$4(12,000) + \$3(6,000)
= \$66,000

C) (16000,0) Profit = \$4(16,000) + \$3(0)
= \$64,000

D) (10000,0) Profit = \$4(10,000) + \$3(0)
= \$40,000

The maximum profit occurs at point B; the maximum profit of \$66,000 will be obtained if the company publishes 6,000 paperbacks and 12,000 hard covered editions.

• PROBLEM 1-11

A boy wants to open a drink stand. His mother says he cannot sell more than four gallons of drinks. The boy sells lemonade and a fruit juice. He sells the lemonade for \$2 a gallon and the fruit juice for \$1.50 a gallon. The lemonade uses 30 lemon slices per gallon and one pound of sugar per gallon. The fruit juice uses 10 lemon slices and two pounds of sugar per gallon. The boy's mother has only 90 lemon slices and 6 pounds of sugar. Find out how many gallons of each type of beverage the boy should make in order to make the most money.

Solution: To find the most profitable solution, graph the boy's constraints, and find a region defined by these constraints. In this region look for the point with the most profit. The profit is found by the formula:

$$\text{Profit} = \$2X + \$1.50Y$$

where X is the number of gallons of lemonade and Y is the number of gallons of fruit juice. The constraints are:

(1) $X \geq 0$ The boy either makes lemonade or not.

(2) $Y \geq 0$ The boy either makes fruit juice or not.

(3) The boy's mother only allows him to make 4 or less gallons. Thus we get the constraint

$$X + Y \leq 4.$$

(4) The lemonade takes 30 lemon slices, and the

fruit juice takes 10 lemon slices per gallon. Since the boy's mother has only 90 lemon slices, we have the constraint

$$30X + 10Y \leq 90.$$

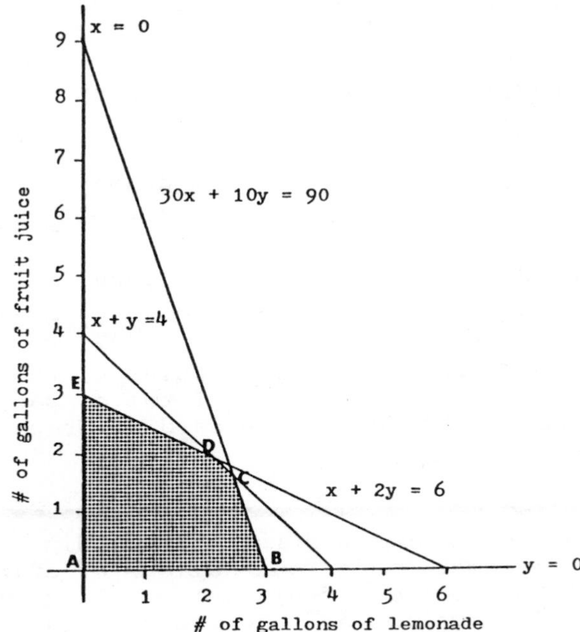

(5) The lemonade takes one pound of sugar, while the fruit juice takes two pounds of sugar per gallon. Thus, the constraint

$$X + 2Y \leq 6.$$

Now graph these constraints and find the "feasible region," i.e., the region where the constraints are met. Within this region look for the point yielding the maximum profit.

The shaded area on the graph is the "feasible region." To find the point with the maximum profit, use a theorem of Linear Programming that states that the point of maximum profits is an intersection of two of the constraint lines. Apply the profit formula to each of the region's corners, and choose the one giving the most profit.

A)	(0,0)	Profit = \$2(0) + \$1.50(0)	= \$0
B)	(3,0)	Profit = \$2(3) + \$1.50(0)	= \$6.00
C)	(2.5,1.5)	Profit = \$2(2.5) + \$1.50(1.5)	= \$7.25
D)	(2,2)	Profit = \$2(2) + \$1.50(2)	= \$7.00
E)	(0,3)	Profit = \$2(0) + \$1.50(3)	= \$4.50

Observe that the maximum profit of $7.25 occurs when the boy makes, and sells, $2\frac{1}{2}$ gallons of lemonade, and 1.5 gallons of fruit juice. (Point C on the graph.)

• PROBLEM 1-12

A company produces two types of mopeds. The low speed moped is produced at their New Jersey plant which can only handle 1,000 mopeds per month. The high speed moped is produced at their Maryland plant which can only handle 850 mopeds per month. The company has a sufficient supply of parts to build 1,175 low speed mopeds or 1,880 high speed mopeds. They also have sufficient labor to build 1,800 low speed mopeds or 1,080 high speed mopeds. A low speed moped yields $100 profit while a high speed moped yields $125 profit. Find what combination of high and low speed mopeds should be produced in order to achieve the maximum profit for one month.

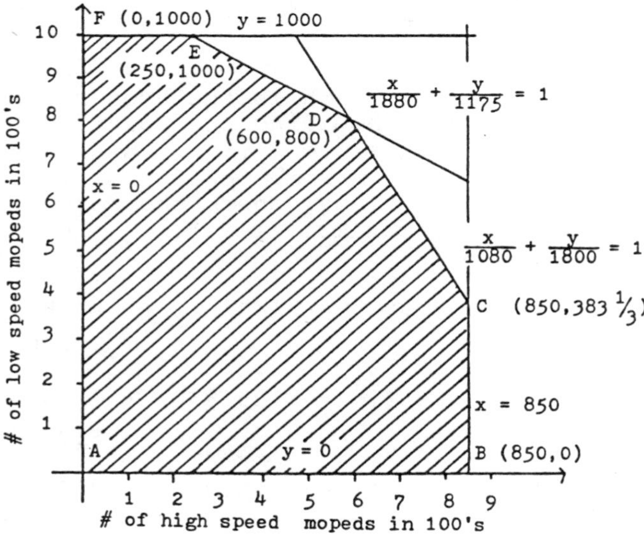

Solution: Take the constraints, and graph them, thus defining a region in which they are satisfied. From this region then choose the point which yields the maximum profits. If we let Y = the low speed mopeds and X = the high speed mopeds, the profit can be found by applying the following formula:

$$\text{Profit} = \$100Y + \$125X.$$

Now find the constraints.

(1) $Y \geq 0$ because low speed mopeds cannot be negative.

(2) $X \geq 0$ because high speed mopeds cannot be negative.

(3) $Y \leq 1{,}000$ for only 1,000 low speed mopeds can be accommodated.

(4) $X \leq 850$ for the plants can only accommodate 850 high speed mopeds.

(5) They have sufficient parts for 1,175 low speed mopeds, or for 1,880 high speed mopeds. Thus if the ratios of the number of high and low speed mopeds produced to the maximum number of each that can be produced are added together, the result cannot be greater than 1 (because if it were greater than 1, we would be using more parts than we have ---1 = 100%).
Thus, the constraint:

$$\frac{Y}{1,175} + \frac{X}{1,880} \leq 1.$$

(6) Similarly, since there is labor sufficient for either 1,800 low speed mopeds or 1,080 high speed mopeds, we have the constraint:

$$\frac{Y}{1,880} + \frac{X}{1,080} \leq 1.$$

Now graph these constraints to find the region defined by them.

The shaded area of the graph is the area which conforms with the constraints. Now find the point in this region which gives the maximum profit. By a theorem of Linear Programming, the maximum profit will occur at a corner of the region. Thus, check the corners to find which one yields the maximum profit.

A) (0,0)	Profit = \$125(0)	+ \$100(0)
		= \$0.00
B) (850,0)	Profit = \$125(850)	+ \$100(0)
		= \$106,250.00
C) (850,383 1/3)	Profit = \$125(850)	+ \$100(383 1/3)
		= \$144,583.33
D) (600,800)	Profit = \$125(600)	+ \$100(800)
		= \$155,000.00
E) (280,1000)	Profit = \$125(280)	+ \$100(1,000)
		= \$135,000.00
F) (0,1000)	Profit = \$125(0)	+ \$100(1,000)
		= \$100,000.00

Thus, the maximum profit, following the constraints, is \$155,000 which is attained at point D on the graph. In order to achieve the maximum profit of \$155,000, the company must produce 800 low speed mopeds and 600 high speed mopeds.

• PROBLEM 1-13

A marketing manager wishes to maximize the number of people exposed to the company's advertising. He may choose television commercials, which reach 20 million people per commercial, or magazine advertising, which reaches 10 million people per advertisement. Magazine advertisements cost $40,000 each while a television advertisement costs $75,000. The manager has a budget of $2,000,000 and must buy at least 20 magazine advertisements. How many units of each type of advertising should be purchased?

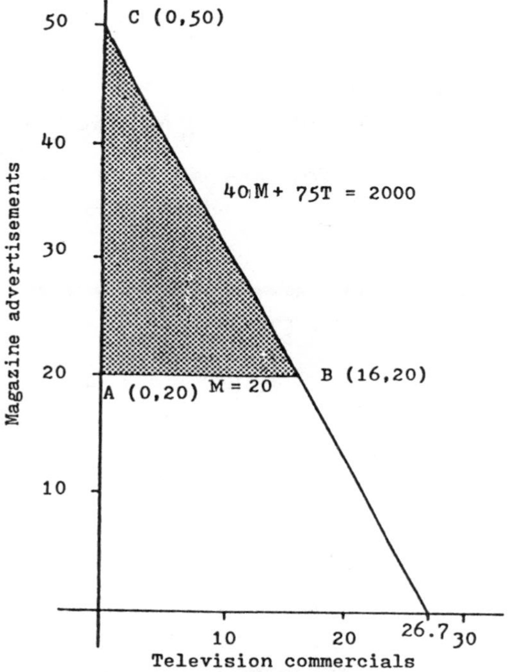

Solution: Find the constraints of the problem, and graph them to find the region defined by them. From this region pick the point which maximizes the number of people exposed to the advertisements.

Let T stand for the number of television commercials and M stand for the number of magazine advertisements.

The constraints are:

(1) $T \geq 0$ There cannot be a negative number of television commercials.

(2) $M \geq 20$ There must be at least twenty magazine advertisements.

(3) This constraint comes from the costs. In thousands the cost of a television commercial is $75 and the cost of a magazine advertisement is $40. He is budgeted to $2,000,000, thus the constraint:

$$40M + 75T \leq 2{,}000.$$

Now graph these constraints to find the region which is defined by them.

The shaded area is the region which is defined by the constraints. The point which yields the highest number of people exposed to the advertisement can be found by a theorem of linear programming which states that the point must be one of the corners of the region.

A) (0,20) number of people = 20 million × T + 10 million × M = 20 million × 0 + 10 million × 20 = 200 million.

B) (16,20) number of people = 20 million × 16 + 10 million × 20 = 520 million.

C) (0,50) number of people = 20 million × 0 + 10 million × 50 = 500 million.

Thus, the best thing for the manager to do is have 16 television commercials and 20 magazine advertisements.

• PROBLEM 1-14

Consider the following problem:

$$\begin{aligned} \text{Minimize} \quad & -2x_1 + 3x_2 \\ \text{Subject to} \quad & -x_1 + 2x_2 \leq 2 \\ & 2x_1 - x_2 \leq 3 \\ & x_2 \geq 4 \\ & x_1, \; x_2 \geq 0 \end{aligned}$$

Solve by the graphical approach.

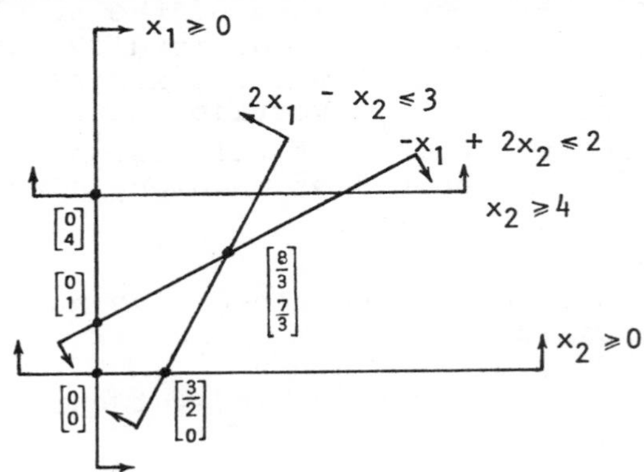

Empty feasible region.

Solution: Examining Figure 1, it is clear that there exists no point (x_1, x_2) satisfying the given inequalities. The problem is said to be infeasible, inconsistent, or with empty feasible region, in this case.

• PROBLEM 1-15

A commercial dairy farmer is interested in feeding his cattle at minimum cost, subject to meeting some constraints. The cattle are fed two feeds: oats and NK-34, a commercial preparation. The constraints are that each cow must get at least 400 grams per day of protein, at least 800 grams per day of carbohydrates, and no more than 100 grams per day of fat. Oats contain 10 percent protein, 80 percent carbohydrates, and 10 percent fat. NK-34 contains 40 percent protein, 60 percent carbohydrates, and no fat. Oats cost $0.20 per 1000 grams, and NK-34 costs $0.50 per 1000 grams.

a. Write a linear programming formulation to solve for the optimal amounts of each type of feed.

b. Solve the problem graphically.

c. Check your solution by finding the three corner points of interest and evaluating the objective function.

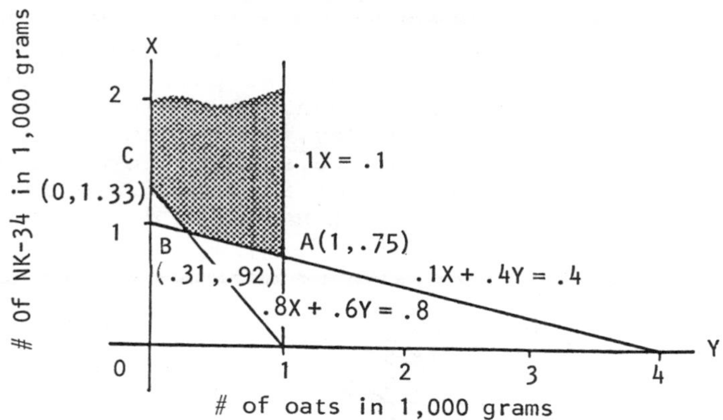

Solution: If X stands for the amount of oats (in 1000 gram units), and Y stands for the amount of NK-34 (in 1000 gram units), then minimize the cost function:

$$\$.20X + \$.50Y.$$

The constraints are the following:

(1) $X \geq 0$
(2) $Y \geq 0$
one cannot feed the cattle negative quantities of oats or NK-34.

(3) $.1X \leq .1$ This is because there is 10% fat in oats, and they must have not more than 100 grams (.1 × 1000) of fat.

(4) Oats are 80% carbohydrates, NK-34 is 60% carbohydrates, and they need at least 800 grams (80% of

1,000 grams), thus we have the constraint:

$$.8X + .6Y \geq .8 .$$

(5) Oats are 10% protein and NK-34 is 40% protein. The cattle require at least 400 grams (40% of 1,000) of protein, giving us the constraint:

$$.1X + .4Y \geq .4 .$$

Now graph these constraints to find the region described by them.

The shaded area in the graph is the region defined by the constraints. The point of minimum cost is known by the theory of linear programming to lie on a corner of the region. Thus, check the corners to find the one with the least cost.

A) (1,.75) Cost = $.20(1) + $.50(.75) = $.575

B) (.31,.92) Cost = $.20(.31) + $.50(.92) = $.522

C) (0,1.33) Cost = $.20(0) + $.50(1.33) = $.67

Thus, the cheapest is point B, .31 kilograms of oats and .92 kilograms of NK-34.

• PROBLEM 1-16

A businessman needs 5 cabinets, 12 desks, and 18 shelves cleaned out. He has two part-time employees Sue and Janet. Sue can clean one cabinet, three desks and three shelves in one day, while Janet can clean one cabinet, two desks and 6 shelves in one day. Sue is paid $25 a day, and Janet is paid $22 a day. In order to minimize the cost, how many days should Sue and Janet be employed?

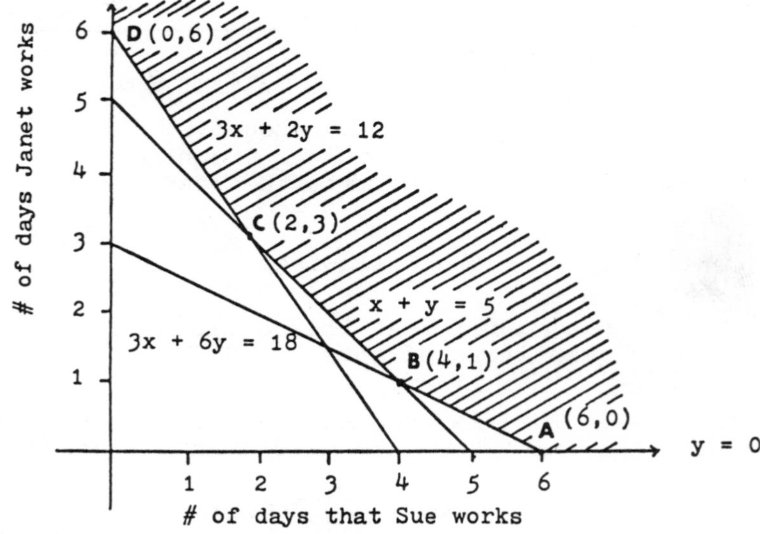

Solution: The businessman wishes to minimize the cost of cleaning out the office. To do this the constraints must be graphed to find the points which gives the minimum cost. To find the cost use the formula:

$$\text{Cost} = \$25\ X + \$22\ Y,$$

where X is the number of days Sue is employed and Y is the number of days Janet is employed. Now find the constraints.

(1) Since Sue can do a cabinet in one day, and Janet can do a cabinet in one day, and there must be at least 5 cabinets cleaned, there is the constraint:

$$X + Y \geq 5.$$

(2) Since Sue can do 3 desks in one day, and Janet can do 2 desks in one day, and 12 desks are required to be cleaned, there is the constraint:

$$3X + 2Y \geq 12.$$

(3) Similarly, the constraint $3X + 6Y \geq 18$ comes from Sue being able to clean 3 shelves and Janet being able to clean 6 shelves in one day.

(4) $X \geq 0$ Sue cannot work a negative number of days.

(5) $Y \geq 0$ Janet cannot work a negative number of days.

Now graph the constraints to find the region described by them.

The shaded area is the region described by the constraints. Note that this is an infinite region, because they can work more days than is needed. To find the minimum point, refer to a theorem of linear programming which states that the minimum cost must oc- occur in one of the corners. Check the four corners to find the one with the least cost.

A) (6,0) $25 (6) + $22 (0) = $150

B) (4,1) $25 (4) + $22 (1) = $122

C) (2,3) $25 (2) + $22 (3) = $116

D) (0,6) $25 (0) + $22 (6) = $132

The minimum cost is, with Janet working 3 days and Sue working 2 days, equal to $116. (Point C on the graph.)

• PROBLEM 1-17

An office is willing to hire up to ten temporary employees to help with the mail. The office has found that a male employee can handle 300 letters and 80 packages per day, and a female employee can handle 400 letters and 50 packages in one day. No less than 3,400 letters and no less than 680 packages in a day are expected. A male employee receives \$25 and a female employee receives \$22 per day. How many male and female helpers should be hired to keep the payroll at a minimum?

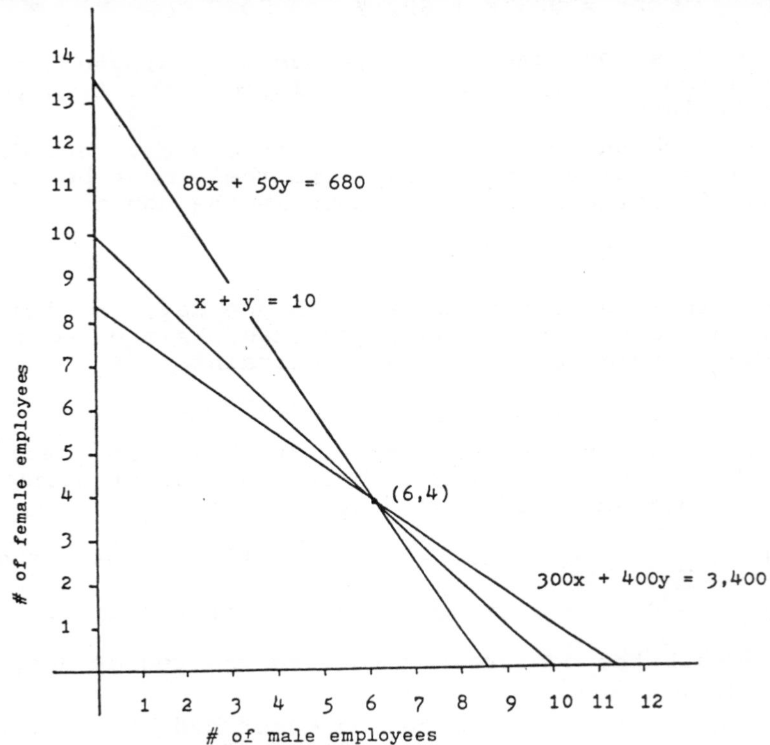

Solution: The office wishes to minimize its expenses while meeting the constraints. To do this, graph the constraints, and choose the point with the minimum cost from the region described. The cost is found by the formula $\$25X + \$22Y = \text{Cost}$,

where X is the number of male employees, and Y is the number of female employees. The constraints are the following:

(1) $X \geq 0$ There cannot be a negative number of male employees.

(2) $Y \geq 0$ There cannot be a negative number of female employees.

(3) Since the office will only hire up to ten temporary employees there is the constraint:

$$X + Y \leq 10.$$

(4) A male employee can handle 300 letters a day, and a female employee can handle 400 letters a day. Since at least 3,400 letters are expected there is the constraint:

$$300X + 400Y \geq 3,400.$$

(5) A male employee can handle 80 packages a day, and a female employee can handle 50 packages in one day. Since at least 680 packages are expected there is the constraint:

$$80X + 50Y \geq 680.$$

Now graph these constraints to find the region which is defined by them. From this region choose the point with the least cost.

The region in this problem is only the single point (6,4). All other points fail to meet at least one of the constraints. Thus the minimum cost is the cost of 6 male and 4 female employees, amounting to

$$\$25(6) + \$22(4) = \$238.$$

• PROBLEM 1-18

The Brown Company has two warehouses and three retail outlets. Warehouse number one (which will be denoted by W_1) has a capacity of 12 units; warehouse number two (W_2) holds 8 units. These warehouses must ship the product to the three outlets, denoted by O_1, O_2, and O_3. O_1 requires 8 units. O_2 requires 7 units, and O_3 requires 5 units. Thus, there is a total storage capacity of 20 units, and also a demand for 20 units. The question is, which warehouse should ship how many units to which outlet? (The objective being, of course, to accomplish this at the least possible cost.)

Costs of shipping from either warehouse to any of the outlets are known and are summarized in the following table, which also sets forth the warehouse capacities and the needs of the retail outlets:

	O_1	O_2	O_3	Capacity
W_1............	\$3.00	\$5.00	\$3.00	12
W_2............	2.00	7.00	1.00	8
Needs (units)	8	7	5	

Solution: This seems to be a linear programming problem with three variables. However, the third variable can be computed from the previous two. Let X be the number of units sent from warehouse 1 to outlet 1. Since outlet 1 requires only 8 units, there is the constraint $X \leq 8$. Also, $X \geq 0$ because one cannot ship negative quantities of the product. Let y be the number of units shipped from warehouse 1, to outlet 2. Similarly,

$$0 \leq y \leq 7$$

is another constraint. Because there are 12 units in warehouse 1, the number of units sent to outlet 3 is

$$12 - X - y.$$

Obviously, this must be larger or equal to zero. Thus,

$$12 - X - y \geq 0 \quad \text{or} \quad X + y \leq 12$$

is a constraint.

The amount of units sent from warehouse 2 to outlet 1 is the original eight less the X that was sent from warehouse 1, or 8 - X. In a similar fashion, find all of the others.

	O_1	O_2	O_3
W_1............	x	y	12 - x - y
W_2............	8 - x	7 - y	x + y - 7

Note that the quantities shipped from both warehouses to Outlet 3 have been determined by simply subtracting the quantities shipped to Outlets 1 and 2 from the total capacities of the warehouses.

The following constraints are obtained:

(1) $X \geq 0$

(2) $y \geq 0$

(3) $X \leq 8$

(4) $y \leq 7$

(5) $X + y \leq 12$

(6) $X + y \geq 7$ (from $O_3 - W_2 \geq 0$).

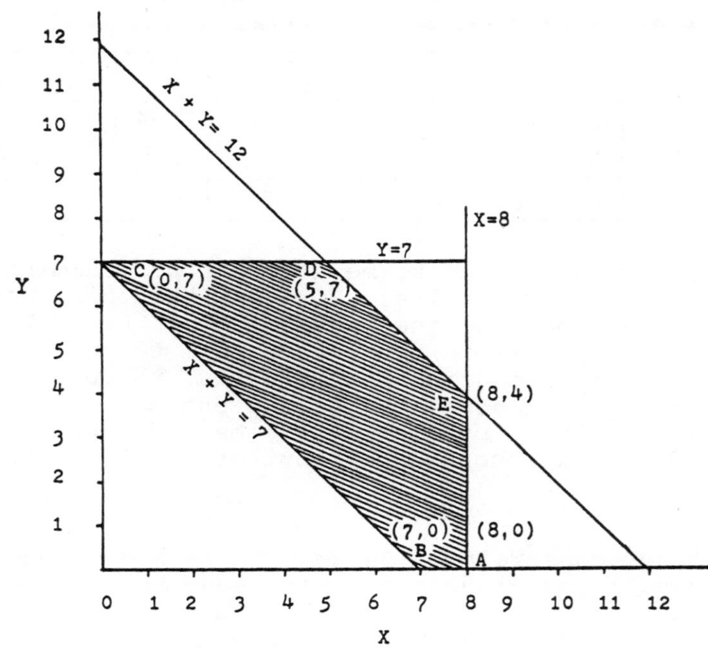

It is desired to minimize the cost function. It can be found by multiplying the number of units sent by their costs.

$$\text{Cost} = 3X + 5y + 3\,(12-X-y) + 2(8-X) + 7(7-y)$$

$$+ 1(X+y-7) = 94 - X - 4y.$$

To minimize this plot the constraints to find the region that is defined by them.

The shaded region is the area that is defined by the constraints. From linear programming it is known that the minimum cost will occur at a corner of this region. Check these corners to pick the best point.

A) (8,0) $94 - 8 = \$86$

B) (7,0) $94 - 7 = \$87$

C) (0,7) $94 - 0 - (4 \times 7) = \$66$

D) (5,7) $94 - 5 - (4 \times 7) = \$61$

E) (8,4) $94 - 8 - (4 \times 4) = \$70$

Thus the point with the least cost is point D. So for the lowest cost the shipping schedule should be

	O_1	O_2	O_3	
W_1...........	5	7	0	12
W_2...........	3	0	5	8
	8	7	5	

• PROBLEM 1-19

Consider the following problem:

$$\text{Maximize} \quad P = 5x_1 + 8x_2 \qquad (1)$$

subject to

$$2x_1 + x_2 \leq 14$$

$$x_1 + 3x_2 \leq 12 \qquad (2)$$

$$x_2 \leq 3$$

$$x_1 \geq 0,\ x_2 \geq 0.$$

Suppose that an additional constraint on x_1 and x_2 is imposed:

$$x_1 + x_2 \leq K \qquad (3)$$

where K is some unspecified amount. How does the solution of (1), (2) and (3) change as K varies from zero to very large values?

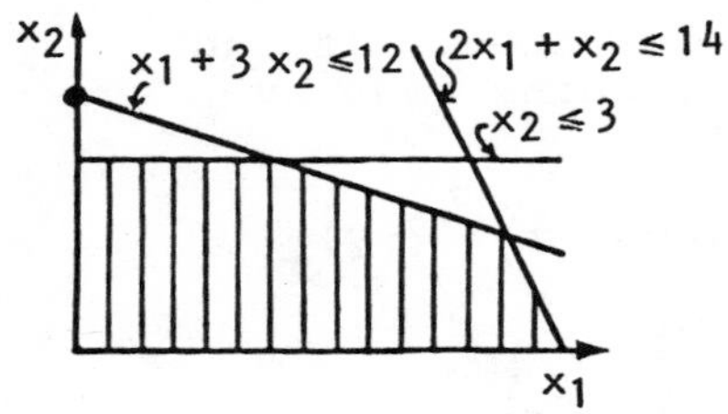

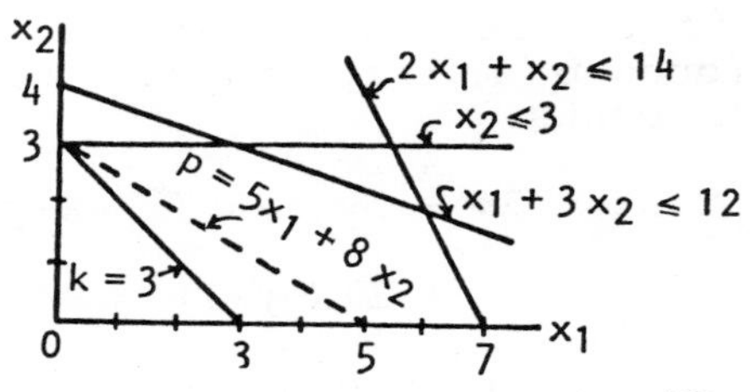

Fig. 1

Fig. 2

Solution: First graph the problem (1), (2), as in Fig. 1.

Assume the first two constraints represent time used on machine 1 and machine 2, respectively, to produce units of products x_1 and x_2. The third constraint indicates that not more than three units of product x_2 can be sold. Now consider the additional constraint $x_1 + x_2 \leq K$. This states that the total amount of working capital used must be less than an unspecified amount, K. If K = 0 the only solution is that of no production and $x_1 = x_2 = 0$. As K increases to one, the first dollar of working capital is used to produce one unit of x_2 since x_2 is the more profitable product. Since each unit of K spent on x_2 produces \$8 of profit as K increases, only x_2 is produced until the situation in Fig. 2 is reached.

When K > 3, the market constraint ($x_2 \leq 3$) becomes binding, and additional units of x_2 cannot be produced. Hence, production of x_1 now begins. Each dollar of working capital has an incremental value of \$5, the profit associated with selling one unit of x_1. Production of x_1 continues until the situation in Fig. 3 is reached.

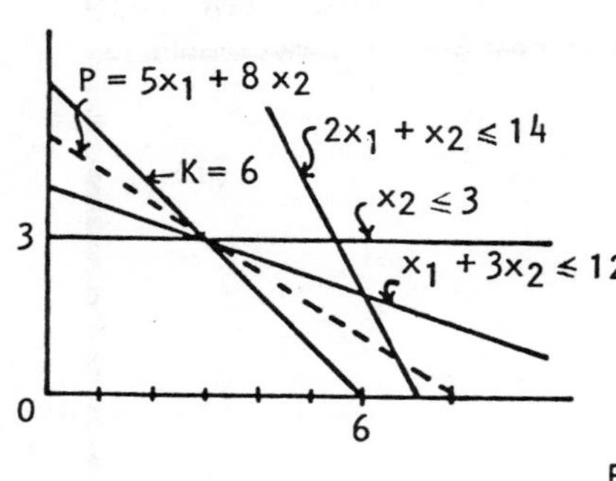

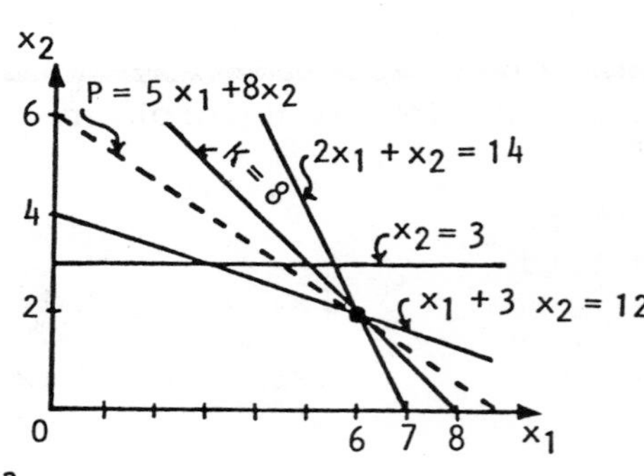

Fig. 3

Fig. 4

In Fig. 3, the constraint on time available on machine 2 also becomes binding, at the point at which six units of K are available. Now, three units of x_1 and 3 units of x_2 are produced for a total profit of \$39. Note that P can still be increased by moving down the $x_1 + 3x_2 = 12$ constraint. But now each unit of working capital contributes only \$3.50 profit. To see this, observe that one unit of x_2 can be substituted for three units of x_1 yielding an additional profit of \$5(3) - \$8(1) = \$7. But this substitution requires three units for the new x_1 less one unit for reduced x_2.

Hence the marginal value of K is $7/2 = $3.50. Finally, the situation portrayed in Fig. 4 is reached. Here the constraints on both machine times are binding. Increasing the working capital, K, beyond this point would have no effect on the solution. This sort of analysis is useful to a business man who is trying to decide how much working capital to invest in this production operation. He would not invest more than $8. However, he might invest even less if he had profitable alternative uses for his funds. For example, if he could use the working capital elsewhere to return him $4 per unit, then he would not invest more than six units. If he could get a return of $6 per unit, he would not use more than 3 units.

• PROBLEM 1-20

A certain textile mill finishes cotton cloth obtained from weaving mills. The mill turns out two styles of cloth, a lightly printed style and a heavily printed one. The mill's output during a week is limited only by the capacity of its equipment for two of the finishing operations--printing and bleaching--and not by demand considerations. The maximum weekly output of the printing machinery is 800 thousand yards of cloth if the light pattern is printed exclusively, 400 thousand yards if the heavy pattern is printed exclusively, or any combination on the printing line L + 2H = 800 (where L represents light pattern and H heavy pattern). In a week, the maximum the bleaching equipment can handle is 500 thousand yards of the light-patterned cloth exclusively, 550 thousand yards of the heavy-patterned cloth exclusively, or any combination on the bleaching line, 1.1 L + H = 550. The mill gained $300 and $290 per thousand yards of the light -- and heavy-patterned cloths, respectively.

1) Draw the graph of the two lines described above.

2) Solve the linear programming problem of maximizing the gain from a week's production.

Solution: 1)

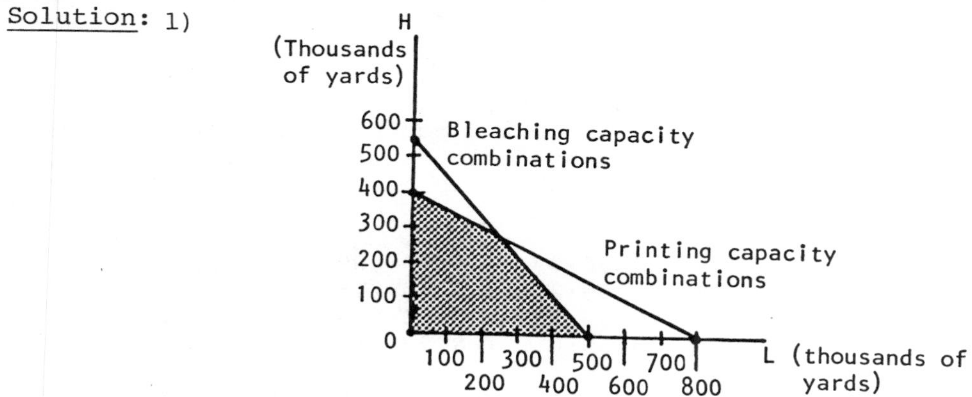

2) Use the graphical approach to solve this linear programming problem. Utilize the graph above. Looking at the graph, notice that any combination of L and H

that falls in the area between the two axes and the printing line can be printed during a week. Again, any combination of L and H that falls in the area between the two axes and the bleaching line can be bleached in one week.

The rules for solving a linear programming problem through a graphical approach are:
i) Graph all the constraining inequalities to obtain a picture of the feasible region.
ii) Solve the corresponding equations to find the vertices, or corners of the feasible area.
iii) Find the vertex point which yields the maximum (or minimum) value of the function under consideration.

Thus, the vertices are:

Output (Thousands of Yards)	
Light Pattern	Heavy Pattern
0	400
250	275
500	0
0	0

The vertices (0,400), (500,0), (0,0) are obtained easily from the graph. The fourth vertex (250,275) is obtained from the simultaneous equations:

$$L + 2H = 800$$

$$1.1L + H = 550$$

From the first equation, L = 800 - 2H. Substituting this into the second equation yields

$$1.1(800 - 2H) + H = 550$$

or

$$880 - 2.2H + H = 550$$

$$-1.2H = -330$$

$$1.2H = 330$$

$$H = 330/1.2$$

$$H = 275$$

Thus, L + 2H = 800 becomes L + 2 × 275 = 800, L = 250. The mill gained \$300 and \$290 per thousand yards of the light- and heavy-patterned cloths, respectively. Thus, for the four vertices, the gain from the week's production is:

at (0,400): $\$300 \cdot 0 + \$290 \cdot 400 = \$116,000$
at (250,275): $\$300 \cdot 250 + \$290 \cdot 275 = \$155,000$
at (500,0): $\$300 \cdot 500 + \$290 \cdot 0 = \$150,000$
at (0,0): $\$300 \cdot 0 + \$290 \cdot 0 = \$0$.

Thus, if the textile mill wants to obtain the highest possible gain from the week's operations, the combination 250 light pattern, 275 heavy pattern should be selected.

Assume a firm produces certain products and stores them in warehouses S_1 and S_2 situated in two different towns. The firm receives orders from customers living in three other towns, D_1, D_2, and D_3. (S signifies supply and D demand.) The unit costs of shipping from each warehouse to each customer are shown in the table below, as well as the capacities of the warehouses and the requirements of the customers. Thus it costs $4 per unit to ship from S_1 to D_1, $5 per unit to ship from S_2 to D_3, and so on.

	D_1	D_2	D_3	Capacity
S_1	$4	$2	$1	15
S_2	$1	$3	$5	25
Requirements	10	20	10	(40)

The margins of this table are to be read as follows: Supply depot 1 has a capacity of 15, supply depot 2 a capacity of 25, customer 1 has a demand of 10, customer 2 a demand of 20, customer 3 a demand of 10.

The objective is to find a shipping program which meets all requirements at least cost. Let x represent the amount shipped from S_1 to customer 1, and y the amount shipped from S_1 to customer 2. Then write all other amounts shipped in terms of x and y, as follows:

	D_1	D_2	D_3
S_1	x	y	$15 - x - y$
S_2	$10 - x$	$20 - y$	$-5 + x + y$

Since all amounts shipped must be nonnegative, our problem is subject to the following constraints, one for each cell in the table above:

$$x \geq 0, \quad y \geq 0, \quad x + y \leq 15$$

$$x \leq 10, \quad y \leq 20, \quad x + y \geq 5$$

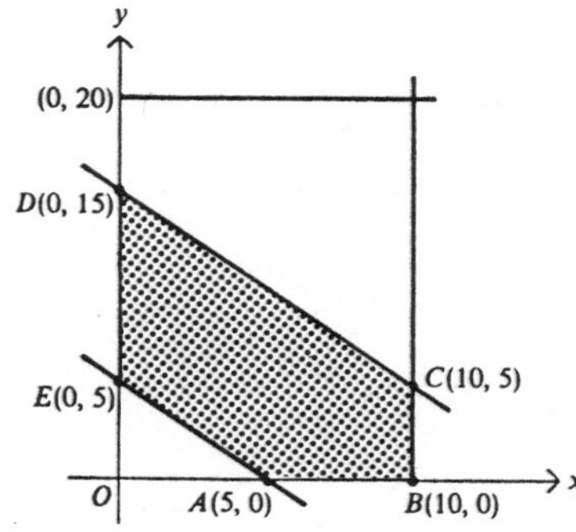

Fig. 1

Solution: The total cost of shipping is

$$C = 4x + 1(10 - x) + 2y + 3(20 - y) + 1(15 - x - y)$$

$$+ 5(-5 + x + y) = 7x + 3y + 60$$

The objective is to minimize this function, subject to the above constraints. The graphical solution to this problem follows.

Figure 1 exhibits the region of feasibility. Construct the region by drawing the limiting line associated with each constraint and then shading the relevant side of each line. Because several of the limiting lines are parallel, read off the feasible corners directly from the graph. They are (5,0), (10,0), (10,5), (0,15), (0,5). In the following table we evaluate the homogeneous form C' = 7x + 3y at each feasible corner:

Corner	Value of $C' = 7x + 3y$
$A(5, 0)$	35
$B(10, 0)$	70
$C(10, 5)$	85
$D(0, 15)$	45
$E(0, 5)$	15

Corner E is the optimal corner. At this corner C' = 15 and hence C = 15 + 60 = 75. Since x = 0 and y = 5 at corner E, use these values to fill in the optimal plan of shipment, as given in the schedule below.

	D_1	D_2	D_3
S_1	0	5	10
S_2	10	15	0

• PROBLEM 1-22

Maximize P = 6x + 2y + 77

subject to the usual nonnegativity constraints on x and y, and the following constraints:

$$3x + y \leq 48$$

$$3x + 4y \leq 120$$

$$3x + y \geq 36$$

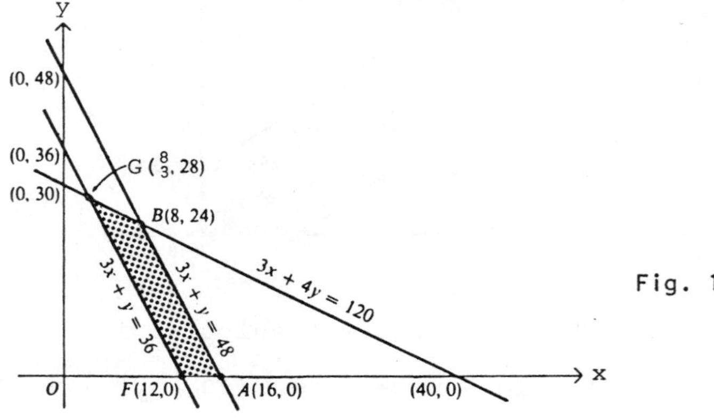

Fig. 1

Solution: The maximum of P occurs at those values (x_0, y_0) which maximize the homogeneous part of P, namely, H = 6x + 2y. The constant part of P, that is, 77, is best thought of as a "fixed return," having no effect on the point where P is maximized.

The region of feasibility for this problem has already been drawn in Figure 1. It is the set of points within and on the boundary of the quadrilateral FABG. To solve this problem, determine the value of H = 6x + 2y at the corners of the region of feasibility. These feasible corners, their coordinates, and the corresponding values of H are:

Corner	Value of H = 6x + 2y
F(12,0)	72
A(16,0)	96
B(8,24)	96
G($\frac{8}{3}$,28)	72

The maximum value of H is 96 and hence the maximum value of P is 96 + 77 = 173. Furthermore, this maximum is obtained at both corners A and B, so that all points on the segment AB represent optimal solutions.

• PROBLEM 1-23

Manufacturing and marketing data for a production situation are summarized in Table 1. Three products compete for the available production time. The objective is to determine the quantity of product A, the quantity of product B, and the quantity of product C to produce so that total profit will be maximized.

Formulate the problem as a linear program. Discuss its graphical representation and find the optimal solution.

TABLE 1
Manufacturing and Marketing Data for Three Products

Department	Product *A*	Product *B*	Product *C*	Capacity
Punch press	2.4	3.0	2.0	1,200
Welding	0.0	2.5	1.5	600
Assembly	5.0	0.0	2.5	1,500
Profit	$0.60	$0.70	$0.50	

Solution: In graphical maximization, when three activities compete for scarce resources, a three-dimensional space is involved. Each restriction is a plane in this space, and all restrictions taken together identify a volume of feasible solutions. The effectiveness function is also a plane, its distance from the origin being proportional to its value. The optimum value for the effectiveness function occurs when this plane is located so that it is at the extreme point of the volume of feasible solutions.

This will require maximizing

$$TP = \$0.60A + \$0.70B + \$0.50C$$

subject to

$$2.4A + 3.0B + 2.0C \leq 1{,}200$$

$$0.0A + 2.5B + 1.5C \leq 600$$

$$5.0A + 0.0B + 2.5C \leq 1{,}500$$

$$A \geq 0,\ B \geq 0,\ \text{and } C \geq 0.$$

The graphical equivalent of the algebraic statement of this three-product production situation is shown in Figure 1. The set of restricting planes defines a volume of feasible solutions. This region lies below 2.4A + 3.0B + 2.0C = 1,200 and is restricted further by the requirement that 2.5B + 1.5C ≤ 600, 5.0A + 2.5C ≤ 1,500, and that A, B, and C be nonnegative. Thus, the scarce resources determine which combinations of the activities are feasible and which are not feasible.

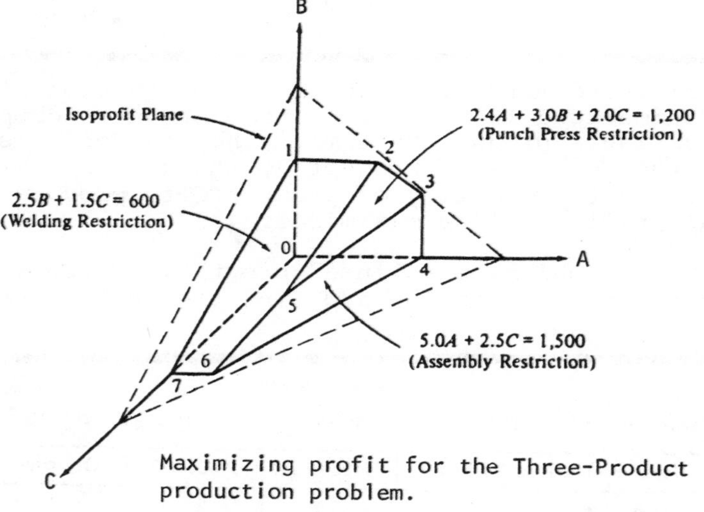

Maximizing profit for the Three-Product production problem. Fig. 1

The production quantity combinations of A, B, and C that fall within the volume of feasible solutions constitute feasible production programs. That combination or combinations of A, B, and C which maximizes total profit is sought. The expression 0.60A + 0.70B + 0.50C gives the relationship among A, B, and C based on the relative profit of each product. The total profit realized will depend upon the production quantity combination chosen. Thus, there exists a family of isoprofit planes, one for each value of total profit. One of these planes will have at least one point in the volume of feasible solutions and will be a maximum distance from the origin. The plane that maximizes profit will intersect the volume at an extreme point.

This calls for the computation of total profit at each extreme point as given in Table 2. The coordinates of each extreme point were found from the restricting planes, and the associated profit was calculated from the total profit equation.

TABLE 2 **Total Profit Computations at Extreme Points of Figure 1**

Point	Coordinate *A*	*B*	*C*	Profit
0	0	0	0	$ 0
1	0	240	0	$168.00
2	200	240	0	$288.00
3	300	160	0	$292.00
4	300	0	0	$180.00
5	180	96	240	$295.20
6	100	0	400	$260.00
7	0	0	400	$200.00

Inspection of the total profit values in Table 2 indicates that profit is maximized at point 5 which has the coordinates 180,96, and 240. This means that if 180 units of product A, 96 units of product B, and 240 units of product C are produced, profit will be maximized. No other production quantity combination will result in a higher profit. Also, no alternate optimum solutions exist, since the total profit plane intersects the volume of feasible solutions at only a single point.

CHAPTER 2

LINEAR PROGRAMMING(LP) - INTRODUCTION

PROBLEM FORMULATION AND APPLICATIONS OF LP

• PROBLEM 2-1

The Marvel Toy Company wishes to make three models of boats for the most profit. They found that a model of a steamship takes the cutter one hour, the painter 2 hours, and the assembler 4 hours of work. It produces $6 of profit. Their model of a four-mast sailboat takes the cutter 3 hours, the painter 3 hours, and the assembler 2 hours. It produces $3 of profit. Their model of a two-mast sailboat takes the cutter one hour, the painter three hours, and the assembler one hour. It produces $2 of profit. The cutter is only available for 45 hours, the painter for 50 hours, and the assembler for 60 hours. Assuming that they can sell all the models that are built, find the constraints of the problem and describe how the solution is obtained.

Solution: To find the constraints for this problem, let X be the number of models of steamships, Y the number of models of four-mast sailboats, Z the number of two-mast sailboats. The constraints are:

(1) $X \geq 0$ There cannot be a negative number of models of steamships.

(2) $Y \geq 0$ There cannot be a negative number of models of four-mast sailboats.

(3) $Z \geq 0$ There cannot be a negative number of models of two-mast sailboats.

(4) A steamship takes one hour of the cutter's time, a four-mast sailboat takes three hours of the cutter's time, and a two-mast sailboat takes one hour of the cutter's time. Since the cutter has only 45 hours available there is the constraint:

$$X + 3Y + Z \leq 45.$$

(5) A steamship takes two hours of the painter's time, a four-mast sailboat takes three hours of the painter's time, and a two-mast sailboat takes three hours of the painter's time. Since the painter has only 50 hours of time available, there is the constraint:

$$2X + 3Y + 3Z \leq 50.$$

(6) A steamship takes four hours of the assembler's time, a four-mast sailboat takes 2 hours of the assembler's time, and a two-mast sailboat takes one hour of the assembler's time. Since the assembler can work only 60 hours, there is the constraint:

$$4X + 2Y + Z \leq 60.$$

Since there are three unknowns, a three dimensional graph is required to plot the constraints. However, it is known from a theorem of Linear Programming that the point of maximum profit lies on the intersection of three lines of constraints (the same number of constraints as the number of unknowns). Thus, to solve this, break up the six constraints into all groups of three that are possible. Then solve each group of three equations for the three unknowns. There is now a group of points. Take from that group of points those that meet the conditions set by all of the constraints. Then take from that new group the point which yields the most profit. That point is the solution to the problem. To find which point yields the most profit, use the following equation for the profit:

$$\text{Profit} = \$6X + \$3Y + \$2Z.$$

After following the above procedure it is found that, in order to make the most profit, the company should produce 13 steamships, no four-mast sailboats, and 8 two-mast sailboats. This will yield a profit of $94.

• PROBLEM 2-2

Given the inconsistent system

$$x - y = 7$$

$$2x + 3y = 5$$

$$3x + y = -1$$

find the best approximate Tchebycheff solution which minimize the sum of all three discrepancies and satisfies the further condition that the coordinates equivalent to the minimizing the sum

$$S = d_1 + d_2 + d_3,$$

where

$$d_1 = | x - y - 7 |$$

$$d_2 = |2x + 3y - 5|$$

$$d_3 = |3x + y + 1|$$

Solution: S can be minimized by solving the following linear program involving six nontrivial constraints:

Minimize $\quad S = d_1 + d_2 + d_3$

where all variables are nonnegative and

$$
\begin{aligned}
x - y - d_1 &= 7 \\
-x + y - d_1 &= -7 \\
2x + 3y - d_2 &= 5 \\
-2x - 3y - d_2 &= -5 \\
3x + y - d_3 &= -1 \\
-3x - y - d_3 &= 1
\end{aligned}
$$

The optimal solution of this program is

$$x = 0,\ y = \frac{5}{3},\ d_1 = \frac{26}{3},\ d_2 = 0,\ d_3 = \frac{8}{3},$$

which gives $\frac{34}{3}$ as the sum of the absolute errors.

If the nonnegativity restriction on x and y is removed, the best approximate solution becomes

$$x = -\frac{8}{7},\ y = \frac{17}{7},\ d_1 = \frac{74}{7},\ d_2 = 0,\ d_3 = 0.$$

The corresponding absolute errors are

$$
\begin{aligned}
|x - y - 7| &= \left| -\frac{8}{7} - \frac{17}{7} - 7\right| = \frac{74}{7} \\
|2x + 3y - 5| &= \left| -\frac{16}{7} + 3\left(\frac{17}{7}\right) - 5\right| = 0 \\
|3x + y + 1| &= \left|3\left(-\frac{8}{7}\right) + \frac{17}{7} + 1\right| = 0
\end{aligned}
$$

The sum of these absolute errors is $\frac{74}{7}$. The sum of the discrepancies decreased when x and y were allowed to be free variables.

The Reggio Advertising Company wishes to plan an advertising campaign in three different media--television, radio, and magazines. The purpose of the advertising program is to reach as many potential customers as possible. Results of a market study are given below:

	Television			
	Day Time	Prime Time	Radio	Magazines
Cost of an advertising unit	\$ 40,000	\$ 75,000	\$ 30,000	\$ 15,000
Number of potential customers reached per unit	400,000	900,000	500,000	200,000
Number of women customers reached per unit	300,000	400,000	200,000	100,000

The company does not want to spend more than \$800,000 on advertising. It further requires that (1) at least 2 million exposures take place among women; (2) advertising on television be limited to \$500,000; (3) at least 3 advertising units be bought on daytime television, and two units during prime time; and (4) the number of advertising units on radio and magazine should each be between 5 and 10. Formulate into a linear programming problem.

Solution: Let x_1, x_2, x_3, and x_4 be the number of advertising units bought in daytime television, prime-time television, radio, and magazines, respectively.

The total number of potential customers reached (in thousands) = $400x_1 + 900x_2 + 500x_3 + 200\ x_4$. The restriction on the advertising budget is represented by:

$$40{,}000x_1 + 75{,}000x_2 + 30{,}000x_3 + 15{,}000x_4 \leq 800{,}000.$$

The constraint on the number of women customers reached by the advertising campaign becomes:

$$300{,}000x_1 + 400{,}000x_2 + 200{,}000x_3 + 100{,}000x_4 \geq 2{,}00{,}000.$$

The constraints on television advertising are:

$$40{,}000x_1 + 75{,}000x_2 \leq 500{,}000$$

$$x_1 \geq 3$$

$$x_2 \geq 2.$$

Since advertising units on radio and magazines should each be between 5 and 10, one gets the following constraints:

$$5 \leqq x_3 \leqq 10$$

$$5 \leqq x_4 \leqq 10.$$

The complete linear programming problem with some minor simplification is given below:

Maximize: $Z = 400x_1 + 900x_2 + 500x_3 + 200x_4$

Subject to:

$$40x_1 + 75x_2 + 30x_3 + 15x_4 \leqq 800$$

$$30x_1 + 40x_2 + 20x_3 + 10x_4 \geqq 200$$

$$40x_1 + 75x_2 \leqq 500$$

$$x_1 \geqq 3$$

$$x_2 \geqq 2$$

$$x_3 \geqq 5$$

$$x_3 \leqq 10$$

$$x_4 \geqq 5$$

$$x_4 \leqq 10.$$

• PROBLEM 2-4

A tomato cannery has 5000 pounds of grade A tomatoes and 10,000 pounds of grade B tomatoes, from which they will make whole canned tomatoes and tomato paste. Whole tomatoes must be composed of at least 80 percent grade A tomatoes, whereas tomato paste must be made with at least 10 percent grade A tomatoes. Whole tomatoes sell for \$0.08 per pound and paste sells for \$0.05 per pound. Formulate a linear program to solve for how much of each product to make, if the company wants to maximize revenue. (Hint: Let x_{WA} = pounds of A grade tomatoes used in whole tomatoes, x_{WB} = pounds of B grade tomatoes used in whole tomatoes; the amount of whole tomatoes produced can be found as $x_{WA} + x_{WB}$ after x_{WA} and x_{WB} are chosen.)

Solution: The constraints are the following:

Let X_{WA} stand for the number of pounds of grade A tomatoes used in whole tomatoes, X_{WB} = pounds of grade B tomatoes in whole tomatoes, X_{PA} = number of pounds of grade A tomatoes in paste, X_{PB} = number of pounds of grade B tomatoes in paste.

Since there cannot be a negative number of pounds of tomatoes the following constraints apply:

$$X_{WA} \geq 0 \quad (1)$$

$$X_{WB} \geq 0 \quad (2)$$

$$X_{PA} \geq 0 \quad (3)$$

$$X_{PB} \geq 0 \quad (4)$$

Since there are 5,000 pounds of grade A tomatoes, there is the constraint

$$X_{WA} + X_{PA} \leq 5{,}000 . \quad (5)$$

Since there are 10,000 pounds of grade B tomatoes, there is the constraint

$$X_{WB} + X_{PB} \leq 10{,}000 . \quad (6)$$

Whole tomatoes must be composed of at least 80% grade A tomatoes. The amount of whole tomatoes is $X_{WA} + X_{WB}$, thus, the constraint

$$\frac{X_{WA}}{X_{WA} + X_{WB}} \geq .80 \quad \text{or rewriting} \quad (7)$$

$$X_{WA} \geq .80\ X_{WA} + .80\ X_{WB} \quad \text{or}$$

$$X_{WA} - .80\ X_{WA} - .80\ X_{WB} \geq 0 \quad \text{or finally}$$

$$.2\ X_{WA} - .8\ X_{WB} \geq 0.$$

The last constraint is found from knowing that grade A tomatoes must be at least 10% of the paste. Since the total number of pounds of paste is

$$X_{PA} + X_{PB},$$

the last constraint is:

$$\frac{X_{PA}}{X_{PA} + X_{PB}} \geq .10 \text{ or rewriting}$$

$$X_{PA} \geq .1\ X_{PA} + .1\ X_{PB} \quad \text{or finally}$$

$$.9\ X_{PA} - .1\ X_{PB} \geq 0. \quad (8)$$

Given these constraints it is desired to maximize the revenue. The formula of the revenue is:

$$\$.08\ (X_{WA} + X_{WB}) + \$.05\ (X_{PA} + X_{PB}).$$

Then use more advanced linear programming techniques to solve this problem.

• PROBLEM 2-5

In order to produce 1000 tons of non-oxidizing steel for engine valves, at least the following units of manganese, chromium and molybdenum, will be needed weekly: 10 units of manganese, 12 units of chromium, and 14 units of molybdenum (1 unit is 10 pounds). These metals are obtainable from dealers in non-ferrous metals, who, to attract markets make them available in cases of three sizes, S, M and L. One S case costs \$9 and contains 2 units of manganese, 2 units of chromium and 1 unit of molybdenum. One M case costs \$12 and contains 2 units of manganese, 3 units of chromium, and 1 unit of molybdenum. One L case costs \$15 and contains 1 unit of manganese, 1 unit of chromium and 5 units of molybdenum.

How many cases of each kind should be purchased weekly so that the needed amounts of manganese, chromium and molybdenum are obtained at the smallest possible cost? What is the smallest possible cost? Formulate and solve by linear programming.

Solution: The general linear programming problem has the following form:

$$\text{Minimize} \quad z = c_1x_1 + c_2x_2 + \ldots + c_nx_n \tag{1}$$

Subject to:

$$a_{11}x_1 + a_{12}x_2 + \ldots + a_{1n}x_n \geq b_1 \tag{2}$$

$$\vdots \qquad\qquad\qquad\qquad \vdots$$

$$a_{m1}x_1 + a_{m2}x_2 + \ldots + a_{mn}x_n \geq b_m$$

$x_i \geq 0$ $(i = 1, 2, \ldots, n)$.

The linear function (1) is called the objective function while the inequalities (2) represent the constraints.

To cast the above problem into this form, first find the objective function. Since cases are being bought, it is desired to minimize:

$$z = 9S + 12M + 15L. \tag{3}$$

To obtain the constraints, at least 10 units of manganese are required. Each small case contains 2 units, each medium case contains 2 units and each large case contains 1 unit. Thus, the manganese constraint is

$$2S + 2M + L \geq 10.$$

Similarly, the constraints on chromium and molybdenum are obtained:

$$2S + 3M + L \geq 12$$

$$S + M + 5L \geq 14.$$

Thus the problem is:

$$\text{Minimize} \qquad z = 9S + 12M + 15L \qquad (3)$$

Subject to:

$$2S + 2M + L \geq 10 \qquad (4)$$

$$2S + 3M + L \geq 12 \qquad (5)$$

$$S + M + 5L \geq 14 \qquad (6)$$

$$S \geq 0,\ M \geq 0,\ L \geq 0. \qquad (7)$$

The region common to the constraints (4)-(7) is called the feasible region. From the theory of linear programming it is known that a point at which the objective function is optimized must be on the boundary. Hence, convert the inequalities in (4)-(7) to equations. A fundamental theorem of linear programming is that if a solution exists it must be at a point of intersection of three equations. There are 6 constraints and three unknowns; hence the number of possible solutions is $\binom{6}{3}$ or 20. For example, the point (0,0,0), corresponding to the solution set of $S = M = L = 0$, is a possible solution. But since it fails to satisfy the constraints (4)-(6) it is not a feasible solution. On the other hand, the solution to $S = 0$, $2S + 2M + L = 10$ and $2S + 3M + L = 12$ is (0,2,6) which is a feasible point. Substituting into the objective function (3):

$$z = 9(0) + 12(2) + 15(6) = \$114.$$

Proceeding in this way for every triplet of equations it is found that the solution to (4)-(6) is (2,2,2). This point satisfies all the contraints, i.e., it is feasible. Substituting $S = 2$, $M = 2$ and $L = 2$ in (3):

$$z = 9(2) + 12(2) + 15(2) = \$72.$$

This is the minimum cost and is the solution to the problem. Two small cases, 2 medium cases and 2 large cases should be bought to obtain this minimum cost.

• PROBLEM 2-6

For its Sanford to Marksville short run, Sutland Airlines has first class, tourist class, and coach accommodations. Packets of three tickets each, called 3-Paks, are available at a special discount. If tickets are sold in accordance with seating capacity, because of "no shows" it often happens that flights are not made at full capacity, thus losing money for Sutland. If Sutland oversells a flight and there are not enough cancellations or "no shows" to balance the oversubscription, then some passengers are going to be inconvenienced until new arrangements are made. It has been found that passengers thus inconvenienced exhibit essentially three kinds of reaction: I. The passenger who heartily curses Sutland and then forgets all about his ordeal after new arrangements have been made; II. The passenger who becomes so angry that he never flies Sutland again; and III. The passenger whose anger is so great that he never flies Sutland again and campaigns to stop other people from flying Sutland.

The effects of these reactions have been thoroughly studied, and an annoyance scale has been developed so that these effects can be described in quantitative terms. For a given flight 15 points of reaction I (measured on the annoyance scale), 12 points of reaction II, and 9 points of reaction III can be tolerated at most. Table 1 was developed and distributed to the executives of Sutland who are involved in customer relations. From an analysis of the past earnings of Sutland Airlines, the expected profit on a 3-Pak of first class tickets is $10, the expected profit on a 3-Pak of tourist class tickets is $12, and a 3-Pak of coach tickets nets $14.

Of concern to Sutland Airlines is the question: By how many 3-Paks of each type of accommodation should a flight be oversold if the tolerance levels on the annoyance scale are not to be exceeded and the largest possible profit is to be obtained? Of course, Sutland will break up a 3-Pak when necessary. Find the constraints, and explain how the problem should be solved.

Table 1

	First Class	Tourist Class	Coach
Reaction I	1	1	5
Reaction II	2	3	1
Reaction III	2	2	1

Number of points of reaction for different classes of 3-paks as measured on the annoyance scale.

<u>Solution</u>: To find the constraints for this problem, let X be the number of oversold first class "3-Paks", let Y be the number of oversold tourist class "3-Paks", and let Z be the number of oversold coach "3-Paks".

The constraints are:

(1) $X \geq 0$ Either they overbook first class or they don't.

(2) $Y \geq 0$ Either they overbook tourist class or they don't.

(3) $Z \geq 0$ Either they overbook coach or they don't.

(4) First class has one point for Reaction I, tourist class has one point for Reaction I, and coach has 5 points for Reaction I. Since the maximum tolerable limit is 15 points for Reaction I, there is the constraint

$$X + Y + 5Z \leq 15.$$

(5) First class has 2 points for Reaction II, tourist class has three points for reaction II, and coach has one point for Reaction II. Since the maximum tolerable limit is 12 points for Reaction II, there is the constraint

$$2X + 3Y + Z \leq 12.$$

(6) First class has two points for Reaction III, tourist class has two points for Reaction III, and coach has one point for Reaction III. Since the maximum tolerable limit is 9 points for Reaction III, there is the constraint

$$2X + 2Y + Z \leq 9.$$

These constraints cannot be plotted for there are three unknown quantities and, therefore, would require a three-dimensional graph. However, it is known from a theorem of Linear Programming, that the point of maximum profit lies on the intersection of three constraints (the same number of constraints as the number of unknowns). Thus, to solve this problem break up the six constraints into all the possible groups of three constraints. Then solve each group of three equations (taken from the three contraints) for the three unknowns. Now there is a group of points. Take from that group of points those that meet the conditions set by all of the constraints. Then apply the profit formula to that set of points to obtain the point yielding the highest profit. The profit formula is

$$\text{Profit} = \$10X + \$12Y + \$14Z.$$

After following the above procedure it is found that in order to make the most profit, the company should overbook 1/3 of a first-class "3-Pak", 3 tourist class "3-Paks", 7/3 of coach "3-Paks" (1 first class ticket, 9 tourist tickets, and 7 coach tickets). This yields the maximum profit of

$$\$10(1/3) + \$12(3) + \$14(7/3) = \$10/3 + \$36 + \$98/3$$

$$= \$108/3 + \$36 = \$36 + \$36 = \$72.$$

• PROBLEM 2-7

Mazarini Butchers, Inc., is a large-scale distributor of dressed meats which specializes in the hotel market and runs a highly technological operation. Schneider Hotels, Inc. placed an order for a ground meatloaf (mixed ground beef, pork, and veal) for 1,000 pounds according to the following specifications:

a. The ground beef is to be no less than 400 pounds and not more than 600 pounds.
b. The ground pork must be between 200 and 300 pounds.
c. The ground veal must weigh between 100 and 400 pounds.
d. The weight of ground pork must be no more than one and one half times the weight of veal.

The negotiated contract provides that Scheider Hotels will pay Mazarini Butchers $1,200 for supplying the meatloaf. An analysis indicated that the cost per pound of beef, pork, and veal would be, respectively, $0.70, $0.60, and $0.80. The problem is one of maximizing contribution to overhead and profit subject to the specified constraints on flavor proportions and the demand constraint of 1,000 pounds. How can this problem be modeled? Can you suggest an easy solution?

Solution to Blending Problem

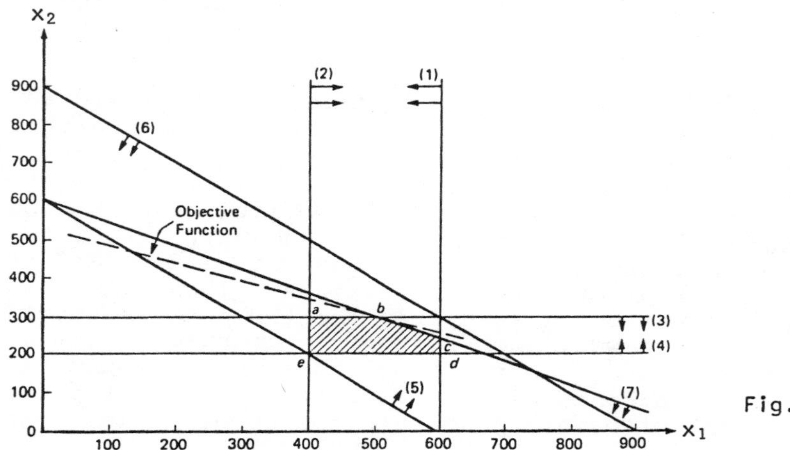

Fig. 1

<u>Solution</u>: Let

x_1 = pounds of ground beef;

x_2 = pounds of ground pork;

x_3 = pounds of ground veal.

At first, the problem appears to consist of three variables, which would make for a rather cumbersome graphical solution. The demand constraint, however, allows for the tacit elimination of any one variable, say x_3; that is

$$x_1 + x_2 + x_3 = 1{,}000$$

may be rewritten as

$$x_3 = 1{,}000 - x_1 - x_2.$$

This expression may be substituted into the objective function and constraints wherever x_3 appears. The complete problem may be stated as

maximize:

$$z = \text{Revenue} - \text{Variable costs}$$
$$= 1{,}200 - 0.70x_1 - 0.60x_2 - 0.80x_3$$
$$= 1{,}200 - 0.70x_1 - 0.60x_2 - 0.80(1{,}000 - x_1 - x_2)$$
$$= 400 + 0.10x_1 + 0.20x_2$$

subject to:

$$x_1 \leq 600$$
$$x_1 \geq 400 \quad (1)$$
$$x_2 \leq 300 \quad (2)$$
$$x_2 \geq 200 \quad (3)$$
$$x_3 \leq 400 \quad (4)$$

$$1{,}000 - x_1 - x_2 \leq 400$$
$$x_1 + x_2 \geq 600 \quad (5)$$
$$x_3 \geq 100$$
$$1{,}000 - x_1 - x_2 \geq 100$$
$$x_1 + x_2 \leq 900 \quad (6)$$
$$x_2 \leq 1.5x_3$$
$$x_2 \leq 1.5(1{,}000 - x_1 - x_2)$$
$$1.5x_1 + 2.5x_2 \leq 1{,}500 \quad (7)$$
$$x_1, x_2 \geq 0.$$

Figure 1 is a graph for the seven constraints and the objective function. Note that constraints (5) and (6) are redundant constraints. Redundant constraints are those which contribute nothing to the determination of the solution space. The solution space is given by the polygon abcde. The objective function has a slope of $-\frac{1}{2}$ and is maximized at extreme point b. The coordinates (500, 300) for point b are determined from constraints (3) and (7). The optimal solution, therefore, is to send a meatloaf mixture consisting of 500 pounds of ground beef, 300 pounds of ground pork and 200 pounds of ground veal. The contribution to overhead and profit is maximized at

$$z = 400 + 0.10(500) + 0.20(300)$$
$$= \$510.$$

A canning company operates two canning plants. Three growers are willing to supply fresh fruits in the following amounts:

Harry	200 tons at \$10/ton
Frank	300 tons at \$9/ton
Tom	400 tons at \$8/ton

Shipping costs in dollars per ton are:

	To	
From	Plant A	Plant B
Harry	2	2.5
Frank	1	1.5
Tom	5	3

Plant capacities and labor costs are:

	Plant A	Plant B
Capacity	450 tons	550 tons
Labor cost	\$25/tons	\$20/tons

The canned fruits are sold at \$50/ton to the distributors. The company can sell at this price all they can produce. How should the company plan its operations at the two plants so as to maximize its profits? Formulate as a linear program.

Table 1

	Plant A	Plant B	
HARRY	13	17.5	200
FRANK	15	19.5	300
TOM	12	19	400
DUMMY	0	0	100
	450	550	

Solution: To formulate this as a linear program, define:

x_{HA} = quantity shipped from Harry to Plant A

x_{HB} = quantity shipped from Harry to Plant B

x_{FA} = quantity shipped from Frank to Plant A

x_{FB} = quantity shipped from Frank to Plant B

x_{TA} = quantity shipped from Tom to Plant A

x_{TB} = quantity shipped from Tom to Plant B.

The supply constraints are given by:

$$x_{HA} + x_{HB} \leqq 200$$

$$x_{FA} + x_{FB} \leqq 300$$

$$x_{TA} + x_{TB} \leqq 400.$$

The constraints on plant capacities are:

$$x_{HA} + x_{FA} + x_{TA} \leqq 450$$

$$x_{HB} + x_{FB} + x_{TB} \leqq 550.$$

All the variables are restricted to be nonnegative. To compute the net profit for each of the variables, the cost of fresh fruits, shipping, and labor costs must be subtracted from the selling price. For example, the profit on variable x_{HA} (fruits bought from Harry and processed at Plant A) is given by:

$$P_{HA} = 50 - (10 + 2 + 25) = \$13/\text{ton}.$$

Similarly, the other profits can be calculated, and the objective function is to maximize:

$$Z = 13x_{HA} + 17.5x_{HB} + 15x_{FA} + 19.5x_{FB} + 12x_{TA} + 19x_{TB}$$

The above linear program is an unbalanced transportation problem where the total supply is less than the total demand. Table 1 gives the equivalent (standard) transportation formulation with the addition of a dummy grower.

• PROBLEM 2-9

An investor has \$100 with him on Monday. He has the following investment option available each day: if he invests 2 units of money on one day, and 1 unit the next day, then on the following day, he can get a return of 4 units. The investor wants to determine the optimal investment policy that will maximize the money he has on Saturday of the same week. Formulate the problem into a linear program.

Solution: Since it is not given explicitly at what time of the day the various investments are made and returns are due, assume that any returns due that day may be used for investment immediately on the same day.

On each day, the investor has the following activities:

1. Follow up yesterday's investment with an additional 50%.
2. Initiate a fresh investment that day.
3. Save or hold cash for future investments.

Note that he has no choice regarding activity 1 if he wants to get a return from the investment initiated the previous day. But, regarding 2 and 3, he has full flexibility. So, two decision variables each day are needed--one to represent fresh investment initiated that day, and the other to represent money saved that day:

x_1 = Fresh investment on Monday

s_1 = Money saved on Monday

x_2 = Fresh investment on Tuesday

s_2 = Money saved on Tuesday

x_3 = Fresh investment on Wednesday

s_3 = Money saved on Wednesday

x_4 = Fresh investment on Thursday

s_4 = Money saved on Thursday

s_5 = Money saved on Friday.

No fresh investment is started on Friday since the return from that investment will not reach the investor before Sunday.

The constraints guarantee that on each day the following relationship is true: Total money invested (follow up or fresh investment) + Money saved = Total cash available.

For Monday: $x_1 + s_1 = 100$

For Tuesday: $\frac{x_1}{2} + x_2 + s_2 = s_1$

For Wednesday: $\frac{x_2}{2} + x_3 + s_3 = s_2 + 2x_1$

For Thursday: $\frac{x_3}{2} + x_4 + s_4 = s_3 + 2x_2$

For Friday: $\frac{x_4}{2} + s_5 = s_4 + 2x_3$.

The total cash on hand on Saturday equals $s_5 + 2x_4$. Hence the objective function is to

Maximize $Z = s_5 + 2x_4$.

• PROBLEM 2-10

A machine shop has one drill press and five milling machines, which are to be used to produce an assembly consisting of two parts, 1 and 2. The productivity of each machine for the two parts is given below:

Production Time in minutes per piece

Part	Drill	Mill
1	3	20
2	5	15

It is desired to maintain a balanced loading on all machines such that no machine runs more than 30 minutes per day longer than any other machine (assume that the milling load is split evenly among all five milling machines).

Formulate a linear program to divide the work time of each machine to obtain the maximum number of completed assemblies assuming an 8-hour working day.

Solution: Let x_1 = number of Part 1 produced per day,

and

x_2 = number of Part 2 produced per day.

The load on each milling machine (in minutes) =

$$\frac{20x_1 + 15x_2}{5} = 4x_1 + 3x_2,$$

whereas the load on the drill press (in minutes) = $3x_1 + 5x_2$. Thus the time restriction on each milling machine is:

$$4x_1 + 3x_2 \leqq (8)(60) = 480.$$

Similarly, for the drill press

$$3x_1 + 5x_2 \leqq 480.$$

The machine balance constraint can be represented by

$$|(4x_1 + 3x_2) - (3x_1 + 5x_2)| \leqq 30$$

or

$$|x_1 - 2x_2| \leqq 30.$$

This is a nonlinear constraint which can be replaced by the following two linear constraints:

$$x_1 - 2x_2 \leq 30$$

$$-x_1 + 2x_2 \leq 30.$$

The number of completed assemblies cannot exceed the smaller value of Part 1 and Part 2 produced. Thus, the objective function is to maximize Z = minimum (x_1, x_2). This is again a nonlinear function. However, another trick can be used to represent it as a linear function. Let y = minimum of (x_1, x_2) where y represents the number of completed assemblies.

This means that:

$$x_1 \geq y$$
$$x_2 \geq y$$

and the objective is to maximize Z = y. Thus, the complete linear programming formulation becomes:

$$\begin{aligned}
\text{Maximize: } & Z = y \\
\text{Subject to: } & 4x_1 + 3x_2 \leq 480 \\
& 3x_1 + 5x_2 \leq 480 \\
& x_1 - 2x_2 \leq 30 \\
& -x_1 + 2x_2 \leq 30 \\
& x_1 - y \geq 0 \\
& x_2 - y \geq 0 \\
& x_1 \geq 0, \quad x_2 \geq 0, \quad y \geq 0.
\end{aligned}$$

• PROBLEM 2-11

Consider the scaffold system shown in figure 1. Wires 1 and 2 can hold up 300 lb each, but wires 3 and 4 can support only 100 lb. each, and wires 5 and 6 are capable of supporting no more than 50 lb each. Neglecting the weight of the beams and wires and assuming that weights are placed only at the position shown, formulate a linear program to find the greatest total weight $y_1 + y_2 + y_3$ that can be supported.

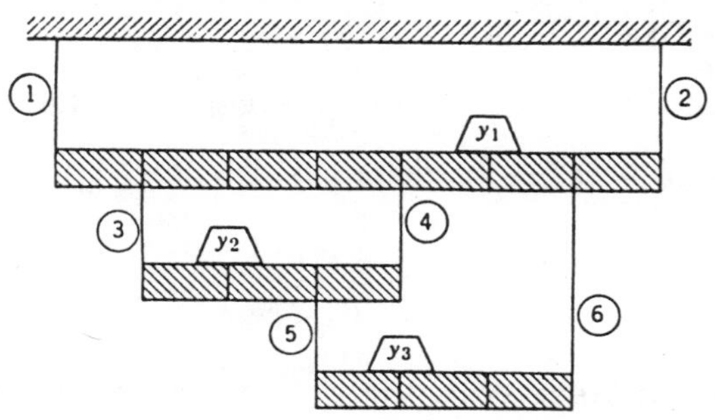

Scaffold system. Fig. 1

Solution: Using a force balance equation and a torque balance equation for each beam, find the force F_i exerted by wire i as a function of the weights y_1, y_2, and y_3. These forces turn out to be:

$$F_1 = \frac{2}{7} y_1 + \frac{5}{7} y_2 + \frac{3}{7} y_3,$$

$$F_2 = \frac{5}{7} y_1 + \frac{2}{7} y_2 + \frac{4}{7} y_3,$$

$$F_3 = \frac{2}{3} y_2 + \frac{2}{9} y_3,$$

$$F_4 = \frac{1}{3} y_2 + \frac{4}{9} y_3,$$

$$F_5 = \frac{2}{3} y_3,$$

$$F_6 = \frac{1}{3} y_3.$$

Hence the problem consists of maximizing the linear function:

$$W = y_1 + y_2 + y_3$$

subject to the linear constraints:

$$\frac{2}{7} y_1 + \frac{5}{7} y_2 + \frac{3}{7} y_3 \le 300,$$

$$\frac{5}{7} y_1 + \frac{2}{7} y_2 + \frac{4}{7} y_3 \le 300,$$

$$\frac{2}{3} y_2 + \frac{2}{9} y_3 \le 100,$$

$$\frac{1}{3} y_2 + \frac{4}{9} y_3 \le 100,$$

$$\frac{2}{3} y_3 \le 50,$$

$$\frac{1}{3} y_3 \le 50.$$

Application of the simplex method gives the solution:

$y_1 = 360$ lb, $y_2 = 150$ lb, $y_3 = 0$ lb, $W = 510$ lb.

Consider a simplified aviation gasoline blending problem faced by an oil company. This company sells two grades of aviation gasolines: low grade L and high grade H. These gasolines are blended from four different blending stocks produced in the refinery: alkylate, catalytic cracked gasoline, straight-run gasoline, and isopentane. Any excess of blending stocks from the aviation gasoline blending process is used as input into the motor gasoline blending process. The latter process is not considered an integral part of this problem, but only enters into it insofar as it absorbs any excess blending stocks. This approximation can be justified by the fact that these unused blending stocks constitute only a small fraction of the total input into the motor gasoline blending process. This situation is depicted in the flow diagram in Fig. 1.

Each grade of aviation gasoline has certain specifications as to the maximum permissible vapor pressure (VP) and the minimum required octane number (ON). For each aviation gasoline there exists a certain daily demand that must be met exactly. No specifications for motor gasolines are stated, since this blending process is not part of the problem. Furthermore, since the total demand for motor gasolines is very large compared to the total volume of excess blending stocks from the aviation gasoline blending process, it can be assumed that it is unlimited. Table 1 lists the specifications for VP and ON, as well as the daily demands for the two grades of aviation gasoline, and the sales revenue per barrel. Each blending stock exhibits an average value for vapor pressure and octane number. The octane number of a gasoline can be improved by adding small quantities of tetraethyl-lead (TEL). Unfortunately, the increase in the octane number is not proportional to the amount of TEL added. In order to get around this problem of nonlinearity assume that aviation gasoline L is leaded at a TEL level of 1.2 ml/gal., whereas aviation gasoline H is leaded at a TEL level of 4 ml/gal. Table 2 lists properties of VP and ON at 1.2 and 4.ml/gal. for each blending stock, as well as their availability in barrels per day and their cost per barrel exclusive of TEL.

Given the properties, availabilities, and costs of each blending stock, the blending problem is to detèrmine how much of each blending stock to allocate to each aviation gasoline, so that the demand for each gasoline is met exactly and their specifications for VP and ON are satisfied. Assuming that the objective is to maximize profits, the optimal allocation is the one that maximizes the difference between net revenue and total cost. Formulate this problem as a linear program.

Solution: First define the decision variables. The blending problem consists of allocating blending stocks to finished products. The decision variables will, therefore, be the number in barrels per day of each blending stock allocated to each aviation gasoline. Table 3 lists the variables used, where columns refer to inputs and rows refer to outputs.

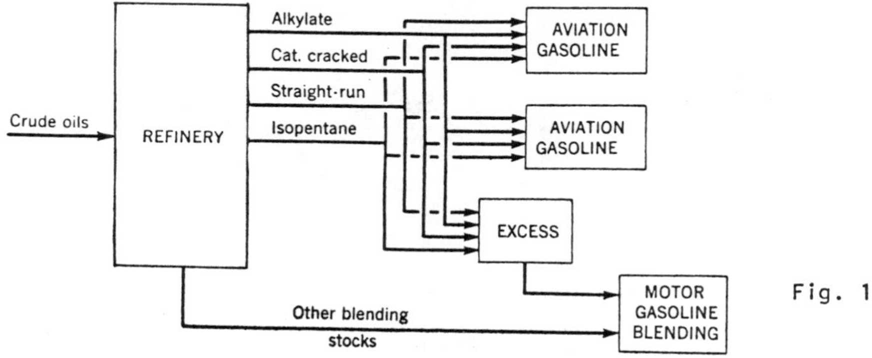

Fig. 1

There are three types of constraints: blending stock availability, product demand, and product specification constraints.

Blending stock availability constraints: Take any blending stock. There is a certain number of barrels available per day. Hence the number of barrels that go into aviation gasoline L and H cannot exceed this availability. This yields the following four constraints:

$$\text{ALL} + \text{ALH} \leq 700 \tag{1}$$

$$\text{CCL} + \text{CCH} \leq 600 \tag{2}$$

$$\text{SRL} + \text{SRH} \leq 900 \tag{3}$$

$$\text{ISL} + \text{ISH} \leq 500\ . \tag{4}$$

Product demand constraints: Remember that the gasoline demands have to be met exactly. Each gasoline can be blended from four different stocks. The sum of the amounts coming from each of these four stocks has to be equal to a given number of barrels per day. This yields the following two equality constraints:

$$\text{ALL} + \text{CCL} + \text{SRL} + \text{ISL} = 1{,}300 \tag{5}$$

$$\text{ALH} + \text{CCH} + \text{SRH} + \text{ISH} = 800\ . \tag{6}$$

Product specification constraints: Assume that the properties of the blended gasolines are approximately given by the volumetric average of the properties of the blending stocks used. Applying this rule to the VP property of gasoline A, the average VP is equal to the following ratio:

$$\frac{5\ \text{ALL} + 6.5\ \text{CCL} + 4\ \text{SRL} + 18\ \text{ISL}}{\text{ALL} + \text{CCL} + \text{SRL} + \text{ISL}}$$

It is required that this ratio not exceed the value 7. Hence, there is the following constraint:

$$\frac{5\ ALL + 6.5\ CCL + 4\ SRL + 18\ ISL}{ALL + CCL + SRL + ISL} \leq 7\ .$$

This constraint is not in a form that is acceptable for linear programming. However, by multiplying both sides of the inequality through by the denominator of this ratio, it changes into a form that is already much closer to what is desired:

$$5\ ALL + 6.5\ CCL + 4\ SRL + 18\ ISL \leq$$
$$7(ALL + CCL + SRL + ISL)\ .$$

By bringing all variables to the left-hand side of the inequality the desired LP constraint for the VP property of gasoline is obtained:

$$-2\ ALL - 0.5\ CCL - 3\ SRL + 11\ ISL \leq 0. \qquad (7)$$

Similarly, for the VP property of aviation gasoline H:

$$-2\ ALH - 0.5\ CCH - 3\ SRH + 11\ ISH \leq 0. \qquad (8)$$

Take now the ON specifications. Assuming again that the average ON property of gasoline L is given by the volumetric average of the ON properties of the blending stocks used, and given that this average has to be at least equal to 90 ON, the following constraint is obtained:

$$\frac{98\ ALL + 87\ CCL + 80\ SRL + 100\ ISL}{ALL + CCL + SRL + ISL} \geq 90$$

Multiplying both sides of this inequality through by the denominator of the left-hand side, and rearranging the resulting inequality into the desired LP form, the ON constraint for gasoline L becomes:

$$8\ ALL - 3\ CCL - 10\ SRL + 10\ ISL \geq 0. \qquad (9)$$

Similarly, for the ON property of aviation gasoline H:

$$8\ ALH - 6\ CCH - 13\ SRH + 8\ ISH \geq 0. \qquad (10)$$

With the exception of the non-negativity conditions, all constraints on the decision variables are thus formulated.

Now formulate the objective function. The concern is with only the aviation gasoline blending process and for this reason, all other operations of the firm are ignored. Thus, the motor gasoline blending process will be ignored in terms of its ramification on the firm's profits. The total profit derived from the aviation gasoline blending process is given by the difference between the sales revenue and the cost of the blending stocks used. Total sales revenue is equal to the number of barrels sold of each type of aviation gasoline, multiplied by the corresponding sales price per barrel and the summed over both types of gasolines. The amounts of gasoline L and H sold are given by constraints (5) and (6) as 1,300 and 800 bbl./day, respectively. Total sales revenue is thus equal to the following constant:

$$6.5(1{,}300) + 7.5(800) = 14{,}450. \qquad (11)$$

The total cost of the blending stocks used is equal to the product of the amount of each blending stock allocated to each aviation gasoline and the corresponding cost per barrel, summed over all allocations:

$$7.2(ALL + ALH) + 4.35(CCL + CCH) + 3.8(SRL + SRH)$$
$$+ 4.3(ISL + ISH). \qquad (12)$$

Subtracting (11) from (12), the following objective function is obtained:

$$14{,}450 - 7.2(ALL + ALH) - 4.35(CCL + CCH)$$
$$- 3.8(SRL + SRH) - 4.3(ISL + ISH). \qquad (13)$$

It is desired to maximize expression (13). Note that the constant term in (13) is immaterial as far as determining the optimal values of the decision variables is concerned, since they will be the same if the constant term is ignored so simply maximize the remaining variable terms. Let the sum of the variable terms be denoted by (-z). Hence the new objective function becomes:

$$-z = -7.2(ALL + ALH) - 4.35(CCL + CCH)$$
$$- 3.8(SRL + SRH) - 4.3(ISL + ISH) \qquad (14)$$

which is to be maximized. The maximization of expression (14) is equivalent to the minimization of the negative of the same expression. Given that the total sales revenue produced is a constant, profit maximization is equivalent to cost minimization. The final objective function to be minimized reads thus:

$$\min z = 7.2\ ALL + 7.2\ ALH + 4.35\ CCL + 4.35\ CCH + 3.8\ SRL + 3.8\ SRH + 4.3\ ISL + 4.3\ ISH \qquad (15)$$

which completes the formulation.

Product	VP	ON	Demand in Bbl./Day	Sales Revenue ($/Bbl.)
Aviation gasoline L	7	90	1,300	6.50
Aviation gasoline H	7	100	800	7.50
Motor gasoline	-	-	unlimited	-

Table 1

Blending Stock	VP	ON at 1.2	ON at 4	Supply in Bbl./Day	Cost $/Bbl.
Alkylate	5	98	108	700	7.20
Catalytic cracked	6.5	87	94	600	4.35
Straight-run	4	80	87	900	3.80
Isopentane	18	100	108	500	4.30

Table 2

	Inputs			
Outputs	Alkylate	Cat. Cracked Gasoline	Straight-Run Gasoline	Isopentane
Aviation Gas. L	ALL	CCL	SRL	ISL
Aviation Gas. H	ALH	CCH	SRH	ISH

Table 3

• PROBLEM 2-13

A quantity y is known to depend upon another quantity x. A set of corresponding values has been collected for x and y and are presented in the accompanying table. Construct mathematical programming models that would

(1) fit the 'best' straight line $y = bx + a$ to this set of data points. The objective is to minimize the sum of absolute deviations of each observed value of y from the value predicted by the linear relationship;

(2) fit the 'best' straight line where the objective is to minimize the maximum deviation of all the observed values of y from the value predicted by the linear relationship;

(3) fit the 'best' quadratic curve $y = cx^2 + bx + a$ to this set of data points using the same objectives as in (1) and (2).

TABLE

x	0.0	0.5	1.0	1.5	1.9	2.5	3.0	3.5	4.0	4.5	5.0	5.5	6.0	6.6
y	1.0	0.9	0.7	1.5	2.0	2.4	3.2	2.0	2.7	3.5	1.0	4.0	3.6	2.7

x	7.0	7.6	8.5	9.0	10.0
y	5.7	4.6	6.0	6.8	7.3

Solution: This is an application of the goal programming type of formulation. Each pair of corresponding data values (x_i, y_i) gives rise to a constraint. For (1) and (2) these constraints are:

$$bx_i + a + u_i - v_i = y_i \qquad i = 1, 2, \ldots, 19$$

x_i and y_i are constants (the given values) b, a, u_i, and v_i are variables. u_i and v_i give the amounts by which the values of y_i proposed by the linear expression differs from that observed. It is important to allow a and b to be 'free' variables, i.e. they can be allowed to take negative as well as positive values.

In case (1) the objective is to minimize

$$\sum_i u_i + \sum_i v_i$$

This model has 19 constraints and 40 variables.

In case (2) it is necessary to introduce another variable z together with 38 more constraints:

$$z - u_i \geq 0$$

$$z - v_i \geq 0 \quad i = 1, 2, . . ., 19$$

The objective, in this case, is simply to minimize z. This minimum value of z will clearly be exactly equal to the maximum value of v_i and u_i.

In case (3) it is necessary to introduce a new (free) variable c into the first set of constraints to give:

$$cx_i^2 + bx_i + a + u_i - v_i = y_i \quad i = 1, 2, . . ., 19$$

The same objective functions as in (1) and (2) will apply.

It is much more usual in statistical problems to minimize the sum of squares of the deviations as the resultant curve often has desirable statistical properties. There are, however, some circumstances in which a sum of absolute deviations is acceptable or even more desirable. Moreover, the possibility of solving this type of problem by linear programming makes it computationally easy to deal with large quantities of data.

Minimizing the maximum deviation has certain attractions from the point of view of presentation. The possibility of a single data point appearing a long way off the fitted curve is minimized.

Computer solutions of the models are as follows:

(1) The 'best' straight line which minimizes the sum of absolute deviations is:

$$y = 0.6375x + 0.5812$$

This is line 1 shown in Figure 1. The sum of absolute deviations resulting from this line is 11.46.

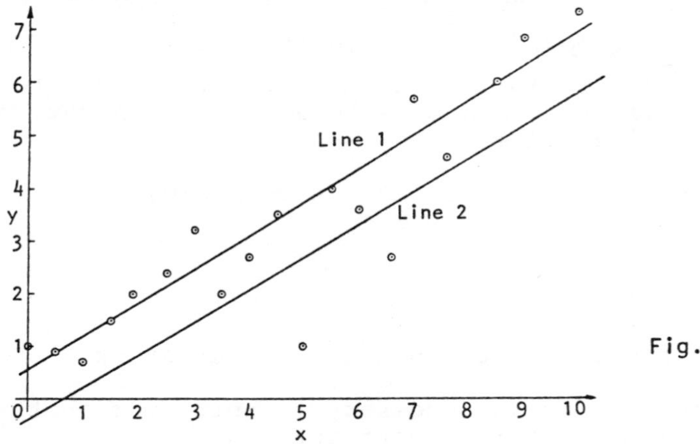

Fig. 1

(2) The 'best' straight line which minimizes the maximum absolute deviation is:

$$y = 0.625x - 0.4.$$

This is line 2 shown in Figure 1. The maximum absolute deviation resulting from this line is 1.725 (points (3.0, 3.2), (5.0, 1.0), and (7.0, 5.7) all have this absolute deviation from the line.)

In contrast line 1 allows point (5.0, 1.0) to have an absolute deviation of 2.77. On the other hand although line 2 allows no point to have an absolute deviation of more than 1.725 the sum of absolute deviations is 19.95 compared with the 11.46 resulting from line 1.

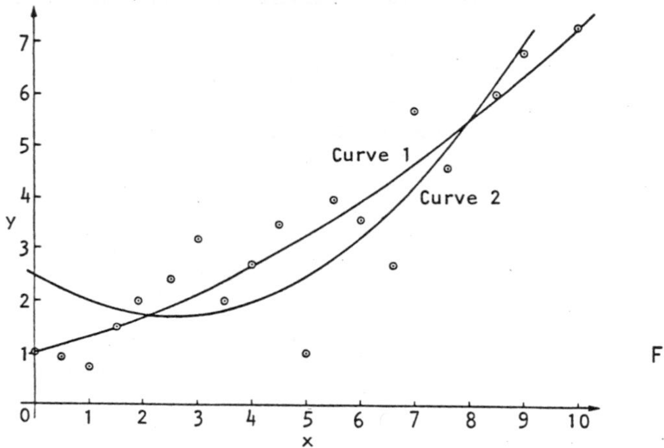

Fig. 2

(3) The 'best' quadratic curve which minimizes the sum of absolute deviations is:

$$y = 0.0337x^2 + 0.2945x + 0.9823$$

This is the curve 1 shown in Figure 2. The sum of absolute deviations resulting from this curve is 10.45.

The 'best' quadratic curve which minimizes the maximum absolute deviation is:

$$y = 0.125x^2 - 0.625x + 2.475$$

This is the curve 2 shown in Figure 2. The maximum absolute deviation resulting from this curve is 1.475 (points (0.0, 1.1) and (5.0, 1.0) both have this absolute deviation from the curve.)

• **PROBLEM 2-14**

In an integer programming problem the following constraint occurs:

$$9x_1 + 13x_2 - 14x_3 + 17x_4 + 13x_5 - 19x_6 + 23x_7 + 21x_8 \leq 37$$

All variables occuring in this constraint are 0-1 variables, i.e., they can only take the value of 0 or 1.

Construct a mathematical model to find the 'simplest' version of this constraint. The objective is to set up a model that would find another constraint involving these variables which is logically equivalent to the original constraint but which has the smallest possible absolute value of the right-hand side (with all coefficients of similar signs to the original coefficients).

If the objective were to find an equivalent constraint where the sum of the absolute values of the coefficients (apart from the right-hand side coefficient) were a minimum what would be the result?

Solution: A procedure for simplifying a single 0-1 constraint is, using a linear programming model. It is convenient to consider the constraint in a standard form with positive coefficients in descending order of magnitude. This can be achieved by the transformation:

$$y_1 = x_7, \quad y_2 = x_8, \quad y = 1 - x_6, \quad y_4 = x_4,$$

$$y_5 = 1 - x_3, \quad y_6 = x_5, \quad y_7 = x_2, \quad y_8 = x_1$$

giving:

$$23y_1 + 21y_2 + 19y_3 + 17y_4 + 14y_5 + 13y_6 + 13y_7 + 9y_8 \leq 70.$$

One wishes to find another, equivalent constraint of the form:

$$a_1y_1 + a_2y_2 + a_3y_3 + a_4y_4 + a_5y_5 + a_6y_6 + a_7y_7 + a_8y_8 \leq a_0.$$

The a_i coefficients become variables in the linear programming model. In order to capture the total logical import of the original constraint search for subsets of the indices known as 'roofs' and 'ceilings'. 'Ceilings' are 'maximal' subsets of the indices of the variables for which the sum of the corresponding coefficients does not exceed the right-hand side coefficient. Such a subset is maximal in the sense that no subset properly containing it, or to the left in the implied lexicographical ordering can also be a ceiling. For example, the subset {1,2,4,8} is a ceiling, $23 + 21 + 17 + 9 \leq 70$ but any subset properly containing it (e.g., {1,2,4,7,8}) or to the 'left' of it (e.g., {1,2,4,7}) is not a ceiling. 'Roofs' are 'minimal' subsets of the indices for which the sum of the corresponding coefficients exceeds the right-hand side coefficient. Such a subset is 'minimal' in the same sense as a subset is 'maximal'. For example, {2,3,4,5} is a roof. 21 + 19 + 17 + 14 > 70 but any subset properly contained in it, (e.g., {3,4,5}) or to the 'right' of it (e.g., {2,3,4,6}) is not a roof.

If $\{i_1, i_2, \ldots, i_r\}$ is a 'ceiling' the following condition among the new coefficients a_i is implied:

$$a_{i_1} + a_{i_2} + \ldots a_{ir} \leq a_0$$

If $\{i_1, i_2, \ldots, i_r\}$ is a 'roof' the following condition among the new coefficients a_i is implied:

$$a_{i_1} + a_{i_2} + \ldots a_{ir} \geq a_0 + 1 .$$

It is also necessary to guarantee the ordering of the coefficients. This can be done by the series of constraints:

$$a_1 \geq a_2 \geq a_3 \geq \ldots \geq a_8 .$$

If these constraints are given together with each constraint corresponding to a roof or ceiling then this is a sufficient set of conditions to guarantee that the new 0-1 constraint has exactly the same set of feasible 0-1 solutions as the original 0-1 constraint.

In order to pursue the first objective minimize $a_0 - a_3 - a_5$ subject to these constraints.

For the second objective minimize $\sum_{i=1}^{8} ai$

For this example the set of ceilings is:

{1,2,3}, {1,2,4,8}, {1,2,6,7}, {1,3,5,6} ,

{2,3,4,6}, {2,5,6,7,8}.

The set of roofs is:

{1,2,3,8}, {1,2,5,7}, {1,3,4,7}, {1,5,6,7,8},

{2,3,4,5}, {3,4,6,7,8}.

The resultant model has 19 constraints and 9 variables.

The computer gives the 'simplest' version of this constraint (with minimum right-hand side coefficient) as:

$$6x_1 + 9x_2 - 10x_3 + 12x_4 + 9x_5 - 13x_6 + 16x_7 + 14x_8$$

$$\leq 25 .$$

This is also the equivalent constraint with the minimum sum of absolute values of the coefficients.

• PROBLEM 2-15

Consider a reduced economy which has only three industries: I, II, and a third which consists of all others. With the aid of an input-output table, the interrelationships of these industries to one another and to other sectors of the economy can be analyzed. See Table 1. To read the table, note that each row details how the output of each industry is used, while the columns denote the inputs required by each industry. Thus, reading across the row for industry I, notice that I's output was used as follows: \$10 billion by I, \$15 billion by II, \$25 billion by other, and \$15 billion by final demand. Reading down the column for II, notice that industry II used \$15 billion of input from I, \$4 billion of input from II, and \$8 billion of input from other. The final demand category includes exports, government purchases, inventory accumulation, and payments to households. (Because this sector is outside the production economy in the sense that final products are "exported" to the inhabitants of the final demand sector, the model is said to be open. Variations in which labor is treated as a produced commodity, i.e., included in the set of producing industries, are said to be closed.) The total output column is simply the sum across each row of the outputs. (Note: The total output column can be summed to generate the total gross output for the economy.) However, this is not the same as gross national product (GNP) because the input-output table includes all transactions in the economy, so that some double counting may occur. On the other hand, GNP is computed so that double counting is eliminated.

Table 1. Input-output table

	Inputs				
Outputs	I	II	Other	Final Demand	Total Output
I	10†	15	25	15	65
II	5	4	18	23	50
Other	22	8	77	18	125

†All figures are in billions of dollars.

Using Table 1, set up a table of input-output coefficients which gives the amount of inputs required from each industry to generate one dollar's worth of the output of that industry. Then, assuming the input-output coefficients are constant in time, given a projected set of final demands (alias, bill of goods), determine the level of production in each industry which can satisfy these demands.

Assuming labor as a produced commodity to be the only primary factor used in this economy (i.e., all other factors are produced by the economy), let a_{0j} units of labor be required to produce 1 unit of output from industry j. Set up a simple linear programming problem out of the "Leontief model", which would minimize the labor required to produce the bill of goods $\vec{y} = (15,23,18)$. Let the labor requirements be 10, 7.5, and 15 units, respectively to produce 1 unit of output in industries I, II and other. What is the labor required to produce the given bill of goods?

Solution: The input-output coefficients can be computed as follows. Let the elements of an input-output table be denoted by:

t_{ij} = output (dollars) of industry i used by industry j; i,j = 1,...,m

t_i = total output of industry i.

Thus t_{11} = \$10 billion is the output of industry I used by industry I and t_{32} = \$8 billion is the output of industry III (other) used by industry II.

Now, let the input-output coefficients be denoted by:

a_{ij} = number of dollars' worth of industry i's output required by industry j to produce one dollar's worth of output; i,j = 1,...,m .

It is known that t_j is the total output of industry j, so that inputs of $t_{1j} + t_{2j} + \dots + t_{mj}$ are required to produce the output of industry j. (In other words, read Table 1 down the columns.) Normalize these outputs by dividing by t_j, which would then tell how much input from each industry is required to produce one dollar's worth of output from industry j. But these quantities are defined as the coefficients a_{ij}. Hence:

$$a_{ij} = \frac{t_{ij}}{t_j}$$

for $i = 1, \ldots, m$.

The coefficients for the three industry economy are given in Table 2. As with Table 1, this table should be read down the columns. For example,

a_{11} = amount of industry I input to produce \$1 of industry I output

$$= \frac{\$10 \text{ billion}}{\$65 \text{ billion}} = \$0.154$$

(Note: Some industries must use some of their own output; for example, the steel industry requires steel to make plants and buildings, etc.)

a_{21} = amount of industry II input to produce \$1 of industry I output

$$= \frac{\$5 \text{ billion}}{\$65 \text{ billion}} = \$0.077$$

a_{31} = amount of industry III (other) input to produce \$1 of industry I output

$$= \frac{\$22 \text{ billion}}{\$65 \text{ billion}} = \$0.338 \ .$$

Thus, the total input from all industries required to produce one dollar's worth of industry I output is \$0.154 + \$0.077 + \$0.338 = \$0.569.

Table 2. Input-output coefficient table (dollars)

	Purchasing industry		
	I	II	Other
Producing industry			
I	0.154	0.300	0.200
II	0.077	0.080	0.144
Other	0.338	0.160	0.616

Since the input-output coefficients are constant, there will be no significant change in time. Then given a projected set of final demands (bill of goods), determine the production in each industry which can accomplish these demands. Let:

x_i = output from industry $i, i = 1,\ldots,m$

y_i = final demand for each industry's output, $i = 1,\ldots,m$.

Now, for the reduced economy, it must be true that:

$$x_1 = y_1 + a_{11} x_1 + a_{12} x_2 + a_{13} x_3$$

$$x_2 = y_2 + a_{21} x_1 + a_{22} x_2 + a_{23} x_3$$

$$x_3 = y_3 + a_{31} x_1 + a_{32} x_2 + a_{33} x_3 .$$

These equations state that the output from any given industry (x_i) must go either to final demand (y_i) or as inputs to the three industries to be used to manufacture their outputs ($a_{i1}x_1 + a_{i2}x_2 + a_{i3}x_3$). The system of equations can be written in vector notation as:

$$\vec{x} = \vec{y} + A\vec{x}$$

or

$$(I - A)\vec{x} = \vec{y}$$

where

$$\vec{y} = \begin{bmatrix} y_1 \\ y_2 \\ y_3 \end{bmatrix}$$

$$A = \left[a_{ij} \right]$$

$$\vec{x} = \begin{bmatrix} x_1 \\ x_2 \\ x_3 \end{bmatrix}$$

The matrix I - A is known as a Leontief matrix. Thus, the question of what outputs are required to produce a given bill of goods becomes:

Find $\vec{x} \geq \vec{0}$

such that $(I - A)\vec{x} = \vec{y}$.

Now, for an open model, it can be shown that $a_{ij} \geq 0$ and also $\Sigma_{i=1}^{m} a_{ij} < 1$ for $j = 1,2,\ldots,m$. Moreover, it can be shown that if a matrix $B = [b_{ij}]$ satisfies the condition

$$\sum_{i=1}^{m} |b_{ij}| < 1 \qquad \text{for} \qquad j = 1,\ldots,m$$

then I-B is nonsingular. This condition is obviously satisfied by A, so I-A is nonsingular. Hence it is true that:

$$\vec{x} = (I-A)^{-1} \vec{y} .$$

For the reduced economy:

$$(I-A)^{-1} = \begin{bmatrix} I.727 & 0.77 & 1.186 \\ 0.409 & 1.345 & 0.715 \\ 1.696 & 1.241 & 3.953 \end{bmatrix}.$$

This matrix has some interesting economic interpretations. First, it can be shown that if for a matrix B:

$$\lim_{n\to\infty} B^n = 0$$

then

$$(I-B)^{-1} = \sum_{n=1}^{\infty} B^n = 1 + B + B^2 + \ldots$$

But it is known that

$$\sum_{i=1}^{m} a_{ij} < 1 \text{ for } j = 1,\ldots m.$$

This is sufficient to ensure that

$$\lim_{n\to\infty} A^n = 0.$$

Hence, it must be true that

$$(I-A)^{-1} = I + A + A^2 + \ldots$$

This implies that

$$\vec{x} = (I-A)^{-1}\,\vec{y} = I\vec{y} + A\vec{y} + A^2\vec{y} + \ldots$$

The interpretation is as follows. To produce the bill of goods $\vec{y}$, total production must consist of $\vec{y}$ itself plus an additional amount $A\vec{y}$ to be used as inputs by the industries. To produce $A\vec{y}$, however, requires the production of the additional amount $A(A\vec{y}) = A^2\vec{y}$, and so on. Hence, the 1.727 in the first position of $(I-A)^{-1}$ indicates that for each dollar's worth of industry I products delivered to the final demand sector, total intraindustry transactions will be an additional 72.7 cents (because when I produces, it requires input from II, which requires input from I, and so forth). Also, to provide that extra dollar's worth of output by I, II's output will increase by 77 cents and other's output will increase by $1.186.

The series expansion also shows that every element of $(I-A)^{-1}$ is nonnegative (because the original a_{ij} are nonnegative). Thus, for every $\vec{y} \geq \vec{0}$, the resulting $\vec{x}$ is producible if one assumes unlimited resources.

Often it is assumed that labor is the only primary factor used in an economy described by a Leontief model: i.e., all other productive factors are produced by the economy. Note that to produce 1 unit of output from industry j, some a_{0j} units of labor is required. Then given a total output $\vec{x}$, the labor required is $\vec{a}_0\vec{x}$, where $\vec{a}_0 = (a_{01}, a_{02}, \ldots, a_{0m})$. Since

$$\vec{x} = (I-A)^{-1}\,\vec{y}$$

the labor requirement becomes

$$\vec{a}_0(I-A)^{-1}\,\vec{y}\ .$$

If labor is a scarce resource, with a limit of (say) l, then a bill of goods is producible only if

$$\vec{a}_0(I-A)^{-1}\,\vec{y} \leq l$$

Putting the Leontief model as a simple linear programming problem: it is desired to minimize the labor required to produce the bill of goods $\vec{y}$ (or more than $\vec{y}$). In symbols:

Minimize $\qquad f = \vec{a}_0 \vec{x}$

subject to $\qquad (I-A)\vec{x} \geq \vec{y}$

$$\vec{x} \geq \vec{0} \ .$$

The solution is:

$$\vec{x} = (I-A)^{-1} y$$

with

$$f = \vec{a}_0 (I-A)^{-1} \vec{y} \ .$$

Consider the reduced economy with $(I-A)^{-1}$. Given the bill of goods $\vec{y} = (15,23,18)$, the production required to produce this bill of goods must be given by:

$$\vec{x} = (I-A)^{-1} \vec{y}$$

$$= \begin{bmatrix} 1.727 & 0.77 & 1.186 \\ 0.409 & 1.345 & 0.715 \\ 1.696 & 1.241 & 3.953 \end{bmatrix} \times \begin{bmatrix} 15 \\ 23 \\ 18 \end{bmatrix}$$

or $\quad \vec{x} = \begin{bmatrix} 64.96 \\ 49.94 \\ 125.14 \end{bmatrix} \simeq \begin{bmatrix} 65 \\ 50 \\ 125 \end{bmatrix}.$

The labor requirements are 10, 7.5, and 15 units, to produce 1 unit of output in industries I, II, and other. Then the labor required to produce the given bill of goods is $\vec{a}_0\vec{x}$, or:

$$[10 \quad 7.5 \quad 15] \begin{bmatrix} 65 \\ 50 \\ 125 \end{bmatrix} = 2900 \text{ units of labor.}$$

It is also possible to extend Leontief models to the dynamic case (as opposed to the static model studied). In this case, capital stocks are allowed to change.

CONVEXITY

• PROBLEM 2-16

Show algebraically that $S = \{(x_1, x_2) \in R^2 | x_1 + x_2 \geq 2\}$ is convex.

Solution: If S is convex, then all points on the line that connect any two points in S are also in S.

S is convex, a fact obvious from a graph of S. To prove this algebraically, take any two points $P = (p_1, p_2)$ and $Q = (q_1, q_2)$ in S. Then $p_1 + p_2 \geq 2$ and $q_1 + q_2 \geq 2$. Take any point:

$$tP + (1 - t)Q = [tp_1 + (1 - t)q_1, tp_2 + (1 - t)q_2],$$

$$0 \leq t \leq 1$$

on the line segment between P and Q. Then,

$$tp_1 + (1 - t)q_1 + tp_2 + (1 - t)q_2$$

$$= t(p_1 + p_2) + (1 - t)(q_1 + q_2)$$

$$\geq 2t + 2(1 - t) = 2$$

using the fact that t and 1 - t are nonnegative. Thus $tP + (1 - t)Q$ is in S and, therefore, this is an algebraic proof that S is convex.

• PROBLEM 2-17

Find the extreme points of the polyhedral convex set $Ax \leq b$ where:

$$A = \begin{pmatrix} -2 & -1 \\ 1 & -3 \\ 1 & 2 \end{pmatrix}, \quad b = \begin{pmatrix} 9 \\ 6 \\ 3 \end{pmatrix}$$

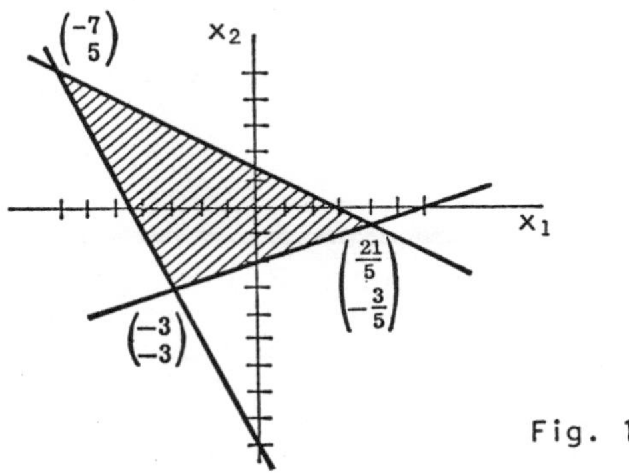

Fig. 1

Solution: A sketch of the three half planes, Figure 1, shows that the set is a triangle.

Find the extreme points by changing the inequalities to equalities in pairs and solving three sets of simultaneous equations. Obtain in this way the points:

$$\begin{pmatrix} -3 \\ -3 \end{pmatrix}, \quad \begin{pmatrix} -7 \\ 5 \end{pmatrix},$$

and

$$\begin{pmatrix} \frac{21}{5} \\ -\frac{3}{5} \end{pmatrix},$$

which are the extreme points of the set.

• PROBLEM 2-18

Is the function f(x) = 7x + 4 convex or concave?

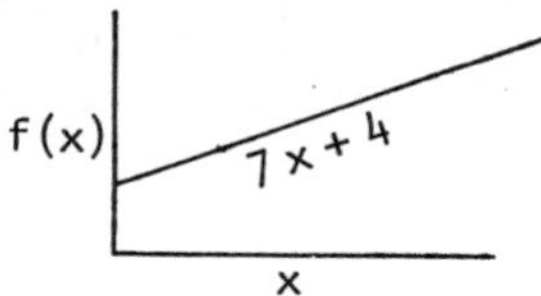

Solution:

$$\frac{df}{dx} = +7$$

$$\frac{d^2f}{dx^2} = 0$$

Since $\frac{d^2f}{dx^2} = 0$, the function is both convex and concave.

• PROBLEM 2-19

The feasible region of a LP model is convex. There are circumstances, however, in non-linear programming problems where it is desired to have a non-convex feasible region. Consider the feasible region ABCDEFGO of Figure 1. This is a non-convex region bounded by a series of straight lines. Such a region may have arisen through the problem considered or represent a piecewise linear approximation to a non-convex region bounded by curves.

Form a set of constraints that would depict the region in Figure 1 as a feasible and operable convex region for an LP problem.

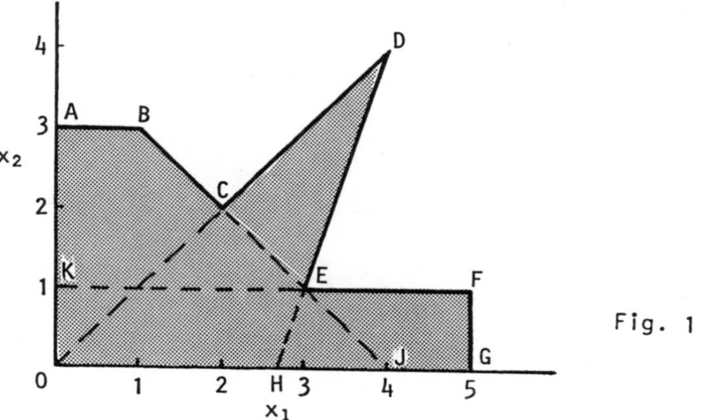

Fig. 1

Solution: Think of the region ABCDEFGO as made up of the union of the three convex regions ABJO, ODH and KFGO as shown in Figure 1. The fact that these regions overlap will not matter.

Region ABJO is defined by the constraints:

$$\begin{aligned} x_2 &\le 3 \\ x_1 + x_2 &\le 4. \end{aligned} \tag{1}$$

Region ODH is defined by the constraints:

$$\begin{aligned} -x_1 + x_2 &\le 0 \\ 3x_1 - x_2 &\le 8. \end{aligned} \tag{2}$$

Region KFGO is defined by the constraints:

$$\begin{aligned} x_2 &\le 1 \\ x_1 &\le 5. \end{aligned} \tag{3}$$

Introduce indicator variables δ_1, δ_2, and δ_3 to use in the following conditions:

$$\delta_1 = 1 \rightarrow (x_2 \le 3)\cdot(x_1 + x_2 \le 4) \tag{4}$$

$$\delta_2 = 1 \rightarrow (-x_1 + x_2 \leq 0) \cdot (3x_1 - x_2 \leq 8) \quad (5)$$

$$\delta_3 = 1 \rightarrow (x_2 \leq 1) \; (x_1 \leq 5) \quad (6)$$

(4), (5) and (6) are respectively imposed by the following constraints:

$$x_2 + \delta_1 \leq 4$$

$$x_1 + x_2 + 5\delta_1 \leq 9$$

$$-x_1 + x_2 + 4\delta_2 \leq 4$$

$$3x_1 - x_2 + \delta_2 \leq 15$$

$$x_2 + 3\delta_3 \leq 4$$

$$x_1 \leq 5.$$

Finally, it is now necessary to impose the condition that at least one of the set (1), (2) or (3) must hold. This is done by the constraint:

$$\delta_1 + \delta_2 + \delta_3 \geq 1.$$

It would also be possible to cope with a situation in which the feasible region was disconnected in this way.

CANONICAL AND STANDARD FORMS

• PROBLEM 2-20

Consider the linear programming problem:

minimize $x_0 = 3x_1 - 3x_2 + 7x_3$

subject to

$$x_1 + x_2 + 3x_3 \leq 40$$

$$x_1 + 9x_2 - 7x_3 \geq 50$$

$$5x_1 + 3x_2 = 20$$

$$|5x_2 + 8x_3| \leq 100$$

$$x_1 \geq 0, \; x_2 \geq 0$$

x_3 is unconstrained in sign.

Find its canonical form.

Solution: The characteristics of canonical form are:

1. All decision variables are nonnegative.
2. All constraints are of the $\leq$ type.
3. The objective function is of the maximization type.

This problem can be put in the canonical form as follows:

$$|5x_2 + 8x_3| \leq 100$$

is equivalent to

$$5x_2 + 8x_3 \leq 100$$

and

$$5x_2 + 8x_3 \geq -100.$$

Also,

$$x_3 = x_3^+ - x_3^-$$

where $x_3^+ \geq 0$ and $x_3^- \geq 0$. Finally, if the objective function is transformed to maximization, the canonical form becomes:

$$\text{maximize} \quad g_0 = (-x_0) = -3x_1 + 3x_2 - 7(x_3^+ - x_3^-)$$

subject to

$$x_1 + x_2 + 3(x_3^+ - x_3^-) \leq 40$$
$$-x_1 - 9x_2 + 7(x_3^+ - x_3^-) \leq -50$$
$$5x_1 + 3x_2 \leq 20$$
$$-5x_1 - 3x_2 \leq -20$$
$$5x_2 + 8(x_3^+ - x_3^-) \leq 100$$
$$-5x_2 - 8(x_3^+ - x_3^-) \leq 100$$

$$x_1 \geq 0, \quad x_2 \geq 0, \quad x_3^+ \geq 0, \quad x_3^- \geq 0 .$$

The only difference between the original and the canonical forms in the above problem occurs in the objective function where x_0 in the original problem becomes equal to $(-g_0)$ in the canonical form. The values of the variables are the same in both cases, since the constraints are mathematically equivalent.

• PROBLEM 2-21

Put the following linear programming problem into canonical form:

$$\text{minimize} \quad 6B + 3E + 2M$$

subject to:

$$B \geq 0$$

$$E \geq 0$$

$$M \geq 0$$

$$B + 3E + M \geq 45$$

$$2B + 3E + 3M \leq 50$$

$$4B + 2E + M \leq 60 \ .$$

Solution: Maximize $-6B - 3E - 2M + 0S_1 + 0S_2 + 0S_3$

$$-B - 3E - M \leq -45$$

$$2B + 3E + 3M \leq 50$$

$$4B + 2E + M \leq 60$$

$$B \geq 0,\ E \geq 0,\ M \geq 0,\ S_1 \geq 0,\ S_2 \geq 0,\ S_3 \geq 0$$

• PROBLEM 2-22

Consider the following problem:

minimize $\quad z = 2x_1 + 4x_2$

subject to

$$x_1 + 5x_2 \leq 80 \qquad (1)$$

$$4x_1 + 2x_2 \geq 20 \qquad (2)$$

$$x_1 + x_2 = 10 \qquad (3)$$

$$x_1, x_2 \geq 0$$

Find the canonical form.

Solution: A function will be minimized if one maximizes the negative of the function. Thus, the objective function above will be minimized if the canonical objective function below is maximized:

$$z_c = -z = -2x_1 - 4x_2.$$

An equality constraint can be replaced by two inequality constraints of opposite sense. Constraint (3) can be replaced by the two constraints:

$$x_1 + x_2 \leq 10 \qquad (4)$$

$$x_1 + x_2 \geq 10 \qquad (5)$$

Constraint inequalities can be reversed by multiplying both sides of the inequality by minus one. Constraints (5) and (2) can be converted to ($\leq$) types by multiplying both sides by (-1), thus,

$$-x_1 - x_2 \leq -10 \qquad (6)$$

$$-4x_1 - 2x_2 \leq -20 \qquad (7)$$

Note that the simplex method requires that all right-hand-side constants be nonnegative. Thus, canonical form is not suitable for use in the simplex algorithm.

The statement of the original problem in canonical form is given below:

maximize $\qquad z_c = -2x_1 - 4x_2$

subject to

$$\begin{aligned} x_1 + 5x_2 &\leq 80 \\ -4x_1 - 2x_2 &\leq -20 \\ x_1 + x_2 &\leq 10 \\ -x_1 - x_2 &\leq -10 \\ x_1, x_2 &\geq 0 . \end{aligned}$$

• PROBLEM 2-23

Put the following linear programming problem into canonical form:

Minimize $\qquad 4M + 4T + W$

subject to:

$M \geq 0$

$$T \geq 0$$

$$W \geq 0$$

$$M + T + W \geq 10$$

$$M + T + 2W \geq 6 .$$

Solution: The corresponding system of equations in canonical form is:

$$\text{Maximize } -4M - 4T - W$$

subject to:

$$-M - T - W \leq -10$$

$$-M - T - 2W \leq -6$$

$$M,T,W \geq 0, \qquad S_1, S_2, S_3 \geq 0 .$$

• PROBLEM 2-24

Maximize $5x_1 + 10x_2 + 8x_3$ subject to:

$$x_1 + 2x_2 + x_3 \geq -6$$

$$3x_1 + 2x_2 + x_3 \geq 8$$

$$2x_1 + 3x_2 + 5x_3 \geq 12$$

$$x_j \geq 0 \qquad j = 1,2,3 .$$

Put into canonical form.

Solution: The related canonical problem is:

Maximize $5x_1 + 10x_2 + 8x_3$

subject to:

$$-(x_1 + 2x_2 + x_3) \leq 6$$

$$-(3x_1 + 2x_2 + x_3) \leq -8$$

$$-(2x_1 + 3x_2 + 5x_3) \leq -12$$

$$x_j \geq 0 \qquad j = 1, 2, 3.$$

• PROBLEM 2-25

Maximize $x_0 = 4x_1 + 3x_2$

subject to:
$$2x_1 + 3x_2 \le 6$$
$$-3x_1 + 2x_2 \le 3$$
$$2x_2 \le 5$$
$$2x_1 + x_2 \le 4$$
$$x_1, x_2 \ge 0 .$$

Find the standard form of this linear programming problem.

Solution: The characteristics of the standard form are:

1. All constraints are equations except for the nonnegative constraints which remain inequalities (≥ 0).
2. The right-hand side element of each constraint equation is nonnegative.
3. All variables are nonnegative.
4. The objective function is of the maximization or the minimization type.

Thus the standard form of the above problem is:

Maximize $x_0 = 4x_1 + 3x_2$

subject to:

$$\begin{aligned} 2x_1 + 3x_2 + S_1 \qquad\qquad\quad &= 6 \\ -3x_1 + 2x_2 \quad + S_2 \qquad\quad &= 3 \\ 2x_2 \qquad\quad + S_3 \quad &= 5 \\ 2x_1 + x_2 \qquad\qquad + S_4 &= 4 \end{aligned}$$

$$x_1, x_2, S_1, S_2, S_3, S_4 \ge 0 .$$

• PROBLEM 2-26

Convert the following canonical linear programming problem to standard form:

Maximize

$$8x_1 + 15x_2 + 6x_3 + 20x_4$$

subject to:

$$x_1 + 3x_2 + x_3 + 2x_4 \le 9$$

$$2x_1 + 2x_2 + 2x_3 + 3x_4 \le 12$$

$$3x_1 + 3x_2 + 2x_3 + 5x_4 \le 16$$

$$x_1, x_2, x_3, x_4 \ge 0 .$$

Solution: The general canonical linear programming problem takes the form

$$\text{Max} \quad f(x_1,\ldots,x_n) = b_1x_1 + b_2x_2 + \ldots + b_nx_n \qquad (1)$$

subject to:

$$\begin{aligned} a_{11}x_1 + a_{12}x_2 + \ldots + a_{1n}x_n &\le c_1 \\ a_{21}x_1 + a_{22}x_2 + \ldots + a_{2n}x_n &\le c_2 \\ \vdots \qquad \vdots \qquad\qquad \vdots\ & \\ a_{m1}x_1 + a_{m2}x_2 + \ldots + a_{mn}x_n &\le c_n \end{aligned} \qquad (2)$$

and

$$x_i \ge 0 \quad (i = 1,2,\ldots,n). \qquad (3)$$

The function $f(x_1,\ldots,x_n)$ is the objective function. It is a real-valued function whose argument comes from the set of all n-tuples that satisfy (2) and (3).

Rewrite the above program in matrix form. Thus,

$$\text{Max} \qquad f(X) = BX$$

subject to:

$$AX \le C, \quad X \ge 0,$$

where

$$B = (b_1,\ldots,b_n),\ X = (x_1,x_2,\ldots,x_n),\ C = (c_1,\ldots,c_n)$$

and

$$A = \begin{bmatrix} a_{11} & a_{12} & \cdots & a_{1n} \\ a_{21} & & & \\ \cdot & & & \cdot \\ \cdot & & & \cdot \\ \cdot & & & \cdot \\ a_{m1} & a_{m2} & \cdots & a_{mn} \end{bmatrix} .$$

The solution of the problem is facilitated by converting the inequalities to equalities. Do this by introducing m new variables, one for each of the inequalities. Thus, let:

$$\begin{array}{lcl} x_{n+1} & = & c_1 - (a_{11}x_1 + a_{12}x_2 + \ldots + a_{1n}x_n) \\ \cdot & & \cdot \\ \cdot & & \cdot \\ \cdot & & \cdot \\ x_{n+m} & = & c_m - (a_{m1}x_1 + a_{m2}x_2 + \ldots + a_{mn}x_n) . \end{array}$$

Then the system of inequalities (2) becomes the system of equalities:

$$\begin{array}{lcl} a_{11}x_1 + a_{12}x_2 + \ldots + a_{1n}x_n + x_{n+1} & = & c_1 \\ a_{21}x_1 + a_{22}x_2 + \ldots + a_{2n}x_n + x_{n+2} & = & c_2 \\ \cdot & & \cdot \\ \cdot & & \cdot \\ \cdot & & \cdot \\ a_{m1}x_1 + a_{m2}x_2 + \ldots + a_{mn}x_n + x_{n+m} & = & c_m . \end{array}$$

By increasing the number of unknowns from n to n+m, a system of equalities is obtained. The analysis of such systems is much more developed than the study of systems of inequalities. When the inequalities in the constraint inequations are converted to equalities, the program is in standard form.

The given problem in standard form is:

Maximize

$$8x_1 + 15x_2 + 6x_3 + 20x_4$$

subject to:

$$x_1 + 3x_2 + x_3 + 2x_4 + x_5 = 9$$

$$2x_1 + 2x_2 + 2x_3 + 3x_4 + x_6 = 12$$

$$3x_1 + 3x_2 + 2x_3 + 5x_4 + x_7 = 16$$

$$x_i \geq 0 \ (i = 1, 2, \ldots, 7).$$

• PROBLEM 2-27

Consider the system: Minimize

$$x_1 + x_2 + \frac{1}{2}x_3 - \frac{13}{3}x_4$$

subject to:

$$\begin{aligned}
2x_1 - \tfrac{1}{2}x_2 + x_3 + x_4 &\leq 2 \\
x_1 + 2x_2 + 2x_3 - 3x_4 + x_5 &\geq 3 \\
x_1 - x_3 + x_4 - x_5 &\geq \tfrac{2}{3} \\
3x_1 - x_2 + 2x_4 - \tfrac{3}{2}x_5 &= 1 \\
x_i \geq 0, i = 1, \ldots, 5
\end{aligned}$$

and put into standard form.

Solution: Let x_6 be a slack variable, and x_7 and x_8 surplus variables; then the system becomes:

Minimize

$$x_1 + x_2 + \frac{1}{2}x_3 - \frac{13}{3}x_4$$

subject to:

$$\begin{aligned}
2x_1 - \tfrac{1}{2}x_2 + x_3 + x_4 + x_6 &= 2 \\
x_1 + 2x_2 + 2x_3 - 3x_4 + x_5 - x_7 &= 3 \\
x_1 - x_3 + x_4 - x_5 - x_8 &= \tfrac{2}{3} \\
3x_1 - x_2 + 2x_4 - \tfrac{3}{2}x_5 &= 1 \\
x_i \geq 0, i=1, \ldots, 8.
\end{aligned}$$

• PROBLEM 2-28

Consider the problem:

minimize

$$x_1 + 3x_2 + 4x_3$$

subject to:

$$x_1 + 2x_2 + x_3 = 5$$

$$2x_1 + 3x_2 + x_3 = 6$$

$$x_2 \geq 0, \quad x_3 \geq 0.$$

Put this program into standard form.

Solution: Since x_1 is free, solve for it from the first constraint, obtaining:

$$x_1 = 5 - 2x_2 - x_3. \tag{1}$$

Substituting this into the objective and the second constraint, obtain the equivalent problem (subtracting five from the objective):

minimize

$$x_2 + 3x_3$$

subject to:

$$x_2 + x_3 = 4$$

$$x_2 \geq 0, \quad x_3 \geq 0,$$

which is a problem in standard form. After the smaller problem is solved (the answer is $x_2 = 4$, $x_3 = 0$) the value for x_1 ($x_1 = -3$) can be found from (1).

• PROBLEM 2-29

Put into standard form:

Maximize $3x + y$

subject to:

$$x \geq 0$$

$$y \geq 0$$

$$2x - y \leq -10$$

$$x + 2y \leq 14$$

$$x \leq 12.$$

Solution: Maximize

$$3x + y + 0S_1 + 0S_2 + 0S_3$$

subject to:

$$-2x + y - S_1 = 10$$

$$x + 2y + S_2 = 14$$

$$x + S_3 = 12$$

$$x \geq 0, \quad 4 \geq 0, \quad S_1 \; S_2 \; S_3 \geq 0$$

where S_1, S_2, S_3 are the slack variables.

• PROBLEM 2-30

Consider the following problem:

Minimize

$$4x_1 + 5x_2 + 3x_3 + 6x_4$$

subject to:

$$x_1 + 3x_2 + x_3 + 2x_4 \leq 2$$

$$3x_1 + 3x_2 + 2x_3 + 2x_4 \leq 4$$

$$3x_1 + 2x_2 + 4x_3 + 5x_4 \leq 6.$$

$$x_j \geq 0 \qquad j = 1, \ldots, 4$$

Put into standard form.

Solution: The related problem is:

Minimize

$$4x_1 + 5x_2 + 3x_3 + 6x_4$$

subject to:

$$x_1 + 3x_2 + x_3 + 2x_4 + x_5 = 2$$

$$3x_1 + 3x_2 + 2x_3 + 2x_4 + x_6 = 4$$

$$3x_1 + 2x_2 + 4x_3 + 5x_4 + x_7 = 6$$

$$x_j \geq 0 \qquad j = 1, \ldots, 7.$$

BASIC FEASIBLE SOLUTION

• PROBLEM 2-31

A certain manufacturer produces four different types of gears. In the production of the gears he uses milling machines, lathes, and presses. He has 9 milling machines, 12 lathes, and 16 presses. Table 1 indicates how many minutes on each kind of machine are needed to produce a gear of each of the four types. The manufacturer realizes a profit of 8 cents on each gear of type 1, 15 cents on each one of type 2, 6 cents on each of type 3, and 20 cents on each gear of type 4. Find a feasible solution to the problem.

TABLE 1

Number of Minutes Required on	Types of Gears			
	1	2	3	4
Milling Machine	1	3	1	2
Lathe	2	2	2	3
Press	3	3	2	5

Solution: Let x_i denote the number of gears of type i, i = 1, 2, 3, 4, produced per minute. The quantity to be minimized --the profit per minute--is:

$$8x_1 + 15x_2 + 6x_3 + 20x_4.$$

The number of milling machines used during any minute is:

$$x_1 + 3x_2 + x_3 + 2x_4,$$

and this number must not exceed 9. The number:

$$2x_1 + 2x_2 + 2x_3 + 3x_4$$

of lathes used per minute must not exceed 12, and the number:

$$3x_1 + 3x_2 + 2x_3 + 5x_4$$

of presses used per minute must not exceed 16. The manufacturer's problem can be stated in the form of a linear programming problem as follows: Find nonnegative numbers x_1, x_2, x_3, x_4 which maximize

$$8x_1 + 15x_2 + 6x_3 + 20x_4$$

subject to:

$$x_1 + 3x_2 + x_3 + 2x_4 \leq 9$$

$$2x_1 + 2x_2 + 2x_3 + 3x_4 \leq 12$$

$$3x_1 + 3x_2 + 2x_3 + 5x_4 \le 16.$$

Equating $x_1 = 0$ and solving the constraint equations simultaneously, it is found that:

$$x_1 = 0, \; x_2 = 13/9, \; x_3 = 0, \; x_4 = 7/3$$

is a feasible solution of the problem.

• PROBLEM 2-32

Maximize

$$z = 7x_1 + 10x_2$$

subject to:

$$5x_1 + 4x_2 \le 24$$

$$2x_1 + 5x_2 \le 13$$

$$x_1, \; x_2 \ge 0.$$

Find an initial feasible solution.

Solution:

$$1z - 7x_1 - 10x_2 - 0S_1 - 0S_2 = 0$$

$$0z + 5x_1 + 4x_2 + 1S_1 + 0S_2 = 24$$

$$0z + 2x_1 + 5x_2 + 0S_1 + 1S_2 = 13.$$

In tableau form this is expressed as:

Basis	z	x_1	x_2	S_1	S_2	b_i
—	1	−7	−10	0	0	0
S_1	0	5	4	1	0	24
S_2	0	2	5	0	1	13

The variables in the basis are indicated in the first column of the tableau. The selection of S_1 and S_2 for the basis is equivalent to setting x_1 and x_2 to zero; hence, the system of three equations is reduced to:

$$1z + 0S_1 + 0S_2 = 0$$

$$0z + 1S_1 + 0S_2 = 24$$

$$0z + 0S_1 + 1S_2 = 13$$

which provides an immediate solution of $z = 0$, $S_1 = 24$, and $S_2 = 13$.

• PROBLEM 2-33

Consider the polyhedral set defined by the following inequalities:

$x_1 + x_2 \leq 6$

$x_2 \leq 3$

$x_1, x_2 \geq 0.$

Find all basic solutions and distinguish basic feasible solutions (b.f.s.) from them, using the computational approach.

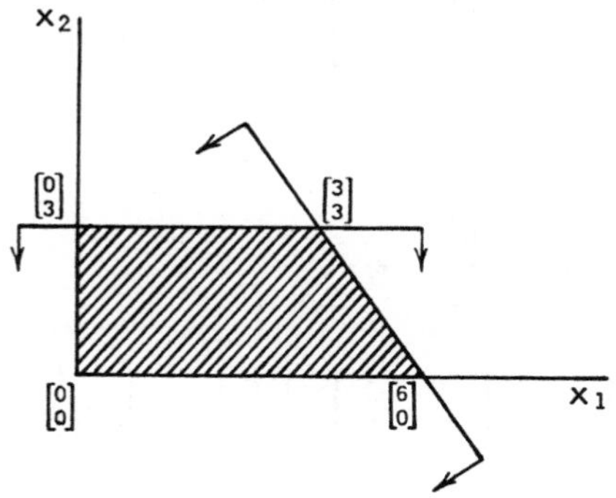

Fig. 1

Solution: By introducing the slack variables x_3 and x_4, the problem is put in the following standard format:

$$x_1 + x_2 + x_3 = 6$$

$$x_2 + x_4 = 3$$

$$x_1, x_2, x_3, x_4 \geq 0.$$

Note the constraint matrix $A = [a_1, a_2, a_3, a_4] =$

$$\begin{bmatrix} 1 & 1 & 1 & 0 \\ 0 & 1 & 0 & 1 \end{bmatrix}.$$

Basic feasible solutions correspond to finding a 2 X 2 basis B with nonnegative $B^{-1}b$. The following are the possible ways of extracting B out of A.

1. $B = [a_1, a_2] = \begin{bmatrix} 1 & 1 \\ 0 & 1 \end{bmatrix}$

$$X_B = \begin{bmatrix} x_1 \\ x_2 \end{bmatrix} = B^{-1}b = \begin{bmatrix} 1 & -1 \\ 0 & 1 \end{bmatrix} \begin{bmatrix} 6 \\ 3 \end{bmatrix} = \begin{bmatrix} 3 \\ 3 \end{bmatrix},$$

$$X_N = \begin{bmatrix} x_3 \\ x_4 \end{bmatrix} = \begin{bmatrix} 0 \\ 0 \end{bmatrix}$$

2. $B = [a_1, a_4] = \begin{bmatrix} 1 & 0 \\ 0 & 1 \end{bmatrix}$

$$X_B = \begin{bmatrix} x_1 \\ x_4 \end{bmatrix} = B^{-1}b = \begin{bmatrix} 1 & 0 \\ 0 & 1 \end{bmatrix} \begin{bmatrix} 6 \\ 3 \end{bmatrix} = \begin{bmatrix} 6 \\ 3 \end{bmatrix},$$

$$X_N = \begin{bmatrix} x_2 \\ x_3 \end{bmatrix} = \begin{bmatrix} 0 \\ 0 \end{bmatrix}$$

3. $B = [a_2, a_3] = \begin{bmatrix} 1 & 1 \\ 1 & 0 \end{bmatrix}$

$$X_B = \begin{bmatrix} x_2 \\ x_3 \end{bmatrix} = B^{-1}b = \begin{bmatrix} 0 & 1 \\ 1 & -1 \end{bmatrix} \begin{bmatrix} 6 \\ 3 \end{bmatrix} = \begin{bmatrix} 3 \\ 3 \end{bmatrix},$$

$$X_N = \begin{bmatrix} x_1 \\ x_4 \end{bmatrix} = \begin{matrix} 0 \\ 0 \end{matrix}$$

4. $B = [a_2, a_4] = \begin{bmatrix} 1 & 0 \\ 1 & 1 \end{bmatrix}$

$$X_B = \begin{bmatrix} x_2 \\ x_4 \end{bmatrix} = B^{-1}b = \begin{bmatrix} 1 & 0 \\ -1 & 1 \end{bmatrix} \begin{bmatrix} 6 \\ 3 \end{bmatrix} = \begin{bmatrix} 6 \\ -3 \end{bmatrix},$$

$$X_N = \begin{bmatrix} x_1 \\ x_3 \end{bmatrix} = \begin{bmatrix} 0 \\ 0 \end{bmatrix}$$

5. $B = [a_3, a_4] = \begin{bmatrix} 1 & 0 \\ 0 & 1 \end{bmatrix}$

$$X_B = \begin{bmatrix} x_3 \\ x_4 \end{bmatrix} = B^{-1}b = \begin{bmatrix} 1 & 0 \\ 0 & 1 \end{bmatrix} \begin{bmatrix} 6 \\ 3 \end{bmatrix} = \begin{bmatrix} 6 \\ 3 \end{bmatrix},$$

$$X_N = \begin{bmatrix} x_1 \\ x_2 \end{bmatrix} = \begin{bmatrix} 0 \\ 0 \end{bmatrix}$$

Note that the points corresponding to 1, 2, 3, and 5 above are basic feasible solutions. The point obtained in 4 is a basic solution, but is not feasible because it violates the nonnegativity restrictions. In other words, there are four basic feasible solutions, namely:

$$x_1 = \begin{bmatrix} 3 \\ 3 \\ 0 \\ 0 \end{bmatrix}, \quad x_2 = \begin{bmatrix} 6 \\ 0 \\ 0 \\ 3 \end{bmatrix}, \quad x_3 = \begin{bmatrix} 0 \\ 3 \\ 3 \\ 0 \end{bmatrix}, \quad x_4 = \begin{bmatrix} 0 \\ 0 \\ 6 \\ 3 \end{bmatrix}.$$

These points belong to E^4 since after introducing the slack variables there are four variables. These basic feasible solutions, projected in E^2--that is, in the (x_1,x_2) space--give rise to the following four points:

$$\begin{bmatrix} 3 \\ 3 \end{bmatrix}, \quad \begin{bmatrix} 6 \\ 0 \end{bmatrix}, \quad \begin{bmatrix} 0 \\ 3 \end{bmatrix}, \quad \begin{bmatrix} 0 \\ 0 \end{bmatrix}.$$

These four points are illustrated in Figure 1. Note that these points are precisely the extreme points of the feasible region.

The possible number of basic feasible solutions is bounded by the number of ways of extracting two columns out of four columns to form the basis. Therefore, the number of basic feasible solutions is less or equal to:

$$\binom{4}{2} = \frac{4!}{2!2!} = 6.$$

Out of these six possibilities, one point violates the nonnegativity of $B^{-1}b$. Furthermore, a_1 and a_3 could not have been used to form a basis since $a_1 = a_3 = \begin{bmatrix} 1 \\ 0 \end{bmatrix}$ are linearly dependent, and hence the matrix $\begin{bmatrix} 1 & 1 \\ 0 & 0 \end{bmatrix}$ does not qualify as a basis. This leaves four basic feasible solutions.

There is another intuitive way of viewing basic solutions and basic feasible solutions. Each constraint, including the nonnegativity constraints, can be associated uniquely with a certain variable. Thus $x_1 \geq 0$ can be associated with the variable x_1, and the line $x_1 = 0$ is the boundary of the halfspace corresponding to $x_1 \geq 0$. Also, $x_1 + x_2 \leq 6$ can be associated with the variable x_3, and $x_3 = 0$ is the boundary of the halfspace corresponding to $x_1 + x_2 \leq 6$. Graphically portraying the boundary of the various constraints, one gets the graph of Figure 2. Now, basic solutions correspond to the intersection of two lines in this graph. The lines correspond to the nonbasic variables. In the graph there are five intersections corresponding to five basic solutions. Note that there is no intersection of the lines $x_2 = 0$ and $x_4 = 0$ and thus no basic solution corresponding to these two variables being nonbasic. As soon as the feasible region is identified, the basic solutions can be distinguished from those that are also basic feasible solutions.

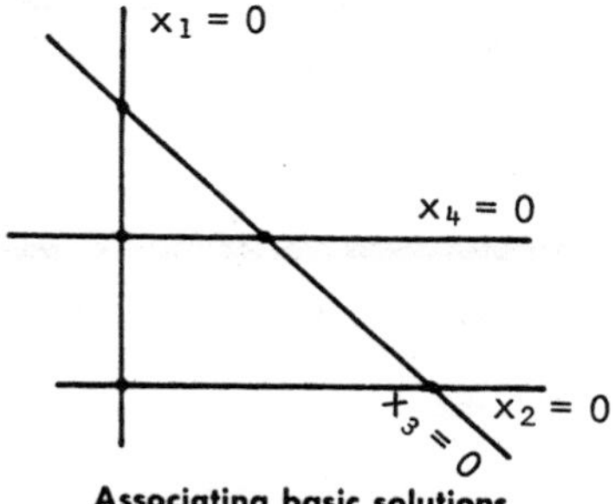

Associating basic solutions with nonbasic variables.

Fig. 2

• PROBLEM 2-34

Show that an upper bound for the number of basic points (and, thus, basic feasible points) is given by:

$$\text{Upper bound} = \frac{(m + n)!}{m!n!}$$

where m and n are as depicted in the below LP:

Minimize

$$u = \sum_{j=1}^{n} c_j x_j$$

subject to:

$$\sum_{j=1}^{n} a_{ij} x_j \geq b_i; \quad i = 1, \ldots, m$$

$$x_j \geq 0 \qquad j=1, \ldots, n.$$

Solution: The equations contain (m+n) unknowns (or variables). To find a possible basic point, set n variables equal to zero and then attempt to solve the resulting system of m equations in m unknowns. If a unique solution results, a basic point is found. Notice thus, that an upper bound for the number of basic points is just the number of ways of choosing n variables (and setting them equal to zero) from a total of (m + n) variables. Thus, the upper bound is none other than C(m + n, n)--the number of combinations of (m + n) things taken n at a time; the latter is equal to $(m + n)!/m!n!$ Thus:

$$\text{Upper bound} = C(m + n, n) = \frac{(m + n)!}{m!n!}$$

Since the number of basic points is at least as great as the number of basic feasible points, the above number is also an upper bound for the number of basic feasible points.

• PROBLEM 2-35

Consider the following standard maximum problem:

$$\text{Maximize} \quad u = 4x + 2y + z \tag{1}$$

subject to: $x + y \leq 1$

$$x + z \leq 1 \tag{2}$$

and

$$x \geq 0, \; y \geq 0, \; z \geq 0. \tag{3}$$

Identify the basic feasible points (extreme points) of the constraint set. Determine which ones, if any are degenerate.

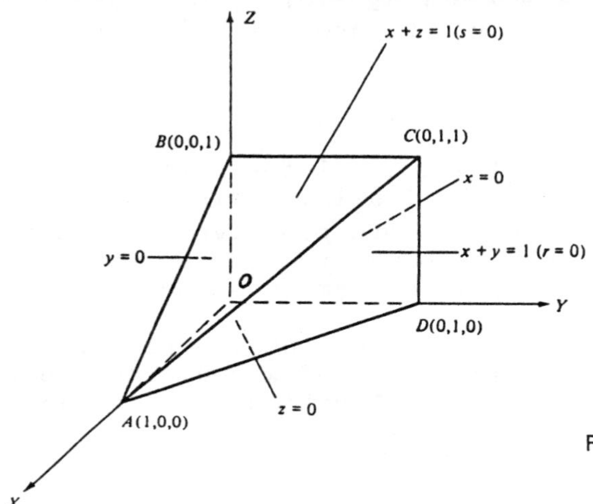

Fig. 1

Solution: Note that the function to be maximized is really irrelevant to the solution of the problem, i.e., the constraint set is determined solely from (2) and (3).

If slack variables r and s are introduced, then rewrite (2) and (3) as:

$$x + y - 1 = -r \tag{4}$$

$$x + z - 1 = -s \tag{5}$$

and

$$x \geq 0$$

$$y \geq 0$$

$$z \geq 0$$

$$r \geq 0$$

$$s \geq 0.$$

The sketch of the constraint set for this problem is given in Figure 1. Plot the bounding planes $x + y = 1$ (or $r = 0$) and $x + z = 1$ (or $s = 0$) as well as $x = 0$, $y = 0$, and $z = 0$. The constraint set consists of those points within and on the surface of the pyramid shown. This is a case of a bounded constraint set.

Note that $x + y = 1$ is parallel to the Z axis because

the variable z is missing from it, while $x + z = 1$ is parallel to the Y axis because here the variable y is missing. The plane labeled $x = 0$ is none other than the yz plane. Similarly, $y = 0$ and $z = 0$ are coordinate planes.

The extreme points (or basic feasible points) can be determined by inspection of Figure 1 and by using Equations (4) and (5). Thus, point B is located at the intersection of $x + z = 1$ $(s = 0)$, $y = 0$, and $x = 0$. Thus, setting $x = 0$, $y = 0$, and $s = 0$ in Equations (4) and (5) yields

$-1 = -r$ and $z - 1 = 0$.

This results in $r = 1$ and $z = 1$ for point B. Thus, B is a nondegenerate basic feasible point because the solved-for variables are both positive. Notice that $n = 3$ variables are set equal to zero and the remaining $m = 2$ variables are solved from equations (4) and (5).

Point C is located at the intersection of $x + z = 1$ $(s = 0)$, $x + y = 1 (r = 0)$, and $x = 0$. Thus, setting $x = 0$, $r = 0$, and $s = 0$ in Equations (4) and (5) yields:

$y - 1 = 0$ and $z - 1 = 0$.

This results in $y = 1$ and $z = 1$ for point C. Thus, point C is also a nondegenerate basic feasible point.

As a final calculation, consider point A, which lies at the intersection of $x + y = 1 (r = 0)$, $y = 0$, and $z = 0$. Thus, setting $r = 0$, $y = 0$, and $z = 0$ in Equations (4) and (5) yields:

$x - 1 = 0$ and $x - 1 = -s$.

This results in $x = 1$ and $s = 0$ for point A. Thus, note that point A is a degenerate basic feasible point because one of the solved-for variables is equal to zero.

The following table indicates the values of the five variables (three original plus two slack variables) for the five basic feasible points of this problem. Only one--point A--is a degenerate basic feasible point:

Basic feasible point	x	y	z	r	s	u
O	0	0	0	1	1	0
A (degenerate)	1	0	0	0	0	4
B	0	0	1	1	0	1
C	0	1	1	0	0	3
D	0	1	0	0	1	2

There are geometrical interpretations to nondegenerate and degenerate basic feasible points. For a standard problem a bounding hyperplane (in the case just considered, an ordinary plane) can be represented by an equation of the form:

Variable = 0.

In a three-dimensional problem such as the problem above, (see Figure 1), a nondegenerate basic feasible point occurs at a point where exactly three of the bounding planes intersect, i.e., at a point where exactly three of the variables equal zero, the other two variables being positive at this point. This is what happens at points O, B, C, and D of the problem.

On the other hand, basic feasible point A occurs at the intersection of four bounding planes, i.e., four variables equal zero, the remaining variable being positive. Thus, for the case where n = 3, a degenerate basic feasible point is a point of intersection of more than three bounding planes.

In a standard linear programming problem, a degenerate basic feasible point may be interpreted as a point solution in the constraint set where more than n bounding hyperplanes intersect. If exactly n bounding hyperplanes intersect at a solution in the constraint set, then such a solution would be a nondegenerate basic feasible solution.

• PROBLEM 2-36

Minimize $x_1 + x_2$

Subject to: $x_1 + 2x_2 \leq 4$

$x_2 \leq 1$

$x_1, x_2 \geq 0.$

Find a basic feasible solution to the above problem, starting from a b.f.s. with x_1 and x_2 in the basis.

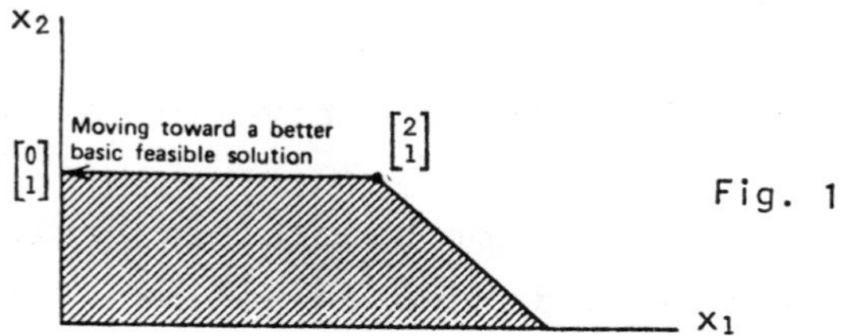

Fig. 1

Improving a basic feasible solution

Solution: Introduce the slack variables x_3 and x_4 to put the problem in a standard form. This leads to the following constraint matrix $\vec{A}$:

$$\vec{A} = [\vec{a}_1, \vec{a}_2, \vec{a}_3, \vec{a}_4] = \begin{bmatrix} 1 & 2 & 1 & 0 \\ 0 & 1 & 0 & 1 \end{bmatrix} .$$

Considering the basic feasible solution corresponding to $\vec{B} = [\vec{a}_1, \vec{a}_2]$ (in other words, x_1 and x_2 are the basic variables while x_3 and x_4 are the nonbasic variables), one gets:

$$\vec{X}_B = \begin{bmatrix} x_1 \\ x_2 \end{bmatrix} = \vec{B}^{-1}\vec{b} = \begin{bmatrix} 1 & 2 \\ 0 & 1 \end{bmatrix}^{-1} \begin{bmatrix} 4 \\ 1 \end{bmatrix} = \begin{bmatrix} 1 & -2 \\ 0 & 1 \end{bmatrix} \begin{bmatrix} 4 \\ 1 \end{bmatrix} = \begin{bmatrix} 2 \\ 1 \end{bmatrix}$$

$$\vec{X}_N = \begin{bmatrix} x_3 \\ x_4 \end{bmatrix} = \begin{bmatrix} 0 \\ 0 \end{bmatrix} .$$

This point is shown in Figure 1. In order to improve this basic feasible solution, calculate $z_j - c_j$ for the nonbasic variables:

$$\begin{aligned} z_3 - c_3 &= \vec{c}_B\vec{B}^{-1}\vec{a}_3 - c_3 \\ &= (1,1) \begin{bmatrix} 1 & -2 \\ 0 & 1 \end{bmatrix} \begin{pmatrix} 1 \\ 0 \end{pmatrix} - 0 \\ &= (1,1) \begin{pmatrix} 1 \\ 0 \end{pmatrix} - 0 \\ &= 1 \end{aligned}$$

$$\begin{aligned} z_4 - c_4 &= \vec{c}_B\vec{B}^{-1}\vec{a}_4 - c_4 \\ &= (1,1) \begin{bmatrix} 1 & -2 \\ 0 & 1 \end{bmatrix} \begin{pmatrix} 0 \\ 1 \end{pmatrix} - 0 \\ &= (1,1) \begin{pmatrix} -2 \\ 1 \end{pmatrix} - 0 \\ &= -1 \end{aligned}$$

Since $z_3 - c_3 > 0$, then the objective improves by increasing x_3.

The criterion $z_k - c_k > 0$ for a nonbasic variable x_k to enter the basis is justified as follows. Note that $z = \vec{c}_B\vec{b} - (z_k - c_k)x_k$, where

$$z_k = \vec{c}_B\vec{B}^{-1}\vec{a}_k = \vec{c}_B\vec{y}_k = \sum_{i=1}^{m} c_{B_i} y_{ik} \qquad (1)$$

and c_{B_i} is the cost of the ith basic variable. Note that if x_k is raised from zero level, while the other nonbasic variables are kept at zero level, then the basic variables $x_{B_1}, x_{B_2}, \ldots, x_{Bm}$ must be modified. In other words, if x_k is increased by 1 unit, then x_{B_1},

x_{B_2}, . . . , and x_{B_m} will be decreased respectively by y_{1k}, y_{2k}, . . . , y_{mk} units (if $y_{ik} < 0$, then x_{B_i} will be increased). The saving (a negative saving means more cost) that results from the modification of the basic variables, as a result of increasing x_k by 1 unit, is therefore, $\Sigma_{i=1}^{m} c_{B_i} y_{ik}$, which is z_k (see Equation 1). However, the cost of increasing x_k itself by 1 unit is c_k. Hence $z_k - c_k$ is the saving minus the cost of increasing x_k by 1 unit. Naturally, if $z_k - c_k$ is positive, it will be advantageous to increase x_k. For each unit of x_k, the cost will be reduced by an amount $z_k - c_k$ and hence it will be advantageous to increase x_k as much as possible. On the other hand, if $z_k - c_k < 0$, then by increasing x_k, the net saving is negative, and this action will result in a larger cost. So this action is prohibited. Finally, if $z_k - c_k = 0$, then increasing x_k will lead to a different solution, with the same cost. So whether x_k is kept at zero level, or increased, no change in cost takes place.

Now suppose that x_k is a basic variable. In particular, suppose that x_k is the tth basic variable, that is, $x_k = x_{B_t}$, $c_k = c_{B_t}$, and $\vec{a}_k = \vec{a}_{B_t}$. Recall that $z_k = \vec{c}_B \vec{B}^{-1} \vec{a}_k = \vec{c}_B \vec{B}^{-1} \vec{a}_{B_t}$. But $\vec{B}^{-1} \vec{a}_{B_t}$ is a vector of zeros except for one at the tth position. Therefore, $z_k = c_{B_t}$, and hence $z_k - c_k = c_{B_t} - c_{B_t} = 0$. The modified solution is given by:

$$\vec{X}_B = \vec{B}^{-1} \vec{b} - \vec{B}^{-1} \vec{a}_3 x_3$$

$$\begin{bmatrix} x_1 \\ x_2 \end{bmatrix} = \begin{bmatrix} 2 \\ 1 \end{bmatrix} - \begin{bmatrix} 1 \\ 0 \end{bmatrix} x_3$$

The maximum value of x_3 is 2 (any larger value of x_3 will force x_1 to be negative). Therefore the new basic feasible solution is:

$$(x_1, x_2, x_3, x_4) = (0,1,2,0).$$

Here x_3 enters the basis and x_1 leaves the basis. Note that the new point has an objective value equal to 1, which is an improvement over the previous objective value of 3. The improvement is precisely $(z_3 - c_3)x_3 = 2$.

• PROBLEM 2-37

Consider:

Minimize $2x_1 - x_2$

Subject to: $-x_1 + x_2 \leq 2$

$2x_1 + x_2 \leq 6$

$x_1, x_2 \geq 0$.

Determine an improved basic feasible solution starting from the b.f.s. with basis

$$\vec{B} = [\vec{a}_1, \vec{a}_2].$$

Identify the blocking variable?

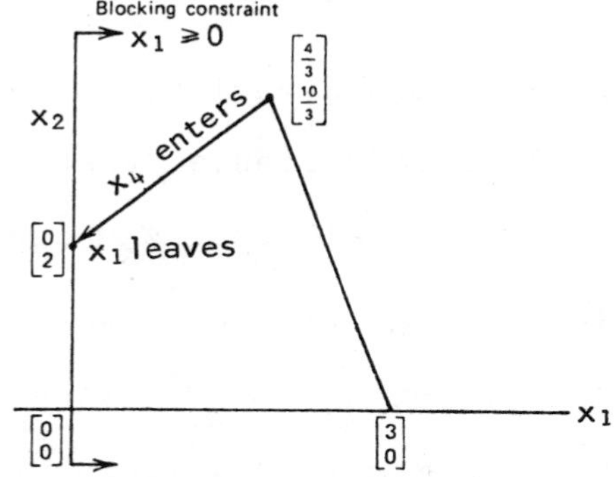

Fig. 1

Blocking variable (Constraint).

Solution: Introduce the slack variables x_3 and x_4. This leads to the following constraints:

$$-x_1 + x_2 + x_3 = 2$$

$$2x_1 + x_2 + x_4 = 6$$

$$x_1, x_2, x_3, x_4 \geq 0 .$$

Considering the basic feasible solution with basis

$$\vec{B} = [\vec{a}_1, \vec{a}_2] = \begin{bmatrix} -1 & 1 \\ 2 & 1 \end{bmatrix}$$

and

$$\vec{B}^{-1} = \begin{bmatrix} -\frac{1}{3} & \frac{1}{3} \\ \frac{2}{3} & \frac{1}{3} \end{bmatrix}$$

$$\vec{X}_B = \vec{B}^{-1}\vec{b} - \vec{B}^{-1}\vec{N}\vec{x}_N$$

$$\begin{bmatrix} X_{B_1} \\ X_{B_2} \end{bmatrix} = \begin{bmatrix} x_1 \\ x_2 \end{bmatrix} =$$

$$\begin{bmatrix} -\frac{1}{3} & \frac{1}{3} \\ \frac{2}{3} & \frac{1}{3} \end{bmatrix} \begin{bmatrix} 2 \\ 6 \end{bmatrix} - \begin{bmatrix} -\frac{1}{3} & \frac{1}{3} \\ \frac{2}{3} & \frac{1}{3} \end{bmatrix} \begin{bmatrix} 1 & 0 \\ 0 & 1 \end{bmatrix} \begin{bmatrix} x_3 \\ x_4 \end{bmatrix}$$

$$= \begin{bmatrix} \frac{4}{3} \\ \frac{10}{3} \end{bmatrix} - \begin{bmatrix} -\frac{1}{3} \\ \frac{2}{3} \end{bmatrix} x_3 - \begin{bmatrix} \frac{1}{3} \\ \frac{1}{3} \end{bmatrix} x_4 \qquad (1)$$

Currently

$$x_3 = x_4 = 0,$$

$$x_1 = \frac{4}{3}$$

and

$$x_2 = \frac{10}{3} .$$

Note that:

$$z_4 - c_4 = \vec{c}_B \vec{B}^{-1} \vec{a}_4 - c_4 = (2, -1) \begin{bmatrix} -\frac{1}{3} & \frac{1}{3} \\ \frac{2}{3} & \frac{1}{3} \end{bmatrix} \begin{bmatrix} 0 \\ 1 \end{bmatrix} - 0$$

$$= \frac{1}{3} > 0 .$$

Hence, the objective improves by introducing x_4 in the basis. Then x_3 is kept at zero level, x_4 is increased, and x_1 and x_2 are modified according to Equation (1). Notice that x_4 can be increased to 4, at which instant x_1 drops to zero. Any further increase of x_4 results in violating the nonnegativity of x_1, and so x_1 is the blocking variable. With $x_4 = 4$ and $x_3 = 0$, the modified values of x_1 and x_2 are 0 and 2 respectively. The new basic feasible solution is:

$$(x_1, x_2, x_3, x_4) = (0,2,0,4).$$

Note that $\vec{a}_4$ replaces $\vec{a}_1$: that is, x_1 drops from the basis and x_4 enters the basis. The new set of basic and nonbasic variables are given below:

$$\vec{X}_B = \begin{bmatrix} x_{B_1} \\ x_{B_2} \end{bmatrix} = \begin{bmatrix} x_4 \\ x_2 \end{bmatrix} = \begin{bmatrix} 4 \\ 2 \end{bmatrix},$$

$$X_N = \begin{bmatrix} x_3 \\ x_1 \end{bmatrix} = \begin{bmatrix} 0 \\ 0 \end{bmatrix}.$$

Moving from the old to the new basic feasible solution is illustrated in Figure 1. Note that as x_4 increases by 1 unit, x_1 decreases by $\frac{1}{3}$ unit and x_2 decreases by $\frac{1}{3}$ unit; that is, it moves in the direction $(-\frac{1}{3}, -\frac{1}{3})$ in the (x_1,x_2) space. This continues until it is blocked by the nonnegativity restriction $x_1 \geq 0$. At this point x_1 drops to zero and leaves the basis.

• PROBLEM 2-38

Consider the following system of inequalities:

$$\begin{aligned} x_1 + x_2 &\leq 6 \\ x_2 &\leq 3 \\ x_1 + 2x_2 &\leq 9 \\ x_1, x_2 &\geq 0 . \end{aligned}$$

Compute basic feasible solutions and identify degenerate basic feasible solutions.

Solution: This system is illustrated in Figure 1. After adding the slack variables x_3, x_4, and x_5, one obtains

$$x_1 + x_2 + x_3 = 6$$

$$x_2 \qquad + x_4 \qquad = 3$$

$$x_1 + 2x_2 \qquad + x_5 = 9$$

$$x_1, x_2, x_3, x_4, x_5 \geqq 0 .$$

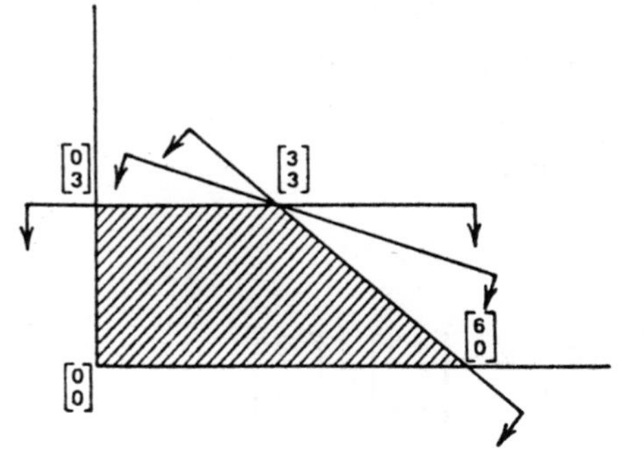

Fig. 1

Degenerate basic feasible solutions.

Note that:

$$\vec{A} = [\vec{a}_1, \vec{a}_2, \vec{a}_3, \vec{a}_4, \vec{a}_5] = \begin{bmatrix} 1 & 1 & 1 & 0 & 0 \\ 0 & 1 & 0 & 1 & 0 \\ 1 & 2 & 0 & 0 & 1 \end{bmatrix} .$$

Consider the basic feasible solution with

$$\vec{B} = [\vec{a}_1, \vec{a}_2, \vec{a}_3]:$$

$$\vec{X}_B = \begin{bmatrix} x_1 \\ x_2 \\ x_3 \end{bmatrix} = \begin{bmatrix} 1 & 1 & 0 \\ 0 & 1 & 0 \\ 1 & 2 & 0 \end{bmatrix}^{-1} \begin{bmatrix} 6 \\ 3 \\ 9 \end{bmatrix} = \begin{bmatrix} 0 & -2 & 1 \\ 0 & 1 & 0 \\ 1 & 1 & -1 \end{bmatrix} \begin{bmatrix} 6 \\ 3 \\ 9 \end{bmatrix} = \begin{bmatrix} 3 \\ 3 \\ 0 \end{bmatrix}$$

$$\vec{X}_N = \begin{bmatrix} x_4 \\ x_5 \end{bmatrix} = \begin{bmatrix} 0 \\ 0 \end{bmatrix} .$$

Note that this basic feasible solution is degenerate since the basic variable $x_3 = 0$. Now consider the basic feasible solution with

$$\vec{B} = [\vec{a}_1, \vec{a}_2, \vec{a}_3]:$$

$$\vec{X}_B = \begin{bmatrix} x_1 \\ x_2 \\ x_4 \end{bmatrix} = \begin{bmatrix} 1 & 1 & 0 \\ 0 & 1 & 1 \\ 1 & 2 & 0 \end{bmatrix}^{-1} , \begin{bmatrix} 6 \\ 3 \\ 9 \end{bmatrix} = \begin{bmatrix} 2 & 0 & -1 \\ -1 & 0 & 1 \\ 1 & 1 & -1 \end{bmatrix} \begin{bmatrix} 6 \\ 3 \\ 9 \end{bmatrix} = \begin{bmatrix} 3 \\ 3 \\ 0 \end{bmatrix}$$

$$\vec{X}_N = \begin{bmatrix} x_3 \\ x_5 \end{bmatrix} = \begin{bmatrix} 0 \\ 0 \end{bmatrix}.$$

Note that this basic feasible solution gives rise to the same point obtained by $\vec{B} = [\vec{a}_1, \vec{a}_2, \vec{a}_3]$. It can be also checked that the basic feasible solution with basis $\vec{B} = [\vec{a}_1, \vec{a}_2, \vec{a}_5]$ is given by:

$$\vec{X}_B = \begin{bmatrix} x_1 \\ x_2 \\ x_5 \end{bmatrix} = \begin{bmatrix} 3 \\ 3 \\ 0 \end{bmatrix} \qquad \vec{X}_N = \begin{bmatrix} x_3 \\ x_4 \end{bmatrix} = \begin{bmatrix} 0 \\ 0 \end{bmatrix}.$$

Note that all three of the foregoing basic feasible solutions with different bases are represented by the single extreme point $(x_1, x_2, x_3, x_4, x_5) = (3,3,0,0,0)$. Each of the three basic feasible solutions is degenerate since each contains a basic variable at level zero. The remaining extreme points of Figure 1 correspond to nondegenerate basic feasible solutions.

• PROBLEM 2-39

Consider

Maximize

$$x_1 + x_2 + x_3$$

subject to

$$x_1 + 2x_2 + x_3 \leqq 4, \quad x_j \geqq 0, \tag{1}$$

$$-x_1 + x_2 - 2x_3 \leqq -2.$$

with

$$\bar{A} = \begin{pmatrix} 1 & 2 & 1 & 1 & 0 \\ -1 & 1 & -2 & 0 & 1 \end{pmatrix}, \qquad b = \begin{pmatrix} 4 \\ -2 \end{pmatrix}$$

and

$$p^T = (1,1,1).$$

Let $\tilde{x} \in R$ and define

$$M(\tilde{x}) = \{i \mid a_i^T \tilde{x} = b_i\} = \{i \mid \tilde{y}_i = 0\},$$

$$N(\tilde{x}) = \{j \mid \tilde{x}_j = 0\}.$$

The index sets $M(\tilde{x}) \subset M$ and $N(\tilde{x}) \subset N$ may be empty. A direction s in $\tilde{x}$ is called feasible if by making a small step in that direction one does not leave the feasible region, i.e.

$$s \text{ feasible in } \tilde{x} \Leftrightarrow \exists \tilde{\lambda} > 0 \forall \lambda,$$

$$0 \leq \lambda \leq \tilde{\lambda}:$$

$$(\tilde{x} + \lambda s \in R)$$

For s to be feasible in $\tilde{x}$ it is necessary and sufficient that

(1) $\forall_i \in M(\tilde{x}) \, (a_i^T s \leq 0)$,

(2) $\forall_j \in N(\tilde{x}) \, (s_j \geq 0)$,

i.e., s should make a non-acute angle with the outward pointing normals

a_i, $i \in M(\tilde{x})$

and

$-e_j$, $j \in N(\tilde{x})$ in $\tilde{x}$.

Define

$$S(\tilde{x}) = \{s \mid a_i^T s \leq 0, \; i \in M(\tilde{x}); \; s_j \geq 0,$$
$$j \in N(\tilde{x})\},$$

the cone of feasible directions in $\tilde{x}$. Then any feasible direction in $\tilde{x}$ should satisfy $s \in S(\tilde{x})$. If, in addition, $p^T s > 0$ one does make progress when moving in the direction s; such a direction will be called usable. Hence

$$s \text{ usable in } \tilde{x} \Leftrightarrow s \in S(\tilde{x}), \; p^T s > 0.$$

A feasible solution $\tilde{x}$ will be optimal if there is no usable direction in $\tilde{x}$. For, suppose there is an $\hat{x} \in R$ with $p^T \hat{x} > p^T \tilde{x}$, then $s = \hat{x} - \tilde{x}$ will be usable in $\tilde{x}$.

By determining successive usable directions and by making steps in those directions, try to solve the linear programming problem (1).

Start with $B = \begin{pmatrix} 1 & 1 \\ -1 & -2 \end{pmatrix}$

or

$$B = \begin{pmatrix} 1 & 1 \\ -2 & 0 \end{pmatrix},$$

where B is the basic vector

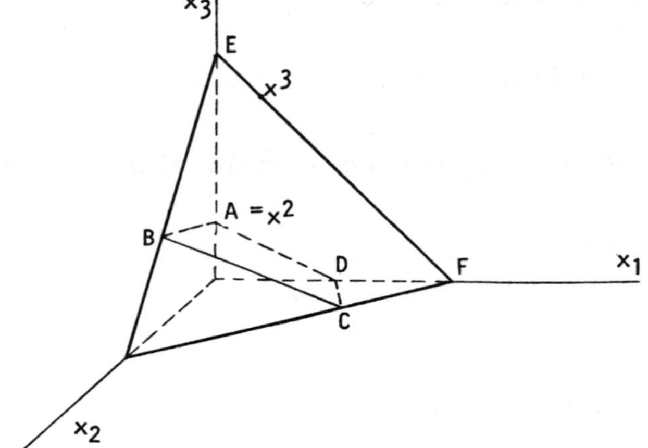

Solution: Choose

$$B = \begin{pmatrix} 1 & 1 \\ -1 & -2 \end{pmatrix},$$

the first and third column;

$$B^{-1} = \begin{pmatrix} 2 & 1 \\ -1 & -1 \end{pmatrix}, \qquad B^{-1}b = \begin{pmatrix} 6 \\ -2 \end{pmatrix}.$$

Hence B is not a feasible basis. Choose

$$B = \begin{pmatrix} 1 & 1 \\ -2 & 0 \end{pmatrix}$$

the third and fourth column;

$$B^{-1} = \begin{pmatrix} 0 & -\frac{1}{2} \\ 1 & \frac{1}{2} \end{pmatrix}, \qquad B^{-1}b = \begin{pmatrix} 1 \\ 3 \end{pmatrix}.$$

The corresponding basic solution is $x_3 = 1$, $y_1 = 3$, $x_1 = x_2 = y_2 = 0$, a feasible solution with value $V = 1$.

Hence, $x^1 = (0,0,1)^T$ with value $V(x^1) = 1$; $M(x^1) = \{2\}$, $N(x^1) = \{1,2\}$.

Hence, one has to require

$$-s_1 + s_2 - 2s_3 \leqq 0, \quad s_1 \geqq 0, \quad s_2 \geqq 0 \text{ and } s_1 + s_2 + s_3 > 0.$$

A solution of this system, hence a usable direction is $s^1 = (1,1,1)^T$ (there are many other ones). Now calculate the maximum value of λ for which $x = x^1 + \lambda s^1$ is feasible. One has $x^1 + \lambda s^1 = (\lambda,\lambda,1+\lambda)^T$, so that λ will be determined by the first inequality $x_1 + 2x_2 + x_3 \leqq 4$ (the other inequalities are satisfied for all $\lambda \geqq 0$). Hence $4\lambda + 1 = 4$, $\lambda_1 = 3/4$. The new solution is

$$x^2 = \begin{pmatrix} 3/4 \\ 3/4 \\ 7/4 \end{pmatrix}, \quad V(x^2) = 13/4, \quad M(x^2) = \{1\}, \; N(x^2) = \phi, \quad y^2 = \begin{pmatrix} 0 \\ 3/2 \end{pmatrix}$$

One now has to require

$$s_1 + 2s_2 + s_3 \leqq 0, \qquad s_1 + s_2 + s_3 > 0.$$

These relations are for instance satisfied by $s^2 = (0,-1,2)^T$. The steplength will now be determined by the requirement $x_2 \geqq 0$, hence $\lambda_2 = 3/4$. This gives

$$x^3 = \begin{pmatrix} 3/4 \\ 0 \\ 13/4 \end{pmatrix}, \quad V(x^3) = 4, \quad M(x^3) = \{1\}, \quad N(x^3) = \{2\}, \quad y^3 = \begin{pmatrix} 0 \\ 21/4 \end{pmatrix}$$

One has to require

$$s_1 + 2s_2 + s_3 \leqq 0, \qquad s_2 \geqq 0, \qquad s_1 + s_2 + s_3 > 0.$$

This is an inconsistent system since $s_1 + 2s_2 + s_3 = (s_1 + s_2 + s_3) + s_2 > 0$ according to the latter two relations and ≤ 0 according to the first one. Hence, there is no usable direction, so that one has arrived at a maximum.

R is the region ABCDEF (see Fig.), $x^1 = A$. The maximum x^3 obtained is not a vertex but situated on the edge. There are two optimal vertices, viz.

$$E = \begin{pmatrix} 0 \\ 0 \\ 4 \end{pmatrix} \quad \text{and} \quad F = \begin{pmatrix} 4 \\ 0 \\ 0 \end{pmatrix}.$$

Any point on the edge EF is optimal as well.

Here, a "trial and error" method to solve the linear programming problem has been demonstrated. There is no guarantee that a maximum will be reached unless the method to find a usable direction is systematized.

FINDING DUALS

• PROBLEM 2-40

Consider the problem:

$$\text{maximize } x_1 + 3x_2$$

subject to:

$$\begin{aligned} 6x_1 + 19x_2 &\leq 100 \\ 3x_1 + 5x_2 &\leq 40 \\ x_1 - 3x_2 &\leq 33 \\ x_2 &\leq 25 \\ x_1 &\leq 42 \\ x_1, x_2 &\geq 0 . \end{aligned}$$

Find its dual problem.

Solution: The dual problem is constructed from the primal problem (the primal can be constructed from the dual similarly) as follows:

1. Each constraint in one problem corresponds to a variable in the other problem.

2. The elements of the right-hand side of the constraints in one problem are equal to the respective coefficients of the objective function in the other problem.

3. One problem seeks maximization and the other seeks minimization.

4. The maximization problem has ($\leq$) constraints and the minimization problem has ($\geq$) constraints.

5. The variables in both problems are nonnegative.

The dual for this problem is constructed as follows.

Designate y_1, y_2, y_3, y_4, and y_5 as the dual variables associated with the first, second, third, fourth and fifth primal constraints. The dual problem is:

minimize

$$100y_1 + 40y_2 + 33y_3 + 25y_4 + 42y_5$$

subject to:

$$6y_1 + 3y_2 + y_3 \qquad + y_5 \geq 1$$

$$19y_1 + 5y_2 - 3y_3 + y_4 \qquad \geq 3$$

$$y_1, y_2, y_3, y_4, y_5 \geq 0$$

In this case, the number of constraints in the dual problem are less than those in the primal problem. Thus, it is easier to solve the dual problem computationally, for an optimal solution. In LP problems computational difficulty depends on the number of constraints rather than the number of variables.

• PROBLEM 2-41

Find the dual to:

$$\text{Maximize} \quad P = x_1 + 2x_2$$

where:

$$x_1 \geq 0, \; x_2 \geq 0$$

and

$$x_1 + 2x_2 \leq 10$$

$$-x_1 - x_2 \leq -30 .$$

Solution: The dual is

$$\text{Minimize } C = 10y_1 - 30y_2$$

where:

$y_1 \geq 0, \ y_2 \geq 0$

and

$$y_1 - y_2 \geq 1$$

$$2y_1 - y_2 \geq 2 \ .$$

These constraints put no restrictions on y_2, and hence C can be made arbitrarily small.

• PROBLEM 2-42

Find the dual to:

$$\max \quad 2x_1 + x_2 + x_3 - x_4$$

subject to:

$$\begin{aligned} x_1 - x_2 + 2x_3 + 2x_4 &\leq 3 \\ 2x_1 + 2x_2 - x_3 &= 4 \\ x_1 - 2x_2 + 3x_3 + 4x_4 &\geq 5 \\ x_1, x_2, x_3 &\geq 0, \end{aligned}$$

x_4 unrestricted.

Solution:

$$\min \ 3y_1 + 4y_2 + 5y_3$$

subject to:

$$\begin{aligned} y_1 + 2y_2 + y_3 &\geq 2 \\ -y_1 + 2y_2 - 2y_3 &\geq 1 \\ 2y_1 - y_2 + 3y_3 &\geq 1 \\ 2y_1 + 4y_3 &= -1 \\ y_1 &\geq 0 \end{aligned}$$

y_2 unrestricted

$$y_3 \leq 0 \ .$$

• PROBLEM 2-43

Find the dual of the following problem:

$$\text{maximize } x_0 = 15x_1 + 3x_2 + 16x_3$$

subject to:

$$x_1 + x_2 - x_3 \le 2$$
$$x_1 + 13x_2 + x_3 = 2$$
$$x_1, x_2, x_3 \ge 0 \quad .$$

Solution: The standard form of this problem is:

$$\text{maximize } x_0 = 15x_1 + 3x_2 + 16x_3 + 0S_1$$

subject to:

$$x_1 + x_2 - x_3 + S_1 = 2$$
$$x_1 + 13x_2 + x_3 + 0S_1 = 2$$
$$x_1, x_2, x_3, S_1 \ge 0 \ .$$

The dual is then given by:

$$\text{minimize } y_0 = 2y_1 + 2y_2$$

subject to:

$$y_1 + y_2 \ge 15$$
$$y_1 + 13y_2 \ge 3$$
$$-y_1 + y_2 \ge 16$$
$$y_1 \ge 0$$

y_2 unrestricted in sign.

• PROBLEM 2-44

Find the dual to the following problem:

Maximize

$$4x_1 + 5x_2 + 3x_3 + 6x_4$$

subject to:

$$x_1 + 3x_2 + x_3 + 2x_4 \le 2$$
$$3x_1 + 3x_2 + 2x_3 + 2x_4 \le 4$$
$$3x_1 + 2x_2 + 4x_3 + 5x_4 \le 6$$
$$x_1, x_2, x_3, x_4 \ge 0$$

Solution: The dual of the given problem is:

Minimize

$$2y_1 + 4y_2 + 6y_3$$

Subject to

$$y_1 + 3y_2 + 3y_3 \geq 4$$

$$3y_1 + 3y_2 + 2y_3 \geq 5$$

$$y_1 + 2y_2 + 4y_3 \geq 3$$

$$2y_1 + 2y_2 + 5y_3 \geq 6$$

$$y_1, y_2, y_3 \geq 0$$

• PROBLEM 2-45

Find the dual to the following primal problem:

Maximize $z = x_1 + 1.5x_2$

subject to:

$$2x_1 + 3x_2 \leq 25$$

$$x_1 + x_2 \geq 1$$

$$x_1 - 2x_2 = 1$$

$$x_1, x_2 \geq 0$$

Solution: It may be rewritten as:

Maximize $z = x_1 + 1.5x_2$

subject to:

$$2x_1 + 3x_2 \leq 25$$

$$-x_1 - x_2 \leq -1$$

$$x_1 - 2x_2 \leq 1$$

$$-x_1 + 2x_2 \leq -1$$

$$x_1, x_2 \geq 0$$

by multiplying the second constraint by -1 and representing the third constraint as two inequalities. The dual of the rewritten problem is then the following:

Minimize $z = 25y_1 - y_2 + y_3 - y_4$

Subject to:
$$2y_1 - y_2 + y_3 - y_4 \geq 1$$
$$3y_1 - y_2 - 2y_3 + 2y_4 \geq 1.5$$
$$y_1, y_2, y_3, y_4 \geq 0 .$$

Since $y_3 - y_4$ appears in every constraint and objective function, it can be replaced with an unrestricted variable (y_5), as follows:

$$\text{Minimize } z = 25y_1 - y_2 + y_5$$
$$\text{subject to: } 2y_1 - y_2 + y_5 \geq 1$$
$$3y_1 - y_2 - 2y_5 \geq 1.5$$
$$y_1, y_2 \geq 0,$$
y_5 unrestricted in sign.

• PROBLEM 2-46

Find the dual to this primal problem and derive conclusions as to the implications of the dual:

$$\text{Maximize: } x_0 = 2x_1 + 3x_3$$
$$\text{Subject to: } -3x_1 + x_2 + 2x_3 \leqq 5$$
$$-2x_1 - x_2 \leqq 1$$
$$x_1, x_2, x_3 \geqq 0$$

Solution: Dual

$$\text{Minimize: } y_0 = 5y_1 + y_2$$
$$\text{Subject to: } 3y_1 - 2y_2 \geqq 2$$
$$y_1 - y_2 \geqq 0$$
$$2y_1 \geqq 3$$
$$y_1, y_2 \geqq 0$$

$x_1 = x_2 = x_3 = 0$ is a feasible solution to the primal problem. But the dual problem is infeasible since the constraint $-3y_1 - 2y_2 \geq 2$ is inconsistent. (For all nonnegative values of y_1 and y_2, the left-hand side is nonpositive while the right-hand side is strictly positive.) The primal problem has an unbounded solution such that maximum x_0 tends to infinity when the dual is infeasible.

• **PROBLEM 2-47**

The optimum solution to the problem:

$$\text{Maximize} \quad P = 12x_1 + 9x_2 \tag{1}$$

subject to:

$$3x_1 + 2x_2 \le 7$$

$$3x_1 + x_2 \le 4 \tag{2}$$

$$x_1 \ge 0, \; x_2 \ge 0$$

is $P = 9(7/2) = 31\frac{1}{2}$. The solution to the dual is $y_1 = 4\frac{1}{2}$, $y_2 = 0$. Now assume the first constraint of (2) is changed from 7 to 8, i.e.,

$$3x_1 + 2x_2 \le 8.$$

Find the increase in P. What is the dual for this new problem?

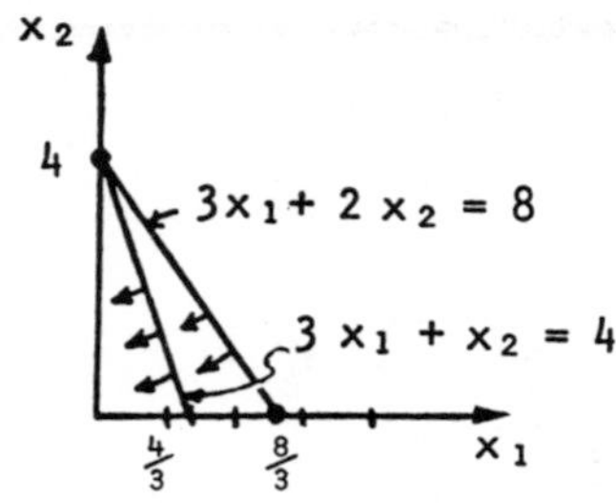

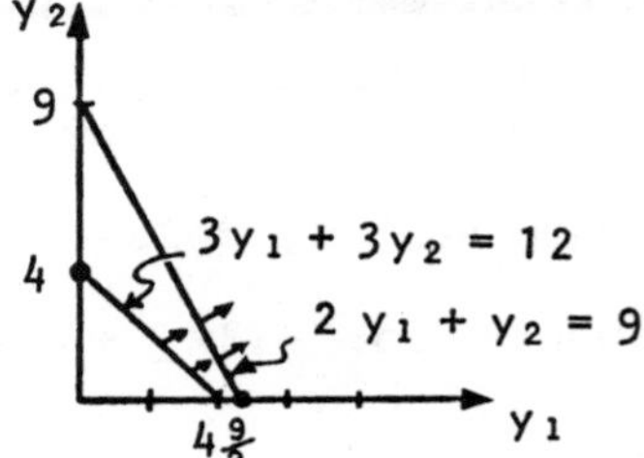

Solution: The new problem is:

$$\text{Maximize} \quad P = 12x_1 + 9x_2$$

subject to:

$$3x_1 + 2x_2 \le 8$$

$$3x_1 + x_2 \le 4$$

$$x_1 \ge 0, \; x_2 \ge 0.$$

The dual to this problem is:

$$\text{Minimize} \quad C = 8y_1 + 4y_2$$

subject to:

$$3y_1 + 3y_2 \ge 12$$

$$2y_1 + y_2 \ge 9$$

$$y_1, y_2 \ge 0.$$

Graph the new program and its dual: (See fig.)

If a program has an optimal solution it has an optimal solution at the intersection of two constraints. From the graph of the primal, P is maximized when $x_1 = 0$ and $x_2 = 4$. The value of P is:

$$P = 9(4) = 36.$$

Note that P has increased by 4½ units as predicted by the dual value $y_1 = 4\frac{1}{2}$. But, examining the graph of the new dual there is no unique optimal solution, since any values for y_1 and y_2 on the line going from $y_1 = 4\frac{1}{2}$ to $y_2 = 9$ will satisfy the constraints.

Assume that another unit is added to the first constraint in the primal which now becomes:

Maximize $\quad P = 12x_1 + 9x_2$

subject to

$$3x_1 + 2x_2 \le 9$$

$$3x_1 + x_2 \le 4$$

$$x_1 \ge 0, \; x_2 \ge 0.$$

The optimum value of P is still 36. The value does not change, since the other unchanged restraint acts to prevent an improvement unless both restraints are changed. The solution is degenerate; of the two primal ordinary variables (x_1 and x_2) and the two primal slack variables, only one of these four variables (x_2) is positive even though there are two constraints.

• PROBLEM 2-48

A: Maximize $\quad f = 4x_1 + 3x_2$

subject to: $\quad -2x_1 - x_2 \le -4$

$$2x_1 - 2x_2 \le 5$$

$$x_1, x_2 \ge 0.$$

This problem is unbounded.

B: Maximize $\quad f = 3x_1 + 5x_2$

subject to: $\quad x_1 - x_2 \le -2$

$$-x_1 + x_2 \le -2$$

$$x_1, x_2 \ge 0.$$

Now the second constraint can be rewritten as:

$$x_1 - x_2 \ge 2$$

(by multiplying through by -1). There are no points which can possibly satisfy these two conflicting constraints, so the primal is infeasible.

Give the dual problems and their optimal solutions.

Solutions:

A: The dual is:

$$\text{Minimize} \quad g = -4y_1 + 5y_2$$

$$\text{subject to:} \quad -2y_1 + 2y_2 \geq 4$$

$$-y_1 - 2y_2 \geq 3$$

$$y_1, y_2 \geq 0.$$

Rewrite the second constraint as:

$$y_1 + y_2 \leq -3$$

which is clearly impossible to satisfy for nonnegative y_1 and y_2. Thus, the dual is infeasible.

B: The dual is:

$$\text{Minimize} \quad g = -2y_1 - 2y_2$$

$$\text{subject to:} \quad y_1 - y_2 \geq 3$$

$$-y_1 + y_2 \geq 5$$

$$y_1, y_2 \geq 0.$$

If one rewrites the second constraint as

$$y_1 - y_2 \leq -5$$

it is apparent that the dual is also infeasible.

• PROBLEM 2-49

A rigid, weightless, four-sided plate is supported at its four corners.

The following, idealized assumptions are made. The supports are rigid. They may be subjected to an arbitrarily high load by tension (the plate is firmly connected to the supports, so that it cannot be lifted off). They may be subjected to loading by compression up to a creep limit, F_j, $j = 1, \ldots, 4$. Thus the jth support remains rigid and unchanged in length while subject to a force P with $-\infty < P \leq F_j$. If P exceeds the creep limit F_j, the support collapses.

The problem is to find the greatest load any point T of the plate may be subjected without causing a collapse of the supports. This maximum admissible load is called the limit load P* at the point T, and naturally depends on the location of T.

Formulate this question as a Linear Programming problem and construct its dual. Derive conclusions as to the physical implications of the dual. Note that; even if one support collapses, if the forces at the other corners are still $P_j < F_j$, the supported plate will not yet collapse; for then there is the (statically determined) case of a loaded plate supported at three corners. Only when the force acting at a second corner exceeds the creep limit will a collapse result (which consists of a rotation about the axis connecting the two remainig corners).

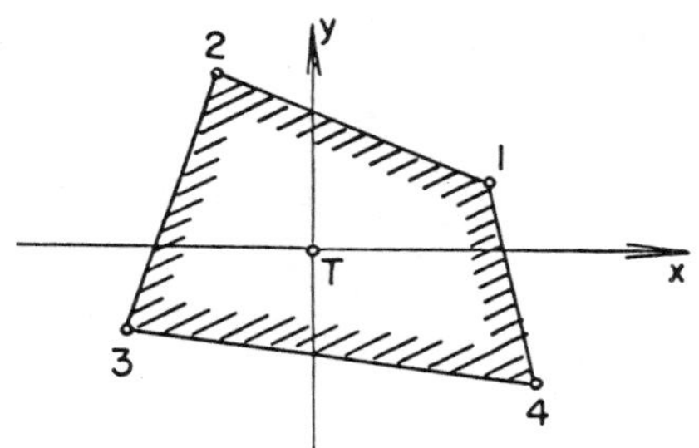

Fig. 1

A plate supported at four places.

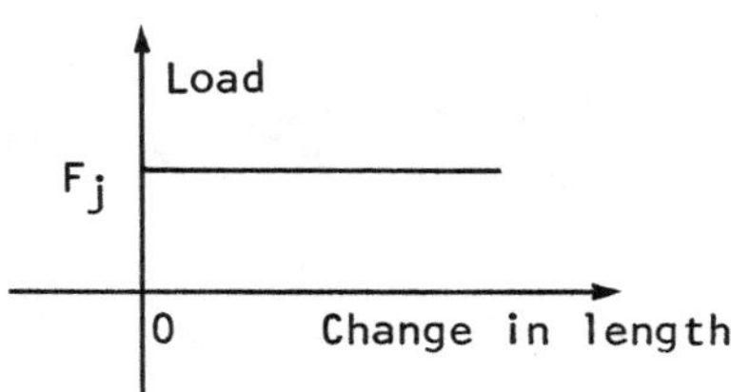

Behavior of a support under load Fig. 2

<u>Solution</u>: Let P_j, j = 1, . . ., 4, denote the force acting on the jth support. As the load P at point T increases from zero, the force $P_j = F_j$ at some corner is eventually reached.

Choose the coordinate system so that T is the origin and the corners of the quadrilateral have coordinates (ξ, η_j), j = 1, . . ., 4. If P is the load at the point T, there are the equilibrium constraints:

$$P = \sum_{j=1}^{4} P_j, \tag{1}$$

$$\sum_{j=1}^{4} P_j \xi_j = 0, \quad \sum_{j=1}^{4} P_j \eta_j = 0. \tag{2}$$

It is desired to find the maximal value P^* of P for which there still exist P_j satisfying (1), (2), and

$$P_j \le F_j \quad (j = 1, \ldots, 4),$$

so that the creep limits are not exceeded. This is, therefore, a linear optimization problem in four variables P_j, without positivity constraints, and six constraints, two equalities and four inequalities. Using the notation (for obtaining the dual of a LP problem with equality and inequality constraints, as well as restricted and unrestricted signs for variables):

$$\underset{\sim}{A} = \begin{pmatrix} \underset{\sim}{A}_{11} & \underset{\sim}{A}_{12} \\ \underset{\sim}{A}_{21} & \underset{\sim}{A}_{22} \end{pmatrix} \begin{matrix} m_1 \text{ rows} \\ m_2 \text{ rows} \end{matrix}$$
$$\qquad \begin{matrix} n_1 & n_2 \\ \text{columns} & \text{columns} \end{matrix}$$

where $m_1 + m_2 = m$ and $n_1 + n_2 = n$. Here, $m_1 < n$, and the matrix $(\underset{\sim}{A}_{11} | \underset{\sim}{A}_{12})$ has rank m_1. Let there also be given the vectors:

$$\underset{\sim}{b} = \begin{pmatrix} \underset{\sim}{b}^1 \\ \underset{\sim}{b}^2 \end{pmatrix}, \quad \underset{\sim}{p} = \begin{pmatrix} \underset{\sim}{p}^1 \\ \underset{\sim}{p}^2 \end{pmatrix},$$

with $\underset{\sim}{b}^1 \in R^{m_1}$, $\underset{\sim}{b}^2 \in R^{m_2}$, $\underset{\sim}{p}^1 \in R^{n_1}$, $\underset{\sim}{p}^2 \in R^{n_2}$. The two problems which will prove to be primal and dual are:

$\tilde{D}^0$: Find $\underset{\sim}{x} = \begin{pmatrix} \underset{\sim}{x}^1 \\ \underset{\sim}{x}^2 \end{pmatrix} (\underset{\sim}{x}^1 \in R^{n_1}, \underset{\sim}{x}^2 \in R^{n_2})$ such that:

$$\underset{\sim}{A}_{11}\underset{\sim}{x}^1 + \underset{\sim}{A}_{12}\underset{\sim}{x}^2 = \underset{\sim}{b}^1, \qquad \underset{\sim}{x}^1 \ge \underset{\sim}{0},$$

$$\underset{\sim}{A}_{21}\underset{\sim}{x}^1 + \underset{\sim}{A}_{22}\underset{\sim}{x}^2 \ge \underset{\sim}{b}^2, \qquad \underset{\sim}{x}^2 \text{ unrestricted in sign}$$

$$\underset{\sim}{p}'\underset{\sim}{x} = \underset{\sim}{p}^{1\prime}\underset{\sim}{x}^1 + \underset{\sim}{p}^{2\prime}\underset{\sim}{x}^2 = \text{Min!}$$

$\tilde{D}^1$: Find $\underset{\sim}{w} = \begin{pmatrix} \underset{\sim}{w}^1 \\ \underset{\sim}{w}^2 \end{pmatrix} (\underset{\sim}{w}^1 \in R^{m_1}, \underset{\sim}{w}^2 \in R^{m_2})$ such that:

$$\underset{\sim}{A}'_{11}\underset{\sim}{w}^1 + \underset{\sim}{A}'_{21}\underset{\sim}{w}^2 \le \underset{\sim}{p}^1, \qquad \underset{\sim}{w}^1 \text{ unrestricted in sign}$$

$$\underset{\sim}{A}'_{12}\underset{\sim}{w}^1 + \underset{\sim}{A}'_{22}\underset{\sim}{w}^2 = \underset{\sim}{p}^2, \qquad \underset{\sim}{w}^2 \ge \underset{\sim}{0},$$

$$\underset{\sim}{w}'\underset{\sim}{b} = \underset{\sim}{w}^{1\prime}\underset{\sim}{b}^1 + \underset{\sim}{w}^{2\prime}\underset{\sim}{b}^2 = \text{Max!}$$

Write the problem in form $\tilde{D}^1$, where

$$\underset{\sim}{w}^1 = \begin{bmatrix} P_1 \\ P_2 \\ P_3 \\ P_4 \end{bmatrix}, \quad \underset{\sim}{A}'_{11} = \begin{bmatrix} 1 & 0 & 0 & 0 \\ 0 & 1 & 0 & 0 \\ 0 & 0 & 1 & 0 \\ 0 & 0 & 0 & 1 \end{bmatrix}, \quad \underset{\sim}{A}'_{12} = \begin{pmatrix} \xi_1 & \xi_2 & \xi_3 & \xi_4 \\ \eta_1 & \eta_2 & \eta_3 & \eta_4 \end{pmatrix}$$

$$\underset{\sim}{p}^1 = \begin{bmatrix} F_1 \\ F_2 \\ F_3 \\ F_4 \end{bmatrix}, \quad \underset{\sim}{p}^2 = \begin{pmatrix} 0 \\ 0 \end{pmatrix}, \quad \underset{\sim}{b}^1 = \begin{bmatrix} 1 \\ 1 \\ 1 \\ 1 \end{bmatrix},$$

and $\underset{\sim}{w}^2$, $\underset{\sim}{A}'_{21}$, $\underset{\sim}{A}'_{22}$, and $\underset{\sim}{b}^2$ do not appear (so $m_2 = 0$, $n_1 = 4$, $n_2 = 2$, and $m_1 = 4$):

$$\underset{\sim}{A}'_{11}\underset{\sim}{w}^1 \leq \underset{\sim}{p}^1, \quad \underset{\sim}{A}'_{12}\underset{\sim}{w}^1 = \underset{\sim}{p}^2, \quad P = \underset{\sim}{w}^{1'}\underset{\sim}{b}^1 = \text{Max!}.$$

The dual problem then is to find an $\underset{\sim}{x} = \begin{pmatrix} \underset{\sim}{x}^1 \\ \underset{\sim}{x}^2 \end{pmatrix}$

$(\underset{\sim}{x}^1 \in R^4, \underset{\sim}{x}^2 \in R^2)$ with $\underset{\sim}{A}_{11}x^1 + \underset{\sim}{A}_{12}x^2 = \underset{\sim}{b}^1$, $\underset{\sim}{x}^1 \geq \underset{\sim}{0}$, $\underset{\sim}{p}^{1'}\underset{\sim}{x}^1 + \underset{\sim}{p}^{2'}\underset{\sim}{x}^2 = \text{Min!}$.

Setting $\underset{\sim}{x}^1 = (v_1, v_2, v_3, v_4)'$, $\underset{\sim}{x}^2 = (\omega_x, \omega_y)'$, the problem is obtained:

$$\left.\begin{aligned} v_j + \xi_j\omega_x + \eta_j\omega_y &= 1 \\ v_j &\geq 0 \end{aligned}\right\}(j = 1, \ldots, 4), \qquad \begin{matrix}(3)\\(4)\end{matrix}$$

$$\sum_{j=1}^{4} F_j v_j = \text{Min!} \qquad (5)$$

where v_j can be interpreted as the virtual deflection at the jth corner, ω_x as the virtual rotation about the axis $x = 0$, and ω_y as the virtual rotation about the axis $y = 0$. (3) is a consequence of the assumption that the plate is rigid, if the point T (the origin of the coordinate system) is subjected to a virtual deflection $v = 1$, in the direction of the applied load, and the corners are subjected to a virtual deflection v_j and also to virtual rotations ω_x and ω_y. $v_j \geq 0$ follows from the assumption that the supports may be subjected to arbitrarily high loads by tension without a change in length. A positive deflection $v_j > 0$ can only occur if the force acting at the jth corner is F_j, since the supports remain rigid under a smaller load. The virtual work (= force times virtual deflection) at the corners thus adds to $\sum_{j=1}^{4} F_j v_j$, while at the point T the virtual work is $Pv = P$, since $v = 1$.

By the principle of virtual work,

$$P = \sum_{j=1}^{4} F_j v_j.$$

(5) requires that the smallest load $P = P^{**}$, for which a positive virtual deflection $v = 1$ is possible at the point T, be found. For $P < P^{**}$ any such virtual deflection is impossible, and the system remains rigid.

Duality theorem (for $\tilde{D}^0$ and $\tilde{D}^1$) yields the conclusion that $P^* = P^{**}$, and this is just shown by physical arguments. In addition, given a solution $P = P^* = P^{**}$ of the dual problems, v_j can be greater than zero only if $P_j = F_j$ (at the corner in question).

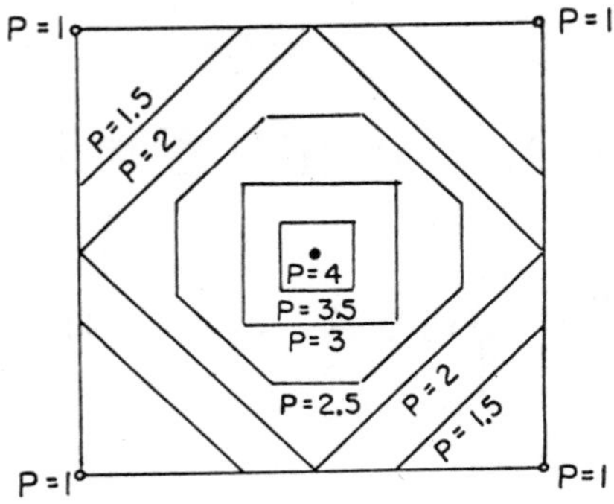

Fig. 3

Square plate with creep limits $F_j = 1$

The case of a square plate with equal creep limits $F_j = 1$, $j = 1, \ldots, 4$, at all four corners and the positivity constraints $P_j \geq 0$, $j = 1, \ldots, 4$, is shown in Figure 3.

CHAPTER 3

LINEAR PROGRAMMING - THE SIMPLEX METHOD

ROW OPERATIONS

• **PROBLEM 3-1**

Assume the following system of equations:

$$\begin{cases} 5x_1 + 4x_2 + 3x_3 = 8 \\ 2x_1 + 7x_2 + 5x_3 = 5 \\ 4x_1 + 4x_2 + 2x_3 = 4. \end{cases}$$

Solve for x_1, x_2, x_3 using elementary row operations.

Solution:

Step 1. Select the variable farthest to the right, x_3.

Step 2. Multiply the last equation by 1/2:

$$\begin{cases} 5x_1 + 4x_2 + 3x_3 = 8 \\ 2x_1 + 7x_2 + 5x_3 = 5 \\ 2x_1 + 2x_2 + x_3 = 2 . \end{cases}$$

Step 3. Eliminate x_3 from all equations above it. Multiply the third equation by five and subtract it from the second:

$$\begin{cases} 5x_1 + 4x_2 + 3x_3 = 8 \\ -8x_1 - 3x_2 = -5 \\ 2x_1 + 2x_2 + x_3 = 2\ . \end{cases}$$

Multiply the third equation by three and subtract it from the first:

$$\begin{cases} -\ x_1 - 2x_1 = 2 \\ -8x_1 - 3x_2 = -5 \\ 2x_1 + 2x_2 + x_3 = 2\ . \end{cases}$$

Step 4. Temporarily strike out the last equation and the last variable (which already has been eliminated from the first two equations):

$$\begin{cases} -\ x_1 - 2x_2 \qquad = 2 \\ -8x_1 - 3x_2 \qquad = -5 \\ 2x_1 + 2x_2 + x_3 = 2\ . \end{cases}$$

Now proceed by Steps 1-3 to deal with the smaller system. First multiply the second equation by -1/3:

$$\begin{cases} -x_1 - 2x_2 = 2 \\ +8/3x_1 + x_2 = 5/3 \\ 2x_1 + 2x_2 + x_3 = 2\ . \end{cases}$$

Multiply the second equation by two and add to the first:

$$\begin{cases} 13/3x_1 = 16/3 \\ 8/3x_1 + x_2 = 5/3 \\ 2x_1 + 2x_2 + x_3 = 2\ . \end{cases}$$

Step 5. Strike out the second equation:

$$\begin{cases} 13/3x_1 = 16/3 \\ \sout{8/3x_1 + x_2 = 5/3} \\ \sout{2x_1 + 2x_2 + x_3 = 2} \end{cases}$$

Multiply the first equation by 3/13:

$$\begin{cases} x_1 = 16/13 \\ 8/3x_1 + x_2 = 5/3 \\ 2x_1 + 2x_2 + x_3 = 2 \end{cases}$$

Now all coefficients above the main diagonal have been eliminated and all coefficients on the main diagonal are equal to one.

Step 6. Eliminate all coefficients below the main diagonal. Multiply the first equation by 8/3 and subtract from the second equation:

$$\begin{cases} x_1 = 16/13 \\ x_2 = -21/13 \\ 2x_1 + 2x_2 + x_3 = 2 \ . \end{cases}$$

Multiply the first equation by two and subtract it from the third equation:

$$\begin{cases} x_1 = 16/13 \\ x_2 = -21/13 \\ 2x_2 + x_3 = -6/13 \ . \end{cases}$$

Multiply the second equation by two and subtract from the third:

$$\begin{cases} x_1 & = 16/13 \\ \quad x_2 & = -21/13 \\ \qquad x_3 & = 36/13 \end{cases}$$

The solution is now complete.

• PROBLEM 3-2

Use row operations to solve for X, Y and Z in the following system of equations:

$$2X + 4Y + 2Z = 16$$

$$2X - Y - 2Z = -6$$

$$4X + Y - 2Z = 0$$

Solution:

1a. $2X + 4Y + 2Z = 16$

2a. $2X - Y - 2Z = -6$

3a. $4X + Y - 2Z = 0$

Subtract 1a from equation 2a to obtain a new equation 2b. Multiply equation 1a by 2 and subtract from equation 3a to obtain new equation 3b.

1b. $2X + 4Y + 2Z = 16$

2b. $- 5Y - 4Z = -22$

3b. $- 7Y - 6Z = -32$

Multiply equation 2b by (7/5) and subtract from equation 3b to form new equation 3c.

1c. $2X + 4Y + 2Z = 16$

2c. $-5Y - 4Z = -22$

3c. $-\frac{2}{5}Z = -\frac{6}{5}$

These final three equations are in echelon form.

The next step is to solve for the roots.

$-\frac{2}{5}Z = -\frac{6}{5}$	Solve equation 3c for Z.
$Z = 3$	Substitute this value for Z into equation 2c.
$-5Y-4(3)=-22$	Solve equation 2c for Y.
$-5Y=-10$	
$Y=2$	Substitute this value for Y and the value for Z into equation 1c.
$2x+4(2)+2(3)=16$	Solve equation 1c for X.
$2X=2$	
$X=1$	This completes the three roots:

$$X = 1,\ Y=2,\ Z=3.$$

• PROBLEM 3-3

Use row operations to solve:

$$x_1 + 4x_2 + x_3 = 2$$

$$2x_1 + 3x_2 = -1$$

$$8x_1 + 2x_3 = 0 .$$

Solution: Denote the first row by R_1, the second by R_2, and the third by R_3 .

Step	Operation	Result
1	$R_2 - 2R_1$	$x_1+4x_2+x_3=2$ $-5x_2-2x_3=-5$ $8x_1+2x_3=0$
2	$R_3 - 8R_1$	$x_1+4x_2+x_3=2$ $-5x_2-2x_3=-5$ $-32x_2-6x_3=-16$
3	$R_1 + \frac{4}{5}R_2$	$x_1 - \frac{3}{5}x_3=-2$ $-5x_2-2x_3=-5$ $-32x_2-6x_3=-16$
4	$R_2 - \frac{5}{32}R_3$	$x_1 - \frac{3}{5}x_3=-2$ $-\frac{17}{16}x_3=-\frac{5}{2}$ $-32x_2-6x_3=-16$
5	$R_3 - \frac{96}{17}R_2$	$x_1 - \frac{3}{5}x_3=-2$ $-\frac{17}{16}x_3=-\frac{5}{2}$ $-32x_2=-\frac{32}{17}$

6	$R_1 - \frac{48}{85} R_2$	$x_1 \quad\quad = -\frac{10}{17}$
		$-\frac{17}{16}x_3 = -\frac{5}{2}$
		$-32x_2 \quad = 16$

TABLE 1

• PROBLEM 3-4

Find a solution using row operations on the given (A, b),

$$\begin{pmatrix} 1 & -2 & 1 & 1 & 3 \\ \boxed{2} & 0 & -1 & -1 & 4 \\ 0 & 1 & 1 & -1 & 4 \\ 1 & 1 & 1 & -4 & 0 \end{pmatrix} . \tag{1}$$

Solution: Work from left to right and top to bottom. There is already a 1 in the (1,1) position of matrix (1). To obtain a 0 where the 2 presently exists in the (2,1) position, multiply row 1 by -2 and add, term by term, to row 2, obtaining a new row 2. After that the array appears as:

$$\begin{matrix} 1 & -2 & 1 & 1 & 3 \\ 0 & 4 & -3 & -4 & -4 \\ \boxed{0} & 1 & 1 & -1 & 4 \\ 1 & 1 & 1 & -4 & 0 . \end{matrix} \tag{2}$$

Still looking at column 1 of (2), one finds the (3,1) element already 0; so observe the (4,1) element, where there is a 1, and multiply row 1 by -1, add term by term to row 4, and obtain a new row 4 with a 0 in location (4,1):

$$\begin{matrix} 1 & -2 & 1 & 1 & 3 \\ 0 & \boxed{4} & -3 & -4 & -4 \\ 0 & 1 & 1 & -1 & 4 \\ 0 & 3 & 0 & -5 & -3 . \end{matrix} \tag{3}$$

Having completed column 1, proceed to column 2. Note, a 1 in position (2,2) and 0's in (3,2) and (4,2) is needed. The 1 is obtained first; therefore, multiply row 2 of (3) by $\frac{1}{4}$. Thus what is obtained is:

$$\begin{matrix} 1 & -2 & 1 & 1 & 3 \\ 0 & 1 & -\frac{3}{4} & -1 & -1 \\ 0 & 1 & 1 & -1 & 4 \\ 0 & 3 & 0 & -5 & -3 \end{matrix} \tag{4}$$

and next set about obtaining 0's in locations (3,2) and (4,2) in (4).

Continuing the process to the end, eventually the following array is obtained

$$\begin{array}{ccccc} 1 & -2 & 1 & 1 & 3 \\ 0 & 1 & -\frac{3}{4} & -1 & -1 \\ 0 & 0 & 1 & 0 & \frac{20}{7} \\ 0 & 0 & 0 & 1 & \frac{45}{14} \end{array}$$

which gives the solution:

$$x_4 = \frac{45}{14}$$

$$x_3 = \frac{20}{7}$$

$$x_2 = -1 + \frac{45}{14} + \frac{3}{4}\left(\frac{20}{7}\right) = \frac{61}{14}$$

$$x_1 = 3 - \frac{45}{14} - \frac{20}{7} + 2\left(\frac{61}{14}\right) = \frac{79}{14}$$

• PROBLEM 3-5

Consider the following three linear equations in three unknowns:

$$x_1 + 4x_2 + 3x_3 = 1 \quad (1)$$

$$2x_1 + 5x_2 + 4x_3 = 4 \quad (2)$$

$$x_1 - 3x_2 - 2x_3 = 5 \ . \quad (3)$$

Use elementary row operations to solve for x_1, x_2, and x_3.

Solution: The method of solving the linear equations above is the following. First use equation (1) to eliminate the variable x_1 from equations (2) and (3); i.e., subtract 2 times (1) from (2) and then subtract (1) from (3), giving

$$x_1 + 4x_2 + 3x_3 = 1 \quad (4)$$

$$- 3x_2 - 2x_3 = 2 \quad (5)$$

$$- 7x_2 - 5x_3 = 4 \ . \quad (6)$$

Next divide equation (5) through by the coefficient of x_2, namely, -3, obtaining $x_2 + \frac{2}{3}x_3 = -\frac{2}{3}$. Use this equation to eliminate x_2 from each of the other two equations. To do this, subtract 4 times this equation from (4) and add 7 times this equation to (6), obtaining:

$$x_1 + 0 + \frac{1}{3}x_3 = \frac{11}{3} \qquad (7)$$

$$x_2 + \frac{2}{3}x_3 = -\frac{2}{3} \qquad (8)$$

$$-\frac{1}{3}x_3 = -\frac{2}{3} \qquad (9)$$

The last step is to divide through (9) by $-\frac{1}{3}$, which is the coefficient of x_3, obtaining the equation $x_3 = 2$; use this equation to eliminate x_3 from the first two equations as follows:

$$x_1 + 0 + 0 = 3 \qquad (10)$$

$$x_2 + 0 = -2 \qquad (11)$$

$$x_3 = 2 \, . \qquad (12)$$

The solution can now be read from these equations as $x_1 = 3$, $x_2 = -2$, and $x_3 = 2$.

• PROBLEM 3-6

Consider the following linear equations:

$$x_1 - 2x_2 - 3x_3 = 2 \qquad (1)$$

$$x_1 - 4x_2 - 13x_3 = 14 \qquad (2)$$

$$-3x_1 + 5x_2 + 4x_3 = 0 \, . \qquad (3)$$

Solve for x_1, x_2, x_3 using elementary row operations.

Solution: Use equation (1) to eliminate the variable x_1 from the other two equations:

$$x_1 - 2x_2 - 3x_3 = 2 \qquad (4)$$

$$-2x_2 - 10x_3 = 12 \qquad (5)$$

$$-x_2 - 5x_3 = 6 \, . \qquad (6)$$

Divide equation (5) by -2, obtaining the equation $x_2 + 5x_3 = -6$. Use this equation to elminate the variable x_2 from each of the other equations--namely, add twice this equation to (4) and then add the equation to (6):

$$x_1 + 0 + 7x_3 = -10 \tag{7}$$

$$x_2 + 5x_3 = -6 \tag{8}$$

$$0 = 0 . \tag{9}$$

The last equation has been eliminated completely. Notice that the variable x_3 can be chosen completely arbitrarily in these equations. Move the terms involving x_3 to the right-hand side, giving:

$$x_1 = -10 - 7x_3 \tag{10}$$

$$x_2 = - 6 - 5x_3 \tag{11}$$

Substitute particular values for x_3 to obtain numerical solutions. Thus if one assumes $x_3 = 1, 0, -2$, respectively, and the resulting numbers are computed, using (10) and (11), the following numerical solutions are obtained:

$$x_1 = -17, \quad x_2 = -11, \quad x_3 = 1$$

$$x_1 = -10, \quad x_2 = -6, \quad x_3 = 0$$

$$x_1 = 4, \quad x_2 = 4, \quad x_3 = -2 .$$

To summarize, the problem has an infinite number of solutions, one for each numerical value of x_3 which is substituted into equations (10) and (11).

• PROBLEM 3-7

Solve, using row operations:

$$\begin{pmatrix} 1 & 4 & 3 \\ 2 & 5 & 4 \\ 1 & -3 & -2 \end{pmatrix} \begin{pmatrix} x_1 \\ x_2 \\ x_3 \end{pmatrix} = \begin{pmatrix} 1 \\ 4 \\ 5 \end{pmatrix} \quad \text{and} = \begin{pmatrix} -1 \\ 0 \\ 2 \end{pmatrix}$$

Solution: It is possible to solve both sets of simultaneous equations at once. The following series of tableaus illustrate this:

$$\left(\begin{array}{ccc|cc} 1 & 4 & 3 & 1 & -1 \\ 2 & 5 & 4 & 4 & 0 \\ 1 & -3 & -2 & 5 & 2 \end{array}\right)$$

(Continued on the following page)

$$\left(\begin{array}{ccc|cc} 1 & 4 & 3 & 1 & -1 \\ 0 & -3 & -2 & 2 & 2 \\ 0 & -7 & -5 & 4 & 3 \end{array}\right)$$

$$\left(\begin{array}{ccc|cc} 1 & 0 & \frac{1}{3} & \frac{11}{3} & \frac{5}{3} \\ 0 & 1 & \frac{2}{3} & -\frac{2}{3} & -\frac{2}{3} \\ 0 & 0 & -\frac{1}{3} & -\frac{2}{3} & -\frac{5}{3} \end{array}\right)$$

$$\left(\begin{array}{ccc|cc} 1 & 0 & 0 & 3 & 0 \\ 0 & 1 & 0 & -2 & -4 \\ 0 & 0 & 1 & 2 & 5 \end{array}\right)$$

Thus, these answers are found:

$$x_1 = 3, \qquad x_2 = -2, \qquad x_3 = 2$$

to the first set of equations and the answers:

$$x_1 = 0, \qquad x_2 = -4, \qquad x_3 = 5$$

to the second set of equations.

SIMPLEX METHOD

• PROBLEM 3-8

Interchange the variables y and r in Tableau 1 by means of the pivot transformation. Interpret the resulting tableau. Determine what basic point corresponds to the resulting tableau. Do a check calculation.

x	y	z	1	
1	$\frac{2}{3}^{*}$	$\frac{1}{4}$	-900	= -r
0	$\frac{1}{3}$	$\frac{3}{4}$	-600	= -s
$\frac{1}{4}$	$\frac{2}{5}$	$\frac{1}{2}$	0	= u

(T.1)

Solution: Since it is desired to interchange the nonbasic variable y and the basic variable r, the pivot entry is thus

$p = \frac{2}{3}$, i.e., the entry label a_{12} with an asterisk next to it.

The resulting tableau-Tableau 2-is as follows

x	y	z	1	
$\frac{3}{2}$	$\frac{3}{2}$	$\frac{3}{8}$	-1350	= -y
$-\frac{1}{2}$	$-\frac{1}{2}$	$\frac{5}{8}$	-150	= -s
$-\frac{7}{20}$	$-\frac{3}{5}$	$\frac{7}{20}$	540	= u

(T.2)

Notice that the variables y and r have been interchanged, but that all other variables remained unchanged.

Pivot entry: $\frac{2}{3}$ to $\frac{3}{2}$.

Other entries in pivot row (row 1):

$$1 \text{ to } \frac{1}{\frac{2}{3}} = \frac{3}{2} , \quad \frac{1}{4} \text{ to } \frac{\frac{1}{4}}{\frac{2}{3}} = \frac{3}{8} ,$$

and

$$-900 \text{ to } \frac{-900}{\frac{2}{3}} = \frac{-2700}{2} = -1350.$$

Note that dividing by $\frac{2}{3}$ is equivalent to multiplying by $\frac{3}{2}$. Thus, for example,

$$\frac{1}{4} \cdot \frac{3}{2} = \frac{3}{8} .$$

Other entries in pivot column (column 2):

$$\frac{1}{3} \text{ to } \frac{\frac{1}{3}}{-\frac{2}{3}} = -\frac{1}{2}$$

and

$$\frac{2}{5} \text{ to } \frac{\frac{2}{5}}{-\frac{2}{3}} = -\frac{3}{5} .$$

If instead of dividing by $-\frac{2}{3}$ the pivot column (column 2) is multiplied by $-\frac{3}{2}$, the calculations would give the same results. For example, with respect to the second calculation it would be:

$$\frac{2}{5} \text{ to } \frac{2}{5} \cdot \frac{-3}{2} = \frac{-3}{5} \ .$$

Now work on the remaining entries, which are all type s entries:

Row 2:

$$0 \text{ to } 0 - \frac{1 \cdot \frac{1}{3}}{\frac{2}{3}} = - 1 \cdot \frac{1}{3} \cdot \frac{3}{2} = - \frac{1}{2} \ .$$

$$\frac{3}{4} \text{ to } \frac{3}{4} - \frac{\frac{1}{4} \cdot \frac{1}{3}}{\frac{2}{3}} = \frac{3}{4} - \frac{1}{4} \cdot \frac{1}{3} \cdot \frac{3}{2} = \frac{6}{8} - \frac{1}{8} = \frac{5}{8} \ .$$

$$-600 \text{ to } -600 - \frac{(-900) \cdot \frac{1}{3}}{\frac{2}{3}} = -600 + 450 = -150.$$

Bottom Row:

$$\frac{1}{4} \text{ to } \frac{1}{4} - \frac{1 \cdot \frac{2}{5}}{\frac{2}{3}} = \frac{1}{4} - 1 \cdot \frac{2}{5} \cdot \frac{3}{2} = \frac{1}{4} - \frac{3}{5} = \frac{5-12}{20} = \frac{-7}{20} \ .$$

$$\frac{1}{2} \text{ to } \frac{1}{2} - \frac{\frac{1}{4} \cdot \frac{2}{5}}{\frac{2}{3}} = \frac{1}{2} - \frac{1}{4} \cdot \frac{2}{5} \cdot \frac{3}{2} = \frac{1}{2} - \frac{3}{20} = \frac{7}{20} \ .$$

$$0 \text{ to } 0 - \frac{(-900) \cdot \frac{2}{5}}{\frac{2}{3}} = +900 \cdot \frac{2}{5} \cdot \frac{3}{2} = 90 \cdot 2 \cdot 3 = 540.$$

Now translate the shorthand of Tableau 2 into equations:

$$\frac{3}{2}x + \frac{3}{2}r + \frac{3}{8}z - 1350 = -y \qquad (2')$$

$$- \frac{1}{2}x - \frac{1}{2}r + \frac{5}{8}z - 150 = -s \qquad (3')$$

$$- \frac{7}{20} x - \frac{3}{5}r + \frac{7}{20} z + 540 = u \ . \qquad (1')$$

Note that the Tableau 2 equations are indicated by primes.

It is now easy to determine coordinates of another basic point by working with the Tableau 2 equations. Set the non-basic variables x, r, and z equal to zero. Immediately obtain:

$$y = 1350, \qquad s = 150, \qquad \text{and } u = 540.$$

The point is a basic feasible point, since the two variables y and s are positive.

It is easy to make arithmetical errors in carrying out the pivot transformation calculations. Thus, a check procedure is useful. One such check is obtained by seeing if the coordinates of the basic point corresponding to Tableau 1 satisfy the equations of Tableau 2. From Tableau 1

if

$$x = y = z = 0,$$

then

$$r = 900, \; s = 600, \text{ and } u = 0.$$

Substituting these into the equations of Tableau 2, the following is obtained:

$$\frac{3}{2} \cdot 0 + \frac{3}{2} \cdot 900 + \frac{3}{8} \cdot 0 - 1350 = 1350 - 1350 = 0 = -y. \qquad (2')$$

Thus,

$$y = 0.$$

$$-\frac{1}{2} \cdot 0 - \frac{1}{2} \cdot 900 + \frac{5}{8} \cdot 0 - 150 = -450 - 150 = -600 = -s. \qquad (3')$$

Thus,

$$s = 600.$$

$$-\frac{7}{20} \cdot 0 - \frac{3}{5} \cdot 900 + \frac{7}{20} \cdot 0 + 540 = -3 \cdot 180 + 540 = 0 = u. \qquad (1')$$

Thus,

$$u = 0.$$

Hence, notice that all the equations of Tableau 2 check out, and this is a partial confirmation that the numbers in Tableau 2 are correct.

Find a basic feasible solution to the problem:

Maximize

$$x_1 + 2x_2 + 3x_3 + 4x_4 \qquad (1)$$

satisfying the conditions:

$$\begin{aligned} x_1 + 2x_2 + x_3 + x_4 &= 3 \\ x_1 - x_2 + 2x_3 + x_4 &= 4 \\ x_1 + x_2 - x_3 - x_4 &= -1 . \end{aligned} \qquad (2)$$

$x_1, x_2, x_3, x_4 \geq 0.$

Solution: This problem can be solved using the simplex method. Note that the number of equations, 3, is less than the number of unknowns, 4. The system of linear equations can be written in vector form as:

$$x_1\begin{pmatrix}1\\1\\1\end{pmatrix} + x_2\begin{pmatrix}2\\-1\\1\end{pmatrix} + x_3\begin{pmatrix}1\\2\\-1\end{pmatrix} + x_4\begin{pmatrix}1\\1\\-1\end{pmatrix}$$

$$= \begin{pmatrix}3\\4\\-1\end{pmatrix} \qquad (3)$$

Any three of the vectors on the left can be used as a basis for R^3. Thus, by setting either $x_1 = 0$, or $x_2 = 0$ or $x_4 = 0$ one can still find x_i, x_j, x_k (i,j,k = 1 or 2 or 4) that satisfy (3). Such solutions are called basic solutions, since they depend on the particular basis chosen when one of the x_i's is set equal to zero. A basic feasible solution (non-negative x_i), when substituted into the objective function will yield some value, not necessarily optimal. Now, the number of basic solutions is the number of ways of selecting a basis for R^3 from a set of four vectors, i.e.,

$$\begin{pmatrix}4\\3\end{pmatrix} = \frac{4!}{3!1!} = 4 .$$

According to the theory of linear programming, if an optimal solution to (1) and (2) exists, then an optimal basic solution exists. Thus the optimal solution can be found by using one of the four bases of R^3.

Let $v_1 = [1,1,1]$, $v_2 = [2,-1,1]$, $v_3 = [1,2,-1]$ and $v_4 = [1,1,-1]$.

Let $b = [3,4,-1]$. Then the system (3) becomes

$$x_1v_1 + x_2v_2 + x_3v_3 + x_4v_4 = b.$$

Letting $x_2 = 0$, note that

$$x_1 = 1,\ x_2 = 0,\ x_3 = 1,\ x_4 = 1$$

is a basic feasible solution which depends on

$$\{v_1,\ v_3,\ v_4\}.$$

Corresponding to this solution a simplex tableau can be constructed. The general form of the simplex tableau is as follows:

	v_1	v_2	. . . . .	v_q	. . .	v_n	b
v_{k1}	s_{11}	s_{12}	. . . . .	s_{1q}	. . .	s_{1n}	x_{k1}
v_{k2}	s_{21}	s_{22}	. . . . .	s_{2q}	. . .	s_{2n}	x_{k2}
.	.						.
.	.						.
.	.						.
v_{kr}	s_{r1}	s_{r2}	. . . . .	s_{rq}	. . .	s_{rn}	x_{kr}
	d_1	d_2	. . . . .	d_q	. . .	d_n	D

The column vectors $v_1,\ldots,v_n$ can all be expressed as linear combinations of the basic vectors $v_{k1}, v_{k2},\ldots,v_{kr}$. The coordinates (s_{ij}), $i = 1,\ldots,r$, $j = 1,\ldots,n$ form the main body of the table. The numbers $d_1,d_2,\ldots,d_n$, D in the last row of the table are defined as follows:

$$d_j = (c_{k1}s_{1j} + c_{k2}s_{2j} + \ldots + c_{kr}s_{rj}) - c_j \ ,$$

$$j = 1,\ldots,n \ .$$

$$D = c_{k1}x_{k1} + c_{k2}x_{k2} + \ldots + c_{kr}x_{kr}$$

$$= c_1x_1 + c_2x_2 + \ldots + c_nx_n \ .$$

The c_i $(i = 1,2,\ldots,n)$ represents the coefficients of the objective function, $z = c_1x_1 + c_2x_2 + \ldots + c_nx_n$. The

c_{kr} are the coeffficients of the x_{kr} which are the coefficients of the basis $\{v_{k1},\ldots,v_{kr}\}$ chosen from $v_1, v_2,\ldots,v_n$. D is the quantity to be maximized. The d_j indicate when the solution is optimal or how to proceed to a more nearly optimal solution. Returning to the problem,

$$b = v_1 + v_3 + v_4;\ v_1 = 1v_1 + 0v_3 + 0v_4;$$

$$v_2 = 3/2\ v_1 - 3v_3 + 7/2\ v_4;\ v_3 = 0v_1 + 1v_3 + 0v_4;$$

$$v_4 = 0v_1 + 0v_3 + 1v_4$$

$$d_1 = c_1 1 + c_3(0) + c_4(0) - c_1 = 0$$

$$d_2 = c_1(3/2) + c_3(-3) + c_4(7/2) - c_2 = 9/2$$

$$d_3 = c_1(0) + c_3(1) + c_4(0) - c_3 = 0$$

$$d_4 = c_1(0) + c_3(0) + c_4(1) - c_4 = 0$$

$$D = c_1x_1 + c_2x_2 + c_3x_3 + c_4x_4 = 8$$

The simplex tableau for this solution is:

	v_1	v_2	v_3	v_4	b
v_1	1	3/2	0	0	1
v_3	0	-3	1	0	1
v_4	0	7/2	0	1	1
	0	9/2	0	0	8

Next, choose another basis for the basic solution and construct another tableau. If the new value of D were greater than before proceed using another new basis. This is the simplex method. Notice that rules for choosing a new basis and for deciding when a solution is optimal are needed. It is important to note the following criteria:

(1) If the numbers $d_1, d_2,\ldots,d_n$ are all non-negative, then the solution is optimal.

(2) If, for some index q, d_q is negative and $s_{1q}, s_{2q},\ldots,s_{rq}$ are all non-positive, then the problem does not have an optimal solution.

• PROBLEM 3-10

Consider the system in standard form:

$$\begin{array}{llllllll} x_1 & & & + \; x_4 & + \; x_5 & - \; x_6 & = & 5 \\ & x_2 & & + \; 2x_4 & - \; 3x_5 & + \; x_6 & = & 3 \\ & & x_3 & - \; x_4 & + \; 2x_5 & - \; x_6 & = & -1 \end{array}$$

Set up the system of equations in tableau form, obtain a basic feasible solution having x_4 x_5, x_6 as basic variables.

Solution: Set up the coefficient array below:

x_1	x_2	x_3	x_4	x_5	x_6	
1	0	0	(1)	-1	1	5
0	1	0	2	-3	1	3
0	0	1	-1	2	-1	-1

The circle indicated is the first pivot element and corresponds to the replacement of x_1 by x_4 as a basic variable. After pivoting the following array is obtained:

x_1	x_2	x_3	x_4	x_5	x_6	
1	0	0	1	-1	-1	5
-2	1	0	0	(-5)	3	-7
1	0	1	0	3	-2	4

and again the next pivot element is circled, indicating the intention to replace x_2 by x_5 . Then the following is obtained:

x_1	x_2	x_3	x_4	x_5	x_6	
3/5	1/5	0	1	0	-2/5	18/5
2/5	-1/5	0	0	1	-3/5	7/5
-1/5	3/5	1	0	0	(-1/5)	-1/5

Continuing, there results:

x_1	x_2	x_3	x_4	x_5	x_6	
1	-1	-1	1	0	0	4
1	-2	-3	0	1	0	2
1	-3	-5	0	0	1	1

From this last standard form the new basic solution is:

$$x_4 = 4 \qquad x_5 = 2 \qquad x_6 = 1 .$$

• PROBLEM 3-11

Find a basic feasible solution to:

$$2x_1 + x_2 + 2x_3 = 4$$

$$3x_1 + 3x_2 + x_3 = 3$$

$$x_1 \geq 0, \qquad x_2 \geq 0, \qquad x_3 \geq 0 .$$

Solution: Introduce artificial variables $x_4 \geq 0$, $x_5 \geq 0$ and an objective function $x_4 + x_5$. The initial tableau is:

x_1	x_2	x_3	x_4	x_5	b
2	1	2	1	0	4
3	3	1	0	1	3
0	0	0	1	1	0

Initial Tableau

A basic feasible solution to the expanded system is given by the artificial variables. To initiate the simplex procedure, update the last row so that it has zero components under the basic variables. This yields:

2	1	2	1	0	4
(3)	3	1	0	1	3
-5	-4	-3	0	0	-7

First Tableau

Pivoting in the column having the most negative bottom row component as indicated, the following is obtained:

0	-1	(4/3)	1	-2/3	2
1	1	1/3	0	1/3	1
0	1	-4/3	0	5/3	-2

Second Tableau

In the second tableau there is only one choice for pivot, and it leads to the final tableau shown:

0	-3/4	1	3/4	-1/2	3/2
1	5/4	0	-1/4	1/2	1/2
0	0	0	1	1	0

Final Tableau

Both of the artificial variables have been driven out of the basis, thus reducing the value of the objective function to zero and leading to the basic feasible solution to the original problem:

$$x_1 = 1/2 , \qquad x_2 = 0 , \qquad x_3 = 3/2 .$$

• PROBLEM 3-12

Consider:

Minimize $-2x_1 - 4x_2$

Subject to:

$$x_1 + 2x_2 + x_3 = 4$$

$$-x_1 + x_2 + x_4 = 1$$

$$x_1, \quad x_2, \quad x_3, \quad x_4 \geq 0 .$$

Find the optimal solution, starting with the basis

$$\vec{B} = [\vec{a}_1, \vec{a}_4],$$

utilizing simplex method.

Solution: The basic feasible solution with basis

$$\vec{B} = [\vec{a}_1, \vec{a}_4] = \begin{bmatrix} 1 & 0 \\ -1 & 1 \end{bmatrix} \quad \text{and } \vec{B}^{-1} = \begin{bmatrix} 1 & 0 \\ 1 & 1 \end{bmatrix}$$

The corresponding point is given by:

$$\vec{x}_B = \begin{bmatrix} x_1 \\ x_4 \end{bmatrix} = \vec{B}^{-1}\vec{b} = \begin{bmatrix} 1 & 0 \\ 1 & 1 \end{bmatrix}\begin{bmatrix} 4 \\ 1 \end{bmatrix} = \begin{bmatrix} 4 \\ 5 \end{bmatrix}$$

$$\vec{x}_N = \begin{bmatrix} x_2 \\ x_3 \end{bmatrix} = \begin{bmatrix} 0 \\ 0 \end{bmatrix}.$$

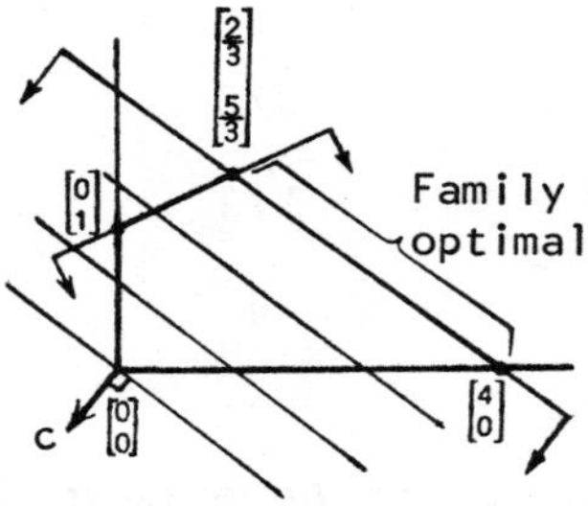

Termination Criterion: Alternative optima.

The objective value is -8. Calculate $z_2 - c_2$ and $z_3 - c_3$ as follows:

$$z_2 - c_2 = \vec{c}_B\vec{B}^{-1}\vec{a}_2 - c_2$$

$$= (-2, 0)\begin{bmatrix} 2 \\ 2 \end{bmatrix} + 4$$

$$= 0$$

$$z_3 - c_3 = \vec{c}_B\vec{B}^{-1}\vec{a}_3 - c_3$$

$$= (-2, 0)\begin{bmatrix} 1 \\ 1 \end{bmatrix} - 0$$

$$= -2$$

In this case, the given basic feasible solution is optimal, but it is not a unique optimal solution. By increasing x_2, a class of optimal solutions is obtained. Actually, if x_2 is increased, $x_3 = 0$ is kept, and x_1 and x_4 are modified, the following is obtained.

$$\begin{bmatrix} x_1 \\ x_4 \end{bmatrix} = \vec{B}^{-1}\vec{b} - \vec{B}^{-1}\vec{a}_2 x_2$$

$$= \begin{bmatrix} 4 \\ 5 \end{bmatrix} - \begin{bmatrix} 2 \\ 3 \end{bmatrix} x_2 .$$

For any $x_2 \leq \frac{5}{3}$, the solution:

$$\begin{bmatrix} x_1 \\ x_2 \\ x_3 \\ x_4 \end{bmatrix} = \begin{bmatrix} 4 - 2x_2 \\ x_2 \\ 0 \\ 5 - 3x_2 \end{bmatrix}$$

is an optimal solution with objective -8. In particular, if $x_2 = \frac{5}{3}$, an alternative basic feasible optimal solution is obtained where x_4 drops from the basis. This is illustrated in the figure. Note that the new objective function lines are parallel to the hyperplane $x_1 + x_2 = 4$ corresponding to the first constraint. That is why alternative optimal solutions are obtained.

• PROBLEM 3-13

Consider:

Minimize $-x_1 - 3x_2$

Subject to:

$$x_1 - 2x_2 \leq 4$$

$$-x_1 + x_2 \leq 3$$

$$x_1, \; x_2 \geq 0 \; .$$

Solve by simplex method.

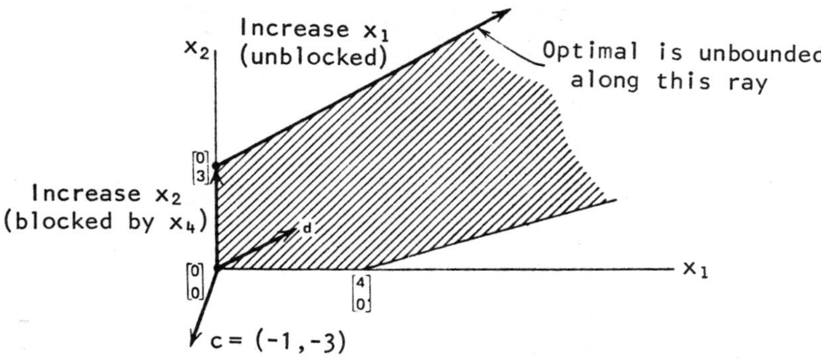

Unbounded optimal.

Solution: The problem is illustrated in the figure. After introducing the slack variables x_3 and x_4, follows the constraint matrix

$$\vec{A} = \begin{bmatrix} 1 & -2 & 1 & 0 \\ -1 & 1 & 0 & 1 \end{bmatrix} .$$

Now consider the basic feasible solution whose basis

$$\vec{B} \text{ is } [\vec{a}_3, \vec{a}_4] = \begin{bmatrix} 1 & 0 \\ 0 & 1 \end{bmatrix}.$$

$$\vec{X}_B = \begin{bmatrix} x_3 \\ x_4 \end{bmatrix} = \begin{bmatrix} 1 & 0 \\ 0 & 1 \end{bmatrix} \begin{bmatrix} 4 \\ 3 \end{bmatrix} = \begin{bmatrix} 4 \\ 3 \end{bmatrix}.$$

$$\vec{X}_N = \begin{bmatrix} x_1 \\ x_2 \end{bmatrix} = \begin{bmatrix} 0 \\ 0 \end{bmatrix}.$$

Calculate $z_1 - c_1$ and $z_2 - c_2$ as follows:

$$z_1 - c_1 = \vec{c}_B \vec{B}^{-1} \vec{a}_1 - c_1$$

$$= (0,0) \begin{bmatrix} 1 \\ -1 \end{bmatrix} + 1$$

$$= 1$$

$$z_2 - c_2 = \vec{c}_B \vec{B}^{-1} \vec{a}_2 - c_2$$

$$= (0,0) \begin{bmatrix} -2 \\ 1 \end{bmatrix} + 3$$

$$= 3 .$$

Increase x_2 with the most positive $z_j - c_j$. Note that

$$\vec{X}_B = \vec{B}^{-1} \vec{b} - \vec{B}^{-1} \vec{a}_2 x_2 ,$$

and hence:

$$\begin{bmatrix} x_3 \\ x_4 \end{bmatrix} = \begin{bmatrix} 4 \\ 3 \end{bmatrix} - \begin{bmatrix} -2 \\ 1 \end{bmatrix} x_2 .$$

The maximum value of x_2 is 3, at which instant x_4 drops to zero. Therefore, the new basic feasible solution is

$$(x_1, x_2, x_3, x_4) = (0,3,10,0).$$

The new basis $\vec{B}$ is

$$[\vec{a}_3, \vec{a}_2] = \begin{bmatrix} 1 & -2 \\ 0 & 1 \end{bmatrix}$$

with inverse

$$\begin{bmatrix} 1 & 2 \\ 0 & 1 \end{bmatrix} .$$

Calculate $z_1 - c_1$ and $z_4 - c_4$ as follows:

$$z_1 - c_1 = \vec{c}_B \vec{B}^{-1} \vec{a}_1 - c_1$$

$$= (0, -3) \begin{bmatrix} 1 & 2 \\ 0 & 2 \end{bmatrix} \begin{bmatrix} 1 \\ -1 \end{bmatrix} + 1$$

$$= (0, -3) \begin{bmatrix} -1 \\ -1 \end{bmatrix} + 1$$

$$= 4$$

$$z_4 - c_4 = \vec{c}_B \vec{B}^{-1} \vec{a}_4 - c_4$$

$$= (0, -3) \begin{bmatrix} 1 & 2 \\ 0 & 1 \end{bmatrix} \begin{bmatrix} 0 \\ 1 \end{bmatrix} - 0$$

$$= (0, -3) \begin{bmatrix} 2 \\ 1 \end{bmatrix}$$

$$= -3 .$$

If there is a basic feasible solution $z_k - c_k > 0$ for some nonbasic variable x_k, and meanwhile $\vec{y}_k \leq \vec{0}$, $\vec{x}_B = \vec{B}^{-1} \vec{b} - \vec{y}_k x_k$ then the optimal is unbounded with objective $-\infty$. This is obtained by increasing x_k indefinitely and adjusting the values of the current basic variables, and is equivalent to moving along the ray:

$$\left\{ \begin{bmatrix} \vec{B}^{-1}\vec{b} \\ \hline 0 \\ \vdots \\ 0 \\ \vdots \\ 0 \end{bmatrix} + x_k \begin{bmatrix} -\vec{y}_k \\ \hline 0 \\ \vdots \\ 1 \\ \vdots \\ 0 \end{bmatrix} : x_k \geq 0 \right\}.$$

Note that the vertex of the ray is the current basic feasible solution

$$\begin{pmatrix} \vec{B}^{-1}\vec{b} \\ \\ \vec{0} \end{pmatrix}$$

and the direction of the ray is:

$$\vec{d} = \begin{bmatrix} -\vec{y}_k \\ 0 \\ \vdots \\ 1 \\ \vdots \\ 0 \end{bmatrix}$$

where the 1 appears in the kth position. It may be noted that:

$$\vec{c}\vec{d} = (\vec{c}_B, \vec{c}_N)\vec{d} = -\vec{c}_B\vec{y}_k + c_k = -z_k + c_k$$

and since $c_k - z_k < 0$ (because x_k was eligible to enter the basis), then $\vec{c}\vec{d} < 0$, is the necessary and sufficient condition for unboundedness.

Note that $z_1 - c_1 > 0$ and $\vec{y}_1 = \vec{B}^{-1}\vec{a}_1 =$

$$\begin{bmatrix} -1 \\ -1 \end{bmatrix} \leq \begin{bmatrix} 0 \\ 0 \end{bmatrix}.$$

Therefore, the optimal solution is unbounded. In this case, if x_1 is increased and x_4 is kept zero, the following solution is obtained:

$$\vec{X}_B = \vec{B}^{-1}\vec{b} - \vec{B}^{-1}\vec{a}_1 x_1$$

$$\begin{bmatrix} x_3 \\ x_2 \end{bmatrix} = \begin{bmatrix} 10 \\ 3 \end{bmatrix} - \begin{bmatrix} -1 \\ -1 \end{bmatrix} x_1 = \begin{bmatrix} 10 + x_1 \\ 3 + x_1 \end{bmatrix}$$

$$x_4 = 0$$

Note that this solution is feasible for all $x_1 \geq 0$. In particular:

$$x_1 - 2x_2 + x_3 = x_1 - 2(3 + x_1) + (10 + x_1) = 4 .$$

and

$$-x_1 + x_2 + x_4 = -x_1 + (3 + x_1) + 0 = 3 .$$

Furthermore, $z = -9 - 4x_1$, which approaches $-\infty$ as x_1 approaches ∞. Therefore, the optimal solution is unbounded by moving along the ray:

$$\{(0,3,10,0) + x_1(1,1,1,0) : x \geq 0\}.$$

Again note that the necessary and sufficient condition for unboundedness holds, namely:

$$\vec{c}\vec{d} = (-1, -3,0,0) \begin{bmatrix} 1 \\ 1 \\ 1 \\ 0 \end{bmatrix} = -4 < 0.$$

• PROBLEM 3-14

The Red Tomato Company operates two plants for canning their tomatoes and has three warehouses for storing the finished products until they are purchased by retailers. The Company wants to arrange its shipments from the plants to the warehouses so that the requirements of the warehouses are met and so that shipping costs are kept at a minimum. The schedule below represents the per case shipping cost from plant to warehouse: (Table a).

Each week, plant I can produce up to 850 cases and plantII can produce up to 650 cases of tomatoes. Also, each week warehouse A requires 300 cases, warehouse B, 400 cases, and warehouse C, 500 cases. If the number of cases shipped from plant I to warehouse A is represented by x_1, from plant I to warehouse B by x_2, and so on, the above data can be represented by the table: (Table b).
Solve by the Simplex Method.

TABLE (a)

	A	B	C
Plant I	\$.25	\$.17	\$.18
Plant II	\$.25	\$.18	\$.14

TABLE (b)

	Warehouse A	B	C
Plant I	x_1	x_2	x_3
Plant II	x_4	x_5	x_6
Total Demand	300	400	500

Solution: The linear programming problem is stated as follows: Minimize the cost function:

$$C = .25x_1 + .17x_2 + .18x_3 + .25x_4 + .18x_5 + .14x_6$$

subject to the conditions:

$$\begin{array}{ll} x_1 + x_2 + x_3 \le 850 & x_1 \ge 0,\ x_2 \ge 0 \\ x_4 + x_5 + x_6 \le 650 & x_3 \ge 0,\ x_4 \ge 0 \\ x_1 + x_4 = 300 & x_5 \ge 0,\ x_6 \ge 0 \\ x_2 + x_5 = 400 & \\ x_3 + x_6 = 500 & \end{array} \qquad (1)$$

Before finding a solution, notice that the linear objective function contains six variables. Also, the number of constraints is eleven. The simplex method requires that the constraints of a linear programming problem be given as linear equations, not as linear inequalities. Thus, before proceeding further, change the inequalities of (1) to equalities. To do this, introduce slack variables. For example, since $x_1 + x_2 + x_3 \le 850$, there is some nonnegative real number x_7, so that $x_1 + x_2 + x_3 + x_7 = 850$, $x_7 \ge 0$. Here x_7 is a slack variable. Similarly, there is a nonnegative integer x_8 so that $x_4 + x_5 + x_6 + x_8 = 650$, $x_8 \ge 0$.

Thus, by introducing slack variables, the linear programming problem can be restated as: Minimize the cost function:

$$C = .25x_1 + .17x_2 + .18x_3 + .25x_4 + .18x_5 + .14x_6$$

subject to the conditions:

$$\begin{array}{ll} x_1 + x_2 + x_3 + x_7 = 850, & x_1 \ge 0,\ x_2 \ge 0 \\ x_4 + x_5 + x_6 + x_8 = 650, & x_3 \ge 0,\ x_4 \ge 0 \\ x_1 + x_4 = 300, & x_5 \ge 0,\ x_6 \ge 0 \\ x_2 + x_5 = 400, & x_7 \ge 0,\ x_8 \ge 0 \\ x_3 + x_6 = 500 . & \end{array} \qquad (2)$$

Now the constraints have been expressed as linear equalities. Physically, the two slack variables x_7 and x_8 can be interpreted as cases of tomatoes produced at plant I and plant II, respectively, but not shipped to any warehouse. It is clear that the shipping cost of not shipping is zero so that the slack variables introduced cannot affect the objective (cost) function to be minimized. From the system of equations (2) there is:

$$x_1 = 300 - x_4$$

$$x_2 = 400 - x_5$$

$$x_6 = 500 - x_3$$

Now, $x_1 = 850 - x_2 - x_3 - x_7$ but $x_1 = 300 - x_4$, $x_2 = 400 - x_5$. Therefore, $x_7 = 850 - 300 + x_4 - 400 + x_5 - x_3$ so, $x_7 = 150 - x_3 + x_4 + x_5$. Also, $x_8 = 650 - x_4 - x_5 - x_6$ but $x_6 = 500 - x_3$, thus,

$$x_8 = 650 - x_4 - x_5 - 500 + x_3$$

$$x_8 = 150 + x_3 - x_4 - x_5 .$$

The cost function C then becomes $C = .25x_1 + .17x_2 + .18x_3 + .25x_4 + .18x_5 + .14x_6$ but $x_1 = 300 - x_4$, $x_2 = 400 - x_5$, and $x_6 = 500 - x_3$. Therefore $C = .25(300 - x_4) + .17(400 - x_5) + .18x_3 + .25x_4 + .18x_5 + .14(500 - x_3)$. $C = 75 - .25x_4 + 68 - .17x_5 + .18x_3 + .25x_4 + .18x_5 + 70 - .14x_3$. $C = 213 + .04x_3 + .01x_5$. Therefore, minimize $C = 213 + .04x_3 + .01x_5$ subject to:

$$x_1 = 300 - x_4$$

$$x_2 = 400 - x_5$$

$$x_6 = 500 - x_3$$

$$x_7 = 150 - x_3 + x_4 + x_5$$

$x_8 = 150 + x_3 - x_4 - x_5$ in which each variable is ≥ 0. The matrix representing the linear programming problem is:

	1	x_3	x_4	x_5
$-C$	-213	-.04	0	-.01
x_1	300	0	-1	0
x_2	400	0	0	-1
x_6	500	-1	0	0
x_7	150	-1	1	1
x_8	150	-1	-1	-1

in which -C is to be maximized. Since every entry in the -C row is negative or zero, go no further. The maximum value for -C is -213. The minimum cost C is then $213. The values x_1, x_2, x_3, x_4, x_5, x_6 giving the minimum cost of $213 are:

$$x_1 = 300$$

$$x_2 = 400$$

$$x_3 = 0$$

$$x_4 = 0$$

$$x_5 = 0$$

$$x_6 = 500 \ .$$

• PROBLEM 3-15

Find nonnegative numbers x_1, x_2, x_3, x_4 which maximize

$$3x_1 + x_2 + 9x_3 - 9x_4$$

and satisfy the conditions

$$x_1 + x_2 + x_3 - 5x_4 = 4$$
$$(1)$$
$$x_1 - x_2 + 3x_3 + x_4 = 0 \ .$$

Use the simplex algorithm to solve the problem.

Solution:
The calculations are conveniently set forth in the form of a table.

c_j	solution variables	solution values	3 x_1	1 x_2	9 x_3	-9 x_4
3	x_1	4	1	1	1	-5
1	x_2	0	1	-1	3	1
	z_j					
	$c_j - z_j$					

Under each column (x_1, x_2, x_3, x_4) are written the coefficients from the constraint equations of the variables found in the heading. For example, under x_3 is written (1,3). Under the column headed solution values, the constants of the constraints are written. The first row in the heading of the table contains the c_j's or the profit per unit (the coefficients of the variables in the profit equation).

Before filling in the rest of the table, identify an initial solution. Find a basic feasible solution by making nonbasic variables zero and by satisfying the constraints (1)

$x_1 = x_2 = 2,\ x_3 = x_4 = 0$.

The value associated with this solution is 3(2) + (1)2 + 9(0) - 9(0) = 8. The terms x_1, x_2 are entered in the simplex table under the solution variables column, and their per-unit profits are entered in the first column under the c_j heading.

Finally, consider the computation of the z_j's and $c_j - z_j$'s. The z_j total of a column is the amount of profit which is given up by replacing some of the present solution mix with one unit of the item heading the column. It is found by multiplying the c_j of the row by the number in the row and jth column (the substitution coefficient) and adding.

c_j	solution variables	solution values	3 x_1	1 x_2	9 x_3	-9 x_4
3	x_1	4	1	1	1	-5
1	x_2	0	1	-1	3	1
	z_j	8	4	2	6	-14
	$c_j - z_j$		-1	-1	3	5

The $c_j - z_j$ now represents the net profit that is added by one unit of the product. x_3 and x_4 are the only positive profits. Therefore, replace some of x_1 or x_2 with one or more units of x_3 . The next step is to determine which row (x_1 or x_2) is to be replaced by x_3 . Divide each amount in the "Solution values" column by the amount in the comparable row of the x_3 column:

for x_1 row: $\frac{-4}{5}$

for x_2 row: $\frac{0}{1}$.

Since negative ratios don't count, choose x_2 for elimination, i.e., pivot on 1. To obtain a new table, convert all other elements in the x_4 column to zero.

c_j	solution variables	solution values	3 x_1	1 x_2	9 x_3	-9 x_4
3	x_1	4	6	-4	16	0
9	x_3	0	1	-1	3	1
	z_j	12	27	-21	75	9
	$c_j - z_j$		-24	22	-66	-18

The z_j and $c_j - z_j$ are calculated as before. If all the $c_j - z_j$ were negative or zero, the solution would be optimal. But the column headed x_2 has a positive amount. On the other hand, both elements in this column are negative indicating that no pivoting is possible.

By the rules of the simplex algorithm the problem has no optimal solution.

• PROBLEM 3-16

A small-trailer manufacturer wishes to determine how many camper units and how many house trailers he should produce in order to make optimal use of his available resources. Suppose he has available 11 units of aluminum, 40 units of wood, and 52 person-weeks of work. (The preceding data are expressed in convenient units. Assume that all other needed resources are available and have no effect on his decision.) The table below gives the amount of each resource needed to manufacture each camper and each trailer.

	Aluminum	Wood	Person-weeks
Per camper	2	1	7
Per trailer	1	8	8

Assume further that based on his previous year's sales record the manufacturer has decided to make no more than 5 campers. If the manufacturer realized a profit of $300 on a camper and $400 on a trailer, what should be his production in order to maximize his profit?

Solution: Letting x_1 represent the number of camper units, and x_2 the number of house trailers, consider first the constraints. From the table note that the manufacturer uses 2 units of aluminum per camper and 1 unit of aluminum per trailer. Thus he needs a total of $2x_1 + x_2$ units of aluminum. This fact, along with the fact that he has available only 11 units of aluminum, gives the inequality $2x_1 + x_2 \leq 11$. Similarly, he needs a total of $x_1 + 8x_2$ units of wood. And since he has available only 40 units of wood, $x_1 + 8x_2 \leq 40$ is obtained. The total number of person-weeks needed to build x_1 campers and x_2 trailers is $7x_1 + 8x_2$. Since only 52 weeks are available, $7x_1 + 8x_2 \leq 52$. He wants to produce no more than 5 campers, therefore, $x_1 \leq 5$. Finally, there exists a constraint that is unrelated to the numbers actually appearing in the statement of the problem. Certainly it is physically impossible for the manufacturer to produce a negative number of campers or trailers, thus $x_1, x_2 \geq 0$. It is desired to maximize the total profit attained from x_1 campers and x_2 trailers, namely $300x_1 + 400x_2$. Thus, the problem is reduced to the following:

Maximize $300x_1 + 400x_2$ subject to the conditions that:

$$\begin{aligned} 2x_1 + x_2 &\leq 11 \\ x_1 + 8x_2 &\leq 40 \\ 7x_1 + 8x_2 &\leq 52 \\ x_1 &\leq 5 \\ x_1, x_2 &\geq 0. \end{aligned} \tag{1}$$

Now, determine the extreme points of the feasible solution set. One way to make the process of finding the extreme points efficient is to introduce slack variables. The purpose is to convert the inequalities of (1) to equalities. Specifically, let $x_3 = 11 - (2x_1 + x_2)$, $x_4 = 40 - (x_1 + 8x_2)$, $x_5 = 52 - (7x_1 + 8x_2)$, and $x_6 = 5 - x_1$, and consider the system of equations:

$$
\begin{aligned}
2x_1 + x_2 + x_3 &= 11 \\
x_1 + 8x_2 + x_4 &= 40 \\
7x_1 + 8x_2 + x_5 &= 52 \\
x_1 + x_6 &= 5
\end{aligned}
\qquad (2)
$$

and still requiring that $x_1, x_2 \geq 0$. Moreover, the original inequality constraints will be satisfied if $x_3, x_4, x_5, x_6 \geq 0$ is also required. Observe, for example, that $x_3 = 11 - (2x_1 + x_2) \geq 0$ if and only if $2x_1 + x_3 \leq 11$. First form the augmented matrix for (2). The function written below the matrix is a reminder for what must be maximized:

$$
\begin{bmatrix}
2 & 1 & 1 & 0 & 0 & 0 & 11 \\
1 & 8 & 0 & 1 & 0 & 0 & 40 \\
7 & 8 & 0 & 0 & 1 & 0 & 52 \\
1 & 0 & 0 & 0 & 0 & 1 & 5
\end{bmatrix}
$$

$$300x_1 + 400x_2 + 0x_3 + 0x_4 + 0x_5 + 0x_6 \ .$$

Thus the starting tableau is:

	x_1	x_2	x_3	x_4	x_5	x_6		
x_3	2	1	1	0	0	0	11	11/1 = 11
x_4	1	(8)	0	1	0	0	40	40/8 = 5
x_5	7	8	0	0	1	0	52	52/8 = 6.5
x_6	1	0	0	0	0	1	5	
	-300	-400	0	0	0	0	0	

To determine the pivot element: The elements of the last row of the tableau are called indicators. Begin by finding the negative indicator having the largest absolute value. In the tableau above the indicator is clearly -400, which appears in the second column. Therefore, call the second column the pivot column. Now consider the ratio of each element in the last column to the corresponding element in the pivot column, if the pivot column is positive. The row associated with the smallest of these ratios is called the pivot row. The pivot column contains three positive elements: a 1 in the first row, an 8 in the second row, and an 8 in the third row. Thus the ratios that must be compared are 11/1 = 11, 40/8 = 5 and 52/8 = 6.5. Since 5 is the smallest of the ratios, the second row is the pivot row. The pivot element is the element common to the pivot column and the pivot row, namely the 8 that is circled in the tableau above. Now, use elementary row operations to transform the tableau into one having a 1 in the place of the pivot element and 0's elsewhere in the pivot column. To accomplish this, first multiply each element in the pivot row by the reciprocal of the pivot element to get:

	x_1	x_2	x_3	x_4	x_5	x_6	
x_3	2	1	1	0	0	0	11
x_4	1/8	1	0	1/8	0	0	5
x_5	7	8	0	0	1	0	52
x_6	1	0	0	0	0	1	5
	-300	-400	0	0	0	0	0

Then, multiply the pivot row by -1 and add it to the first row, by -8 and add it to the third row, and by 400 and add it to the fifth row. The result is:

	x_1	x_2	x_3	x_4	x_5	x_6		
x_3	15/8	0	1	-1/8	0	0	6	$6/\frac{15}{8} = 16/5$
x_2	1/8	1	0	1/8	0	0	5	$5/\frac{1}{8} = 40$
x_5	6	0	0	-1	1	0	12	12/6 = 2
x_6	1	0	0	0	0	1	5	5/1 = 5
	-250	0	0	50	0	0	2000	

In the tableau the x_4 in the notation column is replaced by x_2 . This replacement indicates that the x_2 variable was brought into the solution and the x_4 variable was eliminated. Now, examine the last row of the tableau above. Since -250 is the only negative indicator, the first column is the pivot column. Comparing:

$$6\Big/\frac{15}{8} = \frac{16}{5}, \quad 5\Big/\frac{1}{8} = 40, \quad \frac{12}{6} = 2, \text{ and } 5/1 = 5,$$

see that the third row is the pivot row. Thus the pivot element is 6, which is circled in the tableau above. First multiply the pivot row by 1/6 so a 1 appears in the pivot position. Then, multiply this new pivot row by -15/8, -1/8, -1, and 250, adding the results to the first, second, fourth, and fifth rows, respectively, to get the following tableau:

	x_1	x_2	x_3	x_4	x_5	x_6	
x_3	0	0	1	3/16	-5/16	0	9/4
x_2	0	1	0	7/48	-1/48	0	19/4
x_1	1	0	0	-1/6	1/6	0	2
x_6	0	0	0	1/6	-1/6	1	3
	0	0	0	25/3	125/3	0	2500

Note in the tableau above: Since the pivot element was in the first column and third row, x_1 is placed in the third row of the notation column. Since the tableau above include no negative indicators, it is done. Thus, $x_1 = 2$, $x_2 = 19/4$ is the point at which the function assumes its maximum value, namely, 2500.

Assume that a small company produces two types of paint, paint x_1 and paint x_2. Paint x_1 produces a net profit of \$6 per hundred gallons and paint x_2 gives \$8 per hundred gallons. The amount of paint of either type produced is limited by both raw material availability and labor hours. Assume that both paints use the same scarce raw material, however, paint x_1 requires four units per hundred gallons while paint x_2 requires only one unit of the raw material per hunded gallons. Further, paint x_1 requires one hour, per hundred gallons produced, of labor while paint x_2 requires four hours, per hundred gallons. Finally, there are 20 units of raw material and 40 hours of labor available each week. The problem is then, in mathematical form:

$$Z_{max} = 6x_1 + 8x_2 \qquad \text{(the profit objective)}$$

subject to

$$4x_1 + x_2 \leq 20 \qquad \text{(materials constraint)}$$

$$x_1 + 4x_2 \leq 40 \ . \qquad \text{(labor constraint)}$$

Solve using the Simplex Method.

Solution: Add slack variables S_1 and S_2 to put equations into standard form.

$$Z_{max} = 6x_1 + 8x_2 + 0S_1 + 0S_2$$

subject to:

$$4x_1 + x_2 + S_1 + 0S_2 = 20$$

$$x_1 + 4x_2 + 0S_1 + S_2 = 40 \ .$$

Tableau 1

	$c_j \rightarrow$	6	8	0	0		
		Coefficients of					
Stub	*Basic Variable*	x_1	x_2	S_1	S_2	*Right Hand Side* (b_i)	θ
		in the constraints					
0	S_1	4	1	1	0	20	
0	S_2	1	4	0	1	40	
	Index Row →	-6	-8	0	0	0	

This completes the set up of the initial tableau. The next steps involve checking for optimality, and if the solution is not optimal, determining an improved solution.

1. Determine an entering variable by choosing the variable associated with the most negative value in the index row (x_2 with -8 in the problem).

2. Determine the departing variable by calculating θ for each constraint row.

$$\theta_i = b_i / a_{ie} \text{ (for } a_{ie} > 0)$$

Where a_{ie} is the constraint coefficient under the entering variable in the ith constraint. For the problem there is $\theta_1 = 20/1$, $\theta_2 = 40/4$. The departing variable is the present basic variable associated with the row having the smallest (nonnegative) value of θ .

3. Circle the departing row elements and the entering column elements as shown in Tableau 2.

Tableau 2

	$C_j \rightarrow$	6	8	0	0		
Stub	Basic Variable	x_1	x_2	S_1	S_2	Right Hand Side	θ
0	S_1	4	1	1	0	20	20
0	S_2	1	4	0	1	40	10
	Index Row →	-6	-8	0	0		

Call the matrix element at the intersection of the departing row and entering column the "key" element. This is the element "4" in row 2, column 2 of Tableau 2.

4. Construct the next simplex tableau where the departing vasic variable S_2 is now replaced by x_2, the entering variable, as shown in Tableau 3.

Tableau 3

	$C_j \rightarrow$	6	8	0	0		
Stub	Basic Variable	x_1	x_2	S_1	S_2	Right Hand Side	θ
0	S_1						
8	x_2						
	Index Row →						

Divide the departing row elements in the previous tableau each by the key element and enter the resulting elements in the new simplex tableau as shown in Tableau 4.

Tableau 4

	$C_j \rightarrow$	6	8	0	0		
Stub	Basic Variable	x_1	x_2	S_1	S_2	Right Hand Side	θ
0	S_1						
8	x_2	1/4	1	0	1/4	10	
	Index Row →						

The basic variables are each associated with a column of exactly one 1-element and all the rest of the elements are zeros. The 1-element is associated with the constraint or row for which that variable is basic. The example is shown in Tableau 5.

Tableau 5

	$C_j \rightarrow$	6	8	0	0		
Stub	*Basic Variable*	*Coefficients of* x_1	x_2	S_1	S_2	*Right Hand Side*	θ
0	S_1		0	1			
8	x_2	1/4	1	0	1/4	10	
	Index Row →		0	0			

The remaining elements are found via the following relationship:

$$\hat{a}_{ij} = a_{ij} - \frac{a_{i,key} \cdot a_{key,j}}{\text{key element}}$$

where

$\hat{a}_{ij}$ is the new matrix element.

a_{ij} is the matrix element value from the previous tableau.

$a_{i,key}$ is the matrix element in the entering column for row i--from the previous tableau.

$a_{key,j}$ is the matrix element in the departing row for column j--from the previous tableau.

The key element is the element at the intersection of the entering column and departing row--from the previous tableau.

Tableau 6

	$C_j \rightarrow$	6	8	0	0		
Stub	*Basic Variable*	*Coefficients of* x_1	x_2	S_1	S_2	*Right Hand Side*	θ
0	S_1	3-3/4	0	1	−1/4	10	
8	x_2	1/4	1	0	1/4	10	
	Index Row →	−4	0	0	2	80	

Tableau 7

	$C_j \rightarrow$	6	8	0	0		
Stub	*Basic Variable*	*Coefficients of* x_1	x_2	S_1	S_2	*Right Hand Side*	θ
6	x_1	1	0	4/15	−1/15	8/3	
8	x_2	0	1	−1/15	16/60	28/3	
	Index Row →	0	0	16/15	26/15	90-2/3	

$x_1^* = 8/3$ (optimal production of x_1) $x_2^* = 28/3$ (optimal production of x_2), and $Z^* = \$90\text{-}2/3$ (optimal weekly profit). Z is the value of the objective function for the given solution.

Then fill in the remaining elements. This is shown in Tableau 6.

5. Repeat steps 1 through 4 until the solution found is optimal. In this problem, the solution of $x_2 = 10$, $S_1 = 10$ is not yet optimal, and x_1 is the next entering variable. The final simplex tableau is shown in Tableau 7.

• PROBLEM 3-18

Maximize $3x_1 + x_2 + 3x_3$ subject to:

$$2x_1 + x_2 + x_3 \leq 2$$

$$x_1 + 2x_2 + 3x_3 \leq 5$$

$$2x_1 + 2x_2 + x_3 \leq 6$$

$$x_1 \geq 0, \quad x_2 \geq 0, \quad x_3 \geq 0.$$

Find the optimal solution to this linear program by using the simplex method.

Solution: To transform the problem into standard form so that the simplex procedure can be applied, change the maximization to minimization by multiplying the objective function by minus one, and introduce three nonnegative slack variables x_4, x_5, x_6. Thus, the initial tableau is obtained.

a_1	a_2	a_3	a_4	a_5	a_6	b
(2)	(1)	1	1	0	0	2
1	2	(3)	0	1	0	5
2	2	1	0	0	1	6
-3	-1	-3	0	0	0	0

First tableau

The problem is already in standard form with the three slack variables serving as the basic variables. There is at this point $r_j = c_j - z_j = c_j$, since the costs of the slacks are zero. Application of the criterion for selecting a column in which to pivot shows that any of the first three columns would yield an improved solution. In each of these columns the appropriate pivot element is determined by computing the ratios y_{i0}/y_{ij} and selecting the smallest positive one. The three allowable pivots are all circled on the tableau. Select a pivot that will minimize the amount of division required. Thus, for this problem select (1).

2	1	1	1	0	0	2
-3	0	(1)	-2	1	0	1
-2	0	-1	-2	0	1	2
-1	0	-2	1	0	0	1

Second tableau

Note that the objective function--the negative of the original one--has decreased from zero to minus two. Again pivot on (1).

(5)	1	0	3	-1	0	1
-3	0	1	-2	1	0	1
-5	0	0	-4	1	1	3
-7	0	0	-3	2	0	4

Third tableau

The value of the objective function has now decreased to minus four and may pivot in either the first or fourth column. Select (5).

1	1/5	0	3/5	-1/5	0	1/5
0	3/5	1	-1/5	2/5	0	8/5
0	1	0	-1	0	1	4
0	7/5	0	6/5	3/5	0	27/5

Fourth tableau

Since the last row has no negative elements, the solution corresponding to the fourth tableau is optimal. Thus, $x_1 = \frac{1}{5}$, $x_2 = 0$, $x_3 = \frac{8}{5}$, $x_4 = 0$, $x_5 = 0$, $x_6 = 4$ is the optimal solution with a corresponding value of the negative objective of $-\frac{27}{5}$.

• PROBLEM 3-19

Maximize:

$$Z = 8x_1 + 4x_2$$

subject to:

$$x_1 + x_2 \leq 10$$

$$5x_1 + x_2 \leq 15,$$

by the simplex method.

Solution: The simplex solution is shown in Tableaux 1, 2, and 3.

Tableau 1

Stub	Basic Variable	x_1	x_2	S_1	S_2	Right Hand Side	θ
$C_j\rightarrow$		8	4	0	0		
0	S_1	1	1	1	0	10	10
0	S_2	5	1	0	1	15	3
	Index Row →	−8	−4	0	0	0	

Tableau 2

Stub	Basic Variable	x_1	x_2	S_1	S_2	Right Hand Side	θ
$C_j\rightarrow$		8	4	0	0		
0	S_1	0	4/5	1	−1/5	7	35/4
8	x_1	1	1/5	0	1/5	3	15
	Index Row →	0	−12/5	0	8/5	24	

Tableau 3

Stub	Basic Variable	x_1	x_2	S_1	S_2	Right Hand Side	θ
$C_j\rightarrow$		8	4	0	0		
4	x_2	0	1	5/4	−1/4	35/4	
8	x_1	1	0	−1/4	1/4	5/4	
	Index Row →	0	0	3	1	45	

The solution to the problem is then:

$$x_1^* = 5/4$$

$$x_2^* = 35/4$$

$$Z^* = 45 .$$

• PROBLEM 3-20

Find an optimal solution to this maximization problem using the simplex technique.

$$\text{maximize } x_0 = 3x_1 + 2x_2 + 5x_3$$

subject to:

$$x_1 + 2x_2 + x_3 \le 430$$

$$3x_1 + 2x_3 \le 460$$

$$x_1 + 4x_2 \le 420$$

$$x_1, x_2, x_3 \ge 0$$

Solution: This is expressed in tableau form as follows:

Starting Tableau:

Basic	x_0	x_1	x_2	x_3	S_1	S_2	S_3	Solution
x_0	①	-3	-2	-5	0	0	0	0
S_1	0	1	2	1	①	0	0	430
S_2	0	3	0	2	0	①	0	460
S_3	0	1	4	0	0	0	①	420

First Iteration. x_3 is the entering variable. By taking ratios,

Current basic Solution	Ratios to coefficients of x_3
$S_1 = 430$	$430/1 = 430$
$S_2 = 460$	$460/2 = 230 \leftarrow S_2 = 0, x_3 = 230$
$S_3 = 420$	$420/0 = -$

S_2 becomes the leaving variable. The new tableau is thus given by

Basic	x_0	x_1	x_2	x_3	S_1	S_2	S_3	Solution
x_0	①	9/2	-2	0	0	5/2	0	1150
S_1	0	-1/2	2	0	①	-1/2	0	200
x_3	0	3/2	0	①	0	1/2	0	230
S_3	0	1	4	0	0	0	①	420

Second iteration. x_2 is the entering variable. By taking ratios,

Current basic Solution	Ratios to coefficients of x_2
$S_1 = 200$	$200/2 = 100 \leftarrow S_1 = 0, x_2 = 100$
$x_3 = 230$	$230/0 = -$
$S_3 = 420$	$420/4 = 105$

S_1 leaves the solution. The new tableau is

Basic	x_0	x_1	x_2	x_3	S_1	S_2	S_3	Solution
x_0	①	4	0	0	1	2	0	1350
x_2	0	-1/4	①	0	1/2	-1/4	0	100
x_3	0	3/2	0	①	0	1/2	0	230
S_3	0	2	0	0	-2	1	①	20

This is optimal since all the coefficients in the x_0-equation are nonnegative. The optimal solution is $x_1 = 0$, $x_2 = 100$, $x_3 = 230$, $S_1 = 0$, $S_2 = 0$, $S_3 = 20$, and $x_0 = 1350$.

Consider:

$$\min z = 11 - x_3 - x_4 - x_5$$

subject to:

$$x_1 + x_3 - x_4 + 2x_5 = 2,$$

$$x_2 - x_3 + 2x_4 - x_5 = 1,$$

$$x_j \geq 0 \quad (j = 1,\ldots,5).$$

This can be written as:

$$-z \quad - x_3 - x_4 - x_5 = -11,$$

$$x_1 \quad + x_3 - x_4 + 2x_5 = 2,$$

$$x_2 - x_3 + 2x_4 - x_5 = 1 .$$

Solve by the simplex method.

Solution: This is already in diagonal form with respect to $-z$, x_1, and x_2. Write x_1 and x_2 to the left of Tableau 1 to indicate that they are the basic variables of this tableau. A feasible solution is always ready at hand by setting the basic variables equal to the constants in the 0th column.

Tableau 1

	1	x_1	x_2	x_3	x_4	x_5
$-z$	-11	0	0	-1	-1	-1
x_1	2	1	0	1	-1	2
x_2	1	0	1	-1	2*	-1

Tableau 2

	1	x_1	x_2	x_3	x_4	x_5
$-z$	$-2\frac{1}{2}$	0	1/2	-3/2	0	- 3/2
x_1	5/2	1	1/2	1/2*	0	3/2
x_4	1/2	0	1/2	-1/2	1	-1/2

Now in the 0th row, there are three negative coefficients of the same magnitude. Arbitrarily, choose the column under x_4.

In the column under x_4 there is only one positive coefficient, namely $a_{24} = 2$; so choose a_{24} to be the pivot. This is indicated by an * on the upper right corner of a_{24} . Then make a_{24} equal to 1 by dividing all elements in the row containing the pivot by the pivot and performing Gauss elimination on rows to make $a_{i4} = 0$ $(i = 0,1)$. The result is shown in Tableau 2.

Note in this tabulation that x_4 has replaced x_2 as a basic variable.

Among the negative coefficients in the 0th row, either choose the column under x_3 or the column under x_5 . Arbitrarily, choose the third column. In the third column only $a_{13} = \frac{1}{2}$ is positive, so it is chosen as the pivot. The result of the pivot operation is shown in Tableau 3.

Tableau 3

	1	x_1	x_2	x_3	x_4	x_5
$-z$	3	3	2	0	0	3
x_3	5	2	1	1	0	3
x_4	3	1	1	0	1	1

Note that x_3 has replaced x_1 as a basic variable. In Tableau 3 there are no negative constants $a_{0j} \geq 0$ $(j = 1,\ldots,n)$, so it is optimum. The optimum solution is $x_3 = 5$, $x_4 = 3$, $x_1 = x_2 = x_5 = 0$, $z = 3$.

• PROBLEM 3-22

Maximize $x_0 = 3x_1 + 9x_2$

subject to:

$$x_1 + 4x_2 \leq 8$$
$$x_1 + 2x_2 \leq 4$$
$$x_1, x_2 \geq 0$$

Use the simplex technique to solve.

Solution:

Starting Tableau:

Basic	x_0	x_1	x_2	S_1	S_2	Solution
x_0	①	−3	−9	0	0	0
S_1	0	1	4	①	0	8
S_2	0	1	2	0	①	4

First Iteration: Introduce x_2 and drop S_1.

Basic	x_0	x_1	x_2	S_1	S_2	Solution
x_0	①	−3/4	0	9/4	0	18
x_2	0	1/4	①	1/4	0	2
S_2	0	1/2	0	−1/2	①	0

Second Iteration: Introduce x_1 and drop S_2.

Basic	x_0	x_1	x_2	S_1	S_2	Solution
x_0	①	0	0	3/2	3/2	18
x_2	0	0	①	1/2	−1/2	2
x_1	0	①	0	−1	2	0

The optimal solution is $x_1 = 0$, $x_2 = 2$, and $x_0 = 18$.

Maximize

$$u = 2x + y \tag{1}$$

subject to:

$$x + y \le 1 \tag{2}$$

$$x + 2y \ge 4 \tag{3}$$

$$x \ge 0 \tag{4}$$

$$y \ge 0 . \tag{5}$$

Solve by the simplex method.

Solution: Introduce nonnegative slack variables r and s into (2) and (3) and obtain

$$x + y - 1 = -r \tag{2'}$$

$$-x - 2y + 4 = -s . \tag{3'}$$

Use Equations (1), (2'), and (3') to form the following starting tableau:

x	y	1		
1	1	−1	$= -r$	b.p. $O(0,0)$. (T.1)
−1	−2*	+4	$= -s$	
2	1	0	$= u$	

Either $a_{21} = -1$ or $a_{22} = -2$ is an acceptable pivot entry.

Choose the latter and thereby obtain Tableau 2:

x	s	1		
$\frac{1}{2}$	$\frac{1}{2}$	+1	$= -r$	b.p. $A(0,2)$ (T.2)
$\frac{1}{2}$	$-\frac{1}{2}$	−2	$= -y$	
$\frac{3}{2}$	$\frac{1}{2}$	2	$= u$	

$-b = +1$ is positive. However, neither a_{12} are acceptable pivot entries, since they are both positive. Row 1 of Tableau 2 implies that the problem is infeasible. The equation corresponding to row 1 is

$$-r = \frac{1}{2}x + \frac{1}{2}s + 1$$

or

$$r = -\frac{x}{2} - \frac{s}{2} - 1 \qquad (6)$$

Assume there is a point such that all the constraints are satisfied. In particular, for this point $x \geq 0$, $y \geq 0$, $r \geq 0$, and $s \geq 0$. However, the coordinates x, s, and r are related by Equation (6). Furthermore, the first two terms on the right-hand side are nonpositive, while the third term (-1) is negative. Thus, the right-hand side of (6) is negative. However, this contradicts the fact that the left-hand side (namely, r) has to be nonnegative. This contradiction means that there are no points for which all the constraints are satisfied, i.e., the problem is infeasible.

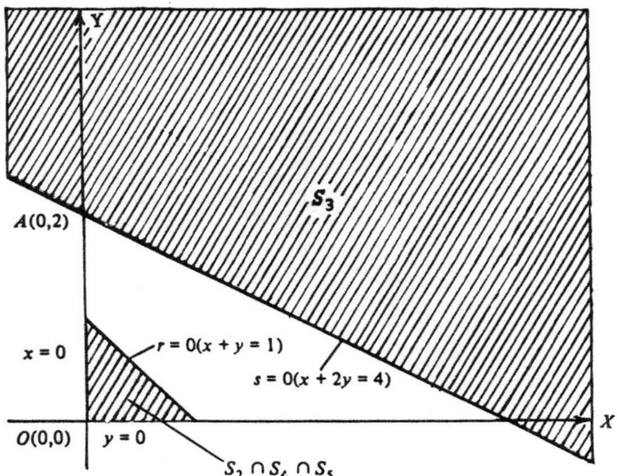

An interesting graphical analysis of this problem is now given. In the figure, the set S_3 is the set of points which satisfy Inequality (3). The set $S_2 \cap S_4 \cap S_5$ (the triangle by the origin) is the set of points for which Inequalities (2), (4), and (5) are satisfied. The constraint set S_c is the intersection set of sets S_2, S_3, S_4, and S_5. As a result of the commutative and associative properties of set intersection, S_c can be expressed as follows:

$$S_c = S_3 \quad (S_2 \quad S_4 \quad S_5). \qquad (7)$$

It is clear from the figure that this set is the empty set, i.e., there is no point that is simultaneously in the region S_3 and the region $S_2 \cap S_4 \cap S_5$. This implies that the problem is infeasible.

Note that the transition from Tableau 1 to Tableau 2 corresponds to movement from basic point O(0,0) to basic point A(0,2).

Consider the maximization problem

$$\max z = 3x_1 + 2x_2 + x_3$$

subject to:

$$\begin{aligned} 2x_1 + x_2 + 2x_3 &\le 4 \\ x_1 + x_2 \quad\quad &\le 1 \qquad\qquad (1) \\ x_1, x_2, x_3 &\ge 0 . \end{aligned}$$

Solve by the Simplex Method.

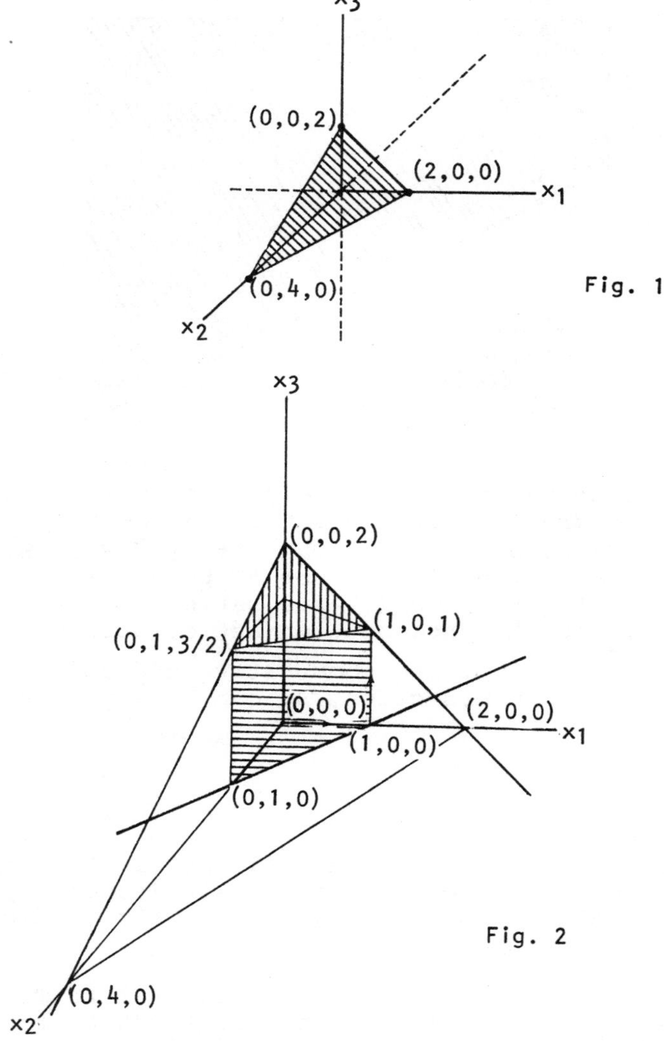

Solution: By setting all possible pairs of variables to zero in $2x_1 + x_2 + 2x_3 = 4$, determine three points lying on the constraining plane, and therefore determine it uniquely. These points and the nonnegativity restrictions give the three-dimensional shaded figure in Figure 1.

When the constraint $x_1 + x_2 \leq 1$ is considered, then the feasible region is reduced to the three-dimensional shaded figure in Figure 2, whose six extreme points have been labeled.

To solve the problem, first obtain the equivalent problem by adding slack variables:

$$\max z = 3x_1 + 2x_2 + x_3.$$

subject to

$$\begin{aligned} 2x_1 + x_2 + 2x_3 + x_4 \quad &= 4 \\ x_1 + x_2 \quad + x_5 &= 1 \\ x_1, \ldots, x_5 &\geq 0 \end{aligned} \qquad (2)$$

The initial tableau is

c_j	Basis	P_1	P_2	P_3	P_4	P_5	b
0	P_4	2	1	2	1	0	4
0	P_5	1	1	0	0	1	1
$c_j - z_j$		3	2	1	0	0	

Initial basic feasible solution corresponds to the extreme point (0,0,0). P_1 is to come in, and P_5 leaves the basis, giving:

c_j	Basis	P_1	P_2	P_3	P_4	P_5	b
0	P_4	0	−1	2	1	−2	2
3	P_1	1	1	0	0	1	1
$c_j - z_j$		0	−1	1	0	−3	

The solution here, $x_1 = 1$, $x_4 = 2$, $x_2 = x_3 = x_5 = 0$, corresponds to the extreme point (1,0,0). P_3 is next to enter and P_4 is removed, giving:

c_j	Basis	P_1	P_2	P_3	P_4	P_5	b
1	P_3	0	$-\frac{1}{2}$	1	$\frac{1}{2}$	−1	1
3	P_1	1	1	0	0	1	1
$c_j - z_j$		0	$-\frac{1}{2}$	0	$-\frac{1}{2}$	−2	

So $x_1 = 1, x_3 = 1, x_2 = 0$ is an optimal solution to the original problem, and the extreme point is (1,0,1).

Figure 2 illustrates the manner in which the solution has moved about the boundary of the feasible region, from extreme point to extreme point as indicated by the arrows. Notice that the simplex technique has always proceeded along what might be called "edges" of the set, never across one of its faces. This is the rule with the simplex technique.

Use the simplex method to solve:

$$\text{Max } Z = 3x + 5y + 4z$$

subject to the restrictions:

$$2x + 3y \leq 8$$

$$2y + 5z \leq 10$$

$$3x + 2y + 4z \leq 15.$$

Solution: Rename the variables x, y, z as x_1, x_2, x_3, and call the slack variables x_4, x_5, x_6. Then the problem becomes one of maximizing:

$$Z = 3x_1 + 5x_2 + 4x_3$$

subject to the restrictions:

$$2x_1 + 3x_2 + x_4 = 8$$

$$2x_2 + 5x_3 + x_5 = 10$$

$$3x_1 + 2x_2 + 4x_3 + x_6 = 15.$$

The first tableau becomes:

$C_{[i]}$	$P_{[i]}$		P_1	P_2	P_3	P_4	P_5	P_6	P_0	
0	P_4		2	3	0	1	0	0	8	
0	P_5		0	2	5	0	1	0	10	
0	P_6		3	2	4	0	0	1	15	
		$C_j \rightarrow$	3	5	4	0	0	0		
		Solution	0	0	0	8	10	15		$(Z = 0)$
		Δ_j	3	5	4	—	—	—		
		$b_i/a_{i,2}$	—	—	—	$\frac{8}{3}$	$\frac{10}{2}$	$\frac{15}{2}$		
				↑ Entering variable		↓ Departing variable				

To obtain the second tableau, first calculate the intermediate coefficient matrix:

$\frac{2}{3}$	1	0	$\frac{1}{3}$	0	0	$\frac{8}{3}$
0	2	5	0	1	0	10
3	2	4	0	0	1	15

and by row operations the coefficient matrix for the second tableau is obtained:

$\frac{2}{3}$	1	0	$\frac{1}{3}$	0	0	$\frac{8}{3}$
$-\frac{4}{3}$	0	5	$-\frac{2}{3}$	1	0	$\frac{14}{3}$
$\frac{5}{3}$	0	4	$-\frac{2}{3}$	0	1	$\frac{29}{3}$

Second Tableau

$C_{[i]}$	$P_{[i]}$	P_1	P_2	P_3	P_4	P_5	P_6	P_0	
5	P_2	$\frac{2}{3}$	1	0	$\frac{1}{3}$	0	0	$\frac{8}{3}$	
0	P_5	$-\frac{4}{3}$	0	5	$-\frac{2}{3}$	1	0	$\frac{14}{3}$	
0	P_6	$\frac{5}{3}$	0	4	$-\frac{2}{3}$	0	1	$\frac{29}{3}$	
	C_j	3	5	4	0	0	0	0	
	Solution	0	$\frac{8}{3}$	0	0	$\frac{14}{3}$	$\frac{29}{3}$		$(Z = \frac{40}{3})$
	Δ_j	$-\frac{1}{3}$	—	4	$-\frac{5}{3}$	—	—		
	b_i/a_{ir}	—	∞	—	—	$\frac{14}{15}$	$\frac{29}{12}$		
				↑ Entering variable		↓ Departing variable			

Third Tableau

$C_{[i]}$	$P_{[i]}$	P_1	P_2	P_3	P_4	P_5	P_6	P_0	
5	P_2	$\frac{2}{3}$	1	0	$\frac{1}{3}$	0	0	$\frac{8}{3}$	
4	P_3	$-\frac{4}{15}$	0	1	$-\frac{2}{15}$	$\frac{1}{5}$	0	$\frac{14}{15}$	
0	P_6	$\frac{41}{15}$	0	0	$-\frac{2}{15}$	$-\frac{4}{5}$	1	$\frac{89}{15}$	
	$C_j \rightarrow$	3	5	4	0	0	0		
	Solution	0	$\frac{8}{3}$	$\frac{14}{15}$	0	0	$\frac{89}{15}$		$(Z = \frac{256}{15})$
	Δ_j	$\frac{11}{15}$	—	—	$-\frac{17}{15}$	$-\frac{4}{5}$			
	b_i/a_{ir}	—	4	$-\frac{7}{2}$	—	—	$\frac{89}{41}$		
		↑ Entering variable					↓ Departing variable		

Fourth Tableau

$C_{[i]}$	$P_{[i]}$	P_1	P_2	P_3	P_4	P_5	P_6	P_0	
5	P_2	0	1	0	$\frac{15}{41}$	$\frac{8}{41}$	$-\frac{10}{41}$	$\frac{50}{41}$	
4	P_3	0	0	1	$-\frac{6}{41}$	$\frac{5}{41}$	$\frac{4}{41}$	$\frac{62}{41}$	
3	P_1	1	0	0	$-\frac{2}{41}$	$-\frac{12}{41}$	$\frac{15}{41}$	$\frac{89}{41}$	
	$C_j \rightarrow$	3	5	4	0	0	0		
	Solution	$\frac{89}{41}$	$\frac{50}{41}$	$\frac{62}{41}$	0	0	0		$(Z = \frac{765}{41})$
	Δ_j	—	—	—	$-\frac{45}{41}$	$-\frac{24}{41}$	$-\frac{11}{41}$		

Since all the Δ_j are non-positive, the fourth tableau yields an optimum. The optimal solution is (89/41, 50/41, 62/41), giving a Z of 765/41.

Maximize:

$$P = 2x_1 + 4x_2 + 3x_3$$

where

$$x_1 \geq 0, \quad x_2 \geq 0, \quad x_3 \geq 0$$

and

$$x_1 + 2x_2 \leq 4$$

$$x_2 + 3x_3 \leq 6$$

$$2x_1 + x_2 + 2x_3 \leq 10.$$

Solve by the Simplex Method. Check the solution by direct calculation, as well.

Solution: Use x_4, x_5, and x_6 to denote slack variables. The solution is as follows:

Tableau 1

	x_1	x_2	x_3	x_4	x_5	x_6	$-P$		
x_4	1	②	0	1	0	0	0	4	←(2)
x_5	0	1	3	0	1	0	0	6	(6)
x_6	2	1	2	0	0	1	0	10	(10)
$-P$	2	4	3	0	0	0	1	0	
		↑							

Tableau 2

	x_1	x_2	x_3	x_4	x_5	x_6	$-P$		
x_2	$\frac{1}{2}$	1	0	$\frac{1}{2}$	0	0	0	2	
x_5	$-\frac{1}{2}$	0	③	$-\frac{1}{2}$	1	0	0	4	←($\frac{4}{3}$)
x_6	$\frac{3}{2}$	0	2	$-\frac{1}{2}$	0	1	0	8	(4)
$-P$	0	0	3	-2	0	0	1	-8	
			↑						

Tableau 3

	x_1	x_2	x_3	x_4	x_5	x_6	$-P$		
x_2	$\frac{1}{2}$	1	0	$\frac{1}{2}$	0	0	0	2	(4)
x_3	$-\frac{1}{6}$	0	1	$-\frac{1}{6}$	$\frac{1}{3}$	0	0	$\frac{4}{3}$	
x_6	($\frac{11}{6}$)	0	0	$-\frac{1}{6}$	$-\frac{2}{3}$	1	0	$\frac{16}{3}$	←($\frac{32}{11}$)
$-P$	$\frac{1}{2}$	0	0	$-\frac{3}{2}$	-1	0	1	-12	
	↑								

Tableau 4

	x_1	x_2	x_3	x_4	x_5	x_6	$-P$	
x_2	0	1	0	$\frac{6}{11}$	$\frac{2}{11}$	$-\frac{3}{11}$	0	$\frac{6}{11}$
x_3	0	0	1	$-\frac{2}{11}$	$\frac{3}{11}$	$\frac{1}{11}$	0	$\frac{20}{11}$
x_1	1	0	0	$-\frac{1}{11}$	$-\frac{4}{11}$	$\frac{6}{11}$	0	$\frac{32}{11}$
$-P$	0	0	0	$-\frac{16}{11}$	$-\frac{9}{11}$	$-\frac{3}{11}$	1	$-13\frac{5}{11}$

Tableau 4 gives the optimal solution.

To check the above calculations, consider the passage from Tableau 1 to Tableau 3. The multiplier vectors of Tableau 3 are:

$$\vec{\mu}_1 = \left(\frac{1}{2}, 0,0,0\right)$$

$$\vec{\mu}_2 = \left(-\frac{1}{6}, \frac{1}{3}, 0,0\right)$$

$$\vec{\mu}_3 = \left(-\frac{1}{6}, -\frac{2}{3}, 1,0\right)$$

$$\vec{\mu}_4 = \left(-\frac{3}{2}, -1,0,1\right) .$$

Consider the products $\vec{\mu}_i \cdot \vec{k}_2$, where $\vec{k}_2$ is the second column of Tableau 1, for i = 1,2,3,4:

$$\vec{\mu}_1 \cdot \vec{k}_2 = \left(\frac{1}{2}, 0,0,0\right) \begin{pmatrix} 2 \\ 1 \\ 1 \\ 4 \end{pmatrix} = 1$$

$$\vec{\mu}_2 \cdot \vec{k}_2 = 0$$

$$\vec{\mu}_3 \cdot \vec{k}_2 = 0$$

$$\vec{\mu}_4 \cdot \vec{k}_2 = 0 .$$

These four products must equal the entries in the successive rows of column 2, Tableau 3.

Now form $\vec{\mu}_i \cdot \vec{b}$, for i = 1,2,3,4, where b is the stub of Tableau 1:

$$\vec{\mu}_1 \cdot \vec{b} = (\tfrac{1}{2}, 0, 0, 0) \begin{pmatrix} 4 \\ 6 \\ 10 \\ 0 \end{pmatrix} = 2$$

$$\vec{\mu}_2 \cdot \vec{b} = -\frac{4}{6} + 2 = \frac{4}{3}$$

$$\vec{\mu}_3 \cdot \vec{b} = -\frac{4}{6} + 4 = 10 = \frac{16}{3}$$

$$\vec{\mu}_4 \cdot \vec{b} = -12.$$

These four products equal the entries in the stub of Tableau 3.

• PROBLEM 3-27

Solve the following linear-programming problem by means of the simplex procedure:

Minimize

$$x_2 - 3x_3 \qquad + 2x_5$$

subject to:

$$\begin{aligned} x_1 + 3x_2 - x_3 \qquad + 2x_5 \qquad &= 7 \\ -2x_2 + 4x_3 + x_4 \qquad\qquad &= 12 \\ -4x_2 + 3x_3 \qquad + 8x_5 + x_6 &= 10 \\ x_j &\geq 0 . \end{aligned}$$

Initial Step

i	Basis	c		0	1	−3	0	2	0	
			P_0	P_1	P_2	P_3	P_4	P_5	P_6	θ
1	P_1	0	7	1	3	−1	0	2	0	—
2	P_4	0	12	0	−2	(4)	1	0	0	12/4 = 3
3	P_6	0	10	0	−4	3	0	8	1	$10/3 = 3\frac{1}{3}$
4			0	0	−1	3	0	−2	0	

Second Step

			P_0	P_1	P_2	P_3	P_4	P_5	P_6	
1	P_1	0	10	1	$(\frac{5}{2})$	0	$\frac{1}{4}$	2	0	$10/\frac{5}{2} = 4$
2	P_3	−3	3	0	$-\frac{1}{2}$	1	$\frac{1}{4}$	0	0	—
3	P_6	0	1	0	$-\frac{5}{2}$	0	$-\frac{3}{4}$	8	1	—
4			−9	0	$\frac{1}{2}$	0	$-\frac{3}{4}$	−2	0	

Third Step

			P_0	P_1	P_2	P_3	P_4	P_5	P_6
1	P_2	1	4	$\frac{2}{5}$	1	0	$\frac{1}{10}$	$\frac{4}{5}$	0
2	P_3	−3	5	$\frac{1}{5}$	0	1	$\frac{3}{10}$	$\frac{2}{5}$	0
3	P_6	0	11	1	0	0	$-\frac{1}{2}$	10	1
4			−11	$-\frac{1}{5}$	0	0	$-\frac{4}{5}$	$-\frac{12}{5}$	0

Solution: The initial basis (see Tableau 1) consists of P_1, P_4, P_6, and the corresponding solution is

$$\vec{X}_0 = (x_1, x_4, x_6) = (7, 12, 10).$$

Since

$$c_1 = c_4 = c_6 = 0$$

the corresponding value of the objective function z_0, equals zero. P_3 is selected to go into the basis, since

$$\max_j (z_j - c_j) = z_3 - c_3 = 3 > 0$$

θ_0 is the minimum of x_{i0}/x_{i3} for $x_{i3} > 0$, that is,

$$\min\left(\frac{12}{4}, \frac{10}{3}\right) = \frac{12}{4} = \theta_0$$

and hence P_4 is eliminated. Transform the tableau (see Second Step, Tableau 1) and obtain a new solution

$$\vec{X}_0' = (x_1, x_3, x_6) = (10,3,1)$$

and the value of the objective function is -9. In the second step, since:

$$\max_j (z'_j - c_j) = z'_2 - c_2 = \frac{1}{2} > 0 .$$

and

$$\theta_0 = \frac{10}{\frac{5}{2}}$$

P_2 is introduced into the basis and P_1 is eliminated. Transform the second-step values of Tableau 1 and obtain the third solution

$$\vec{X}_0'' = (x_2, x_3, x_6) = (4,5,11)$$

with a value of the objective function equal to -11. Since

$$\max (z_j'' - c_j) = 0$$

this solution is a minimum feasible solution.

• PROBLEM 3-28

Maximize

$$f = 3x_1 + 2x_2$$

subject to:

$$6x_1 + 4x_2 \le 24$$

$$10x_1 + 3x_2 \le 30$$

$$x_1, x_2 \ge 0$$

Solve by the Simplex Method to find the optimal solution(s).

Solution: The initial and final simplex tableaux are shown in Figs. 1 and 2. The tableau shown in Fig. 2 reflects an optimal solution because the reduced costs are negative or zero for the non-basic variables (x_3 and x_4). Therefore, the solution

$$x_1^* = \frac{24}{11} \qquad x_2^* = \frac{30}{11} \qquad f^* = \$12$$

is optimal. However, since $c_4 - z_4$ equals zero, x_4 can be brought into the basis to generate a new solution with the same value of the objective function.

Initial Tableau

Maximize			3	2	0	0		
i	c_B	x_B	x_1	x_2	x_3	x_4	b_i	θ_i
1	2	x_3	6	4	1	0	24	4
2	0	x_4	(10)	3	0	1	30	3 → Out
		z_j	0	0	0	0	0	
		$c_j - z_j$	3	2	0	0		
			↑ In					

Fig. 1

Final Tableau

Maximize			3	2	0	0		
i	c_B	x_B	x_1	x_2	x_3	x_4	b_i	θ_i
1	2	x_2	0	1	$\frac{5}{11}$	$-\frac{3}{11}$	$\frac{30}{11}$	–
2	3	x_1	1	0	$-\frac{3}{22}$	($\frac{2}{11}$)	$\frac{24}{11}$	12 → Out
		z_j	3	2	$\frac{1}{2}$	0	12	
		$c_j - z_j$	0	0	$-\frac{1}{2}$	0		
						↑ In		

Fig. 2

Note that the optimal solution of a linear programming problem need not be unique. When the objective function is parallel to a non-redundant (binding) constraint, then there may exist more than one optimal solution. When this occurs, the problem has alternate optima. Alternate optima can be detected easily in the final (optimal) simplex tableau: when at least one non-basic variable has a $c_j - z_j$ value equal to zero, then the optimal solution is nonunique. The reason is that each such nonbasic variable can be pivoted into the basis (which changes the values of the basic variables) without changing the value of the objective function.

Alternate Optimal Solution

Maximize			3	2	0	0	
i	c_B	x_B	x_1	x_2	x_3	x_4	b_i
1	2	x_2	$\frac{3}{2}$	1	$\frac{1}{4}$	0	6
2	0	x_4	$\frac{11}{2}$	0	$-\frac{3}{4}$	1	12
		z_j	3	2	$\frac{1}{2}$	0	12
		$c_j - z_j$	0	0	$-\frac{1}{2}$	0	

Fig. 3

The alternate solution is shown in Fig. 3. In this tableau, the optimal solution is:

$$x_1^* = 0 \qquad x_2^* = 6 \qquad f^* = \$12$$

(Note that in Fig. 3, x_1 has a reduced cost of zero. If you bring x_1 into the basis, you will obtain the tableau shown in Fig. 2. This means there are only two alternate optimal solutions to this problem.)

The graphical solution is reproduced in Fig. 4. The set of feasible solutions is OABC. The optimal solutions occur at points A and B or any point in between them.

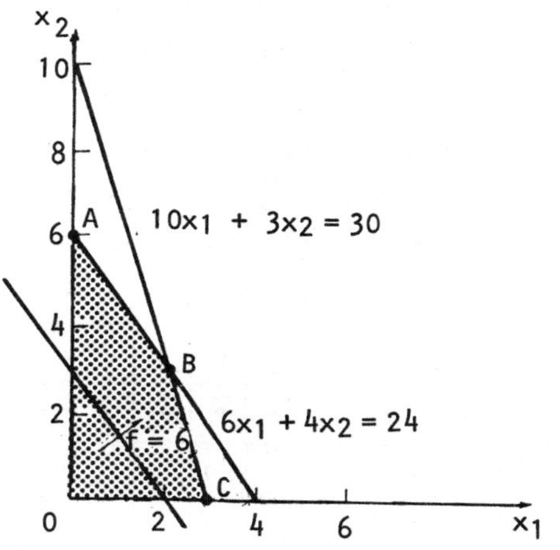

Fig. 4

Graphical solution

Alternate optima provide a very interesting situation for the decision-maker: subjective or secondary considerations may be used to choose the best alternative. For instance, the decision-maker may decide that producing both x_1 and x_2 is preferable to producing only x_2 because of market conditions or perhaps because it leads to more employment.

• PROBLEM 3-29

Minimize

$$2x_1 + x_2$$

subject to:

$$3x_1 + x_2 - x_3 = 3$$

$$4x_1 + 3x_2 - x_4 = 6$$

$$x_1 + 2x_2 - x_5 = 2$$

and

$$x_j \geq 0 .$$

Solve by the Simplex Method.

Solution: Since the given system does not contain any unit vectors and as all elements of $\vec{P}_0$ are strictly positive, the system needs to be augmented with a full artificial basis of three vectors. Denote these vectors as $\vec{P}_6$, $\vec{P}_7$, $\vec{P}_8$ and develop the first solution (see Tableau 1). The first (artificial) solution is then $\vec{X}_0 = (x_6, x_7, x_8) = (3,6,2)$ with a value of the objective function equal to 11. The z_j elements are obtained by taking the inner product of $\vec{P}_j$ with the cost column $\vec{c}$. For example, $z_1 - c_1 = \vec{c}\vec{P}_1 - c_1 = 3w + 4w + 1w - 2 = 8w - 2$, with the coefficient of w noted in the fifth (m + 2) row of the tableau and the -2 in the fourth (m + 1) row under column $\vec{P}_1$. Vector $\vec{P}_1$ is selected to enter the basis as the maximum (m + 2,j) element is (m + 2,1) = 8.

Initial Step

i	Basis	$\vec{c}$	$\vec{P}_0$	2	1	0	0	0	w	w	w	
				$\vec{P}_1$	$\vec{P}_2$	$\vec{P}_3$	$\vec{P}_4$	$\vec{P}_5$	$\vec{P}_6$	$\vec{P}_7$	$\vec{P}_8$	θ
1	$\vec{P}_6$	w	3	(3)	1	−1	0	0	1	0	0	$3/3 = 1$
2	$\vec{P}_7$	w	6	4	3	0	−1	0	0	1	0	$6/4 = 1\frac{1}{2}$
3	$\vec{P}_8$	w	2	1	2	0	0	−1	0	0	1	$2/1 = 2$
4			0	−2	−1	0	0	0	0	0	0	
5			11	8	6	−1	−1	−1	0	0	0	

Second Step

Basis	$\vec{c}$	$\vec{P}_0$	$\vec{P}_1$	$\vec{P}_2$	$\vec{P}_3$	$\vec{P}_4$	$\vec{P}_5$	$\vec{P}_6$	$\vec{P}_7$	$\vec{P}_8$	θ
$\vec{P}_1$	2	1	1	$\frac{1}{3}$	$-\frac{1}{3}$	0	0		0	0	$1/\frac{1}{3} = 3$
$\vec{P}_7$	w	2	0	$\frac{5}{3}$	$\frac{4}{3}$	−1	0		1	0	$2/\frac{5}{3} = 1\frac{1}{5}$
$\vec{P}_8$	w	1	0	($\frac{5}{3}$)	$\frac{1}{3}$	0	−1		0	1	$1/\frac{5}{3} = \frac{3}{5}$
		2	0	$-\frac{1}{3}$	$-\frac{2}{3}$	0	0		0	0	
		3	0	$\frac{10}{3}$	$\frac{5}{3}$	−1	−1		0	0	

Third Step

Basis	$\vec{c}$	$\vec{P}_0$	$\vec{P}_1$	$\vec{P}_2$	$\vec{P}_3$	$\vec{P}_4$	$\vec{P}_5$	$\vec{P}_6$	$\vec{P}_7$	$\vec{P}_8$	θ
$\vec{P}_1$	2	$\frac{4}{5}$	1	0	$-\frac{2}{5}$	0	$\frac{1}{5}$		0		—
$\vec{P}_7$	w	1	0	0	(1)	−1	1		1		$1/1 = 1$
$\vec{P}_2$	1	$\frac{3}{5}$	0	1	$\frac{1}{5}$	0	$-\frac{3}{5}$		0		$\frac{3}{5}/\frac{1}{5} = 3$
		$\frac{11}{5}$	0	0	$-\frac{3}{5}$	0	$-\frac{1}{5}$		0		
		1	0	0	1	−1	1		0		

Fourth Step

Basis	$\vec{c}$	$\vec{P}_0$	$\vec{P}_1$	$\vec{P}_2$	$\vec{P}_3$	$\vec{P}_4$	$\vec{P}_5$	θ
$\vec{P}_1$	2	$\frac{6}{5}$	1	0	0	$-\frac{2}{5}$	$\frac{3}{5}$	$\frac{6}{5}/\frac{3}{5} = 2$
$\vec{P}_3$	0	1	0	0	1	−1	(1)	$1/1 = 1$
$\vec{P}_2$	1	$\frac{2}{5}$	0	1	0	$\frac{1}{5}$	$-\frac{4}{5}$	—
		$\frac{14}{5}$	0	0	0	$-\frac{3}{5}$	$\frac{2}{5}$	
		0	0	0	0	0	0	

Fifth Step

Basis	$\vec{c}$	$\vec{P}_0$	$\vec{P}_1$	$\vec{P}_2$	$\vec{P}_3$	$\vec{P}_4$	$\vec{P}_5$
$\vec{P}_1$	2	$\frac{3}{5}$	1	0	$-\frac{3}{5}$	$\frac{1}{5}$	0
$\vec{P}_5$	0	1	0	0	1	−1	1
$\vec{P}_2$	1	$\frac{6}{5}$	0	1	$\frac{4}{5}$	$-\frac{3}{5}$	0
		$\frac{12}{5}$	0	0	$-\frac{2}{5}$	$-\frac{1}{5}$	0

The corresponding $\theta_0 = \frac{3}{3} = 1$, and the artificial vector $\vec{P}_6$ is eliminated. Next transform all the elements of the initial step (Tableau 1), except the artificial vector columns, by the elmination formulas. The new solution, as shown in the second step, is $\vec{X}_0' = (x_1, x_7, x_8) = (1,2,1)$, with a value of the objective function of 3w + 2. Vector $\vec{P}_2$ goes into the basis next, and the artificial vector $\vec{P}_8$ is removed. The new solution of the third step is $\vec{X}_0'' = (x_1, x_7, x_2) = \left(\frac{4}{5}, 1, \frac{3}{5}\right)$ with the objective function equal to $w + \frac{11}{5}$. Both the elements in the positions (m + 2,3) and (m + 2,5) equal 1; i.e., $z_3 - c_3 = w - \frac{3}{5}$ and $z_j - c_j = w - \frac{1}{5}$. One can choose either vector to enter the basis, and arbitrarily choose $\vec{P}_3$, eliminating the last artificial vector $\vec{P}_7$ to obtain the fourth step solution $\vec{X}_0''' = (x_1, x_3, x_2) = \left(\frac{6}{5}, 1, \frac{2}{5}\right)$, with the objective function equal to $\frac{14}{5}$. The first feasible solution, i.e., a solution which involves only the variables $(x_1, x_2, x_3, x_4, x_5)$ and satisfies the given constraints, has been found.

In the fourth step, as all the artificial variables have been eliminated, use the usual simplex criterion to select the vector to enter the basis, i.e., maximum (m + 1,j) element. Thus, $\vec{P}_5$ is introduced and $\vec{P}_3$ removed. As the new basis of $(\vec{P}_1, \vec{P}_5, \vec{P}_2)$ causes all the (m + 1,j) elements to be nonpositive, i.e., all $z_j - c_j \leq 0$, the fifth step contains the optimum feasible solution of $\vec{X}_0'''' = (x_1, x_5, x_2) = \left(\frac{3}{5}, 1, \frac{6}{5}\right)$ with the minimum of the objective function $2x_1 + x_2$ equal to $\frac{12}{5}$.

• PROBLEM 3-30

In order to manufacture three products, X, Y, and Z, assume that three resources must be utilized, namely, time on machines I and II, and specialized labor. Within a production period, at most 48 units of time are available on machine I, at most 120 units of time on machine II, and exactly 80 units of special man-time.

The production of 1 unit of product X requires 3 units of time on machine I, 3 units of time on machine II, and 2 units of special man-time; the production of a unit of Y requires 1 unit of time on machine I, 4 units of time on machine II, and 4 units of special man-time; the production of 1 unit of Z requires 2 units of time on machine I, 3 units of time on machine II, and 1 unit of special man-time.

Let x denote units of product X, y denote units of product Y, and z denote units of product Z. Then the constraints on production are:

$$3x + y + 2z + s_1 = 48$$

$$3x + 4y + 3z + s_2 = 120$$

$$2x + 4y + 1z + s_3 = 80$$

where all variables are nonnegative; s_1 and s_2 denote slack on machines I and II, respectively, and s_3 denotes unutilized man-time.

As for contributions to profit, product X contributes 5 monetary units; product Y, 6 monetary units; and product Z, 14 monetary units--but, by contractual agreement, for every unit of unutilized man-time, the company must pay 4 monetary units to the guild of specialists. The objective is to maximize:

$$P = 5x + 6y + 14z - 4s_3$$

subject to the given production constraints.

Solution: The above constraints and objective function can be expressed in tableau form.

Tableau 0

	x	y	z	s_1	s_2	s_3	
s_1	3	1	2	1	0	0	48
s_2	3	4	3	0	1	0	120
s_3	2	4	1	0	0	1	80
	5	6	14	0	0	−4	P

Tableau 1

	x	y	z	s_1	s_2	s_3		
s_1	3	1	2	1	0	0	48	(48)
s_2	3	4	3	0	1	0	120	(30)
s_3	2	④	1	0	0	1	80	←(20)
	13	22 ↑	18	0	0	0	$P + 320$	

Tableau 2

	x	y	z	s_1	s_2	s_3		
s_1	$\frac{5}{2}$	0	($\frac{7}{4}$)	1	0	$-\frac{1}{4}$	28	←(16)
s_2	1	0	2	0	1	−1	40	(20)
y	$\frac{1}{2}$	1	$\frac{1}{4}$	0	0	$\frac{1}{4}$	20	(80)
	2	0	$\frac{25}{2}$ ↑	0	0	$-\frac{11}{2}$	$P - 120$	

Tableau 3

	x	y	z	s_1	s_2	s_3	
z	$\frac{10}{7}$	0	1	$\frac{4}{7}$	0	$-\frac{1}{7}$	16
s_2	$-\frac{13}{7}$	0	0	$-\frac{8}{7}$	1	$-\frac{5}{7}$	8
y	$\frac{1}{7}$	1	0	$-\frac{1}{7}$	0	$\frac{2}{7}$	16
	$-\frac{111}{7}$	0	0	$-\frac{50}{7}$	0	$-\frac{26}{7}$	$P - 320$

This is tableau zero because it is nonadjusted--the objective function is not expressed solely as a function of the current corner variables. In order to adjust eliminate s_3 from P, as follows:

$$\begin{aligned} P &= 5x + 6y + 14z - 4s_3 \\ &= 5x + 6y + 14z - 4(80 - 2x - 4y - z) \\ &= 13x + 22y + 18z - 320. \end{aligned}$$

A tableau-type rule for determining whether or not P is adjusted is to look down the columns of the basic variables and check to see if all the objective coefficients in these columns are zero. If these coefficients are not all zero, adjustment must be made before beginning to apply the simplex algorithm. Adjust Tableau 0 by adding 4 times row 3 to the objective row--or equivalently by pivoting on the unit entry in the s_3 row and s_3 column. Thus obtain the adjusted Tableau 1.

Now apply the simplex algorithm. Obtain the following sequence of adjusted tableaux.

Tableau 3 is terminal.

• PROBLEM 3-31

A manufacturer wishes to maximize the profits associated with producing two products, R and S. Products R and S are manufactured by a 2-stage process in which all initial operations are performed in machine center I and all final operations may be performed in either machine center A or in machine center B. Machine centers A and B are different from each other in the sense that, in general, for any given product they yield different unit rates and different unit profits. Assume that a certain amount of overtime has been made available in machine center A for the manufacture of products R and S. Since the use of overtime results in changes (decreases) in unit profits denote separately, by machine center AA, any overtime use of machine center A.

The unit times required to manufacture products R and S, the hours available in each machine center, and the unit profits are given in Table 1.

Table 1

		Product R			Product S			
Operation	Machine Center	R_1	R_2	R_3	S_1	S_2	S_3	Hours Available
1	I	0.01	0.01	0.01	0.03	0.03	0.03	850
2	A	0.02			0.05			700
	AA		0.02			0.05		100
	B			0.03			0.08	900
Profit per part (in dollars)		0.40	0.28	0.32	0.72	0.64	0.60	

In this table, R_1, R_2, and R_3 are introduced to denote the three possible combinations for producing R, and similarly, S_1, S_2, and S_3 are defined for product S.

The problem is to determine how much of each product should be made through the use of each possible combination of machine centers so as to maximize the total profits, keeping in mind the prescribed limitations on the capacities of the machine centers.

Rephrase the problem in mathematical form. If X_1, X_2, X_3, X_4, X_5, X_6 denote the amounts to be made of products $R_1, R_2, R_3, S_1, S_2, S_3$ respectively, then the total profit Z will be given by (see Table 1)

$$Z = 0.40X_1 + 0.28X_2 + 0.32X_3 + 0.72X_4 + 0.64X_5 + 0.60X_6$$

The restrictions to the problem will be given by

$$\begin{aligned} 0.01X_1 + 0.01X_2 + 0.01X_3 + 0.03X_4 + 0.03X_5 + 0.03X_6 &\leq 850 \\ 0.02X_1 + 0.05X_4 &\leq 700 \\ 0.02X_2 + 0.05X_5 &\leq 100 \\ 0.03X_3 + 0.08X_6 &\leq 900 . \end{aligned}$$

The problem now follows: Determine the values of $X_j \geq 0$ (where $j = 1,2,\ldots,6$) which maximize

$$Z = 0.40X_1 + 0.28X_2 + 0.32X_3 + 0.72X_4 + 0.64X_5 + 0.60X_6 \quad (1)$$

subject to the restrictions

$$\begin{aligned} 0.01X_1 + 0.01X_2 + 0.01X_3 + 0.03X_4 + 0.03X_5 + 0.03X_6 &\leq 850 \\ 0.02X_1 + 0.05X_4 &\leq 700 \quad (2) \\ 0.02X_2 + 0.05X_5 &\leq 100 \\ 0.03X_3 + 0.08X_6 &\leq 900 \end{aligned}$$

Solution: To proceed toward a simplex technique solution, the system of inequations 2 is reduced to an equivalent system of equations by introducing new nonnegative slack variables X_7, X_8, X_9, X_{10} so that

$$\begin{aligned} 0.01X_1 + 0.01X_2 + 0.01X_3 + 0.03X_4 & \\ + 0.03X_5 + 0.03X_6 + X_7 &= 850 \\ 0.02X_1 + 0.05X_4 + X_8 &= 700 \quad (3) \\ 0.02X_2 + 0.05X_5 + X_9 &= 100 \\ 0.03X_3 + 0.08X_6 + X_{10} &= 900 . \end{aligned}$$

In this problem, it can be seen that positive values of these slack variables represent underutilization of capacity in machine centers I,A,AA, and B respectively.

To complete the transformation of the present set of equations (1 and 3) into the standard form used in the simplex technique, and also to achieve a much desired compactness, a final set of transformations is now made. Assume one rearranges eqs. 3 so that corresponding X_j's appear in the same column. Then, treating all blanks as zeros, one would have for X_1, for example, the column of coefficients: 0.01, 0.02, 0, 0, reading from top to bottom. The final set of transformations is that which lets the symbol P_j denote the column of coefficients of X_j ($j = 1,2,\ldots,10$) and P_0 denote the right-hand column of numbers in the system of eqs. 3.

The P_j's (and P_0) are such that multiplication of P_j (or P_0) by a real number means that each component of the column is to be multiplied by that real number. Thus, referring back to the coefficients of X_1

$$X_1P_1 = X_1 \begin{pmatrix} 0.01 \\ 0.02 \\ 0 \\ 0 \end{pmatrix} = \begin{pmatrix} 0.01X_1 \\ 0.02X_1 \\ 0 \\ 0 \end{pmatrix} \tag{4}$$

Finally, if P_1 and P_2 are two such "vectors," then

$$X_1P_1 + X_2P_2 = X_2P_2 + X_1P_1 \tag{5}$$

The linear programming problem may now be restated using the symbols P_j as follows: Determine the values of a set of nonnegative X_j (where $j = 1,2,\ldots,10$) which maximize the linear form (functional)

$$Z = 0.40X_1 + 0.28X_2 + 0.32X_3 + 0.72X_4 + 0.64X_5$$
$$+ 0.60X_6 + 0\cdot X_7 + 0\cdot X_8 + 0\cdot X_9 + 0\cdot X_{10}$$

subject to the restrictions

$$\sum_{j=1}^{10} X_jP_j = P_0 .$$

Now carry out its solution by means of the simplex technique. The first step consists of exhibiting the column vectors P_j in a systematic form. This is done in

Tableau 2 by means of eqs. 3, all blank spaces in the table representing zeros.

Tableau 2

P_1	P_2	P_3	P_4	P_5	P_6	P_7	P_8	P_9	P_{10}	P_0
0.01	0.01	0.01	0.03	0.03	0.03	1				850
0.02			0.05				1			700
	0.02			0.05				1		100
		0.03			0.08				1	900

Tableau 3

C							0.40	0.28	0.32	0.72	0.64	0.60
	Basis	P_0	P_7	P_8	P_9	P_{10}	P_1	P_2	P_3	P_4	P_5	P_6
	P_7	850	1				0.01	0.01	0.01	0.03	0.03	0.03
←	P_8	700		1			0.02			0.05		
	P_9	100			1			0.02			0.05	
	P_{10}	900				1			0.03			0.08
	Z_j											
	$Z_j - C_j$						−0.40	−0.28	−0.32	−0.72*	−0.64	−0.60

Tableau 4

	P_7	430	1	−0.6			−0.002	0.01	0.01		0.03	0.03
→ 0.72	P_4	14,000		20			0.4			1		
←	P_9	100			1			0.02			0.05	
	P_{10}	900				1			0.03			0.08
	Z_j	10,080		14.4			0.288			0.72		
	$Z_j - C_j$	10,080		14.4			−0.112	−0.28	−0.32		−0.64*	−0.60

Tableau 5

C							0.40	0.28	0.32	0.72	0.64	0.60
	Basis	P_0	P_7	P_8	P_9	P_{10}	P_1	P_2	P_3	P_4	P_5	P_6
	P_7	370	1	−0.6	−0.6		−0.002	−0.002	0.01			0.03
0.72	P_4	14.000		20			0.4			1		
→ 0.64	P_5	2.000			20			0.4			1	
←	P_{10}	900				1			0.03			0.08
	$Z_j - C_j$	11.360		14.4	12.8		−0.112	−0.024	−0.32			−0.60*

Tableau 6

	P_7	32.5	1	−0.6	−0.6	$-\frac{3}{8}$	−0.002	−0.002	$\frac{-1}{800}$			
← 0.72	P_4	14,000		20			[0.4]			1		
0.64	P_5	2.000			20			0.4			1	
→ 0.60	P_6	11.250				$12\frac{1}{2}$			$\frac{3}{8}$			1
	$Z_j - C_j$	18.110		14.4	12.8	$7\frac{1}{2}$	−0.112*	−0.024	−0.095			

Tableau 7

C							0.40	0.28	0.32	0.72	0.64	0.60
	Basis	P_0	P_7	P_8	P_9	P_{10}	P_1	P_2	P_3	P_4	P_5	P_6
	P_7	102.5	1	$-\frac{1}{2}$	−0.6	$-\frac{3}{8}$		−0.002	$-\frac{1}{800}$	0.005		
→ 0.40	P_1	35,000		50			1			$\frac{5}{2}$		
0.64	P_5	2,000			20			0.4			1	
← 0.60	P_6	11,250				$\frac{100}{8}$			[$\frac{3}{8}$]			1
	$Z_j - C_j$	22,030		20	12.8	$7\frac{1}{2}$		−0.024	−0.095*	0.28		

Tableau 8

	P_7	140	1	$-\frac{1}{2}$	−0.6	$-\frac{1}{3}$		−0.002		0.005		$\frac{1}{300}$
0.40	P_1	35,000		50			1			$\frac{5}{2}$		
← 0.64	P_5	2,000			20			[0.4]			1	
→ 0.32	P_3	30,000				$\frac{100}{3}$			1			$\frac{8}{3}$
	$Z_j - C_j$	24,880		20	12.8	$\frac{32}{3}$		−0.024*		0.28		$0.25\frac{1}{3}$

For the simplex calculational procedure which follows, these columns are now rearranged as shown in Tableau 3. Then, a column labeled "Basis" is inserted to the left of the P_0 column and, in this column, the basis vectors are listed. Next, a row of C_j's are added, where the C_j's are defined as the coefficients of the corresponding X_j's in the expression for Z given in eq. 1. Then, a column of C_i's are added, these corresponding to the C_j's. The expression for Z can now be written as

$$Z = \sum_{j=1}^{10} C_j X_j \tag{6}$$

Tableau 9

C							0.40	0.28	0.32	0.72	0.64	0.60
	Basis	P_0	P_7	P_8	P_9	P_{10}	P_1	P_2	P_3	P_4	P_5	P_6
	P_7	150	1	$-\frac{1}{2}$	$-\frac{1}{2}$	$-\frac{1}{3}$				$\frac{1}{200}$	$\frac{1}{200}$	$\frac{1}{300}$
0.40	P_1	35,000		50			1			$\frac{5}{2}$		
0.28	P_2	5,000			50			1			$\frac{5}{2}$	
0.32	P_3	30,000				$\frac{100}{3}$			1			$\frac{8}{3}$
	$Z_j - C_j$	25,000		20	14	$10\frac{2}{3}$				0.28	0.06	$0.25\frac{1}{3}$

Having entered the equations and the C_j's into the table, now add a row of numbers labeled Z_j, where j denotes the appropriate column. These Z_j's are determined as follows. Letting X_{ij} denote the element in the ith row and jth column of the table, then the Z_j's (including Z_0) are defined by

$$Z_j = \sum_i C_i X_{ij} \tag{7}$$

Finally, a row labeled $Z_j - C_j$ is entered into the table and for any column, say j_0, consists of the corresponding C_{j0} subtracted from the value of Z_{j0} which was entered in the previous row.

This completes the listing process (Tableau 3) and constitutes the first full set of calculations. One now has a feasible solution to the problem, where this solution is given by the column vector P_0 in terms of the basis vectors P_7, P_8, P_9, P_{10}, namely

$$X_7 = 850; \quad X_8 = 700; \quad X_9 = 100; \quad X_{10} = 900 \tag{8}$$

resulting in a net profit of $Z = 0$.

In the problem (Tableau 3), $Z_1 - C_1 < 0$ (as are $Z_2 - C_2$ through $Z_6 - C_6$) and some of the coefficients under P_1 are greater than zero. Hence, further calculations are required.

The procedure is as follows: Of all the $Z_j - C_j < 0$, choose the most negative of these. (In the particular problem, this is $Z_4 - C_4 = -0.72$ and is so indicated by an asterisk in Tableau 3.) This determines a particular P_j (namely, P_4) which will be introduced into the column labeled "Basis" in Tableau 4. To determine the vector which this P_j will replace, one first divides each of the positive X_{ij} appearing in the P_j column into the corresponding X_{i0} which appears in the same row under P_0. The smallest of these ratios then determines the vector to be replaced. In the present problem, P_4 is to replace one of the vectors P_7, P_8, P_9, or P_{10}. Under P_4, there are two positive X_{ij}, $X_{74} = 0.03$ and $X_{84} = 0.05$. The division of these X_{ij} into the corresponding X_{i0}'s which appear under P_0 gives a minimum of 14,000 (i.e., 700/0.05). Thus, P_8 is the vector to be replaced by P_4, so that a new basis is formed consisting of the vectors P_7, P_4, P_9, and P_{10}.

If one now lets

Subscript k denote "coming in"

Subscript r denote "going out"

X_{ij}' denote the elements of the new matrix, and

$$\phi = \min_i \frac{X_{i0}}{X_{ik}}, \qquad X_{ik} > 0 \tag{9}$$

then the elements of the new matrix (X_{ij}') are calculated as follows: for the elements of the row corresponding to the vector just entered into the unit basis

$$X_{kj}' = \frac{X_{rj}}{X_{rk}} \tag{10}$$

while the other elements (X_{ij}') of the new matrix are calculated by

$$X_{ij}' = X_{ij} - \left(\frac{X_{rj}}{X_{rk}}\right) X_{ik} \tag{11}$$

where eq. 11 also applies to the X_{i0}'s appearing under P_0 and to the $Z_j - C_j$ in the entire bottom row (but not to the Z_j's in the second last row). Furthermore, the new value of the profit function will be given by

$$Z_0' = Z_0 - \phi(Z_k - C_k) \quad (12)$$

or, since $C_0 = 0$, the profit function will be given by

$$(Z_0 - C_0)' = (Z_0 - C_0) - \phi(Z_k - C_k) \quad (13)$$

For example, starting with Tableau 3 and proceeding to Tableau 4, the most negative $Z_j - C_j$ is $Z_4 - C_4 = -0.72$. Therefore k = 4. From eq. 9

$$\phi = \underset{i}{\text{Min}} \frac{X_{i0}}{x_{i4}} \text{ for all } X_{i4} > 0$$

i.e.

$$\phi = \text{Min}\left(\frac{850}{0.03} = 28,333; \quad \frac{700}{0.05} = 14,000\right) = 14,000$$

Therefore, P_4 will replace P_8; or, in the equations, k = 4, r = 8.

The elements in the P_4 row of Tableau 4 are then computed by (see eq. 10)

$$X_{4j}' = \frac{X_{8j}}{X_{84}} = \frac{X_{8j}}{0.05}$$

Therefore,

$$X_{40}' = \frac{X_{80}}{0.05} = \frac{700}{0.05} = 14,000$$

$$X_{41} = \frac{X_{81}}{0.05} = \frac{0.02}{0.05} = 0.4, \text{ etc.}$$

For the elements of the other rows (where k = 4, r = 8 are substituted into eq. 11):

$$X_{ij}' = X_{ij} - \left(\frac{X_{8j}}{X_{84}}\right) X_{i4} = X_{ij} - \left(\frac{X_{8j}}{0.05}\right) X_{i4}$$

Therefore,

$$X_{70}' = X_{70} - \left(\frac{X_{80}}{0.05}\right) (X_{74}) = 850 - \left(\frac{700}{0.05}\right)(0.03)$$

$$= 850 - (14,000)(0.03) = 850 - 420 = 430$$

and

$$(Z_1 - C_1)' = (Z_1 - C_1) - \left(\frac{X_{81}}{X_{84}}\right)(Z_4 - C_4)$$

$$= (-0.40) - \left(\frac{0.02}{0.05}\right)(-0.72)$$

$$= (-0.4) - (0.4)(-0.72) = -0.4 + 0.288 = -0.112.$$

Finally, the new value of the profit functional will be given by

$$(Z_0 - C_0)' = (Z_0 - C_0) - \phi(Z_4 - C_4)$$

$$= 0 - 14{,}000(-0.72) = +10{,}080.$$

This procedure is carried out in Tableaus 3-9. This process is repeated until all the values in the $Z_j - C_j$ are positive. For the present problem, the solution is obtained after six iterations. The final tableau, Tableau 9, yields the optimal solution. This optimal solution is also stated, both in terms of the number of parts and hours required, in Tables 10 and 11.

Table 10

Optimum Program (number of parts)

Product R		Product S	
R_1 (Centers I–A)	35,000 parts	S_1	0 parts
R_2 (I–AA)	5,000 parts	S_2	0 parts
R_3 (I–B)	30,000 parts	S_3	0 parts
Total	R = 70,000 parts	S = 0	
Total profit	\$25,000 + · 0 = \$25,000		

Table 11

Optimum Program (Hours)

Operation	Machine Center	Product R: R_1	R_2	R_3	Product S: S_1	S_2	S_3	Hours Used	Hours Avail.	Surplus Hours
1	I	350	50	300	0	0	0	700	850	150
2	A	700			0			700	700	0
	AA		100			0		100	100	0
	B			900			0	900	900	0

The optimal program under the prescribed conditions consists of manufacturing 70,000 units of product R to the complete exclusion of product S. By eq. 1 and also by $(Z_0 - C_0)$ in the optimum tableau, the total profits will be

$$Z = 0.40(35,000) + 0.28(5000) + 0.32(30,000) + 0.72(0)$$
$$+ 0.64(0) + 0.60(0)$$
$$= \$25,000.$$

• PROBLEM 3-32

Solve the following problem by the Simplex Method:

Maximize

$$u = 4x + 2y + z$$

subject to:

$$x + y \leq 1$$

$$x + z \leq 1$$

and

$$x \geq 0, \quad y \geq 0, \quad z \geq 0.$$

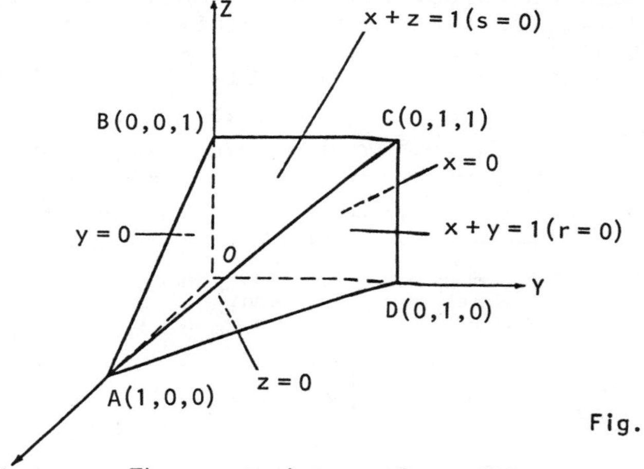

Fig. 1

The constraint set for problem

Solution: The problem, restated in terms of nonnegative slack variables r and s, is as follows:

Maximize

$$u = 4x + 2y + z \tag{1}$$

subject to:

$$x + y - 1 = -r \tag{2}$$

$$x + z - 1 = -s \tag{3}$$

and

$$x \geq 0,\ y \geq 0,\ z \geq 0,\ r \geq 0,\ s \geq 0\ .$$

The initial tableau, which corresponds to the origin in Figure 1, is as follows:

x	y	z	1			
1	1	0	-1	$= -r$		
1*	0	1	-1	$= -s$	$O(0,0,0)$.	(T.1)
4	2	1	0	$= u$		

The first column is a suitable pivot column. Both a_{11} and a_{21} qualify as the pivot entry; because of this the next tableau will be degenerate. Choosing a_{21} as the pivot entry gives rise to Tableau 2:

s	y	z	1			
-1	1*	-1	0	$= -r$		
1	0	1	-1	$= -x$	$A(1,0,0)$.	(T.2)
-4	$+2$	-3	4	$= u$		

Tableau 2 is degenerate since $-b_1 = 0$. Graphically, this corresponds to the planes s = 0, y = 0, z = 0, and r = 0 intersecting at point A of Figure 1. Tableau 2 is not terminal; pivoting on a_{12} produces Tableau 3:

s	r	z	1			
-1	1	-1	0	$= -y$		
1	0	1	-1	$= -x$	$A(1,0,0)$.	(T.3)
-2	-2	-1	4	$= u$		

Tableau 3 is a terminal tableau, since all the c_j's are negative. Note that both Tableau 2 and Tableau 3 correspond to the point A, where the degeneracy occurs. The b.f.p. path is thus from O to A to A. This behavior is typical of what happens when a degenerate b.f.p. is the solution point. Note that Max u = 4.

One way of resolving degeneracy from a theoretical point of view is through the perturbation approach. Note that this method is not usually recommended as a computational device.

In Tableau 2 above, replace the 0 in the right-hand column by $-\varepsilon$, where the "perturbation" ε denotes a small positive number. Thus Tableau 2'is obtained:

s	y	z	1			
-1	1*	-1	$-\epsilon$	$= -r'$		
1	0	1	-1	$= -x$	$A(1,0,0)$.	(T.2')
-4	$+2$	-3	4	$= u$		

Note that the second tableau (in this case, Tableau 2') is no longer degenerate. To obtain a graphical interpretation, write out the equation for r':

$$-r' = -s + y - z - \varepsilon.$$

Substituting for -s from Equation (3), obtain:

$$-r' = x + y - (1 + \varepsilon).$$

The plane $r' = 0$ is thus equivalent to $x + y = 1 + \varepsilon$. Now construct the constraint set $S_{C,\varepsilon}$ that applies to the perturbed problem. This appears in Figure 2. Notice that the degenerate basic feasible point A of Figure 1 has been split into the two nondegenerate basic feasible points A and A'. Both are intersection points of exactly three bounding planes.

Pivoting in Tableau 2' with a_{12} as the pivot entry results in Tableau 3, which is a terminal tableau:

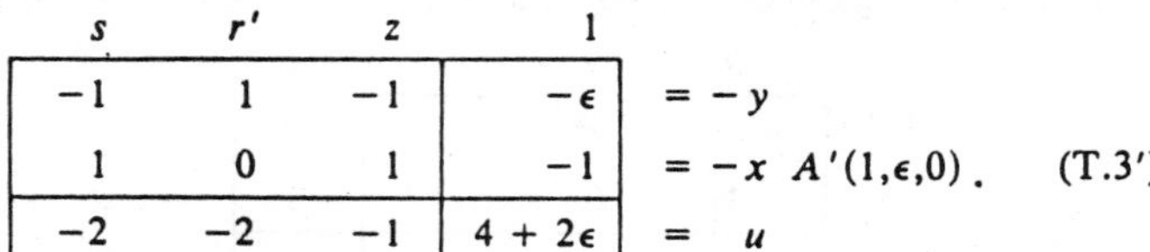

s	r'	z	1		
-1	1	-1	$-\epsilon$	$= -y$	
1	0	1	-1	$= -x$	$A'(1,\epsilon,0)$. (T.3')
-2	-2	-1	$4 + 2\epsilon$	$= u$	

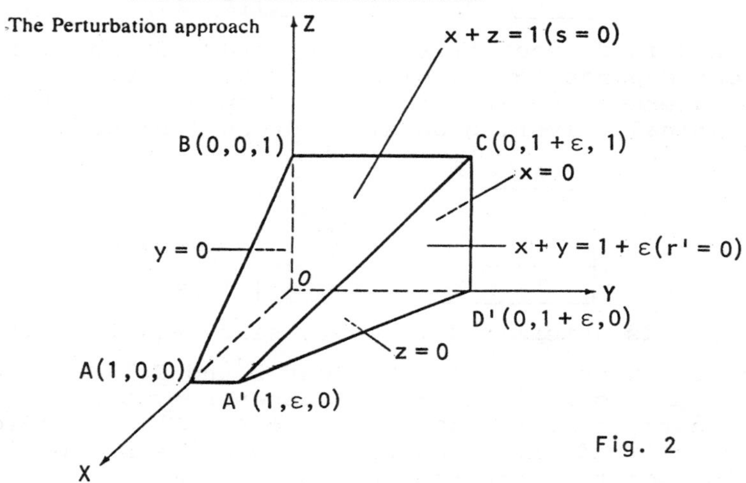

Fig. 2

The b.f.p. corresponding to Tableau 3' is the solution point A' of the perturbed problem:

$$x = 1,\ y = \varepsilon,\ z = 0,$$

and

$$\text{Max } u = 4 + 2\varepsilon.$$

The solution to the original unperturbed (but degenerate) problem is obtained by letting ε approach zero. This results in $x = 1$, $y = 0$, $z = 0$ (point A as before), and Max $u = 4$.

This problem illustrates the perturbation approach. When a zero first appears in the right-hand column, it is replaced by $-\varepsilon$, which represents a small negative number. If another zero appears in the right-hand column, perhaps of a subsequent tableau, it is replaced by $-\varepsilon^2$, etc. In the terminal tableau of the perturbed, but nondegenerate, problem, the solution will be in terms of ε. The solution of the original unperturbed problem is obtained by letting ε approach zero.

A mutual fund is deciding how to divide its investments among bonds, preferred stock, and speculative stock. It does not want to exceed a combined risk rate of 3 when the bonds have been assigned a risk rate of 1, the preferred stock, 3, and the speculative stock, 5. However, the fund does want a total annual yield of at least 10 percent. If the interest rate of the bonds is 8 percent, of the preferred stock is 12 percent, and of the speculative stock is 20 percent, how should the assets be distributed for the greatest annual yield?

Solution: The total amount to be invested does not matter. Let x,y, and z be the fractions of the whole that will be invested in bonds, preferred stock, and speculative stock, respectively. Clearly these fractions must total the whole portfolio: $x + y + z = 1$. The other two constraints indicate the restrictions on the risk rate and total yield:

$$x + 3y + 5z \leq 3 \text{ (risk rate constraint)}$$

$$8x + 12y + 20z \geq 10 \text{ (annual yield constraint).}$$

The annual yield constraint can be omitted, since whether it is there or not, the left side of the inequality can be made as large as possible. If it must be less than 10, there is no feasible solution to the problem as stated, and the fund must reconsider its goals. If it can equal or exceed 10 subject to the other constraints, that constraint is automatically satisfied. Thus, summarize the problem:

$$\text{Maximize } P = 8x + 12y + 12z$$

subject to $x + y + z = 1$ and $x + 3y + 5z \leq 3$. The non-negativity constraints, as usual, are assumed. The first constraint needs no slack variable, but it does need an artificial variable. Recall that a slack variable s_i is used to convert the ith inequality to an equality. An artificial variable is introduced to make the number of unknowns in each row the same. This makes it possible to start with the basic feasible solution $x = y = z = 0$ while not violating the constraints.

The second is given a slack variable as usual:

$$x + y + z + a = 1$$

$$x + 3y + 5z + s = 3$$

Step 1: The first project is to rid the problem of a, since it has no real-world interpretation. This may be achieved by finding the minimum of $A = a$ (which minimum had better be zero), or, equivalently, by finding the maximum of $-A = -a$. It may be written:

	x	y	z	s	a	Solution
a	(1)	1	1	0	1	1
s	1	3	5	1	0	3
-A	0	0	0	0	-1	0
-A	1	1	1	0	0	1

The row above the dashed line is a summary of the equation -A = -a. There is a non-zero number in the last row of the a-column. This is not allowed, because a is a basic variable, and each basic variable must have 1 in its column and the rest of the numbers 0. To obtain a 0 in the last row in the a-column, add the a-row to the last row and write the sum below; then cross out the original row. Since all three positive numbers in the last row are equal, any one of the first three columns may become the pivot column. Choose the first column to be the pivot column. Now, divide the positive elements of the inner rectangle in the pivot column into their corresponding elements in the "solutions" column. Since 1/1 < 3/1, then the first row is the pivot row. Thus, the 1 in the upper left is the pivot. Now in the next table, replace the letter to the left of the pivot row by the letter above the pivot column. Thus x replaces a; a must leave. The pivot row is divided by the pivot. Add the second row of the inner rectangle to -1x the first row of the inner rectangle. Replace the second row with this result.

	x	y	z	s	a	Solution
x	1	1	1	0	1	1
s	0	2	(4)	1	-1	2
-A	0	0	0	0	-1	0

Thus, since the present objective function, A is 0, proceed to Step 2 where the objective function in the original problem was

$$P = 8x + 12y + 20z.$$

Thus, the table is now:

	x	y	z	s	Solution
x	1	1	1	0	1
s	0	2	4	1	2
P	8	12	20	0	0

Since the largest entry in the last row is 20, the z-column is the pivot column. Since 2/4 < 1/1, the s-row is the pivot row and thus the 4 is the pivot. Now the letter must be replaced to the left of the pivot row (s) by the letter above the pivot column (z). Divide the pivot row by the pivot, 4.

	x	y	z	s	Solution
x	1	1	1	0	1
z	0	1/2	1	1/4	1/2
P	8	12	20	0	0

Now, it is left to add the appropriate multiples of the pivot row to the other rows of numbers in such a way as to obtain zeros in the rest of the pivot column. First of all, add the P row to (-1)·x-row to obtain:

	x	y	z	s	Solution
x	1	1	1	0	1
z	0	1/2	1	1/4	1/2
P	0	4	12	0	-8

Now add the P-row to (-12) ·z-row. Add the x-row to (-1) ·z-row.

	x	y	z	s	Solution
x	1	1/2	0	-1/4	1/2
z	0	1/2	1	1/4	1/2
P	0	-2	0	-3	-14

Since there are no positive numbers in the bottom row, the optimum solution has been obtained. It is $P_{max} = 14$ for $x = \frac{1}{2}$, $y = 0$, and $z = \frac{1}{2}$.

Thus, the maximum possible yield under these conditions is 14 percent, well above the 10 percent desired minimum.

• PROBLEM 3-34

Maximize

$$P = 5u + 6v$$

where

$$3u + v \le 1$$

$$3u + 4v \le 0.$$

Here u and v are unconstrained.

<u>Solution</u>: One way to solve this problem is to let $u = u_1 - u_2$, $v = v_1 - v_2$, where $u_1 \ge 0$, $u_2 \ge 0$, $v_1 \ge 0$, $v_2 \ge 0$. Then this problem is transformed into the following auxiliary problem.

Maximize

$$P = 5u_1 - 5u_2 + 6v_1 - 6v_2$$

where all variables are nonnegative:

and

$$3u_1 - 3u_2 + v_1 - v_2 \le 1 \qquad (1)$$

$$3u_1 - 3u_2 + 4v_1 - 4v_2 \le 0. \qquad (2)$$

This problem will be solved by the simplex algorithm.

In the following tableaux, s_1 and s_2 denote slack in Eqs. (1) and (2), respectively.

Tableau 1

	u_1	u_2	v_1	v_2	s_1	s_2		
s_1	3	−3	1	−1	1	0	1	(1)
s_2	3	−3	④	−4	0	1	0	←(0)
	5	−5	6 ↑	−6	0	0	P	

Tableau 2

	u_1	u_2	v_1	v_2	s_1	s_2		
s_1	$\frac{9}{4}$	$-\frac{9}{4}$	0	0	1	$-\frac{1}{4}$	1	$(\frac{4}{9})$
v_1	$(\frac{3}{4})$ circled	$-\frac{3}{4}$	1	−1	0	$\frac{1}{4}$	0	←(0)
	$\frac{2}{4}$ ↑	$-\frac{2}{4}$	0	0	0	$-\frac{3}{2}$	P	

Tableau 3

	u_1	u_2	v_1	v_2	s_1	s_2		
s_1	0	0	−3	③	1	−1	1	←$(\frac{1}{3})$
u_1	1	−1	$\frac{4}{3}$	$-\frac{4}{3}$	0	$\frac{1}{3}$	0	
	0	0	$-\frac{2}{3}$	$\frac{2}{3}$ ↑	0	$-\frac{5}{3}$	P	

Tableau 4

	u_1	u_2	v_1	v_2	s_1	s_2	
v_2	0	0	−1	1	$\frac{1}{3}$	$-\frac{1}{3}$	$\frac{1}{3}$
u_1	1	−1	0	0	$\frac{4}{9}$	$-\frac{1}{9}$	$\frac{4}{9}$
	0	0	0	0	$-\frac{2}{9}$	$-\frac{13}{9}$	$P-\frac{2}{9}$

Tableau 4 is terminal. The optimum solution to the auxiliary problem is $u_1 = \frac{4}{9}$, $u_2 = 0$, $v_1 = 0$, $v_2 = \frac{1}{3}$, and $P = \frac{2}{9}$. Hence the optimum solution to the original problem is $u = u_1 - u_2 = \frac{4}{9}$, $v = v_1 - v_2 = 0 - \frac{1}{3} = -\frac{1}{3}$, and $P = \frac{2}{9}$.

• PROBLEM 3-35

Consider the following problem:

Maximize $x_0 = 3x_1 + 5y + 2x_3$

subject to:

$$x_1 + 2y + 2x_3 \le 14$$
$$2x_1 + 4y + 3x_3 \le 23$$

$0 \le x_1 \le 4,\ 2 \le y \le 5,\ 0 \le x_3 \le 3.$

Solve by the Simplex Method.

Solution: In a Linear Program, if some (or all) variables are bounded from above and below, in addition to the regular constraints, the following procedure can be used to solve the problem:

At every iteration, one guarantees that the solution is feasible as follows: let x_J be a nonbasic variable at zero level which is selected to enter the solution (every nonbasic variable can always be put at zero level.) Let $(\vec{X}_B)_i = (\vec{X}_B^*)_i$ be the ith variable of the current basic solution $\vec{X}_B$. Thus, introducing x_J into the solution gives,

$$(\vec{X}_B)_i = (\vec{X}_B^*)_i - \alpha_i^J x_J$$

where α_i^J is the ith element of $\vec{\alpha}^J = \vec{B}^{-1} \vec{P}_J$. $\vec{B}^{-1}$ being the coefficients' matrix in the current basic solution of the simplex tableau, corresponds to the variables in the starting solution, and $\vec{P}_J$ is the vector of $(\vec{A},\vec{I})$ corresponding to x_J ($(\vec{A},\vec{I})\vec{X} = \vec{P}_0$ representing the regular constraints' matrix).

Now, x_J remains feasible if

$$0 \le x_J \le u_J$$

(the upper and lower binding constraints' matrix equation being $\vec{L} \le \vec{X} \le \vec{U}$, where:

$$\vec{U} = \begin{pmatrix} u_1 \\ u_2 \\ \cdot \\ \cdot \\ \cdot \\ u_{n+m} \end{pmatrix} \quad \text{and} \quad \vec{L} = \begin{pmatrix} \ell_1 \\ \ell_2 \\ \cdot \\ \cdot \\ \cdot \\ \ell_{n+m} \end{pmatrix}$$

n,m: number of nonbasic and basic variables, respectively).

While $(\vec{X}_B^*)_i$ remains feasible if

$$0 \le (\vec{X}_B^*)_i - \alpha^J{}_i n_J \le u_i \ , \ i = 1,2,\ldots,m.$$

Since the introduction of x_J into the solution implies that it must be nonnegative, the feasibility condition about the nonnegativity and upper bound constraints of the entering variable are satisfied. Now, consider the nonnegativity and upper bound constraints for those basic variables may be affected by introducing the entering variable. From the nonnegativity condition

$$(\vec{X}_B)_i = (\vec{X}_B^*)_i - \alpha_i^J x_J \geq 0,$$

it follows that only $\alpha_i^J > 0$ may cause $(\vec{X}_B)_i$ to be negative. Let θ_1 represent the maximum value of x_J resulting from this condition. Thus,

$$\theta_1 = \min_i \left\{ \frac{(\vec{X}_B^*)_i}{\alpha_i^J}, \quad \alpha_i^J > 0 \right\}.$$

This actually is the same as the feasibility condition of the regular simplex method.

In order to guarantee that $(\vec{X}_B)_i$ will not exceed its upper bound, it is necessary that:

$$(\vec{X}_B)_i = (\vec{X}_B^*)_i + (-\alpha_i^J)x_j \leq u_i .$$

This condition can be violated if α_i^J is negative. Thus, by letting θ_2 represent the maximum value of x_J resulting from this condition

$$\theta_2 = \min_i \left\{ \frac{u_i - (\vec{X}_B^*)_i}{-\alpha_i^J}, \quad \alpha_i^J < 0 \right\} .$$

Let θ denote the maximum value of x_J which does not violate any of the above conditions. Then

$$\theta = \min\{\theta_1, \theta_2, u_J\} .$$

It is noticed that an old basic variable $(\vec{X}_B)_i$ can become nonbasic only if the introduction of the entering variable $\vec{x}_J$ at level Θ causes $(\vec{X}_B)_i$ to be at zero level or at its upper bound. This means that if $\theta = u_J, x_J$ cannot be made basic since no $(\vec{X}_B)_i$ can be dropped from the solution and thus x_J should remain nonbasic but at its upper bound. (If $\theta = u_J = \theta_1 = \theta_2$, the tie may be broken arbitrarily.)

In the above derivation, the entering variable x_J is assumed to be at zero level before it is introduced into the solution. To maintain the validity of the above results, every nonbasic variable x_k at upper bound can be put at zero level by the substitution

$$x_k = u_k - x_k'$$

where

$$0 \leq x_k' \leq u_k .$$

Using the above ideas, one can effect the changes in the current basic solution as follows. Let $(\vec{X}_B)_r$ be the variable corresponding to $\theta = \min\{\theta_1, \theta_2, u_j\}$, then

1. if $\theta = \theta_1$, $(\vec{X}_B)_r$ leaves the solution and x_J enters by using the regular row operations of the simplex method,

2. if $\theta = \theta_2$, $(\vec{X}_B)_r$ leaves and x_J enters; then $(\vec{X}_B)_r$ being nonbasic at its upper bound must be substituted out by using $(\vec{X}_B)_r = u_r - (X_B)_r'$,

3. if $\theta = u_J, x_J$ is substituted at its upper bound $u_J - x_J'$ but remains nonbasic.

Considering the problem above, since y has a positive lower bound, it must be substituted at its lower bound. Let $y = x_2 \leq 5 - 2 = 3$ and the problem becomes

Starting tableau:

Basic	x_0	x_1	x_2	x_3	S_1	S_2	Solution
x_0	(1)	-3	-5	-2	0	0	10
S_1	0	1	2	2	(1)	0	10
S_2	0	2	4	3	0	(1)	15

First Iteration:

Select x_2 as the entering variable $(z_2 - c_2 = -5)$. Thus

$$\vec{\alpha}^2 = \begin{pmatrix} 2 \\ 4 \end{pmatrix} > \vec{0}$$

and

$$\theta_1 = \min\{10/2, 15/4\} = 3.75$$

Since all $\alpha_i^2 > 0$, it follows that $\theta_2 = \infty$. Consequently, $\theta = \min\{3.75, \infty , 3\} = 3$.

Because $\theta = u_2, x_2$ is substituted at its upper limit but it remains nonbasic. Thus putting $x_2 = u_2 - x_2' = 3 - x_2'$, the new tableau becomes:

Basic	x_0	x_1	x_2'	x_3	S_1	S_2	Solution
x_0	①	−3	5	−2	0	0	25
S_1	0	1	−2	2	①	0	4
S_2	0	2	−4	3	0	①	3

Second Iteration:

Select x_1 as the entering variable $(z_1 - c_1 = -3)$. Thus,

$$\vec{\alpha}^1 = \begin{pmatrix} 1 \\ 2 \end{pmatrix}$$

$$\theta_1 = \min\{4/1, 3/2\} = 3/2, \text{ corresponding to } S_2$$

$$\theta_2 = \infty$$

Hence, $\theta = \min\{3/2, \infty, 4\} = 3/2$. Since $\theta = \theta_1$, introduce x_1 and drop S_2. This yields

Basic	x_0	x_1	x_2'	x_3	S_1	S_2	Solution
x_0	①	0	−1	5/2	0	3/2	59/2
S_1	0	0	0	1/2	①	−1/2	5/2
x_1	0	①	−2	3/2	0	1/2	3/2

Third Iteration:

Select x_2' as the entering variable. Since

$$\vec{\alpha}^2 = \begin{pmatrix} 0 \\ -2 \end{pmatrix} \leq 0$$

$$\theta_1 = \infty$$

$$\theta_2 = \frac{4 - 3/2}{-(-2)} = \frac{5}{4}, \text{ corresponding to } x_1$$

Thus, $\theta = \min\{\infty, 5/4, 3\} = 5/4$. Since $\theta = \theta_2$, introduce x_2' into basis and drop x_1 then substitute it out at its upper bound $(4 - x_1')$. Thus, by removing x_1 and introducing x_2' the tableau becomes

Basic	x_0	x_1	x_2'	x_3	S_1	S_2	Solution
x_0	①	−1/2	0	7/4	0	5/4	115/4
S_1	0	0	0	1/2	①	−1/2	5/2
x_2'	0	−1/2	①	−3/4	0	−1/4	−3/4

Now, by substituting for $x_1 = 4 - x_1'$, the final tableau becomes

Basic	x_0	x_1'	x_2'	x_3	S_1	S_2	Solution
x_0	①	1/2	0	7/4	0	5/4	123/4
S_1	0	0	0	1/2	①	−1/2	5/2
x_2'	0	1/2	①	−3/4	0	−1/4	5/4

which is now optimal and feasible.

The optimal solution in terms of the original variables x_1, x_2, and x_3 is found as follows. Since $x_1' = 0$, it follows that $x_1 = 4$. Also, since $x_2' = 5/4$, $x_2 = 3 - 5/4 = 7/4$ and $y = 2 + 7/4 = 15/4$. Finally x_3 equals 0. These values yield $x_0 = 123/4$ as shown in the optimal tableau.

• PROBLEM 3-36

A function f(x) takes the following values:

at x =	-1	0	1
f(x) =	-8	-4	6

Formulate as a linear programming problem so as to,

a) find $g(x) = t_o + t_1x$ so that the largest possible deviation between f(x) and g(x) at the given points is as small as possible,

b) find $h(x) = s_o + s_1x$ so that the sum of deviations between f(x) and h(x) is as small as possible,

c) solve (b) with the further condition that the (algebraic) sum of deviations should equal zero;

Use the simplex method to obtain solutions.

Solution:

(a) Minimize m, where $g(x_i) - f(x_i) \le m$,

$f(x_i) - g(x_i) \le m$,

i.e. $m + t_o - t_1 \ge -8 \qquad m - t_o + t_1 \ge 8$

$m + t_o \ge -4 \qquad m - t_o \ge 4$

$m + t_o + t_1 \ge 6 \qquad m - t_o - t_1 \ge -6$

t_o, t_1 not sign-restricted; $m \ge 0$ automatically.

Insert $t_o = -4 - m + y_2$

in remaining inequalities.

$t_1 = 4 - y_1 + y_2$

$y_1, \ldots, y_6$ slack variables.

Final tableau

	y_1	y_3	y_5	
y_2	$-\frac{1}{2}$	$-\frac{1}{2}$	0	3
y_4	$\frac{1}{2}$	$-\frac{1}{2}$	-1	3
m	$-\frac{1}{4}$	$-\frac{1}{4}$	$-\frac{1}{2}$	$\frac{3}{2}$
y_6	$-\frac{1}{2}$	$\frac{1}{2}$	-1	3
	$-\frac{1}{4}$	$-\frac{1}{4}$	$-\frac{1}{2}$	$\frac{3}{2}$

i.e. $t_0 = -\frac{5}{2}$, $t_1 = 7$.

x	- 1	0	1
g(x)	$-\frac{19}{2}$	$-\frac{5}{2}$	$\frac{9}{2}$
$\lvert g(x) - f(x)\rvert$	$\frac{3}{2}$	$\frac{3}{2}$	$\frac{3}{2}$

(b) Minimize $z_1 + z_2 + z_3 + z_4 + z_5 + z_6$,

subject to
$$t_0 - t_1 + z_1 - z_4 = -8$$
$$t_0 + z_2 - z_5 = -4$$
$$t_0 + t_1 + z_3 - z_6 = 6$$

t_0, t_1 not sign-restricted,

$t_0 = -4 - z_2 + z_5$, $\quad t_1 = 10 + z_2 - z_3 - z_5 + z_6$

$t_0 - t_1 = -14 -2z_2 + z_3 + 2z_5 - z_6$,

so that the constraints reduce to the single constraint

$z_1 -2z_2 + z_3 - z_4 +2z_5 - z_6 = 6$.

Answer: $z_5 = 3$, hence $t_0 = -1$, $t_1 = 7$

x	-1	0	1
h(x)	-8	-1	6
$\lvert f(x) - h(x)\rvert$	0	3	0

(c) Further constraint: $z_1 + z_2 + z_3 - z_4 - z_5 - z_6 = 0$.
Solution: $s_0 = -2$, $s_1 = 8$.

h(x)	-10	-2	6
f(x) - h(x)	2	-2	0 (adding up to 0).

Consider the following minimization problem:

$$\min z = 2x_1 + x_2 - x_3$$

subject to:

$$x_1 + x_2 + x_3 \le 3 \qquad (1)$$

$$x_2 + x_3 \ge 2$$

$$x_1 + x_3 = 1$$

$$x_1, x_2, x_3 \ge 0$$

Find an initial basic feasible solution.

Solution: Converting to the equivalent equality-constrained problem, there follows:

$$\min z = 2x_1 + x_2 - x_3$$

subject to:

$$x_1 + x_2 + x_3 + x_4 = 3 \qquad (2)$$

$$x_2 + x_3 - x_5 = 2$$

$$x_1 + x_3 = 1$$

$$x_1, \ldots, x_5 \ge 0$$

Add a different nonnegative variable, x_6 and x_7, not appearing elsewhere, in each of the last two equations of problem (2). Thus:

$$x_1 + x_2 + x_3 + x_4 = 3 \qquad (3)$$

$$x_2 + x_3 - x_5 + x_6 = 2$$

$$x_1 + x_3 + x_7 = 1$$

$$x_1, \ldots, x_7 \ge 0$$

Now, an initial basic solution is easily obtained: $x_1 = x_2 = x_3 = x_5 = 0$, $x_4 = 3$, $x_6 = 2$, $x_7 = 1$. The difficulty, however, is that this solution is not feasible, for it implies:

$$x_1 + x_2 + x_3 = 0$$

$$x_2 + x_3 = 0$$

$$x_1 + x_3 = 0$$

and, therefore, the constraints given in (1) are not satisfied, and neither are those of (2). Since this is not feasible, artificial variables must be added to the program and then their values reduced to zero.

To achieve removalof artificials fromthe basic solution, one associates with each variable a cost so undesirable that the technique will drive these variables to zero, since it is an optimization technique. Thus in a max (min) problem one assigns a large negative (positive) cost to each artificial variable. These costs will be sufficiently large to dominate any expression in which they appear in the computation. It is conventional to employ a symbol as this cost, and M or -M, is frequently used for the min (max) problem, where M is taken to be positive.

Thus the problem becomes:

$$\min z = 2x_1 + x_2 + x_3 + Mx_6 + Mx_7$$

subject to:

$$\begin{aligned} x_1 + x_2 + x_3 + x_4 \qquad\qquad &= 3 \\ x_2 + x_3 \quad - x_5 + x_6 \qquad &= 2 \\ x_1 \quad + x_3 \qquad\qquad + x_7 &= 1 \\ x_1, \ldots, x_7 &\geq 0 \end{aligned}$$

The initial tableau becomes:

Tableau 1

c_j	Basis	P_1	P_2	P_3	P_4	P_5	P_6	P_7	b
0	P_4	1	1	1	1	0	0	0	3
M	P_6	0	1	1	0	-1	1	0	2
M	P_7	1	0	1	0	0	0	1	1
$c_j - z_j$		2- M	1 -M	- 1-2M	0	M	0	0	

P_3 should come into the basis, since -1 -2M is the most negative $c_j - z_j$ available, by virtue of M's dominance. P_7, then, will leave the basis, yielding the tableau:

Tableau 2

c_j	Basis	P_1	P_2	P_3	P_4	P_5	P_6	P_7	b
0	P_4	1	1	0	1	0	0	-1	2
M	P_6	-1	1	0	0	-1	1	-1	1
-1	P_3	1	0	1	0	0	0	1	1
$c_j - z_j$		3 + M	1 -M	0	0	M	0	1+2M	

P_2 should enter and P_6 should be removed, yielding the tableau:

Tableau 3

c_j	Basis	P_1	P_2	P_3	P_4	P_5	P_6	P_7	b
0	P_4	1	0	0	1	1	-1	0	1
1	P_2	-1	1	0	0	-1	1	-1	1
-1	P_3	1	0	1	0	0	0	1	1

In tableau 3 both artificial variables are zero, and $x_4 = 1$, $x_2 = 1$, $x_1 = x_5 = 0$, which is a feasible solution for (2); this then is selected as the initial basic feasible solution.

BIG - M METHOD

• PROBLEM 3-38

Maximize $\quad f = 3x_1 + 2x_2 + x_3$

subject to: $\quad 2x_1 + 5x_2 + x_3 \le 12$

$6x_1 + 8x_2 \le 22$

$x_3 \ge 0$

x_1 unrestricted.

Solve by the Simplex method.

	Maximize		3	-3	2	1	0	0	
i	c_B	y_B	y_1	y_2	y_3	y_4	y_5	y_6	b_i
1	1	y_4	0	0	$\frac{7}{3}$	1	1	$-\frac{1}{3}$	$\frac{14}{3}$
2	3	y_1	1	-1	$\frac{4}{3}$	0	0	$\frac{1}{6}$	$\frac{11}{3}$
		z_j	3	-3	$\frac{19}{3}$	1	1	$\frac{1}{6}$	$\frac{47}{3}$
		$c_j - z_j$	0	0	$-\frac{13}{3}$	0	-1	$-\frac{1}{6}$	

Final Tableau

Solution: To solve this problem, replace x_1 by x_1' and x_1'', where $x_1 = x_1' - x_1''$. The transformed problem is:

Maximize $\quad f = 3x_1' - 3x_1'' + 2x_2 + x_3$

subject to: $\quad 2x_1' - 2x_1'' + 5x_2 + x_3 \le 12$

$6x_1' - 6x_1'' + 8x_2 \le 22$

$x_1', x_1'', x_2, x_3 \ge 0.$

Note that a_1' and a_1'' (the columns of x_1' and x_1'', respectively) are identical except for their signs. Because of this, the two columns are linearly dependent.
Therefore, x_1' and x_1'' cannot appear in any basis simultaneously. One of them always has a value of zero, (this is true in general for any pair x_j' and x_j''.)

Simplify this problem by letting:

$$y_1 = x_1' \qquad y_3 = x_2$$

$$y_2 = x_1'' \qquad y_4 = x_3$$

which yields:

Maximize: $\quad f = 3y_1 - 3y_2 + 2y_3 + y_4$

subject to: $\quad 2y_1 - 2y_2 + 5y_3 + y_4 \le 12$

$$6y_1 - 6y_2 + 8y_3 \le 22$$

$$y_1, y_2, y_3, y_4 \ge 0.$$

The optimal solution is shown in the diagram. The optimal values are:

$$y_1^* = \frac{11}{3} \qquad y_4^* = \frac{14}{3} \qquad f^* = \frac{47}{3}.$$

In terms of the original variables, the solution is:

$$x_1^* = \frac{11}{3} \qquad x_3^* = \frac{14}{3}.$$

• PROBLEM 3-39

Maximize $\quad f = 2x_1 + 3x_2$

subject to: $\quad x_1 + x_2 \ge 3$

$$x - 2x \le 4$$

$$x_1, x_2 \ge 0$$

Solve by the Simplex Method, applying the Big-M technique.

Maximize			2	3	0	0	$-M$			
i	c_B	x_B	x_1	x_2	x_3	x_4	x_5	b_i	θ_i	
1	$-M$	x_5	1	①	-1	0	1	3	3	Out →
2	0	x_4	1	-2	0	1	0	4	-	
		z_j	$-M$	$-M$	M	0	$-M$	$-3M$		
		$c_j - z_j$	2+M	3+M	-M	0	0			
				↑In						

(a) Initial Tableau

Maximize			2	3	0	0			
i	c_B	x_B	x_1	x_2	x_3	x_4	b_i	θ_i	
1	3	x_2	1	1	-1	0	3	-	?
2	0	x_4	3	0	-2	1	10	-	?
		z_j	3	3	-3	0	9		
		$c_j - z_j$	-1	0	3	0			
					↑In				

Fig. 1 (b) Second Tableau

Solution: The first and second simplex tableaus are shown in Fig. 1 a and b. Consider the second tableau. The basic solution shown cannot be optimal because x_3 should be brought into the basis. However, there is no variable to leave: both $a_{1,3}$ and $a_{2,3}$ are negative, so neither can be the pivot element. In practical terms, as x_3 increases, so do x_2 and x_4. Thus, nonnegativity does not identify a variable to leave the basis; in fact, neither variable (x_2 or x_4) can be pivoted out without violating nonnegativity. The reason is that there is no limit to the size of x_3 because there is no limit to either x_2 or x_4. Therefore, maximum profit can be made.

This can be demonstrated simply by writing the equations that correspond to rows 1 and 2 in Fig. 1b. Row 1 tells us:

$$x_1 + x_2 - x_3 = 3$$

or

$$x_2 = 3 + x_3 - x_1$$

and row 2 yields

$$3x_1 - 2x_3 + x_4 = 10$$

or

$$x_4 = 10 + 2x_3 - 3x_1$$

Now x_1 is non-basic, so it has a value of zero. Eliminating x_1 from the above leaves:

$$x_2 = 3 + x_3$$

$$x_4 = 10 + 2x_3$$

Thus, as x_3 increases, so do x_2 and x_4.

Of course, the "real world" does not permit an infinite profit. When such a result occurs in a linear programming model, it invariably indicates a defect in the model. Perhaps one or more constraints were left out, or the situation may require a nonlinear model.

• PROBLEM 3-40

The following problem is an illustration of the condition of "degeneracy."

Maximize $\quad P = 4x_1 + 3x_2 \qquad (1)$

subject to:

$$4x_1 + 2x_2 \le 10.0$$

$$2x_1 + 8/3x_2 \le 8.0 \qquad (2)$$

$$x_1 \ge 0, \; x_2 \ge 1.8$$

What are the signs of degeneracy:
a) in the simplex tableau
b) graphically?

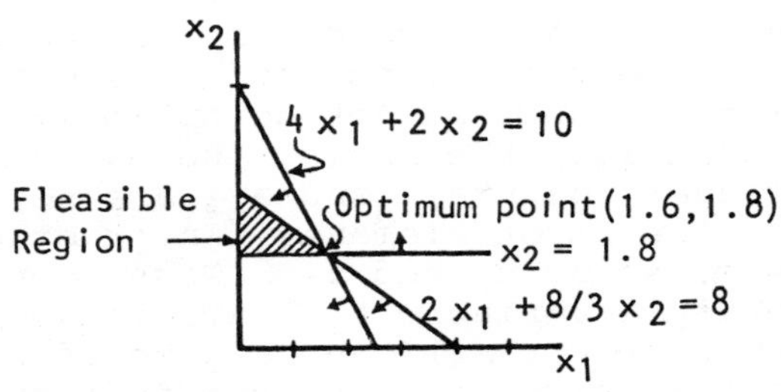

Solution: To apply the simplex method convert the inequalities in (2) to equalities by the addition of artificial and slack variables. In maximization problems, artificial variables are introduced so as to facilitate the simplex method of solution. One of the requirements of the method is that every equation contain a variable whose coefficient is 1 in that equation and zero in every other equation. Thus, the system (2) becomes:

$$4x_1 + 2x_2 + x_3 = 10$$
$$2x_1 + 8/3\,x_2 + x_4 = 8$$
$$x_2 + x_5 - x_6 = 1.8$$

Here x_3, x_4 and x_6 are slack variables, while x_5 is an artificial variable. To ensure that it will not appear in the final solution, assign it a profit factor coefficient of $-M$, where M is a very large number.

The initial simplex tableau with $x_1 = x_2 = x_6 = 0$ is:

c_j	Solution variables	Solution values	4 x_1	3 x_2	0 x_3	0 x_4	$-M$ x_5	0 x_6
0	x_3	10	4	2	1	0	0	0
0	x_4	8	2	8/3	0	1	0	0
$-M$	→ x_5	1.8	0	(1)	0	0	1	−1
	z_j	−1.8M	0	−M	0	0	−M	M
	$c_j - z_j$		4	M+3 ↑	0	0	0	−M

Replace x_5 by x_2; i.e., pivot on 1.

c_j	Solution variables	Solution values	4 x_1	3 x_2	x_3	x_4	x_5	x_6
0	x_3	6.4	4	0	1	0	−2	2
0	x_4	3.2	2	0	0	1	−8/3	8/3
3	x_2	1.8	0	1	0	0	1	−1
	z_j		0	3	0	0	3	−3
	$c_j - z_j$		4 ↑	0	0	0	−M−3	3

Here, both row x_3 and row x_4 are minimum ratios: $\frac{6.4}{4} = \frac{3.2}{2} = 1.6$. This is the signal that degeneracy exists. By the rules of the simplex algorithm, arbitrarily replace either row. If the chosen row eventually leads to no solution (the simplex tables begin to repeat themselves), then choose the other row at the point where the degeneracy was discovered.

In the present problem, replacing row x_4 with x_1 leads immediately to the final simplex tableau and optimal solution $x_1 = 1.6$, $x_2 = 1 \cdot 8$ and $P = 11.8$

Replacing row x_3 with x_1 yields the same result but after an additional iteration.

b) The degeneracy situation can also be identified by examining the graph of the problem. (See fig.)

The optimum point occurs at the intersection of the three constraint equations. Since all the constraints are satisfied exactly, there is no slack in any constraint. In a nondegenerate case, at least one of these slack variables would be non-zero.

• PROBLEM 3-41

Maximize: $Z = 3x_1 + x_2$

subject to $2x_1 + x_2 \geq 4$

and $x_2 \geq 2$.

Solution: Putting into canonical form, the system becomes:

Maximize $z = 3x_1 + x_2 + 0S_1 + 0S_2 + MA_1 + MA_2$

subject to $2x_1 + x_2 - S_1 + A_1 = 4$

$x_2 - S_2 + A_2 = 2$.

To facilitate the simplex method of solution, Tableau 1 reads:

Tableau 1

	$C_j \rightarrow$	3	1	0	0	-M	-M		
Stub	Basic Variable	Coefficients of x_1	x_2	S_1	S_2	A_1	A_2	Right Hand Side	θ
-M	A_1	2	1	-1	0	1	0	4	2
-M	A_2	0	1	0	-1	0	1	2	$+\infty$
	Index Row →	-2M-3	-2M-1	M	M	0	0	-6M	

Tableau 2

Stub	Basic Variable	x_1	x_2	S_1	S_2	A_1	A_2	Right Hand Side	θ
$c_j \rightarrow$		3	1	0	0	−M	−M		
3	x_1	1	1/2	−1/2	0	1/2	0	2	
−M	A_2	0	1	0	−1	0	1	2	
	Index Row →	0	$\frac{-2M+1}{2}$	$-\frac{3}{2}$	M	$\frac{2M+3}{2}$	0	6−2M	

At this iteration (Tableau 2) one may observe that, under the nonbasic variable S_1, there is a negative index row coefficient [−(3/2)], but the elements in the column above this number are either zero or negative. There is no need to go further, the problem is unbounded.

• PROBLEM 3-42

Maximize: $Z = 6x_1 + 4x_2$

subject to $x_1 + x_2 \leq 10$

$2x_1 + x_2 \geq 4,$

using the Simplex method.

Tableau 1

Stub	Basic Variable	x_1	x_2	S_1	S_2	A_1	Right Hand Side	θ
$c_j \rightarrow$		6	4	0	0	−M		
0	S_1	1	1	1	0	0	10	10
−M	A_1	2	1	0	−1	1	4	2
	Index Row →	−2M−6	−M−4	0	M	0	−4M	

Tableau 2

Stub	Basic Variable	x_1	x_2	S_1	S_2	A_1	Right Hand Side	θ
$c_j \rightarrow$		6	4	0	0	−M		
0	S_1	0	1/2	1	1/2	−1/2	8	16
6	x_1	1	1/2	0	−1/2	1/2	2	−4
	Index Row →	0	−1	0	−3	M+3	12	

Tableau 3

Stub	Basic Variable	x_1	x_2	S_1	S_2	A_1	Right Hand Side	θ
$c_j \rightarrow$		6	4	0	0	−M		
0	S_2	0	1	2	1	−1	16	
6	x_1	1	1	1	0	0	10	
	Index Row →	0	2	6	0	M	60	

$x_1^* = 10, x_2^* = 0$, and $Z^* = 60$.

Solution: Converting by addition of slacks and artificials:

maximize $Z = 6x_1 + 4x_2 + 0S_1 + 0S_2 - MA_1$

subject to: $x_1 + x_2 + S_1 + 0S_2 + 0A_1 = 10$

$2x_1 + x_2 + 0S_1 - S_2 + A_1 = 4.$

The iterations via simplex are shown in Tableaus 1, 2, and 3.

• PROBLEM 3-43

The L. H. & D. Chemical Corporation must produce 1,000 pounds of a special mixture for a customer which consists of ingredients 01X, 02X, and 03X. Ingredient 01X costs \$5 per pound, 02X costs \$6 per pound, and 03X costs \$7 per pound. No more than 300 pounds of 01X can be used and at least 150 pounds of 02X must be used. In addition, at least 200 pounds of 03X is required. Since the firm desires to minimize costs, the problem is determining what amount of each ingredient the firm should include in the mixture.

Solution: The problem first must be stated in mathematical form. Based on data given, the equality and inequalities are:

Minimize cost = $\$5X_1 + \$6X_2 + \$7X_3$

Subject to:

$$X_1 + X_2 + X_3 = 1{,}000 \text{ pounds}$$

$$X_1 \leq 300 \text{ pounds}$$

$$X_2 \geq 150 \text{ pounds}$$

$$X_3 \geq 200 \text{ pounds}$$

Where

X_1 = number of pounds for ingredient 01X

X_2 = number of pounds for ingredient 02X

X_3 = number of pounds for ingredient 03X.

Minimize cost = $\$5X_1 + \$6X_2 + \$7X_3 + \$MA_1 + \$0S_1 + \$0S_2 + \$MA_2 + \$0S_3 + \$MA_3$

Subject to:

$$X_1 + X_2 + X_3 + A_1 + 0S_1 + 0S_2 + 0A_2 + 0S_3 + 0A_3 = 1{,}000 \quad (1)$$

$$X_1 + 0X_2 + 0X_3 + 0A_1 + S_1 + 0S_2 + 0A_2 + 0S_3 + 0A_3 = 300 \quad (2)$$

$$0X_1 + X_2 + 0X_3 + 0A_1 + 0S_1 - S_2 + A_2 + 0S_3 + 0A_3 = 150 \quad (3)$$

$$0X_1 + 0X_2 + X_3 + 0A_1 + 0S_1 + 0S_2 + 0A_2 - S_3 + A_3 = 200 \quad (4)$$

Tableau 1

Intersectional elements

C_j	Product Mix	Quantity	\$5 X_1	\$6 X_2	\$7 X_3	\$M A_1	\$0 S_1	\$0 S_2	\$M A_2	\$0 S_3	\$M A_3
Step 4 → \$M	A_1	1,000	1	(1)	1	1	0	0	0	0	0
Step 4 → \$0	S_1	300	1	(0)	0	0	1	0	0	0	0
Replaced row Steps 2 and 3 → \$M	A_2	150	0	(1)	0	0	0	−1	1	0	0
Step 4 → \$M	A_3	200	0	(0)	1	0	0	0	0	−1	1
	Z_j	\$1,350M	\$M	\$2M	\$2M	\$M	\$0	−\$M	\$M	−\$M	\$M
	$C_j - Z_j$		\$5 − M	\$6 − 2M	\$7 − 2M	\$0	\$0	\$M	\$0	\$M	\$0
				↑ Step 1							

Since the optimum solution is concerned with minimizing costs, the optimum column is found by choosing the one that has the largest negative value in the $C_j - Z_j$ row and not the largest plus value as in a maximization problem. The most negative column is selected because this value will decrease costs the most. Upon inspection of Tableau 1, the most negative value (assuming that M equals \$100) is \$6 - 2M; thus X_2 is the optimum column (first step). Note the relatively high cost of the solution, \$1,350M.

Calculations for the last two rows in Tableau 1 that were needed in this first step are:

Z_j row

Z Total = \$M(1,000) + \$0(300) + \$M(150) + \$M(200) = \$1,350M.

ZX_1 = \$M(1) + \$0(1) +\$M(0) + \$M(0) = \$M

ZX_2 = \$M(1) + \$0(0) +\$M(1) + \$M(0) = \$2M

ZX_3 = \$M(1) + \$0(0) + \$M(0) + \$M(1) = \$2M

ZA_1 = \$M(1) + \$0(0) + \$M(0) + \$M(0) = \$M

ZS_1 = \$M(0) + \$0(1) + \$M(0) + \$M(0) = \$0

ZS_2 = \$M(0) + \$0(0) + \$M(-1) + \$M(0) = -\$M

ZA_2 = \$M(0) + \$0(0) + \$M(1) + \$M(0) = \$M

ZS_3 = \$M(0) + \$0(0) + \$M(0) + \$M(-1) = -\$M

ZA_3 = \$M(0) + \$0(0) + \$M(0) + \$M(1) = \$M

$C_j - Z_j$ row

$CX_1 - ZX_1$ = \$5 - \$M = \$5 - \$M

$CX_2 - ZX_2$ = \$6 - \$2M = \$6 - \$2M

$CX_3 - ZX_3$ = \$7 - \$2M = \$7 - \$2M

$CA_1 - ZA_1 = \$M - \$M = \$0$

$CS_1 - ZS_1 = \$0 - \$0 = \$0$

$CS_2 - ZS_2 = \$0 - (-\$M) = \$M$

$CA_2 - ZA_2 = \$M - \$M = \$0$

$CS_3 - ZS_3 = \$0 - (-\$M) = \$M$

$CA_3 - ZA_3 = \$M - \$M = \$0$

In the second step, the replaced row is found by dividing the values in the quantity column by their corresponding intersectional elements in the optimum column and selecting the row with the smallest number of units. These values are calculated as follows:

$A_1 \text{ row} = \frac{1,000}{1} = 1,000$

$S_1 \text{ row} = \frac{300}{0}$ = Not defined; therefore it is ignored

$A_2 \text{ row} = \frac{150}{1} = 150$

$A_3 \text{ row} = \frac{200}{0}$ = Not defined; therefore it is ignored.

The A_2 row, the smaller value of the two, is designated as the replaced row.

For the third step, the replacing row (X_2) is determined by dividing each value in the replaced row (A_2) by the intersectional element of the replaced row (A_2). Since the intersectional element is 1, the values remain the same. Only the variable A_2 needs to be changed to X_2.

In the fourth and final step, new values for the A_1, S_1, and A_3 rows must be calculated for Tableau 2: The formula is:

Former element in the remaining row - (Former intersectional element of remaining row X New corresponding element in replacing row) =

New value for remaining row.

The calculations for the new rows are:

A_1 Row	S_1 Row	A_3 Row
$1,000 - (1 \times 150) = 850$	$300 - (0 \times 150) = 300$	$200 - (0 \times 150) = 200$
$1 - (1 \times 0) = 1$	$1 - (0 \times 0) = 1$	$0 - (0 \times 0) = 0$
$1 - (1 \times 1) = 0$	$0 - (0 \times 1) = 0$	$0 - (0 \times 1) = 0$
$1 - (1 \times 0) = 1$	$0 - (0 \times 0) = 0$	$1 - (0 \times 0) = 1$
$1 - (1 \times 0) = 1$	$0 - (0 \times 0) = 0$	$0 - (0 \times 0) = 0$
$0 - (1 \times 0) = 0$	$1 - (0 \times 0) = 1$	$0 - (0 \times 0) = 0$
$0 - (1 \times -1) = 1$	$0 - (0 \times -1) = 0$	$0 - (0 \times -1) = 0$
$0 - (1 \times 1) = -1$	$0 - (0 \times 1) = 0$	$0 - (0 \times 1) = 0$
$0 - (1 \times 0) = 0$	$0 - (0 \times 0) = 0$	$-1 - (0 \times 0) = -1$
$0 - (1 \times 0) = 0$	$0 - (0 \times 0) = 0$	$1 - (0 \times 0) = 1$

When the intersectional element is zero, such as for the S_1 row and the A_3 row, the values of the new row are the same as the old row. This condition is true of all succeeding tableaus in which an intersectional element of a row is zero.

Tableau 2

Intersectional elements

	C_j	Product Mix	Quantity	$5 X_1	$6 X_2	$7 X_3	$M A_1	$0 S_1	$0 S_2	$M A_2	$0 S_3	$M A_3
Step 4	→ $M	A_1	850	1	0	(1)	1	0	1	−1	0	0
Step 4	→ $0	S_1	300	1	0	(0)	0	1	0	0	0	0
Step 4	→ $6	X_2	150	0	1	(0)	0	0	−1	1	0	0
Replaced row Steps 2 and 3	→ $M	A_3	200	0	0	(1)	0	0	0	0	−1	1
		Z_j	$1,050M +	$M	$6	$2M	$M	$0	$M − 6	−$M + 6	−$M	$M
		$C_j - Z_j$	$900	$5 − $M	$0	$7 − 2M	$0	$0	−$M + 6	$2M − 6	$M	$0
						↑ Step 1						

Tableau 3

Intersectional elements

Minimization Problem

	C_j	Product Mix	Quantity	$5 X_1	$6 X_2	$7 X_3	$M A_1	$0 S_1	$0 S_2	$M A_2	$0 S_3	$M A_3
Step 4	→ $M	A_1	650	(1)	0	0	1	0	1	−1	1	−1
Replaced row Steps 2 and 3	→ $0	S_1	300	(1)	0	0	0	1	0	0	0	0
Step 4	→ $6	X_2	150	(0)	1	0	0	0	−1	1	0	0
Step 4	→ $7	X_3	200	(0)	0	1	0	0	0	0	−1	1
		Z_j	$650M +	$M	$6	$7	$M	$0	$M − 6	−$M + 6	$M − 7	−$M + 7
		$C_j - Z_j$	$2,300	−$M + 5	$0	$0	$0	$0	−$M + 6	$2M − 6	−$M + 7	$2M − 7
				↑ Step 1								

Tableau 4

Intersectional elements

	C_j	Product Mix	Quantity	$5 X_1	$6 X_2	$7 X_3	$M A_1	$0 S_1	$0 S_2	$M A_2	$0 S_3	$M A_3
Replaced row Steps 2 and 3	→ $M	A_1	350	0	0	0	1	−1	(1)	−1	1	−1
Step 4	→ $5	X_1	300	1	0	0	0	1	(0)	0	0	0
Step 4	→ $6	X_2	150	0	1	0	0	0	(−1)	1	0	0
Step 4	→ $7	X_3	200	0	0	1	0	0	(0)	0	−1	1
		Z_j	$350M +	$5	$6	$7	$M	−$M + 5	$M − 6	−$M + 6	$M − 7	−$M + 7
		$C_j - Z_j$	$3,800	$0	$0	$0	$0	$M − 5	−$M + 6	$2M − 6	−$M + 7	$2M − 7
									↑ Step 1			

Inspection of Tableau 2 reveals the optimum column to be X_3. The replaced row is A_3 and the replacing row is X_3 in the next tableau. Notice that the total cost has decreased from $1,350M to $1,050M + $900 between the first two tableaus. The optimum column in Tableau 3 is X_1 and the replaced row is S_1. These changes are reflected in Tableau 4. Again the cost has decreased from the preceding tableaus.

In Tableau 4, there is presently $350M in the total cost function. Nevertheless, total cost is still declining. The optimum column is S_2. When the calculation is made for the replaced row, the value for the X_2 row is -150 [150/(-1)]. This is not a feasible solution since there cannot be a negative quantity in the final solution. Therefore it is discarded as a possibility for the replaced row. The only positive quantity for the replaced row is A_1(350). Again, new rows are determined in Tableau 5.

Tableau 5

C_j	Product Mix	Quantity	\$5 X_1	\$6 X_2	\$7 X_3	\$M A_1	\$0 S_1	\$0 S_2	\$M A_2	\$0 S_3	\$M A_3
\$0	S_2	350	0	0	0	1	−1	1	−1	1	−1
\$5	X_1	300	1	0	0	0	1	0	0	0	0
\$6	X_2	500	0	1	0	1	−1	0	0	1	−1
\$7	X_3	200	0	0	1	0	0	0	0	−1	1
	Z_j	\$5,900	\$5	\$6	\$7	\$6	−\$1	\$0	\$0	−\$1	\$1
	$C_j - Z_j$		\$0	\$0	\$0	\$M − 6	\$1	\$0	\$M	\$1	\$M − 1

Step 1 – since there are zeros and plus values in the $C_j - Z_j$ row, the final solution has been reached.

Inspection of the $C_j - Z_j$ row reveals that no negative values remain. The optimum solution has been reached. Moreover, the total cost solution no longer contains an artificial variable (M). In addition, it is necessary to make certain that the values for the variables X_1, X_2, X_3, and S_2 in the tableau satisfy the original restrictions. Reviewing the original constraint equations, they are:

$$X_1 + X_2 + X_3 + A_1 = 1{,}000 \tag{1}$$

$$X_1 + S_1 = 300 \tag{2}$$

$$X_2 - S_2 + A_2 = 150 \tag{3}$$

$$X_3 - S_3 + A_3 = 200. \tag{4}$$

Substituting the values into the equations, it will be seen that the constraints of the problem are still satisfied when $X_1 = 300$, $X_2 = 500$, $X_3 = 200$, and $S_2 = 350$. All other variables have a value of zero.

$$300 + 500 + 200 = 1{,}000 \tag{1}$$

$$1{,}000 = 1{,}000$$

$$300 + 0 = 300 \tag{2}$$

$$300 = 300$$

$$500 - 350 + 0 = 150 \tag{3}$$

$$150 = 150$$

$$200 - 0 + 0 = 200 \tag{4}$$

$$200 = 200$$

• PROBLEM 3-44

Use the simplex method for the problem:

$$\text{Maximize} \quad P = 4x + 3y + 7z$$

$$\text{where} \quad x \geq 0, \quad y \geq 0, \quad z \geq 0$$

$$\text{and} \quad 2x + y + 3z \leq 120$$

$$x + 3y + 2x = 120$$

Solution: This problem will be solved by considering the auxiliary problem.

$$\text{Maximize} \quad P = 4x + 3y + 7z - MA$$

where all variables are nonnegative

$$\text{and} \quad 2x + y + 3z + s = 120$$

$$x + 3y + 2z + A = 120.$$

In this problem, s is a slack variable and A an artificial variable. The sequence of tableaux which solve this problem is the following:

Tableau 0

	x	y	z	s	A	
s	2	1	3	1	0	120
A	1	3	2	0	①	120
	4	3	7	0	0	P
	0	0	0	0	$-M$	

Tableau 0 is not adjusted. After adjustment, follows:

Tableau 1

	x	y	z	s	A		
s	2	1	3	1	0	120	(120)
A	1	③	2	0	1	120	←(40)
	4	3	7	0	0	P	
	M	$3M$	$2M$	0	0	$120M$	
		↑					

Tableau 2

	x	y	z	s	A		
s	$\frac{5}{3}$	0	$\left(\frac{7}{3}\right)$	1	$-\frac{1}{3}$	80	←$\left(\frac{240}{7}\right)$
y	$\frac{1}{3}$	1	$\frac{2}{3}$	0	$\frac{1}{3}$	40	(60)
	3	0	5	0	-1	$P - 120$	
	0	0	0	0	$-M$	0	
			↑				

Tableau 2 does not give the optimal solution of the auxiliary problem but it signifies the end of "Phase I" of this problem. After pivoting as indicated above, one obtains

Tableau 3

	x	y	z	s	A	
z	$\frac{5}{7}$	0	1	$\frac{3}{7}$	...	$\frac{240}{7}$
y	$-\frac{1}{7}$	1	0	$-\frac{2}{7}$	...	$\frac{120}{7}$
	$-\frac{4}{7}$	0	0	$-\frac{15}{7}$	...	$P - \frac{2040}{7}$

Tableau 3 exhibits the solution to the original problem.

• PROBLEM 3-45

Maximize: $z = 2x_1 + 3x_2$

subject to: $x_1 + x_2 \leq 10$ (1)

$x_1 + x_2 \geq 20$ (2)

$x_1, x_2 \geq 0.$

Solve by the simplex method.

	Basis	z	x_1	x_2	E_2	S_1	A_2	b_i	Row No.	r_i
Tableau I	I	1	−2−M	−3−M	M	0	0	−20M	(0)	—
	S_1	0	1	①	0	[1]	0	10	(1)	10*
	A_2	0	1	1	−1	0	[1]	20	(2)	20
Tableau II	II	1	1	0	M	3+M	0	30−10M	(0)	—
	x_2	0	1	[1]	0	1	0	10	(1)	
	A_2	0	0	0	−1	−1	[1]	10	(2)	

Solution:

Note that the lack of negative coefficients in Row (0) of Tableau II implies that the optimal solution has been reached. A positive value for the artificial variable ($A_2 = 10$), however indicates that constraint (2) has not been satisfied; hence, the solution is not feasible.

When an artificial variables appears in the final solution (basis) at a positive level, the problem has no feasible solution.

• **PROBLEM 3-46**

Maximize $P = 19x_1 + 6x_2$

where $x_1 \geq 0$, $x_2 \geq 0$

and $3x_1 + x_2 \leq 48$

$3x_1 + 4x_2 \geq 120$

by the Big-M method.

Solution: In the tableaux below s_1 and s_2 represent slack variables, A_2 represents an artificial variable, and $-P$ and $-P_M$ are both placed on the top. The column heading $-P$ corresponds to ordinary profits, the column heading $-P_M$ corresponds to M profits, and the use of these two columns allows one to associate a multiplier with each of the four rows of the tableaux.

Tableau 0

	x_1	x_2	s_1	s_2	A_2	$-P$	$-P_M$	
s_1	3	1	1	0	0	0	0	48
A_2	3	4	0	-1	①	0	0	120
$-P$	19	6	0	0	0	1	0	0
$-P_M$	0	0	0	0	$-M$	0	1	0

Tableau 0 must first be adjusted:

Tableau 1

	x_1	x_2	s_1	s_2	A_2	$-P$	$-P_M$		
s_1	3	1	1	0	0	0	0	48	(48)
A_2	3	④	0	-1	1	0	0	120	←(30)
$-P$	19	6	0	0	0	1	0	0	
$-P_M$	$3M$	$4M$	0	$-M$	0	0	1	$120M$	
		↑							

Tableau 1 is the initial tableau. The arrows indicate the pivot row and pivot column. The distinct unit columns bear the headings s_1, A_2, $-P$, and $-P_M$, in that order. Note that the initial value of $-P_M$ is not 0 but rather 120M. If the present problem is not contradictory, no trace of M can appear in the optimum value of $-P_M$, in which case the inner product of the terminal simplex multiplier for row 4 and the initial stub must be $-120M$.

Tableau 2

	x_1	x_2	s_1	s_2	A_2	$-P$	$-P_M$		
s_1	($\frac{9}{4}$)	0	1	$\frac{1}{4}$	$-\frac{1}{4}$	0	0	18	←(8)
x_2	$\frac{3}{4}$	1	0	$-\frac{1}{4}$	$\frac{1}{4}$	0	0	30	(40)
$-P$	$\frac{29}{2}$	0	0	$\frac{3}{2}$	$-\frac{3}{2}$	1	0	-180	
$-P_M$	0	0	0	0	$-M$	0	1	0	
	↑								

Phase I has been completed, but for illustrative purposes the A_2 column is carried in all subsequent tableaux.

Tableau 3

	x_1	x_2	s_1	s_2	A_2	$-P$	$-P_M$	
x_1	1	0	$\frac{4}{9}$	$\frac{1}{9}$	$-\frac{1}{9}$	0	0	8
x_2	0	1	$-\frac{1}{3}$	$-\frac{1}{3}$	$\frac{1}{3}$	0	0	24
$-P$	0	0	$-\frac{58}{9}$	$-\frac{1}{9}$	$\frac{1}{9}$	1	0	-296
$-P_M$	0	0	0	0	$-M$	0	1	0

Tableau 3 is terminal. As contended earlier, the inner product of the stub of Tableau 1 with the vector of simplex multipliers for the fourth row of Tableau 3 is equal to $-120M$.

• PROBLEM 3-47

Minimize $x_1 - 2x_2$

Subject to $x_1 + x_2 \geq 2$

$$-x_1 + x_2 \geq 1$$

$$x_2 \leq 3$$

$$x_1,\ x_2 \geq 0$$

Solve by the two-phase method.

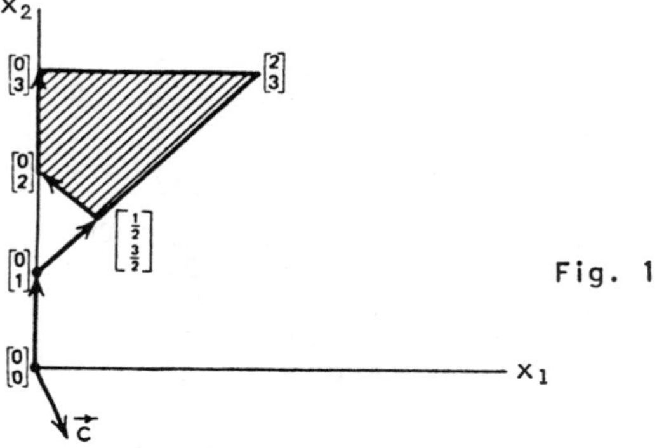

Fig. 1

Solution: The feasible region and the path taken by phase I and phase II to reach the optimal point are shown in Figure 1. After introducing slack variables x_3 x_4, x_5, the following problem is obtained.

Minimize $x_1 - 2x_2$

Subject to: $x_1 + x_2 - x_3 = 2$

$$-x_1 + x_2 - x_4 = 1$$

$$x_2 + x_5 = 3$$

$$x_1,\ x_2,\ x_3,\ x_4,\ x_5 \geq 0.$$

An initial identity is not available. So introduce the

artificial variables x_6 and x_7 (note that the last constraint does not need an artificial variable). Phase I starts by minimizing $x_0 = x_6 + x_7$.

Phase I

x_0	x_1	x_2	x_3	x_4	x_5	x_6 (ARTIFICIALS)	x_7	RHS
1	0	0	0	0	0	−1	−1	0
0	1	1	−1	0	0	1	0	2
0	−1	1	0	−1	0	0	1	1
0	0	1	0	0	1	0	0	3

Add rows 1 and 2 to row 0 so that $z_6 - c_6 = z_7 - c_7 = 0$ will be displayed.

	x_0	x_1	x_2	x_3	x_4	x_5	x_6	x_7	RHS
x_0	1	0	2	−1	−1	0	0	0	3
x_6	0	1	1	−1	0	0	1	0	2
x_7	0	−1	(1)	0	−1	0	0	1	1
x_5	0	0	1	0	0	1	0	0	3

	x_0	x_1	x_2	x_3	x_4	x_5	x_6	x_7	RHS
x_0	1	2	0	−1	1	0	0	−2	1
x_6	0	(2)	0	−1	1	0	1	−1	1
x_2	0	−1	1	0	−1	0	0	1	1
x_5	0	1	0	0	1	1	0	−1	2

	x_0	x_1	x_2	x_3	x_4	x_5	x_6	x_7	RHS
x_0	1	0	0	0	0	0	−1	−1	0
x_1	0	1	0	$-\frac{1}{2}$	$\frac{1}{2}$	0	$\frac{1}{2}$	$-\frac{1}{2}$	$\frac{1}{2}$
x_2	0	0	1	$-\frac{1}{2}$	$-\frac{1}{2}$	0	$\frac{1}{2}$	$\frac{1}{2}$	$\frac{3}{2}$
x_5	0	0	0	$\frac{1}{2}$	$\frac{1}{2}$	1	$-\frac{1}{2}$	$-\frac{1}{2}$	$\frac{3}{2}$

This is the end of phase I. The starting basic feasible solution is $(x_1, x_2) = (1/2, 3/2)$. Now start phase II, where the original objective is minimized starting from the extreme point (1/2, 3/2) (see Figure 1). The artificial variables are disregarded from any further consideration.

Phase II

z	x_1	x_2	x_3	x_4	x_5	RHS
1	−1	2	0	0	0	0
0	1	0	$-\frac{1}{2}$	$\frac{1}{2}$	0	$\frac{1}{2}$
0	0	1	$-\frac{1}{2}$	$-\frac{1}{2}$	0	$\frac{3}{2}$
0	0	0	$\frac{1}{2}$	$\frac{1}{2}$	1	$\frac{3}{2}$

Multiply rows 1 and 2 by 1 and -2 respectively and add to row 0 producing $z_1 - c_1 = z_2 - c_2 = 0$.

	z	x_1	x_2	x_3	x_4	x_5	RHS
z	1	0	0	$\frac{1}{2}$	$\frac{3}{2}$	0	$-\frac{5}{2}$
x_1	0	1	0	$-\frac{1}{2}$	($\frac{1}{2}$)	0	$\frac{1}{2}$
x_2	0	0	1	$-\frac{1}{2}$	$-\frac{1}{2}$	0	$\frac{3}{2}$
x_5	0	0	0	$\frac{1}{2}$	$\frac{1}{2}$	1	$\frac{3}{2}$

	z	x_1	x_2	x_3	x_4	x_5	RHS
z	1	−3	0	2	0	0	−4
x_4	0	2	0	−1	1	0	1
x_2	0	1	1	−1	0	0	2
x_5	0	−1	0	(1)	0	1	1

	z	x_1	x_2	x_3	x_4	x_5	RHS
z	1	−1	0	0	0	−2	−6
x_4	0	1	0	0	1	1	2
x_2	0	0	1	0	0	1	3
x_3	0	−1	0	1	0	1	1

Since $z_j - c_j \le 0$ for all nonbasic variables, the optimal point (0, 3) with objective -6 is reached. Note that phase I moved from the infeasible point (0, 0), to the infeasible point (0, 1), and finally to the feasible point (1/2, 3/2). From this extreme point, phase II moved to the feasible point (0, 2), and finally to the optimal point (0, 3). This is illustrated in Figure 1. The purpose of phase I is to get to an extreme point of the feasible region, while phase II goes from this feasible point to the optimal point.

TWO PHASE METHOD

• **PROBLEM** 3-48

Solve by using the two-phase technique.

Maximize

$$Z = x_1 + 2x_2 + 3x_3,$$

subject to:

$$\begin{aligned} x_1 + 2x_2 + 3x_3 &= 15, \\ 2x_1 + x_2 + 5x_3 &= 20, \\ x_1 + 2x_2 + x_3 + x_4 &= 10, \\ x_1, x_2, x_3, x_4 &\ge 0. \end{aligned} \tag{1}$$

Solution: To find the initial basis, introduce artificial variables y_1, y_2:

$$\begin{aligned} x_1 + 2x_2 + 3x_3 \quad + y_1 &= 15, \\ 2x_1 + x_2 + 5x_3 \quad + y_2 &= 20, \\ x_1 + 2x_2 + x_3 + x_4 &= 10. \end{aligned} \tag{2}$$

Phase I

First assign a price - 1 to all artificial variables

and a price zero to all other variables. In phase I maximize $Z = -y_1 - y_2$ subject to (1) (Tableau 1). If (1) has a feasible solution, then the maximum value of Z, will be zero, which is possible only if y_1 and y_2 each are zero. Then phase I provides a basic feasible solution for the given problem.

Tableau 1
Phase I

Basis	c_i	0 x_1	0 x_2	0 x_3	0 x_4	−1 y_1	−1 y_2	b
y_1	−1	1	2	3	0	1	0	15
y_2	−1	2	1	5	0	0	1	20
x_4	0	1	2	1	1	0	0	10
z_j^*		3	3	8	—	—	—	35

As x_3 is the highest, x_3 enters into the basis. Now compute $\min \frac{b_i}{a_{ir}}, (a_{ir} > 0) = \frac{b_2}{a_{23}}$. Therefore y_2 leaves the basis. Tableau 2 is obtained.

Tableau 2
Phase I

Basis	c_i	0 x_1	0 x_2	0 x_3	0 x_4	−1 y_1	−1 y_2	b
y_1	−1	−1/5	7/5	0	0	1	−3/5	3
x_3	0	2/5	1/5	1	0	0	1/5	4
x_4	0	3/5	9/5	0	1	0	−1/5	6
z_j^*		−1/5	7/5	—	—	—	(3/5+1)	3

Repeating the procedure, arrive at Tableau 3.

Tableau 3
Phase I

Basis	c_i	0 x_1	0 x_2	0 x_3	0 x_4	−1 y_1	−1 y_2	b
x_2	0	−1/7	1	0	0	5/7	−3.7	15/7
x_3	0	3/7	0	1	0	−1/7	2/7	25/7
x_4	0	6/7	0	0	1	−9/7	4/7	15/7
z_j^*		0	—	—	—	−1	−1	0

Since max $z^* = 0$, no artificial variables appear in the basis. Consequently the original problem has a basic feasible solution. Now go into phase II to find an optimal solution. Assign actual prices c_j to all variables and the function to be optimized is the actual objective function Z. Pass on to Tableau 4.

Tableau 4
Phase II

Basis	c_i	1 x_1	2 x_2	3 x_3	−1 x_4	b
x_2	2	−1/7	1	0	0	15/7
x_3	3	3/7	0	1	0	25/7
x_4	−1	6/7	0	0	1	15/7
z_j		6/7	—	—	—	90/7

Again repeating the procedure yields Tableau 5.

Since all $z_i = 0$, an optimal solution to the given problem is $x_1 = 5/2 = x_2 = x_3$ and $x_4 = 0$ and max Z = 15.

Tableau 5
Phase II

Basis	c_i	1 a_1	2 a_2	3 a_3	−1 a_4	b
a_2	2	0	1	0	1/6	5/2
a_3	3	0	0	1	−3/6	5/2
a_1	1	1	0	0	7/9	5/2
z_j		—	—	—	0	15

• PROBLEM 3-49

Solve the problem below by the two-phase method.

$$\text{Maximize } z = x_1 + x_2$$

$$\text{subject to: } 3x_1 + 2x_2 \leq 20$$

$$2x_1 + 3x_2 \leq 20$$

$$x_1 + 2x_2 \geq 2$$

$$x_1, x_2 \geq 0.$$

Solution: Add the slack and artificial variables as follows:

Phase 1: Maximize $z_1 = \qquad - x_a$

Phase 2: Maximize $z_2 = x_1 + x_2$

subject to: $3x_1 + 2x_2 + x_3 = 20$

$2x_1 + 3x_2 + x_4 = 20$

$x_1 + 2x_2 - x_5 + x_a = 2$

Putting the problem into tableau form yields Tableau 0.

Tableau 0

		x_1	x_2	x_3	x_4	x_5	x_a
z(phase 1)	0	0	0	0	0	0	1
z(phase 2)	0	-1	-1	0	0	0	0
x_3	20	3	2	1	0	0	0
x_4	20	2	3	0	1	0	0
x_a	2	1	2	0	0	-1	[1]

The basic representation must be made complete; hence, the partial iteration on the dashed pivotal element must be undertaken to yield Tableau 1.

Tableau 1

		x_1	↓ x_2	x_3	x_4	x_5	x_a	
z(phase 1)	-2	-1	-2	0	0	1	0	
z(phase 2)	0	-1	-1	0	0	0	0	
x_3	20	3	2	1	0	0	0	
x_4	20	2	3	0	1	0	0	
x_a	2	1	$\boxed{2}$	0	0	-1	1	→

Using the phase 1 objective function, x_2 is selected to enter the basis replacing x_a and yielding Tableau 2.

Tableau 2

		x_1	x_2	x_3	x_4	↓ x_5	x_a	
z(phase 1)	0	0	0	0	0	0	1	
z(phase 2)	1	$-\frac{1}{2}$	0	0	0	$-\frac{1}{2}$	$\frac{1}{2}$	
x_3	18	2	0	1	0	1	-1	
x_4	17	$\frac{1}{2}$	0	0	1	$\boxed{\frac{3}{2}}$	$-\frac{3}{2}$	→
x_2	1	$\frac{1}{2}$	1	0	0	$-\frac{1}{2}$	$\frac{1}{2}$	

Variable x_a can now be dropped. Since the phase 1 objective function is zero, the phase 1 objective function can also be dropped.

Proceed to phase 2. Introducing x_5 (choosing x_5 arbitrarily instead of x_1) into the basis to replace x_4, and then introducing x_1 into the basis to replace x_3, leads to the following tableaus.

Tableau 3

		↓ x_1	x_2	x_3	x_4	x_5	
z(phase 2)	$\frac{20}{3}$	$-\frac{1}{3}$	0	0	$\frac{1}{3}$	0	
x_3	$\frac{20}{3}$	$\boxed{\frac{5}{3}}$	0	1	$-\frac{2}{3}$	0	→
x_5	$\frac{34}{3}$	$\frac{1}{3}$	0	0	$\frac{2}{3}$	1	
x_2	$\frac{20}{3}$	$\frac{2}{3}$	1	0	$\frac{1}{3}$	0	

Tableau 4

		x_1	x_2	x_3	x_4	x_5
z(phase 2)	8	0	0	$\frac{1}{5}$	$\frac{1}{5}$	0
x_1	4	1	0	$\frac{3}{5}$	$-\frac{2}{5}$	0
x_5	10	0	0	$-\frac{1}{5}$	$\frac{4}{5}$	1
x_2	4	0	1	$-\frac{2}{5}$	$\frac{3}{5}$	0

Tableau 4 is optimal.

• PROBLEM 3-50

Consider the problem shown here. It has a redundant constraint because the third constraint is simply the sum of the first two. Solve by the two-phase simplex method without eliminating any constraint.

Minimize $\quad f = -x_1 + 2x_2 - 3x_3$

Subject to:

$$x_1 + x_2 + x_3 = 6$$

$$-x_1 + x_2 + 2x_3 = 4$$

$$2x_2 + 3x_3 = 10$$

$$x_3 \le 2$$

$$x_1, x_2, x_3 \ge 0.$$

Tableau 1

		(Minimize)	(−1	2	−3	0)					
		Minimize	0	0	0	0	1	1	1		
i	c_B	x_B	x_1	x_2	x_3	x_4	x_5	x_6	x_7	b_i	θ_i
1	1	x_5	1	1	1	0	1	0	0	6	6
2	1	x_6	−1	1	2	0	0	1	0	4	2
3	1	x_7	0	2	3	0	0	0	1	10	$\frac{10}{3}$
4	0	x_4	0	0	(1)	1	0	0	0	2	2 → Out
		z'_j	0	4	6	0	1	1	1	20	
		$c'_j - z'_j$	0	−4	−6 ↑ In	0	0	0	0		

Tableau 2

		(Minimize)	(−1	2	−3	0)					
		Minimize	0	0	0	0	1	1	1		
i	c_B	x_B	x_1	x_2	x_3	x_4	x_5	x_6	x_7	b_i	θ_i
1	1	x_5	1	1	0	−1	1	0	0	4	4
2	1	x_6	−1	(1)	0	−2	0	1	0	0	0 → Out
3	1	x_7	0	2	0	−3	0	0	1	4	2
4	0	x_3	0	0	1	1	0	0	0	2	–
		z'_j	0	4	0	−6	1	1	1	8	
		$c'_j - z'_j$	0	−4 ↑ In	0	6	0	0	0		

Tableau 3

		(Minimize)	(−1	2	−3	0)					
		Minimize	0	0	0	0	1	1	1		
i	c_B	x_B	x_1	x_2	x_3	x_4	x_5	x_6	x_7	b_i	θ_i
1	1	x_5	(2)	0	0	1	1	−1	0	4	2 → Out
2	0	x_2	−1	1	0	−2	0	1	0	0	–
3	1	x_7	2	0	0	1	0	−2	1	4	2
4	0	x_3	0	0	1	1	0	0	0	2	–
		z'_j	4	0	0	2	1	−3	1	8	
		$c'_j - z'_j$	−4 ↑ In	0	0	−2	0	4	0		

Solution: Adding a slack variable, x_4, and three artificial variables, x_5, x_6, and x_7, leads to the initial Tableau 1 shown. The remaining tableaux for phase I are from 2 to 4. In Tableau 4, note that an artificial variable (x_7) appears in the basis with the value zero. Moreover, no legitimate variable (x_1, x_2, x_3, or x_4) appears on the third row. Thus, this row is redundant and can be eliminated. The initial tableau for phase II is shown in Tableau 5. The third row and all the artificial variables have been eliminated. The solution is optimal, so that $x_1^* = 2$, $x_2^* = 2$, $x_3^* = 2$, and $f^* = -4$.

Tableau 4

	(Minimize)		(−1	2	−3	0)				
	Minimize		0	0	0	0	1	1	1	
i	c_B	x_B	x_1	x_2	x_3	x_4	x_5	x_6	x_7	b_i
1	0	x_1	1	0	0	$\frac{1}{2}$	$\frac{1}{2}$	$-\frac{1}{2}$	0	2
2	0	x_2	0	1	0	$-\frac{3}{2}$	$\frac{1}{2}$	$\frac{1}{2}$	0	2
3	1	x_7	0	0	0	0	−1	−1	1	0
4	0	x_3	0	0	1	1	0	0	0	2
		z_j'	0	0	0	0	−1	−1	1	0
		$c_j' - z_j'$	0	0	0	0	2	2	0	

Tableau 5

	Minimize		−1	2	−3	0	
i	c_B	x_B	x_1	x_2	x_3	x_4	b_i
1	−1	x_1	1	0	0	$\frac{1}{2}$	2
2	2	x_2	0	1	0	$-\frac{3}{2}$	2
3	−3	x_3	0	0	1	1	2
		z_j	−1	2	−3	$-\frac{13}{2}$	−4
		$c_j - z_j$	0	0	0	$\frac{13}{2}$	

• PROBLEM 3-51

Consider the model in standard form

$$x_1 + 4x_2 - 3x_3 - x_4 - 2 = 0$$
$$-x_1 - x_2 + 4x_3 + 2x_4 - 3 = 0$$
$$+ x_3 - x_5 - 4 = 0$$
$$x_1 + 3x_4 + x_9 - 20 = 0$$
$$-9x_1 - 11x_2 + 28x_3 + 14x_4 + 1 = z \text{ min.} \quad (1)$$

Solve by the two-phase simplex method.

Solution: Note that, in the construction of the initial simplex tableau a primal basic variable must have a coefficient of + 1 in one equation and 0 in all the other equations. Thus in (1), x_9 is basic (and so is $-z$, as usual) but no other variable is considered basic; x_5 is not, because its coefficient is negative. In order to form the usual tableau, every equation must contain a basic variable. Consequently artificial variables x_6, x_7^0, x_8^0 are added to the left members of the first three equations of (1). Then the tableau (2) can be formed.

1	x_1	x_2	x_3	x_4	x_5	1
x_6^0	1	4*	-3	-1	0	-2
x_7^0	-1	-1	4	2	0	-3
x_8^0	0	0	1	0	-1	-4
x_9	1	0	0	3	0	-20
$-z$	-9	-11	28	14	0	1
$-z^0$	0	-3	-2	-1	1	9

(2)

All variables (with the possible exception of z) are required to be nonnegative in the optimal solution, and x_6^0, x_7^0, x_8^0 must be zero.

The "infeasibility form" is defined by

$$z^0 = x_6^0 + x_7^0 + x_8^0 \tag{3}$$

which implies that the last row of (2) is obtained as the negative of the sum of the three rows of (2) that have artificial variables as labels; negative, because the labels are $+ x_i^0$ but $- z^0$. Thus the constant term in the row $- z^0$ is always nonnegative. The other coefficients in row $- z^0$ are denoted by g_j for $j = 1, 2, \ldots, n, 0$: $g_j = -\Sigma_i\{a_{ij};\ x_i^0 \text{ is artificial}\}$ where $a_{i0} \triangleq b_i$.

In Phase 1, z^0 is used as the objective function while z may or may not have a role. Of course, neither the coefficients of z^0 nor of z are eligible to be pivots in either phase. The most negative coefficient of z^0 is $- 3$ in column 2; this column also gives the minimum of the ratios:

$$c_j/(-g_j) = - 11/3,\ 28/2,\ 14/1.$$

The only positive pivot available in this column is $a_{62} = 4$. Exchanging x_6^0 and x_2 gives

4	x_1	x_6^0	x_3	x_4	x_5	1
x_2	1	1	-3	-1	0	-2
x_7^0	-3	1	13*	7	0	-14
x_8^0	0	0	4	0	-4	-16
x_9	4	0	0	12	0	-80
$-z$	-25	11	79	45	0	-18
$-z^0$	3	3	-17	-7	4	30

(4)

Now - 17 is the most negative coefficient of z^0 and it also yields the minimum of $c_j/(-g_j) = 79/17, 45/7$. Then the minimum of $-b_i/a_{i3} = 14/13, 16/4$ gives $a_{23} = 13$ (over 4) as the next pivot.

13	x_1	x_6^0	x_7^0	x_4	x_5	1
x_2	1	4	3	2	0	-17
x_3	-3	1	4	7	0	-14
x_8^0	3*	-1	-4	-7	-13	-38
x_9	13	0	0	39	0	-260
$-z$	-22	16	-79	8	0	218
$-z^0$	-3	14	17	7	13	38

(5)

In column 1 there are three possible pivots, of which the 3 in row 8 gives the minimum ratio:

3	x_8^0	x_6^0	x_7^0	x_4	x_5	1
x_2	-1	1	1	1	1*	-1
x_3	3	0	0	0	-3	-12
x_1	13	-1	-4	-7	-13	-38
x_9	-13	1	4	16	13	-22
$-z$	22	2	-25	-10	-22	-14
$-z^0$	3	3	3	0	0	0

(6)

This completes Phase 1. The tableau is now truly feasible because the artificial variables are zero in the basic solution. However, the termination criterion for Phase 1 is that one row $-z^0$ no longer contains any negative coefficients: in fact it merely reproduces the definition (3) in the present case.

In Phase 2, now turn to the objective function z. It has three negative coefficients corresponding to the variables x_7^0, x_4, x_5. However, since the only feasible value of x_7^0 is zero, its negative coefficient does not afford any opportunity to reduce z and it is therefore ignored. In general one has the following rule.

Artificial-Column Exclusion Rule. In Phase 1 or 2 one never chooses a pivot in a column j whose label is artificial, or whose entry g_j in row $-z^0$ was positive (not zero) at the end of Phase 1. Indeed, there is the possibility of dropping these columns out of the tableau.

This rule is desirable in Phase 1, but in Phase 2 it is a necessary and sufficient condition that z^0 (which is assumed to be zero before any Phase 2 is attempted) is not inadvertently increased during Phase 2; it cannot decrease because the artificial variables (like the others) are kept nonnegative in Phase 2. This ban may apply to some nonartificial variables, in the event that some artificial variables are still basic, although necessarily of value zero. Such nonartificial variables must be distinguished in some way, such as by giving them a superscript value other than zero since they are like the artificial variable in having the feasible other than zero. As soon as such provision is made for obeying the above rule, the row $-z^0$ is dropped at the end of Phase 1.

In (6) only the negative coefficients -10/3 and -22/3 in z can be considered; the latter, in column 5, isthe more negative.Of the twopositive pivots in this column, 1 is chosen because 1/1<22/13. This pivot step yields the final tableau

1	x_8^0	x_6^0	x_7^0	x_4	x_2	1
x_5	-1	1	1	1	3	-1
x_3	0	1	1	1	3	-5
x_1	0	4	3	2	13	-17
x_9	0	-4	-3	1	-13	-3
$-z$	0	8	-1	4	22	-12

(7)

Thus, the optimal feasible solution for (1), with all the x_h included is $\vec{x}^* = (17, 0, 5, 0, 1, 0, 0, 0, 3)$, $\vec{z}^* = -12$.

• PROBLEM 3-52

Solve by the two-phase simplex method, starting with the Phase I problem:

Minimize: $W = x_6 + x_7$

Subject to:

$$\begin{aligned} x_1 - 2x_2 + x_3 + x_4 &= 11 \\ -4x_1 + x_2 + 2x_3 - x_5 + x_6 &= 3 \\ -2x_1 + x_3 + x_7 &= 1 \\ x_1 \geq 0, \ldots, x_7 &\geq 0. \end{aligned}$$

The original objective function is Min $Z = -3x_1 + x_2 + x_3$.

Solution: The initial basic feasible solution for the Phase 1 problem is given below:

Tableau 1

(PHASE I)

C_B	Basis \ C_j	0	0	0	0	0	1	1	Constants
		x_1	x_2	x_3	x_4	x_5	x_6	x_7	
0	x_4	1	−2	1	1	0	0	0	11
1	x_6	−4	1	2	0	−1	1	0	3
1	x_7	−2	0	(1)	0	0	0	1	1
$\bar{C}$ Row		6	−1	−3	0	1	0	0	W = 4

The objective function can be reduced further by replacing x_7 by x_3 as follows:

Tableau 2

(PHASE I)

C_B	Basis \ C_j	0	0	0	0	0	1	1	Constants
		x_1	x_2	x_3	x_4	x_5	x_6	x_7	
0	x_4	3	−2	0	1	0	0	−1	10
1	x_6	0	(1)	0	0	−1	1	−2	1
0	x_3	−2	0	1	0	0	0	1	1
$\bar{C}$ Row		0	−1	0	0	1	0	3	W = 1

Tableau 2 is not optimal. The variable x_2 enters the basis to replace the artificial variable x_6.

Tableau 3

(PHASE I)

C_B	Basis \ C_j	0	0	0	0	0	1	1	Constants
		x_1	x_2	x_3	x_4	x_5	x_6	x_7	
0	x_4	3	0	0	1	−2	2	−5	12
0	x_2	0	1	0	0	−1	1	−2	1
0	x_3	−2	0	1	0	0	0	1	1
$\bar{C}$ Row		0	0	0	0	0	1	1	W = 0

There is now an optimal solution to the Phase I linear program given by $x_1=0$, $x_2=1$, $x_3=1$, $x_4=12$, $x_5=0$, $x_6=0$, $x_7=0$ and minimum $W = 0$. Since the artificial variables x_6 and $x_7 = 0$, this tableau represents a basic feasible solution to the original problem. Now begin Phase II of the simplex method to find the optimal solution to the original problem. The initial tableau for Phase II is constructed by deleting the columns corresponding to the artificial variables, and computing the new $\bar{C}$-row coefficients with respect to the original objective function, $Z = -3x_1 + x_2 + x_3$, as shown in Tableau 4.

Tableau 4

(PHASE II)

C_B	Basis \ C_j	-3 x_1	1 x_2	1 x_3	0 x_4	0 x_5	Constants
0	x_4	③	0	0	1	-2	12
1	x_2	0	1	0	0	-1	1
1	x_3	-2	0	1	0	0	1
$\bar{C}$ Row		-1	0	0	0	1	$Z=2$

In Tableau 4,

$$\bar{c}_1 = -3 - (0, 1, 1)(3, 0, -2)^T = -3$$

$$\bar{c}_5 = 0 - (0, 1, 1)(-2, -1, 0)^T = 1$$

and

$$\bar{c}_2 = \bar{c}_3 = \bar{c}_4 = 0$$

Since the objective is to minimize Z, Tableau 4 is not optimal. The nonbasic variable x_1 replaces the basic variable x_4 to reduce the value of Z further:

Tableau 5

(PHASE II)

C_B	Basis \ C_j	-3 x_1	1 x_2	1 x_3	0 x_4	0 x_5	Constants
-3	x_1	1	0	0	1/3	-2/3	4
1	x_2	0	1	0	0	-1	1
1	x_3	0	0	1	2/3	-4/3	9
$\bar{C}$ Row		0	0	0	1/3	1/3	$Z=-2$

An optimal solution has been reached, and it is given by $x_1 = 4$, $x_2 = 1$, $x_3 = 9$, $x_4 = 0$, $x_5 = 0$, and mimimum $Z = -2$.

• PROBLEM 3-53

Maximize:

$$Z = 3x_1 - x_2,$$

Subject to:

$2x_1 + x_2 \geq 2$, $x_1 + 3x_2 \leq 3$, $x_2 \leq 4$, and $x_j \geq 0$, $j = 1, 2, \ldots$

Solution: Introducing slack and surplus variables, the constraints become:

$$2x_1 + x_2 - x_3 = 2,$$

$$x_1 + 3x_2 \qquad + x_4 = 3,$$

$$x_2 \qquad + x_5 \qquad = 4. \tag{1}$$

To obtain the initial basis, introduce artificial variable A_1, and associate a large negative value - M to it in the objective function. Now the above problem becomes:

$$\text{Maximize} \quad 3x_1 - x_2 - MA_1 \tag{2}$$

subject to:

$$2x_1 + x_2 - x_3 \qquad + A_1 = 2$$

$$x_1 + 3x_2 \qquad + x_4 = 3$$

$$x_2 \qquad + x_5 = 4$$

$$x_1, x_2, x_3, x_4, x_5, A_1 \geq 0.$$

Now, if the system of equations (1) has a solution, then there is a basic feasible solution for (2) which has no artificial variable in the bases at positive level.

The sequence of tableaux which solve this problem is the following:

Tableau 1

Basis	c_j	3	−1	0	0	0	−M	
		x_1	x_2	x_3	x_4	x_5	A_1	b
A_1	−M	2	1	−1	0	0	1	2
x_4	0	1	3	0	1	0	0	3
x_5	0	0	1	0	0	1	0	4
z_j		3+2M ↑ highest	−1+M	M	—	—	—	−2M

Here not all z_j are non-negative, so enter x_j into the basis corresponding to most positive z_j, viz. here $z_1 = 3 + 2M$. Therefore, variable x_1 enters the basis. Computing the ratios $\frac{b_i}{a_{i12}}$, notice that variable A_1 is departed from the basis. Thus, Tableau 2,

Tableau 2

Basis	c_j	3	−1	0	0	0	−M	
		x_1	x_2	x_3	x_4	x_5	A_1	b
x_1	3	1	1/2	−1/2	0	0	1/2	1
x_4	0	5/2	5/2	1/2	1	0	−1/2	2
x_5	0	0	1	0	0	1	0	4
z_j	—	—	−5/2	3/2	—	—	−(3/2+M)	3

Repeating the procedure, Tableau 3 is obtained.

Tableau 3

Basis	c_j	3	−1	0	0	0	−M	
		x_1	x_2	x_3	x_4	x_5	A_1	b
x_1	3	1	3	0	1	0	0	3
x_3	0	0	5	1	2	0	−1	4
x_5	0	0	1	0	0	1	0	4
z_j	—	–	−10	–	−3	–	−M	9

Since all $z_j \leq 0$, therefore the optimal solution is obtained with:

$$x_1 = 3, \; x_3 = 4, \; x_5 = 4$$

$$x_2 = x_4 = 0$$

$$\text{Max } Z = 9$$

• PROBLEM 3-54

Consider:

Minimize $-3x_1 + 4x_2$

Subject to: $x_1 + x_2 \leq 4$

$2x_1 + 3x_2 \geq 18$

$x_1, x_2 \geq 0.$

Solve by the two-phase method.

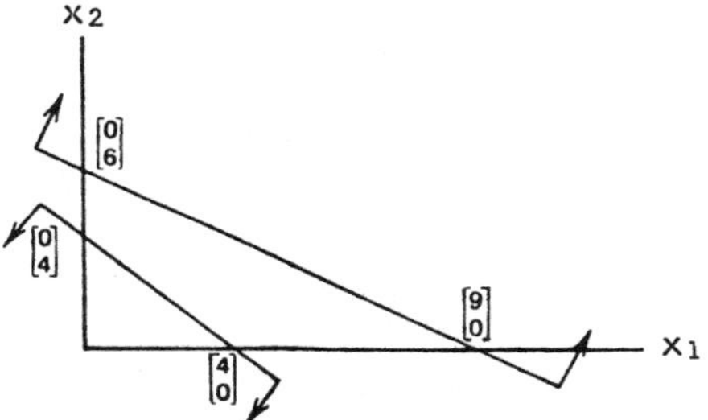

Fig. 1

Empty feasible region.

Solution: The constraints admit no feasible points, as shown in Figure 1. This will be detected by phase 1. Introducing the slack variables x_3 and x_4, thus the following constraints in standard form:

$$x_1 + x_2 + x_3 = 4$$

$$2x_1 + 3x_2 - x_4 = 18$$

$$x_1, x_2, x_3, x_4 \geq 0$$

Since no convenient basis exists, introduce the artificial

variable x_5 into the second constraint. Phase I is used to get rid of the artificial.

Phase I

x_0	x_1	x_2	x_3	x_4	x_5	RHS
1	0	0	0	0	– 1	0
0	1	1	1	0	0	4
0	2	3	0	– 1	1	18

Add row 2 to row 0 so that $z_5 - c_5 = 0$ is displayed.

	x_0	x_1	x_2	x_3	x_4	x_5	RHS
x_0	1	2	3	0	– 1	0	18
x_3	0	1	(1)	1	0	0	4
x_5	0	2	3	0	– 1	1	18

	x_0	x_1	x_2	x_3	x_4	x_5	RHS
x_0	1	– 1	0	– 3	– 1	0	6
x_2	0	1	1	1	0	0	4
x_5	0	– 1	0	– 3	– 1	1	6

The optimality criterion of the simplex method, namely $z_j - c_j \le 0$, holds for all variables; but the artificial $x_5 > 0$. Therefore the original problem has no feasible solutions.

• PROBLEM 3-55

Consider:

Minimize $- x_1 + 2x_2 - 3x_3$

Subject to:

$$x_1 + x_2 + x_3 = 6$$

$$-x_1 + x_2 + 2x_3 = 4$$

$$2x_2 + 3x_3 = 10$$

$$x_3 \le 2$$

$$x_1, x_2, x_3 \ge 0.$$

Solve by the two-phase method.

Solution: A slack variable x_4 needs to be introduced. The constraint matrix $\vec{A}$ is given below:

$$\vec{A} = \begin{bmatrix} 1 & 1 & 1 & 0 \\ -1 & 1 & 2 & 0 \\ 0 & 2 & 3 & 0 \\ 0 & 0 & 1 & 1 \end{bmatrix}$$

Note that the matrix is of full rank. The sum of the first two rows of $\vec{A}$ is equal to the third row; that is, any one of the first three constraints is redundant and can be eliminated. Assume this fact is not known, however, and introduce the artificial variables x_5, x_6, and x_7. The phase I objective is: Minimize $x_0 = x_5 + x_6 + x_7$. Phase I proceeds as follows.

Phase I

x_0	x_1	x_2	x_3	x_4	x_5	x_6	x_7	RHS
1	0	0	0	0	−1	−1	−1	0
1	1	1	1	0	1	0	0	6
0	−1	1	2	0	0	1	0	4
0	0	2	3	0	0	0	1	10
0	0	0	1	1	0	0	0	2

Add rows 1, 2, and 3 to row 0, to display $z_5 - c_5 = z_6 - c_6 = z_7 - c_7 - 0$.

	x_0	x_1	x_2	x_3	x_4	x_5	x_6	x_7	RHS
x_0	1	0	4	6	0	0	0	0	20
x_5	0	1	1	1	0	1	0	0	6
x_6	0	−1	1	2	0	0	1	0	4
x_7	0	0	2	3	0	0	0	1	10
x_4	0	0	0	(1)	1	0	0	0	2

	x_0	x_1	x_2	x_3	x_4	x_5	x_6	x_7	RHS
x_0	1	0	4	0	−6	0	0	0	8
x_5	0	1	1	0	−1	1	0	0	4
x_6	0	−1	(1)	0	−2	0	1	0	0
x_7	0	0	2	0	−3	0	0	1	4
x_4	0	0	0	1	1	0	0	0	2

	x_0	x_1	x_2	x_3	x_4	x_5	x_6	x_7	RHS
x_0	1	4	0	0	2	0	−4	0	8
x_5	0	(2)	0	0	1	1	−1	0	4
x_2	0	−1	1	0	−2	0	1	0	0
x_7	0	2	0	0	1	0	−2	1	4
x_3	0	0	0	1	1	0	0	0	2

	x_0	x_1	x_2	x_3	x_4	x_5	x_6	x_7	RHS
x_0	1	0	0	0	0	−2	−2	0	0
x_1	0	1	0	0	$\frac{1}{2}$	$\frac{1}{2}$	$-\frac{1}{2}$	0	2
x_2	0	0	1	0	$-\frac{3}{2}$	$\frac{1}{2}$	$\frac{1}{2}$	0	2
x_7	0	0	0	0	0	−1	−1	1	0
x_3	0	0	0	1	1	0	0	0	2

Since all the artificial variables are at level zero, proceed to phase II with a basic feasible solution of the original problem. Either proceed directly with the artificial x_7 into the basis at zero level, or attempt to eliminate x_7 from the basis. The only legitimate nonbasic variable is x_4, and it has zero coefficient in row 3 corresponding to x_7. This shows that the third row (constraint of the original problem) is redundant and can be eliminated. This will be done while moving to phase II.

PHASE II

Obviously $z_1 - c_1 = z_2 - c_2 = z_3 - c_3 = 0$. Thus x_5 and x_6 are nonbasic artificial variables and wll not be introduced in the phase II problem. In order to complete row 0 calculate $z_4 - c_4$:

$$z_4 - c_4 = \vec{c}_B \vec{B}^{-1} \vec{a}_4 - c_4$$

$$= (-1,\ 2,\ -3) \begin{bmatrix} \frac{1}{2} \\ -\frac{3}{2} \\ 1 \end{bmatrix} - 0$$

$$= -\frac{13}{2}$$

Since the objective is minimization and $z_4 - c_4 \leq 0$ for the only nonbasic variable, the stop; the solution obtained from phase I is optimal. The tableau below displays the optimal solution.

	z	x_1	x_2	x_3	x_4	RHS
z	1	0	0	0	$-\frac{13}{2}$	-4
x_1	0	1	0	0	$\frac{1}{2}$	2
x_2	0	0	1	0	$-\frac{3}{2}$	2
x_3	0	0	0	1	1	2

CHAPTER 4

LINEAR PROGRAMMING - ADVANCED METHODS

DUALITY

• PROBLEM 4-1

Consider the problem

$$\text{maximize} \quad x_0 = 5x_1 + 12x_2 + 4x_3$$

$$\text{subject to} \quad x_1 + 2x_2 + x_3 \leq 5$$

$$2x_1 - x_2 + 3x_3 = 2$$

$$x_1, x_2, x_3 \geq 0$$

Solve the primal and dual problems by the Simplex method. Compare the results.

Solution: The dual is given by

$$\text{minimize} \quad y_0 = 5y_1 + 2y_2$$

subject to

$$y_1 + 2y_2 \geq 5$$

$$2y_1 - y_2 \geq 12$$

$$y_1 + 3y_2 \geq 4$$

$$y_1 \geq 0$$

y_2 unrestricted in sign

Notice that the last constraint, $y_1 \geq 0$, corresponds to S_1 in the primal. This same result could have been obtained from the original problem where y_1 corresponds to ($\leq$) constraint and y_2 corresponds to (=) constraint.

Inspection yields the solutions ($x_1 = 1$, $x_2 = 1$, $x_3 = 1/3$, and $y_1 = 7$, $y_2 = 2$) are feasible for the primal and dual problems. These give $x_0 = 18\frac{1}{3}$ and $y_0 = 39$ which shows that $x_0 < y_0$. From the property that x_0

$\leq y_0$, this result reveals the immediate information that the optimal value of the objective function lies between $18\frac{1}{3}$ and 39.

The standard form of this problem is

$$\text{maximize} \quad x_0 = 5x_1 + 12x_2 + 4x_3 + 0S_1$$

$$\text{subject to} \quad x_1 + 2x_2 + x_3 + S_1 = 5$$

$$2x_1 - x_2 + 3x_3 + 0S_1 = 2$$

$$x_1, x_2, x_3, S_1 \geq 0$$

Although the canonical and standard forms always yield equivalent duals, the standard form is more useful since it is the basis of all linear programming calculations, namely, the simplex method. The starting tableau for the primal problem is obtained from the standard form. Expressing the x_0-equation in terms of the nonbasic variables gives (R_1 is an artificial variable; artificial variables are nonnegative variables added to the left-hand side of each of the equations corresponding to constraints of the types ($\geq$) and (=) and their addition causes violation of the corresponding constraints. This difficulty is overcome by ensuring that the artificial variables will be zero (=0) in the final solution, (provided the solution of the problem exists. If the problem does not have a solution, at least one of the artificial variables will appear in the final solution at a positive level.)

Basic	x_0	x_1	x_2	x_3	S_1	R_1	Solution
x_0	①	$-5-2M$	$-12+M$	$-4-3M$	0	0	$-2M$
S_1	0	1	2	1	①	0	5
R_1	0	2	-1	3	0	①	2

First Iteration: Introduce x_3 and drop R_1.

Basic	x_0	x_1	x_2	x_3	S_1	R_1	Solution
x_0	①	$-7/3$	$-40/3$	0	0	$4/3+M$	8/3
S_1	0	1/3	7/3	0	①	$-1/3$	13/3
x_3	0	2/3	$-1/3$	①	0	1/3	2/3

Second Iteration: Introduce x_2 and drop S_1.

Basic	x_0	x_1	x_2	x_3	S_1	R_1	Solution
x_0	①	$-3/7$	0	0	40/7	$-4/7+M$	192/7
x_2	0	1/7	①	0	3/7	$-1/7$	13/7
x_3	0	5/7	0	①	1/7	2/7	9/7

Third Iteration: Introduce x_1 and drop x_3.

Basic	x_0	x_1	x_2	x_3	S_1	R_1	Solution
x_0	(1)	0	0	3/5	29/5	$-2/5 + M$	$28\frac{1}{5}$
x_2	0	0	(1)	$-1/5$	2/5	$-1/5$	8/5
x_1	0	(1)	0	7/5	1/5	2/5	9/5

which is the optimal solution with $x_1 = 9/5$, $x_2 = 8/5$, $x_3 = 0$, and $x_0 = 28\frac{1}{5}$.

The dual problem will now be solved. Since y_2 is unrestricted in sign, it is replaced by $y_2^+ - y_2^-$ in the simplex tableau where $y_2^+ \geq 0$ and $y_2^- \geq 0$. Thus, adding the artificial variables R_1, R_2, and R_3 and expressing the y_0- equation in terms of the nonbasic variables, the starting tableau becomes

Basic	y_0	y_1	y_2^+	y_2^-	S_1	S_2	S_3	R_1	R_2	R_3	Solution
y_0	(1)	$-5 + 4M$	$-2 + 4M$	$2 - 4M$	$-M$	$-M$	$-M$	0	0	0	$21M$
R_1	0	1	2	-2	-1	0	0	(1)	0	0	5
R_2	0	2	-1	1	0	-1	0	0	(1)	0	12
R_3	0	1	3	-3	0	0	-1	0	0	(1)	4

Noting that this is a minimization problem, one obtains the optimal solution in five iterations. Its simplex tableau is given by

Basic	y_0	y_1	y_2^+	y_2^-	S_1	S_2	S_3	R_1	R_2	R_3	Solution
y_0	(1)	0	0	0	$-9/5$	$-8/5$	0	$9/5 - M$	$8/5 - M$	$-M$	$28\frac{1}{5}$
S_3	0	0	0	0	$-7/5$	1/5	(1)	7/5	$-1/5$	-1	3/5
y_2^-	0	0	-1	(1)	2/5	$-1/5$	0	$-2/5$	1/5	0	2/5
y_1	0	(1)	0	0	$-1/5$	$-2/5$	0	1/5	2/5	0	29/5

This yields $y_1 = 29/5$, $y_2^+ = 0$, $y_2^- = 2/5$ and $y_0 = 28\frac{1}{5}$. Thus, $y_2 = y_2^+ - y_2^- = 0 - 2/5 = -2/5$. (Notice that y_2 is unrestricted in sign.)

A comparison of the primal and dual solutions shows that

$$\max x_0 = 28\tfrac{1}{5} = \min y_0$$

Notice that the optimal values of the objective function $(= 28\frac{1}{5})$ lies between the previously estimated values, $18\frac{1}{3}$ and 39.

Investigation of the optimal tableaus of the primal and the dual reveals the following results. Consider the variables of the starting solution in the primal. These are S_1 and R_1. The dual variables y_1 and y_2 correspond to the primal constraint equations containing S_1 and R_1, respectively. Now consider the coefficient of S_1 and R_1 in the x_0-equation of the optimal primal tableau. These are given by

Starting solution variables (primal)	S_1	R_1
x_0-equation coefficients	29/5	$(-2/5) + M$
Corresponding dual variables	y_1	y_2

Ignoring the constant M for the moment, one sees that the resulting coefficients 29/5 and -2/5 directly give the optimal solution of the dual problem. This means that optimal y_1 equals 29/5 and optimal y_2 equals -2/5, which is the same result obtained by solving the dual problem independently.

Similar investigation of the coefficients of the starting variables R_1, R_2, and R_3 in the y_0-equation of the optimal dual tableau gives

Starting solution variables (dual)	R_1	R_2	R_3
y_0-equation coefficients	$9/5 - M$	$8/5 - M$	$0 - M$
Corresponding dual variables	x_1	x_2	x_3

Again ignoring the constant M, one sees that these coefficients give directly the optimal primal solution $x_1 = 9/5$, $x_2 = 8/5$ and $x_3 = 0$. This is the same result obtained from the direct solution of the primal.

• PROBLEM 4-2

Consider the following problem

Minimize $2x_1 + 3x_2 + 5x_3 + 2x_4 + 3x_5$

Subject to
$$x_1 + x_2 + 2x_3 + x_4 + 3x_5 \geq 4$$
$$2x_1 - 2x_2 + 3x_3 + x_4 + x_5 \geq 3$$
$$x_1, \quad x_2, \quad x_3, \quad x_4, \quad x_5 \geq 0$$

Find the optimal solution by using the graphical approach.

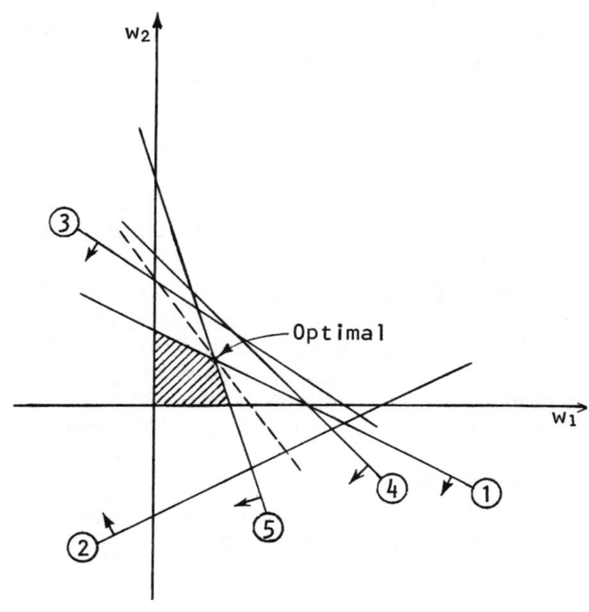

Solution: Since the dual has only two variables, solve it graphically as shown in the figure. The dual problem is as follows:

$$\begin{array}{lrcl} \text{Maximize} & 4w_1 + 3w_2 & & \\ \text{Subject to} & w_1 + 2w_2 & \leq & 2 \\ & w_1 - 2w_2 & \leq & 3 \\ & 2w_1 + 3w_2 & \leq & 5 \\ & w_1 + w_2 & \leq & 2 \\ & 3w_1 + w_2 & \leq & 3 \\ & w_1, \quad w_2 & \geq & 0 \end{array}$$

The optimal solution to the dual is $w_1^* = \frac{4}{5}$, $w_2^* = \frac{3}{5}$ with objective 5. Immediately it is known that $z^* = 5$. Utilizing the weak theorem of complementary slackness, it is further known that $x_2^* = x_3^* = x_4^* = 0$ since none of the corresponding complementary dual constraints are tight. Since $w_1^*, w_2^* > 0$, then $x_1^* + 3x_5^* = 4$ and $2x_1^* + x_5^* = 3$. From these two equations one gets $x_1^* = 1$ and $x_5^* = 1$. Thus the primal optimal point is obtained from the duality theorems and the dual optimal point.

• PROBLEM 4-3

Kopek Products, Inc. produces two kinds of products: Ak Pup dog food is a blend of one pound of cereal and one and a half pounds of meat, it utilizes one unit of Ak Pup packaging capacity, and it generates a contribution to overhead and profits of \$.56 per package. Similarly, Kara Hound is a blend of two pounds of cereal and one pound of meat and generates a contribution to overhead and profits of \$.42 per package. The associated resources are 240,000 pounds of cereal, 180,000 pounds of meat, and packaging equipment that can package at most 110,000 packages of Ak Pup dog food a month. Construct a linear programming model that would maximize the profit by deciding how much to produce of each product. Then formulate the dual problem and interpret the variables and relations used. Solve the dual.

Solution: The problem is formulated as follows

$$\begin{array}{lrcl} \text{Maximize } z = .56x_1 + .42x_2 & & & \\ \text{subject to:} & x_1 + 2x_2 & \leq & 240{,}000 \\ & 1.5x_1 + x_2 & \leq & 180{,}000 \\ & x_1 & \leq & 110{,}000 \\ & x_1, \ x_2 & \geq & 0 \end{array}$$

The optimal solution is to produce 60,000 packages of Ak Pup dog food (x_1) and 90,000 packages of Kara Hound dog food (x_2). The contribution to overhead and profits thereby generated is $71,400 per month.

The dual problem can be stated as finding a set of prices or rents for resources such that the total value of all the resources is minimized subject to constraints requiring that the rents or prices be set in a manner consistent with alternative uses for the resources.

Given the same setting as the above problem, now focus on the dual problem, a pricing problem. Seek to determine prices at which one should value the resources so that the minimum total value can be determined at which one would be willing to lease or sell the resources, as appropriate. One would be willing to sell cereal or meat, and would be willing to rent capacity on the Ak Pup packaging equipment.

Designate as y_1 and y_2 the prices per pound to be charged for cereal and meat respectively, and as y_3 the rent per unit to be charged for Ak Pup packaging capacity. Given the availability of the resources, the total monthly sales and rentals are

$$240{,}000y_1 + 180{,}000y_2 + 110{,}000y_3$$

The lowest value of this objective is desired so that one may intelligently view any bids to buy or lease all the resources as a total package; therefore, one wishes to minimize the sum of rentals and raw materials sales.

Consider next the constraints. The prices (the term prices henceforth includes both prices and rents) should all be zero or greater. Obviously, no resource should have a negative price, since any resource sold (henceforth the verb sell means either sell or rent) at a negative price could be more profitably left idle. Accordingly, the following constraints must be satisfied:

$$y_1, y_2, y_3 \geq 0$$

The other conditions to be satisfied in the other constraints are that the prices should be competitive with available alternatives. For example, since one pound of cereal plus one and a half pounds of meat plus one unit of Ak Pup packaging capacity can be employed to produce one package of Ak Pup dog food, the value in terms of resource prices of a unit of Ak Pup dog food is

$$y_1 + 1.5y_2 + y_3$$

That price should be at least as great as what is obtained when a unit of Ak Pup dog food is produced--namely, a contribution to overhead and profit of $.56. In other words,

$$y_1 + 1.5y_2 + y_3 \geq .56$$

Similarly, two pounds of cereal together with one pound of meat can be employed to produce a package of Kara Hound dog food and thereby generate a contribution to overhead and profits of \$.42. Hence, the following inequality should also be satisfied:

$$2y_1 + y_2 \geq .42$$

There are no further restrictions, so now formulate the objective function, which is to find the total minimum value of all the resources. The problem then is

Minimize $z = 240{,}000y_1 + 180{,}000y_2 + 110{,}000y_3$

subject to:

$$\begin{aligned} y_1 + 1.5y_2 + y_3 &\geq .56 \\ 2y_1 + y_2 &\geq .42 \\ y_1, y_2, y_3 &\geq 0 \end{aligned}$$

For the solution, first formulate it as a maximizing problem by maximizing the negative of the objective function. In other words, the objective function becomes

$$\text{Maximize } z = -240{,}000y_1 - 180{,}000y_2 - 110{,}000y_3$$

Employ a method that uses a single artificial variable in all constraints having greater than or equal inequalities, add an artificial variable (y_a).

This method reduces the number of artificial variables required when there is more than one constraint of the form

(1) $\sum a_{ij}x_j \geq b_i (b_i > 0)$

The reduction is accomplished as follows:

1. Add artificial variables, one per constraint, to all equality constraints.
2. Add slack variables to all inequalities.
3. Use one additional artificial variable, adding that variable to every constraint originally of the form (1). Of the constraints originally of the form (1), choose one with b_i maximum. Designate the artificial variable as basic in that constraint.
4. The starting basis consists of artificial variables for equality constraints (one for each constraint) plus one additional artificial variable basic in one of the constraints of the form (1) as selected in step 3. All other basic variables are slack variables.

The constraints of the form (1) in which slacks are basic must be multiplied by -1 to obtain the starting tableau. The resulting problem, including slack and artificial variables, is as follows:

$$\text{Maximize } z = -240{,}000y_1 - 180{,}000y_2 - 110{,}000y_3 - My_a$$

subject to:

$$y_1 + 1.5y_2 + y_3 - y_4 + \boxed{y_a} = .56$$

$$2y_1 + y_2 \quad \boxed{- y_5} + y_a = .42$$

Tableau 1

		y_1	y_2 ↓	y_3	y_4	y_5	y_a	
z	-.56 M	2.4-M	1.8-1.5M	1.1 -M	M	0	0	
y_a	.56	1	1.5	1	-1	0	1	
y_5	.14	-1	[.5]	1	-1	1	0	→

Tableau 2

		y_1 ↓	y_2	y_3	y_4	y_5	y_a	
	-.504-.14M	6 - 4M	0	-2.5 + 2M	-3.6 - 2M	-3.6 + 3M	0	
y_a	.14	[4]	0	-2	2	-3	1	→
y_2	.28	-2	1	2	-2	2	0	

Tableau 3

		y_1	y_2	y_3	y_4	y_5	y_a
	-.714	0	0	.5	.6	.9	M - 1.5
y_1	.035	1	0	-.5	.5	-.75	.25
y_2	.35	0	1	3	-1	.5	.5

Fig. 1

Pivoting y_a into the first equation and then multiplying the second equation by -1 yields the starting tableau. The solution is given in Figure 1, where the entries in the original objective function have been divided by 100,000 for convenience.

Tableau 3 is optimal, and the corresponding solution is that the optimal price of cereal, y_1, be \$.035 per pound, and that the price of meat, y_2, be \$.35 per pound. The optimal price of Ak Pup packaging capacity, y_3, which is not in the basis, is \$.00. Finally note that the minimum monthly value of the resources is \$71,400, exactly the same as the maximum profit attainable by producing dog food. The relationship between the original linear program (the primal) and the dual is so strong that they are in a sense two sides of the same problem. In fact, when either problem is solved using standard methods, e.g., the simplex method, the solution to the other problem is obtained as a by-product.

Find a solution to the following problem by solving its dual:

$$\text{Minimize} \quad 9x_1 + 12x_2 + 15x_3 \tag{1}$$

subject to

$$\begin{aligned} 2x_1 + 2x_2 + x_3 &\geq 10 \\ 2x_1 + 3x_2 + x_3 &\geq 12 \\ x_1 + x_2 + 5x_3 &\geq 14 \end{aligned} \tag{2}$$

$$x_1 \geq 0,\ x_2 \geq 0,\ x_3 \geq 0. \tag{3}$$

Solution: The dual to (1), (2) and (3) is

$$\text{Maximize} \quad 10y_1 + 12y_2 + 14y_3 \tag{4}$$

subject to

$$\begin{aligned} 2y_1 + 2y_2 + y_3 &\leq 9 \\ 2y_1 + 3y_2 + Y_3 &\leq 12 \\ y_1 + y_2 + 5y_3 &\leq 15 \end{aligned} \tag{5}$$

$$y_1 \geq 0,\ y_2 \geq 0,\ y_3 \geq 0. \tag{6}$$

This problem can be solved using the Simplex method. Converting the inequalities to equalities by adding slack variables

$$\begin{aligned} 2y_1 + 2y_2 + y_3 + y_4 &= 9 \\ 2y_1 + 3y_2 + y_3 + y_5 &= 12 \\ y_1 + y_2 + 5y_3 + y_6 &= 15 . \end{aligned}$$

This may be rewritten in vector form as:

$$y_1 \begin{bmatrix} 2 \\ 2 \\ 1 \end{bmatrix} + y_2 \begin{bmatrix} 2 \\ 3 \\ 1 \end{bmatrix} + y_3 \begin{bmatrix} 1 \\ 1 \\ 5 \end{bmatrix} + y_4 \begin{bmatrix} 1 \\ 0 \\ 0 \end{bmatrix} + y_5 \begin{bmatrix} 0 \\ 1 \\ 0 \end{bmatrix} + y_6 \begin{bmatrix} 0 \\ 0 \\ 1 \end{bmatrix} = \begin{bmatrix} 9 \\ 12 \\ 15 \end{bmatrix} . \tag{7}$$

Since there are three equations in six unknowns, a basic feasible solution can be obtained by setting any three of the y_i's to zero. Let

$$v_1 = \begin{bmatrix} 2 \\ 2 \\ 1 \end{bmatrix},\quad v_2 = \begin{bmatrix} 2 \\ 3 \\ 1 \end{bmatrix},\quad v_3 = \begin{bmatrix} 1 \\ 1 \\ 5 \end{bmatrix},\quad v_4 = \begin{bmatrix} 1 \\ 0 \\ 0 \end{bmatrix},$$

$$v_5 = \begin{bmatrix} 0 \\ 1 \\ 0 \end{bmatrix},\quad v_6 = \begin{bmatrix} 0 \\ 0 \\ 1 \end{bmatrix}$$

and

$$b = \begin{bmatrix} 9 \\ 12 \\ 15 \end{bmatrix}.$$ Let $d_1 = 10$, $d_2 = 12$, $d_3 = 14$. Setting $y_1 = y_2 = y_3 = 0$, a basic feasible solution is $y_4 = 9$, $y_5 = 12$, $y_6 = 15$. Start the Simplex algorithm with v_4, v_5 and v_6 in the basis.

	v_1	v_2	v_3	b	v_4	v_5	v_6
v_4	2	2	1	9	1	0	0
v_5	2	3	1	12	0	1	0
v_6	1	1	5	15	0	0	1
d	-10	-12	-14	0	0	0	0
				↑ D			

To increase the value of D, choose another vector for the basis. Choose the column which has the most negative value in the row labelled 'd'. Here v_3 is the chosen column. Next decide which vector in the basis to discard. The rule here is to choose that row for which the ratio of b to v_3 is the smallest. Here the ratios are 9/1, 12/1 and 15/5. Hence replace v_6 by v_3, by pivoting on 5. The process of conversion is carried out by first converting the 5 to a 1 and then using elementary row operations to reduce every other element under v_3 to zero. Thus obtain the new tableau

	v_1	v_2	v_3	b	v_4	v_5	v_6
v_4	9/5	9/5	0	6	1	0	-1/5
v_5	9/5	14/5	0	9	0	1	-1/5
v_3	1/5	1/5	1	3	0	0	1/5
d	-36/5	-46/5	0	42	0	0	14/5

The value 42 was obtained by using $b = c_1y_1 + c_2y_2 + c_3y_3 + c_4y_4 + c_5y_5 + c_6y_6$ where the y_i are the coefficients of the vectors in the basis. Here the basis vectors are v_4, v_5, v_6. The coefficients are, from (4), $c_1 = 10$, $c_2 = 12$, $c_3 = 14$, $c_4 = c_5 = c_6 = 0$ and the y_i are obtained from the column labelled b. Hence

$$D = c_4(6) + c_5(9) + c_3(3) = 0(6) + 0(9) + 14(3) = 42.$$

Since the row d still contains negative entries repeat the above procedure by pivoting on 14/5. One obtains

	v_1	v_2	v_3	b	v_4	v_5	v_6
v_4	9/14	0	0	3/14	1	-9/14	-1/14
v_2	9/14	1	0	45/14	0	5/14	-1/14
v_3	1/14	0	1	33/14	0	-1/14	3/14
d	-9/7	0	0	501/7	0	23/7	15/7

Next, pivot on the first element in the first column, i.e., 9/14. The final Simplex tableau is

	v_1	v_2	v_3	b	v_4	v_5	v_6
v_1	1	0	0	1/3	14/9	-1	-1/9
v_2	0	1	0	3	-1	1	0
v_3	0	0	1	7/3	-1/9	0	2/9
d	0	0	0	72	2	2	2

Thus the solution to the maximization problem (the dual of the given problem) is

$$y_1 = 1/3,\ y_2 = 3,\ y_3 = 7/3$$

with value 72. It is known from duality theory that if a program has an optimal feasible point then so does its dual and both programs have the same value. The dual of (4), (5), (6) is (1), (2), (3). Thus the solution to the minimization problem has value 72. But what are the values of x_1, x_2, x_3 at this optimum point? From the Complementary Slackness Theorem of duality theory, these values are the values of the slack variables in the final Simplex tableau of the dual problem. Thus $x_1 = 2$, $x_2 = 2$, $x_3 = 2$ is the required solution.

• PROBLEM 4-5

Minimize 9S + 12M + 15L

subject to

$$S \geq 0$$
$$M \geq 0$$
$$L \geq 0$$
$$2S + 2M + L \geq 10$$
$$2S + 3M + L \geq 12$$
$$S + M + 5L \geq 14$$

Find a solution to the above problem by solving its dual.

Solution: The dual of this Linear Program is

Maximize 10X + 12Y + 14Z

subject to

$$X \geq 0$$
$$Y \geq 0$$
$$Z \geq 0$$
$$2X + 2Y + Z \leq 9$$
$$2X + 3Y + Z \leq 12$$
$$X + Y + 5Z \leq 15$$

2	2	1	1	0	0	9	(T_0)	-14 is the most negative number in the extra row and $\frac{15}{5}$ is the smallest ratio, in the crresponding column.
2	3	1	0	1	0	12		
1	1	(5)	0	0	1	15		
−10	−12	−14	0	0	0	0		

$\frac{9}{5}$	$\frac{9}{5}$	0	1	0	$-\frac{1}{5}$	6	(T_1)	$-\frac{46}{5}$ is the most negative number in the extra row and $9/\frac{14}{5}$ is the smallest ratio, in the corresponding column.
$\frac{9}{5}$	($\frac{14}{5}$)	0	0	1	$-\frac{1}{5}$	9		
$\frac{1}{5}$	$\frac{1}{5}$	1	0	0	$\frac{1}{5}$	3		
$\frac{-36}{5}$	$\frac{-46}{5}$	0	0	0	$\frac{14}{5}$	42		

($\frac{9}{14}$)	0	0	1	$-\frac{9}{14}$	$-\frac{1}{14}$	$\frac{3}{14}$	(T_2)	$\frac{-9}{7}$ is the only negative number in the extra row and $\frac{3}{14}/\frac{9}{14}$ is the smallest ratio.
$\frac{9}{14}$	1	0	0	$\frac{5}{14}$	$-\frac{1}{14}$	$\frac{45}{14}$		
$\frac{1}{14}$	0	1	0	$-\frac{1}{14}$	$\frac{3}{14}$	$\frac{33}{14}$		
$\frac{-9}{7}$	0	0	0	$\frac{23}{7}$	$\frac{15}{7}$	$\frac{501}{7}$		

1	0	0	$\frac{14}{9}$	−1	$-\frac{1}{9}$	$\frac{1}{3}$	(T_3)	There are no negative numbers in the extra row so we stop.
0	1	0	−1	1	0	3		
0	0	1	$-\frac{1}{9}$	0	$\frac{2}{9}$	$\frac{7}{3}$		
0	0	0	2	2	2	72		

Solution of the maximum Linear Program (the last column, $\frac{1}{3}, 3, \frac{7}{3}$)

Solution of the minimum dual (the Linear Program of interest) (the extra row entries 2, 2, 2)

Value (72)

Fig. 1

To solve this maximum Linear Program introduce the system of equations

$$
\begin{aligned}
2X + 2Y + Z + S_1 &= 9 \\
2X + 3Y + Z + S_2 &= 12 \\
X + Y + 5Z + S_3 &= 15
\end{aligned}
$$

The sequence of tableaux which solves this problem is illustrated in Fig. 1. The solution of the minimum program is (2, 2, 2) read off from the extra row of tableau T_3 of Fig. 1.

DUAL SIMPLEX METHOD

• PROBLEM 4-6

Minimize $z = 10x_1 + 5x_2 + 4x_3$

subject to

$$
\begin{aligned}
3x_1 + 2x_2 - 3x_3 &\geq 3 \\
4x_1 + 2x_3 &\geq 10 \\
x_1, x_2, x_3 &\geq 0 \qquad (1)
\end{aligned}
$$

Solve the primal problem by applying the Dual Simplex algorithm. Also, solve the dual problem by the Simplex method.

Solution: The primal problem: Adding slack variables x_4 and x_5, one gets

$$\begin{aligned} 3x_1 + 2x_2 - 3x_3 - x_4 \quad &= 3 \\ 4x_1 \quad + 2x_3 \quad - x_5 &= 10 \\ 10x_1 + 5x_2 + 4x_3 \quad &= z \end{aligned}$$

To apply the Simplex process to this problem, add two artificial variables and proceed on. On the other hand, by multiplying the two constraints by (-1), the following is obtained.

$$\begin{aligned} -3x_1 - 2x_2 + 3x_3 + x_4 \quad &= -3 \\ -4x_1 \quad -2x_3 \quad + x_5 &= -10 \\ 10x_1 + 5x_2 + 4x_3 \quad &= z \end{aligned} \tag{2}$$

The system of constraints is in standard form with basic variables x_4 and x_5, the objective function is expressed in terms of the nonbasic variables x_1, x_2, and x_3, and the associated coefficients 10, 5, and 4 are nonnegative, but the associated basic solution $x_1 = x_2 = x_3 = 0$, $x_4 = -3$, $x_5 = -10$ is not feasible.

The basic step of the Dual Simplex algorithm which is intimately related to the dual problem of the linear programming problem, is the pivot operation. Dual Simplex algorithm differs from the standard Simplex process by the rules used to determine the pivot term at each step.

Consider the tableau presentation in Table 1 of the problem as stated in (2).

Table 1

	x_1	x_2	x_3	x_4	x_5	
x_4	−3	−2	3	1	0	−3
x_5	−4	0	−2	0	1	−10
	10	5	4	0	0	0

To apply the Dual Simplex algorithm, determine first the row to pivot in. According to the algorithm, the pivot term can be in any row with a negative constant term. In this tableau, $b_1 = -3$ and $b_2 = -10$; therefore the pivot term can come from either row. An arbitrary rule to use in such a case is to pivot in that row with the smallest b_i term, and so, here, to pivot in the second row, extracting x_5 from the basis.

Next determine what column to pivot in. The algorithm dictates that the pivot term be at a negative a_{ij} entry, and so, here, the pivot term will be either at $a_{21} = -4$ or $a_{23} = -2$. To determine at which entry one pivots, the ratios c_j/a_{rj} must be considered for those $a_{rj} < 0$ (where r is the pivoting row), and the pivot term be in that column, say column s, for which

$$\frac{c_s}{a_{rs}} = \text{Max}\left\{\frac{c_j}{a_{rj}} \,\middle|\, a_{rj} < 0\right\}$$

In this case compare $c_1/a_{21} = \frac{10}{-4} = -\frac{5}{2}$ with $c_3/a_{23} = \frac{4}{-2} = -2$. The maximum occurs in the third column, and therefore pivot at $a_{23} = -2$. (Note that here one is comparing two nonpositive ratios and seeking the maximum, and therefore is actually seeking that ratio of minimum absolute value. By nature of the algorithm, this will always be the case.)

Pivoting here, the tableaux of Table 2 is obtained.

Table 2

	x_1	x_2	x_3	x_4	x_5	
x_4	−3	−2	3	1	0	−3
x_5	−4	0	(−2)	0	1	−10
	10	5	4	0	0	0
x_4	−9	−2	0	1	$\frac{3}{2}$	−18
x_3	2	0	1	0	$-\frac{1}{2}$	5
	2	5	0	0	2	−20

Notice that the c_j^* entries, the 2, 5, 0, 0, and 2, remain nonnegative. The choice of pivoting column guarantees this. Now proceed on. In the second tableau, $b_1^* = -18$ is the only negative constant term, so pivot in the first row. Comparing those ratios corresponding to negative a_{rj}^* terms, one gets $c_1^*/a_{11}^* = -2/9 > c_2^*/a_{12}^* = -5/2$, and so pivot at the $a_{11}^* = -9$ term. The resulting tableau is in Table 3.

Note that after this step, the constant term column entries are nonnegative. In fact, with the original problem presented in this form, one has reached the resolution of the problem. The minimum value of the objective function is 24 and is attained at the point (2,0,1,0,0).

The dual problem is to maximize v with

$$\begin{aligned} 3y_1 + 4y_2 &\le 10 \\ 2y_1 &\le 5 \\ -3y_1 + 2y_2 &\le 4 \\ 3y_1 + 10y_2 &= v \\ y_1, y_2 &\ge 0 \end{aligned}$$

Table 3

	x_1	x_2	x_3	x_4	x_5	
x_4	(−9)	−2	0	1	$\frac{3}{2}$	−18
x_3	2	0	1	0	$-\frac{1}{2}$	5
	2	5	0	0	2	−20
x_1	1	$\frac{2}{9}$	0	$-\frac{1}{9}$	$-\frac{1}{6}$	2
x_3	0	$-\frac{4}{9}$	1	$\frac{2}{9}$	$-\frac{1}{6}$	1
	0	$\frac{41}{9}$	0	$\frac{2}{9}$	$\frac{7}{3}$	−24

The solution is given by the tableaux in Table 4. The optimal result is 24 as for the primal problem.

Table 4

	y_1	y_2	y_3	y_4	y_5	
y_3	3	4	1	0	0	10
y_4	2	0	0	1	0	5
y_5	−3	(2)	0	0	1	4
	−3	−10	0	0	0	0
y_3	(9)	0	1	0	−2	2
y_4	2	0	0	1	0	5
y_2	$-\frac{3}{2}$	1	0	0	$\frac{1}{2}$	2
	−18	0	0	0	5	20
y_1	1	0	$\frac{1}{9}$	0	$-\frac{2}{9}$	$\frac{2}{9}$
y_4	0	0	$-\frac{2}{9}$	1	$\frac{4}{9}$	$\frac{41}{9}$
y_2	0	1	$\frac{1}{6}$	0	$\frac{1}{6}$	$\frac{7}{3}$
	0	0	2	0	1	24

• PROBLEM 4-7

$$\text{Minimize } x_0 = 2x_1 + x_2$$

subject to

$$3x_1 + x_2 \geq 3$$
$$4x_1 + 3x_2 \geq 6$$
$$x_1 + 2x_2 \leq 3$$
$$x_1, x_2 \geq 0$$

Solve by the Dual Simplex method.

Solution: The Dual Simplex method applies to problems which start dual feasible (that is, optimal but infeasible). Such a situation is recognized by first expressing the constraints as ($\leq$) as in the canonical form. The objective function may be in either the maximization or the minimization form. After adding the slack variables and putting the problem in the tableau form, if any right-hand side element is negative and if the optimality condition is satisfied, the problem can be solved by the dual simplex method. Notice that a negative element in the right-hand side signifies that the corresponding slack variable is negative. This means that the problem starts optimal but infeasible as required by the Dual Simplex procedure. At the iteration where the basic solution becomes feasible, this will be the optimal basic feasible solution.

By putting the constraints in the form ($\leq$) and adding the slack variables, the corresponding starting tableau is given by

Basic	x_0	x_1	x_2	S_1	S_2	S_3	Solution
x_0	①	−2	−1	0	0	0	0
S_1	0	−3	−1	①	0	0	−3
S_2	0	−4	−3	0	①	0	−6
S_3	0	1	2	0	0	①	3

The starting solution is $S_1 = -3$, $S_2 = -6$, and $S_3 = 3$. This solution is infeasible since at least one basic variable is negative. In the meantime, the x_0-equation is optimal since all its coefficients are nonpositive (minimization problem). This problem is typical of the type that can be handled by the Dual Simplex method.

As in the regular simplex method, the method of solution is based on the optimality and feasibility conditions. The optimality condition guarantees that the solution remains always optimal, while the feasibility condition forces the basic solutions toward the feasible space.

Feasibility Condition: The leaving variable is the basic variable having the most negative value. (Break ties arbitrarily.) If all the basic variables are nonnegative the process ends and the feasible (optimal) solution is reached.

Optimality Condition: The entering variable is selected from among the nonbasic variables as follows. Take the ratios of the left-hand side coefficients of the x_0-equation to the corresponding coefficients in the equation associated with the leaving variable. Ignore the ratios associated with positive or zero denominators. The entering variable is the one with the smallest ratio if the problem is minimization, or the smallest absolute value of the ratios if the problem is maximization. (Break ties arbitrarily.) If all the denominators are zero or positive, the problem has no feasible solution.

After selecting the entering and the leaving variables, row operations are applied to obtain the next iteration of the solution.

The leaving variable in the above tableau is S_2 (= -6) since it has the most negative value. For the entering variable, the ratios are given by

Variable	x_1	x_2	S_1	S_2	S_3
x_0-equation	−2	−1	0	0	0
S_2-equation	−4	−3	0	1	0
Ratios	1/2	1/3	–	–	–

The entering variable is x_2 since it corresponds to the smallest ratio 1/3. By applying row operations, one finds the new tableau.

Basic	x_0	x_1	x_2	S_1	S_2	S_3	Solution
x_0	(1)	−2/3	0	0	−1/3	0	2
S_1	0	−5/3	0	(1)	−1/3	0	−1
x_2	0	4/3	(1)	0	−1/3	0	2
S_3	0	−5/3	0	0	2/3	(1)	−1

The new solution is still optimal but infeasible (S_1 = -1, S_3 = -1). If S_1 is arbitrarily selected to leave the solution, x_1 becomes the entering variable. This gives

Basic	x_0	x_1	x_2	S_1	S_2	S_3	Solution
x_0	(1)	0	0	−2/5	−1/5	0	12/5
x_1	0	(1)	0	−3/5	1/5	0	3/5
x_2	0	0	(1)	4/5	−3/5	0	6/5
S_3	0	0	0	−1	1	(1)	0

which is now optimal and feasible.

• PROBLEM 4-8

Consider this problem:

Minimize $f = 12x_1 + 5x_2$

subject to
$$4x_1 + 2x_2 \geq 80$$
$$2x_1 + 3x_2 \geq 90$$
$$x_1, x_2 \geq 0$$

Use the Dual Simplex method to solve this linear programming problem.

Solution: Step 1: Conversion to standard form gives:

Minimize $f = 12x_1 + 5x_2 + 0x_3 + 0x_4$

subject to
$$4x_1 + 2x_2 - x_3 = 80$$
$$2x_1 + 3x_2 - x_4 = 90$$
$$x_1, x_2, x_3, x_4 \geq 0$$

Step 2: The starting basis consists of x_3 and x_4, the surplus variables. This basis is obviously infeasible, but it also has an objective-function value of zero which must be less than the optimal value.

Now, before writing the initial tableau, multiply each constraint by -1 to convert the coefficients of the basic variables x_3 and x_4 to the proper sign. This must be done whenever the initial basis consists of surplus variables. The initial tableau is shown in Fig. 1.

Minimize			12	5	0	0		
i	c_B	x_B	x_1	x_2	x_3	x_4	b_i	
1	0	x_3	−4	−2	1	0	−80	
2	0	x_4	−2	(−3)	0	1	−90	Out →
		z_j	0	0	0	0	0	
		$c_j - z_j$	12	5	0	0		
		θ_j	$\frac{12}{2}$	$\frac{5}{3}$	–	–		
				↑ In				

Fig. 1

Step 3: Select x_4 as the outgoing variable because it is more negative than x_3.

Step 4: Compute the θ_j ratios for the non-basic variables:

$$\theta_1 = \frac{c_1 - z_1}{-a_{21}} = \frac{12}{2} = 6$$

$$\theta_2 = \frac{c_2 - z_2}{-a_{22}} = \frac{5}{3} = 1\frac{2}{3}$$

Since θ_2 is less than θ_1, select x_2 as the entering variable. The pivot element is $a_{22} = -3$.

Step 5: Perform the pivot. The new tableau is shown in Fig. 2. Note that in this tableau the reduced costs of all the non-basic variables are still positive; i.e., the basic solution shown is optimal, but not feasible.

Minimize			12	5	0	0		
i	c_B	x_B	x_1	x_2	x_3	x_4	b_i	
1	0	x_3	$-\frac{8}{3}$	0	1	($-\frac{2}{3}$)	−20	Out →
2	5	x_2	$\frac{2}{3}$	1	0	$-\frac{1}{3}$	30	
		z_j	$\frac{10}{3}$	5	0	$-\frac{5}{3}$	150	
		$c_j - z_j$	$\frac{26}{3}$	0	0	$\frac{5}{3}$		
		θ_j	$\frac{26}{8}$	–	–	$\frac{5}{2}$		
						↑ In		

Fig. 2

Step 3: Select x_3 as the outgoing variable because it is the only negative variable.

Step 4: Computing the θ_j ratios gives

$$\theta_1 = \frac{c_1 - z_1}{-a_{11}} = \frac{\frac{26}{3}}{\frac{8}{3}} = \frac{26}{8} = 3.25$$

$$\theta_4 = \frac{c_4 - z_4}{-a_{14}} = \frac{\frac{5}{3}}{\frac{2}{3}} = \frac{5}{2} = 2.50$$

The minimum ratio is θ_4, so x_4 enters. The pivot element is $a_{14} = -2/3$.

Step 5: Perform the pivot. The result is shown in Fig. 3.

Minimize			12	5	0	0	
i	c_B	x_B	x_1	x_2	x_3	x_4	b_i
1	0	x_4	4	0	$-\frac{3}{2}$	1	30
2	5	x_2	2	1	$-\frac{1}{2}$	0	40
		z_j	10	5	$-\frac{5}{2}$	0	200
		$c_j - z_j$	2	0	$\frac{5}{2}$	0	

Fig. 3

Step 3: The basic solution of Fig. 3 is optimal. The values are

$$x_1^* = 0 \qquad x_3^* = 0$$

$$x_2^* = 40 \qquad x_4^* = 30$$

$$f^* = \$200$$

• PROBLEM 4-9

$$\text{Minimize } Y = 50Z_1 + 40Z_2$$

subject to

$$3Z_1 + 2Z_2 \geq 35$$

$$5Z_1 + 6Z_2 \geq 60$$

$$2Z_1 + 3Z_2 \geq 30$$

$$Z_1, \quad Z_2 \geq 0$$

Solve by the Dual Simplex method.

Solution: Assume that a canonical form is generated through the introduction of slack variables $\bar{S}_1$, $\bar{S}_2$, and $\bar{S}_3$ such that

$$-3Z_1 - 2Z_2 + \bar{S}_1 = -35$$

$$-5Z_1 - 6Z_2 + \bar{S}_2 = -60$$

$$-2Z_1 - 3Z_2 + \bar{S}_3 = -30$$

so that an initial simplex tableau is as follows:

	50	40	0	0	0	
	Z_1	Z_2	$\bar{S}_1$	$\bar{S}_2$	$\bar{S}_3$	
$\bar{S}_1$	−3	−2	1	0	0	−35
$\bar{S}_2$	−5	−6	0	1	0	−60
$\bar{S}_3$	−2	−3	0	0	1	−30
V_j	50	40				

Note that the optimality criteria ($v_1, v_2 \geq 0$) is satisfied but the solution is infeasible. Choose $\bar{S}_2$ to leave the basis. Note that Z_1 and Z_2 are both candidates for entering the basis. Since $-\frac{50}{5} < -\frac{40}{6}$, choose Z_2 to enter the basis.

	50	40				
	z_1	z_2	$\bar{\xi}_1$	$\bar{\xi}_2$	$\bar{\xi}_3$	
$\bar{\xi}_1$	-4/3	0	1	-1/3	0	-15
z_2	5/6	1	0	-1/6	0	10
$\bar{\xi}_3$	1/2	0	0	-1/2	1	0
y_j	100/6	0	0	40/6	0	400

	50	40				
	z_1	z_2	$\bar{\xi}_1$	$\bar{\xi}_2$	$\bar{\xi}_3$	
z_1	1	0	-3/4	1/4	0	45/4
z_2	0	1	5/8	-9/24	0	5/8
$\bar{\xi}_3$	0	0	3/8	-5/8	1	-45/8
y_j	0	0	25/2	5/2	0	1175/2

	50	40				
	z_1	z_2	$\bar{\xi}_1$	$\bar{\xi}_2$	$\bar{\xi}_3$	
z_1	1	0	-3/5	0	2/5	9
z_2	0	1	2/5	0	-3/5	4
$\bar{\xi}_2$	0	0	-3/5	1	-8/5	9
y_j	0	0	14	0	4	610

The final solution is given by $Z_1 = 9$, $Z_2 = 4$, and $Y = 610$.

• PROBLEM 4-10

A company owns mines A and B. Mine A is capable of producing 1 ton of high-grade ore, 4 tons of medium-grade ore, and 6 tons of low-grade ore per day. Mine B can produce 2 tons of each of the three grades ore per day. The company requires at least 60 tons of high-grade ore, 120 tons of medium-grade ore, and 150 tons of low-grade ore. If it costs $200 per day to work mine A and $300 per day to work mine B, how many days should each mine be operated if the company wishes to minimize costs? Solve the dual problem by the Dual Simplex method.

Solution: The primal problem is

$$\text{Minimize} \quad w = 200y_1 + 300y_2$$

$$\text{subject to} \quad y_1 + 2y_2 \geq 60$$

$$4y_1 + 2y_2 \geq 120$$

$$6y_1 + 2y_2 \geq 150$$

$$\text{and} \quad y_1, y_2 \geq 0$$

The corresponding dual problem is

$$\text{Maximize} \quad u = 60x_1 + 120x_2 + 150x_3$$

$$\text{subject to} \quad x_1 + 4x_2 + 6x_3 \leq 200$$

$$2x_1 + 2x_2 + 2x_3 \leq 300$$

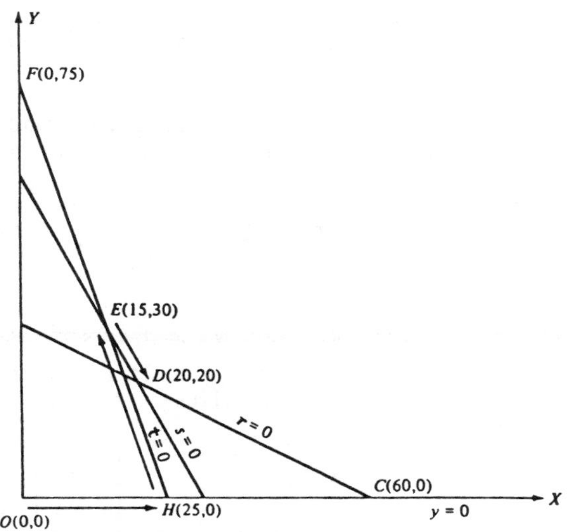

Basic point path (indicated by arrows) $r = 0$ is also $x + 2y = 60$. $s = 0$ is also $4x + 2y = 120$. $t = 0$ is also $6x + 2y = 150$.

Initial tableau for the dual problem is

	x_1	x_2	x_3	1	
y_1	1	4	6	-200	$= -t_1$
y_2	2*	2	2	-300	$= -t_2$
-1	60	120	150	0	$= u$
	$= v_1$	$= v_2$	$= v_3$	$= -w$	

(T.1)

Choosing column 1 as the pivot column leads to $a_{21} = 2$ as the pivot element. Pivoting then results in Tableau 2:

	t_2	x_2	x_3	1	
y_1	$-\frac{1}{2}$	3*	5	-50	$= -t_1$
v_1	$\frac{1}{2}$	1	1	-150	$= -x_1$
-1	-30	60	90	9000	$= u$
	$= y_2$	$= v_2$	$= v_3$	$= -w$	

(T.2)

Note that y_2 and v_1 were interchanged simultaneously with x_1 and t_2. Tableau 2 corresponds to the point on the vertical axis of the Figure shown where $x = 0$ ($y_1 = 0$) and $r = 0$ ($v_1 = 0$). Choosing column 2 as the pivot column yields $a_{12} = 3$ as the pivot element in T.2. Pivoting then results in Tableau 3:

	t_2	t_1	x_3	1	
v_2	$-\frac{1}{6}$	$\frac{1}{3}$	$\frac{5}{3}$	$-\frac{50}{3}$	$= -x_2$
v_1	$\frac{2}{3}$	$-\frac{1}{3}$	$-\frac{2}{3}$	$-\frac{400}{3}$	$= -x_1$
-1	-20	-20	-10	10,000	$= u$
	$= y_2$	$= y_1$	$= v_3$	$= -w$	

(T.3)

This tableau is a terminal tableau. Read off the solution of this minimum problem by setting $v_1 = v_2 = 0$. Thus, one gets $y_1 = 20$, $y_2 = 20$, $v_3 = 10$, and Min $w =$ \$10,000.

Note that this method required only three tableaus, while the primal simplex solution requires four tableaus.

The solution to the dual maximum problem is read off from the row system of Tableau 3 by setting the nonbasic variables equal to zero. Thus, $x_1 = \frac{400}{3}$, $x_2 = \frac{50}{3}$, $x_3 = 0$, $t_1 = t_2 = 0$ and Max u = \$10,000.

• PROBLEM 4-11

Apply the Dual Simplex algorithm to the following dual tableau to obtain a terminal tableau:

	s_1	s_2	1	
q_1	$-\frac{2}{3}$	$-\frac{1}{3}$*	12	$= -r_1$
q_2	$\frac{4}{3}$	$\frac{1}{3}$	-60	$= -r_2$
-1	$-\frac{20}{3}$	$-\frac{5}{3}$	200	$= u$
	$= p_1$	$= p_2$	$= -w$	

(T.k)

Solution: When there is an intermediate dual tableau where the maximum problem is lined up by the rows and the minimum problem by columns, as above, one can apply the Dual Simplex algorithm if all the c_j's are nonpositive, but at least one of the $-b_i$'s is positive.

Focus on a row for which $-b_i$ is positive. Compute c_j/a_{ij} for all those a_{ij}'s in the row that are negative. These ratios will thus be positive or zero in value, since $c_j \le 0$ for all j. Pick the a_{ij} for which c_j/a_{ij} is a minimum. This a_{ij} is then the pivot element (in case of ties, choose any of the eligible a_{ij}'s). In the typical pivot operation, s_j and r_i are interchanged in the maximum problem, while q_i and p_j are interchanged in the minimum problem (it is possible that all the a_{ij}'s in the row under focus are either positive or zero. This indicates that the minimum problem is unbounded).

In the next tableau, after the pivot transformation has been effected, the c_j's will again be nonpositive, and usually the $-b_i$'s will be less positive in character. A terminal tableau that is a solution tableau is achieved when the $-b_i$'s have all become nonpositive.

Clearly, Dual Simplex algorithm applies because both c_1 and c_2 are negative, while $-b_1$ is positive. Tableau k corresponds to feasibility with respect to the minimum problem (at the b.f.p., $q_1 = q_2 = 0$, $p_1 = \frac{20}{3}$, $p_2 =$

$\frac{5}{3}$, and w = 200). Compute the relevant c/a ratios for row 1:

$$\frac{c_1}{a_{11}} = \frac{(-\frac{20}{3})}{(-\frac{2}{3})} = +10$$

$$\frac{c_2}{a_{12}} = \frac{(-\frac{5}{3})}{(-\frac{1}{3})} = +5.$$

Thus, a_{12} is the pivot element in Tableau k. Carrying out the pivot transformation leads to Tableau k + 1, in which s_2 and r_1 (maximum problem) and q_1 and p_2 (minimum problem), respectively, have been exchanged:

	s_1	r_1	1		
p_2	2	−3	−36	$= -s_2$	
q_2	$\frac{2}{3}$	1	−48	$= -r_2$	(T.k + 1)
−1	$-\frac{10}{3}$	−5	140	$= u$	
	$= p_1$	$= q_1$	$= -w$		

This is a terminal tableau; the solutions of the respective problems are easily read off:

Maximum problem:

$$s_1 = r_1 = 0, \quad s_2 = 36, \quad r_2 = 36, \text{ and Max } u = 140.$$

Minimum problem:

$$p_2 = q_2 = 0, \quad p_1 = \frac{10}{3}, \quad q_1 = 5, \text{ and Min } w = 140.$$

• PROBLEM 4-12

Minimize $x_1 - x_2$,

subject to

$$x_1 + 2x_2 + x_3 = 4$$
$$3x_1 - x_2 - x_4 = 1$$
$$x_1 + 3x_2 = 4,$$

all x_j non-negative.

Solve by the Big-M method, applying the Dual Simplex algorithm.

Solution: If the problem is in neither of the standard forms and cannot be transformed into one of them, proceed as follows.

First, multiply both sides of those constraints by -1, in which b_i is negative. The resulting coefficients of

x_{n+i} $(i = 1,\ldots,m)$ are then 1, -1, or 0.
In the latter two cases add an "artificial" variable a_i to the left-hand side, and add Ma_i to the objective function to be minimized (or subtract Ma_i from the objective function to be maximized); M is considered to be a value larger than any other with which it is compared during the calculations. The following shows the procedure.

Tableau:

	x_1	x_2	x_4	
x_3	1	2	0	4
a_1	3*	-1	-1	1
a_2	1	3	0	4
	-1	1	0	0
(M)	4	2	-1	5

The last row arises from the artificial variables by using the checking rule, and its entries are to be multiplied by M. The sum of the last two rows is the row of the objective function $x_1 - x_2 + M(a_1 + a_2)$. The successive tableaus are as follows:

	a_1	x_2	x_4	
x_3		$\frac{7}{3}$	$\frac{1}{3}$	$\frac{11}{3}$
x_1		$-\frac{1}{3}$	$-\frac{1}{3}$	$\frac{1}{3}$
a_2		$\frac{10}{3}$*	$\frac{1}{3}$	$\frac{11}{3}$
		$\frac{2}{3}$	$-\frac{1}{3}$	$\frac{1}{3}$
(M)		$\frac{10}{3}$	$\frac{1}{3}$	$\frac{11}{3}$

The a_1 column is of no interest and is omitted.

Final Tableau

	x_4	
x_3	$\frac{1}{10}$	$\frac{11}{10}$
x_1	$-\frac{3}{10}$	$\frac{7}{10}$
x_2	$\frac{1}{10}$	$\frac{11}{10}$
	$-\frac{4}{5}$	$-\frac{2}{5}$

If it is not possible to make the artificial variables eventually equal to zero, this is an indication that the original constraints were contradictory. It is possible, though, for an artificial variable to remain in the final basis, with value zero. This happens if a constraint is redundant.

• PROBLEM 4-13

Solve the following problem using the Dual Simplex method:

Maximize $z = -2x_1 - 2x_2$

subject to: $2x_1 + x_2 \geq 6$

$x_1 + 2x_2 \geq 6$

$x_1, x_2 \geq 0$

Solution: Denoting the slack variables as x_3 and x_4, one gets the starting tableau, Tableau 1.

Tableau 1

		↓ x_1	x_2	x_3	x_4	
z	0	2	2	0	0	
x_3	-6	[-2]	-1	1	0	→
x_4	-6	-1	-2	0	1	

The problem is dual feasible, i.e., all $a_{0j} \geq 0$, but not primal feasible, i.e., some $a_{i0} < 0$. Hence use the Dual Simplex method. Choose x_3 to leave the basis. The choice of variables to enter the basis is x_1 because

$$\frac{b_1}{|a_{r1}|} = \frac{2}{|-2|} < \frac{b_2}{|a_{r2}|} = \frac{2}{|-1|}$$

Performing the iteration leads to Tableau 2.

Tableau 2

		x_1	↓ x_2	x_3	x_4	
z	-6	0	1	1	0	
x_1	3	1	.5	-.5	0	
x_4	-3	0	[-1.5]	-.5	1	→

In Tableau 2, x_4 is chosen to leave the basis and x_2 is the variable which must enter because

$$\frac{b_2}{|a_{r2}|} = \frac{1}{|-1.5|} < \frac{b_3}{|a_{r3}|} = \frac{1}{|-.5|}$$

The indicated iteration is performed, leading to Tableau 3, for which the solution is feasible and therefore optimal.

Tableau 3

		x_1	x_2	x_3	x_4
z	-8	0	0	$\frac{2}{3}$	$\frac{2}{3}$
x_1	2	1	0	$-\frac{2}{3}$	$-\frac{1}{3}$
x_2	2	0	1	$\frac{1}{3}$	$-\frac{2}{3}$

• PROBLEM 4-14

Minimize $x_1 - 2x_2$,

subject to
$$x_1 - x_2 \geq 5$$
$$x_1 + x_2 \leq 6$$
$$x_1, x_2 \geq 0.$$

Try solving by the Simplex method. If it is not appropriate, solve by applying the Self-dual parametric algorithm.

Solution: A method of dealing with a situation where the problem cannot be transformed into either of the two standard forms is that of the "self-dual parametric algorithm".
After introducing the slack variables x_3 and x_4, the first tableau will be

	x_1	x_2	
x_3	-1	1	-5
x_4	1	1	2
	-1	2	0

This is neither (primal) feasible nor is it dual feasible. Determine the smallest constant, t say, which, when added to the negative b_i and subtracted from the positive c_j, makes the tableau primal as well as dual feasible. In the present case,

	x_1	x_2	
x_3	-1*	1	-5 + t
x_4	1	1	6
	-1	2-t	0

take t = 5. The tableau ceases to be feasible, but not to be dual feasible, if t is just smaller than 5. In such a case, say if t = 4.9, the Dual Simplex method would be appropriate; this is the method to be used to obtain

	x_3	x_2	
x_1	-1	-1	5-t
x_4	1	2*	1+t
	-1	1-t	5-t

If t = 0 made the tableau feasible, and dual feasible, then one would have finished. In the present case this is not so, and therefore continue. If t is just smaller than 1, then the tableau is not dual feasible but feasible, and the Simplex method is appropriate.

	x_3	x_4	
x_1	$-\frac{1}{2}$	$\frac{1}{2}$	(11-t)/2
x_2	$\frac{1}{2}$	$\frac{1}{2}$	(1+t)/2
	(-3+t)/2	(-1+t)/2	$\frac{9}{2} + t^2 - t$

This tableau is feasible, and dual feasible when t = 0; thus one has reached the optimal answer: $x_1 = \frac{11}{2}$, $x_2 = \frac{1}{2}$, $x_1 - 2x_2 = \frac{9}{2}$.

REVISED SIMPLEX METHOD

• PROBLEM 4-15

$$\text{Maximize} \quad x_0 = 3x_1 + 2x_2 + 5x_3$$

subject to

$$x_1 + 2x_2 + x_3 \le 430$$

$$3x_1 + 2x_3 \le 460$$

$$x_1 + 4x_2 \le 420$$

$$x_1, x_2, x_3 \ge 0$$

Solve by the Revised Simplex method.

Solution: The general linear programming problem in standard form can be expressed as follows.

$$\text{Maximize} \quad x_0 = \vec{C}\vec{X}$$

subject to

$$(\vec{A}, \vec{I})\vec{X} = \vec{P}_0, \quad \vec{P}_0 \ge \vec{0}$$

$$\vec{X} \ge \vec{0}$$

where $\vec{X} = (x_1, x_2, \ldots, x_{m+n})^T$

$\vec{C} = (c_1, c_2, \ldots, c_{m+n})$

$\vec{P}_0 = (b_1, b_2, \ldots, b_m)^T$

$$\vec{A} = \begin{pmatrix} a_{11} & a_{12} & \cdots & a_{1n} \\ a_{21} & a_{22} & \cdots & a_{2n} \\ \vdots & \vdots & & \vdots \\ a_{m1} & a_{m2} & \cdots & a_{mn} \end{pmatrix}$$

$\vec{I}$ is the m-identity matrix

The constraints $(\vec{A}, \vec{I})\vec{X} = \vec{P}_0$ may also be written as

$$\sum_{j=1}^{m+n} x_j \vec{P}_j = \vec{P}_0$$

where $\vec{P}_j$ represents the jth column-vector of the matrix $(\vec{A}, \vec{I})$.

Let $\vec{C} = (\vec{C}_I, \vec{C}_{II})$, where $\vec{C}_{II}$ represents the coefficients of the objective function corresponding to the starting solution. Hence, at any iteration, the Simplex tableau form is expressed as

Basic	x_0	$\vec{X}_I^T$	$\vec{X}_{II}^T$	Solution
x_0	1	$\vec{C}_B\vec{B}^{-1}\vec{A} - \vec{C}_I$	$\vec{C}_B\vec{B}^{-1} - \vec{C}_{II}$	$\vec{C}_B\vec{B}^{-1}\vec{P}_0$
$\vec{X}_B$	$\vec{0}$	$\vec{B}^{-1}\vec{A}$	$\vec{B}^{-1}$	$\vec{B}^{-1}\vec{P}_0$

It is noted that $\vec{B}^{-1}$ for the first iteration in the Simplex method is always given by an identity matrix. Consequently, throughout the iterations of the Revised Simplex method, it will not be necessary to invert any matrices.

The Revised Simplex method procedure is now summarized in three basic steps. Let $\vec{B}^{-1} = \vec{B}^{-1}_{starting} = \vec{I}$, and define starting $\vec{C}_B$ accordingly. (Keep in mind that these steps are essentially the same as in the regular Simplex method.) $\vec{C}_B$ is the element of $\vec{C}$ associated with $\vec{X}_B$. $\vec{X}_B$ is the basic vector associated to $\vec{B}$.

Step 1. Determination of the entering vector $\vec{P}_j$.

$$z_j - c_j = \vec{C}_B\vec{B}^{-1}\vec{P}_j - c_j = (1, \vec{C}_B\vec{B}^{-1})\begin{pmatrix} -c_j \\ \vec{P}_j \end{pmatrix}$$

The vector having the most negative $z_j - c_j$ should enter the solution. Otherwise, if all $z_j - c_j \geq 0$, the optimal solution is attained.

Step 2. Determination of the leaving vector $\vec{P}_r$. Given the entering vector $\vec{P}_j$ and the current basic solution $x_k = (\vec{B}^{-1}\vec{P}_0)_k (k = 1,2,\ldots,m)$, then the leaving vector must correspond to

$$\theta = \min_k \left\{ \frac{(\vec{B}^{-1}\vec{P}_0)_k}{\alpha_k^j} \text{ , } \alpha_k^j > 0 \right\}$$

where α_k^j is the kth element of $\vec{\alpha}^j = \vec{B}^{-1}\vec{P}_j$. If all $\alpha_k^j \leq 0$, the problem has no bounded solution.

Step 3. Determination of the next basic solution. The procedure for determining $\vec{B}^{-1}_{next}$ from $\vec{B}$ is summarized as follows. Let the identity matrix $\vec{I}_m$ be represented as

$$\vec{I}_m = (\vec{e}_1, \vec{e}_2, \ldots, \vec{e}_m)$$

where $\vec{e}_i$ is a unit column-vector with a one-element at the ith place and zero elements elsewhere. Also, let x_j and x_r be the entering and leaving variables. The next inverse $\vec{B}^{-1}_{next}$ can then be computed from the formula

$$\vec{B}^{-1}_{next} = \vec{E}\vec{B}^{-1}$$

where $$\vec{E} = (\vec{e}_1, \ldots, \vec{e}_{r-1}, \vec{\xi}, \vec{e}_{r+1}, \ldots, \vec{e}_m)$$

and $$\vec{\xi} = \begin{pmatrix} -\alpha_1^j/\alpha_r^j \\ -\alpha_2^j/\alpha_r^j \\ \cdot \\ \cdot \\ \cdot \\ +1/\alpha_r^j \\ \cdot \\ \cdot \\ \cdot \\ -\alpha_m^j/\alpha_r^j \end{pmatrix} \begin{matrix} \\ \\ \\ \\ \\ \leftarrow \text{ rth place} \\ \\ \\ \\ \\ \end{matrix}$$

where $\vec{\alpha}^j = \vec{B}^{-1}\vec{P}_j$. In other words, $\vec{E}$ is obtained from $\vec{I}_m$ by replacing its rth column-vector by $\vec{\xi}$.

The next basic solution is given by

$$x_0 = \vec{C}_B \vec{B}^{-1}_{next} \vec{P}_0 \quad \text{and} \quad \vec{X}_B = \vec{B}^{-1}_{next} \vec{P}_0$$

Let $\vec{B}^{-1} = \vec{B}^{-1}_{next}$, and define new $\vec{C}_B$ according to $\vec{X}_B$; then go to Step 1. Applying the revised simplex algorithm to the problem:

The starting basic solution is given by

$$\vec{X}_B = \begin{pmatrix} x_4 \\ x_5 \\ x_6 \end{pmatrix} = \begin{pmatrix} 430 \\ 460 \\ 420 \end{pmatrix}$$

Since

$$\vec{C}_B = (0,0,0) \quad \text{and} \quad \vec{B}^{-1} = \begin{pmatrix} 1 & 0 & 0 \\ 0 & 1 & 0 \\ 0 & 0 & 1 \end{pmatrix}$$

then

$$\vec{C}_B \vec{B}^{-1} = (0,0,0)$$

First Iteration:

Step 1. Computations of $(z_j - c_j)$ for $\vec{P}_1$, $\vec{P}_2$, and $\vec{P}_3$.

$$\{z_j - c_j\} = (1, \vec{C}_B \vec{B}^{-1}) \begin{pmatrix} -c_1 & -c_2 & -c_3 \\ \vec{P}_1 & \vec{P}_2 & \vec{P}_3 \end{pmatrix}$$

$$= (1,0,0,0) \begin{pmatrix} -3 & -2 & -5 \\ 1 & 2 & 1 \\ 3 & 0 & 2 \\ 1 & 4 & 0 \end{pmatrix} = (-3, -2, -5)$$

Hence $\vec{P}_3$ enters the solution.

Step 2. Determination of the leaving vector given the entering vector is $\vec{P}_3$.

$$\vec{\alpha}^3 = \begin{pmatrix} \alpha_4^3 \\ \alpha_5^3 \\ \alpha_6^3 \end{pmatrix} = \vec{B}^{-1} \vec{P}_3 = \begin{pmatrix} 1 & 0 & 0 \\ 0 & 1 & 0 \\ 0 & 0 & 1 \end{pmatrix} \begin{pmatrix} 1 \\ 2 \\ 0 \end{pmatrix} = \begin{pmatrix} 1 \\ 2 \\ 0 \end{pmatrix}$$

Hence, for k = 4, 5, and 6,

$$\theta = \min \left\{ \frac{430}{1}, \frac{460}{2}, \text{—} \right\} = 230$$

which corresponds to $\vec{P}_5$. Thus $\vec{P}_5$ leaves the solution.

Step 3. Determination of the new solution.

$$\vec{X}_B = (x_4, x_3, x_6)^T$$

$$\vec{C}_B = (0,5,0)$$

$$\vec{\xi} = \begin{pmatrix} -\alpha_4^3/\alpha_5^3 \\ +1/\alpha_5^3 \\ -\alpha_6^3/\alpha_5^3 \end{pmatrix} = \begin{pmatrix} -1/2 \\ +1/2 \\ -0/2 \end{pmatrix} = \begin{pmatrix} -1/2 \\ 1/2 \\ 0 \end{pmatrix}$$

Then

$$\vec{B}^{-1}_{next} = \vec{E}\vec{B}^{-1} = \begin{pmatrix} 1 & -1/2 & 0 \\ 0 & 1/2 & 0 \\ 0 & 0 & 1 \end{pmatrix} \begin{pmatrix} 1 & 0 & 0 \\ 0 & 1 & 0 \\ 0 & 0 & 1 \end{pmatrix} = \begin{pmatrix} 1 & -1/2 & 0 \\ 0 & 1/2 & 0 \\ 0 & 0 & 1 \end{pmatrix}$$

and

$$\vec{C}_B \vec{B}^{-1}_{next} = (0,5/2,0)$$

The new solution is

$$x_0 = (0,5/2,0)(430,460,420)^T = 1150$$

$$\vec{X}_B = \begin{pmatrix} x_4 \\ x_3 \\ x_6 \end{pmatrix} = \begin{pmatrix} 1 & -1/2 & 0 \\ 0 & 1/2 & 0 \\ 0 & 0 & 1 \end{pmatrix} \begin{pmatrix} 430 \\ 460 \\ 420 \end{pmatrix} = \begin{pmatrix} 200 \\ 230 \\ 420 \end{pmatrix}$$

Second Iteration:

Step 1. Computations of $z_j - c_j$ for $\vec{P}_1$, $\vec{P}_2$, and $\vec{P}_5$.

$$\{z_j - c_j\} = (1,0,5/2,0) \begin{pmatrix} -3 & -2 & 0 \\ 1 & 2 & 0 \\ 3 & 0 & 1 \\ 1 & 4 & 0 \end{pmatrix} = (9/2,-2,5/2)$$

And $\vec{P}_2$ is the entering vector.

Step 2. Determination of the leaving vector given the entering vector is $\vec{P}_2$.

$$\vec{\alpha}^2 = \begin{pmatrix} \alpha_4^2 \\ \alpha_3^2 \\ \alpha_6^2 \end{pmatrix} = \begin{pmatrix} 1 & -1/2 & 0 \\ 0 & 1/2 & 0 \\ 0 & 0 & 1 \end{pmatrix} \begin{pmatrix} 2 \\ 0 \\ 4 \end{pmatrix} = \begin{pmatrix} 2 \\ 0 \\ 4 \end{pmatrix}$$

Hence, for k = 4, 3, and 6,

$$\theta = \min\left\{\frac{200}{2}, \text{——}, \frac{420}{4}\right\} = 100$$

which corresponds to the leaving vector $\vec{P}_4$.

Step 3. Determination of the new solution.

$$\vec{X}_B = (x_2, x_3, x_6)^T$$

$$\vec{C}_B = (2,5,0)$$

$$\vec{\xi} = \begin{pmatrix} +1/\alpha_4^2 \\ -\alpha_3^2/\alpha_4^2 \\ -\alpha_6^2/\alpha_4^2 \end{pmatrix} = \begin{pmatrix} 1/2 \\ -0/2 \\ -4/2 \end{pmatrix} = \begin{pmatrix} 1/2 \\ 0 \\ -2 \end{pmatrix}$$

$$\vec{B}^{-1}_{next} = \begin{pmatrix} 1/2 & 0 & 0 \\ 0 & 1 & 0 \\ -2 & 0 & 1 \end{pmatrix}\begin{pmatrix} 1 & -1/2 & 0 \\ 0 & 1/2 & 0 \\ 0 & 0 & 1 \end{pmatrix} = \begin{pmatrix} 1/2 & -1/4 & 0 \\ 0 & 1/2 & 0 \\ -2 & 1 & 1 \end{pmatrix}$$

$$\vec{C}_B\vec{B}^{-1}_{next} = (1,2,0)$$

Then the new solution is

$$x_0 = (1,2,0)(430,460,420)^T = 1350$$

$$\vec{X}_B = \begin{pmatrix} x_2 \\ x_3 \\ x_6 \end{pmatrix} = \begin{pmatrix} 1/2 & -1/4 & 0 \\ 0 & 1/2 & 0 \\ -2 & 1 & 1 \end{pmatrix}\begin{pmatrix} 430 \\ 460 \\ 420 \end{pmatrix} = \begin{pmatrix} 100 \\ 230 \\ 20 \end{pmatrix}$$

Third Iteration:

Step 1. Computation of $z_j - c_j$ for $\vec{P}_1$, $\vec{P}_4$, and $\vec{P}_5$.

$$\{z_j - c_j\} = (1,1,2,0)\begin{pmatrix} -3 & 0 & 0 \\ 1 & 1 & 0 \\ 3 & 0 & 1 \\ 1 & 0 & 0 \end{pmatrix} = (4,1,2)$$

Since all $z_j - c_j > 0$, the last solution is optimal.

• PROBLEM 4-16

Consider the following problem:

$$\max x_0$$

subject to

$$x_0 \qquad + 2x_3 - 2x_4 - x_5 = 0,$$

$$x_1 \quad - 2x_3 + x_4 + x_5 = 4,$$

$$x_2 + 3x_3 - x_4 + 2x_5 = 2.$$

Solve by the Simplex Method and the Revised Simplex Method.

Tableau 1

	x_0	x_1	x_2	x_3	x_4	x_5	Constant
Cost row x_0	1			2	−2	−1	0
Basic x_1		1		−2	1	1	4
Variables x_2			1	3	−1	2	2

Tableau 2

	x_0	x_1	x_2	x_3	x_4	x_5	Constant
Cost row x_0	1			2	−2	−1	0
x_1		1		−2	1*	1	4
x_2			1	3	−1	2	2

Tableau 3

	x_0	x_1	x_2	x_3	x_4	x_5	Constant
Cost row x_0	1	2	0	−2	0	1	8
x_4	0	1	0	−2	1	1	4
x_2	0	1	1	1*	0	3	6

Tableau 4

	x_0	x_1	x_2	x_3	x_4	x_5	Constant	
Cost row x_0	1	4	2	0	0	7	20	$x_0 = 20$
x_4	0	3	2	0	1	7	16	$x_4 = 16$
x_3	0	1	1	1	0	3	6	$x_3 = 6$

Solution: The starting tableau is Tableau 1. The numerical solution by the simplex method is as shown in Tableaux 2, 3, and 4. Asterisks indicate pivots.

To show the general structure of the Revised Simplex algorithm, we shall rewrite only part of the starting tableau as if it were in the kth iteration and show how the rest of the tableaux can be generated from the present data (Tableau 5) and the starting tableau.

Tableau 5

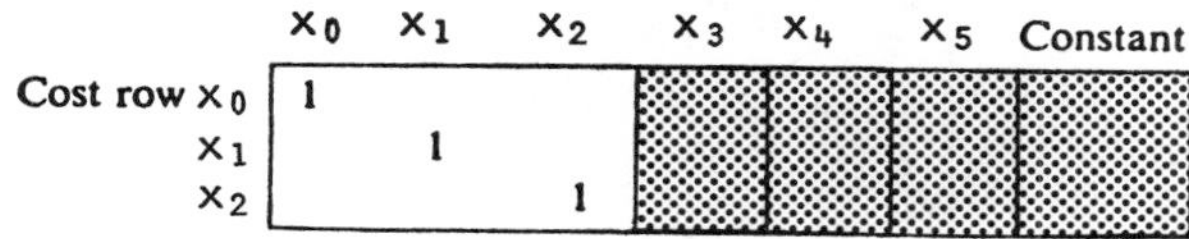

	x_0	x_1	x_2	x_3	x_4	x_5	Constant
Cost row x_0	1						
x_1		1					
x_2			1				

One gets

$$\vec{B}^* = \begin{bmatrix} 1 & 0 & 0 \\ 0 & 1 & 0 \\ 0 & 0 & 1 \end{bmatrix}$$

$$\bar{c}_3 = c_3 - \vec{\pi}\vec{a}_3 = \vec{\beta}_0[c_3, \vec{a}_3] = (1,0,0)[2,-2,3] = 2,$$

$$\bar{c}_4 = c_4 - \vec{\pi}\vec{a}_4 = (1,0,0)[-2,1,-1] = -2,$$

$$\bar{c}_5 = c_5 - \vec{\pi}\vec{a}_5 = (1,0,0)[-1,1,2] = -1.$$

Therefore, bring in $\vec{\bar{a}}_4^*$, where

$$\vec{\bar{a}}_4^* = \vec{B}^{*-1}\vec{a}_4^* = \begin{bmatrix} 1 & 0 & 0 \\ 0 & 1 & 0 \\ 0 & 0 & 1 \end{bmatrix} \begin{bmatrix} -2 \\ 1 \\ -1 \end{bmatrix} = \begin{bmatrix} -2 \\ 1 \\ -1 \end{bmatrix},$$

$$\vec{\bar{b}}^* = \vec{B}^{*-1}\vec{b}^* = \begin{bmatrix} 1 & 0 & 0 \\ 0 & 1 & 0 \\ 0 & 0 & 1 \end{bmatrix} \begin{bmatrix} 0 \\ 4 \\ 2 \end{bmatrix} = \begin{bmatrix} 0 \\ 4 \\ 2 \end{bmatrix}$$

Since in $\vec{\bar{a}}_4^*$, $\bar{a}_{14} = 1$ is the only positive coefficient, drop $\vec{a}_1$ from the basis. Using row elimination with $\bar{a}_{14}$ as the pivot is equivalent to multiplying on the left by

$$\begin{bmatrix} 1 & -(-2/1) & 0 \\ 0 & +(1/1) & 0 \\ 0 & -(-1/1) & 1 \end{bmatrix} = \begin{bmatrix} 1 & 2 & 0 \\ 0 & 1 & 0 \\ 0 & 1 & 1 \end{bmatrix},$$

$$\begin{bmatrix} 1 & 2 & 0 \\ 0 & 1 & 0 \\ 0 & 1 & 1 \end{bmatrix} \left[\begin{array}{ccc|c} 1 & 0 & 0 & 0 \\ 0 & 1 & 0 & 4 \\ 0 & 0 & 1 & 2 \end{array}\right] = \left[\begin{array}{ccc|c} 1 & 2 & 0 & 8 \\ 0 & 1 & 0 & 4 \\ 0 & 1 & 1 & 6 \end{array}\right] = [\vec{B}^{*-1} | \vec{b}^*].$$

Therefore, the new tableau is Tableau 6. Now the inverse of the new basis is

$$\begin{bmatrix} 1 & 2 & 0 \\ 0 & 1 & 0 \\ 0 & 1 & 1 \end{bmatrix},$$

$$\bar{c}_1 = (1,2,0)[0,1,0] = 2,$$

$$\bar{c}_3 = (1,2,0)[2,-2,3] = -2,$$

$$\bar{c}_5 = (1,2,0)[-1,1,2] = 1.$$

As a check

$$\bar{c}_2 = (1,2,0)[0,0,1] = 0,$$

$$\bar{c}_4 = (1,2,0)[-2,1,-1] = 0.$$

Tableau 6

	x_0	x_1	x_2	x_3	x_4	x_5	Constant
Cost row	**1**	**2**	**0**				**8**
x_4	**0**	**1**	**0**				**4**
x_2	**0**	**1**	**1**				**6**

Therefore, bring $\vec{a}_3$ into the basis:

$$\vec{a}_3^* = \begin{bmatrix} 1 & 2 & 0 \\ 0 & 1 & 0 \\ 0 & 1 & 1 \end{bmatrix} \begin{bmatrix} 2 \\ -2 \\ 3 \end{bmatrix} = \begin{bmatrix} -2 \\ -2 \\ 1 \end{bmatrix}$$

Since $\bar{a}_{23} = 1$ is the only positive element, $\vec{a}_2$ should be dropped. Using row elimination with $\bar{a}_{23}$ as pivot is equivalent to multiplying the matrix on the left by

$$\begin{bmatrix} 1 & 0 & -(-2/1) \\ 0 & 1 & -(-2/1) \\ 0 & 0 & (1/1) \end{bmatrix} = \begin{bmatrix} 1 & 0 & 2 \\ 0 & 1 & 2 \\ 0 & 0 & 1 \end{bmatrix},$$

$$\begin{bmatrix} 1 & 0 & 2 \\ 0 & 1 & 2 \\ 0 & 0 & 1 \end{bmatrix} \left[\begin{array}{ccc|c} 1 & 2 & 0 & 8 \\ 0 & 1 & 0 & 4 \\ 0 & 1 & 1 & 6 \end{array}\right] = \left[\begin{array}{ccc|c} 1 & 4 & 2 & 20 \\ 0 & 3 & 2 & 16 \\ 0 & 1 & 1 & 6 \end{array}\right],$$

$$\bar{c}_1 = (1,4,2)[0,1,0] = 4,$$

$$\bar{c}_2 = (1,4,2)[0,0,1] = 2,$$

$$\bar{c}_5 = (1,4,2)[-1,1,2] = 7.$$

As a check

$$\bar{c}_3 = (1,4,2)[2,-2,3] = 0,$$

$$\bar{c}_4 = (1,4,2)[-2,1,-1] = 0.$$

One obtains as an optimum solution $x_0 = 20$, $x_4 = 16$, $x_3 = 6$. Note that in the Revised Simplex method one need not calculate all $\bar{c}_j$. Once a $\bar{c}_j < 0$ is found, one can immediately bring the column into the basis.

Maximize $z = .56x_1 + .42x_2$

subject to:

$$x_1 + 2x_2 + x_3 = 240,000$$
$$1.5x_1 + x_2 + x_4 = 180,000$$
$$x_1 + x_5 = 110,000$$
$$x_j \geq 0, j = 1,\dots,5$$

Use the Revised Simplex method to solve.

Solution: The following vectors and matrices are defined:

$$\vec{A} = \begin{bmatrix} 1 & 2 & 1 & 0 & 0 \\ 1.5 & 1 & 0 & 1 & 0 \\ 1 & 0 & 0 & 0 & 1 \end{bmatrix} \qquad \vec{b} = \begin{bmatrix} 240,000 \\ 180,000 \\ 110,000 \end{bmatrix}$$

$$\vec{c}' = (.56 \quad .42 \quad 0 \quad 0 \quad 0)$$

$$\vec{B} = \begin{bmatrix} 1 & 0 & 0 \\ 0 & 1 & 0 \\ 0 & 0 & 1 \end{bmatrix} \qquad \vec{x}_B = \begin{bmatrix} x_3 \\ x_4 \\ x_5 \end{bmatrix} \qquad \vec{c}_B = \begin{bmatrix} 0 \\ 0 \\ 0 \end{bmatrix}$$

$$\vec{B}^{-1} = \begin{bmatrix} 1 & 0 & 0 \\ 0 & 1 & 0 \\ 0 & 0 & 1 \end{bmatrix}$$

Iteration 1: Compute

$$\vec{\pi}' = \vec{c}'_B\vec{B}^{-1} = (0 \ 0 \ 0) \begin{bmatrix} 1 & 0 & 0 \\ 0 & 1 & 0 \\ 0 & 0 & 1 \end{bmatrix} = (0 \ 0 \ 0)$$

Evaluate only nonbasic variables:

for x_1: $$z_1 - c_1 = \vec{\pi}'\vec{a}_1 - c_1 = (0 \ 0 \ 0) \begin{bmatrix} 1 \\ 1.5 \\ 1 \end{bmatrix} - .56 = -.56$$

for x_2: $$z_2 - c_2 = \vec{\pi}'\vec{a}_2 - c_2 = (0 \ 0 \ 0) \begin{bmatrix} 2 \\ 1 \\ 0 \end{bmatrix} - .42 = -.42$$

Choose x_1 to enter the basis, since $-.56$ is $\text{Min}(\vec{\pi}'\vec{a}_j - c_j)$. Now compute

$$y = \vec{B}^{-1}\vec{a}_1 = \begin{bmatrix} 1 & 0 & 0 \\ 0 & 1 & 0 \\ 0 & 0 & 1 \end{bmatrix} \begin{bmatrix} 1 \\ 1.5 \\ 1 \end{bmatrix} = \begin{bmatrix} 1 \\ 1.5 \\ 1 \end{bmatrix}$$

Recalling that

$$\vec{b} = \begin{bmatrix} 240,000 \\ 180,000 \\ 110,000 \end{bmatrix}$$

for positive y_j, compute $\theta = b_i/y_i$; choose the minimum

$i = 1,\quad \theta = 240,000/1 \quad = 240,000$

$i = 2,\quad \theta = 180,000/1.5 = 120,000$

$i = 3,\quad \theta = 110,000/1 \quad = 110,000$ → Choose Minimum

Therefore set r = 3.

Determine new inverse and new $\vec{b}$.

$\vec{c}_B$	$\vec{x}_B$	$\vec{b}$	*Old Inverse*	$\vec{y}$
0	x_3	240,000	1 0 0	1
0	x_4	180,000	0 1 0	1.5
0	x_5	110,000	0 0 1	[1]

The entries for the new $\vec{b}$ and the new inverse are found in precisely the same manner as in the Simplex method--by using row operations.

$\vec{c}_B$	$\vec{x}_B$	*New* $\vec{b}$	*New Inverse*	$\vec{y}$	*y for next iteration*
0	x_3	130,000	1 0 −1	0	2
0	x_4	15,000	0 1 −1.5	0	[1]
.56	x_1	110,000	0 0 1	1	0

Iteration 2: Compute

$$\vec{\pi}' = \vec{c}_B'\vec{B}^{-1} = (0 \quad 0 \quad .56) \begin{bmatrix} 1 & 0 & -1 \\ 0 & 1 & -1.5 \\ 0 & 0 & 1 \end{bmatrix} = (0 \quad 0 \quad .56)$$

Evaluate nonbasic variables:

for x_2: $$z_2 - c_2 = \vec{\pi}'\vec{a}_2 - c_2 = (0 \ 0 \ .56) \begin{bmatrix} 2 \\ 1 \\ 0 \end{bmatrix} - .42 = -.42$$

for x_5: $$z_5 - c_5 = \vec{\pi}'\vec{a}_5 - c_5 = (0 \ 0 \ .56) \begin{bmatrix} 0 \\ 0 \\ 1 \end{bmatrix} - 0 = .56$$

Choose x_2 to enter the basis, since −.42 is the minimum $(z_j - c_j)$. Since $-.42 < 0$, compute

$$\vec{y} = \vec{B}^{-1}\vec{a}_2 = \begin{bmatrix} 1 & 0 & -1 \\ 0 & 1 & -1.5 \\ 0 & 0 & 1 \end{bmatrix} \begin{bmatrix} 2 \\ 1 \\ 0 \end{bmatrix} = \begin{bmatrix} 2 \\ 1 \\ 0 \end{bmatrix}$$

Now x_4 is chosen to leave the basis. The iteration is performed to yield the following:

$\vec{c}_B$	$\vec{x}_B$	New $\vec{b}$	New Inverse	$\vec{y}$	$\vec{y}$ for next iteration
0	x_3	100,000	1 −2 2	0	[2]
.42	x_2	15,000	0 1 −1.5	1	−1.5
.56	x_1	110,000	0 0 1	0	1

Iteration 3: Compute

$$\vec{\pi}' = \vec{c}_B'\vec{B}^{-1} = (0 \quad .42 \quad .56)\begin{bmatrix}1 & -2 & 2\\0 & 1 & -1.5\\0 & 0 & 1\end{bmatrix} = (0 \quad .42 \quad -.07)$$

Evaluate nonbasic variables:

$$\text{for } x_4\text{: } z_4 - c_4 = \vec{\pi}'\vec{a}_4 - c_4 = (0 \quad .42 \quad -.07)\begin{bmatrix}0\\1\\0\end{bmatrix} - 0 = .42$$

$$\text{for } x_5\text{: } z_5 - c_5 = \vec{\pi}'\vec{a}_5 - c_5 = (0 \quad .42 \quad -.07)\begin{bmatrix}0\\0\\1\end{bmatrix} - 0 = -.07$$

Choose x_5 to enter the basis. Compute

$$\vec{y} = \vec{B}^{-1}\vec{a}_5 = \begin{bmatrix}1 & -2 & 2\\0 & 1 & -1.5\\0 & 0 & 1\end{bmatrix}\begin{bmatrix}0\\0\\1\end{bmatrix} = \begin{bmatrix}2\\-1.5\\1\end{bmatrix}$$

Next x_3 is chosen to leave the basis, because its ratio b_i/y_i for $y_i > 0$ is minimum.

The iteration is now performed to yield the following:

$\vec{c}_B$	$\vec{x}_B$	New $\vec{b}$	New Inverse	$\vec{y}$
0	x_5	50,000	.5 −1 1	1
.42	x_2	90,000	.75 −.5 0	0
.56	x_1	60,000	−.5 1 0	0

Because the solution is optimal there is no $\vec{y}$ for the next iteration.

Iteration 4: Compute

$$\vec{\pi}' = \vec{c}_B'\vec{B}^{-1} = (0 \ .42 \ .56)\begin{bmatrix}.5 & -1 & 1\\.75 & -.5 & 0\\-.5 & 1 & 0\end{bmatrix} = (.035 \ .35 \ 0)$$

Evaluate nonbasic variables:

$$\text{for } x_3\text{: } z_3 - c_3 = \vec{\pi}'\vec{a}_3 - c_3 = (.035 \ .35 \ 0)\begin{bmatrix}1\\0\\0\end{bmatrix} - 0 = .035$$

$$\text{for } x_4\text{: } z_4 - c_4 = \vec{\pi}'\vec{a}_4 - c_4 = (.035 \ .35 \ 0)\begin{bmatrix}0\\1\\0\end{bmatrix} - 0 = .35$$

The solution is optimal; no further iterations are required. The optimal solution has the objective function value

$$\vec{c}_B'\vec{B}^{-1}\vec{b} = (0\ .42\ .56)\begin{bmatrix}50,000\\90,000\\60,000\end{bmatrix} = 71,400$$

• PROBLEM 4-18

Assume the following tableau.

	V_0	P_1	P_2	P_3	P_4	P_5	b
Row 0	1	1	-3	2	0	0	0
Row 1	0	3	-1	2	1	0	7
Row 2	0	-2	4	0	0	1	12

Solve using the Revised Simplex method.

Solution: First Iteration.

Step I. Initially $B_0 = I$.

$$z_j - c_j = (B_0^{-1})_0 \begin{bmatrix}c_j\\ \bar{P}_j\end{bmatrix} \quad \text{for } j = 1,2,3$$

$$= \begin{bmatrix}1 & 0 & 0\end{bmatrix}\begin{bmatrix}1 & -3 & 2\\3 & -1 & 2\\-2 & 4 & 0\end{bmatrix} = (1,-3,2)$$

Hence the vector associated with x_2 enters the basis since the only negative $z_j - c_j$ component is $z_2 - c_2$.

Step II. Next determine θ_r the minimum nonnegative ratio of the right-hand coefficients to the positive components of the updated vector P_2.

Thus

$$B_0^{-1}\begin{bmatrix}-c_2\\ \bar{P}_2\end{bmatrix} = \begin{bmatrix}-3\\-1\\4\end{bmatrix} \qquad B_0^{-1}\begin{bmatrix}0\\7\\12\end{bmatrix} = \begin{bmatrix}0\\7\\12\end{bmatrix}$$

Therefore $\theta_r = \min(12/4)$ with $r = 2$, and the pivot element is 4.

Step III.

$$\eta = \frac{1}{x_{rk}} \begin{bmatrix} -(z_k - c_k) \\ -x_{1k} \\ \vdots \\ 1 \\ -x_{r+1,k} \\ \vdots \end{bmatrix}$$

$$\eta_1 = \frac{1}{4} \begin{bmatrix} -(-3) \\ -(-1) \\ 1 \end{bmatrix} = \begin{bmatrix} 3/4 \\ 1/4 \\ 1/4 \end{bmatrix}$$

so that

$$E_1 = \begin{bmatrix} 1 & 0 & 3/4 \\ 0 & 1 & 1/4 \\ 0 & 0 & 1/4 \end{bmatrix}$$

and $B_1^{-1} = E_1 B_0^{-1} = E_1$. This completes one iteration.

Second Iteration

Step I. Now x_1, x_3, and x_5 are nonbasic, and one gets the following consequences

$$(B_1^{-1})_0 \begin{bmatrix} -c_1 \\ \bar{P}_1 \end{bmatrix} = [1,0,3/4] \begin{bmatrix} 1 \\ 3 \\ -2 \end{bmatrix} = -1/2 \quad \text{for } j = 1$$

$$(B_1^{-1})_0 \begin{bmatrix} -c_3 \\ \bar{P}_3 \end{bmatrix} = 2 \quad \text{for } j = 3$$

$$(B_1^{-1})_0 \begin{bmatrix} -c_5 \\ \bar{P}_5 \end{bmatrix} = 3/4 \quad \text{for } j = 5$$

implying that P_1 enters the basis.

Step II.

$$B_1^{-1} \begin{bmatrix} -c_1 \\ \bar{P}_1 \end{bmatrix} = \begin{bmatrix} 1 & 0 & 3/4 \\ 0 & 1 & 1/4 \\ 0 & 0 & 1/4 \end{bmatrix} \begin{bmatrix} 1 \\ 3 \\ -2 \end{bmatrix} = \begin{bmatrix} -1/2 \\ 5/2 \\ -1/2 \end{bmatrix}$$

and the updated right-hand side is

$$B_1^{-1}P_0 = \begin{bmatrix} 9 \\ 10 \\ 3 \end{bmatrix}$$

giving $\theta_r = \theta_1 = 4$.

Step III.

$$\eta_2 = \frac{2}{5}\begin{bmatrix} -(-1/2) \\ 1 \\ -(-1/2) \end{bmatrix} = \begin{bmatrix} 1/5 \\ 2/5 \\ 1/5 \end{bmatrix} \qquad E_2 = \begin{bmatrix} 1 & 1/5 & 0 \\ 0 & 2/5 & 0 \\ 0 & 1/5 & 1 \end{bmatrix}$$

Therefore

$$B_2^{-1} = E_2 B_1^{-1}$$

$$= \begin{bmatrix} 1 & 1/5 & 0 \\ 0 & 2/5 & 0 \\ 0 & 1/5 & 1 \end{bmatrix}\begin{bmatrix} 1 & 0 & 3/4 \\ 0 & 1 & 1/4 \\ 0 & 0 & 1/4 \end{bmatrix} = \begin{bmatrix} 1 & 1/5 & 4/5 \\ 0 & 2/5 & 1/10 \\ 0 & 1/5 & 3/10 \end{bmatrix}$$

This completes the second iteration.

Third Iteration

Step I. The nonbasic variables are x_3, x_4, and x_5. Hence

$$(B_2^{-1})_0 \begin{bmatrix} -c_3 \\ \bar{P}_3 \end{bmatrix} = [1, 1/5, 4/5]\begin{bmatrix} 2 \\ 2 \\ 0 \end{bmatrix} = 12/5 \quad \text{for } j = 3$$

$$(B_2^{-1})_0 \begin{bmatrix} -c_4 \\ \bar{P}_4 \end{bmatrix} = 1/5 \quad \text{for } j = 4$$

$$(B_2^{-1})_0 \begin{bmatrix} -c_5 \\ \bar{P}_5 \end{bmatrix} = 4/5 \quad \text{for } j = 5$$

Since all $z_j - c_j$ are nonnegative, an optimal solution is given by

$$\begin{bmatrix} z^0 \\ x^0 \end{bmatrix} = B_2^{-1}\begin{bmatrix} 0 \\ b \end{bmatrix} = \begin{bmatrix} 1 & 1/5 & 4/5 \\ 0 & 2/5 & 1/10 \\ 0 & 1/5 & 3/10 \end{bmatrix}\begin{bmatrix} 0 \\ 7 \\ 12 \end{bmatrix} = \begin{bmatrix} 11 \\ 4 \\ 5 \end{bmatrix}$$

• PROBLEM 4-19

Maximize $3x_1 + 5x_2$

subject to

$$x_1 \leq 4$$

$$3x_1 + 2x_2 \leq 18$$

$$x_1, \; x_2 \geq 0$$

Use the Revised Simplex method to solve.

Solution: Converting the problem to tableau form, after introducing two slack variables x_3^S and x_4^S, one obtains

$$\begin{array}{llr} \text{Row } 0 & z_0 - 3x_1 - 5x_2 & = 0 \\ \text{Row } 1 & x_1 + x_3^S & = 4 \\ \text{Row } 2 & 3x_1 + 2x_2 + x_4^S & = 18 \end{array}$$

Since $z_2 - c_2 = -5$, the vector associated with x_2 enters the basis and the vector associated with x_4 leaves the basis, giving the final tableau.

$$\begin{array}{llr} \text{Row } 0 & z_0 + (9/2)x_1 + (5/2)x_4^S & = 45 \\ \text{Row } 1 & x_1 + x_3^S & = 4 \\ \text{Row } 2 & (3/2)x_1 + x_2 \quad (1/2)x_4^S & = 9 \end{array}$$

In this problem

$$\vec{\eta} = \frac{1}{x_{rk}} \begin{bmatrix} -(z_k - c_k) \\ -x_{1k} \\ \cdot \\ \cdot \\ \cdot \\ 1 \\ -x_{r+1,k} \\ \cdot \\ \cdot \\ \cdot \end{bmatrix}$$

$$\vec{\eta}_1 = \frac{1}{2} \begin{bmatrix} -(-5) \\ -0 \\ 1 \end{bmatrix} = \begin{bmatrix} 5/2 \\ 0 \\ 1/2 \end{bmatrix}$$

since the pivot element is 2 and $\vec{\eta}$ is constructed from the vector corresponding to P. Hence

$$\vec{B} = \begin{bmatrix} 1 & 0 & 3/2 \\ 0 & 1 & 0 \\ 0 & 0 & 1/2 \end{bmatrix}$$

where $\vec{\eta}$ is positioned in the rth column of $\vec{E}$ and r is the basic row of the leaving variable. In this case, $\vec{E} = \vec{B}_1^{-1}$, which corresponds to vectors $\vec{V}_0$, $\vec{P}_4$, and $\vec{P}_2$ in the final tableau.

• PROBLEM 4-20

Maximize $3x_1 + x_2 + 3x_3$ subject to

$$2x_1 + x_2 + x_3 \le 2$$

$$x_1 + 2x_2 + 3x_3 \le 5$$

$$2x_1 + 2x_2 + x_3 \le 6$$

$$x_1 \ge 0, \quad x_2 \ge 0, \quad x_3 \ge 0.$$

Solve by the Revised Simplex method.

Solution: Start with an initial basic feasible solution and corresponding $\vec{B}^{-1}$ as shown in the tableau below

Variable	$\vec{B}^{-1}$			$\vec{x}_B$
4	1	0	0	2
5	0	1	0	5
6	0	0	1	6

Compute

$$\vec{\lambda} = [0,0,0]\vec{B}^{-1} = [0,0,0]$$

and then

$$\vec{c}_D - \lambda\vec{D} = [-3,-1,-3].$$

Decide to bring $\vec{a}_2$ into the basis in order to simplify the calculation (although it violates the rule of selecting the most negative relative cost). Its current representation is found by multiplying $\vec{B}^{-1}$; thus one gets

Variable	$\vec{B}^{-1}$			$\vec{x}_B$	$\vec{y}_2$
4	1	0	0	2	(1)
5	0	1	0	5	2
6	0	0	1	6	2

After computing the ratios using the formula y_{io}/y_{ij} (where $y_{20} = 1$, $y_{21} = 1$, $y_{22} = 2$, $y_{23} = 2$), select the pivot indicated. The updated tableau becomes

Variable	$\vec{B}^{-1}$			$\vec{x}_B$
2	1	0	0	2
5	-2	1	0	1
6	-2	0	1	2

then

$$\vec{\lambda} = [-1,0,0]\vec{B}^{-1} = [-1,0,0]$$

$$c_1 - z_1 = -1, \quad c_3 - z_3 = -2, \quad c_4 - z_4 = 1.$$

Select $\vec{a}_3$ to enter. The tableau obtained is

Variable	$\vec{B}^{-1}$			$\vec{x}_B$	$\vec{y}_3$
2	1	0	0	2	1
5	-2	1	0	1	(1)
6	-2	0	1	2	-1

Using the pivot indicated, obtain

Variable	$\vec{B}^{-1}$			$\vec{x}_B$
2	3	-1	0	1
3	-2	1	0	1
6	-4	1	1	3

Now

$$\vec{\lambda} = [-1,-3,0]\vec{B}^{-1} = [3,-2,0]$$

and

$$c_1 - z_1 = -7, \quad c_4 - z_4 = -3, \quad c_5 - z_5 = 2.$$

Select $\vec{a}_1$ to enter the basis. The tableau is

Variable	$\vec{B}^{-1}$			$\vec{x}_B$	$\vec{y}_1$
2	3	-1	0	1	(5)
3	-2	1	0	1	-3
6	-4	1	1	3	-5

Using the pivot indicated, obtain

Variable	$\vec{B}^{-1}$			$\vec{x}_B$
1	3/5	-1/5	0	1/5
3	-1/5	2/5	0	8/5
6	-1	0	1	4

Now

$$\vec{\lambda} = [-3,-3,0]\vec{B}^{-1} = [-6/5,-3/5,0]$$

and

$$c_2 - z_2 = 7/5, \quad c_4 - z_4 = 6/5, \quad c_5 - z_5 = 3/5.$$

Since the $c_i - z_i$'s are all nonnegative, the solution $\vec{x} = (1/5,0,8/5,0,0,4)$ is optimal.

• PROBLEM 4-21

Maximize $x_1 + 2x_2 + 3x_3 - x_4$

subject to

$$x_1 + 2x_2 + 3x_3 = 15$$

$$2x_1 + x_2 + 5x_3 = 20$$

$$x_1 + 2x_2 + x_3 + x_4 = 10$$

and $x_j \geq 0$.

Solve by the Revised Simplex method.

Solution: Here m = 3 and n = 4. The objective function for the corresponding minimization problem is $-x_1 - 2x_2 - 3x_3 + x_4$.

For the revised procedure with a full artificial basis rewrite the problem to read: Maximize

$$x_8$$

subject to

$$\begin{aligned}
x_1 + 2x_2 + 3x_3 \quad\quad + x_5 \quad\quad\quad\quad\quad\quad &= 15 \\
2x_1 + x_2 + 5x_3 \quad\quad\quad + x_6 \quad\quad\quad\quad &= 20 \\
x_1 + 2x_2 + x_3 + x_4 \quad\quad\quad + x_7 \quad\quad &= 10 \\
-x_1 - 2x_2 - 3x_3 + x_4 \quad\quad\quad\quad + x_8 \quad &= 0 \\
-4x_1 - 5x_2 - 9x_3 - x_4 \quad\quad\quad\quad\quad + x_9 &= -45
\end{aligned}$$

The coefficients of the first four variables for the fourth row are equal to the corresponding c_j as written in the original objective function to be minimized. The coefficients of variables x_1, x_2, x_3, x_4 and the right side of the fifth equation were obtained by the formula

$$a_{m+2,1}x_1 + a_{m+2,2}x_2 + \ldots + a_{m+2,n}x_n + x_{m+n+2} = b_{m+2}$$

where

$$a_{m+2,j} = -\sum_{i=1}^{m} a_{ij} \; (j=1,2,\ldots n), \quad b_{m+2} = -\sum_{i=1}^{m} b_i$$

The $\bar{A}$ and U matrices for the problem are

$$\bar{A} = \begin{pmatrix} 1 & 2 & 3 & 0 \\ 2 & 1 & 5 & 0 \\ 1 & 2 & 1 & 1 \\ -1 & -2 & -3 & 1 \\ -4 & -5 & -9 & -1 \end{pmatrix}$$

and

$$U = \begin{pmatrix} 1 & 0 & 0 & 0 & 0 \\ 0 & 1 & 0 & 0 & 0 \\ 0 & 0 & 1 & 0 & 0 \\ 0 & 0 & 0 & 1 & 0 \\ 0 & 0 & 0 & 0 & 1 \end{pmatrix}$$

The starting tableau and the sequence of iterations are as shown.

Row index of tableau	Index of variables in solution	Value of variables	Matrix U					x_{ik}
1. Starting Tableau								
1	5	15	1	0	0	0	0	3
2	6	20	0	1	0	0	0	**(5)**
3	7	10	0	0	1	0	0	1
4	8	0	0	0	0	1	0	-3
5	9	-45	0	0	0	0	1	-9
2. Second Iteration								
1	5	3	1	$-\frac{3}{5}$	0	0	0	**($\frac{7}{5}$)**
2	3	4	0	$\frac{1}{5}$	0	0	0	$\frac{1}{5}$
3	7	6	0	$-\frac{1}{5}$	1	0	0	$\frac{9}{5}$
4	8	$+12$	0	$\frac{3}{5}$	0	1	0	$-\frac{7}{5}$
5	9	-9	0	$\frac{9}{5}$	0	0	1	$-\frac{16}{5}$
3. Third Iteration								
1	2	$\frac{15}{7}$	$\frac{5}{7}$	$-\frac{3}{7}$	0	0	0	0
2	3	$\frac{25}{7}$	$-\frac{1}{7}$	$\frac{2}{7}$	0	0	0	0
3	7	$\frac{15}{7}$	$-\frac{9}{7}$	$\frac{4}{7}$	1	0	0	**(1)**
4	8	$+15$	1	0	0	1	0	1
5	9	$-\frac{15}{7}$	$\frac{16}{7}$	$\frac{3}{7}$	0	0	1	-1
4. Fourth Iteration								
1	2	$\frac{15}{7}$	$\frac{5}{7}$	$-\frac{3}{7}$	0	0	0	$-\frac{1}{7}$
2	3	$\frac{25}{7}$	$-\frac{1}{7}$	$\frac{2}{7}$	0	0	0	$\frac{3}{7}$
3	4	$\frac{15}{7}$	$-\frac{9}{7}$	$\frac{4}{7}$	1	0	0	**($\frac{6}{7}$)**
4	8	$+\frac{90}{7}$	$\frac{16}{7}$	$-\frac{4}{7}$	-1	1	0	$-\frac{6}{7}$
5	9	0	1	1	1	0	1	0
5. Fifth Iteration								
1	2	$\frac{5}{2}$	$\frac{3}{6}$	$-\frac{2}{6}$	$\frac{1}{6}$	0	0	
2	3	$\frac{5}{2}$	$\frac{3}{6}$	0	$-\frac{3}{6}$	0	0	
3	1	$\frac{5}{2}$	$-\frac{9}{6}$	$\frac{4}{6}$	$\frac{7}{6}$	0	0	
4	8	$+15$	1	0	0	1	0	
5	9	0	1	1	1	0	1	

Phase I

$$\delta_k = \delta_3 = U_{m+2}\bar{A}_3 = -9$$

$$\theta_0 = \frac{x_6}{x_{63}} = \frac{20}{5} = 4$$

$$\delta_k = \delta_2 = U_{m+2}\bar{A}_2 = -\frac{16}{5}$$

$$\theta_0 = \frac{x_5}{x_{52}} = \frac{15}{7}$$

$$\delta_k = \delta_4 = U_{m+2}\bar{A}_4 = -1$$

$$\theta_0 = \frac{x_7}{x_{74}} = \frac{15}{7}$$

Phase II

$$x_9 = 0$$

$$\gamma_k = \gamma_1 = U_{m+1}\bar{A}_1 = -\frac{6}{7}$$

$$\theta_0 = \frac{x_4}{x_{41}} = \frac{5}{2}$$

All $\gamma_i \geq 0$

Optimum solution:

$$x_1 = x_2 = x_3 = \frac{5}{2}, x_4 = 0$$

Value of objective function:

$$x_8 = 15$$

• PROBLEM 4-22

> Minimize $x_1 + x_2 + x_3$
>
> subject to
> $$\begin{aligned} x_1 \quad - x_4 \quad\quad - 2x_6 &= 5, \\ x_2 + 2x_4 - 3x_5 + x_6 &= 3, \\ x_3 + 2x_4 - 5x_5 + 6x_6 &= 5; \end{aligned}$$
> $$x_j \geq 0,\ 1 \leq j \leq 6.$$
>
> Use the Revised Simplex method.

Solution: Here
$$\vec{A} = \begin{bmatrix} 1 & 0 & 0 & -1 & 0 & -2 \\ 0 & 1 & 0 & 2 & -3 & 1 \\ 0 & 0 & 1 & 2 & -5 & 6 \end{bmatrix}$$

$$\vec{B} = [5 \quad 3 \quad 5]', \quad \vec{C} = [1 \quad 1 \quad 1 \quad 0 \quad 0 \quad 0]$$

Iteration 1. A b.f.s. which provides the starting point is

$$x_1 = 5,\ x_2 = 3,\ x_3 = 5,\ x_4 = x_5 = x_6 = 0,$$

with $\vec{A}_0^{-1} = \vec{A}_0 = \begin{bmatrix} 1 & 0 & 0 \\ 0 & 1 & 0 \\ 0 & 0 & 1 \end{bmatrix}$, $\vec{C}_0 = [1 \quad 1 \quad 1]$.

$$[\pi_1 \quad \pi_2 \quad \pi_3] = -\vec{C}_0\vec{A}_0^{-1} = [-1 \quad -1 \quad -1].$$

$$c_4' = c_4 + \sum_{i=1}^{3} a_{i4}\pi_i = -3,$$

$$c_5' = c_5 + \sum_{i=1}^{3} a_{i5}\pi_i = 8,$$

$$c_6' = c_6 + \sum_{i=1}^{3} a_{i6}\pi_i = -5.$$

Since c_6' is negative, choose $r = 6$. As $\vec{A}_0^{-1}$ is a unit matrix, from

$$\begin{bmatrix} a_{1r}' \\ a_{2r}' \\ \cdot \\ \cdot \\ \cdot \\ a_{mr}' \end{bmatrix} = \vec{A}_0^{-1} \begin{bmatrix} a_{1r} \\ a_{2r} \\ \cdot \\ \cdot \\ \cdot \\ a_{mr} \end{bmatrix}, \quad \begin{bmatrix} b_1' \\ b_2' \\ \cdot \\ \cdot \\ \cdot \\ b_m' \end{bmatrix} = \vec{A}_0^{-1} \begin{bmatrix} b_1 \\ b_2 \\ \cdot \\ \cdot \\ \cdot \\ b_m \end{bmatrix}$$

$$[a_{16}' \quad a_{26}' \quad a_{36}'] = [a_{16} \quad a_{26} \quad a_{36}] = [-2 \quad 1 \quad 6],$$

and $[b_1' \quad b_2' \quad b_3'] = [b_1 \quad b_2 \quad b_3] = [5 \quad 3 \quad 5]$.

Now $\min b_i'/a_{i6}' = b_3'/a_{36}'$. So choose $p = 3$.

Hence, from

$$\vec{E}_p = \begin{bmatrix} 1 & 0 & \cdots & -a_{1r}'/a_{pr}' & \cdots & 0 \\ 0 & 1 & \cdots & -a_{2r}'/a_{pr}' & \cdots & 0 \\ \cdot & \cdot & \cdots & \cdot\cdot \quad \cdot\cdot & \cdots & \cdot \\ 0 & 0 & \cdots & 1/a_{pr}' & \cdots & 0 \\ \cdot & \cdot & \cdots & \cdot\cdot \quad \cdot\cdot & \cdots & \cdot \\ 0 & 0 & \cdots & -a_{mr}'/a_{pr}' & \cdots & 1 \end{bmatrix},$$

$$\vec{E}_p = \begin{bmatrix} 1 & 0 & 2/6 \\ 0 & 1 & -1/6 \\ 0 & 0 & 1/6 \end{bmatrix}$$

Iteration 2. The new basis is x_1, x_2, x_6 with new $\vec{A}_0^{-1}$ given by

$$\vec{A}_{0r}^{-1} = \vec{E}_p \vec{A}_{0p}^{-1}$$

as

$$\vec{A}_0^{-1} = \begin{bmatrix} 1 & 0 & 2/6 \\ 0 & 1 & -1/6 \\ 0 & 0 & 1/6 \end{bmatrix}$$

The new $\vec{C}_0$ is $[1 \quad 1 \quad 0]$.

Now $[\pi_1 \quad \pi_2 \quad \pi_3] = [-1 \quad -1 \quad -1/6]$, and so $c_3' = 5/6$, $c_4' = -8/6$, $c_5' = 23/6$. c_4' is negative. So $r = 4$.

$$\begin{bmatrix} a_{14}' \\ a_{24}' \\ a_{34}' \end{bmatrix} = \begin{bmatrix} 1 & 0 & 2/6 \\ 0 & 1 & -1/6 \\ 0 & 0 & 1/6 \end{bmatrix} \begin{bmatrix} -1 \\ 2 \\ 2 \end{bmatrix} = \begin{bmatrix} -1/3 \\ 5/3 \\ 1/3 \end{bmatrix}$$

$$\begin{bmatrix} b_1' \\ b_2' \\ b_3' \end{bmatrix} = \begin{bmatrix} 1 & 0 & 2/6 \\ 0 & 1 & -1/6 \\ 0 & 0 & 1/6 \end{bmatrix} \begin{bmatrix} 5 \\ 3 \\ 5 \end{bmatrix} = \begin{bmatrix} 40/6 \\ 13/6 \\ 5/6 \end{bmatrix}$$

$$\min \frac{b_i'}{a_{i4}'} = \frac{b_2'}{a_{24}'} . \quad \text{So } p = 2.$$

$$\vec{E}_p = \begin{bmatrix} 1 & 1/5 & 0 \\ 0 & 3/5 & 0 \\ 0 & -1/5 & 1 \end{bmatrix}$$

Iteration 3. The new basis is x_1, x_4, x_6 with

$$\vec{A}_0^{-1} = \begin{bmatrix} 1 & 1/5 & 0 \\ 0 & 3/5 & 0 \\ 0 & -1/5 & 1 \end{bmatrix} \begin{bmatrix} 1 & 0 & 2/6 \\ 0 & 1 & -1/6 \\ 0 & 0 & 1/6 \end{bmatrix} = \begin{bmatrix} 1 & 1/5 & 9/30 \\ 0 & 3/5 & -3/30 \\ 0 & -1/5 & 6/30 \end{bmatrix}$$

$$\vec{C}_0 = [1 \quad 0 \quad 0], \quad [\pi_1 \quad \pi_2 \quad \pi_3] = [-1 \quad -1/5 \quad -9/30]$$

$$c_2' = 1/2, \quad c_3' = 21/30, \quad c_5' = 21/10.$$

All these three are nonnegative. Therefore the present basis is optimal. The values of the basic variables are

$$\begin{bmatrix} b_1' \\ b_2' \\ b_3' \end{bmatrix} = \begin{bmatrix} 1 & 1/5 & 9/30 \\ 0 & 3/5 & -3/30 \\ 0 & -1/5 & 6/30 \end{bmatrix} \begin{bmatrix} 5 \\ 3 \\ 5 \end{bmatrix} = \begin{bmatrix} 71/10 \\ 13/10 \\ 2/5 \end{bmatrix}$$

So $x_1 = 71/10$, $x_2 = 0$, $x_3 = 0$, $x_4 = 13/10$, $x_5 = 0$, $x_6 = 2/5$, is the optimal solution and the optimum value of the objective function is 71/10.

Solve the problem by Revised Simplex. The problem in standard form is:

Maximize $f = 12x_1 + 8x_2 + 0x_3 + 0x_4 + 0x_5$

subject to
$$5x_1 + 2x_2 + 1x_3 + 0x_4 + 0x_5 = 150$$
$$2x_1 + 3x_2 + 0x_3 + 1x_4 + 0x_5 = 100$$
$$4x_1 + 2x_2 + 0x_3 + 0x_4 + 1x_5 = 80$$
$$x_1, x_2, x_3, x_4, x_5 \geq 0$$

Solution: Use the slack variables x_3, x_4, and x_5 to form the initial basis. Then

$$\vec{B}^{-1} = \vec{B} = I_3 = \begin{bmatrix} 1 & 0 & 0 \\ 0 & 1 & 0 \\ 0 & 0 & 1 \end{bmatrix} \qquad \vec{c}_B = \begin{bmatrix} 0 \\ 0 \\ 0 \end{bmatrix}$$

$$\vec{x}_B = B^{-1}\vec{b} = \vec{b} = \begin{bmatrix} 150 \\ 100 \\ 80 \end{bmatrix}$$

and $$\vec{y}' = \vec{c}_B'\vec{B}^{-1} = [0 \quad 0 \quad 0] \begin{bmatrix} 1 & 0 & 0 \\ 0 & 1 & 0 \\ 0 & 0 & 1 \end{bmatrix} = [0 \quad 0 \quad 0]$$

The initial tableau is Tableau 1.

Tableau 1

x_B	B^{-1}			$\underline{b}$	y	$\underline{a}_1$	θ_i	
x_3	1	0	0	150	0	5	30	
x_4	0	1	0	100	0	2	50	
x_5	0	0	1	80	0	(4)	20	→ Out

The non-basic variables are x_1 and x_2. Then

$$c_1 - z_1 = 12 - \vec{y}'\vec{a}_1 = 12 - [0 \quad 0 \quad 0] \begin{bmatrix} 5 \\ 2 \\ 4 \end{bmatrix} = 12$$

and $$c_2 - z_2 = 8 - \vec{y}'\vec{a}_2 = 8 - [0 \quad 0 \quad 0] \begin{bmatrix} 2 \\ 3 \\ 2 \end{bmatrix} = 8$$

Hence x_1 should enter the basis.

$$\text{Compute } \underline{\vec{a}}_1 = \vec{B}^{-1} a_1 = \begin{bmatrix} 1 & 0 & 0 \\ 0 & 1 & 0 \\ 0 & 0 & 1 \end{bmatrix} \begin{bmatrix} 5 \\ 2 \\ 4 \end{bmatrix} = \begin{bmatrix} 5 \\ 2 \\ 4 \end{bmatrix}$$

Then

$$\theta_1 = \frac{\underline{b}_1}{\underline{a}_{11}} = \frac{150}{5} = 30$$

$$\theta_2 = \frac{\underline{b}_2}{\underline{a}_{21}} = \frac{100}{2} = 50$$

$$\theta_3 = \frac{\underline{b}_3}{\underline{a}_{31}} = \frac{80}{4} = 20$$

The minimum ratio is $\theta_3 = 20$, so that x_5 is the outgoing variable and $\underline{a}_{31} = 4$ is the pivot element.

Tableau 2

x_B	B^{-1}			$\underline{b}$	y	$\underline{a}_2$	θ	
x_3	1	0	$-\frac{5}{4}$	50	0	$-\frac{1}{2}$	–	
x_4	0	1	$-\frac{1}{2}$	60	0	(2)	30	Out →
x_1	0	0	$\frac{1}{4}$	20	3	$\frac{1}{2}$	40	

Perform the pivot, but only to update $\vec{B}^{-1}$. Then, as shown in Tableau 2,

$$\vec{B}^{-1} = \begin{bmatrix} 1 & 0 & -5/4 \\ 0 & 1 & -1/2 \\ 0 & 0 & 1/4 \end{bmatrix}$$

so $$\vec{y}' = \vec{c}_B'\vec{B}^{-1} = [0 \quad 0 \quad 12] \begin{bmatrix} 1 & 0 & -5/4 \\ 0 & 1 & -1/2 \\ 0 & 0 & 1/4 \end{bmatrix} = [0 \quad 0 \quad 3]$$

and $$\underline{\vec{b}} = \vec{B}^{-1}\vec{b} = \begin{bmatrix} 1 & 0 & -5/4 \\ 0 & 1 & -1/2 \\ 0 & 0 & 1/4 \end{bmatrix} \begin{bmatrix} 150 \\ 100 \\ 80 \end{bmatrix} = \begin{bmatrix} 150 - 100 \\ 100 - 40 \\ 20 \end{bmatrix} = \begin{bmatrix} 50 \\ 60 \\ 20 \end{bmatrix}$$

The non-basic variables are x_2 and x_5, so that

$$c_2 - z_2 = 8 - \vec{y}'\vec{a}_2 = 8 - [0 \quad 0 \quad 3]\begin{bmatrix}2\\3\\2\end{bmatrix} = 8 - 6 = 2$$

and $$c_5 - z_5 = 0 - \vec{y}'\vec{a}_5 = 0 - [0 \; 0 \; 3]\begin{bmatrix}0\\0\\1\end{bmatrix} = 0 - 3 = -3$$

Thus, x_2 should enter the basis.

One needs

$$\underline{\vec{a}}_2 = \vec{B}^{-1}\vec{a}_2 = \begin{bmatrix}1 & 0 & -5/4\\0 & 1 & -1/2\\0 & 0 & 1/4\end{bmatrix}\begin{bmatrix}2\\3\\2\end{bmatrix} = \begin{bmatrix}2 - 5/2\\3 - 1\\1/2\end{bmatrix} = \begin{bmatrix}-1/2\\2\\1/2\end{bmatrix}$$

Hence, the θ_i ratios are as shown, which means the smallest ratio is $\theta_2 = 30$. The outgoing variable is x_4, and the pivot element is $\underline{a}_{22} = 2$. Then

$$\vec{B}^{-1} = \begin{bmatrix}1 & 1/4 & -11/8\\0 & 1/2 & -1/4\\0 & -1/4 & 3/8\end{bmatrix}$$

so that

$$\underline{\vec{b}} = \vec{B}^{-1}\vec{b} = \begin{bmatrix}1 & 1/4 & -11/8\\0 & 1/2 & -1/4\\0 & -1/4 & 3/8\end{bmatrix}\begin{bmatrix}150\\100\\80\end{bmatrix}$$

$$= \begin{bmatrix}150 + 25 - 110\\0 + 50 - 20\\0 - 25 + 30\end{bmatrix} = \begin{bmatrix}65\\30\\5\end{bmatrix}$$

and

$$\vec{y}' = \vec{c}_B'\vec{B}^{-1} = [0 \quad 8 \quad 12]\begin{bmatrix}1 & 1/4 & -11/8\\0 & 1/2 & -1/4\\0 & -1/4 & 3/8\end{bmatrix} = [0 \quad 1 \quad 5/2]$$

The new tableau is

Tableau 3

x_B	B^{-1}			b	y	a_k	θ_i
x_3	1	$\frac{1}{4}$	$-\frac{11}{8}$	65	0		
x_2	0	$\frac{1}{2}$	$-\frac{1}{4}$	30	1		
x_1	0	$-\frac{1}{4}$	$\frac{3}{8}$	5	$\frac{5}{2}$		

The non-basic variables are x_4 and x_5. Then

$$c_4 - z_4 = 0 - \vec{y}'\vec{a}_4 = 0 - [0 \quad 1 \quad 5/2]\begin{bmatrix}0\\1\\0\end{bmatrix} = -1$$

and $$c_5 - z_5 = 0 - \vec{y}'\vec{a}_5 = 0 - [0 \quad 1 \quad 5/2]\begin{bmatrix}0\\0\\1\end{bmatrix} = -5/2$$

Hence the current solution is optimal, with $x_1^* = 5$, $x_2^* = 30$, and $f^* = \$12 \times 5 + \$8 \times 30 = \$300$.

• PROBLEM 4-24

Minimize $\quad -45x_1 - 80x_2$

subject to

$$x_1 + 4x_2 + x_3 = 80$$

$$2x_1 + 3x_2 + x_4 = 90$$

$$x_j \geq 0$$

Solve by Revised Simplex method.

Solution: Here

$$\vec{c} = (-45, -80, 0, 0)$$

$$\vec{A} = (\vec{P}_1\vec{P}_2\vec{P}_3\vec{P}_4) = \begin{pmatrix}1 & 4 & 1 & 0\\2 & 3 & 0 & 1\end{pmatrix}$$

$$\vec{b} = \begin{pmatrix}80\\90\end{pmatrix}$$

The first feasible basis $\vec{B}$ is given by the unit vectors $\vec{P}_3$ and $\vec{P}_4$; thus

$$\vec{B} = \begin{pmatrix}1 & 0\\0 & 1\end{pmatrix} \qquad \vec{B}^{-1} = \begin{pmatrix}1 & 0\\0 & 1\end{pmatrix} \qquad \vec{c}_0 = (0,0)$$

and

$$X_0 = \vec{B}^{-1}\vec{b} = \begin{pmatrix}1 & 0\\0 & 1\end{pmatrix}\begin{pmatrix}80\\90\end{pmatrix} = \begin{pmatrix}80\\90\end{pmatrix} = (x_3, x_4)$$

The corresponding pricing vector is

$$\pi = c_0\vec{B}^{-1} = (0 \quad 0)\begin{pmatrix} 1 & 0 \\ 0 & 1 \end{pmatrix} = (0,0)$$

Price out the vectors $\vec{P}_1$ and $\vec{P}_2$ not in the basis by computing the $z_j - c_j$ using

$$\pi\vec{P}_1 - c_1 = (0,0)\begin{pmatrix} 1 \\ 2 \end{pmatrix} + 45 = 45$$

$$\pi\vec{P}_2 - c_2 = (0,0)\begin{pmatrix} 4 \\ 3 \end{pmatrix} + 80 = 80$$

Then select vector $\vec{P}_2$ to enter the basis because it corresponds to the maximum $z_j - c_j$. As the vector $\vec{X}_2$ is needed, which is the representation of $\vec{P}_2$ in terms of the current basis $\vec{B}$, compute

$$\vec{X}_2 = \vec{B}^{-1}\vec{P}_2 = \begin{pmatrix} 1 & 0 \\ 0 & 1 \end{pmatrix}\begin{pmatrix} 4 \\ 3 \end{pmatrix} = \begin{pmatrix} 4 \\ 3 \end{pmatrix}$$

Next, determine the vector to be eliminated by calculating the corresponding θ ratios of 80:4 and 90:3. As the former ratio is the minimum and corresponds to x_3, vector $\vec{P}_3$ is eliminated from the basis and is replaced by vector $\vec{P}_2$. To compute the inverse of the new basis $(\vec{P}_2\vec{P}_4)$ apply the elimination formula

$$\bar{b}_{ij} = b_{ij} - \frac{b_{\ell j}}{x_{\ell k}} x_{ik} \quad \text{for } i \neq 1, \quad \bar{b}_{\ell j} = \frac{b_{\ell j}}{x_{\ell k}}$$

to the matrix

$$\begin{array}{c|cc} \vec{X}_2 & \vec{B}^{-1} & \\ \hline \textcircled{4} & 1 & 0 \\ 3 & 0 & 1 \end{array}$$

to obtain the new inverse

$$(\vec{P}_2\vec{P}_4)^{-1} = \begin{pmatrix} 1/4 & 0 \\ -3/4 & 1 \end{pmatrix}$$

Repeat the process and denote the new basis by $\vec{B} = (\vec{P}_2\vec{P}_4)$ with

$$\vec{B} = \begin{pmatrix} 4 & 0 \\ 3 & 1 \end{pmatrix} \quad \vec{B}^{-1} = \begin{pmatrix} 1/4 & 0 \\ -3/4 & 1 \end{pmatrix} \quad \vec{c}_0 = (-80,0)$$

and

$$\vec{X}_0 = \vec{B}^{-1}\vec{b} = \begin{pmatrix} 1/4 & 0 \\ -3/4 & 1 \end{pmatrix}\begin{pmatrix} 80 \\ 90 \end{pmatrix} = \begin{pmatrix} 20 \\ 30 \end{pmatrix} = (x_2, x_4)$$

The corresponding pricing vector is

$$\pi = \vec{c}_0\vec{B}^{-1} = (-80, 0)\begin{pmatrix} 1/4 & 0 \\ -3/4 & 1 \end{pmatrix} = (-20, 0)$$

Price out vectors $\vec{P}_1$ and $\vec{P}_3$ which are not in the current basis and obtain

$$\pi\vec{P}_1 - c_1 = (-20, 0)\begin{pmatrix} 1 \\ 2 \end{pmatrix} + 45 = 25$$

$$\pi\vec{P}_3 - c_3 = (-20, 0)\begin{pmatrix} 1 \\ 0 \end{pmatrix} - 0 = -20$$

Thus, vector $\vec{P}_1$ is selected to enter the basis and compute

$$\vec{X}_1 = \vec{B}^{-1}\vec{P}_1 = \begin{pmatrix} 1/4 & 0 \\ -3/4 & 1 \end{pmatrix}\begin{pmatrix} 1 \\ 2 \end{pmatrix} = \begin{pmatrix} 1/4 \\ 5/4 \end{pmatrix}$$

with the corresponding θ ratios of $20:\frac{1}{4}$ and $30:\frac{5}{4}$; vector $\vec{P}_4$ is eliminated from the basis. The new basis is $\vec{B} = (\vec{P}_2\vec{P}_1)$, and the inverse is obtained by applying the elimination formulas to the matrix

$$\begin{array}{c|cc} \vec{X}_1 & \vec{B}^{-1} & \\ \hline \frac{1}{4} & \frac{1}{4} & 0 \\ \textcircled{\frac{5}{4}} & -\frac{3}{4} & 1 \end{array}$$

i.e., the new $\vec{B}^{-1} = (\vec{P}_2\vec{P}_1)^{-1} = \begin{pmatrix} 2/5 & -1/5 \\ -3/5 & 4/5 \end{pmatrix}$.

Finally, using the new inverse one sees that the vectors $\vec{P}_3$ and $\vec{P}_4$ not in the basis price out negatively and the optimal solution is

$$\vec{X}_0 = \vec{B}^{-1}\vec{b} = \begin{pmatrix} 2/5 & -1/5 \\ -3/5 & 4/5 \end{pmatrix}\begin{pmatrix} 80 \\ 90 \end{pmatrix} = \begin{pmatrix} 14 \\ 24 \end{pmatrix} = (x_2, x_1)$$

with the minimum value of the objective function

$$z_0 = \vec{c}_0\vec{X}_0 = \vec{c}_0(\vec{B}^{-1}\vec{b}) = (\vec{c}_0\vec{B}^{-1})\vec{b} = \pi\vec{b}$$

$$= (-5, -20)\begin{pmatrix} 80 \\ 90 \end{pmatrix} = -2{,}200$$

• PROBLEM 4-25

Minimize: $Z = -3x_1 + x_2 + x_3$

Subject to:

$$x_1 - 2x_2 + x_3 \leqq 11$$
$$-4x_1 + x_2 + 2x_3 \geqq 3$$
$$2x_1 - x_3 = -1$$
$$x_1, x_2, x_3 \geqq 0$$

Solve by Revised Simplex method.

Solution: In standard form, the problem reduces to

Minimize: $Z = -3x_1 + x_2 + x_3$

Subject to:

$$x_1 - 2x_2 + x_3 + x_4 = 11$$
$$-4x_1 + x_2 + 2x_3 - x_5 = 3$$
$$-2x_1 + x_3 = 1$$
$$x_1, \ldots, x_5 \geqq 0$$

Since there are no basic variables in the second and third equations, artificial variables x_6 and x_7 are added as shown below:

$$x_1 - 2x_2 + x_3 + x_4 = 11$$
$$-4x_1 + x_2 + 2x_3 - x_5 + x_6 = 3$$
$$-2x_1 + x_3 + x_7 = 1$$
$$x_1, \ldots, x_7 \geqq 0$$

Using the Big M method, the objective function becomes

$$\text{Minimize } Z = -3x_1 + x_2 + x_3 + Mx_6 + Mx_7$$

Let $\vec{P}_1, \ldots, \vec{P}_7$ and $\vec{b}$ denote the columns corresponding to $x_1, \ldots, x_7$ and the right-hand side. Thus,

$$\vec{P}_1 = \begin{bmatrix} 1 \\ -4 \\ -2 \end{bmatrix}, \quad \vec{P}_2 = \begin{bmatrix} -2 \\ 1 \\ 0 \end{bmatrix}, \quad \vec{P}_3 = \begin{bmatrix} 1 \\ 2 \\ 1 \end{bmatrix}, \quad \vec{P}_4 = \begin{bmatrix} 1 \\ 0 \\ 0 \end{bmatrix}, \quad \vec{P}_5 = \begin{bmatrix} 0 \\ -1 \\ 0 \end{bmatrix}$$

$$\vec{P}_6 = \begin{bmatrix} 0 \\ 1 \\ 0 \end{bmatrix}, \quad \vec{P}_7 = \begin{bmatrix} 0 \\ 0 \\ 1 \end{bmatrix}, \quad \text{and} \quad \vec{b} = \begin{bmatrix} 11 \\ 3 \\ 1 \end{bmatrix}$$

Since (x_4, x_6, x_7) form the initial basis,

$$\underset{(3\times 3)}{\vec{B}} = [\vec{P}_4,\vec{P}_6,\vec{P}_7] = \begin{bmatrix} 1 & 0 & 0 \\ 0 & 1 & 0 \\ 0 & 0 & 1 \end{bmatrix} = \vec{I}$$

Hence

$$\vec{B}^{-1} = \vec{I} \quad \text{and} \quad \vec{\bar{b}} = \vec{B}^{-1}\vec{b} = \vec{b}$$

The initial tableau of the revised simplex method is given below.

Tableau 1

Basis	$\vec{B}^{-1}$			Constants	Variable to Enter	Pivot Column
x_4	1	0	0	11		1
x_6	0	1	0	3	x_3	2
x_7	0	0	1	1		①

The simplex multipliers are

$$\vec{\pi} = (\pi_1,\pi_2,\pi_3) = \vec{c}_B\vec{B}^{-1} = (0,M,M)\begin{bmatrix} 1 & 0 & 0 \\ 0 & 1 & 0 \\ 0 & 0 & 1 \end{bmatrix} = (0,M,M)$$

Since $\bar{c}_j = c_j - \vec{\pi}\vec{P}_j$ for $j = 1,2,3,5$ one gets,

$$\bar{c}_1 = -3-(0,M,M)\begin{bmatrix} 1 \\ -4 \\ -2 \end{bmatrix} = 6M - 3$$

$$\bar{c}_2 = 1-(0,M,M)\begin{bmatrix} -2 \\ 1 \\ 0 \end{bmatrix} = 1 - M$$

$$\bar{c}_3 = 1-(0,M,M)\begin{bmatrix} 1 \\ 2 \\ 1 \end{bmatrix} = 1 - 3M$$

$$\bar{c}_5 = 0-(0,M,M)\begin{bmatrix} 0 \\ -1 \\ 0 \end{bmatrix} = M$$

Since $\bar{c}_3$ is most negative, x_3 enters the basis. The pivot column is

$$\vec{\bar{P}}_3 = \vec{B}^{-1}\vec{P}_3 = \begin{bmatrix} 1 & 0 & 0 \\ 0 & 1 & 0 \\ 0 & 0 & 1 \end{bmatrix}\begin{bmatrix} 1 \\ 2 \\ 1 \end{bmatrix} = \begin{bmatrix} 1 \\ 2 \\ 1 \end{bmatrix}$$

(The entering variable x_3 and the pivot column elements are now entered in Tableau 1.) Applying the minimum ratio rule, the ratios are (11/1, 3/2, 1/1). Hence x_3 replaces the artificial variable x_7 from the basis.

This is shown by circling the pivot element in Tableau 1. Using the pivot column, the pivot operation is done on Tableau 1 as follows:

1. Multiply row 3 by -1, and add it to row 1.
2. Multiply row 3 by -2, and add it to row 2.

The new $\vec{B}^{-1}$, and the constants are given below:

Tableau 2

Basis	$\vec{B}^{-1}$			Constants	Variable to Enter	Pivot Column
x_4	1	0	−1	10		−2
x_6	0	1	−2	1	x_2	①
x_3	0	0	1	1		0

The simplex multipliers corresponding to Tableau 2 are

$$\vec{\pi} = (0,M,1)\begin{bmatrix} 1 & 0 & -1 \\ 0 & 1 & -2 \\ 0 & 0 & 1 \end{bmatrix} = (0,M,-2M + 1)$$

The $\bar{c}_j$ elements are given by $\bar{c}_1$ =-1, $\bar{c}_2$ = 1 - M and $\bar{c}_5$ = M. ($\bar{c}_7$ is not calculated because x_7 is an artificial variable). Since $\bar{c}_2$ is the most negative, x_2 enters the basis and the pivot column becomes

$$\vec{P}_2 = \vec{B}^{-1}\vec{P_2} = \begin{bmatrix} 1 & 0 & -1 \\ 0 & 1 & -2 \\ 0 & 0 & 1 \end{bmatrix} \begin{bmatrix} -2 \\ 1 \\ 0 \end{bmatrix} = \begin{bmatrix} -2 \\ 1 \\ 0 \end{bmatrix}$$

The ratios are (∞,1/1,∞). Hence x_2 replaces the artificial variable x_6 from the basis. Performing the pivot operation the new basic feasible solution shown in Tableau 3 is obtained.

Tableau 3

Basis	$\vec{B}^{-1}$			Constants	Variable to Enter	Pivot Column
x_4	1	2	−5	12		③
x_2	0	1	−2	1	x_1	0
x_3	0	0	1	1		−2

The simplex multipliers of Tableau 3 are

$$\vec{\pi} = (0,1,1) \begin{bmatrix} 1 & 2 & -5 \\ 0 & 1 & -2 \\ 0 & 0 & 1 \end{bmatrix} = (0,1,-1)$$

The $\bar{c}_j$ elements of the nonbasic variables are given by

$$\bar{c}_1 = -1 \quad \text{and} \quad \bar{c}_5 = 1$$

Thus x_1 enters the basis. The pivot column becomes

$$\vec{P}_1 = \begin{bmatrix} 1 & 2 & -5 \\ 0 & 1 & -2 \\ 0 & 0 & 1 \end{bmatrix} \begin{bmatrix} 1 \\ -4 \\ -2 \end{bmatrix} = \begin{bmatrix} 3 \\ 0 \\ -2 \end{bmatrix}$$

By the minimum ratio rule, x_1 replaces x_4 from the basis, and the new tableau after the pivot operation is given below:

Tableau 4

Basis	$\vec{B}^{-1}$			Constants
x_1	$\frac{1}{3}$	$\frac{2}{3}$	$-\frac{5}{3}$	4
x_2	0	1	-2	1
x_3	$\frac{2}{3}$	$\frac{4}{3}$	$-\frac{7}{3}$	9

The simplex multipliers of Tableau 4 are

$$\vec{\pi} = [-3,1,1] \begin{bmatrix} \frac{1}{3} & \frac{2}{3} & -\frac{5}{3} \\ 0 & 1 & -2 \\ \frac{2}{3} & \frac{4}{3} & -\frac{7}{3} \end{bmatrix} = \left[-\frac{1}{3}, \frac{1}{3}, \frac{2}{3}\right]$$

and

$$\bar{c}_4 = 0 - \left[-\frac{1}{3}, \frac{1}{3}, \frac{2}{3}\right] \begin{bmatrix} 1 \\ 0 \\ 0 \end{bmatrix} = \frac{1}{3}$$

$$\bar{c}_5 = 0 - \left[-\frac{1}{3}, \frac{1}{3}, \frac{2}{3}\right] \begin{bmatrix} 0 \\ -1 \\ 0 \end{bmatrix} = \frac{1}{3}$$

Hence Tableau 4 is optimal, and the unique optimal solution is given by

$$x_1 = 4, \quad x_2 = 1, \quad x_3 = 9, \quad x_4 = 0, \quad \text{and} \quad x_5 = 0$$

The optimal value of the objective function is

$$z = \vec{c}_B \vec{b} = (-3,1,1) \begin{bmatrix} 4 \\ 1 \\ 9 \end{bmatrix} = -2$$

PRIMAL - DUAL METHOD

• PROBLEM 4-26

Maximize $3x_1 + 4x_2 + x_3 + 2x_4 + 2x_5 + x_6$,

subject to $x_1 - 2x_3 + x_4 - x_6 \leq \frac{5}{2}$,

$$x_1 - 2x_2 \qquad + 2x_4 - x_5 + x_6 \geq \frac{1}{2},$$

$$x_2 + x_3 \qquad = 1,$$

$$x_4 + x_5 + x_6 = 1,$$

$$x_j \geq 0, \; j = 1,\ldots,6.$$

Solve this problem by the Primal-Dual method. Take $u_1 = 4$, $u_2 = 0$, $u_3 = 9$, $u_4 = 5$ as the initial solution, where u_i stand for the variables of the dual problem.

Solution: Description of the Primal-Dual method: Assume that the linear programming problem is of the form:

$$\text{Max}\{p^T x \mid Ax = b, \; x \geq 0\}, \tag{1}$$

so that its dual is

$$\text{Min}\{b^T u \mid A^T u \geq p\}. \tag{2}$$

Also assume

$$b \geq 0. \tag{3}$$

This is no restriction since any equation in (1) can be multiplied by -1, if necessary.

In the Primal-Dual method one goes from one dual feasible solution u* to another one with lower value:

$$b^T u^{**} < b^T u^*.$$

One therefore has to start with a dual feasible solution, which may or may not be a basic solution. If such a dual feasible solution is not available an artifice has to be used, which can be easily developed. Let $v = A^T u - p$ and define

$$N^* = \{j \in N \mid v_j^* = 0\}, \tag{4}$$

where N is the set of indices of u.

Now solve the restricted primal problem

$$\text{Max}\left\{-\sum_{i=1}^{m} z_i \;\middle|\; \sum_{j \in N^*} a_{ij}x_j + z_i = b_i, \; x_j \geq 0, \; z_i \geq 0\right\}, \tag{5}$$

leading to an optimal solution x_j^*, $j \in N^*$, z_i^*, $i = 1,\ldots,m$ with their final d-figures $d^*(z_i)$ and $d^*(x_j)$. Define $x_j^* = 0$ if $j \notin N^*$. There are two possibilities:

$$(1) \qquad \sum_{i=1}^{m} z_i^* = 0.$$

The vector x* will then satisfy $Ax^* = b, x^* \geqq 0$ and $(v^*)^T x^* = 0$, so it follows that x* will solve (1), while u* will solve (2).

$$(2) \qquad \sum_{i=1}^{m} z_i^* > 0.$$

The problem dual to (5) is:

$$\text{Min}\left\{ \sum_{i=1}^{m} b_i s_i \,\middle|\, \sum_{i=1}^{m} a_{ij} s_i \geqq 0,\ j \in N^*;\ s_i \geqq -1 \right\}. \quad (6)$$

It will have the optimal solution:

$$s_i^* = d^*(z_i) - 1,\ t_j^* = \sum_{i=1}^{m} a_{ij} s_i^* = d^*(x_j), j \in N^*.$$

One gets

$$-\sum_{i=1}^{m} z_i^* = \sum_{i=1}^{m} b_i \{d^*(z_i) - 1\} < 0. \quad (7)$$

Moreover,

$$0 \leqq d^*(x_j) = t_j^* = \sum_{i=1}^{m} a_{ij} \{d^*(z_i) - 1\},\ j \in N^*. \quad (8)$$

Now let

$$u_i = u_i^* + \lambda\{d^*(z_i) - 1\}$$

and

$$\lambda^* = \text{Max}\left\{ \lambda \,\middle|\, \sum_{i=1}^{m} a_{ij} u_i \geqq p_j \right\},$$

then $\lambda^* > 0$ by (8). If $\lambda^* = \infty$, then (2) will have an infinite solution since (7) holds, so that (1) will not be feasible.

Let

$$u^{**} = u^* + \lambda^*\{d^*(z_i) - 1\},$$

then u** will be dual feasible and $b^T u^{**} < b^T u^*$. Moreover, since $\lambda^* > 0$, one has for at least one value of j $v_j^{**} = 0$ which $v_j^* > 0$.

Hence $N^{**} \neq N^*$. One can now formulate a new restricted primal problem. Under the non-degeneracy assumption one shall necessarily have $\sum_{i=1}^{m} z_i^{**} < \sum_{k=1}^{m} z_i^*$. Any basis in a restricted primal problem of type (5) is an m by m submatrix of the matrix (A,I). With each basis a certain value $\sum z_i$ is associated. It follows that no basis can ever repeat. Hence after a finite number of steps $\sum z_i = 0$ will hold.

Applying the algorithm to the problem:

Primal equations:

$$\begin{aligned}
x_1 \qquad\quad - 2x_3 + x_4 \qquad - x_6 + y_1 \qquad &= \tfrac{5}{2} \\
x_1 - 2x_2 \qquad + 2x_4 - x_5 + x_6 \qquad - y_2 &= \tfrac{1}{2} \\
x_2 + x_3 \qquad\qquad\qquad\qquad &= 1 \\
x_4 + x_5 + x_6 \qquad\qquad &= 1
\end{aligned}$$

$$x_j \geqq 0, \quad y_i \geqq 0$$

$$3x_1 + 4x_2 + x_3 + 2x_4 + 2x_5 + x_6 \text{ to be maximized.}$$

Dual inequalities:

$$\begin{aligned}
&(1) \quad u_1 + u_2 \geqq 3 \\
&(2) \quad -2u_2 + u_3 \geqq 4 \\
&(3) \quad -2u_1 + u_3 \geqq 1 \\
&(4) \quad u_1 + 2u_2 + u_4 \geqq 2 \\
&(5) \quad - u_2 + u_4 \geqq 2 \\
&(6) \quad -u_1 + u_2 + u_4 \geqq 1 \\
&(7) \quad u_1 \geqq 0 \\
&(8) \quad - u_2 \geqq 0
\end{aligned}$$

$$\tfrac{5}{2}u_1 + \tfrac{1}{2}u_2 + u_3 + u_4 \text{ to be maximized.}$$

As initial solution, take

$u_1 = 4, \quad u_2 = 0, \quad u_3 = 9, \quad u_4 = 5.$

Value: $\sum b_i u = 24.$

$v_1 = 1, \quad v_2 = 5, \quad v_3 = 0, \quad v_4 = 4,$

$v_5 = 3, \quad v_6 = 0, \quad v_7 = 4, \quad v_8 = 0.$

$N^* = \{3,6,8\}.$

Restricted primal problem:

		x_3	x_6	y_2
z_1	$\frac{5}{2}$	-2	-1	
z_2	$\frac{1}{2}$		$\boxed{1}$	-1
z_3	1	1		
z_4	1		1	
	-5	1	-1	1

→

		x_3	z_2	y_2
z_1	3	-2	1	-1
x_6	$\frac{1}{2}$		1	-1
z_3	1	1		
z_4	$\frac{1}{2}$		-1	1
	$-4\frac{1}{2}$	1	1	0

Hence,

$$d^*(z_1) - 1 = -1, \quad d^*(z_2) - 1 = 0,$$

$$d^*(z_3) - 1 = -1, \quad d^*(z_4) - 1 = -1;$$

$$u_1 = 4 - \lambda, \quad u_2 = 0, \quad u_3 = 9 - \lambda, \quad u_4 = 5 - \lambda.$$

It follows: $\lambda = 1$ ($v_1 = 1$, $\sum_{i=1}^{4} a_{i1}s_i = -1$).

New solution: $u_1 = 3$, $u_2 = 0$, $u_3 = 8$, $u_4 = 4$.

Value: $\sum b_i u_i = \frac{39}{2}$ $(= 24 - 1\cdot\frac{9}{2})$.

$$v_1 = 0, \quad v_2 = 4, \quad v_3 = 1, \quad v_4 = 5,$$

$$v_5 = 2, \quad v_6 = 0, \quad v_7 = 3, \quad v_8 = 0.$$

$$N^* = \{1,6,8\}.$$

New restricted primal problem:

		x_1	x_6	y_2
z_1	$\frac{5}{2}$	1	-1	
z_2	$\frac{1}{2}$	1	$\boxed{1}$	-1
z_3	1			
z_4	1		1	
	-5	-2	-1	1

→

		z_2	x_6	y_2
z_1	2	-1	-2	$\boxed{1}$
x_1	$\frac{1}{2}$	1	1	-1
z_3	1			
z_4	1		1	
	-4	2	1	-1

→

		z_2	x_6	z_1
y_2	2	-1	-2	1
x_1	$\frac{5}{2}$		-1	1
z_3	1			
z_4	1		$\boxed{1}$	
	-2	1	-1	1

→

		z_2	z_4	z_1
y_2	4	-1	2	1
x_1	$\frac{7}{2}$		1	1
z_3	1			
x_6	1		1	
	-1	1	1	1

Hence, $d^*(z_1) - 1 = 0$, $d^*(z_2) - 1 = 0$, $d^*(z_3) - 1 = -1$, $d^*(z_4) - 1 = 0$; $u_1 = 3$, $u_2 = 0$, $u_3 = 8 - \lambda$, $u_4 = 4$.

It follows: $\lambda = 1 (v_3 = 1, \sum_{i=1}^{4} a_{i3}s_i = -1)$.

New solution: $u_1 = 3$, $u_2 = 0$, $u_3 = 7$, $u_4 = 4$, $v_1 = 0$, $v_2 = 3$, $v_3 = 0$, $v_4 = 5$, $v_5 = 2$, $v_6 = 0$, $v_7 = 3$, $v_8 = 0$.

Value: $\sum b_i u_i = \frac{37}{2}$ $(= \frac{39}{2} - 1 \cdot 1)$.

$$N^* = \{1,3,6,8\}.$$

New restricted primal problem:

		x_1	x_3	x_6	y_2
z_1	$\frac{5}{2}$	1	-2	-1	
z_2	$\frac{1}{2}$	1		1	-1
z_3	1		1		
z_4	1			1	
	-5	-2	1	-1	1

→

		z_2	z_3	z_4	z_1
y_2	6	-1	2	2	1
x_1	$\frac{11}{2}$		2	1	1
x_3	1		1		
x_6	1			1	
	0	1	1	1	1

$\sum z_i = 0$, hence optimal solution obtained: $x_1 = \frac{11}{2}$, $x_2 = 0$, $x_3 = 1$, $x_4 = 0$, $x_5 = 0$, $x_6 = 1$ with value $\frac{37}{2}$.

• PROBLEM 4-27

In the problem

$$\text{maximize} \quad x_0 = 5x_1 + 12x_2 + 4x_3$$

$$\text{subject to} \quad x_1 + 2x_2 + x_3 \le 5$$

$$2x_1 - x_2 + 3x_3 = 2$$

$$x_1, x_2, x_3 \ge 0$$

with the final optimal tableau:

Basic	x_0	x_1	x_2	x_3	S_1	R_1	Solution
x_0	①	0	0	3/5	29/5	$-2/5 + M$	$28\frac{1}{5}$
x_2	0	0	①	−1/5	2/5	−1/5	8/5
x_1	0	①	0	7/5	1/5	2/5	9/5

how would the current optimal solution be affected if the right-hand side of the constraints is changed from $\begin{pmatrix}5\\2\end{pmatrix}$ to $\begin{pmatrix}7\\2\end{pmatrix}$? to $\begin{pmatrix}3\\10\end{pmatrix}$? Which resource should be increased in order to achieve the best marginal increase in the value of the objective function? by how much? How will the solution be affected if the coefficients (in the objective function) of x_1 and x_2 are changed from 5 and 12 to 4 and 10? Coefficient of x_3 is changed from 4 to 8? All of the objective coefficients were changed simulstaneously, to the above mentioned values? if the technological coefficients (in the constraints set) of x_3 are changed from

$$\begin{pmatrix}1\\3\end{pmatrix} \quad \text{to} \quad \begin{pmatrix}-5\\2\end{pmatrix} \quad ?$$

Consider the dual and relationships of the dual with the primal.

Solution: For a dual problem obtained from the standard form of the primal, the following properties prevail:

Property I: At any iteration of either the primal or the dual, the matrix under the variables of the starting solution (not including the objective equation row) can be used to generate the objective-equation coefficients corresponding to the starting solution. This is achieved as follows:

Step 1. Identify the original coefficients of the objective function corresponding to the basic variables of the current iteration and arrange them in a row-vector in the same order of their respective rows in the simplex tableau.

Step 2. Multiply the resulting vector by the matrix defined above.

Step 3. Subtract the original coefficients of the objective function corresponding to the variables of the starting solution from the respective coefficients obtained in Step 2. This will directly give the result indicated by the property.

The results of Step 2, if they correspond to the optimal iteration, will give the optimal values of the other problem directly. In general, the values obtained at Step 2 are referred to as the "simplex multipliers." At the optimal iteration, these simplex multipliers give the optimal solution to the other problem.

Property II. At any iteration of the simplex solution, by substituting the corresponding simplex multipliers for the respective variables in the dual constraints, the coefficients of the x_0-equation in the primal are given by the differences between the left-hand and the right-hand sides of the corresponding dual constraints. This property is equally applicable to generating the coefficients of the y_0-equation from the primal constraints.

This property reveals a very important result. Notice that a negative coefficient in the x_0-equation of the primal implies that the solution is not optimal. Since this coefficient represents the difference between the left and the right sides of the dual constraints, it is seen from the direction of the inequality that such a negative coefficient indicates that the corresponding dual constraint is not satisfied. This leads to the conclusion that when the primal is nonoptimal the dual is infeasible and vice versa. Another remark can also be made here. Since the coefficient of every basic variable in the x_0-equation is always zero, the difference between the left- and right-hand sides of the associated dual constraint must be zero. This means that the dual constraint corresponding to a basic variable must be satisfied in equation form.

The above result implies that while the primal problem starts feasible but nonoptimal and continues to be feasible until the optimal solution is reached, the dual problem starts infeasible but better-than-optimal and continues to be infeasible until the "true" optimal solution is reached. In other words, while the primal problem is seeking optimality the dual problem is automatically seeking feasibility. This result suggests that it is possible to construct a procedure similar to the simplex method for solving dual-type problems. The solution starts optimal (or actually better-than-optimal) and infeasible and remains infeasible until the "true" optimal is reached, at which point the solution becomes feasible.

PropertyII gives an interesting interpretation of the dual variables. Consider the jth dual constraint for a maximization primal problem. This is given by

$$a_{1j}y_1 + a_{2j}y_2 + \dots + a_{mj}y_m \geq c_j$$

where a_{ij} is the per unit requirement of the jth primal variable x_j from the ith scarce resource and c_j is the coefficient of x_j in the objective function. Let z_j designate the left-hand side of the above dual constraint. By Property II, $z_j - c_j$ gives the coefficient of x_j in the x_0-equation. According to the optimality condition, x_j is a promising variable if $z_j - c_j < 0$. Since in this case the primal is a maximization problem, c_j may be regarded as "profit" while z_j (with an opposite sign) may be taken as "cost." Thus, the smaller the value of z_j, the more attractive x_j will be. From the economic point of view, z_j is regarded as the "imputed price" per unit of x_j. The dual variables y_i thus define the worth per unit of the requirement a_{ij}. A nonbasic variable x_j is thus a promising candidate for the optimum solution as long as its "profit" per unit c_j exceeds its "imputed price" per unit z_j, that is, $c_j > z_j$, or $z_j - c_j < 0$. When $z_j = c_j$, the corresponding variable cannot change the present value of the objective function. Finally, when z_j exceeds c_j, that is, $z_j - c_j > 0$, the variable x_j becomes nonpromising and hence should remain nonbasic (at zero level). This remark also implies that for a basic variable, z_j must equal c_j indicating that the corresponding variable has been used to the fullest extent and as such cannot improve the solution any further.

Property III. At any iteration of the primal or the dual, the corresponding values of the basic variables can be obtained by multiplying the matrix defined in Property I by the column-vector comprising the original elements of the right-hand side of the constraints.

Property IV. At any iteration of the primal or the dual, the constraint coefficients under any variable (including those of the starting solution) can be obtained by multiplying the matrix defined in Property I by the column-vector comprising the original elements of the constraints coefficients under the designated variable.

The above properties indicate that, at any iteration, given the original problem, all elements of the simplex tableau can be generated from the matrix under the starting solution. This makes it possible to check the computations at any iteration.

A change from $\begin{pmatrix}5\\2\end{pmatrix}$ to $\begin{pmatrix}7\\2\end{pmatrix}$ can only affect the right-hand side of the final tableau and hence the feasibility of the problem. Thus, the new values of the current basic variables are

$$\begin{pmatrix} x_2 \\ x_1 \end{pmatrix} = \begin{pmatrix} 2/5 & -1/5 \\ 1/5 & 2/5 \end{pmatrix}\begin{pmatrix} 7 \\ 2 \end{pmatrix} = \begin{pmatrix} 12/5 \\ 11/5 \end{pmatrix}$$

Since both x_1 and x_2 are nonnegative, the current basic solution (consisting of x_1 and x_2) remains feasible and optimal at the new values, $x_1 = 11/5$, $x_2 = 12/5$, while x_3 remains zero. The new value of x_0 is $5(11/5) + 12(12/5) + 4(0) = 199/5$.

Consider the case where the new right-hand side of the primal constraints is

$$\begin{pmatrix} 3 \\ 10 \end{pmatrix} \quad \text{instead of} \begin{pmatrix} 5 \\ 2 \end{pmatrix}$$

Then
$$\begin{pmatrix} x_2 \\ x_1 \end{pmatrix} = \begin{pmatrix} 2/5 & -1/5 \\ 1/5 & 2/5 \end{pmatrix}\begin{pmatrix} 3 \\ 10 \end{pmatrix} = \begin{pmatrix} -4/5 \\ 23/5 \end{pmatrix}$$

x_2 becomes infeasible (<0). The first constraint, thus, is not satisfied and the change leaves the current optimal solution infeasible. Here the dual simplex method becomes useful in restoring the feasibility of the problem. First the right-hand side of the (primal) optimal tableau is changed to the new values of x_0 and the current basic variables. Since, new $x_0 = 5(23/5) + 12(-4/5) + 4(0) = 67/5$, the changes in the (primal) optimal tableau appear as follows.

Basic	x_0	x_1	x_2	x_3	S_1	R_1	Solution
x_0							67/5
x_2							−4/5
x_1							23/5

All the other elements of the tableau remain unchanged as given by the optimal primal solution. Since the x_0-equation is optimal (all nonnegative coefficients, maximization) and the basic solution is infeasible ($x_2 = -4/5$), the dual simplex method is used to clear the infeasibility with x_2 as the leaving variable and x_3 as the entering variable.

Which resource should be increased in order to achieve the best marginal increase in the value of the objective function: the answer calls for considering the dual objective function given by

$$y_0 = 5y_1 + 2y_2$$

where $y_1 = 29/5$ and $y_2 = -2/5$ are the dual optimal values. Thus, the first resource should be increased since each additional unit increases the value of the objective function by 29/5 while each additional unit of the second resource decreases it by 2/5. The next question is: How much can one increase the first resource while maintaining the property that each additional unit contributes 29/5 to the value of the objective function? The value 29/5 will remain correct as long as the primal problem remains feasible. Thus, if Δ represents the increase in the first resource, the maximum value of Δ can be determined from the following conditions.

$$\begin{pmatrix} x_2 \\ x_1 \end{pmatrix} = \begin{pmatrix} 2/5 & -1/5 \\ 1/5 & 2/5 \end{pmatrix} \begin{pmatrix} 5+\Delta \\ 2 \end{pmatrix} = \begin{pmatrix} (8+2\Delta)/5 \\ (9+\Delta)/5 \end{pmatrix} \geq \begin{pmatrix} 0 \\ 0 \end{pmatrix}$$

This shows that x_1 and x_2 will remain feasible (≥ 0) for any $\Delta > 0$, indicating that the first resource can be increased indefinitely while maintaining the property that each additional unit will contribute 29/5 to the objective function.

To illustrate the case where there is an upper limit on the value of Δ, assume Δ represents the decrease in the value of the second resource. Then the current solution remains basic and feasible so long as

$$\begin{pmatrix} x_2 \\ x_1 \end{pmatrix} = \begin{pmatrix} 2/5 & -1/5 \\ 1/5 & 2/5 \end{pmatrix} \begin{pmatrix} 5 \\ 2-\Delta \end{pmatrix} = \begin{pmatrix} (8+\Delta)/5 \\ (9-2\Delta)/5 \end{pmatrix} \geq \begin{pmatrix} 0 \\ 0 \end{pmatrix}$$

The second inequality shows that the given solution remains feasible at the new values for all $\Delta \leq 9/2$. For $\Delta > 9/2$, x_1 becomes negative and must leave the solution.

Changes in the coefficients of the objective function can only affect the coefficients of the x_0-equation and hence the optimality of the problem. In order to carry out sensitivity analysis, differentiation is made between the cases where these changes occur in the basic or nonbasic coefficients. In the case of basic coefficients, the simplex multipliers (dual values) change (Property I) and must be recomputed before the optimality of the problem is checked. In the other case, the simplex multipliers remain unchanged and the optimality can be checked directly.

Coefficients of x_1, x_2 changed to 4 and 10 (Basic Coefficients): According to Property I, the simplex multipliers are dependent on the coefficients of the basic variables in the objective function. In order for the current solution to remain optimal, the new simplex multipliers must yield a new objective equation with all its left-hand side coefficients satisfying the optimality condition.

By Property I, the new simplex multipliers are (notice the order of coefficients in the row-vector; x_2, x_1)

$$(10,4)\begin{pmatrix} 2/5 & -1/5 \\ 1/5 & 2/5 \end{pmatrix} = (24/5, -2/5)$$

Hence the new coefficients of S_1 and R_1 in the objective equation are

$$\text{coefficient of } S_1 = 24/5 - (0) = 24/5 > 0$$

$$\text{coefficient of } R_1 = -2/5 - (-M) = -2/5 + M > 0$$

which both satisfy the optimality condition. (It is not necessary actually to check R_1.)

Now, the remaining coefficients of the objective equation will be checked using Property II by checking the feasibility of the corresponding new dual constraints. Thus,

$$\text{coefficient of } x_1 = 1(24/5) + 2(-2/5) - 4 = 0$$

$$\text{coefficient of } x_2 = 2(24/5) - 1(-2/5) - 10 = 0$$

$$\text{coefficient of } x_3 = 1(24/5) + 3(-2/5) - 4$$

$$= -2/5 \ (<0)$$

Since the coefficient of x_3 is negative, the current optimal solution is no longer optimal and must be changed. This is done by applying the regular simplex to the current optimal tableau after changing its x_0-equation coefficients to show the new changes. These changes appear as follows.

Basic	x_0	x_1	x_2	x_3	S_1	R_1	Solution
x_0		0	0	$-2/5$	24/5	$-2/5 + M$	116/5
x_2 x_1							

where the new value of $x_0 = 4(9/5) + 10(8/5) + 4(0) = 116/5$ and all the other elements in the tableau remain unchanged. According to the regular simplex method, the variable x_3 enters the solution. The feasibility condition then shows that x_1 is the leaving variable. The simplex method is applied until optimality is attained.

Coefficient of x_3 is changed from 4 to 8 (Nonbasic Coefficients): This type of change does not affect the simplex multipliers. Consequently, the available multipliers can be used directly to check the objective-equation coefficients. This is done by checking the feasibility of the corresponding new dual constraints with their right-hand sides changed to the new values. The corresponding dual constraint is changed from $y_1 + 3y_2 \geq 4$ to $y_1 + 3y_2 \geq 8$. The simplex multipliers $y_1 = 29/5$ and $y_2 = -2/5$ show that the new constraint is not satisfied. Thus the new coefficient of x_3 in the x_0-equation is $1(29/5) + 3(-2/5) - 8 = -17/5$. This will be the only change in the optimal tableau and the variable x_3 becomes the entering variable.

Basic and Nonbasic Coefficients changed simultaneously:

Simultaneous changes in basic and nonbasic coefficients can be dealt with by combining the above two procedures. First, the new simplex multipliers are determined, and the coefficients of the starting basic variables in the objective equation are checked for nonoptimality. Second, the new dual constraints are checked for feasibility.
The old objective function

$$\text{maximize} \quad x_0 = 5x_1 + 12x_2 + 4x_3$$

is changed to

$$\text{maximize} \quad x_0 = 4x_1 + 10x_2 + 8x_3$$

The computations due to the above changes are

$$\text{new simplex multipliers} = (10,4)\begin{pmatrix} 2/5 & -1/5 \\ 1/5 & 2/5 \end{pmatrix} = (24/5,-2/5)$$

$$\text{coefficient of } R_1 = -2/5 - (-M) = -2/5 + M$$

$$\text{coefficient of } S_1 = 24/5 - (0) = 24/5$$

$$\text{coefficient of } x_3 = 1(24/5) + 3(-2/5) - 8 = -22/5$$

$$\text{coefficient of } x_1 = \text{coefficient of } x_2 = 0$$

The coefficient of x_3 is now -22/5 compared with -17/5 when the basic and nonbasic coefficients are considered separately. This indicates that the combined effect of basic and nonbasic changes may lead in general to completely different solutions.

Technological coefficients of x_3 are changed from $\begin{pmatrix} 1 \\ 3 \end{pmatrix}$ to $\begin{pmatrix} -5 \\ 2 \end{pmatrix}$: Property II reveals that changes in the technological coefficients of the problem can affect the left-hand side of its dual constraints and hence the feasibility of the dual (or equivalently the optimality of the primal). The important point is that changes in the technological coefficients of a basic variable will directly affect the elements of the matrix under the starting solution. Since this matrix plays the important role in all sensitivity analysis computations, the new changes may cause the current solution to be infeasible or nonoptimal or it may even cease to be basic at all. Except in very special cases, such problems make it difficult to consider systematically the effect of changes in the technological coefficients of the basic variables on the optimal solution. Even in the special cases that can be dealt with, the analysis does not yield immediate information concerning the optimality or the feasibility of the new problem.

The change suggested above is in the nonbasic variables.
The new dual constraint corresponding to x_3 becomes

$$-5y_1 + 2y_2 \geq 4$$

The values of the simplex multipliers remain unchanged. The new coefficient of x_3 in the x_0-equation is $-5(29/5) + 2(-2/5) - 4 = -169/5$. This shows that the current solution is no longer optimal. Thus the changes in the coefficients under x_3 must be introduced in the optimal tableau and the regular simplex method is then applied to obtain a new optimal solution. The changes in the optimal tableau are given by

Basic	x_0	x_1	x_2	x_3	S_1	R_1	Solution
x_0				$-169/5$			
x_2				$-12/5$			
x_1				$-1/5$			

All other elements remain unchanged. The new technological coefficients of x_3, obtained by using Property IV, are

$$\begin{pmatrix} 2/5 & -1/5 \\ 1/5 & 2/5 \end{pmatrix}\begin{pmatrix} -5 \\ 2 \end{pmatrix} = \begin{pmatrix} -12/5 \\ -\ 1/5 \end{pmatrix}$$

(The new problem has no bounded solution since all the constraint coefficients are negative.)

• PROBLEM 4-28

Consider the problem, minimize z with

$$-6x_1 + x_3 - 2x_4 + 2x_5 = 6$$

$$-3x_1 + x_2 + 5x_4 + 3x_5 = 15$$

$$5x_1 + 3x_4 - 2x_5 = -21 + z$$

$$x_1, x_2, x_3, x_4, x_5 \geq 0$$

Find the optimal solution by utilizing the simplex method. Assume a new variable x_6 is introduced with the problem becoming the following.

Minimize z with $x_i \geq 0$, $1 \leq i \leq 6$

$$-6x_1 + x_3 - 2x_4 + 2x_5 - 4x_6 = 6$$

$$-3x_1 + x_2 + 5x_4 + 3x_5 + 6x_6 = 15$$

$$5x_1 + 3x_4 - 2x_5 + x_6 = -21 + z$$

Accommodate this change in the final tableau of the original problem and compute a new optimal value.

Solution: The initial simplex tableau for the first problem is as follows:

Table 1

	x_1	x_2	x_3	x_4	x_5	
x_3	−6	0	1	−2	2	6
x_2	−3	1	0	5	3	15
	5	0	0	3	−2	−21

The first column gives the basic variables. The first two rows correspond to the system of constraints, with the constant terms given in the last column. The last row corresponds to the equation defining the objective function, with the constant term on the right-hand side of that equation in the last column and the z term suppressed from the tableau as it remains fixed throughout the simplex method.

The -2 in the x_5 column of the last row indicates that one should pivot in that column. To determine the pivoting row, compare the ratios b_i/a_{is}, for $a_{is} > 0$,

Table 2

	x_1	x_2	x_3	x_4	x_5	
x_3	−6	0	1	−2	(2)	6
x_2	−3	1	0	5	3	15
	5	0	0	3	−2	−21
x_5	−3	0	$\frac{1}{2}$	−1	1	3
x_2	(6)	1	$-\frac{3}{2}$	8	0	6
	−1	0	1	1	0	−15

and find that row in which the minimum is attained. In this case $\frac{6}{2}$ is less than $\frac{15}{3}$ and, therefore, pivot at the 2 in the first row, replacing the basic variable x_3 with the variable x_5. The tableau representing the result of this pivot operation can be constructed from the present tableau by dividing the first row by 2 and then adding multiples of this row to the remaining rows in such a way as to generate zeros in the x_5 column. It is illustrated in Table 2, by placing this new tableau directly below the original tableau. The associated basic feasible solution is (0,6,0,0,3), and the value of the objective function at this point is the negative of the constant in the lower right-hand corner of the tableau, -(-15) = 15.

Pivoting now at the 6 in the x_1 column of the second row gives the tableau of Table 3.

Table 3

x_5	0	$\frac{1}{2}$	$-\frac{1}{4}$	3	1	6
x_1	1	$\frac{1}{6}$	$-\frac{1}{4}$	$\frac{4}{3}$	0	1
	0	$\frac{1}{6}$	$\frac{3}{4}$	$\frac{7}{3}$	0	−14

Since all the constants in the last row, excluding the -14, are nonnegative, the minimum value of the objective function has been attained. This value, -(-14) = 14, is attained at the basic feasible solution (1,0,0,0,6), as can be read from the final tableau.

Since the optimal value for the original problem is attained at the point (1,0,0,0,6), a basic feasible solution for this expanded problem is (1,0,0,0,6,0). This solution remains optimal if $c_6^* \geq 0$. Now,

$$c_6^* = c_6 - c_B B^{-1} A^{(6)}$$

$$= 1 - [-2,5] \begin{bmatrix} -\frac{1}{4} & \frac{1}{2} \\ -\frac{1}{4} & \frac{1}{6} \end{bmatrix} \begin{bmatrix} -4 \\ 6 \end{bmatrix} = -1$$

Thus (1,0,0,0,6,0) is no longer optimal, and $A^{*(6)}$ must be calculated. Now

$$A^{*(6)} = B^{-1} A^{(6)}$$

$$= \begin{bmatrix} -\frac{1}{4} & \frac{1}{2} \\ -\frac{1}{4} & \frac{1}{6} \end{bmatrix} \begin{bmatrix} -4 \\ 6 \end{bmatrix} = \begin{bmatrix} 4 \\ 2 \end{bmatrix}$$

To complete the problem, expand the final tableau of Table 3 to include this new column, and use the simplex algorithm. The resulting tableaux are given in Table 4. The minimum value of z is now $13\frac{1}{2}$, and is attained at the point $(0,0,0,0,4,\frac{1}{2})$.

Table 4

	x_1	x_2	x_3	x_4	x_5	x_6	
x_5	0	$\frac{1}{2}$	$-\frac{1}{4}$	3	1	4	6
x_1	1	$\frac{1}{6}$	$-\frac{1}{4}$	$\frac{4}{3}$	0	(2)	1
	0	$\frac{1}{6}$	$\frac{3}{4}$	$\frac{7}{3}$	0	-1	-14
x_5	-2	$\frac{1}{6}$	$\frac{1}{4}$	$\frac{1}{3}$	1	0	4
x_6	$\frac{1}{2}$	$\frac{1}{12}$	$-\frac{1}{8}$	$\frac{2}{3}$	0	1	$\frac{1}{2}$
	$\frac{1}{2}$	$\frac{1}{4}$	$\frac{5}{8}$	3	0	0	$-13\frac{1}{2}$

• PROBLEM 4-29

Minimize $-4x_1 + x_2 + 30x_3 - 11x_4 - 2x_5 + 3x_6$

subject to

$-2x_1 + 6x_3 + 2x_4 - 3x_6 + x_7 = 20$

$$-4x_1 + x_2 + 7x_3 + x_4 - x_6 = 10$$

$$-5x_3 + 3x_4 + x_5 - x_6 = 60$$

$x_j \geq 0,\ j = 1,\ldots,7$

Solve by the Simplex Method. Assume that b_1 is decreased by 2 units and b_2 increased by 3; that is,

$$b = \begin{bmatrix} 20 \\ 10 \\ 60 \end{bmatrix}, \quad q = \begin{bmatrix} -2 \\ 3 \\ 0 \end{bmatrix}, \quad \text{and } \bar{b} = b + q = \begin{bmatrix} 18 \\ 13 \\ 60 \end{bmatrix}$$

How will the final solution be affected? Assume b_2 were to be increased by 4 units instead; that is,

$$\bar{b} = \begin{bmatrix} 18 \\ 14 \\ 60 \end{bmatrix}$$

How will the final solution change, in this case?

Solution: The simplex solution to the original problem, in tableau form is as follows:

Table 1

	x_1	x_2	x_3	x_4	x_5	x_6	x_7	
x_7	−2	0	6	2	0	−3	1	20
x_2	−4	1	7	(1)	0	−1	0	10
x_5	0	0	−5	3	1	−1	0	60
	0	0	13	−6	0	2	0	110
x_7	(6)	−2	−8	0	0	−1	1	0
x_4	−4	1	7	1	0	−1	0	10
x_5	12	−3	−26	0	1	2	0	30
	−24	6	55	0	0	−4	0	170
x_1	1	$-\frac{1}{3}$	$-\frac{4}{3}$	0	0	$-\frac{1}{6}$	$\frac{1}{6}$	0
x_4	0	$-\frac{1}{3}$	$\frac{5}{3}$	1	0	$-\frac{5}{3}$	$\frac{2}{3}$	10
x_5	0	1	−10	0	1	(4)	−2	30
	0	−2	23	0	0	−8	4	170
x_1	1	$-\frac{7}{24}$	$-\frac{7}{4}$	0	$\frac{1}{24}$	0	$\frac{1}{12}$	$\frac{5}{4}$
x_4	0	$\frac{1}{12}$	$-\frac{5}{2}$	1	$\frac{5}{12}$	0	$-\frac{1}{6}$	$\frac{45}{2}$
x_6	0	$\frac{1}{4}$	$-\frac{5}{2}$	0	$\frac{1}{4}$	1	$-\frac{1}{2}$	$\frac{15}{2}$
	0	0	3	0	2	0	0	230

Now consider

$$\bar{b} = \begin{bmatrix} 18 \\ 13 \\ 60 \end{bmatrix}$$

From the final tableau of Table 1, using the entries of the seventh, second, and fifth columns, one gets

$$B^{-1} = \begin{bmatrix} \frac{1}{12} & -\frac{7}{24} & \frac{1}{24} \\ -\frac{1}{6} & \frac{1}{12} & \frac{5}{12} \\ -\frac{1}{2} & \frac{1}{4} & \frac{1}{4} \end{bmatrix}$$

and so

$$\bar{b}^* = b^* + B^{-1}q$$

$$= \begin{bmatrix} \frac{5}{4} \\ \frac{45}{2} \\ \frac{15}{2} \end{bmatrix} + \begin{bmatrix} \frac{1}{12} & -\frac{7}{24} & \frac{1}{24} \\ -\frac{1}{6} & \frac{1}{12} & \frac{5}{12} \\ -\frac{1}{2} & \frac{1}{4} & \frac{1}{4} \end{bmatrix} \begin{bmatrix} -2 \\ 3 \\ 0 \end{bmatrix} = \begin{bmatrix} \frac{5}{24} \\ \frac{277}{12} \\ \frac{37}{4} \end{bmatrix} \geq \begin{bmatrix} 0 \\ 0 \\ 0 \end{bmatrix}$$

Therefore the final tableau of Table 1, with the b^* entries replaced with these $\bar{b}^*$ entries and z_0^* value corrected, provides the final tableau for the modified problem. The optimal value of the objective function is now attained at the point $(\frac{5}{24},0,0,\frac{277}{12},0,\frac{37}{4},0)$. The new optimal value can be easily determined by simply evaluating the original objective function at this solution point. This value is -227.

If b_2 were to be increased by 4 units, one would have

$$\bar{b}^* = b^* + B^{-1} \begin{bmatrix} -2 \\ 4 \\ 0 \end{bmatrix} = \begin{bmatrix} -\frac{1}{12} \\ \frac{139}{6} \\ \frac{19}{2} \end{bmatrix}$$

Thus the point $(-\frac{1}{12},0,0,\frac{139}{6},0,\frac{19}{2},0)$ is a solution to this new system of constraints, but not a feasible solution. Note that now how to proceed is not at all clear. Since the Simplex method must move from one feasible solution to another feasible solution, it would seem that one is forced to initiate the simplex algorithm on the problem but with this new constant term column of 18, 14, 60, one cannot make use of the data of final tableau of Table 1. However, the Dual Simplex Algorithm can be used to resolve the difficulty of negative entries in the constant term column.

Using the data from the final tableau of Table 1, an equivalent form of this problem is represented by the tableau in Table 2.

Table 2

	x_1	x_2	x_3	x_4	x_5	x_6	x_7	
x_1	1	$-\frac{7}{24}$	$-\frac{7}{4}$	0	$\frac{1}{24}$	0	$\frac{1}{12}$	$-\frac{1}{12}$
x_4	0	$\frac{1}{12}$	$-\frac{5}{2}$	1	$\frac{5}{12}$	0	$-\frac{1}{6}$	$\frac{139}{6}$
x_6	0	$\frac{1}{4}$	$-\frac{5}{2}$	0	$\frac{1}{4}$	1	$-\frac{1}{2}$	$\frac{19}{2}$
	0	0	3	0	2	0	0	226

The $\bar{z}_0^* = 226$ is simply the negative of the value of the objective function at the point $(-\frac{1}{12},0,0,\frac{139}{6},0,\frac{19}{2},0)$. Applying the Dual Simplex algorithm, one gets the tableaux of Table 3.

Thus the problem is resolved after only one iteration. The minimal value of the objective function is -226 and is attained at the point $(0,\frac{2}{7},0,\frac{162}{7},0,\frac{66}{7},0)$.

Table 3

	x_1	x_2	x_3	x_4	x_5	x_6	x_7	
x_1	1	$\boxed{-\frac{7}{24}}$	$-\frac{7}{4}$	0	$\frac{1}{24}$	0	$\frac{1}{12}$	$-\frac{1}{12}$
x_4	0	$\frac{1}{12}$	$-\frac{5}{2}$	1	$\frac{5}{12}$	0	$-\frac{1}{6}$	$\frac{139}{6}$
x_6	0	$\frac{1}{4}$	$-\frac{5}{2}$	0	$\frac{1}{4}$	1	$-\frac{1}{2}$	$\frac{19}{2}$
	0	0	3	0	2	0	0	226
x_2	$-\frac{24}{7}$	1	6	0	$-\frac{1}{7}$	0	$-\frac{2}{7}$	$\frac{2}{7}$
x_4	$\frac{2}{7}$	0	-3	1	$\frac{3}{7}$	0	$-\frac{1}{7}$	$\frac{162}{7}$
x_6	$\frac{6}{7}$	0	-4	0	$\frac{2}{7}$	1	$-\frac{3}{7}$	$\frac{66}{7}$
	0	0	3	0	2	0	0	226

• PROBLEM 4-30

Consider the problem

Minimize $-2x_1 + x_2 - x_3$

Subject to $x_1 + x_2 + x_3 \le 6$

$-x_1 + 2x_2 \le 4$

$x_1, x_2, x_3 \ge 0$

with the optimal tableau

	z	x_1	x_2	x_3	x_4	x_5	RHS
z	1	0	-3	-1	-2	0	-12
x_1	0	1	1	1	1	0	6
x_5	0	0	3	1	1	1	10

How would the optimal tableau change if
a) $c_2 = 1$ in the cost vector is replaced by -3,
b) $c_1 = -2$ is replaced by zero,
c) the right-hand side of the problem is replaced by $\begin{pmatrix}3\\4\end{pmatrix}$,
d) a new constraint, $-x_1 + 2x_3 \geq 2$ is introduced?

Solution: a) $c_2 = 1$ in the cost vector is replaced by -3. x_2 is nonbasic. In this case $\vec{c}_B$ is not affected, and hence $z_j = \vec{c}_B \vec{B}^{-1}\vec{a}_j$ is not changed for any j. Thus $z_k - c_k$ is replaced by $z_k - c'_k$. Note that $z_k - c_k \leq 0$ since the current point was an optimal solution of the original problem. If $z_k - c'_k = (z_k - c_k) + (c_k - c'_k)$ is positive, then x_k must be introduced into the basis and the (primal) simplex method is continued. Otherwise the old solution is still optimal with respect to the new problem.
$z_2 - c'_2 = (z_2 - c_2) + (c_2 - c'_2) = -3 + 4 = 1$, and all other $z_j - c_j$ are unaffected. Hence x_2 enters the basis. The optimal tableau will change as follows.

	z	x_1	x_2	x_3	x_4	x_5	RHS
z	1	0	1	-1	-2	0	-12
x_1	0	1	1	1	1	0	6
x_5	0	0	(3)	1	1	1	10

b) $c_1 = -2$ in the cost vector is replaced by zero. $x_k = x_1$ is a basic variable in this case. Here c_{B_t} is replaced by c'_{B_t}. Let the new value of z_j be z'_j. Then $z'_j - c_j$ is calculated as follows:

$$z'_j - c_j = \vec{c}'_B \vec{B}^{-1}\vec{a}_j - c_j = (\vec{c}_B \vec{B}^{-1}\vec{a}_j - c_j)$$

$$+ (0, 0, \ldots, c'_{B_t} - c_{B_t}, 0, \ldots, 0)\vec{y}_j$$

$$= (z_j - c_j) + (c'_{B_t} - c_{B_t})y_{tj} \quad \text{for all j}$$

In particular for $j = k$, $z_k - c_k = 0$, and $y_{tk} = 1$, and hence $z'_k - c_k = c'_k - c_k$. As expected, $z'_k - c'_k$ is still equal to zero. Therefore the cost row can be updated by adding the net change in the cost of $x_{B_t} \equiv x_k$ times the current t row of the final tableau, to the original cost row. Then $z'_k - c_k$ is updated to $z'_k - c'_k = 0$.

Of course the new objective value $\vec{c}'_B\vec{B}^{-1}\vec{b} = \vec{c}_B\vec{B}^{-1}\vec{b} + (c'_{B_t} - c_{B_t})\bar{b}_t$ will be obtained in the process.

The new cost row, except $z_1 - c_1$, is obtained by multiplying the row of x_1 by the net change in c_1 [that is, $0 - (-2) = 2$] and adding to the old cost row. The new $z_1 - c_1$ remains zero. Note that the new $z_3 - c_3$ is now positive and so x_3 enters the basis. The optimal tableau is:

	z	x_1	x_2	x_3	x_4	x_5	RHS
z	1	0	-1	1	0	0	0
x_1	0	1	1	(1)	1	0	6
x_5	0	0	3	1	1	1	10

c) The right-hand side is replaced by $\begin{pmatrix}3\\4\end{pmatrix}$. If the right-hand-side vector $\vec{b}$ is replaced by $\vec{b}'$, then $\vec{B}^{-1}\vec{b}$ will be replaced by $\vec{B}^{-1}\vec{b}'$. The new right-hand side can be calculated without explicitly evaluating $\vec{B}^{-1}\vec{b}'$. This is evident by noting that $\vec{B}^{-1}\vec{b}' = \vec{B}^{-1}\vec{b} + \vec{B}^{-1}(\vec{b}' - \vec{b})$. If the first m columns originally form the identity, then $\vec{B}^{-1}(\vec{b}' - \vec{b}) = \sum_{j=1}^{m}\vec{y}_j(b'_j - b_j)$ and hence $\vec{B}^{-1}\vec{b}' = \vec{b} + \sum_{j=1}^{m}\vec{y}_j(b'_j - b_j)$. Since $z_j - c_j \le 0$ for all nonbasic variables (for a minimum problem), the only possible violation of optimality is that the new vector $\vec{B}^{-1}\vec{b}'$ may have some negative entries. If $\vec{B}^{-1}\vec{b}' \ge \vec{0}$, then the same basis remains optimal, and the values of the basic variables are $\vec{B}^{-1}\vec{b}'$ and the objective has value $\vec{c}_B\vec{B}^{-1}\vec{b}'$. Otherwise the dual simplex method is used to find the new optimal solution by restoring feasibility.

In this case $\vec{B}^{-1} = \begin{bmatrix}1 & 0\\1 & 1\end{bmatrix}$ and hence $\vec{B}^{-1}\vec{b}' = \begin{bmatrix}1 & 0\\1 & 1\end{bmatrix}\begin{bmatrix}3\\4\end{bmatrix} = \begin{bmatrix}3\\7\end{bmatrix}$. Then $\vec{B}^{-1}\vec{b}' \ge \vec{0}$ and hence the new optimal solution is $x_1 = 3$, $x_5 = 7$, $x_2 = x_3 = x_4 = 0$.

d) A new constraint, $-x_1 + 2x_3 \ge 2$ is added. If the optimal solution to the original problem satisfies the added constraint, it is then obvious that the point is also an optimal solution of the new problem. If, on the other hand, the point does not satisfy the new constraint, that is, if the constraint "cuts away" the optimal point, use the dual simplex method to find the new optimal solution. These two cases are illustrated in the figure shown.

Assume that $\vec{B}$ is the optimal basis before the constraint $\vec{a}^{m+1}\vec{x} \le b_{m+1}$ is added. The corresponding tableau is shown below.

$$z + (\vec{c}_B\vec{B}^{-1}\vec{N} - \vec{c}_N)\vec{x}_N = \vec{c}_B\vec{B}^{-1}\vec{b}$$

$$\vec{x}_B + \vec{B}^{-1}\vec{N}\vec{x}_N = \vec{B}^{-1}\vec{b} \qquad (1)$$

The constraint $\vec{a}^{m+1}\vec{x} \leq b_{m+1}$ is rewritten as $\vec{a}_B^{m+1}\vec{x}_B + \vec{a}_N^{m+1}\vec{x}_N + x_{n+1} = b_{m+1}$,

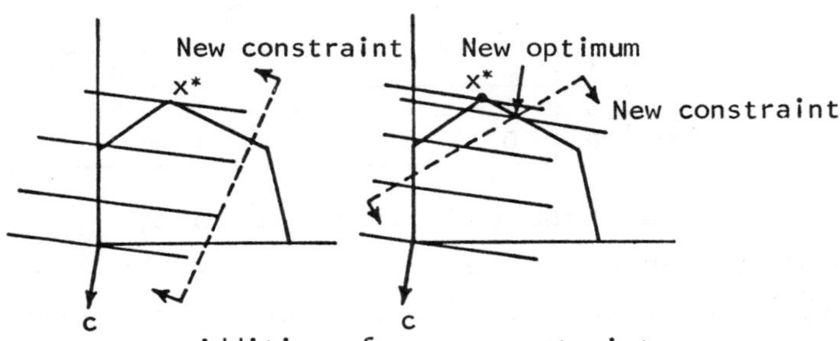

Addition of a new constraint

where $\vec{a}^{m+1}$ is decomposed into $(\vec{a}_B^{m+1}, \vec{a}_N^{m+1})$ and x_{n+1} is a nonnegative slack variable. Multiplying Equation (1) by $\vec{a}_B^{m+1}$ and subtracting from the new constraint gives the following system:

$$z + (\vec{c}_B\vec{B}^{-1}\vec{N} - \vec{c}_N)\vec{x}_N = \vec{c}_B\vec{B}^{-1}\vec{b}$$

$$\vec{x}_B + \vec{B}^{-1}\vec{N}\vec{x}_N = \vec{B}^{-1}\vec{b}$$

$$(\vec{a}_N^{m+1} - \vec{a}_B^{m+1}\vec{B}^{-1}\vec{N})\vec{x}_N + x_{n+1} = b_{m+1} - \vec{a}_B^{m+1}\vec{B}^{-1}\vec{b}$$

These equations give us a basic solution of the new system. The only possible violation of optimality of the new problem is the sign of $b_{m+1} - \vec{a}_B^{m+1}\vec{B}^{-1}\vec{b}$. So if $b_{m+1} - \vec{a}_B^{m+1}\vec{B}^{-1}\vec{b} \geq 0$, then the current solution is optimal. Otherwise, if $b_{m+1} - \vec{a}_B^{m+1}\vec{B}^{-1}\vec{b} < 0$, then the dual simplex method is used to restore feasibility.

In this case, the optimal point $(x_1,x_2,x_3) = (6,0,0)$ does not satisfy this constraint. The constraint $-x_1 + 2x_3 \geq 2$ is rewritten as $x_1 - 2x_3 + x_6 = -2$, where x_6 is a nonnegative slack variable. This row is added to the initial optimal simplex tableau to obtain the following tableau.

	z	x_1	x_2	x_3	x_4	x_5	x_6	RHS
z	1	0	-3	-1	-2	0	0	-12
x_1	0	1	1	1	1	0	0	6
x_5	0	0	3	1	1	1	0	10
x_6	0	1	0	-2	0	0	1	-2

Multiply row 1 by -1 and add to row 3 in order to restore column x_1 to a unit vector. The dual simplex method can then be applied to the resulting tableau below.

	z	x_1	x_2	x_3	x_4	x_5	x_6	RHS
z	1	0	-3	-1	-2	0	0	-12
x_1	0	1	1	1	1	0	0	6
x_5	0	0	3	1	1	1	0	10
x_6	0	0	-1	(-3)	1	0	1	-8

Note that adding a new constraint in the primal problem is equivalent to adding a new variable in the dual problem and vice versa.

• PROBLEM 4-31

Consider the problem

$$\text{Minimize} \quad -2x_1 + x_2 - x_3$$

$$\text{Subject to} \quad x_1 + x_2 + x_3 \le 6$$

$$-x_1 + 2x_2 \le 4$$

$$x_1, x_2, x_3 \ge 0$$

with the optimal tableau

	z	x_1	x_2	x_3	x_4	x_5	RHS
z	1	0	-3	-1	-2	0	-12
x_1	0	1	1	1	1	0	6
x_5	0	0	3	1	1	1	10

How would the optimal tableau change if

a) a_2 in the constraint matrix $\vec{A}$ is changed from $\begin{pmatrix}1\\2\end{pmatrix}$ to $\begin{pmatrix}2\\5\end{pmatrix}$.

b) $\vec{a}_1$ is changed from $\begin{pmatrix}1\\-1\end{pmatrix}$ to $\begin{pmatrix}0\\-1\end{pmatrix}$.

c) $\vec{a}_1$ is changed from $\begin{pmatrix}1\\-1\end{pmatrix}$ to $\begin{pmatrix}3\\6\end{pmatrix}$.

d) a new activity $x_6 \ge 0$ with $c_6 = 1$ and $\vec{a}_6 = -\frac{1}{2}$ is introduced?

<u>Solution</u>: a) a_2 is changed from $\begin{pmatrix}1\\2\end{pmatrix}$ to $\begin{pmatrix}2\\5\end{pmatrix}$. That is, the nonbasic column $\vec{a}_j$ is modified to $\vec{a}_j'$. Then the new updated column is $\vec{B}^{-1}\vec{a}_j'$ and $z_j' - c_j = \vec{c}_B\vec{B}^{-1}\vec{a}_j' - c_j$. If $z_j' - c_j \le 0$, then the old solution is optimal; otherwise the simplex method is continued, after column j of the tableau is updated, by introducing the nonbasic variable x_j. Thus,

$$\vec{y}_2' - \vec{B}^{-1}\vec{a}_2' = \begin{pmatrix}1 & 0\\ 1 & 1\end{pmatrix}\begin{pmatrix}2\\5\end{pmatrix} = \begin{pmatrix}2\\7\end{pmatrix}$$

$$\vec{c}_B \vec{B}^{-1} \vec{a}_2' - c_2 = (-2,0)\begin{pmatrix} 2 \\ 7 \end{pmatrix} - 1 = -5$$

The current optimal tableau remains optimal with column x_2 replaced by $(-5,2,7)^t$.

b) $\vec{a}_1$ is changed from $\begin{pmatrix} 1 \\ -1 \end{pmatrix}$ to $\begin{pmatrix} 0 \\ -1 \end{pmatrix}$. That is, a basic column $\vec{a}_j$ is modified to $\vec{a}_j'$. It is possible that the current set of basic vectors no longer form a basis after the change. Even if this does not occur, a change in the activity vector for a single basic column will change $\vec{B}^{-1}$ and thus the entries in every column. Assume that the basic columns are ordered from 1 to m. Let the activity vector for basic column j change from $\vec{a}_j$ to $\vec{a}_j'$. Compute $\vec{y}_j' = \vec{B}^{-1}\vec{a}_j'$ where $\vec{B}^{-1}$ is the current basis inverse. There are two possibilities. If $y_{jj}' = 0$, the current set of basic vectors no longer forms a basis. In this case it is probably best to add an artificial variable to take the place of x_j in the basis and resort to the two-phase method or the big-M method. However, if $y_{jj}' \neq 0$, replace column j, which is currently a unit vector, by $\vec{y}_j'$ and pivot on y_{jj}'. The current basis continues to be a basis. However, upon pivoting both primal and dual feasibility may have been destroyed and, if so, must resort to one of the artificial variable (primal or dual) techniques.

Then

$$\vec{y}_1' = \vec{B}^{-1}\vec{a}_1' = \begin{pmatrix} 1 & 0 \\ 1 & 1 \end{pmatrix}\begin{pmatrix} 0 \\ -1 \end{pmatrix} = \begin{pmatrix} 0 \\ -1 \end{pmatrix}$$

$$\vec{c}_B \vec{B}^{-1}\vec{a}_1' - c_1 = (-2,0)\begin{pmatrix} 0 \\ -1 \end{pmatrix} - (-2) = 2$$

Here the entry in the x_1 row of y_1' is zero, and so the current basic columns no longer span the space. Replacing column x_1 by $(2,0,-1)^t$ and adding the artificial variable x_6 to replace x_1 in the basis, one gets the following tableau.

	z	x_1	x_2	x_3	x_4	x_5	x_6	RHS
z	1	2	-3	-1	-2	0	-M	-12
x_6	0	0	1	1	1	0	①	6
x_5	0	-1	3	1	1	1	0	10

After preliminary pivoting at row x_6 and column x_6 to get $z_6 - c_6 = 0$, that is, to get the tableau in basic form, proceed with the big-M method.

c) Column $\vec{a}_1$ is changed from $\begin{pmatrix} 1 \\ -1 \end{pmatrix}$ to $\begin{pmatrix} 3 \\ 6 \end{pmatrix}$. Then

$$\vec{y}_1' = \vec{B}^{-1}\vec{a}_1' = \begin{pmatrix} 1 & 0 \\ 1 & 1 \end{pmatrix}\begin{pmatrix} 3 \\ 6 \end{pmatrix} = \begin{pmatrix} 3 \\ 9 \end{pmatrix}$$

$$\vec{c}_B\vec{B}^{-1}\vec{a}_1' - c_1 = (-2,0)\begin{pmatrix} 3 \\ 9 \end{pmatrix} - (-2) = -4$$

In this case the entry in the x_1 row of $\vec{y}_1'$ is nonzero and so, replace column x_1 by $(-4,3,9)^t$, pivot in the x_1 column and x_1 row, and proceed.

	z	x_1	x_2	x_3	x_4	x_5	RHS
z	1	−4	−3	−1	−2	0	−12
x_1	0	(3)	1	1	1	0	6
x_5	0	9	3	1	1	1	10

d) A new activity $x_6 \geq 0$ with $c_6 = 1$ and $\vec{a}_6 = \begin{pmatrix} -1 \\ 2 \end{pmatrix}$ is introduced. That is, a new activity x_{n+1} with unit cost c_{n+1} and consumption column a_{n+1} is considered for possible production. Without resolving the problem, it can easily be determined whether producing x_{n+1} is worthwhile. First calculate $z_{n+1} - c_{n+1}$. If $z_{n+1} - c_{n+1} \leq 0$ (for a minimization problem), then $x^*_{n+1} = 0$ and the current solution is optimal. On the other hand, if $z_{n+1} - c_{n+1} > 0$, then x_{n+1} is introduced into the basis and the simplex method continues to find the new optimal solution.

First calculate $z_6 - c_6$:

$$z_6 - c_6 = \vec{w}\vec{a}_6 - c_6$$

$$= (-2,0)\begin{pmatrix} -1 \\ 2 \end{pmatrix} - 1 = 1$$

$$\vec{y}_6 = \vec{B}^{-1}\vec{a}_6 = \begin{bmatrix} 1 & 0 \\ 1 & 1 \end{bmatrix}\begin{bmatrix} -1 \\ 2 \end{bmatrix} = \begin{pmatrix} -1 \\ 1 \end{pmatrix}$$

Therefore x_6 is introduced in the basis by pivoting at the x_5 row and the x_6 column.

	z	x_1	x_2	x_3	x_4	x_5	x_6	RHS
z	1	0	−3	−1	−2	0	1	−12
x_1	0	1	1	1	1	0	−1	6
x_5	0	0	3	1	1	1	(1)	10

Consider the following linear programming problem:

Maximize $f = 15x_1 + 5x_2$ (1)

subject to $2x_1 + 3x_2 \leq 54$ (2)

$4x_1 + 2x_2 \leq 40$ (3)

$x_1, x_2 \geq 0$

The solution to this problem is $x_1^* = 10$, $x_2^* = 0$, and $f^* = 150$.

a) How would the optimal solution change for ranging values of the coefficient of x_2 in the objective function (c_2)?

b) Assume that Eq. (2) is changed to

$$3.5x_1 + 2x_2 \leq 40$$

(perhaps because of some improvement in methods or equipment). How would the problem be affected? How would the problem be affected if $a_{11} = 2$ was changed?

c) Change the right-hand side of (2), b_1, from 54 to 60; then change b_2 from 40 to 44. What is the effect in each case?

d) Assume the constraint

$$4x_1 + 1.5x_2 = 36$$

is appended to the problem. Does it affect the optimal solution?

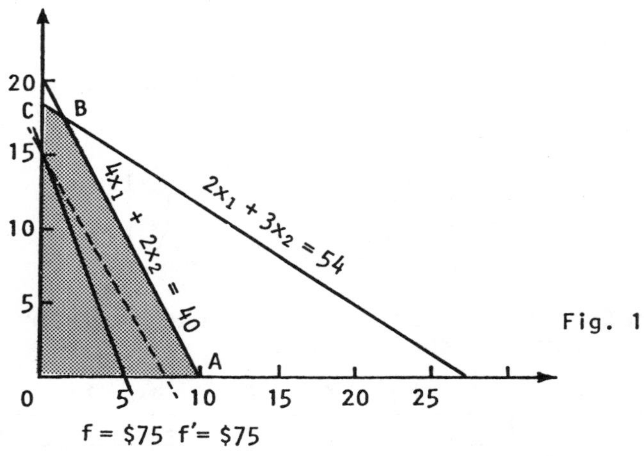

Fig. 1

Change in objective-function coefficients.

Solution: a) Assume that the profitability of variable x_2 increases by $2.50. Since only the objective function is changed, clearly the set of feasible solutions OABC in Fig. 1 is unchanged. However, the slope of the isoprofit lines is changed. The dotted line f' = $75 shows a new isoprofit line. In this case, all points on line AB are optimal, where B = (1.5,17).

If the coefficient of x_2 in the objective function, c_2, is increased further, then point B will be the unique optimal solution, up to the point at which c_2 = $22.50. At this point, both points B and C will be optimal. Finally, when $c_2 >$ $22.50, point C will be optimal. Thus, as long as c_2 is less than $7.50, point A will be optimal. When c_2 is between $7.50 and $22.50, point B will be optimal. When c_2 is greater than $22.50, point C will be optimal. (Alternate optima exist when c_2 = $7.50 or c_2 = $22.50.) Of course, the optimal value of the objective function changes whenever c_2 does. However, the optimal values of the decision variables change only at certain values of c_2. Management can thus assess the significance of a change in the value of an objective-function coefficient.

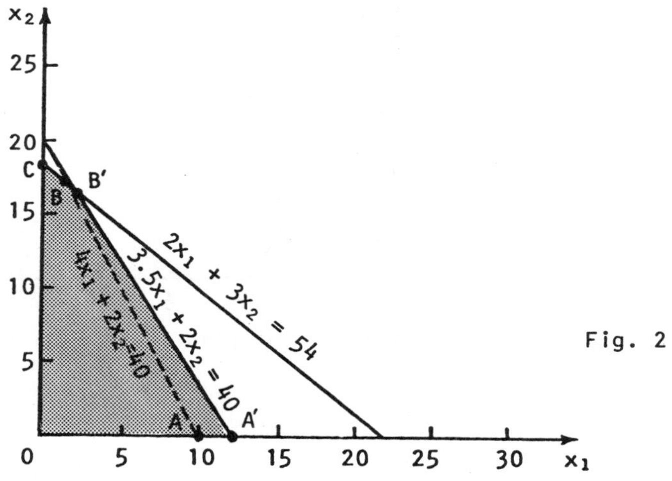

Fig. 2

Change in a technological coefficient.

b) The dotted line in Fig. 2 shows the original constraint (2). The new optimal solution occurs at point A' = (11.43,0) instead of point A = (10,0). The new optimal value of the objective function is 11.43 × $15 = $171.45, an increase of $21.45. Notice that the set of feasible solutions has changed from OABC to OA'B'C'. Consider a change in the coefficient of x_1 in eq. (2) (a_{11} = 2). This coefficient would have to change rather dramatically before it would have any impact on the optimal solution. In fact, if a_{11} were to decrease (assuming it remains positive), then no change whatsoever would occur, while it could increase to a value of 5.4 without any effect.

It should be clear that changing the value of a technological coefficient involves a rotation of the affected constraint. This rotation will (generally) change the set of feasible solutions, but it may have no effect on the optimal solution.

c) A change in a right-hand-side constant involves moving the affected constraint parallel to its original position. This may or may not change the value of the optimal solution.

The right-hand side of eq. 2, b_1, is changed from 54 to 60: The result is shown in Fig. 3. The optimal solution is unchanged; the set of feasible solutions is OAC'. Consider b_2 (the right-hand side of eq. 2)to be changed from 40 to 44: The optimal solution becomes $x_1^* = 11$, $x_2^* = 0$, and $f^* = 165$. This is shown in Fig. 4. The new set of feasible solutions is OA'B'C.

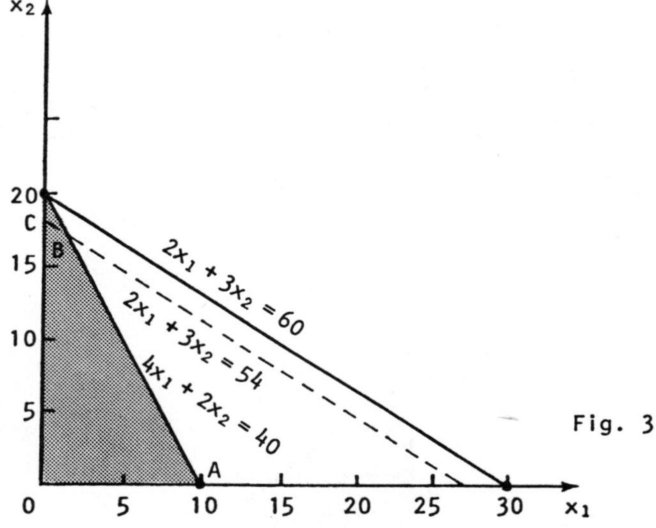

Fig. 3

Change in the right-hand side insignificant.

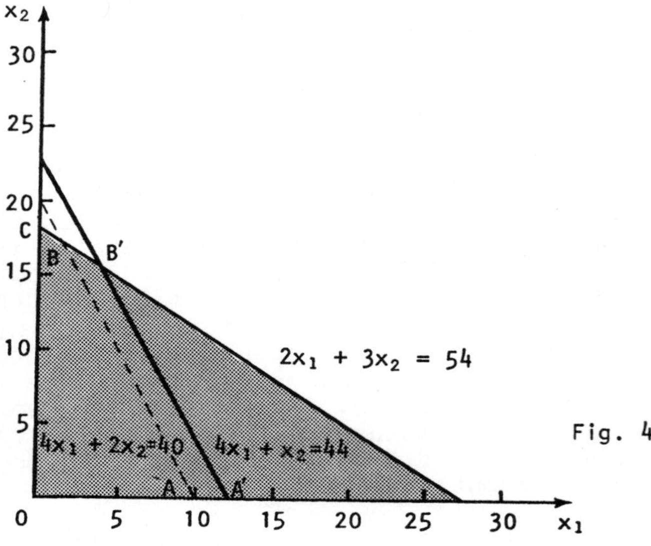

Fig. 4

Change in the right-hand side significant.

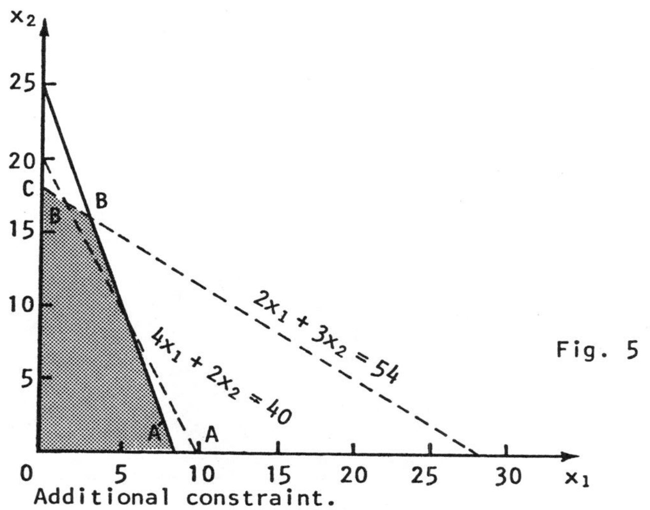

Additional constraint.

(d) Simply check to see if the optimal solution satisfies the new constraint. If it does, then no change occurs. However, as is shown in Fig. 5, the optimal solution $x_1 = 10$, $x_2 = 0$ violates the new constraint. The new optimal solution is $x_1^* = 9$, $x_2^* = 0$, and $f^* = 135$. The new set of feasible solutions changed from OABC to OA'B'C.

• PROBLEM 4-33

A cabinetmaker considers producing two types of bathroom cabinets: Modern and Provincial. These cabinets would be sold through a chain of department stores, and there is, for all practical purposes, an unlimited market for any mix of these cabinets, at least within the cabinetmaker's production capacity. The cabinets have to go through four basic operations: cutting of the lumber, gluing, sanding and priming, and finishing. The last operation introduces the necessary variety as to colors and final finish. Table 1 contains all relevant information concerning production times per cabinet produced and production capacities for each operation per day, as well as the net revenue per unit (after subtracting variable material cost). The cabinetmaker would like to determine a product mix that maximizes his daily net revenue.

CABINETMAKER'S PRODUCT MIX PROBLEM

Product	Cutting in Hours/ Cabinet	Gluing in Hours/ Cabinet	Sanding in Hours/ Cabinet	Finishing in Hours/ Cabinet	Net Revenue/ Cabinet*
Modern	$\frac{2}{5}$	1	$\frac{1}{3}$	$2\frac{2}{3}$	15
Provincial	$\frac{3}{5}$	$1\frac{1}{2}$	1	2	15
Capacity in hours	8	15	8	32	

* After subtracting all materials cost.

Construct a graphical representation of the problem and determine the optimal solution. What if one hour of additional time were offered in each of the cabinetmaker's four departments? How much should he be willing to pay for each?

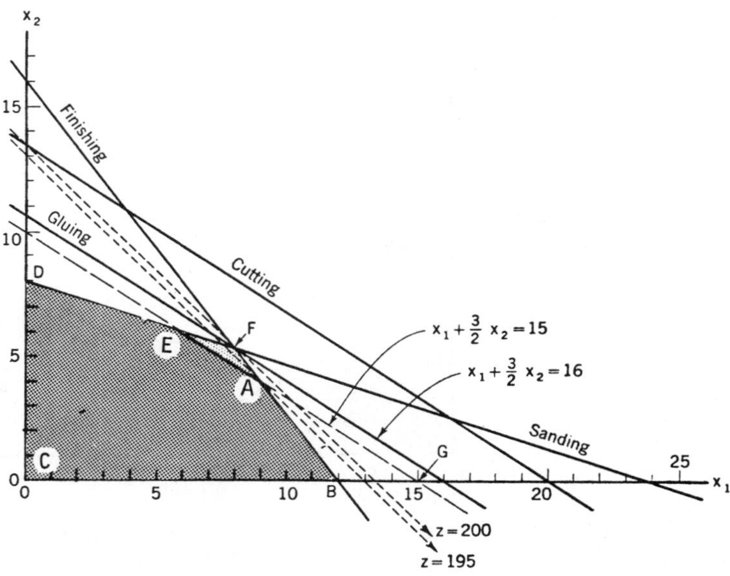

Solution: The graphical representation is given in Figure 1. The feasible region is determined by ABODE and the optimal point is A with objective function value z = 195.

Next, consider the case when one hour of additional time in each of the cabinetmaker's four departments is offered. First of all, he should not pay anything for an extra hour of something when there is already enough, in fact too much, available. This is the case for the total cutting or sanding time availability. They are not used up entirely in the optimal solution. But how about additional gluing or finishing time made available? Analyze graphically the effect on the optimal solution of an additional hour of gluing time available beyond the initial 15, keeping all other inputs unchanged. In Fig. 1 the original gluing constraint boundary is shown as the broken line going through points G and A, and the new boundary of the gluing constraint for 16 hours of gluing time as the solid line going through point F on the graph, parallel to the broken line. A change in the value of an RHS parameter of a constraint causes that constraint to shift parallel to itself. It does not cause a change in its slope. Such a shift may also cause the feasible region to change. For this case, the additional hour of gluing time added the dark gray triangle with corners A, E, and F to the feasible region. But now the original optimal objective function for z = 195 has a segment that is completely inside the new feasible region. Hence, the new optimal solution occurs at point F where z = 200. At point F the optimal production consists of 8 modern cabinets and $5\frac{1}{3}$ provincial cabinets. $1\frac{1}{3}$ more provincial cabinets are worth \$20 and one fewer modern cabinets diminishes this by \$15 for a net increase of \$5, which explains the change of the optimal objective function value from \$195 to \$200. One can conclude that, since an additional hour of gluing time results in an increase in profits of \$5, the cabinet-maker would be willing to pay up to \$5 for an additional hour of gluing time. Note that the new gluing constraint has now only one point in common with the new feasible region, namely point F. From this follows immediately that if the gluing time available is increased beyond 16, the gluing constraint shifts completely outside the new feasible region and hence becomes redundant. This means that further increase in the gluing constraint has no further effect on the optimal solution. Beyond 16 hours, the value of additional gluing time drops to zero.

Each additional hour of finishing time made available beyond the original 32 hours, keeping all other inputs at their original values, results in an increase in profits of \$3.75 up to a total of 8 additional hours. Beyond a total availability of 40 hours of finishing time no further changes occur.

• PROBLEM 4-34

The problem is to determine a maximal profit production schedule in the manufacturing and selling of rowboats and canoes utilizing limited resources of aluminum, machine time, and labor. Letting R and C denote the number of rowboats and canoes, respectively, to be manufactured, the linear programming problem is to

$$\text{Maximize} \quad z = 50R + 60C$$

subject to

$$\begin{aligned} 50R + 30C &\leq 2000 \\ 6R + 5C &\leq 300 \\ 3R + 5C &\leq 200 \\ R, C &\geq 0 \end{aligned} \tag{1}$$

The constant terms of the constraints come from the limits on the resources of aluminum (2000 lb), machine time (300 min), and labor (200 hr). The maximum possible profit is \$2750 earned in the production of 25 rowboats and 25 canoes.

Assume that the boat manufacturer has the opportunity to purchase more aluminum. With additional aluminum available, (possibly) more boats can be produced. But the manufacturer needs to know how the profits from the additional sales would compare with the cost of the extra aluminum. In other words, how much should he be willing to pay for more aluminum? Make the same analysis for machine time and labor.

Solution: In terms of the original problem of (1), what is needed is a measure of the effect of a change in the constant of the first inequality on the maximum value of the objective function. To determine this consider the dual to the problem of (1), and its solution. The dual is to

$$\text{Minimize } v = 2000y_1 + 300y_2 + 200y_3$$

subject to

$$50y_1 + 6y_2 + 3y_3 \geq 50$$
$$30y_1 + 5y_2 + 5y_3 \geq 60$$
$$y_1, y_2, y_3 \geq 0$$

The optimal value of v is 2750 attained at $y_1 = \frac{7}{16}$, $y_2 = 0$, $y_3 = \frac{75}{8}$. Note that the coefficients of the dual objective function v are, by definition, the constant terms from the original constraints. In fact, from the Duality Theorem, one has that

$$\text{Max } z = \text{Min } v = 2000(\tfrac{7}{16}) + 300(0) + 200(\tfrac{75}{8})$$

It follows that as long as $(\frac{7}{16}, 0, \frac{75}{8})$ is an optimal solution point for the dual, the minimum of v and therefore the maximum profit will increase by $\$(\frac{7}{16}) \cong 44$ cents for each available pound of aluminum above the original 2000 pounds. One can now answer the original question. Since the profit figures of \$50 for a rowboat and \$60 for a canoe would be determined by subtracting the cost of the required aluminum, machine time, and labor for each from the selling price, the manufacturer should be willing to pay for additional aluminum up to about 44 cents/lb more than he paid for the original 2000 lb of aluminum. For example, if he can purchase 48 lb for only \$15 more than the original cost of 48 lb of aluminum, he can increase his sales by $\$(\frac{7}{16})48 = \$21$ and, therefore, have a net gain of \$6.

This analysis can be extended to the other resources. Since $y_3 = \frac{75}{8} \cong 9.38$ in the optimal solution to the dual, each additional hour of finishing labor would increase profits by \$9.38. Similarly, $y_2 = 0$ implies that an increase in available machine time over the original 300 min will provide no increase in profits. Actually, one could have reasoned to this by examining the original optimal solution to (1). As can be easily calculated, the production schedule of R = C = 25 utilizes all 2000 lb of aluminum and 200 hr of labor, but only 275 of the available 300 min of machine time. Thus production is restricted by the limited amounts of aluminum and labor available. Machine time is an underutilized resource, so increasing its availability has no effect on profits.

In sum, the solution $(\frac{7}{16}, 0, \frac{75}{8})$ to the dual has provided estimates on the effects changes in the constant terms of the problem have on the optimal value of the objective function. These numbers are sometimes called the shadow prices or marginal values of the constraints, since each provides some indication of the worth or cost on the optimal value of the objective function of a unit of the resource or demand generating the associated constraint. Certainly, however, there are limitations on their use. For example, the boat manufacturer would not be able to make unlimited profits even if there were available an unlimited supply of aluminum, because the other two constraints would still restrict the total production. Thus the estimate of an increased profit of 44 cents/lb for each additional pound of aluminum available is accurate only to some upper limit. Once the change or changes in the constant terms of the original problem effect a change in the optimal solution point to the dual, these marginal values will change.

• PROBLEM 4-35

Let the profit to be maximized be

$$2x_1 + 6x_2 + 3x_3,$$

subject to

$$x_1 + 2x_2 + 2x_3 \le 5$$
$$2x_1 + x_2 + 3x_3 \le 6,$$

where x_1, x_2 and x_3 are some non-negative levels of activities, and the right-hand sides of the constraints are the available upper limits of some facilities.

The optimal tableau turns out to be

	x_1	x_3	x_4	
x_2	$\frac{1}{2}$	1	$\frac{1}{2}$	$\frac{5}{2}$
x_5	$\frac{3}{2}$	2	$-\frac{1}{2}$	$\frac{7}{2}$
	1	3	3	15

One would therefore be prepared to pay (not more than) 3 for a unit increase in the amount of either the first or the second facility. But how much should one be prepared to buy of the first facility?

Solution: Take the dual of the last tableau:

	y_2	y_5	
y_1	$-\frac{1}{2}$	$-\frac{3}{2}$	1
y_3	-1	-2	3
y_4	$-\frac{1}{2}$	$\frac{1}{2}$	3
	$-\frac{5}{2}$	$-\frac{7}{2}$	15

If the right-hand side of the first constraint, and accordingly the coefficient of y_4 in the objective function of the dual, is increased by D, then the checking rule produces the bottom row

$$-(5 + D)/2 \quad (-7 + D)/2 \quad 15 + 3D.$$

The tableau remains optimal as long as D does not exceed 7, hence this is the largest amount that should be bought at a price of 3. The profit would thereby increase by 3 times 7. If more is bought, the price should be less per unit. A further iteration of the tableau which ceases to be optimal shows how much the price for further increases might be.

PARAMETRIC PROGRAMMING

• PROBLEM 4-36

Consider the following problem.

Minimize $-x_1 - 3x_2$

Subject to
$$x_1 + x_2 \leq 6$$
$$-x_1 + 2x_2 \leq 6$$
$$x_1, \quad x_2 \geq 0$$

It is desired to find the optimal solutions and optimal objective values of the class of problems whose objective function is $(-1 + 2\lambda, -3 + \lambda)$ for $\lambda \geq 0$.

Solution: The procedure of solution for a problem of the form

$$\text{Minimize} \quad \vec{c}\vec{x}$$

$$\text{Subject to} \quad \vec{A}\vec{x} = \vec{b}$$

$$\vec{x} \geq \vec{0}$$

when the cost vector is perturbed, is as follows. Assume that $\vec{B}$ is an optimal basis. Suppose that the cost vector $\vec{c}$ is perturbed along the cost direction $\vec{c}'$, that is, $\vec{c}$ is replaced by $\vec{c} + \lambda\vec{c}'$ where $\lambda \geq 0$. One is interested in finding the optimal points and corresponding objective values as a function of $\lambda \geq 0$. Decomposing $\vec{A}$ into $[\vec{B},\vec{N}]$, $\vec{c}$ into $(\vec{c}_B,\vec{c}_N)$ and $\vec{c}'$ into $(\vec{c}'_B,\vec{c}'_N)$, one gets

$$z - (\vec{c}_B + \lambda\vec{c}'_B)\vec{x}_B - (\vec{c}_N + \lambda\vec{c}'_N)\vec{x}_N = 0$$

$$\vec{B}\vec{x}_B + \vec{N}\vec{x}_N = \vec{b}$$

Updating the tableau and denoting $\vec{c}_B'\vec{y}_j$ by z_j', one gets

$$z + \sum_{j \in R} [(z_j - c_j) + \lambda(z_j' - c_j')]x_j = \vec{c}_B\vec{\bar{b}} + \lambda\vec{c}_B'\vec{\bar{b}}$$

$$\vec{x}_B + \sum_{j \in R} \vec{y}_j x_j = \vec{\bar{b}}$$

where R is the set of current indices associated with the nonbasic variables. The current tableau has $\lambda = 0$ and gives an optimal basic feasible solution of the original problem without perturbation. One would like to find out how far one can move in the direction $\vec{c}'$ while still maintaining optimality of the current point. Let $S = \{j:(z_j' - c_j') > 0\}$. If $S = \phi$, then the current solution is optimal for all values of $\lambda \geq 0$. Otherwise calculate $\hat{\lambda}$ as follows:

$$\hat{\lambda} = \underset{j \in S}{\text{Minimum}} \left\{ \frac{-(z_j - c_j)}{z_j' - c_j'} \right\} = \frac{-(z_k - c_k)}{z_k' - c_k'} \tag{1}$$

Let $\lambda_1 = \hat{\lambda}$. For $\lambda \in [0,\lambda_1]$ the current solution is optimal and the optimal objective value is given by $\vec{c}_B\vec{\bar{b}} + \lambda\vec{c}_B'\vec{\bar{b}} = \vec{c}_B\vec{B}^{-1}\vec{b} + \lambda\vec{c}_B'\vec{B}^{-1}\vec{b}$. For $\lambda \in [0,\lambda_1]$, the shadow prices in the simplex tableau are replaced by $(z_j - c_j) + \lambda(z_j' - c_j')$. At $\lambda = \lambda_1$, x_k is introduced into the basis (if a blocking variable exists.) After the tableau is updated, the process is repeated by recalculating S and $\hat{\lambda}$ and letting $\lambda_2 = \hat{\lambda}$. For $\lambda \in [\lambda_1,\lambda_2]$ the new current solution is optimal and its objective value is given by $\vec{c}_B\vec{\bar{b}} + \lambda\vec{c}_B'\vec{\bar{b}} = \vec{c}_B\vec{B}^{-1}\vec{b} + \lambda\vec{c}_B'\vec{B}^{-1}\vec{b}$ where $\vec{B}$ is the current basis. The process is repeated until S becomes empty. If there is no blocking variable when x_k enters the basis, then the problem is unbounded for all values of λ greater than the current value.

Perturb the cost vector along the vector (2,1). First solve the problem with $\lambda = 0$ where x_3 and x_4 are the slack variables. The optimal tableau for $\lambda = 0$ is given by the following.

	z	x_1	x_2	x_3	x_4	RHS
z	1	0	0	$-\frac{5}{3}$	$-\frac{2}{3}$	-14
x_1	0	1	0	$\frac{2}{3}$	$-\frac{1}{3}$	2
x_2	0	0	1	$\frac{1}{3}$	$\frac{1}{3}$	4

In order to find the range over which this tableau is optimal, first find $\vec{c}_B'\vec{B}^{-1}\vec{N} - \vec{c}_N'$:

$$\vec{c}_B'\vec{B}^{-1}\vec{N} - \vec{c}_N' = \vec{c}_B'(\vec{y}_3,\vec{y}_4) - (c_3',c_4')$$

$$= (2,1) \begin{bmatrix} \frac{2}{3} & -\frac{1}{3} \\ \frac{1}{3} & \frac{1}{3} \end{bmatrix} - (0,0)$$

$$= (\tfrac{5}{3}, -\tfrac{1}{3}) \qquad (2)$$

Therefore S = {3} and from Equation (1) $\hat{\lambda}$ is given by

$$\hat{\lambda} = \frac{-(z_3 - c_3)}{z_3' = c_3'} = \frac{-(-\frac{5}{3})}{\frac{5}{3}} = 1$$

Therefore $\lambda_1 = 1$ and for $\lambda \in [0,1]$ the basis $[\vec{a}_1, \vec{a}_2]$ remains optimal. The optimal objective value $z(\lambda)$ in this interval is given by

$$z(\lambda) = \vec{c}_B \vec{b} + \lambda \vec{c}_B' \vec{b}$$

$$= -14 + \lambda(2,1)\begin{pmatrix} 2 \\ 4 \end{pmatrix} = -14 + 8\lambda$$

Noting Equation (2), the shadow prices of the nonbasic variables x_3 and x_4 are given by

$$(z_3 - c_3) + \lambda(z_3' - c_3') = -\frac{5}{3} + \frac{5}{3}\lambda$$

$$(z_4 - c_4) + \lambda(z_4' - c_4') = -\frac{2}{3} - \frac{1}{3}\lambda$$

Hence the optimal solution for any λ in the interval [0,1] is given by the following tableau.

	z	x_1	x_2	x_3	x_4	RHS
z	1	0	0	$-\frac{5}{3} + \frac{5}{3}\lambda$	$-\frac{2}{3} - \frac{1}{3}\lambda$	$-14 + 8\lambda$
x_1	0	1	0	$\frac{2}{3}$	$-\frac{1}{3}$	2
x_2	0	0	1	$\frac{1}{3}$	$\frac{1}{3}$	4

At $\lambda = 1$ the coefficient of x_3 in row 0 is equal to 0 and x_3 is introduced in the basis leading to the following new tableau.

	z	x_1	x_2	x_3	x_4	RHS
z	1	0	0	0	-1	-6
x_3	0	$\frac{3}{2}$	0	1	$-\frac{1}{2}$	3
x_2	0	$-\frac{1}{2}$	1	0	$\frac{1}{2}$	3

Now find the interval $[1, \lambda_2]$ over which the foregoing tableau is optimal. Note that

$$z_1 - c_1 = \vec{c}_B \vec{y}_1 - c_1 = (0,-3)\begin{pmatrix} \frac{3}{2} \\ -\frac{1}{2} \end{pmatrix} + 1 = \frac{5}{2}$$

$$z_4 - c_4 = \vec{c}_B \vec{y}_4 - c_4 = (0,-3)\begin{pmatrix} -\frac{1}{2} \\ \frac{1}{2} \end{pmatrix} - 0 = -\frac{3}{2}$$

$$z_1' - c_1' = \vec{c}_B' \vec{y}_1 - c_1' = (0,1)\begin{pmatrix} \frac{3}{2} \\ -\frac{1}{2} \end{pmatrix} - 2 = -\frac{5}{2}$$

$$z_4' - c_4' = \vec{c}_B' \vec{y}_4 - c_4' = (0,1)\begin{pmatrix} -\frac{1}{2} \\ \frac{1}{2} \end{pmatrix} - 0 = \frac{1}{2}$$

Therefore the shadow prices for the nonbasic variables x_1 and x_4 are given by

$$(z_1 - c_1) + \lambda(z_1' - c_1') = \frac{5}{2} - \frac{5}{2}\lambda$$

$$(z_4 - c_4) + \lambda(z_4' - c_4') = -\frac{3}{2} + \frac{1}{2}\lambda$$

Therefore for λ in the interval [1,3] the shadow prices are nonpositive and the basis consisting of $\vec{a}_3$ and $\vec{a}_2$ is optimal. Note that $\lambda = 3$ can also be determined as follows:

$$S = \{4\} \text{ and } \lambda = \frac{-(z_4 - c_4)}{z_4' - c_4'} = \frac{\frac{3}{2}}{\frac{1}{2}} = 3$$

Over the interval [1,3] the objective function $z(\lambda)$ is given by

$$z(\lambda) = \vec{c}_B \vec{\bar{b}} + \lambda \vec{c}_B' \vec{\bar{b}}$$

$$= (0,-3)\begin{pmatrix} 3 \\ 3 \end{pmatrix} + \lambda(0,1)\begin{pmatrix} 3 \\ 3 \end{pmatrix} = -9 + 3\lambda$$

Hence the optimal tableau for $\lambda \in [1,3]$ is given below.

	z	x_1	x_2	x_3	x_4	RHS
z	1	$\frac{5}{2} - \frac{5}{2}\lambda$	0	0	$-\frac{3}{2} + \frac{1}{2}\lambda$	$-9 + 3\lambda$
x_3	0	$\frac{3}{2}$	0	1	$-\frac{1}{2}$	3
x_2	0	$-\frac{1}{2}$	1	0	$\frac{1}{2}$	3

At $\lambda = 3$ the coefficient of x_4 in row 0 is equal to zero, and x_4 is introduced in the basis leading to the following tableau.

	z	x_1	x_2	x_3	x_4	RHS
z	1	-5	0	0	0	0
x_3	0	1	1	1	0	6
x_4	0	-1	2	0	1	6

Calculate the interval over which the foregoing tableau is optimal. First calculate

$$z_1' - c_1' = \vec{c}_B'\vec{y}_1 - c_1' = -2$$

$$z_2' - c_2' = \vec{c}_B'\vec{y}_2 - c_2' = -1$$

Therefore $S = \phi$ and hence the basis $[\vec{a}_3, \vec{a}_4]$ is optimal for all $\lambda \in [3,\infty]$. Figure 1 shows the optimal points and the optimal objective as a function of λ. Note that this function is piecewise-linear and concave. The break points correspond to the value of λ at which alternative optimal solutions exist.

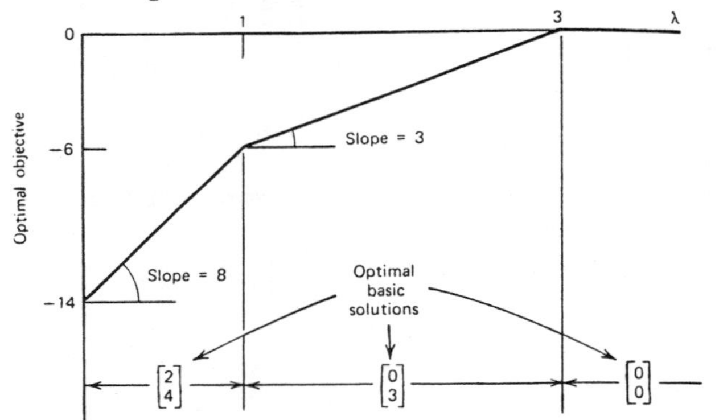

Fig. 1

Optimal objectives and optimal points as a function of λ.

• PROBLEM 4-37

Determine x_1 as a function of c in the optimal solutions of the following two problems:

$$\text{minimize} \quad cx_1 + 4x_2,$$

$$\text{subject to} \quad 3x_1 + 6x_2 \geq 2$$

$$2x_1 + 4x_2 \geq 3$$

$$6x_1 + 2x_2 \geq 2,$$

where c is positive, and

(a) all $x_j \geq 0$, (b) the x_j are not sign-restricted.

Solution: (a) Start with

	x_1	x_2			x_4	x_2	
x_3	-3	-6	-2	x_3	$-\frac{3}{2}$	0	$\frac{5}{2}$
x_4	-2*	-4	-3	x_1	$-\frac{1}{2}$	2	$\frac{3}{2}$
x_5	-6	-2	-2	x_5	-3	10*	7
	-c	-4	0		-c/2	-4+2c	3c/2

Optimal if $c \leq 2$.

	x_4	x_5	
x_3	$-\frac{3}{2}$	0	$\frac{5}{2}$
x_1	$\frac{1}{10}$*	$-\frac{1}{5}$	$\frac{1}{10}$
x_2	$-\frac{3}{10}$	$\frac{1}{10}$	$\frac{7}{10}$
	$\frac{c-12}{10}$	$\frac{2-c}{5}$	$\frac{c+28}{10}$

Optimal if $2 \leq c \leq 12$

	x_1	x_5	
x_3	15	-3	4
x_4	10	-2	1
x_2	3	$-\frac{1}{2}$	1
	12-c	-2	4

Optimal if $c \geq 12$.

(b) Dual

Maximize $2y_3 + 3y_4 + 2y_5$,

subject to
$$3y_3 + 2y_4 + 6y_5 = c$$
$$6y_3 + 4y_4 + 2y_5 = 4$$
$$y_3, y_4, y_5 \geq 0$$

It follows that $c = 2 + 5y_5$, and $y_5 \leq 2$. Therefore only feasible if $2 \leq c \leq 12$.

If $c \leq 2$, then in primal $x_1 = \infty, x_2 = -\infty$ (by inspection);

$c \geq 12$, then in primal $x_1 = -\infty, x_2 = \infty$ (by inspection).

Write primal:

Minimize $c(u_1 - u_2) + 4(v_1 - v_2)$,

subject to
$$3(u_1 - u_2) + 6(v_1 - v_2) \geq 2$$
$$2(u_1 - u_2) + 4(v_1 - v_2) \geq 3$$
$$6(u_1 - u_2) + 2(v_1 - v_2) \geq 2$$
$$u_1, u_2, v_1, v_2 \geq 0.$$

Final tableau:

	x_4	u_2	x_5	v_2	
x_3	$-\frac{3}{2}$	0	0	0	$\frac{5}{2}$
u_1	$\frac{1}{10}$	-1	$-\frac{1}{5}$	0	$\frac{1}{10}$
v_1	$-\frac{3}{10}$	0	$\frac{1}{10}$	-1	$\frac{7}{10}$
	(c-12)/10	0	(2-c)/5	0	(28+c)/10

i.e. $x_1 = \frac{1}{10}$, $x_2 = \frac{7}{10}$.

• PROBLEM 4-38

Find nonnegative x_1, x_2, which maximize

$$Z = c_1 x_1 + x_2 \quad (1)$$

and which satisfy the constraints:

$$2x_1 + x_2 \leq 10 \quad (2)$$

$$x_1 + x_2 \leq 8 \quad (3)$$

$$x_1 \leq 3; \quad x_2 \leq 7 \quad (4)$$

For what values of c_1 will an optimal solution be achieved?

Solution: An initial basic feasible solution for this problem is immediately at hand since the basic set can be selected to consist of the slack variables $\bar{S}_1$-$\bar{S}_4$, corresponding to the constraints (2)-(4), respectively. This produces the tableau of Fig. 1(a), which clearly cannot be an optimal solution for any value of c_1, since the sensitivity coefficient for x_2 is positive. Therefore, select x_2 to enter the basis, replacing $\bar{S}_4$, with the results shown in Fig. 1(b). The basis for this tableau will be optimal as long as c_1 is negative, for then all the sensitivity coefficients will be negative. When c_1 becomes positive, the sensitivity coefficient for x_1 also becomes positive, and the solution can be improved by replacing $\bar{S}_2$ with x_1 in the basic set, producing the tableau of Fig. 1(c). Since now the sensitivity coefficients for $\bar{S}_2$ and $\bar{S}_4$ will remain nonpositive if c_1 is respectively nonnegative and not greater than 1, the basis for this tableau is optimal in the range $0 \leq c_1 \leq 1$. When c_1 exceeds a value of +1, $\bar{S}_4$ is made a basic variable with the results shown in Fig. 1(d). Continuing in this manner, compute the tableau of Fig. 1(e), which remains the optimal solution for all values of c_1 greater than 2.

	c_1	1					
	x_1	x_2	$\bar{s}_1$	$\bar{s}_2$	$\bar{s}_3$	$\bar{s}_4$	
$\bar{s}_1$	2	1	1	0	0	0	10
$\bar{s}_2$	1	1	0	1	0	0	8
$\bar{s}_3$	1	0	0	0	1	0	3
$\bar{s}_4$	0	1	0	0	0	1	7
	$+c_1$	+1	0	0	0	0	0

Fig. 1(a)

Initial tableau, nonoptimal for all values of c_1

$\bar{s}_1$	2	0	1	0	0	-1	3
$\bar{s}_2$	1	0	0	1	0	-1	1
$\bar{s}_3$	1	0	0	0	1	0	3
x_2	0	1	0	0	0	1	7
	$+c_1$	0	0	0	0	-1	7

Fig. 1(b)

Optimal solution for $c_1 < 0$

$\bar{s}_1$	0	0	1	-2	0	1	1
x_1	1	0	0	1	0	-1	1
$\bar{s}_3$	0	0	0	-1	1	1	2
$\bar{s}_2$	0	1	0	0	0	1	7
	0	0	0	$-c_1$	0	$c_1 - 1$	$7 + c_1$

Fig. 1(c)

Optimal solution in the range $0 \leq c_1 \leq 1$

$\bar{s}_4$	0	0	-1	-2	0	1	1
x_1	1	0	1	-1	0	0	2
$\bar{s}_1$	0	0	-1	1	1	0	1
$\bar{s}_2$	0	1	-1	2	0	0	6
	0	0	$1 - c_1$	$c_1 - 2$	0	-1	$6 + 2c_1$

Fig. 1(d)

Optimal solution in the range $1 \leq c_1 \leq 2$

$\bar{s}_4$	0	0	-1	0	2	1	3
x_1	1	0	0	0	1	0	3
$\bar{s}_2$	0	0	-1	1	1	0	1
$\bar{s}_3$	0	1	1	0	-2	0	4
	0	0	-1	0	$2 - c_1$	0	$4 + 3c_1$

Fig. 1(e)

Optimal solution for $c_1 \geq 2$

Although this simple problem can be worked by hand, most parametric programming must be performed on a digital computer, since it requires that numerous simplex iterations be performed on the full tableau.

• PROBLEM 4-39

Solve the parametric programming problem

Minimize $(2 + t)x_1 + (7 - t)x_2 - (2 + 3t)x_3$,

subject to
$$x_1 + 2x_2 + x_3 \leq 1 + s$$
$$-4x_1 - 2x_2 + 3x_3 \leq 2$$
$$x_1, x_2, x_3 \geq 0,$$

where t varies between -3 and 1, and s varies between -1 and 2.

Solution: The first tableau

	x_1	x_2	x_3	
x_4	1	2	1	1+s
x_5	-4	-2	3	2
	-2-t	-7+t	2+3t	0

is optimal for all s in its range, and for $-2 \leq t \leq -\frac{2}{3}$. When t = -2, then pivot on the 1 in the x_1-column and obtain

	x_4	x_2	x_3	
x_1	1	2	1	1+s
x_5	4	6	7	6+4s
	2+t	-3+3t	4+4t	(1+s)(2+t).

This is optimal for all s, and for $t \leq -2$.

On the other hand, if $t = -\frac{2}{3}$, then pivot on 1 in the x_3-column if $s \leq -\frac{1}{3}$ (Case a), or on 3 in the x_3-column if $s \geq -\frac{1}{3}$ (Case b). One obtains the optimal tableaus, respectively,

(a)

	x_1	x_2	x_4	
x_3	1	2	1	1+s
x_5	-7	-8	-3	-1-3s
	-4-4t	-11-5t	-2-3t	(-1-s)(2+3t)

(b)

	x_1	x_2	x_5	
x_4	$\frac{7}{3}$	$\frac{8}{3}$	$-\frac{1}{3}$	(1+3s)/3
x_3	$-\frac{4}{3}$	$-\frac{2}{3}$	$\frac{1}{3}$	$\frac{2}{3}$
	$\frac{2+9t}{3}$	$\frac{-17+9t}{3}$	$\frac{-2-3t}{3}$	$\frac{-(4+6t)}{3}$

• PROBLEM 4-40

Find the values of c_1 and c_2 which produce the several optimal basic solutions of the problem:

$$\text{maximize} \quad c_1x_1 + c_2x_2 + x_3,$$

$$\text{subject to} \quad 3x_1 + 5x_2 + x_3 = 4$$

$$7x_1 - 2x_2 + 4x_3 = 11$$

$$x_1, x_2, x_3 \text{ non-negative.}$$

Solution: Solve for (x_1, x_3), answer clearly feasible.

	x_2			x_1	
x_1	$\frac{22}{5}$	1	x_2	$\frac{5}{22}$	$\frac{5}{22}$
x_3	$-\frac{41}{5}$	1	x_3	$\frac{41}{22}$	$\frac{63}{22}$
	$\frac{22c_1 - 5c_2 - 41}{5}$	c_1+1		$\frac{41 + 5c_2 - 22c_1}{22}$	$\frac{63+5c_2}{22}$

Optimal if

$$22c_1 - 5c_2 - 41 \geq 0.$$

Optimal if

$$22c_1 - 5c_2 - 41 \leq 0.$$

If $x_3 = 0$, answer not feasible.

• PROBLEM 4-41

Consider the following problem.

$$\text{Minimize} \quad -x_1 - 3x_2$$

$$\text{Subject to} \quad x_1 + x_2 \leq 6$$

$$-x_1 + 2x_2 \leq 6$$

$$x_1, \quad x_2 \geq 0$$

It is desired to find the optimal solution and optimal basis as the right-hand-side is perturbed along direction $\begin{pmatrix}-1\\1\end{pmatrix}$.

Solution: Perturbation of the right-hand-side means that the right-hand-side vector $\vec{b}$ is replaced by $\vec{b} + \lambda\vec{b}'$ where $\lambda \geq 0$. Since the right-hand side of the primal problem is the objective of the dual problem, perturbing the right-hand side can be analyzed as perturbing the objective function of the dual problem, as well.

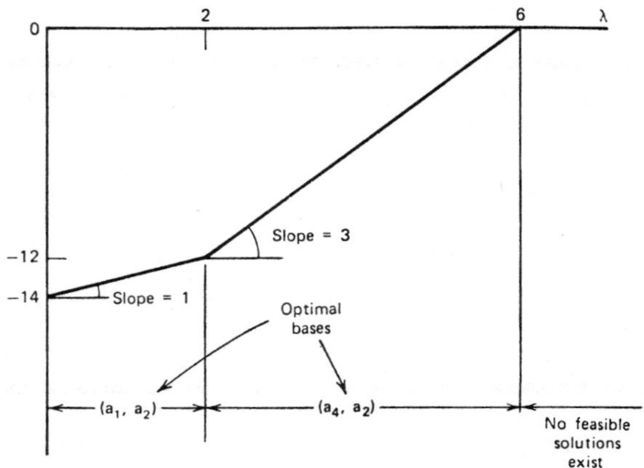

Optimal objectives and bases as a function of λ. Fig. 1

Assume an optimal basis $\vec{B}$ of the original problem, that is, with $\lambda = 0$. The corresponding tableau is given by

$$z + (\vec{c}_B\vec{B}^{-1}\vec{N} - \vec{c}_N)\vec{x}_N = \vec{c}_B\vec{B}^{-1}\vec{b}$$

$$\vec{x}_B + \vec{B}^{-1}\vec{N}\vec{x}_N = \vec{B}^{-1}\vec{b}$$

where $\vec{c}_B\vec{B}^{-1}\vec{N} - \vec{c}_N \leq \vec{0}$. If $\vec{b}$ is replaced by $\vec{b} + \lambda\vec{b}'$, the vector $\vec{c}_B\vec{B}^{-1}\vec{N} - \vec{c}_N$ will not be affected; that is, dual feasibility will not be affected. The only change is that $\vec{B}^{-1}\vec{b}$ will be replaced by $\vec{B}^{-1}(\vec{b} + \lambda\vec{b}')$, and accordingly the objective becomes $\vec{c}_B\vec{B}^{-1}(\vec{b} + \lambda\vec{b}')$. As long as $\vec{B}^{-1}(\vec{b} + \lambda\vec{b}')$ is nonnegative, the current basis remains optimal. The value of λ at which another basis becomes optimal, can therefore, be determined as follows. Let $S = \{i:\bar{b}'_i < 0\}$ where $\vec{\bar{b}}' = \vec{B}^{-1}\vec{b}'$.

If $S = \phi$, then the current basis is optimal for all values of $\lambda \geq 0$. Otherwise let

$$\hat{\lambda} = \underset{i \in S}{\text{Minimum}} \left\{ \frac{\bar{b}_i}{-\bar{b}'_i} \right\} = \frac{\bar{b}_r}{-\bar{b}'_r} \qquad (1)$$

Let $\lambda_1 = \hat{\lambda}$. For $\lambda \in [0,\lambda_1]$ the current basis is optimal, where $\vec{x}_B = \vec{B}^{-1}(\vec{b} + \lambda\vec{b}')$ and the optimal objective is $\vec{c}_B\vec{B}^{-1}(\vec{b} + \lambda\vec{b}')$. At λ_1 the right-hand side is replaced by $\vec{B}^{-1}(\vec{b} + \lambda_1\vec{b}')$, x_{B_r} is removed from the basis, and an appropriate variable (according to dual simplex method criterion) enters the basis. After the tableau is updated, the process is repeated in order to find the range $[\lambda_1,\lambda_2]$ over which the new basis is optimal, where $\lambda_2 = \hat{\lambda}$ from Equation (1). The process is terminated when either S is empty, in which case the current basis is optimal for all values of λ greater than or equal to the last value of λ, or else when all the entries in the row whose right-hand side dropped to zero, are nonnegative. In this latter case no feasible solutions exist for all values of λ greater than the current value.

For the above problem, $\vec{b} = \begin{pmatrix} 6 \\ 6 \end{pmatrix}$ is replaced by $\vec{b} + \lambda\vec{b}'$ $= \begin{pmatrix} 6 \\ 6 \end{pmatrix} + \lambda \begin{pmatrix} -1 \\ 1 \end{pmatrix}$ for $\lambda \geq 0$. The optimal solution with $\lambda = 0$ is shown below where x_3 and x_4 are the slack variables.

	z	x_1	x_2	x_3	x_4	RHS
z	1	0	0	$-\frac{5}{3}$	$-\frac{2}{3}$	-14
x_1	0	1	0	$\frac{2}{3}$	$-\frac{1}{3}$	2
x_2	0	0	1	$\frac{1}{3}$	$\frac{1}{3}$	4

In order to find the range over which the above basis is optimal, first calculate $\vec{\bar{b}}'$:

$$\vec{\bar{b}}' = \vec{B}^{-1}\vec{b}'$$

$$= \begin{bmatrix} \frac{2}{3} & -\frac{1}{3} \\ \frac{1}{3} & \frac{1}{3} \end{bmatrix} \begin{bmatrix} -1 \\ 1 \end{bmatrix} = \begin{bmatrix} -1 \\ 0 \end{bmatrix}$$

Therefore $S = \{1\}$ and from Equation (1) λ_1 is given by

$$\lambda_1 = \frac{\bar{b}_1}{-\bar{b}'_1} = \frac{2}{-(-1)} = 2$$

Therefore the basis $[\vec{a}_1, \vec{a}_2]$ remains optimal over the interval $[0,2]$. In particular, for any $\lambda \in [0,2]$ the objective value and the right-hand-side are given by

$$z(\lambda) = \vec{c}_B\vec{\bar{b}} + \lambda\vec{c}_B\vec{\bar{b}}'$$

$$= (-1,-3)\begin{pmatrix} 2 \\ 4 \end{pmatrix} + \lambda(-1,-3)\begin{pmatrix} -1 \\ 0 \end{pmatrix}$$

$$= -14 + \lambda$$

$$\vec{\bar{b}} + \lambda\vec{\bar{b}}' = \begin{pmatrix} 2 \\ 4 \end{pmatrix} + \lambda\begin{pmatrix} -1 \\ 0 \end{pmatrix}$$

$$= \begin{pmatrix} 2 - \lambda \\ 4 \end{pmatrix}$$

	z	x_1	x_2	x_3	x_4	RHS
z	1	0	0	$-\frac{5}{3}$	$-\frac{2}{3}$	$-14+\lambda$
x_1	0	1	0	$\frac{2}{3}$	$-\frac{1}{3}$	$2-\lambda$
x_2	0	0	1	$\frac{1}{3}$	$\frac{1}{3}$	4

At $\lambda = 2$, $x_{B_r} = x_1$ drops to zero. A dual simplex pivot is performed so that x_1 leaves the basis and x_4 enters the basis leading to the following tableau.

	z	x_1	x_2	x_3	x_4	RHS
z	1	-2	0	-3	0	-12
x_4	0	-3	0	-2	1	0
x_2	0	1	1	1	0	4

In order to find the range $[2,\lambda_2]$ over which this tableau is optimal, first find $\vec{\bar{b}}$ and $\vec{\bar{b}}'$:

$$\vec{\bar{b}} = \vec{B}^{-1}\vec{b} = \begin{bmatrix} -2 & 1 \\ 1 & 0 \end{bmatrix} \begin{bmatrix} 6 \\ 6 \end{bmatrix} = \begin{bmatrix} -6 \\ 6 \end{bmatrix}$$

$$\vec{\bar{b}}' = \vec{B}^{-1}\vec{b}' = \begin{bmatrix} -2 & 1 \\ 1 & 0 \end{bmatrix} \begin{bmatrix} -1 \\ 1 \end{bmatrix} = \begin{bmatrix} 3 \\ -1 \end{bmatrix}$$

Therefore $S = \{2\}$ and λ_2 is given by

$$\lambda_2 = \frac{\bar{b}_2}{-\bar{b}_2'} = \frac{6}{-(-1)} = 6$$

For λ in the interval [2,6] the optimal objective value and the right-hand-side are given by

$$z(\lambda) = c_B\vec{\bar{b}} + \lambda\vec{c}_B\vec{\bar{b}}'$$

$$= (0,-3)\begin{pmatrix} -6 \\ 6 \end{pmatrix} + \lambda(0,-3)\begin{pmatrix} 3 \\ -1 \end{pmatrix}$$

$$= -18 + 3\lambda$$

$$\vec{\bar{b}} + \lambda\vec{\bar{b}}' = \begin{bmatrix} -6 \\ 6 \end{bmatrix} + \lambda\begin{bmatrix} 3 \\ -1 \end{bmatrix}$$

$$= \begin{bmatrix} -6 + 3\lambda \\ 6 - \lambda \end{bmatrix}$$

The optimal tableau over the interval [2,6] is depicted below.

	z	x_1	x_2	x_3	x_4	RHS
z	1	-2	0	-3	0	$-18+3\lambda$
x_4	0	-3	0	-2	1	$-6+3\lambda$
x_2	0	1	1	1	0	$6-\lambda$

At $\lambda = 6$, x_2 drops to zero. Since all entries in the x_2 row are nonnegative, stop with the conclusion that for $\lambda > 6$ there exist no feasible solutions. Figure 1 summarizes the optimal bases and corresponding objectives for $\lambda \geq 0$. Note that the optimal objective as a function of λ is piecewise-linear and convex. The break points correspond to the values of λ for which alternative optimal dual solutions exist.

• PROBLEM 4-42

Two variables x and y are constrained as follows:

$$-x + y \leq 8, \quad (1)$$

$$x + 2y \leq 22, \quad (2)$$

$$x + y \leq 14, \quad (3)$$

$$x + 1/2y \leq 11, \quad (4)$$

$$x + 1/4y \leq 10.5. \quad (5)$$

The objective is to maximize y. Figure 1 depicts the feasible solution space to this problem. Simple inspection will show that the optimum solution to this problem is at point A, with an objective function value of 10. Now add a new constraint:

$$x \geq c, \quad (6)$$

and let c increase from 0 to 12. Analyze the changes that will occur in this parametric linear programming problem.

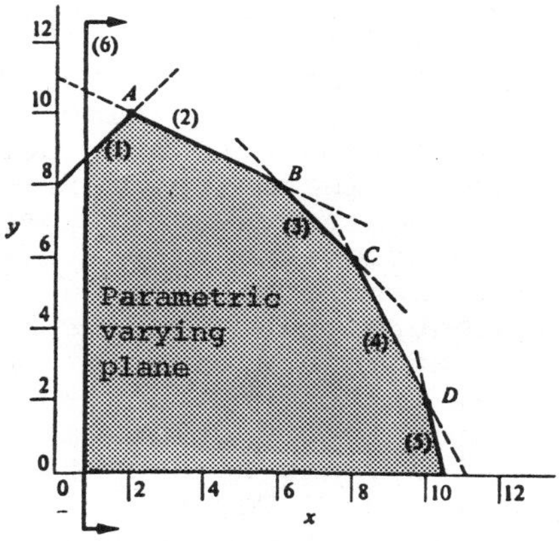

Graphical description of the parametric linear programming procedure.

Fig. 1

Solution: Addition of the new constraint is equivalent to driving a vertical line through the solution space in an easterly direction. This movement shrinks the solution space, since feasible solutions can exist only to the right of the (6) line.

When increasing c from 0 upward, nothing happens until c reaches 2, because the optimum solution is y = 10, x = 2. Expression (6) is not limiting for c between 0 and 2.

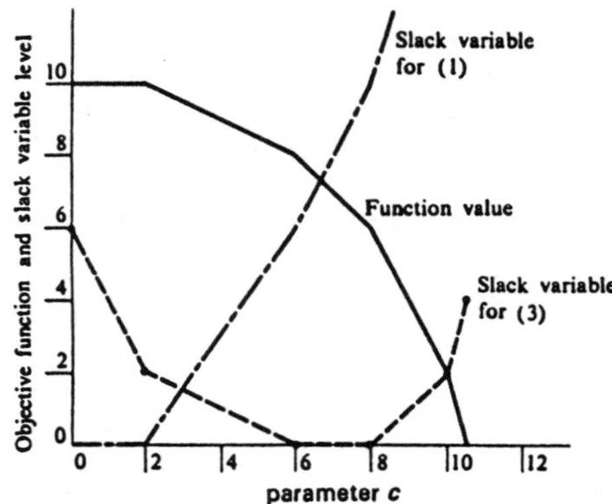

The function value and magnitude of slack variables as parameter *c* ranges from 0 to 12. Fig. 2

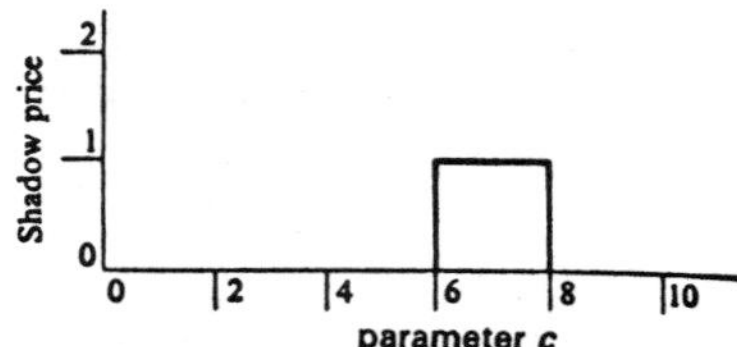

The shadow price for slack 3 as parameter *c* ranges from 0 to 12. Fig. 3

At the original optimal solution, (1) and (2) were limiting; when c reaches 2, (2) and (6) become limiting. When c further increases to 6, (3) and (6) become limiting, etc. Figure 2 shows the value of the objective function and two of the slack variables as the parameter c ranges from 0 to 12. Observe here that as the parameter c increases, different constraints become binding, and when a constraint becomes binding, the magnitude of the associated slack variable becomes 0. At each vertex, therefore, a basis change occurs. The parametric procedure thus jumps from one vertex to another, assuring that each subsequent solution stays feasible and optimal for the current set of constraints. The value of the objective function varies linearly between adjacent vertices, and so does the magnitude of all the problem variables. For example, when c = 4, x = 4, y = 9. The value of the objective is also 9 and the amount of slack for (3) is 14 - 9 - 4 = 1.

While the magnitude of the variables and the objective value vary linearly between adjacent basis changes, the shadow prices are constant for the same variation in parameter. This is so because the shadow prices indicate the rate of change in the objective value if a constraint were raised or lowered. Shadow prices are nonzero only for limiting constraints, and the rate of change in the objective remains constant whether the constraint is just barely binding or doing so severely. In the problem, (3) is binding when the change parameter c ranges from 6 to 8. At the same time, (6), the changing plane, is binding. The optimum solution exists at the intersection of the lines representing (3) and (6). A small positive variation e in (3) causes the intersection of (3) and (6) to slide upward on the (6) line, increasing y and the value of the objective. Note that the rate of change in the objective value is proportional to the rate of change of the constraint for (3). During the parametric linear programming run, therefore, the shadow price for slack variable 3 is as shown in Fig. 3.

In a similar manner, the shadow price for slack variable 1, when (1) and (2) are binding is 0.333. If the constraint value of (1) were raised from 8 to 9, the intersection of (1) and (2) lines would shift from x = 2, y = 10 to x = 1.333, y = 10.333 and the objective value would be 10.333. Thus a change of 1 unit in the constraint causes 0.333 unit difference in the objective value, and hence the shadow price for the slack variable associated with (1) is 0.333 when the optimum solutions lie at the intersection of the (1) and (2) lines. Also, this value is a constant so long as the same set of equations is binding.

• PROBLEM 4-43

Maximize $x_1 + x_2 + 2x_3$,

subject to $x_j \geq 0$ and

$$6x_1 + 3x_2 + 4x_3 \leq c$$

$$x_1 - 5x_2 + x_3 \leq 6$$

Find the solution to the above problem, for all values of c. Use the graph of the dual problem to determine how the model behaves in different regions of c. Then apply the simplex algorithm to the dual problem.

Solution: No solution for negative c.

$c \geq 24$:

Final dual tableau:

	y_2	y_3	
y_1	$-\frac{2}{23}$	$-\frac{33}{23}$	$\frac{45}{23}$
y_4	$-\frac{1}{23}$	$-\frac{5}{23}$	$\frac{11}{23}$
y_5	$\frac{4}{23}$	$-\frac{3}{23}$	$\frac{2}{23}$
	$\frac{24 - c}{23}$	$\frac{-18 - 5c}{23}$	$\frac{12 + 11c}{23}$

$0 \le c \le 24$:

Final dual tableau:

	y_3	y_5	
y_1	$-\frac{3}{2}$	$\frac{1}{2}$	2
y_2	$-\frac{3}{4}$	$\frac{23}{4}$	$\frac{1}{2}$
y_4	$-\frac{1}{4}$	$\frac{1}{4}$	$\frac{1}{2}$
	$-c/4$	$c/4 - 6$	$c/2$

• PROBLEM 4-44

Minimize

$$x_1 + x_2 + 2x_3 + x_4$$

subject to

$$x_1 \quad - 2x_3 - x_4 = 2 - \theta$$

$$x_2 - x_3 + x_4 = -1 + \theta$$

$$x_j \ge 0$$

Solve for all values of θ.

Tableau 1

I. Problem in Simplex Tableau

Basis	$\vec{c}$	$\vec{P}_0$		1 $\vec{P}_1$	1 $\vec{P}_2$	2 $\vec{P}_3$	1 $\vec{P}_4$
$\vec{P}_1$	1	2	−1	1	0	−2	(−1)
$\vec{P}_2$	1	−1	1	0	1	(−1)	1
		1	0	0	0	−5	−1

II. Vector $\vec{P}_4$ Eliminated Vector $\vec{P}_1$ in Step I

$\vec{P}_4$	1	−2	1	−1	0	2	1
$\vec{P}_2$	1	1	0	1	1	−3	0
		−1	1	−1	0	−3	0

III. Vector $\vec{P}_3$ Eliminated Vector $\vec{P}_2$ in Step I

$\vec{P}_1$	1	4	−3	1	−2	0	−3
$\vec{P}_3$	2	1	−1	0	−1	1	−1
		6	−5	0	−5	0	−6

Solution: Develop the simplex tableau as shown in Tableau 1. In Step I, note that the basis $(\vec{P}_1\vec{P}_2)$ has all $z_j - c_j \leq 0$ with $x_1 = q_1 + \theta p_1 = 2 - \theta$ and $x_2 = q_2 - \theta p_2 = -1 + \theta$. (The values of the basis x_i are split into q_i and p_i terms as shown in column $\vec{P}_0$.) If a value of θ can be found so that both x_1 and x_2 are nonnegative, then the basis will also be an optimal feasible basis. Thus, solve the inequalities $2 - \theta \geq 0$ and $-1 + \theta \geq 0$ to determine if they are consistent, i.e., if a θ exists which satisfies both simultaneously. The procedure above shows that this will be true if $1 \leq \theta \leq 2$. The step I optimal, feasible solution is then $x_1 = 2 - \theta$, $x_2 = -1 + \theta$, $x_3 = x_4 = 0$, $z_0 = 1$ for $1 \leq \theta \leq 2$. To determine a solution for $\theta > 2$, the procedure requires vector $\vec{P}_4$ to replace vector $\vec{P}_1$. Note that this calls for a negative pivot element. The resultant solution is shown in Step II. This solution with $x_2 = 1$, $x_4 = -2 + \theta$, $x_1 = x_3 = 0$, and $z_0 = -1 + \theta$ is optimal for $2 \leq \theta \leq +\infty$. To find an optimal feasible solution for $\theta < 1$, go back to Step I and pivot on the second row. Doing this one finds vector $\vec{P}_3$ replacing vector $\vec{P}_2$, with the optimal solution for $-\infty \leq \theta \leq 1$ being $x_1 = 4 - 3\theta$, $x_3 = 1 - \theta$, and $z_0 = 6 - 5\theta$, Step III. The graph of the objective function against values of the parameter θ is shown in Fig. 1.

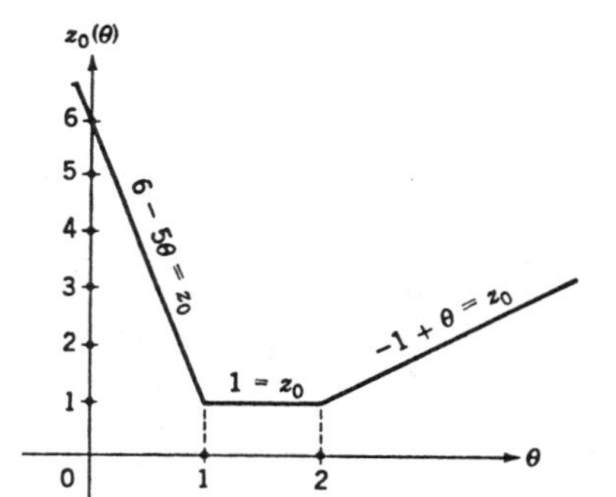

Fig. 1

DECOMPOSITION METHOD

• PROBLEM 4-45

A wood-products company has two divisions, Eastern and Western. The wood is produced at a sawmill in the northwestern part of the country and shipped in the company's own trucks to the divisions. Eastern makes x_1 bobsleds and x_2 playpens each month, using $6x_1 + 2x_2 = x_3$ units of wood. Western makes y_1 desks and y_2 tables each month, using $y_3 = 3y_1 + 5y_2$ units of wood. In a particular month, the main office has 5000 units of wood and 15000 units of truck capacity available. It assigns transfer prices w_1^* and w_2^* to the use of the wood and truck capacity, respectively. Finally, each division has a labor constraint.

The constraints of the main office involve wood and truck capacity as follows:

$$x_3 + y_3 \le 5000 \quad \text{(wood constraint)}$$

$$5x_3 + 2y_3 \le 15000 \quad \text{(truck capacity constraint).}$$

The subproblem faced by Eastern is:

$$\text{Max } 15x_1 + 8x_2 - (w_1^* + 5w_2^*)x_3$$

Subject to:

$$\begin{array}{llll} 6x_1 + 2x_2 - x_3 & \le & 0 & \text{(wood constraint)} \\ 3x_1 + 5x_2 & \le & 4000 & \text{(labor constraint)} \\ x_1 & \ge & 0 & \\ x_2 & \ge & 0 & \end{array} \tag{1}$$

Here, 15 is the gross profit on bobsleds, and 8 is the gross profit on playpens. Similarly, the subproblem faced by Western is:

$$\text{Max } 10y_1 + 11y_2 - (w_1^* + 2w_2^*)y_3$$

Subject to:

$$\begin{array}{llll} 3y_1 + 5y_2 - y_3 & \le & 0 & \text{(wood constraint)} \\ 4y_1 + 4y_2 & \le & 3000 & \text{(labor constraint)} \\ y_1 & \ge & 0 & \\ y_2 & \ge & 0 & \end{array} \tag{2}$$

Ten is the gross profit on desks and 11 the gross profit on tables. Note that the transfer price on wood in each division is determined by the prices that the main office charges for each of the scarce resources, wood and truck capacity, according to the amount of each that is used by each division. Since eastern is far from the wood-supply source, it must pay proportionately more for the use of trucking capacity.

Solve the problem by applying the decomposition method of Dantzig and Wolfe.

Solution: Assume that one has a linear programming problem of the form:

$$\text{Max } c^{(1)}x^{(1)} + c^{(2)}x^{(2)}$$

Subject to:

$$\begin{array}{rl} A^{(1)}x^{(1)} \qquad\qquad\quad & \le b^{(1)} \\ A^{(2)}x^{(2)} & \le b^{(2)} \\ D^{(1)}x^{(1)} + D^{(2)}x^{(2)} & \le r \\ x^{(1)}, x^{(2)} & \ge 0 \end{array} \tag{3}$$

The lowercase letters represent vectors and the uppercase letters, matrices. Dimensions must be appropriate so that the indicated matrix multiplications are well defined.

The structure indicated in (3) might occur in modeling a firm that has two branches, indicated by the superscripts (1) and (2), and a main office that controls a resource vector, r. Each branch of the firm requires certain amounts of the resources r in order to operate; hence, they "compete" for these scarce resources. In addition, each branch has its peculiar own independent constraints. The main office has the problem of coordination--that is, the problem of allocating the proper amounts of the scarce resources so that the operation of each branch will maximize the overall profitability of the firm. One common way to carry out this coordination is to charge each branch "transfer prices" for the use of the scarce resources. Generally just charging transfer prices will not be enough to lead to optimal behavior, but a combination of transfer prices plus resource allocations will be sufficient.

Begin by assuming that the main office has decided to charge a row vector w* of unit transfer prices for each resource. That is, w_i^* is the unit price of resource r_i. Using these prices, define subproblems:

$$\text{Max } c^{(k)}x^{(k)} - w^*D^{(k)}x^{(k)} = (c^{(k)} - w^*D^{(k)})x^{(k)}$$

Subject to: (4)

$$A^{(k)}x^{(k)} \leq b^{(k)}$$

$$x^{(k)} \geq 0$$

for k = 1,2. To see where this problem came from, notice that when the kth branch is operating at level $x^{(k)}$, it demands $D^{(k)}x^{(k)}$ of the scarce resources and the value or transfer cost of these is $w^*D^{(k)}x^{(k)}$. Hence its net "profit" for this level of operation is its gross sales, $c^{(k)}x^{(k)}$, minus the total transfer cost of the scarce resources used. If the kth branch regards itself as a profit center, then it will optimize its behavior by maximizing its profit; that is, it will solve the problem in (4). The problem of the main office is to determine correct transfer prices so that the branch offices will, in fact, end up with behavior that is optimal for the overall corporation.

Suppose that the subproblems (4) have been solved for several choices of transfer prices w*. For each such choice, there will be a basic optimal solution and profit, which shall be indicated by

$$x^{(k,i)} \quad \text{and} \quad p^{(k,i)}, \qquad (5)$$

for $i = 1,\ldots,t$ and $k = 1,2$. Call these optimal solutions proposals. For each transfer price vector w^* given by the main office, a proposal is received back from each of the branch offices. Now turn to the way in which the main office can use these proposals to alter the transfer prices.

It is known that each basic optimal solution $x^{(k,i)}$ of a subproblem is an extreme point of the convex set of feasible solutions of that subproblem. Moreover, every convex combination of such basic solutions is a feasible solution to the subproblem. What shall be done is to set up a master problem for the main office that finds the optimum convex combination of proposals for each branch office in order to maximize the overall profitability of the firm. The master problem is given by

$$\text{Max} \sum_{i=1}^{t} p^{(1,i)}\lambda_i + \sum_{i=1}^{t} p^{(2,i)}\mu_i$$

Subject to

$$\sum_{i=1}^{t} E_1^{(1,i)}\lambda_i + \sum_{i=1}^{t} E^{(2,i)}\mu_i \leq r \qquad (6)$$

$$\sum_{i=1}^{t} \lambda_i = 1$$

$$\sum_{i=1}^{t} \mu_i = 1$$

$$\lambda_i, \mu_i \geq 0$$

Here λ_i is the weight given to proposal $x^{(1,i)}$, μ_i is the weight given to proposal $x^{(2,i)}$, and $E^{(k,i)} = D^{(k)}x^{(k,i)}$ is the demand on the scarce resources made by proposal $x^{(k,i)}$.

The dual problem to the master problem is also of interest. Let w^* be a row vector of dual variables associated with the resource constraints in (6), and let variables w_λ and w_μ be associated with the last two constraints of (6). Then the dual to the master problem is:

$$\text{Min } w^*r + w_\lambda + w_\mu$$

Subject to:

$$w^*E^{(1,i)} + w_\lambda e_\lambda \geq p^{(1,i)} \qquad (7)$$

$$w^*E^{(2,i)} + w_\mu e_\mu \geq p^{(2,i)}$$

$$w^* \geq 0$$

w_λ and w_μ are unrestricted

Here e_λ is a row vector of all 1's with the same number of components as $p^{(1,i)}$, and e_μ is a row vector of all 1's having the same number of components as $p^{(2,i)}$. The solutions to the dual problem have very important interpretations concerning the master problem:

(a) At any stage in the computation the prices of the scarce resources are given by the vector w^* of the solution to the dual problem.

(b) If $w_\lambda < 0$, then the first branch is unprofitable at the current prices for scarce resources.

(c) If $w_\mu < 0$, then the second branch is unprofitable at the current prices for scarce resources.

(d) There is no need to consider a proposal from branch 1 whose profitability is not at least w_λ since it will not improve the solution to the master problem.

(e) Similarly, there is no need to add a new proposal to the master problem from branch 2 whose profitability does not exceed w_μ since it will not improve the solution to the master problem.

Now the steps of the decomposition algorithm are outlined:

(0) Set the resources prices $w^* = 0$. Set $w_\lambda = 0$ and $w_\mu = 0$.

(1) Solve the subproblems (4) for $k = 1,2$. If the corresponding solutions $x^{(k,i)}$ and $p^{(k,i)}$ are more profitable than the corresponding dual prices, include these proposals in the master problem (6). If there are new proposals, go to (2). Otherwise the computation is finished; go to (3).

(2) Solve the new master problem and its dual. Find new dual prices w^*, w_λ, and w_μ. Go to (1).

(3) Use the solution to the last master problem to give allocations to the branch offices so that the resource demands of the branches on scarce resources will be properly coordinated. Use the final dual prices to calculate the transfer prices that will be charged to each of the branches.

As a first observation, notice that both problems (1) and (2) have as a feasible solution all variables set equal to zero--that is shut down the division. This might be a good thing to do if one of the divisions is very much more profitable than the other.

However, each division considered by itself is profitable provided the transfer prices are sufficiently small. Begin by solving each of the divisional problems under the assumption that the transfer prices are zero. It is easy to show that in this case the optimal solution for Eastern is

$$x^{(1)} = \begin{bmatrix} 4000/3 \\ 0 \end{bmatrix}$$

giving profit $p_E^{(1)} = 20{,}000$. However, in order to implement this solution, $x_3 = 8000$, which is more units of wood than the main office has on hand! Also, 40,000 units of truck capacity would be required, which again is more than is on hand.

Similarly, with zero transfer prices, the optimal solution for Western is

$$y^{(1)} = \begin{bmatrix} 0 \\ 750 \end{bmatrix}$$

with profit $p_W^{(1)} = 8250$. Here $y_3 = 3750$ units of wood and 7500 units of truck capacity are needed, both of which are within the current capacity limits.

The main office must now arbitrate between these two proposals and decide what fraction of each it should accept, since obviously not all of either can be kept. Let λ_1 be the fraction of Eastern's proposal 1 that is to be accepted. Then $1 - \lambda_1$ is the fraction of the complete closing of Eastern that is accepted. Similarly, let μ_1 be the fraction of Western's proposal 1 that is to be accepted; then $1 - \mu_1$ is the fraction of the closing down of Western to be accepted. The master problem faced by the main office is

$$\text{Max } 20{,}000\lambda_1 + 8250\mu_1$$

Subject to:

$$\begin{aligned} 8000\lambda_1 + 3750\mu_1 &\le 5000 \\ 40{,}000\lambda_1 + 7500\mu_1 &\le 15{,}000 \\ \lambda_1 &\le 1 \\ \mu_1 &\le 1 \end{aligned}$$

The optimal solution to this problem is given by

$$\lambda_1 = .889, \quad \mu_1 = .208, \quad \text{profit} \quad p_0^{(1)} = 11{,}500,$$

and the dual variables are

$$w_1{}^* = 2 \text{ and } w_2{}^* = .1, \quad w_\lambda = 0, \quad w_\mu = 0.$$

Hence, the main office now charges transfer prices of \$2 on a unit of wood and 10¢ per unit of trucking capacity.

After the main office sends out its new transfer prices to the divisions, they reconsider their optimization problems. Eastern calculates that it must now pay $w_1^* + 5w_2^* = 2.5$ for each unit of wood that it asks for from the main office. Resolving (1) with this total transfer price, it returns with a new proposal,

$$x^{(2)} = \begin{bmatrix} 0 \\ 800 \end{bmatrix}$$

giving profit $p_E^{(2)} = 6400$, exclusive of the transfer cost. Similarly, Western calculates its total transfer price as $w_1^* + 2w_2^* = 2.2$ for each unit of wood. Resolving (2) with this number gives

$$y^{(2)} = \begin{bmatrix} 750 \\ 0 \end{bmatrix}$$

with profit $p_W^{(2)} = 7500$, exclusive of the transfer cost.

After the main office receives the new proposals from both divisions it must set up a new master problem that includes them, since it must decide on what fraction it should accept of each of the proposals made so far. It calculates that $x^{(2)}$ requires 1600 units of wood and 8000 units of trucking capacity, while $y^{(2)}$ requires 3750 units of wood and 7500 units of trucking capacity. Hence the second master problem is:

$$\text{Max } 20{,}000\lambda_1 + 6400\lambda_2 + 8250\mu_1 + 7500\mu_2$$

Subject to:

$$\begin{aligned}
8000\lambda_1 + 1600\lambda_2 + 3750\mu_1 + 2250\mu_2 &\leq 5000 \\
40{,}000\lambda_1 + 8000\lambda_2 + 7500\mu_1 + 4500\mu_2 &\leq 15{,}000 \\
\lambda_1 + \lambda_2 &\leq 1 \\
\mu_1 + \mu_2 &\leq 1
\end{aligned}$$

The solution to this problem is given by

$$\lambda_1 = .078, \quad \lambda_2 = .922, \quad \mu_1 = 1, \quad \mu_2 = 0$$

and with dual prices

$$w_1^* = 0, \quad w_2^* = .425, \quad w_\lambda = 5587.5, \quad w_\mu = 3000.$$

The main office now sends the new transfer prices back to the divisions and asks for new proposals.

Calculating this way, it can be shown that the new proposal of Eastern is the same as $x^{(2)}$, while the new proposal of Western is the same as $y^{(1)}$. Also, the value of Eastern's program is equal to w_λ and the value of Western's program is w_μ. Hence, the computation is terminated.

It should be noted, however, that the main office must not only provide transfer prices, it must also give each division quotas on wood in order to obtain optimal behavior. Notice that it simply tells Western to use its first proposal, but it must give detailed instructions to Eastern to use .078 of its first proposal and .922 of its second proposal. Eastern cannot determine these fractions by solving its own subproblem, since each time it does this it always comes out with one of the previously generated proposals. It thus appears that transfer prices alone are not enough to determine optimal decentralized behavior of a multidivisional firm but that a combination of transfer prices and quotas on raw materials is enough.

There are advantages and disadvantages to the decomposition method. First of all, note that the main office can solve the coordination problem without knowing anything about the technology of the subproblems. For instance, it does not need to know anything about the labor problems of the divisions. Similarly, the divisions do not need to know anything about the main office's resource constraints. The transfer prices are all the division needs to determine optimal proposals. Second, with decomposition techniques, it is possible to solve much bigger problems than would be otherwise possible. Problems with up to 50,000 constraints have been handled in this manner.

However there are also some disadvantages. In actual calculations it has been found that the transfer-price vector tends to fluctuate rather wildly, which causes somewhat erratic computational behavior. Second, the list of proposals tends to become very long--so long that not all can be saved in core memory of a present-day computer. Hence, some kind of a rule for deciding when to drop a proposal is needed. Exactly what rules are used depend on the person who writes the program, and these are frequently held confidential. However, among the rules used are:

(a) Drop a proposal if it becomes unprofitable--that is, if it drops out of the final basis of the master program.

(b) Save the ten best proposals only.

(c) Save as many proposals as possible. When memory space becomes short, drop the least profitable ones.

These rules are somewhat ad hoc in nature.

Still another disadvantage is that some parts of the computation must be repeated several times. For instance, a proposal might enter the list, be dropped as unprofitable, then re-enter later when it becomes profitable again, only to be dropped again, and so on. For this reason, it is usually best to solve a problem with the original simplex method if it is small enough for the core memory. Decomposition remains useful for problems that are too large for core memory.

• PROBLEM 4-46

Minimize $2x_1 - x_2 + x_3 - x_4 = C$,

subject to $x_1 + 3x_2 - x_3 - 2x_4 \leq 10$

and to

$$x_1 + 2x_2 \leq 3$$

$$x_1 - x_2 \leq 1$$

$$x_3 - 3x_4 \leq 7$$

$$2x_3 + x_4 \leq 8,$$

all variables to be non-negative.

Solve by applying the Decomposition Technique.

Solution: Imagine all variables replaced by weighted averages of the coordinates of the vertices of the feasible regions of the blocks in which they appear. If the weights in the two blocks are λ_i and μ_i respectively, then the system is replaced by

$$L(\lambda_i) + M(\mu_i) \leq 10,$$

$$\sum\lambda_i = 1, \quad \sum\mu_i = 1$$

$$\lambda_i \geq 0, \quad \mu_i \geq 0,$$

where L and M are linear forms of their arguments, but where it is not known how many λ_i and μ_i there are, or what their coefficients in the forms are. One shall generate information about them as and when needed. This is the simplest example of a method of "column generation."

The first (inverse) tableau is easily constructed if each feasible region of the blocks has the origin as a vertex. Then the weights of these vertices, say λ_0, μ_0, do not appear in the linking constraints, and the first basic variables can be these, and the slack variables of the linking constraints. In the problem, one gets

						λ_i	μ_i
x_5	1				10	$x_1 + 3x_2$	$-x_3 - 2x_4$
λ_0		1			1	1	0
μ_0			1		1	0	1
C				1	0	$-2x_1+x_2$	$-x_3+x_4$

Also given here are the column of the constants (values of the basic variables) and the columns of any other λ_i and μ_i in which the x_j are the coordinates of the vertex to which the subscript i refers. If there were any other variables in the linking constraints which do not appear in any block, then their columns would also be recorded.

Now a procedure for continuing the computations is described:

If any of the last-mentioned columns, those of variables which appear only in the linking constraints, have a positive value in the bottom row, then introduce this variable in the basis. Also test whether any of the other added columns have a positive value in their last row. To do this, compute the minimum of the expression in the C row for λ_i (or for μ_i) subject to the constraints of the block referring to λ_i (or to μ_i).

The maximum of $-2x_1 + x_2$, subject to

$$x_1 + 2x_2 \leq 3$$

$$x_1 - x_2 \leq 1,$$

is $\frac{3}{2}$ (positive), obtained when $x_1 = 0$ and $x_2 = \frac{3}{2}$. Generate the column λ_1 (say)

$$x_1 + 3x_2 = \frac{9}{2}$$

$$1^*$$

$$0$$

$$-2x_1 + x_2 = \frac{3}{2}$$

and make this variable basic. The pivot is indicated by an asterisk. Then reach the next (inverse) tableau

						λ_i (updated)	μ_i
x_5	1	$-\frac{9}{2}$	0	0	$\frac{11}{2}$	$x_1 + 3x_2 - \frac{9}{2}$	$-x_3 - 2x_4$
λ_1	0	1	0	0	1	1	0
μ_0	0	0	1	0	1	0	1
C	0	$-\frac{3}{2}$	0	1	$-\frac{3}{2}$	$-2x_1 + x_2 - \frac{3}{2}$	$-x_3 + x_4$

The maximum of $-2x_1 + x_2 - \frac{3}{2}$, subject to its block constraints, is 0, and therefore no new λ_i is made basic at this stage. Turn to the μ_i. Maximize $-x_3 + x_4$, subject to $x_3 - 3x_4 \leq 7$, $2x_3 + x_4 \leq 8$. The result is 8, from $x_3 = 0$, $x_4 = 8$. Generate the column

	μ_1 (say)
$-x_3 - 2x_4$	-16
	0
	1^*
$-x_3 + x_4$	8

The next tableau is

						λ_i	μ_i
						(updated)	
x_5	1	$-\frac{1}{3}$	16	0	$\frac{43}{2}$	$x_1+3x_2-\frac{9}{2}$	$-x_3-2x_4+16$
λ_1	0	1	0	0	1	1	0
μ_1	0	0	1	0	1	0	1
C	0	$-\frac{3}{2}$	-8	1	$-\frac{27}{2}$	$-2x_1+x_2-\frac{3}{2}$	$-x_3+x_4-8$

Continuing, one finds that the maximum of $-2x_1 + x_2 - \frac{3}{2}$,

subject to $x_1 + 2x_2 \leq 3$, $x_1 - x_2 \leq 1$

as well as that of $-x_3 + x_4 - 8$,

subject to $x_3 - 3x_4 \leq 7$, $2x_3 + x_4 \leq 8$

is zero, so that the final solution has been reached:

$$x_5 = \frac{43}{2}, \quad \lambda_1 = 1, \quad \mu_1 = 1, \quad C = -\frac{27}{2}.$$

However, one desires to answer in terms of x_1, etc., not of λ_i and μ_i. Now λ_1 was the weight of the vertex $x_1 = 0$, $x_2 = \frac{3}{2}$, and μ_1 that of the vertex $x_3 = 0$, $x_4 = 8$, and these are the optimal values of the variables.

The situation is slightly more complicated if a first basic solution cannot be found by inspection. For

$$\begin{aligned}
\text{minimize} \quad & 2x_1 - x_2, \\
\text{subject to} \quad & x_1 + 3x_2 - x_3 = 4 \\
& x_1 + 2x_2 \leq 3 \\
& x_1 - x_2 \leq 1 \\
& x_1, \; x_2 \geq 0,
\end{aligned}$$

consider the first two inequalities as constituting a block. Two vertices can easily be found: $(x_1, x_2) = (0, \frac{3}{2})$ and $= (\frac{5}{3}, \frac{2}{3})$. Giving them weights λ_1 and λ_2, one gets

$$5\lambda_2/3 + 3(3\lambda_1/2 + 2\lambda_2/3) + \ldots. = 3,$$

i.e.

$$\begin{aligned} 9\lambda_1/2 + 11\lambda_2/3 + \ldots. &= 4 \\ \lambda_1 + \lambda_2 + \ldots. &= 1 \\ 3\lambda_1/2 - 8\lambda_2/3 + C + \ldots &= 0. \end{aligned}$$

To find the values of C, λ_1 and λ_2, invert the matrix

$$\begin{bmatrix} \frac{9}{2} & \frac{11}{3} & 0 \\ 1 & 1 & 0 \\ \frac{3}{2} & -\frac{8}{3} & 1 \end{bmatrix} \quad \text{into} \quad \begin{bmatrix} \frac{6}{5} & -\frac{22}{5} & 0 \\ -\frac{6}{5} & \frac{27}{5} & 0 \\ -5 & 21 & 1 \end{bmatrix}$$

so that

$$\lambda_1 = (\tfrac{6}{5})(4) + (-\tfrac{22}{5})(1) = \tfrac{2}{5}$$

$$\lambda_2 = (-\tfrac{6}{5})(4) + (\tfrac{27}{5})(1) = \tfrac{3}{5}$$

$$C = 1.$$

The original column of x_3 is updated into

$$\begin{matrix} -1 & -\frac{6}{5} \\ 0 & \frac{6}{5}^{*} \\ 0 & 5 \end{matrix}$$

and introduced into the basis, so that the tableau obtained

$$\begin{matrix} \lambda_1 & 0 & 1 & 0 & 1 \\ x_3 & -1 & \frac{9}{2} & 0 & \frac{1}{2} \\ C & 0 & -\frac{3}{2} & 1 & -\frac{3}{2} \end{matrix}$$

is optimal; $x_1 = 0$, $x_2 = \frac{3}{2}$, $x_3 = \frac{1}{2}$.

Consider the linear program

$$\min x_1 + 8x_2 + 5x_1' + 6x_2' + x_3'$$

subject to

$$x_1 + 4x_2 + (1/4)x_1' + 2x_2' + (5/4)x_3' = 7,$$
$$2x_1 + 3x_2 = 5,$$
$$5x_1 + x_2 = 6,$$
$$3x_1' + 4x_2' + 3x_3' = 12,$$
$$x_1, x_2, x_1', x_2', x_3' \geq 0.$$

Solve by the decomposition method.

Solution: Note that this problem is in the form:

$$\min z = \sum_{j=1}^{p} c_j x_j$$

subject to

$$\sum_{j=1}^{p} L_j x_j = b_0$$

$$A_j x_j = b_j \qquad (j = 1,\ldots,p)$$

$$x_j \geq 0$$

so

$$\vec{L}_1 = (1,4), \quad \vec{L}_2 = (1/4,2,5/4),$$

$$\vec{b}_0 = 7, \quad \vec{b}_1 = [5,6], \quad \vec{b}_2 = 12,$$

$$\vec{A}_1 = \begin{bmatrix} 2 & 3 \\ 5 & 1 \end{bmatrix}, \quad \vec{A}_2 = (3,4,3),$$

$$\vec{c}_1 = (1,8), \quad \vec{c}_2 = (5,6,1).$$

The convex set S_1 is a single point with $\vec{x}_{11} = [1,1]$. The convex set S_2 is a plane triangle with $\vec{x}_{12} = [4,0,0]$, $\vec{x}_{22} = [0,3,0]$, and $\vec{x}_{32} = [0,0,4]$ as vertices. In order to have a starting basic solution, $m_0 + p = 1 + 2$ vectors are needed. Therefore, assume that one starts with $\vec{x}_{11}$, $\vec{x}_{12}$, and $\vec{x}_{22}$ (note that $\vec{x}_{32}$ need not be known):

$$\ell_{11} = \vec{L}_1\vec{x}_{11} = (1,4)[1,1] = 5,$$

$$\ell_{12} = \vec{L}_2\vec{x}_{12} = (1/4,2,5/4)[4,0,0] = 1,$$

$$\ell_{22} = \vec{L}_2\vec{x}_{22} = (1/4,2,5/4)[0,3,0] = 6,$$

$$c_{11} = (1,8)[1,1] = 9,$$

$$c_{12} = (5,6,1)[4,0,0] = 20,$$

$$c_{22} = (5,6,1)[0,3,0] = 18.$$

Now put in the form

$$\min z = \sum_{j=1}^{p} \sum_{i=1}^{s_j} c_{ij}\lambda_{ij}$$

$$\text{subject to} \quad \sum_{j=1}^{p} \sum_{i=1}^{s_j} \lambda_{ij}\ell_{ij} = b_0$$

$$\sum_{i=1}^{s_j} \lambda_{ij} = 1 \qquad (j = 1,\ldots,p)$$

$$\lambda_{ij} \geq 0 \qquad (i = 1,\ldots,s)$$

and the problem becomes

$$\min 9\lambda_{11} + 20\lambda_{12} + 18\lambda_{22}$$

subject to

$$5\lambda_{11} + \lambda_{12} + 6\lambda_{22} = 7,$$

$$\lambda_{11} = 1,$$

$$\lambda_{12} + \lambda_{22} = 1.$$

This is a standard linear program with unknown λ_{ij}. In Tableau 1 give zero cost to every artificial variable with the understanding that when the relative cost associated with the artificial variable becomes negative or positive, it does not affect the termination of the simplex algorithm.

Tableau 1

	1	x_1^a	x_2^a	x_3^a	λ_{11}	λ_{12}	λ_{22}	Constant
$-z$	1	0	0	0	9	20	18	0
x_1^a		1			5	1	6	7
x_2^a			1		1	0	0	1
x_3^a				1	0	1	1	1

Tableau 2

	1	x_1^a	x_2^a	x_3^a	λ_{11}	λ_{12}	λ_{22}	Constant
$-z$	1	2/5	−11	−20.4	0	0	0	−28.6
λ_{11}	0	0	1	0	1	0	0	1
λ_{12}	0	−1/5	1	6/5	0	1	0	4/5
λ_{22}	0	1/5	−1	−1/5	0	0	1	1/5

After introducing λ_{11}, λ_{12}, λ_{22} into the basis, Tableau 2 is obtained. From Tableau 2 notice that $(\bar{\pi},\bar{\pi}_1,\bar{\pi}_2) = (-2/5,11,20.4)$.

$$(\vec{c}_1 - \pi\vec{L}_1)\vec{x}_1 = \{(1,8) - (-2/5)(1,4)\}[x_1,x_2]$$

$$= \frac{7}{5}x_1 + \frac{48}{5}x_2.$$

Therefore, in S_1 one has

$$\min \quad \frac{7}{5}x_1 + \frac{48}{5}x_2$$

subject to

$$2x_1 + 3x_2 = 5,$$

$$5x_1 + x_2 = 6,$$

$$x_1,x_2 \geq 0.$$

The solution is $x_1 = 1$, $x_2 = 1$ with

$$(\vec{c}_1 - \pi\vec{L}_1)\vec{x}_1 - \bar{\pi}_1 = \frac{7}{5} \times 1 + \frac{48}{5} \times 1 - 11 = 0.$$

Similarly in S_2

$$(\vec{c}_2 - \pi\vec{L}_2)\vec{x}_2 = \left((5,6,1) - \left(-\frac{2}{5}\right)\left(\frac{1}{4},2,\frac{5}{4}\right)\right) [x_1',x_2',x_3']$$

$$= 5.1x_1' + 6.8x_2' + 1.5x_3',$$

so the linear program becomes

$$\min 5.1x_1' + 6.8x_2' + 1.5x_3'$$

subject to

$$3x_1' + 4x_2' + 3x_3' = 12$$

The solution is $x_1' = 0, x_2' = 0, x_3' = 4$:

$$(\vec{c}_2 - \pi\vec{L}_2)\vec{x}_2 - \bar{\pi}_2 = 5.1 \times 0 + 6.8 \times 0 + 1.5$$

$$\times 4 - \frac{102}{5}$$

$$= 6 - 20.4 = -14.4 < 0,$$

$$\ell_{32} = \vec{L}_2 \vec{x}_{32} = \left(\frac{1}{4}, 2, \frac{5}{4}\right)[0,0,4] = 5.$$

Thus $[\vec{\ell}_{32}, \vec{e}_2] = [5,0,1]$. Before adding this vector to Tableau 2, multiply it by the current $\vec{B}^{-1}$, namely

$$\begin{bmatrix} 0 & 1 & 0 \\ -1/5 & 1 & 6/5 \\ 1/5 & -1 & -1/5 \end{bmatrix} \begin{bmatrix} 5 \\ 0 \\ 1 \end{bmatrix} = \begin{bmatrix} 0 \\ 1/5 \\ 4/5 \end{bmatrix}.$$

This vector [0,1/5,4/5] together with its relative cost -14.4 is added to Tableau 2 and is shown in Tableau 3. A pivot step on Tableau 3 leads to Tableau 4, which is optimum with

$$\lambda_{11} = 1, \qquad \lambda_{12} = 3/4$$

and

$$\lambda_{32} = 1/4$$

Thus

$$\vec{x}_1 = \lambda_{11}[1,1] = [1,1],$$

$$\vec{x}_2 = \frac{3}{4}[4,0,0] + \frac{1}{4}[0,0,4] = [3,0,1].$$

As a check, the constraints are satisfied and

$$z = 1 + 8 \times 1 + 5 \times 3 + 6 \times 0 + 1 \times 1 = 25.$$

Tableau 3

	1	x_1^q	x_2^q	x_3^q	λ_{11}	λ_{12}	λ_{22}	λ_{32}		Constant
$-z$	1	2/5	−11	−20.4	0	0	0	−14.4	...	−28.6
λ_{11}	0	0	1	0	1	0	0	0	...	1
λ_{12}	0	−1/5	1	6/5	0	1	0	1/5	...	4/5
λ_{22}	0	1/5	−1	−1/5	0	0	1	4/5*	...	1/5

Tableau 4

	1	x_1^q	x_2^q	x_3^q	λ_{11}	λ_{12}	λ_{22}	λ_{32}		Constant
$-z$	1	4	−29	−24	0	0	18	0	...	−25
λ_{11}	0	0	1	0	1	0	0	0	...	1
λ_{12}	0	−1/4	5/4	5/4	0	1	−1/4	0	...	3/4
λ_{32}	0	1/4	−5/4	−1/4	0	0	5/4	1	...	1/4

• PROBLEM 4-48

Koltuk Furniture Company has the following linear programming model for its production of chairs (x) and tables (y):

$$\text{Maximize} \quad 5x + 7y$$

$$\begin{aligned} \text{subject to} \quad 2x + 5y &\leq 51 && \text{(materials constraint)} \\ 3x + 2y &\leq 42 && \text{(man-hour constraint)} \\ x + y &\geq 14 && \text{(total number of pieces)} \\ y &\geq 7 && \text{(at least 7 tables)} \\ x, y &\geq 0 \end{aligned}$$

The new manager however, decides to produce seven tables as a goal, as well. Since the reference is to goals, he is specific and states that the "profit goal" is \$100. Furthermore, he estimates the penalty for every table below the goal is \$10 and penalty for every dollar below the goal of \$100 is \$1.

Alter the LP model such that it accommodates these requirements.

Solution: The initial Koltuk Furniture Company problem is such that the company must make at least seven tables. Now, instead of viewing the number of tables as a constraint, the seven tables are a goal. That is, the Koltuk Furniture Company would like to maximize profit and would like to make seven tables subject to constraints on materials, man-hours, and total number of pieces. The two goals are

$$\text{Goal 1} \qquad 5x + 7y = 100$$

and

$$\text{Goal 2} \qquad y = 7$$

The immediate question is how to incorporate the two goals into a linear programming type format. The tools for converting the problem into the proper form are simply the slack and surplus variables. Consider the pair $x = 10$, $y = 4$. Note that (10,4) satisfies the three constraints. With respect to the goals the values are

$$5x + 7y = 50 + 28 = 78 \text{ dollars}$$

and

$$y = 4 \text{ tables}$$

Hence a complete solution must indicate the shortage with respect to both goals. Express Goal 1 as

$$5x + 7y + s_1 = 100$$

where in this particular case s_1 would be 24, the amount below the goal of 100. Furthermore, in general it is possible to be above or below a goal. For this reason both a slack variable and a surplus variable are needed. Thus

$$\text{Goal 1} \qquad 5x + 7y + s_1^- - s_1^+ = 100$$

where s_1^- represents the amount below the goal and s_1^+ represents the amount above the goal. Similarly,

$$\text{Goal 2} \qquad y + s_2^- - s_2^+ = 7$$

and s_2^- is the number of tables produced below seven and s_2^+ is the number of tables produced above seven. Note that all of the new variables that have been added are restricted in sign to being nonnegative.

At this point the two new equations (Goal 1 and Goal 2) are used to define the new variables. Hence they enter the problem as constraints. The problem now, is to define an objective function. First, assume that having a surplus profit or a surplus number of tables does not concern the company. Also, the ratio of penalties between tables and budget is 10 to 1. The objective function must represent this relationship, which is that the cost of being short in tables is ten times the cost of being short in profit. Hence the complete problem is

$$\begin{aligned}
&\text{Minimize} && s_1^- + 10s_2^- \\
&\text{subject to} && 5x + 7y + s_1^- - s_1^+ = 100 && \text{(Goal 1)} \\
& && y + s_2^- - s_2^+ = 7 && \text{(Goal 2)} \\
& && 2x + 5y \le 51 && \text{(materials)} \\
& && 3x + 2y \le 42 && \text{(man-hours)} \\
& && x + y \ge 14 && \text{(total number of pieces)} \\
& && x, y, s_1^-, s_1^+, s_2^-, s_2^+ \ge 0
\end{aligned}$$

This is the required (goal programming) model.

• PROBLEM 4-49

Consider a company which faces uncertain demand for its products that it sells out of inventory. When the inventory level of this product gets low, the company must reorder from its supplier. Now, during the period between when the order is placed and the order arrives (called the lead time), demand may exceed the remaining inventory, causing a stockout. To prevent this (or to lessen its likelihood), the company may choose to maintain extra inventory, called safety stock. Assume that the desired safety stock levels for the various products are known.

Set up a goal programming model which seeks to achieve the safety stock levels within the constraints of limited capital and limited storage space.

Solution: It is obvious that if a firm were blessed with unlimited amounts of capital and storage space, there would be no problem in attaining the safety stock levels. However, this is usually not the case. Define

x_j = amount of product j to stock: $j = 1,2,\ldots,n$

e_j = desired safety stock for product j

x_j^0 = minimum stock level for product j

c = capital resources identified for safety stock decisions

s = space (in cubic feet) available for storing safety stock

a_{cj} = wholesale cost per unit of product j

Then the model becomes:

Minimize $$f = \sum_{j=1}^{n} (P_j^+ d_j^+ + P_j^- d_j^-)$$

subject to $x_j - d_j^+ + d_j^- = e_j$ for $j = 1,2,\ldots,n$

$$\sum_{j=1}^{n} a_{cj} x_j \le c$$

$$\sum_{j=1}^{n} a_{sj} x_j \le s$$

$$x_j \ge x_j^0 \quad \text{for } j = 1,2,\ldots,n$$

Note that when $x_j < e_j$, then d_j^- is positive. The associated penalty incurred is related to underachievement of the service-level goal and the resulting stockout costs. (Service level refers to the probability of demand being satisfied by the inventory on hand during the lead time. Thus, for example, a service level of 99 percent means that there is a probability of .99 that demand will not exceed the available inventory, or, alternately, that the probability of a stockout is only 0.01.) When $x_j > e_j$, then d_j^+ is positive and the total holding cost for the safety stock of product j is higher than desired.

The priorities P_j^- relate to stockout costs per unit and variability of the distribution of forecasting errors. As stockout costs increase, it becomes more important to avoid underachieving the stated goal. As the variance of the forecasting errors increases, the probable size of a stockout increases. Thus, as either costs or variance increase, a higher priority is assigned.

The priorities P_j^+ depend on average demand for each product. The smaller the demand, the more important it is to avoid the overachievement of the service-level goal.

• PROBLEM 4-50

The manager of the only record shop in a college town is not concerned with market competition. Instead, his major decision problem is the sales effort allocation to achieve the maximum profit. The record shop employs five full-time and four part-time salesmen. The average regular working time is 160 hours a month for the full-time salesmen and 80 hours for the part-time salesmen. The average sale of records per hour has been five for the full-time salesmen and two for the part-time salesmen. The average hourly wage rates are \$3.00 for the full-time and \$2.00 for the part-time salesmen.

The average profit from the sale of a record is \$1.50. In view of the past sales records and the increased enrollment at the college, the manager feels that the sales goal for September should be 5,500 records. Since the shop is open six days a week, overtime is often required of salesmen. The manager believes that a good employer-employee relationship is an essential factor of business success. Therefore, he decided that a stable employment level with occasional overtime requirement is a better practice than an unstable employment level with no overtime. However, he also feels that overtime of more than 100 hours for the full-time salesmen should be avoided because of the resulting fatigue.

The relative importance of these goals are as follows: the manager gives the first priority to achievement of the sales goal of 5,500 records in September. Then he wants to limit the overtime of full-time salesmen to 100 hours. The third goal in line is to provide job security to salesmen. The manager feels that full utilization is an important factor for a good employer-employee relationship. However, he is twice as concerned with the full utilization of full-time salesmen as with the utilization of part-time salesmen. The fourth and last concern is to minimize the sum of overtime for both full-time and part-time salesmen. However, differential weights should be assigned to the minimization of overtime for the full-time and part-time salesmen. Between the full-time and part-time salesmen, the sales efficiency ratio is 5 to 2, while the hourly wage rate is \$4.50 (overtime pay) and \$2.00.

The marginal profit per hour of overtime is \$3.00 for the full-time salesmen and \$1.00 for the part-time salesmen. The relative cost of an hour of overtime for the part-time salesmen is three times that of the full-time salesmen.

Set up the goal programming model to solve this problem.

Solution: The model required is constructed as follows:

The following constraints can be formulated:

(1) Sales.--The achievement of the sales goal, which is set at 5,500, is based upon the number of working hours of the full-time and part-time salesmen.

$$5x_1 + 2x_2 + d_1^- + d_1^+ = 5,500$$

where x_1: total full-time salesman hours in the month

x_2: total part-time salesman hours in the month

d_1^-: underachievement of sales goal as set at 5,500 records

d_1^+: overachievement of sales goal beyond 5,500 records

(2) Sales Force.--The salesman hours are determined by the regular working hours and the number of full-time and part-time salesmen.

$$x_1 + d_2^- - d_2^+ = 800$$

$$x_2 + d_3^- - d_3^+ = 320$$

where d_2^-: negative deviation from the regular full-time salesman hours (800 for the month)

d_2^+: overtime given to full-time salesmen in the month

d_3^-: negative deviation from the regular part-time salesman hours (320) for the month

d_3^+: overtime given to part-time salesmen in the month

(3) Overtime.--The manager tries to avoid giving any overtime beyond 100 hours per month to the full-time salesmen.

$$d_2^+ + d_{21}^- - d_{21}^+ = 100$$

where d_{21}^- : negative deviation of overtime hours given to full-time salesmen from 100 hours

d_{21}^+ : overtime hours given to full-time salesmen beyond 100 hours

In addition to the constraints, variables, and constants described above, the following priority factors are to be defined:

P_1: The highest priority factor, P_1, is assigned to

the variable representing the underachievement of sales goal (i.e., d_1).

P_2: The second highest priority, P_2, is assigned to the variable which represents overtime of full-time salesmen beyond 100 hours (i.e., d_{21}).

P_3: $2P_3$ is assigned to the variable representing the under-utilization of full-time salesmen (i.e., d_2^-) and P_3 is assigned to the variable which represents the under-utilization of part-time salesmen (i.e., d_3^-).

P_4: $3P_4$ is assigned to d_3^+, whereas P_4 is assigned to d_2^+.

Now, the model can be formulated. The objective is the minimization of deviations from goals with certain assigned priorities. The deviant variable with the highest priority must be minimized to the fullest possible extent. When no further improvement is possible for the highest goal, the other deviational variables are to be minimized according to their assigned priority factors. The model can be expressed as follows:

Minimize

$$P_1 d_1^- + P_2 d_{21}^+ + 2P_3 d_2^- + P_3 d_3^- + P_4 d_2^+ + 3P_4 d_3^+$$

Subject to:

$$X_1 + X_2 + d_1^- - d_1^+ = 5{,}500$$

$$X_1 + d_2^- - d_2^+ = 800$$

$$X_2 + d_3^- - d_3^+ = 320$$

$$d_{21}^- + d_2^+ - d_{21}^+ = 100$$

$$X_1, X_2, d_1^-, d_2^-, d_3^-, d_{21}^-, d_1^+, d_2^+, d_3^+, d_{21}^+ \geq 0$$

The solution can be derived through the simplex method of linear programming.

The computer solution indicates that the first three goals are achieved but the fourth goal could not be attained. This reflects the everyday sales management problems experienced in business when there are several conflicting goals. To achieve the optimal solution, at the sixth iteration, 900 full-time salesman hours and 500 part-time salesman hours should be employed in September. Hence, the overtime hours allocated to full-time salesmen were 100, whereas the overtime hours to part-time salesmen were 180.

Consider a production planning situation in which a single product is manufactured in a facility. The company is faced with a large demand and fixed capacity in the short run, so that its alternatives include (1) run overtime at a cost of 150 percent of regular production, (2) subcontract, or (3) hire temporary employees. Management is leery of utilizing the last two alternatives because of a reduction in quality as well as increased costs. The basic data are shown in Table 1.

Management has several goals: meeting demand, keeping production costs within budget, and maintaining quality levels. After much discussion, it was decided to use the following priorities:

Priority 1: Meet demand.
Priority 2: Achieve the quality level of 98 percent.
Priority 3: Stay within the production budget of $2200.

How would this problem be modeled by goal programming?

Table 1

DATA FOR PRODUCTION PLANNING

	Normal production	Overtime production	Subcontract	Temporary employees
Hours required per unit	2.0	2.0	2.5	3.0
Cost per hour, $	10	15	8	8
Average quality level, %	99	98	95	90
Hours available: Total of 100 h				
Demand: 100 units				
Required quality level = 98%				

Solution: This problem can be modeled with goal programming as follows. Let

x_1 = number of units produced by normal production

x_2 = number of units produced by overtime

x_3 = number of units produced by subcontract

x_4 = number of units produced by temporary employees

The constraints are:

Demand

$$x_1 + x_2 + x_3 + x_4 + d_1^- - d_1^+ = 100$$

Production hours

$$2x_1 + 2x_2 + d_2^- = 100$$

No positive deviational variable is included because it is physically impossible to exceed 100 h.

Quality

$$0.99x_1 + 0.98x_2 + 0.95x_3 + 0.90x_4 \geq 0.98(x_1 + x_2 + x_3 + x_4)$$

or $$0.01x_1 - 0.03x_3 - 0.08x_4 \geq 0$$

or $$x_1 - 3x_2 - 8x_4 + d_3^- - d_3^+ = 0$$

Budget constraint

$$(2)10x_1 + (2)15x_2 + (2.5)8x_3 + (3)8x_4 \leq 2200$$

or $$20x_1 + 30x_2 + 20x_3 + 24x_4 + d_4^- - d_4^+ = 2200$$

If the established priorities are considered, the objective function is:

Minimize $$f = P_1d_1^- + P_2d_2^- + P_3d_4^+$$

• PROBLEM 4-52

The Lewis Company is considering three new products to replace current models that are being discontinued, so their O.R. Department has been assigned the task of determining which mix of these products should be produced. Management wants primary consideration given to three factors: long-run profit, stability in the work force, and the level of capital investment for new equipment that would be required now. In particular, they have established the goals of (1) achieving a long-run profit (net present value) of at least \$120,000,000 from these products, (2) maintaining the current employment level of 4,000 employees, and (3) holding the capital investment to less than \$60,000,000. However, they realize that it probably won't be possible to attain all of these goals simultaneously, so they have discussed their priorities with the O.R. Department. This has led to setting penalty weights of 5 on missing the profit goal (per million dollars under), 2 for going over the employment goal (per hundred employees), 4 for going under this same goal, and 3 for exceeding the capital investment goal (per million dollars over).

Each new product's contribution to profit, employment level, and capital investment level is proportional to the rate of production that is established. These contributions per unit rate of production are shown in Table 1, along with the goals and penalty weights.

Set up a mathematical programming model that will solve this problem, by utilizing the means of goal programming.

Table 1

Factor	Unit Contribution Product 1	2	3	Goal (units)	Penalty weight
Long-run profit	12	9	15	≥ 120 (millions of dollars)	5
Employment level	5	3	4	= 40 (hundreds of employees)	2(+), 4(−)
Capital investment	5	7	8	≤ 60 (millions of dollars)	3

Solution: The Lewis Company problem includes three types of goals: a lower bound goal (long-run profit), a specific numerical goal (employment level), and an upper bound goal (capital investment). Letting the decision variables x_1, x_2, and x_3 be the production rates of products 1, 2 and 3, respectively, these goals can be stated as

$$12x_1 + 9x_2 + 15x_3 \geq 120 \quad \text{(Profit Goal)}$$

$$5x_1 + 3x_2 + 4x_3 = 40 \quad \text{(Employment Goal)}$$

$$5x_1 + 7x_2 + 8x_3 \leq 60 \quad \text{(Investment Goal)}.$$

Now introduce auxiliary variables,

$$y_1 = 12x_1 + 9x_2 + 15x_3 - 120,$$

$$y_2 = 5x_1 + 3x_2 + 4x_3 - 40,$$

$$y_3 = 5x_1 + 7x_2 + 8x_3 - 60,$$

as well as their positive and negative components,

$$y_1 = y_1^+ - y_1^-, \quad \text{where } y_1^+ \geq 0,\ y_1^- \geq 0,$$

$$y_2 = y_2^+ - y_2^-, \quad \text{where } y_2^+ \geq 0,\ y_2^- \geq 0,$$

$$y_3 = y_3^+ - y_3^-, \quad \text{where } y_3^+ \geq 0,\ y_3^- \geq 0.$$

Since there is no penalty for exceeding the profit goal of 120 or being under the investment goal of 60, neither y_1^+ nor y_3^- should appear in the objective function representing the total penalty for deviations from the goals. However, since it is possible to have $y_1^+ > 0$ and $y_3^- > 0$, both of these variables should appear (along with y_1^-, y_2^+, y_2^-, and y_3^+) in the equality constraints defining the relationship between these six auxiliary variables and the three original decision variables (x_1, x_2, x_3). Using the penalty weights shown in Table 1, this leads to the following linear programming formulation of this goal programming problem:

$$\text{Minimize } Z = 5y_1^- + 2y_2^+ + 4y_2^- + 3y_3^+,$$

subject to

$$12x_1 + 9x_2 + 15x_3 - (y_1^+ - y_1^-) = 120$$

$$5x_1 + 3x_2 + 4x_3 - (y_2^+ - y_2^-) = 40$$

$$5x_1 + 7x_2 + 8x_3 - (y_3^+ - y_3^-) = 60$$

and

$$x_j \geq 0,\ y_k^+ \geq 0,\ y_k^- \geq 0\ (j = 1,2,3;\ k = 1,2,3).$$

• PROBLEM 4-53

Solve the single-goal model below, by graphical means.

Minimize $f = d^-$

subject to

$$12.5x_1 + 10x_2 + d^- - d^+ = 100 \qquad (1)$$

$$0.75x_1 + 2x_2 \leq 6 \qquad (2)$$

$$x_1, x_2, d^-, d^+ \geq 0$$

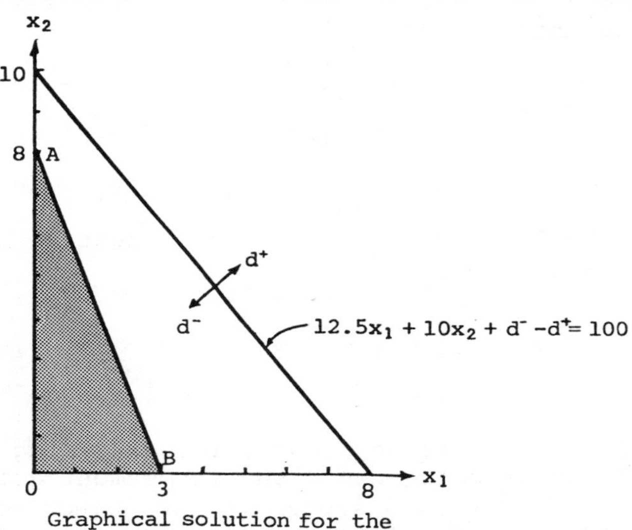

Graphical solution for the model with a single goal.

Solution: The graphical solution is shown in Figure. Any point $\vec{x} = (x_1,x_2) \geq \vec{0}$ will satisfy Equation 1 because points below the line (indicated by d^-), points on the line, and points above the line (indicated by d^+) are feasible. Now consider (2). The set of points which satisfy this constraint is the shaded region OAB. Thus, to minimize d^-, one must find the point(s) in OAB which is closest to line (1). This is point A = (0,8), which means $d^- = 20$.

• PROBLEM 4-54

Consider the model

Minimize $\qquad f = d_1^- + d_2^- + d_3^-$

subject to

$$7.5x_1 + 10x_2 + d_1^- - d_1^+ = 1000$$

$$x_1 + d_2^- - d_2^+ = 10$$

$$x_2 + d_3^- - d_3^+ = 10$$

$$x_1 + 2x_2 \leq 60$$

$$1.5x_1 + 1.5x_2 \leq 60$$

$$x_1, x_2, d_1^-, d_1^+, d_2^-, d_2^+, d_3^-, d_3^+ \geq 0$$

Find the graphical solution to this goal programming problem.

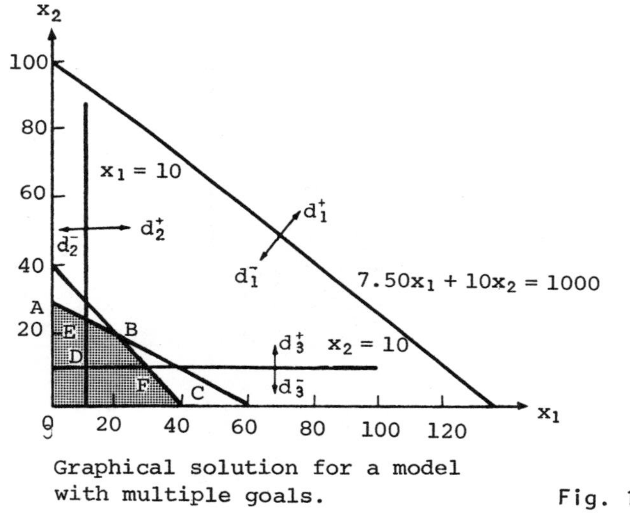

Graphical solution for a model with multiple goals.

Fig. 1

Solution: The graphical solution is shown in Fig. 1. The production constraints require any solution $\vec{x}$ to lie within the feasible region OABC. Within this area, minimize $d_1^- + d_2^- + d_3^-$. Now, any point on or to the right of $x_1 = 10$ will minimize d_2^-, and any point on or above $x_2 = 10$ will minimize d_3^-. Thus, by choosing a point within the area DEBF, it can be ensured that both d_2^- and d_3^- are zero. The problem thus boils down to finding the points within DEBF which minimizes d_1^-. This is obviously point B.

• PROBLEM 4-55

Solve the multiple-conflicting-goals model below, by graphical means.

Minimize $\quad P_1 d_4^+ + 6P_2 d_3^- + 7.5P_2 d_2^- + P_3 d_1^-$

subject to

$$
\begin{aligned}
x_1 + x_2 + d_1^- - d_1^+ &= 10 \\
x_1 + d_2^- - d_2^+ &= 4 \\
x_2 + d_3^- - d_3^+ &= 2 \\
2x_1 + x_2 + d_4^- - d_4^+ &= 7
\end{aligned}
$$

$$x_1, x_2, d_i^-, d_i^+ \geq 0 \qquad i = 1,2,3,4$$

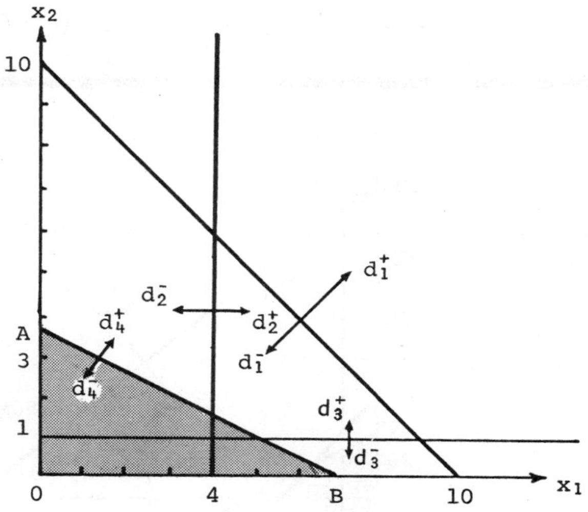

Graphical representation of model with multiple goals. Fig. 1

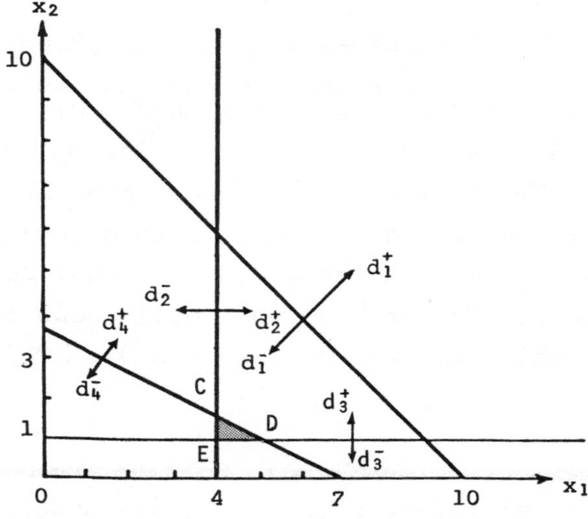

Final analysis for the multiple-conflicting goals model. Fig. 2

Solution: The problem is dealt with in two phases in Figs. 1 and 2. Determine each of the deviational variables in Figure 1. Since there are no standard LP constraints, all of the first quadrant ($\vec{x} \geq \vec{0}$) is considered. The first goal (P_1) is to minimize d_4^+ which gives the shaded area in Figure 1. Do not consider any point outside this region because the most important goal can be achieved only by staying within this region.

The second goal is to minimize $6P_2d_3^- + 7.5P_2d_2^-$ which restricts the feasible region to above of $x_2 = 2$ and right of $x_1 = 4$ lines. This area is shaded in Figure 2.

The third goal is to minimize $P_3d_1^-$. As can be seen from figures, there are no points in the shaded area of Figure 2 that can reduce d_1^- to zero. The best that can be done is to come as close to $x_1 + x_2 = 10$ as possible, which gives point D = (5,1). Do not attempt to achieve the third goal at the expense of the first two goals. (Thus, stay within the area of Fig. 2.)

• PROBLEM 4-56

Consider the goal programming model

$$\text{Minimize } f = P_1d_{41}^+ + P_1d_{51}^+ + P_2d_3^- + P_3d_4^+ + P_3d_5^+ + P_4d_2^- + P_5d_1^-$$

subject to

$$7.5x_1+10x_2+d_1^- -d_1^+ = 500 \quad (1)$$

$$x_1 + d_2^- - d_2^+ = 10 \quad (2)$$

$$x_2 + d_3^- - d_3^+ = 30 \quad (3)$$

$$x_1 + 2x_2 + d_4^- - d_4^+ = 40 \quad (4)$$

$$1.5x_1+1.5x_2 + d_5^- - d_5^+ = 40 \quad (5)$$

$$d_4^+ + d_{41}^- - d_{41}^+ = 20 \quad (6)$$

$$d_5^+ + d_{51}^- - d_{51}^+ = 20 \quad (7)$$

$$x_1, x_2, d_1^-, d_1^+, d_2^-, d_2^+, d_3^-, d_3^+, d_4^-, d_4^+, d_5^-, d_5^+, d_{41}^-, d_{41}^+, d_{51}^- d_{51}^+ \geq 0$$

Solve by graphical means.

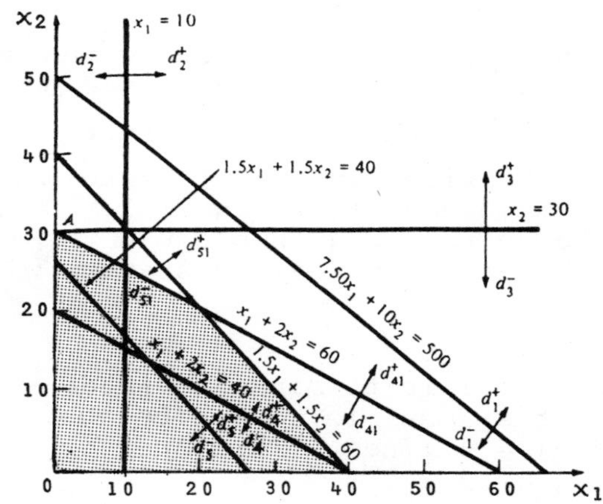

Graphical analysis of multiple conflicting goals. **Fig. 1**

Solution: Note that goal constraints (6) and (7) do not involve the decision variables x_1 and x_2. This is not a problem logically because these constraints are quite reasonable. However, it is a problem with respect to a graphical solution. These constraints must be rewritten so that the decision variables are explicitly included. First, manipulate Eq. (4) to obtain

$$d_4^+ = x_1 + 2x_2 + d_4^- - 40$$

Substituting this expression into Eq. (6) gives

$$x_1 + 2x_2 + d_4^- + d_{41}^- - d_{41}^+ = 60$$

Now, with respect to a goal of 60 units of production, d_4^- is meaningless because it represents underachievement of a goal of 40 units. Hence, eliminate d_4^-, to obtain

$$x_1 + 2x_2 + d_{41}^- - d_{41}^+ = 60 \qquad (6')$$

(d_4^- is not needed in this constraint because d_{41}^- will indicate the amount of underachievement of the goal by itself.)

A similar set of manipulations gives

$$1.5x_1 + 1.5x_2 + d_{51}^- - d_{51}^+ = 60 \qquad (7')$$

The graphical analysis of this problem is shown in Fig. 1. Try to identify the deviational variables and the goal constraints. The first priority is to minimize d_{41}^+ and d_{51}^+. This is accomplished by staying within the shaded area. Next, minimize d_3^-. However, there is only one point within the shaded area at which d_3^- is zero: point A. Thus, point A = (0,30) must be the solution. Any of the remaining goals cannot be considered because only point A will satisfy the first two goals.

In the goal programming problem below

$$\text{Minimize} \quad f(s_1^-, s_2^-)$$

$$\text{subject to} \quad 5x + 7y + s_1^- - s_1^+ = 100$$

$$y + s_2^- - s_2^+ = 7$$

$$2x + 5y \le 51$$

$$x, y, s_1^-, s_1^+, s_2^-, s_2^+ \ge 0$$

$f(s_1^-, s_2^-)$ can be expressed as: first satisfy Goal 1 and if this is accomplished, then satisfy Goal 2.

Find an optimal solution to this problem by the Simplex method, adjusting it to goal programming.

Solution: The objective function can be depicted as

$$\text{Minimize} \quad f(s_1^-, s_2^-) = p_1 s_1^- + p_2 s_2^- \qquad \text{or}$$

$$\text{maximize} \quad -p_1 s_1^- - p_2 s_2^-$$

However, p_1 is not a multiplier but means that p_1 has first priority and p_2 has second priority. Alternatively, it is convenient at times to think of this relationship as $p_2/p_1 \to 0$ (close to zero). Table 1 contains the problem in the form of a tableau. Let s_1^- and s_2^- be the basic variables in rows 1 and 2. (This is easier than addingartificial variables.) However, since s_1^- and s_2^- appear in the last row, perform row operations on the final row so that the columns s_1^- and s_2^- have zeros in every row except the row in which they are basic. This leads to Table 2.

TABLE 1
GOAL PROGRAMMING: First Tableau

Row	Basic	Value	x	y	s_1^-	s_1^+	s_2^-	s_2^+	s_3
1	s_1^-	100	5	7	1	−1	0	0	0
2	s_2^-	7	0	1	0	0	1	−1	0
3	s_3	51	2	5	0	0	0	0	1
			0	0	p_1	0	p_2	0	0

TABLE 2
GOAL PROGRAMMING: Second Tableau

Row	Basic	Value	x	y	s_1^-	s_1^+	s_2^-	s_2^+	s_3
1	s_1^-	100	5	7	1	−1	0	0	0
2	s_2^-	7	0	1	0	0	1	−1	0
3	s_3	51	2	5	0	0	0	0	1
		$-100p_1 - 7p_2$	$-5p_1$	$-7p_1 - p_2$	0	p_1	0	p_2	0

The coefficients in the last row for the nonbasic variables are

Variable	Coefficient
x	$-5p_1$
y	$-7p_1-p_2$
s_1^+	p_1
s_2^+	p_2

This means that if x enters the basis, Goal 1 improves by $5p_1$; if y enters the basis, Goal 1 improves by $7p_1$ and Goal 2 improves by p_2. Similarly, if s_1^+ or s_2^+ enters, Goal 1 and 2 worsen, respectively, by p_1 and p_2. The immediate concern is improving goal 1, since it has the highest priority. Let x enter the basis. The new tableau is given in Table 3. From this tableau it can be seen that the first goal is met. Also, y is the only variable that can improve Goal 2. Therefore let y enter the basis which yields Table 4. From this table it is observed that only s_1^- can improve Goal 2. However, if s_1^- enters the basis Goal 1 will fail. Therefore this is the final solution.

TABLE 3

GOAL PROGRAMMING: Third Tableau

Row	Basic	Value	x	y	s_1^-	s_1^+	s_2^-	s_2^+	s_3
1	x	20	1	$\frac{7}{5}$	$\frac{1}{5}$	$-\frac{1}{5}$	0	0	0
2	s_2^-	7	0	1	0	0	1	-1	0
3	s_3	11	0	$\frac{11}{5}$	$-\frac{2}{5}$	$\frac{2}{5}$	0	0	1
		$-7p_2$	0	$-p_2$	p_1	0	0	p_2	0

TABLE 4

GOAL PROGRAMMING: Final Tableau

Row	Basic	Value	x	y	s_1^-	s_1^+	s_2^-	s_2^+	s_3
1	x	13	1	0	$\frac{5}{11}$	$-\frac{5}{11}$	0	0	$\frac{7}{11}$
2	s_2	2	0	0	$\frac{2}{11}$	$-\frac{2}{11}$	1	-1	$-\frac{5}{11}$
3	y	5	0	1	$-\frac{2}{11}$	$\frac{2}{11}$	0	0	$\frac{5}{11}$
		$2p_2$	0	0	$p_1-\frac{2}{11}p_2$	$\frac{2}{11}p_2$	0	p_2	$\frac{5}{11}p_2$

• PROBLEM 4-58

Consider this problem:

Minimize $f = P_1 d_1^- + P_2 d_2^-$

Subject to

$$x_1 - x_2 + d_1^- - d_1^+ = 50$$

$$-2x_1 + 3x_2 + d_2^- - d_2^+ = 0$$

$$x_1 + x_2 \le 1000$$

$$x_1, x_2, d_1^-, d_1^+, d_2^-, d_2^+ \ge 0$$

Solve by applying the Simplex Method of Goal Programming.

Solution: P_1 and P_2 are preemptive: the deviations with respect to the first goal must be minimized before considering those concerned with the second goal. In order to do this, the simplex criterion $c_j - z_j$ is no longer expressed as a single row below the tableau. Rather, there is a matrix of size k × (n + p + m), where k represents the number of priority levels (two, in this problem) and n + p + m is the total number of variables (seven: two decision variables plus four deviational variables plus one slack variable). Thus, the $c_j - z_j$ matrix will be 2 × 7. Because of this, normally only the $c_j - z_j$ matrix is shown rather than both the z_j and $c_j - z_j$ matrices. (Obviously, if $c_j - z_j$ is 2 × 7, so is z_j.)

initial tableau

Minimize			0	0	P_1	0	P_2	0	0			
i	c_B	x_B	x_1	x_2	d_1^-	d_1^+	d_2^-	d_2^+	s_1	b	θ_i	
1	P_1	d_1^-	(1)	−1	1	−1	0	0	0	50	50	Out →
2	P_2	d_2^-	−2	3	0	0	1	−1	0	0	—	
3	0	s_1	1	1	0	0	0	0	1	1000	1000	
	$c_j - z_j$	P_2	2	−3	0	0	0	1	0	0		
		P_1	−1	1	0	1	0	0	0	$50P_1$		
			↑ In									

Fig. 1

The initial tableau is shown in Fig. 1. An initial basis is easily obtained by using the d_i^- variables. Thus, both decision variables are zero, which means no production. The $c_j - z_j$ matrix is computed for each priority level. For example, consider x_1. Since a_{11} = 1, at the first priority level z_1 = +1 and $c_1 - z_1$ = 0 − 1 = −1. At the second priority level, z_1 = −2 (because a_{21} = −2) so that $c_1 - z_1$ = 0 − (−2) = +2. Thus, entering 1 unit of x_1 decreases the priority 1 deviation and increases the priority 2 deviation. The other variables are evaluated similarly.

Note that deviations from the goals are to be minimized. Moreover, the goals are dealt with in order of priority. Therefore, minimize deviations from the first-priority goal at this point. Because $c_1 - z_1$ = −1 at the P_1 level, choose x_1 to be the entering variable.

The outgoing variable is selected exactly as in linear programming, by choosing the smallest θ_i ratio. Thus, d_1^- becomes the outgoing variable, and a_{11} = 1 is the pivot element.

Second tableau

Minimize			0	0	P_1	0	P_2	0	0			
i	c_B	x_B	x_1	x_2	d_1^-	d_1^+	d_2^-	d_2^+	s_1	b	θ_i	
1	P_1	x_1	1	−1	1	−1	0	0	0	50	—	
2	P_2	d_2^-	0	(1)	2	−2	1	−1	0	100	100	Out →
3	0	s_1	0	2	−1	1	0	0	1	950	475	
	$c_j - z_j$	P_2	0	−1	−2	2	0	1	0	$100P_2$		
		P_1	0	0	1	0	0	0	0	0		
				↑ In								

Fig. 2

The second tableau is shown in Fig. 2. Note the $c_j - z_j$ row for P_1. All entries are zero or positive. This means the first-priority goal is achieved (because d_1^- is now zero). Therefore, consider the second-priority goal by looking at the P_2 row with the proviso to ascertain optimality at the P_1 level. Both x_2 and d_1^- have $c_j - z_j$ coefficients which are negative in the P_2 row. However, the P_1 coefficient is +1 for d_1^-. Therefore this variable cannot enter the basis, because this would destroy the P_1 optimality. (It should be obvious that entering d_1^- would simply reverse the previous pivot and result in the original tableau.) The entering variable is x_2; the outgoing variable is d_2^-.

Third tableau

		Minimize	0	0	P_1	0	P_2	0	0	
i	c_B	x_B	x_1	x_2	d_1^-	d_1^+	d_2^-	d_2^+	s_1	b
1	0	x_1	1	0	3	−3	1	−1	0	150
2	0	x_2	0	1	2	−2	1	−1	0	100
3	0	s_1	0	0	−5	5	−2	2	1	750
	$c_j - z_j$	P_2	0	0	0	0	1	0	0	0
		c P_1	0	0	1	0	0	0	0	0

Fig. 3

The third (and final) tableau is shown in Fig. 3. This tableau is optimal because all entries in the $c_j - z_j$ matrix are nonnegative. The solution is $x_1^* = 150$, $x_2^* = 100$, and $s_1^* = 750$. Both goals have been achieved because d_1^- and d_2^- are both zero.

CHAPTER 5

THE TRANSPORTATION AND ASSIGNMENT PROBLEMS

LEAST COST METHOD

• **PROBLEM** 5-1

Study Table 1

Consider the shipment of steel from two warehouses W_1 and W_2 to two markets M_1 and M_2. The cost of shipping from warehouse W_i to market M_j is given in the ith row and jth column of the table. For example, the cost of shipping from W_1 to M_2 is $c_{12} = 8$ \$/ton. The supplies (a_i) at the warehouses are listed at the right of the table; thus, the supply at W_1 is $a_1 = 15$ tons. The demands (b_j) at the markets are listed at the bottom of the table; thus, the demand at M_1 is $b_1 = 12$ tons. Note that the sum of the supplies equals the sum of the demands:

$$a_1 + a_2 = 20 = b_1 + b_2.$$

Transportation problems in which total supply equals total demand are called balanced.

Let x_{ij} be the amount in tons to be shipped from warehouse W_i to market M_j. The problem is to ship the steel in the least expensive (minimum cost) way and in so doing completely exhaust the supplies at the warehouses and exactly satisfy the demands at the markets.

First, set up the problem in linear programming form and solve it by employing the simplex algorithm. Then, solve by the least cost method.

	M_1	M_2	supplies (tons)
W_1	5	8	15
W_2	4	10	5
demands (tons)	12	8	

Table 1

Solution: The cost in dollars in shipping x_{11} tons from W_1 to M_1 is five times x_{11}, i.e., $5x_{11}$. Thus, express the total shipping cost u in the following way:

$$u = 5x_{11} + 8x_{12} + 4x_{21} + 10x_{22} \quad \text{(to be minimized)}. \tag{1}$$

The requirements pertaining to the warehouses and markets are equation constraints (see the next-to-last paragraph of the problem statement):

$$x_{11} + x_{12} = 15 \tag{2}$$

$$x_{21} + x_{22} = 5 \tag{3}$$

$$x_{11} + x_{21} = 12 \tag{4}$$

$$x_{12} + \quad + x_{22} = 8 \tag{5}$$

and

$$x_{11} \geq 0 \tag{6}$$

$$x_{12} \geq 0 \tag{7}$$

$$x_{21} \geq 0 \tag{8}$$

$$x_{22} \geq 0. \tag{9}$$

Of the four equation constraints, one is redundant. For example, the sum of (2) and (3) minus (4) yields (5). Thus, eliminate (5) as a constraint (any other would do equally as well as the one to be eliminated). This ability to eliminate one of the constraints is a direct consequence of the balanced nature of the problem.

The initial tableau corresponding to (1), (2), (3), and (4) is thus

x_{11}	x_{12}	x_{21}	x_{22}	1	
1*	1	0	0	−15	= −0
0	0	1	1	−5	= −0
1	0	1	0	−12	= −0
5	8	4	10	0	= u

(T.1)

Now replace the zeros in the right-hand margin by basic variables. This is done in Tableaus 2, 3, and 4. In each of these, delete the column with the zero in the top margin. These tableaus, which are very easy to calculate, are as follows:

0	x_{12}	x_{21}	x_{22}	1	
1	1	0	0	−15	= $-x_{11}$
0	0	1	1	−5	= −0
−1	−1	1*	0	3	= −0
−5	3	4	10	75	= u

(T.2)

x_{12}	0	x_{22}	1	
1	0	0	−15	$= -x_{11}$
1	−1	1*	−8	$= -0$
−1	1	0	3	$= -x_{21}$
7	−4	10	63	$= u$

(T.3)

x_{12}	0	1	
1	0	−15	$= -x_{11}$
1	1	−8	$= -x_{22}$
−1*	0	+3	$= -x_{21}$
−3	−10	143	$= u$

(T.4)

Tableau 4 has the appearance of a standard tableau; there are three basic variables and one nonbasic variable. Since $-b_3 = +3$, this tableau is ready for the next stage. Obtain Tableau 5:

x_{21}	1	
1	−12	$= -x_{11}$
1*	−5	$= -x_{22}$
−1	−3	$= -x_{12}$
−3	134	$= u$

(T.5)

Tableau 5 corresponds to a b.f.p. tableau because all the entries in the right-hand column are negative. This leads to the solution tableau for this minimum problem:

x_{22}	1	
−1	−7	$= -x_{11}$
1	−5	$= -x_{21}$
1	−8	$= -x_{12}$
+3	119	$= u$

(T.6)

Read off the optimal solution as:

$$x_{22} = 0,\ x_{11} = 7,\ x_{21} = 5,\ x_{12} = 8, \text{ and Min } u = \$119.$$

Check out the solution by substituting the above x_{ij} values into the original equation for u:

$$u = 5.7 + 8.8 + 4.5 = 119 \quad \text{(check)}.$$

The supply and demand requirements also check out.

Now apply the least Cost Method to the initial table. The calculations and the resulting table are indicated as follows: Locate the least cost option of the initial table. It is 4. Allocate as much units as possible to this option. This amount is smaller than the supply and demand quantities corresponding to the option: min (12, 5) = 5. Subtract 12 - 5 = 7. One still requires to satisfy 7 tons of demand of M_1. Cross out the W_2 row since all its supply is allocated. Now search for the next least cost option and continue this way until all allocations are made.

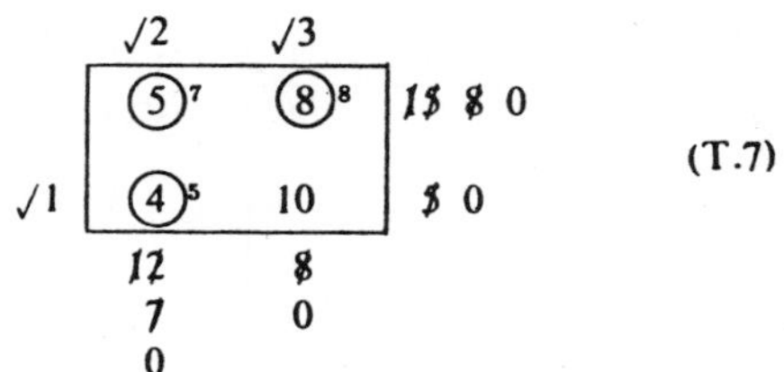

(T.7)

The only relevant cycle is that corresponding to cell (2, 2); the value of cycle is 10 - 4 + 5 - 8 = +3. Thus, the b.f.s. pertaining to Table 7 is an optimal solution. The solution values for the x_{ij}'s are $x_{11} = 7$, $x_{12} = 8$, $x_{21} = 5$, and $x_{22} = 0$. The amount of effort involved in finding the optimal solution is much smaller in the current approach.

• PROBLEM 5-2

Find an initial feasible solution using the Least Minimum Cost Method of Table 1.

Cost, Supply, and Demand Data TABLE 1

Origin (Surplus Area)	*Destination (Shortage Area)*			*Supply*
	1	*2*	*3*	
1	$ 50	100	100	110
2	200	300	200	160
3	100	200	300	150
Demand	140	200	80	420 / 420

TABLE 2

Origin	*Destination*			*Supply*
	1	*2*	*3*	
~~1~~	110 (cost 50)	(cost 100)	(cost 100)	~~110~~
2	(cost 200)	80 (cost 300)	80 (cost 200)	160
3	30 (cost 100)	120 (cost 200)	(cost 300)	150
Demand	~~140~~	200	~~80~~	420 / 420

<u>Solution</u>: Table 2 illustrates the initial solution by the Least Cost Method. To start, the least cost element in the table is identified ($c_{11} = 50$) and the maximum feasible amount is allocated to the corresponding cell ($x_{11} = 110$). Since Row 1 is satisfied, it is crossed out.

The next lowest cost element among feasible cells is

located (c_{31} = 100) and the maximum feasible amount is entered (x_{31} = 30). This eliminates Column 1. The next lowest cost element of 200 is given by either c_{23} or c_{32}. Arbitrarily selecting the former gives x_{23} = 80 and the elimination of Column 3. The solution is completed by entering 80 and 120 in cells (2,2) and (3,2) respectively, to satisfy the requirements of Destination 2. The total cost for this solution is $72,500 (-110 x 50 + 80 x 300 + 80 x 200 + 30 x 100 + 120 x 200).

• PROBLEM 5-3

Assume there are 2 factories and 3 warehouses. Factory I makes 40 widgets. Factory II makes 50 widgets. Warehouse A stores 15 widgets. Warehouse B stores 45 widgets. Warehouse C stores 30 widgets. It costs $80 to ship one widget from Factory I to warehouse A, $75 to ship one widget from Factory I to warehouse B, $60 to ship one widget from Factory I to warehouse C, $65 per widget to ship from Factory II to warehouse A, $70 per widget to ship from Factory II to warehouse B, and $75 per widget to ship from Factory II to warehouse C.

1) Set up the linear programming problem to find the shipping pattern which minimizes the total cost.

2) Find a feasible (but not necessarily optimal) solution to the problem of finding a shipping pattern using the Northwest Corner Algorithm.

3) Use the Least-Cost Method to find a feasible solution to the shipping problem.

Solution: 1) Let x_{11} = number of widgets shipped from Factory I to warehouse A, x_{12}=number of widgets shipped from Factory I to warehouse B, x_{13} = number of widgets shipped from Factory I to warehouse C, x_{21} = number of widgets shipped from Factory II to warehouse A, x_{22} = number of widgets shipped from Factory II to warehouse B, x_{23} = number of widgets shipped from Factory II to warehouse C. Thus, the linear programming problem can be formulated as follows:

$$\text{Minimize} \quad C = 80x_{11} + 75x_{12} + 60x_{13} + 65x_{21} + 70x_{22} + 75x_{23}$$

subject to

$$x_{11} + x_{12} + x_{13} \le 40,$$

$$x_{21} + x_{22} + x_{23} \le 50, \; x_{11} + x_{21} = 15,$$

$$x_{12} + x_{22} = 45$$

and

$$x_{13} + x_{23} = 30.$$

This linear programming problem may be solved using the simplex method.

2) The facts of the problem can be diagrammed in the following table, where the amounts the factories produce are written on the right, the amounts the warehouses can store are written on the bottom, and the numbers in the boxes are the costs of shipping from the factory on the left to the warehouse above.

Warehouse

Factory	A	B	C	
I	80	75	60	40
II	65	70	75	50
	15	45	30	

The Northwest Corner algorithm first al.̵ocates as many widgets as possible to the upper left box (the northwest box). Next, proceed to the nearest box into which something can still be placed, and allocate as much as possible to that one. Then the process continues, each time moving either one box to the right, or one down, or one diagonally down, depending on how the shipments can be made. Since the 15 at the bottom of the first column is less than the 40 at the right of the first row, Factory I can ship only 15 widgets to warehouse A, so write a 15 in the upper left box. Then nothing else can go to warehouse A; that is, nothing else will be written in the boxes of the first column.

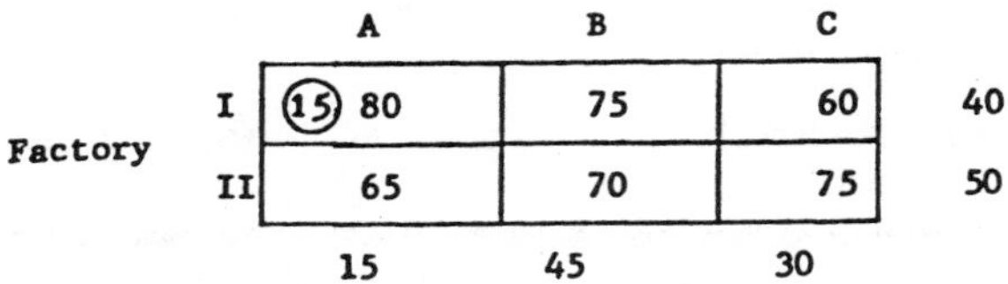

Warehouse

Factory	A	B	C	
I	(15) 80	75	60	40
II	65	70	75	50
	15	45	30	

Thus, move right from 15, making $x_{12} = 40 - 15 = 25$. Now the capacity of factory I has been exhausted, so there can be no more numbers written in the first row. Moving down, next set $x_{22} = 45 - 25 = 20$ to fill warehouse B. Now, move right and set $x_{23} = 50 - 20 = 30$. The results are as follows:

Warehouse

Factory	A	B	C	
I	(15) 80	(25) 75	60	40
II	65	(20) 70	(30) 75	50
	15	45	30	

This table tells that 15 widgets can be shipped from Factory I to warehouse A, 25 widgets from Factory I to warehouse B, 20 widgets from Factory II to warehouse B, and 30 widgets from Factory II to warehouse C. This is not the optimum solution (that is, it is not the cheapest), but it is feasible. The total cost is $C = 15 \cdot 80 + 25 \cdot 75 + 20 \cdot 70 + 30 \cdot 75 = 6725$.

3) The Northwest Corner Algorithm ignores the costs. The Least-Cost Algorithm is another method of finding a feasible solution; unlike the Northwest Corner Algorithm, it does

take the cost into account. The Least-Cost Algorithm finds the cheapest possible rate, and it sends as much as possible at that rate. Again, the problem can be summarized in the following table:

Warehouse

		A	B	C	
Factory	I	80	75	60	40
	II	65	70	75	50
		15	45	30	

Since 60 is the cheapest possible rate, decide to send as much as possible at that rate. Since warehouse C needs 30 widgets and Factory I has 40 widgets, one can send at most 30 widgets from Factory I to warehouse C; do so and write it in the box. To show that all 30 items have been accounted for, of warehouse C cross off the 30. To show that 30 of the 40 items in Factory I have been used, cross off the 40 and write a 10 beside it to show there are 10 items left in Factory I.

Warehouse

		A	B	C		
Factory	I	80	75	(30) 60	~~40~~	10
	II	65	70	75	50	
		15	45	~~30~~		

The next cheapest shipping rate is 65. Since warehouse A needs only 15 widgets, write a 15 in the box with the 65, showing that 15 widgets will be shipped from Factory II to the warehouse A. Cross out the 15 below the first column. And cross out the 50 at the right of the second row and write a 50 - 15 = 35 next to it.

Warehouse

		A	B	C		
Factory	I	80	75	(30) 60	~~40~~	10
	II	(15) 65	70	75	~~50~~	35
		~~15~~	45	~~30~~		

The next cheapest shipping rate is 70. Only 35 of the widgets produced by Factory II remain to be sent to warehouse B, so write a 35 in the box with the 70. Then cross out the 35 at the right of the second row, and replace the 45 below the second column with a 45 - 35 = 10.

Warehouse

		A	B	C		
Factory	I	80	75	(30) 60	~~40~~	10
	II	(15) 65	(35) 70	75	~~50~~	~~35~~
		~~15~~	~~45~~ 10	~~30~~		

Since 75 is the lowest remaining rate, ship the remaining 10 widgets from Factory I to warehouse B and indicate the feasible solution as follows:

Warehouse

Factory		A	B	C	
	I	80	(10) 75	(30) 60	~~40~~ ~~10~~
	II	(15) 65	(35) 70	75	~~50~~ ~~35~~
		~~15~~	~~45~~ ~~10~~	~~30~~	

This shipping pattern yields a cost of 15 · 65 + 35 · 70 + 10 · 75 + 30 · 60 = 5975.

NORTH - WEST CORNER METHOD

• PROBLEM 5-4

Find an initial feasible solution to the transportation problem.

*Negative costs might indicate some sort of bonus, or net profit, realized by the shipping from the corresponding origins to the corresponding destinations.

Destination

		D_1	D_2	D_3	D_4	D_5	D_6
		8	7	12	2	3	10
	O_1:15	10	4	7	2	3	4
	O_2:10	1	1	13	8	7	6
Origin	O_3 : 5	2	8	-1*	5	1	4
	O_4 : 9	7	9	2	7	3	2
	O_5 : 3	3	4	15	7	-2*	5

(1)

Solution: Begin with origin O_1. Allocate from O_1 to destination D_1 until either (1) supply at O_1 is exhausted and demand at D_1 is satisfied, (2) supply at O_1 is exhausted and demand at D_1 is not satisfied, or (3) supply at O_1 is not exhausted and demand at D_1 is satisfied. In case (1) begin a new allocating from O_2 to D_2. In case (2), begin allocating from O_2 to D_1. In case (3), begin allocating from O_1 to D_2.

Again one is led to three cases. The allocation process continues, supplies at origins being exhausted in the order $O_1, O_2, \ldots, O_m$. Simultaneously, demands at destinations are satisfied in the order $D_1, D_2, \ldots, D_n$.

At every step either an origin supply is exhausted or a destination demand is satisfied, or both. Since one has

$$\sum_{i=1}^{m} a_i = \sum_{j=1}^{n} b_j,$$

then at every stage the supply unallocated and the amount of demand not satisfied are identical. Therefore, the last stage must exhaust supply m and satisfy demand n.

Omitting costs from the problem and placing the allocation x_{ij} from origin i to destination j in the block (i,j), the successive stages of the allocation procedure described for the problem are illustrated in the nine steps of Figure 1. The allocation always proceeds from left to right and top to bottom, or from west to east and north to south, thus this technique of obtaining a feasible solution has become known as the northwest-corner method.

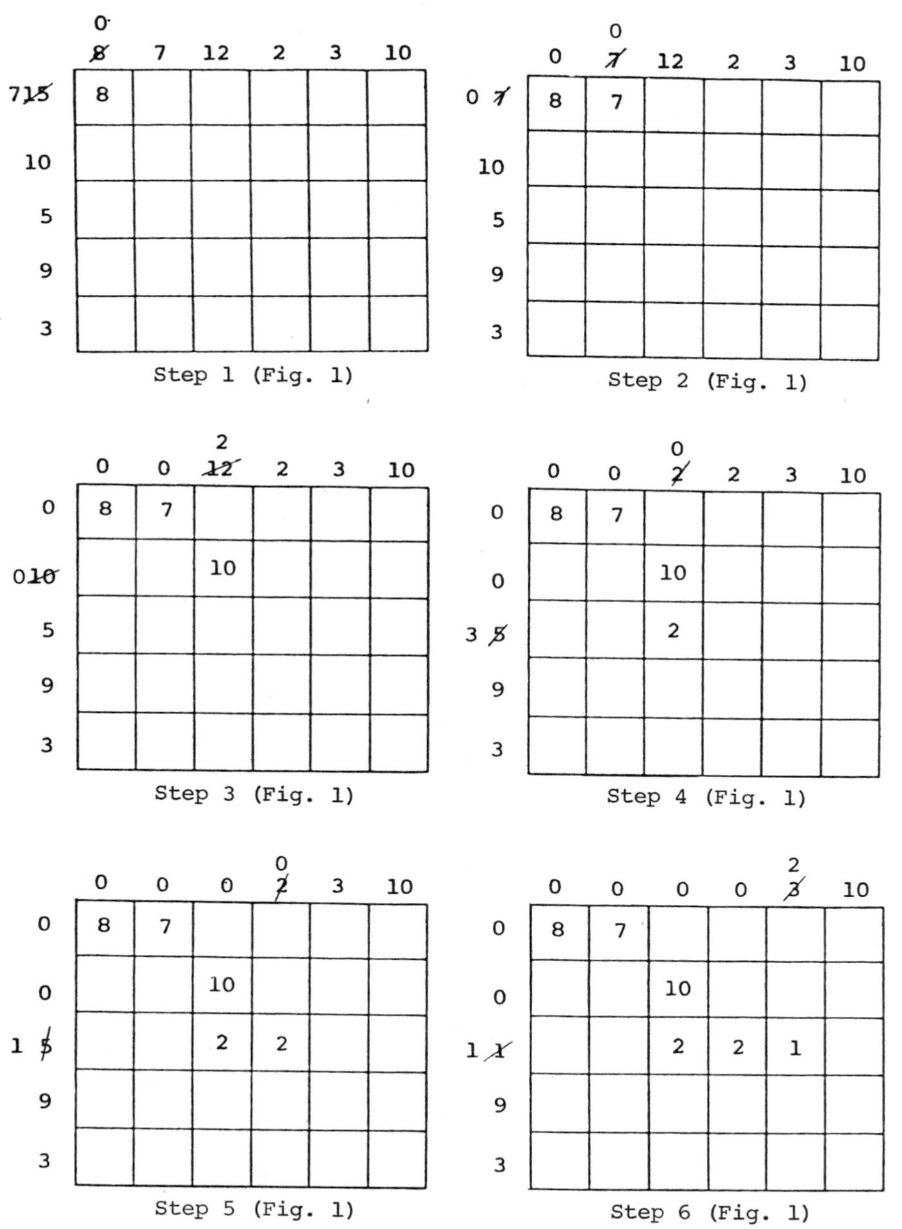

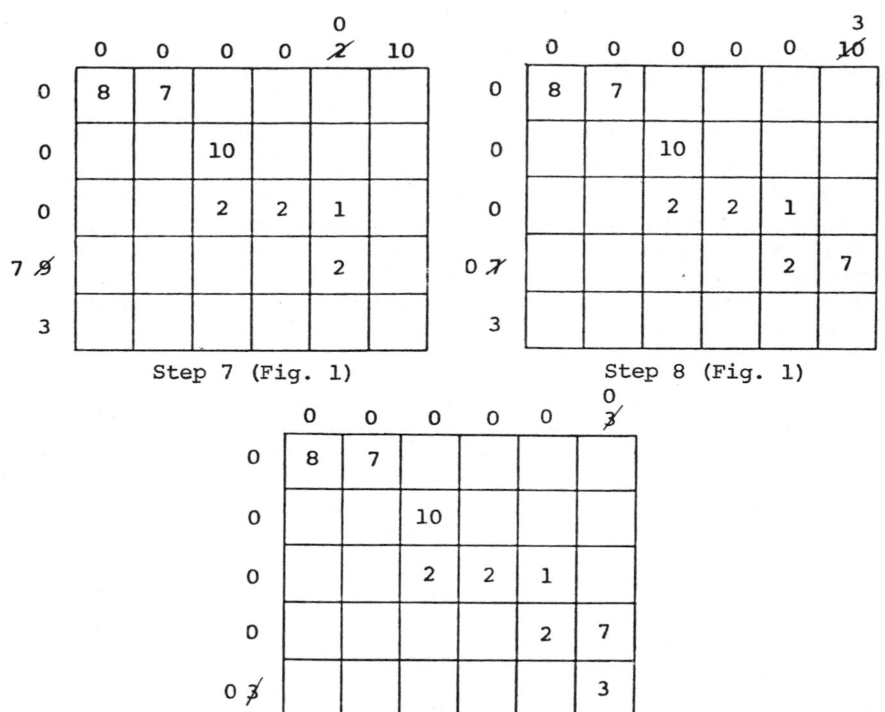

Step 7 (Fig. 1)

Step 8 (Fig. 1)

Step 9 (Fig. 1)

This method has the property that the number of positive variables provided, is at most m + n - 1. To see this, observe that the last step satisfies both the mth supply constraint and the nth demand constraint. Each preceding step satisfies one supply constraint or one demand constraint, or perhaps both. Since there are m + n supply and demand constraints, it must be that at most m + n - 1 positive variables result. Furthermore, one must always end with a positive variable in every row and column.

The feasible solution just obtained is $x_{11} = 8$, $x_{12} = 7$, $x_{23} = 10$, $x_{33} = 2$, $x_{34} = 2$, $x_{35} = 1$, $x_{45} = 2$, $x_{46} = 7$, $x_{56} = 3$, and all other $x_{ij} = 0$. The value of the objective function is $Z = 8(10) + 7(4) + 10(13) + 2(-1) + 2(5) + 1(1) + 2(3) + 7(2) + 3(5) = 282$.

• PROBLEM 5-5

The following problem has m = 3 origins and n = 4 destinations. The supplies at the origins are 18, 5, and 7 units, respectively. The requirements at the destinations are 4, 18, 6, and 2 units, respectively. The problem is balanced because the total supply and total requirements are both 30 units. All this information and the unit shipment costs are represented in Table 1.

Table 1 completely represents the whole transportation problem. Use the northwest corner method to find a feasible solution: a set of shipments x_{ij} such that all supplies are used and all requirements are satisfied exactly.

TABLE 1

	D_1	D_2	D_3	D_4	Supply
O_1	21	36	43	20	18
O_2	60	30	50	43	5
O_3	18	10	48	72	7
Requirements	4	18	6	2	30

Solution:

Step 1: Select the northwest (upper left-hand) corner cell for a shipment.

Step 2: Make as large a shipment as possible. This will completely exhaust either the supply at one origin or the requirement at one destination.

Step 3: Adjust the supply and requirement numbers to reflect the remaining supplies and requirements. If any remain, return to step 1.

Shipments can be indicated in a box within each cell. Supplies and requirements remaining can be entered to the right of the original numbers. Rows corresponding to origins can be lined out after their supply is exhausted. Columns corresponding to destinations can be lined out after their requirements are completely filled.

A transportation problem of size m x n requires m + n - 1 or fewer iterations of these three steps. The first iteration of three steps produces the result.

21 [4]	36	43	20	18,14
60	30	50	43	5
18	10	48	72	7
4,0	18	6	2	

The shipment of 4 units is indicated from O_1 to D_1. The supply remaining at O_1 is 14 units. The requirement at D_1 is filled and so column 1 is lined out. After the next iteration the table looks like

21 [4]	36 [14]	43	20	18,14,0
60	30	50	43	5
18	10	48	72	7
4,0	18,4	6	2	

The northwest corner at the start of this iteration was cell (1,2). The largest shipment possible was 14 units. Now O_1's supply is exhausted and so row 1 is lined out. The new northwest cell in the next iteration is (2,2). Four units is the largest shipment possible. This iteration plus the remaining iterations finally result in the following table:

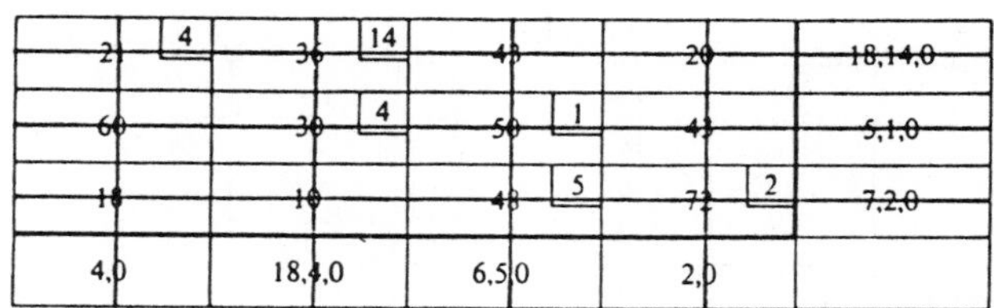

The sixth iteration results in the exhaustion of the supply at O_3 and the simultaneous satisfaction of the requirement at D_4. The six iterations have resulted in six shipments that as a whole constitute a feasible solution. The total cost of this solution is

$$4(21) + 14(36) + 4(30) + 50 + 5(48) + 2(72) = 1142$$

• PROBLEM 5-6

A national truck rental firm, the Eisenthal Trucking Company, is planning for a heavy demand of rental trucks during the month of April. An inventory of its trucks combined with projections for demand indicate that three metropolitan areas will be short of the number of trucks required to satisfy expected demands. Three other metropolitan areas have surpluses of trucks above the number expected to be needed during this period.

In an effort to prepare for the period of heavy demand, company officials wish to relocate trucks from those metropolitan areas expected to have surpluses to those having shortages. Drivers can be hired to drive the trucks between cities, and the company would like to redistribute its trucks at a minimum cost. The costs (in dollars) of driving a truck between cities are provided in Table 1, as well as the surplus and shortage figures for each metropolitan area. The total surplus (supply) and total shortage (demand) are equal at 420 trucks. Find a solution using the Northwest Corner Method.

Cost, supply, and Demand Data — Table 1

Origin (Surplus Area)	*Destination (Shortage Area)* 1	2	3	*Supply (Surplus of Trucks)*
1	$ 50	100	100	110
2	200	300	200	160
3	100	200	300	150
Demand (shortage of trucks)	140	200	80	420 / 420

Solution: To illustrate the Northwest Corner Method, develop an initial solution.

1. The capacity of 110 trucks at Origin 1 is less than the 140 units demanded at Destination 1. Consequently, all

of the capacity at Origin 1 is allocated to cell (1,1). (See Table 2)

2. The exhaustion of the supply at Origin 1 leads to Origin 2. The 160 units available at Origin 2 are compared with the 30 remaining trucks required at Destination 1. This leads to the assignment of 30 trucks to cell (2,1).

3. The assignment in (2) leaves 130 trucks available at Origin 2 and the requirements of Destination 1 satisfied. Moving to the needs of Destination 2, one sees that a comparison of the 200 trucks required with the 130 remaining at Origin 2 results in the assignment of 130 units to cell (2,2).

4. Having exhausted the capacity of Origin 2, one finds the 150 units available at Origin 3 are compared with the 70 units still required at Destination 2. This leads to an assignment of 70 units to cell (3,2).

5. The remaining 80 units at Origin 3 exactly equals the demand at Destination 3. Thus, 80 units are assigned to cell (3,3).

Northwest Corner Method Table 2

Origin	Destination 1		Destination 2		Destination 3		Supply
	Allocation	Cost	Allocation	Cost	Allocation	Cost	
1	110	50		100		100	110
2	30	200	130	300		200	160
3		100	70	200	80	300	150
Demand	140		200		80		420 / 420

Table 3

Basic Variable	Value		Unit Delivery Cost		Contribution to Total Cost
x_{11}	110	×	50	=	$ 5,500
x_{21}	30	×	200	=	6,000
x_{22}	130	×	300	=	39,000
x_{32}	70	×	200	=	14,000
x_{33}	80	×	300	=	24,000
					$88,500

The complete initial solution appears in Table 2. It indicates that 110 trucks should be delivered from the city representing Origin 1 to the city representing Destination 1, 30 from Origin 2 to Destination 1, 130 from Origin 2 to Destination 2, 70 from Origin 3 to Destination 2, and 80 from Origin 3 to Destination 3. Total cost for this redistribution is summarized in Table 3.

• **PROBLEM 5-7**

A company has four warehouses and six stores. The four warehouses altogether have a surplus of 22 units of a given commodity, divided among them as follows:

Warehouse	Surplus
1	5
2	6
3	2
4	9

The six stores altogether need 22 units of the commodity. Individual requirements are:

Store	Requirements
1	4
2	4
3	6
4	2
5	4
6	2

Costs of shipping one unit of the commodity from warehouse i to store j are displayed in the following matrix:

		Store					
		1	2	3	4	5	6
Warehouse	1	9	12	9	6	9	10
	2	7	3	7	7	5	5
	3	6	5	9	11	3	11
	4	6	8	11	2	2	10

Find feasible (not necessarily optimal) solutions, and the cost associated with each:

a) by the Northwest Corner Method and

b) by the Penalty Method.

Solution: a) Northwest Corner Method:

The first step is to draw up a blank m-by-n matrix complete with row and column requirements, as follows:

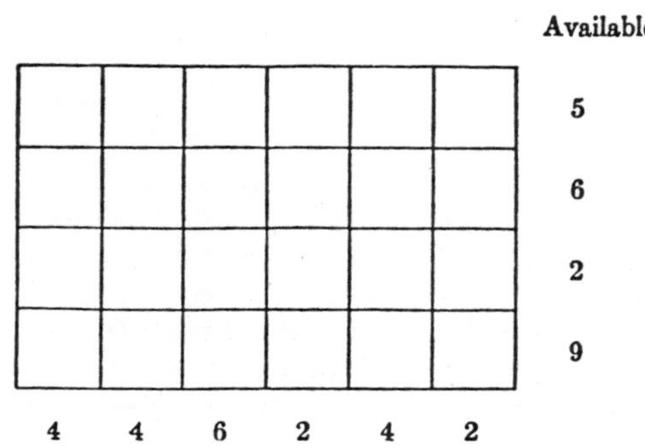

Put a set of allocations in the cells so that row totals and column totals will be as indicated.

Start at the upper left-hand corner, which is cell (1,1), and allocate as much as possible there: in other words, 4. This satisfies the requirement for column 1, and leaves a surplus of 1 unit for row 1; so allocate 1 to cell (1,2). Now the allocations are complete for column 1 and row 1; and there is a remaining deficiency of 3 in column 2. Allocate 3 in position (2,2); now columns 1 and 2 are complete and there is a surplus of 3 in row 2. Continuing in this way, from left to right and top to bottom, eventually complete all the requirements by an allocation in the lower right-hand corner. The resulting feasible solution is:

							Available
	4	1					5
		3	3				6
			2				2
			1	2	4	2	9
Required	4	4	6	2	4	2	

To obtain the cost for the feasible solution, multiply each individual allocation by its corresponding unit cost, and add. The resulting cost is 139.

b) Penalty Method is a better method of finding a feasible solution, in that it usually gives a lower beginning cost. First write down the cost matrix, together with row and column identifications and row and column requirements:

		Store						
		1	2	3	4	5	6	Available
Warehouse	1	9	12	9	6	9	10	5
	2	7	3	7	7	5	5	6
	3	6	5	9	11	3	11	2
	4	6	8	11	2	2	10	9
Required		4	4	6	2	4	2	

The next step is to enter the difference between the smallest and second smallest elements in each column beneath the corresponding column, and the difference between the smallest and second smallest elements of each row to the right of the row. These differences are the numbers in parentheses in the matrix following this paragraph. The first individual allocation will be to the smallest cost of a row or the smallest cost of a column; choose that one for which there is the greatest penalty for not choosing it. That is, choose the minimum cost location in that row or column whose corresponding number in parentheses is the largest. As 5 is the largest number in parentheses, choose column 6 as the line for the first individual allocation, and allocate as much as possible to location (2,6), the minimum cost location in this column. Thus 2 units are allocated to location (2,6) as indicated by the small numeral in the upper left corner of that cell; and this completes the allocations for column 6, so that the other allocations in this column are zero.

Store

Warehouse	1	2	3	4	5	6	Available	
1	9	12	9	6	9	^{0}10	5 (3)	
2	7	3	7	7	5	^{2}5	6 (2)	Completes column 6
3	6	5	9	11	3	^{0}11	2 (2)	
4	6	8	11	2	2	^{0}10	9 (0)	
Required	4 (0)	4 (2)	6 (2)	2 (4)	4 (1)	2 (5) ↑		

The next step is to write down the shrunken cost matrix comprising the rows and columns whose allocations are not yet determined, including revised row and column totals which take into account the allocations already made. Now 4 is the largest unit penalty; this leads to an allocation in the corresponding minimum cost location in column 4: namely cell (4,4). The maximum possible allocation is 2; so allocate 2 units to cell (4,4), and 0 units to the remaining cells in column 4.

Store

Warehouse	1	2	3	4	5	Available	
1	9	12	9	^{0}6	9	5 (3)	
2	7	3	7	^{0}7	5	4 (2)	Completes column 4
3	6	5	9	^{0}11	3	2 (2)	
4	6	8	11	^{2}2	2	9 (0)	
Required	4 (0)	4 (2)	6 (2)	2 (4) ↑	4 (1)		

Next, write down the new cost matrix with column 4 also deleted, and proceed as before. The successive resulting matrices are set down below.

Store

Warehouse	1	2	3	5	Available	
1	9	12	9	^{0}9	5 (0)	
2	7	3	7	^{0}5	4 (2)	Completes column 5
3	6	5	9	^{0}3	2 (2)	
4	6	8	11	^{4}2	7 (4) ←	
Required	4 (0)	4 (2)	6 (2)	4 (1)		

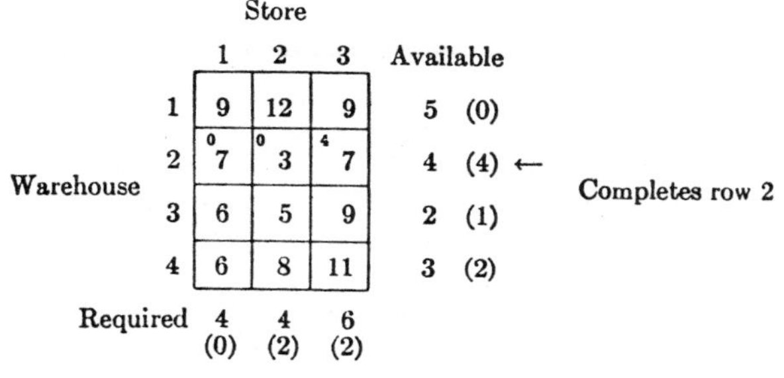

Store

Warehouse	1	2	3	Available	
1	9	12	9	5 (0)	
2	^{0}7	^{0}3	^{4}7	4 (4) ←	Completes row 2
3	6	5	9	2 (1)	
4	6	8	11	3 (2)	
Required	4 (0)	4 (2)	6 (2)		

Store

Warehouse	1	2	3	Available	
1	9	12	9	5 (0)	
3	^{0}6	^{2}5	^{0}9	2 (1)	Completes row 3
4	6	8	11	3 (2)	
Required	4 (0)	4 (3) ↑	2 (0)		

Store

Warehouse	1	2	3	Available	
1	9	^{0}12	9	5 (0)	Completes column 2
4	6	^{2}8	11	3 (2)	
Required	4 (3)	2 (4) ↑	2 (2)		

Store

Warehouse	1	3	Available	
1	^{3}9	^{2}9	5 (0)	Completes matrix.
4	^{1}6	^{0}11	1 (5) ←	
Required	4 (3)	2 (2)		

Copying the various positive allocations as they occur in the successive stages, one obtains as the feasible solution:

Store

Warehouse	1	2	3	4	5	6
1	3		2			
2			4			2
3		2				
4	1	2		2	4	

The cost for this solution turns out to be 127.

The problem is that of moving empty freight cars from "excess" origins to "deficiency" destinations in such a manner that the total cost of the required movement is a minimum, subject, of course, to any restrictions which might be imposed by practical considerations.

Tables 1 and 2 exhibit the physical program requirements (i.e., the given conditions of the problem) and the unit (per freight car) shipping costs.

Table 1 states that origins S_1, S_2, and S_3 have surpluses of 9, 4, and 8 empty freight cars respectively, while destinations D_1, D_2, D_3, D_4, and D_5 are in need of 3, 5, 4, 6, and 3 empties respectively.

Table 2 lists the unit costs C_{ij} of sending an empty freight car from the ith origin to the jth destination. Thus the problem is to obtain values of the X_{ij} (i = 1,2,3; j = 1,2,3,4,5) of Table 1 such that they: 1. satisfy the given stipulated movement requirements, 2. minimize the total cost of so doing.

TABLE 1 Physical Program Requirements

Destinations / Origins	D_1	D_2	D_3	D_4	D_5	Surpluses
S_1	X_{11}	X_{12}	X_{13}	X_{14}	X_{15}	9
S_2	X_{21}	X_{22}	X_{23}	X_{24}	X_{25}	4
S_3	X_{31}	X_{32}	X_{33}	X_{34}	X_{35}	8
Deficiencies	3	5	4	6	3	21

TABLE 2 Unit Shipping Costs

Destinations / Origins	D_1	D_2	D_3	D_4	D_5
S_1	C_{11} −10	C_{12} −20	C_{13} −5	C_{14} −9	C_{15} −10
S_2	C_{21} −2	C_{22} −10	C_{23} −8	C_{24} −30	C_{25} −6
S_3	C_{31} −1	C_{32} −20	C_{33} −7	C_{34} −10	C_{35} −4

TABLE 3 First Feasible Solution

Origins \ Destinations	D_1	D_2	D_3	D_4	D_5	Total surpluses
S_1	(3)	(5)	(1)			9
S_2			(3)	(1)		4
S_3				(5)	(3)	8
Total deficiencies	3	5	4	6	3	21

Solution: In this problem (see Table 3), one proceeds as follows:

1. Set X_{11} equal to 3, namely, the smaller of the amount available at S_1 (9) and that needed at D_1 (3), and

2. Proceed to X_{12}. Compare the number of units still available at S_1 (namely 6) with the amount required at D_2 (5) and, accordingly, let $X_{12} = 5$.

3. Proceed to X_{13} where, here, there is but one unit left at S_1 while four units are required at D_3. Thus set $X_{13} = 1$ and then

4. Proceed to X_{23}. Here $X_{23} = 3$.

5. Continuing, $X_{24} = 1$, $X_{34} = 5$, and, finally, in the southeast corner, $X_{35} = 3$.

The feasible solution obtained by this northwest corner rule is shown in Table 3 by the circled values of the X_{ij}. That this set of values is a feasible solution is easily verified by checking the respective row and column requirements. The corresponding total cost of this solution is obtained by multiplying each circled X_{ij} in Table 3 by its corresponding C_{ij} in Table 2 and summing the products. That is,

$$\text{Total cost} = \sum_{j=1}^{5} \sum_{i=1}^{3} C_{ij}X_{ij} = \sum_{j=1}^{3} \sum_{j=1}^{5} C_{ij}X_{ij}.$$

The total cost associated with the first feasible solution is computed as follows:

$$\text{T.C.} = X_{11}C_{11} + X_{12}C_{12} + X_{13}C_{13} + X_{23}C_{23} + X_{24}C_{24} + X_{34}C_{34} + X_{35}C_{35}$$

$$= (3)(-10) + (5)(-20) + (1)(-5) + (3)(-8) + (1)(-30) + (5)(-10) + (3)(-4)$$

$= -\$251$ (minus sign here means "cost" rather than "profit").

To be able to determine whether a feasible program is optimal, it is necessary to "evaluate" alternative possibilities; i.e., one must evaluate the opportunity costs associated with <u>not</u> using the cells which do not contain circled numbers. Such an evaluation is illustrated by means of the program given in Table 3 and is exhibited in Table 4 (noncircled numbers only). This evaluation is obtained as follows:

1. For any cell in which no circled number appears, describe a <u>path</u> in this manner: Locate the nearest circled-number cell in the same <u>row</u> which is such that another circled value lies in the same <u>column</u>. Thus, in Table 4, if one starts with cell S_3D_1 (row 3, column 1), the value ⑤ at S_3D_5 (row 3, column 4) satisfies this requirement; i.e., it is the closest circled-number cell in the third row which has another circled value, ① at S_2D_4, in the same column (column 4). (Note that the circled number ③ in position S_3D_5 fails to meet this requirement).

TABLE 4 First Feasible Solution (with Evaluations): C = 251

Origins \ Destinations	D_1	D_2	D_3	D_4	D_5	Total
S_1	③	⑤	①	[−18]	−11	9
S_2	−11	−13	③	①	−18	4
S_3	8	17	19	⑤	③	8
Total	3	5	4	6	3	21

2. Make the horizontal and, then, vertical moves so indicated. That is, move from S_3D_1 to S_3D_4 to S_2D_4 (see Table 4).

3. Having made the prescribed horizontal and vertical moves, repeat the procedure outlined in steps 1 and 2. This now gives cells S_2D_3 and S_1D_3 respectively; accordingly, one moves from ① at S_2D_4 to ① at S_1D_3 by way of ③ at S_2D_3.

4. Continue in this manner, moving from one circled number to another by, first, a horizontal move and, then, a vertical move until, by only a horizontal move, that column is reached in which the cell being evaluated is located. Thus, this step is from ① at S_1D_3 to ③ at S_1D_1.

5. Finally, move to the cell being evaluated (here, S_3D_1). This completes the path necessary to evaluate the given cell. (Note: For the purposes of evaluation, the

path ends, rather than starts, with the cell being evaluated).

6. Form the sum, with alternate plus and minus signs, of the unit costs associated with the cells being traversed (these unit costs are given in Table 2). This is the (noncircled) evaluation to be entered into the appropriate cell in Table 4. Thus, one has for the evaluation of cell S_3D_1:

Path (Table 4)	S_3D_4	S_2D_4	S_2D_3	S_1D_3	S_1D_1	S_3D_1
Unit cost (Table 2)	−10	−30	−8	−5	−10	−1
Evaluation (S_3D_1)	+ (−10) − (−30) + (−8) − (−5) + (−10) − (−1) = +8					

Accordingly, one enters +8 in cell S_3D_1 of Table 4.

7. Repeat the procedure outlined until all the cells not containing circled numbers are evaluated.

Having completed the evaluation, one can now determine whether or not an optimal solution has been achieved. If the noncircled numbers (the evaluations) are all nonnegative, then an optimum has been achieved. If one or more noncircled numbers are negative, then further improvement with respect to the objective function is possible.

This improvement is obtained by an iterative procedure in which one proceeds as follows: 1. Of the one or more negative values which appear, select the most negative one, e.g., -N. 2. Retrace the path used to obtain this most negative value. 3. Select those circled values which were preceded by a plus sign in the alternation between plus and minus and, of these, choose the one with the smallest value written in its circle, e.g., m. 4. One is now ready to form a new table, wherein one replaces the most negative value, -N, by this smallest value, m. 5. Circle the number m and then enter all the other circles (except the one which contained the value m in the previous program) in their previous cells, but without any numbers inside.

TABLE 5

Origins \ Destinations	D_1	D_2	D_3	D_4	D_5	Total
S_1	○	○	○	①		9
S_2			○			4
S_3				○	○	8
Total	3	5	4	6	3	21

Thus, in Table 4 the most negative number is -18 and appears in both cells S_1D_4 and S_2D_5 (i.e., -N = -18). For such ties, one may arbitrarily select either of the cells containing this most negative number. Here, cell S_1D_4 is chosen. Retracing the path used to obtain the "-18" value in cell S_1D_4, one obtains, symbolically, $+S_1D_3$, $-S_2D_3$, $+S_2D_4$. Of those preceded by a plus sign, namely S_1D_3 and S_2D_4, both have the circled value ① in their cells. Consequently, either one of these may be chosen as the circled value to be moved. In this case, cell S_2D_4 is arbitrarily chosen. The circled value ① is then entered into cell S_1D_4 (see Table 5), i.e., that cell where -18 appeared in Table 4. The other circles (without numbers) are then entered in the same positions as before (see Table 5).

TABLE 6 Second Feasible Solution: C = 233

Origins \ Destinations	D_1	D_2	D_3	D_4	D_5	Total
S_1	③	⑤	⓪	①	7	9
S_2	−11	[−13]	④	18	0	4
S_3	−10	−1	1	⑤	③	8
Total	3	5	4	6	3	21

TABLE 7 Third Feasible Solution: C = 181

Origins \ Destinations	D_1	D_2	D_4	D_3	D_5	Total
S_1	③	①	④	①	7	9
S_2	2	4	13	31	13	4
S_3	[−10]	−1	1	⑤	③	8
Total	3	5	4	6	3	21

TABLE 8 Fourth Feasible Solution: C = 151

Origins \ Destinations	D_1	D_2	D_3	D_4	D_5	Total
S_1	10	①	④	④	7	9
S_2	12	④	13	31	13	4
S_3	③	[−1]	1	②	③	8
Total	3	5	4	6	3	21

A new feasible solution is obtained by filling in the circles according to the given surplus-deficiency (input-output) specifications. This solution is given by the circled values in Table 6. The program is then evaluated, as before, and negative (noncircled) numbers still appear. Accordingly, the process is successively repeated (Tables 7, 8, and 9) until, finally, in Table 9 the evaluation of the corresponding program given therein results in all (noncircled) numbers being nonnegative. Here, then, an optimal feasible solution, or program, has been reached.

TABLE 9 Optimum Feasible Solution: C = 150

Origins \ Destinations	D_1	D_2	D_3	D_4	D_5	Total
S_1	10	1	(4)	(5)	7	9
S_2	11	(4)	12	30	12	4
S_3	(3)	(1)	1	(1)	(3)	8
Total	3	5	4	6	3	21

Thus the optimal set of movement orders which makes the total cost of movement of the empty freight cars a minimum is given in Table 9. Furthermore, this minimum total cost is $150 as compared with $251 for the original feasible (but obviously nonoptimal) program.

• PROBLEM 5-9

Consider applying the northwest corner rule to Table 1 to find the optimal solution.

Table 1

	1	2	3	4	a_i
1	2	3	4	9	20
2	14	12	5	1	30
3	12	15	9	3	40
b_j	10	10	20	50	

Solution: North-west corner rule gives the following sequence of calculations:

$$x_{11} = \text{Minimum } \{\hat{a}_1, \hat{b}_1\} = \text{Minimum } \{20, 10\} = 10$$

$$\hat{a}_1 = 20 - 10 = 10, \hat{b}_1 = 10 - 10 = 0$$

$$x_{12} = \text{Minimum } \{\hat{a}_1, \hat{b}_2\} = \text{Minimum } \{10, 10\} = 10$$

$$\hat{a}_1 = 10 - 10 = 0, \hat{b}_2 = 10 - 10 = 0$$

At this point one may move to either (2,2), or to (1,3). Assume that one moves to (2,2).

$$x_{22} = \text{minimum } \{\hat{a}_2, \hat{b}_2\} = \text{Minimum } \{30,0\} = 0$$

$\hat{a}_2 = 30 - 0 = 30, \ \hat{b}_2 = 0 - 0 = 0$

$x_{23} = \text{Minimum } \{\hat{a}_2, \hat{b}_3\} = \text{Minimum } \{30,20\} = 20$

$\hat{a}_2 = 30 - 20 = 10, \ \hat{b}_3 = 20 - 20 = 0$

$x_{24} = \text{Minimum } \{\hat{a}_2, \hat{b}_4\} = \text{Minimum } \{10,50\} = 10$

$\hat{a}_2 = 10 - 10 = 0, \ \hat{b}_4 = 50 - 10 = 40$

$x_{34} = \text{Minimum } \{\hat{a}_3, \hat{b}_4\} = \text{Minimum } \{40,40\} = 40$

$\hat{a}_3 = 40 - 40 = 0, \ \hat{b}_4 = 40 - 40 = 0$

All other x_{ij}'s are nonbasic and are assigned value zero.

Table 2

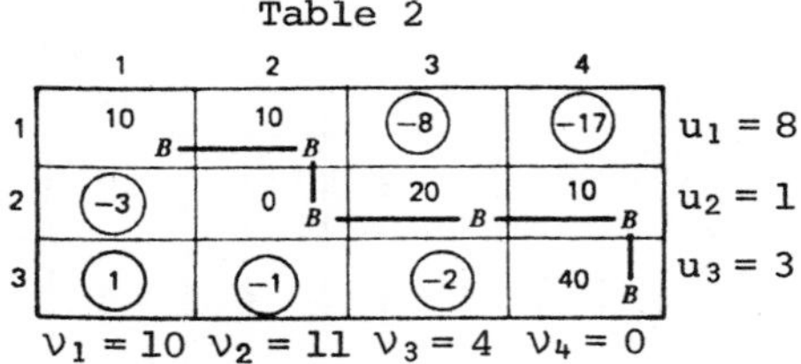

	1	2	3	4	
1	10 B	10 B	(−8)	(−17)	$u_1 = 8$
2	(−3)	0 B	20 B	10 B	$u_2 = 1$
3	(1)	(−1)	(−2)	40 B	$u_3 = 3$
	$v_1 = 10$	$v_2 = 11$	$v_3 = 4$	$v_4 = 0$	

Initial (degenerate) basic feasible solution.

The initial basic feasible solution is given in Table 2. As required there are $m + n - 1 = 3 + 4 - 1 = 6$ basic variables forming a connected tree. Note, however, that the basic feasible solution is degenerate since the basic variable $x_{22} = 0$. A point has been reached where the reduced supply is equal to the reduced demand. That is, at this stage in the application of the northwest corner rule one has

$$x_{k\ell} = \text{Minimum } \{\hat{a}_k, \hat{b}_\ell\} = \hat{a}_k = \hat{b}_\ell$$

where either $\hat{a}_k$ or $\hat{b}_\ell$ was reduced by a previous calculation of $x_{k,\ell-1}$ or $x_{k-1,\ell}$ respectively. Whichever way one goes with the northwest corner rule, the next basic variable will be zero and degeneracy occurs. A practical method for obtaining a starting basis is to proceed in either direction, that is, to $(k,\ell + 1)$ or $(k + 1,\ell)$, and assign either $x_{k,\ell+1}$ or $x_{k+1,\ell}$ as a basic variable at zero level. Basic variables at zero level are treated in exactly the same fashion as other basic variables. This way, northwest corner rule produces a basic feasible solution even in the presence of degeneracy. For each non-basic variable calculate $z_{ij} - c_{ij}$ by either the cycle method or the dual variables method. These values are depicted in circles in Table 2 for the nonbasic variables. Since $z_{31} - c_{31} = 1$, then x_{31} enters the basis. The corresponding cycle is as follows.

x_{31} = Minimum $\{\hat{x}_{11}, \hat{x}_{22}, \hat{x}_{34}\}$ = Minimum $\{10, 0, 40\} = 0$

$x_{11} = 10 - 0 = 10$

$x_{21} = 10 + 0 = 10$

$x_{22} = 0 - 0 = 0$ (leaves the basis)

$x_{24} = 10 + 0 = 10$

$x_{34} = 40 - 0 = 40$

(1, 1) —— (2, 1)
(2, 2) —— (2, 4)
(3, 1) – – – – (3, 4)

Note that x_{22} leaves the basis and x_{31} enters the basis at zero level. One has the same extreme point but a different basis. The new basis and the new $z_{ij} - c_{ij}$'s for the nonbasic variables are shown in Table 3. Since $z_{ij} - c_{ij} \leq 0$ for each nonbasic variable, the current solution is optimal.

Table 3

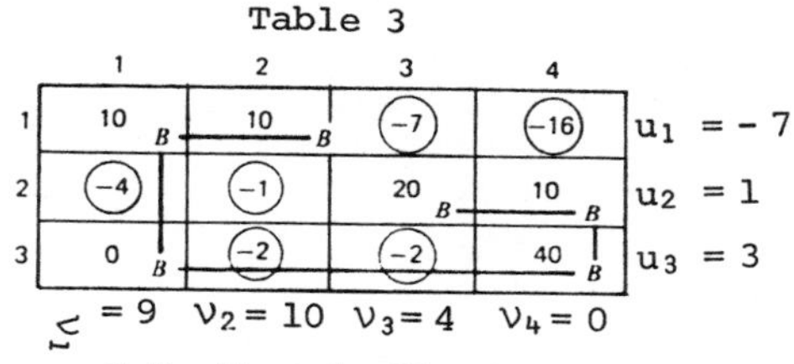

	1	2	3	4	
1	10 B	10 B	(−7)	(−16)	$u_1 = -7$
2	(−4)	(−1)	20 B	10 B	$u_2 = 1$
3	0 B	(−2)	(−2)	40 B	$u_3 = 3$
	$v_1 = 9$	$v_2 = 10$	$v_3 = 4$	$v_4 = 0$	

Optimal basic feasible solution.

Notice that in this problem

$$20 = a_1 = b_1 + b_2 = 10 + 10$$

or, in other words, a subset of the supplies equals a subset of the demands.

VOGEL'S APPROXIMATION METHOD

• PROBLEM 5-10

Use Vogel's Approximation Method to find a solution to this transportation problem.

Solution: The algorithm for Vogel's Approximation Method is:

Step 1: For each row, compute a row penalty which is the difference between the two smallest cost elements in the row. Do the same for each column.

Step 2: Identify the row or column with the largest penalty breaking the ties arbitrarily and assign to the cheapest cell as many units as possible, that is, the smaller of row supply or column demand. If there is only one cell remaining in a row or column, choose this cell and assign as many units as necessary to satisfy the row or column. Reduce the row supply and column demand by the amount assigned.

Sources \ Destinations	New York	Atlanta	LosAngeles	Supplies
Detroit	2.2	2.1	2.4	250
Cleveland	1.8	1.9	2.1	300
Indianapolis	3.0	3.2	3.6	200
Demands	190	240	320	750

Step 3: If a row supply becomes zero, eliminate that row from the tableau and calculate the new column penalties (the other row penalties remain the same). If a column demand becomes zero, eliminate that column from the tableau and calculate the new row penalties. If both a row supply and a column demand become zero, eliminate only the row or only the column but not both. The one remaining will have a supply or demand of zero, which will mean an assignment of zero units at a subsequent step. Any row or column with zero supply or demand should not be used in computing future penalties.

Step 4: a) if exactly one row or one column remains uncrossed out, stop.

b) if only one row (column) with positive supply (demand) remains uncrossed out, determine the basic variables in the row (column) by the least cost method.

c) if all uncrossed out rows and columns have (assigned) zero supply and demand, determine the zero basic variables by the least cost method. Stop.

d) otherwise, recompute the penalties for the uncrossed out rows and columns, then go to step 2.

For the given problem:

Step 1: The row penalties are 2.2 - 2.1 = 0.1,1.9 - 1.8 = 0.1, and 3.2 - 3.0 = 0.2. Similarly, the column penalties are 2.2 - 1.8 = 0.4,2.1 - 1.9 = 0.2, and 2.4 - 2.1 = 0.3. (See Fig. 1).

Steps 2 and 3: The largest penalty is 0.4, associated with column 1 (New York). The cheapest cell is $x_{C,N}$.

Assign min (300,190) = 190 to this cell. Reduce the row by 190 to 110 and the column by 190 to 0. Eliminate the New York column and recompute the row penalties. (See Fig. 2).

Destinations / Sources	New York	Atlanta	LosAngeles	Supplies	Row penalty
Detroit	2.2	2.1	2.4	250	0.1
Cleveland	1.8	1.9	2.1	300	0.1
Indianapolis	3.0	3.2	3.6	200	0.2
Demands	190	240	320	750	
Column penalty	0.4	0.2	0.3		

Fig. 1

Destinations / Sources	New York	Atlanta	LosAngeles	Supplies	Row penalty
Detroit	2.2	2.1	2.4	250	0.3
Cleveland	(190) 1.8	1.9	2.1	~~300~~ 110	0.2
Indianapolis	3.0	3.2	3.6	200	0.4
Demands	~~190~~ 0	240	320	750	
Column penalty	—	0.2	0.3		

Fig. 2

Steps 4,2,3: The largest penalty occurs for the third row (Indianapolis). The cheapest cell is $x_{I,A}$.

Assign min (200,240) = 200 units. Reduce the row by 200 to 0 and the column by 200 to 40. Eliminate the row and recompute the column penalties. (See Fig. 3).

Destinations / Sources	New York	Atlanta	LosAngeles	Supplies	Row penalty
Detroit	2.2	2.1	2.4	250	0.3
Cleveland	(190) 1.8	1.9	2.1	~~300~~ 110	0.2
Indianapolis	3.0	(200) 3.2	3.6	~~200~~ 0	—
Demands	~~190~~ 0	~~240~~ 40	320	750	
Column penalty	—	0.2	0.3		

Fig. 3

Steps 4,2,3 (repeat): The first row and the third column both have a penalty of 0.3. Choose the third column (Los Angeles) arbitrarily. The cheapest cell is $x_{C, L}$. Assign min (110,320) = 110 units. Reduce the row by 110 to 0 and the column by 110 to 210. Eliminate the second row. (See Fig. 4). Note that there is only one cell remaining in the second and in the third columns, so that the penalties cannot be computed.

Destinations / Sources	New York	Atlanta	LosAngeles	Supplies	Row penalty
Detroit	2.2	2.1	2.4	250	0.3
Cleveland	(190) 1.8	1.9	(110) 2.1	~~300~~ ~~110~~ 0	—
Indianapolis	3.0	(200) 3.2	3.6	~~200~~ 0	—
Demands	~~190~~ 0	~~240~~ 40	~~320~~ 210	750	
Column penalty	—				

Fig. 4

Steps 4,2,3: Assign 210 units to $x_{D, L}$ to satisfy the third column and 40 units to $x_{D, A}$ to satisfy the second column. (See Fig. 5). These assignments also satisfy the first row, completing the initial basis. The total cost of this assignment is

$$f = 40 \times \$2.1 + 210 \times \$2.4 + 190 \times \$1.8 + 110 \times \$2.1 + 200 \times \$3.2$$

$$= \$84 + \$504 + \$342 + \$231 + \$640$$

$$= \$1801.$$

Destinations / Sources	New York	Atlanta	LosAngeles	Supplies
Detroit	2.2	(40) 2.1	(210) 2.4	~~250~~ 0
Cleveland	(190) 1.8	1.9	(110) 2.1	~~300~~ ~~110~~ 0
Indianapolis	3.0	(200) 3.2	3.6	~~200~~ 0
Demands	~~190~~ 0	~~240~~ ~~40~~ 0	~~320~~ ~~210~~ 0	750

Fig. 5

This is \$31 cheaper than the least cost solution and \$57 cheaper than the northwest corner solution.

Construct a linear programming model that corresponds to Table 1. Find a feasible solution by Vogel's Approximation method.

Table 1

From	To D	E	F	G	H	Supply
A	$c_{11}=6$	$c_{12}=5$	$c_{13}=3$	$c_{14}=4$	$c_{15}=6$	4
B	$c_{21}=4$	$c_{22}=4$	$c_{23}=7$	$c_{24}=6$	$c_{25}=8$	6
C	$c_{31}=7$	$c_{32}=6$	$c_{33}=5$	$c_{34}=6$	$c_{35}=8$	8
Demand	2	4	3	4	5	

Solution: The LP model is as follows:

The constraints in the problem are stated in the accompanying table,

	Million barrels per year	Production capacity	Demand
$x_{11}+x_{12}+x_{13}+x_{14}+x_{15}$	=4	A	
$x_{21}+x_{22}+x_{23}+x_{24}+x_{25}$	=6	B	
$x_{31}+x_{32}+x_{33}+x_{34}+x_{35}$	=8	C	
$x_{11}+x_{21}+x_{31}$	=2		D
$x_{12}+x_{22}+x_{32}$	=4		E
$x_{13}+x_{23}+x_{33}$	=3		F
$x_{14}+x_{24}+x_{34}$	=4		G
$x_{15}+x_{25}+x_{35}$	=5		H

where $x_{ij} \geq 0$ $(i = 1,2,3;\ j = 1,2,3,4,5)$ indicates the amount of units shipped from the ith source to the jth destination. The objective function is to minimize the total transportation cost z, in thousands of dollars.

$$\text{Minimize } z = 6x_{11} + 5x_{12} + 3x_{13} + 4x_{14} + 6x_{15} + 4x_{21} + 4x_{22} + 7x_{23} + 6x_{24} + 8x_{25} + 7x_{31} + 6x_{32} + 5x_{33} + 6x_{34} + 8x_{35}$$

In Vogel's Approximation method, the basic idea is to assign penalties to a row whenever the lowest entry in that row is not utilized. The penalty is the difference between the lowest and the second-lowest transportation cost in the row. Thus, similar penalties can then be calculated for all rows and columns, where the column penalty is the difference between the lowest and second-lowest cost in a column. To avoid high penalties, the algorithm begins with the highest penalties, and assigns values to the lowest cost in that row or column.

Table 2 includes the penalties for the rows and the columns. The penalty for A's shipping not to the lowest ($c_{13} = 3$) but to the second-lowest ($c_{14} = 4$) is 4 - 3 = 1.

Table 2 Vogel's Approximation Method

Source		2 D	4 E	3 F	4 G	5 H	(1)[a] Penalty	(4)[a] Penalty	(5)[a] Penalty
A	4	6	5	3	4	[6] $x_{15}=4$	1		
B	6	[4] $x_{21}=2$	[4] $x_{22}=4$	7	6	8	0	2	2
C	8	7	6	[5] $x_{33}=3$	[6] $x_{34}=4$	[8] $x_{35}=1$	1	1	0
Penalty (2)[a]		2	1	2	2	2			
Penalty (3)[a]		3	2	2	0	0			

[a]The numbers in parentheses indicate the order of the penalty computations.

Furthermore, the following penalties are obtained for

B $c_{22} - c_{23} = 4 - 4 = 0$

C $c_{32} - c_{33} = 6 - 5 = 1$

D $c_{11} - c_{21} = 6 - 4 = 2$

E $c_{12} - c_{22} = 5 - 4 = 1$

F $c_{33} - c_{13} = 5 - 3 = 2$

G $c_{24} - c_{14} = 6 - 4 = 2$

H $c_{25} - c_{15} = 8 - 6 = 2$

The largest penalty is 2, and H is arbitrarily chosen from among the four destinations with this penalty. To avoid this high penalty of 2, it is best to utilize the lowest channel leading to H, which is $c_{15} = 6$, arriving from A. The largest quantity that can be assigned there is $x_{15} = 4$, which is A's production level, and H still has a remaining demand of 1. The new penalties for the columns are now calculated accordingly. There is no need to calculate new penalties for rows, since there has been no change in the rows.

The new largest row or column penalty is 3 for D. The lowest cost in the column is $c_{21} = 4$, and to avoid the penalty of 3 associated with D, it is necessary to utilize the lowest cost in that column. The amount that can be assigned is D's demand thus $x_{21} = 2$. It appears likely that the new row penalties should be calculated. The highest penalty is now 2, and F is arbitrarily chosen since c_{33} is the lowest cost in the column $x_{33} = 3$, which clears F and leaves C with capacity of 5. The new row penalties are calculated, and the next assingments to be considered are $x_{22} = 4$, $x_{34} = 4$, and $x_{35} = 1$. Therefore, the starting feasible solution that is obtained is as follows:

$x_{15} = 4 \quad x_{21} = 2 \quad x_{22} = 4 \quad x_{33} = 3 \quad x_{34} = 4 \quad x_{35} = 1$

with total transportation cost of

$$z = 6 \cdot 4 + 4 \cdot 2 + 4 \cdot 4 + 5 \cdot 3 + 6 \cdot 4 + 8 \cdot 1 = \$95{,}000.$$

• PROBLEM 5-12

Use Vogel's Approximation Method to find a solution.

Cost, Supply, and Demand Data TABLE 1

Origin (Surplus Area)	Destination (Shortage Area)			Supply
	1	*2*	*3*	
1	$ 50	100	100	110
2	200	300	200	160
3	100	200	300	150
Demand	140	200	80	420 / 420

Solution: If VAM is applied to this problem one obtains the accompanying Vogel numbers:

Row 1: 100 (c_{12}) - 50 (c_{11}) = 50

2: 200 (c_{23}) - 200 (c_{21}) = 0

3: 200 (c_{32}) - 100 (c_{31}) = 100

Column 1: 100 (c_{31}) - 50 (c_{11}) = 50

2: 200 (c_{32}) - 100 (c_{12}) = 100

3: 200 (c_{23}) - 100 (c_{13}) = 100.

Since three Vogel numbers are tied for the maximum of 100, arbitrarily select the first in the list (corresponding to Row 3) and assign 140 trucks to x_{31}. Note that the subscript "31" is based on the lowest cost in Row 3, or c_{31}. The value of "140" is determined using the equation $x_{ij} = \min(s_i, d_j)$ where s_i: supply from source i and d_j: demand from destination J, that is, the minimum of 150 and 140.

In the next pass, Column 1 is ignored (its demand has been satisfied) and the Vogel numbers for Columns 2 and 3 remain unchanged:

Row 1: 100 (c_{13}) - 100 (c_{12}) = 0

2: 300 (c_{22}) - 200 (c_{23}) = 100

3: 300 (c_{33}) - 200 (c_{32}) = 100

Column 2: ... = 100

3: ... = 100

Arbitrarily selecting the first 100 in the list (Row 2) results in an assignment of 80 trucks from Origin 2 to Destination 3 (x_{23} = 80). Since all but one of the column constraints have now been satisfied, all the remaining trucks at Origins 1, 2, and 3 must be assigned to Destination 2, and the initial solution is:

x_{12} = 110

x_{22} = 80

x_{23} = 80

x_{31} = 140

x_{32} = 10

z = $67,000

• PROBLEM 5-13

A manufacturer of a certain good owns three warehouses and supplies three markets. Each warehouse contains known quantities of the good and each market has known demands. In addition, the unit shipping costs from each warehouse to each market are known. These data are best exhibited in the table of Figure 1:

Note that the total supplies in the warehouse add up to 140 tons, which is equal to the sum of the demands at the markets. How shall the manufacturer ship his goods to the markets from the warehouses so that the total transportation cost will be a minimum? Apply Vogel's approximation method to find a feasible solution.

	Market 1	*Market 2*	*Market 3*	Supplies
Warehouse 1	3 $/Ton	2 $/Ton	3 $/Ton	50 T
Warehouse 2	10 $/Ton	5 $/Ton	8 $/Ton	70 T
Warehouse 3	1 $/Ton	3 $/Ton	10 $/Ton	20 T
Demands	50 T	60 T	30 T	140

Fig. 1

Solution: The VAM (Vogel Approximation Method) for obtaining an initial basic solution proceeds as follows.

(1) Compute the difference of the two smallest entries in each row and each column and mark this difference opposite each row and column. (In case there is just one entry in a row or a column, mark that entry.)

(2) Choose the largest difference so marked and utilize the smallest entry in that row or column to empty a warehouse or completely fulfill a market demand.

(3) Delete the line (row or column) corresponding to the used-up warehouse or fully supplied market; in case both of these happen simultaneously (the degenerate case) cross out either the row or the column unless there is exactly one row remaining, in which case cross out the column. Circle or otherwise designate the cost used and mark above the circle the amount shipped by that route. Reduce the supplies and demands in the lines containing the cost used.

(4) If all lines are crossed out, stop; otherwise, return to 1.

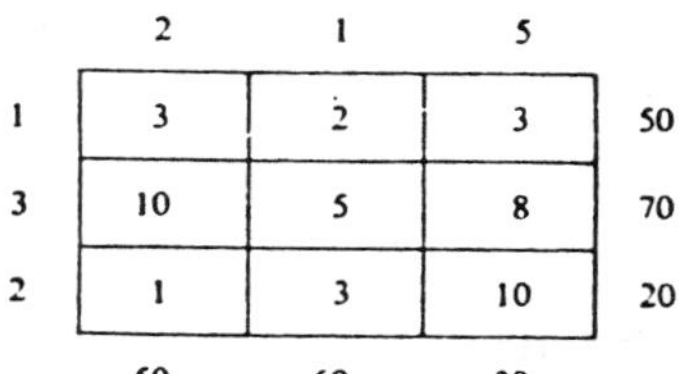

Fig. 2

Consider Figure 1. The row and column differences (of the smallest and next smallest entries) are included in Figure 2. Note that the maximum difference is the 5 in the third column. Hence ship as much as possible using the minimum entry, which is $c_{13} = 3$, in the third column.

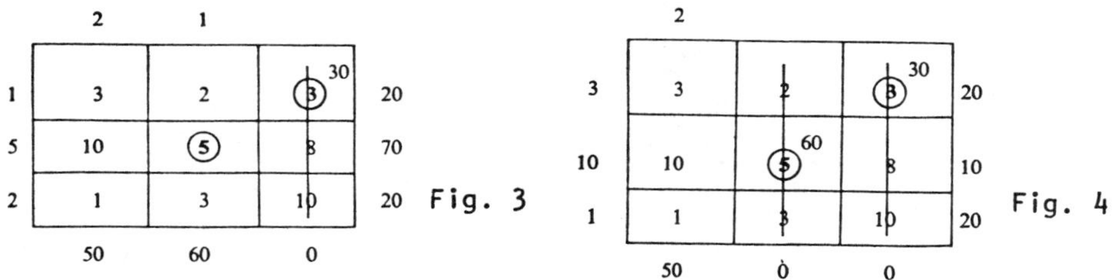

Fig. 3 Fig. 4

The rationale behind this choice is clear; if one doesn't ship via the smallest entry in the third column, at a cost of 3 $/ton, then one will have to use the next higher cost, which is 8 (or perhaps even the cost of 10 eventually); the amount of the difference between the smallest and next smallest cost is a measure of the "regret" one has for not making use of the smallest cost in that column. Now carry out steps (3) and (4), at the same time recomputing the row differences; since a column was struck out on the previous step, the remaining column differences in columns 1 and 2 will be the same. The result is shown in Figure 3. Now the maximum difference occurs in the second row, so ship as much as possible using the minimum-cost entry, namely $c_{22} = 5$. It turns out that one can ship 60 to M_2 from W_2 and completely satisfy its demand. The result is in Figure 4. Since only the first column remains, list it as instructed in (1). The next step is to bring in the 10 entry, followed by the 3 entry and the 1 entry. The final basic solution is displayed in Figure 5. Verify that it is a basis. Its cost is

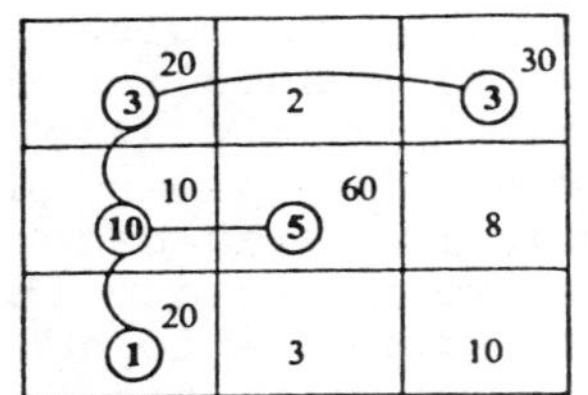

Fig. 5

20 • 3 + 30 • 3 + 10 • 10 + 60 • 5 + 20 • 1 = \$570.

• PROBLEM 5-14

A private carrier must deliver wheat in sacks from the warehouses having the weekly supplies as listed in Table 1.

Delivery must be made to mills which require the quantities in sacks per week as given in Table 2.

The transportation and handling costs (cents per sack) from each warehouse to each mill are given in Table 3.

Use Vogel's approximation method to determine how many sacks should be delivered from each warehouse to each mill in order to achieve the least cost.

Table 1

Warehouse	Supply/week
1	10,000
2	12,000
3	15,000
Total	37,000

Table 2

Mill	Demand/week
A	8,000
B	9,000
C	10,000
D	8,000
Total	35,000

Table 3

Mill	A	B	C	D
Warehouse				
1	13	14	13	20
2	16	13	20	12
3	19	12	17	15

Solution: The data are assembled (adding a nonexistent mill, E, in order to balance quantities) in Table 4.

Table 4

Mill Warehouse	A	B	C	D	E	Supply (000)
1	13	14	13	20	0	10
2	16	13	20	12	0	12
3	19	12	17	15	0	15
Demand (000)	8	9	10	8	2	37

The zero costs within each cell of Column E of Table 4 indicate that it will cost nothing to handle and transport sacks of wheat to a nonexistent mill. Or, 2,000 sacks of wheat per week will remain in the warehouse.

VAM requires that a specific procedure be followed in placing quantities to be shipped from a warehouse to a mill. What cell, and how much to put in it, are determined as follows:

Table 5

Mill / Warehouse	A	B	C	D	E	Supply (000)
1	13	14	8[a] 13	20	2[a] 0	10
2	4[a] 16	13	20	8[a] 12	0	12
3	4[a] 19	9[a] 12	2[a] 17	15	0	15
Demand (000)	8	9	10	8	2	37

Trials	1	2	3	4	5
	13*	1	–	–	–
	12	1	1	3	4*
	12	3	3	5*	2

Trials					
1	3	1	4	3	0
2	3	1	4*	3	–
3	3	1	3	3*	–
4	3	1	3	–	–
5	3	–	3	–	–

Note: The superscript "a" indicates a quantity in thousands of sacks allocated to a box.

In the matrix, Table 5, it is noted that the upper left portion is simply a repeat of the previous table, but with the addition of the quantities of the product. The quantities were derived by means of the trials shown to the right and below the original table. Trial 1 starts in a column--the first to the right of the column headed "Supply"--and continues in a row--the first below the row entitled "Demand." The numbers in the column of Trial 1 were obtained by looking at the five transportation costs in the row marked Warehouse 1, finding the lowest--in this case 0, locating the next lowest, 13, and subtracting one from the other. The same procedure was followed for the remaining two rows. The numbers opposite the row marked Trial 1 were obtained in a similar way. The 3 under the column headed A is the difference between 13, the lowest transportation cost in the column, and 16, the next lowest cost.

The largest number available in Trial 1, row or column, was selected and marked with an asterisk. It was 13. This meant that row 1 was selected for the first allocation. Accordingly, the lowest cost in row 1 was determined, being 0. As many sacks as possible, considering the constraints of supply and demand, were placed in the box with the lowest cost (box 1E). Only 2,000 could be managed since that was as much as this mill demanded. But placing 2 in that box (meaning 2,000 sacks) effectively removed Mill E from further consideration. A vertical line was drawn to indicate this.

The same porcedure was followed for Trial 2, and the 4 (asterisked) of column C was selected as the largest number of the trial. The smallest cost in column C was 13 and, therefore, as much as possible was allocated in that box. It was 8,000 sacks which, with the 2,000 previously assigned to Warehouse 1, exhausted its supply. Therefore, a horizontal line was drawn through all of the boxes of Warehouse 1. The table now consists of 8 boxes.

In Trial 3 no less than 4 equal highest numbers appeared--all 3's. In case of a tie of this kind, the row or column is chosen arbitrarily. Column D was chosen.

Trials 4 and 5 were performed similarly.

The result obtained is as follows: Eight thousand sacks were to go from Warehouse 1 to mill C; 2,000 sacks were to remain in Warehouse 1. Four thousand sacks were to go from Warehouse 2 to mill A; 8,000 sacks were to go from Warehouse 2 to mill D. Four thousand sacks were to go from Warehouse 3 to mill A; 9,000 sacks from Warehouse 3 to mill B; and 2,000 sacks were to go from Warehouse 3 to mill C.

Testing from optimality: In table 6 each box where a quantity appeared was marked with a dot. The "u" column and "v" row were constructed next by so choosing the "u" column number and the "v" row number that they added up to the transportation cost indicated in the box where they intersect. Arbitrarily, Box 1C was chosen as a starter. Its transportation cost is 13 cents per sack. If 13 is written at the end of row 1 under the "u" column, then 0 must be placed at the bottom of "column C" in the "v" row. (The numbers could have been any two that add up to 13, and the final result would not have been affected.) It is now possible to complete the "u" column and the "v" row. Box 1E had a transportation cost of 0, and -13 is placed in the "v" row under the column headed "E". Another "u" is marked opposite row 3 which was determined by observing that a dot appears in row 3 under a dot in row 1. 17 is filled in at the end of row 3, because the 0 at the bottom of column C plus 17 add up to the 17 in the box (the transportation cost).

The remaining "v" and "u" numbers associated with the dotted boxes were filled in, completing the "u" column and the "v" row.

The -2 in box 1A was determined by the rule stating that the "u" number opposite row 1 plus the "v" number under column A (13 + 2 = 15) is subtracted from the transportation cost in the box (13 - 15 = -2). The rest of the empty boxes are similarly completed.

Table 6

	A	B	C	D	E	u
1	−2	+6	.	+9	.	13
2	.	+4	+6	.	−1	14
3	.	.	.	0	−4	17
v	2	−5	0	−2	−13	

If any of the boxes contains a number with a minus sign, the solution is not the best possible. In this case several minuses appear. Therefore, a better, i.e., cheaper, arrangement is possible.

By choosing the box which contained the largest minus number (box 3E), any quantity moved to 3E would reduce the transportation cost by 4 cents per unit. In doing this reallocation, the row and column quantities had to be kept balanced so that the new solution would also be possible.

The question of just how much quantity can be moved to 3E arises. Whatever is done, the rows and columns must be balanced. (This means that one must not exceed the supply and demand quantities associated with each warehouse and each mill, including the fictitious one). This is done by tracing a path starting at box 3E (where the same amount will be subtracted, thus keeping the column balanced), then going to box 1C (where the same quantity will be added, thus keeping row 1 balanced), then moving down to box 3C (where the quantity will be subtracted, thus balancing column C and row 3).

Certainly as much as possible must be moved but no more than greatest amount that can be subtracted in any one box. (Never move negative quantities.) The original table tells that the quantity cannot be more than 2.

Moving 2 into box 3E, making the appropriate adjustments described previously, derive Table 7.

Table 7

	A	B	C	D	E	Supply
1			10		e	10
2	4			8		12
3	4	9			2	15
Demand	8	9	10	8	2	

Subtracting 2 from boxes 1E and 3C, has removed both, causing a difficulty. In Table 7, only six boxes are filled in. "Degeneracy" occurs when the number of rows plus the number of columns less one is more than the number of boxes filled in with quantities. If one tried to test for "optimality," one could not do it because one box (allocation) is lacked. A small letter "e" is placed in either Box 1E or 3C, which disappeared on the last allocation. In Table 7, choose Box 1E arbitrarily. The little "e" may be thought of as a tiny quantity that will not affect the solution, placed as a sort of marker to allow the test for optimality. Box 1E will be treated as though it contains an allocation.

The latest allocation of Table 7 will be tested for optimality by the method previously described. Table 8 results:

Table 8

	A	B	C	D	E	u
1	−6	+2	.	+5	.	13
2	.	+4	+10	.	+3	10
3	.	.	+ 4	0	.	13
v	+6	−1	0	+2	−13	

Table 8 shows that the solution can be improved by moving some quantity into box 1A. Tracing a path that starts at 1A and touches only occupied boxes leads us to 1E, 3E, and 3A, before returning to 1A. The smallest quantity in a box that is negative for this particular path is "e". Therefore, treating "e" exactly as though it were a real quantity, it is moved to 1A and disappears from 1E.

After making the reallocation, filling in all the quantities in their latest position, and performing the test for optimality, derive Table 9:

Table 9

	A	B	C	D	E	Supply	u
1	e	+8	10	+11	+6	10	13
2	4	+4	+4	8	+3	12	16
3	4	9	−2	0	2	15	19
Demand	8	9	10	8	2	37	
v	0	−7	0	−4	−19		

In Table 9, the quantities appear without sign, and the test numbers with a sign. A minus appears, showing that the allocation is not the best solution (appearing in cell 3C). The 0 next to it in cell 3D means that if a quantity were moved to that cell, the total transportation cost would remain unchanged. The smallest quantity must be moved into a minus cell of the path 3C, 1C, 1A, 3A, 3C. The quantity is not "e", but 4, and "e" can be dropped since there are again seven allocations. The allocation appears in Table 10.

The optimality test results in Table 11.

Table 10

	A	B	C	D	E	Supply
1	4		6			10
2	4			8		12
3		9	4		2	15
Demand	8	9	10	8	2	

Table 11

	A	B	C	D	E	u
1	.	+6	.	+11	+4	13
2	.	+2	+4	.	+1	16
3	+2	.	.	+ 2	.	17
v	0	−5	0	−4	−17	

The signs of Table 11 are positive, meaning that the allocation of Table 10 is optimal. The absence of zeros indicates that no other optimal arrangement exists.

The total cost of the best way to ship from warehouses to mills is readily obtained. The quantity given in each occupied box is multiplied by the cost shown in the matrix of Table 12.

Table 12

Box	Quantity (sacks)	Cost/unit ($)	Total Cost ($)
1A	4000	0.13	520
1C	6000	0.13	780
2A	4000	0.16	640
2D	8000	0.12	960
3B	9000	0.12	1080
3C	4000	0.17	680
3E	2000	0.00	0
			4660

Two thousand sacks remain in warehouse 3 at 0 transportation and handling cost. The lowest cost is $4,660 per week.

STEPPING STONE METHOD

• PROBLEM 5-15

Assume there are three factories (F_1, F_2 and F_3) supplying goods to three warehouses (W_1, W_2, W_3). The amounts available in each factory, the amounts needed in each factory and the costs of shipping from factory i to warehouse j are given in the table below:

Source / Destination	F_1	F_2	F_3	Units demanded
W_1	$ .90	$1.00	$1.00	5
W_2	$1.00	$1.40	$ .80	20
W_3	$1.30	$1.00	$ .80	20
units available	20	15	10	45

Find the minimum cost of satisfying warehouse demands given that any factory may supply to any warehouse, using the stepping stone method.

Solution: An initial solution may be found by finding the box that has the lowest value in both its row and column. Place in that box the lower of demand or supply requirements. Next find the next lower value and repeat the placing of units shipped according to demand and supply requirements. Thus obtain

Source / Destination	F_1	F_2	F_3	Units demanded
W_1	.90 / 5	$1.00 / 0	$1.00 / 0	5
W_2	1.00 / 10	1.40 / 0	.80 / 10	20
W_3	1.30 / 5	1.00 / 15	.80 / 0	20
units available	20	15	10	45

The total cost of this program is

(.90)(5) + (1.00)(10) + (1.30)(5) + (1.00)(15) +

(.80)(10) = $44.00.

Now check whether this solution is optimal. Pick a box with zero entry, say W_1F_2. This means that F_2 supplies no goods to W_1. The cost of F_2 directly supplying W_1 is $1.00 per unit. But F_2 is also indirectly supplying W_1 since by supplying W_3 it allows F_1 to supply W_1. What is this indirect cost?

The cost of shipping one unit from F_2 to W_1 by this indirect route is:

+ $1.00 charge for shipping from F_2 to W_3

- $1.30 every unit F_2 sends to W_3 saves the cost of supplying W_3 from F_1

+ $0.90 charge for shipping from F_1 to W_1

+ $0.60

The indirect cost, i.e., the cost currently incurred is $0.60 whereas the direct cost is $1.00. Thus the current solution is cheaper.

The other zero boxes may be evaluated in a comparable manner. For example, the indirect shipment from F_2 to W_2 is the charge from F_2 to W_3 ($1.00) less the W_3F_1 charge ($1.30) plus the W_2F_1 charge ($1.00) = 70¢. Again, this is less than the cost of direct shipment ($1.40), so the current indirect route should be continued. In this way the following table is obtained:

Unused route	Cost of direct route	Cost of indirect route
W_1F_2	$1.00	$0.60
W_1F_3	$1.00	$0.70
W_2F_2	$1.40	$0.70
W_3F_3	$0.80	$1.10

By using W_3F_3 a saving of \$.30 per unit can be obtained. But how many units can be shipped? The answer is the minimum number in any of the connections of the indirect route which must supply units for the transfer. This is five units, from box W_3F_1. Thus 5 units are shipped by the direct route W_3F_3; since F_3 produces only 10 units, this imposes a reduction in the W_2F_3 box to 5. The new pattern is shown in the table below:

Source / Destination	F_1	F_2	F_3	Units demanded
W_1	.90 / 5	1.00 / 0	1.00 / 0	5
W_2	1.00 / 15	1.40 / 0	.80 / 5	20
W_3	1.30 / 0	1.00 / 15	.80 / 5	20
units available	20	15	10	45

Once again, compare the cost of using the direct route to the cost of using the indirect route.

Unused route	Cost of using direct route	Cost of using indirect route
W_3F_1	\$1.30	\$1.00
W_1F_2	\$1.00	\$0.90
W_2F_2	\$1.40	\$1.00
W_1F_3	\$1.00	\$0.70

In every case the cost of using the indirect route is less than the cost of the direct route, indicating that the shipment costs are being minimized. The total cost of shipment from factories to warehouses is:

$$(5)(\$0.90) + (15)(\$1.00) + (15)(\$1.00) + 5(\$0.80) + 5(\$0.80) = \$42.50.$$

• PROBLEM 5-16

Assume that in the course of solving a transportation problem, the following initial feasible solution is computed:

Source / Destination	F_1	F_2	F_3	Units demanded	
W_1	.90 / 0	1.00 / 5	1.00 / 0	5	
W_2	1.00 / 20	1.40 / 0	.80 / 0	20	(1)
W_3	1.30 / 0	1.00 / 10	.80 / 10	20	
	20	15	10	45	

How would you progress further to find the optimal solution? Use the stepping stone method.

Solution: When the number of boxes used in obtaining a trial solution is less than F + W - 1, (number of factories and warehouses minus 1) the problem of degeneracy appears. To improve on an initial solution, one should consider alternative routes. An indirect route is the path a unit would have to follow from a factory to a given warehouse, using only established channels, (i.e., the shipment must avoid zero boxes; otherwise, one is shipping from a box which has no units; or introducing two new boxes into the solution to replace one). When a solution is degenerate, there are too many unused boxes.

To resolve the degeneracy case, record some very small amount, say d, in one of the zero boxes. This d is interpreted as a quantity of goods. The box with the d entry may either ship or receive goods but in the final solution the d is assigned a value of zero if it is still present in the calculations.

For the given initial solution, only 4 boxes are used while W + F - 1 = 5. Put d units in box W_1F_1. Total shipping cost is $43. The zero boxes may now be evaluated in the standard manner.

Source / Destination	F_1	F_2	F_3	Units demanded
W_1	.90 / d	1.00 / 5	1.00 / 0	5
W_2	1.00 / 20	1.40 / 0	.80 / 0	20
W_3	1.30 / 0	1.00 / 10	.80 / 10	20
Supply	20	15	10	45

Consider W_3F_1. The cost of the direct route is $1.30. The indirect route is from F_1W_1, which permits a reduction of shipment from F_2 to W_1; but this in turn requires an increse in the shipment from F_2 to W_3. The costs are $W_1F_1 + W_3F_2 - W_1F_2$ or $.90. Since the indirect route is cheaper than the direct route it should continue to be used. The other zero boxes may be evaluated similarly with the result below:

Source / Destination	F_1	F_2	F_3	
W_1			1.00 / .80	
W_2		1.40 / 1.10	.80 / .90	
W_3	1.30 / .90			

Shipping from F_3 to W_3 has an indirect cost in excess of the direct cost. The maximum amount which can be shifted is five units, since this is the minimum amount in a box which must be reduced (box W_1F_2). The new initial solution is optimal. In this problem degeneracy disappeared in one step. It is possible for degeneracy to remain through several iterations; in fact, the optimal solution may be degenerate.

• PROBLEM 5-17

Assume that costs of transportation between any two cities are proportional to the quantities shipped. Assume that plant capacities, warehouse requirements, and unit transportation costs are those shown in Table 1. Find an optimal solution to this transportation problem, by the stepping stone method.

Table 1 *A Transportation Problem*

Plants	Warehouses 1	2	3	4	Amount Available
1	19	30	50	10	7
2	70	30	40	60	9
3	40	8	70	20	18
Amount required	5	8	7	14	34

Solution: The first step in solving such a problem is to find an allocation that is feasible; then make successive improvements until no further cost reduction is possible.

Let x_{ij} represent the quantity shipped from plant i to warehouse j, and c_{ij} the unit cost of such a shipment.

Table 2

Plants	Warehouses 1	2	3	4	Amount Available
1	5(19)	2(30)			7
2		6(30)	3(40)		9
3			4(70)	14(20)	18
Amount required	5	8	7	14	34

The steps are shown in Table 2. Start with cell (1,1) and find that the largest possible entry (x_{11}) is 5 because that is all that warehouse 1 requires. Make this allocation and proceed to cell (1,2), because no other allocations are required in column 1. The most that can be allocated in this cell is 2, because this is all that is left of plant 1's capacity after $x_{11} = 5$ has been made. Therefore, make $x_{12} = 2$. Now go to cell (2,2) because warehouse 2 still requires 6 units. Allocate this number in (2,2); make $x_{22} = 6$. Now warehouse 2 is taken care of, and proceed to cell (2,3). The most that can be allocated here is the 3 units that are left from plant 2; so make $x_{23} = 3$. Because warehouse 3 still requires 4 units, go to cell (3,3) and allocate the required 4 units; make $x_{33} = 4$. Proceed to cell (3,4) and make $x_{34} = 14$. The cost of the solution shown in Table 2 is

$$5(19) + 2(30) + 6(30) + 3(40) + 4(70) + 14(20) = 1015.$$

A better initial feasible solution can be obtained. The lowest-cost entry (8) in Table 1 is in cell (3,2); therefore, start here and allocate as much as possible, making $x_{32} = 8$. The next lowest cost (10) is in (1,4) where we again allocate as much as possible making $x_{14} = 7$. The next lowest entry (19) is in cell (1,1). Here, make no allocation because the capacity of plant 1 was used up in (1,4). Proceed to cell (3,4) where the most that can be allocated, yields $x_{34} = 7$. Now there are two cells with entries of 30 (1,2) and (2,2), but warehouse 2 has been allocated all that it requires; therefore, proceed to cell (2,3) and make $x_{23} = 7$. Continuing this process, obtain the results shown in Table 3. The total cost of the solution shown in Table 3 is

$$2(70) + 3(40) + 8(8) + 7(40) + 7(10) + 7(20) = 814.$$

Table 3

	Warehouses				
Plants	1	2	3	4	Amount Available
1				7(10)	7
2	2(70)		7(40)		9
3	3(40)	8(8)		7(20)	18
Amount required	5	8	7	14	34

Table 4

	Warehouses					
Plants	1	2	3	4	Available	Penalties
1	19	30	50	10	7	9
2	70	30	40	60	19	10
3	40	8	70	20	18	12
Required	5	8	7	14		
Penalties	21	22	10	10		

This is a reduction in cost of 201 units as compared to the solution shown in Table 2. However, go one step further and apply the penalty method. In the previous procedure we tried to use the smallest costs but could not always do so. Recall that one could not make an allocation to cell (1,1), which has the third lowest cost in the matrix. An allocation in at least one cell of each row and in at least one cell of each column must be made. Therefore, in the following procedure examine the penalties associated with not using the lowest cost in each row and column. The penalties are the differences between the lowest cost in a row or column and the second lowest cost. These are shown in Table 4.

Start with the cell that has the largest penalty, cell (3,2) with a penalty of 22, and allocate as much as possible, making $x_{32} = 8$. Now eliminate column 2, which necessitates our recomputing the new penalties and correcting the amount available from plant 3. The results are shown in Table 5.

Table 5

	Warehouses				
Plants	1	3	4	Available	Penalties
1	19	50	10	7	9
2	70	40	60	9	20
3	40	70	20	10	20
Required	5	7	14		
Penalties	21	10	10		

The largest penalty (21) is now associated with cell (1,1); therefore, allocate here as much as possible, making $x_{11} = 5$. This eliminates column 1, requiring recalculation of row penalties and the amount available from plant 1 as is shown in Table 6.

Table 6

	Warehouses			
Plants	3	4	Available	Penalties
1	50	10	2	40
2	40	60	9	20
3	70	20	10	50
Required	7	14		
Penalties	10	10		

The largest penalty (50) is now associated with (3,4); therefore, make $x_{34} = 10$ and reduce and adjust the matrix as shown in Table 7.

Table 7

	Warehouses			
Plants	3	4	Available	Penalties
1	50	10	2	40
2	40	60	9	20
Required	7	4		
Penalties	10	50		

The largest penalty (50) is now associated with (1,4); therefore, make $x_{14} = 2$. This leaves only plant 2 with 9 units available and warehouses 3 and 4 requiring 7 and 2 units, respectively. Therefore, make $x_{23} = 7$ and $x_{24} = 2$. The resulting initial feasible allocation is shown in Table 8 and involves a cost of

$$5(19) + 8(8) + 7(40) + 2(10) + 2(60) + 10(20) = 779,$$

Table 8

Plants	Warehouses 1	2	3	4	Available
1	5(19)			2(10)	7
2			7(40)	2(60)	9
3		8(8)		10(20)	18
Required	5	8	7	14	

which is 35 cost units less than the previous initial feasible solution.

Even the solution shown in Table 8 is not the best that is possible. To determine whether a feasible solution minimizes costs, find how costs would be affected if one unit was allocated using a source-destination (i.e., plant-warehouse) pair that is not used in the feasible solution. To see how this can be done, begin with the feasible solution shown in Table 3. That solution and the relevant data appear in Table 9.

Table 9

Plants	Warehouses 1	2	3	4	Available
1	(19)	(30)	(50)	7(10)	7
2	2(70)	(30)	7(40)	(60)	9
3	3(40)	8(8)	(70)	7(20)	18
Required	5	8	7	14	

Assume one wishes to ship a unit from plant 1 to warehouse 1. Thus, subtract 1 unit from (1,4) to keep the row total the same, that is, make $x_{14} = 6$. The unit removed from (1,4) will have to be moved to another cell in the solution: to (3,4), making $x_{34} = 8$. Now remove one unit from row 3 and, if possible, put it into (1,1). This can be done by moving a unit from (3,1) to (1,1), making $x_{31} = 2$. The net change in cost, which is represented by d_{11}, is equal to

$$d_{11} = c_{11} - c_{14} + c_{34} - c_{31} = 19 - 10 + 20 - 40 = -11.$$

Call $d_{11} = -11$ the evaluation of cell (1,1). This evaluation shows that 11 cost units can be saved for each unit that is allocated to (1,1). But before making such an allocation, evaluate each empty cell. The evaluations are as follows:

$$d_{12} = c_{12} - c_{14} + c_{34} - c_{32} = 32$$

$$d_{13} = c_{13} - c_{14} + c_{34} - c_{31} + c_{21} - c_{23} = 50$$

$$d_{22} = c_{22} - c_{21} + c_{31} - c_{32} = -8$$

$$d_{24} = c_{24} - c_{21} + c_{31} - c_{34} = 10$$

$$d_{33} = c_{33} - c_{31} + c_{21} - c_{23} = 60.$$

From these results it is clear that one can improve by reallocating to (1,1) or (2,2), but that one can improve most by the use of (1,1). The largest number of units that can be moved into (1,1) is 3 from (3,1). To do so, move 3 units from (1,4) to (3,4). The results of so doing is shown in Table 10. The net saving obtained is 3(11) = 33.

Table 10

Plant	Warehouses 1	2	3	4	Available
1	3(19)	(30)	(50)	4(10)	7
2	2(70)	(30)	7(40)	(60)	
3	(40)	8(8)	(70)	10(20)	
Required	5	8	7	14	

Now reevaluate each of the empty cells. The results are as follows:

$$d_{12} = c_{12} - c_{14} + c_{34} - c_{32} = 32$$

$$d_{13} = c_{13} - c_{11} + c_{21} - c_{23} = 61$$

$$d_{22} = c_{22} - c_{21} + c_{11} - c_{14} + c_{34} - c_{32} = -19$$

$$d_{24} = c_{24} - c_{21} + c_{11} - c_{14} = -1$$

$$d_{31} = c_{31} - c_{34} + c_{14} - c_{11} = 11$$

$$d_{33} = c_{33} - c_{34} + c_{14} - c_{11} + c_{21} - c_{23} = 71.$$

Because savings are still possible, in (2,2) and (2,4), take the larger one and reallocate. The most that can be moved into (2,2) is determined by the most that can be moved out of row 2 into a solution cell, which is 2 out of (2,1). The result of doing so is shown in Table 11. The net saving is 2(19) = 38.

Table 11 *Optimal Solution*

Plant	Warehouses 1	2	3	4	Available
1	5(19)	(30)	(50)	2(10)	
2	(70)	2(30)	7(40)	(60)	9
3	(40)	6(8)	(70)	12(20)	18
Required	5	8	7	14	

Once again reevaluate the empty cells. The results are as follows:

$$d_{12} = c_{12} - c_{14} + c_{34} - c_{32} = 21$$

$$d_{13} = c_{13} - c_{14} + c_{34} - c_{32} + c_{22} - c_{23} = 50$$

$$d_{21} = c_{21} - c_{22} + c_{32} - c_{34} + c_{14} - c_{11} = 11$$

$$d_{24} = c_{24} - c_{22} + c_{32} - c_{34} = 18$$

$$d_{31} = c_{31} - c_{34} + c_{14} - c_{11} = 11$$

$$d_{33} = c_{33} - c_{32} + c_{22} - c_{23} = 52.$$

Since no further improvements are possible (because of the absence of any further possible net reductions in cost), the solution shown in Table 11 is optimal. Its cost is

$$5(19) + 2(30) + 6(8) + 7(40) + 2(10) + 12(20) = 743.$$

• PROBLEM 5-18

What is the optimum shipping plan for this transportation problem with the given initial feasible solution?

Solve by the Stepping-Stone Method.

Tableau 1

Warehouse:	D	C	F	G	E	B	A	Slack	Factory Capacity
Factory: R	\$4 4,000	\$5 3,000	\$6	\$5	\$8	\$7	\$6	\$0	7,000
S	\$5	\$4 1,500	\$3 2,500	\$2	\$4	\$5	\$10	\$0	4,000
T	\$6	\$3	\$9 1,000	\$4 3,000	\$5 2,000	\$5 2,000	\$9 1,000	\$0 1,000	10,000
Warehouse Requirements	4,000	4,500	3,500	3,000	2,000	2,000	1,000	1,000	21,000

Total transportation costs \$94,500.

Solution: To determine a better shipping schedule, evaluate the unfilled cells or those cells which do not have scheduled shipments. Each cell that is not used must be evaluated. This evaluation method shows the net total cost effect of adding one unit to the cell route. Unfilled cells SD and TD of Tableau 1 will be used to illustrate this procedure.

Tableau 2

Warehouse	D	C	All Other	Slack	Factory Capacity
Factory: R	\$4 3,999 →	\$5 3,001			7,000
S	\$5 ↑ 1	\$4 ↓ ← 1,499	2,500		4,000
T			9,000	1,000	10,000
Warehouse Requirements	4,000	4,500	11,500	1,000	21,000

If one unit is added to cell SD, it will cost the firm $5. Since row and column requirements must be satisfied, if one unit is added to cell SD, a unit must be subtracted from RD in order that the D column cells still total 4,000 units. The unit subtracted from RD saves the firm a shipping cost of $4. Likewise, as a unit is subtracted from RD, a unit must be added to RC in order that the shipments of factory R still equal 7,000 units. This costs the firm $5. Now that column C has one too many units, one unit must be subtracted from SC, which saves the firm $4. This is shown in Tableau 2. In effect, a unit has been added to SD, subtracted from RD, added to RC, and subtracted from SC, thereby satisfying the row and column requirements. If this change did take place, the cost factor is of utmost importance since $5 has been added (SD). $4 has been subtracted (RD), $5 has been added (RC), and $4 has been subtracted (SC) for net cost of $2 per unit (+$5 - $4 + $5 - $4 = +$2) to the firm. This means that every unit added to route SD will cost the firm an additional $2 per unit. It would certainly not be worthwhile for the firm to use this route if this were the only choice available.

An evaluation of cell TD in Tableau 1 is longer than the previous example. Adding one unit to cell TD costs the firm $6. In order to satisfy the row and column requirements, one unit must be subtracted from cell RD for savings of $4. Similarly, for warehouse C, one unit must be added to cell RC (cost of $5) and one unit must be subtracted from cell SC (savings of $4). For warehouse F, one unit must be added to cell SF (cost of $3) and one unit must be subtracted from cell TF (savings of $9). The net result is a savings of $3 per unit (+$6 - $4 + $5 - $4 + $3 - $9 = -$3). It would pay the firm to use this route, shown in Tableau 3.

Tableau 3

Warehouse:	D	C	F	All Other	Slack	Factory Capacity
Factory: R	$4 3,999	$5 →3,001				7,000
S	↑	$4 ↓ 1,499	$3 2,501			4,000
T	$6 1 ←		$9 ↓ 999	8,000	1,000	10,000
Warehouse Requirements	4,000	4,500	3,500	8,000	1,000	21,000

The two examples show that it is necessary to have three filled cells to evaluate unfilled cell SD and five filled cells to evaluate unfilled cell TD, because the row and column requirements must be met. If, for example, one unit is moved from RD to RC, the row requirement of 7,000 units would be met, but not the column requirements of 4,000 for warehouse D and 4,500 for warehouse C. Thus movements were at right antles or at 90-degree angles in order to satisfy the requirements of the problem.

Only filled cells or stepping-stones can be used in the

evaluation of an unfilled cell. It should be pointed out that it is allowable to jump over cells (filled or unfilled) when forming a closed route to evaluate an unfilled cell.

Now that the evaluation of the cost values are complete (a plus sign denotes a cost penalty or higher transportation costs, whereas a negative sign denotes additional cost savings or lower transportation costs), the third step is to select the highest negative figure. This will enable the firm to ship at lower costs. Based upon the values found in Tableau 1, cell TC offers the best opportunity to reduce transportation costs further. Thus, this cell with a negative value of 7 is selected.

Warehouse:	Before C	Before F	After C	After F
Factory:				
S	1,500	2,500	−1,000	+5,000
T		1,000	+2,500	−1,500

The next step of this method is moving as large a quantity as possible into the selected unfilled cell. Based upon the quantities shown in Tableau 1, the largest quantity is 2,500 in the three filled cells that were used to evaluate unfilled cell TC. The following example will demonstrate the feasibility or nonfeasibility of moving 2,500 units:

Based on this analysis, it is not feasible to move 2,500 units into cell TC since two negative figures would appear in the adjoining cells. The same condition results in trying to move the second largest quantity or 1,500 units. Thus only 1,000 units can be moved into cell TC, as reflected in Tableau 4.

Tableau 4

Warehouse	D	C	F	G	E	B	A	Slack	Factory Capacity
Factory: *R*	$4 4,000	$5 3,000	$6 + $2	$5 − $1	$8 + $1	$7 $0	$6 − $5	$0 − $2	7,000
S	$5 + $2	$4 1,500 − 1,000 = 500	$3 2,500 + 1,000 = 3,500	$2 − $3	$4 − $2	$5 − $1	$10 $0	$0 − $1	4,000
T	$6 + $4	$3 + 1,000 = 1,000	$9 1,000 − 1,000 = + $7	$4 3,000	$5 2,000	$5 2,000	$9 1,000	$0 1,000	10,000
Warehouse Requirements	4,000	4,500	3,500	3,000	2,000	2,000	1,000	1,000	21,000

The computations for the unused cells in Tableau 1 are shown in Table 1.

To test for degeneracy, does m + n - 1 equal the number of filled cells? The number of filled cells, 10, equals 3 + 8 - 1. Since degeneracy is not applicable, the next step is to re-evaluate all unfilled cells in the manner shown for Tableau 1. The results are shown in Tableau 4. If an unfilled cell can be evaluated by more than one set of routes, the highest minus or lowest plus amount is inserted. However, this was not the case in Tableaux 3 and 4. Selecting the highest minus value in all of the unfilled cells results in moving products to cell RA for lower transportation costs.

Again, the largest quantity will be moved into the unfilled cell as in Tableau 5.

Table 1

Unfilled Cells		Cost: Penalty	Cost: Savings
$SD = +\ 5 - 4 + 5 - 4$ (per above)	=	+2	
$TD = +\ 6 - 4 + 5 - 4 + 3 - 9$ (per above)	=		−3
$TC = +\ 3 - 4 + 3 - 9$	=		−7
$RF = +\ 6 - 3 + 4 - 5$	=	+2	
$RG = +\ 5 - 4 + 9 - 3 + 4 - 5$	=	+6	
$SG = +\ 2 - 4 + 9 - 3$	=	+4	
$RE = +\ 8 - 5 + 9 - 3 + 4 - 5$	=	+8	
$SE = +\ 4 - 5 + 9 - 3$	=	+5	
$RB = +\ 7 - 5 + 9 - 3 + 4 - 5$	=	+7	
$SB = +\ 5 - 5 + 9 - 3$	=	+6	
$RA = +\ 6 - 9 + 9 - 3 + 4 - 5$	=	+2	
$SA = +10 - 9 + 9 - 3$	=	+7	
R Slack $= +\ 0 - 0 + 9 - 3 + 4 - 5$	=	+5	
S Slack $= +\ 0 - 0 + 9 - 3$	=	+6	

Tableau 5

Warehouse:	*D*	*C*	*F*	*G*	*E*	*B*	*A*	Slack	Factory Capacity
Factory: *R*	$4 4,000	$5 (3,000 − 1,000) 2,000	$6 + $2	$5 − $1	$8 + $1	$7 $0	$6 (+ 1,000) 1,000	$0 − $2	7,000
S	$5 + $2	$4 500	$3 3,500	$2 − $3	$4 − $2	$5 − $1	$10 + $5	$0 − $1	4,000
T	$6 + $4	$3 (1,000 + 1,000) 2,000	$9 + $7	$4 3,000	$5 2,000	$5 2,000	$9 (1,000 − 1,000) + $5	$0 1,000	10,000
Warehouse Requirements	4,000	4,500	3,500	3,000	2,000	2,000	1,000	1,000	21,000

Again, the first step in the succeeding tableaux is to test for degeneracy. Then the unfilled cells are evaluated, resulting in cell SG with the largest minus value. The movement of units is shown in Tableau 6.

Tableau 6

Warehouse:	*D*	*C*	*F*	*G*	*E*	*B*	*A*	Slack	Factory Capacity
Factory: *R*	$4 4,000	$5 2,000	$6 − $1	$5 − $1	$8 + $1	$7 $0	$6 1,000	$0 − $2	7,000
S	$5 + $5	$4 (500 − 500) + $3	$3 3,500	$2 (+ 500) 500	$4 + $1	$5 + $2	$10 + $8	$0 + $2	4,000
T	$6 + $4	$3 (2,000 + 500) 2,500	$9 + $4	$4 (3,000 − 500) 2,500	$5 2,000	$5 2,000	$9 + $5	$0 1,000	10,000
Warehouse Requirements	4,000	4,500	3,500	3,000	2,000	2,000	1,000	1,000	21,000

Tableau 7

Warehouse:	D	C	F	G	E	B	A	Slack	Factory Capacity
Factory: R	$4 4,000	$5 (2,000 − 1,000) 1,000	$6 − $1	$5 − $1	$8 + $1	$7 $0	$6 1,000	$0 (+ 1,000) 1,000	7,000
S	$5 + $5	$4 + $3	$3 3,500	$2 500	$4 + $1	$5 + $2	$10 + $8	$0 + $4	4,000
T	$6 + $4	$3 (2,500 + 1,000) 3,500	$9 + $4	$4 2,500	$5 2,000	$5 2,000	$9 + $5	$0 (1,000 − 1,000) + $2	10,000
Warehouse Requirements	4,000	4,500	3,500	3,000	2,000	2,000	1,000	1,000	21,000

Following the same steps as for the previous tableaux, results in allocating units to an unfilled cell, R slack, in Tableau 7. Inspection of this table indicates two minus amounts of the same value. Unfilled cell RG was randomly selected since either cell RF or RG could have been used.

Tableau 8

Warehouse:	D	C	F	G	E	B	A	Slack	Factory Capacity
Factory: R	$4 4,000	$5 (1,000 − 1,000) + $1	$6 $0	$5 (+ 1,000) 1,000	$8 + $2	$7 + $1	$6 1,000	$0 1,000	7,000
S	$5 + $4	$4 + $3	$3 3,500	$2 500	$4 + $1	$5 + $2	$10 + $7	$0 + $3	4,000
T	$6 + $3	$3 (3,500 + 1,000) 4,500	$9 + $4	$4 (2,500 − 1,000) 1,500	$5 2,000	$5 2,000	$9 + $4	$0 + $1	10,000
Warehouse Requirements	4,000	4,500	3,500	3,000	2,000	2,000	1,000	1,000	21,000

The optimal solution is reached in Tableau 8 since there are no minus signs to denote further cost savings. The final shipping schedule is:

Route	No. of Units	Cost per Unit	Total Monthly Transportation Costs
RD	4,000	$4	$16,000
RG	1,000	5	5,000
RA	1,000	6	6,000
R Slack	1,000	0	—
SF	3,500	3	10,500
SG	500	2	1,000
TC	4,500	3	13,500
TG	1,500	4	6,000
TE	2,000	5	10,000
TB	2,000	5	10,000
	21,000		$78,000

• **PROBLEM 5-19**

Find an optimal solution for Table 1 with cost = 410. Use the Stepping Stone Method.

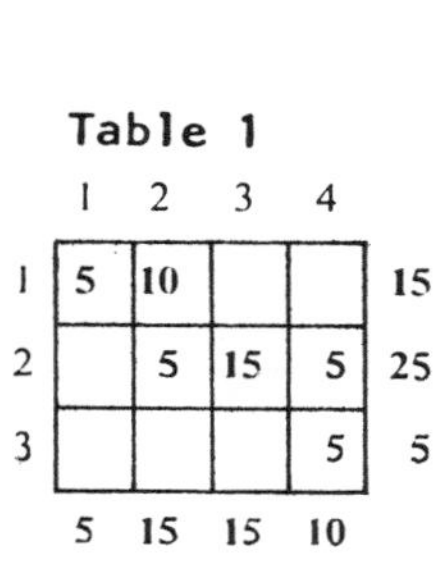

	1	2	3	4	
1	5	10			15
2		5	15	5	25
3				5	5
	5	15	15	10	

Table 1

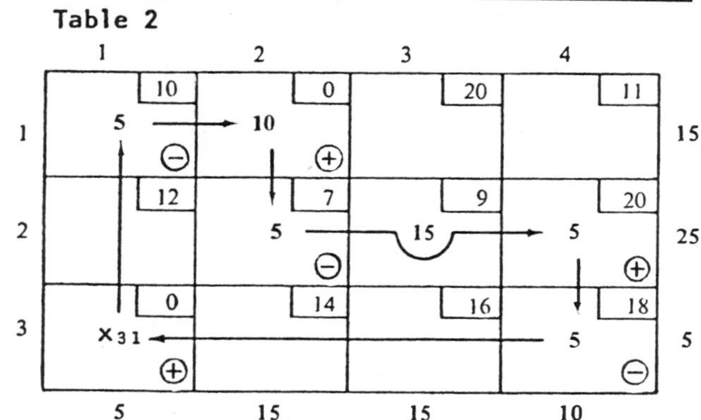

Table 2

Solution: Let $\bar{C}_{31}$ be the net increase or decrease in cost as a result of increasing X_{31} by one unit. Then

$$\bar{C}_{31} = C_{31} - C_{11} + C_{12} - C_{22} + C_{24} - C_{34}$$

$$= 0 - 10 + 0 - 7 + 20 - 18$$

$$= -\$15$$

It is promising to increase X_{31} above zero level, since each unit increase will reduce the transportation cost by \$15. By using the loops for the other non-basic variables, the net increase or decrease in cost per unit increase in each of the remaining nonbasic variables are as follows.

$\bar{C}_{13} = +\$18$, $\bar{C}_{14} = -\$2$.

$\bar{C}_{21} = -\$5$, $\bar{C}_{32} = +\$9$,

and

$\bar{C}_{33} = +\$9$.

Since X_{31} yields the largest per unit decrease in cost ($\bar{C}_{31} = -\$15$), it is selected as the entering variable.

The leaving variable is selected from among the corner variables of the loop which will decrease when the entering variable X_{31} increases above zero level. These are indicated in Table 2 by the variables in the square labeled by minus signs ⊖ . From Table 2, X_{11}, X_{22}, and X_{34} are the basic variables that will decrease when X_{31} increases. The leaving variable is then selected as the one having the smallest value, since it will be the first to reach zero value and any further decrease will cause it to be negative. In this problem, the three ⊖ variables X_{11}, X_{22}, and X_{34} have the same value (=5), in which case any one of them can be selected as a leaving variable. Assume X_{34} is taken as the leaving variable; then the value of X_{31} is increased to 5 and the values of the corner (basic) variables are adjusted accordingly (that is, each increased or decreased by 5 depending on whether it has ⊕ or ⊖ associated with it). The new solution is given in Table 3. Its new cost is

$$0 \times 10 + 15 \times 0 + 0 \times 7 + 15 \times 9 + 10 \times 20 + 5 \times 0$$

$$= \$335.$$

Table 3

	1	2	3	4	
1	[10] 0	[0] 15	[20]	[11]	15
2	[12]	[7] 0	[9] 15	[20] 10	25
3	[0] 5	[14]	[16]	[18]	5
	5	15	15	10	

This cost differs from the one associated with the solution in Table 1 by 410 - 335 = \$75, which is equal to the number of units assigned to X_{31} (=5) multiplied by the decrease in cost per unit (=\$15).

The basic solution in Table 3 is degenerate, since the basic variables X_{11} and X_{22} are zero. Degeneracy, however, needs no special provisions, and the zero basic variables are treated as any other positive basic variables.

Table 4

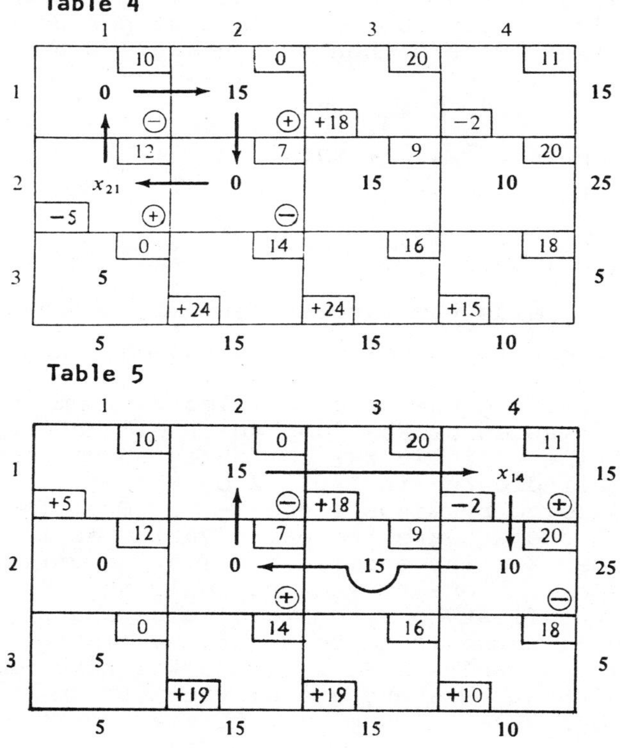

	1	2	3	4	
1	[10] 0 ⊖	[0] 15 ⊕	[20] +18	[11] −2	15
2	[12] x_{21} ⊕ −5	[7] 0 ⊖	[9] 15	[20] 10	25
3	[0] 5	[14] +24	[16] +24	[18] +15	5
	5	15	15	10	

Table 5

	1	2	3	4	
1	[10] +5	[0] 15 ⊖	[20] +18	[11] x_{14} ⊕ −2	15
2	[12] 0	[7] 0 ⊕	[9] 15	[20] 10 ⊖	25
3	[0] 5	[14] +19	[16] +19	[18] +10	5
	5	15	15	10	

The new nonbasic variables are checked for the possibility of improving the current solution. The procedure given with Table 2 is repeated for Table 3 by determining the loops and then checking each nonbasic variable for optimality. The numbers in the southwest corner of each nonbasic square in Table 4 summarize whether a unit increase in the variable can increase or decrease the total transportation cost. For example, a unit increase in X_{14} decreases total cost by $2. As evident from Table 4, X_{21} is the entering variable. The loop associated with X_{21} shows that either X_{11} or X_{22} is the leaving variable. Since both are equal (=0), select X_{11} (arbitrarily) to leave the basic solution. Table 5 gives the new basic solution together with the evaluation of the associated nonbasic variables, which shows that X_{14} is the entering variable and X_{24} is the leaving variable.

Table 6

	1	2	3	4	
1	[10] +5	[0] 5	[20] +18	[11] 10	15
2	[12] 0	[7] 10	[9] 15	[20] +2	25
3	[0] 5	[14] +19	[16] +19	[18] +12	5
	5	15	15	10	

When X_{14} enters the solution and X_{24} leaves the solution, the new solution in Table 6 results. Evaluation of all the nonbasic variables shows that the solution is optimal, since an increase in the value of any nonbasic variable above its current zero value will increase the total costs.

The optimal solution is summarized as follows. Ship 5 units from (source) 1 to (destination) 2 at $5 \times 0 = \$0$, 10 units from 1 to 4 at $10 \times 11 = \$110$, 10 units from 2 to 2 at $10 \times 7 = \$70$, 15 units from 2 to 3 at $15 \times 9 = \$135$, and 5 units from 3 to 1 at $5 \times 0 = \$0$. The total transportation cost of the schedule is $315.

• PROBLEM 5-20

Find the optimum shipping plan for the relevant data, using the Stepping Stone Method.

	D_1	D_2	D_3	*Capacities*
S_1	$3	$17	$11	4
S_2	$12	$18	$10	12
S_3	$10	$25	$24	8
Requirements	10	9	5	(24)

Solution: Seek an extreme solution by trying to construct a plan with at most $m + n - 1 = 5$ occupied cells. Thus, consider the plan

Table 1

	D_1	D_2	D_3	
S_1	[3] 4	[17]	[11]	4
S_2	[12]	[18] 7	[10] 5	12
S_3	[10] 6	[25] 2	[24]	8
	10	9	5	24

This plan has five occupied cells and is clearly feasible. The variables corresponding to empty cells are X_{12}, X_{13}, X_{21}, and X_{33}, and the solution under consideration will certainly be a corner point if the system which remains when these variables are set equal to 0 possesses only one solution. Thus, consider the defining system

$$X_{11} + X_{12} + X_{13} = 4 \quad (r_1)$$

$$X_{21} + X_{22} + X_{23} = 12 \quad (r_2)$$

$$X_{31} + X_{32} + X_{33} = 8 \quad (r_3)$$

$$X_{11} + X_{21} + X_{31} = 10 \quad (k_1)$$

$$X_{12} + X_{22} + X_{32} = 9 \quad (k_2)$$

$$X_{13} + X_{23} + X_{33} = 5 \quad (k_3)$$

Now set $X_{12} = X_{13} = X_{21} = X_{33} = 0$, and then solve for the remaining variables. One obtains the unique feasible solution shown in Table 1. Since it is unique it must correspond to an extreme point.

Now, to test whether Table 1 can be improved, first determine the consequences of entering its four empty cells, namely, cells (1,2), (1,3), (2,1), and (3,3). Sketched below are the unique exchange loops that determine the adjustments attendant upon occupying each of these empty cells.

(1) Occupying cell (1,2)

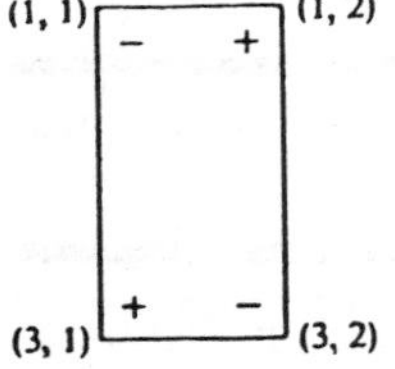

The corners of this loop designate those cells whose allocations must be readjusted when one occupies cell (1,2). If a corner (i,j) carries a plus sign, increase X_{ij}, but if it carries a minus sign, decrease X_{ij}. Furthermore, the loop shows that the effect on cost of increasing X_{12} by 1 unit is to increase cost by

$c_{12} - c_{32} + c_{31} - c_{11} = 17 - 25 + 10 - 3 = -1$

This simple calculation is the exact equivalent of calculating the cost of entering cell (i,j) in terms of direct and indirect effect--because the cost relation

$$c_{12} - (c_{32} - c_{31} + c_{11})$$

mimics the direct-minus-indirect effect corresponding to the exchange ralation

$$x_{12} - (x_{32} - x_{31} + x_{11})$$

(2) Occupying cell (1,3)

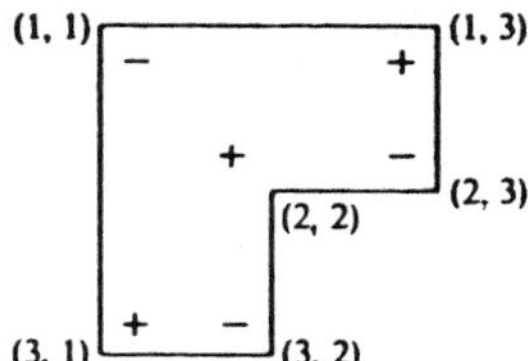

This loop shows that if X_{13} is increased by 1 unit, C will increase by

$$c_{13} - c_{23} + c_{22} - c_{32} + c_{31} - c_{11} = 11 - 10 + 18 - 25 + 10 - 3 = +1$$

(3) Occupying cell (2,1).

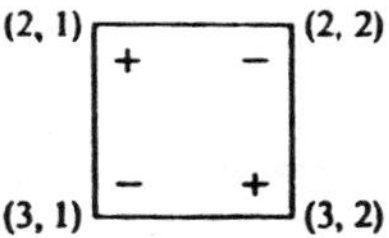

The increase in cost is

$$c_{21} - c_{22} + c_{32} - c_{31} = 12 - 18 + 25 - 10 = +9$$

(4) Occupying cell (3,3).

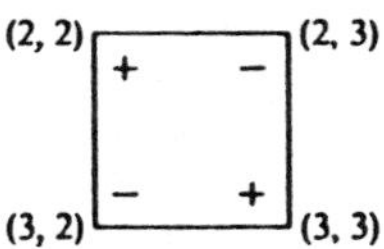

If X_{33} is increased by 1, then C will be increased by

$$c_{33} - c_{32} + c_{22} - c_{23} = 24 - 25 + 18 - 10 = +7$$

The examination of all empty cells is now complete and shows that one should increase X_{12} to the maximum possible extent. Moreover, examination of the appropriate loop indicates that the amount contained in cell (3,2) puts a limit of 2 units on the allowable increase in X_{12}. The updated shipping plan is

Table 2

	D_1	D_2	D_3	
S_1	[3] 2	[17] 2	[11]	4
S_2	[12]	[18] 7	[10] 5	12
S_3	[10] 8	[25]	[24]	8
	10	9	5	24

The table gives a cost of shipping equal to 296. The increases in cost associated with occupying the empty cells of Table 2 are as follows:

Occupy	Increase in cost
Cell (1,3)	+2
Cell (2,1)	+8
Cell (3,2)	+1
Cell (3,3)	+8

This shows that Table 2 is optimal.

• PROBLEM 5-21

A car rental agency serving seven cities has a surplus of cares in three cities (labeled W_1, W_2 and W_3) and a need for cars in four cities (labeled M_1, M_2, M_3, and M_4. The excess of cars in W_1, W_2, and W_3 is 20, 20, and 32, respectively. The table of distances (in miles) between the cities and the rim conditions are as follows:

	M_1	M_2	M_3	M_4	
W_1	17	23	20	M	20
W_2	23	15	23	20	20
W_3	25	M	13	21	32
	16	20	20	16	

The two occurrences of M's in the cells (1,4) and (3,2) indicates that it is not possible to transport cars from W_1 to M_4 or from W_3 to M_4 because of, e.g., road-repair work. Thus, M denotes an extremely large distance. How should the agency transport its cars to satisfy the demands and minimize the total distance driven? Solve by using the Stepping-Stone Method. If there are alternate optimal solutions, find them.

Solution: The quantity to be minimized is total distance; denote this by w. First use the Least Cost Method to find an initial b.f.s.

Tables 1a and 1b indicate the sequence of operations involved in employing the Least Cost Method:

	√3		√1			
	⑰ 16	23	20	M	~~20~~ 4	
√2	23	⑮ 20	23	20	~~20~~ 0	(T.1a)
	25	M	⑬ 20	21	~~32~~ 12	
	~~16~~ 0	~~20~~ 0	~~20~~ 0	16		

	√3	√5	√1	√6		
	⑰ 16	㉓ 0	20	Ⓜ 4	~~4~~ ~~4~~ 0	
√2	23	⑮ 20	23	20	0	(T.1b)
√4	25	M	⑬ 20	㉑ 12	~~12~~ 0	
	0	~~0~~ 0	0	~~16~~ ~~4~~ 0		

The initial b.f.s. is depicted in Table 1b. Note that it is degenerate ($x_{12}=0$) and also that it contains a prohibited route, namely, cell (1,4). The number of cells in the basis (6) is, of course, equal to m + n - 1 as it should be. The evaluation of cells not in the basis is carried out and the cycle values are given in parentheses in Table 1'.

⑰ 16	㉓ 0	20(28 − M)	Ⓜ 4	
23(14)	⑮ 20	23(39 − M)	20(28 − M)	(T.1')
25(−13 + M)	M(2M − 44)	⑬ 20	㉑ 12	

A cycle C is a subset of cells of the initial, data matrix with the property that each row and each column of the original data matrix contains either zero or two cells of C; Let C(p,q) be the unique cycle formed when cell (p,q) is combined with cells of the basis B. Starting with cell (p,q) and going around the cycle (in either direction), alternately label cells "getter" and "giver" cells, where (p,q) is a getter cell. The value of the cycle denoted by v_{pq} is the sum of the costs associated with the cells in C(p,q) where the costs of the getter cells are given plus signs and the costs of the giver cells are given minus signs.

In Table 1 , three cells have negative cycle values, namely, (1,3), (2,3), and (2,4). This is so because of the presence of the large negative number -M. The cycle generated by cell (2,3) is interesting. It contains, in alternating getter-giver order, the cells (2,3), (3,3), (3,4), (1,4), (1,2), and (2,2).

Now introduce cell (2,4) into the initial basis. Since cell (1,4) is the minimum giver cell on the cycle formed by (2,4), it leaves the basis. The resulting basis, together with the new cycle values for nonbasis cells, appears in Table 2:

⑰ 16	㉓ 4	20(0)	$M(M-28)$	
23(14)	⑮ 16	23(11)	⑳ 4	(T.2)
25(15)	$M(M-16)$	⑬ 20	㉑ 12	

The cycle generated by cell (1,3) is interesting. It contains, in alternating getter-giver order, the following cells: (1,3), (3,3), (3,4), (2,4), 2,2), and (1,2). In Table 2, all cycle values for nonbasis cells are nonnegative. Thus, the b.f.s. pertaining to Table 2 is an optimal solution. The pertinent x_{ij} values and the minimum total distance are as follows:

$x_{11} = 16,\ x_{12} = 4,\ x_{22} = 16,$

$x_{24} = 4,\ x_{33} = 20,\ x_{34}=12,$

and

$\text{Min } w = 17 \cdot 16 + 23 \cdot 4 + \ldots + 21 \cdot 12 = 1196$ miles.

One of the cycle values in Tableau 2 is a zero; this means that there is another optimal b.f.s. to the problem.

The alternate optimal b.f.s. is determined by introducing cell (1,3) into the basis, since the cycle value for this cell is zero. The minimum giver cells in the cycle formed by cell (1,3) are (2,4) and (1,2), each of which can give four. Removing the latter cell from the basis and then adjusting shipments via the Method for Change in Basis and Shipping Pattern: (the only shipments that are affected are those associated with cells in the cycle determined by candidate cell (p,q)

a. x'_{pq} = minimum x_{ij} of giver cells in cycle.

b. For getter cells, $x'_{ij} = x_{ij} + x'_{pq}$

For giver cells, $x'_{ij} = x_{ij} - x'_{pq}$

c. The cell (p,q) is introduced into the basis, and a minimum giver cell (i.e., a giver cell with a minimum x_{ij}) is removed from the basis, leads to the basis given in Table 3:

⑰ 16	23(0)	⑳ 4	$M(M-28)$	
23(14)	⑮ 20	23(11)	⑳ 0	(T.3)
25(15)	$M(M-16)$	⑬ 16	㉑ 16	

Since all the relevant cycle values in Table 3 are non-negative, this table corresponds to an optimal b.f.s.

The alternate optimal x_{ij}'s are read off from Table 3 as follows:

$$x_{11} = 16, \; x_{13} = 4, \; x_{22} = 20, \; x_{24} = 0, \; x_{33} = 16,$$

and

$$x_{34} = 16.$$

Note that this b.f.s. is degenerate. The value for w corresponding to this b.f.s. should be the same as the other solution. Again calculating w (as a check), obtain

$$\text{Min } w = 17 \cdot 16 + 20 \cdot 4 + \ldots + 21 \cdot 16 = 1196 \text{ miles.}$$

Note that the value of the cycle formed by cell (1,2), which just left the basis, is zero.

METHOD OF MULTIPLIERS

• PROBLEM 5-22

Obtain an optimal solution to the transportation problem shown in Fig. 1, with the given initial feasible solution. The check mark indicates the position of the empty cell for which the opportunity cost turned out to be negative. Use the Method of Multipliers.

							Available
	[9] 3	[12]	[9] 2	[6]	[9]	[10]	5
	[7]	[3] ✓	[7] 4	[7]	[5]	[5] 2	6
	[6]	[5] 2	[9]	[11]	[3]	[11]	2
	[6] 1	[8] 2	[11]	[2] 2	[2] 4	[10]	9
Required	4	4	6	2	4	2	

Initial feasible solution —cost 127

Fig. 1

Solution: An evaluation of opportunity cost of -N for an empty cell means that an allocation of +1 unit to that cell will reduce the achieved cost by N. If it is possible to allocate +2 units to that cell without making any of the other allocations negative, the achieved cost will be reduced by 2N, and so on. Since the aim of the iteration is to arrive at the minimum cost as quickly as possible, allocate as much as possible to the empty cell with the negative evaluation (or, in general, to the empty cell with the highest negative evaluation).

To perform this re-allocation, first identify the loop joining the empty cell to occupied cells, as indicated below.

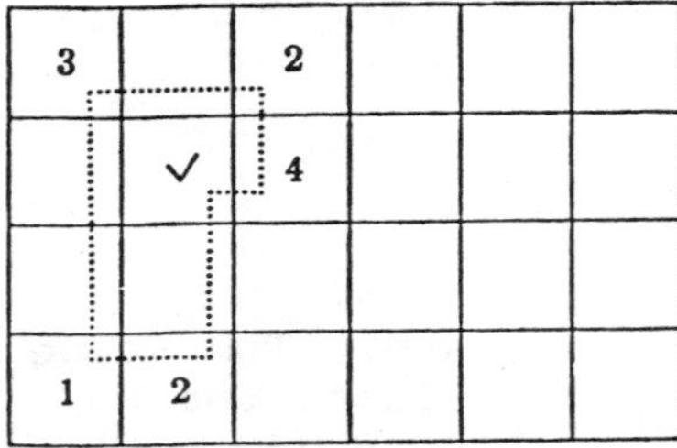

Loop joining cell (2,2) to occupied cells

It is seen that one can allocate at most 2 units to cell (2,2) and still satisfy the row-and-column-total and non-negativity restrictions on the allocations. The effect of allocating 2 units to this empty cell is

1		4			
	2	2			
3	0				

Re-allocation among cells of loop

The four allocations which do not belong to the loop are carried forward without change, and the new feasible solution becomes

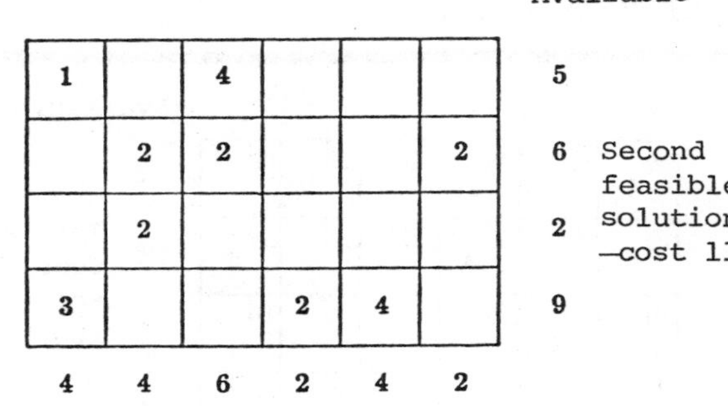

							Avaliable
	1		4				5
		2	2			2	6
		2					2
	3			2	4		9
Required	4	4	6	2	4	2	

Second feasible solution —cost 115

The cost for this new feasible solution is computed to be 115, which is 12 less than the cost for the initial solution; a reduction of this size is anticipated because 2 units are being allocated to a cell where each unit results in a cost change of -6.

The second feasible solution again has 9 allocations in independent positions, and the optimality test is applicable. From the equation for multipliers u_i and v_j,

$u_i + v_j = c_{ij}$, $\quad v_2 + v_3 = 7$,

$u_1 + v_1 = c_{11}$ (=9), $\quad u_1 + v_3 = 9$,

$u_4 + v_1 = c_{41}$ (=6) $\quad u_4 + v_4 = 2$,

$u_3 + v_2 = 5$, $\quad u_4 + v_5 = 2$,

$u_2 + v_2 = 3$, $\quad u_2 + v_6 = 5$.

Let $u_4 = 0$. Then $v_5 = 2$, $v_4 = 2$, $v_1 = 6$, $u_1 = 3$, $v_3 = 6$, $u_2 = 1$, $v_6 = 4$, $v_2 = 2$, $u_3 = 3$. In tableau form:

						u_i
9		9				3
	3	7			5	1
	5					3
6			2	2		0
6	2	6	2	2	4	v_j

Determination of u_i and v_j from $u_i + v_j = c_{iJ}$ for variables in the basis.

Now that one has the costs for each alternative, one can find the opportunity costs, in the same way as in the Stepping-Stone Method. Thus, one gets the matrix:

•	5	•	5	5	7
7	•	•	3	3	•
9	•	9	5	5	7
•	2	6	•	•	4

Determination of $q_{pq} = c_{pq} - u_p - v_q$ for each non-basic variable x_{pq}

•	7	•	1	4	3
0	•	•	4	2	•
−3	•	0	6	−2	4
•	6	5	•	•	6

Opportunity cost matrix for the second feasible solution.

The solution is still not optimal.

The steps for the next iteration, which turns out to yield an optimal solution, are:

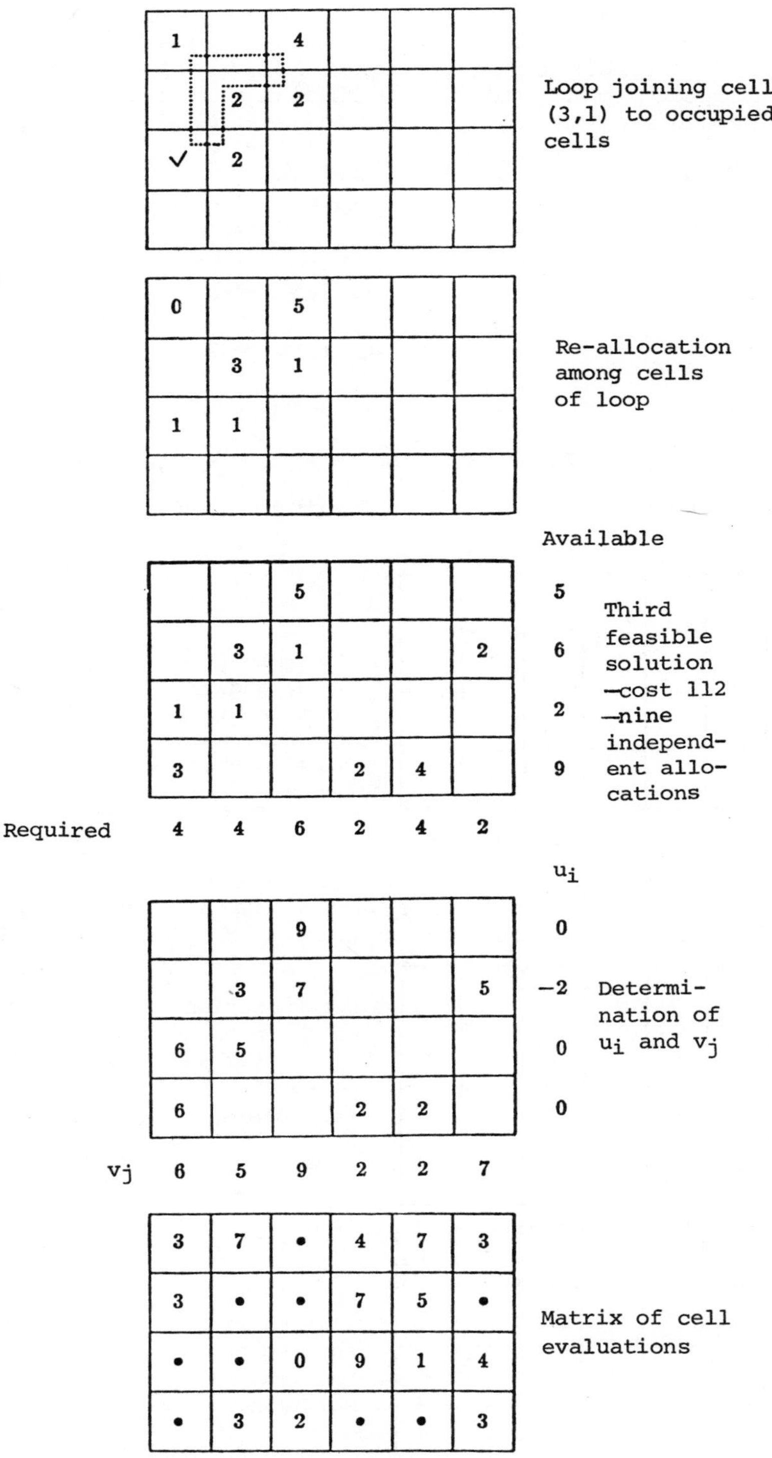

Loop joining cell (3,1) to occupied cells

1		4			
	2	2			
✓	2				

Re-allocation among cells of loop

0		5			
	3	1			
1	1				

Third feasible solution —cost 112 —nine independent allocations

							Available
			5				5
		3	1			2	6
	1	1					2
	3			2	4		9
Required	4	4	6	2	4	2	

Determination of u_i and v_j

							u_i
			9				0
		3	7			5	−2
	6	5					0
	6			2	2		0
v_j	6	5	9	2	2	7	

Matrix of cell evaluations

3	7	•	4	7	3
3	•	•	7	5	•
•	•	0	9	1	4
•	3	2	•	•	3

Since all the cell evaluations are non-negative, the third feasible solution is optimal, and 112 is the corresponding minimum cost.

• PROBLEM 5-23

Consider a "current solution" as in Table 1. Use the Multiplier Method to find an entering variable in Table 1.

Table 1

[10] 0	[0] 15	[20]	[11]	15
[12]	[7] 0	[9] 15	[20] 10	25
[0] 5	[14]	[16]	[18]	5
5	15	15	10	

Solution: The procedure for determining an entering variable is: Assign multipliers u_i and v_j for all rows i and columns j.

Then for each cell which has an assignment (i.e., a basic variable), set up an equation of the form $u_i + v_j = c_{ij}$ where c_{ij} stands for the cost located at the upper right corner of the ij-th cell. Since these multipliers are relative quantities, their values can be determined by assigning an arbitrary value to one of them. (usually $u_1 \equiv 0$) and solving for others through simultaneous equations. This done, nonbasic variables are evaluated by

$$q_{pr} = c_{pr} - u_p - v_r$$

and the entering variable is the one with the lowest q_{pr}

For the data in Table

x_{11}: $u_1 + v_1 = c_{11} = 10$

x_{12}: $u_1 + v_2 = c_{12} = 0$

x_{22}: $u_2 + v_2 = c_{22} = 7$

x_{23}: $u_2 + v_3 = c_{23} = 9$

x_{24}: $u_2 - v_4 = c_{24} = 20$

x_{31}: $u_3 + v_1 = c_{31} = 0$

Let $u_1 \equiv 0$. Values of multipliers are $v_1 = 10$, $v_2 = 0$, $u_2 = 7$, $v_3 = 2$, $v_4 = 13$, and $u_3 = -10$. Values for nonbasic variables are

$q_{13} = c_{13} - u_1 - v_3 = 20 - 0 - 2 = 18$

$q_{14} = c_{14} - u_1 - v_4 = 11 - 0 - 13 = -2$

$q_{21} = c_{21} - u_2 - v_1 = 12 - 7 - 10 = \boxed{-5}$

$$q_{32} = c_{32} - u_3 - v_2 = 14 - (-10) - 0 = 24$$

$$q_{33} = c_{33} - u_3 - v_3 = 16 - (-10) - 2 = 24$$

$$q_{34} = c_{34} - u_3 - v_4 = 18 - (-10) - 13 = 15$$

Therefore, x_{21} is the entering variable. The leaving variable is calculated by using a loop associated with x_{21}, as in the Stepping Stone Method.

• PROBLEM 5-24

Find an optimal solution for the following transportation problem. Use the Method of Multipliers.

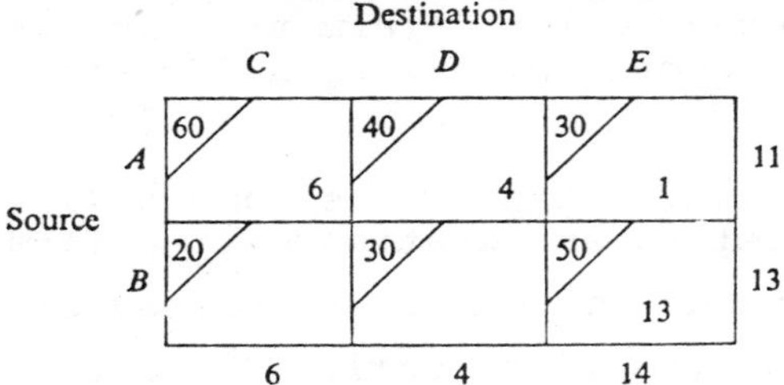

Destination
C
D
E
60
40
30
A
11
6
4
1
Source
20
30
50
B
13
13
6
4
14

Solution: Choose $u_1 = 0$ (arbitrarily).

For basic cells, $u_i + v_j = c_{ij}$

$$u_1 + v_1 = 60 \rightarrow v_1 = 60$$

$$u_1 + v_2 = 40 \rightarrow v_2 = 40$$

$$u_1 + v_3 = 30 \rightarrow v_3 = 3$$

$$u_2 + v_3 = 50 \rightarrow u_2 = 20$$

Tableau 1

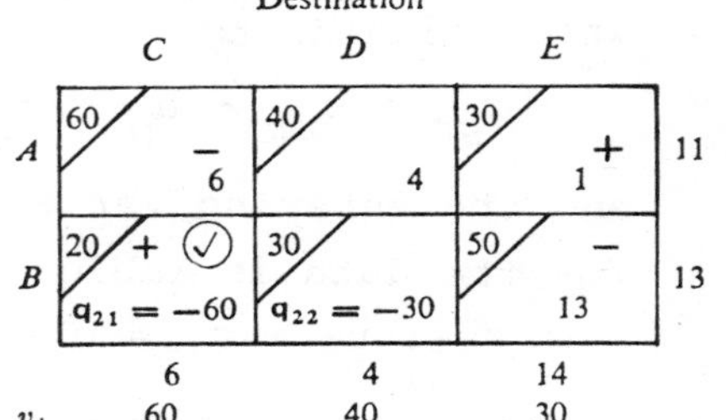

For nonbasic cells, compute $q_{ij} = c_{ij} - u_i - v_j$

$$q_{21} = c_{21} - u_2 - v_1 = 20 - 20 - 60 = -60$$

$$q_{22} = c_{22} - u_2 - v_2 = 30 - 20 - 40 = -30$$

Hence cell (2,1) will enter the basis.

The loop is from (2,1) to (2,3) to (1,3) to (1,1) to (2,1). Put a plus in cell (2,1), a minus in cell (2,3), a plus in cell (1,3), and a minus in cell (1,1).

The minimum quantity in a minus cell is 6, in cell (1,1). Since it is unique, cell (1,1) will leave the basis.

Add 6 to the plus cells and subtract 6 from the minus cells.

Drop (1,1) from the basis. The result is Tableau 2.

Choose $u_1 = 0$ artibrarily.

For basic cells $u_i + v_j = c_{ij}$

Tableau 2

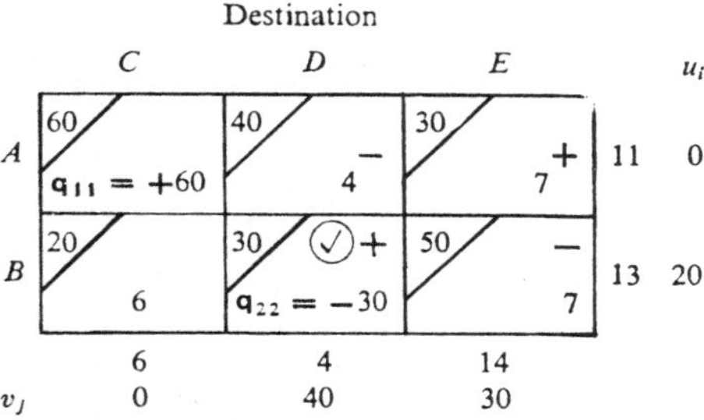

$$u_1 + v_2 = 40 \rightarrow v_2 = 40$$

$$u_1 + v_3 = 30 \rightarrow v_3 = 30$$

$$u_2 + v_3 = 50 \rightarrow u_2 = 20$$

$$u_2 + v_1 = 20 \rightarrow v_1 = 0$$

For nonbasic cells, compute $q_{ij} = c_{ij} - u_i - v_j$

$$q_{11} = c_{11} - u_1 - v_1 = 60 - 0 - 0 = 60$$

$$q_{22} = c_{22} - u_2 - v_2 = 30 - 20 - 40 = -30$$

Hence, cell (2,2) will enter the basis (indicated by a check ✓). The loop is from (2,2) to (2,3) to (1,3) to (1,2) to (2,2).

Put a plus in cell (2,2), a minus in cell (2,3), a plus in cell (1,3), and a minus in cell (1,2).

The minimum quantity in a minus cell is 4, in cell (2,1). Since it is unique, cell (2,1) will leave the basis.

Add 4 to the plus cells and subtract 4 from the minus cells.

Drop cell (2,1) from the basis. The result is Tableau 3.

Choose $u_2 = 0$ (arbitrarily).

Tableau 3

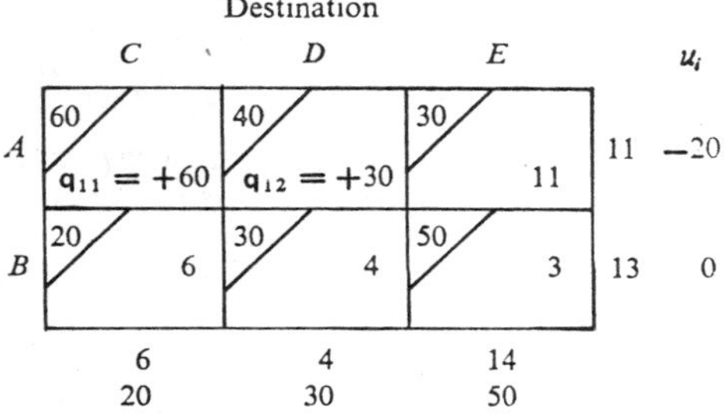

$$u_2 + v_1 = 20 \rightarrow v_1 = 20$$

$$u_2 + v_2 = 30 \rightarrow v_2 = 30$$

$$u_2 + v_3 = 50 \rightarrow v_3 = 50$$

$$u_1 + v_3 = 30 \rightarrow u_1 = -20$$

For nonbasic cells, compute $q_{ij} = c_{ij} - u_i - v_j$

$$q_{11} = c_{11} - u_1 - v_1 = 60 - (-20) - 20 = 60$$

$$q_{12} = c_{12} - u_1 - v_2 = 40 - (-20) - 30 = 30$$

Thus, the optimal allocation is as in Tableau 3.

• PROBLEM 5-25

Solve the following transportation problem by the Method of Multipliers.

Table 1

	D_1	D_2	D_3	
S_1	4 10	2 5	1	15
S_2	1	3 15	5 10	25
	10	20	10	40

Solution: To determine the exact objective function at a given corner, eliminate the basic variables from the universal objective function by equating the relevant coefficients to 0. The occupied cells of Table 1 show that x_{11}, x_{12}, x_{22}, and x_{23} are basic variables, and hence the coefficients of these variables in the universal form of C should be 0. Thus consider the system of equations, where the notation "Eq. (i,j)" signifies that x_{ij} is basic:

$$(O_1)\quad \begin{cases} u_1 + v_1 = 4 & (1) \\ u_1 + v_2 = 2 & (2) \\ u_2 + v_2 = 3 & (3) \\ u_2 + v_3 = 5 & (4) \end{cases}$$

(Call this system (O_1); O for orthogonal, 1 for Table 1.) With each such system (O_n), associate a derived system of numbers, the (Q_n) system. The numbers in this system equal the coefficients of the current nonbasic variables appearing in the objective function. Thus

$$(Q_1)\quad \begin{cases} q_{13} = c_{13} - (u_1 + v_3) = 1 - (u_1 + v_3) \\ q_{21} = c_{21} - (u_2 + v_1) = 1 - (u_2 + v_1) \end{cases}$$

Note that system (O_1) contains more unknowns than equations.

It is necessary to determine the values of the combinations of u_i's and v_j's which appear in system (Q_1). These sums turn out to be constant for any solution to system (O_1).

For example, if the following combination of equations is formed in system (O_1):

Eq. (2) - Eq. (3) + Eq. (4)

the relation

$u_1 + v_3 = 4$ is obtained.

Similarly, the combination

$$Eq. (3) - Eq. (2) + Eq. (1)$$

gives the relation

$$u_2 + v_1 = 5$$

These relations suggest that the key sums $u_1 + v_3$ and $u_2 + v_1$ are determined by first finding any numerical solution to system (O_1), and afterward using the numerical values obtained to calculate the values of the key sums. Accordingly, let $v_1 = 0$ in system (O_1). Then it follows that:

$$\begin{aligned} v_1 &= 0 \\ u_1 &= 4 \\ v_2 &= -2 \qquad [v_1 = 0] \\ u_2 &= 5 \\ v_3 &= 0 \end{aligned}$$

On the other hand, if in system (O_1) it is specified that $u_1 = 0$, the following solution is obtained:

$$\begin{aligned} u_1 &= 0 \\ v_1 &= 4 \\ v_2 &= 2 \qquad [u_1 = 0] \\ u_2 &= 1 \\ u_3 &= 4 \end{aligned}$$

Once the value of any unknown in system (O_1) is determined, the remaining 4 × 4 system is triangular and can be solved by sight, simply by substituting back from one equation to another. Whatever the numerical solution obtained it will always follow that

$$u_1 \qquad + v_3 = 4$$

$$u_2 + v_1 \qquad = 5$$

From these two key sums the (Q_1) system of numbers can be determined immediately, as

$$(Q_1) \quad \begin{cases} q_{13} = c_{13} - (u_1 + v_3) = 1 - 4 = -3 \\ \\ q_{21} = c_{21} - (u_2 + v_1) = 1 - 5 = -4 \end{cases}$$

This shows that entering cell (2,1) will decrease C at the fastest per-unit rate.

Now construct the unique exchange loop which describes the consequences of entering cell (2,1). This loop shows that the maximum number of units that can be shipped into cell (2,1) is 10. This takes us to the updated table

Table 2

	D_1	D_2	D_3	
S_1	[4] 0	[2] 15	[1] 0	15
S_2	[1] 10	[3] 5	[5] 10	25
	10	20	10	(40)

Now apply the multiplier method to Table 2, by writing down the system (O_2) of basic equations corresponding to its occupied cells. This gives

$$(O_2)\quad \begin{cases} u_1 + v_2 = c_{12} = 2 \\ u_2 + v_1 = c_{21} = 1 \\ u_2 + v_2 = c_{22} = 3 \\ u_2 + v_3 = c_{23} = 5 \end{cases}$$

If $u_1 = 0$, then $v_2 = 2$, $u_2 = 1$, $v_1 = 0$, $v_3 = 4$. From this particular solution the (Q_2) system is obtained:

$$(Q_2)\quad \begin{cases} q_{11} = c_{11} - (u_1 + v_1) = 4 - (0 + 0) = +4 \\ q_{13} = c_{13} - (u_1 + v_3) = 1 - (0 + 4) = -3 \end{cases}$$

It pays to enter cell (1,3). Only now the appropriate stepping-stone loop is constructed. The following updated table is obtained:

The (O_3) system corresponding to Table 3 is

$$(O_3)\quad \begin{cases} u_1 + v_2 = c_{12} = 2 \\ u_1 + v_3 = c_{13} = 1 \\ u_2 + v_1 = c_{21} = 1 \\ u_2 + v_2 = c_{22} = 3 \end{cases}$$

Let $u_1 = 0$. Then a particular solution to (O_3) is $u_1 = 0$, $v_2 = 2$, $v_3 = 1$, $u_2 = 1$, $v_1 = 0$. This fixes the entries in the (Q_3) system, namely,

Table 3

	D_1	D_2	D_3	
S_1	[4]	[2] 5	[1] 10	15
S_2	[1] 10	[3] 15	[5]	25
	10	20	10	

$$(Q_3)\begin{cases} q_{11} = c_{11} - (u_1 + v_1) = 4 - 0 = +4 \\ q_{23} = c_{23} - (u_2 + v_3) = 5 - 2 = +3 \end{cases}$$

Since all q_{ij} in system (Q_3) are nonnegative, Table 3 must be optimal.

• PROBLEM 5-26

In this transportation problem there are three origins, with availabilities of $a_1 = 6$, $a_2 = 8$, and $a_3 = 10$, and four destinations, with requirements of $b_1 = 4$, $b_2 = 6$, $b_3 = 8$, and $b_4 = 6$. Note that $\sum_i a_i = \sum_j b_j = 24$. The costs between each origin and destination are given in the following cost matrix.

Find an optimal solution applying the Method of Multipliers.

Destinations

Origins	1	2	3	4
1	1	2	3	4
2	4	3	2	0
3	0	2	2	1

$= (c_{ij})$

Solution: Using the northwest-corner rule, one obtains the first feasible solution:

$(x_{ij}) =$

4	2			6
	4	4		8
		4	6	10
4	6	8	6	

where $x_{11} = 4$, $x_{12} = 2$, $x_{22} = 4$, $x_{23} = 4$, $x_{33} = 4$, $x_{34} = 6$, and all the other $x_{ij} = 0$. The value of the objective function is 42. Since this is a nondegenerate basic feasible solution, the first solution does not require our perturbing the problem. When a degenerate solution occurs, select from the two variables that can be in the solution with a value of zero, the one having the smaller c_{ij}. Always keep track of a solution with exactly m + n - 1 nonnegative variables.

Determine, for those variables in the basic solution, m numbers u_i and n numbers v_j such that

$$\begin{aligned} u_1 + v_1 &= c_{11} = 1 \\ u_1 + v_2 &= c_{12} = 2 \\ u_2 + v_2 &= c_{22} = 3 \\ u_2 + v_3 &= c_{23} = 2 \\ u_3 + v_3 &= c_{33} = 2 \\ u_3 + v_4 &= c_{34} = 1 \end{aligned} \qquad (1)$$

Here there are seven variables in six (that is, m + n - 1) equations. Since (1) is an underdetermined set of linear equations (i.e., the number of unknowns exceeds the number of equations), this system has an infinite number of solutions. Determine a solution by arbitrarily letting any one of the variables equal its corresponding c_{ij}. This reduces the number of unknowns by one and forces a unique solution of the m + n - 1 equations in the remaining m + n - 1 variables.

Following the discussion above, in (1) let $u_1 = 0$; then it is an easy matter to solve for the remaining u_i and v_j. With $u_1 = 0$, then $v_1 = 1$ and $v_2 = 2$; with $v_2 = 2$ then $u_2 = 1$; with $u_2 = 1$ then $v_3 = 1$; with $v_3 = 1$ then $u_3 = 1$; and finally, with $u_3 = 1$ then $v_4 = 0$. This computation can be readily accomplished by setting up the following table containing the cost coefficients (in bold type) of the variables in the basic solution:

u \ v				
	1	**2**		
		3	**2**	
			2	**1**

By letting $u_1 = 0$, compute, as was done above, the resulting u_i and v_j and enter them in the corresponding positions as follows:

u \ v	1	2	1	0
0	**1**	**2**		
1		**3**	**2**	
1			**2**	**1**

Since all the equations of (1) are satisfied, obtain $u_i + v_j = c_{ij}$ for those x_{ij} in the basic feasible solution. Then compute $q_{ij} = u_i + v_j$ for all combinations (i,j) and place these figures in their corresponding cells of the indirect-cost table, ($q_{ij} = c_{ij}$ for all x_{ij} in the solution.) The indirect-cost table (q_{ij}) for the first solution, along with a copy of the direct-cost table (c_{ij}), follows:

$(q_{ij}) =$

1	2	1	0
2	3	2	1
2	3	2	1

1	2	3	4
4	3	2	0
0	2	2	1

$= (c_{ij})$

For example, $q_{14} = u_1 + v_4 = 0$. Next compute the difference $q_{ij} - c_{ij}$. If all $q_{ij} - c_{ij} \leq 0$, then the solution that yielded the indirect-cost table is a minimum feasible solution. If at least one $q_{ij} - c_{ij} > 0$, a minimum solution has not been found. One can, as will be described below, readily obtain a new basic feasible solution which contains a variable associated with a $q_{ij} - c_{ij} > 0$. Select for entry into the new basis the variable corresponding to $q_{pq} - c_{pq} = \max\,(q_{ij} - c_{ij} > 0)$. This scheme will yeild a new basic solution whose value of the objective function will be less than the value for the preceding solution.

For the first solution, one finds that $q_{pq} - c_{pq} = q_{31} - c_{31} = 2$. Select $x_{pq} = x_{31}$ to be introduced into the solution. Now one wishes to determine a new basic feasible solution which contains x_{31}. From the first solution matrix (x_{ij}) and with $x_{pq} = x_{31} = \theta \geq 0$, now solve the transportation problem with origin and destination quantities given by

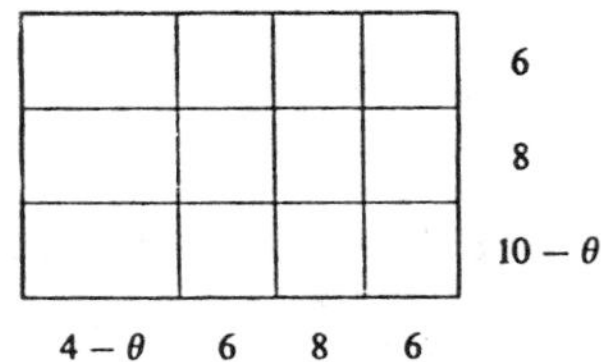

with the values of the nonzero x_{ij}'s restricted to those in the first solution. Start the process by first determining the largest possible value of a variable which appears by itself in either a row or a column, here x_{11} or x_{34}. The values of the remaining variables are obtained by selecting values which eliminate a row or column from further consideration, each time preserving the row or column balance. For the first restricted problem one has the new values of the variables in terms of θ given by

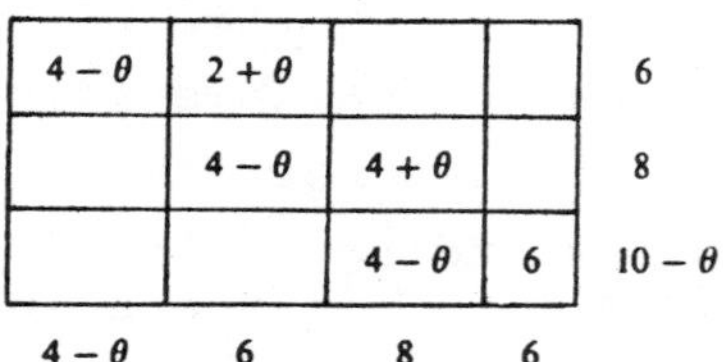

$4-\theta$	$2+\theta$			6
	$4-\theta$	$4+\theta$		8
		$4-\theta$	6	$10-\theta$
$4-\theta$	6	8	6	

Note that the size of θ is restricted by those x_{ij} from which it is subtracted. θ cannot be larger than the smallest x_{ij} from which it is subtracted. Here θ must be less than or equal to 4 and must be greater than zero in order to preserve feasiblity. Since one wishes to eliminate one of the variables from the old solution and to introduce x_{31}, let $\theta = 4$. However, since $x_{11} - \theta = x_{22} - \theta = x_{33} - \theta = 4 - \theta$, one would eliminate three variables and obtain a degenerate solution with four positive variables. To keep a solution with exactly $m + n - 1$ nonnegative variables, retain two of these three variables with values of zero. Select x_{11} and x_{33}, because they correspond to the smaller c_{ij}. The new solution with $\theta = x_{31} = 4$ is

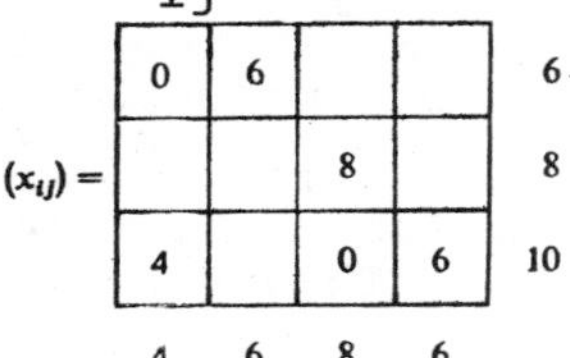

$(x_{ij}) =$

0	6			6
		8		8
4		0	6	10
4	6	8	6	

The objective function for this solution is equal to

$$42 - [\max (q_{ij} - c_{ij} > 0)]\theta = 42 - (2)(4) = 34$$

The corresponding combined (u_i, v_j) table and q_{ij} matrix for this solution is given in the following table:

$(q_{ij}) =$

u \ v	1	2	3	2
0	**1**	**2**	3	2
−1	0	1	**2**	1
−1	**0**	1	**2**	**1**

1	2	3	4
4	3	2	0
0	2	2	1

$= (c_{ij})$

where the bold numbers correspond to the c_{ij} for the basis vectors. Note that $\max (q_{ij} - c_{ij} > 0) = q_{24} - c_{24} = 1$ and introduce $x_{24} = \theta \geq 0$ into cell (2,4). Thus use the old solution tableau to introduce θ into the appropriate cell positions, and for the current step add and subtract $\theta = x_{24}$ from the previous x_{ij} as follows:

0	6			6
		$8-\theta$	θ	8
4		$0+\theta$	$6-\theta$	10
4	6	8	6	

One has $\theta = 6$; x_{34} is eliminated, and x_{24} is introduced with a value of $\theta = 6$. The new value of the objective function is

$$34 - (q_{24} - c_{24})\theta = 34 - (1)(6) = 28$$

The new solution is

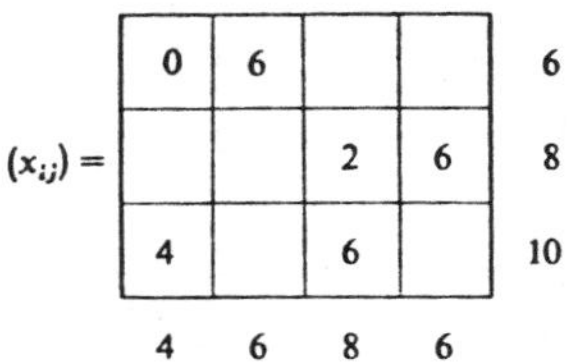

$(x_{ij}) =$

0	6			6
		2	6	8
4		6		10
4	6	8	6	

The corresponding (u_i, v_j) table and (q_{ij}) matrix is given by

$(q_{ij}) =$

u \ v	1	2	3	1
0	1	2	3	1
−1	0	1	2	0
−1	0	1	2	0

$= (c_{ij})$

1	2	3	4
4	3	2	0
0	2	2	1

Here, all $q_{ij} - c_{ij} \le 0$, and this last solution ($x_{11} = 0$, $x_{12} = 6$, $x_{23} = 2$, $x_{24} = 6$, $x_{31} = 4$, $x_{33} = 6$, and all other $x_{ij} = 0$) is a degenerate minimum feasible solution. The value of the objective function is 28. Note that $q_{13} - c_{13} = 0$ and that x_{13} is not in the solution. Then introduce x_{13} into this last solution and obtain an alternate minimum solution. Put $\theta \ge 0$ into cell (1,3) and obtain

$0 - \theta$	6	θ		6
		2	6	8
$4 + \theta$		$6 - \theta$		10
4	6	8	6	

Then $x_{13} = \theta = 0$ and a new degenerate basic minimum solution is obtained as follows:

$(x_{ij}) =$

	6	0		6
		2	6	8
4		6		10
4	6	8	6	

The value of the objective function is 28.

• PROBLEM 5-27

Test the feasible solution for optimality. Cost = 127. With the cost matrix of:

		Store						
		1	2	3	4	5	6	Available
Warehouse	1	3		2				5
	2			4			2	6
	3		2					2
	4	1	2		2	4		9
Required		4	4	6	2	4	2	

		Store					
		1	2	3	4	5	6
Warehouse	1	9	12	9	6	9	10
	2	7	3	7	7	5	5
	3	6	5	9	11	3	11
	4	6	8	11	2	2	10

Solution: The allocations for the feasible solution with cost 127 fall in the following positions:

•		•			
		•			•
	•				
•	•		•	•	

Apply the Method of Multipliers. The positions are seen to be independent, and there are 9 of them (M + N - 1); so the optimality test routine is applicable. Since the u_i and v_j are to be determined by means of the unit costs in the occupied cells only, write in the corresponding unit costs:

9		9			
		7			5
	5				
6	8		2	2	

Matrix of unit costs (empty cells only)

•	12	•	6	9	10
7	3	•	7	5	•
6	•	9	11	3	11
•	•	11	•	•	10

Matrix of $(u_i + v_j)$

•	11	•	5	5	7
7	9	•	3	3	•
3	•	3	−1	−1	1
•	•	6	•	•	4

Matrix of cell evaluations

•	1	•	1	4	3
0	−6	•	4	2	•
3	•	6	12	4	10
•	•	5	•	•	6

Since one of the cell evaluations turns out to be negative, the feasible solution under test is not optimal. Assign an arbitrary value to an arbitrary u_i; thus u_4 is taken as 0. Since it is desired, $u_i + v_j$ to equal c_{ij} for occupied cells (i,j), this value for u_4 leads to $v_1 = 6$, $v_2 = 8$, $v_4 = 2$, and $v_5 = 2$. The subset of the u_i and v_j already determined leads successively to $u_1 = 3$, $u_3 = -3$, $v_3 = 6$, $u_2 = 1$, $v_6 = 4$. Our complete set of u_i and v_j becomes

							u_i
	9		9				3
			7			5	1
		5					−3
	6	8		2	2		0
v_j	6	8	6	2	2	4	

To compute the matrix of cell evaluations, it is convenient to write down the matrix of the corresponding unit costs, and and the matrix of the numbers $(u_i + v_j)$, and then subtract the latter matrix from the former.

• PROBLEM 5-28

Using the Method of Multipliers, check the initial feasible solution for the transportation problem, for optimality.

Table 1 Shipment costs.

	D_1	D_2	D_3	D_4	Supply
O_1	[21] 4	[36] 6	[43] 6	[20] 2	18
O_2	[60]	[30] 5	[50]	[43]	5
O_3	[18]	[10] 7	[48]	[72]	7
Requirements	4	18	6	2	30

Solution: The process begins by listing the cells with non-zero shipments and their unit costs. The equation follows. In the next column the order of steps is given; the last column gives the results of the steps.

Table 2 Organization of Calculations.

Cell	c_{ij}	$c_{ij} = u_i + v_j$	Step	Result
(1,1)	21	$21 = u_1 + v_1$	1	Set $u_1 = 0$, then $v_1 = 21$
(1,2)	36	$36 = u_1 + v_2$	2	$v_2 = 36$
(2,2)	30	$30 = u_2 + v_2$	3	$u_2 = -6$
(3,2)	10	$10 = u_3 + v_2$	4	$u_3 = -26$
(1,3)	43	$43 = u_1 + v_3$	5	$v_3 = 43$
(1,4)	20	$20 = u_1 + v_4$	6	$v_4 = 20$

Table 3 Table of Equations: $c_{ij} - u_i - v_j = q_{ij}$

$21 - 0 - 21 = 0$ $60 + 6 - 21 = 45$ $18 + 26 - 21 = 23$	$36 - 0 - 36 = 0$ $30 + 6 - 36 = 0$ $10 + 26 - 36 = 0$	$43 - 0 - 43 = 0$ $50 + 6 - 43 = 13$ $48 + 26 - 43 = 31$	$20 - 0 - 20 = 0$ $43 + 6 - 20 = 29$ $72 + 26 - 20 = 78$	$u_1 = 0$ $u_2 = -6$ $u_3 = -26$
$v_1 = 21$	$v_2 = 36$	$v_3 = 43$	$v_4 = 20$	

Next construct a table to display the results in terms of q (Table 3). The results show that all q_{ij} are zero for the nonzero cells of the current solution, as required, and furthermore that all other q_{ij} values are positive. Therefore all other solution have higher total costs. The additional fact that no zero shipment cell has a zero value of q_{ij} implies that this solution is the unique optimum; no other solution is as good.

• PROBLEM 5-29

A company has four warehouses a, b, c and d. It is required to deliver a product from these warehouses to three customers, A, B, and C. The warehouses have the following amounts in stock:

a	15 units
b	16 units
c	11 units
d	13 units
	55 units

The customers' requirements are:

A	17 units
B	20 units
C	18 units
	55 units

Table 1

		Warehouses			
		a	b	c	d
Customers	A	8	9	6	3
	B	6	11	5	10
	C	3	8	7	9

Transportation costs per unit

The costs of transporting one unit of the product from any warehouse a, b, c or d, to any customer A, B or C are given in Table 1.

The problem is to meet the customers' requirements while keeping the total transportation cost to a minimum.

Solution: The method of solution is to find, first, a feasible solution to the problem, i.e., a method of transporting the product which satisfies the customers' requirements while not violating the restrictions of availability. This solution is then tested to see whether it is the cheapest solution. If not, a cheaper solution is found, and retested in a similar manner. This process is repeated until no further reduction in cost is possible.

In the above problem the number of units available equals the number required and hence any feasible solution meets each customer's requirement and leaves each warehouse empty. There are several ways of obtaining a feasible solution to the problem. A reasonable way is to allocate first as much as possible to that route having the least transportaton cost per unit. There are two routes which have a unit transportation cost of 3. Start by allocating as much as possible to route dA. The maximum that can be allocated to this route is 13--the amount initially held at warehouse d. Doing this leaves customer A requiring 4 units from any of the three remaining warehouses. The cheapest way customer A can receive these additional four units is from warehouse c--route cA having a unit transportation cost of 6.

Allocating four units to this route satisfies customer A's requirement and reduces the amount held at warehouse c to 7 units. It is now cheaper to send the remaining 7 units at warehouse c to customer B than to customer C. Allocating 7 units to route cB exhausts the supply at warehouse c and reduces customer B's requirement from 20 units to 13. The cheapest way customer B can receive this amount is from warehouse a. Allocating 13 units to route aB satisfies customer B's requirement and reduces the amount at warehouse a to 2 units. These remaining 2 units at warehouse a, plus the 16 units at warehouse b, must finally go to customer C via routes aC and bC respectively. Table 2 illustrates this feasible solution.

Table 2

		Warehouses a	b	c	d	*Required*
Customers	*A*	[8]	[9]	4 [6]	13 [3]	~~17~~ ~~4~~
	B	13 [6]	[11]	7 [5]	[10]	~~20~~ ~~13~~
	C	2 [3]	16 [8]	[7]	[9]	~~18~~
Available		~~15~~ ~~2~~	~~16~~	~~11~~ ~~7~~	~~13~~	55

First determine the cost of transporting the product in this way. This is obtained by multiplying the cost of each route by the number of units transported along it, and summing for all routes as follows:

In order to see whether or not there is an alternative solution with a lower total transportation cost, examine in turn each unused route to see whether or not the cost could be reduced by bringing it into use.

Consider the possibility of sending one unit along route aA. In order to achieve this, some modification to the remainder of the allocations is necessary. One unit must be subtracted from either of the routes aB or aC so that the restriction of there being only 15 units initially at warehouse a is not violated. If we reduce by one unit the amount sent along route aB, one unit must be added to route cB to maintain customer B's requirement of 20. Finally, to comply with the restriction of only 11 units at warehouse c, one unit must be subtracted from route cA. This last subtraction compensates for the initial modification of sending one unit along the new route aA by maintaining customer A's requirement of 17 units. These changes can be seen to have no effect on the feasibility of the initial allocation (see Table 3).

Table 3

		Warehouses			
	a	*b*	*c*	*d*	*Required*
Customers *A*	$^{+1}$ [8]	[9]	4^{-1} [6]	13 [3]	17
B	13^{-1} [6]	[11]	7^{+1} [5]	[10]	20
C	2 [3]	16 [8]	[7]	[9]	18
Available	15	16	11	13	55

The effect of the change is that customer A receives one more unit from warehouse a and one less from warehousec while customer B receives one more from c and one less from a. The former has the effect of increasing the transportation cost by 2--the unit cost of route aA being 8 compare with 6 of route cA while the latter reduces the transportation cost by 1. The net result is that the modified solution shows an increase rather than a decrease in the total transportation cost.

If c_{aA} is the unit transportation cost from warehouse a to customer A, c_{bA} is the unit transportation cost from warehouse b to customer A, etc., the change in cost in the above modification is given by $c_{aA} - c_{cA} + c_{cB} - c_{aB}$. This equals 8 - 6 + 5 - 6 = 1. A positive sign represents an increase in cost while a negative sign represents a decrease.

The above inspection procedure could be repeated for each unused route in turn to test whether or not the initial solution can be improved. A short cut to this rather laborious method is provided by the concept of shadow costs. Shadow costs are obtained by assuming that the transportation cost for all used routes is made up of two parts--a cost of despatch, a, b, c or d and a cost of reception, A, B or C--such that the unit cost $c_{cA} = c + A$, $c_{dA} = d + A$, etc. Under this assumption, by assigning an arbitrary value to one of the shadow costs, for example A, the remaining ones, a, b, c, d, B and C may be uniquely determined provided that the solution employs exactly six routes, i.e., one route for each shadow cost required. The initial allocation does use exactly six routes and therefore the shadow costs may be determined from the following six equations:

$$c + A = 6,\ d + A = 3,\ a + B = 6,\ c + B = 5,\ a + C = 3,$$

$$\text{and } b + C = 8$$

If A is made equal to zero, these equations may be solved to give a = 7, b = 12, c = 6, d = 3, B = - 1, and C = - 4. Table 4 shows, along with the initial allocation, these shadow costs.

Table 4

		Warehouses				
		a	b	c	d	
	Shadow costs	7	12	6	3	Required
Customers A	0	[8]	[9]	4 [6]	13 [3]	17
Customers B	−1	13 [6]	[11]	7 [5]	[10]	20
Customers C	−4	2 [3]	16 [8]	[7]	[9]	18
Available		15	16	11	13	55

It was shown earlier, how introducing the route aA into the solution, and sending one unit along it, increased the total transportation cost by $c_{aA} - c_{cA} + c_{cB} - C_{aB}$. In terms of shadow costs this is equivalent to

$$c_{aA} - (c + A) + (c + B) - (a + B),$$

which simplifies to $c_{aA} - (a + A)$. This illustrates a general result, that the sending of one unit along a previously unoccupied route increases the total transportation cost by the unit transportation cost of the new route minus the sum of the shadow costs for that route. Thus if this difference is negative for any unused route, a saving in cost, equal to this difference, will be made for each unit that can be transferred to this route. Now evaluate this difference for each unused route in the initial allocation as follows:

$$c_{aA} - (a + A) = 8 - (7 + 0) = 1$$

(This confirms the previous analysis of this route.)

$$c_{bA} - (b + A) = 9 - (12 + 0) = - 3$$

$$c_{bB} - (b + B) = 11 - (12 - 1) = 0$$

$$c_{dB} - (d + B) = 10 - (3 - 1) = 8$$

$$c_{cC} - (c + C) = 7 - (6 - 4) = 5$$

$$c_{dC} - (d + C) = 9 - (3 - 4) = 10$$

These results are entered in the top left-hand corner of the appropriate squares in Table 5.

Table 5

			Warehouses				
			a	b	c	d	
		Shadow costs	7	12	6	3	Required
Customers	A	0	(1) [8]	(−3) [9]	4 [6]	13 [3]	17
	B	−1	13 [6]	(0) [11]	7 [5]	(8) [10]	20
	C	−4	2 [3]	16 [8]	(5) [7]	(10) [9]	18
Available			15	16	11	13	55

Note that a saving of 3 can be made for each unit that can be sent along route bA. The next step is to utilize this new route as fully as possible while still satisfying the movement requirements. Table 6 illustrates how this is achieved.

Assume x units are sent along route bA. In order not to exceed the number initially held at warehouse b, the number sent along route bC must be reduced to 16 - x. However, this reduces by x the number of units sent to customer C, and so the amount sent along route aC must be increased to 2 + x units. By a similar chain of reasoning the numbers sent along routes aB, cB and cA are seen to be 13 - x, 7 + x and 4 - x respectively. Reference to Table 6 will show that this modification in no way affects the feasibility of the solution, provided that x is not so large that any route allocation becomes negative. The value of x is actually chosen so that the amount sent along one of the previously used routes falls to zero. This occurs along route cA when x takes the value 4. Substituting 4 for x in Table 6 yields the improved solution of Table 7.

Table 6

			Warehouses				
			a	b	c	d	
		Shadow costs	7	12	6	3	Required
Customers	A	0	(1) [8]	(−3) +x [9]	4−x [6]	13 [3]	17
	B	−1	13−x [6]	(0) [11]	7+x [5]	(8) [10]	20
	C	−4	2+x [3]	16−x [8]	(5) [7]	(10) [9]	18
Available			15	16	11	13	55

Table 7

		Warehouses				
		a	b	c	d	Required
Customers	A	[8]	4 [9]	[6]	13 [3]	17
	B	9 [6]	[11]	11 [5]	[10]	20
	C	6 [3]	12 [8]	[7]	[9]	18
Available		15	16	11	13	55

Sending 4 items along a route whose potential saving is 3 per unit, reduces the total transportation cost by 12. This saving may be verified by evaluating the new total transportation cost as follows:

Route	Cost/unit	No. of units	Cost/route
bA	9	4	36
dA	3	13	39
aB	6	9	54
cB	5	11	55
aC	3	6	18
bC	8	12	96
		Total transportation cost	$298

In order to determine whether further improvement to the solution is possible, new shadow costs are calculated for the second feasible solution and the test procedure repeated. This re-iterative process is continued until no further improvement is possible. In practice, all the calculations necessary within an iteration can be carried out using one table--Table 6--constructed via Tables 2, 4, and 5. The second iteration of the present problem is illustrated in Table 8.

Table 8

		Warehouses a	b	c	d	
	Shadow costs	4	9	3	3	*Required*
Customers A	0	(4) [8]	4 [9]	(3) [6]	13 [3]	17
B	2	9 [6]	(0) [11]	11 [5]	(5) [10]	20
C	−1	6 [3]	12 [8]	(5) [7]	(7) [9]	18
Available		15	16	11	13	55

Arbitrarily assigning the value of zero to shadow cost A, the new shadow costs, a, b, c, d, B and C, obtained by solving the following equations:

$b + A = 9$, $d + A = 3$, $a + B = 6$, $c + B = 5$, $a + C = 3$,

and $b + C = 8$

are 4, 9, 3, 3, 2 and - 1 respectively. Also, the differences between the unit transportation costs and the sum of the shadow costs for the unused routes, aA, cA, bB, dB, cC and dC, are 4, 3, 0, 5, 5 and 7. None is negative, and therefore no further improvement to the solution is possible. The minimum cost allocation is 298.

• PROBLEM 5-30

Find the shipping plan with the least time for the transportation problem with three warehouses and four markets with supplies and demands $s_1 = 3$, $s_2 = 7$, $s_3 = 5$, $d_1 = 4$, $d_2 = 3$, $d_3 = 4$, and $d_4 = 4$. The transportation time is given below:

	M_1	M_2	M_3	M_4
W_1	2	2	2	1
W_2	10	8	5	4
W_3	7	6	6	8

Solution: Table 1 gives an initial basic feasible solution using the least-cost rule.
The corresponding shipping time

$$T = \max\,[t_{14}, t_{21}, t_{23}, t_{24}, t_{31}, t_{32}] = t_{21} = 10$$

Since all the nonbasic cells in Table 1 have $t_{ij} < 10$, none of them will be crossed out. The basic variable x_{21} has the largest transportation time. A $-\theta$ is placed in that cell and a closed loop using cells (2,2), (3,1), and (3,2) is found. The maximum θ is 2, and the nonbasic variable x_{22} replaces x_{21} in the basis. The new basic feasible solution is given by Table 2.

Table 1

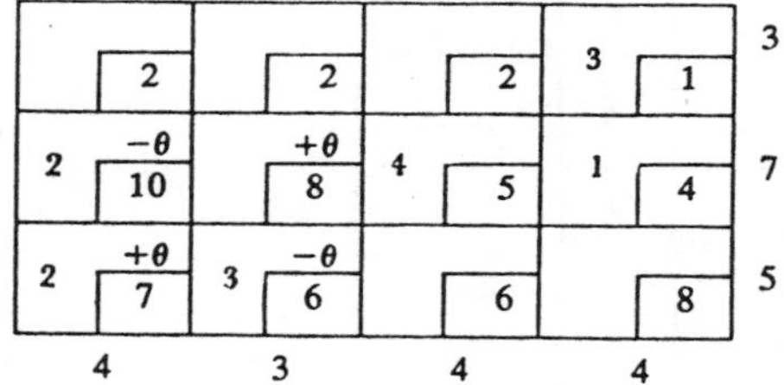

Table 2

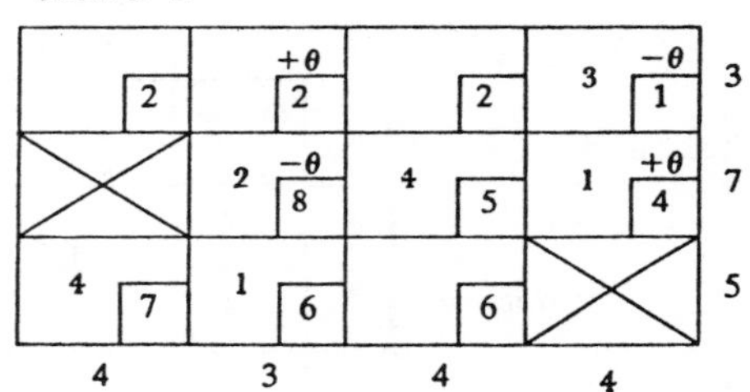

The shipment time now is 8, which corresponds to the cell (2,2). The nonbasic cells (2,1) and (3,4) of Table 2 are crossed out since their t_{ij}'s are not better than 8. Another closed loop is formed using cells (2,2),(2,4),(1,4), and (1,2). Maximum $\theta = 2$, and the new basic feasible solution is shown in Table 3.

Table 3

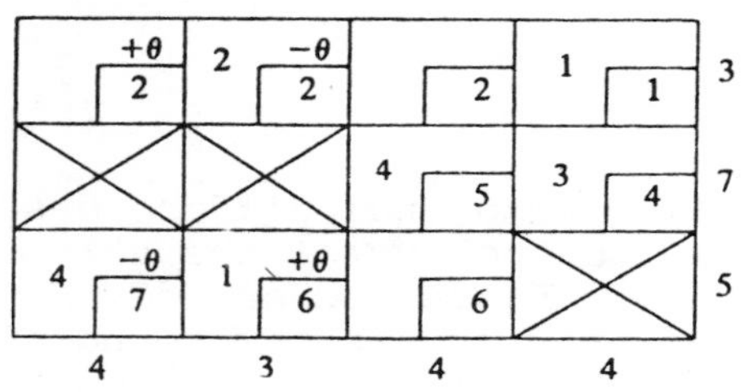

Table 4

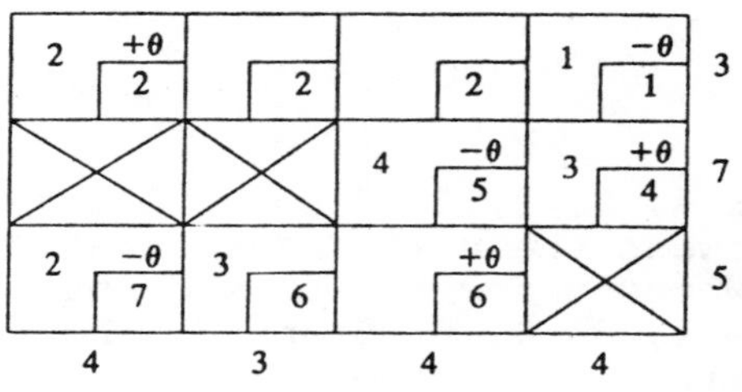

The solution from Table 3 gives T = 7, which corresponds to the basic variable x_{31}. A closed loop using cells (3,1), (3,2), (1,2), and (1,1) is formed. Maximum $\theta = 2$, implying x_{12} leaves the basis. The basic variable with the largest transportation time, namely x_{31}, still remains in the basis. Hence the new basic feasible solution does not result in a reduction in the value of T as shown in Table 4.

The value of T is still 7. Once again a closed loop using the cells (3,1), (1,1), (1,4), (2,4), and (3,3) is formed; maximum $\theta = 1$. The basic variable x_{14} is replaced by x_{33}. Table 5 gives a new shipping plan.

Table 5

3 [2]	[2]	[2]	[1]	3
X	X	3 [5]	4 [4]	7
1 [7]	3 [6]	1 [6]	X	5
4	3	4	4	

The value of T has not changed, and it corresponds to the basic variable x_{31}. Referring to Table 5, a $-\theta$ in cell (3,1) results in a $+\theta$ in cell (1,1). This has to be compensated by a $-\theta$ in one of the remaining cells in the first row. Since these are nonbasic variables at zero, a positive value cannot be subtracted without making the solution infeasible. Hence no closed loop can be formed, and Table 5 represents an optimal solution.

An optimal plan is to ship

3 units from W_1 to M_1

3 units from W_2 to M_3

4 units from W_2 to M_4

1 unit from W_3 to M_1

3 units from W_3 to M_2

1 unit from W_3 to M_3

The least possible time for completing all the shipments is 7.

ASSIGNMENT PROBLEM

• PROBLEM 5-31

Assume that four draftsmen are available for assignment to four drafting jobs. Although all four men can perform the work, their relative efficiencies vary for each job. The goal will be to assign the men to minimize overall drafting cost. On the basis of past performance, the unit-cost data is shown in matrix 1.

$$
1 = \begin{array}{c} \\ J_1 \\ J_2 \\ J_3 \\ J_4 \end{array}
\begin{array}{c}
\begin{array}{cccc} M_1 & M_2 & M_3 & M_4 \end{array} \\
\begin{bmatrix} 8 & 7 & 9 & 9 \\ 5 & 2 & 7 & 8 \\ 6 & 1 & 4 & 9 \\ 2 & 3 & 2 & 6 \end{bmatrix}
\end{array}
$$

<u>Solution</u>: Step 1: In the first row of numbers, find the smallest number in the row, and write it at the right of the row. Repeat for the other rows.

$$
1 = \begin{bmatrix} 8 & 7 & 9 & 9 \\ 5 & 2 & 7 & 8 \\ 6 & 1 & 4 & 9 \\ 2 & 3 & 2 & 6 \end{bmatrix} \begin{array}{c} 7 \\ 2 \\ 1 \\ 2 \end{array}
\qquad
2 = \begin{bmatrix} 1 & 0 & 2 & 2 \\ 3 & 0 & 5 & 6 \\ 5 & 0 & 3 & 8 \\ 0 & 1 & 0 & 4 \end{bmatrix}
\qquad
2 = \begin{bmatrix} 1 & \boxed{0} & 2 & 2 \\ 3 & 0 & 5 & 6 \\ 5 & 0 & 3 & 8 \\ \boxed{0} & 1 & 0 & 4 \end{bmatrix}
$$

Step 2: Make a new matrix 2 from 1 by subtracting the row minimum (7 for the first row) from each number in the first row of 1, and writing each of the remainders in matrix 2 to form the first row.
Repeat for the second, third, and fourth rows, using their minimums. Check 2; there should be at least one zero in each row.
Step 3: Find whether the matrix will give a complete basis for making the optimum assignments of men by first picking out a pattern of zeros in the matrix in such a way that no row or column (in the pattern) contains more than one zero. Identify this pattern by putting a square around each zero selected. (In many cases, as in this one, there is more than one pattern of "squared" zeros. Any one of these patterns is acceptable for this step.) In this particular case, the pattern of zeros is easily found by trial and error.
Step 4: Starting with the matrix constructed in Step 3 examine each row until one is found that has only one zero. Make a square around that zero. If there are any other zeros in the same column as the zero just "squared," put X's through them. Repeat until every row with just one zero is marked. In the problem, the first row is the only one with just one zero.

$$
2 = \begin{bmatrix} 1 & \boxed{0} & 2 & 2 \\ 3 & \cancel{0} & 5 & 6 \\ 5 & \cancel{0} & 3 & 8 \\ 0 & 1 & 0 & 4 \end{bmatrix}
\qquad
2 = \begin{bmatrix} 1 & \boxed{0} & 2 & 2 \\ 3 & \cancel{0} & 5 & 6 \\ 5 & \cancel{0} & 3 & 8 \\ \boxed{0} & 1 & \cancel{0} & 4 \end{bmatrix}
\qquad
2 = \begin{array}{c} \begin{bmatrix} 1 & 0 & 2 & 2 \\ 3 & 0 & 5 & 6 \\ 5 & 0 & 3 & 8 \\ 0 & 1 & 0 & 4 \end{bmatrix} \\ \begin{array}{cccc} 0 & 0 & 0 & 2 \end{array} \end{array}
$$

Step 5: Now examine columns until one is found that has only one unmarked zero. Make a square around it, and put an X through any other zeros in the same row. Repeat until all columns have been examined. In the example, the first column is the only one with just one zero in it.
If the result of Step 3 is a pattern of zeros with exactly

one "squared" zero in every row and column, then the matrix is an optimum solution. In this particular case 2 is not optimum. If it were optimum, Steps 5 through 10 could be skipped.

Step 6: In matrix 2 write the minimum number in each column under the column. (A minimum number can be zero as well as any other number.)

Step 7: Perform the same operations on columns which were performed on rows in Step 2 to form a new matrix 3. Check matrix 3. There is at least one zero in every column, which is as it should be.

$$3 = \begin{bmatrix} 1 & 0 & 2 & 0 \\ 3 & 0 & 5 & 4 \\ 5 & 0 & 3 & 6 \\ 0 & 1 & 0 & 2 \end{bmatrix} \qquad 3 = \begin{bmatrix} 1 & 0 & 2 & \boxed{0} \\ 3 & \boxed{0} & 5 & 4 \\ 5 & 0 & 3 & 6 \\ \boxed{0} & 1 & 0 & 2 \end{bmatrix} \qquad 3 = \begin{array}{c} \left[\begin{array}{cccc} 1 & 0 & 2 & \boxed{0} \\ 3 & \boxed{0} & 5 & 4 \\ 5 & 0 & 3 & 6 \\ \boxed{0} & 1 & 0 & 2 \end{array}\right]\begin{array}{c} \\ \\ \checkmark \\ \\ \end{array} \\ \begin{array}{cccc} & \checkmark & & \end{array} \end{array}$$

Step 8: Repeat Steps 3 - 7 to determine whether matrix 3 is an optimum solution. (It is not.)

Step 9: In the previous figure put a check mark at the right of each row which has no squared zero in it. (In the problem, this is Row 3 only.) Put a checkmark under each column which has a zero in a checked row.

Step 10: Make a check mark at the right of each row which has a <u>squared</u> zero in a checked column. All rows and columns which can be marked with a check are now marked. If they were not, Steps 9 and 10 would be repeated until all rows and columns which could be checked were checked.

$$3 = \begin{array}{c} \left[\begin{array}{cccc} 1 & 0 & 2 & \boxed{0} \\ 3 & \boxed{0} & 5 & 4 \\ 5 & 0 & 3 & 6 \\ \boxed{0} & 1 & 0 & 2 \end{array}\right]\begin{array}{c} \\ \checkmark \\ \checkmark \\ \\ \end{array} \\ \begin{array}{cccc} & \checkmark & & \end{array} \end{array} \qquad 3 = \begin{array}{c} \begin{bmatrix} 1 & 0 & 2 & \boxed{0} \\ 3 & \boxed{0} & 5 & 4 \\ 5 & 0 & 3 & 6 \\ \boxed{0} & 1 & 0 & 2 \end{bmatrix} \\ \begin{array}{cccc} & \checkmark & & \end{array} \end{array} \qquad 4 = \begin{bmatrix} 1 & 3 & 2 & 0 \\ 0 & 0 & 2 & 1 \\ 2 & 0 & 0 & 3 \\ 0 & 4 & 0 & 2 \end{bmatrix}$$

Step 11: Draw lines through all <u>un</u>checked rows and all <u>checked</u> columns. The number of lines should be the same as the number of squared zeros.

Step 12: Start to form a new matrix 4. If a number in the previous matrix has only one line through it, copy it into the same position in matrix 4. Repeat for every number in 3 which has just one line through it.

Step 13: Find the smallest number in matrix 3 with no line through it. (In this problem, the number is 3.)

Step 14: For each number in 3, with no line through it, subtract 3 (the number of Step 13) from it, and enter the remainder in the same position in 4.

Step 15: For each number in 3 which is at the intersection of two lines, add (the number of Step 13) to it, and enter the sum in the same position in 4.

Step 16: Test matrix 4 as in Steps 3-6. This time, it is an optimum solution.

$$4 = \begin{bmatrix} 1 & 3 & 2 & \boxed{0} \\ \boxed{0} & 0 & 2 & 1 \\ 2 & \boxed{0} & 0 & 3 \\ 0 & 4 & \boxed{0} & 2 \end{bmatrix} \qquad 5 = \begin{bmatrix} - & - & - & 9 \\ 5 & - & - & - \\ - & 1 & - & - \\ - & - & 2 & - \end{bmatrix}$$

Step 17: Go back to matrix 1. The "squared" zeros in 4 show which numbers to pick out of matrix 1. Put these numbers into a matrix 5 by themselves. This new matrix indicates that one optimum solution for the problem is to assign job J_1 to man M_4, job J_2 to man M_1, and so on. The numbers in the matrix show the cost-per-unit-of-output for each assignment indicated. The sum of these numbers, 17 cents, is the minimum total cost. This sum is the same for any of the optimum assignment patterns, if there is more than one.

• PROBLEM 5-32

Solve the following Assignment Problem.

original table			
40	60	60	70
10	60	70	30
20	50	40	20
30	20	10	40

Solution: Step 1a:

Select the smallest element in each row and subtract it from each row element. Repeat this for all rows.

Step 1b:

Select the smallest element in each column and subtract it from each column element. Repeat this procedure for the other columns.

Notice that at the end of Step 1a there is at least one zero element in each row, and at the end of Step 1b there is at least one zero element in each column.

In order to perform Step 1a, subtract 40 from the first row, 10 from the second row, 20 from the third row, and 10 from the fourth row. This is illustrated as follows.

subtraction	table at end of Step 1a			
−40	0	20	20	30
−10	0	50	60	20
−20	0	30	20	0
−10	20	10	0	30

In Step 1b it is not necessary to subtract 0 from the first, third, or fourth columns, but only 10 from the second column:

					table at end of Step 1b			
	0	20	20	30	0	10	20	30
	0	50	60	20	0	40	60	20
	0	30	20	0	0	20	20	0
	20	10	0	20	20	0	0	30
subtraction	−0	−10	−0	−0				

Step 2:

Next, cover the zeros with the smallest possible number of horizontal and vertical lines. For this problem, if n = 4 lines are necessary, an optimal solution has been reached. If less than four lines are used, proceed to Step 3.

Step 2 is verified by the following procedure. Determine the maximum number of possible zero assignments. This number is always equal to the number of minimal lines required to cover the zeros.

For example, the possible zero assignments are enclosed in a box in the following matrix:

[0]	10	20	30
0	40	60	20
0	20	20	[0]
20	[0]	0	30

Three zeros are assigned for n = 4. Thus all zeros can then be covered by three lines, as follows:

0	10	20	30
0	40	60	20
0	20	20	0
20	0	0	30

Three lines (one horizontal and two vertical) are required to cover the zeros. If at any iteration the number of lines is not equal to the number of possible zero assignments, this indicates either an arithmetic error, an error in locating the zero assignments, or an error in placing the covering lines.

Step 3:

For this step, which is used if less than n lines are drawn in Step 2, find the smallest uncovered number in the matrix. Add it to the elements in the covered rows and columns, and subtract it from all of the matrix elements. This step generates new zero elements, which provide additional possibilities for zero assignments.

The smallest uncovered number is 10. It is then necessary to add 10 to the fourth row and the first and fourth columns, and to subtract it from the entire matrix:

0	(10)	20	30	
0	40	60	20	
0	20	20	0	
20	0	0	30	+10

after adding 10 to row 4				after adding 10 to columns 1 and 4			
0	10	20	30	10	10	20	40
0	40	60	20	10	40	60	30
0	20	20	0	10	20	20	10
30	10	10	40	40	10	10	50
+10			+10				

After subtracting 10 from the matrix it appears as

0	0	10	30
0	30	50	20
0	10	10	0
30	0	0	40

Step 3 can be shortened by subtracting 10 from the uncovered numbers and adding it to the numers covered twice. The result is the same.
At the end of Step 3, Step 2 should be repeated. In Step 2 the minimal number of covering lines are drawn, which in this case is four.

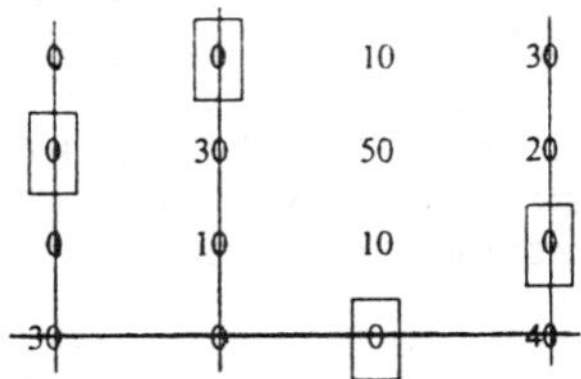

An optimal solution has now been reached. The solution of the assignment problem in terms of the original costs is

$$A2 + B1 + C4 + D3 = 60 + 10 + 20 + 10 = 100.$$

• PROBLEM 5-33

Seven projects are to be completed, and seven different contractors are requested to submit bids. Each contractor is capable of performing any of the projects, but can complete only one. It may be further noted that the bid of contractor i on each project j is c_{ij}. The bids are submitted in thousands of dollars, as

It is important to remember that each contractor can complete only one job. The objective function is to subcontract the jobs at a minimal cost.

Solve the Assignment Problem.

Contractor	Project 1	2	3	4	5	6	7
A	2	4	6	3	5	4	5
B	4	3	1	2	4	1	3
C	2	1	5	7	1	8	3
D	9	2	1	4	5	2	3
E	8	6	4	3	2	2	1
F	4	4	8	6	4	3	6
G	4	3	2	8	7	5	4

Solution: Step 1a:

Subtract 2, 1, 1, 1, 1, 3, 2 from the respective rows.

Step 1b:

Subtract 0, 0, 0, 1, 0, 0, 0 from the respective columns. The new cost matrix is

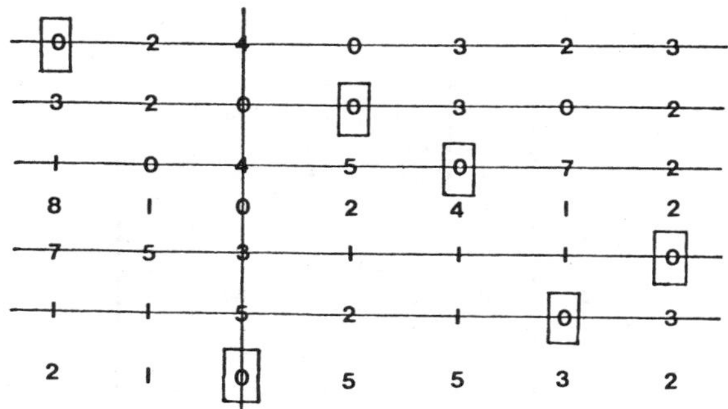

Step 2:

To cover the zeros only six lines are used. Since seven lines are necessary to provide an optimal solution, proceed to step 3.

Step 3:

The smallest uncovered number is 1. Therefore, subtract 1 from all uncovered numbers and add 1 to all numbers covered twice. The new cost matrix is

0	2	5	0	3	2	3
3	2	1	0	3	0	2
1	0	5	5	0	7	2
7	0	0	1	3	0	1
7	5	4	1	1	1	0
1	1	6	2	1	0	3
1	0	0	4	4	2	1

It is now possible to cover the zeros with seven lines, and an optimal solution has been reached. In terms of the original costs, the optimal solution is

$$A1 + B4 + C5 + D2 + E7 + F6 + G3$$

$$= 2 + 2 + 1 + 2 + 1 + 3 + 2 = 13 \quad \text{or} \quad \$13{,}000.$$

Note that the total row subtractions in Step 1a are 2 + 1 + 1 + 1 + 1 + 3 + 2 = 11, the column subtraction in Step 1b is 1, and the additional subtraction in Step 3 is 1, which results in a total of 11 + 1 + 1 = 13. The value subtracted from the rows and columns is always equal to the optimal solution.

• PROBLEM 5-34

A car hire company has one car at each of five depots a, b, c, d and e. A customer in each of the five towns A, B, C, D and E requires a car. The distances between the depots and the towns where the customers are, are given in Table 1.

How should the cars be assigned to the customers so as to minimize the distance travelled?

Table 1

	a	*b*	*c*	*d*	*e*
A	160	130	175	190	200
B	135	120	130	160	175
C	140	110	155	170	185
D	50	50	80	80	110
E	55	35	70	80	105

Distances between depots and customers (miles)

Solution: This problem could be solved using the transportation technique. However, only five of the routes will be used and so an additional four routes would have to be included at zero level in order to determine shadow costs and thus test for optimality.

The problem is to select five elements from the matrix of Table 1 such that there is one element in each row, one in each column, and the sum is the minimum possible.

Step 1. Subtract the smallest element in each row from every element in that row. This yields the following new matrix of distances:

Table 2

	a	*b*	*c*	*d*	*e*
A	30	0	45	60	70
B	15	0	10	40	55
C	30	0	45	60	75
D	0	0	30	30	60
E	20	0	35	45	70

Step 2. Subtract the smallest element in each column of Table 2 from every element in that column. This yields the following distance matrix:

Table 3

	a	*b*	*c*	*d*	*e*
A	30	0	35	30	15
B	15	0	0	10	0
C	30	0	35	30	20
D	0	0	20	0	5
E	20	0	25	15	15

Step 3. Test whether it is possible to make an assignment using only zero distances. If this is possible, clearly the assignment must be an optimal one, since no element in the matrix of Table 3 is negative. It can be shown that a "zero assignment" can only be made if the minimum number of horizon-

tal and vertical lines necessary to cover all zeros in the matrix equals the number of rows in the matrix--5 in this case. Applying this test to the matrix of Table 3, we find that three lines, suitably chosen, cover all zeros (see Table 4).

Table 4

	a	b	c	d	e
A	30	0	35	30	15
B	15	0	0	10	0
C	30	0	35	30	20
D	0	0	20	0	5
E	20	0	25	15	15

Table 5

	a	b	c	d	e
A	15	0	20	15	0
B	15	15	0	10	0
C	15	0	20	15	5
D	0	15	20	0	5
E	5	0	10	0	0

Thus a zero assignment is not possible at this stage.

Step 4.

(i) Find the smallest uncovered element as a result of Step 3. Call this element x.

(ii) Subtract x from every element in the matrix.

(iii) Re-add x to every element in all rows and columns covered by lines.

(iv) Re-apply the test of Step 3 to the resulting matrix. The effect of (ii) and (iii) above is to:

Subtract x from all uncovered elements, add x to elements at the intersection of two lines, and leave unchanged elements covered by one line.

Applying Step 4 to the matrix of Table 3 it is noted that x = 15, and the new matrix is given in Table 5.

The zeros in this matrix cannot be covered by fewer than five lines and hence a zero assignment is now possible. This is indicated below:

Table 6

	a	b	c	d	e
A	15	ø	20	15	**0**
B	15	15	**0**	10	ø
C	15	**0**	20	15	5
D	**0**	15	20	ø	5
E	5	ø	10	**0**	ø

To reach this assignment proceed as follows:

Columns 1 and 3 each contain only one zero. These zeros must, therefore, form part of the optimal assignment and are indicated in bold type. The additional zeros in rows 2 and 4 can now be crossed out as they cannot feature in the final assignment. This leaves column 4 with one zero remaining. This is indicated in bold type, the two other zeros in row 5 are crossed out. Column 5 now has one zero remaining and, when this is eliminated, the zero at the intersection of row 3 and column 2 completes the assignment.

The minimum assignment is therefore:

Route	Distance
Ae	200 miles
Bc	130
Cb	110
Da	50
Ed	80

Total distance travelled: 570 miles.

• PROBLEM 5-35

Find an optimal solution for this Assignment Problem.

5	4	6
9	3	7
3	2	1

Solution: For each row select the smallest number in that row and then subtract it from every element in that row. Repeat this step for all rows, entering the results in a new matrix.

The resulting new matrix is

1	0	2
6	0	4
2	1	0

For each column select the smallest number in that column and subtract it from every element in that column. Repeat for all columns, entering the results in a new matrix.

0	0	2
5	0	4
1	1	0

Search for a solution having all zero-cost assignments. If one is found, it is the optimum solution. The next part of this step is a procedure to determine that the current matrix does not have a solution with all zero-cost assignments.

Draw a set of lines through the rows or columns (each line covering one row or one column) such that all zero elements are covered using as few lines as possible. Let m represent the minimum number of lines that cover all zero elements at least once. If m < n then a solution with all zero-cost assignments is not present.

It is easy to find a zero cost in matrix (1). The solution is marked by circles around the elements used in the assignment:

(0)	0	2
5	(0)	4
1	1	(0)

This is an optimal solution. A quick search for other zero-cost solutions indicates that it is the unique optimum. The real total cost of this solution can be obtained most efficiently from the original cost matrix: 5 + 3 + 1 = 9. An alternative way to obtain it is by summation of all the subtractions performed up to this point: 4 + 3 + 1 + 1 + 0 + 0 = 9.

• PROBLEM 5-36

A department head has four subordinates, and four tasks to be performed. The subordinates differ in efficiency, and the tasks differ in their intrinsic difficulty. His estimate of the times each person would take to perform each task is given in the effectiveness matrix below. How should the tasks be allocated, one to a person, so as to minimize the total man-hours?

		Man			
		I	II	III	IV
Task	A	8	26	17	11
	B	13	28	4	26
	C	38	19	18	15
	D	19	26	24	10

Solution: Choose the smallest number in row A and subtract it from each element in the row. The result is:

0	18	9	3
13	28	4	26
38	19	18	15
19	26	24	10

Now proceed to subtract the minimum element in each row from all the elements in its row, yielding

0	18	9	3
9	24	0	22
23	4	3	0
9	16	14	0

Next, subtract the minimum element in each column from all the elements in its column, obtaining

0	14	9	3
9	20	0	22
23	0	3	0
9	12	14	0

The final step depends on the fact that, so long as the matrix consists of positive or zero elements, the total effectiveness cannot be negative for any assignment. If an assignment that has a zero total can be chosen, there cannot be an assignment with a lower total. In other words the total is certain to be minimum if all assignments can be made to positions where elements are zero.
Thus the following assignments are made:

A-I, B-III, C-II, D-IV.

These assignments will minimize the total number of man-hours for the original matrix.

• PROBLEM 5-37

Find two optimal solutions to the assignment problem of machines to jobs, with the given cost matrix.

	J_1	J_2	J_3	J_4
m_1	12	8	7	8
m_2	6	6	4	8
m_3	3	5	7	4
m_4	1	3	5	4

Solution: Subtract the minimum element in each row (or column) from all the elements in that row. In this way, the "reduced-cost" matrix given below is obtained.

	J_1	J_2	J_3	J_4
m_1	5	1	0	1
m_2	2	2	0	4
m_3	0	2	4	1
m_4	0	2	4	3

Jobs J_1 and J_3 have zero costs in machines m_3, m_4 and m_1, m_2, respectively. Assigning jobs to machines using only zero costs is not possible at this stage. Subtract the minimum element of each column (or row this time) which does not have any zeros.

	J_1	J_2	J_3	J_4
m_1	5	0	0	0
m_2	2	1	0	4
m_3	0	1	3	1
m_4	0	1	3	3

A feasible assignment is still not possible, because only three jobs can be assigned zero costs. At this stage, draw the minimum number of horizontal or vertical lines to cover all the zeros in the matrix. The number of lines gives the number of feasible assignments:

	J_1	J_2	J_3	J_4
m_1	5	0	0	0
m_2	2	1	0	4
m_3	0	1	3	1
m_4	0	1	3	3

From this matrix select the lowest uncrossed element, add it to those elements at the intersections of lines, and subtract it from all uncrossed elements:

	J_1	J_2	J_3	J_4
m_1	6	0	1	0
m_2	2	0	0	4
m_3	0	0	3	1
m_4	0	0	3	3

Now, feasible assignments are possible. One solution is $m_1 - J_4$, $m_2 - J_3$, $m_3 - J_2$, $m_4 - J_1$. Another solution is $m_1 - J_4$, $m_2 - J_3$, $m_3 - J_1$, $m_4 - J_2$.

• PROBLEM 5-38

A realtor has five purchasers for six sites. The ith purchaser is willing to pay price P_{ij} (or less) for the jth site. The values of P_{ij} are given in the following matrix. The realtor wishes to know which site to offer to each purchaser at what price so as to maximize his total receipts. Find the answer for him, and find his total revenue.

Purchaser \ Site	1	2	3	4	5	6
1	6	7	6	2	9	4
2	0	5	8	1	1	10
3	5	10	6	5	10	3
4	2	7	12	4	10	7
5	6	9	9	5	7	9

Solution: The first step in solving this problem is to balance it by adding a dummy purchaser. The site assigned to this fictitious purchaser will, in reality, go unsold. Therefore a profit of zero is generated. The dummy row will contain all zeros. The next step is to observe that the matrix represents profits, not costs, and the objective function is to be maximized. Therefore the conversion must be performed to reverse the magnitude. The largest entry is 12. The new cost matrix has entries obtained from the original matrix by subtraction from 12:

	1	2	3	4	5	6
1	6	5	6	10	3	8
2	12	7	4	11	11	2
3	7	2	6	7	2	9
4	10	5	0	8	2	5
5	6	3	3	7	5	3
6	12	12	12	12	12	12

Next row and column subtractions are performed. The result is

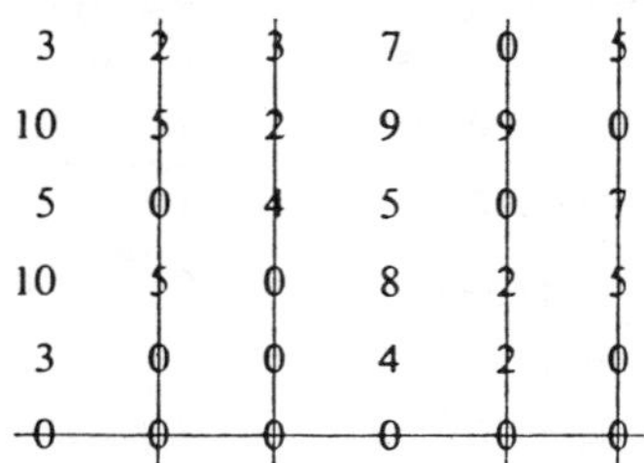

The minimum number of lines to cover all zero entries is 5, as shown. Therefore there is no solution present among the zero entries. The smallest uncovered entry is a 3. Subtract 3 from all uncovered elements. Add it to all twice covered elements. Do not change the singly covered elements.

[0]	2	3	4	(0)	5
7	5	2	6	9	[(0)]
2	(0)	4	2	[0]	7
7	5	[(0)]	5	2	5
(0)	[0]	0	1	2	0
0	3	3	[(0)]	3	3

Two optimal solutions are now present: One is marked by circles and the other by squares. Both give a total revenue of 47.

Find an optimal solution for the following Assignment Problem with initial costs:

-1	-2	3	4	5	1
2	-4	3	5	10	-1
4	3	-6	7	8	-1
3	2	5	7	9	4
2	4	0	3	7	-1
4	-3	0	2	7	8

and with the objective to maximize .

$$\sum_{i=1}^{6} \sum_{j=1}^{6} c_{ij}x_{ij}.$$

Solution: Transforming the cost array, using row and column operations, an equivalent minimization problem is obtained, and the beginning array then is

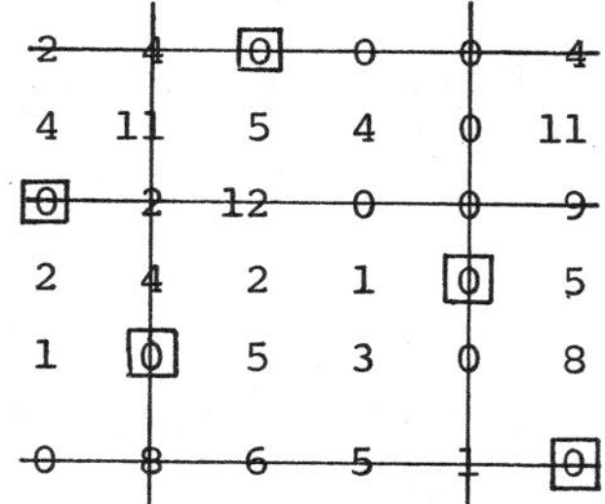

where have been indicated a minimal cover and a maximal independent subset.

The minimal uncovered element is 1, so subtract it from every uncovered row and add it to every covered column, obtaining

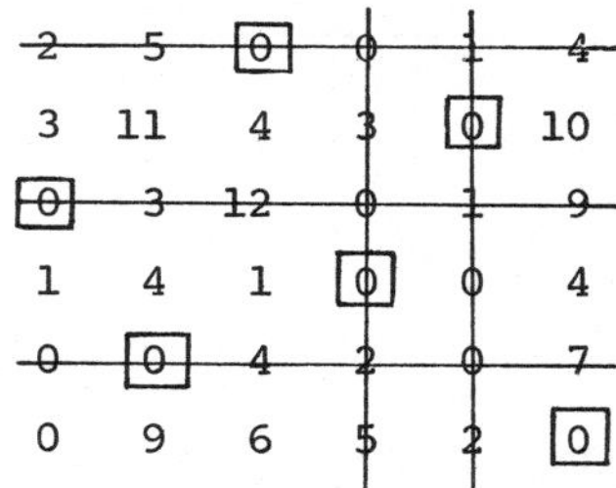

For this array, a minimal cover, one of which has been shown, has six elements. Also show a maximal independent set of zero positions. An optimal solution is
$x^*_{13} = x^*_{25} = x^*_{31} = x^*_{44} = x^*_{52} = x^*_{66} = 1$

$x^*_{ij} = 0$, all other i,j

and the optimal objective function value is 3 + 10 + 4 + 7 + 4 + 8 = 36.

Solve the assignment problem for which the cost matrix is

Jobs

Persons	1	2	3	4	5
1	5	3	4	7	1
2	2	3	7	6	5
3	4	1	5	2	4
4	6	8	1	2	3
5	4	2	5	7	1

Solution: Step I

Subtract minimum element in each row from every element in its row. One gets

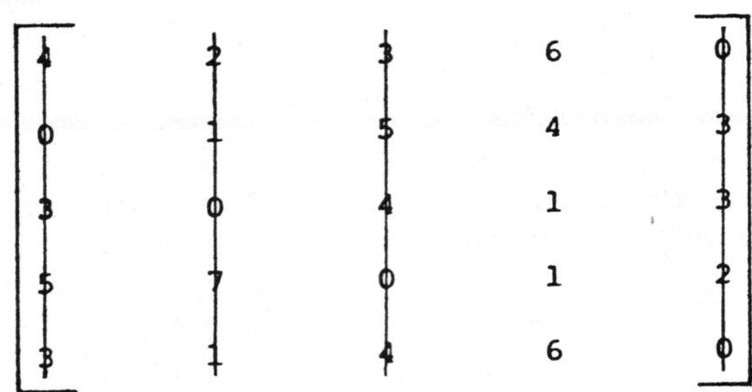

here $n_1 = 4 < n = 5$.

Step II

Subtract the minimum element in each column from every element in its column.

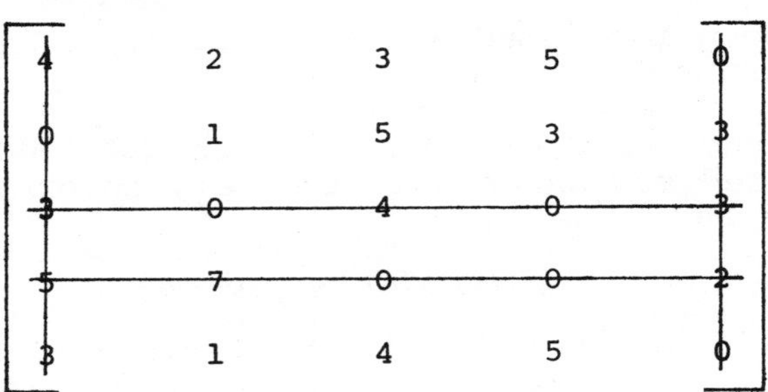

here $n_2 = 4 < n = 5$.

Step III

The minimum element not covered by any line is 1. Subtract 1 from the elements not covered by any line and add it to those which lie at the intersection of lines. The matrix thus obtained is

$$\begin{vmatrix} 4 & 1 & 2 & 4 & (0) \\ (0) & 0 & 4 & 2 & 3 \\ 4 & 0 & 4 & (0) & 4 \\ 0 & 7 & (0) & 0 & 3 \\ 3 & (0) & 3 & 4 & 0 \end{vmatrix}$$

Here $n_3 = 5 = n$, and a solution to assignment problem is given by the bracketted (0)'s which are obtained as follows: assign job 1 to person 2, job 2 to person 5, job 3 to person 4, job 4 to person 3, and job 5 to person 1.

The minimum cost for this assignment is

$$= 2 + 2 + 1 + 2 + 1 = 8.$$

• PROBLEM 5-41

Find a feasible solution for the assignment problem:

Table 1

	Jobs					
Men	1	2	3	4	5	Available
1	2	9	2	7	1	1
2	6	8	7	6	1	1
3	4	6	5	3	1	1
4	4	2	7	3	1	1
5	5	3	9	5	1	1
Required	1	1	1	1	1	5

Solution: Start by subtracting the smallest element from each row, and then do the same for each column. The results are shown in Table 2. A total of 10 was subtracted from the rows and columns. Therefore, any solution that is obtained by using Table 2 must have 10 added to it for its proper evaluation.

First look for a solution involving only those cells in Table 2 that have zero entries, for such a solution would be the best one possible. There may be several solutions, however, that are equally good. In this case, no such solution can be found. A feasible solution is indicated in Table 2b by the cells whose entries are enclosed in parentheses. But to determine whether an improvement is possible, the following procedure can be used.

Draw the minimum number of horizontal and vertical lines necessary to cover all zeros at least once. Carrying out this step on Table 2 gives the result shown in Table 3.

Table 2

	(a)							(b)					
	1	2	3	4	5	Subtracted		1	2	3	4	5	Subtracted
1	1	8	1	6	0	1	1	0	7	(0)	4	0	1
2	5	7	6	5	0	1	2	(4)	6	5	3	0	1
3	3	5	4	2	0	1	3	2	4	3	(0)	0	1
4	3	1	6	2	0	1	4	2	(0)	5	0	0	1
5	4	2	8	4	0	1	5	3	1	7	2	(0)	1
						Subtracted		1	1	1	2	1	

Table 3

	1	2	3	4	5
1	0	7	0	4	0
2	4	6	5	3	0
3	2	4	3	0	0
4	2	0	5	0	0
5	3	1	7	2	0

Note that only four lines are used; hence there is no optimal solution among the zero cells.

Select the smallest number that does not have a line through it. In this problem, it is 1 in (5,2).

Subtract this number from all elements that have no lines through them and add it to all elements that have two lines through them. In this problem this yields the result shown in Table 4. This procedure must add a zero where one did not previously exist; in this case in (5,2).

Try for a solution among the new set of zeros. (In this case one cannot be found.) If one cannot be found, continue until a solution is found. Continuing the problem, the results shown in Table 5 are obtained.

Table 4

	1	2	3	4	5
1	0	7	0	4	1
2	3	5	4	2	0
3	2	4	3	0	1
4	2	0	5	0	1
5	2	0	6	1	0

Table 5

	1	2	3	4	5
1	0	7	0	4	1
2	3	5	4	2	0
3	2	4	3	0	1
4	2	0	5	0	1
5	2	0	6	1	0

Table 6

	1	2	3	4	5
1	0	9	(0)	6	3
2	1	5	2	2	(0)
3	0	4	1	(0)	1
4	0	(0)	3	0	1
5	(0)	0	4	1	0

The smallest uncovered number is now 2. Therefore, next obtain Table 6. A solution, as indicated by the parenthesis, can be found here. Its value is 13, which is an improvement of 1 over the initial feasible solution.

• PROBLEM 5-42

Find the optimum solution to this assignment problem:

3	5	7	1
9	8	12	10
13	8	14	2
5	7	10	6

Solution: After doing the first two steps, row and column subtractions, the cost matrix then becomes the following:

2	4	2	0
1	0	0	2
11	6	8	0
0	2	1	1

The zero elements of this matrix can be covered by three lines but not by two. Hence $m = 3$ while $n = 4$. Since $m < n$, then a zero-cost solution is not present.

Select the smallest uncovered element. Subtract it from all uncovered elements. Add it to all twice-covered elements. Do not change the singly covered elements.

The smallest uncovered element in this matrix is a 2. This

yields

0	2	(0)	0
1	(0)	0	4
9	4	6	(0)
(0)	2	1	3

Now a zero-cost solution is found. Examination for alternative assignments shows that this solution is the unique optimum. Its total cost, by reference to the original matrix, is 5 + 8 + 7 + 2 = 22.

• PROBLEM 5-43

Find an optimal solution for the assignment problem in Table 1.

TABLE 1

	1	2	3	4
1	4	8	12	6
2	18	7	10	9
3	8	5	11	7
4	16	7	8	5

Solution: Using row operations, obtain Table 2.

Using column operations, obtain Table 3.

TABLE 2

	1	2	3	4
1	0	4	8	2
2	11	0	3	2
3	3	0	6	2
4	11	2	3	0

TABLE 3

	1	2	3	4
1	0	4	5	2
2	11	0	0	2
3	3	0	3	2
4	11	2	0	0

TABLE 4

	1	2	3	4
1	0	4	5	2
2	11	0	0	2
3	3	0	3	2
4	11	2	0	0

TABLE 5

	1	2	3	4
1	[0]	4	5	2
2	11	0	[0]	2
3	3	[0]	3	2
4	11	2	0	[0]

A feasible assignment to the zero elements is possible in this case. When one draws a minimum number of lines through some of the rows and columns such that all zeros are crossed out, one gets four lines of such sort. Thus, Table 4 implies the assignments in Table 5, denoted by boxes.

CHAPTER 6

INTEGER PROGRAMMING

PROBLEM FORMULATION

• PROBLEM 6-1

An assembly line consisting of a collection of work stations has to perform a series of jobs in order to assemble a product. At each work station one or more of the jobs may be performed. Normally there are some restrictions on the order in which jobs may be done. These are called precedence relations, and there is a limit on the time a product can stay at any particular work station. Consider a product with 5 jobs. The decision involves allocating each job to a work station so that the number of work stations is minimized. Table 1 gives the jobs, any precedence relations that exist, and the time needed to complete each job.

Job i is either done at station j, or it is not done at station j. This is an either/or type situation which fits in well with zero-one variables.

$$\text{Let } x_{ij} = \begin{cases} 1 & \text{if i is done at station j} \\ 0 & \text{if i is not done at station j.} \end{cases}$$

Forumulate as an integer program.

Table 1

Data for assembly line balancing.

Job i	Time (p_i) in minutes	Predecessors
1	6	—
2	5	—
3	7	—
4	6	3
5	5	2,4

Solution: Assume that there are 4 stations and the maximum time at each work station is 12 minutes. There is the following time constraint on each solution:

$$\sum_{i=1}^{5} p_i x_{ij} \leq 12, \qquad j = 1,\ldots,4 \tag{1}$$

(i.e., the time taken for jobs assigned to station j must be less than 12 minutes.) Equations (1) expand to

$$\begin{aligned}
6x_{11} + 5x_{21} + 7x_{31} + 6x_{41} + 5x_{51} &\leq 12 \\
6x_{12} + 5x_{22} + 7x_{32} + 6x_{42} + 5x_{52} &\leq 12 \\
6x_{13} + 5x_{23} + 7x_{33} + 6x_{43} + 5x_{53} &\leq 12 \\
6x_{14} + 5x_{24} + 7x_{34} + 6x_{44} + 5x_{54} &\leq 12.
\end{aligned} \tag{2}$$

Next, handle precedence relations between jobs. By saying that job 3 must be done before job 4, that means that job 3 must be performed either at the same station as job 4 or at a prior station. Job i has been done at or before station k, if

$$\sum_{j=1}^{k} x_{ij} = 1,$$

and has not been done if

$$\sum_{j=1}^{k} x_{ij} = 0.$$

At station k, if

$$\sum_{j=1}^{k} x_{4j} \leq \sum_{j=1}^{k} x_{3j},$$

then job 4 cannot be done unless job 3 has been done because

$$\sum_{j=1}^{k} x_{4j} = 1$$

only if

$$\sum_{j=1}^{k} x_{3j} = 1.$$

For the precedence relations to be satisfied this must hold at all stations. Therefore

$$\sum_{j=1}^{k} x_{4j} \le \sum_{j=1}^{k} x_{3j}, \qquad k = 1,\ldots,4. \tag{3}$$

If neither job is done by station k, expression (3) holds trivially (i.e., $0 \le 0$), and it also holds if both jobs have been done (i.e., $1 \le 1$).

The precedence relations for job 5 are

$$\left.\begin{aligned} \sum_{j=1}^{k} x_{5j} &\le \sum_{j=1}^{k} x_{2j} \\ \sum_{j=1}^{k} x_{5j} &\le \sum_{j=1}^{k} x_{4j} \end{aligned}\right\} \qquad k = 1,\ldots,4. \tag{4}$$

It is also necessary to ensure that each job is done once and only once:

$$\sum_{j=1}^{k} x_{ij} = 1, \qquad i = 1,\ldots,5. \tag{5}$$

The objective is to find the minimum number of stations to set up. This is achieved by allocating a lower "cost" to job i if it is done at station 1 than if it is done at station 2, etc. By minimizing these costs, the jobs are forced to the earliest possible work stations. The costs are arbitrary if a cost of j is given to x_{ij} (= job i done at station j). Thus

$$\text{minimize } z = \sum_{i=1}^{5} x_{i1} + 2\sum_{i=1}^{5} x_{i2} + 3\sum_{i=1}^{5} x_{i3} + 4\sum_{i=1}^{5} x_{i4} \tag{6}$$

The collection of equations (2) to (6), together with the nonnegativity and integrality conditions on the variables

$$x_{ij} \ge 0 \text{ and integer}$$

make up the integer program for this problem. There is no need to put an upper limit of 1 on each x_{ij}; equation (4) does that implicitly.

• PROBLEM 6-2

A large company wishes to move some of its departments out of Boston. There are benefits to be derived from doing this (cheaper housing, government incentives, easier recruitment, etc.) which have been costed. Also, however, there will be greater costs of communication between departments. These have also been costed for all possible locations of each department.

The company comprises 5 departments (A,B,C,D,E). The possible cities for reallocation are Newark, Stamford or a department may be kept in Boston. None of these cities (including Boston) may be the location of more than 3 of the departments.

Benefits to be derived from each relocation are given below (in thousands of dollars per year).

	A	B	C	D	E
Newark	10	15	10	20	5
Stamford	10	20	15	15	15

Communication costs are of the form $C_{ik}D_{jl}$, where

C_{ik} = quantity of communication between departments i and k per year

D_{jl} = cost per unit of communication between cities j and l

C_{ik} and D_{jl} are given by the tables below:

Quantities of communication C_{ik} (in thousands of units)

	A	B	C	D	E
A		0·0	1·0	1·5	0·0
B			1·4	1·2	0·0
C				0·0	2·0
D					0·7

Costs per unit of communication D_{jl} (in $)

	Newark	Stamford	Boston
Newark	5	14	13
Stamford		5	9
Boston			10

Formulate this problem as a zero-one integer programming problem to answer the question of where each department should be located so as to minimize overall yearly cost.

Solution: This is a modified form of the quadratic assignment problem. It can be solved by linearizing the quadratic terms and reducing the problem to a 0-1 integer programming problem.

Variables:

$$\delta_{ij} = \begin{cases} 1 & \text{if department } i \text{ is located in city } j \text{ (i=A,B,C,D,E, j=L (Boston), S (Newark), G (Stamford))} \\ 0 & \text{otherwise} \end{cases}$$

There are 15 such 0-1 variables.

$$\gamma_{ijkl} = \begin{cases} 1 & \text{if } \delta_{ij} = 1 \text{ and } \delta_{kl} = 1 \\ 0 & \text{otherwise} \end{cases}$$

γ_{ijkl} is only defined for $i < k$ and $C_{ik} \neq 0$.

There are 54 such 0-1 variables.

Constraints:

Each department must be located in exactly one city. This gives constraints:

$$\sum_j \delta_{ij} = 1 \quad \text{for all } i.$$

There are 5 such constraints.

No city may be the location for more than 3 departments. This gives constraints:

$$\sum_i \delta_{ij} \leq 3 \quad \text{for all } j.$$

There are 3 such constraints.

Using the variables δ_{ij} together with the two types of constraint above one could formulate a model with an objective function involving some quadratic terms δ_{ij}, δ_{kl}. Instead these terms are replaced by the 0-1 variables γ_{ijkl} giving a linear objective function. It is, however, necessary to relate these new variables to the δ_{ij} variables correctly. To do this, model the relations:

$$\gamma_{ijkl} = 1 \rightarrow \delta_{ij} = 1, \delta_{kl} = 1$$

and

$$\delta_{ij} = 1, \delta_{kl} = 1 \rightarrow \gamma_{ijkl} = 1$$

The first conditions can be achieved by the following constraints:

$$\gamma_{ijkl} - \delta_{ij} \leq 0 \quad \text{for all } i, j, k, l$$

$$\gamma_{ijkl} - \delta_{kl} \leq 0 \quad \text{for all } i, j, k, l$$

There are 108 such constraints.

The second conditions are achieved by the constraints:

$$\delta_{ij} + \delta_{kl} - \gamma_{ijkl} \leq 1 \quad \text{for all } i, j, k, l.$$

There are 54 such constraints.

Objective:

The objective is to minimize:

$$-\sum_{i,j} G_{ij}\delta_{ij} + \sum_{i,j,k,l} C_{ik}D_{jl}\gamma_{ijkl}$$

where G_{ij} is the benefit to be gained from locating department i in city j (for j = L (Boston) G_{ij} = 0).

This model has 170 constraints and 69 variables (all 0-1).

The problem can be modeled more compactly and the branching strategy can be used to avoid expanding other constraints. The optimal solution is:

Locate departments A and D in Newark

Locate departments B, C, and E in Stamford.

This results in a yearly benefit of $80,000 but communications costs of $65,100. It is interesting to note that communication costs are also reduced by moving out of Boston in this problem since they would have been $78,000 if each department had remained in Boston.

The net yearly benefit (benefits less communication costs) is therefore $14,900.

• PROBLEM 6-3

A company is planning its capital spending for the next T periods. There are N projects which compete for the limited capital B_i available for investment in period i. Each project requires a certain investment in each period once it is selected. Let a_{ij} be the required investment in project j for period i. The value of the project is measured in terms of the associated cash flows in each period discounted for inflation. This is called the net present value (NPV). Let v_j denote the NPV for project j. The problem is to select the proper projects for investment which will maximize the total value (NPV) of all the projects selected.

Solution: To formulate this as an integer program, introduce a binary variable for each project to denote whether it is selected or not.

Let

$x_j = 1$ if project j is selected

$x_j = 0$ if project j is not selected.

The following pure integer program will represent the capital budgeting problem:

$$\text{Maximize} \quad Z = \sum_{j=1}^{N} v_j x_j$$

$$\text{Subject to} \quad \sum_{j=1}^{N} a_{ij} x_j \leq B_i \qquad \text{for } i = 1, \ldots, T$$

$0 \leq x_j \leq 1$, x_j a binary variable for all $j = 1, \ldots, N$.

• PROBLEM 6-4

Logical circuits have a given number of inputs and one output. Impulses may be applied to the inputs of a given logical circuit and it will either respond by giving an output (signal 1) or will give no output (signal 0). The imput impulses are of the same kind as the outputs, i.e., (positive input) or 0 (no input).

In this problem a logical circuit is to be built up of NOR gates. A NOR gate is a device with 2 inputs and 1 output. It has the property that there is positive output (signal 1) if and only if neither input is positive, i.e. both inputs have value 0. By connecting such gates together with outputs from one gate possibly being inputs into another gate it is possible to construct a circuit to perform any desired logical function. For example the circuit illustrated in Figure 1 will respond to the inputs A and B in the way indicated by the truth table.

The problem is to construct a circuit using the minimum number of NOR gates which will perform the logical function specified by the truth table in Figure 2. Set up an integer programming model that will solve this problem.

'Fan-in' and 'fan-out' are not permitted. That is, more than one output from a nor gate cannot lead into one input. Nor can one output lead into more than one input.

It may be assumed throughout that the optimal design is a 'subnet' of the 'maximal' net shown in Figure 3.

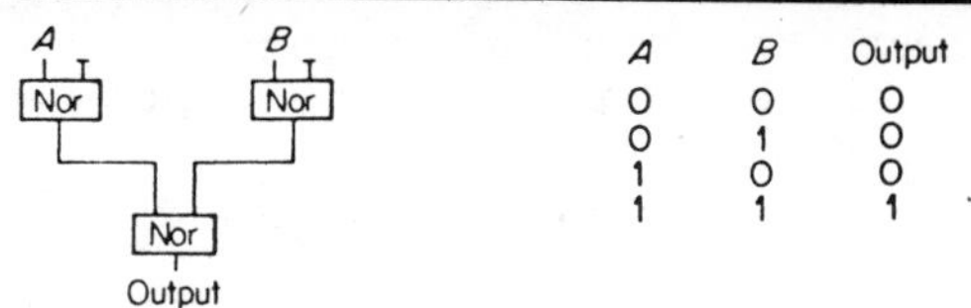

A	B	Output
0	0	0
0	1	0
1	0	0
1	1	1

Fig. 1

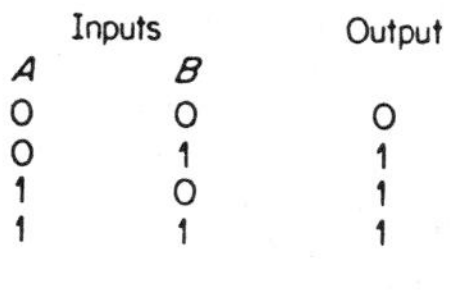

Fig. 2

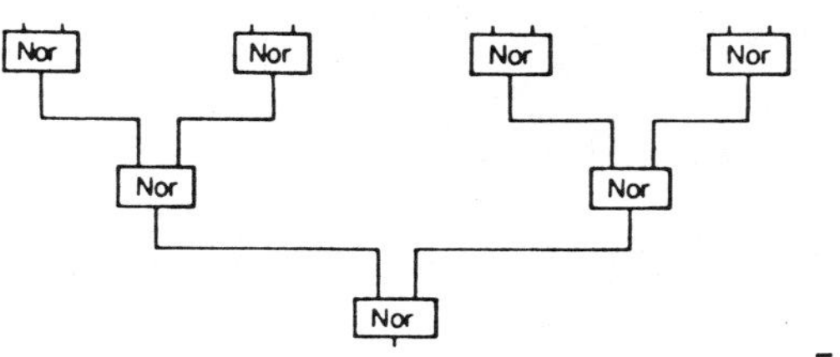

Fig. 3

Solution: The following 0-1 integer variables are used:

$$s_i = \begin{cases} 1 & \text{if NOR gate } i \text{ exists, } i = 1, 2, \ldots, 7 \\ 0 & \text{otherwise} \end{cases}$$

$$t_{i1} = \begin{cases} 1 & \text{if external input A is an input to gate } i \\ 0 & \text{otherwise} \end{cases}$$

$$t_{i2} = \begin{cases} 1 & \text{if external input B is an input to gate } i \\ 0 & \text{otherwise} \end{cases}$$

x_{ij} = output from gate i for the combination of external input signals specified in the jth row of the truth table.

The following constraints are imposed.

A NOR gate can only have an external input if it exists. These conditions are imposed by the constraints:

$$s_i - t_{i1} \le 0$$

$$s_i - t_{i2} \le 0 \qquad i = 1, 2, \ldots, 7.$$

If a NOR gate has one (or two) external inputs leading into it only one (or no) NOR gates can feed into it. These conditions are imposed by the constraints:

$$s_j + s_k + t_{i1} + t_{i2} \le 2 \qquad i = 1, 2, 3$$

where j and k are the two NOR gates leading into i in Figure 3.

The output signal from NOR gate i must be the correct logical function (nor) of the input signals into gate i if gate i exists. Let α_j (a constant) be the value of the external input signal A in the jth row of the truth table. Similarly α_{2j} corresponds to the external input signal B. These restrictions give:

$$x_{j\ell} + x_{i\ell} \leq 1$$

$$x_{k\ell} + x_{i\ell} \leq 1$$

$$\alpha_{1\ell} t_i{}^{\ell} + x_i{}^{\ell} \leq 1 \qquad i = 1, 2, \ldots, 7$$

$$\alpha_{2\ell} t_{i2} + x_{i\ell} \leq 1 \qquad \ell = 1, 2, 3, 4$$

where j and k are the two NOR gates leading into gate i in Figure 3. Since the α_{ij} are constants some of the above constraints are redundant for particular values of ℓ and may be ignored.

If there is an output signal of 1 from a particular NOR gate for any combination of the input signals then that gate must exist.

$$s_i - x_{i\ell} \geq 0 \qquad i = 1, 2, \ldots, 7 \quad \ell = 1, 2, 3, 4$$

The objective is to minimize $\Sigma_i s_i$.

This model has 114 constraints and 45 variables (all 0-1).

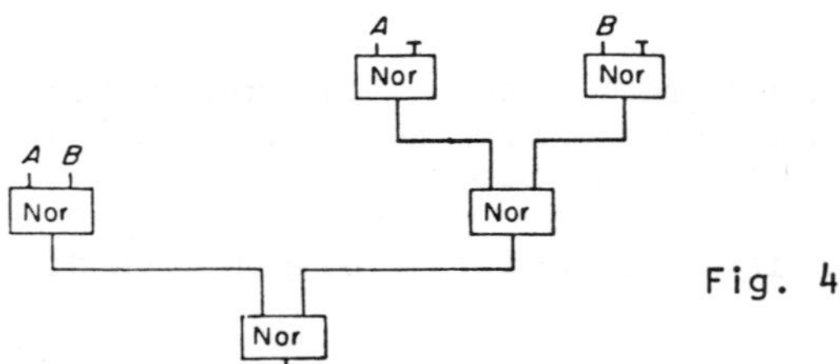

Fig. 4

• PROBLEM 6-5

Twenty-seven cells are arranged in a (3 x 3 x 3)-dimensional array as shown in Figure 1.

Three cells are regarded as lying in the same line if they are on the same horizontal or vertical line or the same diagonal. Diagonals exist on each horizontal and vertical section and connecting opposite vertices of the cube. (There are 49 lines altogether.)

Given 13 white balls (noughts) and 14 black balls (crosses), construct an integer programming model that would arrange them, one to a cell, so as to minimize the number of lines with balls all of one color.

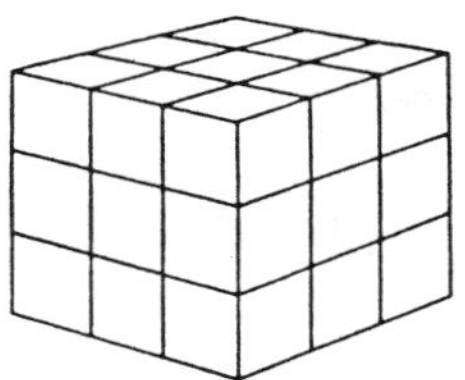

Fig. 1

Solution: This "pure" problem typifies the combinatorial character of quite a lot of integer programming problems. Clearly there are an enormous number of ways of arranging the balls in the three-dimensional array. Such problems often prove difficult to solve as integer programming models. There is an advantage to using a heuristic solution first. This solution can then be used to obtain a cut-off value for the branch and bound tree search. A formulation is described as follows:

Variables:

The cells are numbered 1 to 27. It is convenient to number sequentially row by row and section by section. Associated with each cell a 0-1 variable δ_j is introduced with the following interpretation :

$$\delta_j = \begin{cases} 1 & \text{if cell j contains a black ball} \\ 0 & \text{if cell j contains a white ball} \end{cases}$$

There are 27 such 0-1 variables.

There are 49 possible lines in the cube. With each of these lines a 0-1 variable γ_i is associated with the following interpretations:

$$\gamma_i = \begin{cases} 1 & \text{if all the balls in the line i are of the same color} \\ 0 & \text{if there are a mixture of colors of ball in line i} \end{cases}$$

There are 49 such 0-1 variables.

Constraints:

To ensure that the values of the variables γ_i truly represent the conditions above, we have to model the condition:

$$\gamma_i = 0 \rightarrow \delta_{i1} + \delta_{i2} + \delta_{i3} \geq 1 \quad \text{and}$$

$$\delta_{i1} + \delta_{i2} + \delta_{i3} \leq 2$$

where i1, i2, and i3 are the numbers of the cells in line i.

This condition can be modelled by the constraints

$$\delta_{i1} + \delta_{i2} + \delta_{i3} - \gamma_i \leq 2$$

$$\delta_{i1} + \delta_{i2} + \delta_{i3} + \gamma_i \geq 1$$

$$i = 1,2,\ldots,49$$

In fact these constraints do not ensure that if $\gamma_i = 1$ all balls will be of the same color in the line. When the objective is formulated it will be clear that this condition will be guaranteed by optimality.

In order to limit the black balls to 14 we impose the constraint:

$$\sum_j \delta_j = 14.$$

There are a total of 99 constraints.

Objective:

In order to minimize the number of lines with balls of a similar color we minimize

$$\sum_j \gamma_j.$$

In total this model has 99 constraints and 76 0-1 variables. The model is completed.

The computer solution to the model is:

The minimum number of lines of the same color is 4. There are many alternative solutions one of which is given in Figure 2, where the top, middle, and bottom sections of the cube are given. Cells with black balls are shaded.

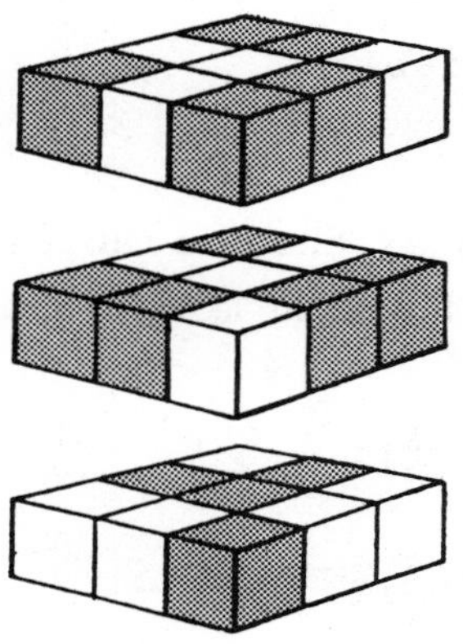

Fig. 2

• PROBLEM 6-6

Solve the following problem in integer programming:

Find non-negative integers X_{ij} which will

Minimize $200X_{11} + 300X_{12} + 250X_{21} + 100\ X_{22} + 250\ X_{31} + 250X_{32}$

subject to:

$$X_{11} + X_{21} + X_{31} \geq 30$$

$$X_{12} + X_{22} + X_{32} \geq 20$$

$$-X_{11} - X_{12} \geq -20$$

$$-X_{21} - X_{22} \geq -20$$

$$-X_{31} - X_{32} \geq -20.$$

Solution: Since some of the constraints are negative the simplex algorithm cannot be applied to the given problem. However, the dual, which is a maximization problem, is receptive to the simplex technique. The dual is

Maximize $30y_1 + 20y_2 - 20y_3 - 20y_4 - 20y_5$

subject to:

$$y_1 - y_3 \leq 200$$

$$y_2 - y_3 \leq 300$$

$$y_1 - y_4 \leq 250$$

$$y_2 - y_4 \leq 100$$

$$y_1 - y_5 \leq 250$$

$$y_2 - y_5 \leq 250$$

$$y_1, y_2, \ldots, y_5 \geq 0.$$

The inequalities cannot be converted to equalities by adding six slack variables

$y_6, y_7, y_8, y_9, y_{10}, y_{11}$.

An initial basic feasible solution is obtained by setting $y_1 = y_2 = y_3 = y_4 = y_5 = 0$. The simplex tableau is then

	v_1	v_2	v_3	v_4	v_5	v_6	v_7	v_8	v_9	v_{10}	v_{11}	b
v_6	1	0	-1	0	0	1	0	0	0	0	0	200
v_7	0	1	-1	0	0	0	1	0	0	0	0	300
v_8	1	0	0	-1	0	0	0	1	0	0	0	250
v_9	0	1	0	-1	0	0	0	0	1	0	0	100
v_{10}	1	0	0	0	-1	0	0	0	0	1	0	250
v_{11}	0	1	0	0	-1	0	0	0	0	0	1	250
d	-30	-20	20	20	20	0	0	0	0	0	0	0

Since -30 is the largest negative entry and 200/1 is the minimum positive ratio, replace v_6 by v_1 in the basis on the left. Thus pivoting on the first element in the first column to obtain

	v_1	v_2	v_3	v_4	v_5	v_6	v_7	v_8	v_9	v_{10}	v_{11}	b
v_1	1	0	-1	0	0	1	0	0	0	0	0	200
v_7	0	1	-1	0	0	0	1	0	0	0	0	300
v_8	0	0	1	-1	0	-1	0	1	0	0	0	50
v_9	0	(1)	0	-1	0	0	0	0	1	0	0	100
v_{10}	0	0	1	0	-1	-1	0	0	0	1	0	50
v_{11}	0	1	0	0	-1	0	0	0	0	0	0	250
d	0	-20	-10	20	20	30	0	0	0	0	0	6,000

Now replace v_9 by v_2 to obtain a new basic feasible solution. Pivoting on the encircled element:

	v_1	v_2	v_3	v_4	v_5	v_6	v_7	v_8	v_9	v_{10}	v_{11}	b
v_1	1	0	-1	0	0	1	0	0	0	0	0	200
v_7	0	0	-1	1	0	0	1	0	-1	0	0	200
v_8	0	0	1	-1	0	-1	0	1	0	0	0	50
v_2	0	1	0	-1	0	0	0	0	1	0	0	100
v_{10}	0	0	(1)	0	-1	-1	0	0	0	1	0	50
v_{11}	0	0	0	1	-1	0	0	0	-1	0	1	50
d	0	0	-10	0	20	30	0	0	20	0	0	8,000

The only negative entry is under v_3. Notice that the ratios of b to v_8 and of b to v_{10} are both the same, i.e. 50/1. By the rules of the simplex algorithm, choose either v_8 or v_{10} for liquidation. Choose to replace

v_{10} by v_3 and hence pivot on the encircled element. The next tableau is

	v_1	v_2	v_3	v_4	v_5	v_6	v_7	v_8	v_9	v_{10}	v_{11}	b
v_1	1	0	0	0	-1	0	0	0	0	1	0	250
v_7	0	0	0	1	-1	-1	1	0	1	1	0	250
v_8	0	0	0	-1	1	0	0	1	0	-1	0	0
v_2	0	1	0	-1	0	0	0	0	1	0	0	100
v_3	0	0	1	0	-1	-1	0	0	0	1	0	50
v_{11}	0	0	0	1	-1	0	0	0	-1	0	1	50
d	0	0	0	0	10	20	0	0	20	10	0	8,500

Since there are no more negative entries in the last row the algorithm has converged to a solution. The maximum feasible solution is 8,500. Therefore the mimimum feasible solution is also 8,500. At this value, the values of X_{ij} are read off from the slack variable values in the last row. Thus, $x_{11}=20$, $x_{12}= 0$, $x_{21}= 0$, $x_{22}= 22$, $x_{31}= 10$, $z_{32}= 0$. Note that the main body of the simplex tableau consisted only of ones and of zeros. It makes pivoting easier and also ensures that the solution values will be integers.

• PROBLEM 6-7

A railway management runs trains with

(a) 4 first-class and 4 second-class carriages

6 " " 3 " " "

2 " " 5 " " "

and the income from these types of trains is in the proportion 5 : 6 : 4. The management has altogether 22 first-class and 25 second-class carriages at its disposal. How many trains of each type should be run?

(b) Solve the same problem with types

6 first-class and 4 second-class carriages

6 " " 6 " " "

5 " " 7 " " "

when the income is in the proportions 26 : 30 : 19, and the management has 33 first-class and 37 second-class carriages at its disposal. Solve by the simplex method.

Solution: Formulations:

(a) $4x_1 + 6x_2 + 2x_3 \leq 22$ (b) $6x_1 + 6x_2 + 5x_3 \leq 33$

$4x_1 + 3x_2 + 5x_3 \leq 25$ $4x_1 + 6x_2 + 7x_3 \leq 37$

Maximize $5x_1 + 6x_2 + 4x_3$, Maximize $26x_1 + 30x_2 + 19x_3$,

$x_j \geq 0$, integer. $x_j \geq 0$, integer.

Answers:

$x_1 = 1,\ x_2 = 2,\ x_3 = 3$ $x_1 = 0,\ x_2 = 5,\ x_3 = 0$.

or $x_1 = 5,\ x_2 = 0,\ x_3 = 1$.

Objective function: 29. Objective function: 150.

All carriages are used in case (a).

In case (b), not all carriages are being used. The management could make up 1 train of the first type, 2 trains of the second type, and 3 trains of the third type, thus using all available carriages, but the income would be 143 against 150 in the optimal solution.

• PROBLEM 6-8

Maximize $f(x_1, x_2) = 3x_1 + 13x_2$

subject to:

$2x_1 + 9x_2 \leq 40$

$11x_1 - 8x_2 \leq 82$

$x_1, x_2 \geq 0$ and integer.

Solve by the simplex method first, ignoring the integer requirements. Try to approximate an integer solution by using the result of the simplex algorithm. Also solve by graphical means, and compare with the continuous solution obtained from the simplex tableaux.

Solution: If the integer restrictions are ignored the simplex algorithm can be applied (after adding slack variables x_3 and x_4). From the tableaux of Table 1, the maximum value of f for the simple linear programming problem is $58\frac{4}{5}$ and is attained at the point $(9\frac{1}{5}, 2\frac{2}{5})$. Now, for the original problem with the integer restricted variables, if would seem reasonable that the above solution point $(9\frac{1}{2}, 2\frac{2}{5})$ be rounded off to (9, 2) or maybe (10, 2), or (10, 3) or (9, 3). However none of these four points are feasible; the first three do not satisfy the second inequality, and the last two do not satisfy the first. Thus the simplex algorithm has provided us with no useful information, and it is not all clear how one could proceed in general.

Table 1

	x_1	x_2	x_3	x_4	
x_3	2	(9)	1	0	40
x_4	11	-8	0	1	82
	-3	-13	0	0	0
x_2	$\frac{2}{9}$	1	$\frac{1}{9}$	0	$4\frac{4}{9}$
x_4	($\frac{115}{9}$)	0	$\frac{8}{9}$	1	$117\frac{5}{9}$
	$-\frac{1}{9}$	0	$\frac{13}{9}$	0	$57\frac{7}{9}$
x_2	0	1	$\frac{11}{115}$	$-\frac{2}{115}$	$2\frac{2}{5}$
x_1	1	0	$\frac{8}{115}$	$\frac{9}{115}$	$9\frac{1}{5}$
	0	0	$\frac{167}{115}$	$\frac{1}{115}$	$58\frac{4}{5}$

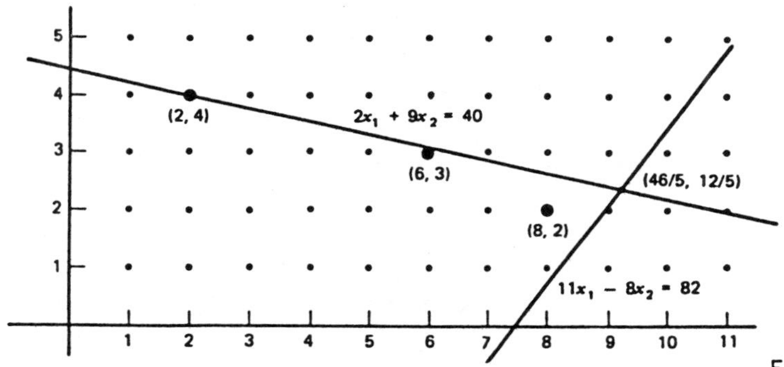

Fig. 1

The graph for the problem is sketched in Figure 1. There are 36 lattice points (points with both coordinates integer) in the region bounded by the constraints. Since the coefficients of the objective finction are positive, htere can be no lattice points in the feasible region that are to the right or above the point at which the maximal value of the objectine finction is attained, and so the optimal value of f must occur at either (2, 4), (6, 3), or (8, 2). Now f(2, 4) = 58, f(6, 3) = 57, and f(8, 2) = 50, so the maximal value of f is 58 and is attained at the point (2, 4). Contrast here the proximites of the feasible lattice point (8, 2) and the actual solution point (2, 4) to the solution point of the noninteger restricted problem, $(9\ \frac{1}{5},\ 2\ \frac{2}{5})$, and the difference in values of f at these two points, 50 and 58.

• PROBLEM 6-9

For the picture galleries the plans of which are given in Fig. 1, find the smallest number of attendants who, if placed in the various doorways connect two adjacent rooms, can supervise all rooms. Use integer programming and the simplex method to solve.

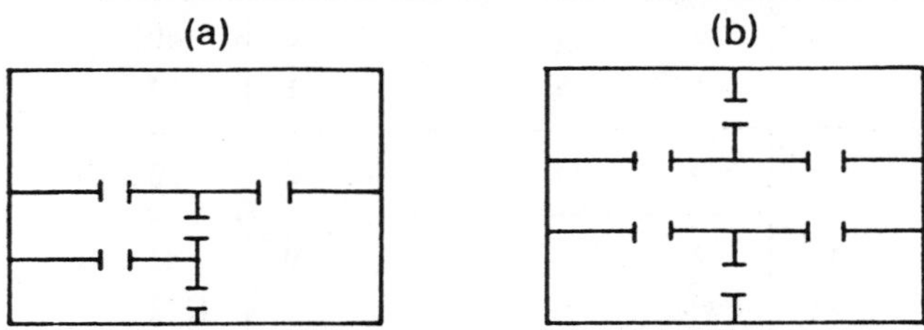

Fig. 1

Solution:

(a) Minimize $x_1 + x_2 + x_3 + x_4 + x_5$,

subject to: $x_1 + x_2 \geq 1, \quad x_1 + x_4 \geq 1,$

$x_4 + x_5 \geq 1, \quad x_2 + x_3 + x_5 \geq 1.$

$x_j = 1$ or 0, $j = 1, \ldots, 5$.

(b) Minimize $x_1 + x_2 + x_3 + x_4 + x_5 + x_6$,

subject to: $x_1 + x_2 \geq 1, \quad x_1 + x_3 \geq 1$

$x_2 + x_3 + x_4 + x_5 \geq 1$

$x_4 + x_6 \geq 1, \quad x_5 + x_6 \geq 1$

$x_j = 1$ or $0 \quad j = 1, \ldots, 6$.

Answers (Fig. 2):

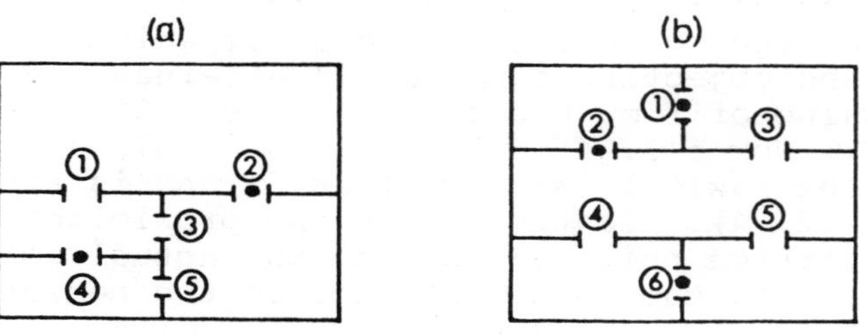

Fig. 2

BRANCH AND BOUND METHOD

• PROBLEM 6-10

Consider the following integer programming problem:

$$\text{Maximize} \quad P = 6x_1 + 3x_2 + x_3 + 2x_4 \tag{1}$$

subject to:

$$\begin{aligned} x_1 + x_2 + x_3 + x_4 &\le 8 \\ 2x_1 + x_2 + 3x_3 &\le 12 \\ 5x_2 + x_3 + 3x_4 &\le 6 \\ x_1 &\le 1 \\ x_2 &\le 1 \\ x_3 &\le 4 \\ x_4 &\le 2 \end{aligned} \tag{2}$$

x_1, x_2, x_3, x_4 all non-negative integers. Use the branch and bound algorithm to solve this problem.

Solution: When a problem is required to have an integer solution, this means that there are a finite number of possible solution points. It is theoretically possible to enumerate and evaluate every possible solution to find the optimum.

List all possible solutions to the given problem by means of a tree diagram. The constraints $x_1 \le 1$, $x_2 \le 1$ imply that x_1 and x_2 can take on only the values zero or one. x_3 can take on five values while x_4 can take on 3 values. Thus, there are $2 \times 2 \times 5 \times 3 = 60$ possible solutions.

Some of the possible solutions will not satisfy the remaining constraints. For example, the solution $x_2 = 1$, $x_3 = 3$ and $x_4 = 2$ fails to satisfy the constraint $5x_2 + x_3 + 3x_4 \le 6$. The branch and bound approach reduces the search by eliminating whole branches of the above tree. The principle used is: A branch can be eliminated if it can be shown to contain no feasible solution better than the one already obtained.

Solving the problem as a linear programming problem (L. P.) yields an upper limit or bound on the possible integer solution. If the simplex method is used to solve the given problem the solution is obtained:

$$x_1 = 1; \quad x_2 = 0; \quad x_3 = 3.33; \; x_4 = 0.89$$

and P = 11.11. The integer solution must therefore be less than or equal to P = 11. An initial feasible integer solution is $x_1 = x_2 = x_3 = x_4 = 0$ and P = 0.

Now select an arbitrary variable and construct branches. Select x_4 for branching. Since the L. P. solution was $x_4 = .89$, let $x_4 = 0$ or $x_4 \geq 1$.

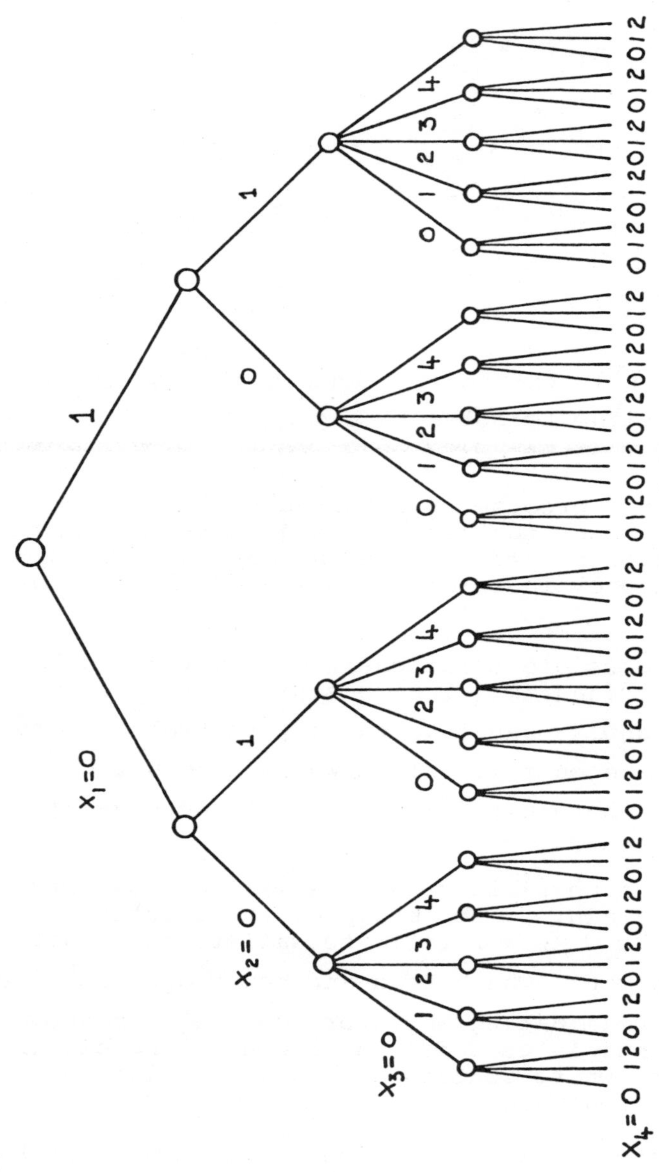

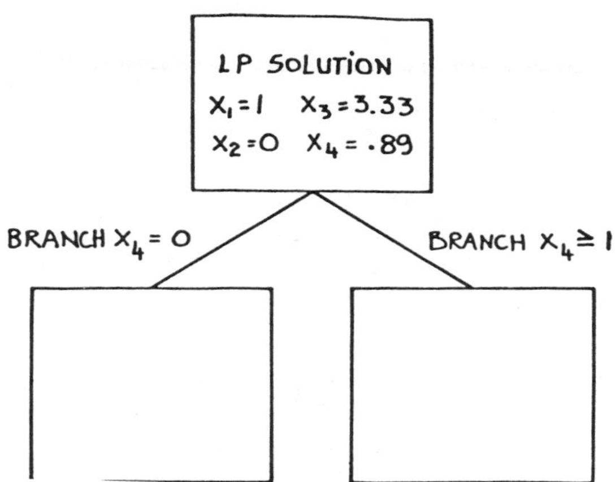

Consider the branch $x_4 = 0$. Replace the last constraint in the original problem ($x_4 \leq 2$) by the constraint $x_4 = 0$. Considered as a linear programming problem, the solution is $x_1 = 1$, $x_2 = .57$, $x_3 = 3.14$, $x_4 = 0$ and $P = 10.85$.

Now select x_2 as the branch variable. The two possible branches are $x_2 = 1$ and $x_2 = 0$. Let $x_2 = 1$ in the original problem (1), (2). The solution to the L. P. problem is $x_1 = 1$, $x_2 = 1$, $x_3 = 1$, $x_4 = 0$ and $P = 10$. This is better than the original feasible solution $P = 0$.

Letting $x_2 = 0$ we obtain $P = 9.33$. Since the bound on profit in this branch is less than 10, eliminate this branch.

Now move back to the branch $x_4 \geq 1$. The solution to the L. P. is

$$x_1 = 1, \quad x_2 = 0, \quad x_3 = 3, \quad x_4 = 1 \quad \text{and} \quad P = 11.$$

This is the optimal solution since all branches have been searched.

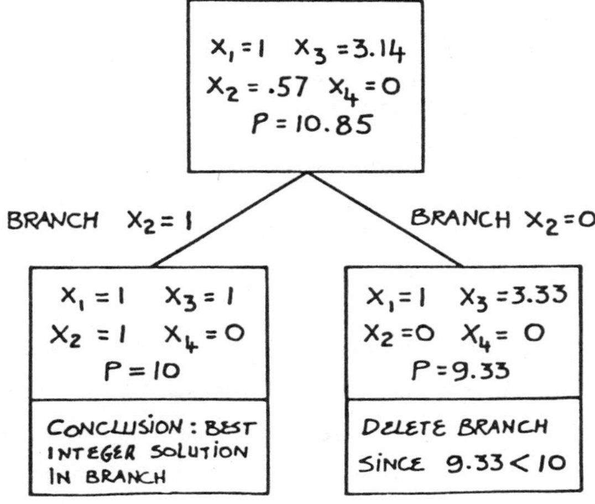

• PROBLEM 6-11

Use the branch and bound method to solve the integer programming problem

$$\text{Maximize} \quad P = 2x_1 + 3x_2 + x_3 + 2x_4$$

subject to:

$$5x_1 + 2x_2 + x_3 + x_4 \leq 15$$

$$2x_1 + 6x_2 + 10x_3 + 8x_4 \leq 60$$

$$x_1 + x_2 + x_3 + x_4 \leq 8$$

$$2x_1 + 2x_2 + 3x_3 + 3x_4 \leq 16$$

$x_1 \leq 3, \quad x_2 \leq 7, \quad x_3 \leq 5, \; x_4 \leq 5.$

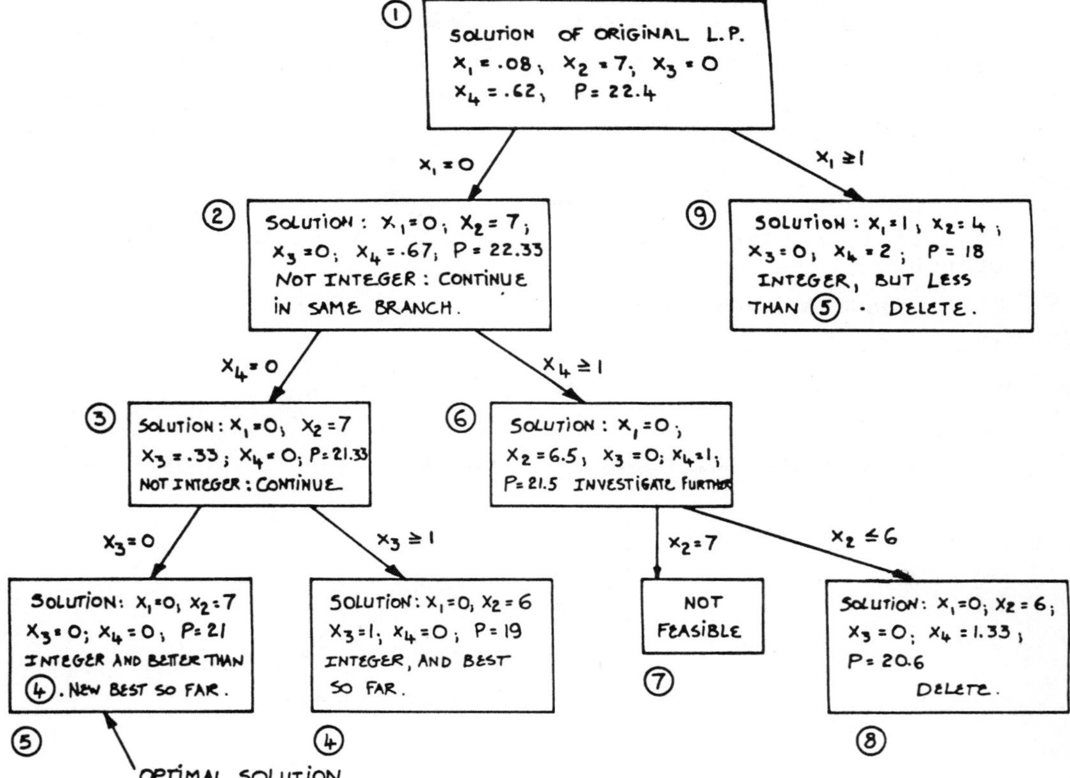

Solution: x_1 can take on any of the four values 0, 1, 2, or 3. Similarly, there are eight possibilities for x_2, six for x_3 and six for x_4. By the Fundamental Principle of Counting there are $4 \times 8 \times 6 \times 6 = 1{,}152$ possible solutions.

The branch and bound procedure eliminates non-optimal solutions and thus reduces the amount of calculation. The steps in the procedure are as follows:

1) Find an initial feasible integer solution.

2) Branch: Select a variable and divide the possible solutions into two groups. Select one branch for investigation.

3) Find an upper bound or maximum value for the problem defined by the branch selected. This bound can be found by considering the problem as a linear programming problem.

4) Compare: Compare the bound obtained for the branch being considered with the best solution so far for the previous branches examined. If the bound is less, delete the whole new branch. If the bound is greater and an integer it becomes the new best solution so far. If the bound is greater but not an integer, continue in this same branch by branching further (Step 2).

5) Completion: When all branches have been examined, the best solution so far is the optimal solution.

The general approach is illustrated for the given problem in the figure.

Thus the optimal solution to the integer program is $x_1 = 0$, $x_2 = 7$, $x_3 = 0$, $x_4 = 0$ and $P = 21$. When first selecting a variable for branching, a good rule to follow is to choose a variable whose linear programming solution is non-integer.

• PROBLEM 6-12

The graphical representation of the following integer programming problem is shown in Figure 1, use branch-and-bound method.

Maximize

$$z = 40x_1 + 90x_2$$

subject to:

$$9x_1 + 7x_2 \le 56$$

$$7x_1 + 20x_2 \le 70$$

$$x_1,\ x_2 = \text{nonnegative integers}$$

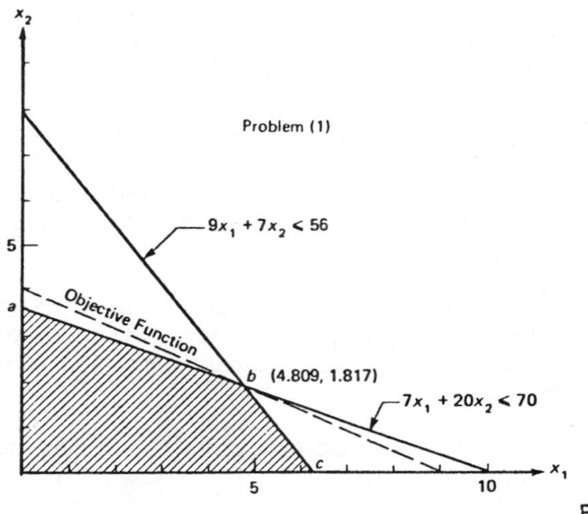

Fig. 1

Solution: Note that the optimal simplex solution occurs at point b with neither variable assuming an integer value ($x_1 = 4.809$, $x_2 = 1.817$, and $z = 355.890$).

The branch-and-bound algorithm focuses upon one of the noninteger decision variables (the choice is arbitrary). For instance focus upon $x_1 = 4.809$. The optimal integer solution will have an integer value assigned to x_1 such that $x_1 \leq 4$ or $x_1 \geq 5$. The noninteger region between $x_1 = 4$ and $x_1 = 5$ is not feasible in the integer version of the problem. Consequently, the branch-and-bound algorithm branches from the original problem, or partitions it into two further constrained problems which eliminate this noninteger area. Figure 2 illustrates the graphic representation of these two problems. Number the original problem as problem (1) and descendant problems as problems (2), (3), and so forth.

Partitioned Descendants from Problem(1)

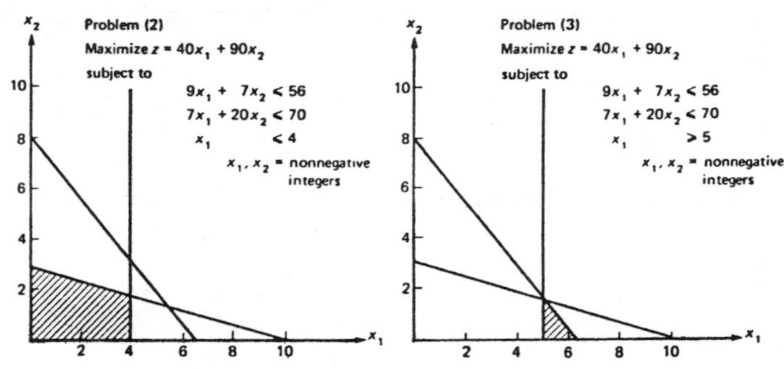

Fig. 2

Solving each of the newly formed problems by the simplex method as if they were continuous (noninteger) problems yields the following solutions:

Problem (2)		Problem (3)	
z =	349.000	z =	341.390
x_1 =	4.000	x_1 =	5.000
x_2 =	2.100	x_2 =	1.571

Again, neither solution is all-integer, but both have led to integer values for x_1. Since no feasible integer solution points was excluded in creating these two problems, the values of 349.000 and 341.390 act as upper bounds for any feasible integer solutions. That is, integer values of four of less for x_1 cannot possibly result in a z value greater than 349.000 and values of five of more for x_1 cannot exceed 341.390 for z.

The branch-and-bound algorithm works on the principle of searching problem subsets to find teasible solutions, but discarding (not searching) subsets that cannot produce results superior to those already attained. Continuing the analysis, partition from either problem (2) or problem (3) in an effort to integerize x_2. However, the "potential" associated with partitioning from problem (2) is more promising. This is because the upper bound on any descendant problem which further constrains problem (2) is z = 349.000, whereas the best that can be expected from descendants of problem (3) is z = 341.390. Thus, the next step begins with problem (2) by adding the constraints $x_2 \leq 2$ (problem 4) and $x_2 \geq 3$ (problem 5). In this subset of problems the noniteger area between $x_2 = 2$ and $x_2 = 3$ is excluded, since $x_2 = 2.1$ in the solution to Problem (2).

Summary of Branch-and-Bound Solution

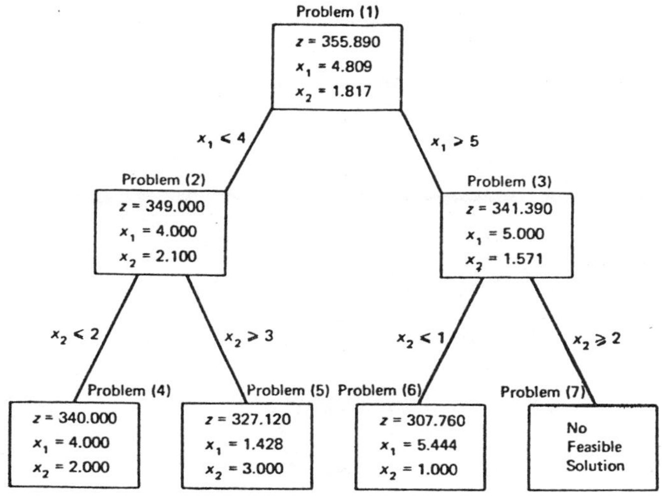

Fig. 3

Figure 3 summarizes the remaining steps leading to the identification of the optimal integer solution. In problem (4) an all-integer solution is identified with an objective function valued at 340. In problem (5), the other descendant problem from problem (2), the optimal solution is not integer. However, since any descendant problems cannot produce z values greater than 327.120, discard problem (5) and its descendants from further considerations.

One might be inclined to conclude that the optimal integer solution has been found. However, there is potentially a better solution from one of the descendants of problem (3). The value of z = 341.390 is greater than the 340 found in problem (4). Therefore it is necessary to partition problem (3) into problems (6) and (7) by adding the constraints $x_2 \leq 1$ and $x_2 \geq 2$, respectively. As can be seen in Figure 3, the results for these two problems are inferior to the solution found in problem (4). Any descendants from problem (6) would have optimal values for z no greater than 307.76 and any descendants of problem (7) would be infeasible. Thus, the optimal integer solution is $x_1 = 4$, $x_2 = 2$, and z = 340.

• PROBLEM 6-13

Maximize $P = 10x + 20y$

subject to:

$$5x + 8y \leq 60$$
$$x \leq 8$$
$$y \leq 4$$
$$x, y \geq 0 \text{ and integer.}$$

with a solution of

$$x = 5.6 \qquad y = 4 \qquad P = 136.$$

The profit P = 136 is an upper bound for the problem simply because any additional restriction of integrality can only reduce the solution from P = 136. Solve this branch and bound problem.

Solution: While y = 4 is an integer, the value for x = 5.6 violates the integrality restriction. A branching process is now performed by forming two new problems P_2 and P_3 for $x \leq 5$ and $x \geq 6$ as follows:

P_2: Maximize $P = 10x + 20y$

subject to: $5x + 8y \leq 60$

$$x \leq 8$$

$$y \leq 4$$
$$x \leq 5$$
$$x, y \geq 0.$$

P_3: Maximize $P = 10x + 20y$

subject to: $5x + 8y \leq 60$
$$x \leq 8$$
$$y \leq 4$$
$$x \geq 6$$
$$x, y \geq 0.$$

Also, notice that in P_2, $x \leq 8$ is redundant to $x \leq 5$. The two problems P_2 and P_3 are not solved as LP problems. The solution for P_2 is

$$x = 5 \qquad y = 4 \qquad P = 130$$

and for P_3

$$x = 6 \qquad y = 3.75 \qquad P = 135.$$

In effect, the solution for P_2 is integer and is feasible for the original problem. It should be emphasized that the value $P = 130$ is a lower bound for the original problem and it is possible that other integer programming (IP) solutions may exist in the range 130 - 136.

The solution pertaining to P_3 now provides us with a new upper bound of $P = 135$. As indicated before, the optimal solution is at least 130 and at most 135.

Since $y = 3.75$ in P_3 a new branching process is used to determine a solution by using either $y \leq 3$ or $y \geq 4$. Consequently, two new problems are structured, such as P_4 and P_5:

P_4: Maximize $10x + 20y$

subject to: $5x + 8y \leq 60$
$$x \leq 8$$
$$y \leq 4$$
$$x \geq 6$$
$$y \geq 4$$
$$x, y \geq 0.$$

P_5: Maximize $10x + 20y$

subject to: $5x + 8y \leq 60$

$$x \leq 8$$

$$y \leq 4$$

$$x \geq 6$$

$$y \leq 3$$

$$x, y \geq 0.$$

Notice that whenever a branching is performed and new problems are formulated, all the restrictions imposed on the problems are maintained. For example, $x \geq 6$ was imposed on P_3, and is therefore maintained as a constraint when P_3 is partitioned into P_4 and P_5. Here, however, other factors appear to surface that are related to the problem, such as that the solution for P_4 is infeasible and no further consideration is given to the branches beyond P_4, since any new restrictions cannot change the infeasibility condition.

The solution to P_5 is

$x = 7.2 \qquad y = 3 \qquad P = 132.$

Therefore, the new upper bound has been reduced from 135 to 132 and the optimal solution is somewhere between 130 and 132. Since $x = 7.2$ in P_5, a new branching step is required. It is taken with respect to x (since $y = 3$ is an integer). Moreover, P_5 is now partitioned into P_6 and P_7 with either $x < 7$ or $x \geq 8$ and presented as follows:

P_6: Maximize $10\,x + 20y$

subject to: $5x + 8x \leq 60$

$$x \leq 8$$

$$y \leq 4$$

$$x \geq 6$$

$$y \leq 3$$

$$x \leq 7$$

$$x, y \geq 0.$$

P_7: Maximize $10x + 20y$

subject to: $5x + 8y \leq 60$

$$x \leq 8$$

$$y \leq 4$$

$$x \geq 6$$

$$y \leq 3$$
$$x \geq 8$$
$$x, y \geq 0$$

The lists of constraints of P_6 can be stated as

$5x + 8y \leq 60 \quad 6 \leq x \leq 7 \quad y \leq 3 \quad x,y \geq 0$

and for P_7 the constraints are

$5x + 8y \leq 60 \quad x = 8 \quad y \leq 3 \quad x,y \geq 0.$

The solution to P_7 is

$x = 8 \quad y = 2.5 \quad P = 130$

and the solution to P_6 is

$x = 7 \quad y = 3 \quad P = 130.$

The new upper bound has been reduced from 132 to 130, which means that the lower bound is 130 and the upper bound is 130, and consequently the optimal solution must be 130. A solution with a value of 130 has already been determined in P_2. Thus x = 5, y = 4, P = 130 of P_2 is an optimal solution. However, in this particular case, it just happened that another optimal solution is found in P_6 which is

$x = 7 \quad y = 3 \quad P = 130.$

Any further partitioning of P_7 with $y \leq 2$ or $y \geq 3$ can provide integer solutions that are worse than P_7 or lower than P = 130, which is inferior to what already exist.

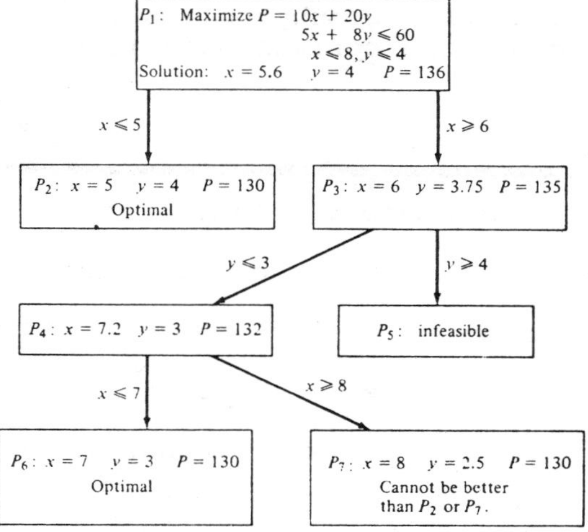

Fig. 1

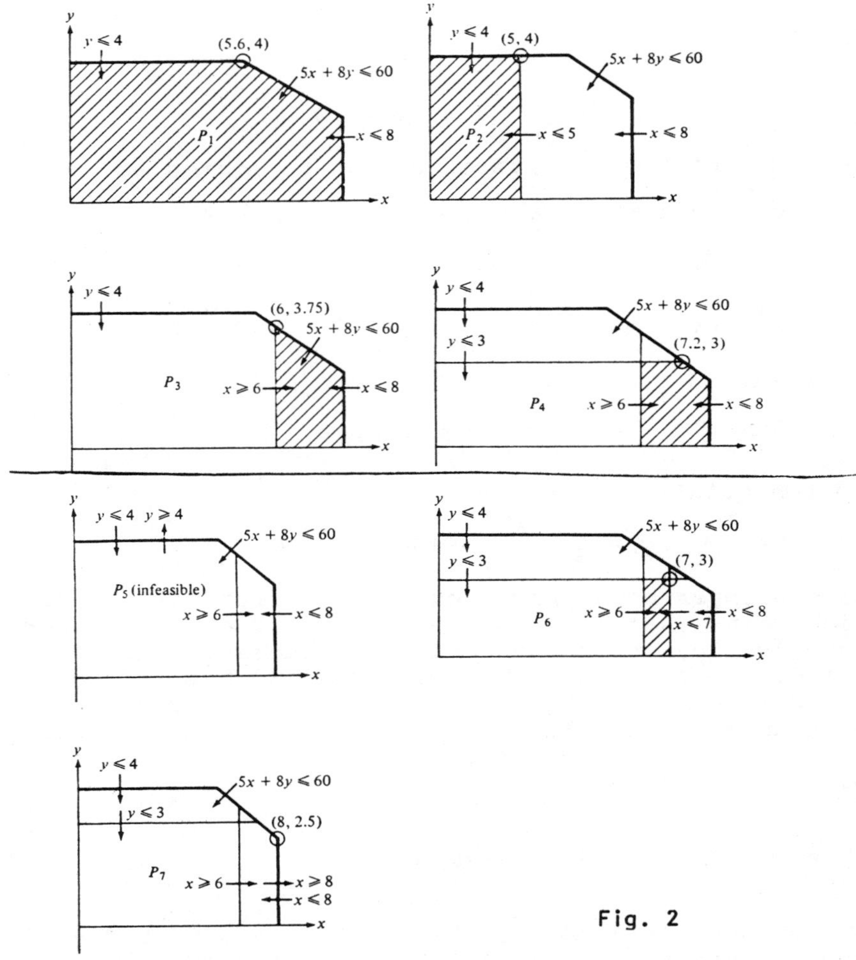

Fig. 2

The branch and bound solution is summarized in Figures 1 and 2, which demonstrate the various steps of the algorithm, the six linear programming subproblems (seven LP problems), and feasible regions and optimal solutions.

• PROBLEM 6-14

Solve the branch and bound problem:

$$\text{Minimize} \qquad c = 2x + 3y$$

$$\text{subject to:} \qquad x + 3y \geq 5$$

$$2x + y \geq 6$$

$$x, y \geq 0 \text{ and integer}$$

with a solution of

$$x = 2.6 \qquad y = 0.8 \qquad c = 7.6.$$

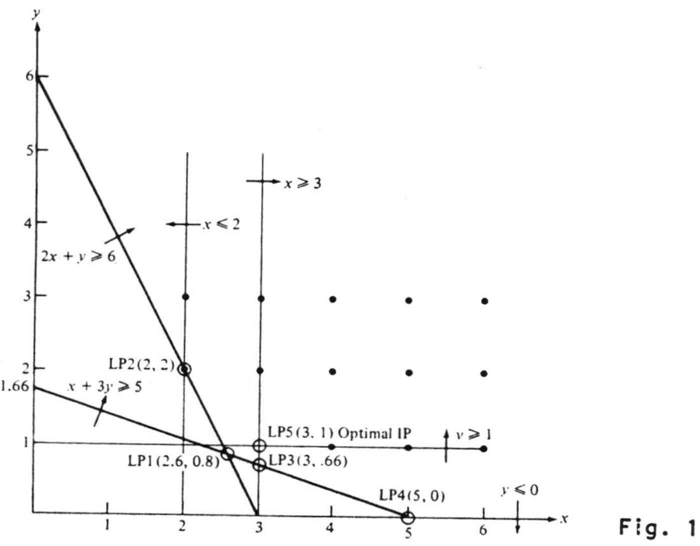

Fig. 1

Solution: The graphical solution of the problem is illustrated in Figure 1. The value c = 7.6 is a lower bound for the integer programming problem.

The first branch is around the integer x, which cannot be x = 2.6 but must be either $x \leq 2$ or $x \geq 3$. Thus, problems P_2 and P_3 are constructed as

P_2: Minimize $c = 2x + 3y$

subject to:

$$x + 3y \geq 5$$
$$2x + y \geq 6$$
$$x \leq 2$$
$$x, y \geq 0.$$

P_3: Minimize $c = 2x + 3y$

subject to:

$$x + 3y \geq 5$$
$$2x + y \geq 6$$
$$x \geq 3$$
$$x, y \geq 0.$$

The solution to P_2 is x = 2, y = 2, c = 10, and to P_3 is x = 3, y = 2/3, c = 8. Therefore, the value c = 8 from P_3 is a new lower bound that replaces c = 7.6. The solution to P_2 is an integer with an upper bound to the problem of c = 10. The optimal solution is at best c = 8 and at worst c = 10. The next branch is from P_3 around y = 2/3 with either $y \leq 0$ or $y \geq 1$. This branching process generates the two problems depicted by P_4 and P_5 as

P_4: Minimize $c = 2x + 3y$

$$\text{subject to:} \quad \begin{aligned} x + 3y &\geq 5 \\ 2x + y &\geq 6 \\ x &\geq 3 \\ y &\leq 0 \\ x, y &\geq 0. \end{aligned}$$

P_5: Minimize $c = 2x + 3y$

$$\text{subject to:} \quad \begin{aligned} x + 3y &\geq 5 \\ 2x + y &\geq 6 \\ x &\geq 3 \\ y &\geq 1 \\ x, y &\geq 0. \end{aligned}$$

P_1: minimize $c = 2x + 3y$
$x + 3y \geq 5$
$2x + y \geq 6$
$x, y \geq 0$
Solution: $x = 2.6$ $y = .8$ $c = 7.6$

$x \leq 2$ | $x \geq 3$

P_2: $x = 2$ $y = 2$ $c = 10$

P_3: $x = 3$ $y = \frac{2}{3}$ $c = 8$

$y \leq 0$ | $y \geq 1$

P_4: $x = 5$ $y = 0$ $c = 10$

P_5: $x = 3$ $y = 1$ $c = 9$
Optimal

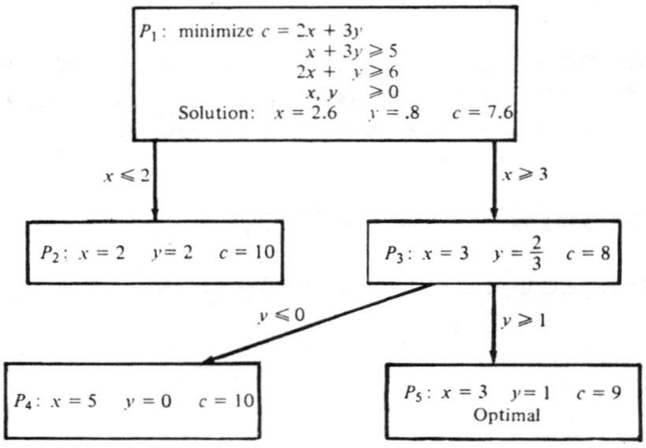

Fig. 2

The solution to P_4 is $x = 5$, $y = 0$, $c = 10$ and to P_5 it is $x = 3$, $y = 1$, $c = 9$. Moreover, the solution to the linear programming problem P_5 is $c = 9$, which is a new lower bound. However, the solution to P_5 is also an integer, and therefore it is also an upper bound. Since $c = 9$ is both an upper and lower bound, then $x = 3$, $y = 1$, $c = 9$ is also the optimal solution. In addition, P_4 also happens to be an integer solution but its value $c = 10$ is worse than $c = 9$. Thus the problem may be expressed as the branching process summarized in Figure 2.

• PROBLEM 6-15

Consider the problem,

Maximize $3x_1 + 4x_2$

subject to: $\frac{2}{5}x_1 + x_2 \leq 3$

$$\frac{2}{5}x_1 - \frac{2}{5}x_2 \leq 1$$

$$\left.\begin{array}{l} x_1 \leq M \\ x_2 \leq M \end{array}\right\} \text{ or } \left\{\begin{array}{l} x_1 + x_5 = M \\ x_2 + x_6 = M \end{array}\right.$$

$M = 1000$ (a large positive integer)

$x_1, x_2, x_5, x_6 \geq 0$ and integer.

Solve by the Branch and Bound Method.

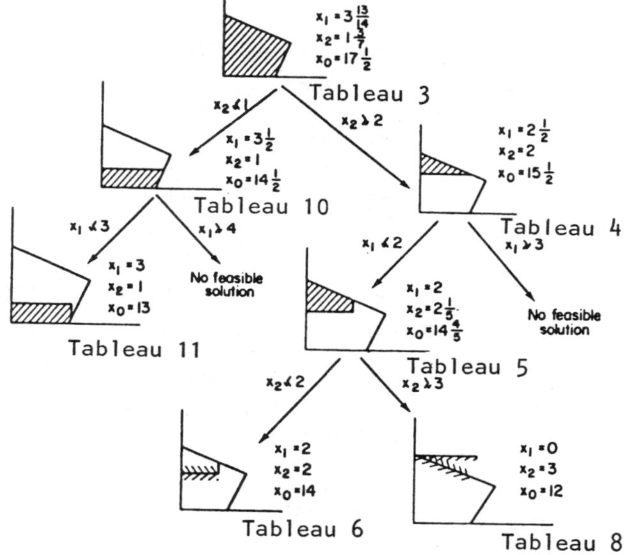

Fig. 1

Solution: A very simple variable choice strategy (choose last non integer variable) is employed and the (nodes) subproblems are selected on last-in-first-out basis. The tableaux (set up in Tucker-Beale form) 1 to 11 illustrate how the exploration of the solution space corresponds with the exploration of the tree; also see Fig. 1. In Tableau 3 the two penalties on the variable x_2, may be calculated from the equations for the "up" and "down" penalties.

$$\text{Pen}_u = \min_{J,\bar{a}_{pJ}<0} \bar{a}_{0J}(1 - f_k) \,/\, |\bar{a}_{pJ}|, \quad J \in N,$$

$$\text{Pen}_d = \min_{J,\bar{a}_{pJ}>0} \bar{}_{0J} f_k \,/\, \bar{a}_{pJ}, \quad J \in N,$$

where $\bar{a}_{0J}$ represents the reduced cost coefficient, $\bar{a}_{pJ}$ updated row entry for the tableau under consideration, $f_k = x_k - \beta_k$, with β_k being the integer part of the value of the variable.

Thus,

$$\text{Pen}_u = (4/7 \times 1/2)/(1/7) = 2,$$

the penalty for setting the bound $x_2 \geq 2$; and

$$\text{Pen}_d = (3/7 \times 1)/(1/7) = 3,$$

the penalty for setting the bound $x_2 \leq 1$.

Now, branch on the variable with the highest penalty and develop the node in the other direction.

		$-x_1$	$-x_2$
x_0	0	-3	-4
x_3	15	2	(5)
x_4	5	2	-2
x_5	1000	1	0
x_6	1000	0	1
x_1	0	-1	0
x_2	0	0	-1

Tableau 1

		$-x_1$	$-x_2$
x_0	12	$-7/5$	4/5
x_3	0	0	-1
x_4	11	(14/5)	2/5
x_5	1000	1	0
x_6	997	$-2/5$	$-1/5$
x_1	0	-1	0
x_2	3	2/5	1/5

Tableau 2

		$-x_4$	$-x_3$
x_0	35/2	1/2	1
x_3	0	0	-1
x_4	0	-1	0
x_5	$996^1/14$	$-5/14$	$-1/7$
x_6	$998^4/7$	1/7	$-1/7$
x_1	55/14	5/14	1/7
x_2	10/7	$-1/7$	1/7

Tableau 3

Continuous optimum solution Branch on variable x_2 and and store $x_2 \leqslant 1$ and explore $x_2 \geqslant 2$ TABLEAU 4

Rewrite x_2 row as L.B.2$|\, x_2 = -4/7 - 1/7(-x_4) + 1/7(-x_3)$

		$-x_2$	$-x_3$	
x_0	31/2	7/2	3/2	
x_3	0	0	-1	
x_4	4	-7	-1	$x_1 \leqslant 2$
x_5	$997^1/2$	$-5/2$	$-1/2$	i.e. infeasibility row
x_6	998	1	0	$x_5 = -1/2$
x_1	5/2	5/2	1/2	$-5/2(-x_2)$
LB2→ x_2	0	-1	0	$-1/2(x_3)$

(pivot: $-x_4$ → $-x_2$)

Tableau 4 — Pivot

Now branch on x_1 and $x_1 \geqslant 3$ is not feasible. So explore $x_1 \leqslant 2$

		$-x_5$	$-x_3$	
x_0	74/5	7/5	4/5	
x_3	0	0	-1	
x_4	27/5	$-14/5$	2/5	
x_5	0	-1	0	
x_6	$997^4/5$	2/5	$-1/5$	$x_6 = -1/5$
x_1	2	1	0	$+ 2/5(-x_5)$
LB2 x_2	1/5	$-2/5$	1/5	$-1/5(-x_3)$

Tableau 5 — Pivot

List $x_2 \geqslant 3$ and explore $x_2 \leqslant 2$

		$-x_5$	$-x_6$	
x_0	14	3	4	
x_3	1	-2	-5	
x_4	5	-2	2	
x_5	0	-1	0	
x_6	0	0	-1	UB = 2
x_1	2	1	0	
LB2 x_2	0	0	1	

Tableau 6

		$-x_5$	$-x_3$
x_0	74/5	7/5	4/5
x_3	0	0	−1
x_4	27/5	−14/5	2/5
x_5	0	−1	0
x_6	997⁴/5	2/5	−1/5
x_1	2	1	0
LB → 3 x_2	−4/5	−2/5	1/5

Tableau 7

		$-x_4$	$-x_3$	
x_0	35/2	1/2	1	
x_3	0	−0	−1	
x_4	0	−1	0	
x_5	996¹/14	−5/14	−1/7	
x_6	−3/7	1/7	(−1/7)	UB = 1
x_1	55/14	5/14	1/7	
x_2	10/7	−1/7	1/7	

Tableau 9

		$-x_2$	$-x_3$
x_0	12	7/2	3/2
x_3	0	0	−1
x_4	11	−7	−1
x_5	2	1	0
x_6	997	1	0
x_1	0	5/2	1/2
LB3 → x_2	0	−1	0

Tableau 8

Integer feasible but worse than the best solution. Extract another problem from the list, Tableau 3 set $x_2 \leq 1$.

		$-x_4$	$-x_6$
x_0	29/2	3/2	7
x_3	3	−1	−7
x_4	0	−1	0
x_5	996½	−1/2	−1
x_6	0	0	−1
x_1	7/2	1/2	1
x_2	1	0	1

$x_5 = -1/2 - 1/2$

$(-x_4) - (-x_6)$

Add $x_1 \leq 1$ to 1

Tableau 10

UB = 1

$x_1 \geq 2$ leads to no feasible solution.

Tableau 10

		$-x_5$	$-x_6$	
x_0	13	3	4	
x_3	4	−2	−5	
x_4	1	−2	2	
x_5	0	−1	0	UB = 3
x_6	0	0	−1	
x_1	3	1	0	
x_2	1	0	1	

Tableau 11

Less than the currently best integer solution.

No problem left in the list; the search is completed.

Tableau 6 is integer feasible so its objective function value 14 is taken as the value of the currently best integer solution. Extract the last problem from the list (Tableau 5; set lower bound $x_2 \geq 3$)

• PROBLEM 6-16

Maximize $z = 5x_1 + 2x_2$

subject to:
$$2x_1 + 2x_2 + x_3 = 9$$
$$3x_1 + x_2 + x_4 = 11$$
$$x_1,\ x_2,\ x_3,\ x_4,\ \geq 0 \text{ and integer.}$$

The optimal noninteger solution is given in Tableau 1.

Solve this Branch and Bound problem.

Tableau 1

		x_1	x_2	x_3	x_4
z	18.75	0	0	.25	1.5
x_2	1.25	0	1	.75	−.50
x_1	3.25	1	0	−.25	.50

optimal noninteger solution to the problem

<u>Solution</u>: Since it is not integer, proceed and arbitrarily choose x_2 as the variable to be made integer. By adjoining $x_2 \leq 1$ and using the method of upper bounds, with $\bar{x}_2$ as the complement of x_2, obtain the solution given in Tableau 2. (To perform the iteration, replace x_2 by $1 - \bar{x}_2$ and perform a dual simplex iteration.)

Tableau 2

		x_1	$\bar{x}_2$	x_3	x_4
z	18.67	0	0.33	0	1.67
x_3	0.33	0	−1.33	1	−0.67
x_1	3.33	1	−0.33	0	0.33

optimal solution to partial problem ($x_2 \leq 1$)
$\bar{x}_2$ is the complement of x_2 in the bound constraint $x_2 \leq 1$

By adjoining $x_2 \geq 2$ to the solution of Tableau 1 and performing the necessary iteration, we obtain the solution given in Tableau 3.

Tableau 3

		x_1	x_2'	x_3	x_4
z	16.5	0	3	2.5	0
x_4	1.5	0	−2	−1.5	1
x_1	2.5	1	1	0.5	0

optimal solution to partial problem ($x_2 \geq 2$)
x_2' is the excess of x_2 above 2

Neither of these solutions is integer, but since both are feasible they are stored in the list. The solution of Tableau 2 is next selected from the list. By choosing x_1 as the branching variable and adjoining $x_1 \leq 3$, obtain the solution of Tableau 4.

Tableau 4

		$\bar{x}_1$	$\bar{x}_2$	x_3	x_4
z	17	5	2	0	0
x_3	1	−2	−2	1	0
x_4	1	−3	−1	0	1

optimal solution to the partial ($x_2 \leq 1, x_1 \leq 3$)
$\bar{x}_j$ is the complement of x_j

Since the solution of Tableau 4 is integer, no solutions with objective functions less than 17 need be considered, and so the partial solution corresponding to Tableau 3 may be deleted from the list. By adjoining the constraint $x_1 \geq 4$ to Tableau 2, note that there is no feasible solution to that problem. Hence, only the solution in Tableau 4 is added to the list. Next the solution of Tableau 4 is selected from the list. Since it is integer, it is optimal. A tree for this problem's solution is given in Figure 1.

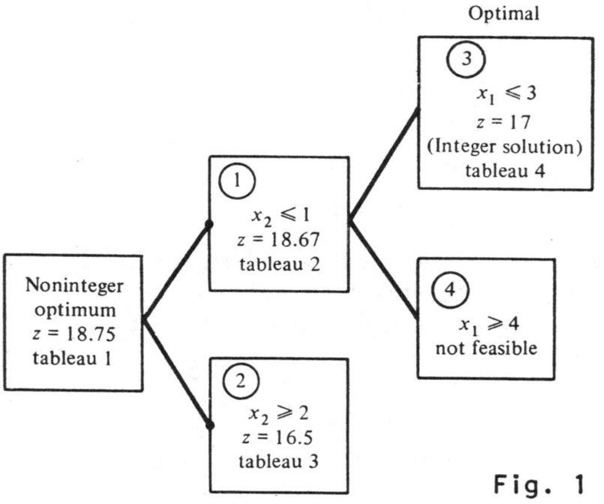

Fig. 1

• PROBLEM 6-17

$$\text{Max } x_0 = -7x_1 - 3x_2 - 4x_3$$

$$x_1 + 2x_2 + 3x_3 - x_4 = 8$$

$$3x_1 + x_2 + x_3 - x_5 = 5$$

$$x_1 \ldots\ldots x_5 \geq 0 \quad \text{integer.}$$

Use the Branch and Bound method to solve.

Table 1

		$-x_3$	$-x_4$	$-x_5$
x_0	$-\frac{71}{5}$	$\frac{3}{5}$	$\frac{2}{5}$	$\frac{11}{5}$
x_1	$\frac{2}{5}$	$-\frac{1}{5}$	$\frac{1}{5}$	$-\frac{2}{5}$
x_2	$\frac{19}{5}$	$\frac{8}{5}$	$-\frac{3}{5}$	$\frac{1}{5}$

Solution: Solve the corresponding LP. The optimal LP tableau is given in Table 1.

The solution is not all-integer and $\bar{z}_0$, the integer approximation to x_0, is $[-71/5] = -15$. Now partition node 0 based on x_1 or x_2 and arbitrarily choose x_2. The resulting tree is shown in Figure 1.

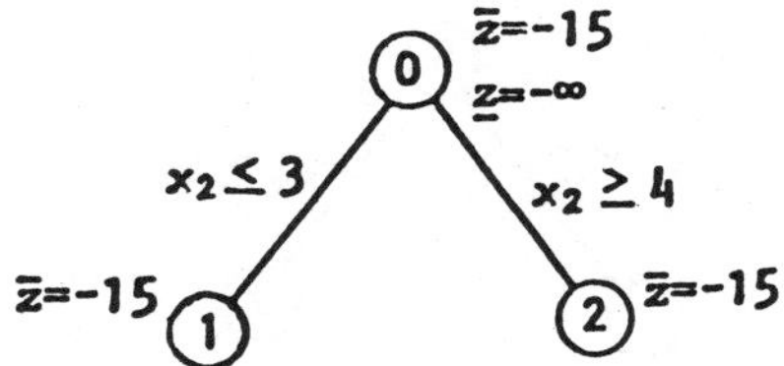

Fig. 1

Taking the left branch add the constraint $x_2 \leq 3$. The first dual simplex iteration yields Table 2.

Table 2

		$\overset{*}{-x_2}$	$-x_4$	$-x_5$	
x_0	$-\frac{29}{2}$	$-\frac{3}{8}$	$\frac{5}{8}$	$\frac{17}{8}$	
x_1	$\frac{1}{2}$	$\frac{1}{8}$	$\frac{1}{8}$	$-\frac{3}{8}$	$x_2 = 3$
x_3	$\frac{1}{2}$	$\frac{5}{8}$	$-\frac{3}{8}$	$\frac{1}{8}$	

The solution in Table 2 is primal feasible but not integer. There is no change in the bounds at vertex 1 or vertex 2, and we choose to partition at node 1, using x_1 as in Figure 2.

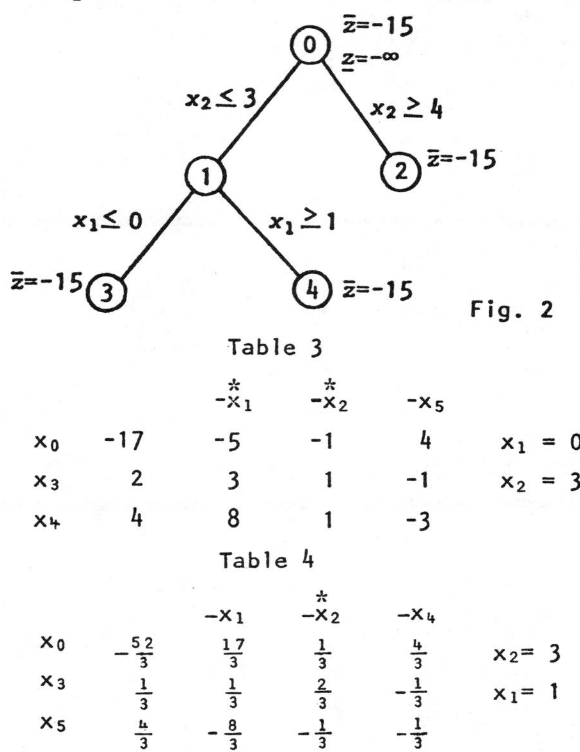

Fig. 2

Table 3

		$\overset{*}{-x_1}$	$\overset{*}{-x_2}$	$-x_5$	
x_0	-17	-5	-1	4	$x_1 = 0$
x_3	2	3	1	-1	$x_2 = 3$
x_4	4	8	1	-3	

Table 4

		$-x_1$	$\overset{*}{-x_2}$	$-x_4$	
x_0	$-\frac{52}{3}$	$\frac{17}{3}$	$\frac{1}{3}$	$\frac{4}{3}$	$x_2 = 3$
x_3	$\frac{1}{3}$	$\frac{1}{3}$	$\frac{2}{3}$	$-\frac{1}{3}$	$x_1 = 1$
x_5	$\frac{4}{3}$	$-\frac{8}{3}$	$-\frac{1}{3}$	$-\frac{1}{3}$	

Taking the left branch and solving the LP, obtain Table 3, which is primal feasible and all-integer. Thus $z_0 = z_3 = -17$. Also, vertex 3 is fathomed, but vertex 2 and vertex 4 remain live. Branch to vertex 4. Two dual simplex iterations yield Table 4. Thus $\bar{z}_4 = -18 < \underline{z}_0$ and vertex 4 is fathomed. The resulting tree is in Figure 3. The only live vertex is vertex 2.

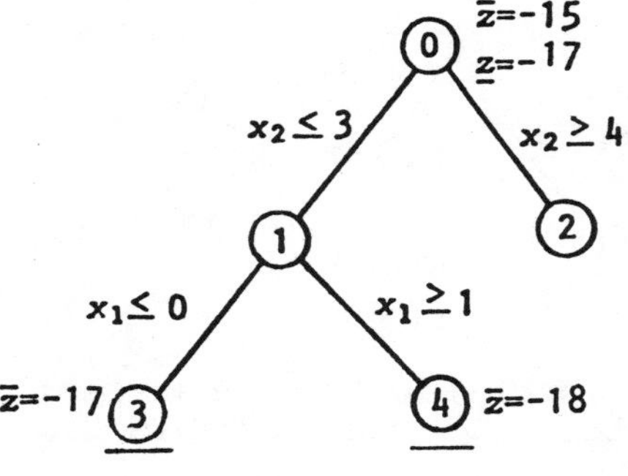

Fig. 3

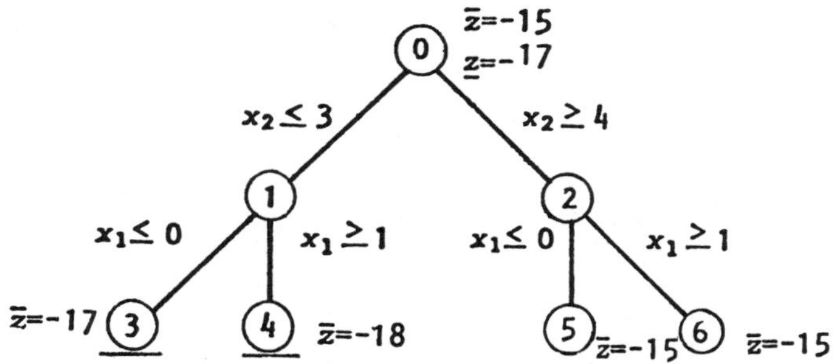

Fig. 4

Table 5

		$-x_2$	$-x_3$	$-x_5$	
x_0	$-\frac{43}{3}$	$\frac{2}{3}$	$\frac{5}{3}$	$\frac{7}{3}$	
x_1	$\frac{1}{3}$	$\frac{1}{3}$	$\frac{1}{3}$	$-\frac{1}{3}$	$x_2 = 4$
x_4	$\frac{1}{3}$	$-\frac{5}{3}$	$-\frac{8}{3}$	$-\frac{1}{3}$	

Table 6

		$\overset{*}{-x_1}$	$-x_3$	$-x_5$	
x_0	-15	-2	1	3	
x_2	5	3	1	-1	$x_1 = 0$
x_4	2	5	-1	-2	

Adding $x_2 \geq 4$ to Table 1 and doing one dual simplex iteration, obtain Table 5. The resulting tree is in Figure 4 and we choose to branch on x_1. Taking the left branch, one dual simplex iteration yields Table 6.

The solution in Table 6 is primal feasible and integer. Thus $\underline{z}_0 = \underline{z}_5 = -15$, and vertex 5 and vertex 6 are fathomed. An optimal solution is $x_1 = 0$, $x_2 = 5$, $x_3 = 0$, $x_4 = 2$, $x_5 = 0$, and $x_0 = -15$.

• PROBLEM 6-18

Consider the integer programming problem

Minimize $z = x_1 - 2x_2$

subject to:

$$2x_1 + x_2 \leq 5$$

$$-4x_1 + 4x_2 \leq 5$$

$$x_1, x_2 \geq 0 \text{ and integer.}$$

Use the Branch and Bound algorithm to solve.

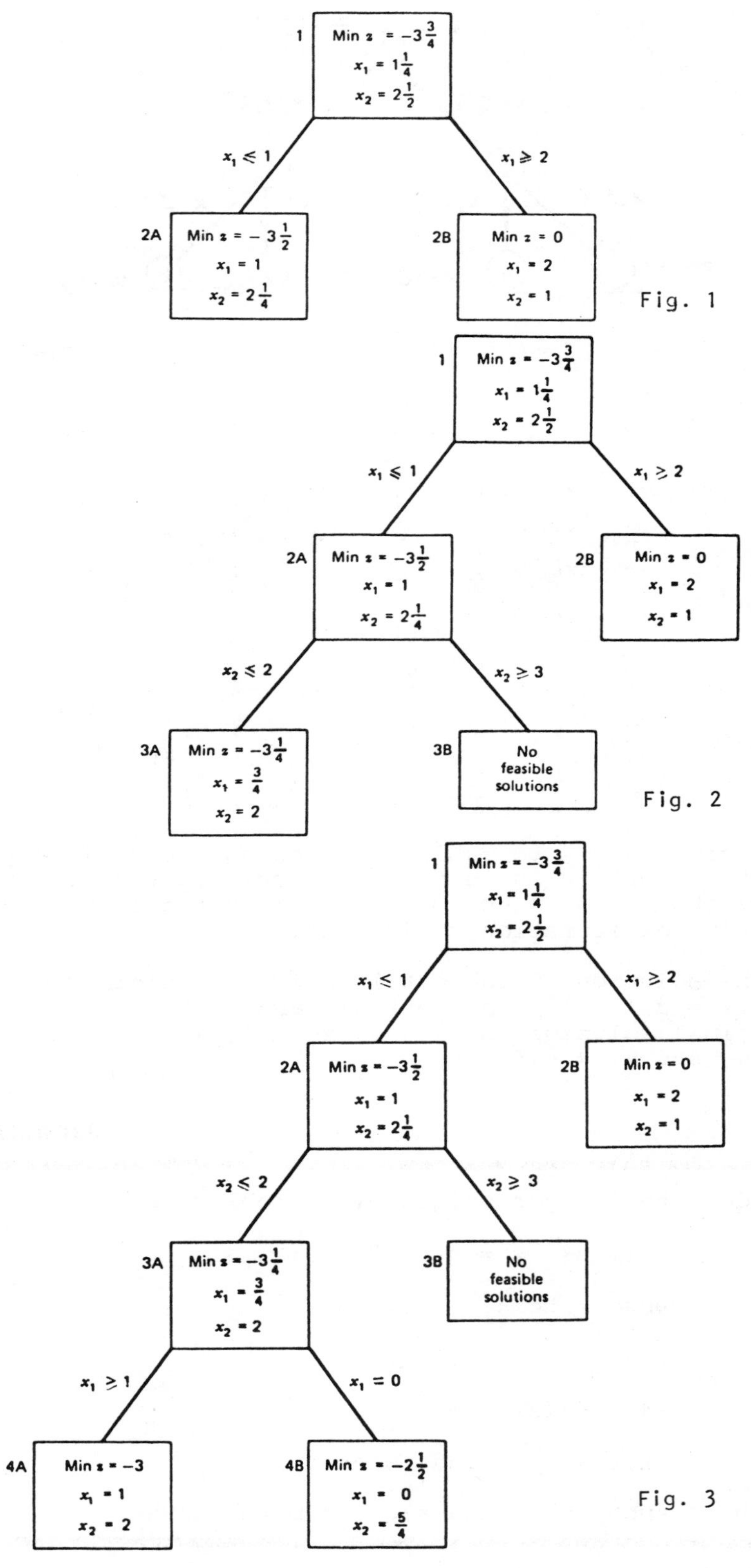

Fig. 1

Fig. 2

Fig. 3

Solution: The solution with the integer restrictions ignored in Min $z = -3\ 3/4$ attained at $x_1 = 1\ 1/4$ $x_2 = 2\ 1/2$. Using the branch and bound algorithm, formulate two new problems here by restricting either the x_1 or the x_2 variable. Arbitrarily select the x_1 variable and use the constraints $x_1 \leq 1$ and $x_1 \geq 2$ to form two new problems. This branching process is denoted in Figure 1. The first box in the figure corresponds to the original problem: its solution, with the integer restrictions ignored, is inside. The boxes labeled 2A and 2B correspond to the two new problems, with the new constraints indicated on the branches leading to the respective boxes. The solutions to these problems, again with the integer restrictions ignored, could be determined by using the Dual Simplex Algorithm in conjunction with the final tableau solution to the original problem, because in each, a constraint has been added to a completed problem. These solutions are listed in the appropriate boxes. Problem 2A has an optimal solution of Min $z = -\ 3\ 1/2$ at $x_1 = 1$, $x_2 = 2\ 1/4$. The optimal value for this problem is greater than the optimal value for Problem 1, as would be expected, because a constraint has been added and therefore the solution set of feasible points on which to minimize the objective function has been reduced. Problem 2B provides a feasible integer solution $x_1 = 2$, $x_2 = 1$ to the constraints of the original problem and an upper bound of 0 for the optimal value of the integer restricted problem. Since better integer solutions may be contained in Problem 2A, branch again off Problem 2A using the x_2 variable, as illustrated in Figure 2. The branch to Problem 3B terminates here, since this problem has no feasible solutions. However, continue by branching at Problem 3A. See Figure 3. Problem 4A yields the integer feasible solution of $x_1 = 1$, $x_2 = 2$ with the optimal value of $z = -3$. The optimal value for Problem 4B is $-\ 2\ 1/2$, and so further branching here can lead only to solutions with value greater than $-2\ 1/2$. Since an integer solution to the constraints of the original problem has already been obtained at which the value of the objective function is -3, there is no need to branch at Problem 4B. No other problems remain to be considered. The original integer programming problem must have an optimal value of -3 attained at $x_1 = 1$, $x_2 = 2$, the optimal solution to Problem 4A. Note that here, the calculations could cease once the solution to Problem 4A had been found, because the objective function has integer coefficients; it follows from the optimal solution to Problem 1 that the smallest value the objective function can possibly attain at a feasible integer solution is -3, and the solution to Problem 4A provides a lattice point at which this value is attained.

• PROBLEM 6-19

Maximize $z = 8x_1 + 15x_2$

subject to:

$10x_1 + 21x_2 \leq 156$

$$2x_1 + x_2 \leq 22$$

$$x_1, x_2 \geq 0 \text{ and integer}$$

Solve by Branch and Bound algorithm of the integer programming problem.

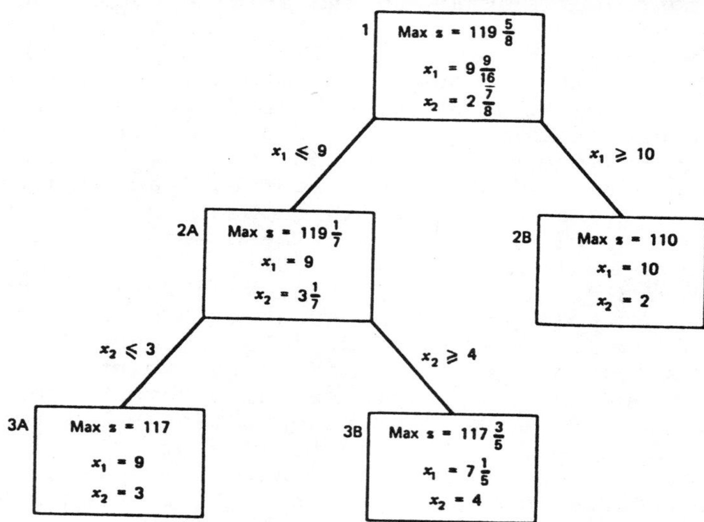

Solution: The Figure contains the completed branch and bound diagram. Upon solving the original problem, Problem 1 of the diagram, the optimal value of z restricted to integer feasible solutions is at most 119. Arbitrarily selecting the x_1 variable, create Problems 2A and 2B. Problem 2B provides a feasible integral solution to the original constraints and a lower bound of 110 for the final maximal value of z. Restrictions on x_2 lead to Problems 3A and 3B from Problem 2A. The integer solution to Problem 3A yields the improved lower bound of 117 for the optimal value of z. The optimal value for Problem 3B exceeds 117, but only by a fraction, and so the value of z at any integer solution to the constraints of Problem 3B cannot exceed 117. Thus the algorithm terminates. The optimal value for the objective function for the integer restricted problem is 117, and one point at which this value is attained is $x_1 = 9$, $x_2 = 3$.

• PROBLEM 6-20

Consider the problem

Maximize $z = 3x_1 + 13x_2$

subject to:

$$2x_1 + 9x_2 \leq 40$$

$$11x_1 - 8x_2 \leq 82$$

$x_1, x_2 \geq 0$ and integer

Solve by branch and bound algorithm.

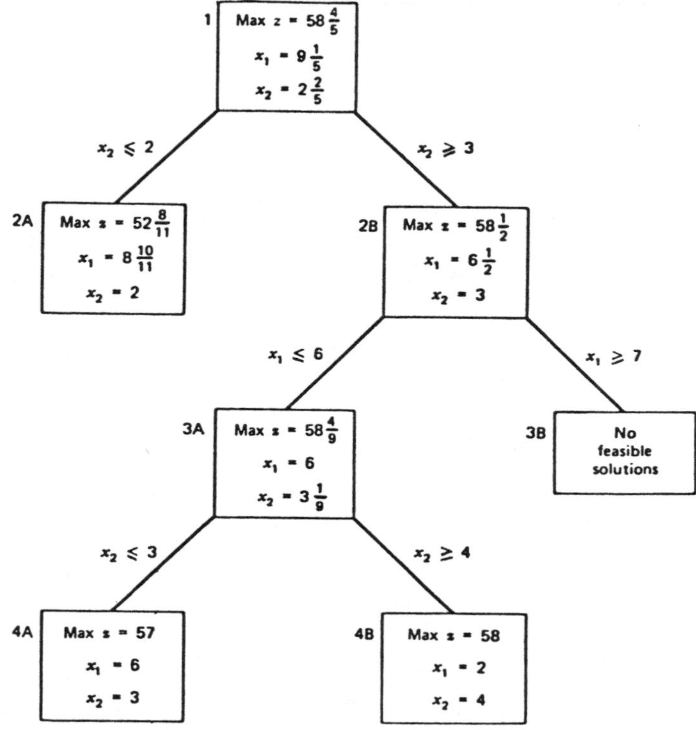

Solution:

Figure contains the completed branch and bound diagram. Note that after branching from Problem 1 to Problems 2A and 2B, and solving these problems, there is the choice of problems from which to work. The maximal value of the objective function under the constraints of Problem 2B is 58 1/2, but under the constraints of 2A is only 52 8/11. Thus, at this time work from Problem 2B and hold Problem 2A in abeyance for future consideration. But then the optimal value for z of 58 in Problem 4B attained at the feasible integer solution x = 2, x = 4 makes further consideration of Problem 2A unnecessary, and the algorithm terminates with this solution as the optimal solution to the interger programming problem.

• PROBLEM 6-21

Maximize $-x_1 + 15x_2$,

Subject to:

$-x_1 + 10x_2 \leq 10$

$x_1 + x_2 \leq 6$

$x_1, x_2 \geq 0$, integer

Solve by Branch and Bound method.

Solution: The Simplex method produces

	x_3	x_4	
x_1	$-\frac{1}{11}$	$\frac{10}{11}$	$\frac{50}{11}$
x_2	$\frac{1}{11}$	$\frac{1}{11}$	$\frac{16}{11}$
	$\frac{16}{11}$	$\frac{5}{11}$	$\frac{190}{11}$

The value of x_1 is between 4 and 5. The first row shows that, in orded to make $x_1 = 4$, x_4 has to be increased. We deal with this by exchanging x_1 and x_4, to obtain

	x_3	x_1	
x_4	$-\frac{1}{10}$	$\frac{11}{10}$	5
x_2	$\frac{1}{10}$	$-\frac{1}{10}$	1
	$\frac{3}{2}$	$-\frac{1}{2}$	15

This means that, if $x_1 = 4$, $x_2 = 7/5$, $x_4 = 3/5$, and the objective function has value 17. The value of x_2 is between 1 and 2. For x_2 to be 1, less than now, x_3 must be increased. Exchange x_2 and x_3;

	x_2	x_1	
x_4	1	1	6
x_3	10	- 1	10
	- 15	1	0

This means that if $x_1 = 4$, $x_2 = 1$, then $x_4 = 1$, $x_3 = 4$, and the objective function has value 11. All variables are integers.

However, also consider $x_1 = 4$ and $x_2 = 2$. To obtain this, x_1 must be increased. But then x_4 would be negative, and this branch need not be continued.

Go back to the final Simplex tableau and investigate the case $x_1 = 5$. This is brought about by increasing x_3. An exchange of x_1 and x_3 produces

x_1 x_4

x_3	-11	-10	-50
x_5	1	1	6
	16	15	90.

For x_1 to be 5, we take $x_3 = 5$, $x_2 = 1$, and the objective function equals 10. All variables are integers, but 10 is less than 11, which can be obtained with integer variables when x_1 was 4. This also means that it is not necessary to consider higher values for x_1, but lower values than 4 might be useful. In fact, if they are investigated, it will turn out that one must go down to $x_1 = 0$, and then reach the optimal answer which is $x_1 = 0$, $x_2 = 1$, $x_3 = 0$, $x_4 = 5$, objective function 15.

• PROBLEM 6-22

Consider the following problem

$$\text{Maximize } f(x) = 9x_1 + 6x_2 + 5x_3$$

subject to:

$$2x_1 + 3x_2 + 7x_3 \leq \frac{35}{2}$$

$$4x_1 + 9x_3 \leq 15$$

$$x_1, x_2, x_3 \geq 0 \text{ and are integers.}$$

Solve by branch-and-bound method of integer programming.

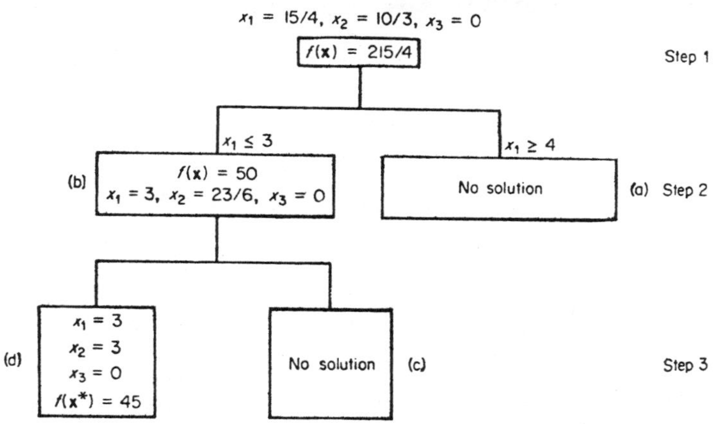

Fig. 1

Solution:

Step 1: First obtain the following linear programming solution.

$x_1 = \frac{15}{4}$, $x_2 = \frac{10}{3}$, $x_3 = 0$, $f(x) = \frac{215}{4}$ (not all integers).

Step 2: Choosing the variable x_1, create two new problems, (a) and (b). One has no feasible solution and one generates the following solution:

$x_1 = 3$, $x_2 = \frac{23}{6}$, $x_3 = 0$, $f(x) = 50$.

Step 3: The problem (b) of step 2 can be divided into two more problems.

(c) Maximize

$$f(x) = 9x_1 + 6x_2 + 5x_3$$

subject to:

$$2x_1 + 3x_2 + 7x_3 \leq \frac{35}{2}$$

$$4x_1 + 9x_3 \leq 15$$

$$0 \leq x_1 \leq 3$$

$$x_2 \geq 4$$

$$x_3 \geq 0$$

(d) Maximize

$$f(x) = 9x_1 + 6x_2 + 5x_3$$

subject to:

$$2x_1 + 3x_2 + 7x_3 \leq \frac{35}{2}$$

$$4x_1 + 9x_3 \leq 15$$

$$0 \leq x_1 \leq 3$$

$$0 \leq x_2 \leq 3$$

$$x_3 \geq 0.$$

Problem (c) has no feasible solution, while the solution to problem (d) is given by $x_1 = 3$, $x_2 = 3$, $x_3 = 0$, $f(x^*) = 45$.

Since this solution is all-integer, the procedure terminates. For a summary of the branch-and-bound procedures, see Fig. 1.

Maximize $f(x) = 9x_1 + 6x_2 + 5x_3$

subject to:

$$2x_1 + 3x_2 + 7x_3 \le \frac{35}{2}$$

$$4x_1 + 9x_3 \le 15$$

x_1 nonnegative integer.

Solve by branch-and-bound technique of integer programming.

Solution:

Step 1: Solve the problem as an ordinary linear program.

x_0	x_1	x_2	x_3	x_4	x_4	RHS
1	−9	−6	−5	0	0	0
0	2	3	7	1	0	35/2
0	4	0	9	0	1	15

x_0	x_1	x_2	x_3	x_4	x_5	RHS
1	0	15/2	53/2	9/2	0	35/4 x 9
0	1	3/2	7/2	1/2	0	35/4
0	0	−6	−5	−2	1	−20

x_0	x_1	x_2	x_3	x_4	x_5	RHS
1	0	0	81/4	2	5/4	35/4 x 9 − 10/3 x 15/2
0	1	0	23/4	0	1/4	15/4
0	0	1	5/6	1/3	−1/6	10/3

$x_1 = 15/4,\ x_2 = 10/3,\ x_3 = 0,\ f(\mathbf{x}) = 215/4$

Step 2: This solution does not satisfy the integer restrictions, so divide the original problem into two mutually exclusive and exhaustive subproblems.

(a) Maximize

$$f(x) = 9x_1 + 6x_2 + 5x_3$$

subject to:

$$2x_1 + 3x_2 + 7x_3 \le \frac{35}{2}$$

$$4x_1 \qquad + 9x_3 \le 15$$

$$x_1 \qquad \ge 4 \text{ (integer)}$$

$$x_2,\ x_3 \ge 0.$$

(b) Maximize

$$f(x) = 9x_1 + 6x_2 + 5x_3$$

subject to:

$$2x_1 + 3x_2 + 7x_3 \le \frac{35}{2}$$

$$4x_1 \qquad + 9x_3 \le 15$$

$$0 \le x_1 \qquad \le 3 \text{ (integer)}$$

$$x_2, x_3 \ge 0.$$

It is clear that problem (a) has no feasible solution. The solution to problem (b) is given by: $x_1 = 3$, $x_2 = \frac{23}{6}$, $x_3 = 0$.

$$f(x) = 50.$$

Since this satisfies all problem restrictions, it is a feasible and optimal solution.

• PROBLEM 6-24

Maximize $f(\vec{x}) = 3x_1 + 2x_2$

subject to:

$$5x_1 + 4x_2 \le 23.7$$

$$x_1,\ x_2 \text{ integer} \qquad \vec{x} \ge 0.$$

Formulate as a zero-one, integer program and solve by Branch-and-Bound algorithm.

Solution: Due to the integrality requirements on the solution variable, the following constraints are implied:

$$x_1 \le 4 \quad \text{and} \quad x_2 \le 5.$$

Since the upper bounds on x_1 and x_2 are $U_1 = 4$ and $U_2 = 5$, reformulate the problem as follows. Consider replacing x_1 with two binary variables; that is, $k = 1$. From the above,

$$2^{k+1} \geq U_1 + 1 \geq 5$$

or

$$2^2 = 4 \geq 5.$$

Since the inequality is not satisfied, k = 2 is required; that is,

$$2^3 = 8 \geq 5$$

hence

$$x_1 = \sum_{\ell=0}^{2} 2^{\ell} Y_{\ell} = Y_0 + 2Y_1 + 4Y_2 .$$

In a similar manner, the transformation of x_2 in terms of a binary vector Z is given by:

$$x_2 = Z_0 + 2Z_1.$$

The new problem is formulated as follows:

$$\text{maximize } f(\vec{Y}, \vec{Z}) = 3Y_0 + 6Y_1 + 12Y_2 + 2Z_0 + 4Z_1$$

subject to:

$$5Y_0 + 10Y_1 + 20Y_1 + 4Z_0 + 8Z_1 \leq 23.7$$

$$\vec{Y}, \vec{Z} \geq 0$$

$$\vec{Y}, \vec{Z}, \text{ binary.}$$

The solution is given by

$$Y_0 = 1, \quad Y_1 = 1, \quad Y_2 = 0$$

$$Z_0 = 0, \quad Z_1 = 1, \; f^*(\vec{Y}, \vec{Z}) = 13.$$

Transforming back to the original solution space, we obtain the following:

$$x_1^* = 3, \quad x_2^* = 2, \; f^*(x) = 13.$$

CUTTING PLANE METHOD

• PROBLEM 6-25

Consider the integer linear programming problem,

$$\text{maximize } x_0 = 7x_1 + 9x_2$$

subject to: $-x_1 + 3x_2 \leq 6$

$$7x_1 + x_2 \leq 35$$

x_1, x_2 nonnegative integers.

The optimal continuous solution is given by

Basic	x_0	x_1	x_2	x_3	x_4	Solution
x_0	①	0	0	28/11	15/11	63
x_2	0	0	①	7/22	1/22	7/2
x_1	0	①	0	−1/22	3/22	9/2

Solve by the cutting plane method.

Solution: Note that a basic requirement for the application of this algorithm is that all the coefficients and the right-hand side constraint must be integer. For example, the constraint

$$x_1 + \frac{1}{3} x_2 \le \frac{13}{2}$$

must be transformed to

$$6x_1 + 2x_2 \le 39$$

where no fractions are present. The latter is achieved by multiplying both sides of the original constraint by the least common multiple of the denominators.

The above requirement is imposed since, as will be shown later, the pure integer algorithm does not differentiate between the regular and slack variables of the problem in the sense that all variables must be integers. The presence of fractional coefficients in the constraints thus may not allow the slack variables to assume integer values. In this case, the fractional algorithm may indicate that no feasible solution exists, even though the problem may have a feasible integer solution in terms of nonslack variables.

The fractional algorithm is as follows: First, the problem is solved as a regular linear programming problem: that is, disregarding the integrality condition. If the optimal solution happens to be integer, there is nothing more to be done. Otherwise, the secondary constraints which will force the solution toward the integer solution are developed as follows. Let the final optimal tableau for the linear program be given by:

Basic	x_0	x_1	$\cdots$	x_i	$\cdots$	x_m	w_1	$\cdots$	w_j	$\cdots$	w_n	Solution
x_0	①	0	$\cdots$	0	$\cdots$	0	$\bar{c}_1$	$\cdots$	$\bar{c}_j$	$\cdots$	$\bar{c}_n$	β_0
x_1	0	①	$\cdots$	0	$\cdots$	0	α_1^1	$\cdots$	α_1^j	$\cdots$	α_1^n	β_1
$\vdots$	$\vdots$	$\vdots$		$\vdots$		$\vdots$	$\vdots$		$\vdots$		$\vdots$	$\vdots$
x_i	0	0	$\cdots$	①	$\cdots$	0	α_i^1	$\cdots$	α_i^j	$\cdots$	α_i^n	β_i
$\vdots$	$\vdots$	$\vdots$		$\vdots$		$\vdots$	$\vdots$		$\vdots$		$\vdots$	$\vdots$
x_m	0	0	$\cdots$	0	$\cdots$	①	α_m^1	$\cdots$	α_m^j	$\cdots$	α_m^n	β_m

The variables x_i $(i = 1, 2, \ldots, m)$ represent the basic variables while the variables w_j $(j = 1, 2, \ldots, n)$ are the nonbasic variables. These variables have been arranged as such for convenience.

Consider the ith equation where the basic variable x_i assumes a noninteger value.

$$x_i = \beta_i - \sum_{j=1}^{n} \alpha_i^j w_j \qquad \beta_i \text{ noninteger (Source row)}$$

Any such equation will be referred to as a source row. Since in general the coefficients of the objective function can be made integer, the variable x_0 is also integer and the x_0-equation may be selected as a source row. Indeed, the convergence proof of the algorithm requires that x_0 be integer.

Let

$$\beta_i = [\beta_i] + f_i$$

$$\alpha_i^j = [\alpha_i^j] + f_{ij}$$

where $N = [a]$ is the largest integer such that $N \leq a$. It follows that $0 < f_i < 1$ and $0 \leq f_{ij} < 1$; that is, f_i is a strictly positive fraction and f_{ij} is a nonnegative fraction. For example,

a	$[a]$	$f = a - [a]$
$1\frac{1}{2}$	1	1/2
$-2\frac{1}{3}$	-3	2/3
-1	-1	0
$-2/5$	-1	3/5

The source row thus yields

$$f_i - \sum_{j=1}^{n} f_{ij} w_j = x_i - [\beta_i] + \sum_{j=1}^{n} [\alpha_i^j] w_j$$

In order for all the variables x_i and w_j to be integer, the right-hand side of the above equation must be integer. Given $f_{ij} \geq 0$ and $w_j \geq 0$ for all i and j, it follows that $\Sigma_{j=1}^{n} f_{ij} w_j \geq 0$. Consequently,

$$f_i - \sum_{j=1}^{n} f_{ij} w_j \leq f_i.$$

This means $f_i - \Sigma_{j=1}^{n} f_{ij} w_j < 1$ because $f_i < 1$. Since the left-hand side must be integer, a necessary condition for satisfying the integrality becomes

$$f_i - \sum_{j=1}^{n} f_{ij} w_j \leq 0.$$

The last constraint can be put in the form

$$S_i = \sum_{j=1}^{n} f_{ij} w_j - f_i \qquad \text{(Fractional cut)}$$

where S_i is a nonnegative slack variable which by definition must be an integer. This constraint equation defines the so-called fractional cut. From the last tableau, $w_j = 0$ and thus $S_i = -f_i$, which is infeasible. This means that the new constraint is not satisfied by the given solution. The dual simplex method can then be used to clear this infeasibility, which is equivalent to cutting off the solution space toward the optimal integer solution.

The new tableau after adding the fractional cut will thus become

Basic	x_0	x_1	$\cdots$	x_i	$\cdots$	x_m	w_1	$\cdots$	w_j	$\cdots$	w_n	S_i	Solution
x_0	①	0	$\cdots$	0	$\cdots$	0	$\bar{c}_1$	$\cdots$	$\bar{c}_j$	$\cdots$	$\bar{c}_n$	0	β_0
x_1	0	①	$\cdots$	0	$\cdots$	0	α_1^1	$\cdots$	α_1^j	$\cdots$	α_1^n	0	β_1
$\vdots$	$\vdots$	$\vdots$		$\vdots$		$\vdots$	$\vdots$		$\vdots$		$\vdots$	$\vdots$	$\vdots$
x_i	0	0	$\cdots$	①	$\cdots$	0	α_i^1	$\cdots$	α_i^j	$\cdots$	α_i^n	0	β_i
$\vdots$	$\vdots$	$\vdots$		$\vdots$		$\vdots$	$\vdots$		$\vdots$		$\vdots$	$\vdots$	$\vdots$
x_m	0	0	$\cdots$	0	$\cdots$	①	α_m^1	$\cdots$	α_m^j	$\cdots$	α_m^n	0	β_m
S_i	0	0	$\cdots$	0	$\cdots$	0	$-f_{i1}$	$\cdots$	$-f_{ij}$	$\cdots$	$-f_{in}$	①	$-f_i$

If the new solution (after applying dual simplex method) is integer, the process ends. Otherwise, a new fractional cut is constructed from the resulting tableau and the dual simplex method is used again to clear the infeasiblity. This procedure is repeated until an integer solution is achieved. However, if at any iteration the dual simplex algorithm indicates that no feasible solution exists, the problem has no feasible integer solution.

In the above given problem, since the optimal solution is noninteger, a fractional cut must be added to the tableau. Generally, any of the constraint equations corresponding to a noninteger solution can be selected to generate the cut. However, as a rule of tumb, one usually chooses the equation corresponding to $\max_i \{f_i\}d$.

Since both equations in this problem have the same value of f_i, that is, $f_1 = f_2 = 1/2$, either one may be used. Consider the x_2-equation. This gives:

$$x_2 + \frac{7}{22} x_3 + \frac{1}{22} x_4 = 3\ \frac{1}{2}$$

or

$$x_2 + \left(0 + \frac{7}{22}\right) x_3 + \left(0 + \frac{1}{22}\right) x_4 = \left(3 + \frac{1}{2}\right)$$

Hence, the corresponding fractional cut is given by

$$S_1 - \frac{7}{22}x_3 - \frac{1}{22}x_4 = -\frac{1}{2}$$

This gives the new tableau

Basic	x_0	x_1	x_2	x_3	x_4	S_1	R.H.S.
x_0	(1)	0	0	28/11	15/11	0	63
x_2	0	0	(1)	7/22	1/22	0	$3\frac{1}{2}$
x_1	0	(1)	0	−1/22	3/22	0	$4\frac{1}{2}$
S_1	0	0	0	−7/22	−1/22	(1)	−1/2

The dual simplex method yields

Basic	x_0	x_1	x_2	x_3	x_4	S_1	Solution
x_0	(1)	0	0	0	1	8	59
x_2	0	0	(1)	0	0	1	3
x_1	0	(1)	0	0	1/7	−1/7	$4\frac{4}{7}$
x_3	0	0	0	(1)	1/7	−22/7	$1\frac{4}{7}$

Since the solution is still noninteger, a new cut is constructed. The x_1- equation is written as

$$x_1 + \left(0 + \frac{1}{7}\right)x_4 + \left(-1 + \frac{6}{7}\right)S_1 = \left(4 + \frac{4}{7}\right)$$

which gives the cut

$$S_2 - \frac{1}{7}x_4 - \frac{6}{7}S_1 = -\frac{4}{7}$$

Adding this constraint to the last tableau, one gets

Basic	x_0	x_1	x_2	x_3	x_4	S_1	S_2	R.H.S.
x_0	(1)	0	0	0	1	8	0	59
x_2	0	0	(1)	0	0	1	0	3
x_1	0	(1)	0	0	1/7	−1/7	0	$4\frac{4}{7}$
x_3	0	0	0	(1)	1/7	−22/7	0	$1\frac{4}{7}$
S_2	0	0	0	0	−1/7	−6/7	(1)	−4/7

The dual simplex method now yields:

Basic	x_0	x_1	x_2	x_3	x_4	S_1	S_2	Solution
x_0	(1)	0	0	0	0	2	7	55
x_2	0	0	(1)	0	0	1	0	3
x_1	0	(1)	0	0	0	−1	1	4
x_3	0	0	0	(1)	0	−4	1	1
x_4	0	0	0	0	(1)	6	−7	4

which gives the optimal integer solution $x_0 = 55$, $x_1 = 4$, $x_2 = 3$.

The reader can verify graphically that the addition of the above cuts "cuts" the solution space as desired (see Figure). The first cut

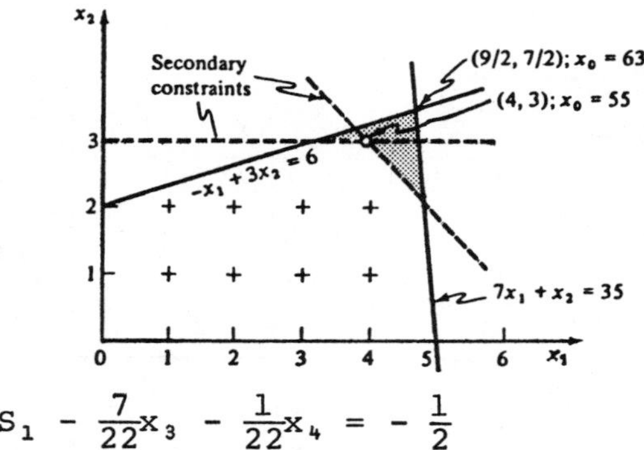

$$S_1 - \frac{7}{22}x_3 - \frac{1}{22}x_4 = -\frac{1}{2}$$

can be expressed in terms of x_1 and x_2 only by using the appropriate substitution as follows:

$$S_1 - \frac{7}{22}(6 + x_1 - 3x_2) - \frac{1}{22}(35 - 7x_1 - x_2) = -\frac{1}{2}$$

or $\qquad S_1 + x_2 = 3$

which is equivalent to

$$x_2 \leq 3.$$

Similarly, for the second cut

$$S_2 - \frac{1}{7}x_4 - \frac{6}{7}S_1 = -\frac{4}{7}$$

the equivalent constraint in terms of x_1 and x_2 is

$$x_1 + x_2 \leq 7.$$

Figure shows that the addition of these two constaints will result in the new (optimal) extreme point (4, 3).

• PROBLEM 6-26

Consider the following integer program.

Minimize $3x_1 + 4x_2$

subject to: $3x_1 + x_2 \geq 4$

$x_1 + 2x_2 \geq 4$

$x_1, x_2 \geq 0$

x_1, x_2 integer

Solve by applying the cutting plane method.

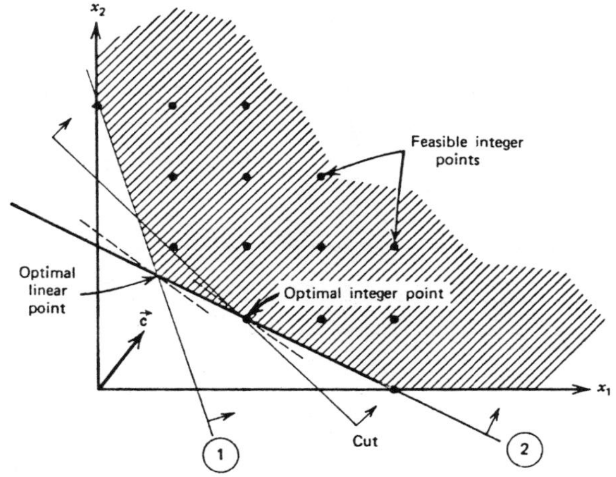

Fig. 1

Solution: In Figure 1 the optimal linear programming and integer programming solutions are shown respectively.

Ignoring the integer conditions, the following tableau gives the optimal linear programming solution.

	z	x_1	x_2	x_3	x_4	RHS
z	1	0	0	$-\frac{2}{5}$	$-\frac{9}{5}$	$\frac{44}{5}$
x_1	0	1	0	$-\frac{2}{5}$	$\frac{1}{5}$	$\frac{4}{5}$
x_2	0	0	1	$\frac{1}{5}$	$-\frac{3}{5}$	$\frac{8}{5}$

Since this solution is noninteger, one may select a non-integer variable for generating a cut (including z). Select x_2. (Note: Selecting different variables may generate different cuts.) The equation for the basic variable x_2 is

$$x_2 + \frac{1}{5}x_3 - \frac{3}{5}x_4 = \frac{8}{5}.$$

From this one gets

$$I_{23} = 0, \qquad I_{24} = -1, \qquad I_2 = 1$$

$$F_{23} = \frac{1}{5}, \qquad F_{24} = \frac{2}{5}, \qquad F_2 = \frac{3}{5}$$

where I_{ij}, F_{ij} are the integer and fractional parts of the coefficient at the ij-th place in the tableau and I_i, F_i are the integer and fractional parts respectively of the right-hand side of the equation concerned.

The additional constraint becomes:

$$\frac{1}{5}x_3 + \frac{2}{5}x_4 \geq \frac{3}{5} \text{ (cut)}$$

Adding this constraint with slack variable x_5 to the tableau and applying the dual simplex method, get the following tableaux:

	z	x_1	x_2	x_3	x_4	x_5	RHS
z	1	0	0	$-\frac{2}{5}$	$-\frac{9}{5}$	0	$\frac{44}{5}$
x_1	0	1	0	$-\frac{2}{5}$	$\frac{1}{5}$	0	$\frac{4}{5}$
x_2	0	0	1	$\frac{1}{5}$	$-\frac{3}{5}$	0	$\frac{8}{5}$
x_3	0	0	0	$\left(-\frac{1}{5}\right)$	$-\frac{2}{5}$	1	$-\frac{3}{5}$

	z	x_1	x_2	x_3	x_4	x_5	RHS
z	1	0	0	0	-1	-2	10
x_1	0	1	0	0	1	-2	2
x_2	0	0	1	0	-1	1	1
x_3	0	0	0	1	2	-5	3

Hence the optimal integer solution $x^* = (2, 1)$ has been obtained with only one cut. In other integer programs the cutting plane process may have to be many times. If in the foregoing tableau some variable had turned out non-integer, one would have generated a new cut and continued.

It is interesting to examine the cut in terms of the original variables. Substituting $x_3 = 3x_1 + x_2 - 4$ and $x_4 = x_1 + 2x_2 - 4$ into $\frac{1}{5}x_3 + \frac{2}{5}x_4 \geq \frac{3}{5}$ and simplifying, obtain:

$$x_1 + x_2 \geq 3 \qquad \text{(cut in terms of } x_1 \text{ and } x_2\text{)}.$$

It can easily be seen that the addition of this constraint to Figure 1 will yield the required integer optimum.

• PROBLEM 6-27

Consider this problem:

Maximize $\quad f = x_1 + 4x_2$

subject to: $\quad 5x_1 + 7x_2 + x_3 = 21$

$-x_1 + 3x_2 + x_4 = 8$

$x_1, x_2, x_3, x_4 \geq 0$ and integer.

Use cuts to solve this integer problem.

Solution: (Variables x_3 and x_4 are slack variables.) The initial tableau is shown in Fig. 1a. Variable x_2 has the most positive reduced cost. Then $\bar{b}_r/\bar{a}_{r_2} = \min(21/7, 8/3) = 8/3$, which means $\bar{a}_{r2} = 3$. Since $\bar{a}_{r2} > 1$, we generate the cut

$$\left[-\frac{1}{3}\right]x_1 + \left[\frac{3}{3}\right]x_2 + s_1 = \left[\frac{8}{3}\right]$$

or $\quad -x_1 + x_2 + s_1 = 2.$

This is added to the original tableau, as shown in Fig. 1b.

The result of the pivot is shown in Fig. 2a. Variable x_1 has a positive reduced cost. Then $\bar{b}_r/\bar{a}_{r1}$ = min (7/12, 2/2) = 7/12 which means $\bar{a}_{r1}$ = 12. Generate the cut

$$\left[\frac{12}{12}\right]x_1 + \left[\frac{-7}{12}\right]s_1 + s_2 = \left[\frac{7}{12}\right]$$

or $\quad x_1 - s_1 + s_2 = 0.$

This cut is added to the second tableau as shown in Fig. 2b.

		Maximize	1	4	0	0	
i	c_B	x_B	x_1	x_2	x_3	x_4	b_i
1	0	x_3	5	7	1	0	21
2	0	x_4	-1	3	0	1	8
		z_j	0	0	0	0	0
		c_j-z_j	1	4	0	0	

(a)

		Maximize	1	4	0	0	0		
i	c_B	x_B	x_1	x_2	x_3	x_4	s_1	b_i	
1	0	x_3	5	7	1	0	0	21	
2	0	x_4	-1	3	0	1	0	8	
3	0	s_1	-1	(1)	0	0	1	2	Out →
		z_j	0	0	0	0	0	0	
		c_j-z_j	1	4	0	0	0		
				↑ In					

(b)

Figure 1.

Maximize			1	4	0	0	0	
i	c_B	x_B	x_1	x_2	x_3	x_4	s_1	b_i
1	0	x_3	12	0	1	0	-7	7
2	0	x_4	2	0	0	1	-3	2
3	4	x_2	-1	1	0	0	1	2
		z_j	-4	4	0	0	4	8
(a)		c_j-z_j	5	0	0	0	-4	

Maximize			1	4	0	0	0	0		
i	C_B	X_B	x_1	x_2	x_3	x_4	s_1	s_2	b_i	
1	0	x_3	12	0	1	0	-7	0	7	
2	0	x_4	2	0	0	1	-3	0	2	
3	4	x_2	-1	1	0	0	1	0	2	
4	0	s_2	(1)	0	0	0	-1	1	0	Out →
		z_j	-4	4	0	0	4	0	8	
(b)		c_j-z_j	5	0	0	0	-4	0		
			In ↑							

Figure 2.

Maximize			1	4	0	0	0	0	
i	c_B	x_B	x_1	x_2	x_3	x_4	s_1	s_2	b_i
1	0	x_3	0	0	1	0	5	-12	7
2	0	x_4	0	0	0	1	-1	-2	2
3	4	x_2	0	1	0	0	0	1	2
4	1	x_1	1	0	0	0	-1	1	0
		z_j	1	4	0	0	-1	5	8
(a)		c_j-z_j	0	0	0	0	1	-5	

		Maximize	1	4	0	0	0	0	0		
i	c_B	x_B	x_1	x_2	x_3	x_4	s_1	s_2	s_3	b_i	
1	0	x_3	0	0	1	0	5	12	0	7	
2	0	x_4	0	0	0	1	-1	-2	0	2	
3	4	x_2	0	1	0	0	0	1	0	2	
4	1	x_1	1	0	0	0	-1	1	0	0	
5	1	s_3	0	0	0	0	(1)	-3	1	1	Out →
		z_j	1	4	0	0	-1	5	0	8	
(b)		c_j-z_j	0	0	0	0	1	-5	0		
							↑ In				

Figure 3.

The result of the pivot is shown in Fig. 3 a. Variable s_1 has a positive reduced cost. Then $\bar{b}_r/\bar{a}_{rs_1}$ = $\min(\frac{7}{5}) = \frac{7}{5}$ which means $\bar{a}_{rs_1} = 5$.

Generate the cut:

$$\left[\frac{5}{5}\right] s_1 + \left[\frac{-12}{5}\right] s_2 + s_3 = \left[\frac{7}{5}\right]$$

or

$$s_1 - 3s_2 + s_3 = 1$$

This is added to the third tableau, as shown in Fig 3b.

The result of the pivot is shown in Fig. 4. This solution is optimal, resulting in $x_1^* = 1$ and $x_2^* = 2$ with $f^* = \$9$.

This problem may be interpreted geometrically. See Fig. 5. The first cut was:

$$-x_1 + x_2 + s_1 = 2$$

or

$$-x_1 + x_2 \leq 2$$

The second cut was:

$$x_1 - s_1 + s_2 = 0$$

but

$$s_1 = 2 + x_1 - x_2.$$

so we have upon substitution $x_2 \leq 2$. The third cut was

$$s_1 - 3s_2 + s_3 = 1.$$

		Maximize	1	4	0	0	0	0	0	
i	c_B	x_B	x_1	x_2	x_3	x_4	s_1	s_2	s_3	b_i
1	0	x_3	0	0	1	0	0	3	-5	2
2	0	x_4	0	0	0	1	0	-5	1	3
3	4	x_2	0	1	0	0	0	1	0	2
4	1	x_1	1	0	0	0	0	-2	1	1
5	0	s_1	0	0	0	0	1	-3	1	1
		z_j	1	4	0	0	0	2	1	9
		c_j-z_j	0	0	0	0	0	-2	-1	

Figure 4.

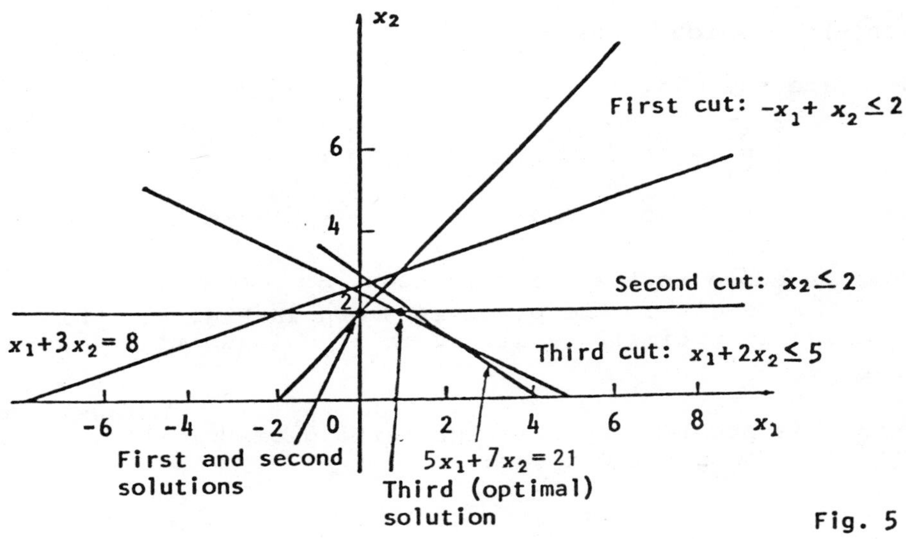

Fig. 5

A similar substitution for the values of s_1 and s_2 yields $x_1 + 2x_2 \leq 5$.

The imposition of the first cut resulted in the first corner point, $x_1 = 0$ and $x_2 = 2$. The imposition of the second cut resulted in a degenerate pivot and the same corner point. Finally, the third cut gave rise to the optimal solution. $x_1^* = 1$ and $x_2^* = 2$.

Consider the problem,

$$\text{Maximize} \quad 3x_1 + 4x_2$$

$$\text{subject to:} \quad \frac{2}{5}x_1 + x_2 \leq 3 \tag{1}$$

$$\frac{2}{5}x_1 - \frac{2}{5}x_2 \leq 1$$

$$x_1,\ x_2 \geq 0 \text{ and integer.}$$

Solve by cutting plane method.

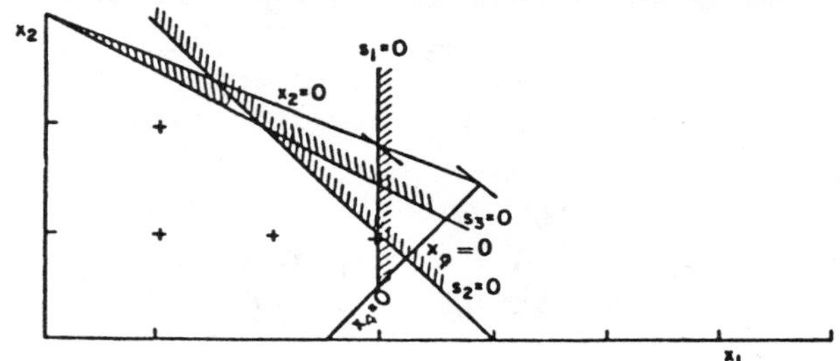

Fig. 1

Solution: Although this problem may be loosely referred to as a pure integer problem, if one introduces the slack variables, the corresponding problem

$$\text{Maximize} \quad 3x_1 + 4x_2$$

$$\text{subject to:} \quad \frac{2}{5}x_1 + x_2 + x_3 = 3$$

$$\frac{2}{5}x_1 - \frac{2}{5}x_2 + x_4 = 1 \tag{2}$$

$$x_1,\ x_2,\ x_3,\ x_4 \geq 0 \text{ and}$$

$$x_1,\ x_2 \text{ integer,}$$

is a mixed integer problem since integer values of x_1, x_2 do not imply that x_3, x_4 must be integer. However, if the two inequalities in (1) are multiplied by the common denominator 5 then this leads to the all-integer problem,

$$\text{Maximize} \quad 3x_1 + 4x_2$$

$$\text{subject to:} \quad 2x_1 + 5x_2 \leq 15 \tag{3}$$

$$2x_1 - 2x_2 \leq 5$$

$x_1, x_2 \geq 0$ and x_1, x_2 integer.

If slack variables x_3, x_4 are introduced, the corresponding problem

$$\text{Maximize} \quad 3x_1 + 4x_2$$

$$\begin{aligned} 2x_1 + 5x_2 + x_3 \quad &= 15 \\ 2x_1 - 2x_2 \quad + x_4 &= 5 \\ x_1, x_2, x_3, x_4 &\geq 0 \\ x_1, x_2 \text{ integer} \end{aligned} \tag{4}$$

is also a pure integer problem since integer values of x_1, x_2 imply x_3, x_4 must also take on integer values.

		$-x_1$	$-x_2$
x_0	0	-3	-4
x_3	15	2	(5)
x_4	5	2	-2
x_1	0	-1	0
x_2	0	0	-1

Tableau 1

		$-x_1$	$-x_3$
x_0	12	$-7/5$	$4/5$
x_3	0	0	-1
x_4	11	$(14/5)$	$2/5$
x_1	0	-1	0
x_2	3	$2/5$	$1/5$

Tableau 2

		$-x_4$	$-x_3$
x_0	$35/2$	$1/2$	1
x_3	0	0	-1
x_4	0	-1	0
x_1	$55/14$	$5/14$	$1/7$
x_2	$10/7$	$-1/7$	$1/7$

Tableau 3

The transformed problem as expressed in the form (4) is set up in Tableau 1. Applying the primal simplex algorithm the continuous optimum solution is obtained as displayed in Tableau 3. The slacks s_1, s_2, s_3 represent the cutting planes introduced in the Tableaux 4, 5, 6, lead to primal infeasibility, and exclude the corresponding optimal solutions. The Tableau 7 contains the optimal integer solution. The slack variables s_1, s_2, s_3 are expressed in terms of structural variables x_1, x_2 (next to the tableau) and the corresponding cutting planes are illustrated in Fig. 1.

		$-x_4$	$-x_3$
x_0	$35/2$	$1/2$	1
x_3	0	0	-1
x_4	0	-1	0
x_1	$55/14$	$5/14$	$1/7$
x_2	$10/7$	$-1/7$	$1/7$
s_1	$-13/14$	$(-5/14)$	$-1/7$

Tableau 4

Cutting plane from the row of x_1 variables

$$5/14x_4 + \frac{x_3}{7} \geq 13/14$$

$$s_1 = -13/14 + 5/14x_4 + \frac{x_3}{7}$$

$$= -13/14 + \frac{5}{14}(5 - 2x_1 + 2x_2) + \frac{1}{7}(15 - 2x_1 - 5x_2)$$

$$= 3 - x_1;\ x_1 + S_1 = 3 \text{ or } x_1 \le 3$$

		$-s_1$	$-x_3$
x_0	81/5	7/5	4/5
x_3	0	0	−1
x_4	13/5	−14/5	2/5
x_1	3	1	0
x_2	9/5	−2/5	1/5
s_2	−4/5	(−3/5)	−1/5

Tableau 5

Cutting plane from the row of x_2 variables

$$\frac{3}{5}s_1 + \frac{x_3}{5} \le 4/5$$

$$s_2 = -4/5 + 3/5s_1 + x_3/5$$

$$= -4/5 + 3/5(3 - x_1) + \frac{1}{5}(15 - 2x_1 - 5x_2)$$

$$= 4 - x_1 - x_2;\ \text{i.e., } x_1 + x_2 \le 4$$

		$-s_2$	$-x_3$	
x_0	43/3	7/3	1/3	
x_3	0	0	−1	
x_4	19/3	−14/3	4/3	
x_1	5/3	5/3	−1/3	
x_2	7/3	−2/3	1/3	←
s_3	−1/3	−1/3	(−1/3)	

Tableau 6

Cutting plane from the row of x_2 variable

$\frac{1}{3}s_2 + \frac{1}{3}x_3 \ge 1/3;$ $\qquad$ $s_3 = -1/3 + s_2/3 + x_3/3$

$$s_3 = 6 - x_1 - 2x_2;\ \text{i.e., } x_1 + 2x_2 \le 6$$

		$-s_2$	$-s_3$
x_0	14	2	1
x_3	1	1	−3
x_4	5	−6	4
x_1	2	2	−1
x_2	2	−1	1

Tableau 7

A company produces reels of paper of width 50 cm, and cuts from it reels of smaller width, dependent on orders it receives. If the width requirement is less than 20 cm, then the technical reasons demand that a reel of 20 cm width must first be cut, from which the reel of smaller width is then obtained by the second cut.

On a certain day the orders received are as follows:

5 reels of width 25, 2 reels of width 18,

6 reels of width 10, 10 reels of width 6.

How should the reels of width 50 cm be cut, so that the trim loss is minimized?

Solution: First, determine how many reels of width 20 cm will be needed. Possible patterns:

(1) Width 18, trim loss 2.

(2) Width 10 + 10, no trim loss.

(3) Width 10 + 6, trim loss 4.

(4) Width 6 + 6 + 6, trim loss 2.

Requirements: $y_1 - z_0 = 2, \quad 2y_2 + y_3 - z_1 = 6$

$$y_3 + 3y_4 - z_2 = 10.$$

Minimize $\quad 2y_1 + 4y_3 + 2y_4 + 10z_1 + 6z_2$

Clearly $y_1 = 2$. Remains to determine y_2, y_3, y_4.

First tableau

	y_2	y_3	y_4	
z_1	-2^*	-1	0	-6
z_2	0	-1	-3	-10
	-20	-20	-20	-120

Third tableau

	z_1	y_3	z_2	
y_2	$\frac{1}{2}$	$\frac{1}{2}$	0	3
y_4	0	$\frac{1}{3}$	$-\frac{1}{3}$	$\frac{10}{3}$

	-10	$-\frac{10}{3}$	$-\frac{20}{3}$	$\frac{20}{3}$
s_1	0	$-\frac{1^*}{3}$	$-\frac{2}{3}$	$-\frac{1}{3}$

Fourth tableau

	z_1	s_1	z_2	
y_2	$-\frac{1}{2}$	$\frac{3}{2}$	-1	$\frac{5}{2}$
y_4	0	1	-1	3
y_3	0	-3	2	1
	-10	-10	0	10
s_2	$-\frac{1}{2}$	$-\frac{1}{2}$	0	$-\frac{1}{2}$

Next tableau gives answer:

either $y_2 = 3, \quad y_3 = 1, \quad y_4 = 3$

or $y_2 = 1, \quad y_3 = 4, \quad y_4 = 2.$

Trim loss 20.

In either case, 7 reels are required, and 2 more for y_1.

5 reels of width 25 and 9 reels of width 20 are to be made up from the following patterns:

(1) 25 + 25, no trim loss;

(2) 25 + 20, trim loss 5;

(3) 20 + 20, trim loss 10.

$$2x_1 + x_2 - t_1 = 5, \qquad x_2 + 2x_3 - t_2 = 9$$

Minimize $5x_2 + 10x_3 + 25t_1 + 20t_2.$

Answer: $x_1 = 2, \quad x_2 = 1, \quad x_3 = 4,$

trim loss 45cm (width of one reel);

or $x_2 = 5, \quad x_3 = 2.$

Trim loss from second cut, 24.

Total trim loss, 69 width.

Notice that one of the possibilities does not use pattern 25 + 25 at all, although this has no trim loss.

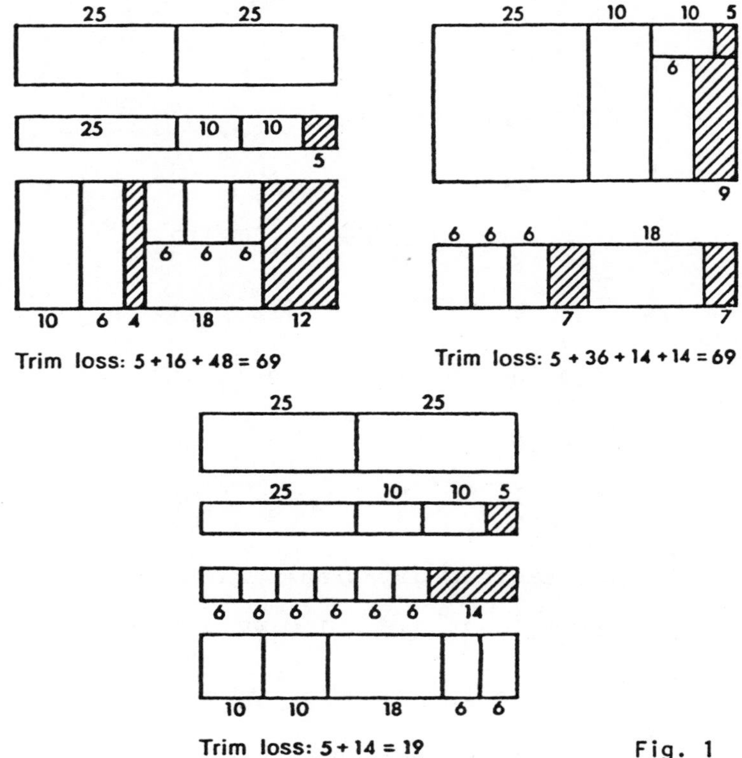

Fig. 1

Of course, if the double cut were not required, the total trim loss would be smaller (see Fig. 1).

• PROBLEM 6-30

Tom wishes to make rice biscuits and requires 16 parts of flour, 8 of ground rice, 12 of sugar, and 12 of margarine. In a supermarket he can buy packets of the following types:

(A) Small packet, containing 4 parts of flour, 3 of sugar, and 2 of margarine.

(B) Small packet, containing 3 parts of ground rice and 4 of sugar.

(C) Large packet, containing 10 parts of flour, 10 of sugar, 8 of margarine, and 5 of ground rice.

(D) Large packet, containing 15 parts of sugar and 10 of margarine.

A large packet costs (a) twice as much, (b) three times a much as a small one, and only entire packets can be bought. Cover the requirements at the cheapest cost.

<u>Solution</u>: Numbers of small packets x_1, x_2

Numbers of large packets y_1, y_2

	x_1	x_2	y_1	y_2	
t_1	-4	0	-10*	0	-16
t_2	0	-3	-5	0	- 8
t_3	-3	-4	-10	-15	-12
t_4	-2	0	-8	-10	-12
	-1	-1	-2	-2	0

	x_1	x_2	t_1	y_2	
y_1	$\frac{2}{5}$	0	$-\frac{1}{10}$	0	$\frac{8}{5}$
t_2	2	-3	$-\frac{1}{2}$	0	0
t_3	1	-4	-1	-15	4
t_4	$\frac{6}{5}$	0	$-\frac{4}{5}$	-10	$\frac{4}{5}$
	$-\frac{1}{5}$	-1	$-\frac{1}{5}$	-2	$\frac{16}{5}$
s_1	$-\frac{1}{5}$	0	$-\frac{1}{5}$*	0	$-\frac{4}{5}$

	x_1	x_2	s_1	y_2	
y_1	$\frac{1}{2}$	0	$-\frac{1}{2}$	0	2
t_2	$\frac{5}{2}$	-3	$-\frac{5}{2}$	0	2
t_3	2	-4	-5	-15	8
t_4	2	0	-4	-10	4
t_1	1	0	-5	0	4
	0	-1	-1	-2	4

Optimal.

(b) Start with last tableau, but with bottom line

	$\frac{1}{2}$	-1	$-\frac{3}{2}$	-3	6
and t_2	$\frac{5^*}{2}$	-3	$-\frac{5}{2}$	0	2

leads to two optimal tableaus:

	s_2	x_2	s_1	y_2	
y_1	$-\frac{1}{2}$	1	0	0	2
x_1	1	-2	-1	0	0
t_3	-2	0	-3	-15	8
t_4	-2	4	-2	-10	4
t_1	-1	2	-4	0	4
t_2	$-\frac{5}{2}$	2	0	0	2
	$-\frac{1}{2}$	0	-1	-3	6

or

	t_2	s_2	s_1	y_2	
y_1	$-\frac{1}{2}$	$\frac{3}{4}$	0	0	1
x_1	1	$-\frac{3}{2}$	-1	0	2
t_3	0	-2	-3	-15	8
t_4	-2	3	-2	-10	0
t_1	-1	$\frac{3}{2}$	-4	0	2
x_2	$\frac{1}{2}$	$-\frac{5}{4}$	0	0	1
	0	$-\frac{1}{2}$	-1	-3	6

Consider the problem:

$$\max x_0 = 2x_1 + x_2$$

$$x_1 + x_2 + x_3 = 5$$

$$-x_1 + x_2 + x_4 = 0$$

$$6x_1 + 2x_2 + x_5 = 21$$

$$x_1, \ldots, x_5 \geq 0, \text{ integer},$$

and use cuts to solve.

Solution: Solve the corresponding LP. This yields the tableau of Table 1.

Table 1

		$-x_3$	$-x_5$
x_0	$\frac{31}{4}$	$\frac{1}{2}$	$\frac{1}{4}$
x_1	$\frac{11}{4}$	$-\frac{1}{2}$	$\frac{1}{4}$
x_2	$\frac{9}{4}$	$\frac{3}{2}$	$-\frac{1}{4}$
x_4	$\frac{1}{2}$	-2	$\frac{1}{2}$

Using the formula $s_i = -f_{i0} + \sum_{j \in r} f_{ij} x_i, \quad s_i \geq 0$

where s_i is a nonnegative slack variable which by definition must be an integer to generate cuts, yeilds:

$$\frac{x_3}{2} + \frac{x_5}{4} \geq \frac{3}{4} \qquad (x_0 \text{ row})$$

$$\frac{x_3}{2} + \frac{x_5}{4} \geq \frac{3}{4} \qquad (x_1 \text{ row})$$

$$\frac{x_3}{2} + \frac{3x_5}{4} \geq \frac{1}{4} \qquad (x_2 \text{ row})$$

$$\frac{x_5}{2} \geq \frac{1}{2} \qquad (x_4 \text{ row})$$

Each row could serve as the source of a cut or simply as a source row. Note, however, that the cuts generated from the first two rows happen to be identical and the cut generated from the third row is weaker than the cut from the first, since any nonnegative (x_3, x_5) that satisfies the first satisfies the third, but not conversely.

The x_4 row cut is equivalent to

$$6x_1 + 2x_2 \leq 20.$$

Similarly,

$$\frac{x_3}{2} + \frac{x_5}{4} \geq \frac{3}{4}$$

is equivalent to

$$2x_1 + x_2 \leq 7.$$

These two cuts together with $Ax = b, x \geq 0$ are shown in Figure 1. If both of these cuts were added to the LP, they would yield the optimal integer solution $(x_1, x_2) = (3,1)$.

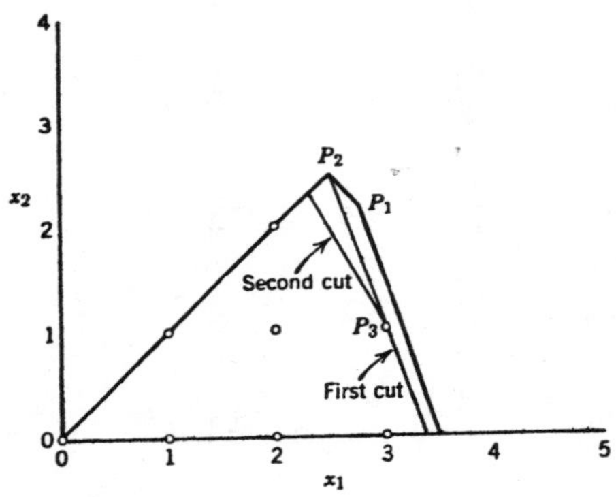

Fig. 1

When adding constraints that exclude the present basic solution to an optimal (primal and dual feasible) tableau, dual feasibility is retained. Thus it is convenient to reoptimize using the dual simplex algorithm. Usually, only one constraint is added at a time.

Suppose the x_4 row cut is appended, or

$$-\frac{x_5}{2} + s_1 = -\frac{1}{2}, \qquad s_1 \geq 0$$

to the tableau of Table 1. This yields Table 2, with $s_1 = -1/2$ as a new basic variable in the dual feasible solution.

Table 2

		$-x_3$	$-x_5$ ↓
x_0	$\frac{31}{4}$	$\frac{1}{2}$	$\frac{1}{4}$
x_1	$\frac{11}{4}$	$-\frac{1}{2}$	$\frac{1}{4}$
x_2	$\frac{9}{4}$	$\frac{3}{2}$	$-\frac{1}{4}$
Source x_4	$\frac{1}{2}$	-2	$\frac{1}{2}$
← Cut s_1	$-\frac{1}{2}$	0	$-\frac{1}{2}$

Following the dual simplex algorithm, s_1 leaves and x_5 enters the basis. After pivoting, Table 3 (excluding the bottom row), is obtained.

Table 3

		$-x_3$ ↓	$-s_1$
x_0	$\frac{30}{4}$	$\frac{1}{2}$	$\frac{1}{2}$
Source x_1	$\frac{10}{4}$	$-\frac{1}{2}$	$\frac{1}{2}$
x_2	$\frac{10}{4}$	$\frac{3}{2}$	$-\frac{1}{2}$
x_4	0	-2	1
x_5	1	0	-1
← Cut s_2	$-\frac{1}{2}$	$-\frac{1}{2}$	$-\frac{1}{2}$

The solution in Table 3 (excluding the bottom row) is primal and dual feasible, but not all-integer. Another constraint must be added. Choose the x_0, x_1, or x_2 row as a source row. Arbitrarily selecting the x_1 row, obtain

$$\frac{x_3}{2} + \frac{s_1}{2} \geq \frac{1}{2} .$$

Thus add the constraint

$$-\frac{x_3}{2} - \frac{s_1}{2} + s_2 = -\frac{1}{2}$$

to Table 3 and reoptimize. The departing variable is s_2. Either x_3 or s_1 can enter, and choose x_3. After pivoting, obtain Table 4.

Table 4

		$-s_2$	$-s_1$
x_0	7	1	0
x_1	3	-1	1
x_2	1	3	-2
x_4	2	-4	3
x_5	1	0	-1
x_3	1	-2	1

The solution in Table 4 is primal and dual feasible, and integer; therefore it is optimal to the Integer Linear Program. The steps from Table 2 to Table 4 are equivalent to going from P_1 to P_2 to P_3 in Figure 1, since the constraint

$$\frac{x_3}{2} + \frac{s_1}{2} \geq \frac{1}{2}$$

is equivalent to

$$2x_1 + x_2 \leq 7.$$

• PROBLEM 6-32

Minimize $x_1 - 3x_2$

subject to:

$$x_1 - x_2 \leq 2$$

$$2x_1 + 4x_2 \leq 15$$

$$x_1, x_2 \geq 0 \text{ and integer.}$$

First solve by the Simplex Method. If integer values cannot be obtained, apply Gomory's Cutting Plane Method.

Solution: Adding integer restricted slack variables x_3 and x_4 and using the simplex algorithm on the associated linear programming problem yields the tableaux of Table 1. The minimal value of the objective function, ignoring the integer constraints, is attained at $x_1 = 0$, $x_2 = 15/4 = 3\ 3/4$ (and $x_3 = 2\ 3/4$, $x_4 = 0$). Since this point has noninteger coordinates, a new constraint needs to be generated.

Table 1

	x_1	x_2	x_3	x_4	
x_3	1	−1	1	0	2
x_4	2	(4)	0	1	15
	1	−3	0	0	0
x_3	$\frac{3}{2}$	0	1	$\frac{1}{4}$	$\frac{23}{4}$
x_2	$\frac{1}{2}$	1	0	$\frac{1}{4}$	$\frac{15}{4}$
	$\frac{5}{2}$	0	0	$\frac{3}{4}$	$\frac{45}{4}$

To generate these new constraints, suppose after solving the associated linear programming problem, the constant term of the ith row of the final tableau is not an integer. Then, in the optimal basic solution corresponding to this final tableau, the value of the basic variable isolated in the ith row will not be integral, and so a new constraint needs to be added.

Attaching back the variables, suppose this ith constraint is

$$\sum_j a_{ij}x_j = b_i. \qquad (1)$$

Letting [a] denote the greatest integer in a (i.e., the greatest integer less than or equal to a, and so [3 4/5] = 3, [1] = 1, [-3 2/5] = -4), define the fractional part of a number a by a - [a]. Thus the fractional part of 3 4/5 is 4/5, of 1 is 0, and of -3 2/5 is -3 2/5 - (-4) = 3/5. Notice that the fractional part of a number must be nonnegative and less than 1. Now let f_{ij} and f_i denote the fractional parts of a_{ij} and b_i, respectively, that is,

$$f_{ij} = a_{ij} - [a_{ij}]$$

$$f_i = b_i - [b_i].$$

Then rewrite (1) as

$$\sum_j ([a_{ij}] + f_{ij})x_j = [b_i] + f_i$$

or

$$\sum_j f_{ij}x_j - f_i = [b_i] - \sum_j [a_{ij}]x_j. \qquad (2)$$

Notice that all the constant terms on the right side of (2) are integer. Thus, for any integer solution to the original system of constraints, the right side, and therefore the left side of (2), must be integer. Moreover, since all variables are nonnegative and f_i is less than 1, the left side of (2) must be greater than or equal to the integer 0. Hence the new constraint:

$$\sum_j f_{ij}x_j - f_i \geq 0 \quad \text{and integer.}$$

To do this work with any constraining equation from the final tableau that has a noninteger constant term, and so, in this case, either equation can be used. Consider the equation defined by the first row of the final tableau

$$\frac{3}{2}x_1 + x_3 + \frac{1}{4}x_4 = \frac{23}{4},$$

separating all constants into their integer and fractional parts

$$(1 + \frac{1}{2})x_1 + x_3 + \frac{1}{4}x_4 = 5 + \frac{3}{4}.$$

Therefore;

$$\frac{1}{2}x_1 + \frac{1}{4}x_4 - \frac{3}{4} = 5 - x_1 - x_3.$$

Now, since only integer solutions are desired, the right side and therefore the left side of this equation must be integer. And, since all variables are nonnegative, the left side must be greater than or equal to -3/4. Combining, we want solutions such that

$$\frac{1}{2}x_1 + \frac{1}{4}x_4 - \frac{3}{4}$$

is a nonnegative integer, say x_5. It is this constraint that is added to the two orginal constraints, giving the appended problem of

Minimizing $\frac{5}{2}x_1 + \frac{3}{4}x_4 - \frac{45}{4}$

subject to:

$$\frac{3}{2}x_1 + x_3 + \frac{1}{4}x_4 = \frac{23}{4}$$

$$\frac{1}{2}x_1 + x_2 + \frac{1}{4}x_4 = \frac{15}{4}$$

$$\frac{1}{2}x_1 + \frac{1}{4}x_4 - x_5 = \frac{3}{4}$$

$$x_1, x_2, x_3, x_4, x_5 \geq 0 \quad \text{and integer.}$$

Here the final tableau data of Table 1 has been used in expressing the original problem. Notice that the optimal solution found above, $x_1 = x_4 = 0$, $x_2 = 15/4$, $x_3 = 23/4$, does not satisfy the new constraint.

Now proceed to solve the corresponding linear programming problem. To do this, add a constraint to a completed problem and use the Dual Simplex Algorithm. After multiplying the new constraint by (-1), there are, as basic variables for the first tableau, the basic variables of the previous final tableau (x_3 and x_2) along with the new variable x_5. The tableaux are presented in Table 2. The solution point here has all integer coordinates, and is therefore the solution to the original integer programming problem. The minimal value of the objective function is -9 and is attained at the point $x_1 = 0$, $x_2 = 3$.

Table 2

	x_1	x_2	x_3	x_4	x_5	
x_3	$\frac{3}{2}$	0	1	$\frac{1}{4}$	0	$\frac{23}{4}$
x_2	$\frac{1}{2}$	1	0	$\frac{1}{4}$	0	$\frac{15}{4}$
x_5	$-\frac{1}{2}$	0	0	$\left(-\frac{1}{4}\right)$	1	$-\frac{3}{4}$
	$\frac{5}{2}$	0	0	$\frac{3}{4}$	0	$\frac{45}{4}$
x_3	1	0	1	0	1	5
x_2	0	1	0	0	1	3
x_4	2	0	0	1	-4	3
	1	0	0	0	3	9

Geometrically, what has happened is the following. The feasible points for the original system of constraints are the lattice points of the hatched region of Figure 1. Now the added constraint can be expressed as

$$\frac{1}{2}x_1 + \frac{1}{4}x_4 - \frac{3}{4} \geq 0.$$

Using $x_4 = 15 - 2x_1 - 4x_2$, this inequality reduces to

$$2x_1 + (15 - 2x_1 - 4x_2) \geq 3,$$

or

$$4x_2 \leq 12,$$

or

$$x_2 \leq 3.$$

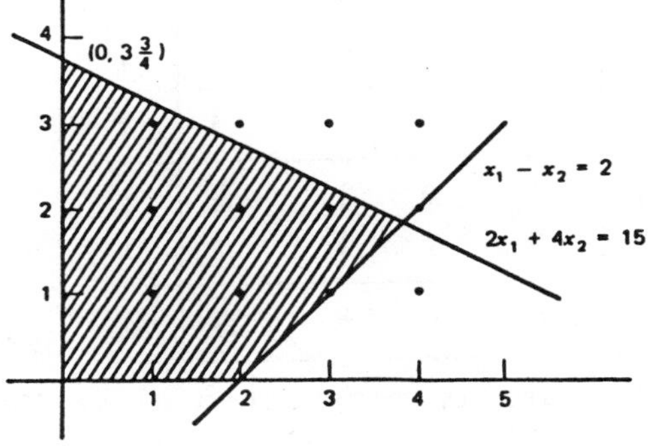

Fig. 1

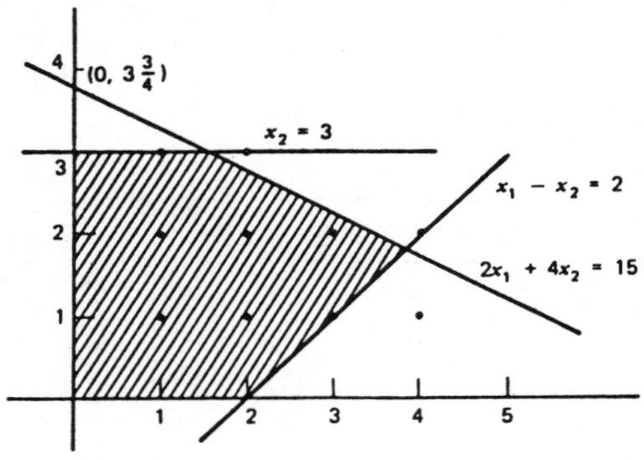

Fig. 2

As can be seen in Figure 2, this new constraint is equivalent to an inequality that cuts off from the feasible set the original nonintegral optimal solution (0, 3 3/4), but does not exclude from consideration any feasible lattice points.

• PROBLEM 6-33

Minimize $x_1 - 2x_2$

subject to:

$$2x_1 + x_2 \leq 5$$

$$-4x_1 + 4x_2 \leq 5$$

$x_1, x_2 \geq 0$ and integer.

Solve by Gomory's Cutting Plane Algorithm.

Table 1

	x_1	x_2	x_3	x_4	
x_3	2	1	1	0	5
x_4	−4	(4)	0	1	5
	1	−2	0	0	0
x_3	(3)	0	1	$-\frac{1}{4}$	$\frac{15}{4}$
x_2	−1	1	0	$\frac{1}{4}$	$\frac{5}{4}$
	−1	0	0	$\frac{1}{2}$	$\frac{5}{2}$
x_1	1	0	$\frac{1}{3}$	$-\frac{1}{12}$	$\frac{5}{4}$
x_2	0	1	$\frac{1}{3}$	$\frac{1}{6}$	$\frac{5}{2}$
	0	0	$\frac{1}{3}$	$\frac{5}{12}$	$\frac{15}{4}$

Solution: Adding integrally restricted slack variables x_3 and x_4 and applying the simplex algorithm, yields the tableaux of Table 1. Both constant terms of the final tableau are nonintegral, but 5/2 has the larger fractional value. The second row of this tableau generates the constraint

$$-\frac{1}{3}x_3 - \frac{1}{6}x_4 + x_5 = -\frac{1}{2}$$

where x_5 is a new slack variable. Adding this equation and using the Dual Simplex Algorithm leads to the tableaux of Table 2. The first row of the final tableau of this table generates the constraint

$$-\frac{3}{4}x_4 + x_6 = -\frac{3}{4},$$

where x_6 is a new slack variable. (Note that $-\frac{1}{4} = [-\frac{1}{4}] = -\frac{1}{4} - (-1) = \frac{3}{4}$

Table 2

	x_1	x_2	x_3	x_4	x_5	
x_1	1	0	$\frac{1}{3}$	$-\frac{1}{12}$	0	$\frac{5}{4}$
x_2	0	1	$\frac{1}{3}$	$\frac{1}{6}$	0	$\frac{5}{2}$
x_5	0	0	($-\frac{1}{3}$)	$-\frac{1}{6}$	1	$-\frac{1}{2}$
	0	0	$\frac{1}{3}$	$\frac{5}{12}$	0	$\frac{15}{4}$
x_1	1	0	0	$-\frac{1}{4}$	1	$\frac{3}{4}$
x_2	0	1	0	0	1	2
x_3	0	0	1	$\frac{1}{2}$	-3	$\frac{3}{2}$
	0	0	0	$\frac{1}{4}$	1	$\frac{13}{4}$

Adding this constraint, yields the tableaux of Table 3. Thus the minimal value of the objective function is -3 and is attained at $x_1 = 1$, $x_2 = 2$.

Table 3

	x_1	x_2	x_3	x_4	x_5	x_6	
x_1	1	0	0	$-\frac{1}{4}$	1	0	$\frac{3}{4}$
x_2	0	1	0	0	1	0	2
x_3	0	0	1	$\frac{1}{2}$	-3	0	$\frac{3}{2}$
x_6	0	0	0	($-\frac{3}{4}$)	0	1	$-\frac{3}{4}$
	0	0	0	$\frac{1}{4}$	1	0	$\frac{13}{4}$
x_1	1	0	0	0	1	$-\frac{1}{3}$	1
x_2	0	1	0	0	1	0	2
x_3	0	0	1	0	-3	$\frac{2}{3}$	1
x_4	0	0	0	1	0	$-\frac{4}{3}$	1
	0	0	0	0	1	$\frac{1}{3}$	3

To show the action of the cutting planes geometrically note that the first constraint added corresponds to

$$\frac{1}{3}x_3 + \frac{1}{6}x_4 - \frac{1}{2} \geq 0,$$

that is,

$$\frac{1}{3}(5 - 2x_1 - x_2) + \frac{1}{6}(5 + 4x_1 - 4x_2) - \frac{1}{2} \geq 0.$$

This reduces to $x_2 \leq 2$. Similarly, the second additional constraint reduces from

$$\frac{3}{4}x_4 - \frac{3}{4} \geq 0$$

to

$$-x_1 + x_2 \leq 1.$$

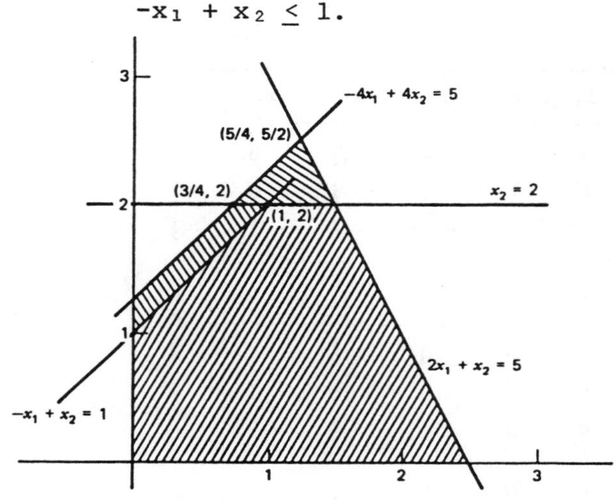

Fig. 1

The graph is sketched in Figure 1.

• PROBLEM 6-34

Maximize $f(x) = x_1 + x_2$

subject to:

$$-2x_1 + 5x_2 \leq 8$$

$$6x_1 + x_2 \leq 30$$

$$x_1, x_2 \geq 0 \text{ and integer.}$$

Use the Gomory cutting plane algorithm to solve this integer program.

Solution:

Step 1: Solve the preceding problem as a continuous linear program.

	x_0	x_1	x_2	s_3	s_4	RHS
	1	-1	-1	0	0	0
s_3	0	-2	5	1	0	8
s_4	0	6	1	0	1	30

	x_0	x_1	x_2	s_3	s_4	RHS
	1	0	- 5/6	0	1/6	5
s_3	0	0	16/3	1	1/3	18
x_1	0	1	1/6	0	1/6	5

	x_0	x_1	x_2	s_3	s_4	RHS
	1	0	0	5/32	7/32	125/16
x_2	0	0	1	3/16	1/16	27/8
x_1	0	1	0	- 1/32	5/32	71/16

The optimal solution is given by:

$$x_1^* = 4\frac{7}{16}$$

$$x_2^* = 3\frac{3}{8}\ .$$

Step 2: Since both solution variables are noninteger, choose one to form a cut. Choose x_1 at random and apply the equation

$$\sum_k (-\bar{\delta}_k)x_k + s = -\bar{\delta}$$

where

$$\bar{\delta}_k = \phi_k - [B_k]$$

and

$$\bar{\delta} = \phi - [b],$$

yields:

$$-\frac{3}{16}S_1 - \frac{1}{16}S_4 + S_1 = -\frac{3}{8}$$

Append this to the second simplex tableau and obtain the following:

	x_0	x_1	x_2	s_3	s_4	s_1	RHS
	1	0	0	5/32	7/32	0	125/16
x_2	0	0	1	3/16	1/16	0	27/8
x_1	0	1	0	-1/32	5/32	0	71/16
s_1	0	0	0	-3/16	-1/16	1	- 3/8

Use the dual simplex procedure to generate the following optimal tableau.

	x_0	x_1	x_2	s_3	s_4	s_1	RHS
	1	0	0	0	1/6	5/6	15/2
x_2	0	0	1	0	0	1	3
x_1	0	1	0	0	1/6	−1/6	9/2
s_3	0	0	0	1	1/3	−16/3	2

The current solution is given by

$$x_2^* = 3, \quad x_1^* = 4\frac{1}{2}, \quad S_3^* = 2.$$

Since x_1^* is noninteger, repeat step 2 using that variable.

Step 2 (repeat):

$$x_1 + \frac{1}{6}S_4 - \frac{1}{6}S_1 = \frac{9}{2} .$$

Use the same equation as above, and obtain the cut:

$$-\frac{1}{6}S_4 - \frac{5}{6}S_1 + S_2 = -\frac{1}{2} .$$

Append this to the previous tableau:

	x_0	x_1	x_2	s_3	s_4	s_1	s_2	RHS
	1	0	0	0	1/6	5/6	0	15/2
x_2	0	0	1	0	0	1	0	3
x_1	0	1	0	0	1/6	− 1/6	0	9/2
s_3	0	0	0	1	1/3	−16/3	0	2
s_2	0	0	0	0	−1/6	−5/6	1	−1/2

Use dual simplex and again reach optimality.

	x_0	x_1	x_2	s_3	s_4	s_1	s_2	RHS
	1	0	0	0	0	0	1	7
x_2	0	0	1	0	0	1	0	3
x_1	0	1	0	0	0	−1	1	4
s_3	0	0	0	1	0	−7	2	1
s_4	0	0	0	0	1	5	−6	3

The answer is

$$x_1^* = 4, \quad x_2^* = 3, \quad x_0^* = 7, \quad S_3^* = 1, \quad S_4^* = 3.$$

Since this solution is all-integer, the procedure is terminated.

An excursion company is considering adding small boats to their fleet. The company has $200,000 to invest in this venture. At present there is an estimated maximum demand of 6,000 customers per season for these tours. The company does not wish to provide capacity in excess of the estimated maximum demand. The basic data are given below for the two types of available boats. The company will make an estimated seasonal profit of $4,000 for each boat of Type 1 and $7,000 for each boat of Type 2. How many boats of each type should the company use to maximize profit?

	Type 1	Type 2
capacity, $\frac{\text{customers}}{\text{season}}$	1,200	2,000
initial cost, $\frac{\$}{\text{boat}}$	25,000	80,000

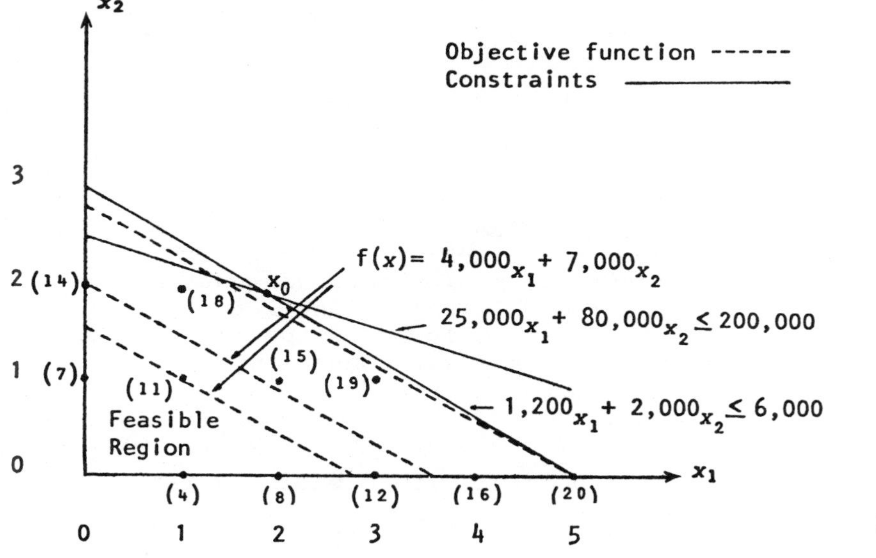

Fig. 1

• Feasible continuations of decision variable values

( ) The value of the objective function in thousands of $

Solution: The linear programming problem (illustrated in Figure 1) is:

$$\text{Maximize} \quad 4{,}000\, x_1 + 7{,}000\, x_2$$

$$\text{Subject to} \quad 1{,}200\, x_1 + 2{,}000\, x_2 \leq 6{,}000$$

$$25{,}000\, x_1 + 80{,}000\, x_2 \leq 200{,}000$$

$x_1, x_2 \geq 0$; x_1 x_2 are integers.

Constraints in the original problem formulation should be transformed so that all coefficients are integers. This is done to facilitate solution of the integer programming problem. No transformation is required in this problem. If there were a constraint such as $(3/4)x_1 + (6/4)x_2 \leq 48/10$, both sides must be multiplied by 20 so that it becomes $15x_1 + 30x_2 \leq 96$. To simplify notation, divide the first constraint by 100 and the objective function and second constraint by 1000 and construct the initial tableau (Tableau 1).

Tableau 1

c_i	BASIS	V_1	V_2	V_3	V_4	b_i
0	x_3	12	20	1	0	60
0	x_4	25	80	0	1	200

The final tableau in the Simplex solution is:

Tableau 2

c_i	BASIS	V_1	V_2	V_3	V_4	b_i	f_{i0}
4	x_1	1	0	0.1739	-0.0435	1.739	0.739
7	x_2	0	1	-0.0543	0.0261	1.956	0.956
Solution (x_0)		0	0	-0.3155	-0.0087	20.65	

Since the solution is noninteger, add cutting planes to reduce the feasible region until an integer solution is obtained. The following steps will be used to develop new cutting planes (or constraints).

1. Add a new column to the final Simplex tableau. This is the f_{i0} column in Tableau 2. For each b_i value associated with a basic variable determine an f_{i0} value, where f_{i0} is a nonnegative fraction greater than or equal to zero but less than one, which when subtracted from a given noninteger will convert to an integer (e.g. 0.739 subtracted from 1.739 will convert it to an integer; 0.25 subtracted from -6.75 will convert it to an integer).

2. The largest f_{io} value will determine the row of the tableau to be used in constructing a cutting plane. In the above tableau $f_{20} = 0.956$ designates the second row to be used for this purpose since $0.956 > 0.739$ (i.e. $f_{20} > f_{10}$). When ties occur, an arbitrary choice among tied rows is made. For each a_{ij} coefficient in this

row determine an f_{ij} value, just as f_{i0} was determined for b_i.

	x_1	x_2	x_3	x_4	b_i
Row 2	0	1	-0.0543	0.0261	1.956
f_{2j} values	0	0	0.9457	0.0261	0.956
Integer value	0	1	-1	0	1

The f_{2j} values give a new constraint

$$0x_1 + 0x_2 + 0.9457x_3 + 0.0261x_4 \geq 0.956.$$

Adding a surplus variable x_5 gives:

$$0x_1 + 0x_2 + 0.9457x_3 + 0.0261x_4 - x_5 = 0.956.$$

Tableau 3

c_i	BASIS	V_1	V_2	V_3	V_4	V_5	b_i	
4	x_1	1	0	0.1739	-0.0435	0	1.739	
7	x_2	0	1	-0.0543	0.0261	0	1.956	
0	x_3	0	0	0.9457	0.0261	-1	0.956	→

3. The new constraint is added to the final Simplex tableau. The incoming variable is the one that will cause the smallest decrease in the objective function as indicated by the x_{0j} values of the final Simplex tableau. An alternative rule (sometimes more efficient) is to select the incoming variable as that having the maximum quotient of x_{0j}/a_{ij} for nonbasic variable j, where $a_{ij} < 0$. The incoming variable will be x_4 with a x_{04} of -0.0087. The outgoing variable, x_5, is always that associated with the constraint just annexed (in this case, row 3).

Apply the Simplex procedure to get the following tableau:

Tableau 4

c_i	BASIS	V_1	V_2	V_3	V_4	V_5	b_i	f_{io}
4	x_1	1	0	1.750	0	-1.667	3.333	.332
7	x_2	0	1	-1	0	1	1.000	.000
0	x_4	0	0	36.234	1	-38.3142	-0.333	- -
	x_0	0	0	0	0	-0.333	20.333	

In the new solution X = (3.333, 1.000). Since x_1 has the maximum f_{i0}, it is used to determine the next cutting plane. Upon adding another column V_6, and another constraint, the next tableau becomes:

Tableau 5

c_i	BASIS	V_1	V_2	V_3	V_4	V_5	V_6	b_i	
4	x_1	1	0	1.750	0	-1.667	0	3.333	
7	x_2	0	1	-1.	0	1	0	1.000	
0	x_4	0	0	36.234	1	-38.3142	0	36.628	
0	x_6	0	0	.750	0	0.333	-1	0.333	→
						↑			

Apply the Simplex procedure to obtain:

Tableau 6

c_i	BASIS	V_1	V_2	V_3	V_4	V_5	V_6	b_i
4	x_1	1	0	5.5	0	0	5	5
7	x_2	0	1	-325.	0	0	3	0
0	x_4	0	0	122.44	1	0	-114.94	74.94
0	x_5	0	0	2.25	0	1	-3	1.00
x_{0j}		0	0	-2197	0	0	-41	20

Tableau 6 gives the optimum integer solution. X* = (5,0).

Let X_1, X_2, X_3, X_4 be four projects under consideration which are "competing" for a scarce resiurce (money for development).

Now, let each project "pay" a return of a unique amount (return = capital + profit to the firm):

e_j = pay-off coefficient for the jth project

$e_1 = \$40$

$e_2 = \$30$

$e_3 = \$50$

$e_4 = \$60.$

Let "costs" also be associated with each project:

c_j = "cost" to develop the jth project

$c_1 = \$30$

$c_2 = \$20$

$c_3 = \$40$

$c_4 = \$50$

and total available capital be \$100.

Formulate and solve the problem to maximize total return, using the special case (0 - 1) of integer programming: if

$x_j = 0$

then project X_j is not accepted for allocation, and if

$x_j = 1$

then X_j receives an allocation of necessary funds for initiating and funding the project. Utilize Gomory's Cutting Plane Method.

<u>Solution</u>: Now, let an objective function, expressing the firm's prospective total return, be written in the form

$$z = \sum_{j=1}^{j} c_j x_j$$

which is to be maximized by integer LP techniques, subject to certain constraints. In this case,

$$z = 40x_1 + 30x_2 + 50\,x_3 + 60x_4$$

The initial constraints are written from the cost coefficients and the initial requirement that each x_i be some number between 0 and 1, but not necessarily either 0 or 1. This latter requirement is to permit optimization with primal simplex rules, in which the optimal solution will be primal optimal but not necessarily integer. The integer constraints will be applied later.

Accordingly, the initial constraints are:

$$\left.\begin{array}{l} R \geq \sum^{j} c_j x_j \\ 30x_1 + 20x_2 + 40x_3 + 50x_4 \leq 100 \end{array}\right\} \text{Resource Limitation}$$

$0 \leq x_j \leq 1\}$ Feasible Projects = + 1 or less.

Introducing the necessary slack variables to convert the constraint inequalities to equations:

$$30x_1 + 20x_2 + 40x_3 + 50x_4 + s_0 = 100$$

$$x_1 + s_1 = 1$$

$$x_2 + s_2 = 1$$

$$x_3 + s_3 = 1.$$

$$x_4 + s_4 = 1.$$

Rewriting the objective function to convert to matrix form:

$$z - 40x_1 - 30x_2 - 50x_3 - 60x_4 + s_0(0) + s_1(0) + s_2(0)$$

$$+ s_3(0) + s_4(0) = 0.$$

The initial tableau, now initially feasible but not optimal, can now be written (Gauss-Jordan Matrix), which is then iterated to an optimal primal solution by the conventional primal simplex rules:

Tableau 1

z	x_1	x_2	x_3	x_4	s_0	s_1	s_2	s_3	s_4	b	θ
	30	20	40	50	1					100	2
	1					1				1	—
		1					1			1	—
			1					1		1	—
				(1)					1	1	1 ← r
1	−40	−30	−50	−60 ↑ k							

$$b'_i = a'_{it}x_t + a'_{ir}x_r + \ . \ . \ . \ + a'_{iq}x_q + x_s.$$

(The prime indicates the equation is from the primal optimal tableau; x_s is the variable in solution.)

Tableau 2

x_1	x_2	x_3	x_4	s_0	s_1	s_2	s_3	s_4	b	θ
30	20	40	0	1				−50	50	$\frac{5}{4}$
1					1				1	—
	1					1			1	—
		(1)					1		1	1 ← r
			1					1	1	—
−40	−30	−50	0 ↑ k					60	60	

Tableau 3

x_1	x_2	x_3	x_4	s_0	s_1	s_2	s_3	s_4	b	θ
30	20	0	0	1			−40	−50	10	$\frac{1}{3}$ ← r
1					1				1	1
	1					1			1	—
		1					1		1	—
			1					1	1	—
−40 ↑ k	−30	0	0				50	60	110	

Tableau 4

x_1	x_2	x_3	x_4	s_0	s_1	s_2	s_3	s_4	b	θ
1	$\frac{2}{3}$	0	0	$\frac{1}{30}$	0	0	$-\frac{4}{3}$	$-\frac{5}{3}$	$\frac{1}{3}$	—
	$-\frac{2}{3}$			$-\frac{1}{30}$	1		$\frac{4}{3}$	($\frac{5}{3}$)	$\frac{2}{3}$	$\frac{2}{5}$ ← r
	1					1			1	—
		1					1		1	—
			1					1	1	1
0	$-\frac{10}{3}$	0	0	$\frac{4}{3}$	0	0	$-\frac{10}{3}$	$-\frac{20}{3}$ ↑ k	$\frac{370}{3}$	

Tableau 5

x_1	x_2	x_3	x_4	s_0	s_1	s_2	s_3	s_4	b	θ
1					1				1	—
	$-\frac{2}{5}$			$-\frac{1}{50}$	$\frac{3}{5}$		$\frac{4}{5}$	1	$\frac{2}{5}$	—
	1					1			1	1 ← r
		1					1		1	—
	$\frac{2}{5}$		1	$\frac{1}{50}$	$-\frac{3}{5}$		$-\frac{4}{5}$		$\frac{3}{5}$	$\frac{3}{2}$
0	$-\frac{18}{3}$	0	0	$\frac{6}{5}$	4	0	2	0	$\frac{378}{3}$	
	↑ k									

Tableau 6

x_1	x_2	x_3	x_4	s_0	s_1	s_2	s_3	s_4	b	θ
1	0	0	0	0	1	0	0	0	1	
0	0	0	0	$-\frac{1}{50}$	$\frac{3}{5}$	$\frac{2}{5}$	$\frac{4}{5}$	1	$\frac{4}{5}$	←
0	1	0	0	0	0	1	0	0	1	
0	0	1	0	0	0	0	1	0	1	
0	0	0	1	$\frac{1}{50}$	$-\frac{3}{5}$	$-\frac{2}{5}$	$-\frac{4}{5}$	0	$\frac{1}{5}$	
0	0	0	0	$\frac{6}{5}$	4	6	2	0	$\frac{396}{3} = 132$	

In Tableau 6, choose the second row (custom is to choose the greatest fractional b_i' since one wishes to remove from the solution the "most infeasible" variable (x_s) whose value is b_i').

Thus:

$$\frac{4}{5} = \frac{4}{5}s_3 + \frac{2}{5}s_2 + \frac{3}{5}s_1 - \frac{1}{50}s_0 + (1)s_4.$$

Rearrange the equation so that all terms except s_4 are on the left-hand side:

$$\frac{4}{5} - \frac{4}{5}s_3 - \frac{2}{5}s_2 - \frac{3}{5}s_1 + \frac{1}{50}s_0 = s_4$$

$s_4$can be constrained to be integer by forcing the left-hand-side to be congruent to zero (from the method of fractional parts: $f(d) = a_i$; $0 \le a < 1$; where $d - a =$ integer):

$$f\left(\frac{4}{5}\right) + f\left(-\frac{4}{5}\right)s_3 + f\left(-\frac{2}{5}\right)s_2 + f\left(-\frac{3}{5}\right)s_1 + f\left(\frac{1}{50}\right)s_0 \equiv 0;$$

or, transposing $f\left(\frac{4}{5}\right)$ to the right-hand side:

$$f\left(-\frac{4}{5}\right)s_3 + f\left(-\frac{2}{5}\right)s_2 + f\left(-\frac{3}{5}\right)s_1 + f\left(\frac{1}{50}\right)s_0 \equiv -f\left(\frac{4}{5}\right)$$

$$\equiv f\left(-\frac{4}{5}\right)$$

Then:

$$f\left(\frac{1}{5}\right)s_3 + f\left(\frac{3}{5}\right)s_2 + f\left(\frac{2}{5}\right)s_1 + f\left(\frac{1}{50}\right)s_0$$

$$\equiv f\left(\frac{1}{5}\right),\ f\left(\frac{6}{5}\right),\ f\left(\frac{4}{5}\right)$$

or

$$\frac{1}{5}s_3 + \frac{3}{5}s_2 + \frac{2}{5}s_1 + \frac{1}{50}s_0 \geq \frac{1}{5}$$

which is the new integer constraint inequality.

To simplify the inequality, multiply through by 50:

Tableau 6 is now the primal, feasible optimum solution since:

(1) no negative e_j remain (→ optimal)

(2) all $b_i \geq 0$ } feasible.

(3) all $s_j \geq 0$ }

However, all x_j are not integer-valued:

$$x_1 = 1$$

$$x_2 = 1$$

$$x_3 = 1$$

$$x_4 = \frac{1}{5}.$$

It is now desired to "force" an integer solution (all x_j = 0, 1), which can be done by the Gomory-Baumol method of introducing an integer constraint and "back-pivoting" to an optimal solution in which all structural variables (x_j) become integers.

This method uses the so-called dual simplex rules for pivoting, which are different from the primal simplex rules. To introduce the new integer constraint and then back-pivot, the solution matrix must first be in dual-feasible form. The first primal matrix which is also dual-feasible is the primal optimal; i.e., the noninteger primal optimal Tableau 6. Once this matrix (primal optimal) has been developed, then the integer constraint can be written and the back-pivoting started.

The new integer constraint is developed as follows:

(1) Choose any row in the primal optimal tableau, for which b_i is noninteger. Rewrite this row

as:

$$10s_3 + 30s_3 + 20s_1 + s_0 \geq 10$$

Subtract a new slack variable, s_5, to convert to an equality:

$$10s_3 + 30s_2 + 20s_1 + s_0 - s_5 = 10$$

and multiply by -1 to convert the new constraining equality to dual-feasible form:

$$-10s_3 - 30s_2 - 20s_1 - s_0 + s_5 = -10.$$

(2) This new constraining equation is now introduced as an additional constraint in the dual-feasible (= primal optimal) Tableau 6. This tableau thus becomes primal infeasible (since $b_i = -10$), but still optimal. In this manner, infeasibility is introduced, while at the same time, optimality is preserved:

Tableau 6A

x_1	x_2	x_3	x_4	s_0	s_1	s_2	s_3	s_4	s_5	b	
				-1	-20	-30	-10		$+1$	-10	The new ← constraint equality
1					1					1	
				$-\frac{1}{50}$	$\frac{3}{5}$	$\frac{2}{5}$	$\frac{4}{5}$	1		$\frac{4}{5}$	
	1									1	
		1								1	
			1	$\frac{1}{50}$	$-\frac{3}{5}$	$-\frac{2}{5}$	$-\frac{4}{5}$			$\frac{1}{5}$	
				$\frac{6}{5}$	4	6	2			132	

One now re-optimizes, hopefully removing the infeasibility by the dual simplex rules.

One chooses the pivot element in Tableau 6B as follows:

Tableau 6B

x_1	x_2	x_3	x_4	s_0	s_1	s_2	s_3	s_4	s_5	b
				-1	-20	-30	-10		1	-10
1					1					1
				$-\frac{1}{50}$	$\frac{3}{5}$	$\frac{2}{5}$	$\frac{4}{5}$	1		$\frac{4}{5}$
	1					1				1
		1					1			1
				$\frac{1}{50}$	$-\frac{3}{5}$	$-\frac{2}{5}$	$-\frac{4}{5}$			$\frac{1}{5}$
				$\frac{6}{5}$	4	6	2			132
	$e_i - f_i$			$-\frac{6}{5}$	$-\frac{1}{5}$	$-\frac{1}{5}$	$-\frac{1}{5}$			$\leftarrow \delta_i$

The pivot element is - 10, at the intersection of the rth row and the kth column.

One can now iterate in the normal primal manner, using primal rules for the iteration:

The Tableau is optimal (all $e_j - z_j \geq 0$)

The Tableau is feasible (all $b_i \geq 0$, all $s_i \geq 0$)

The Tableau is integer (all $x_i = 0, 1$).

The solution variables can now be read out:

$x_1 = 1$ $s_0 = 0$

$x_2 = 1$ $s_1 = 0$

$x_3 = 0$ $s_2 = 0$

$x_4 = 1$ $s_3 = 1$

$s_4 = 0$

$s_5 = 0$

z opt. = \$130.

The original resources constraint is satisfied since

$$(\Sigma c_{ij} x_{ij} + 100) \leq (R = 100).$$

Tableau 7A

z	x_1	x_2	x_3	x_4	s_0	s_1	s_2	s_3	s_4	s_5	b
					$+\frac{1}{10}$	+2	+3	+1		$-\frac{1}{10}$	1
	1					1		0			1
					$-\frac{1}{10}$	−1	−2	0	+1		0
		1					1	0			1
			1		$-\frac{1}{10}$	−2	−3	0		$+\frac{1}{10}$	0
				1	$+\frac{1}{10}$	+1	+2	0		$-\frac{4}{50}$	1
					1	0	0	0	0	$\frac{2}{10}$	130

The conclusion is that Tableau 7A is an optimal, feasible, integer solution to the problem.

Minimize

$$10x_1 + 14x_2 + 21x_3$$

subject to:

$$8x_1 + 11x_2 + 9x_3 - x_4 = 12$$

$$2x_1 + 2x_2 + 7x_3 - x_5 = 14$$

$$9x_1 + 6x_2 + 3x_3 - x_6 = 10$$

$$x_j > 0, \text{ all integer}$$

Solve this integer programming problem by cuts algorithm.

Tableau 1

i	Basis	c	P_0	P_1 (10)	P_2 (14)	P_3 (21)	P_4 (0)	P_5 (0)	P_6 (0)	P_1' (10)	P_2' (14)	P_3' (21)	P_7
0			0	−10	−14	−21	0	0	0	0	0	0	0
1	P_4	0	−12	−8	−11	−9	1	0	0	0	0	0	0
2	P_5	0	−14	−2	−2	−7	0	1	0	0	0	0	0
3	P_6	0	−10	−9	−6	−3	0	0	1	0	0	0	0
4	P_1'	10	0	−1	0	0	0	0	0	1	0	0	0
5	P_2'	14	0	0	−1	0	0	0	0	0	1	0	0
6	P_3'	21	0	0	0	−1	0	0	0	0	0	1	0
7	P_7		−4	(−1)	−1	−2	0	0	0	0	0	0	1

Solution: The set of equations $x_1' = x_1$, $x_2' = x_2$, $x_3' = x_3$ and the conditions $c_j' = c_j$ have been added in Tableau 1, and row 7 has been added for the cutting constraint and column P_7 for the new variable.

The second equation of the system is used to generate the cutting constraint

$$\frac{z_k - c_k}{-1} = \min_{x_{2j}<0} \frac{z_j - c_j}{-1} \quad \frac{z_1 - c_1}{-1} = 10$$

Hence column P_1 is to be the pivot column. To determine the m_j, there is

$$10 \le \frac{10}{m_1} \qquad 10 \le \frac{14}{m_2} \qquad 10 \le \frac{21}{m_3}$$

or $m_1 = 1$, $m_2 = 1$, $m_3 = 2$. The $\lambda_j = - x_{ij}/m_j$ are then

$$\lambda_1 = \frac{2}{1} \qquad \lambda_2 = \frac{2}{1} \qquad \lambda_3 = \frac{7}{2}$$

and

$$\lambda = \max \lambda_j = \frac{7}{2}$$

The new constraint is then given by

$$\left[\frac{-14}{\frac{7}{2}}\right] = \left[\frac{-2}{\frac{7}{2}}\right]x_1 + \left[\frac{-2}{\frac{7}{2}}\right]x_2 + \left[\frac{-7}{\frac{7}{2}}\right]x_3 + x_7$$

$$-4 = -x_1 - x_2 - 2x_3 + x_7.$$

Tableau 2

i	Basis	c	P_0	P_1	P_2	P_3	P_4	P_5	P_6	P'_1	P'_2	P'_3	P_7
0			40	0	−4	−1	0	0	0	0	0	0	−10
1	P_4	0	20	0	−3	7	1	0	0	0	0	0	−8
2	P_5	0	−6	0	0	−3	0	1	0	0	0	0	−2
3	P_6	0	26	0	3	15	0	0	1	0	0	0	−9
4	P'_1	10	4	0	1	2	0	0	0	1	0	0	−1
5	P'_2	14	0	0	−1	0	0	0	0	0	1	0	0
6	P'_3	21	0	0	0	−1	0	0	0	0	0	1	0
7													

Tableau 3

i	Basis	P_0	P_7	P_2	P_3	P_8
0		40	−10	−4	−1	
1	P_4	20	−8	−3	7	
2	P_5	−6	−2	0	−3	
3	P_6	26	−9	3	15	
4	P'_1	4	−1	1	2	
5	P'_2	0	0	−1	0	
6	P'_3	0	0	0	−1	
7	P_8	−2	−1	0	(−1)	1

This equation is shown added to Tableau 1. By applying the elimination transformation with the pivot element as shown, Tableau 2 is obtained. Since all the elements of column P_1 have been reduced to zeros, it can be eliminated from the tableau and column P_7 substituted in its place. In fact, since vectors P_4, P_5, P_6, P'_1, P'_2, P'_3 will not change under the all-integer algorithm transformation, the tableau can be made quite concise as Tableau 3. Note that $x'_1 = x_1$ is still in the basis and now has a value of 4. Here there is only one

row with a negative constant term. The pivot column is P_3 since

$$\frac{-1}{-1} = \min\left(\frac{-10}{-1} \quad \frac{-1}{-1}\right) \qquad 1 \le \frac{10}{m_7} \qquad 1 \le \frac{1}{m_3}$$

or $m_7 \le 10$, $m_3 \le 1$. Hence $\lambda_7 = 2/10$, $\lambda_3 = 3/1$, $\lambda = 3$. The new constraint is given by

$$-2 = -x_7 - x_3 + x_8$$

as shown in Tableau 3. The new solution is shown in Tableau 4.

Tableau 4

i	Basis	P_0	P_7	P_2	P_8	P_9
0		42	−9	−4	−1	
1	P_4	6	−15	−3	7	
2	P_5	0	1	0	−3	
3	P_6	−4	−24	3	15	
4	P'_1	0	−3	1	2	
5	P'_2	0	0	−1	0	
6	P'_3	2	1	0	−1	
7	P_9	−1	(−1)	0	0	1

Tableau 5

i	Basis	P_0	P_9	P_2	P_8	P_{10}
0		51	−9	−4	−1	
1	P_4	21	−15	−3	7	
2	P_5	−1	1	0	−3	
3	P_6	20	−24	3	15	
4	P'_1	3	−3	1	2	
5	P'_2	0	0	−1	0	
6	P'_3	1	1	0	−1	
7	P_{10}	−1	0	0	(−1)	1

Tableau 6

i	Basis	P_0	P_9	P_2	P_{10}
0		52	−9	−4	1
1	P_4	14	−15	−3	7
2	P_5	2	1	0	−3
3	P_6	5	−24	3	15
4	P'_1	1	−3	1	2
5	P'_2	0	0	−1	0
6	P'_3	2	1	0	−1

Selecting row 3 as the row to generate the cutting constraint, there is P_7 as the pivot column and $\lambda = 24$. The new constraint is $-1 = -x_7 + x_9$. The next solution is then given by Tableau 5. With row 2 as the generating row, we have P_8 as the pivot column and $\lambda = 3$. The new constraint is $-1 = -x_8 + x_{10}$. This yields the final Tableau 6 and the optimum solution.

The final solution is given by

$$x_1 = x_1' = 1 \qquad x_2 = x_2' = 0 \qquad x_3 = x_3' = 2$$

$$x_4 = 14 \qquad x_5 = 2 \qquad x_6 = 5 \qquad x_{00} = 52.$$

KNAPSACK PROBLEM

• PROBLEM 6-38

Consider a set of five indivisible items, each having the weight and value units given below:

ITEM NO.	WEIGHT	VALUE
1	18	27
2	12	9
3	15	30
4	16	16
5	13	6.5

The problem is to fill a knapsack with these items so as to maximize its total value without exceeding a total weight of 45 units.

Solution: First arrange these items in terms of their value per unit weight as shown below:

INDEX NO.	ITEM NO.	WEIGHT	VALUE	VALUE/ WEIGHT
1	3	15	30	2
2	1	18	27	1.5
3	4	16	16	1
4	2	12	9	0.75
5	5	13	6.5	0.5

If the items were divisible, then the knapsack could be filled with item number 3, which has the largest value per unit weight, until the weight of the knapsack reached its allowable limit. If this weight limit were not reached, then item number 1 should be put into the knapsack, since it has the second largest value per unit weight. If this procedure was continued, the knapsack contents having the maximum value would comprise all of items 3 and 1 plus 3/4 of item 4. The total weight and value of this knapsack would be 15 + 18 + 3/4(16) = 45 units and 30 + 27 + 3/4(16) = 69 units respectively.

Since the items are indivisible, the above solution is not valid. However, proceed to take the items from the top of the above list until no more undivided items can be taken without exceeding the weight limit. This procedure results in taking all of items 3 and 1, with a total weight and value of 33 and 57 units respectively. This solution is not optimal, since a combination of all of items 3, 1, and 2 results in a total weight and value of 45 and 66 units respectively. Note also that the value of any combination of indivisible items with a total weight limit can always be increased if division of items is allowed.

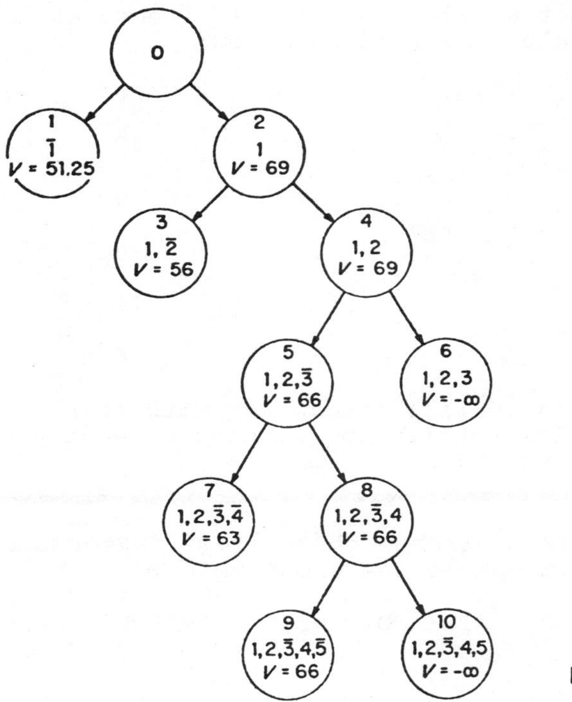

Fig. 1

Figure 1 show the tree of solutions of this problem as created by the branch and bound method. In this figure, a node marked (i, j, $\bar{k}$) represents all possible combinations of items which include indices i and j and exclude index k. The upper bound V of the total value is computed by allowing divisibility of items.

Node 1 contains all possible combinations of items that exclude index 1, and the upper bound V for node 1 is computed as shown below:

Index No.	Item No.	Weight	Value
2	1	18	27
3	4	16	16
4	2	12	9

Now if all of items numbered 1 and 4 and 11/12 of item number 2 are taken, then the total weight of the knapsack becomes 18 + 16 + 11/12(12) = 45 units and the corresponding value V = 27 + 16 + 11/12(9) = 51.25 units.

On the other hand, node 2 represents all possible combinations of items that include index 1, and the upper bound V for node 2 is computed as shown below:

INDEX NO.	ITEM NO.	WEIGHT	VALUE
1	3	15	30
2	1	18	27
3	4	16	16

If all of items 3 and 1 and 3/4 of item 4 are taken, then the total weight of the knapsack is 15 + 18 + 3/4(16) = 45 units and the corresponding value V = 30 + 27 + 3/4(16) = 69 units.

Since the upper bound on the total value at node 2 is larger than at node 1, subdivide node 2 into nodes 3 and 4. Similarly, since node 4 has a higher upper bound, subdivide node 4 into nodes 5 and 6. Node 6 represents an inadmissible combination of items, since it violates the total-weight constraint. Thus, set $V = -\infty$ for node 6 and proceed in this manner until terminal nodes 9 and 10 are reached, where node 9 provides the optimum combination of the given items.

• PROBLEM 6-39

A hiker wishes to go on a camping trip and does not wish to carry more than 60 pounds in his pack. Unfortunately in laying out his equipment he finds its total weight to be 90 pounds. There are three objects he wants to take, so in order to decide which combination is best, he attaches a value to each. Suppose his data are:

Object	Value	Weight	Value/ Weight
1	70	40	1.75
2	50	30	1.67
3	30	20	1.5

Notice that he has listed the objects in order of decreasing value-to-weight ratio.

Formulate a linear programming model to solve this problem. What is the solution obtained by applying the largest-ratio rule?

<u>Solution</u>: In order to solve this problem, he must solve the following integer programming problem:

$$\text{Max } 70x_1 + 50x_2 + 30x_3$$

Subject to:

$$40x_1 + 30x_2 + 20x_3 \leq k = 60$$

$x_1, x_2, x_3 \geq 0$ and integer.

One way of getting a feasible solution to the problem is to take as many units as possible of the most valuable item first (that is, the one with the largest value/weight ratio), then as many of the second as possible, and so on. If this is done for the given problem, the solution is $x_1 = 1$, $x_2 = 0$, $x_3 = 1$, objective function $= 100$. Note that there is an alternative solution with the same objective value for which $x_2 = 2$ and the others are 0. The first solution discussed above is the largest-ratio solution. The largest-ratio rule gives an optimum answer quite often.

TRAVELING SALESMAN PROBLEM

• PROBLEM 6-40

Consider the traveling salesman problem with the following cost data:

		To city				
		1	2	3	4	5
From city	1	*M*	20	4	10	25
	2	20	*M*	5	30	10
	3	4	5	*M*	6	6
	4	10	25	6	*M*	20
	5	35	10	6	20	*M*

Solve.

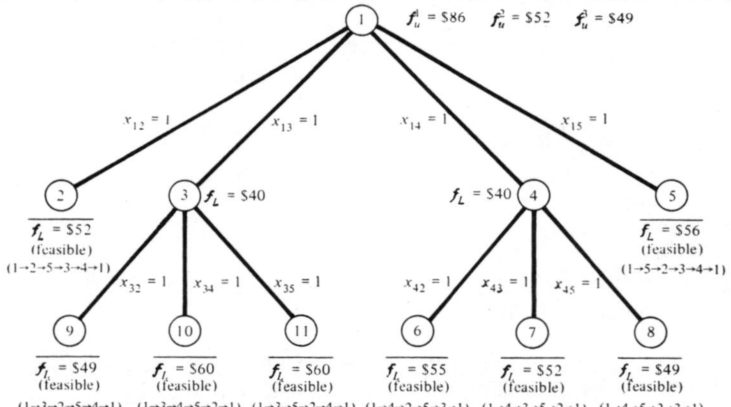

Fig. 1

Solution: The following algorithm is used to solve traveling salesman problems:

Step 1: Solve the original problem as an assignment problem. If the solution is a complete tour, it is optimal. Otherwise, go to step 2.

Step 2: Generate an upper bound on the minimum value of the objective function by finding any feasible tour. Denote this bound by f_U.

Generate the initial branches by setting $x_1 = 1$ for each city j = 2, 3, . . ., n (unless $c_{1j} = M$, indicating the route is infeasible). Compute a lower bound (f_L) on the minimum value of the objective function at each node as follows. From the original data, delete the first row and the jth column. Next, set $c_{j1} = +M$. Solve the resulting assignment problem and add its cost ($\hat{f}$) to c_{1j}, to yield f_L, that is, $f_L = c_{1j} + \hat{f}$. If $f_L > f_U$, fathom the node and go to step 3.

Step 3: If there are no active nodes, the current incumbent solution is optimal. Otherwise, choose the node with smallest value of f_L, and generate new branches by setting $x_{jk} = 1$ for each city k not previously visited on the partial tour. Go to step 4.

Step 4: Generate bounds f_L at each node by deleting row j and column k from the problem solved at the node immediately above the current node, setting $c_{kj} = M$ and then adding the solution cost $\hat{f}$ to c_{jk} and all earlier costs incurred in the partial tour.

The branch-and-bound tree is shown in Fig. 1.

Step 1: The solution to the assignment problem is $x_{13} = x_{34} = x_{41} = 1$ and $x_{25} = x_{52} = 1$, which contains subtours.

Step 2: Notice that the tour $x_{12} = x_{23} = x_{34} = x_{45} = x_{51} = 1$ is feasible with a cost of \$20 + \$5 + \$6 + \$20 + \$35 = \$86, so we set $f_U^1 = \$86$.

Generate the initial branches $x_{12} = 1$ (node 2), $x_{13} = 1$ (node 3), x_{14} = (node 4), and $x_{15} = 1$ (node 5).

At node 2 solve the assignment problem resulting by deleting the first row and second column from the original data data and then settting $c_{21} = M$, which yields the problem:

M	5	30	10
4	M	6	6
10	6	M	20
35	6	20	M

The solution is $x_{25} = x_{53} = x_{34} = x_{41} = 1$ with $\hat{f}$ = \$32. Since it was assumed $x_{12} = 1$ with a cost of \$20, there is a feasible tour with a cost $f_L = \$52$. Set $f_U^2 = \$52$, store this solution as the new incumbent and fathom node 2.

At node 3 delete the first row and third column from the original problem and set c_{31} = M:

20	*M*	30	10
M	5	6	6
10	25	*M*	20
35	10	20	*M*

This yields the problem with the solution $x_{34} = x_{41} = 1$ and $x_{25} = x_{52} = 1$ with $\hat{f} = \$36$. Thus, $f_L = c_{13} + \hat{f} = \$4 + \$36 = \$40$, so $f_L < f_U^2$ and node 3 cannot be fathomed.

At node 4 delete the first row and fourth column and set c_{41} = M to obtain:

20	*M*	5	10
4	5	*M*	6
M	25	6	20
35	10	6	*M*

The solution is $x_{43} = x_{31} = 1$ and $x_{25} = x_{52} = 1$ with $\hat{f} = \$30$. Thus, $f_L = \$10 + \hat{f} = \$40 < f_U^2$, so node 4 cannot be fathomed.

At node 5 delete the first row and fifth column and set c_{51} = M to obtain:

20	*M*	5	30
4	5	*M*	6
10	25	6	*M*
M	10	6	20

The solution is $x_{52} = x_{23} = x_{34} = x_{41} = 1$ which, when coupled with $x_{15} = 1$, completes a tour with a cost of $f_L = \$56$. Thus node 5 can be fathomed.

Step 3: There are two active nodes (3 and 4) with $f_L = \$40$. Choosing node 4 arbitrarily, generate the branches $x_{42} = 1$ (node 6), $x_{43} = 1$ (node 7), and $x_{45} = 1$ (node 8).

Step 4: Generate the bounds at nodes 6, 7, and 8 by modifying the data at node 4, because these nodes are descendants of (derived from) node 4.

At node 6 delete the row for city 4 and the column for city 2, and set c_{21} = M, to obtain:

M	5	10
4	*M*	6
35	6	*M*

with solution $x_{25} = x_{53} = x_{31} = 1$. Coupled with $x_{14} = x_{42} = 1$, this completes a tour with $f_L = \$55$, so fathom node 6.

At node 7 delete the row for city 4 and the column for city 3, and set c_{31} = M, to obtain

20	M	10
M	5	6
35	10	M

with solution $x_{35} = x_{52} = x_{21} = 1$. Coupled with $x_{14} = x_{43} = 1$, this complete a tour with f_L = \$52, so fathom node 7.

At node 8 delete the row for city 4 and the column for city 5, and set $c_{51} = M$, to obtain:

20	M	5
4	5	M
M	10	6

with solution $x_{52} = x_{23} = x_{31} = 1$. Since $x_{14} = x_{45} = 1$ above, there is a feasible tour with f_L = \$49. Since $f_L < f_U^2$, set f_U^3 = \$49 and store the new incumbent.

Step 3: The only remaining active node is node 3. Generate the branches $x_{32} = 1$ (node 9), $x_{34} = 1$ (node 10), and $x_{35} = 1$ (node 11).

Step 4: The calculations for the bounds result in feasible tours at all three nodes, with the values shown. Also find an alternate solution at node 9.

Step 3: There are no active nodes. There are two alternate optimal tours: 1 → 4 → 5 → 2 → 3 → 1, with a cost of \$49, and 1 → 3 → 2 → 5 → 4 → 1, also with a cost of \$49.

• PROBLEM 6-41

To

	A	B	C	D
From A	-	1	4	5
B	3	-	1	2
C	2	4	-	3
D	5	2	6	-

Find the shortest circuit in the above network which meets all nodes.

Solution: Start by reducing the entries in each row by the smallest entry in it. At least these distances will have to be covered, whatever the circuit, since each node will have to be left for some other node. Then do the same for each column. Each node will have to be reached from some other node. Thus the sum of all the reductions is a lower bound of the length of any circuit.

Obtain, first,

	A	B	C	D
(-1)A	-	0	3	4
(-1)B	2	-	0	1
(-2)C	0	2	-	1
(-2)D	3	0	4	-

and then

	A	B	C	D
A	-	0	3	3
B	2	-	0	0
C	0	2	-	0
D	3	0	4	-
				(-1)

The total reduction is 7, and this is a lower bound for the length of a circuit. Now write against all zero entries the sum of the smallest remaining entry in its row and the smallest remaining entry in its column.

	A	B	C	D
A		3		
B			3	0
C	2			0
D		3		

Take one of the largest of these values, 3, in AB say. If AB is not a link in the circuit (denote this decision by $\overline{AB}$) then A will be left for some other node than B, and B will be reached from some other node than A (see Fig. 1). Therefore another 3 can be added to the lower bound in this case. See what happens if AB is used. Exclude from the table the A row and the B column, and also the link BA, because this would return to A, without having been to all nodes.

	A	C	D
B	-	0	0
C	0	-	0
D	3	4	-

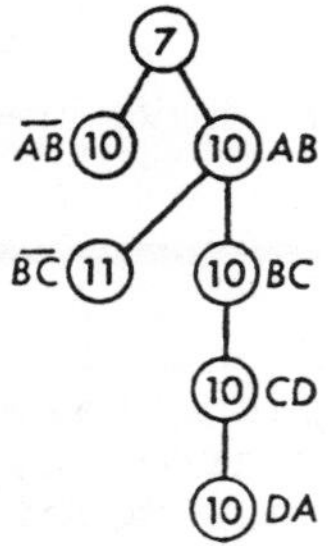

Fig. 1

Reduce the last row by 3, and add this to the lower bound, if AB is used as a link:

	A	C	D			A	C	D
B	-	0	0		B		1	0
C	0	-	0	which leads to	C	0		0
D	0	1	-		D	1		

for the sum of the lowest remaining entries in row and column.

If BC is not taken as a link, then the lower bound is increased by another 1. It is now 11. If BC is taken, then row B, column C and CA are omitted (because this would close the short circuit ABCA).

	A	D
C	-	0
D	0	-

The circuit is closed by CD, DA, total length 10. If BC is not taken, then it is known already that the length of any circuit is at least 11, longer than 10.

Going one step further back, note that a circuit not including AB has a length of at least 10. For alternative circuits of this length, consider this case.

Start again from the original table, but excluding AB.

	A	B	C	D			A	B	C	D
A	-	-	4	5		(-4)A	-	-	0	0
B	3	-	1	2	reduced to	(-1)B	2	-	0	0
C	2	4	-	3		(-2)C	0	2	-	0
D	5	2	6	-		(-2)D	3	0	4	-
										(-1)

Total reduction 10.

The numbers attached to the 0 entries are

	A	B	C	D
A			0	0
B			0	0
C	2			0
D		5		

If DB is not used, then the lower bound is 10 + 5, already too high. So choose DB and exclude BD.

	A	C	D
A	-	0	0
B	2	0	-
C	0	-	0

which leads to

	A	C	D
A		0	0
B		2	
C	2		0

If BC or CA is not chosen, then the lower bound is again too high, therefore choose one of them, and obtain the alternative circuit DBCAD, again of length 10.

CHAPTER 7

DYNAMIC PROGRAMMING

RECURSIONS

• PROBLEM 7-1

Consider the following general resource allocation problem. Assume that a fixed resource can be used for any of N tasks. Let the return from using y units of resource on task k, k= 1,2,...,N be defined by

$$\text{Return} = R(y,k)$$

where the amount of resource utilized on task k is bounded by $0 \leq y \leq Y(k)$. Develop a dynamic programming equation to find the best utilization of B units of resource.

Solution: The dynamic programming formulation can be established as follows. Let

x(k) = amount of resource left to utilize on tasks k, k+1,...,N.

u(k) = amount of resource used on task k.

Then the system equation becomes

$$x(k+1) = x(k) - u(k)$$

i.e., the resource left to utilize on tasks k+1,...,N is the amount left to use on k,...,N less the amount used on k. The performance criterion, which is to be maximized, is the total return, given by

$$J = \sum_{k=1}^{N} R(u,k).$$ The constraints are:

$$0 \leq u(k) \leq Y(k)$$

$$0 \leq x(k) \leq B$$

The iterative equation becomes

$$I(x,k) = \max_{0 \leq u \leq Y(k)} \left(R(u,k) + I(x-u,\ k+1) \right)$$

where the boundary condition is

$$I(x,N) = R(x,N)$$

i.e., if there is any resource remaining at the last task, it will all be used on this task. The best utilization of B units of resource over the N tasks is found by applying the above recursive equation to find I(B,1) and then tracing out the solution from this state and stage.

• PROBLEM 7-2

Mr. Sine has some money which he wants to invest in a number of activities (investment programs) in such a way that the total return is maximized.

Assume that he has $8,000 for allocation and that the investments can only be integral multiples of $1000. Three investment programs are available. The return function for each program is tabulated below:

Return Functions $h_i(x)$

X(000)	0	1	2	3	4	5	6	7	8
$h_1(x)$	0	5	15	40	80	90	95	98	100
$h_2(x)$	0	5	15	40	60	70	73	74	75
$h_3(x)$	0	4	26	40	45	50	51	52	53

Using the principles of dynamic programming, how would the optimal investment in each program be determined so as to maximize total return?

Solution: The problem can be solved recursively, i.e., the optimal solution for one stage is used as input for the next stage.

Step 1: Assume that program 3 is the only program. Then the optimal return from investing

$$X = 0,1,2,\ldots,8$$

in $h_3(x)$ is given by the last row of the table above. In particular, $h_3(8) = 53$ is the optimal return.

Step 2: Now assume only programs 2 and 3 are available and that $d_2(x)$, $d_3(y)$ can be invested in programs 2 and 3, where

$$x = 0,1,\ldots,8 \quad y = 0,1,2,\ldots,8$$

$$\text{and } x + y = 0,1,2,\ldots,8.$$

Thus, with 8 he can invest 0 in 2 and 8 in 3, with 5, 3 in 2 and 2 in 3 and so on. Find the optimum of all these choices for each x in 0,1,2,...,8. The functional equation is

$$f_2(x) = \max_{y = 0,1,\ldots,8-x} \left[g_2(y) + f_3(x)\right]$$

$$x = 0,1,\ldots,8.$$

Step 3: The final stage is the same as the original problem. Now assume all three programs are available. Examine the results of investing z in program 1 and 8 - z units in programs 2 and 3 (the optimal amounts for each 8 - z (z = 0,1,2,...,8) have already been found in Step 2).

The functional equation for the last stage is

$$f_i(x) = \max\,[g_i(z) + f_{i+1}(x - z)]$$

$$x = 0,\ldots,8$$

$$z = 0,1,\ldots,x$$

$$d_i(x) = \text{value of } z \text{ that yields } f_i(x)$$

where $f_i(x)$ is the optimal return from investing x units in programs, i, i + 1,..,3 and $d_i(x)$ is the optimal amount to invest in program i when x units are available to invest in programs i, i + 1,...,3 for i = 1,2,3.

• PROBLEM 7-3

Consider the problem with system equation

$$x(k+1) = x(k) + u(k),$$

performance criterion

$$J = \sum_{k=0}^{2} [x^2(k) + u^2(k)],$$

and constraints

$$0 \le x \le 4$$

$$-1 \le u \le 1.$$

Find the minimum cost function and optimum decision policy as analytical functions of x for k = 0,1,2.

Solution: Note that at stage 2

$$\hat{u}(x,2) = 0$$

$$I(x,2) = x^2.$$

Then examine the recursive equation for stage 1

$$I(x,1) = \min_u \{x^2 + u^2 + I(x + u, 2)\}$$

$$= \min_u \{x^2 + u^2 + (x+u)^2\}.$$

Assume that the constraints do not apply and differentiate, obtain

$$\hat{u}(x,1) = -\frac{1}{2}x$$

$$I(x,1) = \frac{3}{2}x^2.$$

For $0 \le x \le 2$, it follows that $-1 \le \hat{u} \le 0$, and the constraint does not apply. Therefore, the above solution does indeed hold for $0 \le x \le 2$.

Now, for $x > 2$, considering the constraint $-1 \le u \le 0$, note that the quantity in brackets is minimized if $\hat{u} = -1$. Therefore, for $x > 2$

$$\hat{u}(x,1) = -1$$

$$I(x,1) = x^2 + (-1)^2 + (x-1)^2 = 2x^2 - 2x + 2.$$

To summarize:

$$\hat{u}(x,1) = \begin{cases} -\frac{1}{2}x & 2 \ge x \ge 0 \\ -1 & 4 \ge x \ge 2 \end{cases}$$

$$I(x,1) = \begin{cases} \frac{3}{2}x^2, & 2 \ge x \ge 0 \\ 2x^2 - 2x + 2 & 4 \ge x \ge 2. \end{cases}$$

Now examine stage 0. The recursive equation is

$$I(x,0) = \min_u \{x^2 + u + I(x+u, 1)\}$$

Assume that $0 \le x + u \le 2$. Then

$$I(x,0) = \min_u \{x^2 + u^2 + \frac{3}{2}(x+u)^2\}$$

The solution is

$$\hat{u}(x,0) = -\frac{3}{5}x$$

$$I(x,0) = 1\frac{3}{5}x^2.$$

Now, $0 \leq x + \hat{u}(x,0) \leq 2$ only if $0 \leq \frac{2}{5}x \leq 2$, or if $0 \leq x \leq 5$. Since this covers the region $0 \leq x \leq 3$, one sees that if $-1 \leq \hat{u}(x,0) \leq 0$ for $0 \leq x \leq 3$, then the above expression is exact. Note, however, that it holds only for $0 \leq x \leq \frac{5}{3}$.

On the other hand, note that for $x \geq \frac{5}{3}$, $\hat{u}(x,0) = -1$.

First assume $I(x-1,1) = \frac{3}{2}(x-1)^2$. In that case

$$I(x,0) = x^2 + (-1)^2 + \frac{3}{2}(x-1)^2 = \frac{5}{2}x^2 - 3x + \frac{5}{2}.$$

Notice that for $\frac{5}{3} \leq x \leq 3$, $\frac{2}{3} \leq x-1 \leq 2$. Therefore, for

this range of x, the next state falls in the region where $I(x,1) = \frac{3}{2}x^2$, and the above expression is correct.

For $x \geq 3$, note that $x-1 \geq 2$, so that $I(x-1,1)$ is given by $[2(x-1)^2 - 2(x-1) + 2]$. Therefore, for $3 \leq x \leq 4$,

$$\hat{u}(x,0) = -1$$

$$I(x,0) = x^2 + (-1)^2 + 2(x-1)^2 - 2(x-1) + 2$$
$$= 3x^2 - 6x + 7.$$

Thus

$$u(x,0) = \begin{cases} -\frac{3}{5}x & , 0 \leq x \leq \frac{5}{3} \\ -1 & , \frac{5}{3} \leq x \leq 4 \end{cases}$$

$$I(x,0) = \begin{cases} \frac{8}{5}x^2 & , 0 \leq x \leq \frac{5}{3} \\ \frac{5}{2}x^2 - 3x + \frac{5}{2} & , \frac{5}{3} \leq x \leq 3 \\ 3x^2 - 6x + 7 & , 3 \leq x \leq 4 \end{cases}$$

• PROBLEM 7-4

> Write the recurrence relation and obtain an explicit solution for the problem with cost function:
>
> $$J = \sum_{k=0}^{2} [x^2(k) + u^2(k)] + x^2(3),$$
>
> system equation:
>
> $$x(k+1) = x(k) + u(k)$$
>
> and no constraints.

Solution: The recurrence relation can be written immediately as

$$I(x,k) = \min_{\substack{u \\ k=0,1,2}} \{x^2 + u^2 + I(x + u, k+1)\}$$

$$I(x,3) = x^2.$$

Begin by calculating I(x,2)

$$I(x,2) = \min_u \{x^2 + u^2 + (x+u)^2\}.$$

Differentiating the quantity in brackets with respect to u and setting the result equal to 0, yields

$$\frac{d}{du} [x^2 + u^2 + (x+u)^2] = 2u + 2(x+u) = 2x + 4u = 0.$$

Use this result and the convexity of the function $[x^2 + u^2 + (x+u)^2]$ to deduce that the minimizing value of u as $u = -\frac{1}{2} x$. Substituting into the equation for I(x,2), obtain

$$I(x,2) = x^2 + (-\frac{1}{2} x)^2 + x - \frac{1}{2}x)^2 = \frac{3}{2} x^2.$$

To obtain I(x,1), set up the recurrence relation as

$$I(x,1) = \min_u \{x^2 + u^2 + \frac{3}{2} (x+u)^2\}.$$

By following the same procedure, find that the minimizing value of u is $u = -\frac{3}{5} x$. Substituting this value into the recursive relation yields

$$I(x,1) = \frac{8}{5} x^2.$$

Finally, the recursive relation for I(x,0) is

$$I(x,0) = \min_u \{x^2 + u^2 + \frac{8}{5}(x+u)^2\}.$$

The minimizing value of u as $u = -\frac{8}{13}x$ and the resulting minimum cost function as $I(x,0) = \frac{21}{13}x^2$ are thus obtained.

DETERMINISTIC DP

• PROBLEM 7-5

A family is moving from the East to the West Coast. They plan to drive across the country to combine the move with sightseeing. Their point of departure and their destination are fixed, but they have some choice of route segments in between. Each segment is more or less desirable from a sightseeing point of view, and they want to travel the sequence of route segments that will give them the "most" in sightseeing. The total trip will have to be done in four stages, as shown in Fig. 1. The arrows represent the available route segments.

Let the "sightseeing value" of going from Point i to Point j be s_{ij}. Then the problem is to maximize the sum

$$S_{19} = s_{1i} + s_{ij} + s_{jk} + s_{k9},$$

where:

i may be 2 or 3,

j may be 4, 5, or 6, and

k may be 7 or 8.

The values of s_{ij} are given in Table 1.

Table 1

Stage I

	j = 2	j = 3
i = 1	4	2

Stage II

	j = 4	j = 5	j = 6
i = 2	6	1	5
3	3	4	2

Stage III

	j = 7	j = 8
i = 4	2	1
5	6	2
6	3	5

Stage IV

	j = 9
i = 7	2
8	5

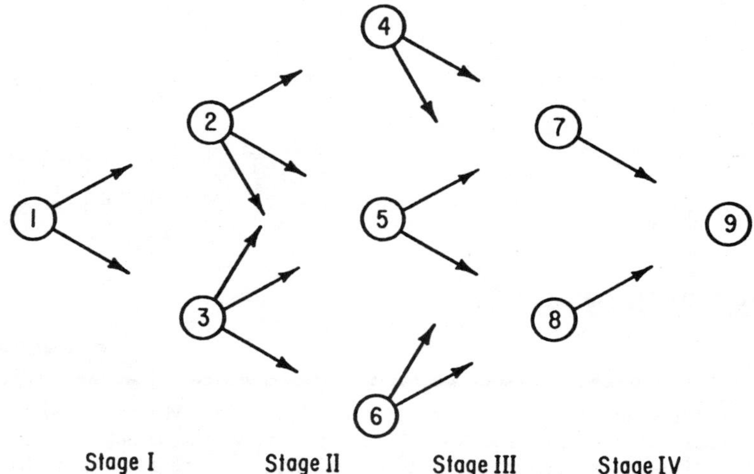

Fig. 1

Solution: Now, if the family chooses the largest value stage after stage, they will, for example, have:

$$S_{19} = s_{12} + s_{24} + s_{47} + s_{79} = 4 + 6 + 2 + 2 = 14.$$

But this is not necessarily the highest total value they can obtain, because sacrificing somewhat at one stage may make the overall result come out higher.

In dynamic programming, a small portion of the problem is first solved and then more and more stages are taken into the solution until the entire span of stages is covered. Usually, the procedure starts from the end.

Stage IV: There are two possibilities for going to Destination 9, given that the family was at either 7 or 8:

$$S_{79} = 2, \quad \text{and} \quad S_{89} = 5.$$

For Stages III and IV, there are six possibilities:

$$S_{49} = \begin{cases} s_{47} + s_{79} = 2 + 2 = 4 \\ s_{48} + s_{89} = 1 + 5 = 6 = S^*_{489} \end{cases}$$

$$S_{59} = \begin{cases} s_{57} + s_{79} = 6 + 2 = 8 = S^*_{579} \\ s_{58} + s_{89} = 2 + 5 = 7 \end{cases}$$

$$S_{69} = \begin{cases} s_{67} + s_{79} = 3 + 2 = 5 \\ s_{68} + s_{89} = 5 + 5 = 10 = S^*_{689} \end{cases}$$

Thus, an "optimal" route selection results for going to the destination, given that the family is at either 4, 5, or 6. The optimal choices for the last two stages are denoted by stars. If this procedure is carried back to the starting point, it will give the overall optimal choice S_{19}^*. Note that, with any succeeding iteration, one need only take into account the starred (optimal) policies of the partial problems before.

Stages II, III, and IV:

$$S_{29} = \begin{cases} s_{24} + S_{489}^* = 6 + 6 = 12 \\ s_{25} + S_{579}^* = 1 + 8 = 9 \\ s_{26} + S_{689}^* = 5 + 10 = 15 = S_{2689}^* \end{cases}$$

$$S_{39} = \begin{cases} s_{34} + S_{489}^* = 3 + 6 = 9 \\ s_{35} + S_{579}^* = 4 + 8 = 12 = S_{3579}^* \\ s_{36} + S_{689}^* = 2 + 10 = 12 = S_{3689}^* \end{cases}$$

At this iteration, the optimal route from 3 to 9 is not unique.

Stages I, II, III, and IV:

$$S_{19} = \begin{cases} s_{12} + S_{2689}^* = 4 + 15 = 19 = S_{12689}^* \\ s_{13} + S_{3579}^* = 2 + 12 = 14 \\ s_{13} + S_{3689}^* = 2 + 12 = 14 \end{cases}$$

This results in the optimal route: 1, 2, 6, 8, 9 with value 19. This is considerably different from choosing the "best" route at each stage successively, which gave a value of only 14.

• PROBLEM 7-6

A traveler wants to go from a fixed origin to a fixed destination. The trip will proceed in four stages because he must stop each night to rest. Several paths of travel are possible. He will stop each night in a city. Each morning he will decide which of several possible cities he will travel to during the day.

The traveler's origin is city C_{41}. The first subscript indicates that there are four stages of travel remaining as he starts the process; the second indicates that this city is the first with that property. The traveler must decide first whether to proceed to city C_{31}, city C_{32}, or city C_{33} next. These are the only possibilities.

The traveler's objective is to minimize the total cost of the whole trip. He knows the cost of traveling from each city to each other city for each stage of the trip. The problem is to consider the total cost of every possible complete trip from the origin to the destination and to select from these the one having minimum total cost.

The complete problem can be described by the diagram in Fig. 1, which shows the possible stop-over cities and the possible travel paths between them. Associated with each path is a travel cost. The stages of travel (days) are numbered backward to indicate the number of future stages remaining. The process begins with stage 4. At the start of stage 4 the traveler must decide his destination for that day, either city C_{31}, C_{32}, or C_{33}. The destination for day 4 is also the starting point for stage 3. Again at the start of stage 3 he must decide whether to travel to city C_{21}, C_{22}, or C_{23}. The destination for stage 3 is the starting point for stage 2 and so on. The final destination is city C_{01}. The traveler will arrive there at the end of the fourth day of travel and the process will then be over.

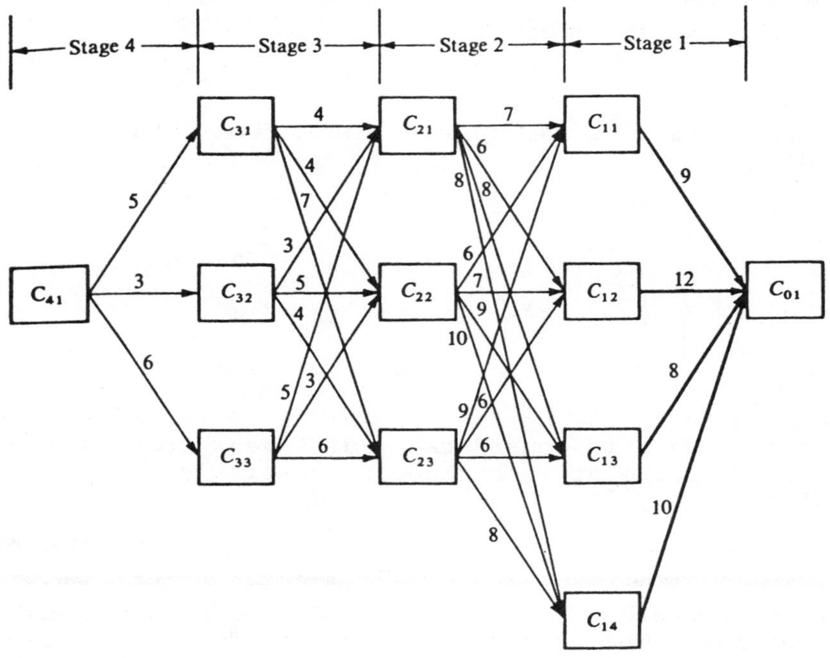

Fig. 1

Solution: Consider the stage 1 decision. Stage 1 begins with the traveler in city C_{11}, C_{12}, C_{13}, or C_{14}. In all these cases there is actually no decision to be made. All that remains of the journey is to proceed to the final destination. The cost of the whole future process starting with stage 1 is

$F_{11} = 9$ if starting from C_{11}

$F_{12} = 12$ if starting from C_{12}

$F_{13} = 8$ if starting from C_{13}

and

$F_{14} = 10$ if starting from C_{14}.

These results can be used in the following way: Replace cities C_{11}, C_{12}, C_{13}, and C_{14} by the symbols F_{11}, F_{12}, F_{13}, and F_{14}, which stand for the entire future process starting from stage 1. Label them with the costs of the future process as just calculated. The new problem is represented by Fig. 2.

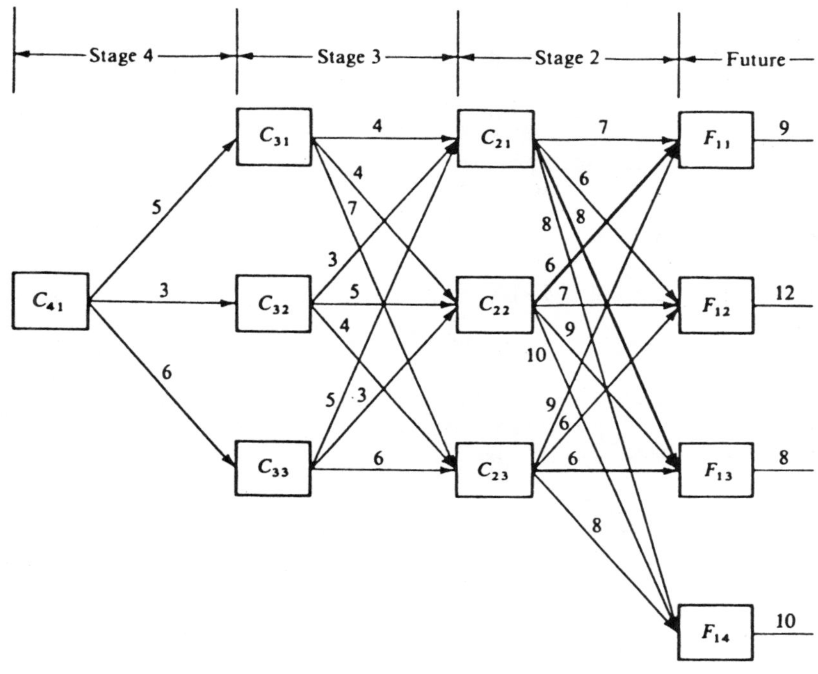

Fig. 2

The stage 2 problem can now be solved. The entire future, beginning from the start of stage 2, is represented in two parts: stage 2 itself plus the future following stage 2. Let F_{21}, F_{22}, and F_{23} represent the total cost of the optimal path from cities C_{21}, C_{22}, and C_{23}, respectively. This can be expressed as the sum of the cost in stage 2 plus the cost of the future following stage 2. For each starting point there are four possible decisions. Their costs, for starting point C_{21}, are

$7 + F_{11} = 7 + 9$ if C_{11} is selected as next destination

$6 + F_{12} = 6 + 12$ if C_{12} is selected

$8 + F_{13} = 8 + 8$ if C_{13} is selected

and

$8 + F_{14} = 8 + 10$ if C_{14} is selected.

The calculation and selection of the best destination can be expressed as

$$F_{21} = \min \{7 + F_{11},\ 6 + F_{12},\ 8 + F_{13},\ 8 + F_{14}\}$$

$$= \min \{16, 18, 16, 18\} = 16.$$

Thus the cost of the optimum path from city C_{21} is 16 and is obtained by setting either C_{11} or C_{13} as the next destination. Similarly, for the starting point C_{22} the optimum cost and decision are found by the following calculations:

$$F_{22} = \min\{6 + F_{11},\ 7 + F_{12},\ 9 + F_{13},\ 10 + F_{14}\}$$

$$= \min\{15,19,17,20\}$$

$$= 15 \quad \text{obtained with destination } C_{11}.$$

The last possible starting point is C_{23}. The total cost of the best path from C_{23} is

$$F_{23} = \min\{9 + F_{11},\ 6 + F_{12},\ 6 + F_{13},\ 8 + F_{14}\}$$

$$= \min\{18,18,14,18\}$$

$$= 14 \quad \text{obtained with destination } C_{13}.$$

The results of the stage 2 calculations, which can be used in the stage 3 calculations, are represented by the diagram in Fig. 3.

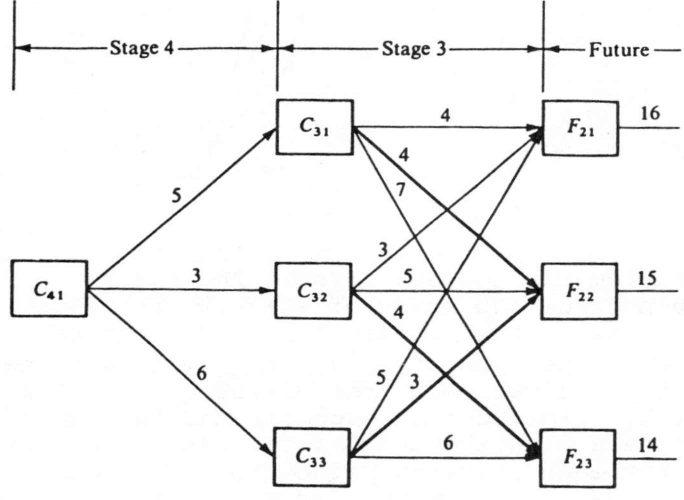

Fig. 3

The stage 3 calculations proceed as follows:

$$F_{31} = \min\{4 + F_{21},\ 4 + F_{22},\ 7 + F_{23}\}$$

$$= \min\{20,19,21\}$$

$$= 19 \quad \text{obtained with destination } C_{22}$$

$$F_{32} = \min\{3 + F_{21},\ 5 + F_{22},\ 4 + F_{23}\}$$

$$= \min\{19,20,18\}$$

$$= 18 \quad \text{obtained with destination } C_{23}$$

$$F_{33} = \min\{5 + F_{21}, \quad 3 + F_{22}, \quad 6 + F_{23}\}$$

$$= \min\{21, 18, 20\}$$

$$= 18 \quad \text{obtained with destination } C_{22}.$$

The results of the stage 3 calculations can be represented as shown in Fig. 4.

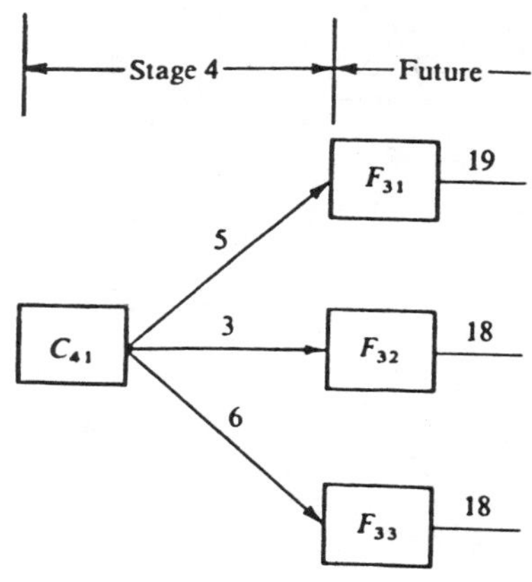

Fig. 4

The stage 4 calculations use the stage 3 results:

$$F_{41} = \min\{5 + F_{31}, \quad 3 + F_{32}, \quad 6 + F_{33}\}$$

$$= \min\{24, 21, 24\}$$

$$- 21 \quad \text{obtained with destination } C_{32}.$$

The complete solution is now known. The best path, shown in Fig. 5, has a total cost of 21 units.

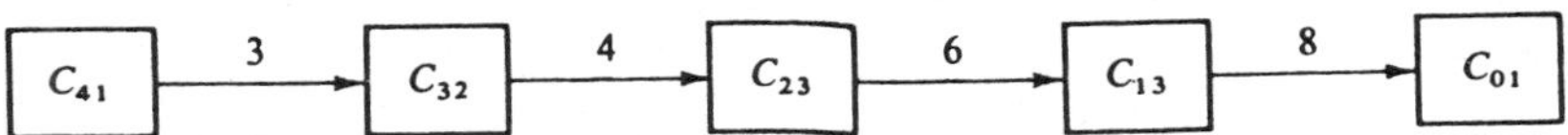

Fig. 5

• PROBLEM 7-7

Consider the following water distribution network construction problem. Based on an analysis of water pressure zones and topological considerations, a set of possible routings of pipe is portrayed in Figure 1. It is desired to find the least costly routing of pipe from point A to point M.

The candidate pipe segments are represented in network theory terminology as directed links between nodes, where the actual physical locations of the nodes A,B,...,M are specified by the designer. Each link has an arrow showing the direction water will flow in the pipe. Each link also has an associated total cost, which includes all costs for materials (pipes, valves, etc.) and construction (acquiring right of way, digging holes, connecting pipes, etc.). The problem is to find that connection of pipes from A to M that has minimum total cost. Use dynamic programming to formulate and solve this problem.

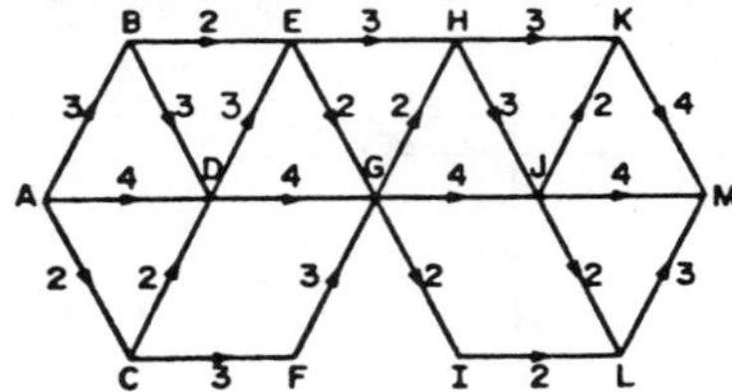

Fig. 1

Solution: The system equations can be thought of here as a "state transition function," which relates to the connection of one node to another node by a link. The quantized "state" is thus the index of the originating node. The quantized "decision" is the index of the link that is installed. The "stage" is merely the ordering of these connections. Thus, the "state-transition function" expresses the next node along a given pipe routing as a function of the present node and the link that is selected.

The single-stage cost function is simply the cost of the link that is selected. The total cost function is the sum of these single-stage costs.

The constraints have already been applied to specify the "states" (nodes) that are admissible and the "decisions" (links) that can be applied at any "state" (node).

To solve the recursive equation for the given network, note that the terminal condition for this case is

$$I(M) = 0$$

Next, try to find nodes for which the recursive equation can be solved. Note that nodes J, K and L all connect to node M. First try to find I(J), the minimum cost of going to the terminal node from node J. This quantity is explicitly

$$I(J) = \min \{2 + I(K),\quad 4 + I(M),\quad 2 + I(L)\}$$

where the first term in each sum is the cost of the next link and the second term is the resulting cost at the terminal end of the link. Since only the value I(M) = 0 has been computed so far, this calculation cannot be completed.

Next try to find I(K). This quantity is

$$I(K) = \min \{4 + I(M)\} = 4.$$

Since there is only one link emanating from K, find its minimum cost immediately. This partial solution is portrayed in Figure 2 by putting the cost for the node in a circle and by indicating with an arrow which link was selected.

Similarly, find for node L that

$$I(L) = \min \{3 + I(M)\} = 3$$

This result is also shown in Figure 2.

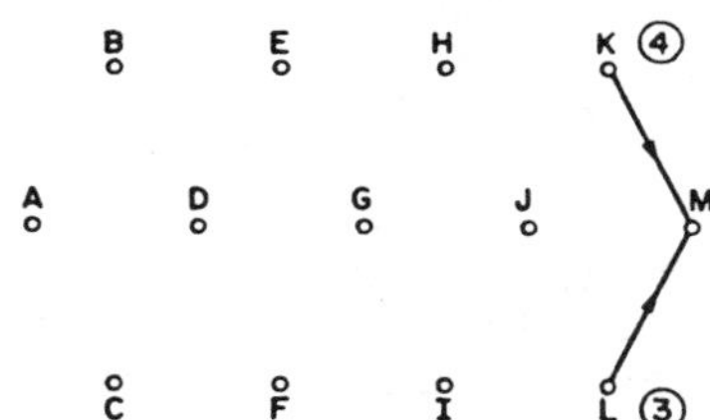

Fig. 2

Next proceed to consider all nodes that connect to any link for which the minimum cost function has been computed. In this case, the nodes for which there are values are K, L, and M, and the nodes connected to them are H, I, and J.

At node H

$$I(H) = \min \{3 + I(K), \quad 3 + I(J)\}.$$

This analysis cannot be completed because I(J) is not yet known. At node I

$$I(I) = \min \{2 + I(L)\}$$

$$= \min \{2 + 3\}$$

$$= 5.$$

The result is entered on Figure 3.

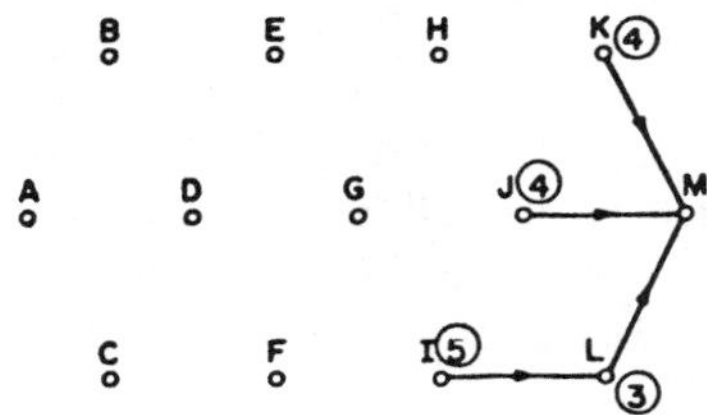

Fig. 3

Proceeding to node J

$$I(J) = \min \{2 + I(K), 4 + I(M), 2 + I(L)\}$$

$$= \min \{2 + 4, 4 + 0, 2 + 3\}$$

$$= \min \{6, 4, 5\}$$

$$= 4.$$

This result is also indicated on Figure 3.

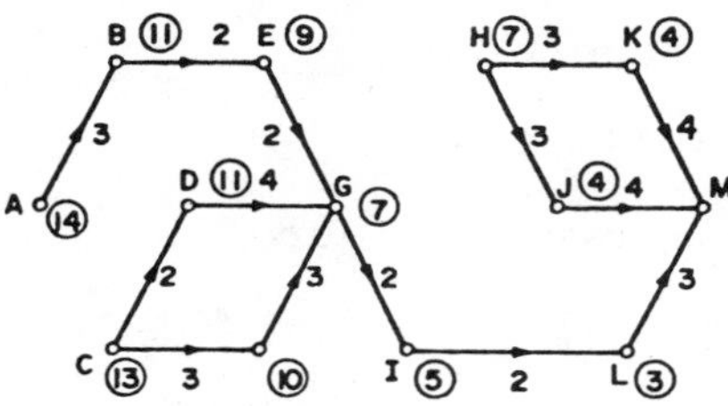

Fig. 4

The results of completing this procedure for the problem are shown in Figure 4. From this solution trace back the optimum routing of the pipes as beginning at node A and passing through nodes B, E, G, I, and L before reaching the terminal node M. The cost of this path is 14 units.

• PROBLEM 7-8

The Ankara shoe store sells rubber shoes for protective use in snow. Past experience has indicated that the selling season is only 6 months long, and lasts from October 1 through March 31. The sales division has forecast the following demands for next year

Month	Demand
October	40
November	20
December	30
January	40
February	30
March	20

All shoes sold by this store are purchased from outside sources. The following information is known about this particular shoe.

Purchasing Conditions: The unit purchasing cost is $4.00 per pair; however, the supplier will only sell in lots of 10, 20, 30, 40, or 50 pair. Any orders for more than 50 or less than 10 will not be accepted.

Quantity Discounts: The following quantity discounts apply on lot size orders

Lot Size	Discount (percent)
10	5
20	5
30	10
40	20
50	25

Ordering Costs: For each order placed, the store incurs a fixed cost of \$2.00. In addition, the supplier charges an average amount of \$8.00 per order to cover transportation costs, insurance, packaging, and so on, irrespective of the amount ordered.

Storage Limitations: Due to large in-process inventories, the store will carry no more than 40 pair of shoes in inventory at the end of any one month. Carrying charges are \$0.20 per pair per month, based on the end-of-month inventory. Since the sale of snowshoes is highly seasonable and subject to design changes, it is desired to have both incoming and outgoing seasonal inventory at zero.

Assuming that demand occurs at a constant rate throughout each month and that the holding cost is based on the end of the month inventory, find an ordering policy which will minimize total seasonal costs.

Solution: Stages: Each month of the 6-month ordering cycle will constitute a single stage. The state diagram will be as shown below.

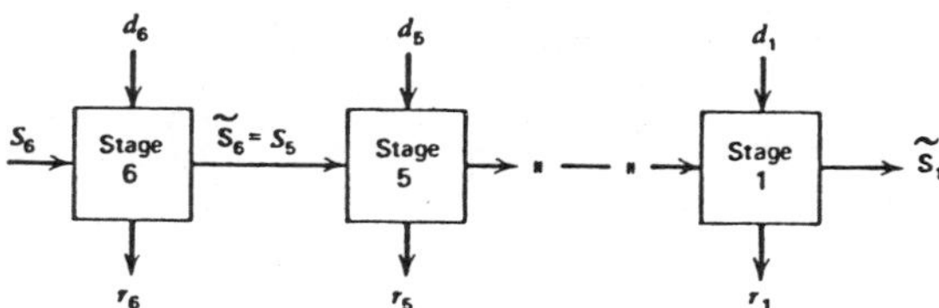

State Variables: At the nth stage, the state variable should be defined as the smount of entering inventory, given that there are n months remaining in the present selling period.

Decision Variables: At the nth stage, the decision to be made is how many pairs of shoes should be ordered to satisfy the demand during stages n,(n-1),...,1.

Transition Function: The transition function must relate the state variable at stage n to the state variable at stage (n-1). This function is given by

$$S_{n-1} = S_n + d_n - D_n \qquad n = 1,2,\ldots,6$$

where

$$S_0 = \tilde{S}_1 \equiv 0$$

$$S_6 \equiv 0$$

S_n = state variable at nth stage (entering material)

d_n = decision variable at nth stage (quantity ordered)

D_n = demand at nth stage.

Note that $(S_n + d_n - D_n)$ will be the quantity of items for which a holding cost of $h_n = \$0.20$, $n = 1,2,\ldots,6$ per unit will be incurred.

Return Function: The return function at each stage should reflect the total cost resulting from the particular decision made at that stage. The return function at the nth stage is given by:

$$r_n(d_n, S_n) = \phi(d_n) + h_n(S_n + d_n - D_n) \qquad n = 1,2,\ldots,6$$

where: $\phi(d_n)$ = order cost function at nth stage. In this problem $\phi(d_n)$; $n = 1,2,\ldots,6$ is composed of a fixed cost of \$10.00 per order, plus a variable cost which depends upon the number of units ordered.

h_n = holding cost per unit per month. This cost is the same for all stages and is equal to \$0.20 per pair; $h_n = \$0.20$, $n = 1,2,\ldots,6$.

The dynamic programming formulation is therefore represented in the following mathematical form:

$$f_n^*(S_n) = \min_{d_n}\{\phi(d_n) + h_n(S_n + d_n - D_n) + f_{n-1}^*(S_{n-1})\}$$

$$n = 1,2,\ldots,6$$

where: $f_0^*(S_0) \equiv 0$

$$S_{n-1} = S_n + d_n - D_n \qquad n = 1,2,\ldots,6$$

$$S_0 \equiv 0$$

$$S_6 \equiv 0.$$

In computing this equation recursively, it will be convenient to refer to the following cost data:

Units Ordered	$\phi(d_n)$	Comment (percent discount)
10	48	5
20	86	5
30	118	10
40	138	20
50	160	25

Stage 1 (March)
Since it is desired to reduce all inventory to zero by the end of March, $S_0 \equiv 0$. Demand for stage 1 is 20 units, so it follows that S_1 will be either 0, 10 or 20 units, and $d_1^* = D_1 - S_1$

$$f_1^*(S_1) = \min_{d_1}\{\phi(d_1)\}$$

S_1	d_1^*	$f_1^*(S_1)$
0	20	86
10	10	48
20	0	0

Stage 2 (February)

$$f_2^*(S_2) = \min_{d_2}\{\phi(d_2) + 0.20(S_2 + d_2 - 30) + f_1^*(S_1)\}$$

where:

$$S_1 = S_2 + d_2 - 30$$

S_2 \ d_2	0	10	20	30	40	50	d_2^*	$f_2^*(S_2)$
0	—	—	—	204	188	164	50	164
10	—	—	172	168	142	—	40	142
20	—	134	136	122	—	—	30	122
30	86	98	90	—	—	—	0	86
40	50	52	—	—	—	—	0	50

Stage 3 (January)

$$f_3^*(S_3) = \min_{d_3}\{\phi(d_3) + 0.20(S_3 + d_3 - 40) + f_2^*(S_2)\}$$

where:

$$S_2 = S_3 + d_3 - 40$$

S_3 \ d_3	0	10	20	30	40	50	d_3^*	$f_3^*(S_3)$
0	—	—	—	—	302	304	40	302
10	—	—	—	282	282	286	30, 40	282
20	—	—	250	262	264	252	20	250
30	—	212	230	244	230	218	10	218
40	164	192	212	210	196	—	0	164

Stage 4 (December)

$$f_4^*(S_4) = \min_{d_4}\{\phi(d_4) + 0.20(S_4 + d_4 - 30) + f_3^*(S_3)\}$$

where:

$$S_3 = S_4 + d_4 - 30$$

S_4 \ d_4	0	10	20	30	40	50	d_4^*	$f_4^*(S_4)$
0	—	—	—	420	422	414	50	414
10	—	—	388	402	392	384	50	384
20	—	350	370	372	362	332	50	332
30	302	332	340	342	310	—	0	302
40	284	302	310	290	—	—	0	284

Stage 5 (November)

$$f_5^*(S_5) = \min_{d_5}\{\phi(d_5) + 0.20(S_5 + d_5 - 20) + f_4^*(S_4)\}$$

where: $S_4 = S_5 + d_5 - 20$

$S_5 \backslash d_5$	0	10	20	30	40	50	d_5^*	$f_5^*(S_5)$
0	—	—	500	504	474	468	50	468
10	—	462	472	454	446	452	40	446
20	414	434	422	426	430	—	0	414
30	386	384	394	410	—	—	10	384
40	336	356	378	—	—	—	0	336

Stage 6 (October)

$$f_6^*(S_6) = \min_{d_6}\{\phi(d_6) + 0.20(S_6 + d_6 - 40) + f_5^*(S_5)\}$$

where: $S_5 = S_6 + d_6 - 40.$

Since the seasonal nature of the problem dictates a zero ending inventory, there will be no inventory carried from stage 6. Hence:

$S_6 \backslash d_6$	0	10	20	30	40	50	d_6^*	$f_6^*(S_6=0)$
0	—	—	—	—	606	608	40	606

From stage 6, the optimal policy is easily recovered from the transition functions and is given by:

$d_6^* = 40$ $\quad d_3^* = 40$

$d_5^* = 50$ $\quad d_2^* = 50$

$d_4^* = 0$ $\quad d_1^* = 0$

$$\text{Total cost} = 138 + \{160 + 0.20(30)\} + 0 + 138 + \{160 + 0.2(20)\}$$

$$\text{Total cost} = 606 = f_6^*(S_6 = 0).$$

• PROBLEM 7-9

Suppose that the work capacity of one truck is required for N years. The work capacity of an individual truck, if properly maintained, remains constant in time. However, its deterioration is reflected in an increasing operating cost and decreasing salvage value. Suppose that a new truck will always cost \$9000. Table 1 gives the operating cost for each successive full year, $C_0(n)$, and the resale value of the truck at the end of each year, $R_s(n)$.

Table 1 Operating Cost and Resale Value

Year (n)	Operating Cost [$C_0(n)$]	Resale Value [$R_s(n)$]
1	1800	6000
2	2100	4000
3	2400	3000
4	2700	2250
5	3000	1500
6	3600	900
7	4500	500
8	5500	200

The objective of the problem is to minimize the total cost of the truck capacity over whatever period of time the truck capacity is needed. The application of dynamic programming to this problem begins with the identification of the stage and the state of the process. The stages are 1-year periods because it is understood that replacement actions are considered only at 1-year intervals. The stage number is the number of future years for which the one-truck capacity will be required. This can be viewed as a planning horizon. The state of the process is the age of the current truck at the start of the stage (year). The decision at the start of each stage is whether to retain the current truck for another year or to replace it and start the new year with a new truck. The notation for the objective function is $f_N(n)$ = total cost of future N stages if the current truck is n years old at the start and if optimum decisions are made in all future stages.

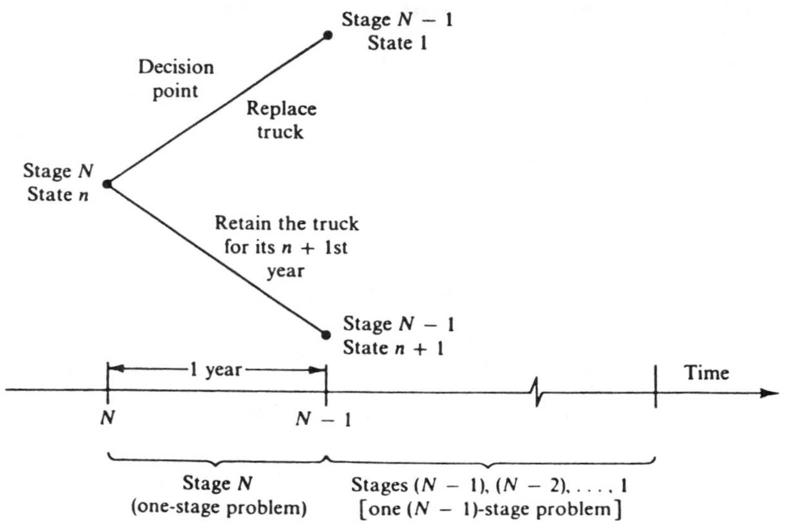

Fig. 1

Solution: Dynamic programming decomposes the N stages into a one-stage problem (Nth) followed by an (N - 1) stage problem. The state at the start of the (N - 1) stage problem depends upon the decision made at the start of stage N. This is illustrated in the diagram in Fig. 1. The dynamic programming equation can be derived from this diagram. Suppose that $f_N(n)$ is to be computed and $f_{N-1}(n)$ is already known. The cost of the next year, stage N, depends upon whether or not the n-year-old truck is replaced at the start. If it is not replaced, the operating cost during the coming year will be $C_0(n + 1)$. The cost of the future N - 1 stages will be $f_{N-1}(n + 1)$. The total cost if it is not replaced will be

$$C_0(n + 1) + f_{N-1}(n + 1).$$

If the truck is replaced at the start of stage N, there will be a purchase cost of $9000 less the resale value $R_s(n)$ of the current n-year-old truck plus the operating cost $C_0(1)$ of the new truck during its first year. The total cost of the future N - 1 stages following this year will be $f_{N-1}(1)$. The total future cost if the truck is replaced is:

$$9000 - R_s(n) + C_0(1) + f_{N-1}(1).$$

The best decision at the start of stage N is that having the lower of these two costs. Thus:

$$f_N(n) = \min \{C_0(n + 1) + f_{N-1}(n + 1),$$

$$9000 - R_s(n) + C_0(1) + f_{N-1}(1)\}.$$

This equation shows how to compute $f_N(n)$ when $f_{N-1}(n)$ is already known. The beginning point for this iterative procedure is N = 1. Then the equation relates $f_1(n)$ to $f_0(n)$. This function $f_0(n)$ is the cost of zero future stages when starting with an n-year-old truck. This is the negative of the resale value of the truck because it is no longer needed.

$$f_0(n) = -R_s(n).$$

Then the equation for $f_1(n)$ is

$$f_1(n) = \min \{C_0(n + 1) - R_s(n + 1),$$

$$9000 - R_s(n) + C_0(1) - R_s(1)\}.$$

This calculation is performed for each n value

$$f_1(1) = \min \{C_0(2) - R_s(2), 9000 - R_s(1) + C_0(1) - R_s(1)\}$$

$$= \min \{2100 - 4000, 9000 - 6000 + 1800 - 6000\}$$

$$= \min \{-1900, -1200\}$$

$$= -1900 \text{ (retain)}.$$

Similarly: $f_1(2) = \min \{2400 - 3000, 9000 - 4000 + 1800 - 6000\}$
$= \min \{-600, 800\}$
$= -600$ (retain).

The results of the next three calculations are

$$f_1(3) = 450 \text{ (retain)}$$

$$f_1(4) = 1500 \text{ (retain)}$$

$$f_1(5) = 2700 \text{ (retain)}.$$

The next calculation shows that a 6-year-old truck should not be kept for its seventh year even when there is just 1 year to go:

$$f_1(6) = \min\{4500 - 500, 9000 - 900 + 1800 - 6000\}$$

$$= \min\{4000, 3900\}$$

$$= 3900 \text{ (replace)}.$$

A truck 6 years old or more would always be replaced because the operating costs continue to increase. The calculations are carried up to n = 7:

$$f_1(7) = 4300 \text{ (replace)}.$$

The equation for stage 2 is

$$f_2(n) = \min\{C_0(n+1) + f_1(n+1),$$

$$9000 - R_s(n) + C_0(1) + f_1(1)\}.$$

Since $f_1(n)$ is now known, $f_2(n)$ can be calculated. For example

$$f_2(1) = \min\{C_0(2) + f_1(2), 9000 - R_s(1) + C_0(1) + f_1(1)\}$$

$$= \min\{2100 - 600, 9000 - 6000 + 1800 - 1900\}$$

$$= \min\{1500, 2900\}$$

$$= 1500 \text{ (retain)}.$$

Similar calculations give

$$f_2(2) = 2850 \text{ (retain)}$$

$$f_2(3) = 4200 \text{ (retain)}$$

$$f_2(4) = 5700 \text{ (retain)}$$

$$f_2(5) = 7400 \text{ (replace)}$$

$$f_2(6) = 8000 \text{ (replace)}$$

$$f_2(7) = 8400 \text{ (replace)}.$$

Now stage 3 can be evaluated. The equation is

$$f_3(n) = \min\{C_0(n+1) + f_2(n+1),$$

$$9000 - R_s(n) + C_0(1) + f_2(1)\}.$$

This repetitive calculation can be organized as shown in Table 2. This shows that with 3 years to go a 3-year-old truck would be retained. However, a truck that is already 4 years old would be replaced and the new truck would be used for the 3-year period.

Table 2

n	$C_0(n+1) + f_2(n+1)$	$[9000 - R_s(n)] + [C_0(1) + f_2(1)]$	$f_3(n)$
1	2100 + 2850 = 4950	3000 + 3300 = 6300	4950 (retain)
2	2400 + 4200 = 6600	5000 + 3300 = 8300	6600 (retain)
3	2700 + 5700 = 8400	6000 + 3300 = 9300	8400 (retain)
4	3000 + 7400 = 10,400	6750 + 3300 = 10,050	10,050 (replace)
5	3600 + 8000 = 11,600	7500 + 3300 = 10,800	10,800 (replace)
6	4500 + 8400 = 12,900	8100 + 3300 = 11,400	11,400 (replace)
7		8500 + 3300 = 11,800	11,800 (replace)

• PROBLEM 7-10

Consider the problem of scheduling a workforce over four quarters (n = 4) for an organization. Each quarter has a projected demand for labor in hours. Assuming that the labor requirements must be met and that overtime is not allowed, management is faced with the cost tradeoff of hiring-firing on the one hand and idle labor on the other. The objective is to propose a workforce schedule which (1) meets requirements for labor of 30,000, 40,000, 35,000, and 50,000 hours in Quarters 1, 2, 3, and 4 respectively, and (2) minimizes the sum of costs associated with changes in the workforce and idle labor over the planning horizon of four quarters.

Assume that the workforce level prior to Quarter 1 stands at 32,000 hours and that an analysis indicates a cost of \$6 per hour for idle labor and a cost associated with workforce changes (hours) equal to 1 percent of the square of the change.

Solution: Working with a backward recursion to facilitate the stage transformations, define the following:

d_i = Demand in Stage i

x_i = hours of workforce hired ($x_i > 0$) or fired ($x_i < 0$) in Stage i

s_i = Workforce level (hours) with i more quarters to go

r_i = Costs (dollars) of idle time and hiring-firing in Stage i.

The transformation function and recursive equation follow easily from the definitions

$$s_{i-1} = s_i + x_i \tag{1}$$

and

$$f_i = \min_{x_i \geq d_i - s_i} [r_i + f^*_{i-1}]$$

or $$f_i = \min_{x_i \geq d_i - s_i} [6(s_{i-1} - d_i) + 0.01x_i^2 + f^*_{i-1}] \quad (2)$$

Substituting Equation (1) into (2) gives

$$f^*_i = \min_{x_i \geq d_i - s_i} [6(s_i - d_i) + 6x_i + 0.01x_i^2 + f^*_{i-1}]. \quad (3)$$

Note that the condition which requires meeting the demand for labor in each quarter is expressed as

$$s_{i-1} \geq d_i \quad (4)$$

$d_1 = 50{,}000$, $d_2 = 35{,}000$, $d_3 = 40{,}000$, and

$d_4 = 30{,}000$

or substituting Equation (1) into Equation (4) as

$$x_i \geq d_i - s_i \quad (5)$$

The unit of measurement for the decision variable (hours) and the availability of part-time labor make x_i and s_i continuous variables.

Stage 1: $f_1 = 6(s_1 - 50{,}000) + 6x_1 + 0.01x_1^2 + 0.$ (6)

The requirement of 50,000 hours in Stage 1 (Period 4) and the nonoptimality of having idle labor in the last period dictate that

$$x_1^* = 50{,}000 - s_1; \quad (7)$$

that is, hire as much as is needed to reach the requirement. Note that an optimal policy necessarily specifies that s_1 never exceed the maximum requirement of 50,000. Plugging Equation (7) into (6) gives the optimal recursion in Stage 1 as

$$f_1^* = 0.01(50{,}000 - s_1)^2. \quad (8)$$

Stage 2: $$f_2 = 6(s_2 - 35{,}000) + 6x_2 + 0.01x_2^2 + 0.01(50{,}000 - s_1)^2. \quad (9)$$

Substituting Equation (1) into (9) f_2 can be expressed strictly in terms of s_2 and x_2, or

$$f_2 = 6(s_2 - 35{,}000) + 6x_2 + 0.01x_2^2 + 0.01(50{,}000 - s_2 - x_2)^2. \quad (10)$$

To find the optimal policy in Stage 2, take the partial derivative of f_2 with respect to x_2, set it to zero, and solve for x_2, giving

$$x_2^* = 24{,}850 - 0.5s_2. \quad (11)$$

The second-order condition identifies x_2^* as a global minimum. Does x_2^* satisfy the constraints imposed by Equation (5)? The answer is yes, as found by plugging Equation (11) in (5) and given that $s_2 \geq 40{,}000$ according to Equation (4), so (11) represents the optimal policy in Stage 2 and the optimal recursion is given by

$$f_2^* = 12,439,550 - 497s_2 + 0.005s_2^2 \quad (12)$$

after substituting Equation (11) into (9) and simplifying.

Stages 3 and 4 proceed in the same manner to arrive at

$$x_3^* = 40,000 - s_3 \quad (13)$$

$$f_3^* = 16,560,000 - 800s_3 + 0.01s_3^2 \quad (14)$$

and

$$x_4^* = 19,850 - 0.5s_4 \quad (15)$$

$$f_4^* = 16,380,000 - 794(s_4 + x_4) + 0.02s_4x_4 + 0.01s_4^2 + 0.02x_4^2. \quad (16)$$

Note that Equation (13) satisfies (5) strictly, which should indicate that the stationary point in Stage 3 did not satisfy (5).

Given that $s_4 = 32,000$, evaluate Equations (15), (13), (11), and (7), making use of (1), to get $x_4^* = 3,850$, $x_3^* = 4,150$, $x_2^* = 4,850$, and $x_1^* = 5,150$; that is, hire 5,150; 4,850; 4,150; and 3,850 hours of labor in Quarters 1, 2, 3, and 4, respectively. Given an optimal hiring-firing policy in each stage, the workforce levels for Quarters 1, 2, 3, and 4 are 35,850; 40,000; 44,850; and 50,000 respectively. The optimal cost, as given by Equation (16), is $915,550 over four quarters.

• PROBLEM 7-11

A man is engaged in buying and selling identical items, each of which required considerable storage space. He operates from a warehouse which has a capacity of 500 items. He can order on the 15th of each month, at the prices shown below, for delivery on the first of the following month. During a month he can sell any amount up to his total stock on hand, at the market prices given below. If he starts the year with 200 items in stock, how much should he plan to purchase and sell each month in order to maximize his profits (cash receipts minus cash expenditures) for the year?

Cost prices $[c_i]$		Sales prices $[p_i]$	
January 15	150	January	165
February 15	155	February	165
March 15	165	March	185
April 15	160	April	175
May 15	160	May	170
June 15	160	June	155
July 15	155	July	155
August 15	150	August	155
September 15	155	September	160
October 15	155	October	170
November 15	150	November	175
December 15	150	December	170

Solution: Call January month 1, February month 2, etc., and introduce the following notation:

x_i = amount to be sold during month i

y_i = amount to be ordered on the 15th of month i

p_i = sales price during month i

c_i = purchase price on the 15th of month i

s_i = stock level on the 1st of month i

H = warehouse capacity.

Each month decide on the values of x_i and y_i. Future cost prices and sale prices act as a basis for these two decisions, the existing inventory level s_i, and the restriction that no future s_i can exceed the warehouse capacity H. (An additional restriction is that no x_i, y_i, or s_i can be negative.)

Define

$f_n(s)$ = maximum achievable return during the remaining n months, if the existing stock level is s.

Thus, f_{12} refers to January, f_{11} to February, etc. On the first day of December, the final month

$$f_1(s_{12}) = \max_{x_{12},\, y_{12}} \{p_{12} x_{12} - c_{12} y_{12}\}$$

where x_{12} and y_{12} are subject to the restrictions

$$0 \le x_{12} \le s_{12}$$

$$0 \le y_{12} \le H - [s_{12} - x_{12}].$$

The solution for December is

$$f_1(s_{12}) = p_{12} s_{12} \qquad (1)$$

Policy: Take $x_{12} = s_{12}$; $y_{12} = 0$.

On November 1, there are two months left and the existing stock level is s_{11}. Thus

$$f_2(s_{11}) = \max_{x_{11},\, y_{11}} \{p_{11} x_{11} - c_{11} y_{11} + f_1(s_{11} + y_{11} - x_{11})\} \qquad (2)$$

subject to:

$$0 \le x_{11} \le s_{11}, \quad 0 \le y_{11} \le H - [s_{11} - x_{11}]. \qquad (3)$$

Solution (1) indicates that $f_1(s_{11} + y_{11} - x_{11})$ has the value

$$p_{12}(s_{11} + y_{11} - x_{11}).$$

Thus:

$$f_2(s_{11}) = \max_{x_{11},\, y_{11}} \{[p_{11} - p_{12}]x_{11} + [p_{12} - c_{11}]y_{11} + p_{12} s_{11}\} \qquad (4)$$

subject to the same restrictions on x_{11} and y_{11}.

Since the expression in brackets in (4) is linear in x_{11} and y_{11}, and the restrictions on x_{11} and y_{11} are also linear, the solution will be at one of the corners of the area satisfying all of the restrictions (3). The restrictions are: $x_{11} \geq 0$, $y_{11} \geq 0$, $x_{11} \leq s_{11}$,

$-x_{11} + y_{11} \leq H - s_{11}$.

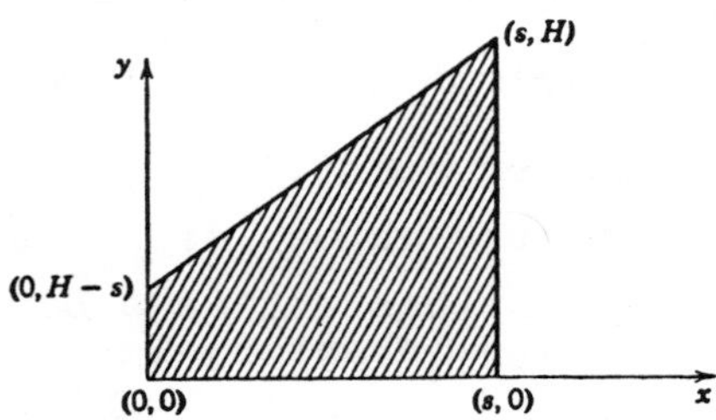

Fig. 1

Figure 1 shows the area including all feasible decisions. The four corners representing possible optima are, for the situation in (4), (0,0), $(0, H-s_{11})$, (s_{11}, H), $s_{11}, 0)$. The actual optimum is obtained by enumeration, yielding a solution for x_{11} and y_{11} in terms of s_{11}. Further, since $s_{12} = s_{11} + y_{11} - x_{11}$, the policy (1) for December can also be stated in terms of s_{11}. Another iteration would give the policies for October, November and December in terms of s_{10}, and so on, until finally the policies for all the months stated in terms of the known initial stock level s_1 were obtained.

The general relationship is

$$f_{n+1}(s) = \max_{\substack{0 \leq x \leq s \\ 0 \leq y \leq H-s+x}} \{p_{12-n}x - c_{12-n}y + f_n(s + y - x)\}$$

Notice that, as $f_1(s)$ is linear in s, each successive $f_n(s)$ is also linear in s. Hence the expression to be minimized is linear in x and y.

Repeated application of this equation yields the following:

December 1: Maximize $170x_{12} - 150y_{12}$
Policy: $x_{12} = s_{12}, y_{12} = 0$
$f_1(s_{12}) = 170s_{12}$

November 1: Maximize $5x_{11} + 20y_{11} + 170s_{11}$
Policy: $x_{11} = s_{11}, y_{11} = H$
$f_2(s_{11}) = 175s_{11} + 20H$

October 1: Maximize $-5x_{10} + 20y_{10} + 175s_{10} + 20H$
Policy: $x_{10} = s_{10}, y_{10} = H$
$f_3(s_{10}) = 170s_{10} + 40H$

September 1: Maximize $-10x_9 + 15y_9 + 170s_9 + 40H$
Policy: $x_9 = s_9, y_9 = H$
$f_4(s_9) = 160s_9 + 55H$

August 1: Maximize $-5x_8 + 10y_8 + 160s_8 + 55H$
Policy: $x_8 = s_8, y_8 = H$
$f_5(s_8) = 155s_8 + 65H$

July 1: Maximize $155s_7 + 65H$
Policy: Any feasible (x_7, y_7)
$f_6(s_7) = 155s_7 + 65H$

June 1: Maximize $-5y_6 + 155s_6 + 65H$
Policy: $y_6 = 0$, any feasible x_6
$f_7(s_6) = 155s_6 + 65H$

May 1: Maximize $15x_5 - 5y_5 + 155s_5 + 65H$
Policy: $x_5 = s_5, y_5 = 0$
$f_8(s_5) = 170s_5 + 65H$

April 1: Maximize $5x_4 + 10y_4 + 170s_4 + 65H$
Policy: $x_4 = s_4, y_4 = H$
$f_9(s_4) = 175s_4 + 75H$

March 1: Maximize $10x_3 + 10y_3 + 175s_3 + 75H$
Policy: $x_3 = s_3, y_3 = H$
$f_{10}(s_3) = 185s_3 + 85H$

February 1: Maximize $-20x_2 + 30y_2 + 185s_2 + 85H$
Policy: $x_2 = s_2, y_2 = H$
$f_{11}(s_2) = 165s_2 + 115H$

January 1: Maximize $-10x_1 + 25y_1 + 165s_1 + 115H$
Policy: $x_1 = s_1, y_1 = H$
$f_{12}(s_1) = 165s_1 + 130H$.

Here $s_1 = 200$, $H = 500$. Thus the maximum achievable return $f_{12}(200)$ is $(165)(200) + (130)(500) = 98{,}000$. This is achieved by means of the optimal policy summarized in Table 1.

TABLE 1

Month	Initial stock (s)	Sell (x)	Buy (y)
January	200	200	500
February	500	500	500
March	500	500	500
April	500	500	500
May	500	500	0
June	0	0	0
July	0	0	$y(\leq 500)$
August	y	y	500
September	500	500	500
October	500	500	500
November	500	500	500
December	500	500	0

• PROBLEM 7-12

Consider a power system in which Unit 1 runs at all times. The cost of starting either Unit 2 or Unit 3 is $25, while the cost of shutting down either unit is 0. Each unit has a capacity of 10. The system day begins at time 0 with Unit 1 on and demand $D(0) = 0$, and it ends at time 5 with Unit 1 on and demand $D(5) = 0$. The demand at other times is given in Table 1. Use dynamic programming and the economic dispatching solutions $f_1(D)$, $f_2(D)$, and $f_3(D)$, to find the start-up costs and operating costs. Also, specify the minimum total cost.

Note that $f_1(D) = \frac{1}{2}D^2 = 0.500D^2$, $f_2(D) = \frac{1}{3}D^2 = .333D^2$ and $f_3(D) = \frac{3}{11}D^2 = .273D^2$.

Table 1 System Demand

k	D(k)
0	0
1	5
2	10
3	15
4	10
5	0

Solution: In the unit commitment problem, both start-up costs and operating costs are considered to determine which units are utilized at each hour of the day and how the demand is distributed over these units. These composite cost curves, $f_1(D)$, $f_2(D)$, and $f_3(D)$, describe the operating costs for 1, 2, and 3 units on. Now all that is needed is a framework for deciding which units to start-up and shut-down at each stage.

The state variable for this problem is the number of units on, i.e.

$$x(k) = 1,\ 2,\ \text{or}\ 3$$

where $x(k) = j$ signifies that j units are on. If $x(k)$ is known the operating costs can be computed at each stage and start-up costs at each stage can be determined for any change in number of units on.

The decision variable is the change in number of units on

$$u(k) = -2,\ -1,\ 0,\ 1,\ \text{or}\ 2$$

where $u(k) = 0$ means no start-up or shut-down, $u(k) = 1$ or 2 means 1 or 2 units are started-up, while $u(k) = -1$ or -2 means 1 or 2 units are shut-down.

The system equation is

$$x(k+1) = x(k) + u(k)$$

$$x(0) = 1.$$

The admissible states and decisions are already quantized

$$X = \{1,\ 2,\ 3\}$$

$$U = \{-2,\ -1,\ 0,\ 1,\ 2\}.$$

The cost function combines start-up costs and operating costs. The operating cost can be written

$$L_1(x,k) = f_x(D(k)),\quad x = 1,2,3.$$

The start-up costs can be summarized as

$$L_2(u,k) = 50, \quad u = 2$$

$$25, \quad u = 1$$

$$0, \quad u = 0, -1, -2.$$

The total cost at each stage is thus

$$L(x,u,k) = L_1(x,k) + L_2(u,k).$$

Because everything is already quantized, a grid can be set up. Since $x(5) = 1$, $D(5) = 0$, and there is no decision $u(5)$, the starting condition can be obtained as shown in Fig. 1.

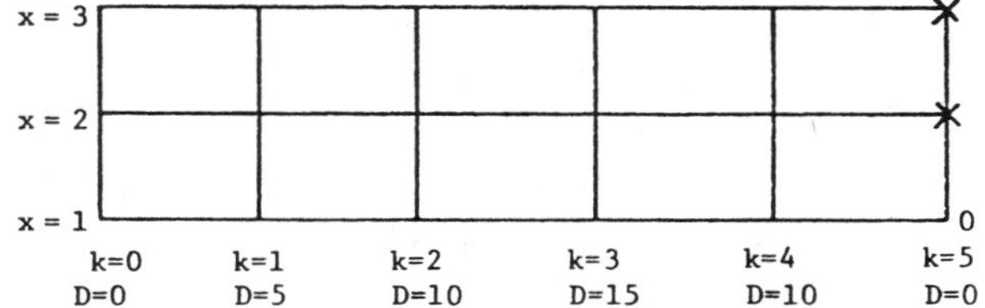

Fig. 1

The calculations can be carried out relatively rapidly by precomputing the functions $L_1(x,k)$ for the allowed values of demands, $D = 0, 5, 10$ and 15.

$$f_1(0) = f_2(0) = f_3(0) = 0$$

$$f_3(5) = 6.8$$

$$f_2(5) = 8.3$$

$$f_1(5) = 12.5$$

$$f_3(10) = 27.3$$

$$f_2(10) = 33.3$$

$$f_1(10) = 50.0$$

$$f_3(15) = 61.4$$

$$f_2(15) = 75.0$$

$$f_1(15) = 111.5.$$

The final grid is as shown in Figure 2.

	k=0 D=0	k=1 D=5	k=2 D=10	k=3 D=15	k=4 D=10	k=5 D=0
x=3	X	122.8 / 0	116.0 / 0	88.7 / 0	27.3 / -2	
x=2	X	149.3 / 1	141.6 / 0	108.3 / 0	33.3 / -1	
x=1	172.8 / 2	178.5 / 2	183.3 / 1	X	50.0 / 0	0

Fig. 2

The number above and to the right of the grid point is $I(x,k)$ and the number below and to the right is $\hat{u}(x,k)$.

The x at x=1, k=3 occurs because the demand 15 exceeds the capacity of a single unit. The x's at x=2, k=0 and x=3, k=0 occur because the initial state is fixed at x(0) = 1.

The minimum cost is 172.8. The optimal decision policy is to turn on all three units at time 1 and to shut them down at time 5. The solution is summarized in Table 2.

Table 2

k	x	u	L_1	L_2	L
0	1	2	0	50	50
1	3	0	6.8	0	6.8
2	3	0	27.3	0	27.3
3	3	0	61.4	0	61.4
4	3	-2	27.3	0	27.3
5	1	--	0	0	0
			122.8	50	172.8

• PROBLEM 7-13

Consider the following electric utility expansion planning problem. New units are available in two sizes, 500 MW and 1,000 MW. One new unit of either type can be bought in 1985, 1990, and 1995. There is an economy-of-scale advantage to the larger unit, and a significant discount rate is assumed. The purchase costs, normalized to 1975 dollars, are shown as a function of time and unit size in Table 1.

The system load is increasing over the planning period. The cumulative increase in system peak load is as shown in Table 2.

If the cumulative capacity of new units installed exceeds cumulative increase in peak demand, operating cost is assumed to be normal. If cumulative capacity falls short by 500 MW or more, the system is not feasible. If the cumulative capacity falls short by an amount less than 500 MW, then it is assumed that the system can still operate, but with a penalty in operating cost given in Table 3:

Find the optimal expansion plan for this system, i.e., determine what size unit (if any) to build in each of years 1985, 1990 and 1995, such that the total capacity cost and total operating cost penalty is minimized. Assume that at most one unit can be purchased in any one year.

Solution: The stage variable for this problem can be taken as k=0 for 1975, k=1 for 1985, k=2 for 1990, and k=3 for 1995. The state variable, x(k), is the total new capacity installed by stage k. The decision variable, u(k), is the amount of new capacity installed just after stage k. The system equation thus becomes

$$x(k+1) = x(k) + u(k), \quad k = 0,1,2$$

where the new capacity installed just after stage k is assumed to be available at stage k+1. The initial capacity is x(0) = 0.

Table 1 Purchase Cost, 1975 dollars ($\times 10^{+6}$)

Unit Size \ Year	1980	1985	1990
500 MW	1.0	0.5	0.25
1000 MW	1.6	0.8	0.4

Table 2 Cumulative Increase System Peak Load Over 1975

YEAR	CUMULATIVE INCREASE
1980	400 MW
1985	800 MW
1990	1200 MW

Table 3 Total Operating Cost Penalty for Cumulative New Capacity Falling Short of Cumulative Increase in Demand, 1975 Dollars

Shortfall \ Year of Shortfall	1980	1985	1990
100	0.2	0.1	0.05
200	0.4	0.2	0.1
300	0.6	0.3	0.15
400	0.8	0.4	0.2

The total capacity can be quantized in increments of 500 MW, because the capacity additions are either 500 MW or 1,000 MW. The maximum capacity that needs to be considered is 1,500 MW, which is the smallest quantized value that exceeds the 1995 demand of 1,200 MW. The set of admissible states is thus X = {0, 500, 1000, 1500}. The set of admissible decisions is U = {0, 500, 1000}.

Table 4

u \ k	0	1	2
0	0.0	0.0	0.0
500	1.0	0.5	0.25
1000	1.6	0.8	0.4

Table 5

x \ k	0	1	2	3
0	0.0	0.8	X	X
500	0.0	0.0	0.3	X
1000	0.0	0.0	0.0	0.1
1500	0.0	0.0	0.0	0.0

X denotes inadmissible state

Table 6

k	$\hat{x}(k)$	$\hat{u}(k)$	$L_1(\hat{u},k)$	$L_2(\hat{x}+\hat{u},k+1)$
0	0	500	1.0	0.0
1	500	500	0.5	0.0
2	1000	0	0.0	0.1
3	1000	--	--	--

The cost function includes two terms, one for capacity additions and one for the penalty due to total capacity falling short of demand. The capacity addition cost can be calculated from Table 1, where the capacity installed just after stage k is assumed to be paid for at stage k+1. Note that this term depends only on the decision variable. If this cost is denoted as $L_1(u,k)$, it can be tabulated as in Table 4. The shortfall penalty term can be calculated using the peak load from Table 2 and the penalty data in Table 3. Note that this term depends only on the state variable. If this cost is denoted as $L_2(x,k)$, it can be tabulated as in Table 5.

The basic recursive equation thus can be written as

$$I(x,k) = \underset{u}{\text{Min}} \{L_1(u,k) + L_2(x,k) + I\,(x+u,\ k+1)\}. \qquad k = 0,1,2$$

$$I(x,3) = L_2(x,3).$$

The initial and final grids are given in Figures 1 and 2 respectively.

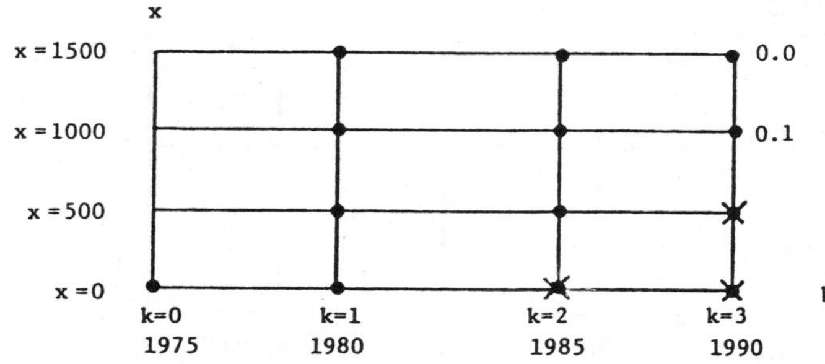

Initial Grid Fig. 1

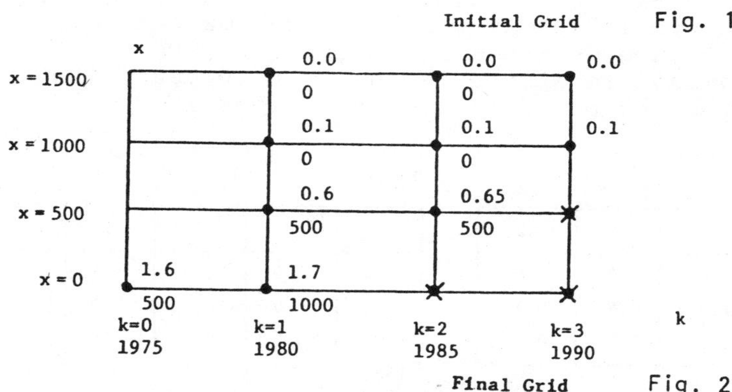

Final Grid Fig. 2

• PROBLEM 7-14

A state government has received proposals for five projects. Table 1 gives the cost of each project and its estimated value. The state budget for new projects is \$15,000, and a legislative subcommittee must decide which of these projects should be approved and funded. The committee would like to maximize the total value that accrues due to project funding.

In mathematical programming terms the problem is expressed as

Maximize $8x_1 + 6x_2 + 2x_3 + 7x_4 + 5x_5$

subject to: $4x_1 + 6x_2 + 5x_3 + 3x_4 + 7x_5 \leq 15$

$$x_j = \begin{cases} 1 & \text{if project } j \text{ is funded} \quad j=1,2,3,4,5. \\ 0 & \text{otherwise} \end{cases}$$

This is an integer programming problem known as a capital budgeting problem. Solve by using dynamic programming.

Table 1

Project (j)	Cost[a] (c_j)	Value (v_j)
1	4	8
2	6	6
3	5	2
4	3	7
5	7	5

[a]In thousands of dollars.

Solution: For this capital budgeting problem let P(j,b) denote the optimal value of a problem with projects j, j+1,...,n and budget b. In other words P(1,15) is the answer to the problem, P(3,7) is the optimal value for a problem with projects 3, 4, and 5 and a budget of 7, and so forth.

There are two possibilities: Project 1 is either funded or not funded. If project 1 is funded, then there remain 15 - 4 = $11,000 for projects 2 through 5, and this $11,000 should be allocated in the best possible way among the last four projects. That is, if project 1 is funded, it requires the solution of P(2,11). The total value would then be 8 for project 1 plus P(2,11). If project 1 is not funded, then there are $15,000 left for funding projects 2 through 5 and this should be done in an optimal fashion; that is, find P(2,15). The total value in this case is 0 for project 1 plus P(2,15). It follows then that the best value for the five-project problem is given by

$$P(1,15) = \text{maximum}\{8 + P(2,11),\ 0 + P(2,15)\}. \quad (1)$$

Notice that inside the braces there are two similar terms, P(2,11) and P(2,15). In order to solve the original problem, solve a four-project problem for two different budgets, $11,000 and $15,000. Once P(2,11) and P(2,15) are known, it is simple to determine P(1,15) according to Equation (1). Thus, solving the four-project problem enables the solving of the five-project problem.

Equation (1) can be rewritten as

$$P(1,15) = \underset{\substack{x_1=0,1 \\ 4x_1 \leq 15.}}{\text{maximum}} \{8x_1 + P(2,15 - 4x_1)\}$$

Now let $b_2 = 15 - c_1x_1$. That is, b_2 is the budget after project 1 is or is not funded. The variable b_2 must be either $15,000 or $11,000 but consider b_2 to be any budget between 0 and \$15,000, which implies that the search is for $P(2,b_2)$. As in the case of Equation (1), project 2 is either funded or not. Hence

$$P(2,b_2) = \underset{\substack{x_2=0,1 \\ 6x_2 \leq b_2}}{\text{maximum}} \{6x_2 + P(3,b_2 - 6x_2)\}.$$

That is, if there are not sufficient funds for the second project ($c_2 > b_2$), then x_2 must be zero. Otherwise, either do or do not fund project 2, depending on whether or not $6 + P(3,b_2-6)$ is larger than $0 + P(3,b_2)$. Again, given $P(3,b_2-6)$ and $P(3,b_2)$ the four-project problem is trivial because it depends only on two three-project problems.

Continuing in this fashion yields the equation

$$P(3,b_3) = \underset{\substack{x_3=0,1 \\ 5x_3 \leq b_3}}{\text{maximum}} \{2x_3 + P(4,b_3 - 5x_3)\}$$

where b_3 is given by $b_3 = b_2 - 6x_2$. Also

$$P(4,b_4) = \underset{\substack{x_4=0,1 \\ 3x_4 \leq b_4}}{\text{maximum}} \{7x_4 + P(5,b_4 - 3x_4)\}$$

where $b_4 = b_3 - 5x_3$. Finally

$$P(5,b_5) = \underset{\substack{x_5=0,1 \\ 7x_5 \leq b_5}}{\text{maximum}} \{5x_5\}$$

where $b_5 = b_4 - 3x_4$.

At this point the original problem is converted into a sequence of five problems, $P(1,15)$, $P(2,b_2)$, $P(3,b_3)$, $P(4,b_4)$, and $P(5,b_5)$. Notice that the last of these problems is the easiest to solve. Very simply, if b_5 is less than 7, then project 5 cannot be funded. If b_5 is 7 or larger, then project 5 can and should be funded. Since it seems so easy to solve the last problem, that of finding $P(5,b_5)$, solve the sequence of five problems by working backward. That is, first find $P(5,b_5)$, then $P(4,b_4)$,..., until $P(1,15)$ is found.

Table 2

	Reward from state 5 if		
b_5	$x_5=0$	$x_5=1$	$P(5, b_5)$
0	0	—	0
1	0	—	0
2	0	—	0
3	0	—	0
4	0	—	0
5	0	—	0
6	0	—	0
7	0	5	5
8	0	5	5
9	0	5	5
10	0	5	5
11	0	5	5
12	0	5	5
13	0	5	5
14	0	5	5
15	0	5	5

There is one minor difficulty with finding $P(5,b_5)$, namely, that the value of b_5 is unknown. For this reason list all possibilities for b_5, keeping track of the solutions to the 16 problems given by $P(5,b_5)$, $b_5 = 0,1,2,\ldots,15$. To keep track of these solutions, they are recorded in Table 2. The entries in the table are v_5x_5 for $x_5 = 0$ or 1, and the last column is the larger of the entries. Where no entry appears, project 5 cannot be budgeted.

The next problem to be solved is that of finding $P(4,b_4)$. As before, the value of b_4 is unknown, so 16 different problems are solved, with b_4 assuming values from 0 to 15. For any one of these problems the solution is rather simple. If project 4 is funded, then the value is $7 + P(5,b_4 - 3)$ where $P(5,b_4 - 3)$ can be found in Table 2. If project 4 is not funded, then the value is $P(5,b_4)$, which again can be found in Table 2.

Table 3

b_4	Reward from state 4 if $x_4=0$	Reward from state 4 if $x_4=1$	$P(4,b_4)$
0	0	—	0
1	0	—	0
2	0	—	0
3	0	7	7
4	0	7	7
5	0	7	7
6	0	7	7
7	5	7	7
8	5	7	7
9	5	7	7
10	5	12	12
11	5	12	12
12	5	12	12
13	5	12	12
14	5	12	12
15	5	12	12

Finally, the larger of $7 + P(5,b_4 - 3)$ and $P(5,b_4)$ is $P(4,b_4)$. For example, if b_4 is 8, then for $x_4 = 0$ the value of $0 + P(5,8) = 0 + 5 = 5$, while if $x_4 = 1$, the value is $7 + P(5,8 - 3) = 7 + P(5,5) = 7 + 0 = 7$. Since 7 is larger than 5, $P(4,8)$ is equal to 7. These computations as well as the computations for all the different b_4's can be found in Table 3.

Table 4

b_3	Reward from state 3 if $x_3=0$	Reward from state 3 if $x_3=1$	$P(3,b_3)$
0	0	—	0
1	0	—	0
2	0	—	0
3	7	—	7
4	7	—	7
5	7	2	7
6	7	2	7
7	7	2	7
8	7	9	9
9	7	9	9
10	12	9	12
11	12	9	12
12	12	9	12
13	12	9	12
14	12	9	12
15	12	14	14

Next, compute $P(3,b_3)$ in the same way for all values of b_3 between 0 and 15. This time use the identity

$$P(3,b_3) = \underset{\substack{x_3=0,1 \\ 5x_3 \le b_3}}{\text{maximum}} \{2x_3 + P(4,b_3 - 5x_3)\}$$

and find $P(4,b_3 - 5x_3)$ from Table 3. The values of $P(3,b_3)$ are presented in Table 4. The 16 values for $P(2,b_2)$ computed from Table 4 are shown in Table 5.

Table 5

	Reward from state 2 if		
b_2	$x_2 = 0$	$x_2 = 1$	$P(2, b_2)$
0	0	—	0
1	0	—	0
2	0	—	0
3	7	—	7
4	7	—	7
5	7	—	7
6	7	6	7
7	7	6	7
8	9	6	9
9	9	13	13
10	12	13	13
11	12	13	13
12	12	13	13
13	12	13	13
14	12	15	15
15	14	15	15

Finally, the original problem given by Equation (1) is solved in order to find $P(1,15)$. Since the budget is known for five projects, only one problem, $P(1,15)$, needs to be solved rather than 16 problems, $P(1,b_1)$ for budgets b_1 ranging from 0 to 15. From Equation (1)

$$\begin{aligned} P(1,15) &= \text{maximum}\{8 + P(2,11),\ 0 + P(2,15)\} \\ &= \text{maximum}\{8 + 13,\ 0 + 15\} \quad \text{(using Table 5)} \\ &= \text{maximum}\{21,15\} \\ &= 21. \end{aligned}$$

Hence, the optimal value for the original problem is 21. Now that the optimal value is known, the next step is to find which projects yield this value. This time the computations are performed in the forward direction. That is, begin with $P(1,15)$ and end with $P(5,b_5)$ for some known b_5.

In the set of equations above, the optimal value of 21 is generated partially by $x_1 = 1$. Thus $x_1 = 1$ is part of the optimal solution and $b_2 = 15 - 4 = 11$. In Table 5 in the row $b_2 = 11$ the better value is 13 and this value appears in the $x_2 = 1$ column. This means that $x_2 = 1$ is part of the optimal solution and therefore $b_3 = 11 - 6 = 5$. In Table 4 for the row $b_3 = 5$ the optimal value is 7 and is given by $x_3 = 0$, which implies that $x_3 = 0$ is part of the optimal solution and $b_4 = 5$. From Table 3, $x_4 = 1$ is also part of the optimal solution and yields the value 7, and b_5 is equal to $5 - 3 = 2$.

Lastly, in Table 2 for b_5 having the value 2, $x_5 = 0$ is the last part of the optimal solution. In summary, the solution is to fund projects 1, 2, and 4 at a cost of $13,000 and with a value equal to 21.

In this case it is optimal not to spend the entire budget. With the information in Table 2 to 5, compute the optimal allocations for any budget from 0 through 15. This is done by creating a table for $P(1,b_1)$ with b_1 varying from 0 to 15 and noting that

$$P(1,b_1) = \underset{\substack{x_1=0,1 \\ 4x_1 \leq b_1}}{\text{maximum}} \{8x_1 + P(2,b_1 - 4x_1)\}$$

The results are presented in Table 6.

Table 6

b_1	Reward from state 1 if $x_1=0$	$x_1=1$	$P(1,b_1)$
0	0	—	0
1	0	—	0
2	0	—	0
3	7	—	7
4	7	8	8
5	7	8	8
6	7	8	8
7	7	15	15
8	9	15	15
9	13	15	15
10	13	15	15
11	13	15	15
12	13	17	17
13	13	21	21
14	15	21	21
15	15	21	21

Another potential advantage of these tables is that if a sixth proposal is added, the answer can be found immediately. For example, if the new project (numbered 0) has a $5000 cost and a value of 7, then for the original $15,000 budget

$$\begin{aligned} P(0,15) &= \text{maximum}\{0 + P(1,15),\ 7 + P(1,10)\} \\ &= \text{maximum}\{0 + 21,\ 7 + 15\} \\ &= \text{maximum}\{21, 22\} \\ &= 22. \end{aligned}$$

Working backward through the tables the optimal solution is:

$$\begin{aligned} x_0 &= 1 & b_1 &= 15 - 5 = 10 \\ x_1 &= 1 & b_2 &= 10 - 4 = 6 \\ x_2 &= 0 & b_3 &= 6 - 0 = 6 \\ x_3 &= 0 & b_4 &= 6 - 0 = 6 \\ x_4 &= 1 & b_5 &= 6 - 3 = 3 \\ x_5 &= 0. \end{aligned}$$

• **PROBLEM 7-15**

Consider the following production planning problem. The Pabutch Sneaker Company has forecast demands for sneakers for the next 4 months. These forecasts are given, in thousands of pairs, in Table 1. The production manager must have a production schedule immediately. That is, he must know how many pairs of sneakers are to be produced during each month from January through April. A schedule then is represented by (x_1,x_2,x_3,x_4) where x_j represents the number of pairs, in thousands, produced during period j. The schedule is feasible if the demands are always met. That is

$$x_1 \geq 4$$

$$x_1 + x_2 \geq 5$$

$$x_1 + x_2 + x_3 \geq 8$$

$$x_1 + x_2 + x_3 + x_4 = 10.$$

The last constraint is expressed as an equality since there is no reason to produce more sneakers than are demanded. (Assume that this product is replaced in May by an improved sneaker.) The costs are \$7 per pair produced, \$40,000 for each month that has a production run (setup cost), and \$10 per month for each pair that is produced but shipped later. For example, the total cost in thousands of dollars due to the schedule (5,0,3,2) would be 5•7 + 0•7 + 3•7 + 2•7 for the units produced plus 3•40 for the three setups in January, March, and April, plus 1•10 for the sneakers produced in January and sold in February.

Table 1

	Month	Demand[a]
January	1	4
February	2	1
March	3	3
April	4	2

[a]In thousands of pairs.

Solution: This problem can be formulated as a dynamic programming problem. Let z_i be the number of units on hand at the beginning of each month (stage) i for i = 1,2,3,4. Then

$$z_1 = 0 \quad z_2 = x_1 - 4 \quad z_3 = z_2 + x_2 - 1$$

$$z_4 = z_3 + x_3 - 3 \quad \text{and} \quad z_5 = z_4 + x_4 - 2$$

which must be zero. The function equation then becomes

$$P_j(z_j) = \underset{\substack{\{x_j : z_j+x_j \geq d_j; \\ z_j+x_j \leq d_j+d_{j+1}+\ldots+d_n\}}}{\text{minimum}} \{7x_j+10(z_j+x_j-d_j)+40\delta(x_j)+P_{j+1}(z_j+x_j-d_j)\}$$

(satisfy demand)

(do not overproduce)

where

$$\delta(x_j) = \begin{cases} 1 & \text{if } x_j > 0 \\ 0 & \text{otherwise.} \end{cases}$$

Working backward, note that z_4 can be either 0, 1, or 2, in which case x_4 must equal $2 - z_4$. The costs are given in Table 2. For the problem of finding $P_3(z_3)$ note that z_3 can be any amount from 0 to 5. Notice that for a given z_3, the amount produced, x_3, is bounded above and below by the two facts that

$$x_3 + z_3 \leq 5 \quad \text{or} \quad x_3 \leq 5 - z_3.$$

and

$$x_3 + z_3 \geq 3 \quad \text{or} \quad x_3 \geq 3 - z_3$$

Table 2

z_4	x_4 0	1	2	$P_4(z_4)$
0	×	×	54	54
1	×	47	×	47
2	0	×	×	0

× indicates an infeasible solution

Now compute the cost table for $P_3(z_3)$. These costs are shown in Table 3; they are given by the equation

$$P_3(z_3) = \begin{cases} 10(z_3 - 3) + P_4(z_3 - 3) & \text{if } x_3 = 0 \\ 40 + 7x_3 + 10(z_3 + x_3 - 3) & \\ \quad + P_4(z_3 + x_3 - 3) & \text{if } x_3 > 0. \end{cases}$$

Table 3

z_3	x_3 0	1	2	3	4	5	$P_3(z_3)$
0	×	×	×	115	125	95	95
1	×	×	108	118	88	×	88
2	×	101	111	81	×	×	81
3	54	104	74	×	×	×	54
4	57	67	×	×	×	×	57
5	20	×	×	×	×	×	20

× indicates an infeasible solution

For example, if z_3 equals 2, then x_3 is 1, 2, or 3. For x_3 equal to 1 the total costs are 40 (setup) + 7 (unit cost) + 0 (holding) + 54 ($P_4(0)$), which totals 101. For $x_3 = 2$ the total costs are 40 (setup) + 14 (unit cost) + $10 (holding one item) + 47 ($P_4(1)$), which totals 111. Similarly, for x_3 equal to 3 the total cost is 81 and since 81 is the smallest value, this is $P_3(2)$.

Using Table 3, compute $P_2(z_2)$ and notice that z_2 and x_2 can each vary from 0 to 6 subject to the constraints that $z_2 + x_2 \geq 1$ and $z_2 + x_2 \leq 6$. The computations for $P_2(z_2)$ can be found in Table 4. Finally, compute $P_1(z_1)$; however, z_1 is zero, so an entire table is not needed but simply one row. Also, x_1 is at least 4, so

x_1 varies from 4 to 10 and the cost when the value x_1 is chosen is given by

Table 4

z_2	x_2 0	1	2	3	4	5	6	$P_2(z_2)$
0	×	142	152	162	152	172	152	142
1	95	145	158	148	165	145	×	95
2	98	148	138	158	138	×	×	98
3	101	131	151	114	×	×	×	101
4	84	144	134	×	×	×	×	84
5	97	117	×	×	×	×	×	97
6	70	×	×	×	×	×	×	70

× indicates an infeasible solution

$$c(x_1) = 40 + 7x_1 + 10(x_1 - 4) + P_2(x_1 - 4).$$

Using this equation and Table 4 note that

x_1	4	5	6	7	8	9	10	$P_1(0)$
cost	210	180	210	220	220	250	240	180

From this row notice that 180 is the minimum cost that $x_1 = 5$, which results in $z_2 = 1$. From Table 4, $P_2(z_2) = 95$, so that $x_2 = 0$ and $z_3 = 2 - 2 = 0$. From Table 3, $P_3(0) = 95$ and $x_3 = 5$, which yields $z_4 = 5 - 5 = 0$ and $x_4 = 0$. The optimal schedule is (5,0,5,0) at a minimum cost of \$180.

• PROBLEM 7-16

Suppose Ali is considering investment in two mutual funds. She has \$10,000 to invest right now and will be able to invest an additional \$1000 per year for each of the next 4 years. At the beginning of each investment period, she must decide how much of her available capital to invest in each fund. Once invested, the money cannot be withdrawn until the end of the 5-year period. The investments will earn money in two different ways: (1) Each fund has a long-term dividend potential realized as a percent return per year on accumulated capital, and the value of any investment left in the fund is expected to increase at this growth rate; (2) each fund also has a short-term interest-dividend rate, and any investment in some period will return cash to her at the end of the period at the particular rate of interest. This cash is available for reinvestment. Any money not invested in one of these funds earns her nothing.

What she needs is a "5-year plan" for investment, the goal being to maximize total investment returns at the end of the fifth year.

Use backward recursion.

Fund	Short-Term Rates (i) 1	2	3	4	5	Long Term Dividend (I)
A	0.020	0.0225	0.0225	0.025	0.025	0.04
B	0.060	0.0475	0.050	0.040	0.040	0.03

Solution:

Define: Stage: each investment period

State: S_n = amount of capital available for investment at beginning of year (6 - n)

Decision: d_n = amount of capital to invest in fund A at beginning of year (6 - n)

$\therefore$ $(S_n - d_n)$ = amount of money for fund B

Return: r_n = future value of long term earnings for stages 5,4,3,2.

r_1 = present value of all earnings for stage 1.

Transition Function:

$$S_{n-1} = i_A d_n + i_B(S_n - d_n) + 1000$$
$$= 1000 + i_B \cdot S_n + d_n(i_A - i_B)$$

for n = 2,3,4,5

and

$$S_5 = 10,000$$

The goal is to

$$\max R = \sum_{n=1}^{5} r_n$$

where

$$r_n = (1 + I_A)^n \cdot d_n + (1 + I_B)^n(S_n - d_n)$$
$$= d_n[(1 + I_A)^n - (1 + I_B)^n] + S_n(1 + I_B)^n$$

for n = 2,3,4,5

$$r_1 = (1 + I_A)^1 d_1 + (1 + I_B)^1(S_1 - d_1) + i_A d_1 + i_B(S_1 - d_1)$$
$$= d_1[I_A - I_B + i_A - i_B] + S_1[1 + I_B + i_B].$$

Stage 1:

$$f_1^*(S_1) = \max_{0 \le d_1 \le S_1} \{d_1(0.04 - 0.03 + 0.025 - 0.040) + S_1(1 + 0.03 + 0.040)\}$$
$$= \max_{d_1} \{1.070S_1 - 0.005d_1\}.$$

The optimal decision is therefore to make d_1 as small as possible. Hence

$$d_1^* = 0$$

$$f_1^*(S_1) = 1.070S_1.$$

Stage 2:

$$f_2^*(S_2) = \max_{0 \leq d_2 \leq S_2} \{r_2 + f_1^*(S_1)\}$$

$$= \max_{d_2}\{d_2(1.04^2 - 1.03^2) + S_2(1.03)^2 + 1.07(1000 + 0.04S_2 - 0.015d_2)\}$$

$$= \max_{d_2}\{1070 + 1.1037S_2 + 0.0046d_2\}.$$

Hence

$$f_2^*(S_2) = 1070 + 1.108S_2 \quad \text{and} \quad d_2^* = S_2.$$

Stage 3:

$$f_3^*(S_3) = \max_{0 \leq d_3 \leq S_3} \{r_3 + f_2^*(S_2)\}$$

$$= \max_{d_3} \{d_3(1.04^3 - 1.03^3) + S_3(1.03)^3 + 1070 + 1.108(1000 + 0.05S_3 - 0.0275d_3)\}$$

$$= \max_{d_3}\{2178 + 1.1481S_3 + 0.0018d_3\}.$$

Hence

$$f_3^*(S_3) = 2178 + 1.15S_3 \quad \text{and} \quad d_3^* = S_3.$$

Stage 4:

$$f_4^*(S_4) = \max_{0 \leq d_4 \leq S_4} \{r_4 + f_3^*(S_3)\}$$

$$= \max_{d_4} \{d_4(1.04^4 - 1.03^4) + S_4(1.03)^4 + 2178 + 1.15(1000 + 0.045S_4 - 0.025d_4)\}$$

$$= \max_{d_4} \{3328 + 1.1772S_4 + 0.0156d_4\}.$$

Hence

$$f_4^*(S_4) = 3328 + 1.193S_4 \quad \text{for} \quad d_4^* = S_4.$$

Stage 5:

$$f_5^*(S_5) = \max_{0 \leq d_5 \leq S_5} \{r_5 + f_4^*(S_4)\}.$$

But

$$S_5 = 10{,}000.$$

Therefore

$$f_5^*(S_5) = \max_{d_5} \{d_5(1.04^5 - 1.03^5) + 10{,}000(1.03)^5 + 3328 + 1.193(1000 + 0.05(10{,}000)) - 0.04d_5)\}$$

or $f_5^*(S_5) = \max_{d_5} \{16,711 + 0.0097d_5\}$.

Hence $f_5^*(S_5) = 16,808$ and $d_5^* = S_5 = 10,000$

Beginning of year	Investment in Fund	
	A	B
1	10,000	0
2	All available funds	0
3	All available funds	0
4	All available funds	0
5	0	All available funds

Optimal total return = $f_5^*(S_5 = \$10,000) = \$16,808$ at end of fifth year.

• PROBLEM 7-17

Consider the system equation

$$x(k+1) = x(k) + u(k) \tag{1}$$

where $x(k)$ = scalar state variable at stage k

$u(k)$ = scalar decision variable at stage k.

The performance criterion, which is to be minimized, is

$$J = \sum_{k=0}^{9} [x^2(k) + u^2(k)] + 2.5[x(10) - 2]^2. \tag{2}$$

The state variable is constrained to lie in the interval

$$0 \leq x \leq 8, \tag{3}$$

while the decision variable is bounded by

$$-2 \leq u \leq 2. \tag{4}$$

The final state of the system at k = 10, is constrained to fall in the interval

$$0 \leq x(10) \leq 2. \tag{5}$$

The state variable is quantized in uniform increments of one, i.e., $\Delta x=1$. Thus, $X=\{0,1,2,3,4,5,6,7,8\}$ is the set of admissible states.

The decision variable is also quantized in uniform increments of 1, so that the set of admissible decisions is

$$U = \{-2, -1, 0, 1, 2\}. \tag{6}$$

Find the minimum cost for k = 9.

Solution: The grid of quantized values of x and k at which computations are to be made is shown in Figure 1. When the computational procedure is about to begin, all final states with $x(10) > 2$ are forbidden by the constraint of Eq. (5). This is denoted by placing x's at all these states. A small circle is placed at $x(10) = 0$, $x(10) = 1$, and $x(10) = 2$ to indicate that a minimum cost can be computed for those points. From Eq. (2) it can be seen that these minimum costs are

$$\begin{aligned} I(0,10) &= 10. \\ I(1,10) &= 2.5 \\ I(2,10) &= 0 \quad . \end{aligned} \tag{7}$$

These values are placed in Figure 1 to the right of the grid points to which they correspond.

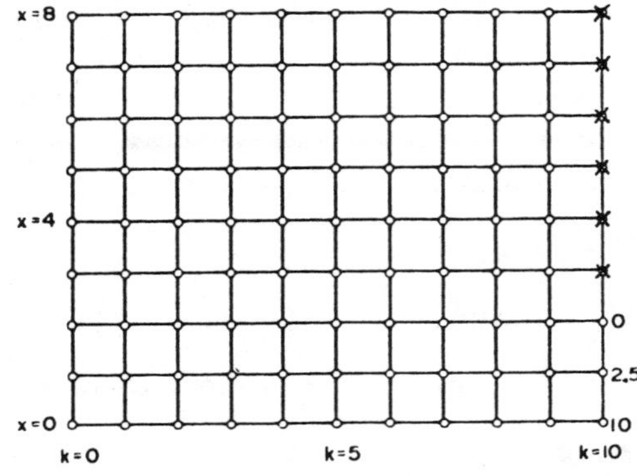

Fig. 1

With the initial values of minimum cost established, it is possible to apply iteratively the functional equation based on the principle of optimality. Making the identifications

$$L[x(k),\ u(k),\ k] = x^2(k) + u^2(k) \quad , \quad (k=0,1,2,\ldots,9) \tag{8}$$

and

$$g[x(k),\ u(k),\ k] = x(k) + u(k) \quad , \quad (k=0,1,2,\ldots,9) \tag{9}$$

the iterative relation becomes

$$I(x,k) = \min_{u \varepsilon U} \{x^2 + u^2 + I(x + u,\ k+1)\} \ , \quad (k=0,1,2,\ldots,9). \tag{10}$$

The set of admissible decisions U is given in Eq. (6). The values I(x,10) in Eq. (7) are used in starting conditions. If an admissible decision results in a next state which is not admissible (the next state either fails to satisfy Eq. (3) or else it has an x placed on it), then that decision is not considered further. If all admissible decisions are rejected on this basis, then an x is placed at such a point, and it is considered an inadmissible state for this stage.

Equation (10) is first applied at k=9, then at k=8, then at k=7, etc., until k=0 is reached. Each time an admissible optimal decision is found, a small circle is drawn at that grid point, the optimal decision is written to the right and below the circle, and the minimum cost is written to the right and above it. These numbers constitute the dynamic programming solution to the problem.

The computations at a given state x for k=9 take place as follows: each decision $u \in U$ is applied and the next state is computed for each decision. If the next state is admissible, the minimum cost of that state is found from Eq. (7). The cost $[x^2(9) + u^2(9)]$, over the next stage is computed and the sum of the two costs is stored. If the next state is not admissible, nothing is stored. From among the stored costs the minimum is picked. This cost becomes the minimum cost at state x, stage k, while the optimal decision is the decision corresponding to the minimum cost.

For x(9) = 0 the computations can be summarized in tabular form as follows:

Table 1 Computations at x=0, k=9

u	g(x,u,k)	I(g,k+1)	L(x,u,k)	Total Cost
-2	-2	x	x	x
-1	-1	x	x	x
0	0	10	$0^2 + 0^2 = 0$	10
1	1	2.5	$0^2 + 1^2 = 1$	3.5
2	2	0	$0^2 + 2^2 = 4$	4

The x's in the table indicate that the next state is not admissible. Comparing the total costs for admissible next states, it is seen that the minimum cost is 3.5, which corresponds to u=1. Note that this minimum utilizes neither the minimum "immediate cost," L(x,u,k) which in this case corresponds to u=0, nor the minimum "next-state cost," I(g,k+1), which in this case corresponds to u=2. It is the combination of these two quantities which must be minimized.

For x(9) = 1, the computations can be abbreviated in the following form

Table 2 Computations at x=1, k=9

u	g(x,u,k)	I(g,k+1)	L(x,u,k)	Total Cost
-2	-1	x	x	x
-1	0	10	$1^2 + (-1)^2 = 2$	12
0	1	2.5	$1^2 + 0^2 = 1$	3.5
1	2	0	$1^2 + 1^2 = 2$	2
2	3	x	x	x

The minimum cost is 2, again corresponding to u=1.

For x(9) = 2,

Table 3 Computations at x=2, k=9

u	g(x,u,k)	I(g,k+1)	L(x,u,k)	Total Cost
-2	0	10	$2^2 + (-2)^2 = 8$	18
-1	1	2.5	$2^2 + (-1)^2 = 5$	7.5
0	2	0	$2^2 + 0^2 = 4$	4
1	3	x	x	x
2	4	x	x	x

The minimum cost is 4, corresponding to u=0.

For x(9) = 3,

Table 4 Computations at x=3, k=9

u	g(x,u,k)	I(g,k+1)	L(x,u,k)	Total Cost
-2	1	2.5	13	15.5
-1	2	0	10	10
0	3	x	x	x
1	4	x	x	x
2	5	x	x	x

The minimum cost is 10, corresponding to u=-1.

For x(9) = 4,

Table 5 Computations at x=4, k=9

u	g(x,u,k)	I(g,k+1)	L(x,u,k)	Total Cost
-2	2	0	20	20
-1	3	x	x	x
0	4	x	x	x
1	5	x	x	x
2	6	x	x	x

The minimum cost is 20, corresponding to u=-2, the only decision which results in an admissible next state.

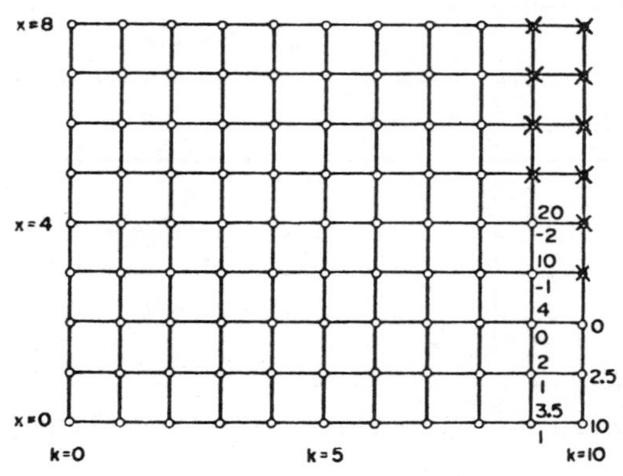

Fig. 2

For $x(9)>4$, there is no decision which results in an admissible next state. Consequently, these states must be regarded as inadmissible. This completes the computations at $k=9$. The results are summarized in Figure 2.

• PROBLEM 7-18

Consider the linear programming problem

$$\text{Maximize } Z = 3x_1 + 5x_2,$$

subject to

$$x_1 \le 4$$

$$2x_2 \le 12$$

$$3x_1 + 2x_2 \le 18$$

and

$$x_1 \ge 0, \quad x_2 \ge 0.$$

Solve this problem by dynamic programming.

Solution: This problem requires making two interrelated decisions, namely, the level of activity 1, x_1, and the level of activity 2, x_2. Therefore, these two activities can be interpreted as the two stages in a dynamic programming formulation. Although they can be taken in either order, let stage n = activity n(n = 1,2). Thus, x_n is the decision variable at stage n.

The right-hand side of these constraints (4, 6, and 18) represent the total available amount of resources 1, 2, and 3, respectively. The state s is the amount of the respective resources remaining to be allocated. Thus,

$$s = (R_1, R_2, R_3),$$

where R_i is the amount of resource i remaining to be allocated (i = 1,2,3).

Therefore, this problem has three state variables rather than one. It is necessary to consider all possible combinations of values of the several state variables. Since the number of combinations, in general, can be as large as the product of the number of possible values of the respective variables, the number of required calculations tend to "blow up" rapidly when additional state variables are introduced. Each of the three state variables is continuous. Therefore, rather than consider each possible combination of values separately, it is necessary to use the approach of solving for the required information as a function of the state of the system.

Thus, interpreting Z as profit, $f_n(R_1,R_2,R_3,x_n)$ is the maximum total profit from stage n onward, given that the state and policy decision at stage n are (R_1, R_2, R_3) and x_n, respectively.

$$f_n(R_1, R_2, R_3, x_n) = c_n x_n + \text{maximum} \sum_{j=n+1}^{2} c_j x_j$$

$$\text{such that} \quad \sum_{j=n}^{2} a_{ij} x_j \leq R_i \quad (i = 1,2,3),$$

$$\text{the } x_j \geq 0,$$

for n = 1,2. In addition:

$$f_n^*(R_1, R_2, R_3) = \max_{x_n} f_n(R_1, R_2, R_3, x_n),$$

where this maximum is taken over the feasible values of x_n. Therefore

$$f_n(R_1, R_2, R_3, x_n) = c_n x_n + f_{n+1}^*(R_1 - a_{1n}x_n, R_2 - a_{2n}x_n, R_3 - a_{3n}x_n)$$

(with f_3^* defined to be zero). These basic relationships are summarized in Fig. 1.

	Stage n		Stage n+1
State:	(R_1, R_2, R_3)	$\xrightarrow{c_n x_n}$	$(R_1 - a_{1n}x_n, R_2 - a_{2n}x_n, R_3 - a_{3n}x_n)$
	$f_n(R_1, R_2, R_3, x_n)$ =sum		$f_{n+1}^*(R_1 - a_{1n}x_n, R_2 - a_{2n}x_n, R_3 - a_{3n}x_n)$

Fig. 1

The last two equations together define the recursive relationship relating f_1^* and f_2^*. To solve at the last stage (n = 2), note that

$$f_2(R_1, R_2, R_3, x_2) = 5x_2 ,$$

where the feasible values of x are those satisfying the set of restrictions $2x_2 \leq R_2$, $2x_2 \leq R_3$, $x_2 \geq 0$. Therefore

$$f_2^*(R_1, R_2, R_3) = \max_{\substack{2x_2 \leq R_2 \\ 2x_2 \leq R_3 \\ x_2 \geq 0}} \{5x_2\}.$$

Thus, the resulting solution is

n = 2 R_1, R_2, R_3	$f_2^*(R_1, R_2, R_3)$	x_2^*
$R_i \geq 0$	$5 \min\left\{\frac{R_2}{2}, \frac{R_3}{2}\right\}$	$\min\left\{\frac{R_2}{2}, \frac{R_3}{2}\right\}$

For the two-stage problem (n = 1)

$$f_1(R_1,R_2,R_3,x_1) = 3x_1 + f_2^*(R_1 - x_1, R_2, R_3 - 3x_1),$$

where the feasible values of x_1 are those satisfying the set of restrictions $x_1 \leq R_1$, $3x_1 \leq R_3$, $x_1 \geq 0$. Therefore, because it is known that $R_1 = 4$, $R_2 = 12$, $R_3 = 18$ at the first stage, the desired recursive relationship is

$$f_1^*(4,12,18) = \max_{\substack{x_1 \leq 4 \\ 3x_1 \leq 18 \\ x_1 \geq 0}} \{3x_1 + f_2^*(4 - x_1, 12, 18 - 3x_1)\}$$

$$= \max_{0 \leq x_1 \leq 4} \left\{3x_1 + 5 \min\left\{\frac{12}{2}, \frac{18 - 3x_1}{2}\right\}\right\} .$$

Notice that

$$\min\left\{\frac{12}{2}, \frac{18 - 3x_1}{2}\right\} = \begin{cases} 6, & \text{if } 0 \leq x_1 \leq 2 \\ 9 - \frac{3}{2}x_1, & \text{if } 2 \leq x_1 \leq 4, \end{cases}$$

so that

$$3x_1 + 5 \min\left\{\frac{12}{2}, \frac{18 - 3x_1}{2}\right\} = \begin{cases} 3x_1 + 30, & \text{if } 0 \leq x_1 \leq 2 \\ 45 - \frac{9}{2}x_1, & \text{if } 2 \leq x_1 \leq 4. \end{cases}$$

Since both

$$\max_{0 \leq x_1 \leq 2} \{3x_1 + 30\} \text{ and } \max_{2 \leq x_1 \leq 4} \left\{45 - \frac{9}{2}x_1\right\}$$

achieve their maximum at $x_1 = 2$, it follows that $x_1^* = 2$, as summarized below.

$n = 1$

R_1,R_2,R_3	$f_1^*(R_1,R_2,R_3)$	x_1^*
4,12,18	36	2

Therefore the optimal solution for this problem is

$$x_1 = 2 \quad \text{and} \quad x_2 = \min\left\{6, \frac{18 - 3(2)}{2}\right\} = 6,$$

with a total profit of 36.

Maximize $\sum_{i=1}^{3} r_i$

Subject to: $S_{i-1} = 3S_i - d_i \quad i = 1,2,3$

$S_i \geqq d_i \geqq 0$

where

$r_1 = 3d_1$

$r_2 = 2d_2$

$r_3 = d_3^2$

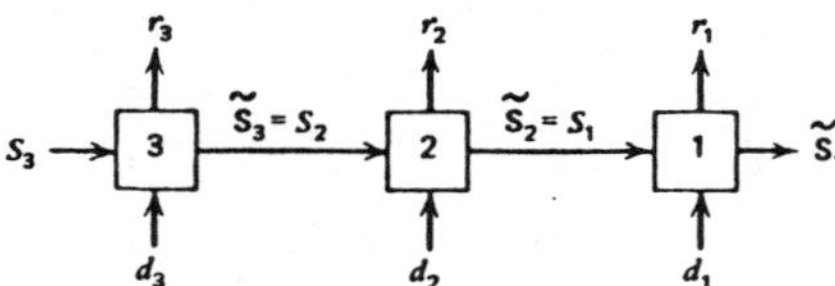

Solution: The problem is one of maximizing the set of three stage returns, where the return at a given stage is a function of the decision made at that stage. The solution is as follows:

Stage 1

$$\max_{S_1 \geqq d_1 \geqq 0} \{r_1\} = \max_{S_1 \geqq d_1 \geqq 0} \{3d_1\}.$$

Since d_1 can assume any value on the range $S_1 \geqq d_1 \geqq 0$, it is obvious that d_1^* (the optimal value of d_1) should be as large as possible. Therefore:

$$d_1^* = S_1$$

$$f_1^*(S_1) = 3S_1$$

Stage 2

$$\max_{S_2 \geqq d_2 \geqq 0} \{r_2 + f_1^*(S_1)\} = \max_{S_2 \geqq d_2 \geqq 0} \{2d_2 + 9S_2 - 3d_2\}$$

$$= \max_{S_2 \geqq d_2 \geqq 0} \{9S_2 - d_2\}$$

$$\therefore \quad d_2^* = 0$$

$$f_2^*(S_2) = 9S_2$$

Stage 3

$$\max_{S_3 \geqq d_3 \geqq 0} \{r_3 + f_2^*(S_2)\} = \max_{S_3 \geqq d_3 \geqq 0} \{d_3^2 + 27S_3 - 9d_3\}.$$

The objective at stage 3 is to maximize the function $f = d_3^2 - 9d_3 + 27S_3$. This is a convex function in d_3 as shown in Fig. 1. From Fig. 1 the optimal decision policy would be:

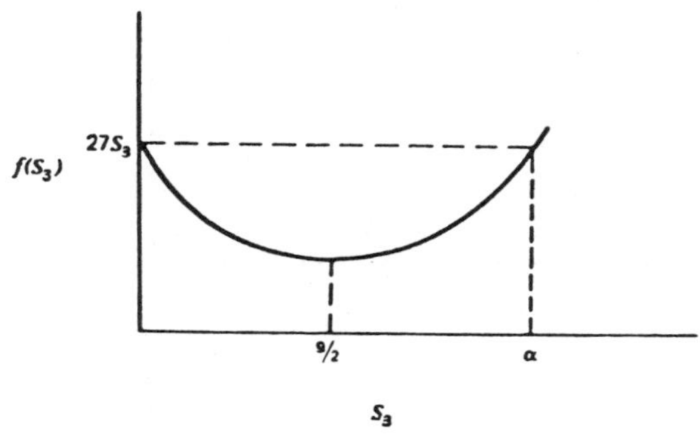

Fig. 1

if:	$S_3 < \alpha$	Then:	$d_3^* = 0$
	$S_3 > \alpha$		$d_3^* = S_3$
	$S_3 = \alpha$		$d_3^* = 0$ or S_3.

The point α is easily found, since

$$27S_3 = \alpha^2 - 9\alpha + 27S_3$$

$$\Rightarrow \alpha = 9.$$

Hence

$$f_3^*(S_3) = \begin{cases} 27S_3 & \text{for} \quad S_3 \leqq 9 \\ S_3^2 + 18S_3 & \text{for} \quad S_3 > 9. \end{cases}$$

The optimal decision policy is now available for any input state S_3. Solution values are given in Table 1 for selected inputs.

Table 1

S_3	d_1^*	d_2^*	d_3^*	Optimal Return $f_3^*(S_3)$
3	27	0	0	81.0
6	54	0	0	162
9	81(54)	0	0(9)	243
12	72	0	12	360

• PROBLEM 7-20

If the year 1975 (year 1) is started with a 2 year old truck, what decision should be made at the start of this year and the start of the next four years in order to maximize the total return.

<u>Solution</u>: This is a problem in dynamic optimization.

Financial estimates for trucks made each year, for the fiscal period under consideration:

YEARS:	1975	1976	1977	1978	1979
Truck made in 1973 (year -1)					
Age	**2**	**3**	**4**	**5**	**6**
Revenue	**10**	**8**	**8**	**6**	**4**
Upkeep	**3**	**3**	**4**	**4**	**5**
Replacement	**25**	**26**	**27**	**28**	**29**
Truck made in 1975 (year 1)					
Age	**0**	**1**	**2**	**3**	**4**
Revenue	**14**	**16**	**16**	**14**	**12**
Upkeep	**1**	**1**	**2**	**2**	**3**
Replacement	**20**	**22**	**24**	**25**	**26**
Truck made in 1976 (year 2)					
Age	**0**	**1**	**2**	**3**	
Revenue	**16**	**14**	**14**	**12**	
Upkeep	**1**	**1**	**2**	**2**	
Replacement	**20**	**22**	**24**	**25**	
Truck made in 1977 (year 3)					
Age	**0**	**1**	**2**		
Revenue	**18**	**16**	**16**		
Upkeep	**1**	**1**	**2**		
Replacement	**20**	**22**	**24**		
Truck made in 1978 (year 4)					
Age	**0**	**1**			
Revenue	**18**	**16**			
Upkeep	**1**	**1**			
Replacement	**21**	**22**			
Truck made in 1979 (year 5)					
Age	**0**				
Revenue	**20**				
Upkeep	**1**				
Replacement	**21**				

A series of decisions must be made over time so as to maximize some chosen quantity. Each decision by itself

may be non-optimal; the optimality of the sequence of decisions is what matters. As an example, suppose X wishes to travel from city A to city F and has the choice of routes ABCF and ADEF. It is possible for AB to cost less than AD and yet ADEF may be cheaper overall (DE is less than BC and Ef is less than CF).
Going back to the initial problem, let

1) $r_i(t)$ = revenue in period i from a truck that was made in year (i - t) and is t years old at the start of period i. For example, revenue in 1976 from a truck made in 1973 is $r_3(3) = 8$.

2) $u_i(t)$ = upkeep in period i on a truck that was made in year (i - t) and is t years old at the start of period i. For example, a truck made in 1975 requires an upkeep of 2 in 1978, i.e., $u_5(3) = 2$.

3) $C_i(t)$ = cost to replace a truck that was made in year (i - t) and is t years old at the start of period i.

4) IT = age of the given truck = 2.

5) $f_i(t)$ = optimal return for periods i, i + 1,...., 5 when the i-th period is started with a truck that is t years old.

6) $X_i(t)$ = decision to make at the start of period i that will yield $f_i(t)$. The only two possible decisions are to keep the old truck or to purchase a new one.

Suppose one decides to keep the current truck until 1979. Then the total revenue is

$$10 + 8 + 8 + 6 + 4 = 36.$$

Total upkeep is

$$3 + 3 + 4 + 4 + 5 = 19.$$

Thus total return is 17. On the other hand, suppose one decides to replace the 1973 truck with a truck made in 1975 at the start of 1975. Then, total revenue is

$$14 + 16 + 16 + 14 + 12 = 72$$

and upkeep costs are

$$1 + 1 + 2 + 2 + 3 = 9.$$

Replacement costs are 25 and hence total return is 38. Of course one could keep the truck for a year and then sell it. The total return in this case works out to 37. Clearly there is a large number of possible choices. The functional equation for period i is

$$f_i(t) = \max \begin{bmatrix} \text{purchase: } r_i(0) - u_i(0) - C_i(t) + f_{i+1}(1) \\ \text{keep: } r_i(t) - u_i(t) + f_{i+1}(t + 1) \end{bmatrix}$$

for i = 1,2,...,5 and t = 1,2,...(i - 1),(i + IT - 1).

Now apply the functional equation working backwards. That is, assume that the fifth year is reached with a truck that is 1, 2, 3, 4, or 6 years old. (Note that a 5 year old truck is not considered; this is because a 5 year old truck at the beginning of 1979 is not a possible alternative since it implies that the truck was purchased in 1974 and used until the end of 1978; whereas the present condition is that we are at 1975 and have a 2 year old truck.)

Thus, for i = 5 and t = 1

$$f_5(1) = \max \begin{bmatrix} \text{Purchase: } r_5(0) - u_5(0) - C_5(1) + f_6(1) \\ \text{Keep: } r_5(1) - u_5(1) + f_6(2) \end{bmatrix}$$

Note that $f_6(j) = 0$ for all j. Then

$$f_5(1) = \max \begin{bmatrix} 20 - 1 - 22 + 0 \\ 16 - 1 + 0 \end{bmatrix} = 15$$

Thus, keep the 1978 truck in 1979, i.e., $x_5(1)$ is Keep.

At t = 2

$$f_5(2) = \max \begin{bmatrix} \text{Purchase: } r_5(0) - u_5(0) - C_5(2) \\ \text{Keep: } r_5(2) - u_5(2) \end{bmatrix}$$

$$= \max \begin{bmatrix} 20 - 1 - 24 \\ 16 - 2 \end{bmatrix} = 14$$

$x_5(2)$ = Keep

t = 3

$$f_5(3) = \max \begin{bmatrix} \text{Purchase: } 20 - 1 - 25 \\ \text{Keep: } 12 - 2 \end{bmatrix} = 10$$

$x_5(3)$ = Keep

t = 4

$$f_5(4) = \max \begin{bmatrix} \text{Purchase: } 20 - 1 - 26 \\ \text{Keep: } 12 - 3 \end{bmatrix} = 9$$

$x_5(4)$ = Keep

t = 6

$$f_5(6) = \max \begin{bmatrix} \text{Purchase:} & 20 - 1 - 29 \\ \text{Keep:} & 4 - 5 \end{bmatrix} = -1$$

$x_5(6)$ = Keep.

Now, assume that the start of the fourth period is reached with a 1, 2, 3, or 5 year old truck. The optimal decision to make in order to maximize the return from the last two periods is given by the functional equation:

$$f_4(t) = \max \begin{bmatrix} P: r_4(0) - u_4(0) - C_4(t) + f_5(1) \\ K: r_4(t) - u_4(t) + f_5(t + 1) \end{bmatrix}$$

$t = 1,2,3,5$

Thus,

$$f_4(1) = \max \begin{bmatrix} P: 18 - 1 - 22 + 15 \\ K: 16 - 1 + 14 \end{bmatrix} = 29$$

$x_4(1)$ = Keep

$$f_4(2) = \max \begin{bmatrix} P: 18 - 1 - 24 + 15 \\ K: 14 - 2 + 10 \end{bmatrix} = 22$$

$x_4(2)$ = Keep

$$f_4(3) = \max \begin{bmatrix} P: 18 - 1 - 25 + 15 \\ K: 14 - 2 + 9 \end{bmatrix} = 21$$

$x_4(3)$ = Keep

$$f_4(5) = \max \begin{bmatrix} P: 18 - 1 - 28 + 15 \\ K: 6 - 4 + (-1) \end{bmatrix} = 4$$

$x_4(5)$ = Purchase

Moving back to the start of the third period and considering the optimal policy over the last three periods when the third period is started with a 1, 2 or 4 year old truck, one has

$$f_3(t) = \max \begin{bmatrix} P: r_3(0) - u_3(0) - C_3(t) + f_4(1) \\ K: r_3(t) - u_3(t) + f_4(t + 1) \end{bmatrix}$$

$t = 1,2,4$

$$f_3(1) = \max \begin{bmatrix} P: 18 - 1 - 22 + 29 \\ K: 14 - 1 + 22 \end{bmatrix} = 35$$

$x_3(1)$ = Keep

$$f_3(2) = \max\begin{bmatrix} P: 18 - 1 - 24 + 29 \\ K: 16 - 2 + 21 \end{bmatrix} = 35$$

$x_3(2)$ = Keep

$$f_3(4) = \max\begin{bmatrix} P: 18 - 1 - 27 + 29 \\ K: 8 - 4 + 4 \end{bmatrix} = 19$$

$x_3(4)$ = Purchase

Now move backwards from period 2 with t = 1,3.

$$f_2(1) = \max\begin{bmatrix} P: 16 - 1 - 22 + 35 \\ K: 16 - 1 + 35 \end{bmatrix} = 50$$

$x_2(1)$ = Keep

$$f_2(3) = \max\begin{bmatrix} P: 16 - 1 - 26 + 35 \\ K: 8 - 3 + 19 \end{bmatrix} = 24$$

$x_2(3)$ = Purchase or Keep

Finally, period 1 is reached where one has a 2-year-old truck. To arrive at a decision whether to keep it or replace it in order to maximize the total return over the next five periods, one has

$$f_1(2) = \max\begin{bmatrix} P: 14 - 1 - 25 + 50 \\ K: 10 - 3 + 24 \end{bmatrix} = 38$$

$x_1(2)$ = Purchase.

Thus, purchase a truck at the start of 1975. Keep this truck in 1976, 1977, 1978 and 1979 in order to maximize total returns over the next four years.

PROBABILISTIC DP

• PROBLEM 7-21

A government space project is conducting research on a certain engineering problem that must be solved before man can fly safely to Venus. Three research teams are currently trying three different approaches for solving this problem. The estimate has been made that, under present circumstances, the probability that the respective teams--call them 1, 2, and 3--will not succeed is 0.40, 0.60, and 0.80, respectively. Thus, the current probability that all three teams will fail is (0.40) (0.60)(0.80) = 0.192. Since the objective is to minimize this probability, the decision has been made to assign two more top scientists among the three teams to lower it as much as possible.

Table 1 gives the estimated probability that the respective teams will fail when 0, 1, or 2 additional scientists are added to that team. The problem is to determine how to allocate the two additional scientists to minimize the probability that all three teams will fail.

Table 1

Data on the government space project problem

No. of new scientists	Probability of failure		
	Team		
	1	2	3
0	0.40	0.60	0.80
1	0.20	0.40	0.50
2	0.15	0.20	0.30

Solution: In this case the stages correspond to the research teams, and the state s is the number of new scientists still available for assignment at that stage. The decision variables x_n (n = 1,2,3) are the number of additional scientists allocated to stage (team) n. Let $p_i(x_i)$ denote the probability of failure for team i if it is assigned x_i additional scientists, as given by Table 1. Letting Π denote multiplication, the government's objective is to choose x_1, x_2, x_3 so as to

$$\text{Minimize} \quad \prod_{i=1}^{3} p_i(x_i) = p_1(x_1)p_2(x_2)p_3(x_3),$$

subject to

$$\sum_{i=1}^{3} x_i = 2$$

and

the x_i are nonnegative integers.

Consequently,

$$f_n(s,x_n) = p_n(x_n)\cdot\text{minimum} \prod_{i=n+1}^{3} p_i(x_i)$$

$$\text{such that } \sum_{i=n}^{3} x_i = s,$$

the x_i are nonnegative integers,

for n = 1,2,3 where $f_n(s,x_n)$ is the minimum total probability from stage n onward, given that the state and policy decision at stage n are s and x_n, respectively. Thus

$$f_n^*(s) = \min_{x_n \le s} f_n(s,x_n).$$

Hence

$$f_n(s,x_n) = p_n(x_n) \cdot f^*_{n+1}(s - x_n)$$

(with f_4^* defined to be one). Fig. 1 summarizes these basic relationships.

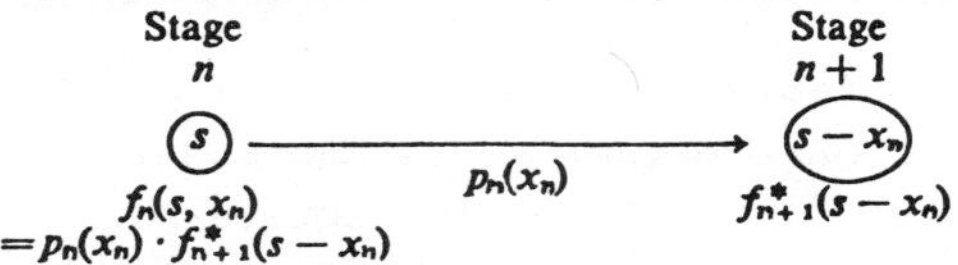

The basic structure for the government space project problem.

Fig. 1

Thus the recursive relationship relating the f_1^*, f_2^*, and f_3^* functions in this case is

$$f_n^*(s) = \min_{x_n \le s} \{p_n(x_n) \cdot f^*_{n+1}(s - x_n)\}, \text{ for } n = 1,2,$$

and, when n = 3,

$$f_3^*(s) = \min_{x_3 \le s} p_3(x_3).$$

The resulting dynamic program calculations are

n = 1

s \ x_1	$f_1(s, x_1) = p_1(x_1) \cdot f_2^*(s - x_1)$: 0	1	2	$f_1^*(s)$	x_1^*
2	0.064	0.060	0.072	0.060	1

n = 2

s \ x_2	$f_2(s, x_2) = p_2(x_2) \cdot f_3^*(s - x_2)$: 0	1	2	$f_2^*(s)$	x_2^*
0	0.48			0.48	0
1	0.30	0.32		0.30	0
2	0.18	0.20	0.16	0.16	2

n = 3

s	$f_3^*(s)$	x_3^*
0	0.80	0
1	0.50	1
2	0.30	2

Therefore the optimal solution must have $x_1^* = 1$, which makes s = 1 at stage 2, so that $x_2^* = 0$, which makes s = 1 at stage 3, so that $x_3^* = 1$. Thus, teams 1 and 3 should each receive one additional scientist. The new probability that all three teams will fail would then be 0.060.

• PROBLEM 7-22

An enterprising young statistician believes that he has developed a system for winning a popular Atlantic City game. His colleagues do not believe that this is possible, so they make a large bet with him that, starting with three chips, he will not have five chips after three plays of the game. Each play of the game involves betting any desired number of available chips and then either winning or losing this number of chips. The statistician believes that his system will give him a probability of 2/3 of winning a given play of the game.

Assuming the statistician is correct, determine his optimal policy regarding how many chips to bet (if any) at each of the three plays of the game. The decision at each play should take into account the results of earlier plays. The objective is to maximize the probability of winning his bet with his colleagues.

Solution: The plays of the game constitute the stages in the dynamic programming formulation. The decision variables x_n (n = 1,2,3) are the number of chips to bet at stage n. The state of the system at any stage is the number of chips available for betting at that stage because this is the information required for making an optimal decision on how many chips to bet.

Since the objective is to maximize the probability that the statistician will win his bet, the objective function to be maximized at each stage must be the probability of finishing the three plays with at least five chips. Therefore $f_n(s,x_n)$ is the maximum of this probability given that the statistician is starting play (stage) n with s chips available. Furthermore,

$$f_n^*(s) = \max_{x_n=0,1,\ldots,s} f_n(s,x_n).$$

The expression for $f_n(s,x_n)$ must reflect the fact that it may still be possible to eventually accumulate five chips even if the statistician should lose the next play. If he should lose, the state at the next stage would be $(s - x_n)$, and the probability of finishing with at least five chips would then be $f_{n+1}^*(s - x_n)$. If he should win the next play instead, the state would become $(s + x_n)$, and the corresponding probability would be $f_{n+1}^*(s + x_n)$. Since the alleged probability of winning a given play is 2/3, it now follows that

$$f_n(s,x_n) = \frac{1}{3} f_{n+1}^*(s - x_n) + \frac{2}{3} f_{n+1}^*(s + x_n)$$

[where $f_4^*(s)$ is defined to be zero for $s < 5$ and 1 for $s \geq 5$]. Thus there is no direct contribution to the objective function from stage n in addition to the effect of being in the next state. These basic relationships are summarized in Fig. 1.

$n=1$	s \ x_1	$f_1(s, x_1) = \frac{1}{3} f_2^*(s - x_1) + \frac{2}{3} f_2^*(s + x_1)$				$f_1^*(s)$	x_1^*
		0	1	2	3		
	3	$\frac{2}{3}$	$\frac{20}{27}$	$\frac{2}{3}$	$\frac{2}{3}$	$\frac{20}{27}$	1

Therefore the optimal policy is

$$x_1^* = 1 \begin{cases} \text{if win, } x_2^* = 1 \begin{cases} \text{if win, } x_3^* = 0 \\ \text{if lose, } x_3^* = 2,3 \end{cases} \\ \text{if lost, } x_2^* = 1 \text{ or } 2 \begin{cases} \text{if win, } x_3^* = \begin{cases} 2,3 \text{ (for } x_2^*=1) \\ 1,2,3,4 \text{ (for } x_2^*=2) \end{cases} \\ \text{if lose, bet is lost.} \end{cases} \end{cases}$$

This policy gives the statistician a probability of 20/27 of winning his bet with his colleagues.

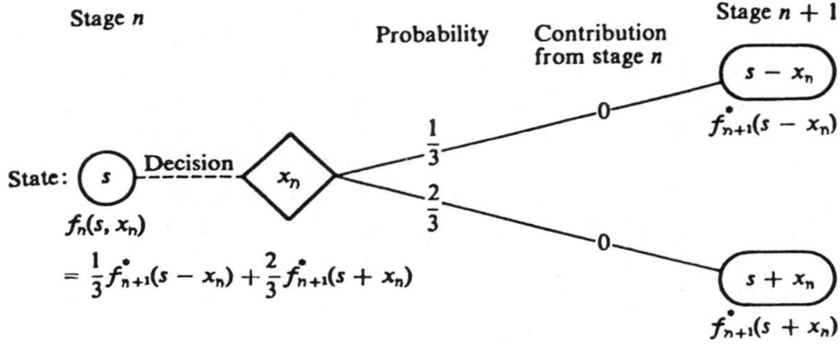

Fig. 1

Therefore the recursive relationship for this problem is:

$$f_n^*(s) = \max_{x_n=0,1,\ldots,s} \left\{ \frac{1}{3} f_{n+1}^*(s - x_n) + \frac{2}{3} f_{n+1}^*(s + x_n) \right\}$$

for n = 1,2,3. This leads to the computational results given below:

$n=3$ s	$f_3^*(s)$	x_3^*
0	0	....
1	0	....
2	0	....
3	$\frac{2}{3}$	2 (or more)
4	$\frac{2}{3}$	1 (or more)
≥ 5	1	0 (or $\leq s-5$)

$n = 2$

s \ x_2	$f_2(s, x_2) = \frac{1}{3} f_3^*(s - x_2) + \frac{2}{3} f_3^*(s + x_2)$					$f_2^*(s)$	x_2^*
	0	1	2	3	4		
0	0					0	....
1	0	0				0	....
2	0	$\frac{4}{9}$	$\frac{4}{9}$			$\frac{4}{9}$	1, 2
3	$\frac{2}{3}$	$\frac{4}{9}$	$\frac{2}{3}$	$\frac{2}{3}$		$\frac{2}{3}$	0, 2, 3
4	$\frac{2}{3}$	$\frac{8}{9}$	$\frac{2}{3}$	$\frac{2}{3}$	$\frac{2}{3}$	$\frac{8}{9}$	1
≥ 5	1					1	0 (or $\leq s - 5$)

CHAPTER 8

NETWORK ANALYSIS AND SCHEDULING

ARROW DIAGRAMS

• **PROBLEM 8-1**

Construct the arrow diagram comprising activities A,B, ..., M,N and O so that the following relationships are fulfilled:

1. A and B (the first activities of this project) can start simultaneously.
2. A precedes D,C.
3. B precedes C,E,F.
4. C and E precede G and I.
5. D and G precede H.
6. F,I precede K and L.
7. K,L precede M and N.
8. L precedes H.
9. H,M precede O.
10. O and N are the terminal activities of the project.

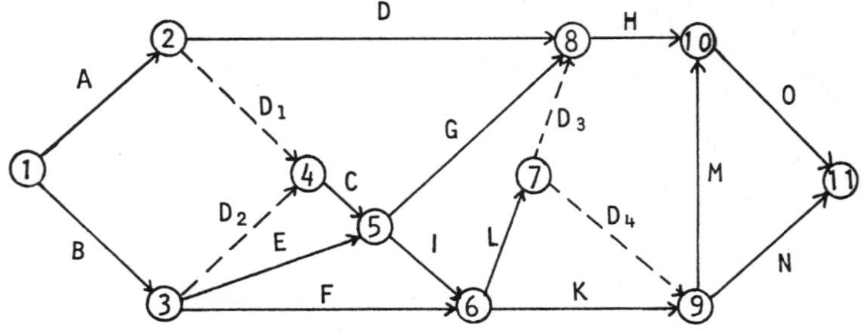

Arrow Diagram

Solution: The arrow diagram constructed from the above information is shown in the figure. The dummy activities (depicted by dashed arrows) are used to establish correct precedence relationships. The events of the project (depicted by circles in the figure) are numbered in ascending order to show the direction of progress.

• PROBLEM 8-2

Write down the flow conservation equations for the network in Figure 1.

Consider the partition

$$\vec{X} = \{1,3,5\} \; , \; \vec{\bar{X}} = \{2,4,6\} \; ,$$

a cutset separating the source and the sink. What is the set of forward arcs, reverse arcs and the capacity of the cutset?

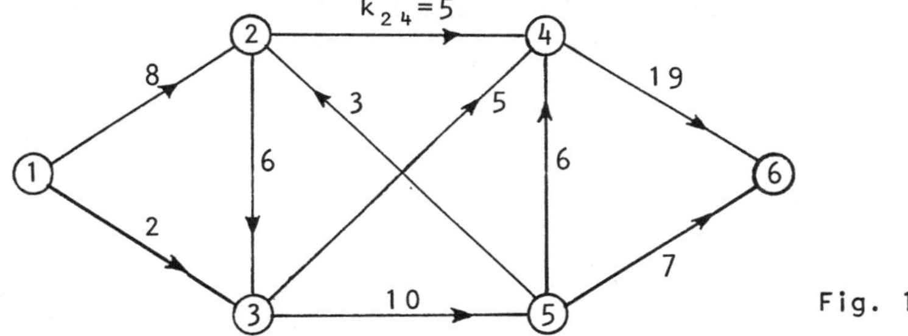

Fig. 1

Network where k_{ij} is the capacity of the arc(i,j)

Solution: The flow conservation equations are as follows:

$$\sum_{j\in\vec{A}_i} f_{ij} - \sum_{j\in\vec{B}_i} f_{ji} = v \qquad \text{if } i \text{ is source}$$

$$= -v \qquad \text{if } i \text{ is sink}$$

$$= 0 \qquad \text{if } i \text{ is an intermediate point}$$

where

$$\vec{A}_i = \{j: j \text{ such that } (i,j) \in T\},$$

$$\vec{B}_i = \{j: j \text{ such that } (j,i) \in T\},$$

where T stands for the set of all arcs and v is the net amount of material leaving the source (and arriving at the sink) is known as the value of the flow vector $f(=f_{ij})$. f specifies the amount of flow on each arc of the network. The equations require that the total amount of material reaching, should be equal to total amount of material leaving, at every intermediate point.

Hence:

Conservation equation for node	f_{12}	f_{13}	f_{23}	f_{24}	f_{52}	f_{34}	f_{35}	f_{54}	f_{46}	f_{56}	$-v =$	
1	1	1									1	0
2	−1		1	1	−1							0
3		−1	−1			1	1					0
4				−1		−1		−1	1			0
5					1		−1	1		1		0
6									−1	−1	−1	0

Letting G be a directed network, $\vec{X}$ a subset of points of G containing the source and not containing the sink, $\bar{\vec{X}}$ the set of all the points of G that are in $\vec{X}$, the partition $\vec{X},\bar{\vec{X}}$ generates "a cutset separating the source and the sink." The set of forward arcs of this cutset is

$$\{(i,j):(i,j) \in T,\ i \in \vec{X},\ j \in \bar{\vec{X}}\}\ .$$

The set of reverse arcs of this cutset is

$$\{(i,j):(i,j) \in T,\ i \in \bar{\vec{X}},\ J \in \vec{X}\}\ .$$

The cutset itself is denoted by $(\vec{X},\bar{\vec{X}})$.

The capacity of the cutset $(\vec{X},\bar{\vec{X}})$ separating the source and the sink is defined as

$$\sum_{(i,j)} k_{ij} - \sum_{(i,j)} \ell_{ij}$$

(Forward arcs) (Reverse arcs)

In Figure 1 the set of forward arcs is

$$\{(1,2),(3,4),(5,2),(5,4),(5,6)\}$$

and the set of reverse arcs is $\{(2,3)\}$ and the capacity of the cutset is 17.

• PROBLEM 8-3

A man is to be dressed as fast as possible, with undershirt, shorts, shirt, tie, trousers, jacket, socks, boots (too large to pass through the trouser legs), and wallet, which must go in the trousers after they are put on. Draw a network, assuming that five aides can work simultaneously and the man either stands on two feet or sits as he is dressed.

Solution:

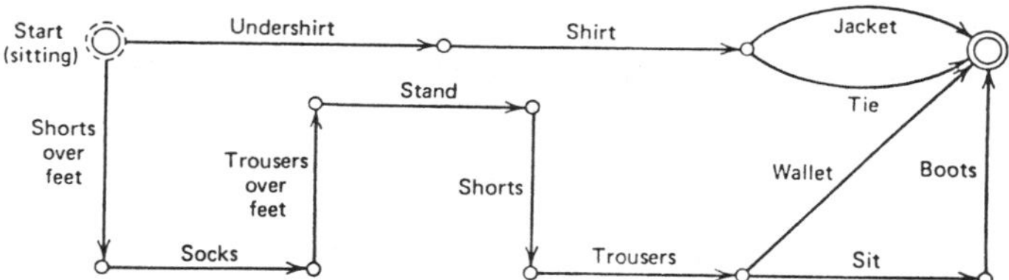

• **PROBLEM 8-4**

A couple must move as quickly as possible from city I to a nearby city II. Both persons are needed for loading and unloading the truck and agreeing on a new apartment. Other tasks, which either can do alone, are packing, cleaning both apartments, renting the truck and returning it to I, driving the truck and their own car, and viewing prospective apartments. Draw a plausible network, leaving such things as meals and sleep to be improvised.

Solution:

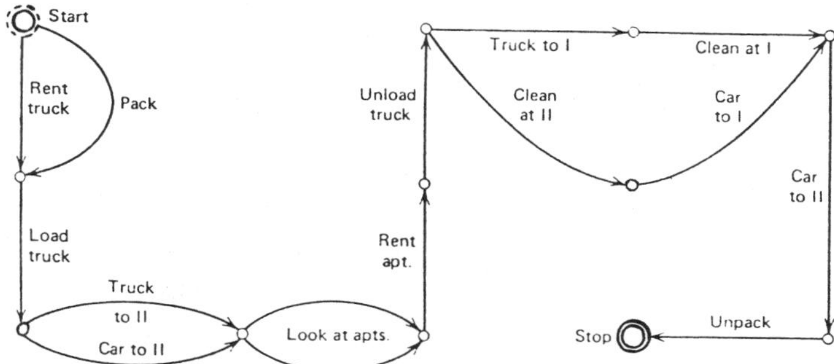

SHORTEST PATH(S)

• **PROBLEM 8-5**

Consider the network shown in Fig. 1. The numbers on the arcs give the distances d_{ij}. Find the shortest route from node 1 to each of the other nodes.

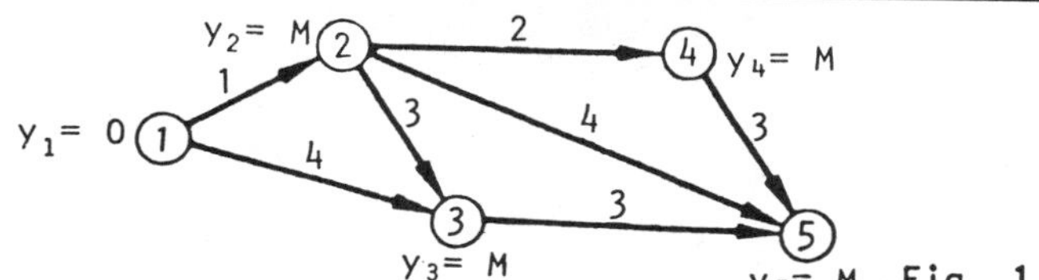

Fig. 1

Solution: Step 1: Set

$$y_1 = 0 \text{ and } y_2 = y_3 = y_4 = y_5 = M.$$

Node 1 is permanently labeled; the others are temporarily labeled. Set i = 1.

Step 2: From node 1, only nodes 2 and 3 can be reached. There are

$$y_2 = \min (M, 0 + 1) = 1 \text{ and } y_3 = \min (M, 0 + 4) = 4.$$

See Fig. 2.

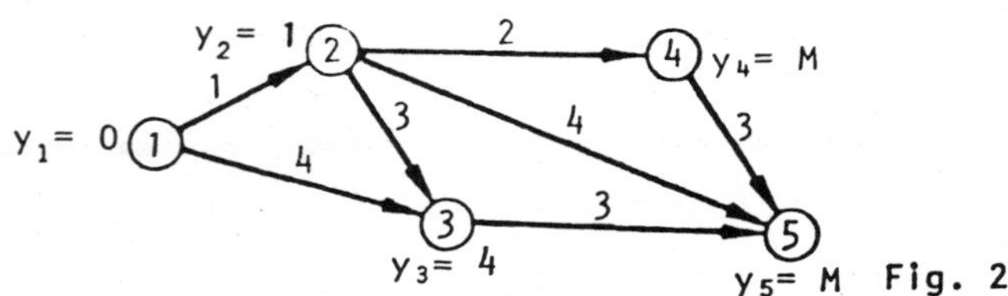

Fig. 2

Step 3: The smallest temporary label is $y_2 = 1$. Node 2 is now permanently labeled (with $y_2 = 1$). Set i = 2.

Step 4: Nodes 3, 4, and 5 still have temporary labels, so continue.

Step 2: From node 2, nodes 3, 4, and 5 can be reached. Thus,

$$y_3 = \min (4, 1 + 3) = 4$$

$$y_4 = \min (M, 1 + 2) = 3$$

$$y_5 = \min (M, 1 + 4) = 5$$

See Fig. 3.

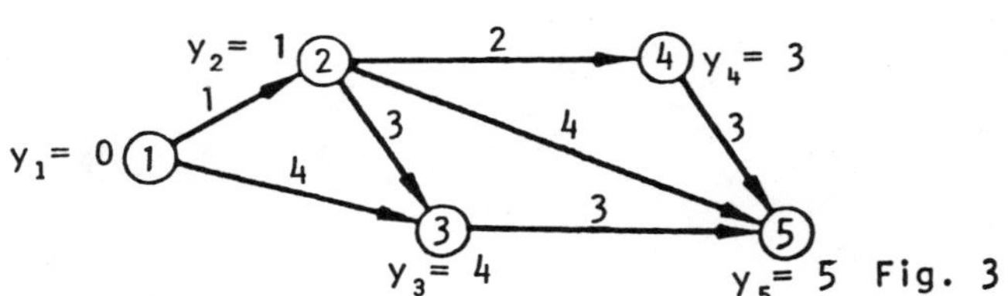

Fig. 3

Step 3: The smallest temporary label is $y_4 = 4$, so node 4 is now permanently labeled. Set i = 4.

Step 4: Nodes 3 and 5 are still temporarily labeled, so continue.

Step 2: From node 4, only node 5 can be reached and $y_5 = \min (5, 3 + 3) = 5$.

Step 3: The smallest temporary label is $y_3 = 4$, so permenently label node 3. Set i = 3.

Step 4: Node 5 still has a temporary label.

Step 2: From node 3, node 5 can be reached and $y_5 = \min (5, 4 + 3) = 5$.

Step 3: The only temporary label is $y_5 = 5$, so permanently label node 5.

Step 4: All nodes are permanently labeled.

The final (permanent) labels y_j give the length of the shortest path from node 1 to node j. Notice that once a node is permanently labeled, arcs are examined leading from it only once.

The answer is shown in Table 1.

Table 1

Node	Length of shortest route from node 1	Arcs in shortest route
2	1	(1,2)
3	4	(1,3)or (1,2),(2,3)
4	3	(1,2),(2,4)
5	5	(1,2),(2,5)

• PROBLEM 8-6

Consider the network shown in Figure 1, with 3 intermediate stages and 3 possible choices of route at all but the last cities.

Which intermediate cities are visited if the time taken to get from P to Z is to be as small as possible?

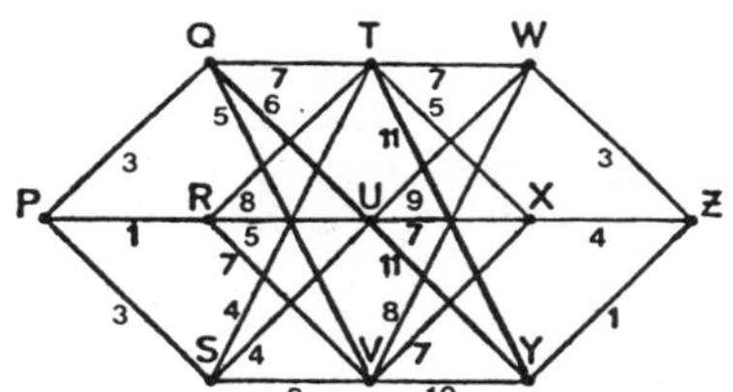

Fig. 1

Solution: Starting from P, consider the problem in stages:

First: Q, R or S?

Second: T, U or V?

Third: W, X or Y?

Final: Best route to Z?

Fist stage: It is not yet known whether the quickest route lies through Q, but if it does the quickest route from P to Q is obviously PQ. Similar statements about getting to R and to S are equally obvious.

Thus

$$\left.\begin{array}{l} P \text{ to } Q = 3 \\ P \text{ to } R = 1 \\ P \text{ to } S = 3 \end{array}\right\} \text{ by the shortest and only route}$$

Second stage. It is not yet known whether the quickest route lies through T, but if it does, would it have gone through Q, R or S? Now the route PQT takes 3 + 7 = 10, PRT takes 1 + 8 = 9 and PST takes 3 + 4 = 7. Therefore the quickest way to T is through S, though T is completely inaccessible, once the overall quickest route is known.

It is not yet known whether the quickest route lies through U rather than T. But if it does, would it have gone through Q, R or S? Now the route PQU takes 3 + 6 = 9, PRU takes 1 + 5 = 6 and PSU takes 3 + 4 = 7. Therefore the quickest way to U is through R, though U is completely inaccessible, once the overall quickest route is known.

To finish the second stage, it is not yet known whether the quickest route lies through V rather than T or U. But if it does, would it have gone through Q, R or S? Now the route PQV takes 3 + 5 = 8, PRV takes 1 + 7 = 8 also, and PSV takes 3 + 6 = 9. Therefore the quickest way to V is through either Q or R, though V is still inaccessible, once the overall quickest route is known.

Thus

$$\left.\begin{array}{l} P \text{ to } T = 7 \\ P \text{ to } U = 6 \\ P \text{ to } V = 8 \end{array}\right\} \text{ by the quickest route.}$$

Third stage. It is not yet known whether the quickest route lies through W, but if it does, would it have gone through T, U or V? Now the route PTW takes 7 + 7 = 14 if T is reached by the quickest route; PUW takes 6 + 9 = 15 if U is reached by the quickest route; PVW takes 8 + 8 = 16 if V is reached by the quickest route. Therefore the quickest way to W is through T, provided that T itself was reached in the quickest way (through S). W, T or S are

completely inaccessible, once the overall quickest route is known.

It is not yet known whether the best route lies through X rather than W. But if it does, would it have gone through T, U or V? Now the route PTX takes 7 + 5 = 12 if T is reached by the quickest route; PUX takes 6 + 7 = 13 if U is reached by the quickest route; PVX takes 8 + 7 = 15 if V is reached by the quickest route. Therefore the quickest way to X is through T, provided that T itself was reached in the quickest way (through S). X, T or S are still not accessible once the overall quickest route is known.

To finish the third stage, it is not yet known whether the best route lies through Y rather than W or X. But if it does, would it have gone through T, U or V? Now the route PTY takes 7 + 11 = 18 if T is reached by the quickest route; PUY takes 6 + 11 = 17 if U is reached by the quickest route; PVY takes 8 + 10 = 18 if V is reached the the quickest route. Therefore the quickest way to Y is through U, provided that U itself was reached in the quickest way (through R). Y, U, or R are still not accessible once the overall quickest route is known.

Thus

$$\left.\begin{array}{l} P \text{ to } W = 14 \\ P \text{ to } X = 12 \\ P \text{ to } Y = 17 \end{array}\right\} \text{ by the quickest route.}$$

Final stage: The quickest route from P to Z can now be calculated. P to W by the quickest route and on to Z takes 14 + 3 = 17; P to X by the quickest route and on to Z takes 12 + 4 = 16; P to Y by the quickest route and on to Z takes 17 + 1 = 18. Therefore the quickest route from P to Z takes 16.

Trace the steps back through the network and determine which intermediate cities lie on the quickest route from P to Z. The final stage of the calculation indicates that X does. This implies (from the third stage) that T also does, since the quickest route from P to X is through T. This in turn implies (from the second stage) that S also is on the quickest route from P to Z, since the quickest route from P to T is through S.

The quickest route, therefore, runs from P through S, T and X to Z, taking a total time of 16. This is also the quickest route from Z to P, since in this problem none of the times depend on the direction of travel.

• PROBLEM 8-7

Consider an undirected network shown in Fig. 1, where numbers along the arcs (i,j) represent distances between nodes i and j. Assume that the distance from i to j is the same as from j to i (i.e., all arcs are two-way streets). Determine the shortest distance and the length of the shortest path from node 1 to node 6.

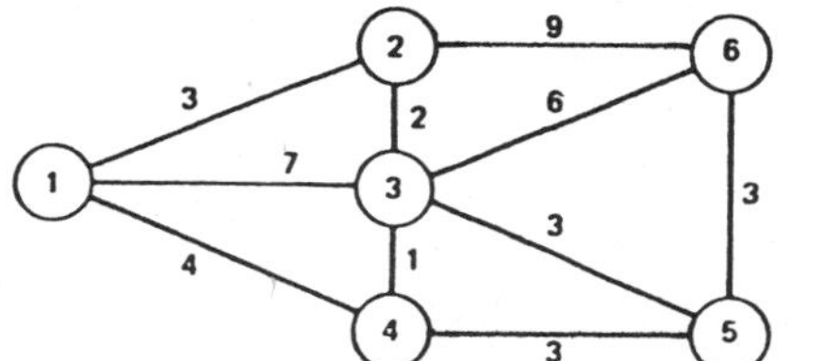

Fig. 1

Solution: Initially node 1 is labeled permanently as zero, and all other nodes are given temporary labels equal to their direct distance from node 1. Thus the node labels at Step 0, denoted by L(0), are

$$L(0) = [\underset{*}{0},3,7,4,\infty,\infty].$$

(An asterisk indicates a permanent label.)

At Step 1 the smallest of the temporary labels is made permanent. Thus node 2 gets a permanent label equal to 3, and it is the shortest distance from node 1 to node 2. To understand the logic behind this step, consider any other path from node 1 to node 2 through an intermediate node j = 3,4,5,6. The shortest distance from node 1 to node j will be at least equal to 3 and d_{j2} is nonnegative since all the distances are assumed to be nonnegative. Hence any other path from node 1 to node 2 cannot have a distance less than 3, and the shortest distance from node 1 to node 2 is 3. Thus at Step 1 the node labels are

$$L(1) = [\overset{*}{0},\overset{*}{3},7,4,\infty,\infty].$$

For each of the remaining nodes j (j = 3,4,5,6), compute a number which is the sum of the permanent label of node 2 and the direct distance from node 2 to node j. Compare this number with the temporary label of node j, and the smaller of the two values becomes the new tentative label for node j. For example, the new temporary label for node 3 is given by

$$\text{minimum of } (3 + 2,7) = 5$$

Similarly, for nodes 4, 5, and 6, the new temporary labels are 4, ∞, and 12, respectively. Once again the minimum of the new temporary labels is made permanent. Thus at Step 2, node 4 gets a permanent label as shown below:

$$L(2) = [\overset{*}{0},\overset{*}{3},5,\overset{*}{4},\infty,12].$$

Now using the permanent label of node 4, the new temporary labels of nodes 3, 5, and 6 are computed as 5, 7, and 12, respectively. Node 3 gets a permanent label and the node labels at Step 3 are

$$L(3) = [\overset{*}{0},\overset{*}{3},\overset{*}{5},\overset{*}{4},7,12].$$

At each step, only the node which has been recently labeled permanent is used for further calculations. Thus at Step 4 the permanent label of node 3 is used to update the temporary labels of nodes 5 and 6 (if possible). Node 5 gets a permanent label and the node labels at Step 4 are

$$L(4) = [\overset{*}{0},\overset{*}{3},\overset{*}{5},\overset{*}{4},\overset{*}{7},11].$$

Using the permanent label of node 5, the temporary label of node 6 is changed to 10 and is made permanent. The algorithm now terminates, and the shortest distance from node 1 to node 6 is 10. The shortest distance from node 1 to every other node in the network is obtained as

$$L(5) = [\overset{*}{0},\overset{*}{3},\overset{*}{5},\overset{*}{4},\overset{*}{7},\overset{*}{10}].$$

To determine the sequence of nodes in the shortest path from node 1 to node 6, work backwards from node 6. Node j (j = 1,2,3,4,5) precedes node 6 if the difference between the permanent labels of nodes 6 and j equals the length of the arc from j to 6. This gives node 5 as its immediate predecessor. Similarly node 4 precedes node 5, and the immediate predecessor of node 4 is node 1. Thus the shortest path from node 1 to node 6 is 1→4→5→6.

• PROBLEM 8-8

Use the algorithm developed by Dijkstra to find the shortest path between nodes 1 and 6.

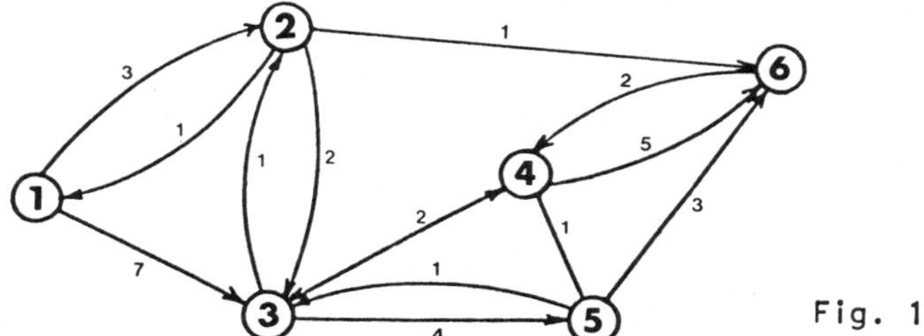

Fig. 1

<u>Solution</u>: The algorithm due to Dijkstra has the advantages that it: (i) requires $3n^3$ elementary operations, where each operation is either an addition or a comparison, and hence is more efficient than the other algorithms; (ii) can be applied in the case of non-symmetric distance matrices, with positive and negative arc lengths, hence it is quite general; and (iii) does not require storing all the data for all arcs simultaneously in the computer, irrespective of the size of the network, but only those for the arcs in sets I and II (described below), and this number is always less than n; hence it is quite economical in its demands on computer memory.

The algorithm follows. It capitalizes on the fact that if $\underline{j}$ is a node on the minimal path from $\underline{s}$ to $\underline{t}$, knowledge of the latter implies knowledge of the minimal path from $\underline{s}$ to $\underline{j}$. In the algorithm, the minimal paths from $\underline{s}$ to other nodes are constructed in order of increasing length until $\underline{t}$ is reached.

In the course of the solution the nodes are subdivided into three sets:

A. the nodes for which the path of minimum length from

s is known; nodes will be added to this set in order of increasing minimum path length from node s.

B. the nodes from which the next node to be added to set A will be selected; this set comprises all those nodes that are connected to at least one node of set A but do not yet belong to A themselves;

C. the remaining nodes.

The arcs are also subdivided into three sets:

I. The arcs occurring in the minimal paths from node s to the nodes in set A;

II. The arcs from which the next arc to be placed in set I will be selected; one and only one arc of this set will lead to each node in set B;

III. The remaining arcs (rejected or not yet considered).

To start with, all nodes are in set C and all arcs are in set III. Now transfer node s to set A and from then onwards repeatedly perform the following steps.

Step 1. Consider all arcs as connecting the node just transferred to set A with nodes j in sets B or C. If node

j belongs to set B, investigate whether the use of arc a gives rise to a shorter path from s to j than the known path that uses the corresponding arc in set II. If this is not so, arc a is rejected; if, however, use of arc a results in a shorter connection between s and j than

hitherto obtained, it replaces the corresponding arc in set II and the latter is rejected. If the node j belongs to set C, it is added to set B and arc a is added to set II.

Step 2. Every node in set B can be connected to node s in only one way if restricted to arcs from set I and one from set II. In this sense each node in set B has a distance from node s: the node with minimum distance from s is transferred from set B to set A, and the corresponding arc is transerred from set II to set I. Then return to step 1 and repeat the process until node t is transferred to set A. Then the solution has been found.

Applying the algorithm to the problem, obtain the calculations in tableau form.

As can be seen, the result is obtained in five iterations and required only 10 comparisons.

Table 1

	A[†]	B	C	I	II*	III*
Start	①		~~1,2,3~~, 4,5,6			~~(1,2)~~ (2,1) (3,2) ~~(1,3)~~ ~~(2,3)~~ ~~(3,4)~~ (4,3) ~~(2,6)~~ ~~(3,5)~~ ~~(4,5)~~ (5,3) ~~(6,4)~~ (4,6) (5,6)
S1.1	①	~~2~~,3	4,5,6		~~(1,2)~~, ~~(1,3)~~	
S2.1	1,②		4,5,~~6~~	(1,2)		
S1.2	1,②	3,~~6~~	4,5	(1,2)	(2,3), ~~(2,6)~~	
S2.2	1,2,⑥	3	~~4~~,5	(1,2),(2,6)	(2,3)	
S1.3	1,2,⑥	~~3~~,4	5	(1,2),(2,6)	~~(2,3)~~,(6,4)	
S2.3	1,2,③, 6	4	5	(1,2),(2,3), (2,6)	(6,4)	
S1.4	1,2,③, 6	~~4~~	5	(1,2),(2,3), (2,6)	~~(6,4)~~,(3,5)	
S2.4	1,2,3, ④,6		~~5~~	(1,2),(2,3), (2,6),(6,4)	(3,5)	
S1.5	1,2,3, ④,6	~~5~~		(1,2),(2,3), (2,6),(6,4)	(3,5),~~(4,5)~~	
S2.5	1,2,3, 4,⑤,6			(1,2),(2,3), (2,6),(6,4), (4,5)	(3,5)	

† The circled node is the node 'just entered' in the set A

* A crossed arc is a 'rejected' arc. Arc (1,3) was rejected in step S1.2 and arc (3,4) was rejected in step S1.4

• PROBLEM 8-9

Consider the network in Fig. 1, where the numbers beside the arcs are the distances. Arcs without arrows are undirected arcs and their distances are symmetric.

Find the shortest distance from node s to node t.

Solution: In the beginning, there is not a single tree arc and N_1, N_2, and N_3 are neighboring nodes of N_s. Give temporary labels $(L'_{s1}, s) = (4,s)$ to N_1, $(3,s)$ to N_2, and $(1,s)$ to N_3. As min $\{4,3,1\} = 1$, $(1,s)$ becomes a permanent label of N_3 and A_{s3} becomes a tree arc. The tree now consists of A_{s3} only.

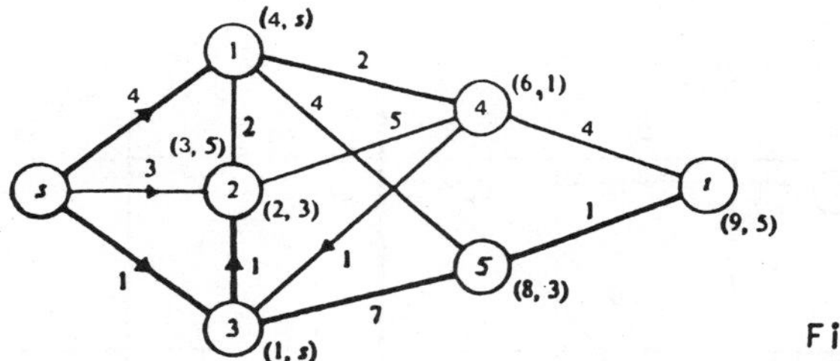

Fig. 1

Now the neighboring nodes of the tree are N_1, N_2, N_4, and N_5:

$$L'_{s1}: = \min(L'_{s1}, L_{s3} + d_{31}) = \min(4, 1 + \infty) = 4,$$

$$L'_{s2}: = \min(L'_{s2}, L_{s3} + d_{32}) = \min(3, 1 + 1) = 2,$$

$$L'_{s4}: = \min(L'_{s4}, L_{s3} + d_{34}) = \min(\infty, 1 + \infty) = \infty,$$

$$L'_{s5}: = \min(L'_{s5}, L_{s3} + d_{35}) = \min(\infty, 8) = 8$$

Since L'_{s2} is the smallest, it becomes a permanent label and A_{32} becomes a tree arc. Now the tree consists of two tree arcs. Continuing,

$$L'_{s1} : = \min(L'_{s1}, L_{s2} + d_{21}) = \min(4, 2 + 2) = 4,$$

$$L'_{s4} : = \min(L'_{s4}, L_{s2} + d_{24}) = \min(\infty, 2 + 5) = 7,$$

$$L'_{s5} : = \min(L'_{s5}, L_{s2} + d_{25}) = \min(8, 2 + \infty) = 8.$$

Since L'_{s1} is the smallest, it now becomes a permanent label and A_{s1} becomes a tree arc. Proceeding,

$$L'_{s4} : = \min(L'_{s4}, L_{s1} + d_{14}) = \min(7, 4 + 2) = 6,$$

$$L'_{s5} : = \min(L'_{s5}, L_{s1} + d_{15}) = \min(8, 4 + 4) = 8.$$

Since L'_{s4} is the smallest, it now becomes a permanent label and A_{14} becomes a tree arc. Continuing,

$$L'_{st} : = \min(L'_{st}, L_{s4} + d_{4t}) = \min(\infty, 6 + 4) = 10,$$

$$L'_{s5} : = \min(L'_{s5}, L_{s4} + d_{45}) = \min(8, 6 + \infty) = 8.$$

Since L'_{s5} is the smallest, it becomes a permanent label and A_{15} or A_{35} becomes a tree arc. Choose A_{35} as the tree arc. Then,

$$L'_{st} := \min(L'_{st}, L_{s5} + d_{5t}) = \min(10, 8+1) = 9.$$

So A_{5t} becomes a tree arc and the computation is completed. In Fig. 1 all tree arcs are drawn as heavy lines and the labels are enclosed in parentheses.

• PROBLEM 8-10

Find the minimum path from v_0 to v_7 in the graph G of figure 1. Notice that it has no circuit whose length is negative.

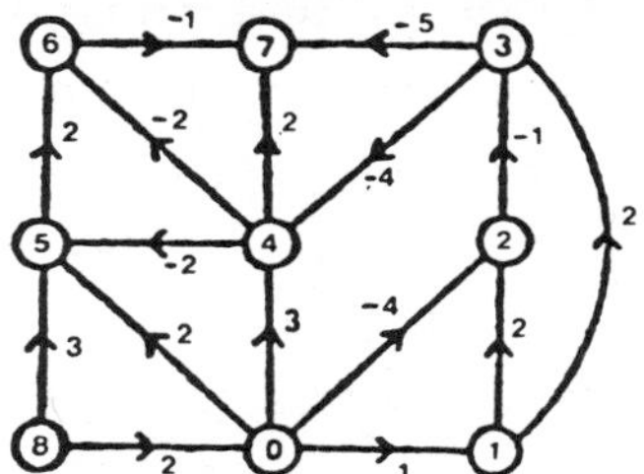

Fig. 1

Solution: An algorithm for arc lengths unrestricted in sign:

Let v_a, v_b be two vertices in the graph G(V,U) whose arc lengths are real numbers, positive, negative or zero. Find the minimum path from v_a to v_b. Assume that there are no circuits in the graph whose arc lengths add up to a negative number. For, if there is any such circuit, one can go round and round it and decrease the length of the path without limit, getting an unbounded solution.

Construct an arborescence $A_1(V_1, U_1)$, $V_1 \subseteq V$, $U_1 \subseteq U$. with center v_a and V_1 containing all those vertices of V which can be reached from v_a along a path, and U_1 containing some arcs of U which are necessary to construct the arborescence. If V_1 contains v_b, a path connects v_a to v_b. In a particular arborescence this path is unique. There may be many arborescences and therefore many paths. A_1 is any one arborescence. If in any problem only one arborescence is possible, there is only one path from v_a to v_b, and that is the solution. If V_1 does not contain v_b, there is no path from v_a to v_b and the problem has no solution.

The method of construction of the arborescence is

straightforward. Mark out the arcs going from v_a. From the vertices so reached mark out the arcs (not necessarily all of them) going out to the other vertices. No vertex should be reached by more than one arc, that is not more than one arc should be incident to any vertex. If there is a vertex to which no arc is incident, it cannot be reached from v_a and so is left out. No arc incident to v_a should be drawn.

Let f_j denote the length of the path from v_a to any vertex v_j in the arborescence. The arborescence determines f_j uniquely for each v_j in V_1, but f_j is not necessarily minimum. Let (v_k, v_j) be an arc in G but not in A_1. Consider the length $f_k + x_{kj}$ and compare it with f_j. If $f_j \leq f_k + x_{kj}$, make no change. If $f_j > f_k + x_{kj}$, delete the arc incident to v_j in A_1 and include instead the arc (v_k, v_j). This modifies the arborescence from A_1 to A_2 and reduces f_j to its new value $f_k + x_{kj}$, the reduction in the value of f_j being $f_j - f_k - x_{kj}$. The lengths of the paths to the vertices going through v_j are also reduced by the same amount. These adjustments are made and thus the new values of f_j for all v_j in A_2 are calculated.

Now repeat the operation in A_2, that is, select a vertex and see if any alternative arc gives a smaller path to it. If yes, modify A_2 to A_3 and adjust f_j accordingly. Ultimately an arborescence A_r is reached which cannot be further changed by the above procedure. A_r marks out the minimum path to each v_j from v_a, and f_b in this arborescence is the minimum path to v_b. The proof is as follows.

Draw an arborescence A_1 (figure 2) with center v_0 consisting of all those vertices of the graph which can be reached from v_0, (v_8 is thus excluded), and the necessary number of arcs. Notice that there can be many such arborescences. A_1 is one of them.

The lengths f_j of the paths from v_0 to different vertices v_j of A_1 are as follows.

$f_0 = 0$, $f_1 = 1$, $f_2 = -4$, $f_3 = 3$, $f_4 = 3$,

$f_5 = 2$, $f_6 = 4$, $f_7 = 5$.

Consider the vertex v_2. There is an arc (v_1, v_2) in G which is not in A_1, such that

$$f_2 = -4 < f_1 + x_{12} = 1 + 2 = 3$$

A_1 is left unchanged.

Now consider the vertex v_3. There is an arc (v_2, v_3) in G which is not in A_1 such that

$$f_3 = 3 > f_2 + x_{23} = -4 - 1 = -5.$$

Delete the arc (v_1, v_3) which is incident to v_3 in A_1 and instead include the arc (v_2, v_3). This gives a new arborescence A_2 with $f_3 = -5$. Since no vertex is reached in A_1 through v_3, all other f_j remain unchanged.

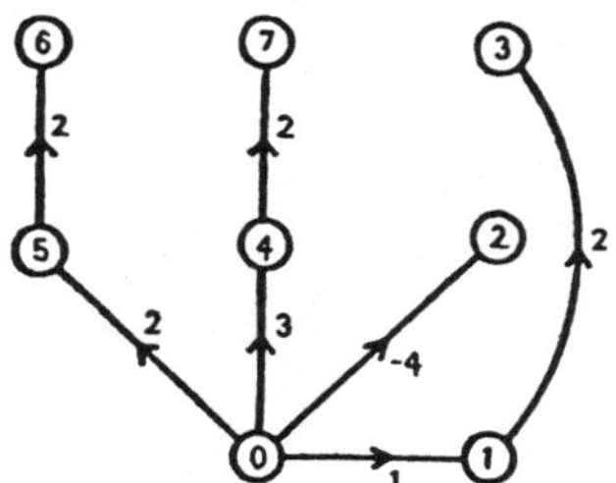

Fig. 2

Coming now to v_4 in A_2 (figure not drawn), arc (v_3, v_4) is in G but not in A_2 such that

$$f_4 = 3 > f_3 + x_{34} = -5 - 4 = -9$$

Delete the arc (v_0, v_4), include (v_3, v_4), get another arborescence A_3 with $f_4 = -9$ and consequently $f_7 = -7$.

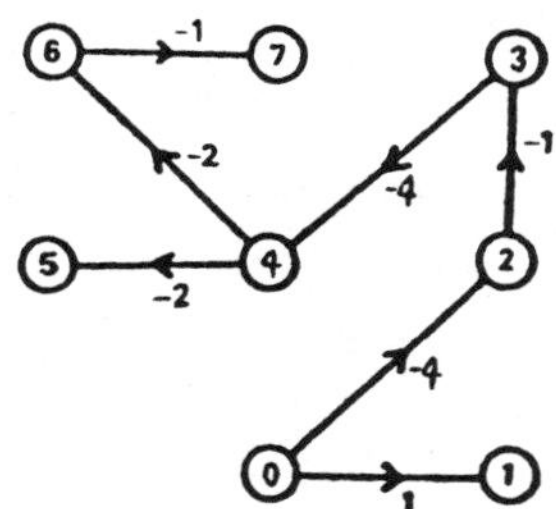

Fig. 3

Continuing like this, get the arborescence (figure 3) which cannot be further modified. No alternative arc decreases the length of the path from v_0 to any vertex. This is seen by testing for every vertex and every possible alternative arc. The minimum path from v_0 to v_7 is

$$(v_0, v_2, v_3, v_4, v_6, v_7)$$

with length -12.

Find the minimum path from v_0 to v_8 in the graph of figure 1 in which the number along a directed arc denotes its length.

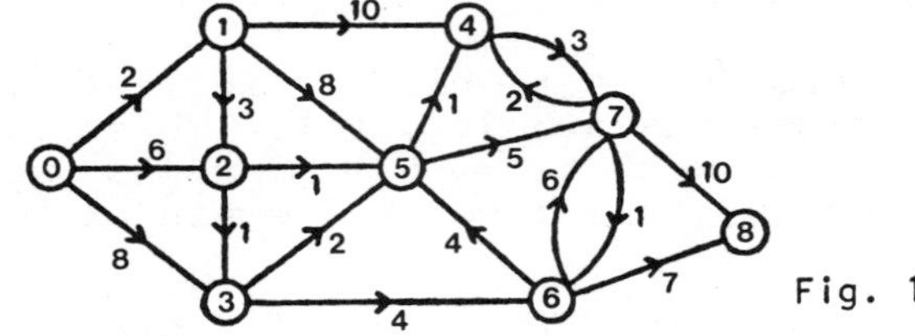

Fig. 1

Solution: Let a number x_{jk} be associated with each arc (v_j, v_k) of a graph $G(V,U)$, and let v_a and v_b be two vertices of the graph. There may be a number of paths from v_a to v_b. For each path define the length of the path as

$$\sum x_{jk}$$

where the summation is over the sequence of arcs forming the path. The problem is to find the path of the smallest length.

An algorithm for all arc lengths nonnegative, is:

Let f_j denote the minimum path from v_a to v_j. Find f_b, where $f_a = 0$.

Let V_p be a subset of V such that v_a is in V_p and v_b is not in V_p. Further assume that f_j for every v_j in V_p has been determined. Now determine $f_j + x_{jk}$ for every v_j in V_p and v_k not in V_p such that (v_j, v_k) is an arc incident from V_p. Let

$$f_r + x_{rs} = \min(f_j + x_{jk})$$

where

$$v_r \in V_p$$

and

$$v_s \notin V_p.$$

Then the minimum path from v_a to v_s is given by:

$$f_s = f_r + x_{rs}$$

This is so because to reach v_s, V_p must be left and $f_r + x_{rs}$ is the least of all paths going out of V_p along single arcs. Any alternative path to v_s can either be along some other single arc going out of V_p to v_s which would be larger, or along some other arc going out of V_p to some other point and then to v_s which would be larger still.

Now form an enlarged subset V_{p+1} of V defined by

$$V_{p+1} = V_p \cup \{v_s\},$$

TABLE 1

p	v_p	f	$\Omega-(V_p)$	x	$f+x$	f_s	ν_s
0	0	0	(0,1)	2	2	2	1
			(0,2)	6	6		
			(0,3)	8	8		
1	0	0	(0,2)	6	6		
			(0,3)	8	8		
	1	2	(1,2)	3	5	5	2
			(1,4)	10	12		
			(1,5)	8	10		
2	0	0	(0,3)	8	8		
	1	2	(1,4)	10	12		
			(1,5)	8	10		
	2	5	(2,3)	1	6	6	3
			(2,5)	1	6	6	5
3	0	0					
	1	2	(1,4)	10	12		
	2	5					
	3	6	(3,6)	4	10		
	5	6	(5,4)	1	7	7	4
			(5,7)	5	11		
4	0	0					
	1	2					
	2	5					
	3	6	(3,6)	4	10	10	6
	4	7	(4,7)	3	10	10	7
	5	6	(5,7)	5	11		
5	0	0					
	1	2					
	2	5					
	3	6					
	4	7					
	5	6					
	6	10	(6,8)	7	17	17	8
	7	10	(7,8)	10	20		

and repeat the operation. Assume the solution begins with $p = 0$ with V_0 consisting of a single vertex v_a and $f_a = 0$. Following the procedure described above the sets V_1,

V_2, ..., V_p, V_{p+1}, ... are formed. As soon as a set in this sequence which includes v_b is arrived at f_b is found. If no such set can be found, there is no path connecting v_a to v_b; Table 1 shows the iterations according to the algorithm explained above. In the V_p column are listed the vertices in the subset v_p, r denoting v_r. Under f are written the least distances to these vertices from v_0.

Ω-(v_p) are the arcs incident from V_p, (v_j, v_k) being written as (j,k). Under x are given the lengths of the arcs. f_s is the minimum of f+x, and v_s is the vertex to which this minimum distance leads and which in the next iteration is included on the enlarged subset V_{p+1}.

The minimum path is found to be of length 17 and goes through the vertices (0,1,2,3,6,8).

• PROBLEM 8-12

Determine the shortest chain from the source to all other nodes of the network in Figure 1,where the distances associated with the arcs and edges are indicated.

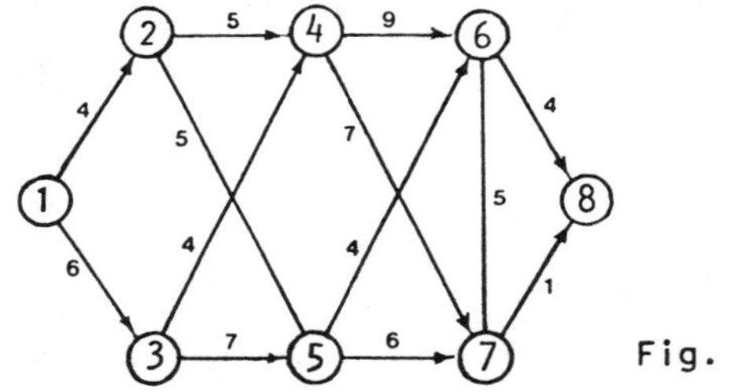

Fig. 1

Solution: The following is Dijkstra's algorithm for finding the shortest chain from the source to all other nodes of a network.

Step 1. Let $L'_{sk} = d_{sk}$. Initially, s (source) is the only node in the tree and $L_{ss} = 0$.

Step 2. $L_{sr} = \min_k L'_{sk} = L_{sj} + d_{jr}$. The k are neighbor nodes of the current tree.

Step 3. Make the arc (j,r) a tree arc.

Step 4. If the number of tree arcs is n - 1, terminate the algorithm. Otherwise, proceed to step 5.

Step 5. $L'_{sk} := \min(L'_{sk}, L_{sr} + d_{rk})$, where: = means to be replaced by. Go to step 2.

The algorithm may be implemented by labeling the nodes. A label of the type (L,i) will be given to each node of the network. The L in the label is the value L'_{sk} or L_{sk}, and i refers to the last node on the shortest chain from the source to node k. There are two types of labels: temporary and permanent. A label is temporary if $L = L'_{sk}$, and it is permanent if $L = L_{sk}$.

Initially, there are no tree arcs and node 1 is the sole tree node. The neighbor nodes of 1 are 2 and 3. Since $L'_{1k} = d_{1k}$, attach the temporary labels (4,1) to node 2 and (6,1) to node 3. By step 1 of the algorithm, $L_{11} = 0$; thus $L_{1r} = \min\{4,6\} = 4$, and (4,1) is a permanent label of 2. In addition, the arc (1,2) is now a tree arc.

The neighbor nodes of the two-node tree are 3, 4, and 5:

$$L'_{13} := \min(L'_{13}, L_{12} + d_{23}) = \min(6, 4 + \infty) = 6$$

$$L'_{14} := \min(L'_{14}, L_{12} + d_{24}) = \min(\infty, 4 + 5) = 9$$

$$L'_{15} := \min(L'_{15}, L_{12} + d_{25}) = \min(\infty, 4 + 5) = 9.$$

Since it is noted that the smallest of the L'_{1k} is L'_{13}, then (6,1) becomes a permanent label for node 3, and (1,3) is a tree arc. The tree now consists of two tree arcs, and there are only five more to determine. The neighbor nodes of the current tree are 4 and 5. Then

$$L'_{14} := \min(L'_{14}, L_{13} + d_{34}) = \min(9, 6 + 4) = 9$$

$$L'_{15} := \min(L'_{15}, L_{13} + d_{35}) = \min(9, 6 + 7) = 9.$$

Since L'_{14} equals L'_{15}, the tie is broken arbitrarily, and (9,2) is selected as a permanent label for node 4. Also, (2,4) is a tree arc. The neighbor nodes of the current tree are 5, 6, and 7. Thus

$$L'_{15} := \min(L'_{15}, L_{14} + d_{45}) = \min(9, 9 + \infty) = 9$$

$$L'_{16} := \min(L'_{16}, L_{14} + d_{46}) = \min(\infty, 9 + 9) = 18$$

$$L'_{17} := \min(L'_{17}, L_{14} + d_{47}) = \min(\infty, 9 + 7) = 16.$$

Since the smallest of the L'_{1k} is L'_{15}, then (9,2) becomes a permanent label for node 5, and (2,5) is a tree arc. The neighbor nodes of the current tree are 6 and 7. Hence

$$L'_{16} := \min(L'_{16}, L_{15} + d_{56}) = \min(18, 9 + 4) = 13$$

$$L'_{17} := \min(L'_{17}, L_{15} + d_{57}) = \min(16, 9 + 6) = 15.$$

Since the smaller of the L'_{1k} is L'_{16}, then (13,5) becomes a permanent label for node 6, and (5,6) is a tree arc. The neighbor nodes of the current tree are 7 and 8. The tree now consists of five tree arcs, and there are only two more to determine. Continuing

$$L'_{17} := \min(L'_{17}, L_{16} + d_{67}) = \min(15, 13 + 5) = 15$$

$$L'_{18} := \min(L'_{18}, L_{16} + d_{68}) = \min(\infty, 13 + 14) = 17.$$

Since L'_{17} is the smaller, then (15,5) becomes a permanent label for node 7, and (5,7) is a tree arc. Finally

$$L'_{18} := \min(L'_{18}, L_{17} + d_{78}) = \min(17, 15 + 1) = 16.$$

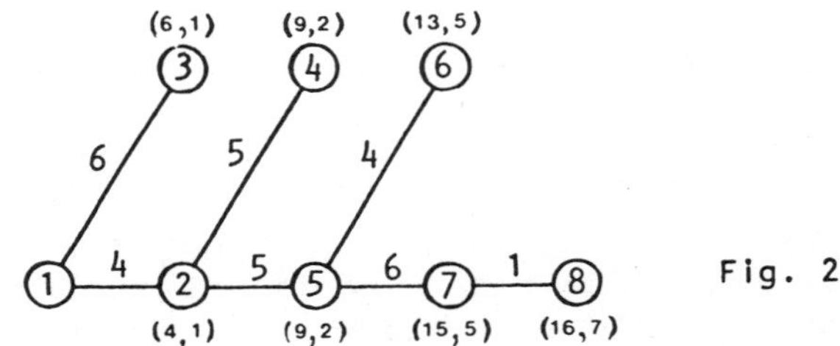

Fig. 2

Thus (7,8) becomes a tree arc, and node 8 receives the permanent label (16,7). There are now seven tree arcs, and the algorithm terminates. Figure 2 illustrates the complete tree where the permanent labels are next to each node.

• PROBLEM 8-13

Given the directed network, find all the shortest paths from node A by Dijkstra's algorithm.

i/j =	A	B	C	D	E	F	G	H	K
(A)	—	9	7	6					
B		—	16	4	11				
C	15	13	—	7		1			
D		2	8	—	12	14	5		
E		10			—	1	4	6	
F			3			—	13		9
G				7		2	—	10	8
H					4		5	—	12
K						11	7	3	—

Solution: Assume all lengths $c_{ij} \geq 0$. Let d_{Ai} denote the shortest path length from some fixed node A to node i; let node A = [1] be the sole member of S_1, and $d_{AA} = 0$. In general let S_r consist of the r nodes i = [1],....,[r] whose shortest path lengths d_{Ai} from A have been determined at stage r, and let $\bar{S}_r$ consist of the remaining nodes. The shortest paths from A to the other nodes of S_r, if unique, form a subtree. Then the r th arc to be added to this subtree is the (i,j) that minimizes:

$$d_{A[r+1]} = \min_{i \in S_r} (d_{Ai} + \min_{i \in \bar{S}_r} c_{ij}) \quad (r = 1,\ldots,p-1). \tag{1}$$

The added node [r + 1] is the j that minimizes (1). Values of (i,j) for which c_{ij} is undefined are ignored or else such c_{ij} are set equal to $+\infty$. To determine the the shortest path lengths d_{iA} to A one uses

$$d_{[r+1]A} = \min_{j \in S_r} (\min_{j \in \bar{S}_r} c_{ij} + d_{jA}) \quad (r = 1,\ldots,p-1) \tag{2}$$

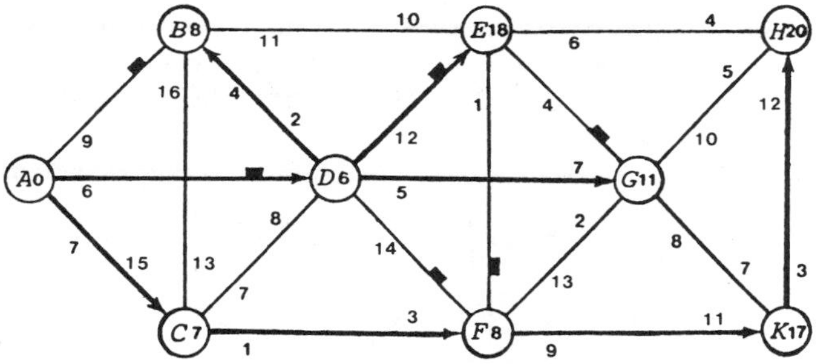

Fig. 1

Shortest paths from A.

In a small network diagram, (1) permits the successive $d_{A[r]}$ to be written down by inspection. In Figure 1 they are included within the circle representing the node, while each c_{ij} labels its arc on the right side near its initial node i. The shortest paths are indicated by heavy lines and arrowheads. Where necessary a small black square indicates a nonexistent directed arc (or infinite cost).

First A is labeled with $d_{AA} = 0$ because it is the given node. The next two labels (for D and C) are determined thus:

$$d_{AD} = 6 = d_{AA} + \min(c_{AB}, c_{AD}, c_{AC}) = 0 + \min(9,6,7).$$

$$d_{AC} = 7 = \min(0 + 7, 6 + 2) = \text{the smaller of } d_{AA}$$

$$+ \min(c_{AB}, c_{AC}) \text{ and } d_{AD} +, \min(c_{DB}, c_{DE}, c_{DG}, c_{DF}, c_{DC}).$$

There is a tie for the next minimum and hence B and F can be labeled in either order or simultaneously:

$$d_{AB} = d_{AF} = 8 = \min(0 + 9, 6 + 2, 7 + 1)$$

where

$$0 + 9 = d_{AA} + c_{AB},\ 6 + 2 = d_{AD} + \min(c_{DB}, c_{DE}, c_{DG}, c_{DF})$$

$$= d_{AD} + c_{DB} \text{ and } 7 + 1 = d_{AC} = c_{CF}.$$

The remaining labels $d_{AG} = 11$, $d_{AK} = 17$, $d_{AE} = 18$ and $d_{AH} = 20$ are determined in that order. The resulting oriented tree of shortest paths with root at A may be recorded compactly as

```
 E
BDA'CFKH.
 G
```

• PROBLEM 8-14

Consider the network in Fig. 1, where the distances of arcs are shown in Table 1. Find the shortest chains between every pair of nodes.

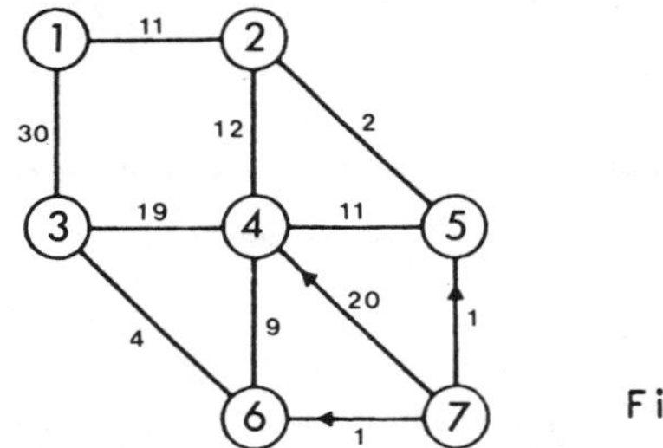

Fig. 1

Solution: Revised Cascade Method will be used. Apply the equation

$$d_{ik} = \min(d_{ik}, d_{ij} + d_{jk})$$

(for all $i \neq k \neq J$). For $j = 1$, check every entry in Table 1 which does not lie in the first column or in the first row. Thus

$$d_{23} := \min(d_{23}, d_{21} + d_{13}) = \min(\infty, 11 + 30) = 41$$

$$d_{32} := \min(d_{32}, d_{31} + d_{12}) = \min(\infty, 30 + 11) = 41.$$

All other entries remain the same. For j = 2 apply the same operation to each of the entries in Table 1 which does not lie in the second column or the second row. The result is (the calculations have been omitted for

Table 1

	①	②	③	④	⑤	⑥	⑦
①	0	11	30	∞	∞	∞	∞
②	11	0	∞	12	2	∞	∞
③	30	∞	0	19	∞	4	∞
④	∞	12	19	0	11	9	∞
⑤	∞	2	∞	11	0	∞	∞
⑥	∞	∞	4	9	∞	0	∞
⑦	∞	∞	∞	20	1	1	0

$d_{43} = d_{34}$, $d_{41} = d_{14}$, $d_{51} = d_{15}$, and $d_{53} = d_{35}$),

$$d_{34} := \min(d_{34}, d_{32} + d_{24}) = \min(19, 41 + 12) = 19,$$

$$d_{14} := \min(d_{14}, d_{12} + d_{24}) = \min(\infty, 11 + 12) = 23,$$

$$d_{15} := \min(d_{15}, d_{12} + d_{25}) = \min(\infty, 11 + 2) = 13,$$

$$d_{35} := \min(d_{35}, d_{32} + d_{25}) = \min(\infty, 41 + 2) = 43,$$

and all other entries remain the same. Note that in the above computation for j = 2, the results for j = 1 have already been used. If the computation is carried through, the result is Table 2, which shows the shortest distances, and Table 3, which shows the actual nodes on the shortest chains. For example, if the shortest chain from N_1 to N_6 is desired, then look at Table 3, where (1,6) = 2. Then look at (2,6) = 4, (4,6) = 6. Therefore, the nodes in the shortest chain are successivly N_1, N_2, N_4, and N_6.

Table 2

	①	②	③	④	⑤	⑥	⑦
①	0	11	30	23	13	32	∞
②	11	0	25	12	2	21	∞
③	30	25	0	13	24	4	∞
④	23	12	13	0	11	9	∞
⑤	13	2	24	11	0	20	∞
⑥	32	21	4	9	20	0	∞
⑦	14	3	5	10	1	1	0

Table 3

	①	②	③	④	⑤	⑥	⑦
①	1	2	3	2	2	2	7
②	1	2	4	4	5	4	7
③	1	6	3	6	6	6	7
④	2	2	6	4	5	6	7
⑤	2	2	4	4	5	4	7
⑥	4	4	3	4	4	6	7
⑦	5	5	6	6	5	6	7

MINIMAL SPANNING TREE

• PROBLEM 8-15

Find the shortest spanning tree in Figure 1, by applying the greedy algorithm.

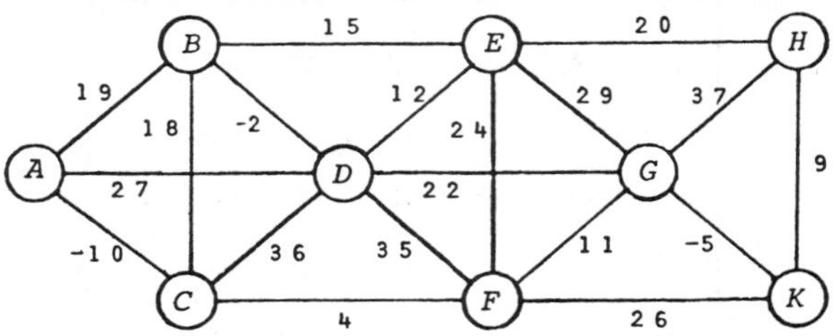

Fig. 1

Solution: The greedy algorithm: One begins with a subtree consisting of only one arbitrarily selected node, which will not affect the length of the final tree; this subtree is expanded by adding one arc at a time (with its incident node) until all p nodes have been connected by means of p - 1 arcs. At each stage the added arc is an arc of shortest length c_{ij} connecting a node i in the subtree with a node j not yet in the subtree. This produces a shortest spanning tree if $c_{ij} = c_{ji}$ and the arcs having finite c_{ij} form a connected graph.

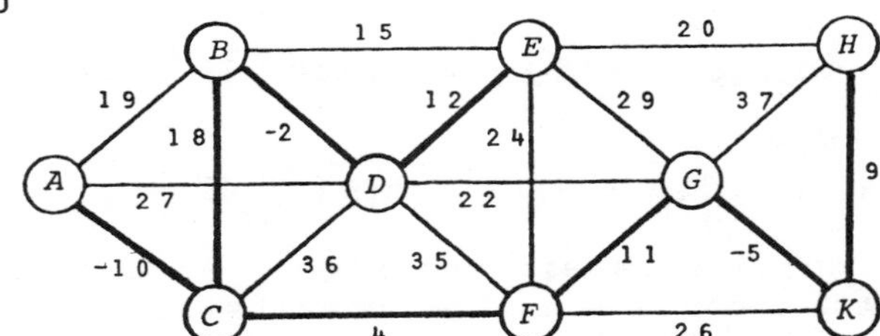

Fig. 2

The algorithm, applied to the problem produces the network in Figure 2 in which the heavy lines indicate the resulting shortest spanning tree of length 37. If one starts at node A one obtains the arc lengths

$$c_{AC} = -10 = \min(c_{AB} = 19,\ c_{AD} = 27,\ c_{AC} = -10)$$

$$c_{CF} = 4 = \min(19,27,18,36,4)$$

$$c_{FG} = 11 = \min(19,27,18,36,35,24,11,26)$$

and so on to GK, KH, CB, BD and DE. The resulting undirected tree may be recorded compactly as:

EDBCFGKH.
A

• PROBLEM 8-16

The planned locations of computer terminals that are to be installed in a multistory building are given in Figure 1. Terminal A is the computer itself and phone cables must be wired along some of the indicated branches in order that there be a connected path from every terminal back to A. The numbers along the arcs represent the costs (in hundreds of dollars) of installing the lines between terminals. Since operating costs are very low, the company would like to find the branches that should be installed in order to minimize total installation costs.

Solve this problem by applying the greedy (next-best) rule.

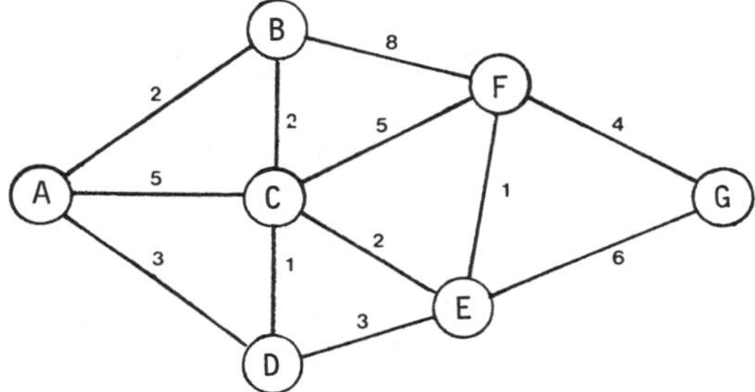

Fig. 1

Solution: Begin at any terminal and find the branch to the nearest unconnected terminal. This branch is part of the tree. From these two terminals find the branch to the nearest unconnected terminal and add this branch to the tree. Continue in this fashion until all terminals are connected.

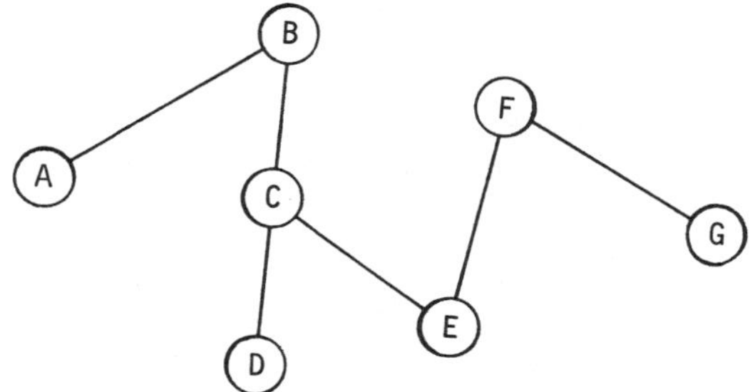

Fig. 2

Beginning arbitrarily at node C in Figure 1, the nearest terminal is D; CD is a branch on the tree. The nearest terminals to both C and D are B and E; arbitrarily choose E. Next, find F closest to C, D, and E, and finally choose B, then A and G. The spanning tree is as given in Figure 2 and the total cost is $1200. This happens to be the optimal solution even though the "next-best" rule has been used to solve the problem. The next-best method always finds the minimum spanning tree.

• **PROBLEM 8-17**

The city park management needs to determine under which roads telephone lines should be installed to connect all stations with a minimum total length of line. Using the data given in Fig. 1 find the shortest spanning tree (spanning tree is defined as a connected subgraph of a network G which contains the same nodes as G but contains no loops).

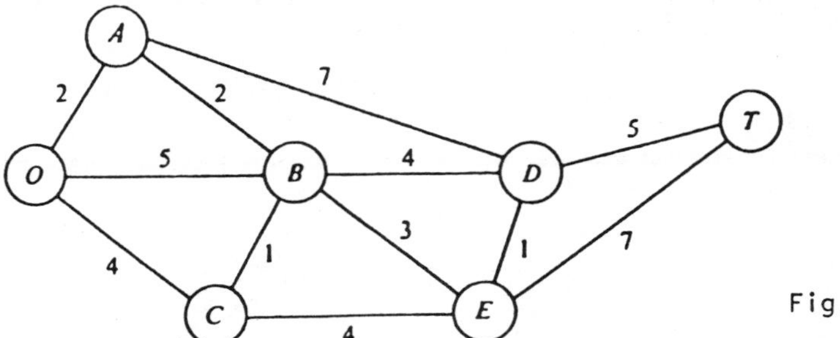

Fig. 1

Solution: Arbitrarily select node O to start. The unconnected node closest to node O is node A. Connect node A to node O.

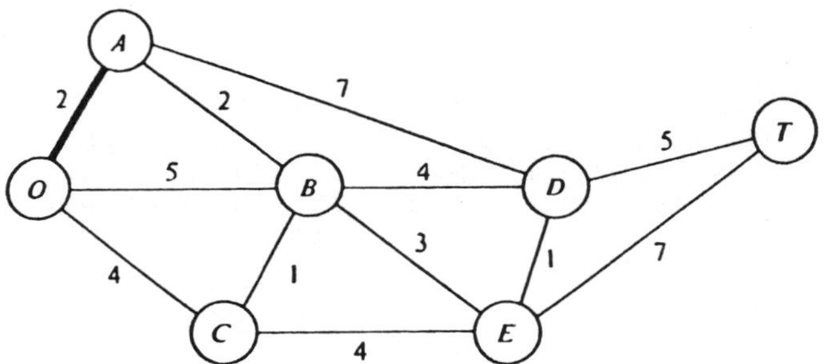

The unconnected node closest to node O or A is node B (closest to A). Connect node B to node A.

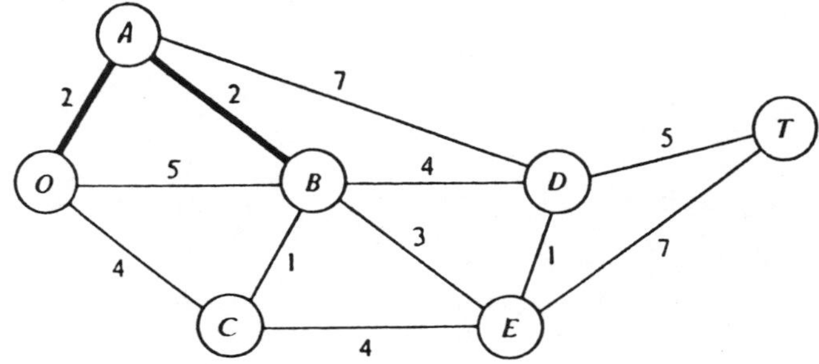

The unconnected node closest to node O, A, or B is node C (closest to B). Connect node C to node B.

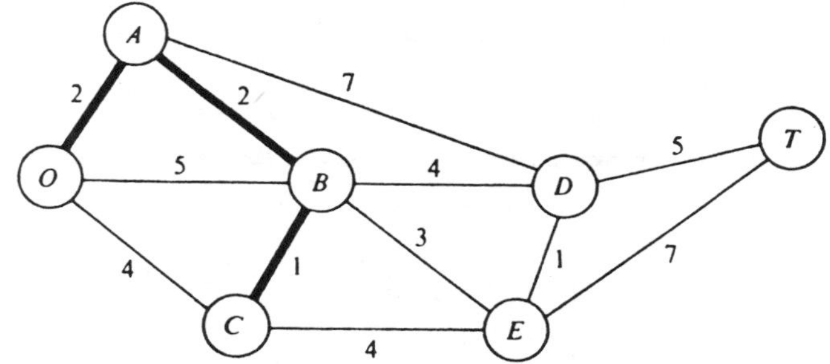

The unconnected node closest to node O, A, B, or C is node E (closest to B). Connect node E to node B.

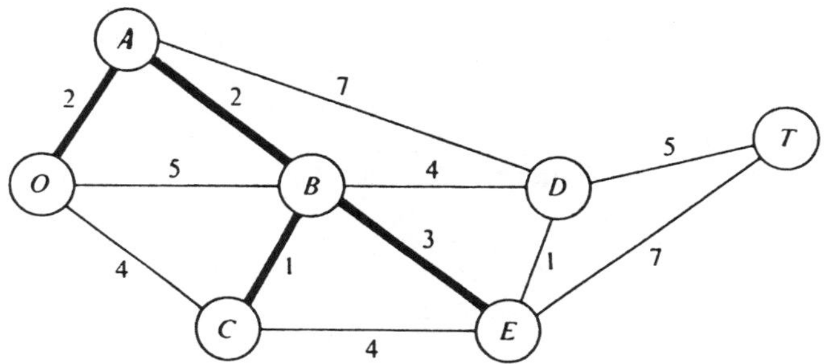

The unconnected node closest to node O, A, B, C or E is node D (closest to E). Connect node D to node E.

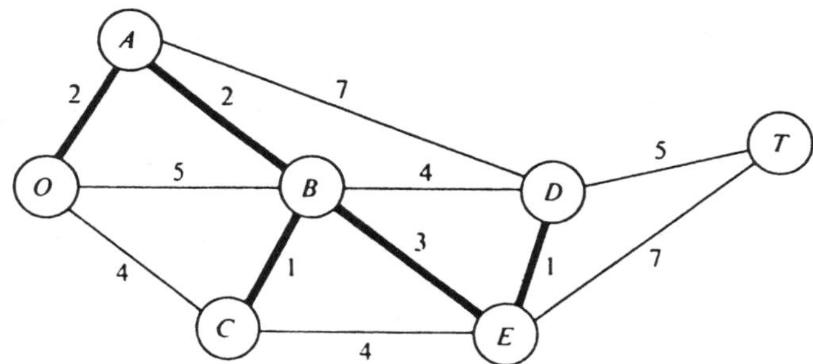

The only remaining unconnected node is node T. It is closest to node D. Connect node T to node D.

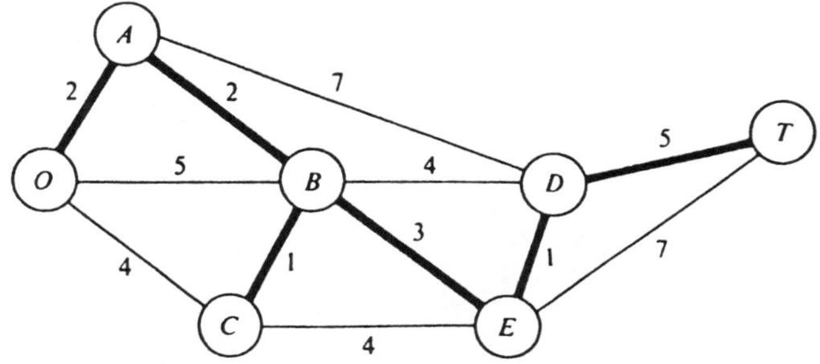

All nodes are now connected, so this is the desired solution to the problem. The total length of the branches is 14 miles.

• **PROBLEM 8-18**

Find the minimum spanning tree of the graph G(V,U) of figure 1. Notice that it is an undirected graph.

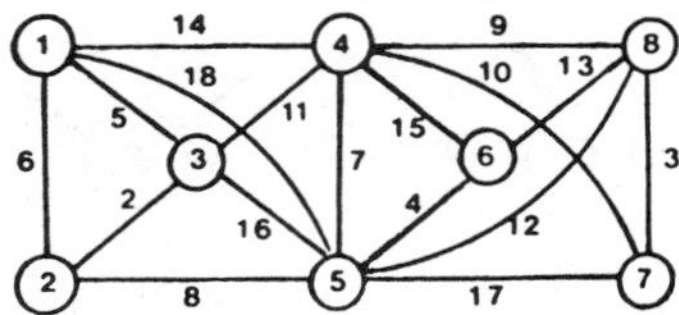

Fig. 1

Solution: Going through all the vertices v_1 to v_8 and drawing the arc connecting each to its nearest neighbor, yields the graph $G_1(V,U_1)$ of figure 2. The nearest neighbor of v_1 is v_3, of v_2 is v_3, of v_3 is v_2, and so on. The graph G_1 is not connected. It has three components, A_1, A_2, A_3. Treat them as three 'vertices'. The arcs of G connecting A_1 to A_2 are of lengths 14,18, 8,16,11, and so the distance between A_1 and A_2 is 8. Similarly the distance between A_2 and A_3 is 9. Also since there is no arc connecting A_1 and A_3, the distance betweem them is ∞. The nearest neighbor of A_1 is A_2 and of A_2 is A_1. Connect the two by arc (v_2,v_5), which measures the distance between the two.

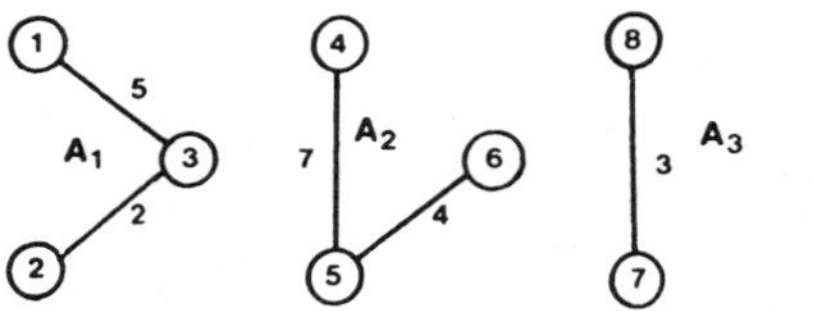

Fig. 2

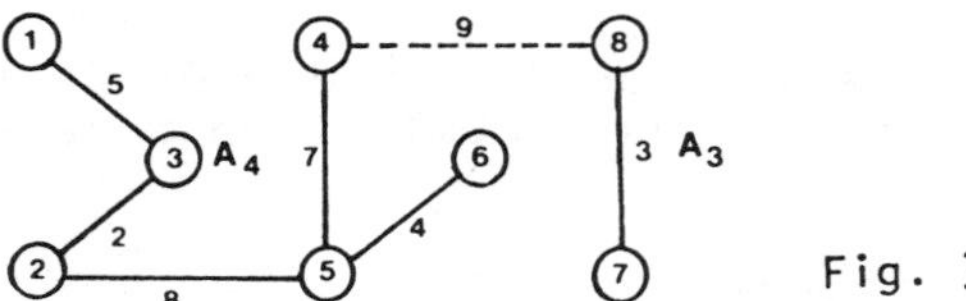

Fig. 3

Thus results the graph $G_2(V,U_2)$ of figure 3 which has two components, A_4 and A_3. Since they are only two, each is the nearest neighbor of the other, and so connect them with the arc (v_4, v_8) (shown dotted) which measures the distance between them. Thus, there is a single connected graph which is the smallest spanning tree. The length of the tree is 38.

MAXIMUM FLOW

• PROBLEM 8-19

In the graph of figure 1, numbers along arcs are values of c_i. Find the maximum flow in the graph.

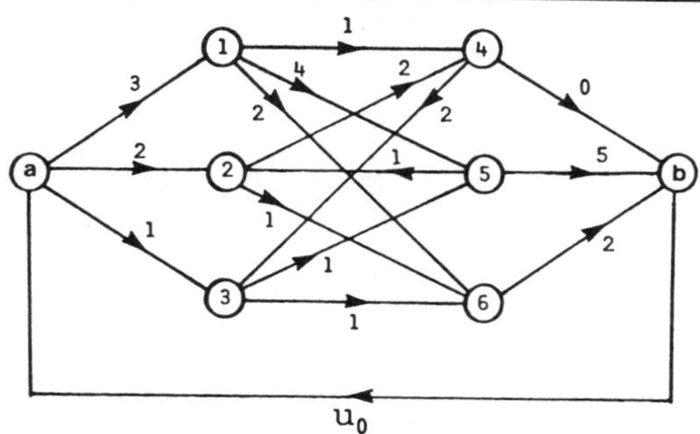

Fig. 1

Solution: Assuming the initial flow as zero in all arcs, let $W_1 = \{v_a\}$, $W_2 = \{$all other nodes$\}$. Now define a criterion (i): if (v_j, v_k) is an arc u and $x_u < c_u$, transfer v_k to W_1.

There is an arc (v_a, v_1) from v_a in W_1 to v_1 in W_2 in which the flow (zero) is less than its capacity 3. Therefore by the criterion (i) transfer v_1 to W_1. Now there is an arc (v_1, v_4) with $v_1 \in W_1$ and $v_4 \in W_2$ such that the flow in it is less than its capacity 1. So transfer v_4 to W_1. In the arc (v_4, v_b), $v_4 \in W_1$, $v_b \in W_2$, the flow is zero which is equal to its capacity, and therefore v_b cannot be transferred to W_1. But there is another arc (v_4, v_3), $v_4 \in W_1$, $v_3 \in W_2$, which is such that v_3 is transferrable to W_1. Further, because the flow in arc (v_3, v_5), $v_3 \in W_1$, $v_5 \in W_2$ is below capacity, v_5 is transferred to W_1, and finally because the arc (v_5, v_b) satisfies the same criterion, v_b is transferred to W_1. Thus it is possible to transfer v_b to W_1 and so the flow is not optimal.

The chain $(v_a, v_1, v_4, v_3, v_5, v_b)$ has been examined. The least capacity in this chain is 1. So in each arc of this chain and also in the return arc (v_b, v_a)increase the flow to 1, keeping the flow as it was in all other arcs. The modified flow is feasible because in each arc it is less than or equal to its capacity, and also at every vertex the flow in equals the flow out.

The above reasoning is repeated with every modified feasible flow until it is not possible to transfer v_b to W_1. The iterations are shown in Table 1. In each feasible flow the bold numbers indicate the chain along which it is possible to proceed to bring v_b into W_1. The asterisk

TABLE 1

Arcs	Capacity c_i	Feasible flows I	II	III	IV	V	VI
(a, 1)	3	0	1	3*	3*	3*	3*
(a, 2)	2	0	0	0	1	2*	2*
(a, 3)	1	0	0	0	0	0	1*
(1, 4)	1	0	1*	1*	1*	1*	0
(1, 5)	4	0	0	2	2	2	3
(1, 6)	2	0	0	0	0	0	0
(2, 4)	2	0	0	0	0	1	1
(2, 6)	1	0	0	0	1*	1*	1*
(3, 5)	1	0	1*	1*	1*	1*	1*
(3, 6)	1	0	0	0	0	1*	1*
(4, 3)	2	0	1	1	1	2	1
(4, b)	0	0*	0*	0*	0*	0*	0*
(5, 2)	1	0	0	0	0	0	0
(5, b)	5	0	1	3	3	3	4
(6, b)	2	0	0	0	1	2*	2*
(b, a)		0	1	3	4	5	6

(*) indicates that the flow in the corresponding arc is equal to its capacity and cannot be further increased.

The change from flow V to flow VI deserves to be followed carefully. The chain in V the flow through which has been modified is $(v_a, v_3, v_4, v_1, v_5, v_b)$. Starting with $W_1 = \{v_a\}$, v_3 can be transferred to W_1 by (i). There is no unsaturated arc going out from v_3, both (v_3, v_6) and (v_3, v_5) carrying capacity flows. But (v_4, v_3) is an arc such that $v_3 \in W_1$, $v_4 \in W_2$, and the flow in it is 2 which is greater than zero. Hence, by criterion (ii) if

$$(v_k, v_j)$$

is an arc u and $x_u > 0$, transfer v_k to W_1, v_4 is transferred to W_1. Again there is an arc (v_1, v_4) with $v_4 \in W_1$ and $v_1 \in W_2$ and with the flow in it greater than zero. So v_1 is also transferred to W_1 by criterion (ii). This time there is an arc (v_1, v_5) with $v_1 \in W_1$, $v_5 \in W_2$ with flow 2 in it which is less than its capacity 4. Consequently, by criterion (i), v_5 is transferred to W_1, and finally, by the same criterion, v_b is transferred to W_1. So the flow is not optimal. In this chain arcs (v_4, v_3) and (v_1, v_4) occur in reverse directions. Reduce flows in them by 1 and increase flows in other arcs of the chain by 1 thereby saturating the arc (v_a, v_3).

The iterations stop at this stage because v_b cannot be brought into W_1. In fact one cannot even proceed one step from the initial position of W_1 containing only one point v_a. This is so because the arcs going out from v_a are all saturated and so neither v_1 nor v_2 nor v_3 can be brought in W_1. The maximum flow in the graph is 6.

• PROBLEM 8-20

Determine the maximal flow through the network in Figure 1.

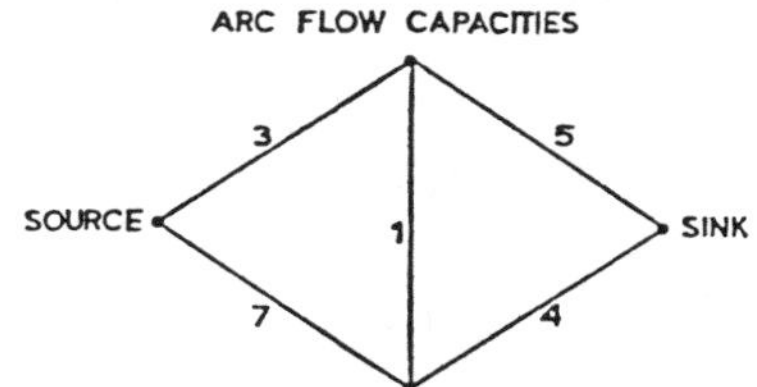

Fig. 1

Solution: There are four cuts, of which the values are

3			+ 7		= 10
	5			+ 4	= 9
3		+ 1		+ 4	= 8
	5	+ 1	+ 7		= 13

The minimal cut is, therefore, 8. The maximal flow is obtained by saturating the arcs concerned, with other arcs flowing at less than full capacity. In this problem there is only one way of getting maximal flow, and this is shown in Figure 2.

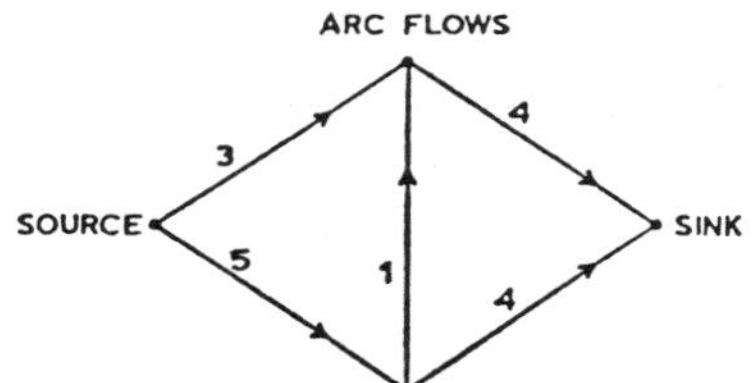

Fig. 2

• PROBLEM 8-21

Consider the network in Figure 1.

Let the capacities of the various arcs be as shown: e.g.,

$c(s,2) = 5$; $c(2,5) = 6$, etc.

Notice that the network is undirected. The problem is to determine the maximal flow between $\underline{s}$ and $\underline{t}$, assuming infinite availability at $\underline{s}$.

Determine the maximal flow between $\underline{s}$ and $\underline{t}$ by the labeling procedure due to Ford and Fulkerson.

Solution: To start the procedure, assume any reasonable flow $\{f(i,j)\} \geq 0$. There is no question of feasibility, since $f(i,j) = 0$ for all (i,j) is certainly feasible. But one can usually do better than that. Start with the

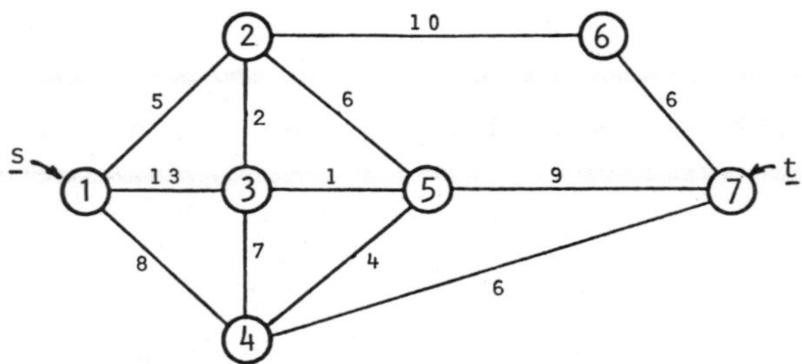

Fig. 1

flow shown in Fig. 2. Each arc carries two numbers (f,r), where f is the flow through the arc, $f(i,j) \leq c(i,j)$, and r is the residual capacity $r(i,j) = c(i,j) - f(i,j) \geq 0$. Notice that branches (s,2), (s,4), (3,5) and (4,t) are saturated, since r = 0 in all of them.

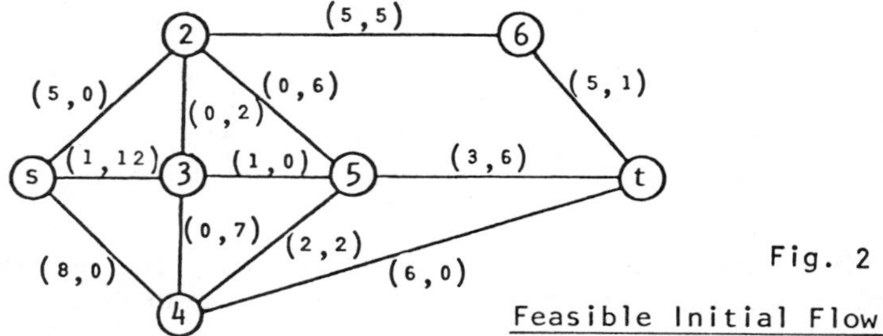

Fig. 2

Feasible Initial Flow

Inspection of Fig. 2 reveals that 12 more units can be transferred from s (which is assumed of infinite availability) to 3 because of the available residual capacity in arc (s,3). This is recorded by labeling node 3 with (12;s) in Figure 3: the first entry gives the quantity that can be transmitted and the second entry the origin of such flow.

When 12 units are available at node 3, it is obvious that two units and no more, due to the capacity of branch (3,2), can be transmitted to node 2 and seven units to node 4. Thus, nodes 2 and 4 can be labeled with (2;3) and (7;3) respectively. Thus, in labeling node j from node 3, j = 2 or 4, the flow is the minimum of two numbers. q_3, the quantity made available at node 3 by previously determined labeling, and r(3,j), the residual capacity in branch (3,j). In general, if node j connects with node i, then node j can be labeled as (q_j, i), where

$$q_j = \min\,[q_i; r(i,j)] \quad \text{if } r(i,j) > 0. \qquad (1)$$

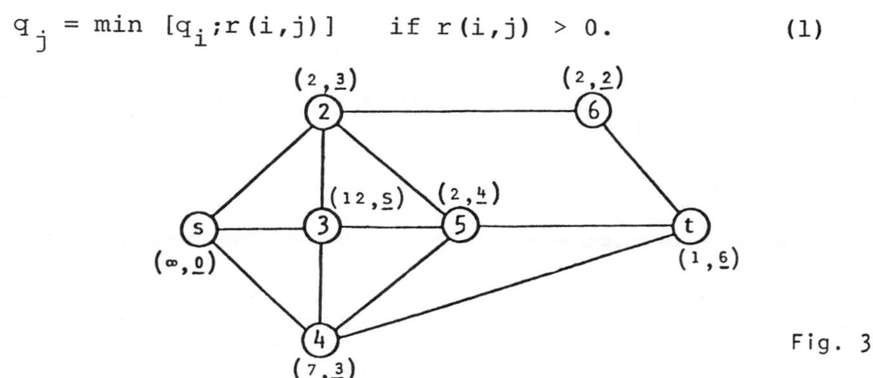

Fig. 3

Naturally, if $r(i,j) = 0$, node j cannot be labeled from node i. Proceeding in this fashion, the complete labeling of Fig. 2 is accomplished, as shown in Fig. 3. It is advisable to proceed in a systematic way such as: at stage k always start with the node bearing the smallest (or largest) number, label all nodes that connect with it which can be labeled and have not been labeled before (following the rule of Eq. 1), then proceed to the next higher (or lower) numbered node and repeat the process until all labeled nodes in stage k are exhausted. Then move to stage k + 1, i.e., to the nodes that have just been labeled from stage k. Once a node is labeled, it is not considered again for labeling.

One of two conditions must be obtained:

1. The terminal t is labeled.

2. The terminal t cannot be labeled.

When the terminal node t is labeled, which is termed a "breakthrough," the flow can be increased by the amount q_t. Tracing backwards from t the chain that leads to such extra flow can be determined. The flow and residual capacities are then adjusted to reflect the increased flow, q_t, along all the branches of the chain.

The cycle of labeling and increasing the flow continues until no breakthrough is possible, i.e., until t cannot be labeled. This stage is reached in Fig. 4c: nodes 3 and 4 are labeled but no other node can be labeled. The maximum flow has been achieved and is equal to the sum of the flow in all branches incident on either s or t; it is equal to 18 units.

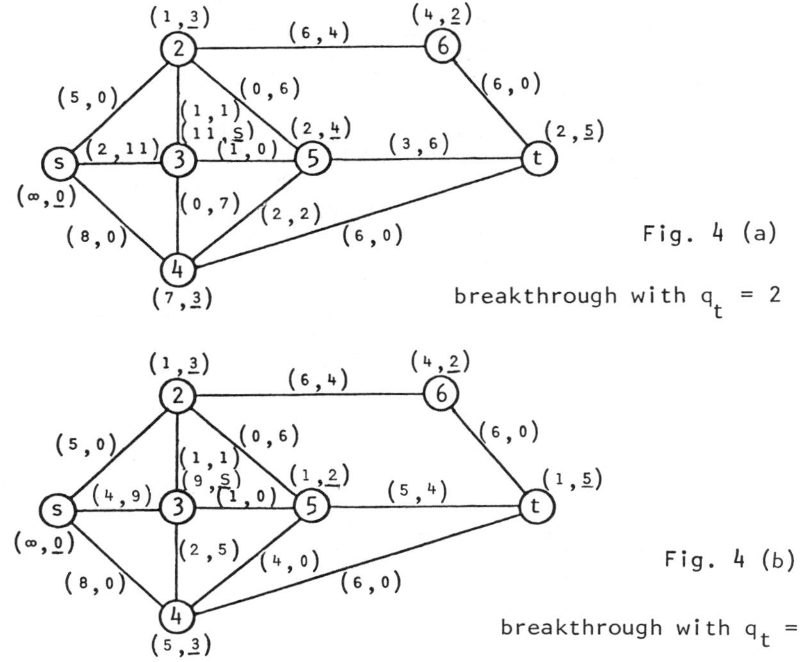

Fig. 4 (a)

breakthrough with $q_t = 2$

Fig. 4 (b)

breakthrough with $q_t = 1$

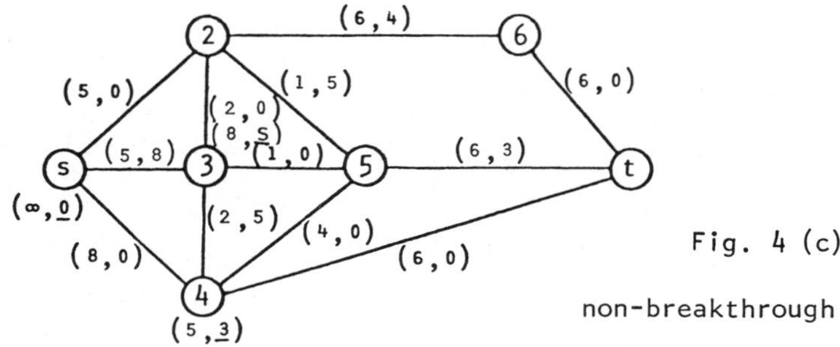

Fig. 4 (c)

non-breakthrough

Consider Fig. 4c for a minute. Node 5 cannot be labeled in spite of the availability of an infinite supply at s, of 8 units at node 3 and 5 units at node 4, because, in a manner of speaking, all "roads are blocked" thereafter. That is, the residual capacities are all equal to zero for all arcs leading from these three nodes. It is an interesting observation that the capacities of these "blocked" branches add up to exactly 18 units, the total flow between s and t.

• PROBLEM 8-22

Consider the network shown in Fig. 1. The problem is to maximize the flow from node 1 to node 6 given the capacities shown on the arcs. Solve by Ford and Fulkerson algorithm.

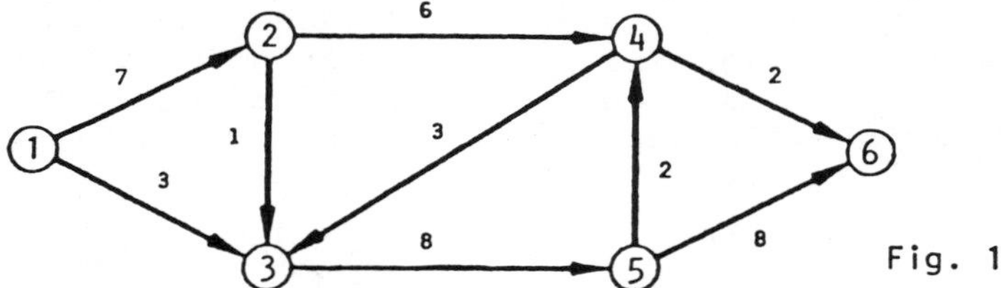

Fig. 1

Solution: An algorithm to find maximal flow is:

Step 1: Label node 1 with (+0,M). +0 indicates there is no predecessor node and M indicates an unlimited supply of additional flow. Node 1 is labeled and unscanned, all other nodes are unlabeled. The initial flow v can be any easily determined amount or zero.

Step 2: Select a labeled and unscanned node, say node i. If all nodes are either labeled and scanned or unlabeled, the current solution is optimal; stop. Otherwise, go to Step 3.

Step 3: Suppose node i is labeled $(\pm k, y_i)$. Then for each unlabeled node j for which an arc (i,j) exists with $x_{i,j} < b_{i,j}$, where $b_{i,j}$ is the capacity of the arc from i to j, $x_{i,j}$ is the initial flow between i and j, assign the label $(+i, y_i)$ to node j, where

y_j is the minimum of $b_{i,j} - x_{i,j}$ and y_i; for each unlabeled node j for which an arc (j,i) exists with $x_{j,i} > 0$, assign the label $(-i, y_j)$ to node j, where y_j is the minimum of $x_{j,i}$ and y_i.

Node i is now scanned; node j is labeled and unscanned.

Step 4: If node n (the destination node) is labeled go to step 5. If node n is unlabeled, go to step 2.

Step 5: Increase the value of the flow by y_n. This is accomplished by using the first component of the labels to go from node n back to node 1. For each arc on the route traced, add y_n to the arc flow when the first component (of the label) is positive and subtract y_n from the arc flow when the first component is negative. Erase all labels and go to step 1.

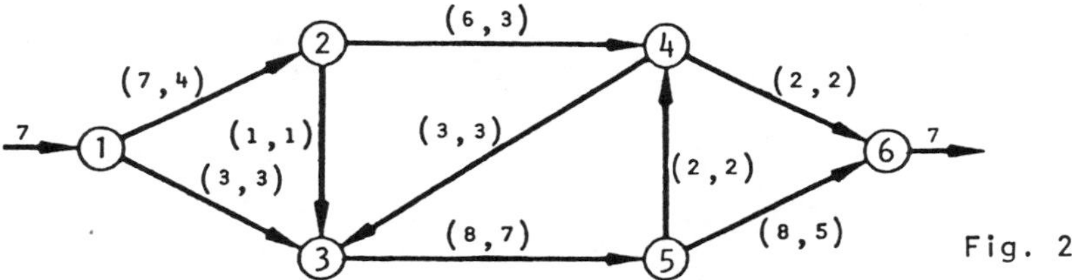

Fig. 2

Assume the initial flow shown in Fig. 2. The numbers on the arcs are (capacity, flow). The value of the initial flow is 7 units.

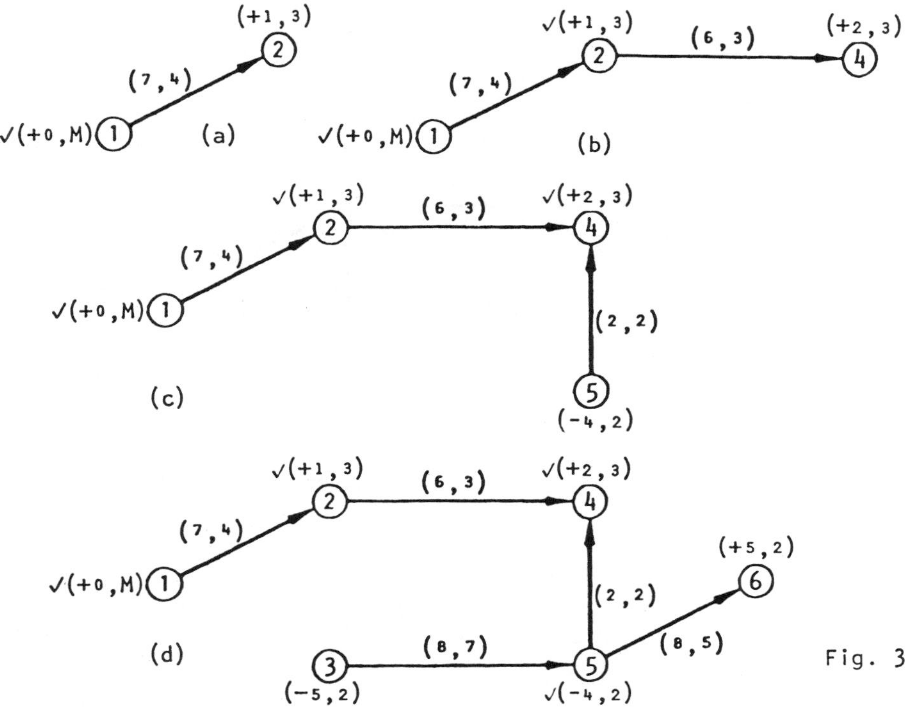

Fig. 3

Step 1: Label node 1 with (+0,M). Node 1 is unscanned, and all other nodes are unlabeled.

Steps 2 and 3: Select node 1. Since $x_{1,2} = 4 < b_{1,2} = 7$, one can label node 2 with (+1,3). See Fig. 3a. Use a check to indicate that node 1 is scanned.

Steps 4,2,3: Node 6 is not labeled, so select node 2. Since $x_{2,4} = 3 < b_{2,4} = 6$, one can label node 4 with (+2,3). Node 2 is now scanned. See Fig. 3b.

Steps 4,2,3: Node 6 is not labeled, so select node 4. Since $x_{5,4} = 2 > 0$, one can label node 5 with (-4,2) (here $x_{ji} = x_{5,4} = 2$ is less than $y_4 = 3$). Node 4 is now scanned. See Fig. 3c.

Steps 4,2,3: Node 6 is not labeled, so select node 5, Since $x_{3,5} = 7 > 0$, one can label node 3 with (-5,2) (here $x_{3,5} = 7$ is greater than $y_5 = 2$). Also, since $x_{5,6} = 5 < b_{5,6} = 8$, one can label node 6 with (+5,2). Node 5 is now scanned. See Fig. 3d.

Steps 4 and 5: Node 6 is labeled, so breakthrough has occurred. Since $y_6 = 2$, one can increase the flow through the network by 2 units as follows. Add 2 units to $x_{5,6}$, subtract 2 units from $x_{5,4}$, add 2 units to $x_{2,4}$, and add 2 units to $x_{1,2}$. The resulting flows are shown in Fig. 4.

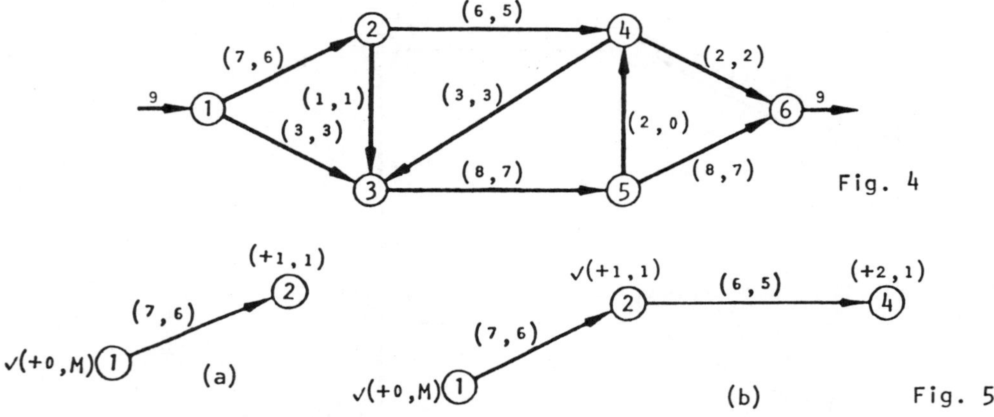

Fig. 4

Fig. 5

Steps 1,2,3: Starting again, label node 1 with (+0,M). Scanning from node 1, see that $x_{1,2} = 6 < b_{1,2} = 7$, so one can label node 2 with (+1,1). Node 1 is scanned. See Fig. 5a.

Steps 4,2,3: Node 6 is not labeled, so select node 2. $x_{2,4} = 5 < b_{2,4} = 6$, so one can label node 4 with (+2,1).

Node 2 is scanned. See Fig. 5b.

Steps 4,2,3: Node 6 is not labeled, so select node 4. Note that $x_{4,3} = 3 = b_{4,3}$ and $x_{4,6} = 2 = b_{4,6}$ and $x_{5,4} = 0$, so that one cannot label from node 4. Node 4 is scanned.

Steps 4 and 2: Node 6 is not labeled. However, all nodes are either labeled and scanned (nodes 1, 2, and 4) or unlabeled, so that current flows are optimal. Thus, the flows shown in Fig. 4 are optimal. The value of the maximal flow is 9 units.

• PROBLEM 8-23

Find the net flow of the pipeline problem. In Figure 1 the excess capacities for an initial flow of zero are shown on each line.

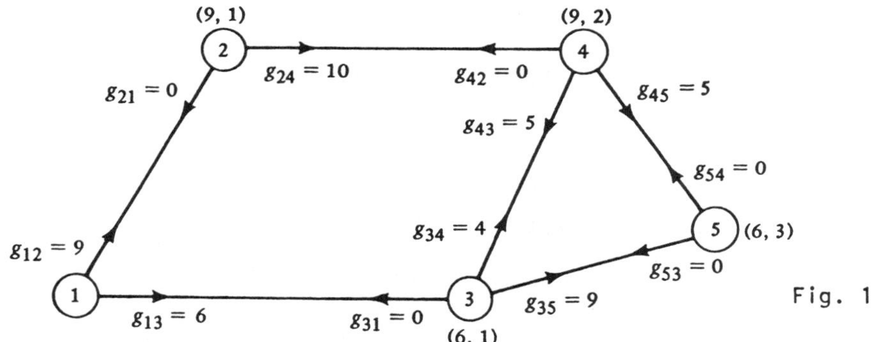

Fig. 1

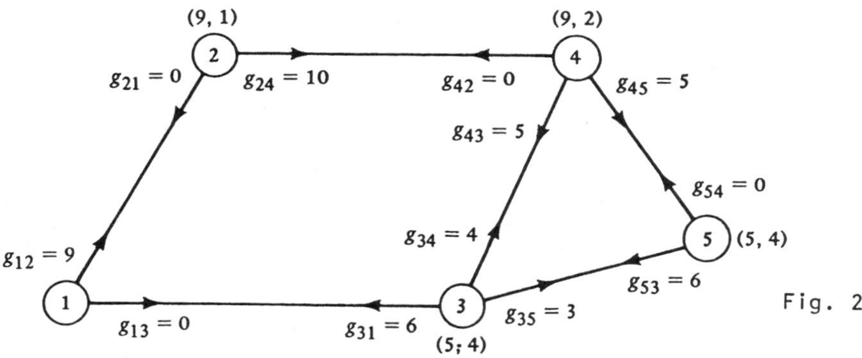

Fig. 2

Solution: Starting at node 1 note that $g_{12} = 9 > 0$. So node 2 is labeled ($\delta_2 = 9$, $\gamma_2 = 1$). Similarly $g_{13} = 6 > 0$, and node 3 is labeled (6,1). Now proceed to the next labled node in ascending numerical order. This is node 2. Since $g_{24} = 10 > 0$, label node 4. The value of δ_4 is found that δ_4 = minimum (9,10) = 9, and $\gamma_4 = 2$. No other nodes can be labeled from node 2. Proceeding to node 3, find

$g_{34} = 4 > 0$, and $g_{35} = 9 > 0$. But since node 4 is already labeled, it cannot be labeled again. Thus, only node 5 can be labeled from node 3, with δ_5 = minimum (6,9) = 6, and $\gamma_5 = 3$. The sink is labeled now and one can find the feasible path by tracing back from node 5. From $\gamma_5 = 3$, note that the prior node in the path is node 3. From $\gamma_3 = 1$, notice that the node prior to node 3 is node 1, the source. So the feasible path is $(1\rightarrow3)$, $(3\rightarrow5)$. The increase in flow through the network is $\delta_5 = 6$.

To find a new flow through the network and the corresponding excess capacities, use the expressions

1) $D\hat{x}_{ij} = x_{ij} + \delta_N$,

2) $\hat{x}_{ij} = x_{ij}$

From 1) obtain $\hat{x}_{13} = 0 + 6 = 6$,

and

$$\hat{x}_{35} = 0 + 6 = 6.$$

From expression 2), obtain

$$\hat{x}_{12} = 0,\ \hat{x}_{24} = 0,\ \hat{x}_{34} = 0,\ \hat{x}_{42} = 0,\ \hat{x}_{43} = 0$$

and

$$\hat{x}_{45} = 0.$$

Since no flow can go into the source, or out of the sink, x_{21}, x_{31}, x_{53} and x_{54} are always zero (they can be ignored). The new flows or updated solution is obtained:

$$x_{12} = 0 \qquad x_{24} = 0 \qquad x_{35} = 6 \qquad x_{43} = 0$$

$$x_{13} = 6 \qquad x_{34} = 0 \qquad x_{42} = 0 \qquad x_{45} = 0.$$

Since $\hat{z} = z + \delta_N$

then

$$\hat{z} = 0 + 6 = 6$$

is the total flow through the network. Expressions 1) and 2) also enable us to update the excess capacities. For instance, from

$$\hat{g}_{13} = 6 - 6 = 0,$$

$$\hat{g}_{31} = 0 + 6 = 6, \text{ etc.},$$

and from 2)

$$\hat{g}_{12} = 9,$$

$$\hat{g}_{21} = 0, \text{ etc.}$$

The whole set of new excess capacities is shown in Figure 2.

At the second iteration, node 3 cannot be labeled from node 1, since $g_{13} = 0$. The labeling technique finds a path through node 2, allowing us to label the sink.

The increase in the flow is $\delta_5 = 5$, and the feasible path is (1→2), (2→4), (4→5). From 1), 2) and

3) $\hat{z} = z + \delta_N$,

$\hat{x}_{12} = 0 + \delta_5 = 5$

$\hat{x}_{24} = 0 + \delta_5 = 5$

$\hat{x}_{35} = 6$

$\hat{x}_{43} = 0$

$\hat{x}_{13} = 6$

$\hat{x}_{34} = 0$

$\hat{x}_{42} = 0$

$\hat{x}_{45} = 0 + \delta_5 = 5$

and

$\hat{z} = 6 + \delta_5 = 11$

The updated excess capacities are given in Figure 3.

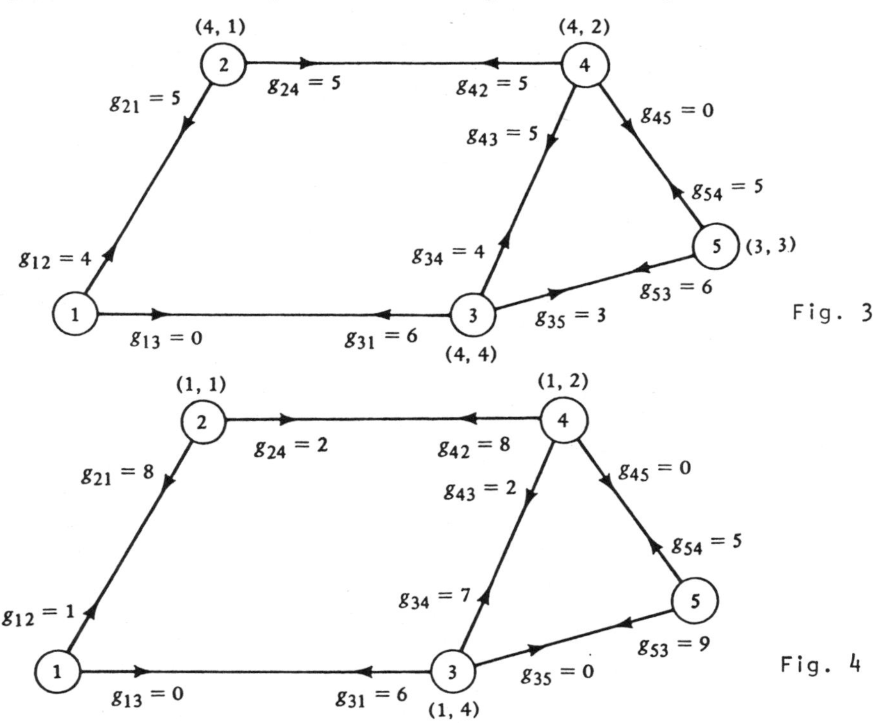

Fig. 3

Fig. 4

The third iteration yields the feasible path (1→2), (2→3), (4→3), (3→5), with $\delta_5 = 3$. By 1), 2) and 3), the new flows are

$\hat{x}_{12} = 8$ $\hat{x}_{24} = 8$ $\hat{x}_{35} = 9$ $\hat{x}_{43} = 3$

$\hat{x}_{13} = 6$ $\hat{x}_{34} = 0$ $\hat{x}_{42} = 0$ $\hat{x}_{45} = 5$

$$\hat{z} = 11 + \delta_5 = 14. \tag{4}$$

At the fourth iteration note from Figure 4 that nodes 2, 3, and 4, can be labeled but not the sink. So there does not exist another feasible path through this network. The solution given by (4) is thus the optimal flow.

• PROBLEM 8-24

The problem facing the Kughulu Park management during the peak season is to determine how to route the various tram trips from the park entrance (station O in Fig. 1) to the scenic wonder (station T) to maximize the number of trips per day. Strict upper limits have been imposed on the number of outgoing trips allowed in each direction on each individual road. These limits are shown in Fig. 1, where the number next to each station and road gives the limit for that road in the direction leading away from that station. Find the route maximizing the number of trips made per day.

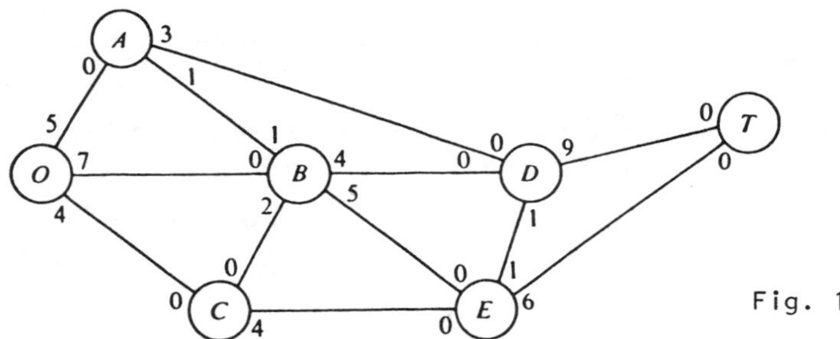

Fig. 1

Solution: Iteration 1:

Assign flow of 5 to O→B→E→T. The resulting network is

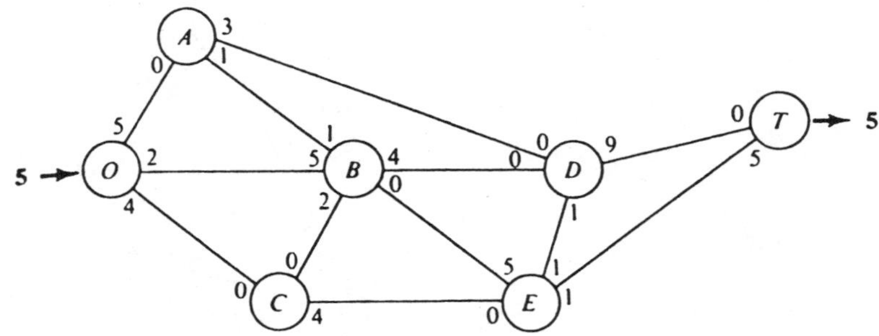

Iteration 2:

Assign flow of 3 to O→A→D→T. The resulting network is

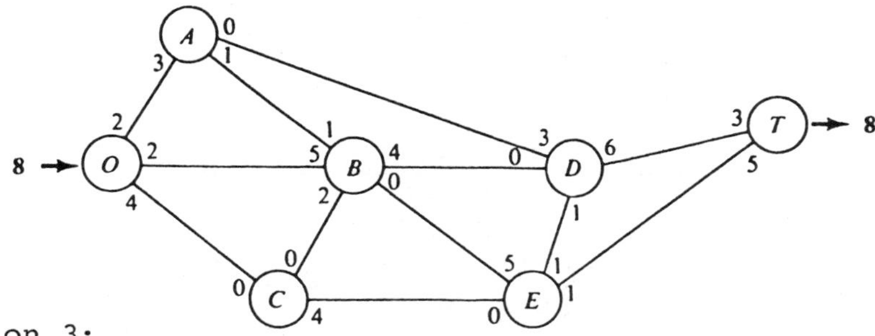

Iteration 3:

Assign flow of 1 to O→A→B→D→T.

Iteration 4:

Assign flow of 2 to O→B→D→T. The resulting network is

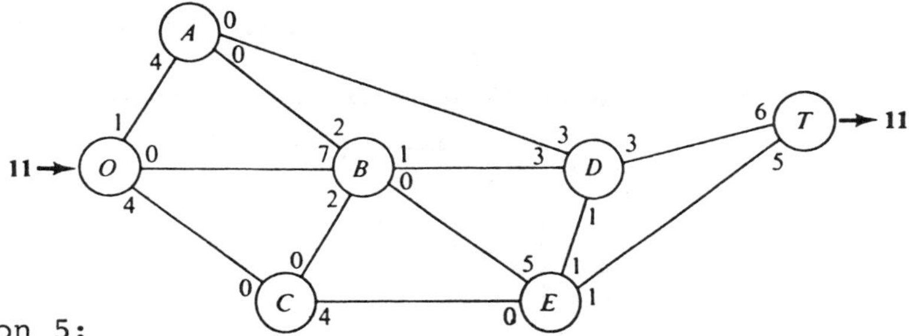

Iteration 5:

Assign flow of 1 to O→C→E→D→T.

Iteration 6:

Assign flow of 1 to O→C→E→T. The resulting network is

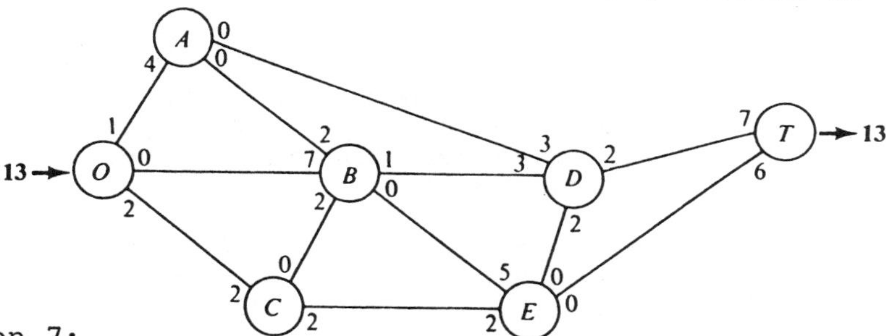

Iteration 7:

Assign flow of 1 to O→C→E→B→D→T. The resulting network is

No paths with strictly positive flow capacity remain.
The current flow pattern is optimal.

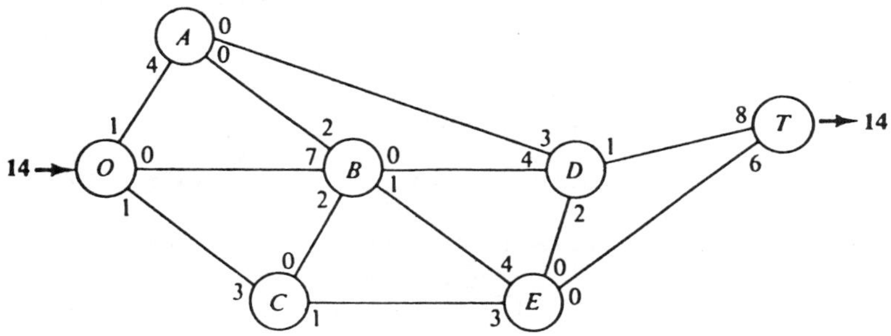

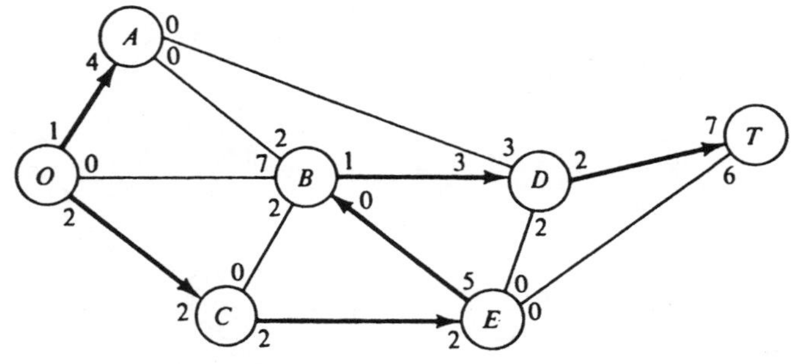

Optimal Route

• PROBLEM 8-25

Find the maximal flow between every pair of nodes in the network below, using the procedure of Gomory and Hu.

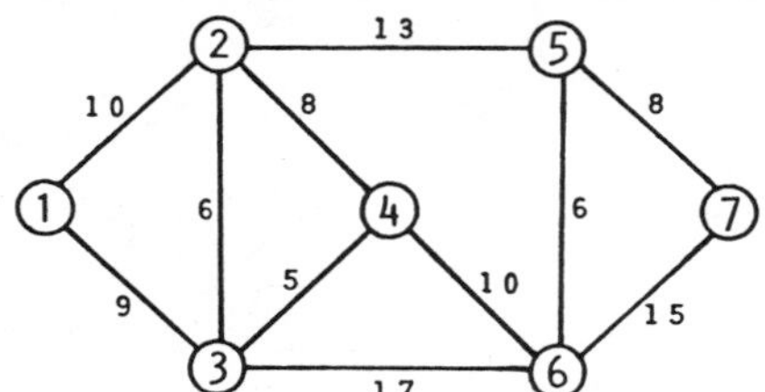

Fig. 1

Solution: The procedure according to Gomory and Hu requires the solution of only n-1 maximal flow problems. It rests on two fundamental, though essentially simple, ideas.

A spanning tree of a connected undirected network G is a connected subgraph of G which contains the same nodes as G but contains no loops. It is easy to prove, e.g., by induction, that a tree contains exactly n-1 arcs, where n is the number of nodes of G.

In general, a graph, connected or not, without cycles, is called a forest; each connected piece of a forest is clearly a tree. Finally, let c(i,j) denote the capacity of the arc between i and j, and for any source-terminal pair (s,t), let v(s,t) denote the value of the maximal flow between s and t. Such maximal flow can be determined by any well known approach.

The two fundamental concepts mentioned above are:

The first is a form of triangular inequality:

$$v(s,t) \geq \min\, [v(s,x),\ v(x,t)];\quad s,x,t \in N. \tag{1}$$

The proof of this inequality relies on the maximum-flow minimum-cut theorem. For, in determining maximum flow between s and t a cut-set $C(\underline{X},\bar{X})$ must be obtained, with $s \varepsilon X$ and $t \in \bar{X}$, such that $c(\underline{X},\bar{X}) = v(s,t)$. Clearly, if $x \in X$, then $v(x,t)$ must be $< c(X,\bar{X})$; on the other hand, if $x \in \bar{X}$, then $v(s,x)$ must be $\leq c(X,\bar{X})$; and the inequality (1) follows. Simple as this inequality may seem, its consequences are far reaching. By simple induction one gets

$$v(s,t) \geq \min [v(s,x_1), v(x_1,x_2), \ldots, v(x_r,t)], \quad (2)$$

where

$$x_1, x_2, \ldots, x_r$$

are any sequence of nodes in N. Furthermore, if the network consists only of three nodes, $\underline{s}$, x, and $\underline{t}$ and only three arcs, then applying (1) to each 'side of the triangle' shows that, among the three maximum flow values appearing in (1), two must be equal and the third no smaller than their common value. As a further consequence of (1) (or (2)) it must be true that in a network of n nodes, the function v can have at most n-1 numerically distinct values.

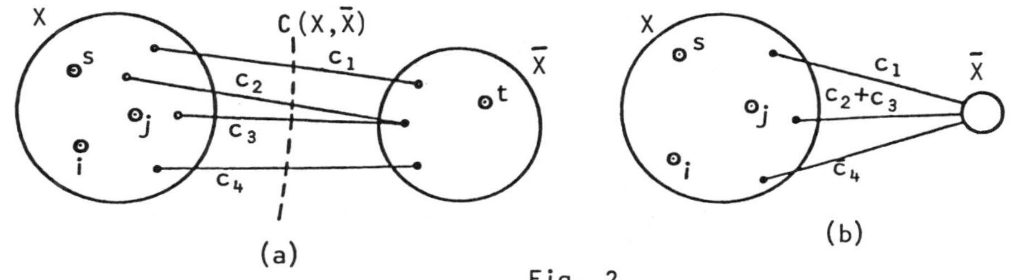

Fig. 2

The second fundamental concept is a 'condensation property'. Suppose that with $\underline{s}$ as source and $\underline{t}$ as sink a maximal flow problem has been solved, thereby locating a minimal cut $C(X,\bar{X})$ with $s \in X$ and $t \in \bar{X}$, see Fig. 2a. Suppose now that it is desired to find $v(i,j)$ where both i and j are on the same side of $C(X,\bar{X})$; say both are in X, as

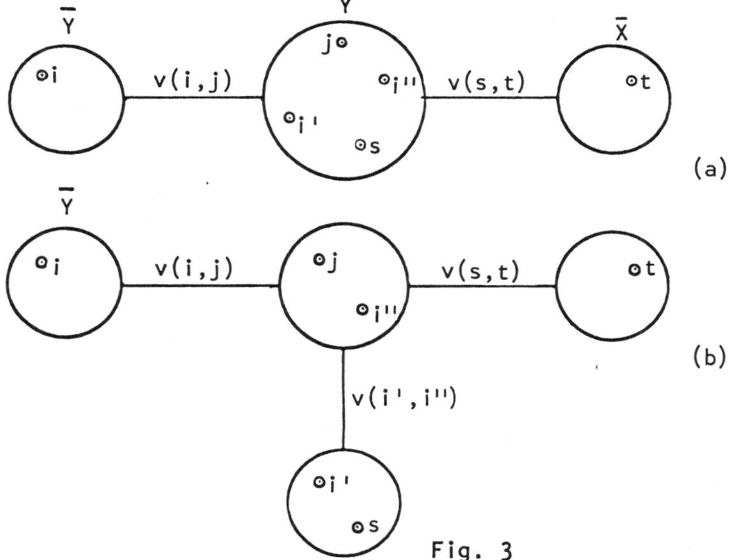

Fig. 3

shown in Fig. 2a. Then for this purpose, all nodes of $\bar{X}$ can be 'condensed' into a single node to which all the arcs of the minimal cut are attached. The resulting network is a condensed network, as shown in Fig. 2b. In a sense, one may think of the condensed network as having accorded an infinite capacity to the arcs joining all pairs of nodes of $\bar{X}$.

The statement is certainly plausible. The formal proof involves the demonstration that all the nodes of $\bar{X}$ must lie on one side of the cut-set between i and j. Consequently, the condensation of all the nodes in $\bar{X}$ cannot affect the value of the maximum flow from i to j.

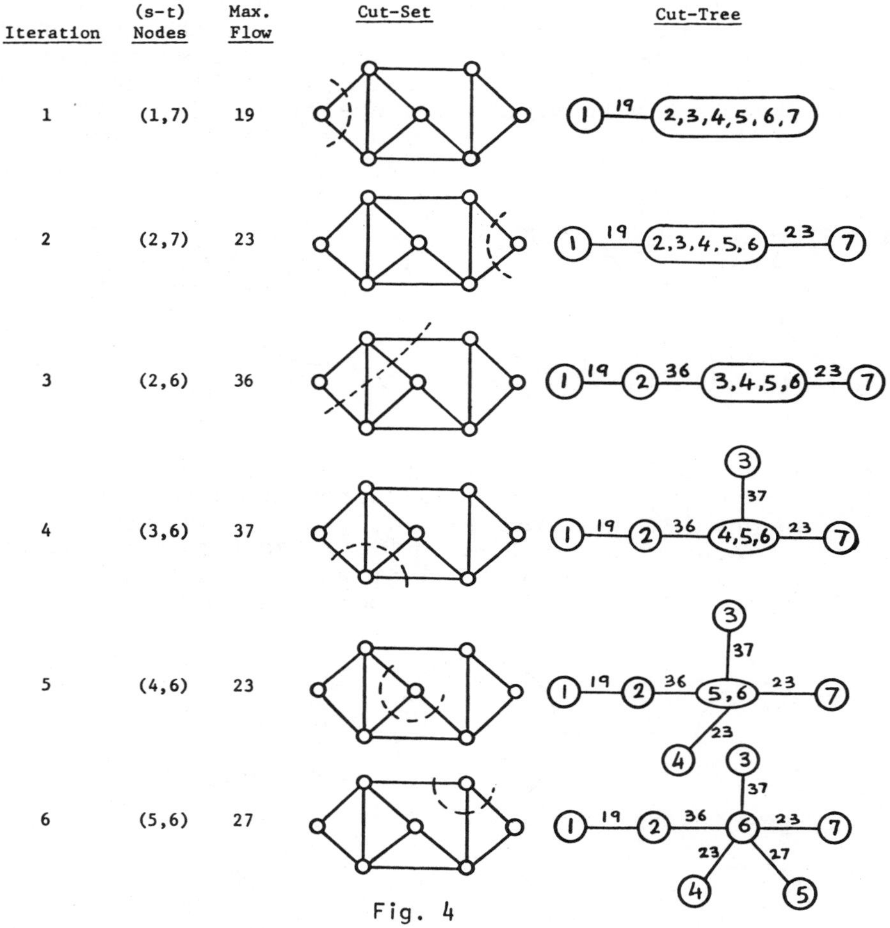

Iteration	(s-t) Nodes	Max. Flow	Cut-Set	Cut-Tree
1	(1,7)	19		1 —19— (2,3,4,5,6,7)
2	(2,7)	23		1 —19— (2,3,4,5,6) —23— 7
3	(2,6)	36		1 —19— 2 —36— (3,4,5,6) —23— 7
4	(3,6)	37		1 —19— 2 —36— (4,5,6) —23— 7; 3 —37— (4,5,6)
5	(4,6)	23		1 —19— 2 —36— (5,6) —23— 7; 3 —37— (5,6); 4 —23— (5,6)
6	(5,6)	27		1 —19— 2 —36— 6 —23— 7; 3 —37— 6; 4 —23— 6; 5 —27— 6

Fig. 4

The Gomory-Hu construction exploits this second property to the extreme. Suppose that after choosing i, j ∈ X as the new source-terminal pair (i or j may be s), the maximal flow v(i,j) and the minimal cut-set $C(Y,\bar{Y})$ between i and j are determined by the standard labeling procedure with all the nodes of the subset $\bar{X}$ condensed into one node. Notice that $\bar{X}$ is on one side of the new cut-set, see Fig. 3a. Next choose two nodes i', i" ∈ Y, say; condense all the nodes in $\bar{X}$ and $\bar{Y}$ to one node each and repeat the maximal flow determination. Continue until each condensed subset contains only one node. Obviously, this requires exactly n-1 maximal flow calculations. Moreover, the resultant is a tree which is called the cut-tree R.

The steps of iteration, the minimal cut-set at each iteration , and the final cut-tree R for network in Fig. 1 are shown in Fig. 4, steps (1) to (6).

Notice that each arc of R represents a cut-set in G, and the number $v(\tau)$ attached to the τth arc of the cut-tree is the capacity of the corresponding cut-set in G.

The remarkable conclusion is that this cut-tree gives the maximal flow between any pair of nodes.

CRITICAL PATH, CPM, PERT

• PROBLEM 8-26

A building activity has been analyzed as follows. v_j stands for a job.

(i) v_1 and v_2 can start simultaneously, each one taking 10 days to finish.

(ii) v_3 can start after 5 days and v_4 after 4 days of starting v_1.

(iii) v_4 can start after 3 days of work on v_3 and 6 days of work on v_2.

(iv) v_5 can start after v_1 is finished and v_2 is half done.

(v) v_3, v_4 and v_5 take respectively 6, 8 and 12 days to finish. Find the critical path and the minimum time for completion.

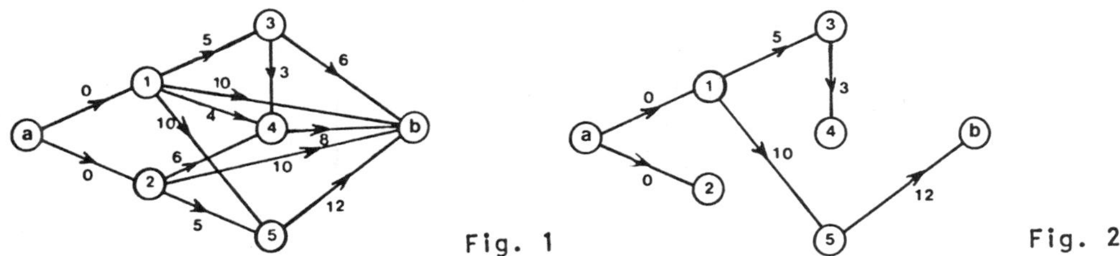

Fig. 1

Fig. 2

Solution: Figure 1 is the graph of the activity, vertices v_a and v_b representing the start and the finish, and the other vertices the jobs to be done in between. The arc lengths denote the time between the start of two jobs.

The aborescence giving the maximum path is shown in figure 2. The critical path is (v_a, v_1, v_5, v_b) of length 22 days which is the minimum time of completion of the work.

• PROBLEM 8-27

Give the earliest and latest occurrence times of each event (A,B ..., H) and the critical path.

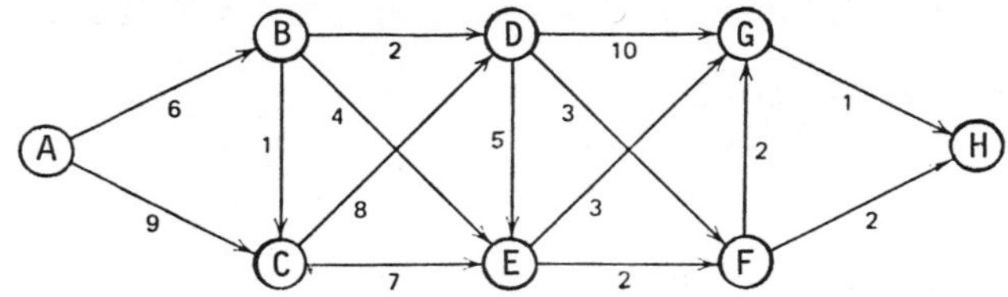

Solution:

Earliest times:

A	B	C	D	E	F	G	H
0	6	9	17	22	24	27	28

Latest times:

0	8	9	17	23	25	27	28

The critical path is ACDGH.

• PROBLEM 8-28

Find the critical path in Figure 1.

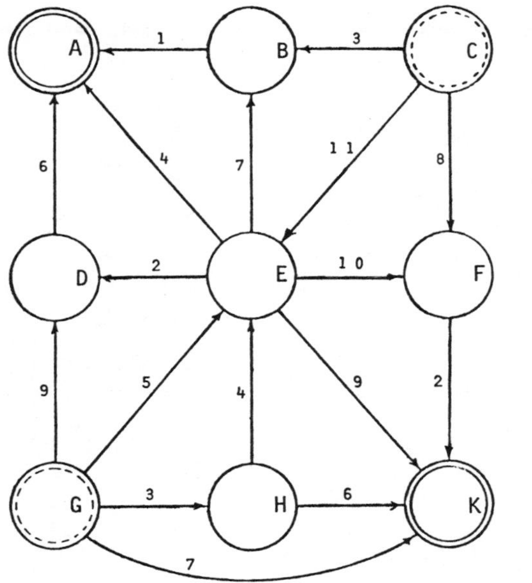

Acyclic network in which C and G are start events and A and K are end events.

Solution: c_{ij}, s_i, t_i stand for: duration of activity between i and j, earliest time event i can occur and latest time of event i, respectively. The algorithm used for finding the critical path is as follows:

1. Index the nodes C = 1, G = 2, etc.

2. Let s_1 and $S_C = 0$.

   Let $t^* = \max s_i$ after using

$$s_j = \max_{i<j} \{s_i + c_{ij}, 0\} \quad \text{for} \quad j = 2,3,\ldots,p.$$

For example, $s_8 = s_A = \max (1 + 18, 6 + 13, 4 + 11, 0) = 19$.

3. Let

$$t_p = t_K = t^* = 23$$

and use

$$t_i = \min_{j>i} \{t_j - c_{ij}, t^*\} \qquad \text{for } i = p - 1,\ldots,2,1.$$

Thus

$$t_2 = t_G = \min (17-9, 11-5, 7-3, 23-7, 23) = 4.$$

4. The set Z of critical nodes is $\{i: s_i = t_i\} = \{C,E,F,K\}$.

5. Critical arcs (i,j) have $i \in z$, $j \in z$, $t_j = s_i + c_{ij}$.

   CE, EF, FK are critical; thus the critical path is CEFK.

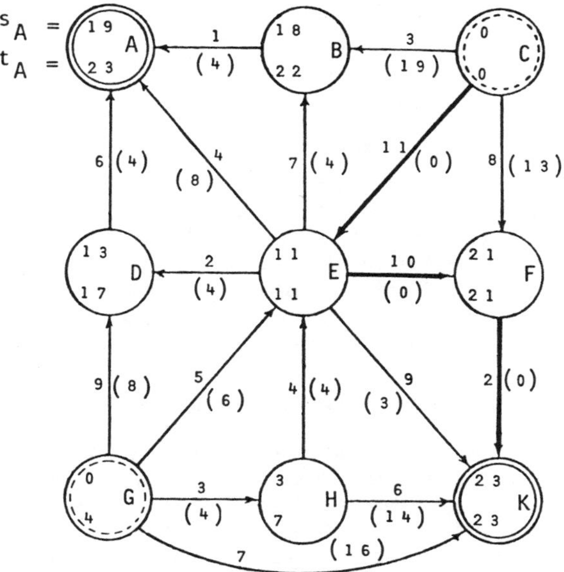

Fig. 2

Critical path CEFK in an acyclic network. Earliest times s_i in order CG,H,E,BDF, AK; then the latest times t_j in the reverse order. Start with $s_C = s_G = 0$, $s_H = 3 + 0$, $s_E = \max(11 + 0, 5 + 0, 4+3) = 11, \ldots, t_A = t_K = t^* = 23$, $t_F = 23 - 2, \ldots, t_H = \min(11 - 4, 23 - 6) = 7, \ldots$ ..The value of the total float $t_j - s_i - c_{ij}$ is in parentheses; it is zero if and only if the arc is critical.

The critical path, earliest times and latest times for each node are demonstrated in Figure 2.

• PROBLEM 8-29

Consider the problem of scheduling a fleet of vehicles to accomplish the shipment of some commodity from supply points to a series of demand points. It is required to know the smallest size and required routing of a fleet of tankers to achieve a prescribed set of deliveries.

There are the shipments shown in Table 1. The commodity shipped must be picked up on the day shown and delivered (unloaded) on the delivery day shown. Because of contractual requirements, the shipments must adhere exactly to the dates. The profits shown are the net of revenues and operating costs. However, there is an additional fixed cost of 4 for bringing a ship into the fleet (only one payment is required no matter how many trips are made).

The transit times (including loading and unloading times) are

From \ To	C	D
A	3	2
B	2	3

The return times (no cargo) are:

From \ To	A	B
C	2	1
D	1	2

The problem is to determine which shipments to make and how many ships to use so as to maximize profits. Thus, construct a network flow diagram with nodes representing specific time and place, which shows all the possibilities of combinations of routes to get the whole job done. Can you suggest different alternatives of fleet sizes-shipments' combinations which will give the most profit?

Solution: By using a network model in which the nodes represent a specific time and place. See Fig. 1. A single source S and a single sink T are shown. The fixed cost of 4 is incurred on each arc leaving the source. The shipments are represented by the heavy arcs. When a ship can return from a delivery in time to make another one, a solid arc is shown. Thus, go from port C on day 3 to port B on day 4 (that is, from shipment 1 to shipment 4). Note, however, that it is impossible to go from port D on day 3 to port B on day 4, so no line is drawn from shipment 3 to shipment 4. Finally, all arcs have unlimited capacities with the exception of the shipment arcs which each have a capacity of 1.

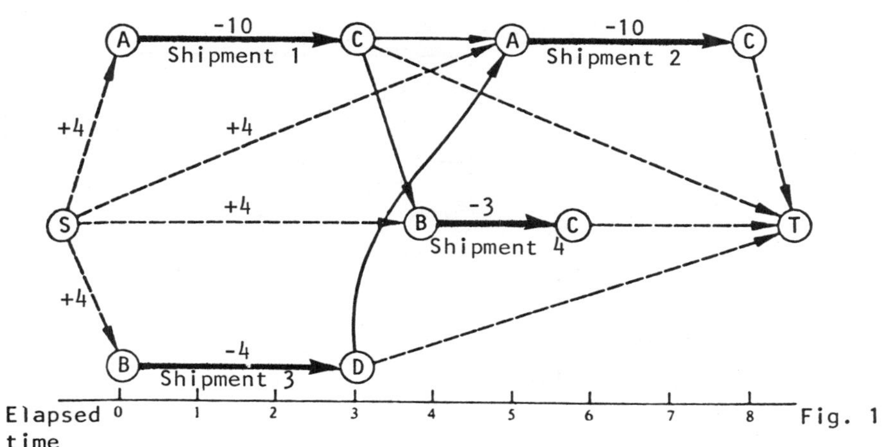

Fig. 1

Tanker scheduling, shipments

Shipment	Origin	Destination	Delivery date	Profit
1	Port A	Port C	3	10
2	Port A	Port C	8	10
3	Port B	Port D	3	4
4	Port B	Port C	6	3

Table 1

Cost of flow as related to fleet size in the tanker scheduling problem

Fleet size	Shipments	Profit
1	1,2	16
2	Ship 1:1,4	9
	Ship 2:3,2	10
		19

Table 2

The problem is to minimize the cost of flow through the network. This can be done for a fixed fleet size, or it can be solved parametrically as a function of fleet size. See the data in Table 2.

• **PROBLEM 8-30**

A maintenance schedule is being drawn up for the partial overhaul of a unit in an oil refinery, and the following list of jobs has been compiled:

Job ref.	Description	Duration hr
	No. 1 Cooler:	
A	Remove tube bundle from shell	16
B	Inspect and gauge shell	16
C	Clean tube bundle	8
D	Replace tube bundle	6
P	Test cooler	36
	No. 2 Cooler:	
E	Pressure test	16
Q	Replace piping after test	12
	Bottom inlets:	
F	Remove and repair	40
R	Re-install	8
	Heat Exchanger:	
H	Remove tube bundle from shell	16
K	Inspect and gauge shell	16
L	Fit replacement tubes to bundle	24
M	Replace tube bundle	8
S	Test and replace piping	16
	Miscellaneous:	
U	General preparation before any work begins	24
G	Regenerate catalyst	24
N	Test auxiliary piping	4
T	Clean up after all work has been completed	8

Work on the two coolers, the bottom inlets, the auxiliary piping and the heat exchanger can go on concurrently, but the last two items only must wait until the catalyst has been regenerated.

The tests must be carefully scheduled. No. 1 Cooler must not be tested until No. 2 has been found satisfactory, although there is no need to wait for the piping to be replaced on No. 2. The heat exchanger test cannot be done until the auxiliary piping has been tested. The shell of a unit cannot be inspected until the tube bundle has been taken out, and no unit can be tested until it has been reassembled.

Give the arrow diagram of the whole project (an arrow diagram represents the individual jobs and events in a project as arrows and nodes respectively. These symbols are arranged into a network according to their logical sequence and systematically labelled for subsequent analysis).

Find earliest start, latest start, earliest finish, latest finish, total and free float times for each job. Determine the critical path.

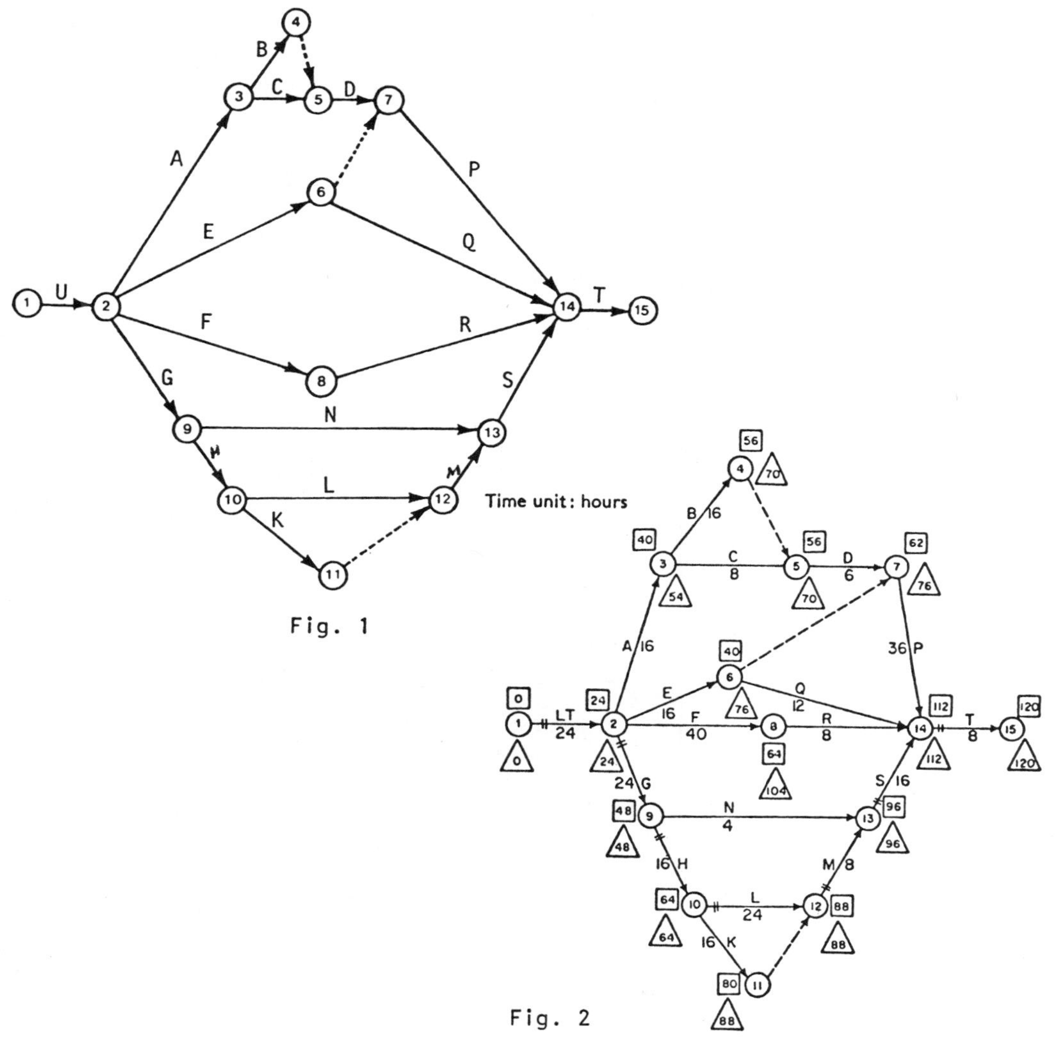

Fig. 1

Fig. 2

Maintenance of oil refinery: event times and critical path

Solution: The arrow diagram (network) for maintenance of an oil refinery is given in Fig. 1.

The required times and critical path are given in Table and Figure 2. In Fig. 2, numbers enclosed in squares give the earliest times for events, in triangles give the latest event times.

TABLE Schedule of Maintenance Project for an Oil Refinery

Events i	Events j	Job Code	Job Description	Duration hr	Earliest Start	Latest Start	Earliest Finish	Latest Finish	Critical Path	Float Total	Float Free
1	2	U	Lead time	24	0	0	24	24	*	0	0
2	3	A	Remove tube bundle	16	24	38	40	54		14	0
2	6	E	Pressure test	16	24	60	40	76		36	0
2	8	F	Remove bottom inlets	40	24	64	64	104		40	0
2	9	G	Regenerate catalyst	24	24	24	48	48	*	0	0
3	4	B	Inspect shell	16	40	54	56	70		14	0
3	5	C	Clean tube bundle	8	40	62	48	70		22	8
4	5		Dummy	0	56	70	56	70		14	0
5	7	D	Replace tube bundle	6	56	70	62	76		14	0
6	7		Dummy	0	40	76	40	76		36	22
6	14	Q	Replace piping	12	40	100	52	112		60	60
7	14	P	Test cooler	36	62	76	98	112		14	14
8	14	R	Re-install bottom inlets	8	64	104	72	112		40	40
9	10	H	Remove tube bundle	16	48	48	64	64	*	0	0
9	13	N	Test auxiliary piping	4	48	92	52	96		44	44
10	11	K	Inspect shell	16	64	72	80	88		8	0
10	12	L	Fit replacement tubes	24	64	64	88	88	*	0	0
11	12		Dummy	0	80	88	80	88		8	8
12	13	M	Replace tube bundle	8	88	88	96	96	*	0	0
13	14	S	Test and replace piping	16	96	96	112	112	*	0	0
14	15	T	Clear up site	8	112	112	120	120	*	0	0

• **PROBLEM 8-31**

Consider the activities in a project given in Table 1. Construct a project network. Find the earliest and latest occurrence times for each event. Find the critical path.

Assume the project has the most likely, optimistic, and pessimistic activity durations shown in columns (1), (2), and (3) respectively, of Table 2.

Compute activity duration means and variances. Applying central limit theorem, find mean and variance of total project duration, probability that the project requires less than 45 time periods, and a 95 percent confidence interval estimate of project completion time.

Table 1

Activity	Duration	Immediate Predecessor
(1, 2)	4	—
(2, 4)	7	(1, 2)
(2, 3)	8	(1, 2)
(2, 5)	6	(1, 2)
(4, 6)	15	(2, 4), (2, 3)
(3, 5)	9	(2, 3)
(5, 6)	12	(2, 5), (3, 5)
(6, 7)	8	(4, 6), (5, 6)

Table 2

ACTIVITY	(1) m_{ij}	(2) a_{ij}	(3) b_{ij}
(1, 2)	4	2	6
(2, 4)	7	4	10
(2, 3)	7	6	14
(2, 5)	6	3	9
(4, 6)	14	12	22
(3, 5)	10	2	12
(5, 6)	9	6	12
(6, 7)	7	5	15

Solution: The notation is as follows:

t_{ij} = duration for activity (i,j)

E_i = earliest occurrence time for event i

L_i = latest occurrence time for event i

$S_{i,j}$ = total slack or float for activity (i,j)

$$E_j = \max \{E_{i1} + t_{i1,j},\ E_{i2} + t_{i2,j},\ \ldots\ E_{in} + t_{in,j}\},\ j > 1 \qquad (1)$$

$$S_{i,j} = L_j - E_i - t_{ij}\ . \qquad (2)$$

The forward pass computations begins with $E_1 = 0$, and then

$E_2 = E_1 + t_{1,2} = 0 + 4 = 4$

$E_3 = E_2 + t_{2,3} = 4 + 8 = 12$

$E_4 = \max \{E_2 + t_{2,4},\ E_3 + t_{3,4}\} =$

$\max \{4 + 7,\ 12 + 0\} = 12$, etc.

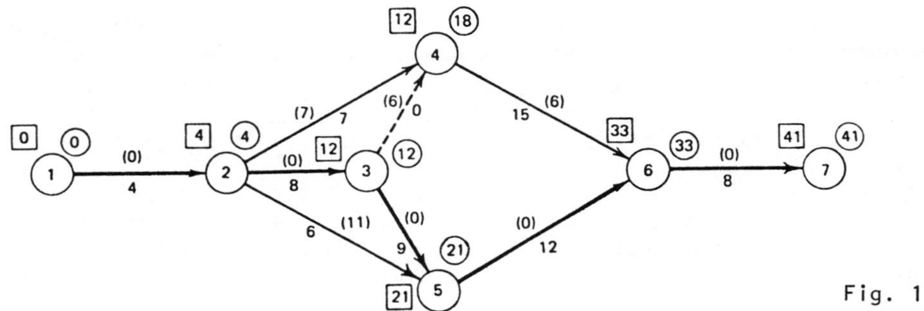

Fig. 1

Project network and VPM calculations.

The values of E_i for the remaining portion of the network are shown in the square boxes to the left of each node in the network in Figure 1. As a result of these calculations, note that the earliest occurrence time for event 7 is 41 time periods. Thus, 41 time periods is the earliest possible completion time for the project. The backward pass calculations for the latest event times begin by setting $L_7 = 41$, and then computing

$$L_6 = L_7 - t_{6,7} = 41 - 8 = 33$$

$$L_5 = L_6 - t_{5,6} = 33 - 12 = 21$$

$$L_4 = L_6 - t_{4,6} = 33 - 15 = 18$$

$$L_3 = \min \{L_4 - t_{3,4}, L_5 - t_{3,5}\} = \{18 - 0, 21 - 9\}$$

$$= 12, \text{ etc.}$$

The remaining values of L_i are shown in circles to the right of each node in the network of Figure 1. The slack times may be computed according to Equation (2). For example, the slack time for activity (4,6) is seen to be:

$$S_{4,6} = L_6 - E_4 - t_{4,6} = 33 - 12 - 15 = 6$$

and the slack time for activity (5,6) is

$$S_{5,6} = L_6 - E_5 - t_{5,6} = 33 - 21 - 12 = 0.$$

The slack for each activity is shown enclosed in parentheses immediately adjacent to the activity. Finally, the critical path is determined as those activities with zero slack, or

$$\{(1,2),(2,3),(3,5),(5,6),(6,7)\}$$

The activity duration means and variances may be computed by Equations (3) and (4) and are shown in columns (2) and (3) of Table 3.

$$\bar{t}_{ij} = \frac{a_{ij} + 4m_{ij} + b_{ij}}{6} \tag{3}$$

$$\sigma_{ij}^2 = \frac{(b_{ij} - a_{ij})^2}{36} \tag{4}$$

Applying equations (5) and (6) and the central limit theorem,

$$\bar{t}_p = \sum_{(i,j)\in u} \bar{t}_{ij} \tag{5}$$

$$\sigma_p^{\,2} = \sum_{(i,j)\in u} \sigma_{ij}^{\,2}\,, \tag{6}$$

the probability distribution of total project duration is approximately normal with mean $\bar{t}_p = 41$ and variance $\sigma_p^{\,2} = 8.778$ respectively. Therefore, the probability that the project requires less than (say) 45 time periods is, approximately

$$\Pr\{E_7 < 45\} = \Pr\left\{Z < \frac{45 - 41}{\sqrt{8.778}}\right\} = \Pr\{Z < 1.350\} \simeq 0.91$$

where E_7 is assumed to be normally distributed with mean 41 and variance 8.778, and Z is the standard normal random variable. From this calculation, note that if 45 times periods is the target completion data for the project, then there is approximately a 91 percent chance of completing the project on time.

To compute an approximate 100(1 - α) percent confidence interval for project completion time, if t is the true project completion time,

$$\Pr\{\bar{t}_p - z_{\alpha/2}\sigma_p \le t \le \bar{t}_p + z_{\alpha/2}\sigma_p\} = 1 - \alpha$$

approximately, where $z_{\alpha/2}$ denotes a percentage point of the standard normal distribution such that

$$\Pr\{Z > z_{\alpha/2}\} = \alpha/2.$$

Thus, the approximate 100(1 - α) percent confidence interval is

$$\bar{t}_p - z_{\alpha/2}\sigma_p \le t \le \bar{t}_p + z_{\alpha/2}\sigma_p.$$

TABLE 3

Activity Duration Means and Variances for Project Network

(1) ACTIVITY	(2) $\bar{t}_{ij}$ (DURATION MEAN)	(3) σ_{ij}^2 (DURATION VARIANCE)
(1, 2)	4	0.444
(2, 4)	7	1.000
(2, 3)	8	1.778
(2, 5)	6	1.000
(4, 6)	15	2.778
(3, 5)	9	2.778
(5, 6)	12	1.000
(6, 7)	8	2.778

The 95 percent confidence interval estimate of project completion time for the project whose activity durations are given in Table 3 is

$$41 - (1.96)(3.682) \le t \le 41 + (1.96)(3.682)$$

or

$$33.783 \le t \le 48.216.$$

• PROBLEM 8-32

Consider the network in Figure 1. The normal and crash points for each activity are given in Table 1. Normal points refer to the time and cost at which an activity can be accomplished without compressing. Crash points give the minimum times an activity can be completed at an increased cost. Compute the different minimum cost-schedules that can occur between normal and crash times.

$$FF_{ij} = ES_j - ES_i - D_{ij}$$

ES_j: Earliest start time of all the activities emanating from event J

D_{ij}: Duration of activity (i,j)

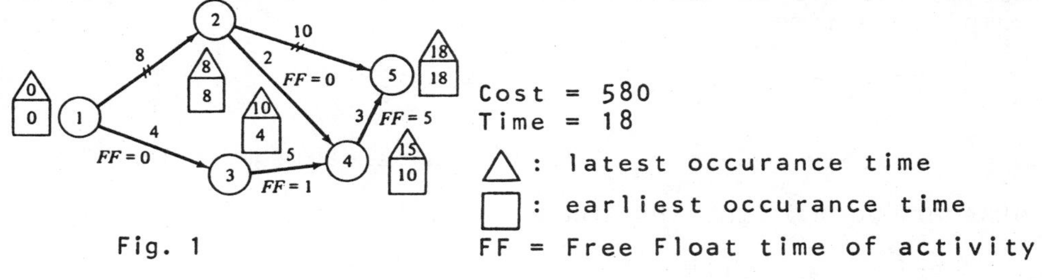

Fig. 1

Table 1

Activity (i, j)	Normal Duration	Normal Cost	Crash Duration	Crash Cost
(1, 2)	8	100	6	200
(1, 3)	4	150	2	350
(2, 4)	2	50	1	90
(2, 5)	10	100	5	400
(3, 4)	5	100	1	200
(4, 5)	3	80	1	100

Solution: The analysis in this problem is mainly dependent on the cost-time slopes for the different activities. These are computed using the following formula:

$$\text{slope} = \frac{C_c - C_n}{D_n - D_c}$$

The slopes for the activities of the above network are summarized in Table 2.

Table 2

Activity	Slope
(1, 2)	50
(1, 3)	100
(2, 4)	40
(2, 5)	60
(3, 4)	25
(4, 5)	10

The first step in the calculation procedure is to assume that all activities occur at normal times. The network in Figure 1 shows the critical path calculations under normal conditions. Activities (1,2) and (2,5) constitute the critical path. The time of the project is 18 and its associated (normal) cost is 580.

The second step is to reduce the time of the project by compressing (as much as possible) the critical activity with the least slope. For the network in Figure 1 there are only two critical activities, (1,2) and (2,5). Activity (1,2) is selected for compression since it has the smaller slope. According to the time-cost curve, this activity can be compressed by two time units; a limit which is specified by its crash point (henceforth called "crash limit"). However, compressing a critical activity to its crash point would not necessarily mean that the duration of the entire project will be reduced by an equivalent amount. This follows since as the critical activity is compressed a new critical path may develop. At this point one must discard the old critical activity and pay attention to the activities of the new critical path.

One way of predicting whether a new critical path will develop before reaching crash point is to consider the free floats for the noncritical activities. By definition, these free floats are independent of the start times of the other activities. Thus if during the compression of a critical activity, a positive free float becomes zero, this critical activity is not to be compressed without further checking since there is a possibility this zero free float activity may become critical. This means that in addition to the "crash limit" one must also consider the "free float limit."

To determine the free float limit, one needs first to reduce the duration of the critical activity selected for compression by one time unit. Then, by recomputing the free floats for all the noncritical activities, one will note which of these activities have reduced their positive free floats by one time unit. The smallest free float (before reduction) of all such activities determines the required free float limit.

Applying this to the network of Figure 1, the free floats (FF) are shown on the respective activities. A reduction of activity (1,2) by one time unit will drop the free float of activity (3,4) from one to zero. The free float of activity (4,5) will remain unchanged at 5. Thus, FF-limit = 1. Since the crash limit for (1,2) is 2, its "compression limit" is equal to the minimum of its crash limit and its FF-limit, that is, min {2,1} = 1. The new schedule is shown in Figure 2. The corresponding project time is 17 and its associated cost is equal to that of the previous schedule plus the additional cost of the compressed time, that is, 580 + (18 - 17) x 50 = 630. Although the free float is binding, the critical path remains the same. This illustrates that it is not always true that a new critical path will arise when the compression limit is specified by the FF-limit.

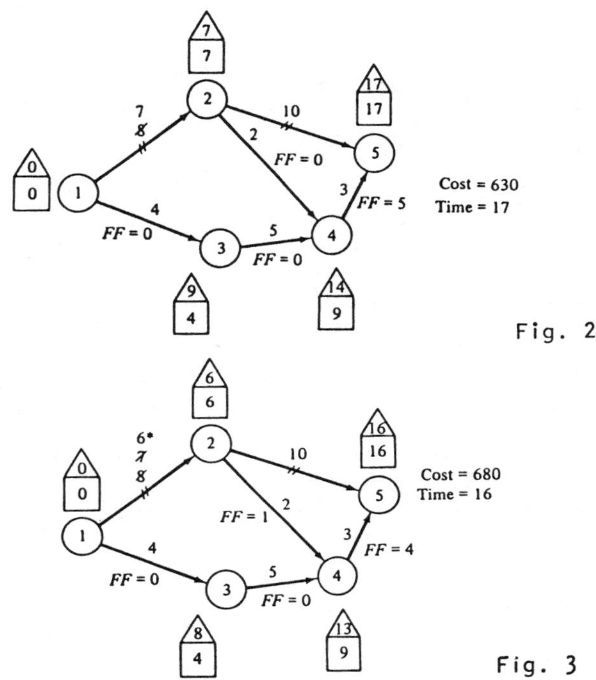

Fig. 2

Fig. 3

•signifies that activity has reached its crash limit

Since activity (1,2) is still the best candidate for compression, its corresponding crash and FF-limits are computed. However, since the crash limit for activity (1,2) is equal to 1, it is not necessary to compute the FF-limit because any positive FF is at least equal to 1. Consequently, activity (1,2) is compressed by one unit thus reaching its crash limit. The resulting computations are shown in Figure 3, which also shows that the critical path remains unchanged. The time of the project is 16 and its associated cost is 630 + (17 - 16) x 50 = 680.

Activity (1,2) can no longer be compressed. Hence, activity (2,5) is selected for compression. Now

crash limit = 10 - 5 = 5

FF-limit = 4, corresponding to activity (4,5)

compression limit = min {5,4} = 4

The resulting computations are shown in Figure 4. There are two critical paths now: (1,2,5) and (1,3,4,5). The time for the new project is 12, and its cost is 680 + (16 - 12) x 60 = 920.

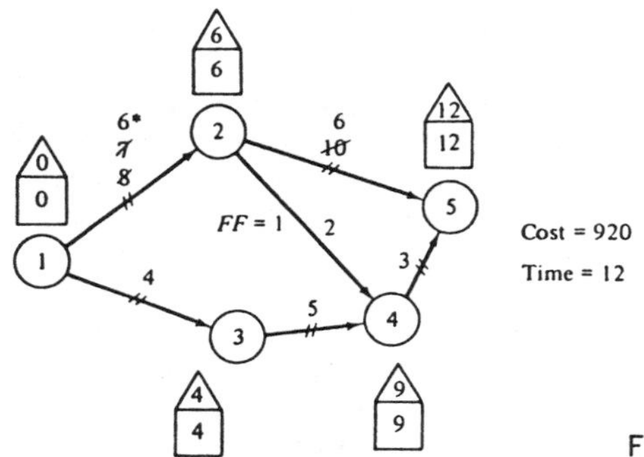

Fig. 4

*signifies that activity has reached its crash limit

The appearance of two critical paths indicates that, in order to reduce the time of the project, it will be necessary to reduce the time of the two critical paths simultaneously. The previous rule for selecting the critical activities to be compressed still applies here. For path (1, 2, 5,) activity (2, 5) can be compressed by one time unit. For path (1, 3, 4, 5,) activity (4, 5) has the least slope and its crash limit is 2. Thus, the crash limit for the two paths is equal to min {1,2} =1. The FF-limit is determined for this case by taking the minimum of the FF-limits obtained by considering each critical path separately. However, since the crash limit is equal to 1, the FF-limit need not be computed.

The new schedule is shown in Figure 5. Its time is 11 and its cost is 920 + (12 - 11) x (10 + 60) = 990.

The two critical paths of the project remain the same. Since all the activities on the critical path (1,2,5) are at crash time, it is no longer possible to reduce the time of the project. The schedule in Figure 5 thus gives the crash schedule.

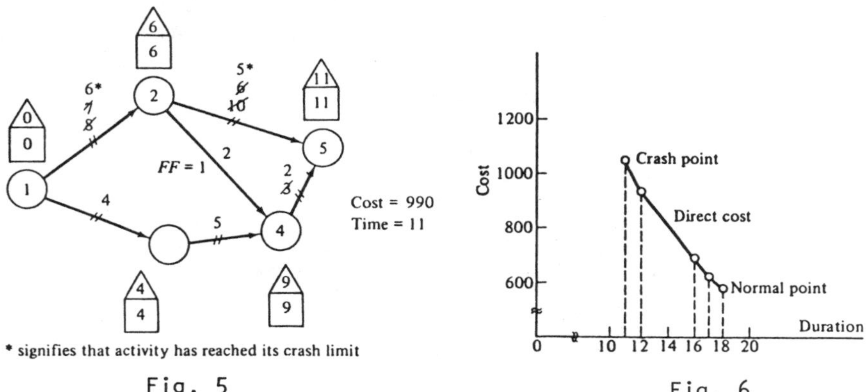

* signifies that activity has reached its crash limit

Fig. 5

Fig. 6

A summary of the above computations is given in Figure 6. This represents the direct cost of the project. By adding the indirect costs corresponding to each schedule one can compute the minimum total cost (or optimum) schedule.

• PROBLEM 8-33

Consider the network in Figure 1 which starts at node 1 and terminates at node 6. The time required to perform each activity is indicated on the arrows.

Find earliest start times, latest completion times, for each node and the critical path. Determine the total and free floats for noncritical activities. Construct the corresponding time chart (schedule) and using Table 1, the manpower requirements for each activity; construct a time schedule which will level the manpower requirements during the project duration.

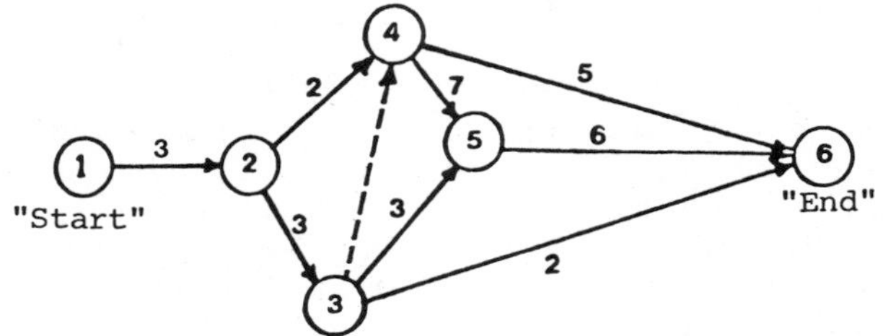

Fig. 1

Table 1

Activity	Number of men	Activity	Number men
1,2	5	3,6	1
1,3	7	4,5	2
2,4	3	4,6	5
3,5	2	5,6	6

Solution: The critical path calculations include two phases. The first phase is called the forward pass where calculations begin from the "start" node and move to the "end" node. At each node a number is computed representing the earliest occurrence time of the corresponding event. These numbers are shown in Figure 2 in squares □ . The second phase, called the backward pass, begins calculations from the "end" node and moves to the "start" node. The number computed at each node (shown in triangles Δ) represents the latest occurrence time of the corresponding event. The forward pass is considered now.

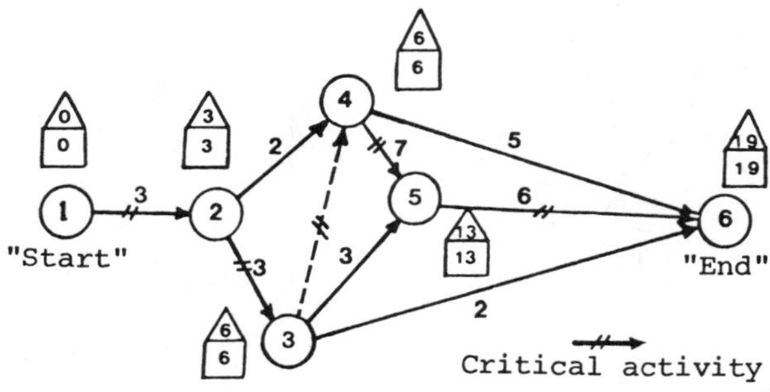

Fig. 2

Let ES_i be the earliest start time of all the activities emanating from event i. Thus, ES_i represents the earliest occurrence time of event i. If i = 1 is the "start" event, then conventionally, for the critical path calculations, $ES_1 = 0$. Let D_{ij} be the duration of activity (i,j). The forward pass calculations are thus obtained from the formula

$$ES_j = \max_i\{ES_i + D_{ij}\}, \text{ for all defined (i,j) activities}$$

where $ES_1 = 0$. Thus, in order to compute ES_j for event j, ES_i for the tail events of all the incoming activities (i,j) must be computed first.

The forward pass calculations applied to Figure 2 yield $ES_1 = 0$ as shown in the square above event 1. Since there is only one incoming activity (1,2) to event 2 with $D_{12} = 3$,

$$ES_2 = ES_1 + D_{12} = 0 + 3 = 3$$

This is entered in the square associated with event 2. The next event to be considered is 3. [Notice that event 4 cannot be considered at this point since ES_3 (event 3) is not yet known.] Thus,

$$ES_3 = ES_2 + D_{23} = 3 + 3 = 6$$

The value of ES_4 can now be obtained. Since there are two incoming activities, (2,4) and (3,4),

$$ES_4 = \max_{i=2,3} \{ES_i + D_{i4}\} = \max \{3 + 2, 6 + 0\} = 6$$

This is entered in the square associated with event 4.

The procedure continues in the same manner until ES_j is computed for all j. Thus,

$$ES_5 = \max_{i=3,4} \{ES_i + D_{i5}\} = \max \{6 + 3, 6 + 7\} = 13$$

$$ES_6 = \max_{i=3,4,5} \{ES_i + D_{i6}\} = \max \{6 + 2, 6 + 5, 13 + 6\} = 19$$

These calculations complete the forward pass.

The backward pass starts from the "end" event. The objective of this phase is to compute LC_i, the latest completion time for all the activities coming into event i. Thus, if i = n is the "end" event, $LC_n = ES_n$ initiates the backward pass. In general, for any node i,

$$LC_i = \min_j \{LC_j - D_{ij}\}, \text{ for all defined (i,j) activities}$$

The values of LC (entered in the triangles Δ) are determined as follows:

$$LC_6 = ES_6 = 19$$

$$LC_5 = LC_6 - D_{56} = 19 - 6 = 13$$

$$LC_4 = \min_{j=5,6} \{LC_j - D_{4j}\} = \min \{13 - 7, 19 - 5\} = 6$$

$$LC_3 = \min_{j=4,5,6} \{LC_j - D_{3j}\} = \min \{6 - 0, 13 - 3, 19 - 2\} = 6$$

$$LC_2 = \min_{j=3,4} \{LC_j - D_{2j}\} = \min \{6 - 3, 6 - 2\} = 3$$

$$LC_1 = LC_2 - D_{12} = 3 - 3 = 0$$

This completes the backward pass calculations.

The critical path activities can now be identified by using the results of the forward and backward passes. An activity (i,j) lies on the critical path if it satisfies the following three conditions,

(i) $ES_i = LC_i$

(ii) $ES_j = LC_j$

(iii) $ES_j - ES_i = LC_j - LC_i = D_{ij}$

These conditions actually indicate that there is no float or slack time between the earliest start (completion) and the latest start (completion) of the activity. Thus, this activity must be critical. In the arrow diagram these activities are characterized by the numbers in □ and Δ being the same at each of the head and the tail events and that the difference between the number in □ (or Δ) at the head event and the number in □ (or Δ) at the tail event is equal to the duration of the activity.

Activities (1,2), (2,3), (3,4), (4,5), and (5,6) define the critical path in Figure 2. This is actually the shortest possible time to complete the project. Notice that activities (2,4), (3,5), (3,6), and (4,6) satisfy conditions (i) and (ii) for critical activities but not condition (iii). Hence, they are not critical. Notice also that the critical path must form a chain of connected activities which spans the network from "start" to "end."

Determination of the floats:

Before showing how floats are determined, it is necessary to define two new times which are associated with each activity. These are the latest start (LS) and the earliest completion (EC) times, which are defined for activity (i,j) by

$$LS_{ij} = LC_j - D_{ij}$$

$$EC_{ij} = ES_i + D_{ij}$$

The total float TF_{ij} for activity (i,j) is the difference between the maximum time available to perform the activity $(= LC_j - ES_i)$ and its duration $(= D_{ij})$; that is,

$$TF_{ij} = LC_j - ES_i - D_{ij} = LC_j - EC_{ij} = LS_{ij} - ES_i$$

The free float is defined by assuming that all the activities start as early as possible. In this case, FF_{ij} for activity (i,j) is the excess of available time $(= ES_j - ES_i)$ over its duration $(= D_{ij})$; that is,

$$FF_{ij} = ES_j - ES_i - D_{ij}$$

Table 2

		Earliest		Latest			
Activity (i,j) (1)	Duration D_{ij} (2)	Start □ ES_i (3)	Completion EC_{ij} (4)	Start LS_{ij} (5)	Completion △ LC_j (6)	Total float TF_{ij} (7)	Free float FF_{ij} (8)
(1, 2)	3	0	3	0	3	0*	0
(2, 3)	3	3	6	3	6	0*	0
(2, 4)	2	3	5	4	6	1	1
(3, 4)	0	6	6	6	6	0*	0
(3, 5)	3	6	9	10	13	4	4
(3, 6)	2	6	8	17	19	11	11
(4, 5)	7	6	13	6	13	0*	0
(4, 6)	5	6	11	14	19	8	8
(5, 6)	6	13	19	13	19	0*	0

*Critical activity

The critical path calculations together with the floats for the noncritical activities can be summarized in the convenient form shown in Table 2. Columns (1), (2), (3), and (6) are obtained from the network calculations. The remaining information can be determined from the above formulas.

Table 2 gives a typical summary of the critical path calculations. It includes all the information necessary to construct the time chart (schedule). Notice that a critical activity, and only a critical activity, must have zero total float. The free float must also be zero when the total float is zero. The converse is not true, however, in the sense that a noncritical activity may have zero free float. Table 2 shows that the total float is the same as the free float. This is accidental since all the events of the project happen to be on the critical path. In general, this may not be true.

Constructing a time chart:

The information necessary to construct the time chart is summarized in Table 2. The first step is to consider the scheduling of the critical activities. Next, the noncritical activities are considered by indicating their ES and LC time limits on the chart. The critical activities are shown with solid lines. The time ranges for the non-critical activities are shown by dotted lines, indicating that such activities may be scheduled anywhere within those ranges provided the precedence relationships are not disturbed.

Figure 3 shows the corresponding time chart.

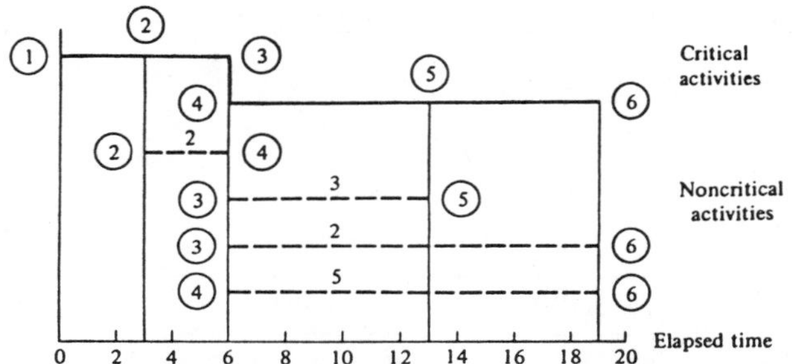

Fig. 3

The dummy activity (3,4) consumes no time and hence is shown by a vertical line. The numbers shown with the noncritical activities represent their durations. If resources are not an effective factor, each noncritical activity should be scheduled as early as possible. This allows taking the utmost advantage of the float in case the execution of any of these activities is delayed unexpectedly.

Constructing a time schedule for leveling the manpower requirements:

Figure 4 (a) shows the manpower requirements over time if the non-critical activities are scheduled as early as possible, while Figure 4 (b) shows the requirements if these activities are scheduled as late as possible. The dotted line shows the requirements for the critical activities which must be satisfied if the project is to be completed on time.

The project requires at least 7 men as indicated by the requirements of the critical activity (2,3). The earliest scheduling of the noncritical activities results in a maximum requirement of 10 men, while the latest scheduling of the same activities sets the maximum requirements at 12 men. This illustrates that the maximum requirements depend on how the total floats of the noncritical activities are used. In Figure 4, however, regardless of how the floats are allocated the maximum requirement cannot be less than 10 men. This follows since the range for activity (2,4) coincides with the time for the critical activity (2,3).

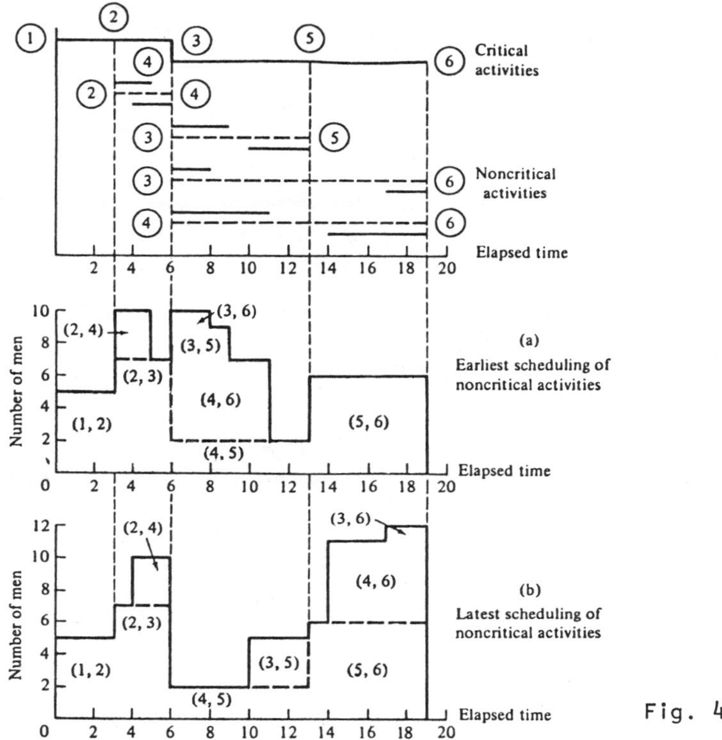

Fig. 4

The manpower requirement using the earliest scheduling can be improved by rescheduling activity (3,5) at its latest possible time and activity (3,6) immediately after activity

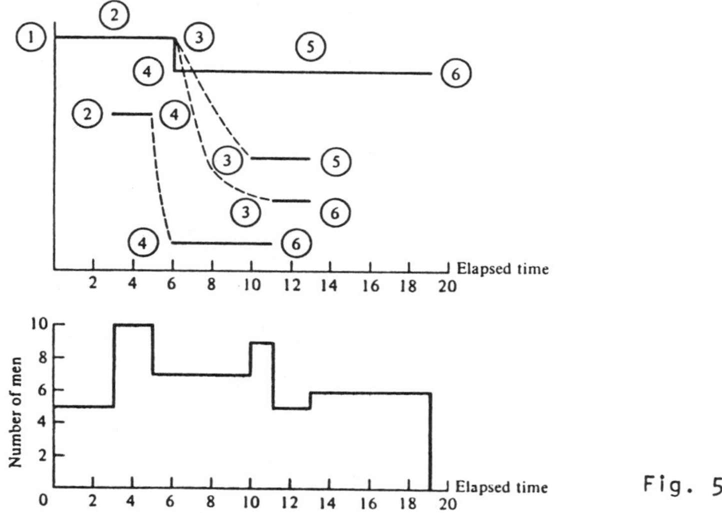

Fig. 5

(4,6) is completed. This new requirement is shown in Figure 5. The new schedule has now resulted in a smoother allocation of resources.

In some projects the objective may be to keep the maximum resource utilization below a certain limit rather than merely leveling the resources. If this cannot be accomplished by rescheduling the noncritical activities, it will be necessary to expand the time for some of the critical activities. This, however, may necessitate that some jobs be executed in segments rather than as an entity.

SCHEDULING

• PROBLEM 8-34

Denis wishes to schedule 6 jobs on a single machine. Suppose that, all jobs are not equally important. Each job has a processing time and an importance weight or value w_i (the larger w_i, the more important the job). These values and ratios of processing time to weight are shown in the table below.

Minimize the mean weighted flow time.

TABLE

JOB	p_i	w_i	p_i/w_i
1	10	5	2.0
2	6	10	0.6
3	5	5	1.0
4	4	1	4.0
5	2	3	0.67
6	8	5	1.6

Solution: A schedule to minimize the mean flow time of n jobs on a single machine may be found by sequencing the jobs in order of nondecreasing processing time, that is, such that

$$p_{[1]} \leq p_{[2]} \leq \cdots \leq p_{[n]}.$$

The flow time of a job in the kth position of an arbitrary sequence is

$$F_{[k]} = \sum_{i=1}^{k} p_{[i]}.$$

The mean flow time of the entire n job sequence is just

$$\bar{F} = \frac{\sum_{k=1}^{n} F_{[k]}}{n} = \frac{\sum_{k=1}^{n} \sum_{i=1}^{k} p_{[i]}}{n}$$

$$= \frac{\sum_{i=1}^{n} (n - i + 1)p_{[i]}}{n}.$$

Denis wishes to schedule a set of n jobs so as to minimize the mean weighted flow time

$$\bar{F}_w = \frac{\sum_{i=1}^{n} w_i F_i}{n} .$$

This may be accomplished by sequencing the jobs so that

$$\frac{p_{[1]}}{w_{[1]}} \le \frac{p_{[2]}}{w_{[2]}} \le \ldots \le \frac{p_{[n]}}{w_{[n]}} .$$

Thus, to minimize $\bar{F}_w$, the jobs should be processed in the sequence {2,5,3,6,1,4}.

• PROBLEM 8-35

Consider an auto repair shop that currently has five cars waiting to be painted. Only one car at a time can be painted. The accompanying table designates the five cars and the length of time it takes to paint each one.

Car	Painting time (hours)
A	6
B	2
C	5
D	4
E	3

The objective is to find the order in which the cars should be painted so that the average time it takes to get a car out of the shop is minimized. Apply the "next-best" (greedy) rule to solve this problem.

Assume each car has a relative importance represented by the weights shown.

Car	Weight
A	2
B	1
C	4
D	1
E	2

What should be the order in this case, with the same algorithm?

Solution: The greedy schedule is as follows: Let t_j represent the processing time for job j. Consider any two jobs i and j and the two sequences ij and ji, where ij indicates that job i immediately precedes job j and ji indicates that job j immediately precedes job i. Let F(s) represent the total completion time of the jobs in the sequence s. Then for adjacent i, j with starting time T_0, $F(ij) = T_0 + t_i + (T_0 + t_i + t_j)$ and $F(ji) = T_0 + t_j + T_0 + t_j + t_i$. Hence $F(ij) - F(ji) = t_i - t_j$. If $t_i - t_j < 0$, then the schedule ij is better than the schedule ji. In other words, if $t_i < t_j$, job i should precede job j. Since this is true for any two adjacent jobs, the optimal schedule is to start with the shortest job, then proceed to the second shortest job, and continue in this way; the longest job is scheduled last.

The optimal schedule is found to be B, E, D, C, A. The completion times are shown in the accompanying table.

Car	Completion time (hours)
B	2
E	5
D	9
C	14
A	20
	50

For the second case, let w_j represent the relative importance of job j, and that the objective is to minimize the sum of the weighted completion times. That is, if T_j is the time at which job j is completed, the objective is to minimize

$$\sum_{j=1}^{n} w_j T_j$$

For any two adjacent jobs i, j with starting time T_0, the weighted completion times $F(ij) = w_i(T_0 + t_i) + w_j(T_0 + t_i + t_j)$ and $F(ji) = w_j(T_0 + t_j) + w_i(T_0 + t_j + t_i)$. Thus $F(ij) - F(ji) = w_j t_i - w_i t_j$, so if $w_j t_i < w_i t_j$, schedule job i before job j. Another way to state this is, if $t_i/w_i < t_j/w_j$, schedule job i before job j.

Compute the (inversely) weighted times (t_j/w_j):

Car	t_j/w_j
A	3
B	2
C	1.25
D	4
E	1.5

The optimal schedule is C,E,B,A,D, with a weighted cost of 98.

• PROBLEM 8-36

There are two machines and six jobs that have to be processed in these machines. Given the processing times of jobs in each machine, in the table below, what is the minimum makespan schedule by using Johnson's algorithm? Draw the Gantt chart for the solution.

TABLE Processing Times

JOB	Machine 1	Machine 2
1	5	2
2	3	4
3	1	2
4	6	4
5	5	8
6	6	6

Solution: By Johnson's algorithm, see that $\min \{p_{ij}\} = 1$ occurs for Job 3 on machine 1. Therefore Job 3 is placed first in the sequence. Eliminating Job 3, find that

$\min_{i \neq 3} \{p_{ij}\} = 2$ occurs for Job 1 on machine 2, so Job 1 is placed last in the sequence. Next $\min_{i \neq 1,3} \{p_{ij}\} = 3$ occurs for Job 2 at machine 1, hence place it second in the sequence. Job 4 is next placed as second from last, Job 5 as third from the beginning. Only Job 6 remains and it is placed between Jobs 5 and 4. Thus the minimum makespan sequence is {3,2,5,6,4,1}. The Gantt chart for this sequence shown in Figure reveals a makespan of 29 time units.

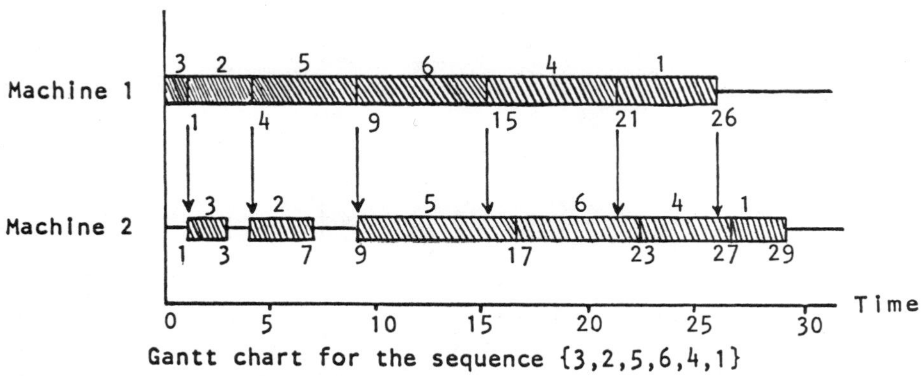

Gantt chart for the sequence {3,2,5,6,4,1}

An early graphical approach to scheduling problems was proposed by Henry L. Gantt. The Gantt chart simply displays job operations as a function of time on each machine. The chart usually consists of a horizontal bar for each machine, with idle and busy periods for a particular schedule designated. Inspection of the Gantt chart allows the schedule to be evaluated for makespan, machine idle time, and job waiting time. While the Gantt chart is an excellent display device, it has serious weakness as a scheduling technique because it does not provide any structured approach to schedule improvement. The analyst must use intuition to find an improved schedule.

• PROBLEM 8-37

Ann has five jobs, each of which must go through the two machines A and B in the order AB. Processing times are given in the table below:

Determine a sequence for the five jobs that will minimize the elapsed time T, using Johnson's algorithm.

Processing Time, HR

Job	Machine A	Machine B
1	5	2
2	1	6
3	9	7
4	3	8
5	10	4

Solution: The smallest processing time is 1 hour for job 2 on machine A. Thus schedule job 2 first:

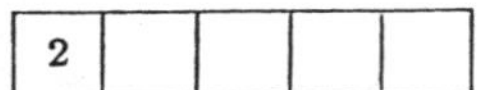

2				

The reduced set of processing times is

Job	A	B
1	5	2
3	9	7
4	3	8
5	10	4

The smallest processing time, 2, is B_1. So schedule job 1 last:

2				1

Continuing

Job	A	B
3	9	7
4	3	8
5	10	4

leading to

2	4			1

Job	A	B
3	9	7
5	10	4

yielding

2	4		5	1

so that the optimal sequence is

2	4	3	5	1

Calculate the elapsed time corresponding to the optimal ordering, using the individual processing times given in the statement of the problem. The details are given in the following table.

Thus the minimum elapsed time is 30 hours. Idle time is 3 hours for machine B, and 2 hours for machine A.

Job	Machine A Time in	Machine A Time out	Machine B Time in	Machine B Time out
2	0	1	1	7
4	1	4	7	15
3	4	13	15	22
5	13	23	23	27
1	23	28	28	30

• PROBLEM 8-38

Consider the four-job, three machine flow shop scheduling problem shown in the table below. Solve by Ignall and Schrage's branch-and-bound algorithm.

TABLE Processing Times

JOB	MACHINE 1	MACHINE 2	MACHINE 3
1	12	5	13
2	6	10	3
3	9	11	18
4	17	16	4

Solution: Ignall and Schrage's branch-and-bound algorithm for the general three-machine flow shop problem requires a description of the problem as a tree, in which each node represents a partial solution. At each node, a lower bound on makespan is computed for all nodes that emanate from it. It is easy to see that the flow shop scheduling problem can be expressed as a tree. The first node in the tree structure corresponds to the initial state, with no jobs scheduled. From this node, there are n branches corresponding to the n possible jobs that can be placed first in the sequence. From each of these nodes, there are n - 1 branches corresponding to the jobs available to be placed second in the sequence. Since there are n! possible sequences, there are 1 + n + n(n - 1) + . . . + n! nodes in the tree.

Each node represents a partial sequence containing from 1 to n jobs. Consider an arbitrary node, say P, with sequence J_r. That is, J_r is a particular subset of size $r(1 \leq r \leq n)$ or the n jobs. Let TIME 1 (J_r), TIME 2 (J_r), and TIME 3 (J_r) be the times at which machine 1, 2, and 3, respectively, complete processing on the jobs in J_r. Then a lower bound on the makespan of all schedules that begin with sequence J_r, is

$$\mathrm{LB}(P) = \mathrm{LB}(J_r) = \max \begin{Bmatrix} \mathrm{TIME1}(J_r) + \sum_{i \notin J_r} p_{i1} + \min_{i \notin J_r} (p_{i2} + p_{i3}) \\ \mathrm{TIME2}(J_r) + \sum_{i \notin J_r} p_{i2} + \min_{i \notin J_r} (p_{i3}) \\ \mathrm{TIME3}(J_r) + \sum_{i \notin J_r} p_{i3} \end{Bmatrix} \quad (1)$$

where $\bar{J}_r$ is the set of n-r jobs that have not been scheduled.

$$\text{TIME 2 (231)} = \max\{\text{TIME 1 (231)} + p_{12}, \text{TIME 2 (23)} + p_{12}\}$$
$$= \max\{27 + 5 = 32, 27 + 5 = 32\} = 32$$
$$\text{TIME 3 (231)} = \max\{\text{TIME 2 (231)} + p_{13}, \text{TIME 3 (23)} + p_{13}\}$$
$$= \max\{32 + 13 = 45, 45 + 13 = 58\} = 58$$
$$\text{TIME 1 (234)} = \text{TIME 1 (23)} + p_{41} = 15 + 17 = 32$$
$$\text{TIME 2 (234)} = \max\{\text{TIME 1(234)} + p_{42}, \text{TIME 2 (23)} + p_{42}\}$$
$$= \max\{32 + 16 = 48, 27 + 16 = 43\} = 48$$
$$\text{TIME 3 (234)} = \max\{\text{TIME 2 (234)} + p_{43}, \text{TIME 3 (23)} + p_{43}\}$$
$$= \max\{48 + 4 = 52, 45 + 4 = 49\} = 52$$

The lower bounds are

$$\text{LB(231)} = \max\begin{Bmatrix} 27 + 17 + 20 = 64 \\ 32 + 16 + \ \ 4 = 52 \\ 58 + \ \ 4 \qquad\ = 62 \end{Bmatrix} = 64$$

and

$$\text{LB(234)} = \max\begin{Bmatrix} 32 + 12 + 18 = 62 \\ 48 + \ \ 5 + 13 = 66 \\ 52 + 13 \qquad\ = 65 \end{Bmatrix} = 66$$

At this point, see that the least lower bound on the tree is LB(341) = 63. Therefore, the optimal sequence is {3, 4, 1, 2} and

$$\text{LB(342)} = \max\begin{Bmatrix} 32 + 12 + 18 = 62 \\ 52 + \ \ 5 + 13 = 70 \\ 55 + 13 \qquad\ = 68 \end{Bmatrix} = 70$$

As LB (2) = 62, still investigate node 2. Notice that

$$\text{TIME 1 (21)} = \text{TIME 1 (2)} + p_{11} = 6 + 12 = 18$$
$$\text{TIME 2 (21)} = \max\{\text{TIME 1 (21)} + p_{12}, \text{TIME 2 (2)} + p_{12}\}$$
$$= \max\{18 + 5 = 23, 16 + 5 = 21\} = 23$$
$$\text{TIME 3 (21)} = \max\{\text{TIME 2 (21)} + p_{13}, \text{TIME 3 (2)} + p_{13}\}$$
$$= \max\{23 + 13 = 36, 19 + 13 = 32\} = 36$$
$$\text{TIME 1 (23)} = \text{TIME 1 (2)} + p_{31} = 6 + 9 = 15$$
$$\text{TIME 2 (23)} = \max\{\text{TIME 1 (23)} + p_{32}, \text{TIME 2 (2)} + p_{32}\}$$
$$= \max\{15 + 11 = 26, 16 + 11 = 27\} = 27$$
$$\text{TIME 3 (23)} = \max\{\text{TIME 2 (23)} + p_{33}, \text{TIME 3 (2)} + p_{33}\}$$

$= \max\{27 + 18 = 45,\ 19 + 18 = 37\} = 45$

$\text{TIME 1 (24)} = \text{TIME 1 (2)} + p_{41} = 6 + 17 = 23$

$\text{TIME 2 (24)} = \max\{\text{TIME 1 (24)} + p_{42},\ \text{TIME 2 (2)} + p_{42}\}$

$= \max\{23 + 16 = 39,\ 16 + 16 = 32\} = 39$

$\text{TIME 3 (24)} = \max\{\text{TIME 2 (24)} + p_{43},\ \text{TIME 3 (2)} + p_{43}\}$

$= \max\{39 + 4 = 43,\ 19 + 4 = 23\} = 43$

and the lower bounds are

$$LB(21) = \max\begin{Bmatrix} 18 + 26 + 20 = 64 \\ 23 + 27 + \ \ 4 = 54 \\ 36 + 22 \qquad\quad = 58 \end{Bmatrix} = 64$$

and

$$LB(23) = \max\begin{Bmatrix} 15 + 29 + 18 = 62 \\ 27 + 21 + \ \ 4 = 52 \\ 45 + 17 \qquad\quad = 62 \end{Bmatrix} = 62$$

$$LB(24) = \max\begin{Bmatrix} 23 + 21 + 18 = 62 \\ 39 + 16 + 13 = 68 \\ 43 + 31 \qquad\quad = 74 \end{Bmatrix} = 74$$

Branch from node 23

$\text{TIME 1 (231)} = \text{TIME 1 (23)} + p_{11} = 15 + 12 = 27.$

Note that

$\text{TIME 1 (132)} = \text{TIME 1 (13)} + p_{21} = 21 + 6 = 27$

$\text{TIME 2 (132)} = \max\{\text{TIME 1 (132)} + p_{22},\ \text{TIME 2 (13)} + p_{22}\}$

$= \max\{27 + 10 = 37,\ 32 + 10 = 42\} = 42$

$\text{TIME 3 (132)} = \max\{\text{TIME 2 (132)} + p_{23},\ \text{TIME 3 (13)} + p_{23}\}$

$= \max\{42 + 3 = 45,\ 50 + 3 = 53\} = 53$

$\text{TIME 1 (134)} = \text{TIME 1 (13)} + p_{41} = 21 + 17 = 38$

$\text{TIME 2 (134)} = \max\{\text{TIME 1 (134)} + p_{42},\ \text{TIME 2 (13)} + p_{42}\}$

$= \max\{38 + 16 = 54,\ 32 + 16 = 48\} = 54$

$\text{TIME 3 (134)} = \max\{\text{TIME 2 (134)} + p_{43},\ \text{TIME 3 (13)} + p_{43}\}$

$= \max\{54 + 4 = 58,\ 50 + 4 = 54\} = 58.$

Since TIME 2 (134) = TIME 2 (314) and TIME 3 (134) = TIME 3(314), node 134 is dominated by node 314. The only lower bound which must be calculated is

$$LB(132) = \max\begin{Bmatrix} 27 + 17 + 20 = 64 \\ 42 + 16 + \ \ 4 = 62 \\ 53 + \ \ 4 \qquad\quad = 57 \end{Bmatrix} = 64$$

At this point, investigate either node 2 or node 34. Arbitrarily choose node 34. Find

$$\text{TIME 1 (341)} = \text{TIME 1 (34)} + p_{11} = 26 + 12 = 38$$

$$\text{TIME 2 (341)} = \max\{\text{TIME 1 (341)} + p_{12}, \text{TIME 2 (34)} + p_{12}\}$$
$$= \max\{38 + 5 = 43, 42 + 5 = 47\} = 47$$

$$\text{TIME 3 (341)} = \max\{\text{TIME 2 (341)} + p_{13}, \text{TIME 3 (34)} + p_{13}\}$$
$$= \max\{47 + 13 = 60, 46 + 13 = 59\} = 60$$

$$\text{TIME 1 (342)} = \text{TIME 1 (34)} + p_{21} = 26 + 6 = 32$$

$$\text{TIME 2 (342)} = \max\{\text{TIME 1 (342)} + p_{22}, \text{TIME 2 (34)} + p_{22}\}$$
$$= \{32 + 10 = 42, 42 + 10 = 52\} = 52$$

$$\text{TIME 3 (342)} = \max\{\text{TIME 2 (342)} + p_{23}, \text{TIME 3 (34)} + p_{23}\}$$
$$= \max\{52 + 3 = 55, 46 + 3 = 49\} = 55$$

and the lower bounds are

$$\text{LB(341)} = \max\begin{Bmatrix} 38 + 6 + 13 = 57 \\ 47 + 10 + 3 = 60 \\ 60 + 3 = 63 \end{Bmatrix} = 63$$

The lower bounds are

$$\text{LB(31)} = \max\begin{Bmatrix} 21 + 23 + 13 = 57 \\ 26 + 26 + 3 = 55 \\ 51 + 7 = 58 \end{Bmatrix} = 58$$

and

$$\text{LB(32)} = \max\begin{Bmatrix} 15 + 29 + 21 = 65 \\ 30 + 21 + 4 = 55 \\ 41 + 17 = 58 \end{Bmatrix} = 65$$

$$\text{LB(34)} = \max\begin{Bmatrix} 26 + 18 + 13 = 57 \\ 42 + 15 + 3 = 60 \\ 46 + 16 = 62 \end{Bmatrix} = 62$$

Since LB(31) is the smallest lower bound, branch from node 31. Note that

$$\text{TIME 1 (312)} = \text{TIME 1 (31)} + p_{21} = 21 + 6 = 27$$

$$\text{TIME 2 (312)} = \max\{\text{TIME 1 (312)} + p_{22}, \text{TIME 2 (31)} + p_{22}\}$$
$$= \max\{27 + 10 = 37, 26 + 10 = 36\} = 37$$

$$\text{TIME 3 (312)} = \max\{\text{TIME 2 (312)} + p_{23}, \text{TIME 3 (31)} + p_{23}\}$$
$$= \max\{37 + 3 = 40, 51 + 3 = 54\} = 54$$

$$\text{TIME 1 (314)} = \text{TIME 1 (31)} + p_{41} = 21 + 17 = 38$$

$$\text{TIME 2 (314)} = \max\{\text{TIME 1 (314)} + p_{42}, \text{TIME 2 (31)} + p_{42}\}$$

$$= \max\{38 + 16 = 54,\ 26 + 16 = 42\} = 54$$

$$\text{TIME 3 (314)} = \max\{\text{TIME 2 (314)} + p_{43},\ \text{TIME 3 (31)} + p_{43}\}$$

$$= \max\{54 + 4 = 58,\ 51 + 4 = 55\} = 58$$

The lower bounds are

$$LB(312) = \max\begin{Bmatrix} 27 + 17 + 20 = 64 \\ 37 + 16 + 4 = 57 \\ 54 + 4 = 58 \end{Bmatrix} = 64$$

and

$$LB(314) = \max\begin{Bmatrix} 38 + 6 + 13 = 57 \\ 54 + 10 + 3 = 67 \\ 58 + 3 = 61 \end{Bmatrix} = 67$$

Since the least lower bound is LB(13) = 61, backtrack to node 13

$$\text{TIME 2 (14)} = \max\{\text{TIME 1 (14)} + p_{42},\ \text{TIME 2 (1)} + p_{42}\}$$

$$= \max\{29 + 16 = 45,\ 17 + 16 = 33\} = 45$$

$$\text{TIME 3 (14)} = \max\{\text{TIME 2 (14)} + p_{43},\ \text{TIME 3 (1)} + p_{43}\}$$

$$= \max\{45 + 4 = 49,\ 30 + 4 = 34\} = 49$$

The lower bounds are

$$LB(12) = \max\begin{Bmatrix} 18 + 26 + 20 = 64 \\ 28 + 27 + 4 = 59 \\ 33 + 22 = 55 \end{Bmatrix} = 64$$

and

$$LB(13) = \max\begin{Bmatrix} 21 + 23 + 13 = 57 \\ 32 + 26 + 3 = 61 \\ 50 + 7 = 57 \end{Bmatrix} = 61$$

$$LB(14) = \max\begin{Bmatrix} 29 + 15 + 13 = 57 \\ 45 + 21 + 3 = 69 \\ 49 + 21 = 70 \end{Bmatrix} = 70$$

Since LB(3) = 58 is now the smallest lower bound, next branch from node 3. The following quantities are needed.

$$\text{TIME 1 (31)} = \text{TIME 1 (3)} + p_{11} = 9 + 12 = 21$$

$$\text{TIME 2 (31)} = \max\{\text{TIME 1 (31)} + p_{12},\ \text{TIME 2(3)} + p_{12}\}$$

$$\max\{21 + 5 = 26,\ 20 + 5 = 25\} = 26$$

$$\text{TIME 3 (31)} = \max\{\text{TIME 2 (31)} + p_{13},\ \text{TIME 3 (3)} + p_{13}\}$$

$$= \max\{26 + 13 = 39,\ 38 + 13 = 51\} = 51$$

$$\text{TIME 1 (32)} = \text{TIME 1 (3)} + p_{21} = 9 + 6 = 15$$

$$\text{TIME 2 (32)} = \max\{\text{TIME 1 (32)} + p_{22}, \text{TIME 2 (3)} + p_{22}\}$$
$$= \max\{15 + 10 = 25, 20 + 10 = 30\} = 30$$
$$\text{TIME 3 (32)} = \max\{\text{TIME 2 (32)} + p_{23}, \text{TIME 3 (3)} + p_{23}\}$$
$$= \max\{30 + 3 = 33, 38 + 3 = 41\} = 41$$
$$\text{TIME 1 (34)} = \text{TIME 1 (3)} + p_{41} = 9 + 17 = 26$$
$$\text{TIME 2 (34)} = \max\{\text{TIME 1 (34)} + p_{42}, \text{TIME 2 (3)} + p_{42}\}$$
$$= \max\{26 + 16 = 42, 20 + 16 = 36\} = 42$$
$$\text{TIME 3 (34)} = \max\{\text{TIME 2 (34)} + p_{43}, \text{TIME 3 (3)} + p_{43}\}$$
$$= \max\{42 + 4 = 46, 38 + 4 = 42\} = 46$$

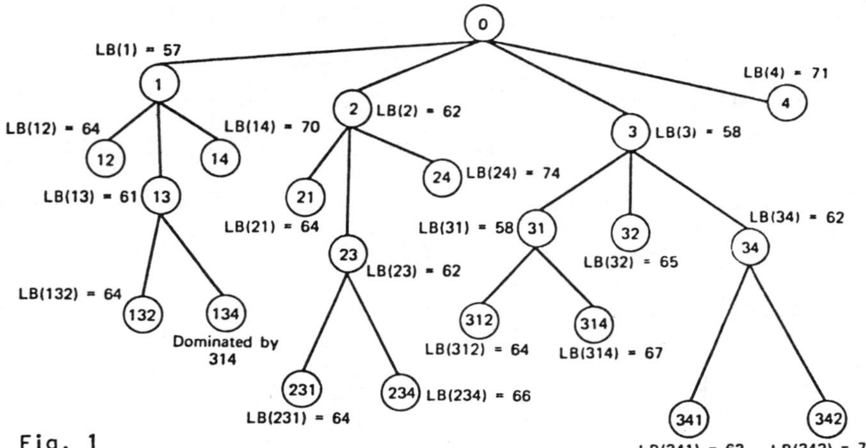

Fig. 1
Tree for the four-job, three-machine problem

$$\text{LB}(4) = \max\begin{Bmatrix} 17 + 27 + 13 = 57 \\ 33 + 26 + \ \ 3 = 62 \\ 37 + 34 \qquad = 71 \end{Bmatrix} = 71$$

As LB(1) is the smallest lower bound, branch from node 1. To compute the lower bounds one needs TIME 1 (12), TIME 2 (12), . . ., TIME 3 (14). These quantities may be computed as follows:

$$\text{TIME 1 (12)} = \text{TIME 1 (1)} + p_{21} = 12 + 6 = 18$$
$$\text{TIME 2 (12)} = \max\{\text{TIME 1 (12)} + p_{22}, \text{TIME 2 (1)} + p_{22}\}$$
$$= \max\{18 + 10 = 28, 17 + 10 = 27\} = 28$$
$$\text{TIME 3 (12)} = \max\{\text{TIME 2 (12)} + p_{23}, \text{TIME 3 (1)} + p_{23}\}$$
$$= \max\{28 + 3 = 31, 30 + 3 = 33\} = 33$$
$$\text{TIME 1 (13)} = \text{TIME 1 (1)} + p_{31} = 12 + 9 = 21$$

$$\text{TIME 2 (13)} = \max\{\text{TIME 1 (13)} + p_{32},\ \text{TIME 2 (1)} + p_{32}\}$$

$$= \max\{21 + 11 = 32,\ 17 + 11 = 28\} = 32$$

$$\text{TIME 3 (13)} = \max\{\text{TIME 2 (13)} + p_{33},\ \text{TIME 3 (1)} + p_{33}\}$$

$$= \max\{32 + 18 = 50,\ 30 + 18 = 48\} = 50$$

$$\text{TIME 1 (14)} = \text{TIME 1 (1)} + p_{41} = 12 + 17 = 29$$

The actual procedure consists of generating the nodes in the tree and computing the lower bounds associated with them. One always branches from the node with the smallest lower bound. To branch from a node, create a new node for every job not yet scheduled by attaching the unscheduled job to the end of the partial sequence of scheduled jobs. The lower bounds can then be computed from Equation 1.

As soon as a node has been found with all n jobs scheduled and a smallest lower bound, the problem is solved and the sequence at that node is optimal. In performing the above steps, dominance can be used to some extent. That is, if J_r and I_r are sequences containing the same r jobs, then if TIME 2 $(J_r) \leq$ TIME 2 (I_r) and TIME 3 $(J_r) \leq$ TIME 3 (I_r), the node associated with sequence I_r can be discarded as soon as J_r is created.

To branch from node 0, construct nodes 1, 2, 3, and 4 as shown in Figure 1. In computing the lower bounds:

TIME 1 (1) = 12, TIME 2 (1) = 17, TIME 3 (1) = 30,

TIME 1 (2) = 6, TIME 2 (2) = 16, TIME 3 (2) = 19,

TIME 1 (3) = 9, TIME 2 (3) = 20, TIME 3 (3) = 38,

TIME 1 (4) = 17, TIME 2 (4) = 33, and TIME 3 (4) = 37.

The lower bounds are:

$$LB(1) = \max\begin{Bmatrix} 12 + 32 + 13 = 57 \\ 17 + 37 + 3 = 57 \\ 30 + 25 = 55 \end{Bmatrix} = 57$$

$$LB(2) = \max\begin{Bmatrix} 6 + 38 + 18 = 62 \\ 16 + 32 + 4 = 52 \\ 19 + 35 = 54 \end{Bmatrix} = 62$$

$$LB(3) = \max\begin{Bmatrix} 9 + 35 + 13 = 57 \\ 20 + 31 + 3 = 54 \\ 38 + 20 = 58 \end{Bmatrix} = 58$$

Find the optimal schedule for the two jobs to be processed in the four machines, with processing times as given in the table. Job 1 must be processed with the technological ordering a, b, c, d. The technological ordering of job 2 is d, b, a, c. Use the Graphical approach sugested by Hardgrave and Nemhauser.

TABLE Processing Times

	MACHINE			
JOB	*a*	*b*	*c*	*d*
1	2	5	3	2
2	3	5	2	6

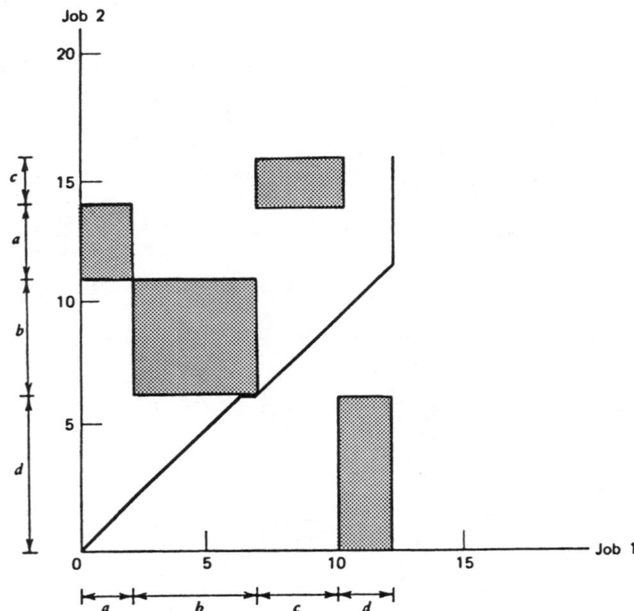

Fig. 1

Solution: There is a simple graphical solution to the two-job, m-machine job shop scheduling problem. The graphical representation of the problem is shown in Figure 1. The axes represent the amount of work completed on the jobs, with the machine times laid out in the proper technological order (hence, the restriction to two jobs). The coordinates represent a possible state of comletion of the two jobs. The Cartesian product of the job 1-job 2 processing times for each machine is shown as a shaded region. Clearly, these shaded regions are infeasible, as they represent simultaneous processing of both jobs on the same machine.

A solution to this problem is any line from the point (0, 0) to the point

$$\left(\sum_{i=1}^{m} p_{i1}, \sum_{i=1}^{m} p_{i2} \right),$$

which does not pass through a shaded region. The line may be composed of horizontal (work on job 1 only), vertical (work on job 2 only), and 45° (simultaneous work on both jobs) segments.

A minimum makespan schedule is a line that minimizes the length of vertical (or horizontal) segment, that is, a schedule that maximizes the amount of simultaneous processing. This schedule must be determined by trial and error. Usually, only a few lines must be drawn before the optimal solution is found. An optimal solution to the problem is shown in Figure 1.

• PROBLEM 8-40

Consider the nine-task problem whose precedence relations are shown in Figure 1 and whose performance times are shown in Table 1.

Using the Kilbridge and Wester procedure for heuristic assembly line balancing, assign the above nine tasks to a minimum number of stations. Let the cycle time be c = 16 time units. First, check if this c is feasible.

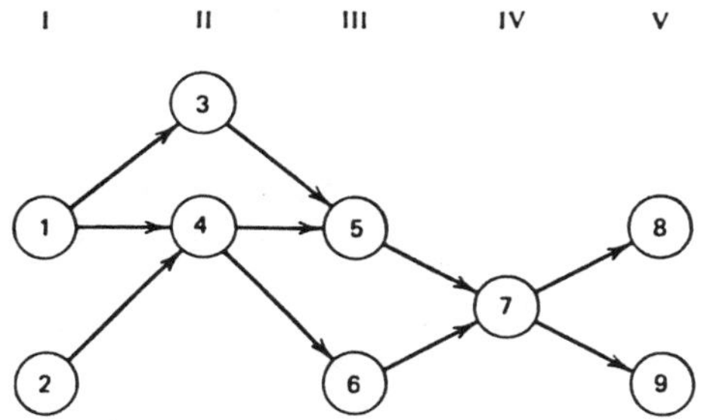

Fig. 1

Precedence diagram

TABLE 1 Performance Times

TASK	PERFORMANCE TIME
1	5
2	3
3	6
4	8
5	$10 = p_{max}$
6	7
7	1
8	5
9	3
	$\sum_{i=1}^{n} p_i = 48$

Solution: The Kilbridge and Wester method requires the addition of colum labels to the precedence diagram. These labels are the Roman numbers in Figure 1. Tasks that have no predecessors are placed in column I, tasks that are preceded directly by those in column I are placed in column II, tasks that are immediately preceded by those in column II are placed in column III, etc. Note that this results in a precedence diagram that places each task as far to the left as possible. Intracolumn movement of tasks is unrestricted, as there are no precedence constraints within a column. Furthermore, many tasks can be moved from their current columns to a column further right without violating precedence constraints.

To determine the possible cycle times for which

$$\sum_{i=1}^{n} p_i/c$$

is an integer, and thus, the possible cycle times yielding a perfect balance, write

$$\sum_{i=1}^{n} p_i$$

as a product of prime numbers. In this problem, since

$$\sum_{i=1}^{n} p_i = 48.$$

Thus

$$2 \times 2 \times 3 \times 2 \times 2 = 48.$$

Since $10 \leq c \leq 48$, it is easily seen that the ratio

$\sum_{i=1}^{n} p_i/c$ is an integer for

$$c_1 = 2 \times 2 \times 3 \times 2 \times 2 = 48$$

$$c_2 = 2 \times 2 \times 2 \times 3 = 24$$

$$c_3 = 2 \times 2 \times 2 \times 2 = 16$$

$$c_4 = 2 \times 2 \times 3 = 12.$$

Thus $c = 16$ is justified.

Then, perfect balance can possibly be achieved with

$$k_1 = \frac{\sum_{i=1}^{n} p_i}{c_1} = \frac{48}{48} = 1 \text{ station (trivial)}$$

$$k_2 = \frac{\sum_{i=1}^{n} p_i}{c_2} = \frac{48}{24} = 2 \text{ stations}$$

$$k_3 = \frac{\sum_{i=1}^{n} p_i}{c_3} = \frac{48}{16} = 3 \text{ stations}$$

$$k_4 = \frac{\sum_{i=1}^{n} p_i}{c_4} = \frac{48}{12} = 4 \text{ stations.}$$

TABLE 2 **Tabular Representation of Precedence Diagram**

COLUMN NUMBER	TASK	p_i	SUM OF p_i	CUMULATIVE SUM OF p_i
I	1	5		
	2	3	8	8
II	3	6		
	4	8	14	22
III	5	10		
	6	7	17	39
IV	7	1	1	40
V	8	5		
	9	3	8	48

Construct a table containing detailed information about the tasks taken from each column of the precedence diagram. This is shown as Table 2. Attempt to assign tasks to station 1. Scan the "cumulative sum" column of Table 2 until the smallest cumulative sum that is greater than or equal to the cycle time, 16 is found. The value found is the cumulative sum of the tasks in columns I and II, that is, 22. Since the tasks in column I require eight units of time and have the fewest predecessors of the available tasks, they will be assigned to station 1. Now c - 8 = 16 - 8 = 8 time units are left. Scan column II and see if any combination of tasks total eight time units. Find that task 4 is acceptable. Therefore, move task 4 to the top of the column II list and assign it to station 1, along with tasks 1 and 2. In general, if a choice between two or more tasks exists, always use the task with the longest performance time first. The status of the solution is now shown by Table 3.

Scan the "cumulative sum" column of Table 3 to find the smallest cumulative sum greater than or equal to 2 x 16 = 32. The cumulative sum for column III is 39. Assigning task 3 to station 2 yields c - 6 = 16 - 6 = 10 units of time available in this station. Search column III for any combination of tasks whose times total 10. Thus, note that task 5 qualifies.

Therefore, also assign task 5 to station 2. The status of the solution is shown in Table 4. Repeating these steps for station 3, it is easily seen that the smallest cumulative sum greater than or equal to 3 x 16 = 48 is the cumulative sum for column V, that is, 48. Since there are exactly 16 time units of unassigned work remaining, tasks 6, 7, 8, and 9 may be assigned to station 3.

TABLE 3 Modified Table 2 After Assignment of Tasks to Station 1

COLUMN NUMBER	TASK	p_i	SUM OF p_i	CUMULATIVE SUM OF p_i	
I	1 2	5 3			Station 1
II	4	8	16	16	Station 1
	3	6	6	22	Unassigned Tasks
III	5 6	10 7	17	39	Unassigned Tasks
IV	7	1	1	40	Unassigned Tasks
V	8 9	5 3	8	48	Unassigned Tasks

TABLE 4 Modified Table 3 After Assignment of Tasks to Station 2

COLUMN NUMBER	TASK	p_i	SUM OF p_i	CUMULATIVE SUM OF p_i	
I	1 2	5 3			Station 1
II	4	8	16	16	Station 1
	3	6			Station 2
III	5	10	16	32	Station 2
	6	7			Unassigned Tasks
IV	7	1	8	40	Unassigned Tasks
V	8 9	5 3	8	48	Unassigned Tasks

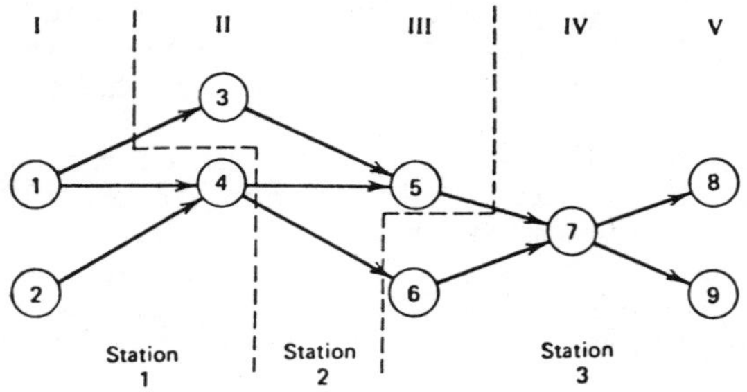

Fig. 2

Final station assignments

The final station assignments are shown in Figure 2. Kilbridge and Wester method has resulted in a perfect balance, as there is no idle time in any station. It may be easily verified that for c = 12 and c = 24, there are no perfect balances using the minimum number of stations. Therefore, the best solution to the problem seems to be the perfect balance attained with c = 16 and k = 3 stations.

CHAPTER 9

NONLINEAR PROGRAMMING - UNCONSTRAINED OPTIMIZATION

CONVEXITY, CONCAVITY

• PROBLEM 9-1

Is the function $f(x) = 2x^3 - x^2 + 2x + 5$ convex or concave?

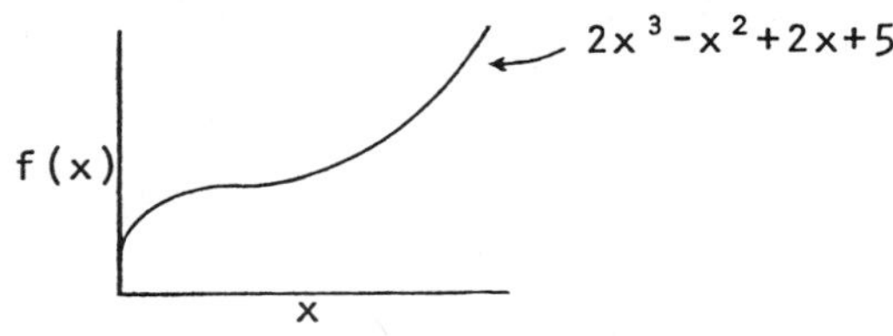

Solution: Let S be a nonempty convex set in E_n, and let $f: S \to E_n$ be twice differentiable on S. Then f is convex if and only if the Hessian matrix is positive semidefinite at each point in S. Note that the entry in row i and column j of the Hessian matrix $H(\bar{x})$ is the second partial derivative $\partial^2 f(\bar{x})/\partial x_i \partial x_j$. Positive semidefiniteness implies, for any $\bar{x}$ in S, one must have $x'H(\bar{x})\, x \geq 0$ for all $x \in E_n$. A function $f: S \to E_n$ is called concave on S if $-f$ is convex.

Hence, for this function:

$$\frac{df}{dx} = 6x^2 - 2x + 2$$

$$\frac{d^2f}{dx^2} = 12x - 2$$

Since $(d^2f/dx^2)x^2$ is not greater than or equal to (or less than or equal to) zero for every x from $-\infty$ to $+\infty$, this function is neither convex nor concave.

• PROBLEM 9-2

Is the function $f(x) = x^2 - 6x + 4$ convex or concave?

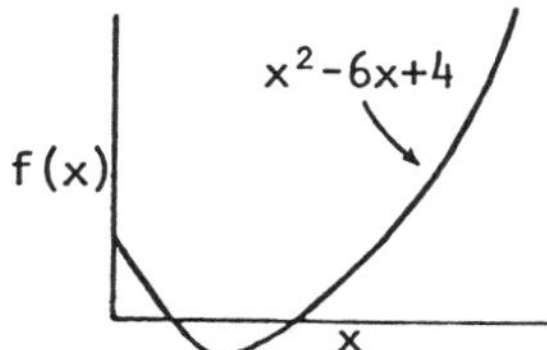

Solution:

$$\frac{df}{dx} = 2x - 6$$

$$\frac{d^2f}{dx^2} = +2$$

Since $d^2f/dx^2 > 0$, f(x) is strictly convex.

• PROBLEM 9-3

Let $f(x_1, x_2) = 3x_1 + 5x_2 - 4x_1^2 + 1x_2^2 - 5x_1x_2$. Find if f is convex, concave, or neither.

Solution: Put f in matrix form for convenience.

$$f(x_1, x_2) = (3\ 5)\begin{pmatrix} x_1 \\ x_2 \end{pmatrix} + \frac{1}{2}(x_1\ x_2)\begin{bmatrix} -8 & -5 \\ -5 & 2 \end{bmatrix}\begin{pmatrix} x_1 \\ x_2 \end{pmatrix}$$

It is required to check whether the Hessian matrix $\vec{H}$ of this function is positive semidefinite or negative semidefinite or neither. Hence, find the eigenvalues by

$$\det(\vec{H} - \lambda\vec{I}) = 0$$

$$\det\begin{bmatrix} -8-\lambda & -5 \\ -5 & 2-\lambda \end{bmatrix} = (-8 - \lambda)(2 - \lambda) + 25$$

$$\lambda^2 + 6\lambda + 9 = 0.$$

The roots of this equation are $\lambda_1 = -3$, and $\lambda_2 = -3$. Since both values of λ are negative, $\vec{H}$ is negative semi-definite, which implies that f is concave.

• PROBLEM 9-4

For each of the following, construct a diagram indicating the set of feasible points. Is the set convex? Assume $x_1 \geq 0$, $x_2 \geq 0$.

(a) $x_1^2 + (x_2 - 1)^2 - 1 \leq 0,$

$(x_1 - 1)^2 + x_2^2 - 1 \leq 0.$

(b) $x_1^2 + (x_2 - 1)^2 - 1 \leq 0,$

$x_1^2 + x_2^2 - 1 \leq 0.$

(c) $x_1^2 + x_2^2 - 1 \leq 0,$

$x_1 + x_2 - \frac{1}{2} \leq 0.$

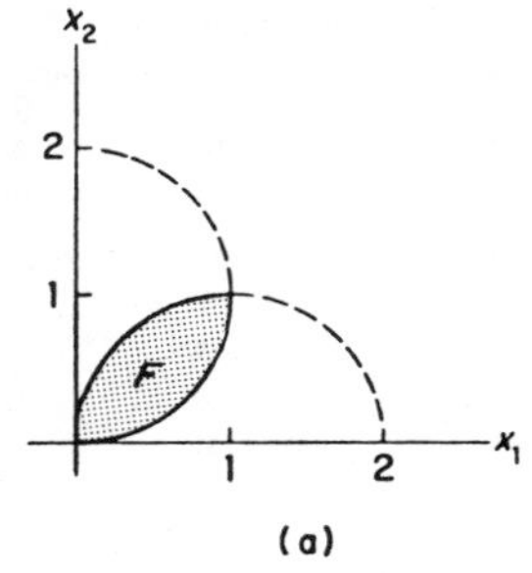

(a)

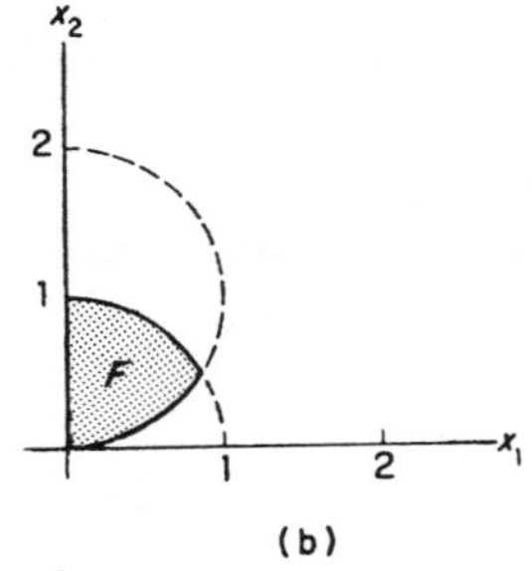

(b)

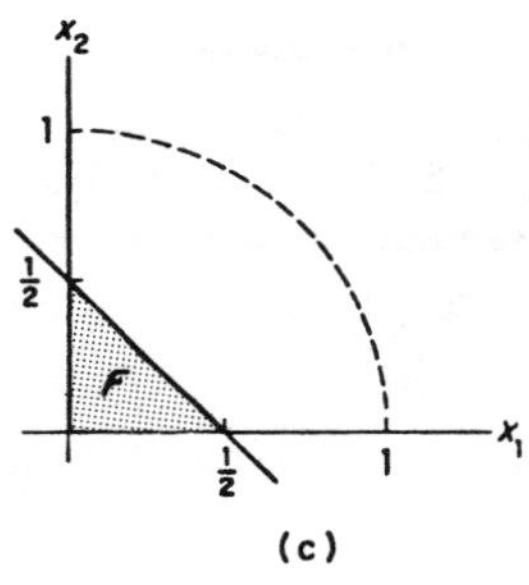

(c)

FIGURE 1

Solution: Definition of convexity: Let S be a nonempty convex set in E_n. The function $f:S \rightarrow E_1$ is said to be convex if

$$f(\lambda\vec{x}_1 + (1 - \lambda)\vec{x}_2) \leq \lambda f(\vec{x}_1) + (1 - \lambda) f(\vec{x}_2)$$

for each $\vec{x}_1$, $\vec{x}_2 \in S$ and for each $\lambda \in [0,1]$. The function f is said to be strictly convex if the above inequality holds as a strict inequality for each distinct $\vec{x}_1$, $\vec{x}_2 \in S$ and for each $\lambda \in (0,1)$.

(a) F is strictly convex, therefore convex. See Fig. 1 (a).

(b) F is convex but not strictly convex. See Fig. 1 (b).

(c) F is convex but not strictly convex. See Fig. 1 (c).

Which curves in Figure 1 are quasi-concave?

Which functions below are quasi-concave?

$$f(x) = \frac{1}{\sqrt{2\pi}} e^{-x^2/2},$$

$$f(x) = x^3,$$

$$f(x) = -3x,$$

$$f(x) = x^3 - 3x,$$

$$f(x_1) = x_1^3, \; g(x_1, x_2) = x_1^3 + x_2.$$

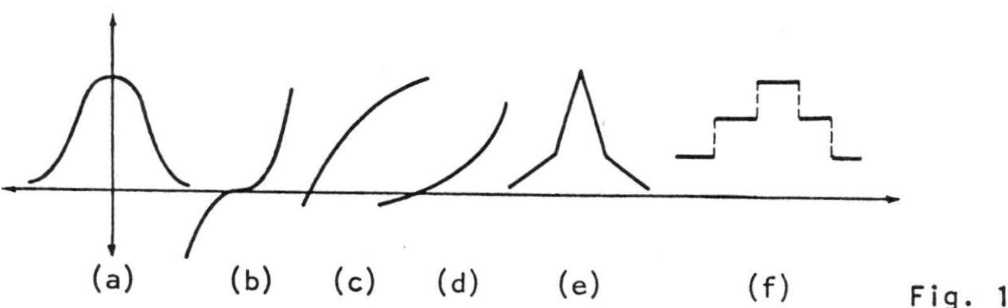

Fig. 1

Solution: A scalar function $f(\vec{x})$ is a quasi-concave function over a convex set X in E^n if for any two points $\vec{x}_1$ and $\vec{x}_2$ in X,

$$f(\lambda\vec{x}_1 + (1 - \lambda)\vec{x}_2) \geq \min\{f(\vec{x}_1), f(\vec{x}_2)\}, \qquad (1)$$

for all λ such that $0 \leq \lambda \leq 1$. Similarly, $f(\vec{x})$ is a quasi-convex function over X if for any $\vec{x}_1$ and $\vec{x}_2$ in X and any λ satisfying $0 \leq \lambda \leq 1$,

$$f(\lambda\vec{x}_1 + (1 - \lambda)\vec{x}_2) \leq \max\{f(\vec{x}_1), f(\vec{x}_2)\}.$$

The first definition implies that if $f(\vec{x})$ is a quasi-concave function, then it is impossible to find three collinear points such that the point in the middle has a smaller objective value than both of the other two. Thus the hypersurface $f(\vec{x})$ cannot have a "pit" or valley (in the ordinary sense of those terms), nor can it have two distinct peaks, although it may have one. For this reason quasi-concave functions are also called unimodal, or "one-humped."

A typical quasi-concave profile is that of the bell-shaped curve 1(a), which represents the unit normal probability density function.

Another kind of quasi-concave shape is illustrated by the curves (b), (c) and (d) in Fig. 1, which have no humps, or at least not in the intervals shown. It should be clear from these curves that any monotonically non-increasing or nondecreasing function is both quasi-concave and quasi-convex. Such a function may in addition be concave, as is (c), or convex, as is (d) -- and, of course, any linear function would be concave, convex, quasi-concave, and quasi-convex.

The last two curves of Fig. 1 illustrate certain pathologies of quasi-concave functions. Although 1(e) does not possess a well-defined derivative at every point and 1(f) is not even continuous, both satisfy the definition (1).

The function

$$f(x) = \frac{1}{\sqrt{2\pi}} e^{-x^2/2}$$

is the unit normal probability density function shown in Fig. 1(a). Note that this function is (strictly) concave in the middle but convex on either side; thus a quasi-concave function is not necessarily concave. However, concavity does imply quasi-concavity.

Although quasi-concave and quasi-convex functions -- those whose derivatives are continuous -- have certain properties that are desirable in mathematical programming, they are not nearly so important or useful as concave and convex functions. One major difficulty in working with them is that the properties of quasi-concavity and quasi-convexity are not necessarily preserved under addition. For example, $f(x) = x^3$ and $g(x) = -3x$ are both quasi-concave for all x, but $h(x) \equiv f(x) + g(x) = x^3 - 3x$ is not, inasmuch as it has a "pit" or local minimum at $x = 1$. The quasi-concavity of a function may even be destroyed by the addition of an "independent" quasi-concave term in some other variable. Thus $f(x_1) = x_1^3$ is quasi-concave everywhere, but $g(x_1, x_2) = x_1^3 + x_2$ is not, as is demonstrated by the following three collinear points:

$$g(0,0) = 0, \quad g(1, -3) = -2, \text{ and } g(2, -6) = 2.$$

As this example might suggest, there are few quasi-concave functions of two or more variables that are not concave as well.

• PROBLEM 9-6

Find the values of x_1 and x_2 that minimize

$$f(x_1, x_2) = e^{x_1 - x_2} + x_1^2 + x_2^2,$$

by using partial differentiation.

Solution: Since $f(x_1, x_2)$ can never be less than zero, its minimum value is finite and the optimal solution must lie at a point that satisfies the necessary conditions:

$$\frac{\partial f(\vec{x})}{\partial x_j} = 0, \quad j = 1,\ldots,n.$$

Thus

$$\frac{\partial f}{\partial x_1} = e^{x_1 - x_2} + 2x_1 = 0.$$

and

$$\frac{\partial f}{\partial x_2} = -e^{x_1 - x_2} + 2x_2 = 0.$$

These equations lead to

$$e^{2x_1} = -2x_1,$$

and, using a log table, discover by trial and error that

$$x_1 = -.2836,$$

$$x_2 = .2836,$$

$$f(x_1, x_2) = .7281.$$

Since this is the only critical point, it must be the global minimum.

• PROBLEM 9-7

Locate the stationary points (values of the independent variables at which the slope of the function is zero) of $f(x)$ and determine whether they are local maxima, local minima or neither.

$$f(X) = x_1^3 - x_1x_2 + x_2^2 - 2x_1 + 3x_2 - 4$$

Solution:

1. $\frac{\partial f}{\partial x_1} = 3x_1^2 - x_2 - 2 = 0.$

2. $\frac{\partial f}{\partial x_2} = -x_1 + 2x_2 + 3 = 0.$

3. From 2,

$x_1 = 2x_2 + 3.$

4. From 1 and 3

$3(2x_2 + 3)^2 - x_2 - 2 = 0$

$3(4x_2^2 + 12x_2 + 9) - x_2 - 2 = 0$

$12x_2^2 + 35x_2 + 25 = 0$

$(3x_2 + 5)(4x_2 + 5) = 0$

$x_2 = -5/3$ or $x_2 = -5/4,$

From 3

if $x_2 = -5/3$, $x_1 = -1/3$

if $x_2 = -5/4$, $x_1 = +1/2$

and the two stationary points are

$X_{01} = [-1/3, -5/3]$

and

$X_{02} = [+1/2, -5/4].$

The gradient vector ∇f and Hessian matrix is defined as follows:

$$\nabla f \equiv \left[\frac{\partial f}{\partial x_1}, \frac{\partial f}{\partial x_2}, \ldots, \frac{\partial f}{\partial x_n}\right]^T$$

$$H \equiv \left[\frac{\partial^2 f}{\partial x_i \partial x_j}\right] \quad (i,j = 1,2, \ldots, n)$$

The preliminary condition for a global maximum (and also a global minimum) is that f(X) should be continuous on a closed (end points of the variables are included in the region) and bounded (all variables have limiting values other than $-\infty$ or $+\infty$) region. If f(X) is to have a local maximum (or minimum) at X^*, ∇f should exist on some -neighborhood (i.e. incremental vicinity) around X^* and $\nabla f|_x = 0$. Also, second partial derivatives matrix, $H|_{x^*}$ should exist and be negative definite (positive definite) for a local maximum (local minimum) point.

The Hessian of f(X) is

$$\frac{\partial^2 f}{\partial x_1^2} = 6x_1 \qquad \frac{\partial^2 f}{\partial x_2^2} = +2$$

$$\frac{\partial f}{\partial x_1 \partial x_2} = \frac{\partial f}{\partial x_2 \partial x_1} = -1$$

$$H_f(x) = \begin{bmatrix} 6x_1 & -1 \\ -1 & +2 \end{bmatrix} .$$

Now to calculate the eigenvalues of the Hessian at each of the stationary points

$$[\lambda I - H] = \begin{bmatrix} \lambda - 6x_1 & +1 \\ +1 & \lambda - 2 \end{bmatrix}$$

At $x_{01} = [-1/3, -5/3]$

$$\det [\lambda I - H] = \begin{vmatrix} \lambda + 2 & +1 \\ +1 & \lambda - 2 \end{vmatrix} = (\lambda+2)(\lambda-2) - 1 = 0$$

$$\lambda^2 - 5 = 0$$

$$\lambda^2 = 5$$

$$\lambda = +\sqrt{5} \quad \text{and} \quad \lambda = -\sqrt{5} .$$

Since one eigenvalue is positive and the other negative, X_{01} is neither a local maximum nor a local minimum.

At $X_{02} = [+1/2, -5/4]$

$$\det [\lambda 1 - H] = \begin{vmatrix} \lambda - 3 & +1 \\ +1 & \lambda - 2 \end{vmatrix} = (\lambda-3)(\lambda-2) - 1 = 0$$

$$\lambda^2 - 5\lambda + 5 = 0$$

$$\frac{-b \pm \sqrt{b^2 - 4ac}}{2a} = \frac{+5 \pm \sqrt{25 - 20}}{2}$$

the solution to this equation is

$$\lambda_1 = \frac{5 + \sqrt{5}}{2} \qquad \lambda_2 = \frac{5 - \sqrt{5}}{2} .$$

Since both eigenvalues are positive, X_{02} is a local minimum.

Notice that when

$$X = [0, +\infty], \quad f(x) = +\infty$$

and when:

$$X = [-\infty, 0], \quad f(x) = -\infty$$

so that the global maximum and global minimum responses occur at extreme values of the decision variables.

• PROBLEM 9-8

Minimize $V(x_1,x_2) = c(x_1^2 + x_2^2 + x_1x_2 - ax_1 + ax_2)^2$

$$+ (1 - bx_1 - bx_2)^2$$

where

$$a = 4, \; b = 4, \; c = 10.$$

Solve by partial differentiation.

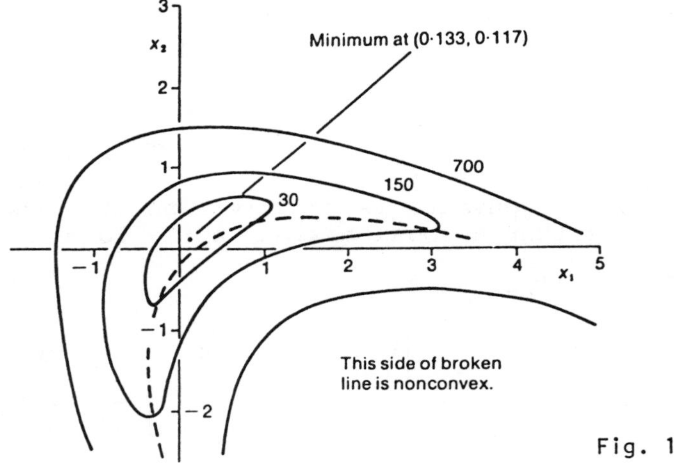

Fig. 1

Contours of constant V.

Solution: To deduce certain basic analytical results the manipulations are simplified if one substitutes

$$y = x_1 + x_2$$

$$x = x_1 - x_2$$

although this transformation will not be used when applying numerical techniques below.

Thus, in terms of the new variables

$$V(x,y) = c(y^2 - ax)^2 + (1 - by)^2$$

Note that:

$$\frac{\partial V}{\partial x} = 2ac(ax - y^2)$$

$$\frac{\partial V}{\partial y} = 4cy(y^2 - ax) - 2b(1 - by)$$

$$\frac{\partial^2 V}{\partial x^2} = 2a^2c$$

$$\frac{\partial^2 V}{\partial y \partial x} = -4acy$$

$$\frac{\partial^2 V}{\partial y^2} = 4c(3y^2 - ax) + 2b^2$$

from which it can be easily deduced that there is a stationary point at $(1/ab^2, 1/b)$. To check convexity, the following matrix must be positive definite

$$A = \begin{bmatrix} \dfrac{\partial^2 V}{\partial x^2} & \dfrac{\partial^2 V}{\partial x \partial y} \\ \dfrac{\partial^2 V}{\partial y \partial x} & \dfrac{\partial^2 V}{\partial y^2} \end{bmatrix}$$

Hence since $\partial^2 V/\partial x^2 > 0$ if $c > 0$, test that

$$|A| = 4a^2c[2c(y^2 - ax) + b^2] \qquad (1)$$

is positive. Assuming c is positive, it follows from Eq. (1) that the function is convex when

$$y^2 > a\left(x - \frac{b^2}{2ac}\right)$$

By substitution of $(1/ab^2, 1/b)$ in Eq. (2), it follows that the function has a single minimum when c is positive. On the other hand, there is a region where the function V is not convex. In terms of the original variables (x_1, x_2) the situation is illustrated in Fig. 1. The minimum value of the function is zero at (0.1328, 0.1172) and contours of V = 30, 150 and 700 are shown. The convexity boundary is indicated by a broken line.

• PROBLEM 9-9

Find the necessary and sufficient conditions for the following unconstrained optimization problem to have a solution:

$$\min\ x_1^4 + 6x_1^2x_2^2 + x_1x_2^3 - 6x_1x_3^3 - x_2x_3 + 4x_3^3 .$$

Solution: Necessary conditions:

$$\frac{\partial f}{\partial x_1} = 4x_1^3 + 12x_1x_2^2 + x_2^3 - 6x_3^3 = 0,$$

$$\frac{\partial f}{\partial x_2} = 12x_1^2x_2 + 3x_1x_2^2 - x_3 = 0,$$

$$\frac{\partial f}{\partial x_3} = -18x_1x_3^2 - x_2 + 12x_3^2 = 0.$$

Sufficient conditions: $\vec{H}$, the Hessian matrix (matrix of second partial derivatives) must be positive definitive. i.e.,

$$\vec{x}^t\ \vec{H}\ \vec{x} > 0$$

for all nonzero $\vec{x}$ in E_n ($\vec{H}$ being an $n \times n$ symmetric matrix). Hence

$$\vec{H} = \begin{bmatrix} f_{11} & f_{12} & f_{13} \\ f_{21} & f_{22} & f_{23} \\ f_{31} & f_{32} & f_{33} \end{bmatrix}$$

where

$$f_{ij} = \frac{\partial f}{\partial_i \partial_j},$$

for $i = i,2,3,;\ j = 1,2,3$

and

$$f_{11} = 12x_1^2 + 12x_2^2, \qquad f_{12} = 24x_1x_2 + 3x_2^2 = f_{21},$$

$$f_{22} = 12x_1^2 + 6x_1x_2, \qquad f_{13} = 18x_3^2 = f_{31},$$

$$f_{33} = -36x_1x_3 + 24x_3, \qquad f_{23} = -1 = f_{32}.$$

• **PROBLEM 9-10**

Consider the function

$$f(x_1,x_2,x_3)=2x_1 + 3x_2 + 3x_3 - x_1x_2 + x_1x_3$$

$$- x_2x_3 - x_1^2 - 3x_2^2 - x_3^2 .$$

Find a maximum point.

Solution: The necessary condition

$$\vec{\nabla}f \ (\vec{x}_0) = \vec{0},$$

gives

$$\frac{\partial f}{\partial x_1} = -2x_1 - x_2 + x_3 + 2 = 0$$

$$\frac{\partial f}{\partial x_2} = -6x_2 - x_2 - x_3 + 3 = 0$$

$$\frac{\partial f}{\partial x_3} = -2x_3 + x_3 - x_2 + 3 = 0.$$

The simultaneous solution yields

$$(\vec{x}_0) = (-7, -1, -16) .$$

To check for sufficiency condition, consider

$$\vec{H}\Big|_{\vec{x}} = \begin{pmatrix} \frac{\partial^2 f}{\partial x_1^2} & \frac{\partial^2 f}{\partial x_1 \partial x_2} & \frac{\partial^2 f}{\partial x_1 \partial x_3} \\ \frac{\partial^2 f}{\partial x_2 \partial x_1} & \frac{\partial^2 f}{\partial x_2^2} & \frac{\partial^2 f}{\partial x_2 \partial x_3} \\ \frac{\partial^2 f}{\partial x_3 \partial x_1} & \frac{\partial^2 f}{\partial x_3 \partial x_2} & \frac{\partial^2 f}{\partial x_3^3} \end{pmatrix}$$

$$= \begin{pmatrix} -2 & -1 & 1 \\ -1 & -6 & -1 \\ 1 & -1 & -2 \end{pmatrix}$$

the principal minor determinants as -2, 11, -17

respectively. Therefore,

$$\vec{H}\Big|_{\vec{x}}$$

is negative definite

and

$$\vec{x} = (-7, -1, -16)$$

is a maximum point.

• PROBLEM 9-11

In E.A.B. Company, production is found to be a function of of two factors x_1 and x_2, the objective is to maximize the yield $f(x) = 8x_1 + 2x_2 - x_1^2 - 4/2x_2^2$.

Solution:

$$\frac{\partial f}{\partial x_1} = 8 - 2x_1 = 0$$

$$\frac{\partial f}{\partial x_2} = 2 - x_2 = 0.$$

Solving these euqations yields a stationary point of $X = [4, 2]$. Now determine the nature of this stationary point;

$$\frac{\partial^2 f}{\partial x_1^2} = -2 \quad \frac{\partial^2 f}{\partial x_2^2} = -1 \qquad \frac{\partial^2 f}{\partial x_1 \partial x_2} = 0$$

$$H = \begin{bmatrix} -2 & 0 \\ 0 & -1 \end{bmatrix}$$

$$|\lambda I - H| = \begin{vmatrix} \lambda + 2 & 0 \\ 0 & \lambda + 1 \end{vmatrix} = (\lambda + 2)(\lambda + 1) = 0$$

See that the values of λ do not depend on X and that $\lambda_1 = -2$, $\lambda_2 = -1$. Since the eigen values are both negative, f(X) is concave and $x_1 = 4\%$, $x_2 = 2\%$ will give the global maximum yield of $f(X) = 78.0\%$.

NEWTON - RAPHSON METHOD

• PROBLEM 9-12

Use the Newton-Raphson method to solve

$$\min_{x_1, x_2} \ 4x_1^2 + 2x_1x_2 + 2x_2^2 + x_1 + x_2.$$

Solution:

$$\vec{\nabla} f(\vec{x}) = \begin{bmatrix} 8x_1 + 2x_2 + 1 \\ \\ 2x_1 + 4x_2 + 1 \end{bmatrix} = \vec{0} ,$$

$$\vec{H}(\vec{x}) = \begin{bmatrix} 8 & 2 \\ \\ 8 & 4 \end{bmatrix} ,$$

$$\vec{H}^{-1}(\vec{x}) = \frac{1}{14} \begin{bmatrix} 2 & -1 \\ -1 & 4 \end{bmatrix} .$$

$$\vec{x}^{n+1} = \vec{x}^n - \vec{H}^{-1} \vec{\nabla} f(\vec{x}^n).$$

Substituting

$$x_1^{n+1} = x_1^n - \frac{1}{14} [16x_1^n + 4x_2^n + 2 - 2x_1^n - 4x_2^n - 1],$$

$$x_2^{n+1} = x_2^n - \frac{1}{14} [-8x_1^n - 2x_2^n - 1 + 8x_1^n + 16x_2^n + 4] ,$$

or

$$x_1^{n+1} = x_1^n - x_1^n - \frac{1}{14} = - \frac{1}{14} ,$$

$$x_2^{n+1} = x_2^n - x_2^n - \frac{3}{14} = - \frac{3}{14} .$$

Thus the Newton-Raphson method solves linear equations in one iteration regardless of the initial estimate $\vec{X}^0$.

• PROBLEM 9-13

Consider the following unconstrained optimization problem:

$$\text{Min } f(x_1, x_2) = x_1^2 + x_1^2 x_2^2 + 3x_2^4 .$$

Solve by applying the Newton-Raphson Method with starting point

$$\vec{x}_0 = (1,1).$$

Find the answer, correct to three decimal places.

Solution: Since $f(x_1, x_2)$ can never be less than zero, its minimum value is finite and must occur at a point where the first partial derivatives vanish:

$$f_1(x_1, x_2) \equiv \frac{\delta f(x_1, x_2)}{\delta x_1} = 2x_1 + 2x_1x_2^2 = 0$$

and

$$f_2(x_1, x_2) \equiv \frac{\delta f(x_1, x_2)}{\delta x_2} = 2x_1^2x_2 + 12x_2^3 = 0.$$

The optimal solution lies at the origin. Now solve this pair of nonlinear equations via Newton-Raphson iteration. The first partial derivatives of f_1 and f_2 are

$$\frac{\delta f_1}{\delta x_1} = 2 + 2x_2^2 \qquad \frac{\delta f_1}{\delta x_2} = 4x_1x_2$$

$$\frac{\delta f_2}{\delta x_1} = 4x_1x_2 \qquad \frac{\delta f_2}{\delta x_2} = 2x_1^2 + 36x_2^2.$$

Taking $x_0 = (1,1)$ as the starting point, the Taylor-expansion equations, truncating after the first-order terms,

$$f_1(\vec{x}_0) + \frac{\delta f_1(\vec{x}_0)}{\delta x_1}\vec{\Delta}x_1 + \frac{\delta f_1(\vec{x}_0)}{\delta x_2}\vec{\Delta}x_2 + \ldots + \frac{\delta f_1(\vec{x}_0)}{\delta x_n}\vec{\Delta}x_n = 0,$$

$$f_2(\vec{x}_0) + \frac{\delta f_2(\vec{x}_0)}{\delta x_1}\vec{\Delta}x_1 + \frac{\delta f_2(\vec{x}_0)}{\delta x_2}\vec{\Delta}x_2 + \ldots + \frac{\delta f_2(\vec{x}_0)}{\delta x_n}\vec{\Delta}x_n = 0,$$

$$\cdots\cdots\cdots\cdots$$

$$f_n(\vec{x}_0) + \frac{\delta f_n(\vec{x}_0)}{\delta x_1}\vec{\Delta}x_1 + \frac{\delta f_n(\vec{x}_0)}{\delta x_2}\vec{\Delta}x_2 \ldots + \frac{\delta f_n(\vec{x}_0)}{\delta x_n}\vec{\Delta}x_n = 0,$$

for a set of equations

$$f_i(\vec{x}) = 0, \quad i = 1,\ldots,n,$$

become

$$4 + 4\vec{\Delta}x_1 + 4\vec{\Delta}x_2 = 0$$

and

$$14 + 4\vec{\Delta}x_1 + 38\vec{\Delta}x_2 = 0.$$

Solving, find

$$\vec{\Delta}x_1 = -12/17,$$

$$\vec{\Delta}x_2 = -5/17,$$

and the new point is therefore

$$\vec{x}_1 = (.294,\ .706),$$

$$\text{with } f(\vec{x}_1) = .874.$$

The next few iterations produce:

$$\vec{x}_2 = (.064,\ .477), \quad f(\vec{x}_2) = .160;$$

$$\vec{x}_3 = (.008,\ .318), \quad f(\vec{x}_3) = .031;$$

$$\vec{x}_4 = (.000,\ .212), \quad f(\vec{x}_4) = .006.$$

After 19 iterations a point $\vec{x}_{19} = (.000,\ .000)$ is obtained that is correct to three decimal places; six further iterations are required to achieve four-place accuracy.

Unfortunately, the method given for solving simulataneous nonlinear equations has a rather severe computational disadvantage: Unless the starting point $\vec{x}_0$ is chosen quite close to one of the solutions, the entire process may fail to converge.

• PROBLEM 9-14

Consider the problem of finding the solution to the system of one "simultaneous" nonlinear equation

$$f_1(x) = xe^{-x} = 0$$

by Newton-Raphson iteration. Determine for which values of the starting point x_0, the function will converge.

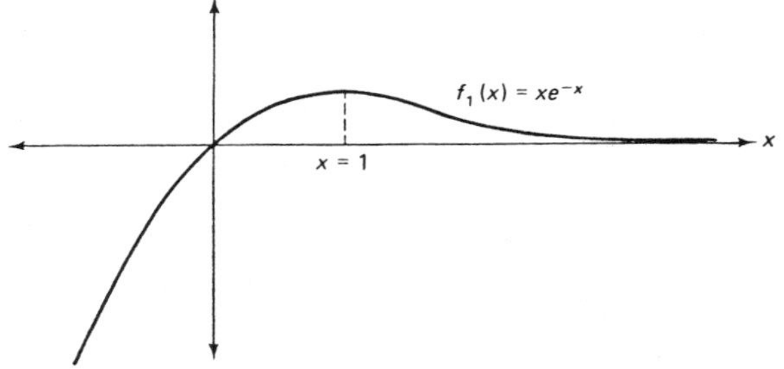

Fig. 1

Solution: The function is graphed in Fig. 1 and has only a single finite root at the origin. The derivative is

$$\frac{df_1}{dx} = (1 - x)e^{-x},$$

so the first-order Taylor expansion

$$f_1(x_0) + \frac{\delta f_1(x_0)}{\delta x_1}\Delta x_1 + \frac{\delta f_1(x_0)}{\delta x_2}\Delta x_2 + \ldots + \frac{\delta f_1(x_0)}{\delta x_n}\Delta x_n = 0$$

becomes

$$x_0 e^{-x_0} + (1 - x_0)e^{-x_0} \Delta x = 0.$$

Given any current point x_0, the correction in x will be

$$\Delta x = \frac{x_0}{x_0 - 1} . \tag{1}$$

Evidently, if the starting point x_0 is greater than 1, the first correction will be positive, so that the new value x_1 will exceed the old; the next correction will again be positive, and so on, with the kth value x_k diverging toward infinity as k increases. On the other hand, if the starting point is less than 1 (including all negative values), the process will eventually converge to the root $x = 0$. This can be verified by repeated application of (1).

Even when convergence to a local optimum occurs in an orderly and well-behaved manner, however, Newton-Raphson iteration is a very laborious procedure for obtaining points at which the partial derivatives of a function vanish. This is principally because each iteration requires the inversion of an n-by-n matrix.

ONE DIMENSIONAL SEARCH WITHOUT USING DERIVATIVES

• PROBLEM 9-15

For the function $f(x) = e^x - 5x$, perform two iterations of the three-point equal-interval search scheme for locating x^* in [1,2]. Since $d^2f/dx^2 = e^x > 0$, f(x) is strictly convex on all finite intervals and hence is unimodal. This function actually attains a minimum at $x^* = \ln 5 = 1.609$.

Apply the golden-section search scheme to locate the minimum of f(x) in the interval [1,2], and compare the result with that of three-point equal interval search.

Find the minimum of f(x) in [1,2] by the quadratic interpolation technique.

Solution: Three-Point-Equal-Interval Search: It is given $a^0 = 1$ and $b^0 = 2$. Choose $x_1^0 = 1.25$, $x_2^0 = 1.5$, and $x_3^0 = 1.75$. By direct computation, $f(1.25) = -2.75$, $f(1.5) = -3.0$, and $f(1.75) = -2.96$. Evidently $f(1.5) = \min[f(1.25), f(1.5), f(1.75)]$. Hence set $a^1 = 1.25$

and $b^1 = 1.75$. Then $(b^1 - a^1)/4 = 0.125$, and choose $x_1^1 = 1.375$, $x_2^1 = 1.5$, and $x_3^1 = 1.625$. The function $f(x_2^1) = f(1.5) = -3.0$ has already been computed. As for the other function values, obtain by direct computation $f(1.375) = -2.95$ and $f(1.625) = -3.03$. Now $f(1.625) = \min [f(1.375), f(1.5), f(1.625)]$. Therefore, set $a^2 = 1.5$ and $b^2 = 1.75$. One can either continue these iterations or take the midpoint of $[a^2, b^2]$, which is 1.625, as an estimate of x^*.

Golden-Section Search: When the three-point equal-interval search scheme is used after five function evaluations $\Delta L = 0.25$ is attained. Now allow five function evaluations for the golden-section search scheme and, obtain the resulting ΔL. Since it is given $a^0 = 1$ and $b^0 = 2$, the intermediate points for the golden-section search scheme are $x_1^0 = 1.382$ and $x_2^0 = 1.618$. By direct computation $f(1.382) = -2.94$ and $f(1.618) = 3.1$. Since $f(x_1^0) > f(x_2^0)$, set $a^1 = x_1^0 = 1.382$ and $b^1 = b^0 = 2$.

In the next iteration set $x_1^1 = x_2^0 = 1.618$ and compute $x_2^1 = 2 - (1 - 0.618)(2 - 1.382) = 1.765$. Then by direct computation, $f(1.765) = -3.0$. Since $f(x_2^1) > f(x_1^1)$, set $a^2 = a^1 = 1.382$ and $b^2 = x_2^1 = 1.765$.

In the third iteration, set $x_2^2 = x_1^1 = 1.618$ and compute $x_1^2 = 1.382 + 0.382\,(1.765 - 1.382) = 1.527$. By direct computation $f(1.527) = -2.0$ and evidently $f(x_1^2) > f(x_2^2)$, so set $a^3 = x_1^2 = 1.527$ and $b^3 = b^2 = 1.765$.

In the fourth iteration set $x_1^3 = x_2^2 = 1.618$ and compute $x_2^3 = 1.765 - 0.382(1.765 - 1.527) = 1.674$. Then by direct computation $f(1.674) = -3.06$, and evidently $f(x_2^3) > f(x_1^3)$, so that $a^4 = a^3 = 1.527$ and $b^4 = x_2^3 = 1.674$. Now five function evaluations have been used up so now compute $\Delta L = (b^4 - a^4)/(b^0 - a^0) = 0.147$. Comparing this value with 0.25 achieved in three-point equal-interval search clearly shows the superiority of the golden-section search scheme over the three-point equal-interval search scheme.

Quadratic Interpolation: $\hat{\lambda}$ - an estimate of λ_1, where λ_1 minimizes $f(x^0 + \lambda v)$ with respect to λ - is given by

$$\hat{\lambda} = \frac{1}{2}\,\frac{g(a)(c^2 - b^2) + g(b)(a^2 - c^2) + g(c)(b^2 - a^2)}{g(a)(c - b) + g(b)(a - c) + g(c)(b - a)}. \tag{1}$$

Using the new variable $\lambda = x - 1$, obtain $g(\lambda) = e^{\lambda+1} - 5(\lambda + 1)$. By direct computation $g(0) = -2.282$ and $g(1) = -2.611$. Since $g(1) < g(0)$, compute $g(2) = 5.086$. Now $g(2) > g(1)$, so set a = 0, b = 1, and c = 2 in (1), obtaining

$$\hat{\lambda} = \frac{1}{2}\left(\frac{-2.282(4-1) + (-2.611)(-4) + 5.086}{-2.282(2-1) + (-2.611)(-2) + 5.086}\right) = 0.531.$$

The exact solution λ^* is given by $\lambda^* = x^* - 1 = 0.609$.

• PROBLEM 9-16

For the function $f(x) = 8x^3 - 2x^2 - 7x + 3$, perform two iterations of the dichotomous search scheme for locating the minimum in [0,1].

In the interval [0,1], apply the three-point equal-interval search scheme and compare the results with the above solution. Applying the quadratic interpolation technique, find $\hat{\lambda}$ from (1) and compare the result with that of dichotomous search:

$$\hat{\lambda} = \frac{1}{2}\left(\frac{g(a)(c^2 - b^2) + g(b)(a^2 - c^2) + g(c)(b^2 - a^2)}{g(a)(c - b) + g(b)(a - c) + g(c)(b - a)}\right) \quad (1)$$

Choose $\varepsilon = 0.1$.

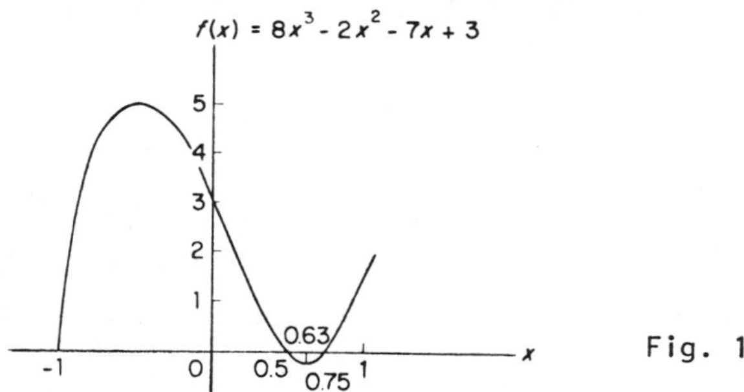

Fig. 1

Solution: One can analytically verify that in the interval [-1,1], f(x) has a maximum of 5 at x = - 0.464 and a minimum of - 0.2 at x = 0.63. The graph of f(x) is shown in Fig. 1.

Dichotomous Search: Set $a^0 = 0$, $b^0 = 1$. Then $c^0 = 0.5$, $x_1^0 = 0.45$, and $x_2^0 = 0.55$. By direct computation obtain $f(0.45) = 0.52$ and $f(0.55) = -0.124$. Since $f(x_1^0) > f(x_2^0)$, set $a^1 = x_1^0 = 0.45$ and $b^1 = b^0 = 1$. Then $c^1 = 0.725$,

$x_1^1 = 0.675$, and $x_2^1 = 0.775$. Again, by direct computation $f(0.675) = -0.17$ and $f(0.775) = 0.076$. Since $f(x_2^1) > f(x_1^1)$, set $a^2 = a^1 = 0.45$ and $b^2 = x_2^1 = 0.775$.

Equal Interval Search: Since $a^0 = 0$ and $b^0 = 1$, choose $x_1^0 = 0.25$, $x_2^0 = 0.5$, and $x_3^0 = 0.75$. By direct computation $f(0.25) = 1.24$, and $f(0.5) = f(0.75) = 0$. Thus either $a^1 = 0.5$ and $b^1 = 1$ or $a^1 = 0.25$ and $b^1 = 0.75$ can be set, and both these intervals contain x^*. In this case $b^1 - a^1 = 0.50$, compared with $b^1 - a^1 = 1 - 0.45 = 0.55$ in dichotomous search. Further reduce the length of the interval containing x^* by noting that $f(x)$ is unimodal and $f(0.5) = f(0.75) < f(0.25)$. Thus set $a^1 = 0.5$ and $b^1 = 0.75$, which results in $b^1 - a^1 = 0.25$ rather than 0.5. However, in this case $f(x)$ must be evaluated three times in the next iteration.

Quadratic Interpolation: Note that $g(0) = 3$ and $g(1) = 2$, i.e., $g(1) < g(0)$. Compute $g(\lambda)$ for $\lambda = 2$ and obtain $g(2) = 45$. Since $g(2) > g(1)$, set $a = 0$, $b = 1$, and $c = 2$. Then by (1):

$$\hat{\lambda} = \frac{1}{2}\left(\frac{3(4-1) + 2(0-4) + 45(1-0)}{3(2-1) + 2(0-2) + 45(1-0)}\right) = 0.52.$$

It is known that $g(\lambda)$ attains a minimum in $[0,1]$ at $\lambda^* = 0.63$, and thus $\hat{\lambda} = 0.52$ is a poor estimate of λ^* although it does require only three function evaluations. Most of the other interval search techniques will yield a better estimate of λ^* with four function evaluations. However, this accuracy may not be needed in the initial stages of an optimization algorithm which uses a one-dimensional search in every iteration.

• PROBLEM 9-17

Perform three iterations of the three-point equal-interval search to minimize

$f(x) = x^2 - 4x + 2$ over the interval $0 \le x \le 10$.

Solution: Evaluating $f(x)$ at three equidistant points on the interval $[0,10]$ yields

$$f(2.5) = -6.75,\ f(5.0) = -3.00,\ f(7.5) = 13.25.$$

Retain the interval $[0,5]$ and evaluate $f(x)$ at three

equidistant points on the interval [0,5], yielding

$$f(1.25) = -3.94, \quad f(2.5) = -6.75, \quad f(3.75) = -6.44.$$

Retain the interval [2.5,5] and evaluate f(x) at three equidistant points on the interval [2.5,5], obtaining

$$f(3.125) = -6.98, \quad f(3.75) = -6.44, \quad f(4.335) = -5.11.$$

Retain the interval [2.5,3.75]. Thus after three iterations consisting of 9 trials, the interval of uncertainty has been reduced to 12.5% of its initial value.

• PROBLEM 9-18

Consider the following problem:

Minimize $\lambda^2 + 2\lambda$

subject to $-3 \leq \lambda \leq 5$

Use the golden Section search to solve. Reduce the interval of uncertainty to one whose length is at most 0.2.

TABLE 1

Iteration k	a_k	b_k	λ_k	μ_k	$\theta(\lambda_k)$	$\theta(\mu_k)$
1	−3.000	5.000	0.056	1.944	0.115*	7.667*
2	−3.000	1.944	−1.112	0.056	−0.987*	0.115
3	−3.000	0.056	−1.832	−1.112	−0.308*	−0.987
4	−1.832	0.056	−1.112	−0.664	−0.987	−0.887*
5	−1.832	−0.664	−1.384	−1.112	−0.853*	−0.987
6	−1.384	−0.664	−1.112	−0.936	−0.987	−0.996*
7	−1.384	−0.936	−1.208	−1.112	−0.957*	−0.987
8	−1.208	−0.936	−1.112	−1.032	−0.987	−0.999*
9	−1.112	−0.936				

Solution: The first step is to choose an allowable final length of uncertainty $\ell > 0$ (given $\ell < 0.2$.) Let $[a_1, b_1]$ be the initial interval of uncertainty, and let $\lambda_1 = a_1 + (1 - \alpha)(b_1 - a_1)$ and $\mu_1 = a_1 + \alpha(b_1 - a_1)$, where $\alpha = 0.618$. Evaluate $\theta(\lambda_1)$ and $\theta(\mu_1)$, let $k = 1$. The function θ to be minimized is strictly quasiconvex, and the initial interval of uncertainty is of length 8. The first two observations are located at

$$\lambda_1 = -3 + 0.382(8) = 0.056 \quad \mu_1 = -3 + 0.618(8) = 1.944$$

The algorithm is as follows:

1. If $b_k - a_k < \ell$, stop; the optimal solution lies in the interval $[a_k, b_k]$. Otherwise, if $\theta(\lambda_k) > \theta(\mu_k)$,

go to step 2, and if $\theta(\lambda_k) \le \theta(\mu_k)$, go to step 3.

2. Let $a_{k+1} = \lambda_k$ and $b_{k+1} = b_k$. Let $\lambda_{k+1} = \mu_k$ and $\mu_{k+1} = a_{k+1} + \alpha(b_{k+1} - a_{k+1})$. Evaluate $\theta(\mu_{k+1})$, and go to step 4.

3. Let $a_{k+1} = a_k$, and $b_{k+1} = \mu_k$. Let $\mu_{k+1} = \lambda_k$ and let $\lambda_{k+1} = a_{k+1} + (1 - \alpha)(b_{k+1} - a_{k+1})$. Evaluate $\theta(\lambda_{k+1})$, and go to step 4.

4. Replace k by k+1, and go to step 1.

Note that $\theta(\lambda_1) < \theta(\mu_1)$. Hence, the interval of uncertainty is [-3,1.944]. The process is repeated, and the computations are summarized in Table 1. The values of θ that are computed at each iteration are indicated by an asterisk. After eight iterations involving nine observations, the interval of uncertainty is [-1.112, -0.936], so that the minimum could be estimated to be the midpoint -1.024. Note that the true minimum is, in fact, -1.0.

• PROBLEM 9-19

Assume that one wishes to reduce an interval $5.11 \le x \le 23.64$ to one only 10% as long, the resolution being 0.545 unit. Use the Fibonacci Search Method to solve.

Solution: Hence

$$I^0 = 18.53, \quad I^n \le 1.853, \qquad \text{and}$$

$$\varepsilon = 0.545/18.53 = 0.0294.$$

The number of observations n is the unique integer satisfying

$$\vec{A}^n((\vec{A}^{n-2}\varepsilon + 1)^{-1} < \frac{\vec{I}^0}{\vec{I}^n} \le \vec{A}^{n+1}(\vec{A}^{n-1}\varepsilon + 1)^{-1}$$

which gives n = 6, since

$$8[3(0.0294) + 1]^{-1} = 7.35 < 10.00 < 13[5(0.0294) + 1]^{-1}$$

$$= 11.33$$

The final interval will be shorter than 1.853, so take the full reduction ratio of 11.33 and have a final interval of length $18.53(11.33)^{-1} = 1.636$. In terms of this final interval, the resolution is

$$\delta = \frac{\varepsilon I^1}{I^6} = (0.0294)(11.33) = 0.334 .$$

Since $\delta < \frac{1}{2}$, there is no danger of having the last two observations too close together.
Fibonacci search places the first observation at

$$5.11 + x^1 = 5.11 + (A^6 - A^{6-2}\delta)I^6$$

$$= 5.11 + [8 - 3(0.334)](1.636)$$
$$= 5.11 + 11.45 = 16.56.$$

The second is placed symmetrically at

$$23.64 - x^1 = 12.19.$$

Assume that $y(16.56) = 8.73$ and $y(12.19) = 9.07.$

Then if the maximum is sought, there is no need to explore values greater than 16.56,

$$5.11 \leq x^* < 16.56.$$

The third measurement is placed symmetrically with respect to the one still in the interval, namely at

$$16.56 - (12.19 - 5.11) = 9.48.$$

Let the result be

$$y(9.48) = 7.89.$$

This eliminates the left portion and implies that

$$9.48 < x^* < 16.56.$$

The best result is still at 12.19.

The fourth is located symmetrically at

$$9.48 + 16.56 - 12.19 = 13.85.$$

If $y(13.85) = 9.32 > y(12.19)$,

then $12.19 < x^* < 16.56$

and the fifth observation is made at

$$12.19 + 16.56 - 13.85 = 14.90.$$

If $y(14.90) = 9.27 < y(13.85)$,

then $12.19 < x^* < 14.90$

and the objective is measured finally at

$$12.19 + 14.90 - 13.85 = 13.24.$$

Notice that this is 0.61 unit from the nearest measurement at 13.85, a close approximation to the desired resolution, 0.545. The discrepancy is due to accumulated error caused by rounding off in the second decimal place.

Assume that the sixth result is $y(13.24) = 9.36 > y(13.85)$. Then the final interval is

$$12.19 < x^* < 13.85.$$

Its length is 1.66, slightly above the predicted 1.64 because of rounding error, but still well below the 1.85 required.

• PROBLEM 9-20

Consider the following problem:

Minimize $\lambda^2 + 2\lambda$

subject to $-3 \leq \lambda \leq 5$

Use the Fibonacci search method to solve. Adopt a

distinguishability constant

$$\varepsilon = 0.01.$$

TABLE 1

Iteration k	a_k	b_k	λ_k	μ_k	$\theta(\lambda_k)$	$\theta(\mu_k)$
1	−3.000000	5.000000	0.054545	1.945454	0.112065*	7.675699*
2	−3.000000	1.945454	−1.109091	0.054545	−0.988099*	0.112065
3	−3.000000	0.054545	−1.836363	−1.109091	−0.300497*	−0.988099
4	−1.836363	0.054545	−1.109091	−0.672727	−0.988099	−0.892892*
5	−1.836363	−0.672727	−1.399999	−1.109091	−0.840001*	−0.988099
6	−1.399999	−0.672727	−1.109091	−0.963636	−0.988099	−0.998677*
7	−1.109091	−0.672727	−0.963636	−0.818182	−0.998677	−0.966942*
8	−1.109091	−0.818182	−0.963636	−0.963636	−0.998677	−0.998677
9	−1.109091	−0.963636	−0.963636	−0.953636	−0.998677	−0.997850*

Solution: The first step is to choose an allowable final length of uncertainty $\ell > 0$ and a distinguishability constant $\varepsilon > 0$. Let a_1, b_1 be the initial interval of uncertainty, and choose the number of observations n to be taken such that

$$F_n > (b_1 - a_1)/\ell$$

Let $$\lambda_1 = a_1 + (F_{n-2}/F_n)(b_1 - a_1),$$

and $$\mu_1 = a_1 + (F_{n-1}/F_n)(b_1 - a_1)$$

Evaluate $\theta(\lambda_1)$ and $\theta(\mu_1)$, let k=1, and go to the main step.

Note that the function is strictly quasiconvex on the interval and that the true minimum occurs at $\lambda = -1$. Reduce the interval of uncertainty to one whose length is, at most, 0.2. Hence,

$$F_n > 8/0.2 = 40,$$

so that n = 9.

The first two observations are located at

$$\lambda_1 = -3 + \frac{F_7}{F_9}(8) = 0.054545$$

$$\mu_1 = -3 + \frac{F_8}{F_9}(8) = 1.945454.$$

Main Step:

1. If $\theta(\lambda_k) > \theta(\mu_k)$, go to step 2, and if $\theta(\lambda_k) \leq \theta(\mu_k)$, go to step 3.

2. Let $a_{k+1} = \lambda k$ and $b_{k+1} = b_k$. Let $\lambda_{k+1} = \mu_k$ and let

$$\mu_{k+1} = a_{k+1} + (F_{n-k-1}/F_{n-k})(b_{k+1} - a_{k+1}).$$

If k = n − 2, go to step 5, otherwise, evaluate $\theta(\mu_{k+1})$ and go to step 4.

3. Let $a_{k+1} = a_k$ and $b_{k+1} = \mu_k$. Let $\mu_{k+1} = \lambda_k$ and let

$$\lambda_{k+1} = a_{k+1} + (F_{n-k-2}/F_{n-k})(b_{k+1} - a_{k+1}).$$

If $k = n - 2$, go to step 5; otherwise, evaluate $\theta(\lambda_{k+1})$, and go to step 4.

4. Replace k by k+1, and go to step 1.

5. Let $\lambda_n = \lambda_{n-1}$, and $\mu_n = \lambda_{n-1} + \varepsilon$.

If $\theta(\lambda_n) > \theta(\mu_n)$ let $a_n = \lambda_n$ and $b_n = b_{n-1}$. Otherwise, if $\theta(\lambda_n) \leq \theta(\mu_n)$, let $a_n = a_{n-1}$ and $b_n = \lambda_n$.

Stop; the optimal solution lies in the interval a_n, b_n .

Note that $\theta(\lambda_1) < \theta(\mu_1)$. Hence the new interval of uncertainty is [-3.000000, 1.945454]. The process is repeated, and the computations are summarized in Table 1. The values of θ that are computed at each iteration are indicated by an asterisk. Note that at k = 8, $\lambda_k = \mu_k = \lambda_{k-1}$, so that no functional evaluations are needed at this stage. For k = 9, $\lambda_k = \lambda_{k-1} = -0.963636$ and $\mu_k = \lambda_k + \varepsilon = -0.953636$.

Since $\theta(\mu_k) > \theta(\lambda_k)$, the final interval of uncertainty

$[a_9, b_9]$ is [-1.109091, -0.963636], whose length $\ell = 0.145455$. Approximate the minimum to be the midpoint -1.036364.

• PROBLEM 9-21

The Scheker Candy Company is beginning the production of a new dietetic candy bar. The production cost is 8.5¢ per bar. The marketing department has suggested that the weekly demand is given by $1000/p^2$ where p is the wholesale price at which the candy bar is sold. Scheker Candy Company is interested in finding the selling price that maximizes its total weekly profits.

Since weekly profit is simply the profit per bar times the number of bars sold, the profit function Z(p) is given by

$$Z(p) = (p - 0.085)1000/p^2.$$

The problem is to find the price, p, that maximizes Z(p).

Assume that the interest is in determining the maximum of $Z(p) = (p - 0.085)1000/p^2$ for $0.0 \leq p \leq 0.60$, but that due to computational cost the function Z(p) can be evaluated only 11 times. That is, the profit for any 11 prices between 0 and 60¢ can be computed.

Apply the Uniform Search method to solve this problem.

TABLE 1 Evaluation of profit

Price p	Demand $1000/p^2$	Profit (loss)/bar $p-0.085$	Total profit (loss) $(p-0.085)1000/p^2$
0	∞	−0.085	$-\infty$
0.06	277,000	−0.025	−6925
0.12	69,444	0.035	2431
0.18	30,864	0.095	2932
0.24	17,361	0.155	2691
0.30	11,111	0.215	2388
0.36	7,716	0.275	2122
0.42	5,668	0.335	1899
0.48	4,340	0.395	1714
0.54	3,429	0.455	1560
0.60	2,777	0.515	1431

Solution: Uniform Search requires that
$Z(p)$ for $p = 0, 0.06, 0.12, 0.18, \ldots, 0.60$
be examined. That is begin at 0¢ and examine points spaced equally apart. These computations have been performed for Scheker Candy problem and the results can be seen in Table 1. Consider the information gained from the uniform search.

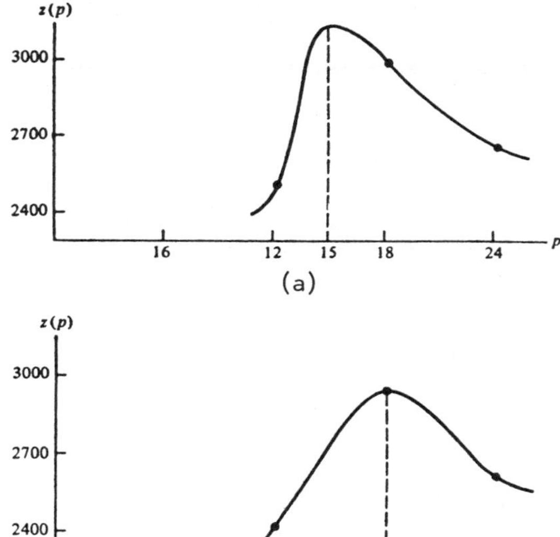

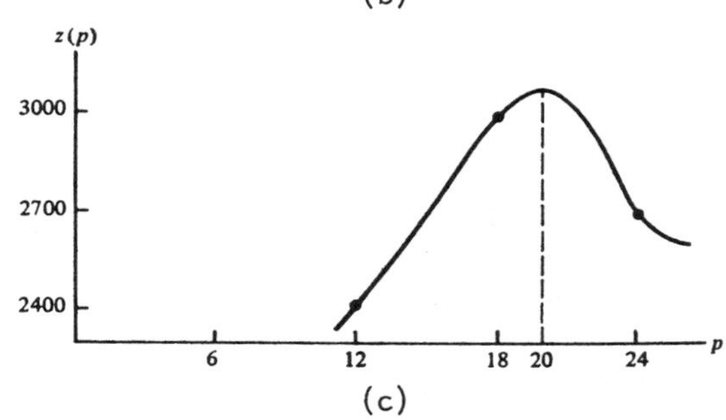

(c)

Possible Shapes of Z(p) Fig. 1

From the table, guess that the best price is near 18¢ and certainly between 12¢ and 24¢. The reason the maximum is not at 18¢ can be seen in Figure 1. For the three values at 12¢, 18¢, and 24¢ it is possible that the function actually appears as any one of the cases in the figure. In Figure 1a, 15 is indicated as the maximum; in 1b, 18 is maximum; and in 1c, 20 is maximum. Actually the safest statement to be made is that "the optimal price lies between 12¢ and 24¢." (Since it is not known whether or not Z(p) is unimodal, by optimal it is meant local.) Of course, the denser the grid, the smaller this interval of uncertainty. Since each interval in the grid has a length of L/(n-1) when n is the number of points searched and L is the size of the domain of the search, the interval of uncertainty is given by 2L/(n-1).

• PROBLEM 9-22

Consider the function $Z(p) = (p - 0.085)1000/p^2$;

assume that the initial interval of uncertainty is [0,0.6]. Examine 11 points by Bisecting Search method in order to find a maximum value. What is the final interval of uncertainty?

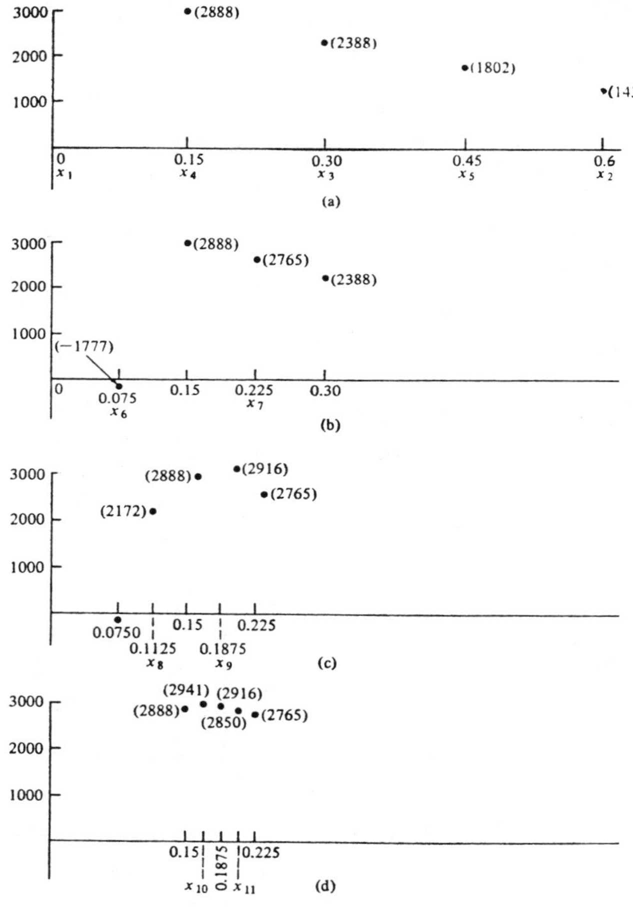

Bisecting Search Method Fig. 1

Solution: In summary, the Bisecting Search method for optimizing a function defined on [a,b] is as follows:

1. Set $x_1 = a, x_2 = a + (b-a)/4, x_3 = (a + b)/2, x_4 = a + 3(b - a)/4$, $x_5 = b$.

2. Compute $f(x_j)$, $j = 1,2,3,4,5$.

3. Let j be such that $f(x_j) = \text{optimum}\ \{f(x_1), f(x_2), \ldots, f(x_5)\}$.

4. If j = 2, 3, or 4, then set $a = x_{j-1}$, $b = x_{j+1}$ and go to Step 7.

5. If j = 1, set $a = x_1$, $b = x_2$ and go to Step 7.

6. If j = 5, set $a = x_4$, $b = x_5$ and go to Step 7.

7. Set the interval of uncertainty equal to L = b - a. If L is less than the predetermined length, stop. Otherwise go to Step 1.

Let $x_1 = 0$ and $x_2 = 0.6$

and evaluate Z at these two boundary points, obtaining

$$Z(0) = -\infty \quad \text{and} \quad Z(0.6) = 1431.$$

A logical point to consider next is the midpoint of the interval [0,0.6]. Hence, let $x_3 = 0.3$ and find that Z(0.3) = 2388. The information available is that the profit begins at minus infinity, reaches at least $2388, and is reduced to $1431 at a price of 60¢. However, it is not known if profit increases to the right of 30¢ or not. The points that might help determine this are the midpoints of the intervals [0,0.30] and [0.30,0.60]. Thus, search x_4 = 15¢ and x_5 = 45¢, respectively, and find that the associated profits are Z(0.15) = 2888 and Z(0.45) = 1802, respectively. Hence, the information appears as in Figure 1a. From the figure it can be determined that the maximum lies between 0 and 30¢. (Again, it is a global maximum if Z is well behaved, a local maximum otherwise.) Hence, after the initial two boundary point evaluations and the three midpoint evaluations, the interval of uncertainty is now one half the length of the original interval of uncertainty. Repeat this process on the new interval, [0,0.30]. The points that must be evaluated are 0¢, 7.5¢, 15¢, 22.5¢ and 30¢. Notice that there already are values for 0¢, 15¢, and 30¢, so that actually only two new points need to be evaluated.

Letting $x_6 = 0.075$ and $x_7 = 0.225$, determine that Z(0.075) = -1777 and Z(0.225) = 2765. The results are plotted in Fig. 1b and one can see that the maximum must lie between 7.5¢ and 22.5¢. Again the interval of uncertainty has been reduced in length by one half. Continuing, one finds that $x_8 = 0.1125$ and $x_9 = 0.1875$ and the respective profits are $Z(x_8) = 2172$ and $Z(x_9) = 2916$. Hence the new interval of uncertainty is between 15¢ and 22.5¢. One last bisection is made, and the evaluation at $x_{10} = 0.16875$ and $x_{11} = 0.20625$ is computed. The values are $Z(x_{10}) = 2941$ and $Z(x_{11}) = 2850$, respectively. The interval of uncertainty is now [0.15,0.1875], which has a length of 0.0375.

ONE DIMENSIONAL SEARCH USING DERIVATIVES

• PROBLEM 9-23

Consider the following problem:

Minimize $\lambda^2 + 2\lambda$

subject to $-3 \leq \lambda \leq 6$

Reduce the interval of uncertainty to an interval whose length ℓ is less than or equal to 0.2. Use the Bisecting Search Method.

TABLE **Summary of Computations for the Bisecting Search Method**

Iteration k	a_k	b_k	λ_k	$\theta'(\lambda_k)$
1	−3.0000	6.0000	1.5000	5.0000
2	−3.0000	1.5000	−0.7500	0.5000
3	−3.0000	−0.7500	−1.8750	−1.7500
4	−1.8750	−0.7500	−1.3125	−0.6250
5	−1.3125	−0.7500	−1.0313	−0.0625
6	−1.0313	−0.7500	−0.8907	0.2186
7	−1.0313	−0.8907		

Solution: The Bisecting Search Method:

At any iteration k, θ' is evaluated at the midpoint of the interval of uncertainty. Based on the value of θ', either stop or construct a new interval of uncertainty whose length is half that of the previous iteration.

The procedure for minimizing a pseudoconvex function θ over a closed and bounded interval is as follows:

Initialization Step: Let $[a_1, b_1]$ be the initial interval of uncertainty, and let ℓ be the allowable final interval of uncertainty. let n be the smallest positive integer such that

$$\left(\frac{1}{2}\right)^n \leq \ell/(b_1 - a_1).$$

Let k = 1, and go to the main step.

Main Step:

1. Let $\lambda_k = \frac{1}{2}(a_k + b_k)$ and evaluate $\theta'(\lambda_k)$. If $\theta'(\lambda_k) = 0$, stop; λ_k is an optimal solution. Otherwise, go to step 2 if $\theta'(\lambda_k) > 0$, and go to step 3 if $\theta'(\lambda_k) < 0$.

2. Let $a_{k+1} = ak$, and $b_{k+1} = \lambda_k$. Go to step 4.

3. Let $a_{k+1} = \lambda_k$, and $b_{k+1} = b_k$. Go to step 4.

4. If k = n, stop; the minimum lies in the interval

$$[a_{n+1}, b_{n+1}].$$

Otherwise, replace k by k + 1, and repeat step 1. Hence, the number of observations n satisfying

$$\left(\frac{1}{2}\right)^n \leq \ell/(b_1 - a_1) = 0.2/9 = 0.0222$$

is given by n = 6. A summary of the computations using the Bisecting Search method is given in the Table. The final interval of uncertainty is [-1.0313, -0.8907], so that the minimum could be taken as the midpoint -0.961.

• PROBLEM 9-24

Consider the function θ defined below:

$$\theta(\lambda) = \begin{cases} 4\lambda^3 - 3\lambda^4 & \text{if } \lambda \geq 0 \\ 4\lambda^3 + 3\lambda^4 & \text{if } \lambda < 0 \end{cases}$$

Note that θ is twice differentiable everywhere. Apply Newton's method, to find if and what value the function converges, starting from two different points: λ_1 = 0.40 and λ_1 = 0.60. ε = 0.003.

TABLE 1 **Summary of Computations for Newton's Method Starting from $\lambda_1 = 0.4$**

Iteration k	λ_k	$\theta'(\lambda_k)$	$\theta''(\lambda_k)$	λ_{k+1}
1	0.400000	1.152000	3.840000	0.100000
2	0.100000	0.108000	2.040000	0.047059
3	0.047059	0.025324	1.049692	0.022934
4	0.022934	0.006167	0.531481	0.011331
5	0.011331	0.001523	0.267322	0.005634
6	0.005634	0.000379	0.134073	0.002807

Solution: Newton's method is based on exploiting the quadratic approximation of the function θ at a given point λ_k. This quadratic approximation q is given by

$$q(\lambda) = \theta(\lambda_k) + \theta'(\lambda_k)(\lambda - \lambda_k) + \frac{1}{2}\theta''(\lambda_k)(\lambda - \lambda_k)^2.$$

The point λ_{k+1} is taken to be the point where the derivative of q is equal to zero. This yields $\theta'(\lambda_k) + \theta''(\lambda_k)(\lambda_{k+1} - \lambda_k) = 0$, so that

$$\lambda_{k+1} = \lambda_k - \frac{\theta'(\lambda_k)}{\theta''(\lambda_k)} .$$

The procedure is terminated when $|\lambda_{k+1} - \lambda_k| < \varepsilon$ or when $|\theta'(\lambda_k)| < \varepsilon$ where ε is a prespecified termination scalar.

Note that the above procedure can only be applied for twice differentiable functions. Furthermore, the procedure is well defined only if $\theta''(\lambda_k) \neq 0$ for each k.

In the first case, $\lambda_1 = 0.40$, and as shown in Table 1, the procedure produced the point 0.002807 after six iterations. It can be verified that the procedure indeed converges to the stationary point $\lambda = 0$. In the second case, $\lambda_1 = 0.60$, and the procedure oscillates between the points 0.60 and -0.60, as shown in Table 2.

TABLE 2 **Summary of Computations for Newton's Method Starting from $\lambda_1 = 0.6$**

Iteration k	λ_k	$\theta'(\lambda_k)$	$\theta''(\lambda_k)$	λ_{k+1}
1	0.600	1.728	1.440	−0.600
2	−0.600	1.728	−1.440	0.600
3	0.600	1.728	1.440	−0.600
4	−0.600	1.728	−1.440	0.600

The method of Newton, in general, does not converge to a stationary point starting with an arbitrary initial point.

MULTIDIMENSIONAL SEARCH WITHOUT USING DERIVATIVES

• PROBLEM 9-25

Consider the following problem:

Minimize $(x_1 - 2)^4 + (x_1 - 2x_2)^2$

Find if and to what values of x_1 and x_2, this function converges, by using the Cyclic Coordinate Method. Start from the initial point (0,3). $\varepsilon = 0.03$.

Solution: The Cyclic Coordinate Method uses the coordinate axes as the search directions. More specifically, the method searches along the directions $\vec{d}_1, \ldots, \vec{d}_n$, where $\vec{d}_j$ is a vector of zeros except for a one at the jth position. Thus, along the search direction $\vec{d}_j$, the variable x_j is changed, while all other variables are kept fixed.

Summary of the Cyclic Coordinate Method:

The termination criterion used, is $||\vec{x}_{k+1} - \vec{x}_k|| < \varepsilon$.

Initialization Step: Choose a scalar $\varepsilon > 0$ to be used for terminating the algorithm, and let $\vec{d}_1, \ldots, \vec{d}_n$ be the coordinate directions. Choose an initial point $\vec{x}_1$, let $\vec{y}_1 = \vec{x}_1$, let $k = j = 1$, and go to the main step.

Main Step:

1. Let λ_j be an optimal solution to the problem to minimize $f(\vec{y}_j + \lambda\vec{d}_j)$ subject to $\lambda \in E_1$, and let $\vec{y}_{j+1} = \vec{y}_j + \lambda_j\vec{d}_j$. If $j < n$, replace j by $j + 1$, and repeat step 1. Otherwise, if $j = n$, go to step 2.

2. Let $\vec{x}_{k+1} = \vec{y}_{n+1}$. If $||\vec{x}_{k+1} - \vec{x}_k|| < \varepsilon$, then stop. Otherwise let $\vec{y}_1 = \vec{x}_{k+1}$, let $j = 1$, replace k by $k + 1$, and repeat step 1.

TABLE 1 **Summary of Computations for the Cyclic Coordinate Method**

Iteration k	$\vec{x}_k$ / $f(\vec{x}_k)$	j	$\vec{d}_j$	$\vec{y}_j$	λ_j	$\vec{y}_{j+1}$
1	(0.00, 3.00)	1	(1.0, 0.0)	(0.00, 3.00)	3.13	(3.13, 3.00)
	52.00	2	(0.0, 1.0)	(3.13, 3.00)	−1.44	(3.13, 1.56)
2	(3.13, 1.56)	1	(1.0, 0.0)	(3.13, 1.56)	−0.50	(2.63, 1.56)
	1.63	2	(0.0, 1.0)	(2.63, 1.56)	−0.25	(2.63, 1.31)
3	(2.63, 1.31)	1	(1.0, 0.0)	(2.63, 1.31)	−0.19	(2.44, 1.31)
	0.16	2	(0.0, 1.0)	(2.44, 1.31)	−0.09	(2.44, 1.22)
4	(2.44, 1.22)	1	(1.0, 0.0)	(2.44, 1.22)	−0.09	(2.35, 1.22)
	0.04	2	(0.0, 1.0)	(2.35, 1.22)	−0.05	(2.35, 1.17)
5	(2.35, 1.17)	1	(1.0, 0.0)	(2.35, 1.17)	−0.06	(2.29, 1.17)
	0.015	2	(0.0, 1.0)	(2.29, 1.17)	−0.03	(2.29, 1.14)
6	(2.29, 1.14)	1	(1.0, 0.0)	(2.29, 1.14)	−0.04	(2.25, 1.14)
	0.007	2	(0.0, 1.0)	(2.25, 1.14)	−0.02	(2.25, 1.12)
7	(2.25, 1.12)	1	(1.0, 0.0)	(2.25, 1.12)	−0.03	(2.22, 1.12)
	0.004	2	(0.0, 1.0)	(2.22, 1.12)	−0.01	(2.22, 1.11)

Note that the optimal solution to the problem is (2,1) with objective value equal to zero. Table 1 gives a summary of computations for the cyclic coordinate method starting from the initial point (0,3). At each iteration, the vectors $\vec{y}_2$ and $\vec{y}_3$ are obtained by performing a line search in the directions (1,0) and (0,1), respectively. Also note that significant progress is made during the first few iterations, whereas much slower progress is made during later iterations. After seven iterations, the point (2.22, 1.11), whose objective value is 0.0023, is reached.

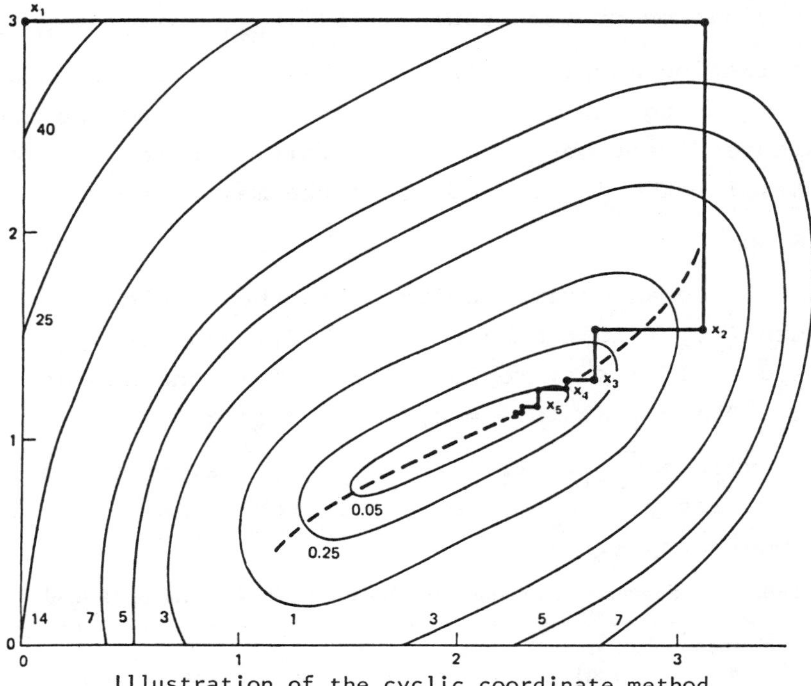

Illustration of the cyclic coordinate method. Fig. 1

In Figure 1, the contours of the objective function are given, and the points generated above by the cyclic coordinate method are shown. Note that at later iterations, slow progress is made because of the short orthogonal movements along the valley indicated by the dotted lines.

• PROBLEM 9-26

Consider the following problem:

Minimize $\quad (x_1 - 2)^4 + (x_1 - 2x_2)^2$

Use the Hooke and Jeeves' method to solve.

TABLE 1

Iteration k	$\vec{x}_k$ $f(\vec{x}_k)$	j	$\vec{y}_j$	$\vec{d}_j$	λ_j	$\vec{y}_{j+1}$	$\vec{d}$	$\hat{\lambda}$	$\vec{y}_3 + \hat{\lambda}\vec{d}$
1	(0.00, 3.00)	1	(0.00, 3.00)	(1.0, 0.0)	3.13	(3.13, 3.00)	—	—	
	52.00	2	(3.13, 3.00)	(0.0, 1.0)	−1.44	(3.13, 1.56)	(3.13, −1.44)	−0.10	(2.82, 1.70)
2	(3.13, 1.56)	1	(2.82, 1.70)	(1.0, 0.0)	−0.12	(2.70, 1.70)	—	—	—
	1.63	2	(2.70, 1.70)	(0.0, 1.0)	−0.35	(2.70, 1.35)	(−0.43, −0.21)	1.50	(2.06, 1.04)
3	(2.70, 1.35)	1	(2.06, 1.04)	(1.0, 0.0)	−0.02	(2.04, 1.04)	—	—	—
	0.24	2	(2.04, 1.04)	(0.0, 1.0)	−0.02	(2.04, 1.02)	(−0.66, −0.33)	0.06	(2.00, 1.00)
4	(2.04, 1.02)	1	(2.00, 1.00)	(1.0, 0.0)	0.00	(2.00, 1.00)	—	—	—
	0.000003	2	(2.00, 1.00)	(0.0, 1.0)	0.00	(2.00, 1.00)			
5	(2.00, 1.00)								
	0.00								

Solution: First choose a scalar $\varepsilon > 0$ to be used in terminating the algorithm. Choose a starting point $\vec{x}_1$, let $\vec{y}_1 = \vec{x}_1$, let $k = j = 1$, and go to the main step.

Main Step:

1. Let λ_j be an optimal solution to the problem to minimize $f(\vec{y}_j + \lambda\vec{d}_j)$ subject to $\lambda \in E_1$, and let $\vec{y}_{j+1} = \vec{y}_j + \lambda_j\vec{d}_j$. If $j < n$, replace j by j + 1, and repeat step 1. Otherwise, if $j = n$, let $\vec{x}_{k+1} = \vec{y}_{n+1}$. If $||\vec{x}_{k+1} - \vec{x}_k|| < \varepsilon$, stop; otherwise go to step 2.

2. Let $\vec{d} = \vec{x}_{k+1} - \vec{x}_k$, and let $\hat{\lambda}$ be an optimal solution to the problem to minimize $f(\vec{x}_{k+1} + \lambda\vec{d})$ subject to $\lambda \in E_1$. Let $\vec{y}_1 = \vec{x}_{k+1} + \hat{\lambda}\vec{d}$, let $j = 1$, replace k by k + 1, and repeat step 1.

Note that the optimal solution is (2.00,1.00) with objective value equal to zero. Table 1 summarizes the computations for the method of Hooke and Jeeves, starting from the initial point (0.00, 3.00). At each iteration, an exploratory search along the coordinate directions gives the points $\vec{y}_2$ and $\vec{y}_3$, and a pattern search along the direction $\vec{d} = \vec{x}_{k+1} - \vec{x}_k$ gives the point $\vec{y}_1$, except at iteration $k = 1$, where $\vec{y}_1 = \vec{x}_1$. Note that four iterations were required to move from the initial point to the optimal point (2.00,1.00) whose objective value is zero. At this point $||\vec{x}_5 - \vec{x}_4|| = 0.002$, and the procedure is terminated.

• PROBLEM 9-27

The objective function

$$f(\vec{x}) = \frac{1}{(x_1 + 1)^2 + x_2^2}$$

is to be maximized starting at $\vec{x}^{(0)} = [2.00 \quad 2.80]^T$, with an initial $\Delta\vec{x}$ of $[0.60 \quad 0.84]^T$. The initial value of f(2.00,2.80) at the base point $\vec{x}^{(0)}$ is 0.059. Use Hooke's and Jeeves' direct search.

Solution: A type I exploratory search is made to define a successful direction (such a move is called a type I exploratory search in contrast to the type II exploratory search that follows a pattern search. After type II exploratory move, a decision is made as to whether the previous pattern moves were a success or failure):

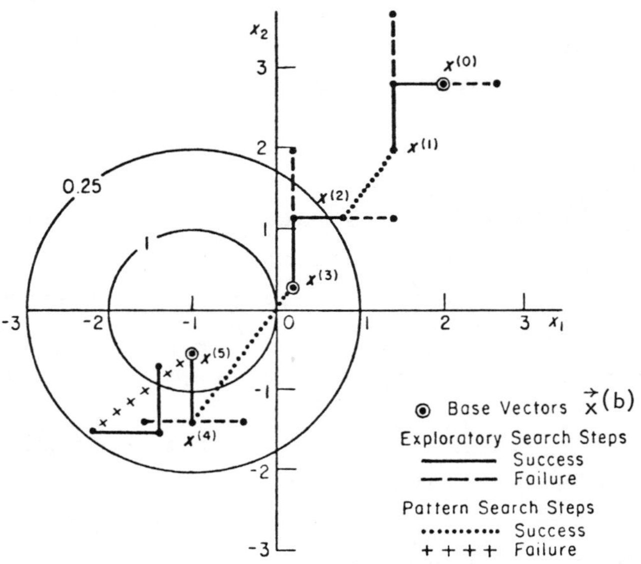

Fig. 1

$x_1^{(1)} = 2.00 + 0.60 = 2.60$ $f(2.60,2.80) = 0.048$ failure

$x_1^{(1)} = 2.00 - 0.60 = 1.40$ $f(1.40,2.80) = 0.073$ success

$x_2^{(1)} = 2.80 + 0.84 = 3.64$ $f(1.40,3.64) = 0.052$ failure

$x_2^{(1)} = 2.80 - 0.84 = 1.96$ $f(1.40,1.96) = 0.104$ success

The exploratory search is a success. Note that the last successful $\vec{x}$ vector is picked up on each search. The new base vector will be (1.40,1.96).

Now a pattern search is made from the point (1.40,1.96) according to the acceleration rule:

$$x_i^{(k+1)} = 2x_i^{(k)} - x_i^{(b)}$$

where $x_i^{(b)}$ is the old base $\vec{x}$ vector, here at the start $\vec{x}^{(0)}$.

$$x_1^{(2)} = 2(1.40) - 2.00 = 0.80$$

$$x_2^{(2)} = 2(1.96) - 2.80 = 1.12$$

$$f(0.8,1.12) = 0.22.$$

Finally, a type II exploratory search is made; failure or success is based on a comparison with f(0.8,1.12) = 0.22.

$x_1^{(3)} = 0.80 + 0.60 = 1.40$ $f(1.40,1.12) = 0.14$ failure

$x_1^{(3)} = 0.80 - 0.60 = 0.20$ $f(0.20,1.12) = 0.38$ success

$x_2^{(3)} = 1.12 + 0.84 = 1.96$ $f(0.20,1.96) = 0.19$ failure

$x_2^{(3)} = 1.12 - 0.84 = 0.28$ $f(0.20,0.28) = 0.67$ success

To determine if the pattern search is a success, $f(0.20,0.28) = 0.67$ is compared with $f(1.40,1.96) = 0.104$. Because the pattern search is a success, the new base point is $\vec{x}^{(3)} = [0.20 \quad 0.28]^T$ and the old base point becomes $\vec{x}^{(1)} = [1.40 \quad 1.96]^T$.

Another pattern search is made.

$$x_1^{(4)} = 2(0.20) - 1.40 = -1.00$$

$$x_2^{(4)} = 2(0.28) - 1.96 = -1.40$$

$$f(-1.00,-1.40) = 0.51.$$

Now a type II exploratory search is carried out.

$x_1^{(5)} = -1.00 + 0.60 = -0.40 \quad f(-0.40,-1.40) = 0.43$ failure

$x_1^{(5)} = -1.00 - 0.60 = -1.60 \quad f(-1.60,-1.40) = 0.43$ failure

$x_2^{(5)} = -1.40 + 0.84 = -0.56 \quad f(-1.00,-0.56) = 3.18$ success.

Since $f(-1.00,-0.56) = 3.18 > f(0.20,0.28) = 0.67$, the pattern move is a success, and $\vec{x}^{(5)} = [-1.00 \quad -0.56]^T$ becomes the new base point and $\vec{x}^{(3)}$ the old base point.

This sequence of steps continues until the conditions are reached in which, at the end of a type II exploratory search, the value of $f(\vec{x})$ is less than the value of $f(\vec{x}^{(b)})$ at the new base point. Then even if the type II exploratory search is a success on one or more of the perturbations, the pattern search is said to fail, and a type I exploratory move is initiated from the old base point to define a new successful direction. To illustrate, continue the search from $\vec{x}^{(5)} = [-1.00 \quad -0.56]^T$.

Pattern search:

$$\left.\begin{aligned} x_1^{(6)} &= 2(-1.00) - 0.20 = -2.20 \\ x_2^{(6)} &= 2(-0.56) - 0.28 = -1.40 \end{aligned}\right\} f(-2.20,-1.40) = 0.29.$$

Type II exploratory search:

$x_1^{(7)} = -2.20 + 0.60 = -1.60 \quad f(-1.60,-1.40) = 0.43$ success

$x_2^{(7)} = -1.40 + 0.84 = -0.56 \quad f(-1.60,-0.56) = 1.49$ success.

However, because $f(-1.60,-0.56) = 1.49 < f(-1.00,-0.56) = 3.18$, even though the type II exploratory search was a success, the pattern move is deemed a failure, and a type I exploratory search is initiated from $\vec{x}^{(5)} = [-1.00 \quad -0.56]^T$.

When the stage is reached in which neither the type I exploratory search nor the pattern search (together with the type II exploratory search) has a success in any coordinate direction, both are said to fail and the perturbation $\Delta\vec{x}$ is reduced as follows:

$$\Delta x_{i,new} = \Delta x_{i,previous} \frac{\Delta x_i^{(0)}}{e^{\xi}}$$

where ξ is the number of consecutive exploratory search failures at the given step size since the last successful exploratory search.

In this problem the maximum of $f(\vec{x}) \to \infty$ as $x_1 \to -1$ and $x_2 \to 0$.

• PROBLEM 9-28

Suppose that the base point $\vec{b}_i$ for the ith local excursion has coordinates (2,3). Let the head point $\vec{b}_{i+1}$ for this pattern (which will be the base point for the next exploration) be at (2.4,2.7). Form a new set of linearly independent orthogonal search directions for the (i + 1) pattern using the Method of Rosenbrock. Also, assuming optimum $\lambda_1 = 2$ and $\lambda_2 = 0.5$, find $\vec{b}_{i+2}$.

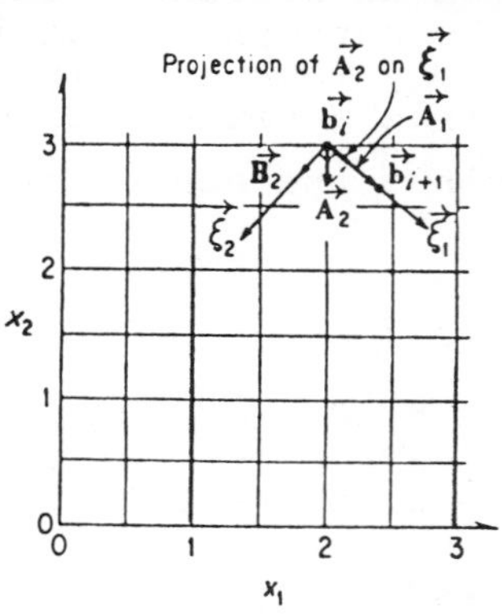

Rotation of coordinates Fig. 1

Solution: According to the Method of Rosenbrock, when there are k independent variables, construct k mutually perpendicular (or orthogonal) vectors $\vec{\xi}_1, \vec{\xi}_2, \ldots, \vec{\xi}_k$ from the k vectors $\vec{A}_1, \vec{A}_2, \ldots, \vec{A}_k$, defined by

$$\vec{A}_1 \equiv (\vec{b}_{i+1} - \vec{b}_i) \equiv (a_1, a_2, \ldots, a_k)$$

$$\vec{A}_2 \equiv (0, a_2, \ldots, a_k)$$

$$\vec{A}_k \equiv (0, 0, \ldots, 0, a_k).$$

The first is obtained by normalizing $\vec{A}_1$:

$$\vec{\xi}_1 \equiv \frac{\vec{A}_1}{[\sum a_i^2]^{1/2}} \equiv (\xi_{11}, \xi_{12}, \ldots, \xi_{ik}).$$

Then use $\vec{A}_2$ to construct a vector $\vec{B}_2$ normal to $\vec{\xi}_1$:

$$\vec{B}_2 \equiv \vec{A}_2 - \vec{\xi}_1 [\sum \xi_{1i} a_i] \equiv (b_{21}, b_{22}, \ldots, b_{2k}).$$

This is normalized to obtain $\vec{\xi}_2$:

$$\vec{\xi}_2 \equiv \frac{\vec{B}_2}{[\sum b_{2i}^2]^{1/2}} \equiv (\xi_{21}, \xi_{22}, \ldots, \xi_{2k}).$$

Continue in this manner, calculating $\vec{B}_3$, $\vec{\xi}_3$, $\vec{B}_4$, $\vec{\xi}_4$, etc. until at the last stage,

$$\vec{B}_k \equiv \vec{A}_k - \vec{\xi}_{k-1} [\sum \xi_{k-1,k} a_k]^{1/2} \equiv (b_{k1}, b_{k2}, \ldots, b_{kk})$$

and

$$\vec{\xi}_k \equiv \frac{\vec{B}_k}{[\sum b_{ki}^2]^{1/2}}$$

This procedure is the Gram-Schmidt orthogonalization process. (It can be used to remove interaction between variables.)

For this problem, one of the axes for the (i + 1) search should be pointed in the direction

$$(\vec{b}_{i+1} - \vec{b}_i) = (0.4, -0.3).$$

Let $\vec{\xi}_1$ be a multiple of this vector, and require that $\vec{\xi}_1$ have unit length relative to the scales of x_1 and x_2

$$|\vec{\xi}_1| = 1.$$

This vector is found simply by normalizing $\vec{b}_{i+1} - \vec{b}_i$, that is, by dividing each component by the total length

$$[(0.4)^2 + (0.3)^2]^{1/2} = 0.5.$$

Then:

$$\vec{\xi}_1 = (0.8, -0.6).$$

The second vector $\vec{\xi}_2$ is constructed from $\vec{\xi}_1$ and the vector $\vec{A}_2$ obtained from $\vec{b}_{i+1} - \vec{b}_i$ by setting the first component equal to zero.

$$\vec{A}_2 \equiv (0, -0.3)$$

First compute the projection of $\vec{A}_2$ on $\vec{\xi}_1$, shown in Fig. 1. This projection, also a vector, is

$$[(0)(0.8) + (-0.3)(-0.6)](0.8, -0.6) = (0.144, -0.108).$$

Subtraction of this projection from $\vec{A}_2$ gives a new vector $\vec{B}_2$ perpendicular to $\vec{\xi}_1$, as shown in the figure.

$$\vec{B}_2 = (0,-0.3) - (0.144,-0.108)$$
$$= (-0.144,-0.192).$$

The second new coordinate axis must be pointed in the same direction as $\vec{B}_2$. Let $\vec{\xi}_2$ be a vector of unit length in this direction. It is obtained by normalizing $\vec{B}_2$ whose length is $[(0.144)^2 + (0.192)^2]^{1/2} = 0.240$.

$$\vec{\xi}_2 = \frac{\vec{B}_2}{0.240} = (-0.6,-0.8)$$

It can be verified that $\vec{\xi}_1$ and $\vec{\xi}_2$ are perpendicular by comparing the slope of the former $(-\frac{3}{4})$ with that of the latter $(\frac{4}{3})$.

To develop the (i + 1) pattern one searches for the maximum in the $\vec{\xi}_1$ direction. The vector equation of this line is

$$\vec{x} = \vec{b}_{i+1} + \lambda_1\vec{\xi}_1 = (2.4,2.7) + \lambda_1(0.8,-0.6)$$

or in parametric form $\quad x_1 = 2.4 + 0.8\lambda_1$

$$x_2 = 2.7 - 0.6\lambda_1$$

where λ_1 is the parameter of the line of search. Letting the optimum value of y on this line to be where $\lambda_1 = 2$, the first temporary head point for this search is at

$$\vec{t}_{i+1,1} = (4.0,1.5).$$

From this temporary head, explore in the perpendicular direction $\vec{\xi}_2$. The parametric equations for the search are

$$x_1 = 4.0 - 0.6\lambda_2$$
$$x_2 = 1.5 - 0.8\lambda_2$$

where λ_2 is the parameter. Letting the optimum value of λ_2 to be 0.5, the second temporary head, which will become the next base point, is given by

$$\vec{t}_{i+1,2} = \vec{b}_{i+2} = (3.7,1.1).$$

From this point and the old base point $\vec{b}_{i+1}$, expressed in terms of the x_1-x_2 coordinates, a new set of rotated coordinates can be calculated as before. Notice that at all times it is a simple matter to express moves in the oblique directions $\vec{\xi}_1$ and $\vec{\xi}_2$ in terms of the original coordinates x_1 and x_2.

• PROBLEM 9-29

Consider the following problem:

Minimize $(x_1 - 2)^4 + (x_1 - 2x_2)^2$

Solve by the Method of Rosenbrock using line search. Start from the initial point (0.0,3.00).

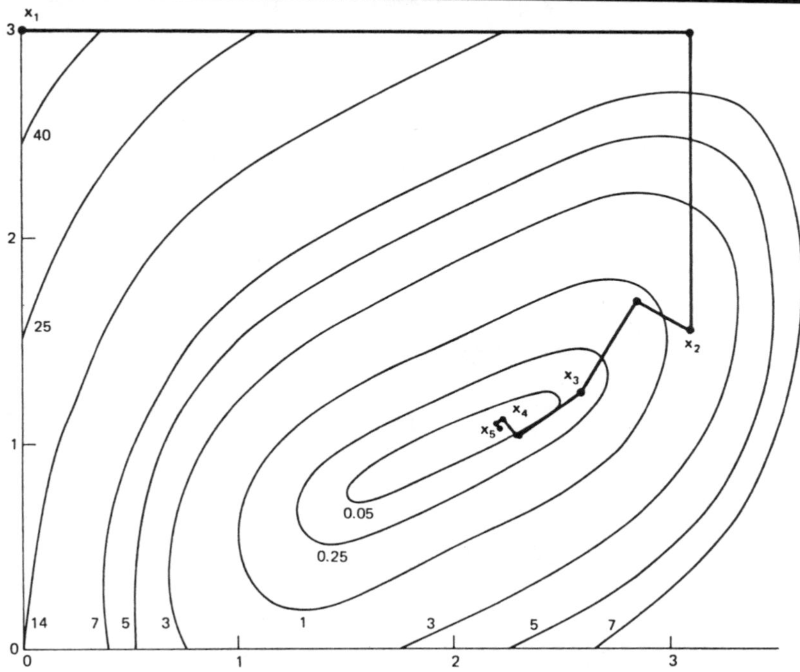

Illustration of the method of Rosenbrock using line search.

Fig. 1

Solution: Summary of Rosenbrock's method using line search for minimizing a function f of several variables. If f is differentiable, then the method converges to a point with zero gradient.

Initialization Step: Let $\varepsilon > 0$ be the termination scalar. Choose $\vec{d}_1, \ldots, \vec{d}_n$ as the coordinate directions. Choose a starting point $\vec{x}_1$, let $\vec{y}_1 = \vec{x}_1$, $k = j = 1$, and go to the main step.

Main Step:

1. Let λ_j be an optimal solution to the problem to minimize $f(\vec{y}_j + \lambda\vec{d}_j)$ subject to $\lambda \in E_1$, and let $\vec{y}_{j+1} = \vec{y}_j + \lambda_j\vec{d}_j$. If $j < n$, replace j by j + 1, and repeat step 1. Otherwise, go to step 2.

2. Let $\vec{x}_{k+1} = \vec{y}_{n+1}$. If $\|\vec{x}_{k+1} - \vec{x}_k\| < \varepsilon$, then stop; otherwise, let $\vec{y}_1 = \vec{x}_{k+1}$, replace k by k + 1, let j = 1,

and go to step 3.

3. Form a new set of linearly independent orthogonal search directions $\vec{d}_1, \ldots, \vec{d}_n$. Let $\vec{d}_1, \ldots, \vec{d}_n$ be linearly independent vectors, each with norm equal to one. Furthermore, suppose that these vectors are mutually orthogonal, that is $\vec{d}_i^{\,t}\vec{d}_j = 0$ for $i \neq j$. Starting from the current vector $\vec{x}_k$, the objective function f is minimized along each of the directions iteratively, resulting in the point $\vec{x}_{k+1}$. In particular, $\vec{x}_{k+1} - \vec{x}_k = \sum_{j=1}^{n} \lambda_j \vec{d}_j$, where λ_j is the distance moved along $\vec{d}_j$. The new collection of directions $\bar{\vec{d}}_1, \ldots, \bar{\vec{d}}_n$ are formed by the Gram-Schmidt procedure as follows:

$$\vec{a}_j = \begin{cases} \vec{d}_j & \text{if } \lambda_j = 0 \\ \sum_{i=j}^{n} \lambda_i \vec{d}_i & \text{if } \lambda_j \neq 0 \end{cases} \tag{1}$$

$$\vec{b}_j = \begin{cases} \vec{a}_j & j = 1 \\ \vec{a}_j - \sum_{i=1}^{j-1} (\vec{a}_j^{\,t}\bar{\vec{d}}_i)\bar{\vec{d}}_i & j \geq 2 \end{cases}$$

$$\bar{\vec{d}}_j = \frac{\vec{b}_j}{\|\vec{b}_j\|} .$$

TABLE 1 Summary of Computations for the Method of Rosenbrock Using Line Search

Iteration k	$\vec{x}_k$ $f(\vec{x}_k)$	j	$\vec{y}_j$ $f(\vec{y}_j)$	$\vec{d}_j$	λ_j	$\vec{y}_{j+1}$ $f(\vec{y}_{j+1})$
1	(0.00, 3.00) 52.00	1	(0.00, 3.00) 52.00	(1.00, 0.00)	3.13	(3.13, 3.00) 9.87
		2	(3.13, 3.00) 9.87	(0.00, 1.00)	−1.44	(3.13, 1.56) 1.63
2	(3.13, 1.56) 1.63	1	(3.13, 1.56) 1.63	(0.91, −0.42)	−0.34	(2.82, 1.70) 0.79
		2	(2.82, 1.70) 0.79	(−0.42, −0.91)	0.51	(2.61, 1.24) 0.16
3	(2.61, 1.24) 0.16	1	(2.61, 1.24) 0.16	(−0.85, −0.52)	0.38	(2.29, 1.04) 0.05
		2	(2.29, 1.04) 0.05	(0.52, −0.85)	−0.10	(2.24, 1.13) 0.004
4	(2.24, 1.13) 0.004	1	(2.24, 1.13) 0.004	(−0.96, −0.28)	0.04	(2.20, 1.12) 0.003
		2	(2.20, 1.12) 0.003	(0.28, −0.96)	0.02	(2.21, 1.10) 0.002

Table 1 summarizes the computations starting from the point (0.00,3.00). The point $\vec{y}_2$ is obtained by optimizing the function along the direction $\vec{d}_1$ starting from $\vec{y}_1$, and $\vec{y}_3$ is obtained by optimizing the function along the direction $\vec{d}_2$ starting from $\vec{y}_2$. After the first iteration, one has $\lambda_1 = 3.13$ and $\lambda_2 = -1.44$. Using (1), the new search directions are (0.91,-0.42) and (-0.42,-0.91). After four iterations, the point (2.21,1.10) is reached, and the corresponding objective function value is 0.002. One now has $||\vec{x}_4 - \vec{x}_3|| = 0.15$ and the procedure is stopped. The progress of the method is shown, in Figure 1.

MULTIDIMENSIONAL SEARCH USING DERIVATIVES

• PROBLEM 9-30

Consider the following problem.

Minimize $\quad (x_1 - 2)^4 + (x_1 - 2x_2)^2$.

Use the method of steepest descent to solve. Start with the point (0.00,3.00).

TABLE 1

Iteration k	$\vec{x}_k$ $f(\vec{x}_k)$	$\vec{\nabla} f(\vec{x}_k)$	$\|\vec{\nabla} f(\vec{x}_k)\|$	$\vec{d}_k = -\vec{\nabla} f(\vec{x}_k)$	λ_k	$\vec{x}_{k+1}$
1	(0.00, 3.00) 52.00	(−44.00, 24.00)	50.12	(44.00, −24.00)	0.062	(2.70, 1.51)
2	(2.70, 1.51) 0.34	(0.73, 1.28)	1.47	(−0.73, −1.28)	0.24	(2.52, 1.20)
3	(2.52, 1.20) 0.09	(0.80, −0.48)	0.93	(−0.80, 0.48)	0.11	(2.43, 1.25)
4	(2.43, 1.25) 0.04	(0.18, 0.28)	0.33	(−0.18, −0.28)	0.31	(2.37, 1.16)
5	(2.37, 1.16) 0.02	(0.30, −0.20)	0.36	(−0.30, 0.20)	0.12	(2.33, 1.18)
6	(2.33, 1.18) 0.01	(0.08, 0.12)	0.14	(−0.08, −0.12)	0.36	(2.30, 1.14)
7	(2.30, 1.14) 0.009	(0.15, −0.08)	0.17	(−0.15. 0.08)	0.13	(2.28, 1.15)
8	(2.28, 1.15) 0.007	(0.05, 0.08)	0.09			

<u>Solution</u>: First, let $\varepsilon > 0$ be the termination scalar. Choose a starting point $\vec{x}_1$, let k = 1, and go to the main step.

Main Step: If $||\vec{\nabla} f(\vec{x}_k)|| < \varepsilon$ stop; otherwise, let $\vec{d}_k = -\vec{\nabla} f(\vec{x}_k)$, and let λ_k be an optimal solution to the problem to minimize $f(\vec{x}_k + \lambda\vec{d}_k)$ subject to $\lambda \geq 0$. Let $\vec{x}_{k+1} = \vec{x}_k + \lambda\vec{d}_k$, replace k by k + 1, and repeat the main step. The summary of the computations are given in Table 1. After seven iterations, the point $\vec{x}_8 = (2.28, 1.15)^t$ is reached. The algorithm is terminated since $\|\vec{\nabla}f(\vec{x}_8)\| = 0.09$ is small. The minimizing point is (2.00,1.00).

• PROBLEM 9-31

Consider

Minimize: $f(\vec{x}) = x_1^2 + 25x_2^2$.

Compute three cycles using a fixed step length λ having a value of unity. Then solve the problem by the steepest descent method. Start from $\vec{x}^{(0)} = \{2,2\}^T$ in each case.

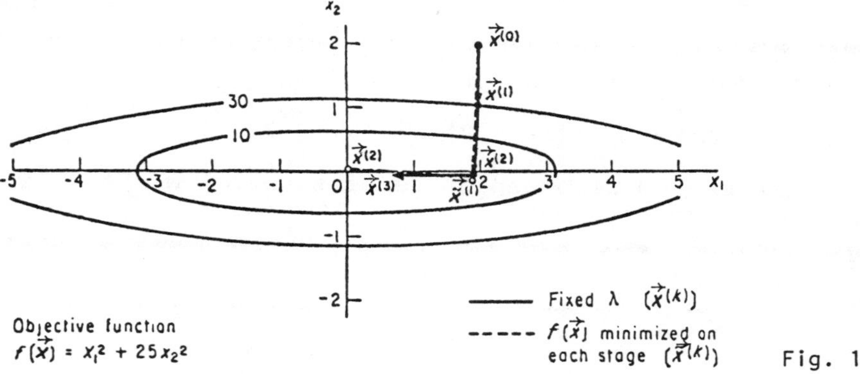

Fig. 1

Solution: Consider first using a fixed step length λ having an initial value of unity. On each stage values of the following functions are required:

$$\frac{\partial f(\vec{x}^{(k)})}{\partial x_1} = 2x_1^{(k)} \qquad \frac{\partial f(x^{(k)})}{\partial x_2} = 50x_2^{(k)}$$

$$\|\vec{\nabla}f(\vec{x}^{(k)})\| = \sqrt{\left(\frac{\partial f(\vec{x}^{(k)})}{\partial x_1}\right)^2 + \left(\frac{\partial f(\vec{x}^{(k)})}{\partial x_2}\right)^2}\ .$$

After starting at $\vec{x}^{(0)} = [2 \quad 2]^T$, the following steps are taken:

Stage	x_1	x_2	$\frac{\partial f(\vec{x}^{(k)})}{\partial x_1}$	$\frac{\partial f(\vec{x}^{(k)})}{\partial x_2}$	$\|\vec{\nabla}f(\vec{x}^{(k)})\|$	*Step to next stage* Δx_1	Δx_2
0	2	2	4	100	~100	−0.04	−1.00
1	1.96	1.00	3.92	50	50.1	−0.078	−1.00
2	1.88	0	3.76	0	3.76	−1.00	0
3	0.88	0					

Refer to Fig. 1 for the trajectory of the path of the search.

For the method to converge, λ usually must be successively reduced by some fraction or the search will oscillate back and forth. Note that at the minimum, $\vec{x} = [0 \quad 0]^T$, $\vec{\nabla} f(\vec{x}) = \vec{0}$.

The results of the three corresponding stages of calculation in which, rather than using a fixed λ, the minimum of $f(\vec{x})$ is sought in the direction of steepest descent are:

Stage k	$\lambda^{(k)}$	x_1	x_2	$\frac{\partial f(\vec{x}^{(k)})}{\partial x_1}$	$\frac{\partial f(\vec{x}^{(k)})}{\partial x_2}$	$f(\vec{x}^{(k)})$
0		2	2	4	100	104
1	2.003	1.92	−0.003	3.84	−0.15	3.19
2	1.850	0.070	0.070	0.14	3.50	0.13
3	0.070	0.070	−0.000			

Observe in Fig. 1 that the gradient of $f(\vec{x})$ does not point in the direction of the minimum at the start of the search because the scale of x_1 and x_2 is quite different. By a change of variable

$$y = 5x_2$$

the function to be minimized becomes

$$f(\vec{x}) = x_1^2 + y^2$$

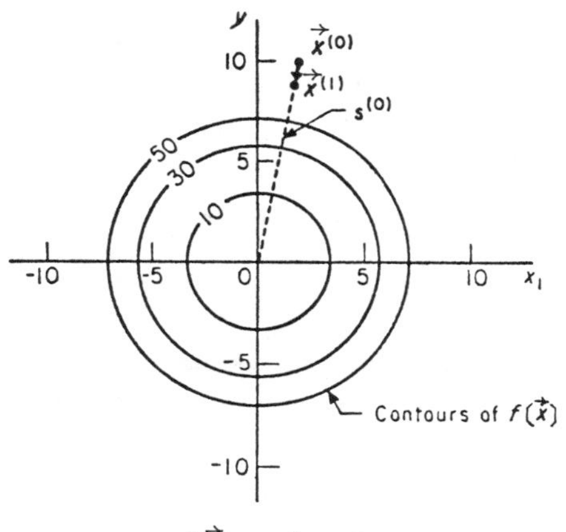

Fig. 2

and the vector at $x_1 = 1$, $y = 5x_2 = 10$, does indeed point to the minimum, because the scales of x_1 and y are now the same; examine Fig. 2.

• PROBLEM 9-32

Find a better solution to the problem below by using optimal steepest ascent method:

$$\text{Maximize} \quad f(x,y,z) = y(x-1)^2 - zx + z^2 - y^2$$

over the region $-3 \leq x \leq 2, -2 \leq y \leq 4, 0 \leq z \leq 15$.

Let $\vec{x}_0 = (-1,0,4)$.

Solution:

$$\vec{\nabla}f(x,y,z) = (2y(x-1) - z, (x-1)^2 - 2y, 2z - x) \qquad (1)$$

$$\vec{\nabla}f(-1,0,4) = (-4,4,9).$$

The half-line generated is

$$H = (-1,0,4) + \lambda(-4,4,9), \ \lambda \geq 0$$

which leaves the region of interest for $\lambda > \frac{1}{2}$. Thus maximize

$$g_1(\lambda) = f(-1 - 4\lambda, 4\lambda, 4 + 9\lambda) \qquad (2)$$

$$= 4\lambda(-2 - 4\lambda)^2 - (4 + 9\lambda)(-1 - 4\lambda) + (4 + 9\lambda)^2 - (4\lambda)^2$$

for $0 \leq \lambda \leq \frac{1}{2}$. Expanding $g_1(\lambda)$, it is found that,

$$g_1(\lambda) = 64\lambda^3 + 165\lambda^2 + 113\lambda + 20$$

which for $0 \leq \lambda \leq \frac{1}{2}$ is strictly increasing. Thus find $\vec{x}_1$ by letting $\lambda = \frac{1}{2}$ and plugging into Eq. (2)

$$x_1 = (-3, 2, 8\tfrac{1}{2})$$

and find $\vec{\nabla}f(\vec{x}_1)$ by plugging the values for $\vec{x}_1$ into Eq. (1).

$$\vec{\nabla}f(\vec{x}_1) = (-24\tfrac{1}{2}, 12, 20)$$

This way, an alternative, better solution to the problem is obtained.

• PROBLEM 9-33

Consider the poorly sealed objective function devised by Rosenbrock, two contours of which ($f(\vec{x}) = 8$ and $f(\vec{x}) = 4$) are illustrated in Figure 1.

$$f(\vec{x}) = 100(x_2 - x_1^2)^2 + (1 - x_1)^2. \qquad (1)$$

Geometrically $f(\vec{x})$ is interpreted as a slowly falling curved valley with its lowest point at $\vec{x}^* = [1,1]^T$, where $f(\vec{x}^*) = 0$.

Carry out the first iterations for the method of steepest descent and Newton's method to solve this function. Start from the point $[-0.5, 0.5]$.

Solution: Method of Steepest Descent:

Consider the point $\vec{x}^{(k)} = [-0.5 \quad 0.5]^T$, at which $f(\vec{x}^{(k)})$

= 8.5. The normalized gradient of $f(\vec{x})$ at $\vec{x}^{(k)}$ = $[-0.5 \quad 0.5]^T$ is

$$\frac{1}{[(\partial f/\partial x_1)^2 + (\partial f/\partial x_2)^2]^{1/2}_{\vec{x}^{(k)}}} \begin{bmatrix} \partial f/\partial x_1 \\ \partial f/\partial x_2 \end{bmatrix}_{\vec{x}^{(k)}} = \frac{1}{68.6}\begin{bmatrix} 47 \\ 50 \end{bmatrix}$$

$$= [0.685 \quad 0.729]^T. \qquad (2)$$

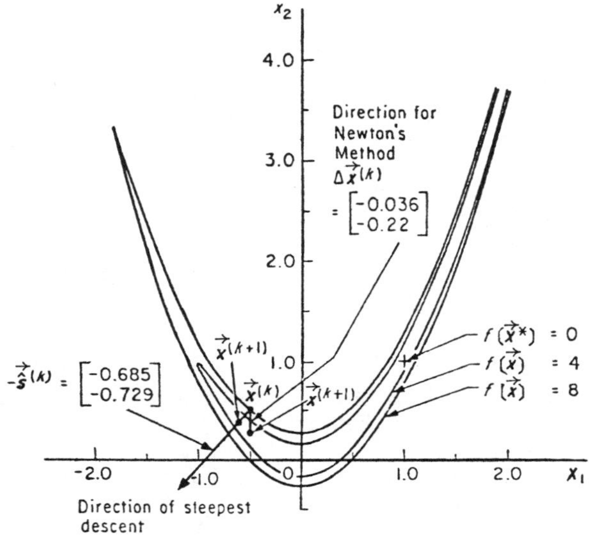

Fig. 1

The negative of the normalized gradient at $\vec{x}^{(k)}$, $\hat{s}^{(k)}$ = $[-0.685,-0.729]^T$, as shown in Fig. 1, points in the direction of steepest descent and is orthogonal to the coutour of $f(\vec{x})$ that passes through $\vec{x}^{(k)}$.

To find the new vector $\vec{x}^{(k+1)}$, it is necessary to select a value for λ. For example, choose a specific value for λ or find that value of λ at which $f(\vec{x})$ achieves its minimum in the direction given by the unit vector $\vec{s}^{(k)}$. At $\vec{x}^{(k)} = [-0.5 \quad 0.5]^T$, the equation

$$\vec{x}^{(k+1)} = \vec{x}^{(k)} + \Delta\vec{x}^{(k)} = \vec{x}^{(k)} + \lambda^{(k)}\hat{s}^{(k)} = \vec{x}^{(k)} + \lambda^{*(k)}\vec{s}^{(k)}$$

where $\Delta\vec{x}^{(k)}$ = vector from $\vec{x}^{(k)}$ to $\vec{x}^{(k+1)}$

$\hat{s}^{(k)}$ = a unit vector in direction $\Delta\vec{x}^{(k)}$

$\vec{s}^{(k)}$ = any vector in direction $\Delta\vec{x}^{k}$

$\lambda^{(k)}, \lambda^{*(k)}$ = scalars such that $\Delta\vec{x}^{(k)} = \lambda^{(k)}\hat{s}^{(k)} = \lambda^{*(k)}\vec{s}^{(k)}$

is:

$$\vec{x}^{(k+1)} = \begin{bmatrix} -0.5 \\ 0.5 \end{bmatrix} - \lambda^{(k)} \begin{bmatrix} 0.685 \\ 0.729 \end{bmatrix} . \qquad (3)$$

Consequently,

$$f(\vec{x}^{(k+1)}) = f(\lambda) = 100[0.5 - 0.729\lambda - (0.5 + 0.685\lambda)^2]^2 + (1.5 + 0.685\lambda)^2. \qquad (4)$$

The minimum of $f(\lambda)$ with respect to λ occurs at λ = 0.164. Introduction of $\lambda^{(k)} = 0.164$ into Eq. (3) gives the new point $\vec{x}^{(k+1)} = [-0.612 \quad 0.381]^T$, at which $f(\vec{x})$ = 2.6. The new $\vec{s}^{(k+1)}$ is determined at $\vec{x}^{(k+1)}$ by the equation

$$\vec{s}^{(k)} = - \frac{\nabla f(\vec{x}^{(k)})}{\|\nabla f(\vec{x}^{(k)})\|}$$

and then $\vec{x}^{(k+2)}$ is found in the direction of $\vec{s}^{(k+1)}$ in the same manner as $\vec{x}^{(k+1)}$ was found. This iterative procedure is continued until it is no longer possible to reduce the value of $f(\vec{x})$ or until some specified convergence criterion has been satisfied.

However, the method of steepest descent is not successful in solving this function (i.e., in rounding the curve in the valley of Rosenbrock's function).

Newton's Method: Starting from the same point, $\vec{x}^{(k)}$ = $[-0.5 \quad 0.5]^T$; $\vec{x}^{(k+1)}$ is found as follows:

$$\vec{\nabla}^2 f(\vec{x}^{(k)}) = \begin{bmatrix} (-400x_2 + 1200x_1^2 + 2) & (-400x_1) \\ (-400x_1) & (200) \end{bmatrix}_{\vec{x}^{(k)}}$$

$$= \begin{bmatrix} 102 & 200 \\ 200 & 200 \end{bmatrix}$$

$$\Delta\vec{x}^{(k)} = -[\vec{\nabla}^2 f(\vec{x}^{(k)})]^{-1}\vec{\nabla} f(\vec{x}^{(k)}) = \frac{1}{98}\begin{bmatrix} 1 & 1 \\ -1 & 0.51 \end{bmatrix}\begin{bmatrix} 47 \\ 50 \end{bmatrix}$$

$$= \begin{bmatrix} -0.03 \\ -0.22 \end{bmatrix}$$

$$\vec{x}^{(k+1)} = \begin{bmatrix} -0.5 \\ 0.5 \end{bmatrix} + \begin{bmatrix} -0.03 \\ -0.22 \end{bmatrix} = \begin{bmatrix} -0.53 \\ 0.28 \end{bmatrix}$$

At $\vec{x}^{(k+1)} = [-0.53 \quad 0.28]^T$, the value of $f(\vec{x})$ if $f(\vec{x})$ = 2.33. The vector $\Delta\vec{x}^{(k)} = [-0.03 \quad -0.22]^T$ is shown in Fig. 1.

The new $\Delta\vec{x}^{(k+1)}$ is evaluated at $\vec{x}^{(k+1)}$ and $\vec{x}^{(k+2)}$.

An alternative procedure would be to compute $\vec{s}^{(k)} = -H^{-1}(\vec{x}^{(k)})\vec{\nabla}f(\vec{x}^{(k)})$ as above but search in the direction of $\vec{s}^{(k)}$ for a λ that minimizes $f(\vec{x})$. In either instance, the iterative procedure is repeated until a specified convergence criterion is satisfied or until it is no longer possible to reduce the value of $f(\vec{x})$.

• PROBLEM 9-34

Identify the global maximum:

$$y = 2x_1 + 5x_2 + x_1x_2 - x_1^2 - x_2^2 + 10.$$

Use the Gradient Method, start from the origin, and conduct four iterations.

TABLE 1

Iterations for Gradient Solution

Iteration	t^*	(x_1,x_2)	y
0		(0.00,0.00)	10.00
1	0.763	(1.53,3.82)	21.07
2	0.372	(2.55,3.40)	22.71
3	0.762	(2.78,3.97)	22.96
4	0.374	(2.93,3.91)	22.99

Solution: The gradient for this function is

$$\vec{\nabla y} = \begin{pmatrix} 2 + x_2 - 2x_1 \\ 5 + x_1 - 2x_2 \end{pmatrix}.$$

The search starts from the origin: $x_1 = x_2 = 0$ (any point can be selected as the starting point).

Evaluating the gradient at the starting point one finds that

$$\vec{\nabla y} = \begin{pmatrix} 2 \\ 5 \end{pmatrix}.$$

This vector implies that from the point $x_1 = x_2 = 0$, the instantaneous rate of increase in y is +2 units for each unit increase in x_1 and +5 units for each unit increase in x_2. Move along the gradient as long as the value of y increases.

Determining the optimal step size, t* is the essential concern. Coordinates of points along the projection of the gradient can be defined as a function of the step size (t) by the following relationship:

$$\vec{x}' = \vec{x} + t\vec{\nabla y}$$

where $\vec{x}'$ is the vector of coordinates for the new point and $\vec{x}$ is the vector of coordinates for the original point.

Thus:

$$\vec{x}' = \begin{pmatrix} x_1' \\ x_2' \end{pmatrix} = \begin{pmatrix} 0 \\ 0 \end{pmatrix} + t\begin{pmatrix} 2 \\ 5 \end{pmatrix}$$

or $\quad x_1' = 0 + 2t \qquad (1)$

and $\quad x_2' = 0 + 5t. \qquad (2)$

If these relationships are substituted for the new coordinates of x_1 and x_2 into the original function, then y becomes a function of the variable t. Differentiate the function with respect to t to determine the value of t which maximizes y:

$$\begin{aligned} y &= 2x_1 + 5x_2 + x_1x_2 - x_1^2 - x_2^2 + 10 \\ &= 2(2t) + 5(5t) + (2t)(5t) - (2t)^2 - (5t)^2 + 10 \\ &= 29t - 19t^2 + 10 \end{aligned}$$

$$\frac{dy}{dt} = 29 - 38t.$$

By setting this first derivative equal to zero, note that y will be maximized at $t^* = 0.763$, or the optimal step size is 0.763. Substituting into (1) and (2), identify the coordinates of the new point to be

$$x_1' = 0 + 2(0.763) = 1.526$$

and

$$x_2' = 0 + 5(0.763) = 3.815.$$

Having reached the point (1.526,3.815), where the value of y is 21.07, determine the direction of steepest ascent from this point by evaluating the gradient at (1.526,3.815):

$$\nabla\vec{y} = \begin{pmatrix} 2.763 \\ -1.104 \end{pmatrix}.$$

Moving along this vector, coordinates of potential stopping points are given by

$$\vec{x}' = \begin{pmatrix} 1.526 \\ 3.815 \end{pmatrix} + t\begin{pmatrix} 2.763 \\ -1.104 \end{pmatrix}$$

or

$$x_1' = 1.526 + 2.763t$$

and

$$x_2' = 3.815 - 1.104t.$$

To determine the optimal step size, these expressions for x_1' and x_2' are substituted into the original equation to yield

$$y = f(t) = -11.903t^2 + 8.853t + 21.066.$$

Differentiating as before, t^* is found to equal 0.372; the coordinates of the new stopping point are (2.554, 3.404), with a value of y equal to 22.71. Table 1 summarizes the first four iterations.

By observation, it is apparent that the gradient approach is converging toward the global optimal point (3, 4), where y is maximized at a value of 23. Note that, given a nonconcave function which has stationary points, the gradient method would converge on a local maximum (which may or may not be the global maximum).

Maximize

$$f(\vec{x}) = f(x_1,x_2)$$

$$= -x_1^2 + 4x_1 + 2x_1x_2 - 2x_2^2$$

starting at the point

$$\vec{x}^0 = \begin{bmatrix} 0 \\ 0 \end{bmatrix}.$$

Use the Gradient Search method. Try to make an intelligent guess as to what integer values does the function converges to, after the fourth iteration.

Solution: Step 1: $\vec{\nabla}f(\vec{x}) = (-2x_1 + 2x_2 + 4,\ 2x_1 - 4x_2)$.

Thus,

$$\nabla f(\vec{x}_0) = (4,0) \qquad \text{for } \vec{x}_0 = \begin{bmatrix} 0 \\ 0 \end{bmatrix}.$$

Step 2:

$$\begin{aligned} f[\vec{x}_0 + s^*\vec{\nabla}f(\vec{x}_0)] &= \max f[(0,0) + s(4,0)] & s>0 \\ &= \max f[4s,0] & s>0 \\ &= \max (-16s^2 + 16s) & s>0. \end{aligned}$$

Since

$$\frac{d}{ds}(-16s^2 + 16s) = -32s + 16 = 0,$$

$$s^* = \frac{1}{2},\ \text{greater than } 0.$$

Step 3:

$$\vec{x}_1 = \vec{x}_0 + s^*\vec{\nabla}f(\vec{x}_0) = \begin{bmatrix} 0 \\ 0 \end{bmatrix} + \frac{1}{2}\begin{bmatrix} 4 \\ 0 \end{bmatrix} = \begin{bmatrix} 2 \\ 0 \end{bmatrix}$$

and

$$\vec{\nabla}f(\vec{x}_1) = (-4 + 4,4) = (0,4).$$

Step 2:

$$\begin{aligned} f[\vec{x}_1 + s^*\vec{\nabla}f(\vec{x}_1)] &= \max f[(2,0) + s(0,4)] & s>0 \\ &= \max f[2,4s] & s>0 \\ &= \max (4 + 16s - 32s^2) & s>0. \end{aligned}$$

Now

$$\frac{d(4 + 16s - 32s^2)}{ds} = 16 - 64s = 0$$

gives

$$s^* = \frac{1}{4}\ \text{(again positive)}.$$

Step 3:

$$\vec{x}_2 = \vec{x}_1 + s^*\vec{\nabla}f(\vec{x}_1) = \begin{bmatrix} 2 \\ 0 \end{bmatrix} + \frac{1}{4}\begin{bmatrix} 0 \\ 4 \end{bmatrix} = \begin{bmatrix} 2 \\ 1 \end{bmatrix}$$

and

$$\nabla f(\vec{x}_2) = (-4 + 2 + 4,4 - 4) = (2,0).$$

Step 2:

$$\begin{aligned} f[\vec{x}_2 + s^*\vec{\nabla}f(\vec{x}_2)] &= \max f[(2,1) + s(2,0)] & s>0 \\ &= \max f[2 + 2s,1] & s>0 \\ &= \max (6 + 4s - 4s^2) & s>0 \end{aligned}$$

and
$$\frac{d(6 + 4s - 4s^2)}{ds} = 4 - 8s = 0$$
gives
$$s^* = \frac{1}{2} .$$

$$\text{Step 3:} \quad \vec{x}_3 = \vec{x}_2 + s^*\vec{\nabla}f(\vec{x}_2) = \begin{bmatrix} 2 \\ 1 \end{bmatrix} + \frac{1}{2}\begin{bmatrix} 2 \\ 0 \end{bmatrix} = \begin{bmatrix} 3 \\ 1 \end{bmatrix}$$

and
$$\vec{\nabla}f(\vec{x}_3) = (-6 + 2 + 4, 6 - 4) = (0,2).$$

$$\begin{aligned} \text{Step 2:} \quad f(\vec{x}_3 + s^*\vec{\nabla}f(\vec{x}_3)] &= \max_{s>0} f[(3,1) + s(0,2)] \\ &= \max_{s>0} f(3, 1 + 2s) \\ &= \max_{s>0} (7 + 4s - 8s^2) \end{aligned}$$

and
$$\frac{d(7 + 4s - 8s^2)}{ds} = 4 - 16s = 0$$
gives
$$s^* = \frac{1}{4} .$$

$$\text{Step 3:} \quad \vec{x}_4 = \vec{x}_3 + s^*\vec{\nabla}f(\vec{x}_3) = \begin{bmatrix} 3 \\ 1 \end{bmatrix} + \frac{1}{4}\begin{bmatrix} 0 \\ 2 \end{bmatrix} = \begin{bmatrix} 3 \\ \frac{3}{2} \end{bmatrix}$$

and
$$\vec{\nabla}f(\vec{x}_4) = (-6 + 3 + 4, 6 - 6) = (1,0).$$

Continuing in this fashion, the algorithm will generate the points

$$\begin{bmatrix} \frac{7}{2} \\ \frac{3}{2} \end{bmatrix}, \begin{bmatrix} \frac{7}{2} \\ \frac{7}{4} \end{bmatrix}, \begin{bmatrix} \frac{15}{4} \\ \frac{7}{4} \end{bmatrix}, \begin{bmatrix} \frac{15}{4} \\ \frac{15}{8} \end{bmatrix} \cdots\cdots$$

These points are converging to the point
$$\vec{x}^* = \begin{pmatrix} 4 \\ 2 \end{pmatrix}$$
which is the optimal solution.

• PROBLEM 9-36

Use the Gradient Search method for the two-variable problem

$$\text{Maximize} \quad f(\vec{x}) = 2x_1x_2 + 2x_2 - x_1^2 - 2x_2^2$$

Start from $\vec{x} = (0,0)$.

Solution: $\frac{\partial f}{\partial x_1} = 2x_2 - 2x_1$, $\qquad \frac{\partial f}{\partial x_2} = 2x_1 + 2 - 4x_2$.

$f(x)$ is concave. To begin the gradient search procedure, $\vec{x} = (0,0)$ is selected as the initial trial solution. Since the respective partial derivatives are 0 and 2 at this point, the gradient is
$$\nabla f(0,0) = (0,2).$$
Therefore, for the first iteration

$$f(\vec{x}' + t\nabla f(\vec{x}')) = f(0 + 0t,\ 0 + 2t) = f(0,2t)$$
$$= 2(0)(2t) + 2(2t) - (0)^2 - 2(2t)^2$$
$$= 4t - 8t^2.$$

Since $\quad f(0,2t^*) = \max_{t \geq 0} f(0,2t) = \max_{t \geq 0}\{4t - 8t^2\},$

and $\quad \frac{d}{dt}\{4t - 8t^2\} = 4 - 16t = 0,$

it follows that $\quad t^* = \frac{1}{4},$

so reset $\vec{x}' = (0,0) + \frac{1}{4}(0,2) = \left(0,\frac{1}{2}\right).$

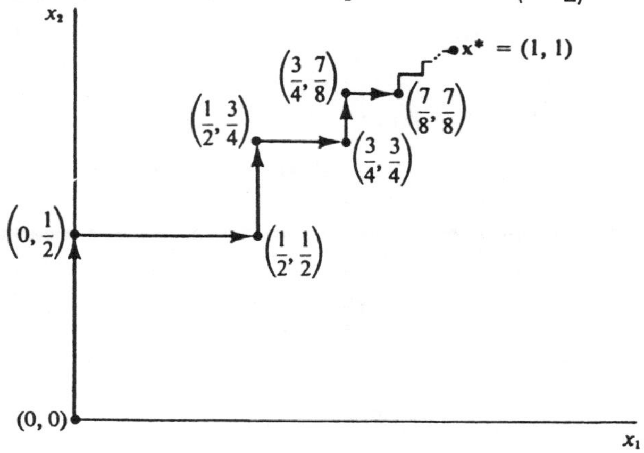

Fig. 1

For this new trial solution, the gradient is

$$\nabla f\left(0,\frac{1}{2}\right) = (1,0).$$

Thus, for the second iteration

$$f(\vec{x}' + t\nabla f(\vec{x}')) = f\left(0 + t, \frac{1}{2} + 0t\right) = f\left(t,\frac{1}{2}\right)$$
$$= (2t)\frac{1}{2} + 2\ \frac{1}{2} - t^2 - 2\left(\frac{1}{2}\right)^2$$
$$= t - t^2 + \frac{1}{2}.$$

$$\text{Reset } \vec{x} = \left(0,\frac{1}{2}\right) + t^*(1,0) = \left(t^*,\frac{1}{2}\right).$$

Since

$$f\left(t^*,\frac{1}{2}\right) = \max_{t \geq 0} f\left(t,\frac{1}{2}\right) = \max_{t \geq 0}\ t - \left\{t^2 + \frac{1}{2}\right\},$$

$$\frac{d}{dt}\left\{t - t^2 + \frac{1}{2}\right\} = 1 - 2t = 0,$$

then $\quad t^* = \frac{1}{2},$

so

$$\text{reset } \vec{x}' = \left(0,\frac{1}{2}\right) + \frac{1}{2}(1,0) = \left(\frac{1}{2},\frac{1}{2}\right).$$

Continuing in this fashion, the subsequent trial solutions would be (1/2,3/4), (3/4,3/4), (3/4,7/8), (7/8, 7/8), ..., as shown in Fig. 1. Since these points are converging to $\vec{x}^* = (1,1)$, this is the optimal solution, as verified by the fact that

$$\nabla f(1,1) = (0,0).$$

However, since this converging sequence of trial solutions never reaches its limit, the procedure actually will stop somewhere (depending on ε, which is a preset value determining the level of accuracy of the solution) slightly below (1,1) as its final approximation of $\vec{x}^*$.

• PROBLEM 9-37

Use the optimal gradient method to solve the following problem:

$$\text{Min } f(x_1,x_2) = (x_1 - 3x_2)^2 + (x_2 - 1)^2.$$

Start with the point $\vec{x}_0 = (2,2)$, and terminate when the gradient vector becomes reasonably small.

Solution: By inspection the optimal solution is $x_1 = 3$, $x_2 = 1$, with $f(3,1) = 0$, but we begin at the point $\vec{x}_0 = (2,2)$, which has an objective value of 17. The gradient vector is given by

$$\vec{\nabla} f(\vec{x}) = \begin{pmatrix} 2x_1 - 6x_2 \\ -6x_1 + 20x_2 - 2 \end{pmatrix},$$

and its value at the starting point is:

$$\vec{\nabla} f(\vec{x}_0) = \begin{pmatrix} -8 \\ 26 \end{pmatrix}.$$

Since this is a minimization problem, move in the direction opposite to the gradient, so

$$\vec{x}_1 = \vec{x}_0 - \theta_0 \vec{\nabla} f(\vec{x}_0) = \begin{pmatrix} 2 \\ 2 \end{pmatrix} - \theta_0 \begin{pmatrix} -8 \\ 26 \end{pmatrix} = \begin{pmatrix} 2 + 8\theta_0 \\ 2 - 26\theta_0 \end{pmatrix},$$

where a positive value of θ_0 is being sought. Given any θ_0, the value of the objective is

$$g(\theta_0) \equiv f(\vec{x}_0 - \theta_0 \vec{\nabla} f(\vec{x}_0)) = f(2 + 8\theta_0, 2 - 26\theta_0)$$

$$= 17 - 740\theta_0 + 8072\theta_0^2.$$

To find the value of θ_0 at which $g(\theta_0)$ stops decreasing, set its derivative equal to zero:

$$\frac{dg(\theta_0)}{d\theta_0} = -740 + 16{,}144\theta_0 = 0.$$

This yields a step length of $\theta_0 = .0458$, so that

$$\vec{x}_1 = \begin{pmatrix} 2.3667 \\ .8082 \end{pmatrix}.$$

The value of the objective has decreased from $f(\vec{x}_0) =$ 17 to $f(\vec{x}_1) = .0402$.

The gradient at $\vec{x}_1$ is

$$\vec{\nabla} f(\vec{x}_1) = \begin{pmatrix} -.1160 \\ -.0357 \end{pmatrix},$$

which is perpendicular to $\vec{\nabla} f(\vec{x}_0)$. Because the gradient still differs significantly from $\vec{0}$, the current point $\vec{x}_1$ is not a local minimum so proceed further. The next point in the sequence is of the form

$$\vec{x}_2 = \vec{x}_1 - \theta_1 \vec{\nabla} f(\vec{x}_1) = \begin{pmatrix} 2.3667 + .1160\theta_1 \\ .8082 + .0357\theta_1 \end{pmatrix},$$

which has an objective value given by

$$g(\theta_1) = .0402 - .0147\theta_1 + .00135\theta_1^2.$$

This function is minimized at $\theta_1 = 5.4413$, yielding

$$\vec{x}_2 = \begin{pmatrix} 2.9976 \\ 1.0024 \end{pmatrix},$$

at which point the objective value is $f(\vec{x}_2) = .000094$ and the gradient is

$$\vec{\nabla} f(\vec{x}_2) = \begin{pmatrix} -.0188 \\ .0612 \end{pmatrix}.$$

A further iteration then produces

$$\vec{x}_3 = \begin{pmatrix} 2.9985 \\ .9995 \end{pmatrix}, \quad f(\vec{x}_3) = 2.2 \times 10^{-7}, \quad \text{and}$$

$$\vec{\nabla} f(\vec{x}_3) = \begin{pmatrix} -.0003 \\ -.0001 \end{pmatrix}.$$

$\vec{x}_i$	$\lvert\vec{x}_i - \vec{x}_{i-1}\rvert$	$f(\vec{x}_i)$	$\vec{\nabla} f(\vec{x}_i)$
x_0 = (2.0000, 2.0000)		17.0000	(−8.0000, 26.0000)
x_1 = (2.3667, .8082)	1.246	0.0402	(−.1160, −.0357)
x_2 = (2.9976, 1.0024)	.660	$\sim 10^{-4}$	(−.0188, .0612)
x_3 = (2.9985, .9995)	.003	$\sim 10^{-7}$	(−.0003, −.0001)

This point would be likely to satisfy whatever criterion is being used for terminating the algorithm, either because $\vec{x}_3$ is so close to $\vec{x}_2$ or because the magnitude of the vector $\vec{\nabla}f(\vec{x}_3)$ is so small.

The progress of the optimal gradient method in converging to the local maximum $\vec{x}_3$ is summarized in the following table, where $|\vec{x}_i - \vec{x}_{i-1}|$ is the Euclidean distance from $\vec{x}_{i-1}$ to $\vec{x}_i$ (this distance equals the product of the step length θ_{i-1} and the magnitude of the gradient vector $\vec{\nabla}f(\vec{x}_{i-1})$):

• PROBLEM 9-38

Consider the problem of maximizing the function $f(x_1,x_2) = x_1^2 - x_2^2$, starting at $\vec{x}_0 = (0,1)$. Use the optimal gradient method to solve.

Solution: The gradient is $\vec{\nabla}f(\vec{x}) = (2x_1,-2x_2)$, so $\vec{\nabla}f(\vec{x}_0) = (0,-2)$, and

$$g(\theta) \equiv f(\vec{x}_0 + \theta\vec{\nabla}f(\vec{x}_0)) = f(0,1 - 2\theta)$$
$$= -(1 - 2\theta)^2.$$

This is maximized at $\theta_m = .5$, and

$$\vec{x}_1 = \vec{x}_0 + \theta_m\vec{\nabla}f(\vec{x}_0) = \begin{bmatrix} 0 \\ 1 \end{bmatrix} + .5\begin{bmatrix} 0 \\ -2 \end{bmatrix} = \begin{bmatrix} 0 \\ 0 \end{bmatrix}.$$

But $\vec{\nabla}f(\vec{x}_1) = (0,0)$, so the algorithm terminates at the origin, which is a stationary point of $f(x_1,x_2)$ but not a local maximum. This is because $\vec{\nabla}f(\vec{x}) = (0,0)$ is satisfied for inflection and saddle points as well. Thus it is not sufficient for identifying extreme points; and it is not possible to check the Hessian matrix's definiteness. Thus an optimum solution can not be proposed.

• PROBLEM 9-39

Apply the deflected gradient method of Fletcher and Powell to the following problem

$$\text{Maximize } y = 2x_1^2 + x_2^2 + 3x_3^2.$$

Start at the point (-1,1,-1), where $\Delta y = (-4,2,-6)$.

Solution: The computations and the final result is given in the table below:

TABLE 1

$\vec{x}_0 = (-1, 1, -1)$ $\quad y\langle\vec{x}_0\rangle = 6.0000$ $\quad \vec{\nabla y}_0 = (-4, 2, -6)$ $\quad \vec{H}_0 = \begin{pmatrix} 1 & & \\ 0 & 1 & \\ 0 & 0 & 1 \end{pmatrix}$

	$n=1$	$n=2$	$n=3$
$\vec{H}_{n-1}\vec{\nabla y}_{n-1}$	-4.0000 2.0000 -6.0000	-1.0612 1.2653 0.6122	0.2641 0.5281 -0.0587
μ_n	0.1944	0.3116	0.4106
$\vec{x}_n$	-0.2222 0.6111 0.1667	0.1084 0.2169 -0.0241	0.0000 0.0000 0.0000
$y\langle\vec{x}_n\rangle$	0.5556	0.0723	0.0000
$\vec{\nabla y}_n$	-0.8889 1.2222 1.0000	0.4337 0.4337 -0.1446	0.0000 0.0000 0.0000
$\vec{g}_n$	0.3111 -0.7778 7.0000	1.3226 -0.7885 -1.1446	-0.4337 -0.4337 0.1446
$\vec{A}_n$	0.0556 -0.0278 0.0139 0.0833 -0.0417 0.1250	0.1131 -0.1349 0.1608 -0.0652 0.0778 0.0377	0.0813 0.1627 0.3253 -0.0181 -0.0361 0.0040
$\vec{B}_n$	-0.1633 0.0408 -0.0102 -0.3673 0.0918 -0.8265	0.6387 0.3553 -0.1976 0.3233 -0.1798 -0.1637	-0.1980 -0.3961 -0.7922 0.0440 0.0880 -0.0098
$\vec{H}_n$	0.8923 0.0130 1.0037 -0.2840 0.0502 0.2985	0.3667 0.2334 0.9669 -0.0259 -0.0519 0.1724	0.2500 0.0000 0.5000 0.0000 0.0000 0.1667

• PROBLEM 9-40

Consider the problem

$$\text{Min } f(x_1, x_2) = x_1^2 + x_1^2 x_2^2 + 3x_2^4.$$

Solve one iteration of Newton's Method by using the starting point $\vec{x}_0 = (1.0, 1.0)$ and the direction of displacement $(-.706, -.294)$.

Solution: From the recursion for Newton's method

$$\vec{x}_{k+1} = \vec{x}_k + \theta[-\vec{H}^{-1}(\vec{x}_k) \cdot \vec{\nabla} f(\vec{x}_k)],$$

where $\vec{H}$ is the Hessian and $\vec{\nabla} f$ is the gradient matrix, seek a point of the form

$$\vec{x}_1 = \begin{pmatrix} 1.0 \\ 1.0 \end{pmatrix} + \theta \begin{pmatrix} -.706 \\ -.294 \end{pmatrix},$$

whose objective value is

$$g(\theta) = f(\vec{x}_1) = f(1.0 - .706\theta, 1.0 - .294\theta)$$

$$= 5.0 - 6.941\theta + 3.470\theta^2 - .720\theta^3 + .066\theta^4.$$

To minimize $g(\theta)$ take its derivative:

$$\frac{dg}{d\theta} = -6.941 + 6.941\theta - 2.161\theta^2 + .262\theta^3 = 0.$$

The only real root is $\theta = 1.755$, which yields

$$\vec{x}_1 = (-.239, .484), \quad \text{with } f(\vec{x}_1) = .235.$$

This point is substantially closer to the optimum (i.e., the origin).

The major advantage of the Newton method over the steepest-ascent algorithm is that it uses a better direction of movement at each stage; thus it generally requires fewer iterations for convergence. However, Newton's method also has two important disadvantages:

1. It calls for a great deal of calculation at each stage, and
2. It may fail to converge.

METHODS USING CONJUGATE DIRECTIONS

• PROBLEM 9-41

Use the Davidon-Fletcher-Powell method for the problem

$$\text{Minimize:} \quad 4(x_1 - 5)^2 + (x_2 - 6)^2.$$

The initial $\vec{x}$ vector is $\vec{x}^{(0)} = [8 \quad 9]^T$, and initial direction matrix $\vec{\eta}^{(0)} = \vec{I}$.

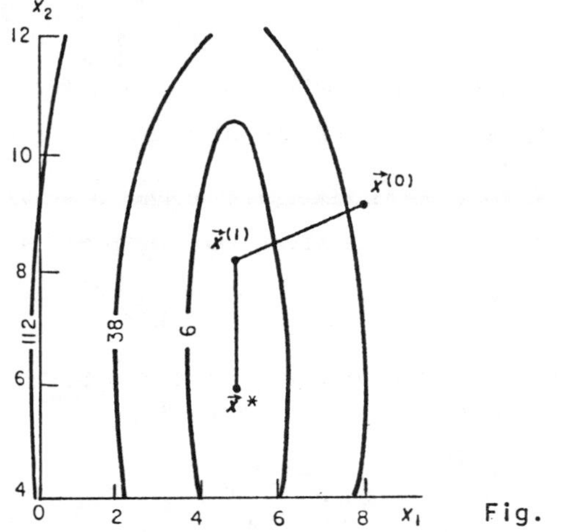

Fig. 1

Solution: The recursion relation to be used is

$$\vec{x}^{(k+1)} = \vec{x}^{(k)} - \lambda^{*(k)}\vec{\eta}^{(k)}\vec{\nabla}f(\vec{x}^{(k)}) \tag{1}$$

where

$$\vec{\nabla}f(\vec{x}^{(k)}) = \begin{bmatrix} 8(x_1 - 5) \\ 2(x_2 - 6) \end{bmatrix} .$$

and $\vec{\eta}^{(k)}$ (the direction matrix representing an approximation to the inverse Hessian matrix) is given by the following equation:

$$\vec{\eta}^{(k+1)} = \vec{\eta}^{(k)} + \vec{A}^{(k)} - \vec{B}^{(k)}$$

$$= \vec{\eta}^{(k)} + \frac{(\Delta x^{(k)})(\Delta x^{(k)})^T}{(\Delta x^{(k)})^T(\Delta g^{(k)})} - \frac{\vec{\eta}^{(k)}(\Delta g^{(k)})(\vec{\eta}^{(k)})^T}{(\Delta g^{(k)})^T\vec{\eta}^{(k)}(\Delta\vec{g}^{(k)})} ,$$

$$\Delta\vec{x}^{(k)} \equiv \vec{x}^{(k+1)} - \vec{x}^{(k)} , \quad \Delta\vec{g}^{(k)} \equiv \vec{\nabla}f(\vec{x}^{(k+1)}) - \vec{\nabla}f(\vec{x}^{(k)}).$$

Since $\vec{\eta}^{(0)} = \vec{I}$ and the initial $\vec{x}$ vector is $\vec{x}^{(0)} = [8 \quad 9]^T$, the new $\vec{x}$ vector $\vec{x}^{(1)}$ is computed from Eq. (1)

$$\begin{bmatrix} x_1^{(1)} \\ x_2^{(1)} \end{bmatrix} = \begin{bmatrix} 8 \\ 9 \end{bmatrix} - \lambda*^{(0)} \begin{bmatrix} 1 & 0 \\ 0 & 1 \end{bmatrix} \begin{bmatrix} 24 \\ 6 \end{bmatrix} .$$

Determine $\lambda*^{(0)}$ by minimizing $f(\vec{x}^{(1)})$ with respect to $\lambda*$, using analytical methods rather than a search

$$f(\vec{x}^{(1)}) = 4[(8 - 24\lambda*) - 5]^2 + [(9 - 6\lambda*) - 6]^2$$

$$\frac{df(\vec{x}^{(1)})}{d\lambda*} = 0 = 51 - 390\lambda*$$

or $\lambda*^{(0)} = 0.1307$, at which stage $\vec{x}^{(1)} = [4.862 \quad 8.215]^T$ and $f(\vec{x}) = 4.985$, as shown in Fig. 1. At $\vec{x}^{(1)}$

$$\vec{\nabla}f(\vec{x}^{(1)}) = [-1.108 \quad 4.431]^T$$

so that

$$(\Delta\vec{g})^{(0)} = [-25.108 \quad -1.569]^T.$$

Next, $\vec{\eta}^{(1)}$ is computed:

$$\vec{\eta}^{(1)} = \begin{bmatrix} 1 & 0 \\ 0 & 1 \end{bmatrix} + \frac{\begin{bmatrix} -3.13 & 0 \\ -0.785 & 0 \end{bmatrix} \begin{bmatrix} -3.13 & -0.785 \\ 0 & 0 \end{bmatrix}}{[-3.13 \quad -0.785] \begin{bmatrix} -25.108 \\ -1.569 \end{bmatrix}}$$

$$- \frac{\begin{bmatrix} 1 & 0 \\ 0 & 1 \end{bmatrix} \begin{bmatrix} -25.108 & 0 \\ 1.569 & 0 \end{bmatrix} \begin{bmatrix} -25.108 & -1.569 \\ 0 & 0 \end{bmatrix} \begin{bmatrix} 1 & 0 \\ 0 & 1 \end{bmatrix}}{[-25.108 \quad -1.569] \begin{bmatrix} 1 & 0 \\ 0 & 1 \end{bmatrix} \begin{bmatrix} -25.108 \\ -1.569 \end{bmatrix}}$$

$$= \begin{bmatrix} 1.270 \times 10^{-1} & -3.149 \times 10^{-2} \\ -3.149 \times 10^{-2} & 1.0038 \end{bmatrix}.$$

Now $\vec{x}^{(2)}$ can be computed using Eq. (1):

$$\begin{bmatrix} x_1^{(2)} \\ x_2^{(2)} \end{bmatrix} = \begin{bmatrix} 4.862 \\ 8.215 \end{bmatrix} - \lambda^{*(1)} \begin{bmatrix} 1.270 \times 10^{-1} & -3.149 \times 10^{-2} \\ -3.149 \times 10^{-2} & 1.0038 \end{bmatrix}$$

$$\times \begin{bmatrix} -1.108 \\ 4.431 \end{bmatrix}.$$

As before, $\lambda^{*(1)}$ is formed by minimizing $f(\vec{x}^{(2)})$ with respect to λ^*. Additional stages of the optimization yield the information in Table 1. Table 2 lists the matrix $\vec{\eta}$ at each stage of the search, which can be compared with the inverse of the Hessian matrix, $\vec{H}^{-1}$, at $\vec{x}^* = [5 \quad 6]^T$:

$$\vec{H} = \begin{bmatrix} 8 & 0 \\ 0 & 2 \end{bmatrix} \quad \text{and} \quad \vec{H}^{-1} = \begin{bmatrix} \frac{1}{8} & 0 \\ 0 & \frac{1}{2} \end{bmatrix}$$

TABLE 1

Stage k	$x_1^{(k)}$	$x_2^{(k)}$	$\frac{\partial f(\vec{x}^{(k)})}{\partial x_1}$	$\frac{\partial f(\vec{x}^{(k)})}{\partial x_2}$	$f(\vec{x}^{(k)})$	$\lambda^{*(k)}$
0	8.000	9.000	24.000	6.000	45.000	0.1307
1	4.862	8.215	-1.108	4.431	4.985	0.4942
2	5.000	6.000	3.81×10^{-7}	2.55×10^{-9}	9.06×10^{-15}	1.000
3	5.000	6.000	0	0	0	

TABLE 2

Stage 0	Stage 1
$\vec{\eta}$ $\begin{bmatrix} 1 & 0 \\ 0 & 1 \end{bmatrix}$	$\begin{bmatrix} 1.270 \times 10^{-1} & -3.149 \times 10^{-2} \\ -3.149 \times 10^{-2} & 1.0038 \end{bmatrix}$

Stage 2	Stage 3
$\begin{bmatrix} 1.250 \times 10^{-1} & -8.882 \times 10^{-16} \\ -8.882 \times 10^{-16} & 5.000 \times 10^{-1} \end{bmatrix}$	$\begin{bmatrix} 1.250 \times 10^{-1} & 1.387 \times 10^{-17} \\ -1.387 \times 10^{-17} & 5.000 \times 10^{-1} \end{bmatrix}$

• PROBLEM 9-42

Use Powell's search method to solve.

Minimize: $y(x) = 3x^2 - 18x + 27.$

Let the accuracy in x = 0.01

accuracy in y[x] = 0.01.

$x^{(1)} = 0, \ \Delta x = 0.5.$

	$x^{(k)}$	$y[x^{(k)}]$
$k = 1$	0	27
$k = 2$	0.5	18.75
$k = 3$	1	12
$\bar{x}_1^*$	3	0
$\bar{x}_2^*$	3	0

Solution: The algorithm to solve this type problem is the following:

Step 1: From the base vector $x^{(1)}$, compute $x^{(2)} = x^{(1)} + \Delta x$.

$$x^{(2)} = x^{(1)} + \Delta x = 0.5$$

Step 2: Compute $y(x^{(1)})$ and $y(x^{(2)})$:

$$y[x^{(1)}] = 27$$

$$y[x^{(2)}] = 18.75.$$

Step 3: If $y(x^{(1)}) > y(x^{(2)})$, let $x^{(3)} = x^{(1)} + 2\Delta x$. If $y(x^{(1)}) < y(x^{(2)})$, let $x^{(3)} = x^{(1)} - \Delta x$:

$$y[x^{(1)}] > y[x^{(2)}] \text{ Let } x^{(3)} = x^{(1)} + 2\Delta x$$

$$= 0 + 2x - 5 = 3.$$

Step 4: Compute $y(x^{(3)})$:

$y[x^{(3)}] = 12.$

Step 5: Estimate the value of x at the minimum of y(x), x* by:

$$x^* = \frac{1\{[x^{(2)}]^2 - [x^{(3)}]^2\}y[x^{(1)}] + \{[x^{(3)}]^2}{2[x^{(2)} - x^{(3)}]y[x^{(1)}] + [x^{(3)} - x^{(1)}]}$$

$$\frac{- [x^{(1)}]^2\}y[x^{(2)}] + \{[x^{(1)}]^2 - [x^{(2)}]^2\}y[x^{(3)}]}{\cdot y[x^{(2)}] + [x^{(1)} - x^{(2)}]y[x^{(3)}]}$$

$$= \frac{1(0.5^2 - 1^2)\cdot 27 + (1 - 0)\cdot 18.75 + (0 - 0.5^2)\cdot 12}{2(0.5 - 1)\cdot 27 + (1 - 0)\cdot 18.75 + (0 - 0.5)\cdot 12}$$

$$= 3.$$

Step 6: If x* and whichever of $x^{(1)}$, $x^{(2)}$, $x^{(3)}$ corresponding to the smallest y(x) differ by less than the prescribed accuracy in x(or y[x]), terminate the search. Otherwise, evaluate y(x*) and discard from the set, $x^{(1)}$, $x^{(2)}$, $x^{(3)}$ the one that corresponds to the greatest current value of y(x); unless the bracket on the minimum of y(x) will be lost by so doing, in which case discard the x so as to maintain the bracket.

$y[x^*] = 0$ accuracy $x > 0.01$

discard $x^{(1)}$ accuracy in $y[x] > 0.01$.

Step 7: Let $x^{(1)} = x^*$, and go back to step 1. Eventually, it will be necessary to successively reduce Δx and the algorithm continues until the desired precision listed in step 6 is obtained.

$$x^* = \frac{1}{2} \cdot \frac{(0.5^2 - 1^2)\cdot 0 + (1 - 3^2)\cdot 18.75 + (3^2 - 0.5^2)\cdot 12}{(0.5 - 1)\cdot 0 + (1 - 3)\cdot 18.75 + (3 - 0.5)\cdot 12}$$

$$= 3 \Rightarrow x^* = 3.$$

• PROBLEM 9-43

Consider the following problem:

Minimize: $(x_1 - 2)^4 + (x_1 - 2x_2)^2$

Solve the problem by the Fletcher and Reeves method. Start with point (0.00,3.00) and terminate when norm of gradient vector becomes less than 0.05.

Solution: First choose a termination scalar $\varepsilon > 0$ and an initial point $\vec{x}_1$. Let $\vec{y}_1 = \vec{x}_1$, $\vec{d}_1 = -\vec{\nabla}f(\vec{y}_1)$, k = j

= 1, and go to the main step.

TABLE 1

Iteration k	$\vec{x}_k$ $f(\vec{x}_k)$	j	$\vec{y}_j$ $f(\vec{y}_j)$	$\vec{\nabla} f(\vec{y}_j)$	$\lVert\vec{\nabla} f(\vec{y}_j)\rVert$	α_1	$\vec{d}_j$	λ_j	$\vec{y}_{j+1}$
1	(0.00, 3.00) 52.00	1	(0.00, 3.00) 52.00	(−44.00, 24.00)	50.12	—	(44.00, −24.00)	0.062	(2.70, 1.51)
		2	(2.70, 1.51) 0.34	(0.73, 1.28)	1.47	0.0009	(−0.69, −1.30)	0.23	(2.54, 1.21)
2	(2.54, 1.21) 0.10	1	(2.54, 1.21) 0.10	(0.87, −0.48)	0.99	—	(−0.87, 0.48)	0.11	(2.44, 1.26)
		2	(2.44, 1.26) 0.04	(0.18, 0.32)	0.37	0.14	(−0.30, −0.25)	0.63	(2.25, 1.10)
3	(2.25, 1.10) 0.008	1	(2.25, 1.10) 0.008	(0.16, −0.20)	0.32	—	(−0.16, 0.20)	0.10	(2.23, 1.12)
		2	(2.23, 1.12) 0.003	(0.03, 0.04)	0.05	0.04	(−0.036, −0.032)	1.02	(2.19, 1.09)
4	(2.19, 1.09) 0.0017	1	(2.19, 1.09) 0.0017	(0.05, −0.04)	0.06	—	(−0.05, 0.04)	0.11	(2.185, 1.094)
		2	(2.185, 1.094) 0.0012	(0.02, 0.01)	0.02				

Main Step:

1. If $\lVert\vec{\nabla} f(\vec{y}_j)\rVert < \varepsilon$, stop. Otherwise, let λ_j be an optimal solution to the problem to minimize $f(\vec{y}_j + \lambda\vec{d}_j)$ subject to $\lambda \geq 0$, and let $\vec{y}_{j+1} = \vec{y}_j + \lambda_j\vec{d}_j$. If $j < n$, go to step 2; otherwise go to step 3.

2. Let $\vec{d}_{j+1} = -\vec{\nabla} f(\vec{y}_{j+1}) + \alpha_j\vec{d}_j$, where $\alpha_j = \lVert\vec{\nabla} f(\vec{y}_{j+1})\rVert^2 / \lVert\vec{\nabla} f(\vec{y}_j)\rVert^2$. Replace j by j + 1 and go to step 1.

3. Let $\vec{y}_1 = \vec{x}_{k+1} = \vec{y}_{n+1}$, and let $\vec{d}_1 = -\vec{\nabla}f(\vec{y}_1)$. Let j = 1, replace k by k + 1, and go to step 1.

The summary of the computations using the method of Fletcher and Reeves is given in Table 1. At each iteration $\vec{d}_1$ was given by $-\vec{\nabla}f(\vec{y}_1)$, and $\vec{d}_2$ was given by $\vec{d}_2 = -\vec{\nabla}f(\vec{y}_2) + \alpha_1\vec{d}_1$, where $\alpha_1 = \|\vec{\nabla}f(\vec{y}_2\|^2/\|\vec{\nabla}f(\vec{y}_1)\|^2$. Furthermore, $\vec{y}_{j+1}$ is obtained by optimizing along $\vec{d}_j$, starting from $\vec{y}_j$. At iteration 4, the point $\vec{y}_2 = (2.185,1.094)^t$, which is very close to the optimal point (2.00,1.00), is reached. Since the norm of the gradient is equal to 0.02, which is small, stop here.

CHAPTER 10

NONLINEAR PROGRAMMING - CONSTRAINED OPTIMIZATION

PROBLEM FORMULATION

• PROBLEM 10-1

A manufacturing process produces x_i items in a given time period at a cost $f_i(x_i)$. In each period there is a demand d_i for the product and a cost $c_i(y_i)$ for holding inventory in amount y_i. The production cannot exceed X in each time period and the inventory cannot exceed Y. If the initial inventory is zero, formulate a nonlinear programming problem for minimizing total cost over n periods.

Solution: The total cost is given by

$$F(\vec{x},\vec{y}) = \sum_{i=1}^{n} [f_i(x_i) + c_i(y_i)].$$

The inventory in any period is given by

$$y_i = y_{i-1} + x_i - d_i ,$$

where $$y_0 = 0, \quad i = 1,2,\ldots,n.$$

The nonlinear programming problem is

$$\min_{x_i, y_i} \sum_{i=1}^{n} [f_i(x_i) + c_i(y_i)]$$

such that

$$y_i = y_{i-1} + x_i - d_i ,$$

$$y_0 = 0, \qquad x_i \le X, \qquad y_i \le Y .$$

Note that the x_i variables can be easily eliminated, so the problem becomes

$$\min_{y_i} \sum_{i=1}^{n} [f_i(y_i - y_{i-1} + d_i) + c_i(y_i)]$$

such that $y_i - y_{i-1} + d_i \leq X,$

$$y_0 = 0,\ y_i \leq Y,\ i = 1,2,\dots,n.$$

• PROBLEM 10-2

A manufacturer makes three products. The sale volume of each product is dependent on its price, and in one case, product 3, sales volume is also dependent on the price of another product. The market forecasting division estimated the following relationship between monthly sales volume x_j (thousands of units) and unit price p_j for each product:

$$x_1 = 10 - p_1$$

$$x_2 = 16 - p_2 \qquad (1)$$

$$x_3 = 6 - \frac{1}{2}p_3 + \frac{1}{4}p_2$$

The variable costs for the three products are \$6, \$7, and \$10 per unit, respectively. Production is limited by available resources, manpower, and machine time.

Each month 1000 machine hours and 2000 man hours are available. Product 1 uses 0.4 machine hour and 0.2 man hour per unit, product 2 uses 0.2 machine hour and 0.4 man hour per unit, and product 3 uses 0.1 hour of each per unit. The manufacturer wishes to find the monthly sales schedule that will maximize profits.

Solution: Total profit for each product is equal to total revenue minus total variable cost for the product. For product 1, total revenue is

$$R_1 = p_1x_1 .$$

From (1),

$$p_1 = 10 - x_1 ,$$

so

$$R_1 = p_1x_1 = 10x_1 - x_1^2 .$$

Total variable cost for product 1 is $V_1 = 6x_1$. So the total profit for product 1 is

$$\pi_1 = R_1 - V_1 = 10x_1 - x_1^2 - 6x_1 = 4x_1 - x_1^2$$

For product 2 the total revenue amounts to

$$R_2 = p_2x_2 = 16x_2 - x_2^2,$$

and the total variable cost $V_2 = 7x_2$, with the difference of

$$\pi_2 = R_2 - V_2 = 16x_2 - x_2^2 - 7x_2 = 9x_2 - x_2^2$$

Product 3 presents a new problem, since x_3 depends on p_2 as well as p_3. Total revenue is

$$R_3 = p_3x_3 = 2(6 - x_3 + \frac{1}{4} p_2)\ x_3$$

Using $p_2 = 16 - x_2$ from expressions (1), obtain

$$R_3 = 2(6 - x_3 + \frac{1}{4}(16 - x_2))x_3 = 20x_3 - 2x_3^2 - \frac{1}{2} x_2x_3$$

Variable cost is $V_3 = 10x_3$. Hence total profit for product 3 is

$$\pi_3 = R_3 - V_3 = 20x_3 - 2x_3^2 - \frac{1}{2} x_2x_3 - 10x_3$$

$$= 10x_3 - 2x_3^2 - \frac{1}{2} x_2x_3$$

Summing π_1, π_2, and π_3, obtain the total profit function

$$\pi = f(x_1,x_2,x_3) = 4x_1 - x_1^2 + 9x_2 - x_2^2 + 10x_3 -$$

$$2x_3^2 - \frac{1}{2} x_2x_3 \qquad (2)$$

It is necessary to find values for x_1, x_2, and x_3 that maximize expression (2) within the monthly machine time and man hour restrictions imposed:

$$4x_1 + 2x_2 + x_3 \leq 10 \text{ (units of 100 machine hours)}$$

$$2x_1 + 4x_2 + x_3 \leq 20 \text{ (units of 100 man hours)}$$

Summarizing, the following programming problem is obtained.

maximize

$$f(x_1,x_2,x_3) = 4x_1 - x_1^2 + 9x_2 - x_2^2 + 10x_3 - 2x_3^2 - \frac{1}{2} x_2x_3$$

subject to

$$4x_1 + 2x_2 + x_3 \leq 10 \qquad \text{(machine time)} \qquad (3)$$

$$2x_1 + 4x_2 + x_3 \leq 20 \qquad \text{(man hours)}$$

$$x_1 \geq 0,$$

$$x_2 \geq 0, \qquad \text{(nonnegativity conditions)}$$

$$x_3 \geq 0$$

Problem (3) is a nonlinear programming problem, since some of its functional relationships are nonlinear.

• PROBLEM 10-3

The peace-loving nation of Amazonia wishes to allocate N antiballistic missiles (ABMs) among its M cities in order to provide optimal deterrence against a possible nuclear attack. The value of the ith city, based on population and industry, is estimated to be V_i. Each ABM can destroy with certainty one attacking missile but can only be used against an attacker aimed at the city where it has been located. Given any deployment of Amazonia ABMs, a potential enemy nation with limited resources could do serious damage merely by buying or building enough offensive missiles to wipe out one city. Since the enemy nation would presumably decide to attack the city at which it could do the most damage per dollar (per offensive missile), how should Amazonia allocate its ABMs in order to minimize this maximum damage per dollar? Treat all variables as continuous.

Set up a mathematical programming model that would solve this problem.

Solution: Let x_i be the number of ABMs deployed at city i; from the problem statement, that city could then be destroyed by $x_i + 1$ offensive missiles, yielding to the attacker a payoff per missile of $V_i/(x_i + 1)$. Amazonia therefore wishes to minimize the maximum of the $V_i/(x_i + 1)$. This can be represented mathematically by letting the variable z equal that (unknown) maximum. The problem then becomes

$$\text{Min } z$$

$$\text{subject to} \qquad \frac{V_i}{x_i + 1} \leqq z, \quad i = 1,\ldots,M,$$

with the additional constraints being

$$\sum_{i=1}^{M} x_i = N \quad \text{and} \quad x_i \geqq 0, \quad i = 1,\ldots,M.$$

In game theory Amazonia's optimal deployment is known as a minimax strategy. It should be added that the problem would be rather more difficult if the realistic constraint that all x_i must be integers were included.

• PROBLEM 10-4

An unmanned rocket of mass M is to travel through outer space from one docking station to another that is exactly 1 million miles away. The rocket has two engines, one capable of exerting up to b units of thrust (i.e., force) in the forward direction and the other capable of up to c units in the reverse direction. At discrete points 100,000 miles apart the thrust exerted by these engines may be altered instantaneously by radio control, but between those points no adjustments are permitted. How should the engines of the rocket be controlled in order to bring it to its destination in the shortest possible time? Assume that no frictional or gravitational forces act on the rocket.

Construct a mathematical programming model to solve this problem.

Solution: Let v_i, $i = 1,\ldots,11$, be the velocity of the rocket in miles per hour as it passes the ith control point, where

$$v_1 = 0 \quad \text{and} \quad v_{11} = 0$$

are required. From the laws of motion one may write

$$v_{i+1} = v_i + a_i t_i, \quad i = 1,\ldots,10, \tag{1}$$

where a_i is the rocket's constant acceleration as it moves from point i to i + 1, and t_i is the total time it takes to cover that 100,000-mile distance. Because the acceleration is constant, the average velocity between points i and i + 1 is

$$\frac{v_i + v_{i+1}}{2} = v_i + \frac{a_i t_i}{2} = \frac{100{,}000}{t_i} .$$

Converting to a quadratic equation and solving for t_i, one finds

$$t_i = \frac{-v_i + (v_i^2 + 200{,}000a_i)^{\frac{1}{2}}}{a_i} .$$

Substitution into (1) then yields

$$v_{i+1} = \left(v_i^2 + 200{,}000a_i\right)^{\frac{1}{2}} .$$

It remains only to substitute force for acceleration in accordance with Newton's law:

$$f_i = Ma_i ,$$

where f_i is the net (algebraic) thrust exerted by the rocket's engines in the forward direction between points i and i + 1. The optimal control problem can now be written as a mathematical program:

$$\text{Min} \sum_{i=1}^{10} \left(\frac{-v_i + (v_i^2 + 200{,}000f_i/M)^{\frac{1}{2}}}{f_i/M}\right)$$

subject to $v_{i+1} = (v_i^2 + 200{,}000f_i/M)^{\frac{1}{2}}$, $i = 1,\ldots,10$,

$v_1 = 0$, $v_{11} = 0$, and $-c \leq f_i \leq b$, $i = 1,\ldots 10$.

Although control problems of this sort can be solved by the techniques of mathematical programming, they are much better suited to dynamic programming methods.

• PROBLEM 10-5

The government of a country wants to decide what prices should be charged for its dairy products milk, butter, and cheese. All these products arise directly or indirectly from the country's raw milk production. This raw milk is usefully divided into the two components of fat and dry matter. After subtracting the quantities of fat and dry matter which are used for making products for export or consumption on the farms there is a total yearly availability of 600,000 tons of fat and 750,000 tons of dry matter. This is all available for producing milk, butter, and two kinds of cheese for domestic consumption.

Table 1

	Fat	Dry matter	Water
Milk	4	9	87
Butter	80	2	18
Cheese 1	35	30	30
Cheese 2	25	40	35

Table 2

	Milk	Butter	Cheese 1	Cheese 2
Domestic Consumption (1000 tons)	4820	320	210	70
Price ($/ton)	297	720	1050	815

The percentage compositions of the products are given in Table 1. For the previous year the domestic consumption and prices for the products are given in Table 2.

Price elasticities of demand, relating consumer demand to the prices of each product have been calculated on the basis of past statistics. The price elasticity E of a product is defined by

$$E = \frac{\text{percentage decrease in demand}}{\text{percentage increase in price}}$$

For the two makes of cheese there will be some degree of substitution in consumer demand depending on relative prices. This is measured by cross elasticity of demand with respect to price. The cross elasticity E_{AB} from a product A to a product B is defined by:

$$E_{AB} = \frac{\text{percentage increase in demand for A}}{\text{percentage increase in price of B}}$$

The elasticities and cross elasticities are given in Table 3.

The objective is to determine what prices and resultant demand will maximize total revenue.

Table 3

Milk	Butter	Cheese 1	Cheese 2	Cheese 1 to Cheese 2	Cheese 2 to Cheese 1
0·4	2·7	1·1	0·4	0·1	0·4

It is, however, politically unacceptable to allow a certain price index. As a result of the way this index is calculated this limitation simply denies that the new prices must be such that the total cost of last year's consumption would not be increased. A particularly important additional requirement is to quantify the economic cost of this political limitation.

Construct a Nonlinear Programming model that would solve this problem. Approximate price-elasticity relationships by linear relationships so as to reduce the number of nonlinearities. How can one put this model into separable programming form?

Solution: Let x_M, x_B, x_{C1}, and x_{C2} be the quantities of milk, butter, cheese 1, and cheese 2 consumed (in thousands of tons) and p_M, p_B, p_{C1}, and p_{C2} their respective prices (in \$1000 per ton).

The limited availabilities of fat and dry matter give the following two constraints:

$$0.04x_M + 0.8\,x_B + 0.35x_{C1} + 0.25x_{C2} \le 600$$

$$0.09x_M + 0.02x_B + 0.3\,x_{C1} + 0.4\,x_{C2} \le 750$$

The price index limitation gives (measured in \$1000)

$$4.82p_M + 0.32p_B + 0.21p_{C1} + 0.07p_{C2} \le 1.939$$

The objective is to maximize

$$\textstyle\sum_i x_i p_i \ .$$

In addition the x variables are related to the p variables through the price elasticity relationships:

$$\frac{dx_M}{x_M} = -E_M \frac{dp_M}{p_M} \ , \quad \frac{dx_B}{x_B} = -\,E_B \frac{dp_B}{p_B}$$

$$\frac{dx_{C1}}{x_{C1}} = -\,E_{C1} \frac{dp_{C1}}{p_{C1}} + E_{C1C2} \frac{dp_{C2}}{p_{C2}},\ \frac{dx_{C2}}{p_{C2}} = -\,E_{C2} \frac{dx_{C2}}{p_{C2}} + E_{C2C1} \frac{dp_{C2}}{p_{C2}}$$

These differential equations can easily be integrated to give the x variables as expressions involving the p variables. If these expressions are substituted in the above constraints and the objective function, non-linearities are introduced into the first two constraints as well as the objective function; the non-linearities could be separated and approximated to by piecewise linear functions.

In order to reduce the number of non-linearities in the model the relationships implied by the differential equations above can be approximated to by the linear relationships:

$$\frac{x_M - \bar{x}_M}{\bar{x}_M} = -E_M \frac{p_M - \bar{p}_M}{\bar{p}_M},$$

$$\frac{x_B - \bar{x}_B}{\bar{x}_B} = -E_B \frac{p_B - \bar{p}_B}{\bar{p}_B}$$

$$\frac{x_{C1} - \bar{x}_{C1}}{\bar{x}_{C1}} = -E_{C1} \frac{p_{C1} - \bar{p}_{C1}}{\bar{p}_{C1}} + E_{C1C2} \frac{p_{C2} - \bar{p}_{C2}}{\bar{p}_{C2}}$$

$$\frac{x_{C2} - \bar{x}_{C2}}{\bar{x}_{C2}} = -E_{C2} \frac{p_{C2} - \bar{p}_{C2}}{\bar{p}_{C2}} + E_{C2C1} \frac{p_{C1} - \bar{p}_{C1}}{\bar{p}_{C1}}$$

$\bar{x}$ and $\bar{p}$ are known quantities consumed with their prices for the previous year. This approximation can be regarded as warranted if the resultant values of x and p do not differ significantly from $\bar{x}$ and $\bar{p}$.

Using the above relationships to substitute for the x variables in the first two constraints and the objective function gives the model: maximize

$$-6491p_M^2 - 1200p^2_B - 220p_{C1}^2 - 34p_{C2}^2 + 53p_{C1}p_{C2}$$

$$+ 6748p_M + 1184p_B + 420p_{C1} + 70p_{C2}$$

subject to

$$260p_M + 960p_B + 70.25p_{C1} - 0.6p_{C2} \geq 782$$

$$584p_M + 24p_B + 58.2p_{C1} + 2.8p_{C2} \geq 248$$

$$4.82p_M = 0.32p_B + 0.21p_{C1} + 0.07p_{C2} \leq 1.939$$

In addition it is necessary to represent explicitly the non-negativity conditions on the x variables. These give:

$$p_M \leq 1.039, \; p_B \leq 0.987$$

$$220p_{C1} - 26p_{C2} \leq 420$$

$$-27p_{C1} + 34p_{C2} \leq 70$$

This is a quadratic programming model as there are quadratic terms in the objective function.

In order to put this model into a separable form it is necessary to remove the term $p_{C1}p_{C2}$. This may be done by introducing a new variable q together with the constraint:

$$p_{C1} - p_{C2} - 0.194q = 0$$

(It is important to allow q to be negative, if necessary, by incorporating it in the model as a 'free' variable.)

The objective function can then be written in the separable form (a sum of non-linear functions of single variables):

$$-6491p_M^2 - 1200p_B^2 - 193.5p_{C1}^2 - 7.5p_{C2}^2 - q^2 + 6748p_M$$

$$+1185p_B + 420p_{C1} + 70p_{C2}$$

This transformation also demonstrates that the model is convex. Using a piecewise linear approximation to the non-linearities, there is therefore no danger of obtaining a local optimum with separable programming. In fact it is sufficient to use the conventional simplex algorithm. This will enable one to obtain a true (global) optimum. The optimal prices by computer solution are:

Milk	\$300/ton
Butter	\$662/ton
Cheese 1	\$950/ton
Cheese 2	\$1163/ton

The resultant yearly revenue will be \$1.99 (1000 million). It is straightforward to calculate the yearly demands which will result from these prices. They are:

Milk	4800 (1000 tons)
Butter	390 (1000 tons)
Cheese 1	241 (1000 tons)
Cheese 2	55 (1000 tons)

The economic cost of imposing a constraint on the price index can be obtained from the shadow price on the constraint. For this problem this shadow price in the optimal solution indicates that each \$1 by which the new prices are allowed to increase the cost of last year's consumption would result in an increased revenue of \$0.54.

GRAPHICAL SOLUTIONS

• PROBLEM 10-6

Consider the following problem:

Minimize $(x_1 - 3)^2 + (x_2 - 2)^2$

subject to
$$x_1^2 - x_2 - 3 \leq 0$$
$$x_2 - 1 \leq 0$$
$$-x_1 \leq 0$$

Give the graphical solution.

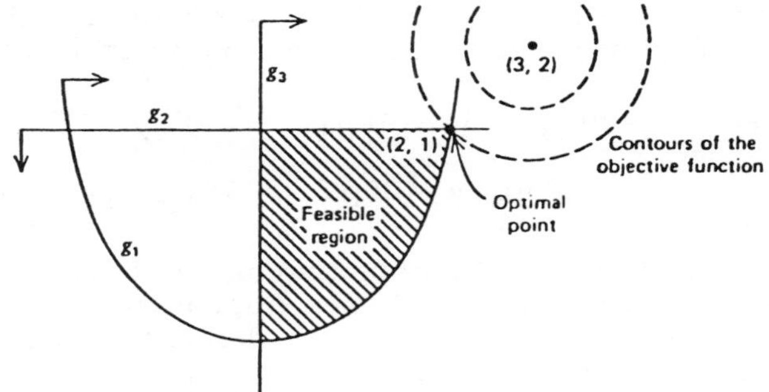

Geometric solution of a nonlinear problem.

Fig. 1

Solution: Figure 1 illustrates the feasible region. The problem, then, is to find the point in the feasible region with the smallest possible

$$(x_1 - 3)^2 + (x_2 - 2)^2.$$

Note that points (x_1, x_2) with

$$(x_1 - 3)^2 + (x_2 - 2)^2 = c$$

represent a circle with radius $\sqrt{c}$ and center (3,2). This circle is called the contour of the objective function having value c. Since one wishes to minimize c, one must find the circle with the smallest radius that intersects the feasible region. As shown in Figure 1, the smallest such circle has c = 2 and intersects the feasible region at the point (2,1). Therefore, the optimal solution occurs at the point (2,1) and has an objective value equal to 2.

The approach used above to find an optimal solution by determining the objective contour with the smallest objective value that intersects the feasible region, is only suitable for small problems and is not practical for problems with more than two variables or those with complicated objective and constraint functions.

Consider the nonlinear programming problem

minimize $z = (x_1 - 3)^2 + (x_2 - 4)^2$

subject to the linear constraints

$$x_1 \geq 0$$
$$x_2 \geq 0$$
$$5 - x_1 - x_2 \geq 0$$
$$-2.5 + x_1 - x_2 \leq 0$$

Solve by using the graphical approach. Change the objective function to

$$z = (x_1 - 2)^2 + (x_2 - 2)^2$$

and solve graphically.

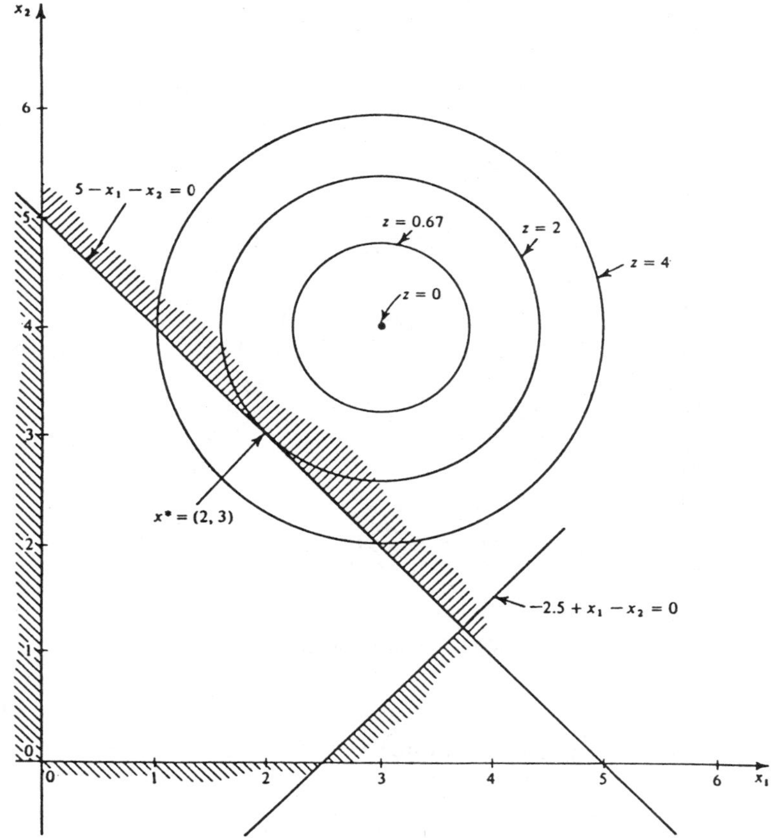

Minimum on boundary of constraint set.

Fig. 1

Solution: The problem is shown graphically in Figure 1. The constraint set is of the linear programming type, having a finite number of corner points. The objective function, being nonlinear, has contours of constant value which are not parallel lines, as in the linear case, but concentric circles. The minimum value of z corresponds to the contour of lowest value having at least one point in common with the constraint set. This is the contour labeled z = 2, and the solution is at its point of tangency with the constraint set, i.e., at

$$x_1^* = 2, \ x_2^* = 3.$$

This is not an extreme point of the set, although it is a boundary point. (Recall that for linear programs the minimum is always at an extreme point.)

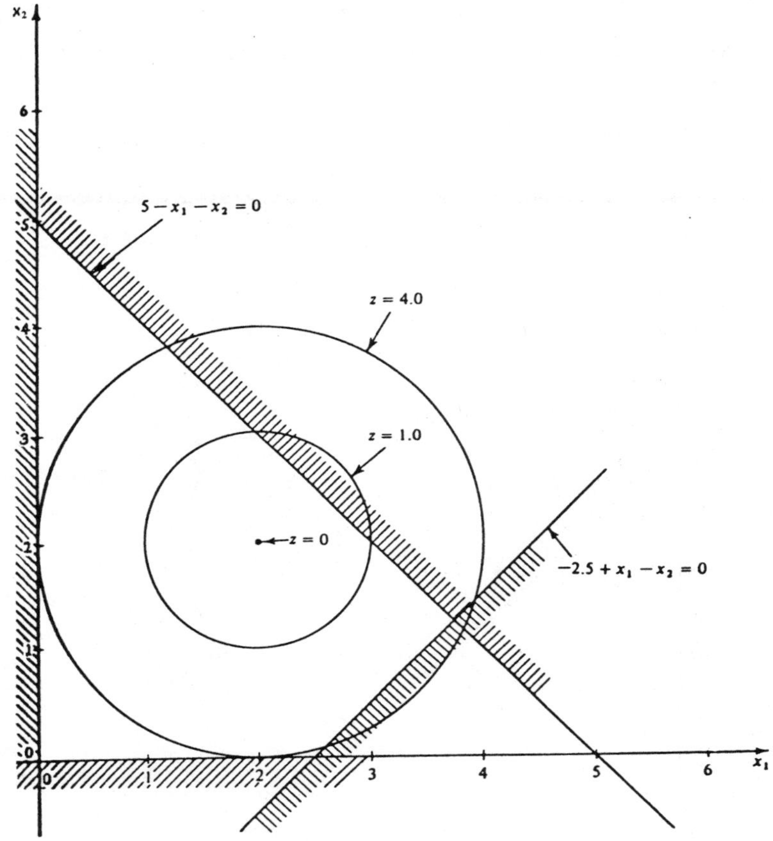

Unconstrained minimum interior to constraint set.

Fig. 2

With the new objective function

$$z = (x_1 - 2)^2 + (x_2 - 2)^2$$

the situation is depicted in Figure 2. The minimum is now at $x_1 = 2$, $x_2 = 2$, which is not even a boundary point of the constraint set. Here the unconstrained minimum of the nonlinear function satisfies the constraints.

• **PROBLEM 10-8**

Consider extremizing the function

$$f(\vec{x}) = \frac{1}{(x_1 - 1)^2 + (x_2 - 1)^2 + 1}$$

where the allowable range of $\vec{x}$ is constrained such that

$$|x_i| \leq \frac{1}{2}, \quad i = 1,2.$$

Determine the value of $\vec{x}$ that maximizes f with respect to the set of allowable values of $\vec{x}$ by utilizing graphical means.

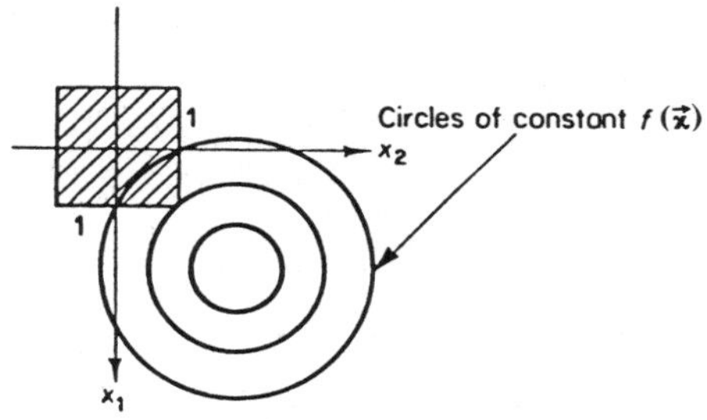

Top view of f showing the region defined by $|x_i| \leq \frac{1}{2}, i = 1, 2.$

Solution: In the figure, it is apparent for this problem that f has an extremum on the boundary of the allowable set of vectors and the maximum is attained at

$$x^T = \left[\frac{1}{2}, \frac{1}{2}\right] .$$

DERIVATIVES

• **PROBLEM 10-9**

Consider the two-dimensional problem

Minimize

$$(x_1 - 3)^2 + (x_2 - 4)^2$$

subject to

$$2x_1 + x_2 = 7$$

Find the global minimum and the optimal value of the function by using differentiation.

Solution: The unconstrained minimum occurs at (3,4) and is equal to zero. One way to find the constrained minimum is by substitution. That is, since

$$x_2 = 7 - 2x_1 ,$$

the problem is to minimize $f(x_1)$ where

$$f(x_1) = (x_1 - 3)^2 + (7 - 2x_1 - 4)^2$$

$$= (x_1 - 3)^2 + (3 - 2x_1)^2$$

$$= x_1^2 - 6x_1 + 9 + 9 - 12x_1 + 4x_1^2$$

$$= 5x_1^2 - 18x_1 + 18$$

Since

$$f'(x_1) = 10x_1 - 18$$

and

$$f''(x_1) = 10 > 0,$$

the global minimum occurs at

$$x_1 = 18/10$$

and

$$x_2 = 7 - 2(1.8) = 3.4$$

The optimal value of the objective function is

$$(1.8 - 3)^2 + (3.4 - 4)^2 = 1.8.$$

• PROBLEM 10-10

Consider the maximization of

$$f(\vec{x}) = \frac{1}{(x_1 - 1)^2 + (x_2 - 1)^2 + 1}$$

subject to the constraint that the Euclidean norm of $\vec{x}$ equals one. Solve the problem by taking derivatives.

Solution: Symbolically the Euclidean norm means that

$$||\vec{x}||^2 = \vec{x}^T\vec{x} = x_1^2 + x_2^2 + \ldots + x_n^2 = \langle\vec{x},\vec{x}\rangle .$$

Since the dimension of the problem is two, the Euclidean norm squared becomes

$$||\vec{x}||^2 = x_1^2 + x_2^2 .$$

One approach to the problem is to solve for x_1 in terms of x_2, then solve for $\Theta = f(\vec{x})$ in terms of x_2 alone. This will then allow one to use the standard scalar procedure. From the given constraint on the length of the Euclidean norm,

$$x_1 = (1 - x_2^2)^{\frac{1}{2}} \quad .$$

Substituting this into the expression for $\Theta(\vec{x})$ find that

$$\Theta(x_2) = \frac{1}{(\pm\sqrt{1 - x_2^2} - 1)^2 + (x_2 - 1)^2 + 1}$$

where $\Theta(x_2)$ has the given constraint imbedded into it. The next step is to differentiate this expression with respect to the remaining variable x_2 and set the result equal to zero. This yields two solutions. The second-derivative test shows that a maximum (which is easily shown to be an absolute maximum) occurs at

$$\vec{x}^T = [0.707, 0.707]$$

and that an (absolute) minimum occurs at

$$\vec{x}^T = [-0.707, -0.707].$$

The figure illustrates $\Theta(x_2)$.

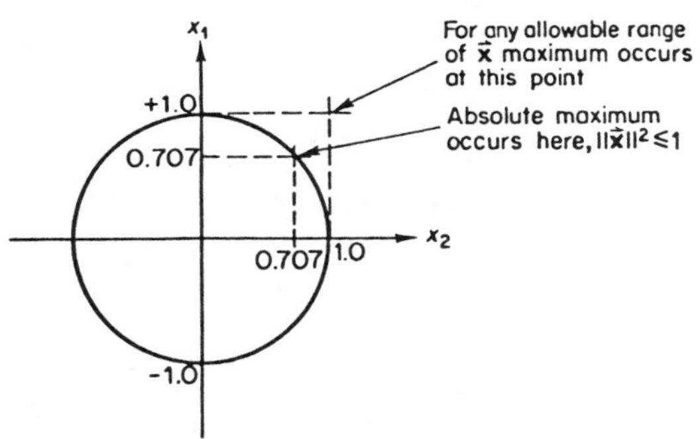

Top view showing the region defined in state space by $||x||^2 < 1$.

Note that, in the absence of the equality constraint, this problem has no relative minimum.

• PROBLEM 10-11

A tin can manufacturer wants to maximize the volume of a certain run of cans subject to the constraint that the area of tin used be a given constant. If a fixed metal thickness is assumed, a volume of tin constraint implies that the cross-sectional area is constrained.

The defining equations for this problem are:

$$\text{Volume} = V(r,\ell) = \pi r^2 \ell \qquad (1)$$

Cross-sectional area =

$$A(r,\ell) = 2\pi r^2 + 2\pi r\ell = A_0 . \tag{2}$$

The problem is to maximize $V(r,\ell)$ subject to keeping

$$A(r,\ell) = A_0 ,$$

where A_0 is a given constant, by using the derivative.

Solution: Solve for ℓ in terms of r (or if preferred, r in terms of ℓ) and then express the volume as a function of r alone, noting that the constraint on the cross-sectional area is now imbedded into the expression for the volume. Then examine the first and second derivatives to discern the character and location of the extrema.

From Eq. (2)

$$\ell = \frac{A_0 - 2\pi r^2}{2\pi r} . \tag{3}$$

By substituting Eq. (3) into Eq. (1), obtain

$$V(r) = \frac{r}{2} A_0 - 2\pi r^2 . \tag{4}$$

Differentiate V with respect to r and set the result to zero to obtain

$$\frac{dV(r)}{dr} = \frac{A_0}{2} - 3\pi r^2 = 0,$$

$$r = \sqrt{\frac{A_0}{6}} . \tag{5}$$

Now substitute Eq. (5) into Eq. (2) and solve for ℓ :

$$\ell = \sqrt{\frac{2A_0}{3\pi}} . \tag{6}$$

It is interesting to obtain the optimum length-to-radius ratio. In doing this, see that, to get maximum volume, one has to make the length of the tin can equal the diameter, keeping cross-sectional area equal to a given constant.

• PROBLEM 10-12

Consider the following mathematical programming problem:

$$\text{Min } f(x_1,x_2) = x_1^2 - 4x_1x_2 + 5x_2^2 + 2x_1 - 6x_2$$

subject to

$$x_1^2 + x_2^2 \leq 9,$$

$$x_1 + x_2 \leq 3,$$

and

$$x_2 \geq 0.$$

Solve by using derivatives.

Solution: The first constraint requires that a convex function be less than or equal to a constant; the set of points satisfying it constitutes a convex set. Since the other two constraints, being linear, also define convex sets, the feasible region must itself be convex. The objective function can be expressed as

$$f(x_1,x_2) = (x_1 - 2x_2)^2 + x_2^2 + 2x_1 - 6x_2 ,$$

and since the quadratic portion is positive definite, the problem is evidently one of minimizing a convex function over a convex set.

See if there are any unconstrained local minima of $f(x_1,x_2)$ in the feasible region. The partial derivatives are

$$\frac{\delta f}{\delta x_1} = 2x_1 - 4x_2 + 2$$

and

$$\frac{\delta f}{\delta x_2} = -4x_1 + 10x_2 - 6 ,$$

both of which vanish at the point (1,1). This point satisfies all the constraints, and a check of the second derivatives shows that it is an unconstrained local minimum, and therefore a constrained local minimum. Then, it must be the (global) optimal solution to the problem.

• PROBLEM 10-13

Minimize $(x_1 - \frac{3}{2})^2 + (x_2 - 5)^2$

subject to

$$\begin{aligned} -x_1 + x_2 &\leq 2 \\ 2x_1 + 3x_2 &\leq 11 \\ -x_1 &\leq 0 \\ -x_2 &\leq 0 \end{aligned}$$

Solve this Nonlinear Programming problem by using differentiation.

Solution: Let S be a nonempty convex set in E_n, and let

$$f: S \to E_1$$

be convex. Then $\vec{\xi}$ is called a subgradient of f at

$$\bar{\vec{x}} \in S$$

if

$$f(\vec{x}) \geq f(\bar{\vec{x}}) + \vec{\xi}'(\vec{x} - \bar{\vec{x}})$$

for all $\vec{x} \in S$

Consider the problem to minimize $f(\vec{x})$ subject to

$$\vec{x} \in S.$$

The point $\bar{\vec{x}} \in S$

is an optimal solution to this problem if and only if f has a subgradient $\vec{\xi}$ at $\bar{\vec{x}}$ such that

$$\vec{\xi}'(\vec{x} - \bar{\vec{x}}) \geq 0$$

for all

$$\vec{x} \in S .$$

Clearly

$$f(x_1,x_2) = (x_1 - \frac{3}{2})^2 + (x_2 - 5)^2$$

is a convex function, which gives the square of the distance from the point

$$(\frac{3}{2} , 5) .$$

The convex polyhedral set S is represented by the four inequalities. The problem is depicted in the figure.

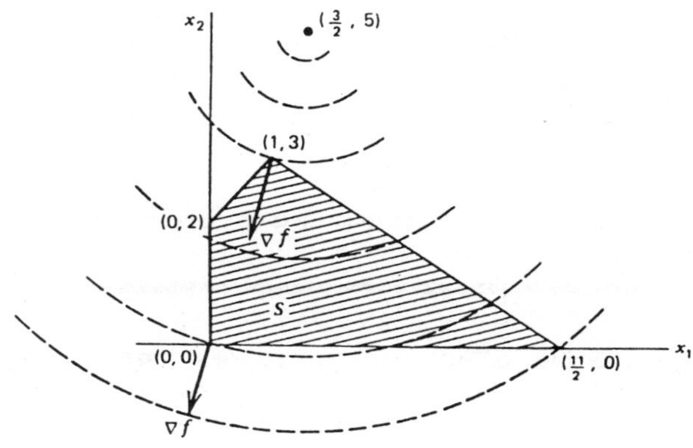

From the figure, clearly the optimal point is (1,3). The gradient vector at the point (1,3) is

$$\vec{\nabla} f(1,3) = (-1, -4)^t$$

One sees geometrically that the vector (-1, -4) makes an angle of $\leq$ 90° with each vector of the form

$$(x_1 - 1, x_2 - 3),$$

where

$$(x_1, x_2) \in S.$$

Thus, the optimality condition stated above is verified.

FRITZ - JOHN OPTIMALITY CONDITIONS

• PROBLEM 10-14

Minimize

$$-x_1$$

subject to

$$x_2 - (1 - x_1)^3 = 0$$

$$-x_2 - (1 - x_1)^3 = 0$$

using Fritz John conditions.

Solution: This problem has only one feasible point, namely

$$\vec{x} = (1,0)^t$$

At this point,

$$\vec{\nabla} f(\vec{x}) = (-1,0)^t$$

$$\vec{\nabla} h_1(\vec{x}) = (0,1)^t$$

$$\vec{\nabla} h_2(\vec{x}) = (0, -1)^t$$

where $f(\vec{x})$ is the objective function, $h_1(\vec{x})$ and $h_2(\vec{x})$, first and second constraints respectively.

The condition

$$u_0 \begin{pmatrix} -1 \\ \\ 0 \end{pmatrix} + v_1 \begin{pmatrix} 0 \\ \\ 1 \end{pmatrix} + v_2 \begin{pmatrix} 0 \\ \\ -1 \end{pmatrix} = \begin{pmatrix} 0 \\ \\ 0 \end{pmatrix}$$

is true only if

$$u_0 = 0$$

and

$$v_1 = v_2 = \alpha,$$

where α is any scalar. Thus the Fritz John necessary conditions for optimality:

$$u_0 \vec{\nabla} f(\vec{\bar{x}}) + \vec{\nabla} h(\vec{\bar{x}})\vec{v} = \vec{0} \qquad u_0 \geq 0$$

$$(u_0, \vec{v}) \neq (0, \vec{0})$$

where $\vec{\nabla} h(\vec{\bar{x}})$

is an $n \times \ell$ matrix whose ith column is

$$\vec{\nabla} h_i(\vec{\bar{x}});$$

also $\vec{v}$ is an ℓ vector denoting the Lagrangian multipliers associated with the equality constraints, are met at the point $\vec{\bar{x}}$.

• PROBLEM 10-15

Minimize

$$(x_1 - 3)^2 + (x_2 - 2)^2$$

subject to

$$x_1{}^2 + x_2{}^2 \leq 5$$

$$x_1 + 2x_2 \leq 4$$

$$-x_1 \leq 0$$

$$-x_2 \leq 0$$

Find the optimal point(s). Check the Fritz John optimality conditions for the points (2,1) and (0,0).

Solution: The Fritz John conditions are given as follows: Let X be a nonempty open set in E_n, and let

$$f: E_n \to E_1,$$

and

$$g_i: E_n \to E_1$$

for $i = 1,\ldots,m$.

Consider Problem P to minimize $f(\vec{x})$ subject to

$$\vec{x} \in X \qquad \text{and} \qquad g_i(\vec{x}) \leq 0$$

for $i = 1,\ldots,m$.

Let $\bar{\vec{x}}$ be a feasible solution, and let

$$I = \{i: g_i(\bar{\vec{x}}) = \vec{0}\}$$

Furthermore, suppose that f and g_i for $i \in I$ are differentiable at $\bar{\vec{x}}$ and that g_i for $i \in I$ are continuous at $\bar{\vec{x}}$. If $\bar{\vec{x}}$ locally solves Problem P, then there exists scalars u_0 and u_i for $i \in I$, such that

$$u_0 \vec{\nabla} f(\bar{\vec{x}}) + \sum_{i \in I} u_i \vec{\nabla} g_i(\bar{\vec{x}}) = \vec{0}$$

$$u_0, u_i \geq 0 \qquad \text{for } i \in I$$

$$(u\ , \vec{u}_I) \neq (0, \vec{0})$$

where $\vec{u}_I$

is the vector whose components are u_i for $i \in I$. Furthermore, if g_i for $i \notin I$ are also differentiable at $\bar{\vec{x}}$, then the Fritz John conditions can be written in the following equivalent form:

$$u_0 \vec{\nabla} f(\bar{\vec{x}}) + \sum_{i=1}^{m} u_i \vec{\nabla} g_i(\bar{\vec{x}}) = \vec{0}$$

$$u_i g_i(\bar{\vec{x}}) = 0 \qquad \text{for } i = 1,\ldots,m$$

$$u_0, u_i \geq 0 \qquad \text{for } i = 1,\ldots,m$$

$$(u_0, \vec{u}) \neq (0, \vec{0})$$

where $\vec{u}$ is the vector whose components are

$$u_i \text{ for } i = 1,\ldots,m.$$

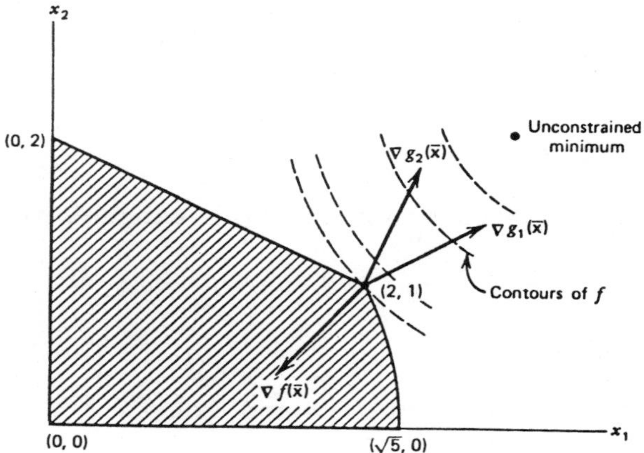

The feasible region for the above problem is illustrated in the figure shown. Now verify that the Fritz John conditions are true at the optimal points (2,1). First note that the set of binding constraints

$$I \text{ at } \vec{\bar{x}} = (2,1)^t$$

is given by $\quad I = \{1,2\}$.

Thus the Lagrangian multipliers u_3 and u_4 associated with $\quad -x_1 \le 0 \quad$ and $\quad -x_2 \le 0$,

respectively, are equal to zero. Note that

$$\vec{\nabla} f(\vec{\bar{x}}) = (-2, -2)^t$$

$$\vec{\nabla} g_1(\vec{\bar{x}}) = (4,2)^t$$

$$\vec{\nabla} g_2(\vec{\bar{x}}) = (1,2)^t$$

Thus, $\quad u_0 = 3, \quad u_1 = 1 \quad$ and $\quad u_2 = 2$

will satisfy the Fritz John conditions, since we now have a nonzero vector

$$(u_0, u_1, u_2) \ge \vec{0}$$

satisfying

$$u_0 \begin{pmatrix} -2 \\ \\ -2 \end{pmatrix} + u_1 \begin{pmatrix} 4 \\ \\ 2 \end{pmatrix} + u_2 \begin{pmatrix} 1 \\ \\ 2 \end{pmatrix} = \begin{pmatrix} 0 \\ \\ 0 \end{pmatrix}$$

Now check whether the Fritz John conditions are true at the point

$$\vec{\bar{x}} = (0,0)^t.$$

Here, the set of binding constraints is

$$I = \{3,4\} ,$$

and thus $u_1 = u_2 = 0.$

Note that

$$\vec{\nabla} f(\vec{\hat{x}}) = (-6, -4)^t$$

$$\vec{\nabla} g_3(\vec{\hat{x}}) = (-1,0)^t$$

$$\vec{\nabla} g_4(\vec{\hat{x}}) = (0, -1)^t$$

Also note that

$$u_0 \begin{pmatrix} -6 \\ \\ -4 \end{pmatrix} + u_3 \begin{pmatrix} -1 \\ \\ 0 \end{pmatrix} + u_4 \begin{pmatrix} 0 \\ \\ -1 \end{pmatrix} = \begin{pmatrix} 0 \\ \\ 0 \end{pmatrix}$$

holds true if and only if

$$u_3 = -6u_0$$

and

$$u_4 = -4u_0 .$$

If $u_0 > 0,$

then $u_3, u_4 < 0,$

contradicting the nonnegativity restrictions. If, on the other hand,

$$u_0 = 0,$$

then

$$u_3 = u_4 = 0,$$

which contradicts the stipulation that the vector

$$(u_0, u_3, u_4)$$

is nonzero. Thus the Fritz John conditions do not hold true at

$$\vec{\hat{x}} = (0,0)^t ,$$

which also shows that the origin is not a local optimal point.

LAGRANGE MULTIPLIERS

• PROBLEM 10-16

Find the extrema for the function

$$x^2 + y^2 + z^2$$

subject to the constraint

$$x^2 + 2y^2 - z^2 - 1 = 0$$

using Lagrangian multipliers.

Solution: The problem is to find the extreme values of a function

$$f(x,y,z)$$

given a constraint

$$G(x,y,z) = k$$

(k a constant). Lagrange's method consists of the formation of the function

$$u = f(x,y,z) + \lambda G(x,y,z)$$

subject to the conditions

$$\frac{\partial u}{\partial x} = 0, \qquad \frac{\partial u}{\partial y} = 0, \qquad \frac{\partial u}{\partial z} = 0.$$

Here x,y,z are treated as independent variables and λ is a constant, independent of x,y,z, called Lagrange's multiplier.

For this method solve the three equations in (1) along with the equation of constraint

$$G(x,y,z) = k$$

to find the values of x,y,z,λ. More than one point (x,y,z) may be found in this way, but among the points so found will be the points of extremal values of F. For this problem

$$f(x,y,z) = x^2 + y^2 + z^2$$

and

$$G(x,y,z) = x^2 + 2y^2 - z^2 = 1 \qquad (1)$$

To apply the method of Lagrange let

$$u = x^2 + y^2 + z^2 + \lambda(x^2 + 2y^2 - z^2).$$

Then

$$\frac{\partial u}{\partial x} = 2x + \lambda 2x = 0 \qquad (2)$$

$$\frac{\partial u}{\partial y} = 2y + \lambda 4y = 0 \qquad (3)$$

$$\frac{\partial u}{\partial z} = 2z - \lambda 2z = 0 \qquad (4)$$

Next, let (x_0, y_0, z_0)

be a solution. If $z_0 \neq 0$,

then from equation (4), $\lambda = 1$. For this to be true in (2) and (3), it is needed

$$x = y = 0.$$

In that case from (1), this gives

$$z_0^2 = -1$$

which is impossible.

Hence, any solution must have

$$z_0 = 0.$$

If $x \neq 0$, then from (2), $\lambda = -1$ and from (3) and (4) for this to be true $y = z = 0$. Then from (1), this yields

$$x_0^2 = 1; \; x_0 = \pm 1.$$

Therefore, two solutions satisfying the conditions have been obtained, namely (1,0,0) and (-1,0,0). Similarly if $y \neq 0$, then from (3) $\lambda = -\frac{1}{2}$

and from (2) and (4), this gives

$$x = z = 0.$$

Hence, from (1),

$$y_0^2 = \frac{1}{2}; \qquad y_0 = \pm\sqrt{\frac{1}{2}}$$

and two more solutions, namely,

$$\left(0, \sqrt{\frac{1}{2}}, 0\right) \quad \text{and} \quad \left(0, -\sqrt{\frac{1}{2}}, 0\right),$$

are found. These four points are therefore the extrema of the function f(x,y,z) subject to the constraint g. If a minimum of f is desired, then direct computation shows that the two points

$$\left(0, \pm\sqrt{\frac{1}{2}}, 0\right)$$

are the only possible solutions. This is because the function

$$f(x,y,z) = x^2 + y^2 + z^2$$

is the square of the distance from the origin. Since the constraint defines a surface, a minimum for f(x,y,z) given the constraint is a point on the surface which is at a minimum distance from the origin. Hence because

$$1 > \frac{1}{2}$$

the points $(0, \pm\sqrt{\frac{1}{2}}, 0)$

are a shorter distance from the origin than the points $(\pm 1, 0, 0)$.

• PROBLEM 10-17

Maximize $f(X) = 5x_1 - 2x_1^2 + 3x_1x_2 - 2x_2^2$

Subject to $x_1 + x_2 \leq 2$.

Use Lagrange's multipliers method to solve.

Solution: First determine if the objective function is concave (as is required for a maximization problem to have a solution):

$$\frac{\partial f}{\partial x_1} = 5 - 4x_1 + 3x_2$$

$$\frac{\partial f}{\partial x_2} = 3x_1 - 4x_2$$

$$\frac{\partial^2 f}{\partial x_1^2} = -4$$

$$\frac{\partial^2 f}{\partial x_2^2} = -4$$

$$\frac{\partial^2 f}{\partial x_1 \partial x_2} = 43$$

$$H_{f(x)} = \begin{bmatrix} -4 & +3 \\ -3 & -4 \end{bmatrix}$$

$$\left|\lambda I - H_{f(x)}\right| = \begin{vmatrix} \lambda + 4 & -3 \\ -3 & \lambda + 4 \end{vmatrix}$$

$$= (\lambda + 4)^2 - 9 = \lambda^2 + 8\lambda + 7 = 0$$

$$\lambda_1 = -7$$

$$\lambda_2 = -1$$

Since both eigenvalues of the Hessian are negative, the objective function is concave.

The Lagrangian is

$$h(X,\lambda) = 5x_1 - 2x_1^2 + 3x_1x_2 - 2x_2^2 - \lambda(x_1 + x_2 - 2)$$

$$\frac{\partial h}{\partial x_1} = 5 - 4x_1 + 3x_2 - \lambda = 0 \qquad (1)$$

$$\frac{\partial h}{\partial x_2} = 3x_1 - 4x_2 - \lambda = 0 \qquad (2)$$

$$\frac{\partial h}{\partial \lambda} = -x_1 - x_2 + 2 = 0 \qquad (3)$$

solving these equations

$$x_1 + x_2 - 2 = 0 \quad \text{or} \quad x_1 = 2 - x_2 ,$$

upon substitution into (2)

$$3(2 - x_2) - 4(x_2) - \lambda = 0$$

$$\lambda = 6 - 7x_2$$

$$x_2 = \frac{6}{7} - (\frac{1}{7})\lambda \cdot$$

From (3)

$$x_1 = 2 - x_2$$

so that

$$x_1 = 2 - (6/7 - \lambda/7)$$

$$x_1 = 8/7 + \lambda/7 .$$

Upon substitution of these expressions for x_1 and x_2 into (1) one can solve for a value of λ:

$$5 - 4(8/7 + \lambda/7) + 3(6/7 - \lambda/7) - \lambda = 0$$

$$3 - 2\lambda = 0$$

$$\lambda = 3/2$$

Finally

$$x_2 = 6/7 - (1/7)\lambda = 6/7 - 1/7(3/2) = 9/14$$

$$x_1 = 8/7 + (1/7)\lambda = 8/7 + 1/7(3/2) = 19/14$$

• **PROBLEM** 10-18

Maximize:

$$f(\vec{x}) = 3x_1^2 + x_2^2 + 2x_1x_2 + 6x_1 + 2x_2$$

Subject to:

$$2x_1 - x_2 = 4$$

Use the Lagrangian function.

Solution: Maximize:

$$L(x_1,x_2,\lambda) = 3x_1^2 + x_2^2 + 2x_1x_2 + 6x_1 + 2x_2 - \lambda[2x_1 - x_2 - 4]$$

$$\frac{\partial L}{\partial x_1} = 6x_1 + 2x_2 + 6 - 2\lambda = 0$$

$$\frac{\partial L}{\partial x_2} = 2x_2 + 2x_1 + 2 + \lambda = 0$$

$$\frac{\partial L}{\partial \lambda} = 2x_1 - x_2 - 4 = 0$$

There are now three equations in three unknowns which can be solved simultaneously; and so, one obtains:

$$x_1^* = \frac{7}{11}$$

$$x_2^* = -\frac{30}{11}$$

$$\lambda^* = \frac{24}{11}$$

The original objective function yields the value:

$$f(x_1^*, x_2^*) = 85.7.$$

Although a stationary point has been found for this maximization problem, there is actually no guarantee that this particular solution vector is the one sought. In fact, any solution vector obtained by this constrained optimization technique might be a maximum, minimum, or a saddle point. If the objective function is concave, and the constraints form a convex set, then the solution will be a global maximum. If the Hessian matrix of a function is negative or negative definite, then the function is concave. From the objective function:

$$H(\vec{x}) = \begin{bmatrix} \dfrac{\partial f}{\partial x_1^2} & \dfrac{\partial f}{\partial x_1 x_2} \\ \\ \dfrac{\partial f}{\partial x_2 x_1} & \dfrac{\partial f}{\partial x_2^2} \end{bmatrix}$$

Hence

$$H(\vec{x}) = \begin{bmatrix} 6 & 2 \\ \\ 2 & 2 \end{bmatrix}$$

Since the matrix is symmetric and all principal diagonals are positive, the Hessian matrix is found to be positive definite. The objective function is thus convex, not concave. In addition, since the constraint is linear, it is convex and forms a convex set. If a convex function is maximized, the solution will be found at an extreme point. In this problem, the Lagrangian has located only a stationary point.

Consider the problem

minimize

$$x_0 = x_1^2 + x_2^2 + x_3^2$$

subject to

$$4x_1 + x_2^2 + 2x_3 - 14 = 0$$

Use Lagrangian Multipliers to solve.

Solution: The Lagrangian function is

$$L(\vec{X},\vec{\lambda}) = x_1^2 + x_2^2 + x_3^2 - \lambda\ (4x_1 + x_2^2 + 2x_3 - 14)$$

This yields the following necessary conditions.

$$\frac{\partial L}{\partial x_1} = 2x_1 - 4\lambda = 0$$

$$\frac{\partial L}{\partial x_2} = 2x_2 - 2\lambda x_2 = 0$$

$$\frac{\partial L}{\partial x_3} = 2x_3 - 2\lambda = 0$$

$$\frac{\partial L}{\partial \lambda} = -(4x_1 + x_2^2 + 2x_3 - 14) = 0$$

whose solution is, by solving the simultaneous equations,

$$(\vec{X}_0,\vec{\lambda}_0)_1 = (2,2,1,1)$$

$$(\vec{X}_0,\vec{\lambda}_0)_2 = (2,\ -2,1,1)$$

$$(\vec{X}_0,\vec{\lambda}_0)_3 = (2.8,\ 0,\ 1.4,\ 1.4)$$

The first sufficiency condition for the Lagrangian method is as follows. Define

$$\vec{H}^B = \left(\begin{array}{c|c} \vec{0} & \vec{P} \\ \hline \vec{P}^T & \vec{Q} \end{array}\right)_{(m+n)\ \times\ (m+n)}$$

where

$$\vec{P} = \begin{pmatrix} \nabla g_1(\vec{X}) \\ \vdots \\ \nabla g_m(\vec{X}) \end{pmatrix}_{m\times n}$$

and

$$\vec{Q} = \left\| \frac{\partial^2 L(\vec{X},\vec{\lambda})}{\partial x_i \ \partial x_j} \right\|_{n\times n}$$

for all i,j

The matrix $\vec{H}^B$ is called the bordered Hessian matrix.

Given the stationary point $(\vec{X}_0,\vec{\lambda}_0)$ for the Lagrangian function $L(\vec{X},\vec{\lambda})$ and the bordered Hessian matrix $\vec{H}^B$ evaluated at $(\vec{X}_0,\vec{\lambda}_0)$ then $\vec{X}_0$ is

1. A maximum point if, starting with the principal minor determinant of order (2m+1), the last (n-m) principal minor determinants of $\vec{H}^B$ have an alternating sign pattern starting with $(-1)^{m+1}$.

2. A minimum point if, starting with the principal minor determinant of order (2m+1), the last (n-m) principal minor determinants of $\vec{H}^B$ have the sign of $(-1)^m$.

The above conditions are sufficient for identifying an extreme point, but not necessary. A stationary point may be an extreme point without satisfying the above conditions. Other conditions which are both necessary and sufficient for identifying extreme points do exist but they are computationally infeasible for most practical purposes.

Applying the first sufficiency condition yields

$$\vec{H}^B = \left(\begin{array}{c|ccc} 0 & 4 & 2x_2 & 2 \\ \hline 4 & 2 & 0 & 0 \\ 2x_2 & 0 & 2-2\lambda & 0 \\ 2 & 0 & 0 & 2 \end{array}\right)$$

Since m = 1 and n = 3, then the signs of the last

$$(3 - 1) = 2$$

principal minor determinants must be that of

$$(-1)^m = -1$$

in order for a stationary point to be a minimum. Thus, for $(\vec{X}_0, \vec{\lambda}_0) = (2,2,1,1)$,

$$\begin{vmatrix} 0 & 4 & 4 \\ 4 & 2 & 0 \\ 4 & 0 & 0 \end{vmatrix} = -32 < 0$$

and

$$\begin{vmatrix} 0 & 4 & 4 & 2 \\ 4 & 2 & 0 & 0 \\ 2 & 0 & 0 & 0 \\ 2 & 0 & 0 & 2 \end{vmatrix} = -64 < 0$$

For $(\vec{X}_0, \vec{\lambda}_0) = (2, -2,1,1)$,

$$\begin{vmatrix} 0 & 4 & -4 \\ 4 & 2 & 0 \\ -4 & 0 & 0 \end{vmatrix} = -32 < 0$$

and

$$\begin{vmatrix} 0 & 4 & -4 & 2 \\ 4 & 2 & 0 & 0 \\ -4 & 0 & 0 & 0 \\ 2 & 0 & 0 & 2 \end{vmatrix} = -64 < 0$$

Finally, for $(\vec{X}_0, \vec{\lambda}_0)_3 = (2.8, 0, 1.4, 1.4)$,

$$\begin{vmatrix} 4 & 4 & 0 \\ 4 & 2 & 0 \\ 0 & 0 & -.8 \end{vmatrix} = 12.8 > 0$$

and

$$\begin{vmatrix} 0 & 4 & 0 & 2 \\ 4 & 2 & 0 & 0 \\ 0 & 0 & -.8 & 0 \\ 2 & 0 & 0 & 2 \end{vmatrix} = 32 > 0$$

This shows $(\vec{X}_0)_1$ and $(\vec{X}_0)_2$ are minimum points. The fact that $(\vec{X}_0)_3$ does not satisfy the sufficiency conditions or a minimum does not necessarily mean it is not an extreme point. This follows since the given conditions, although sufficient, may not be satisfied for every extreme point. In such a case, it is necessary to use the other sufficiency condition.

To use the other sufficiency condition which employs the roots of the polynomial, consider

$$\vec{\Delta} \quad \left(\begin{array}{c|ccc} 0 & 4 & 2x_2 & 2 \\ \hline 4 & 2-\mu & 0 & 0 \\ 2x_2 & 0 & 2-2\lambda-\mu & 0 \\ 2 & 0 & 0 & 2-\mu \end{array}\right)$$

Now, for $(\vec{x}_0, \vec{\lambda}_0)_1 = (2, 2, 1, 1)$,

$$|\vec{\Delta}| = 9\mu^2 - 26\mu + 16 = 0$$

This gives $\mu = 2$ or $8/9$. Since $\mu > 0$, $(\vec{x}_0)_1 = (2, 2, 1,)$ is a minimum point.

Again, for $(\vec{x}_0, \vec{\lambda}_0)_2 = (2, -2, 1, 1)$,

$$|\vec{\Delta}| = 9\mu^2 - 26\mu + 16 = 0$$

which is the same as in the previous case. Hence, $(\vec{x}_0)_2 = (2, -2, 1)$ is a minimum point. Finally,

for $(\vec{x}_0, \vec{\lambda}_0)_3 = (2.8, 0, 1.4)$,

$$|\vec{\Delta}| = 5\mu^2 - 6\mu - 8 = 0$$

• PROBLEM 10-20

The problem is

Minimize

$$(x_1 - 3)^2 + (x_2 - 4)^2$$

subject to

$$2x_1 + x_2 \leq 6$$

Use Lagrangian Multipliers to solve.

Solution: Create the Lagrangian with s the slack variable

$$L(x_1,x_2,\lambda) = (x_1 - 3)^2 + (x_2 - 4)^2 + \lambda(2x_1 + x_2 + s - 6)$$

The partial derivatives are

$$\partial L/\partial x_1 = 2(x_1 - 3) + 2\lambda$$

$$\partial L/\partial x_2 = 2(x_2 - 4) + \lambda$$

$$\partial L/\partial \lambda = 2x_1 + x_2 + s - 6$$

Now if $s > 0$, then L is minimized at $\lambda = -\infty$. Thus if λ is restricted to be at least 0 for the inequality constraint, then L is minimized at $\lambda = 0$. If $s = 0$, then it does not matter what λ is, since

$$L(x_1, x_2, \lambda) = f(x_1, x_2).$$

Hence if (x_1, x_2, λ) minimizes L and $\lambda > 0$, then (x_1, x_2) minimized f and x_1, x_2 is feasible. Hence

$$\lambda(2x_1 + x_2 - 6) = 0,$$

since

$$\lambda = 0$$

or

$$2x_1 + x_2 - 6 = 0.$$

Thus the conditions are

$$\frac{\partial}{\partial x_j} L(x_1, x_2) = 0$$

$$\lambda(2x_1 + x_2 - 6) = 0$$

There are m + n nonlinear equations and (m + n) unknowns. In this case λ is restricted in sign. The equations are

$$2(x_1 - 3) + 2\lambda = 0$$

$$2(x_2 - 4) + \lambda = 0$$

$$\lambda(2x_1 + x_2 - 6) = 0$$

By solving the simultaneous equations, the solution is

$$x_1 = 7/5,$$

$$x_2 = 16/5,$$

and

$$\lambda = 8/5.$$

Consider the problem

Minimize:

$$y = x_1 x_2 \qquad \vec{x} \in E^n$$

subject to:

$$g_1(\vec{x}):\quad 25 - x_1^2 - x_2^2 \geq 0$$

Use Lagrange multipliers to solve.

Solution: The augmented function is

Minimize: $P(\vec{x},\lambda) = x_1x_2 - \lambda_1(25 - x_1^2 - x_2^2 - v_1^2)$ (1)

The necessary conditions are

$$\frac{\partial P}{\partial x_1} = x_2 + 2\lambda_1 x_1 = 0$$

$$\frac{\partial P}{\partial x_2} = x_1 + 2\lambda_1 x_2 = 0$$

$$\frac{\partial P}{\partial \lambda_1} = 25 - x_1^2 - x_2^2 - v_1^2 = 0 \qquad (2)$$

$$\frac{\partial P}{\partial v_1} = 2\lambda_1 v_1 = 0$$

The simultaneous solutions of equations (2) for $\lambda_1 = 0$ and for $\lambda_1 \neq 0$ are listed in Table 1.

Table 1

λ_1	x_1	x_2	Point	v_1	$f(\vec{x})$	Remarks
0	0	0	E	5	0	Saddle
0.5	+3.54	−3.54	D	0	−12.5	Minimum
	−3.54	+3.54	A	0	−12.5	Minimum
−0.5	+3.54	+3.54	B	0	+12.5	Maximum
	−3.54	−3.54	C	0	+12.5	Maximum

The vectors $\vec{x}^*$ are the stationary solutions of the problem. Note that the solutions for $\lambda_1 > 0$ are minima, those for $\lambda_1 < 0$ are maxima, and $\lambda_1 = 0$ is a saddle point of the problem. Figure 1 illustrates the functions in the problem. The contours of the objective functions (hyperbolas) are represented by broken lines, and the feasible region is the shaded area enclosed by the circle $[g_1(\vec{x}) = 0]$.

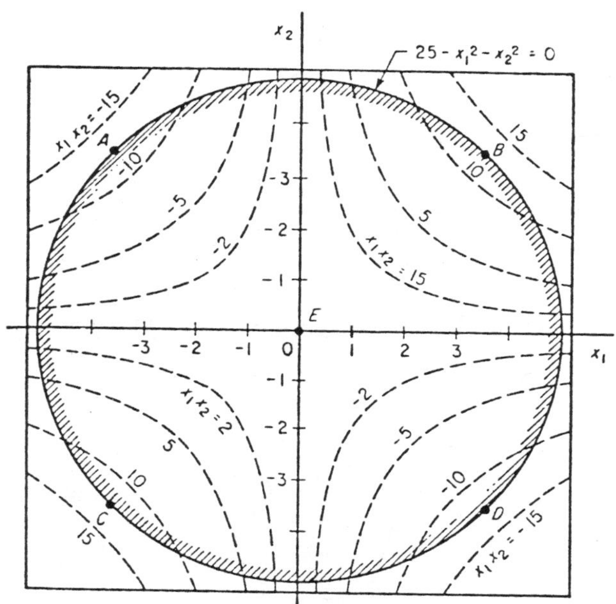

Fig. 1

Points A and D correspond to the two minima, B and C to the two maxima, and E to the saddle point of

$$f(\vec{x}).$$

• PROBLEM 10-22

Consider

$$\min\ (x_1 - 2)^2 + (x_2 - 2)^2$$

such that

$$x_1 + x_2 = 6.$$

Find the solutions for the unconstrained and constrained (use Lagrange multipliers) problem above.

Solution: The unconstrained solution is given by

$$\frac{\partial f}{\partial x_1} = 2(x_1 - 2) = 0,$$

$$\frac{\partial f}{\partial x_2} = 2(x_2 - 2) = 0,$$

from which $x_1^* = 2$, $x_2^* = 2$, and $f(x_1^*, x_2^*) = 0$.

Using the constraint to eliminate x_2, one gets

$$\min\ (x_1 - 2)^2 + (6 - x_1 - 2)^2,$$

$$\frac{\partial f}{\partial x_1} = 2(x_1 - 2) - 2(4 - x_1) = 0,$$

or

$$x_1^* = 3,$$

and

$$x_2^* = 6 - 3 = 3,$$

$$f(x_1^*, x_2^*) = (3 - 2)^2 + (3 - 2)^2 = 2.$$

The constrained and unconstrained solutions are shown in Fig. 1.

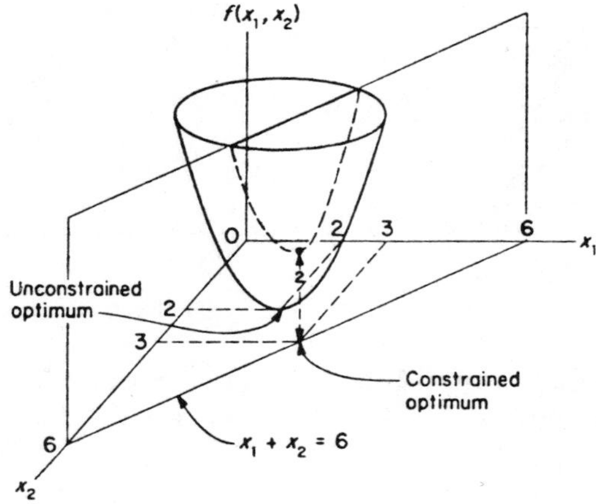

Fig. 1

• **PROBLEM 10-23**

The problem is:

Minimize:

$$f(\vec{x}) = x_1^2 + x_2$$

Subject to:

$$g_1(\vec{x}) = -(x_1^2 + x_2^2) + 9 \geq 0$$

$$g_2(\vec{x}) = -x_1 - x_2 + 1 \geq 0$$

Solution: In the problem, $g_1(\vec{x})$ will be an active constraint, whereas

$$g_2(\vec{x})$$

will be an inactive constraint; refer to Fig. 1.

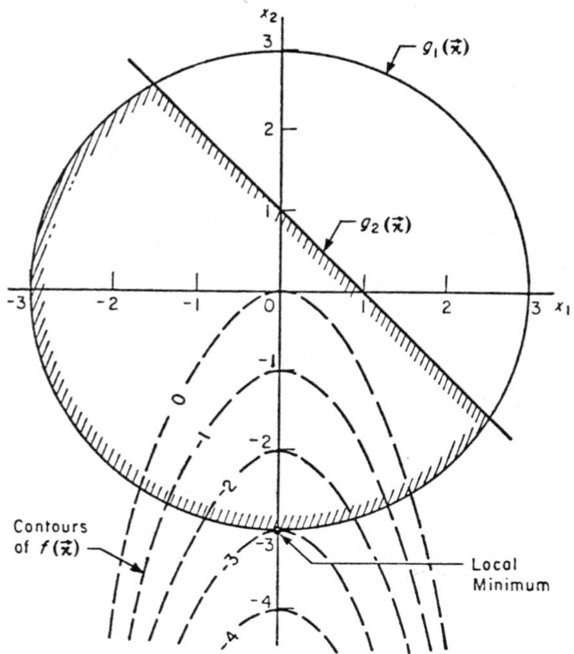

Fig. 1

Note that the functions are twice-differentiable. Because there is only one binding constraint,

$$g_1(\vec{x}),$$

a test does not have to be carried out to satisfy the first- and second-order constraint qualifications.

Show that the vectors $\vec{x}^*$ and $\vec{u}^*$ exist that satisfy the following listed conditions.

Constraints $g_1(\vec{x}^*)$ and $g_2(\vec{x}^*)$ are nonnegative, or

$$\begin{aligned} -x_1^{*2} - x_2^{*2} + 9 &\geq 0 \\ -x_1^* - x_2^* + 1 &\geq 0 \end{aligned} \qquad (1)$$

Any point within or on the boundaries of the shaded region is a feasible $\vec{x}$ vector.

$$1 \begin{bmatrix} 2x_1^* \\ 1 \end{bmatrix} - u_1^* \begin{bmatrix} -2x_1^* \\ -2x_2^* \end{bmatrix} - u_2^* \begin{bmatrix} -1 \\ -1 \end{bmatrix} = \vec{0} \quad (2)$$

or

$$2x_1^* u_1^* + u_2^* = 0$$

$$2x_2^* u_1^* + u_2^* = 0$$

$$u_1^*(-x_1^{*2} - x_2^{*2} + 9) = 0$$
$$u_2^*(-x_1^* - x_2^* + 1) = 0 \tag{3}$$

$$u_1^* \geq 0 \quad \text{and} \quad u_2^* \geq 0 \tag{4}$$

If one assumed from constraints (3) that both u_1^* and u_2^* were zero, a contradiction would arise from constraints (2) because then 1 = 0, hence not all the u*'s may be zero.
Assume one places

$$u_2^* = 0.$$

Then, from the first constraint in (2), either

$$x_1^* = 0$$

or

$$(1 + u_1^*) = 0,$$

the latter being impossible, because u_1^* cannot be negative. Hence

$$x_1^* = 0.$$

From the constraints in (3), because

$$u_1^* \neq 0,$$

$$x_1^{*2} + x_2^{*2} = 9$$

or

$$x_2^* = \pm 3$$

is a possible minimum. However,

$$x_2^* = +3$$

with

$$x_1^* = 0$$

violates the second constraint in (1). Consequently,

one has found an $\vec{x}^*$ vector,

$$\vec{x}^* = [0 \ -3]^T,$$

and a $\vec{u}^*$ vector

$$u_1^* = \frac{1}{6}$$

$$u_2^* = 0$$

that satisfy the constraints (2), (3), and (4). Thus the first-order necessary conditions are fulfilled.
The second-order necessary condition that must be fulfilled is that for

$$[v_1 \ v_2] \begin{bmatrix} -2x_1^* \\ \\ -2x_2^* \end{bmatrix} = 0$$

or

$$v_1(0) + v_2(6) = 0,$$

i.e., v_1 is any value and $v_2 = 0$, the following holds true

$$[v_1 \;\; 0]\vec{\nabla}^2 L(\vec{x}^*,\vec{u}^*) \begin{bmatrix} v_1 \\ \\ 0 \end{bmatrix}$$

Because

$$L = f(\vec{x}) - u_1 g_1(\vec{x}) - u_2 g_2(\vec{x})$$

$$\vec{\nabla}^2 L = \begin{bmatrix} 2(1 + u_1) & 0 \\ \\ 0 & 2u_2 \end{bmatrix}$$

One finds

$$4v_1^2 u_1^*(1 + u_1^*) \geq 0 > 0.$$

Consequently the second-order necessary conditions are satisfied and also the sufficient conditions.

To determine if the alternate sufficient conditions are satisfied, form the jacobian matrix of the functions

$$u_1(-x_1^2 - x_2^2 + 9)$$

$$u_2\;(-x_1 - x_2 + 1)$$

$$x_1 + 2u_1x_1 + u_2$$

$$2u_1x_2 + u_2$$

with respect to x_1, x_2, u_1, and u_2 respectively.
or

$$\vec{J} = \begin{bmatrix} -2x_1u_1 & -2x_2u_1 & (-x_1^2 - x_2^2 + 9) & 0 \\ -u_1 & -u_2 & 0 & (-x_1 - x_2 + 1) \\ (1 + 2u_1) & 0 & 2x_1 & 1 \\ 0 & 2u_1 & 2x_2 & 1 \end{bmatrix}$$

At

$$x_1^* = 0,\; x_2^* = -3$$

and with

$$u_1^* = \frac{1}{6}$$

and

$$u_2^* = 0,$$

$$\det \vec{J} = \det \begin{bmatrix} 0 & 1 & 0 & 0 \\ -\frac{1}{6} & 0 & 0 & 4 \\ \frac{14}{6} & 0 & 0 & 1 \\ 0 & \frac{1}{3} & -6 & 1 \end{bmatrix} \neq 0$$

Thus the alternate sufficient conditions are fulfilled for the vector

$$\vec{x}^* = [0 \quad -3]^T$$

to be a local minimum.

• PROBLEM 10-24

Find the maximum and minimum values of

$$|X|^2, \ X \in E_3,$$

subject to the constraints

$$g_1(X) = \frac{x_1^2}{4} + \frac{x_2^2}{5} + \frac{x_3^2}{25} - 1 = 0 \ ,$$

$$g_2(X) = x_1 + x_2 - x_3 = 0$$

Solution: First form the Lagrangian function

$$F(X) = x_1^2 + x_2^2 + x_3^2 + \lambda_1\left(\frac{x_1^2}{4} + \frac{x_2^2}{5} + \frac{x_3^2}{25} - 1\right) + \lambda_2(x_1 + x_2 - x_3).$$

For stationary values of F(X),

$$\frac{\partial F}{\partial x_1} = 2x_1 + \frac{1}{2}\lambda_1 x_1 + \lambda_2 = 0,$$

$$\frac{\partial F}{\partial x_2} = 2x_2 + \frac{2}{5}\lambda_1 x_2 + \lambda_2 = 0,$$

$$\frac{\partial F}{\partial x_3} = 2x_3 + \frac{2}{25}\lambda_1 x_3 - \lambda_2 = 0,$$

Solving them,

$$x_1 = -\frac{2\lambda_2}{\lambda_1 + 4},$$

$$x_2 = -\frac{5\lambda_2}{2\lambda_1 + 10},$$

$$x_3 = \frac{25\lambda_2}{2\lambda_1 + 50}$$

Substituting in the second constraint,

$$\lambda_2 \left(\frac{2}{\lambda_1 + 4} + \frac{5}{2\lambda_1 + 10} + \frac{25}{2\lambda_1 + 50}\right) = 0 .$$

$\lambda_2 \neq 0$ otherwise the first constraint will not be satisfied. Hence

$$17\lambda_1^2 + 245\lambda_1 + 750 = 0$$

or

$$\lambda_1 = -10,\ -75/17.$$

(i) $\lambda_1 = -10$. Then

$$x_1 = (1/3)\lambda_2,$$
$$x_2 = (1/2)\lambda_2,$$
$$x_3 = (5/6)\lambda_2 .$$

Substituting in the first constraint,

$$\lambda_2 = \pm 6\sqrt{5}/\sqrt{19}.$$

This gives two stationary points

$$\pm(2\sqrt{5}/\sqrt{19},\ 3\sqrt{5}/\sqrt{19},\ 5\sqrt{5}/\sqrt{19}),$$

and corresponding $|X|^2 = 10.$

(ii) $\lambda_1 = -75/17$. Then

$$x_1 = (34/7)\lambda_2,$$
$$x_2 = -(17/4)\lambda_2,$$
$$x_3 = (17/28)\lambda_2 .$$

Again substituting in the first constraint,

$$\lambda_2 = \pm 140/17\sqrt{646},$$

which gives the stationary points as

$$\pm(40/\sqrt{646},\ -35/\sqrt{646},\ 5/\sqrt{646})$$

and so $$|X|^2 = 75/17$$

The required maximum and minimum values are 10 and 75/17 respectively.

Consider the problem of finding the point on the plane

$$Ax_1 + Bx_2 + Cx_3 = D$$

that is closest to the origin in E^3. Solve by utilizing Lagrange multipliers.

Solution: In the functional notation the problem becomes

$$\text{Min } f(\vec{x}) = x_1^2 + x_2^2 + x_3^2$$

subject to

$$g(\vec{x}) = Ax_1 + Bx_2 + Cx_3 = D.$$

Let $\vec{X}_0$ in E^n be any local maximum or minimum of $f(\vec{x})$ subject to the equality constraints

$$g_i(\vec{x}) = b_i, \quad i = 1, \dots, m,$$

where

$$m < n.$$

If it is possible to choose a set of m variables for which the Jacobian matrix

$$[\delta g_i(\vec{x}_0)/\delta \vec{x}_k]$$

has an inverse, then there exists a unique set of Lagrange multiplier values

$$\lambda_1, \dots, \lambda_m$$

satisfying

$$\frac{\delta f(\vec{x}_0)}{\delta x_j} - \sum_{i=1}^{m} \lambda_1 \frac{\delta g_i(\vec{x}_0)}{\delta x_j} = 0, \qquad j = 1, \dots, n. \tag{1}$$

If the constraints

$$g_i(\vec{x}_0) = b_i, \qquad i = 1, \dots, m, \tag{2}$$

are included, (1) and (2) together form a system of m + n equations in m + n unknowns. Each local maximum and minimum, along with its associated Lagrange multiplier values, is among the solutions to this system, and therefore so is the global maximum (assuming it is finite).

From (1) immediately write

$$2x_1 - \lambda A = 0,$$

$$2x_2 - \lambda B = 0,$$

and

$$2x_3 - \lambda C = 0,$$

each of which holds at any local mimimum. Substituting these into the constraint equation produces

$$\lambda \frac{A^2}{2} + \lambda \frac{B^2}{2} + \lambda \frac{C^2}{2} = D.$$

Thus,

$$\lambda = 2D/(A^2 + B^2 + C^2),$$

and find that the only local optimum is

$$x_1 = \frac{AD}{A^2 + B^2 + C^2},$$

$$x_2 = \frac{BD}{A^2 + B^2 + C^2},$$

$$x_3 = \frac{CD}{A^2 + B^2 + C^2}.$$

Since the global minimum sought is finite, it must occur at a local minimum; hence, the point found is the global minimum.

Approach this problem in a different way: By solving the constraint for one of the variables, one can reduce the problem to one of unconstrained minimization. Thus

$$x_3 = \frac{D - Ax_1 - Bx_2}{C},$$

and the function to be minimized becomes

$$\hat{f}(\vec{\hat{x}}) = x_1^2 + x_2^2 + \frac{1}{C^2}(D - Ax_1 - Bx_2)^2.$$

Now take the two partial derivatives, equate them to zero, and manipulate, eventually arriving at the same solution.

Although this second approach may have been slightly more clumsy and time-consuming, it was nevertheless a reasonably satisfactory way of solving this particular problem. The method of Lagrange multipliers is indispensable, however, in dealing with larger problems in which the objective and constraint functions are more complex.

• PROBLEM 10-26

An advertising firm has developed a coordinated program for two products, x_1 and x_2. Based on experience with these products, they estimate an increased profit function of

$$f(X) = -\tfrac{1}{2}x_1^2 - \tfrac{1}{2}x_2^2 + x_1x_2 + 3x_2$$

where x_i is the advertising expenditure on product i (i = 1,2). (Suppose that f(X) and x_i are in units of hundreds of thousands of dollars).

The company has decided to spend exactly $300,000 on advertising. It is required to allocate this money between the two products and estimate increased profits.

$$\text{Max } f(X) = -\tfrac{1}{2}x_1^2 - \tfrac{1}{2}x_2^2 + x_1x_2 + 3x_2$$

subject to

$$x_1 + x_2 = 3$$

or

$$x_1 + x_2 - 3 = 0.$$

Solve by using Lagrangian multipliers.

Solution: First forumulate the Lagrangian function and locate the stationary points.

$$h(X,\lambda) = -\tfrac{1}{2}x_1^2 - \tfrac{1}{2}x_2^2 + x_1x_2 + 3x_2 - \lambda(x_1 + x_2 - 3)$$

$$\frac{\partial h}{\partial x_1} = -x_1 + x_2 - \lambda = 0$$

$$\frac{\partial h}{\partial x_2} = -x_2 + x_1 + 3 - \lambda = 0$$

$$\frac{\partial h}{\partial \lambda} = -x_1 - x_2 + 3 = 0$$

Solving these equations one gets $\lambda = 1.5$, $x_1 = 0.75$, $x_2 = 2.25$. To determine if this is a maximum:

$$\frac{\partial^2 h}{\partial x_1^2} = -1, \quad \frac{\partial^2 h}{\partial x_2^2} = -1, \quad \frac{\partial^2 h}{\partial x_1 \ x_2} = +1, \quad \frac{\partial g}{\partial x_1} = +1, \quad \frac{\partial g}{\partial x_2} = +1.$$

Now evaluation of the determinant, Δe, as shown below, will give a polynomial in e of (n-m) order where there are n variables and m constraining equations. Let

$$\Delta e = \left|\begin{array}{cccc|ccc}
K_{11} - e & K_{12} & \cdots\cdots & K_{1n} & L_{11} & \cdots & L_{m1} \\
K_{21} & K_{22} - e & \cdots\cdots & K_{2n} & L_{12} & \cdots & L_{22} \\
\cdot & \cdot & \cdots\cdots & \cdot & \cdot & \cdots & \cdot \\
\cdot & \cdot & \cdots\cdots & \cdot & \cdot & \cdots & \cdot \\
\cdot & \cdot & \cdots\cdots & \cdot & \cdot & \cdots & \cdot \\
K_{n1} & K_{n2} & \cdots\cdots & K_{nn} - e & L_{1n} & \cdots & L_{mn} \\
\hline
L_{11} & L_{12} & \cdots\cdots & L_{1n} & 0 & \cdots & 0 \\
\cdot & \cdot & \cdot & \cdot & \cdot & \cdot & \cdot \\
\cdot & \cdot & \cdot & \cdot & \cdot & \cdot & \cdot \\
\cdot & \cdot & \cdot & \cdot & \cdot & \cdot & \cdot \\
L_{m1} & L_{m2} & \cdots\cdots & L_{mn} & 0 & \cdots & 0
\end{array}\right|$$

where

$$K_{ij} = \left.\frac{\partial^2 h(X,\lambda)}{\partial x_i \delta x_j}\right|_{X_0} \quad \text{for } i,j = 1,2,\ldots,n$$

$$L_{pi} = \frac{\partial g_p(X)}{\partial x_i}$$

where $p = 1,2,\ldots,m$ and $i = 1,2,\ldots,n$.

Thus: If each root of e in this equation is negative, the point X_0 is a local maximum. If all roots are positive, X_0 is a local minimum. If some are positive and some negative, X_0 is neither a local maximum nor a local minimum.

Note that this analysis does not require convexity of the objective function, or any constraining function.

Therefore,

$$\Delta e = \left|\begin{array}{cc|c} -1-e & +1 & +1 \\ +1 & -1-e & +1 \\ \hline +1 & +1 & 0 \end{array}\right|$$

Expanding along the last column,

$$\Delta e = \begin{vmatrix} +1 & -1-e \\ +1 & +1 \end{vmatrix} - \begin{vmatrix} -1-e & +1 \\ +1 & +1 \end{vmatrix}$$

$$\Delta e = 1 + 1 + e - (-1 - e - 1)$$

$$= 4 + 2e = 0$$

or

$$e = -2.$$

Since the only root of e is negative, the stationary point is a local maximum. Since e does not depend on values of X, this local maximum is also the global maximum and the solution is.

Spend \$75,000 on advertising product 1 and \$225,000 for product 2.

The increased profit will be

$$f(X) = -\tfrac{1}{2}(0.75)^2 - \tfrac{1}{2}(2.25)^2 + 0.75(2.25) - 3(2.25)$$

$$= 5.625, \text{ or } \$562,500 .$$

Consider the optimal allocation of a scarce resource between two processes where the total amount of resource available is b (see Fig. 1). It is required to maximize the return from both processes. Thus, one has

$$\max_{x_1, x_2} \quad f(x_1) + f(x_2)$$

such that

$$x_1 + x_2 = b.$$

Use the Lagrangian Multipliers to solve.

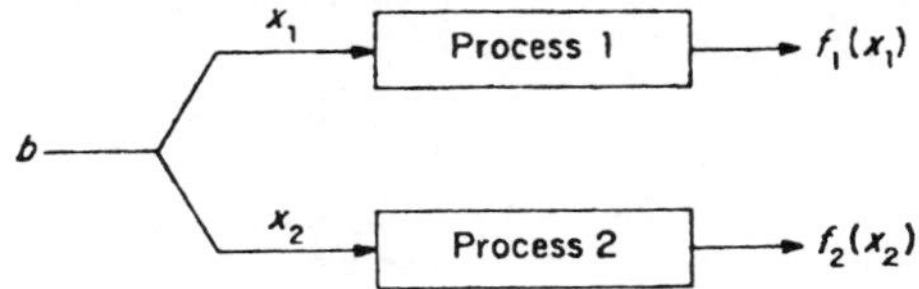

Fig. 1

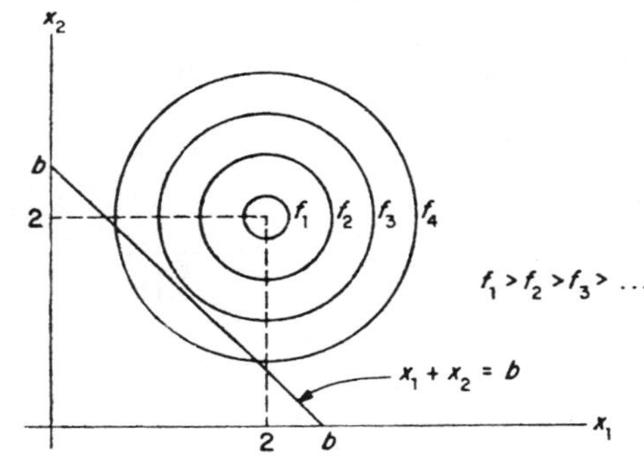

Fig. 2

Solution: If $\quad f(x_1) = 50 - (x_1 - 2)^2$

and $\quad f(x_2) = 50 - (x_2 - 2)^2,$

then (see Fig. 2)

$$L = 100 - (x_1 - 2)^2 - (x_2 - 2)^2 + \lambda[x_1 + x_2 - b],$$

$$\frac{\partial L}{\partial x_1} = -2(x_1 - 2) + \lambda = 0,$$

$$\frac{\partial L}{\partial x_2} = -2(x_2 - 2) + \lambda = 0,$$

$$\frac{\partial L}{\partial \lambda} = x_1 + x_2 - b = 0,$$

and

$$x_1^* = x_2^* = b/2,$$

$$\lambda^* = b - 4.$$

The sensitivity

$$-\lambda^* = \frac{\partial f}{\partial b}(x^*) = 4 - b$$

implies that for $b < 4$ an increase in b would have a positive return, while for $b > 4$ an increase in b would have a negative return or loss. If $b = 4$, then $\lambda^* = 0$, and the solutions to the constrained and the unconstrained problems are identical.

LAGRANGIAN DUALITY

• PROBLEM 10-28

Consider the following problem

$$\text{Minimize} \quad x_1{}^2 + x_2{}^2$$

$$\text{subject to} \quad -x_1 - x_2 + 4 \leq 0$$

$$x_1 + 2x_2 - 8 \leq 0.$$

Use the Lagrangian dual method to solve the problem, starting with the (0,0) point for the Lagrangian dual vector.

Solution: Note that the optimal solution occurs at the point (2,2) where the objective function value is equal to 8. The Lagrangian dual problem is to maximize $\theta(u_1, u_2)$ subject to $u_1, u_2 \geq 0$, where

$$\theta(u_1, u_2) = \underset{x_1, x_2}{\text{minimum}} \{x_1{}^2 + x_2{}^2 + u_1(-x_1 - x_2 + 4) + u_2(x_1 + 2x_2 - 8)\}.$$

The dual problem will be solved by the gradient method.

The algorithm is as follows:

Initialization step: Choose a vector $(\vec{u}_1, \vec{v}_1)$ with $\vec{u}_1 \geq \vec{0}$, let $k = 1$, and go to the main step.

Main Step: 1. Given $(\vec{u}_k, \vec{v}_k)$, solve the following subproblem:

$$\text{Minimize } f(\vec{x}) + \vec{v}_k{}^t\, \vec{g}(\vec{x}) + \vec{v}_k{}^t\, \vec{h}(\vec{x})$$

$$\text{subject to } \vec{x} \in X.$$

Let $\vec{x}_k$ be the unique optimal solution and form the vector $[\vec{\hat{g}}(\vec{x}_k), \vec{h}(\vec{x}_k)]$ using

$$\hat{g}_i(\vec{\bar{x}}) = \begin{cases} g_i(\vec{\bar{x}}) & \text{if } \bar{u}_i > 0 \\ \text{maximum } [0, g_i(\vec{\bar{x}})] & \text{if } u_i = 0 \end{cases}$$

where $\vec{\bar{x}}$ is the optimal solution. If this vector is zero, then stop; $(\vec{u}_k, \vec{v}_k)$ is an optimal solution. Otherwise, go to step 2.

2. Consider the following problem:

$$\text{Maximize} \quad \theta[(\vec{u}_k, \vec{v}_k) + \lambda(\vec{\hat{g}}(\vec{x}_k), \vec{h}(\vec{x}_k)]$$

$$\text{subject to} \quad \vec{u}_k + \lambda\vec{\hat{g}}(\vec{x}_k) \geq \vec{0}$$

$$\lambda \geq 0.$$

Let λ_k be an optimal solution, and let

$$(\vec{u}_{k+1}, \vec{v}_{k+1}) = (\vec{u}_k, \vec{v}_k) + \lambda_k[\vec{\hat{g}}(\vec{x}_k), \vec{h}(\vec{x}_k)],$$

replace k by k + 1, and repeat step 1.

For $\vec{u}_1 = (0,0)^t$, $\theta(\vec{u}_1) = \text{minimum}_{x_1, x_2}\{x_1^2 + x_2^2\} = 0$, and is achieved at the unique optimal point $\vec{x}_1 = (0,0)^t$. $\vec{\nabla}\theta(\vec{0}) = \vec{g}(\vec{x}_1) = (4, -8)^t$. In this case $\vec{\hat{g}}(\vec{x}_1) = (4,0)^t$.

Note that

$$\begin{aligned} \theta(4\lambda, 0) &= \underset{x_1}{\text{minimum}}\ \{x_1^2 - 4\lambda x_1\} + \underset{x_2}{\text{minimum}}\ \{x_2^2 - 4\lambda x_2\} + 16\lambda \\ &= -4\lambda^2 - 4\lambda^2 + 16\lambda \\ &= -8\lambda^2 + 16\lambda. \end{aligned}$$

Hence, the optimal solution to the problem to maximize $\theta(4\lambda, 0)$ subject to $\lambda \geq 0$ is achieved at $\lambda_1 = 1$, so that

$$\vec{u}_2 = \vec{u}_1 + \lambda_1\vec{\hat{g}}(\vec{x}_1) = (0,0)^t + 1(4,0)^t = (4,0)^t.$$

For $\vec{u}_2 = (4,0)^t$, $\theta(\vec{u}_2) =$

$$\text{minimum}_{x_1, x_2}\{x_1^2 + x_2^2 + 4(-x_1 - x_2 + 4)\}$$

$$= 8,$$

and is achieved at the unique optimal point $\vec{x}_2 = (2,2)^t$. $\vec{\nabla}\theta(\vec{u}_2) = \vec{g}(\vec{x}_2) = (0,-2)^t$. In this case $\vec{\hat{g}}(\vec{x}_2) = (0,0)^t$, and hence $\vec{u}_2 = (4,0)^t$ is an optimal solution to the Lagrangian dual problem.

Consider the problem

$$v = \min 3x_1 + 7x_2 + 10x_3$$

$$\text{s.t. } 1x_1 + 3x_2 + 5x_3 \geq 7 \qquad (1)$$

$$x_1, x_2, x_3 = 0 \text{ or } 1$$

Set up and use the Lagrangian dual function to find the optimal solution.

Solution: The Lagrangian function derived from (1) is

$$L(u) = 7u + \min\{(3 - u)x_1 + (7 - 3u)x_2 + (10 - 5u)x_3\}$$

$$x_1, x_2, x_3 = 0 \text{ or } 1.$$

The minimum is calculated simply by setting $x_j = 0$ if its reduced cost coefficient is positive and setting $x_j = 1$ if its reduced cost coefficient is negative. The result is the family of solutions

	x_1	x_2	x_3
$0 \leq u \leq 2$	0	0	0
$2 \leq u \leq 7/3$	0	0	1
$7/3 \leq u \leq 3$	0	1	1
$3 \leq u$	1	1	1

The corresponding Lagrangian is

$$L(u) = \begin{cases} 7u & \text{for } 0 \leq u \leq 2 \\ 2u + 10 & \text{for } 2 \leq u \leq 7/3 \\ -u + 17 & \text{for } 7/3 \leq u \leq 3 \\ -2u + 20 & \text{for } 3 \leq u \end{cases}$$

for which it is clear that the optimal $\bar{u} = 7/3$. This is because L increases to that value and decrease after it.

At $\bar{u}$, there are two optimal solutions in the Lagrangian; $\bar{x}_1 = \bar{x}_2 = 0$, $\bar{x}_3 = 1$ and $\bar{\bar{x}}_1 = 0$, $\bar{\bar{x}}_2 = \bar{\bar{x}}_3 = 1$. The former solution is infeasible and the latter is feasible, but the complementary slackness condition does not hold since $3\bar{\bar{x}}_2 + 5\bar{\bar{x}}_3 = 8 > 7$ and $\bar{u} > 0$. The maximal dual objective function value d = 44/3 which is less than the minimal primal objective function value v = 17. In fact, the solution $\bar{\bar{x}}$ is optimal although the effort to establish this optimality has failed because of the duality gap. This dual approach to the integer programming problem is equivalent to solving the linear programming relaxation which results when $x_j = 0$ or 1 is replaced by $0 \le x_j \le 1$.

• PROBLEM 10-30

Consider the following primal problem:

$$\text{Minimize} \quad x_1^2 + x_2^2$$

$$\text{subject to} \quad -x_1 - x_2 + 4 \le 0$$

$$x_1, x_2 \ge 0.$$

Note that the optimal solution occurs at the point $(x_1, x_2) = (2,2)$, whose objective is equal to 8. Use Lagrangian duality to solve.

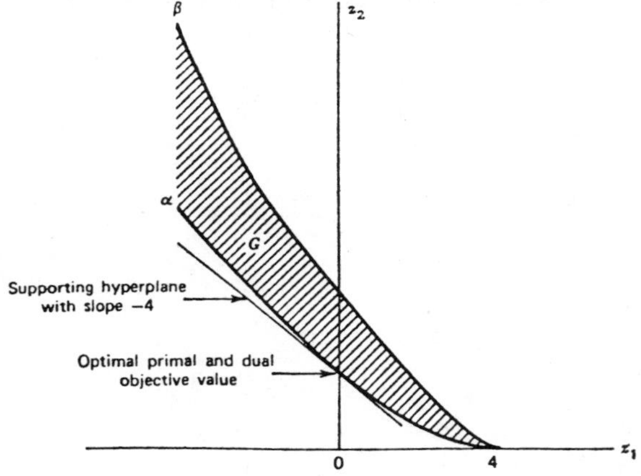

Fig. 1

Solution: Considering the following nonlinear programming problem

$$\text{Minimize } f(\vec{x})$$

$$\text{subject to } g_i(\vec{x}) \le 0 \quad \text{for } i = 1,\ldots,m$$

$$h_i(\vec{x}) = 0 \quad \text{for } i = 1,\ldots,\ell$$

$$\vec{x} \in X,$$

The Lagrangian Dual Problem is given as

Maximize $\theta(\vec{u}, \vec{v})$

subject to $\vec{u} \geq 0$

where $$\theta(\vec{u},\vec{v}) = \inf \{f(\vec{x}) + \sum_{i=1}^{m} (u_i g_i(\vec{x}) + \sum_{i=1}^{\ell} v_i h_i(\vec{x}) : \vec{x} \in X\}.$$

u_i and v_i are the Lagrangian multipliers. This dual problem consists of maximizing the infimum (greatest lower bound). Letting $g(x) = -x_1 - x_2 + 4$ and $X = \{(x_1, x_2): x_1, x_2 \geq 0\}$, the dual function is given by

$$\theta(u) = \inf \{x_1^2 + x_2^2 + u(-x_1 - x_2 + 4): x_1, x_2 \geq 0\}$$

$$= \inf \{x_1^2 - ux_1: x_1 \geq 0\} + \inf\{x_2^2 - ux_2: x \geq 0\} + 4u.$$

Note that the above infima are achieved at

$$x_1 = x_2 = u/2$$

if

$$u \geq 0$$

and at

$$x_1 = x_2 = 0$$

if

$$u < 0.$$

Hence,

$$\theta(u) = \begin{cases} -\tfrac{1}{2}u^2 + 4 & \text{for } u \geq 0 \\ 4u & \text{for } u < 0 \end{cases} .$$

Note that θ is a concave function, and its maximum over $u \geq 0$ occurs at $\bar{u} = 4$. Note also that the optimal primal and dual objectives are both equal to 8.

Now consider the problem in the (z_1, z_2) plane, where

$$z_1 = g(x) \quad \text{and} \quad z_2 = f(x).$$

In Figure 1, the set $\{(z_1, z_2): z_1 = g(\vec{x}), z_2 = f(\vec{x})$ for some $\vec{x} \in X\}$ is denoted by G. Then, G is the image of X under the (g, f) map. The primal problem asks to find a point in G to the left of the z_2 axis with the minimum ordinate. This requires finding G, the image of

$$X = \{(x_1, x_2): x_1 \geq 0, x_2 \geq 0\},$$

under the (g, f) map. This can be done by deriving explicit expressions for the lower and upper envelopes of G, denoted, respectively, by α and β.

Given z_1, note that $\alpha(z_1)$ and $\beta(z_1)$ are the optimal objective values of the following problems P_1 and P_2, respectively.

Problem P_1		Problem P_2	
Minimize	$x_1^2 + x_2^2$	Maximize	$x_1^2 + x_2^2$
subject to	$-x_1 - x_2 + 4 = z_1$	subject to	$-x_1 - x_2 + 4 = z_1$
	$x_1, x_2 \geq 0$		$x_1, x_2 \geq 0.$

$$\alpha(z_1) = (4 - z_1)^2/2$$

and

$$\beta(z_1) = (4 - z_1)^2$$

for

$$z_1 \leq 4.$$

Note that $\vec{x} \in X$ implies that $x_1, x_2 \geq 0$, so that

$$-x_1 - x_2 + 4 \leq 4.$$

Thus, every point $\vec{x} \in X$ corresponds to $z_1 \leq 4$.

Note that the optimal dual solution is $\bar{u} = 4$, which is the negative of the slope of the supporting hyperplane shown in Figure 1. The optimal dual objective is

$$\alpha(0) = 8$$

and is equal to the optimal primal objective.

• PROBLEM 10-31

Solve the following problem P and formulate the dual problem D. Also verify that min P = max D.

$$P: \min(-x^2 - x^3)$$

such that

$$x^2 \leq 1.$$

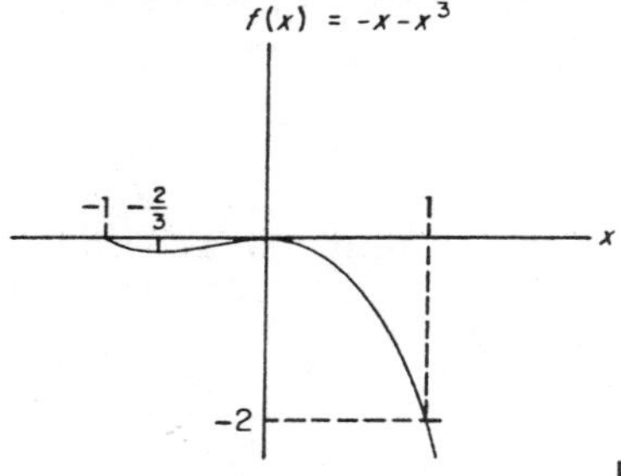

Fig. 1

Solution: Since the constraint implies that $x^* \in [-1, 1]$, a graphical solution $x^* = 1$ is easily obtained from Fig. 1. Now, form the Lagrangian

$$L(x, \lambda) = -x^2 - x^3 + \lambda(x^2 - 1).$$

The stationarity conditions are

$$\frac{\partial L}{\partial x} = -2x - 3x^2 + \lambda(2x) = 0. \tag{1}$$

$$x^2 \leq 1,$$

$$\lambda \geq 0,$$

$$\lambda(x^2 - 1) = 0.$$

If $\lambda = 0$, $x(-2 - 3x) = 0$; so $x = -\frac{2}{3}$ or $x = 0$.

If $x = 1$, $\lambda = \frac{5}{2}$.

If $x = -1$, $\lambda = -\frac{1}{2}$, which does not satisfy $\lambda \geq 0$.

Thus there are three possible solutions,

$$x = -\frac{2}{3}, \qquad x = 0, \qquad x = 1$$

where

$$L(-\frac{2}{3}, 0) = -\frac{4}{27},$$

$$L(0,0) = 0,$$

$$L(1, \frac{5}{2}) = -2,$$

so $x^* = 1$ is the solution which minimizes $L(x,\lambda^*)$, and this agrees with the graphical solution.

From (1) for $x \neq 0$,

$$x = \frac{2}{3}(\lambda - 1).$$

Substituting in $L(x, \lambda)$ yields

$$h(\lambda) = \frac{4}{27}\lambda^3 - \frac{4}{9}\lambda^2 - \frac{5}{9}\lambda - \frac{4}{27}.$$

The dual problem is

$$\max h(\lambda)$$

such that

$$\lambda \geq 0.$$

Thus

$$\frac{\partial h}{\partial \lambda} = \frac{4}{9}\lambda^2 - \frac{8}{9}\lambda - \frac{5}{9} = 0,$$

from which

$$\lambda = -\frac{1}{2} \quad \text{or} \quad \lambda = \frac{5}{2}.$$

Only the positive value satisfies the constraint, so

$$\lambda^* = \frac{5}{2}.$$

Now

$$h(\tfrac{5}{2}) = \frac{4}{27}(\frac{125}{8}) - \frac{4}{9}(\frac{25}{4}) - \frac{5}{9}(\frac{5}{2}) - \frac{4}{27} = -2.$$

and

$$f(1) = -1^2 - 1^3 = -2.$$

KUHN - TUCKER OPTIMALITY CONDITIONS

• PROBLEM 10-32

Solve using Kuhn-Tucker conditions

$$\text{Max } f(\vec{x}) = 3x_1 + x_2$$

$$\text{subject to } g_1(\vec{x}) = x_1^2 + x_2^2 \le 5$$

$$\text{and } g_2(\vec{x}) = x_1 - x_2 \le 1.$$

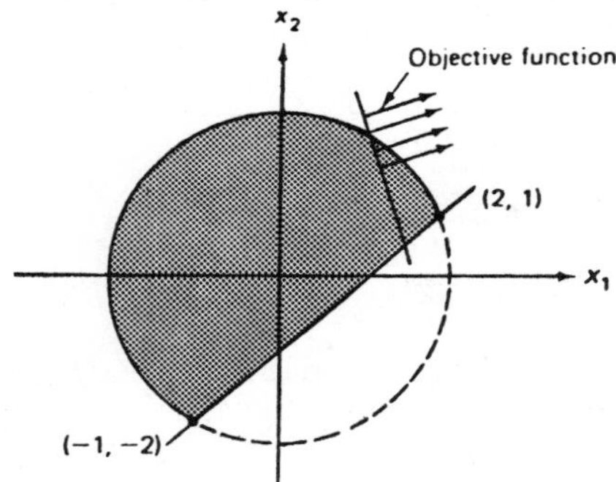

Fig. 1

Solution: The Kuhn-Tucker conditions are formed as follows. Given the problem

Maximize $z = f(\vec{x})$ $\vec{x} = (x_1, \ldots, x_n)$

subject to

$$g_i(\vec{x}) \le b_i \qquad i = 1, \ldots, m$$

The inequality constraints may be converted to equations by the addition of nonnegative slack variables

$$s_i,\ i = 1, \ldots, m$$

producing the following problem:

Maximize $z = f(\vec{x})$

subject to

$$g_i(\vec{x}) + s_i = b_i \qquad i = 1, \ldots, m$$

$$s_i \geq 0 \qquad i = 1,\ldots m$$

Now one can write the Lagrangian function

$$F(\vec{x},\vec{s},\vec{\lambda}) = f(\vec{x}) - \sum_{i=1}^{m} \lambda_i [g_i(\vec{x}) + s_i - b_i]$$

At any constrained local maximum the partial derivatives of the x_j and λ_i should equal zero. Since one of the constrained local maxima is global, the following relationships must all be satisfied by the global maximum

$$(\vec{x}^*, \vec{s}^*, \vec{\lambda}^*):$$

$$\frac{\partial F}{\partial x_j} \equiv \frac{\partial f(\vec{x}^*)}{\partial x_j} - \sum_{i=1}^{m} \lambda_i^* \frac{\partial g_i(\vec{x}^*)}{\partial x_j} = 0 \qquad (1)$$

$$j = 1,\ldots,n$$

$$\frac{\partial F}{\partial \lambda_i} \equiv - [g_i(\vec{x}^*) + s_i^* - b_i] = 0 \qquad (2)$$

$$\frac{\partial F}{\partial s_i} \equiv - \lambda_i^* \leq 0 \qquad i = 1,\ldots,m$$

(2) composes the original constraints. Removing the slack variables and writing all of (1) as a single vector equation, the above reduce to the Kuhn-Tucker necessary conditions;

$$\vec{\nabla} F(\vec{x}^*) - \sum_{i=1}^{m} \lambda_i^* (\vec{\nabla} g_i(\vec{x}^*) = \vec{0} \qquad (3)$$

$$g_i(\vec{x}^*) \leq b_i \qquad i = 1,\ldots,m \qquad (4)$$

$$\lambda_i^* \geq 0 \qquad i = 1,\ldots,m \qquad (5)$$

and

$$\lambda_i^* [b_i - g_i(\vec{x}^*)] = 0 \qquad i = 1,\ldots,m \qquad (6)$$

That is, at the optimal solution $\vec{x}^*$ to problem, there must exist generalized Lagrange multipliers

$$\vec{\lambda}^* = (\lambda_1^*,\ldots,\lambda_m^*)$$

such that (3) to (6) are satisfied.

From the necessary conditions

$$\frac{\partial f}{\partial x_1} = 3 = \lambda_1 (2x_1) + \lambda_2 , \qquad (7)$$

$$\frac{\partial f}{\partial x_2} = 1 = \lambda_1 (2x_2) - \lambda_2 , \qquad (8)$$

$$\lambda_1 (5 - x_1^2 - x_2^2) = 0, \qquad (9)$$

$$\lambda_2 (1 + x_2 - x_1) = 0. \qquad (10)$$

If $\lambda_1 = 0$, two contradictory values for λ_2 arise from (7) and (8); therefore $\lambda_1 \neq 0$, and, from (9)

$$x_1^2 + x_2^2 = 5 . \qquad (11)$$

If $\lambda_2 = 0$, (7) and (8) yield

$$x_1 = \frac{3}{2\lambda_1}$$

and

$$x_2 = \frac{1}{2\lambda_1} ;$$

substituting these into (11) produces nonnegativity of λ_1),

$$\lambda_1 = \sqrt{2}/2$$

(the negative root is forbidden by the nonnegativity of λ_1), so

$$x_1 = 3/\sqrt{2}$$

and

$$x_2 = 1/\sqrt{2}.$$

But these do not satisfy the second constraint; therefore λ_2 must be different from zero, and (10) yields

$$x_1 - x_2 = 1. \qquad (12)$$

There are two solutions to (11) and (12),

$$x_1 = 2, \; x_2 = 1$$

and

$$x_1 = -1, \; x_2 = -2.$$

Substitution of the latter into (7) and (8) leads to

$$\lambda_1 = -\frac{2}{3} ,$$

an impermissible value. Therefore, choose

$$x_1 = 2, \; x_2 = 1,$$

which yields the acceptable values

$$\lambda_1 = \frac{2}{3} , \quad \lambda_2 = \frac{1}{3} ;$$

the maximum value of the objective function is then

$$f(\vec{x}) = 7.$$

• PROBLEM 10-33

Consider the following problem:

$$\text{Max } f(x_1,x_2) = x_2$$

subject to

$$x_1^2 + x_2^2 - 4 \leq 0$$

and

$$-x_1^2 + x_2 \leq 0,$$

using Kuhn-Tucker conditions.

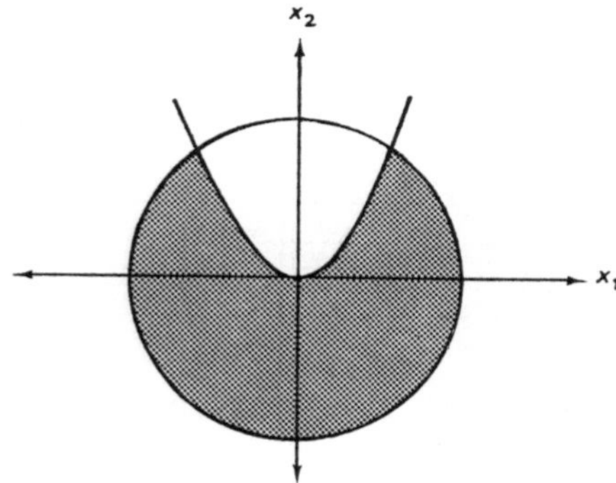

Fig. 1

Solution: The feasible region is diagrammed in Fig. 1. The Kuhn-Tucker conditions are

$$0 - \lambda_1(2x_1) - \lambda_2(-2x_1) = 0,$$

$$1 - \lambda_1(2x_2) - \lambda_2(1) = 0,$$

$$\lambda_1(x_1^2 + x_2^2 - 4) = 0,$$

$$\lambda_2(x_2 - x_1^2) = 0,$$

and

$$\lambda_1, \lambda_2 \geq 0.$$

Note that the feasible point $x_1 = 0$, $x_2 = 0$, along with $\lambda_1 = 0$ and $\lambda_2 = 1$, satisfies all these equations. Yet the origin is obviously not a local maximum of $f(x_1, x_2)$ in the feasible region, since any neighboring point on the parabola $x_2 = x_1^2$ is feasible and yields a greater objective value. So there exists a nonoptimal Kuhn-Tucker point.

• PROBLEM 10-34

Consider the problem of magnetism illustrated in Fig. 1. The Pole of a magnet is located at the co-ordinate point (4,3) on a horizontal surface and the equipotential lines in the (x_1, x_2) plane are defined by the concentric circles

$$\phi(x_1, x_2) = (x_1 - 4)^2 + (x_2 - 3)^2. \qquad (1)$$

Let a steel ball be

(a) free to move in an elliptic path (groove) on this x_1, x_2 plane defined by the equation

$$g(x_1, x_2) = 36(x_1 - 2)^2 + (x_2 - 3)^2 = 9, \qquad (2)$$

or (b) free to move in an elliptic area within the region

$$g(x_1, x_2) = 36(x_1 - 2)^2 + (x_2 - 3)^2 \leq 9. \qquad (3)$$

Minimize $\phi(x)$ subject to (a) and then to (b).

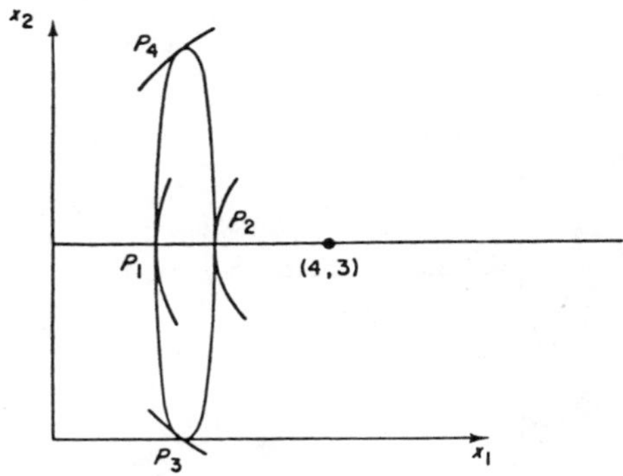

Fig. 1

Solution: The problem of minimizing $\phi(x)$ in (1) subject to (2) is a Lagrangean problem and that of minimizing $f(x)$ in (1) subject to (3) is a Kuhn-Tucker inequality problem. In both the cases the solution of the physical problem of determining the position of rest of the steel ball is sought. In both the cases the Lagrangean function to be investigated is

$$F(x_1, x_2, \lambda) = -\phi(x_1, x_2) - \lambda(g(x_1, x_2) - b). \quad (4)$$

(a) To solve the first problem the following set of three non-linear equations in three variables needs to be solved:

$$\frac{\partial F}{\partial x_1} = -[2(x_1 - 4) + \lambda 72(x_1 - 2)] = 0 \quad (5)$$

$$\frac{\partial F}{\partial x_2} = -[2(x_2 - 3) + 2.\lambda(x_2 - 3)] = 0 \quad (6)$$

$$\frac{\partial F}{\partial \lambda} = -[36(x_1 - 2)^2 + (x_2 - 3)^2 - 9] = 0. \quad (7)$$

From (6) it follows that if $x_2 = 3$ then λ and x_1 must be calculated from the remaining two equations (5) and (7).

Setting $x_2 = 3$ in (7) $x_1 = 3/2$ or $5/2$ and

$$\lambda = -\frac{1}{36}\left(\frac{x_1 - 4}{x_1 - 2}\right) = -\frac{5}{36} \text{ or } +\frac{1}{12}.$$

These correspond to the points

$$P_1: \quad x_1 = \frac{3}{2}, \quad x_2 = 3, \quad \lambda = -\frac{5}{36}$$

and

$$P_2: \quad x_1 = \frac{5}{2}, \quad x_2 = 3, \quad \lambda = \frac{1}{12}.$$

If $x_2 \neq 3$ it follows from (6) that $\lambda = -1$. Substituting $\lambda = -1$ in (5) and (7) it follows that the two points

$$P_3: \quad x_1 = 1.956, \quad x_2 = 0.002, \quad \lambda = -1,$$

and

$$P_4: \quad x_1 = 1.956, \quad x_2 = 5.998, \quad \lambda = -1$$

are obtained.

Of these four stationary points of the Lagrangean, the first two P_1, P_2 are the local optimum of the problem (a) and P_3, P_4 are points of inflexion or points of unstable rest.

In the problem (b), which is the Kuhn-Tucker problem, only the point P_2 satisfies the Kuhn-Tucker condition, i.e.,

$$\lambda = \frac{\partial f}{\partial x_1} = \frac{1}{12} > 0$$

and $g(x) = b$, i.e., $\lambda.(g(x) - b) = 0$. Hence this is an optimum point. The functions $\phi(x)$ and $g(x)$ are convex hence the local optimum in this case is also the global optimum.

• PROBLEM 10-35

Using the Kuhn-Tucker stationarity conditions, solve the problem

$$\min_{\vec{x}} \{f(\vec{x}) = (x_1 - 1)^2 + (x_2 - 2)\}$$

such that

$$x_2 - x_1 = 1,$$

$$x_1 + x_2 \leq 2,$$

$$x_1 \geq 0, \quad x_2 \geq 0,$$

and check the answer graphically.

Solution: Define

$$L(\vec{x}, \vec{\lambda}, \vec{\mu}) = f(\vec{x}) + \vec{\lambda}^T w(x) + \vec{\mu}^T g(\vec{x}).$$

The necessary conditions are

$$\vec{\nabla}_x L(\vec{x}^*, \vec{\lambda}^*, \vec{\mu}^*) \geq \vec{0}, \quad g(\vec{x}^*) \leq \vec{0},$$

$$\vec{x}^* \geq \vec{0}, \quad \vec{\mu}^* \geq \vec{0},$$

$$(\vec{x}^*)^T \vec{\nabla}_x L(\vec{x}^*, \vec{\lambda}^*, \vec{\mu}^*) = 0, \quad (\vec{\mu}^*)^T g(\vec{x}^*) = 0,$$

$$\vec{w}(\vec{x}^*) = \vec{0}.$$

Then

$$L(\vec{x}, \lambda, \mu) = (x_1 - 1)^2 + (x_2 - 2)^2 + \lambda(x_2 - x_1 - 1) + \mu(x_1 + x_2 - 2).$$

Now

$$\frac{\partial L}{\partial x_1} = 2(x_1 - 1) - \lambda + \mu \geq 0. \tag{1}$$

$$\frac{\partial L}{\partial x_2} = 2(x_2 - 2) + \lambda + \mu \geq 0 \tag{2}$$

$$x_1 \geq 0, \quad x_2 \geq 0. \tag{3}$$

$$x_1[2(x_1 - 1) - \lambda + \mu] = 0. \tag{4}$$

$$x_2[2(x_2 - 2) + \lambda + \mu] = 0. \tag{5}$$

$$x_1 + x_2 - 2 \leq 0. \tag{6}$$

$$\mu \geq 0. \tag{7}$$

$$\mu[x_1 + x_2 - 2] = 0. \tag{8}$$

$$x_2 - x_1 - 1 = 0. \tag{9}$$

To solve these equations, first assume $x_1 \neq 0$, $x_2 \neq 0$, and $\mu = 0$. Then solve (3), (4) and (8), i.e.,

$$2(x_1 - 1) - \lambda = 0.$$

$$2(x_2 - 2) + \lambda = 0.$$

$$x_2 - x_1 - 1 = 0.$$

yielding

$$x^*_1 = 1, \; x^*_2 = 2, \text{ and } \lambda^* = 0.$$

But this solution does not satisfy the inequality (5), i.e.,

$$1 + 2 - 2 \leq 0, \quad \text{or } 1 \leq 0.$$

Next let $\mu \neq 0$ and solve (3), (4), (7), and (8) simultaneously:

$$x_1 + x_2 - 2 = 0,$$

$$x_2 - x_1 - 1 = 0,$$

$$2(x_1 - 1) - \lambda + \mu = 0,$$

$$2(x_2 - 2) + \lambda + \mu = 0,$$

yielding

$$x^*_1 = \frac{1}{2}, \quad x^*_2 = \frac{3}{2}, \quad \mu^* = 1, \quad \lambda^* = 0,$$

and

$$f(x^*_1, x^*_2) = \frac{1}{2}.$$

Checking (2) and (6), we see that

$$x^*_1 \geq 0, \quad x^*_2 \geq 0, \text{ and } \mu \geq 0,$$

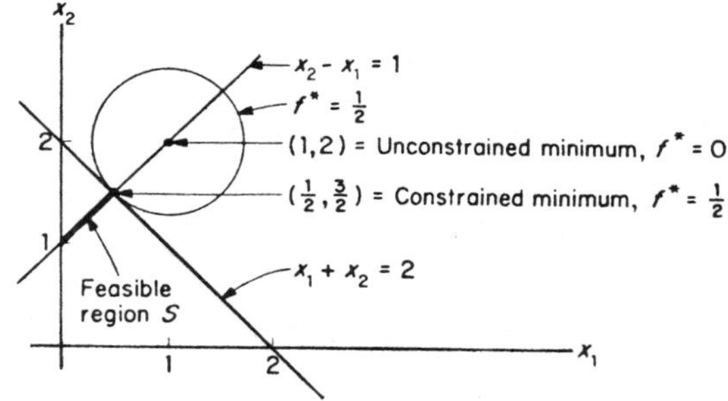

Fig. 1

so the solution is obtained. The solution and the feasible region are shown in Fig. 1.

• PROBLEM 10-36

Are the Kuhn-Tucker conditions satisfied at $x = 6$ for the following problem? Does the Lagrangian have a saddle point there?

$$\max_{x} \ (x - 4)^2$$

such that

$$1 < x < 6.$$

Solution: Write

$$g_1(x) = x - 6 < 0,$$

$$g_2(x) = 1 - x < 0.$$

Then

$$L(x,\lambda_1,\lambda_2) = (x - 4)^2 + \lambda_1(x - 6) + \lambda_2(1 - x),$$

and the stationarity conditions are

$$\frac{\partial L}{\partial x} = 2(x - 4) + \lambda_1 - \lambda_2 = 0,$$

$$x \leq 6, \quad x \geq 1,$$

$$\lambda_1 \leq 0, \quad \lambda_2 \leq 0,$$

$$\lambda_1(x - 6) = 0,$$

$$\lambda_2(1 - x) = 0.$$

At $x = 6$, one gets $\lambda_1 = -4$ and $\lambda_2 = 0$, and the stationarity conditions are satisfied.

Now examine the nature of the Lagrangian at $(6, -4, 0)$. Holding (λ_1, λ_2) fixed, the Hessian with respect to x is

$$\frac{\partial^2 L}{\partial x^2}(6, -4, 0) = 2 > 0,$$

which implies that $L(6, -4, 0)$ has a minimum with respect to x (instead of a maximum as required).

When the primal problem is to be maximized, the dual function is defined as

$$h(\vec{\lambda}) = \max_x L(x, \vec{\lambda}).$$

Since $L(x, \lambda_1, \lambda_2)$ does not possess a maximum at $(6, -4, 0)$, the dual functions does not exist at this stationarity point, and therefore no saddle point exists either.

Thus the stationarity conditions are satisfied at $x = 6$, but the Lagrangian does not have a saddle point there. The reason for this phenomenon is that we are asked to minimize a convex function. The stationarity conditions, being necessary conditions for a local maximum only, are satisfied, while the saddle-point conditions, being sufficient, are not.

• PROBLEM 10-37

Find the minimum of

$$f(X) = (x_1 + 1)^2 + (x_2 - 2)^2$$

subject to

$$g_1(X) = x_1 - 2 \leq 0,$$

$$g_2(X) = x_2 - 1 \leq 0,$$

$$x_1 \geq 0, \qquad x_2 \geq 0,$$

by the use of Kuhn-Tucker conditions.

Solution: The Lagrangian function in this case is

$$F(X, Y) = (x_1 + 1)^2 + (x_2 - 2)^2 + y_1(x_1 - 2) + y_2(x_2 - 1).$$

The Kuhn-Tucker conditions give

$$x_1[2(x_1 + 1) + y_1] = 0,$$

$$x_2[2(x_2 - 2) + y_2] = 0,$$

$$y_1(x_1 - 2) = 0,$$

$$y_2(x_2 - 1) = 0,$$

$$2(x_1 + 1) + y_1 \geq 0,$$

$$2(x_2 - 2) + y_2 \geq 0,$$

$$x_1 - 2 \leq 0, \quad x_2 - 1 \leq 0,$$

$$x_1, x_2, y_1, y_2 \geq 0.$$

The four equations above have the following nine solutions.

	x_1	x_2	y_1	y_2
(i)	0	0	0	0
(ii)	0	1	0	2
(iii)	0	2	0	0
(iv)	2	0	-6	0
(v)	2	1	-6	2
(vi)	2	2	-6	0
(vii)	-1	2	0	0
(viii)	-1	0	0	0
(ix)	-1	1	0	2

Of these solutions (ii) is the only one which satisfies all the inequalities. Hence the minimum of f(X) is 2 at $x_1 = 0$, $x_2 = 1$.

f(X) = constant are circles with center (-1, 2) and the constraints give a rectangular area as the set of feasible solutions.

• PROBLEM 10-38

Consider the nonlinear programming problem

$$\text{minimize } f(x, y) = (x - 2)^2 + (y - 1)^2$$

subject to

$$g_1(x, y) = -y + x^2 \leq 0$$

$$g_2(x, y) = x + y - 2 \leq 0.$$

Find the optimal point and check if Kuhn-Tucker conditions are satisfied - graphically.

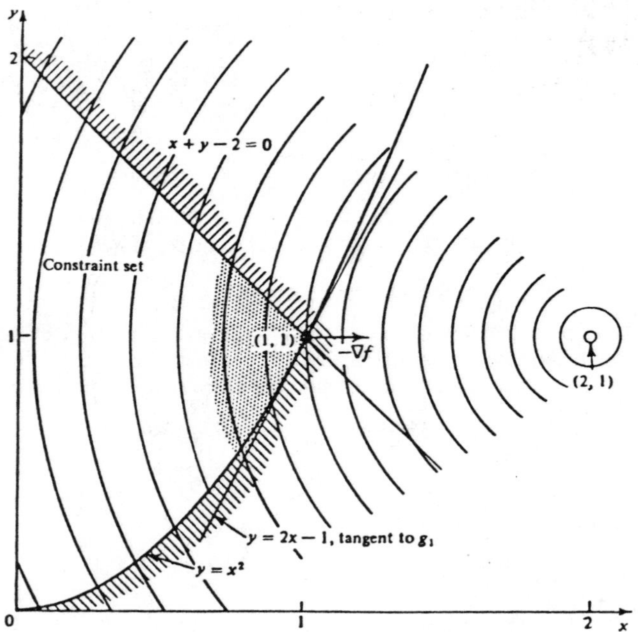

Geometry of constrained optimization problem.

Fig. 1

Solution: The Kuhn-Tucker conditions are predicated on this fact: At any constrained optimum, no (small) allowable change in the problem variables can improve the objective function.

The problem is shown geometrically in Figure 1. It is evident that the optimum is at the intersection of the two constraints at (1,1). Define a feasible direction as a vector such that a small move along that vector violates no constraints. At (1,1), the set of all feasible directions lies between the line

$$x + y - 2 = 0$$

and the tangent line to

$$y = x^2 \quad \text{at} \quad (1,1),$$

i.e., the line

$$y = 2x - 1.$$

In other words, this set is the cone generated by these lines. The vector $-\nabla f$ points in the direction of maximum rate of decrease of f and a small move along any direction making an angle of less than 90° with $-\nabla f$ will decrease f. Thus, at the optimum, no feasible direction can have an angle of less than 90° between it and $-\nabla f$.

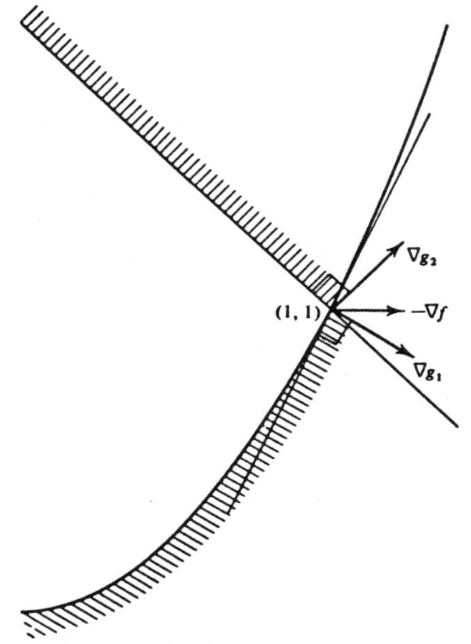

Gradient of objective contained in convex cone.

Fig. 2

Consider Figure 2, in which the gradient vectors ∇g_1 and ∇g_2 are drawn. Note that $-\nabla f$ is contained in the cone generated by ∇g_1 and ∇g_2. What if this were not so? If $-\nabla f$ were slightly above ∇g_2, it would make an angle of less than 90° with a feasible direction just below the line $x + y - 2 = 0$. If $-\nabla f$ were slightly below ∇g_1, it would make an angle of less than 90° with a feasible direction just above the line $y = 2x - 1$. Neither case can occur at an optimal point, and both cases are excluded if and only if $-\nabla f$ lies within the cone generated by ∇g_1 and ∇g_2. Of course, this is the same as requiring that ∇f lie within the cone generated by $-\nabla g_1$ and $-\nabla g_2$. This is the usual statement of the Kuhn-Tucker conditions, i.e., if f and all g_i are differentiable, a necessary condition for a point x^0 to be a constrained minimum of the problem

$$\text{minimize } f(x)$$

subject to

$$g_i(x) \leq 0, \quad i = 1,\ldots,m$$

is that, at x^0, ∇f lie within the cone generated by the negative gradients of the binding constraints. Binding constraints are those which hold as equalities at x^0.

CUTTING PLANE, PENALTY AND BARRIER FUNCTION METHODS

• PROBLEM 10-39

Minimize

$$(x_1 - 2)^2 + \frac{1}{4}x_2^2$$

subject to

$$x_1 - \frac{7}{2}x_2 - 1 \le 0$$

$$2x_1 + 3x_2 = 4.$$

Solve the Nonlinear Programming problem by the Cutting Plane Method. Take the feasible solution

$$\vec{x}_0 = (\frac{5}{4}, \frac{1}{2})^t$$

as the initial point.

Solution: Definition: Given the Primal Problem P

Minimize

$$f(\vec{x})$$

subject to

$$\vec{g}(\vec{x}) \le 0$$

$$\vec{h}(\vec{x}) = \vec{0}$$

$$\vec{x} \in X.$$

Lagrangian Dual Problem D is defined as

Maximize

$$\theta(\vec{u}, \vec{v}) = \inf\{f(\vec{x}) + \vec{u}^t\vec{g}(\vec{x}) + \vec{v}^t\vec{h}(\vec{x}) : \vec{x} \in X\}$$

subject to

$$\vec{u} \ge 0.$$

The cutting plane method as summarized below, is a Lagrangian Dual Method: it is assumed that f, $\vec{g}$, and $\vec{h}$ are continuous, and that X is compact (a set X in E_n is said to be compact if it is closed and bounded; for every sequence $\{\vec{x}_k\}$ in a compact set X, there is a convergent subsequence with a limit in X), so that the set $X(\vec{u}, \vec{v})$ is not empty for each $(\vec{u}, \vec{v})$.

Initialization Step: Find a point $\vec{x}_0 \in X$ such that $\vec{g}(\vec{x}_0) \leq \vec{0}$ and $\vec{h}(\vec{x}_0) = \vec{0}$. Let k = 1, and go to the main step.

Main Step: 1. Solve the following problem, which is usually referred to as the master problem.

Maximize z

subject to

$$z \leq f(\vec{x}_j) + \vec{u}^t\vec{g}(\vec{x}_j) + \vec{v}^t\vec{h}(\vec{x}_j)$$

$$\text{for } j = 0,\ldots,k-1$$

$$\vec{u} \geq \vec{0}.$$

Let $(z_k, \vec{u}_k, \vec{v}_k)$ be an optimal solution and go to step 2.

2. Solve the following subproblem.

Minimize

$$f(\vec{x}) + \vec{u}_k^t\ \vec{g}(\vec{x}) + \vec{v}_k^t\ \vec{h}(\vec{x})$$

subject to

$$\vec{x} \in X.$$

let $\vec{x}_k$ be an optimal point, and let

$$\theta(\vec{u}_k, \vec{v}_k) = f(\vec{x}_k) + \vec{u}_k^t\ \vec{g}(\vec{x}_k) + \vec{v}_k^t\ \vec{h}(\vec{x}_k).$$

If $z_k = \theta(\vec{u}_k, \vec{v}_k)$, then stop; $(\vec{u}_k, \vec{v}_k)$ is an "optimal dual" solution. Otherwise, if $z_k > \theta(\vec{u}_k, \vec{v}_k)$, then replace k by k + 1, and repeat step 1.

At each iteration, a cut (constraint) is added to the master problem, and hence the size of the master problem increases monotonically. If the size of the master problem becomes excessively large, all constraints that are not binding may be eliminated. Also note that the optimal solutions of the master problem form a nonincreasing sequence $\{z_k\}$. Since each z_k is an upper bound on the optimal value of the "dual" problem, one may stop if $z_k - \text{maximum}_{1 \leq j \leq k}\theta(\vec{u}_j, \vec{v}_j) < \varepsilon$, where ε is a small positive number.

The cutting plane algorithm for maximizing the dual function can be interpreted as a tangential approximation technique. By definition of θ, one must have

$$\theta(\vec{u}, \vec{v}) \le f(\vec{x}) + \vec{u}^t\vec{g}(\vec{x}) + \vec{v}^t\vec{h}(\vec{x}) \quad \text{for } \vec{x} \in X.$$

Thus, for any fixed $\vec{x} \in X$, the hyperplane

$$\{(\vec{u}, \vec{v}, \vec{z}): \vec{u} \in E_m, \vec{v} \in E_1, z = f(\vec{x}) + \vec{u}^t\vec{g}(\vec{x}) + \vec{v}^t\vec{h}(\vec{x})\}$$

bounds the function θ from above.

The master problem at iteration k is equivalent to solving the following problem.

$$\text{Maximize} \quad \hat{\theta}(\vec{u}, \vec{v})$$

$$\text{subject to} \quad \vec{u} \ge \vec{0}$$

where $\hat{\theta}(\vec{u}, \vec{v}) = \text{minimum}\{f(\vec{x}_j) + \vec{u}^t\vec{g}(\vec{x}_j) + \vec{v}^t\vec{h}(\vec{x}_j):$ $j = 1,\ldots,k-1\}$. Note that $\hat{\theta}$ is a piecewise linear function that approximates θ by considering only k - 1 of the bounding hyperplanes.

Let the optimal solution to the master problem be $(z_k, \vec{u}_k, \vec{v}_k)$. Now, the subproblem is solved yielding $\theta(\vec{u}_k, \vec{v}_k)$ and $\vec{x}_k$. If $z_k > \theta(\vec{u}_k, \vec{v}_k)$, then the new constraint $z \le f(\vec{x}_k) + \vec{u}^t\vec{g}(\vec{x}_k) + \vec{v}^t\vec{h}(\vec{x}_k)$ is added to the master problem, giving a new and tighter piecewise linear approxaimation to θ. Since $\theta(\vec{u}_k, \vec{v}_k) = f(\vec{x}_k) + \vec{u}_k{}^t\vec{g}(\vec{x}_k) + \vec{v}_k{}^t\vec{h}(\vec{x}_k)$, the hyperplane $\{(z, \vec{u}, \vec{v}): z = f(\vec{x}_k) + \vec{u}^t\vec{g}(\vec{x}_k) + \vec{v}^t\vec{h}(\vec{x}_k)\}$ is tangential to the graph of θ at $(z_k, \vec{u}_k, \vec{v}_k)$.

Let

$$X = \{(x_1,x_2): 2x_1 + 3x_2 = 4\},$$

so that the Lagrangian dual function is given by

$$\theta(u) = \text{minimum} \quad \{(x_1 - 2)^2 + \frac{1}{4}x_2{}^2 + u(x - \frac{7}{2}x_2 - 1): 2x_1 + 3x_2 = 4\} \quad (1)$$

The cutting plane method is initiated with a feasible solution

$$\vec{x}_0 = \left(\frac{5}{4}, \frac{1}{2}\right)^t.$$

At step 1 of the first iteration, solve the following problem:

$$\text{Maximize} \qquad z$$

subject to

$$z \le \frac{5}{8} - \frac{3}{2}u$$

$$u \ge 0$$

The optimal solution is

$$(z_1, u_1) = \left(\frac{5}{8}, 0\right).$$

At step 2, one solves (1) for $u = u_1 = 0$, yielding an optimal solution

$$\vec{x}_1 = (2,0)^t$$

with

$$\theta(u_1) = 0 < z_1 .$$

Hence, more iterations are needed. The summary of the first four iterations are given in Table 1.

Table 1 **Summary of Computations**

Iteration k	Constraint Added	Step 1 Solution	Step 2 Solution	
		(z_k, u_k)	x_k^t	$\theta(u_k)$
1	$z \le \frac{5}{8} - \frac{3}{2}u$	$(\frac{5}{8}, 0)$	$(2, 0)$	0
2	$z \le 0 + u$	$(\frac{1}{4}, \frac{1}{4})$	$(\frac{13}{8}, \frac{1}{4})$	$\frac{3}{32}$
3	$z \le \frac{5}{32} - \frac{1}{4}u$	$(\frac{1}{8}, \frac{1}{8})$	$(\frac{29}{16}, \frac{1}{8})$	$\frac{11}{128}$
4	$z \le \frac{5}{128} + \frac{3}{8}u$	$(\frac{7}{64}, \frac{3}{16})$	$(\frac{55}{32}, \frac{3}{16})$	$\frac{51}{512}$

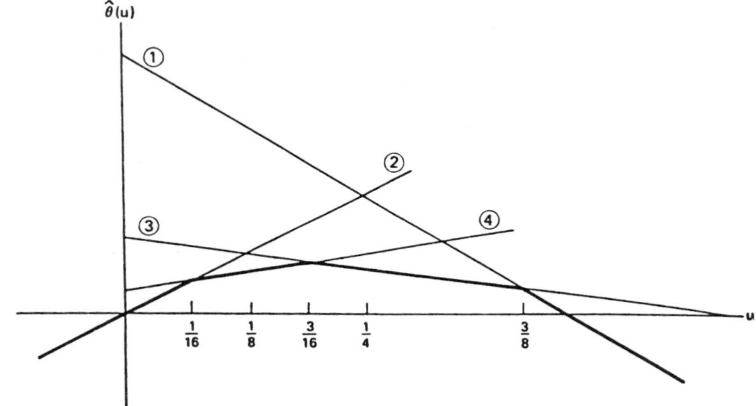

Tangential approximation of θ.

The approximating function $\hat{\theta}$ at the end of the fourth iteration is shown in darkened lines in the figure. One can verify that the Langrangian dual function for this problem is given by

$$\theta(u) = -\frac{5}{2}u^2 + u$$

and that the hyperplanes added at iteration 2 onward are indeed tangential to the graph of θ at the point (z_k, u_k). Incidentally, the dual objective function

is maximized at

$$\bar{u} = \frac{1}{5}$$

with

$$\theta(\bar{u}) = \frac{1}{10} .$$

Note that the sequence $\{u_k\}$ converges to the optimal point

$$\bar{u} = \frac{1}{5} .$$

• PROBLEM 10-40

Consider the following problem

Minimize

$$(x_1 - 2)^4 + (x_1 - 2x_2)^2$$

subject to

$$x_1^2 - x_2 = 0$$

$$X = E_2$$

Use the penalty function to solve.

Solution: Let $\varepsilon > 0$ be a termination scalar. Choose an initial point

$$\vec{x}_1 ,$$

a penalty parameter $\mu_1 > 0$, and a scalar $\beta > 1$. Let $k = 1$ and go to the main step.

Main step.

1. Starting with $\vec{x}_k$ solve the following problem:

Minimize

$$f(\vec{x}) + \mu_k \alpha(\vec{x})$$

subject to

$$\vec{x} \in X$$

Let

$$\vec{x}_{k+1}$$

be an optimal solution, and go to step 2.

2. If

$$\mu_k \alpha(\vec{x}_{k+1}) < \varepsilon$$

stop; otherwise, let

$$\mu_{k+1} = \beta\mu_k ,$$

replace k by k + 1, and go to step 1.

Note that at iteration k, for a given penalty parameter μ_k, the problem to be solved to give

$\vec{x}_{\mu k}$ is

minimize

$$(x_1 - 2)^4 + (x_1 - 2x_2)^2 + \mu_k(x_1^2 - x_2)^2$$

Table 1

Iteration k	μ_k	$\vec{x}_{k+1} = \vec{x}_{\mu_k}$	$f(\vec{x}_{k+1})$	$\alpha(\vec{x}_{\mu_k}) = h^2(\vec{x}_{\mu_k})$	$\theta(\mu_k)$	$\mu_k\alpha(\vec{x}_{\mu_k})$
1	0.1	(1.4539, 0.7608)	0.0935	1.8307	0.2766	0.1831
2	1.0	(1.1687, 0.7407)	0.5753	0.3908	0.9661	0.3908
3	10.0	(0.9906, 0.8425)	1.5203	0.01926	1.7129	0.1926
4	100.0	(0.9507, 0.8875)	1.8917	0.000267	1.9184	0.0267
5	1000.0	(0.9461094, 0.8934414)	1.9405	0.0000028	1.9433	0.0028

Table 1 summarizes the computations using the penalty function method. The starting point is taken as

$$\vec{x} = (2.0,\ 1.0),$$

where the objective function value is 0.0. The initial value of the penalty parameter is taken as

$$\alpha_1 = 0.1.$$

• PROBLEM 10-41

Consider the following problem:

$$\text{Minimize} \qquad x$$

$$\text{subject to} \qquad -x + 2 \leq 0$$

Use the penalty function to solve.

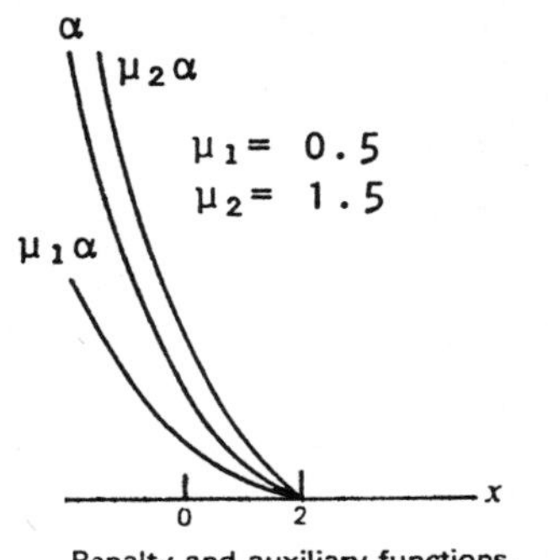

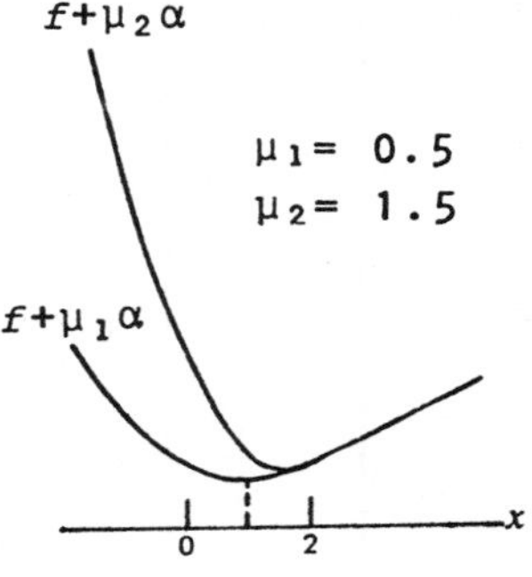

Penalty and auxiliary functions.

Fig. 1

<u>Solution</u>: Let $\alpha(x) = [\text{maximum } \{0, g(x)\}]^2$.

Then

$$\alpha(x) = \begin{cases} 0 & \text{if } x \geq 2 \\ (-x+2)^2 & \text{if } x < 2 \end{cases}$$

Figure 1 shows the penalty and auxiliary functions α and $f + \mu\alpha$. Note that the minimum of $f + \mu\alpha$ occurs at the point

$$2 - \frac{1}{2\mu},$$

and approaches the minimum point $\bar{x} = 2$ of the original problem, as μ approaches ∞.

Show that

$$\lambda_1^* = \lim_{K_1 \to \infty} 2K_1 g_1(x) u_1(g_1)$$

for the problem

$$\min x_1^2 + x_2^2$$

such that

$$g_1(\vec{x}) = 3x_1 + 2x_2 - 6 \geq 0,$$

$$g_2(\vec{x}) = x_1 \geq 0,$$

$$g_3(\vec{x}) = x_2 \geq 0.$$

Apply the penalty function method.

Solution: The Lagrangian is given by

$$L(\vec{x},\vec{\lambda}) = x_1^2 + x_2^2 + \lambda_1(3x_1 + 2x_2 - 6) + \lambda_2 x_1 + \lambda_3 x_2,$$

and the Kuhn-Tucker conditions are

$$\frac{\partial L}{\partial x_1} = 2x_1 + 3\lambda_1 + \lambda_2 = 0$$

$$\frac{\partial L}{\partial x_2} = 2x_1 + 2\lambda_1 + \lambda_3 = 0,$$

$$\frac{\partial L}{\partial \lambda_1} = 3x_1 + 2x_2 - 6 \geq 0,$$

$$\frac{\partial L}{\partial \lambda_2} = x_1 \geq 0,$$

$$\frac{\partial L}{\partial \lambda_3} = x_2 \geq 0,$$

$$\lambda_1(3x_1 + 2x_2 - 6) = 0,$$

$$\lambda_2 x_1 = 0,$$

$$\lambda_3 x_2 = 0.$$

The optimal set of $(\vec{x},\vec{\lambda})$ which satisfies these conditions is

$$\vec{x}^* = \left[\frac{18}{13}, \frac{12}{13}\right]^T,$$

$$\vec{\lambda}^* = \left[-\frac{12}{13}, 0,0\right]^T .$$

Using the penalty function method, the new objective function is given by

$$P(\vec{x};\vec{K}) = x_1^2 + x_2^2 + K_1(3x_1 + 2x_2 - 6)^2 u_1(g_1)$$
$$+ K_2 x_1^2 u_2(g_2) + K_3 x_2^2 u\ (g_3).$$

For x_1, x_2 in the first quadrant but outside the feasible region,

$$u_1(g_1) = 1$$

and

$$u_2(g_2) = u_3(g_3) = 0,$$

and the necessary conditions are

$$\frac{\partial P}{\partial x_1} = 2x_1 + 6K_1(3x_1 + 2x_2 - 6) = 0,$$

$$\frac{\partial P}{\partial x_2} = 2x_2 + 4K_1(3x_1 + 2x_2 - 6) = 0.$$

Solving these two equations, one gets

$$x_1(K_1) = \frac{36K_1}{2 + 26K_1} ,$$

$$x_2(K_1) = \frac{24K_1}{2 + 26K_1} ,$$

so

$$\vec{x}^* = \lim_{K_1 \to \infty} (x_1(K_1), x_2(K_1)) = \left[\frac{18}{13}, \frac{12}{13}\right]^T$$

and

$$2K_1 g_1(x) = 2K_1\ 3\left[\left(\frac{36K_1}{2 + 26K_1}\right) + 2\left(\frac{24K_1}{2 + 26K_1}\right) - 6\right]$$

$$= \frac{-24K_1}{2 + 26K_1}.$$

So

$$\lambda_1^* = \lim_{k_1 \to \infty} \left(\frac{-24K_1}{2 + 26K_1}\right) = -\frac{12}{13} .$$

• PROBLEM 10-43

Show that the penalty function

$$\vec{K}[g(\vec{x})]^2$$

attains the optimal solution to the equality-constrained problem

$$\min\ x_1^2 + x_1^2$$

such that

$$g(\vec{x}) = x_2^2 - (x_1 - 1)^3 = 0,$$

even though the optimal Lagrange multipliers do not exist.

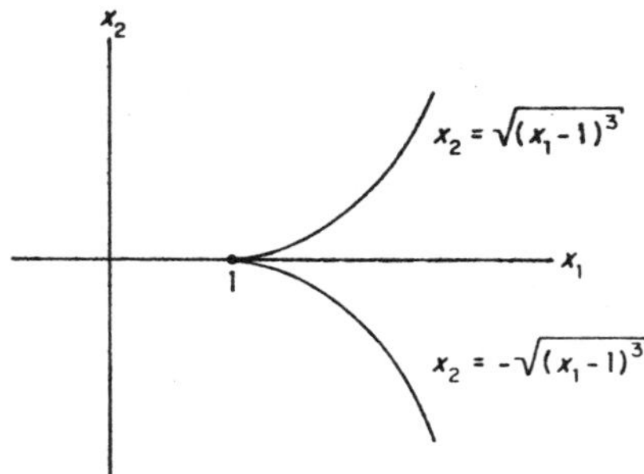

Fig. 1

Solution: By inspection of Fig. 1 the optimal solution is at the point (1,0). The Lagrange multipliers exist if the Jacobian of the constraint matrix has rank 1 at 1,0. But

$$\vec{\nabla}g(1,0) = \begin{bmatrix} -3(x_1 - 1)^2 \\ \\ 2x_2 \end{bmatrix}_{1,0} = \begin{bmatrix} 0 \\ \\ 0 \end{bmatrix},$$

which has rank 0, so the optimal Lagrange multipliers do not exist.

Now by penalty-function methods, the objective function is

$$P(\vec{x};\vec{K}) = x_1^2 + x_2^2 + \vec{K}[x_2^2 - (x_1 - 1)^3]^2,$$

and the necessary conditions are

$$\frac{\partial P}{\partial x_1} = 2x_1 - 6K(x_1 - 1)^2[x_2^2 - (x_1 - 1)^3] = 0$$

$$\frac{\partial P}{\partial x_2} = 2x_2 + 4Kx_2[x_2^2 - (x_1 - 1)^3] = 0.$$

Writing these two equations as

$$(x_1 - 1)^2[x_2^2 - (x_1 - 1)^3] = \frac{x_1}{3K},$$

$$x_2[x_2^2 - (x_1 - 1)^3] = -\frac{x_2}{2K},$$

and taking the limit as $K\to\infty$, it can be seen that

$$x_1^* = 1$$

and

$$x_2^* = 0,$$

which is the optimal solution.

• **PROBLEM 10-44**

Consider the problem:

min ax

subjet to

$$x - 1 \geq 0, \; 2 - x \geq 0,$$

where

$$a > 0.$$

The solution is $x^* = 1$.

Develop the objective functions for the barrier and penalty methods and illustrate them graphically.

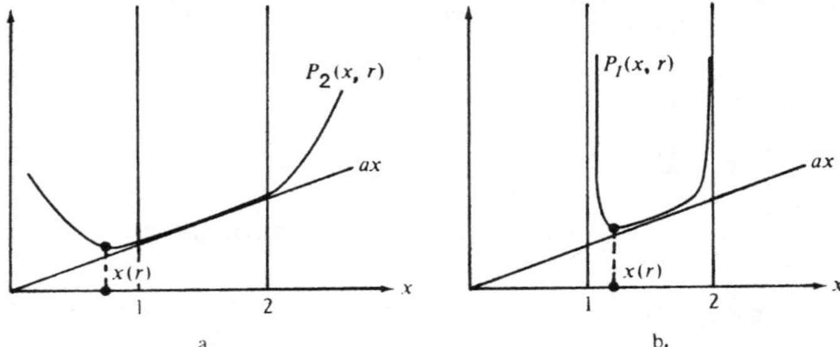

Barrier and penalty functions

Fig. 1

Solution: The two types of transformations that can be developed are:

barrier function

$$P_1(x,r) = ax + r\left(\frac{1}{x-1} + \frac{1}{2-x}\right)$$

and penalty function

$$P_2(x,r) = ax + \frac{1}{r}\{(\min[x-1,0])^2 + (\min[2-x,0)^2\}$$

where $r > 0$ is a perturbation parameter.

Figure 1 illustrates the original problem and transformed functions. Clearly, the transformed function

$$P_1(x,r)$$

sets up a barrier against leaving the feasible region. All solutions $x(r)$ or $\min P_1(x,r)$ are interior points, and it can be expected that under suitable conditions

$$\lim_{r \to 0} x(r) = x^*.$$

Consider the following problem:

Minimize

$$(x_1 - 2)^4 + (x_1 - 2x_2)^2$$

subject to

$$x_1^2 - x_2 \leq 0$$

Solve the problem by using the barrier function method with barrier function

$$B(x) = -1/(x_1^2 - x_2).$$

Start calculations from the point (0.0, 1.0).

Minimize

$$\theta(\mu) = \inf\{f(\vec{x}) + \mu B(\vec{x}) : g(\vec{x}) < \vec{0}, \vec{x} \in X\}$$

subject to

$$\mu \geq 0,$$

$\mu = 10$ and the parameter used to update μ's value, is

$$\beta = 0.10$$

Solution: Described below is a scheme using barrier functions for optimizing a nonlinear programming problem of the form to minimize

$$f(\vec{x})$$

subject to $g(\vec{x}) \leq \vec{0}$ and $\vec{x} \in X$. The barrier function B used must satisfy (1).

$$B(\vec{x}) = \sum_{i=1}^{m} \phi[g_i(\vec{x})] \qquad (1)$$

where ϕ is a function of one variable that is continuous over

$$\{y : y < 0\}$$

and satisfies:

$$\phi(y) \geq \text{ if } y < 0$$

and

$$\lim_{y \to 0^-} \phi(y) = \infty$$

Thus, a typical barrier function is of the form:

$$B(\vec{x}) = \sum_{i=1}^{m} \frac{-1}{g_i(\vec{x})}$$

The problem stated at step 1 below incorporates the constraint

$$g(\vec{x}) < \vec{0}.$$

If

$$g(\vec{x}_k) < \vec{0},$$

and since the barrier function approaches ∞ as the boundary of the region

$$G = \{\vec{x}: g(\vec{x}) < \vec{0}\}$$

is reached, then the constraint

$$g(\vec{x}) < \vec{0}$$

may be ignored, provided that an unconstrained optimization technique is used that will ensure that the resulting optimal point

$$\vec{x}_{k+1} \in G.$$

However, as most line search methods use discrete steps, if we are close to the boundary, a step could lead to a point outside the feasible region where the value of the barrier function B is a large negative number. Therefore, the problem could be treated as an unconstrained optimization problem only if an explicit check for feasibility is made. The algorithm is as follows:

Initialization Step

Let $\varepsilon > 0$ be a termination scalar, and choose a point

$$\vec{x}_1 \in X$$

with

$$g(\vec{x}_1) < \vec{0}.$$

Let

$$\mu_1 > 0, \quad \beta \in (0,1),$$

let

$$k = 1,$$

and go to the main step.

Main Step

1. Starting with $\vec{x}_k$ solve the following problem:

Minimize

$$f(\vec{x}) + \mu_k B(\vec{x})$$

subject to

$$g(\vec{x}) < \vec{0}$$

$$\vec{x} \in X$$

Let

$$\vec{x}_{k+1}$$

be an optimal solution, and go to step 2.

2. If

$$\mu_k B(\vec{x}_{k+1}) < \varepsilon ,$$

stop. Otherwise, let

$$\mu_{k+1} = \beta\mu_k ,$$

replace k by k+1, and repeat step 1.

The summary of the computations is shown in the table and the progress of the algorithm is shown in the figure.

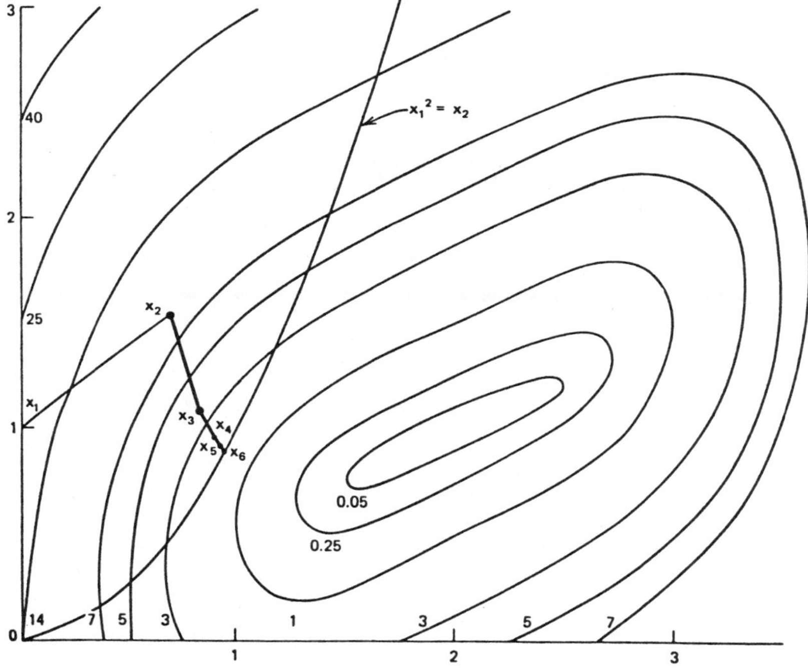

Illustration of the barrier function method.

TABLE Summary of Computations for the Barrier Function Method

Iteration k	μ_k	$\vec{x}_{\mu k} = \vec{x}_{k+1}$	$f(\vec{x}_{k+1})$	$B(\vec{x}_{k+1})$	$\theta(\mu_k)$	$\mu_k B(\vec{x}_{\mu_k})$
1	10.0	(0.7079, 1.5315)	8.3338	0.9705	18.0388	9.705
2	1.0	(0.8282, 1.1098)	3.8214	2.3591	6.1805	2.3591
3	0.1	(0.8989, 0.9638)	2.5282	6.4194	3.1701	0.6419
4	0.01	(0.9294, 0.9162)	2.1291	19.0783	2.3199	0.1908
5	0.001	(0.9403, 0.9011)	2.0039	59.0461	2.0629	0.0590
6	0.0001	(0.94389, 0.89635)	1.9645	184.4451	1.9829	0.0184

After six iterations the point

$$\vec{x}_7^t = (0.94389,\ 0.89635)$$

is reached, where

$$\mu_6 B(\vec{x}_7) = 0.0184$$

and the algorithm is terminated. It can be verified that this point is very close to the optimal. Noting that μ_k is decreasing, it can be observed from the accompanying table that

$$f(\vec{x}_{\mu k})$$

and

$$\theta(\mu_k)$$

are nondecreasing functions of μ_k. Likewise,

$$B(\vec{x}_{\mu k})$$

is a nonincreasing function of μ_k. Furthermore,

$$\mu_k B(\vec{x}_{\mu k})$$

converges to zero.

SEQUENTIAL UNCONSTRAINED MINIMIZATION TECHNIQUE (SUMT)

• PROBLEM 10-46

Consider the two-variable problem

Minimize

$$g(\vec{x}) = \frac{(x_1 + 1)^3}{3} + x_2$$

subject to

$$x_1 \geq 1$$

$$x_2 \geq 0.$$

Solve by Sequential Unconstrained Minimizing Technique.

Solution: The problem contains constraints; therefore it cannot be solved by methods for unconstrained nonlinear problems. But, a simple method can be devised to integrate them to the objective function and solve by an algorithm for the unconstrained case. The new objective function is defined as

$$P(\vec{x};r) = g(\vec{x}) + r\left(\sum_{i=1}^{m} \frac{1}{h_i(\vec{x})} - \sum_{j-1}^{n} \frac{1}{x_j}\right)$$

where

$$h_i(\vec{x})$$

are the constraints other than nonnegativity constraints, and

$$-x_j \leq 0$$

are the nonnegativity constraints.

Thus,

$$h_1(\vec{x}) = x_1 - 1$$

and

$$h_2(\vec{x}) = x_2.$$

Therefore

$$P(\vec{x};r) = \frac{(x_1 + 1)^3}{3} + x_2 + r\left[\frac{1}{x_1 - 1} + \frac{1}{x_2}\right]$$

The minimizing solution of

$$P(\vec{x};r)$$

can be derived analytically:

$$\frac{\partial P}{\partial x_1} = (x_1 + 1)^2 - \frac{r}{(x_1 - 1)^2} = 0,$$

so

$$(x_1^2 - 1)^2 = r,$$

$$\frac{\partial P}{\partial x_2} = 1 - \frac{r}{x_2^2} = 0,$$

so

$$\bar{x}_1 = (\sqrt{r} + 1)^{\frac{1}{2}}, \; \bar{x}_2 = \sqrt{r}.$$

Thus, if the gradient search procedure were still used, it would obtain essentially this solution at each iteration.

A typical sequence of values of r for the interations would be

$$r = 1, 10^{-2}, 10^{-4}, 10^{-6}, \ldots.$$

Using this sequence gives the results summarized in Table 1.

Table 1

Iteration	r	$\bar{x}_1$	$\bar{x}_2$	$g(\bar{x}) - r\sum_{i=1}^{m} \frac{1}{h_i(\bar{x})}$	$g(\bar{x})$
1	1	1.4142	1	2.27	5.69
2	10^{-2}	1.0488	0.1	2.66	2.97
3	10^{-4}	1.0050	0.01	2.67	2.70
4	10^{-6}	1.0005	0.001	2.67	2.67
		↓	↓	↓	↓
		1	0	2.67	2.67

where the last two columns give the lower and upper bound on

$$g(\vec{x}^*).$$

After iteration 4, these two bounds coincide to two decimal places, so

$$\vec{\bar{x}}$$

must be extremely close to optimal. The sequence of solutions is converging to the boundary values of the two variables. Therefore the optimal solution must be

$$\vec{x}^* = (1,0).$$

• PROBLEM 10-47

Solve by the SUMT (Sequential Unconstrained Minimizing Technique) algorithm.

Minimize:

$$f(\vec{x}) = 4x_1 - x_2^2 - 12$$

Subject to:

$$h_1(\vec{x}) = 25 - x_1^2 - x_2^2 = 0$$

$$g_2(\vec{x}) = 10x_1 - x_1^2 + 10x_2 - x_2^2 - 34 \geq 0$$

$$g_3(\vec{x}) = x_1 \geq 0$$

$$g_4(\vec{x}) = x_2 \geq 0$$

Start from

$$\vec{x}^{(0)} = [1\ 1]^T$$

Solution: Starting from

$$\vec{x}^{(0)} = [1\ 1]^T,$$

where

$$f(\vec{x}^{(0)}) = -9,$$

but because

$$\vec{x}^{(0)}$$

is an exterior point, SUMT first locates an interior $\vec{x}$ vector (nonfeasible with respect to $h_1(\vec{x})$

by minimizing the negative of

$g_2(\vec{x})$

subject to $g_3(\vec{x})$ and $g_4(\vec{x})$, which are satisfied. A preliminary P function is formed.

$$P' = -g_2(\vec{x}) + r \sum_{i=3}^{4} \frac{1}{g_i(\vec{x})}$$

$$= -(10x_1 - x_1^2 + 10x_2 - x_2^2 - 34) + (1)\left(\frac{1}{x_1} + \frac{1}{x_2}\right) \qquad (1)$$

At

$$\vec{x}^{(0)} = [1 \ 1]^T, \ -g_2(\vec{x}) = 16,$$

and

$$[(1/x_1) + (1/x_2)] = 2,$$

so that

$$P'(\vec{x}^{(0)}) = 18.$$

The value of the augmented objective function of the dual problem (to be maximized) is

$$E = -g_2(\vec{x}) - r \sum_{i=3}^{4} \frac{1}{g_i(\vec{x})} = 14 \qquad (2)$$

The minimization of this preliminar P' function is carried out by Newton's method. The partial derivatives of P' are

$$\frac{\partial P'}{\partial x_1} = -10 + 2x_1 - \frac{1}{x_1^2}$$

$$\frac{\partial P'}{\partial x_2} = -10 + 2x_2 - \frac{1}{x_2^2}$$

$$\frac{\partial^2 P'}{\partial x_1^2} = 2 + \frac{2}{x_1^3}$$

$$\frac{\partial^2 P'}{\partial x_2^2} = 2 + \frac{2}{x_2^3}$$

$$\frac{\partial^2 P'}{\partial x_1 \partial x_2} = 0$$

The direction and step length to minimize P' are given by

$$\vec{s} = -[\nabla^2 \ P']^{-1} \nabla P'$$

$$= -\begin{bmatrix} 4 & 0 \\ 0 & 4 \end{bmatrix}^{-1} \begin{bmatrix} -9 \\ -9 \end{bmatrix} = \begin{bmatrix} 2.25 \\ 2.25 \end{bmatrix} \qquad (3)$$

A step length of 2.25 is taken in each coordinate direction to give an interior $\vec{x}$ of

$$\vec{x}^{(0)'} = \vec{x}^{(0)} + \vec{s} = \begin{bmatrix} 3.25 \\ \\ 3.25 \end{bmatrix} \qquad (4)$$

where all the inequality constraints are satisfied and

$$f(\vec{x}) = -20.25.$$

Now the regular P function is formed,

$$P = f(\vec{x}) + \frac{h_1^2(\vec{x})}{\sqrt{r}}$$

$$+ r\left(\frac{1}{x_1} + \frac{1}{x_2} + \frac{1}{10x_1 - x_1^2 + 10x_2 - x_2^2 - 34}\right) \qquad (5)$$

that has a value of 529.716 at

$$\vec{x} = [3.25 \quad 3.25]^T \quad \text{for } r = 1.$$

The objective function to be maximized of the dual problem is

$$E = f(\vec{x}) - r\left(\frac{1}{x_1} + \frac{1}{x_2} + \frac{1}{10x_1 - x_1^2 + 10x_2 - x_2^2 - 34}\right)$$

$$+ 2rh_1^2(\vec{x})$$

and has the value of 1047.72 at $\vec{x} = [3.25 \quad 3.25]^T$.

First, the derivatives of P are evaluated at $\vec{x} = [3.25 \quad 3.25]^T$.

$$\frac{\partial P}{\partial x_1} = -46.505, \quad \frac{\partial^2 P}{\partial x_1^2} = 69.084, \quad \frac{\partial^2 P}{\partial x_1 \partial x_2} = 84.525,$$

$$\frac{\partial P}{\partial x_2} = -57.006, \quad \frac{\partial^2 P}{\partial x_2^2} = 69.084, \quad \frac{\partial^2 P}{\partial x_2 \partial x_1} = 84.525.$$

Because the hessian matrix of the P function is not positive definite inasmuch as the leading element is positive but

$$\det \begin{bmatrix} 69.084 & 84.525 \\ \\ 84.525 & 69.084 \end{bmatrix} < 0$$

the search component directions are along the components of negative gradient of the P function. The vector

$$\vec{x}^{(0)'}$$

is changed as follows:

$$\vec{x} = \vec{x}^{(0)'} + \Delta\vec{x}^{(0)}$$

as the initial step, or

$$\begin{bmatrix} 49.755 \\ \\ 60.256 \end{bmatrix} = \begin{bmatrix} 3.25 \\ \\ 3.25 \end{bmatrix} + \begin{bmatrix} 46.505 \\ \\ 57.006 \end{bmatrix}$$

Subsequently, a Fibonacci search is executed to minimize the P function until the vector

$$\vec{x} = [3.516 \quad 3.577]^T$$

is reached (the precision of the search is actually five decimals).

Again the partial derivatives are computed:

$$\frac{\partial P}{\partial x_1} = 6.119 , \qquad \frac{\partial^2 P}{\partial x_1^2} = 99.613 , \qquad \frac{\partial^2 P}{\partial x_1 \partial x_2} = 100.628 ,$$

$$\frac{\partial P}{\partial x_2} = 2.160 , \qquad \frac{\partial^2 P}{\partial x_2^2} = 101.024 , \qquad \frac{\partial^2 P}{\partial x_2 \partial x_1} = 100.628 ,$$

and again the hessian matrix of the P function is not positive definite because

$$\det \begin{bmatrix} 99.613 & 100.628 \\ \\ 100.628 & 101.024 \end{bmatrix} < 0$$

Hence the negative gradiant direction is used again to initiate a Fibonacci search until the

$$\vec{x} \text{ vector } \vec{x} = [2.137 \quad 4.702]^T$$

is reached. The minimization of the P function continues in this fashion.

After 23 successive search directions, the value of r=1 is reduced to r = 0.25. Values of the variables and the

$$f(\vec{x}) , \ P(\vec{x},r) , \text{ and } E(\vec{x},r)$$

functions at each reduction in r are:

Note the characteristic convergence of the values of the P and E functions to that of

$$f(\vec{x}) .$$

Also note the upper bound provided by the P function and the lower bound provided by the E function. Within each stage there are various numbers of function and derivative evaluations ranging from 11 on the first stage to 4 on the last stage, the exact number depending on the preselected precision in the unidimensional search. Figure 1 illustrates the trajectory of the search.

Stage no.	r	$E(\vec{x},r)$	$f(\vec{x})$	$P(\vec{x},r)$	x_1	x_2	$h_1(\vec{x})$
13	1	-32.990	-31.583	-29.400	1.150	4.918	-1.01×10^{-1}
23	1/4	-32.270	-31.807	-30.959	1.073	4.909	-2.53×10^{-1}
33	1/16	-32.065	-31.902	-31.547	1.037	4.904	-1.26×10^{-1}
42	1/64	-32.011	-31.948	-31.788	1.019	4.902	-6.34×10^{-2}
51	1/256	-31.997	-31.970	-31.895	1.010	4.900	-3.17×10^{-2}
55	1/1024	-31.993	-31.944	-31.944	1.006	4.899	-1.58×10^{-2}
62	1/4096	-31.993	-31.987	-31.969	1.004	4.899	-7.94×10^{-3}
68	1/16,384	-31.992	-31.990	-31.981	1.002	4.899	-3.95×10^{-3}

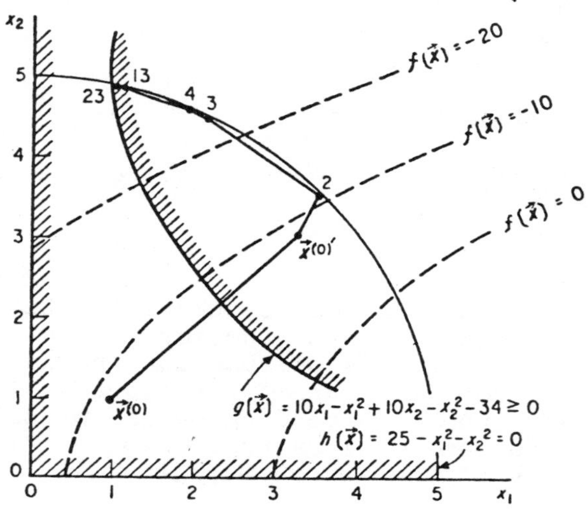

Fig. 1

METHODS OF FEASIBLE DIRECTIONS

• PROBLEM 10-48

Solve the following model, by the method of Zoutendijk:

Minimize

$$2x_1^2 + 2x_2^2 - 2x_1x_2 - 4x_1 - 6x_2$$

subject to

$$\begin{aligned} x_1 + 5x_2 &\le 5 \\ 2x_1^2 - x_2 &\le 0 \\ -x_1 &\le 0 \\ -x_2 &\le 0 \end{aligned}$$

Start from the feasible point

$$\vec{x}_1 = (0.00, 0.75)^t$$

and carry on four iterations.

Solution: Method of Zoutendijk works as follows:

Initialization Step: Select a starting point $\vec{x}_1$ meeting the requirement

$$g_i(\vec{x}_1) \le 0$$

for i = 1,...,m. Let k = 1, go to the main step.

Main Step:

1) Let

$$I = \{i: g_i(\vec{x}_k) = 0\},$$

solve the model

Minimize z

subject to

$$\vec{\nabla}f(\vec{x}_k)^t \vec{d} - z \le 0$$

$$\vec{\nabla}g_i(\vec{x}_k)^t \vec{d} - z \le 0 \qquad \text{for } i \in I$$

$$-1 \le d_j \le 1 \qquad \text{for } j = 1,\ldots,n$$

Assuming $(z_k, \vec{d}_k)$ is the optimal solution, stop if

$z_k = 0$; $\vec{x}_k$ is a Fritz John point. If $z_k < 0$, go to step 2.

2) Solve the line search problem

Minimize $\quad f(\vec{x}_k + \lambda\vec{d}_k)$

subject to $\quad 0 \leq \lambda \leq \lambda_{max}$

where

$$\lambda_{max} = \sup\{\lambda : g_i(\vec{x}_k + \lambda\vec{d}_k) \leq 0 \quad \text{for } i = 1,\ldots,m\}$$

(sup $\{\cdot\}$ is the least upper bound, i.e., the smallest possible scalar α satisfying $\alpha \geq x$ for each $x \in \{\cdot\}$). Assume λ_k be an optimal solution to the above problem. Let

$$\vec{x}_{k+1} = \vec{x}_k + \lambda_k\vec{d}_k$$

and replace k by k+1 and go to step 1.

The algorithm, when applied produces the following:

Iteration 1

Search direction: At $\vec{x}_1 = (0.00, 0.75)^t$ the gradient

$$\vec{\nabla}f(\vec{x}_1) = (4x_1 - 2x_2 - 4,\ 4x_2 - 2x_1 - 6)^t = (-5.50,\ -3.00)^t,$$

and the binding constraints are defined by $I = \{3\}$. Also,

$$\vec{\nabla}g_3 = (-1, 0)^t.$$

The direction finding problem becomes

Minimize z

subject to

$$-5.5d_1 - 3.0d_2 - z \leq 0$$

$$-d_1 - z \leq 0$$

$$-1 \leq d_1 \leq 1 \qquad \text{for } j = 1,2$$

By the simplex method, the optimal solution is obtained as

$$\vec{d}_1 = (1.00, -1.00)^t$$

and

$$z_1 = -1.00.$$

Line Search: A point starting from $\vec{x}_1 = (0.00, 0.75)$ along the direction

$$\vec{d}_1 = (1.00, -1.00)^t$$

can be written in the form

$$\vec{x}_1 + \lambda\vec{d}_i = (\lambda, 0.75 - \lambda)^t,$$

and corresponding value of the objective function is given by

$$f(\vec{x}_1 + \lambda\vec{d}_1) = 6\lambda^2 - 2.5\lambda - 3.375.$$

The maximum value of λ which satisfies the feasibility of $\vec{x}_1 + \lambda\vec{d}_1$ is $\lambda_{max} = 0.414$ where the constraint

$$2x_1^2 - x_2 \leq 0$$

becomes binding. Therefore, the problem that had to be solved for the value of λ_1 is

Minimize $\quad 6\lambda^2 - 2.5\lambda - 3.375$

subject to $\quad 0 \leq \lambda \leq 0.414$

The optimal value turns out to be $\lambda_1 = 0.2083$. As a result,

$$\vec{x}_2 = (\vec{x}_1 + \lambda_1\vec{d}_1) = (0.2083,0.5417)^t.$$

After four iterations the new point is

$$\vec{x}_5 = \vec{x}_4 + \lambda_4\vec{d}_4 = (0.6302,0.8740)^t.$$

The value of the objective function is -6.5443 compared with the value at the optimal point: -6.5590 at $(0.658872,0.868226)^t$.

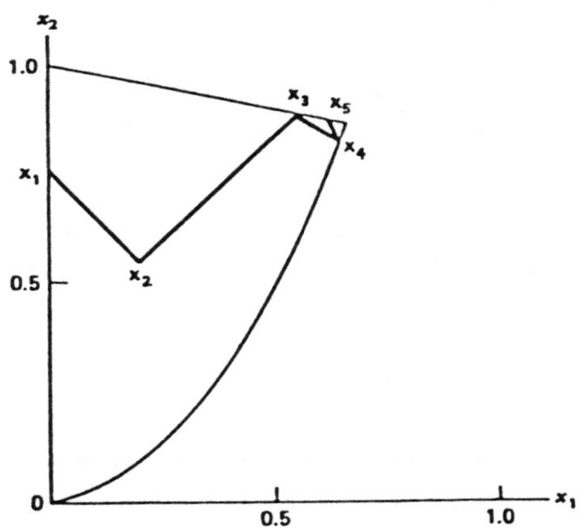

Illustration of the method of Zoutendijk for nonlinear constraints.

Fig. 1

Table 1 gives the data of the four iterations and Figure 1 shows the progress of the algorithm.

Table 1 Summary of Computations for the Method of Zoutendijk with Nonlinear Constraints

Iteration			Search Direction			Line Search		
k	$\vec{x}_k$	$f(\vec{x}_k)$	$\vec{\nabla} f(\vec{x}_k)$	$\vec{d}_k$	$\vec{z}_k$	λ_{max}	λ_1	$\vec{x}_{k+1}$
1	(0.00, 0.75)	-3.3750	(−5.50, −3.00)	(1.0000, −1.0000)	−1.000	0.4140	0.2083	(0.2083, 0.5417)
2	(0.2083, 0.5477)	-3.6354	(−4.25, −4.25)	(1.0000, 1.0000)	-8.500	0.3472	0.3472	(0.55555, 0.8889)
3	(0.5555, 0.8889)	-6.3455	(−3.5558, −3.5554)	(1.0000, −0.5325)	−1.663	0.09245	0.09245	(0.6479, 0.8397)
4	(0.6479, 0.8397)	-6.4681	(−3.0878, −3.9370)	(−0.5171, 1.0000)	−2.340	0.0343	0.0343	(0.6302, 0.8740)

• PROBLEM 10-49

Solve the following model by the gradient projection method of Rosen:

Minimize

$$2x_1^2 + 2x_2^2 - 2x_1x_2 - 4x_1 - 6x_2$$

subject to

$$x_1 + x_2 \le 2$$
$$x_1 + 5x_2 \le 5$$
$$-x_1 \le 0$$
$$-x_2 \le 0$$

Start from the point (0,0).

Solution: Rosen's gradient projection method for a problem of the form

$$\text{minimize} \quad f(\vec{x})$$
$$\text{subject to} \quad \vec{A}\vec{x} \le \vec{b}$$
$$\text{and} \quad \vec{E}\vec{x} = \vec{e}$$

is as follows:

Initialization step: **Choose** a point $\vec{x}_1$ which satisfies $\vec{A}\vec{x}_1 \le \vec{b}$ and $\vec{E}\vec{x} = \vec{e}$. Decompose $\vec{A}^t$ and $\vec{b}^t$ into $(\vec{A}_1^t, \vec{A}_2^t)$ and $(\vec{b}_1^t, \vec{b}_2^t)$ to satisfy $\vec{A}_1\vec{x}_1 = \vec{b}_1$ and $\vec{A}_2\vec{x}_1 < \vec{b}_2$. Let $k = 1$ and go to the main step.

Main Step:

1) Let $\vec{M}^t = (\vec{A}_1^t, \vec{E}^t)$. If $\vec{M}$ is vacuous, let $\vec{P} = \vec{I}$; otherwise, let $\vec{P} = \vec{I} - \vec{M}^t(\vec{M}\vec{M}^t)^{-1}\vec{M}$. Let $\vec{d}_k = -\vec{P}\vec{\nabla}f(\vec{x}_k)$. If $\vec{d}_k \ne \vec{0}$, go to step 2. If $\vec{d}_k = \vec{0}$, stop if $\vec{M}$ is vacuous; otherwise let $\vec{w} = -(\vec{M}\vec{M}^t)^{-1}\vec{M}\vec{\nabla}f(\vec{x}_k)$, and let $\vec{w}(\vec{u}^t, \vec{v}^t)$. If $\vec{u} \ge \vec{0}$, stop; $\vec{x}_k$ is a Kuhn-Tucker point. If $\vec{u} \not\ge \vec{0}$, choose a negative component of $\vec{u}$, u_j. Delete the row of $\vec{A}_1$ that corresponds to u_j, and repeat step 1.

2) Solve the problem

$$\text{Minimize} \quad f(\vec{x}_u + \lambda\vec{d}_k)$$

subject to

$$0 \le \lambda \le \lambda_{max}$$

with

$$\lambda \max = \begin{cases} \text{minimum } \{\hat{b}_i/\hat{d}_i : \hat{d}_i > 0\} & \text{if } \hat{\vec{d}} \not\le \vec{0} \\ \infty & \text{if } \hat{\vec{d}} \le \vec{0} \end{cases}$$

$$\hat{\vec{b}} = \vec{b}_2 - \vec{A}_2\vec{x}_k$$

$$\hat{\vec{d}} = \vec{A}_2\vec{d}_k$$

Let $\vec{x}_{k+1} = \vec{x}_k + \lambda_k \vec{d}_k$ and decompose A^t and b^t into $(\vec{A}_1^t, \vec{A}_2^t)$ and $(\vec{b}_1^t, \vec{b}_2^t)$ such that $\vec{A}_1 \vec{x}_{k+1} = b_1$ and $\vec{A}_2 \vec{x}_{u+1} < \vec{b}_2$. Replace k by k+1, and repeat step 1.

The algorithm, when applied produces the following:

Iteration 1

Search Direction: At $\vec{x}_1 = (0,0)^t$, the gradient

$$\vec{\nabla} f(\vec{x}_1) = (4x_1 - 2x_2 - 4,$$

$$4x_2 - 2x_1 - 6)^t = (-4, -6)^t.$$

Also note that only the nonnegativity constraints are binding at $\vec{x}_1$, so that

$$\vec{A}_1 = \begin{bmatrix} -1 & 0 \\ 0 & -1 \end{bmatrix} \qquad \vec{A}_2 = \begin{bmatrix} 1 & 1 \\ 1 & 5 \end{bmatrix}$$

Then it is true that

$$\vec{P} = \vec{I} - \vec{A}_1{}^t (\vec{A}_1 \vec{A}_1{}^t)^{-1} \vec{A}_1 = \begin{bmatrix} 0 & 0 \\ 0 & 0 \end{bmatrix}$$

and

$$\vec{d}_1 = -\vec{P}\vec{\nabla} f(\vec{x}_1) = (0,0)^t.$$

Note that there are no equality constraints, and compute

$$\vec{w} = \vec{u} = -(\vec{A}_1 \vec{A}_1{}^t)^{-1} \vec{A}_1 \vec{\nabla} f(\vec{x}_1) = (-4,-6)^t$$

Choose $u_4 = -6$, and delete the corresponding gradient of the fourth constraint from $\vec{A}_1$. The matrix $\vec{A}_1$ is modified to give $\hat{A}_1 = (-1,0)$. Then obtain the modified projection matrix

$$\hat{P} = \vec{I} - \hat{A}_1{}^t (\hat{A}_1 \hat{A}_1^t)^{-1} \hat{A}_1 = \begin{bmatrix} 0 & 0 \\ 0 & 1 \end{bmatrix}$$

and the direction $\vec{d}^1$ to move is given by

$$\vec{d}_1 = -\hat{P}\vec{\nabla} f(\vec{x}_1) = \begin{bmatrix} 0 & 0 \\ 0 & 1 \end{bmatrix} \begin{bmatrix} -4 \\ -6 \end{bmatrix} = \begin{bmatrix} 0 \\ 6 \end{bmatrix}$$

Line Search: A point $\vec{x}_2$ in the direction $\vec{d}_1$, starting from the point $\vec{x}_1$ can be written as

$$\vec{x}_2 = \vec{x}_1 + \lambda \vec{d}_1 = (0,6\lambda)^t$$

and the corresponding objective function value is

$$f(\vec{x}_2) = 72\lambda^2 - 36\lambda.$$

The maximum value for which $\vec{x}_1 + \lambda\vec{d}_1$ is feasible is obtained from (1) as

$$\lambda_{max} = \text{Minimum}\left\{\frac{2}{6}, \frac{5}{30}\right\} = \frac{1}{6}$$

Solving for λ_1 in the problem below

$$\text{Minimize} \quad 72\lambda^2 - 36\lambda$$

$$\text{subject to} \quad 0 \le \lambda \le \frac{1}{6},$$

obtain the optimal solution as $\lambda_1 = \frac{1}{6}$ such that

$$\vec{x}_2 = \vec{x}_1 + \lambda_1\vec{d}_1 = (0,1)^t.$$

At the end of the third iteration

$$\vec{u} = -(\vec{A}_1\vec{A}_1{}^t)^{-1}\,\vec{A}_1\vec{\nabla}f(\vec{x}_3) = \frac{32}{31} \ge 0$$

Therefore $\vec{x}_3$ is the optimal point. The gradient of the binding constraint points in the direction opposite to $\nabla f(\vec{x}_3)$. For

$$u_2 = \frac{32}{31}, \quad \vec{\nabla}f(\vec{x}_3) + u_2\,\vec{\nabla}g_2(\vec{x}_3) = \vec{0},$$

so that $\vec{x}_3$ is a Kuhn-Tucker point. In this problem, since f is convex, the point $\vec{x}_3$ is in fact the global optimal point.

• PROBLEM 10-50

Consider the following problem:

$$\text{Minimize } 2x_1^2 + 2x_2^2 - 2x_1x_2 - 4x_1 - 6x_2$$

$$\text{subject to } x_1 + x_2 + x_3 = 2$$

$$x_1 + 5x_2 + x_4 = 5$$

$$x_1, x_2, x_3, x_4 \ge 0$$

Solve this problem using Wolfe's reduced gradient method starting from the point $\vec{x}_1 = (0, 0, 2, 5)^t$. Note that

$$\vec{\nabla}f(\vec{x}) = (4x_1 - 2x_2 - 4,\ 4x_2 - 2x_1 - 6,\ 0,\ 0)^t.$$

Solution: Summary of the algorithm of Wolfe's reduced gradient method:

Initialization Step: Choose a point $\vec{x}$ satisfying $\vec{A}\vec{x}_1 = \vec{b}$, $\vec{x}_1 \ge \vec{0}$. Let k = 1 and go to the main step.

Main Step:

1. Let $\vec{d}_k^t = (\vec{d}_B^t, \vec{d}_N^t)$, where $\vec{d}_N$ and $\vec{d}_B$ are obtained from (4) and (5), respectively. If $\vec{d}_k = \vec{0}$, stop; $\vec{x}_k$ is a Kuhn-Tucker point. Otherwise, go to step 2.

$$I_k = \text{index set of m largest components of } \vec{x}_k \tag{1}$$

$$\vec{B} = \{ \vec{a}_j : j \in I_k \}, \quad \vec{N} = \{ \vec{a}_j : j \notin I_k \} \tag{2}$$

$$\vec{r}^t = \vec{\nabla} f(\vec{x}_k)^t - \vec{\nabla}_B f(\vec{x}_k)^t \vec{B}^{-1} \vec{A} \tag{3}$$

$$d_j = \begin{cases} -r_j & \text{if } j \notin I_k \text{ and } r_j \le 0 \\ -x_j r_j & \text{if } j \notin I_k \text{ and } r_j > 0 \end{cases} \tag{4}$$

$$\vec{d}_B = -\vec{B}^{-1} \vec{N} \vec{d}_N \tag{5}$$

2. Solve the following line search problem:

Minimize $f(\vec{x}_k + \lambda \vec{d}_k)$

subject to $0 \le \lambda \le \lambda_{max}$

where

$$\lambda_{max} = \begin{cases} \underset{1 \le j \le n}{\text{minimum}} \left\{ \dfrac{-x_{jk}}{d_{jk}} : d_{jk} < 0 \right\} & \text{if } \vec{d}_k \ngeq \vec{0} \\ \infty & \text{if } \vec{d}_k \ge \vec{0} \end{cases} \tag{6}$$

and x_{jk}, d_{jk} are the jth components of $\vec{x}_k$ and $\vec{d}_k$, respectively. Let λ_k be an optimal solution, and let $\vec{x}_{k+1} = \vec{x}_k + \lambda_k \vec{d}_k$. Replace k by k + 1, and repeat step 1.

Applying the algorithm:

Iteration 1

Search Direction: At the point $\vec{x}_1 = (0,0,2,5)^t$, one gets $\vec{\nabla} f(\vec{x}_1) = (-4, -6, 0, 0)$. By (1), one gets $I_1 = \{3,4\}$, so that $\vec{B} = [\vec{a}_3, \vec{a}_4]$ and $\vec{N} = [\vec{a}_1, \vec{a}_2]$. From (3), the reduced gradient is given by

$$\vec{r}^t = (-4, -6, 0, 0) - (0, 0) \begin{bmatrix} 1 & 1 & 1 & 0 \\ 1 & 5 & 0 & 1 \end{bmatrix} = (-4, -6, 0, 0)$$

Note that the computations for the reduced gradient are

similar to the computations for the objective row coefficients in the simplex method. Also, $r_i = 0$ for $i \in I_1$. The information at this point is summarized in the tableau below.

		x_1	x_2	x_3	x_4
Solution $\vec{x}_1$		0	0	2	5
$\vec{\nabla} f(\vec{x}_1)$		−4	−6	0	0
$\vec{\nabla}_B f(\vec{x}_1) = \begin{bmatrix} 0 \\ 0 \end{bmatrix}$	x_3	1	1	1	0
	x_4	1	5	0	1
$\vec{r}$		−4	−6	0	0

By (4), then, one gets $\vec{d}_N = (d_1, d_2)^t = (4,6)^t$. Then compute $\vec{d}_B$ using (5) to get

$$\vec{d}_B = (d_3, d_4)^t = -\vec{B}^{-1}\vec{N}\vec{d}_N = -\begin{bmatrix} 1 & 1 \\ 1 & 5 \end{bmatrix}\begin{pmatrix} 4 \\ 6 \end{pmatrix} = (-10, -34)^t$$

Note that $\vec{B}^{-1}\vec{N}$ is recorded under the variables corresponding to $\vec{N}$, namely x_1 and x_2. The direction vector is, then, $\vec{d}_1 = (4, 6, -10, -34)^t$.

Line Search: Start from $\vec{x}_1 = (0, 0, 2, 5)^t$. Now minimize the objective function along the direction $\vec{d}_1 = (4, 6, -10, -34)^t$. The maximum value of λ such that $\vec{x}_1 + \lambda\vec{d}_1$ is feasible is computed using (6), and one gets

$$\lambda_{max} = \text{minimum}\left\{\frac{2}{10}, \frac{5}{34}\right\} = \frac{5}{34}$$

Verify that $f(\vec{x}_1 + \lambda\vec{d}_1) = 56\lambda^2 - 52\lambda$ so that λ_1 is the solution to the following problem:

$$\text{Minimize } 56\lambda^2 - 52\lambda$$
$$\text{subject to } 0 \le \lambda \le \frac{5}{34}$$

Clearly $\lambda_1 = \frac{5}{34}$, so that $\vec{x}_2 = \vec{x}_1 + \lambda_1\vec{d}_1 = (\frac{10}{17}, \frac{15}{17}, \frac{9}{17}, 0)^t$.

Iteration 1 is, thus, completed.

Table 1 **Summary of Computations for the Reduced Gradient Method of Wolfe**

Iteration			Search Direction		Line Search	
k	$\vec{x}_k$	$f(\vec{x}_k)$	$\vec{r}_k$	$\vec{d}_k$	λ_k	$\vec{x}_{k+1}$
1	$(0, 0, 2, 5)$	0.0	$(-4, -6, 0, 0)$	$(4, 6, -10, -34)$	$\frac{5}{34}$	$(\frac{10}{17}, \frac{15}{17}, \frac{9}{17}, 0)$
2	$(\frac{10}{17}, \frac{15}{17}, \frac{9}{17}, 0)$	−6.436	$(0, 0, \frac{57}{17}, \frac{4}{17})$	$(\frac{2565}{1156}, -\frac{513}{1156}, -\frac{513}{289}, 0)$	$\frac{68}{279}$	$(\frac{35}{31}, \frac{24}{31}, \frac{3}{31}, 0)$
3	$(\frac{35}{31}, \frac{24}{31}, \frac{3}{31}, 0)$	−7.16	$(0, 0, 0, 1)$	$(0, 0, 0, 0)$		

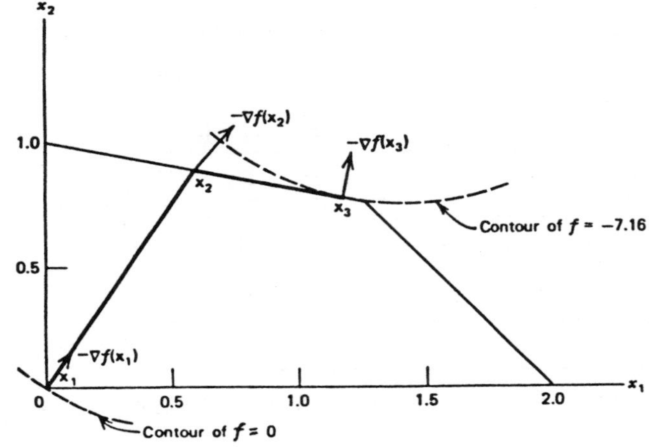

Illustration of the reduced gradient method of Wolfe.

Fig. 1

At iteration 3, from (4), $\vec{d}_N = (d_3, d_4)^t = (0,0)^t$, and from (5), $\vec{d}_B = (d_1, d_2)^t = (0,0)^t$. Hence, $\vec{d} = \vec{0}$, and the solution $\vec{x}_3$ is optimal. Table 1 gives the summary of the computations, and the progress of the algorithm is shown in Figure 1.

• PROBLEM 10- 51

Consider the following problem:

Minimize

$$2x_1^2 + 2x_2^2 - 2x_1x_2 - 4x_1 - 6x_2$$

subject to

$$x_1 + x_2 + x_3 = 2$$

$$x_1 + 5x_2 + x_4 = 5$$

$$x_1, x_2, x_3, x_4 \geq 0$$

Solve the problem using Zangwill's convex simplex method starting from the point $\vec{x}_1 = (0,0,2,5)^t$. Note that

$$\vec{\nabla}f(\vec{x}) = (4x_1 - 2x_2 - 4,\ 4x_2 - 2x_1 - 6,\ 0,\ 0)^t$$

Solution: Summary of Zangwill's convex simplex method is as follows:

Initialization Step: Choose a point $\vec{x}_1$ such that $\vec{A}\vec{x}_1 = \vec{b}$ and $\vec{x}_1 \geq \vec{0}$. Let k = 1, and go to the main step.

Main Step:

1. Give $\vec{x}_k$, identify I_k, $\vec{B}$, $\vec{N}$, and compute $\vec{r}$ as follows:

$$I_k = \text{index set of m largest components of } \vec{x}_k \tag{1}$$

$$\vec{B} = \{\vec{a}_i : j \in I_k\}, \qquad \vec{N} = \{\vec{a}_j : j \notin I_k\} \tag{2}$$

$$\vec{r}^t = \vec{\nabla} f(\vec{x}_k)^t - \vec{\nabla}_B f(\vec{x}_k)^t \vec{B}^{-1} \vec{A} \tag{3}$$

If $\alpha = \beta = 0$, stop. If $\alpha > \beta$, compute $\vec{d}_N$ from (6) and (8). If $\alpha < \beta$, compute $\vec{d}_N$ from (7) and (9). If $\alpha = \beta \neq 0$, compute $\vec{d}_N$ either from (6) and (8) or else from (7) and (9). In all cases, determine $\vec{d}_B$ from (10) and go to step 2.

$$\alpha = \text{maximum } \{-r_j : r_j \leq 0\} \tag{4}$$

$$\beta = \text{maximum } \{x_j r_j : r_j \geq 0\} \tag{5}$$

$$v = \begin{cases} \text{an index such that } \alpha = -r_v & (6) \\ \text{an index such that } \beta = x_v r_v & (7) \end{cases}$$

$$d_j = \begin{cases} 0 & \text{if } j \notin I_k,\ j \neq v \\ 1 & \text{if } j \notin I_k,\ j = v \end{cases} \tag{8}$$

$$d_j = \begin{cases} 0 & \text{if } j \notin I_k,\ j \neq v \\ -1 & \text{if } j \notin I_k,\ j = v \end{cases} \tag{9}$$

$$\vec{d}_B = -\vec{B}^{-1} \vec{N} \vec{d}_N \tag{10}$$

2. Consider the following line search problem:

Minimize

$$f(\vec{x}_k + \lambda \vec{d}_k)$$

subject to

$$0 \leq \lambda \leq \lambda_{max}$$

where

$$\lambda_{max} = \begin{cases} \underset{1 \leq j \leq n}{\text{minimum}} \left\{ \dfrac{-x_{jk}}{d_{jk}} : d_{jk} < 0 \right\} & \text{if } \vec{d}_k \geq \vec{0} \\ \infty & \text{if } \vec{d}_k \not\geq \vec{0} \end{cases} \tag{11}$$

and x_{jk}, d_{jk} are the jth components of $\vec{x}_k$ and $\vec{d}_k$, respectively. Let λ_k be an optimal solution, and let $\vec{x}_{k+1} = \vec{x}_k + \lambda_k\vec{d}_k$. Replace k by k + 1, and go to step 1.

Applying the algorithm:

Iteration 1

Search Direction: At the point $\vec{x}_1 = (0,0,2,5)^t$, one has $\vec{\nabla}f(\vec{x}_1) = (-4,-6,0,0)^t$. From (1), one then has $I_1 = \{3,4\}$, so that $\vec{B} = [\vec{a}_3,\vec{a}_4]$ and $N = [\vec{a}_1,\vec{a}_2]$. The reduced gradient is computed using (3) as follows

$$\vec{r}^t = (-4,-6,0,0) - (0,0)\begin{bmatrix}1 & 1 & 1 & 0\\ 1 & 5 & 0 & 1\end{bmatrix} = (-4,-6,0,0)$$

The tableau at this stage is given below

		x_1	x_2	x_3	x_4
Solution $\vec{x}_1$		0	0	2	5
$\vec{\nabla}f(\vec{x}_1)$		−4	−6	0	0
$\vec{\nabla}_B f(\vec{x}_1) = \begin{bmatrix}0\\0\end{bmatrix}$	x_3	1	1	1	0
	x_4	1	5	0	1
$\vec{r}$		−4	−6	0	0

Now from (4), α = maximum $\{-r_1, -r_2, -r_3, -r_4\} = -r_2 = 6$. Also from (5), β = maximum $\{x_3r_3, x_4r_4\} = 0$, and hence from (6) $v = 2$. Note that $-r_2 = 6$ implies that x_2 can be increased to yield a reduced objective function value. The search direction is given by (8) and (10). From (8), one gets $\vec{d}_N^t = (d_1, d_2) = (0,1)$, and from (10) one gets $d_B^t = (d_3,d_4) = -(1,5)$. Note that $\vec{d}_B$ is the negative of the column of x_2 in the above tableau. Hence $\vec{d}_1 = (0,1,-1,-5)^t$.

Line Search: Starting from the point $\vec{x}_1 = (0,0,2,5)^t$, search along the direction $\vec{d}_1 = (0,1,-1,-5)^t$. The maximum value of λ such that $\vec{x}_1 + \lambda\vec{d}_1$ is feasible is given by (11). In this case,

$$\lambda_{max} = \text{minimum}\left\{\frac{2}{1}, \frac{5}{5}\right\} = 1$$

Also, $f(\vec{x}_1 + \lambda\vec{d}_1) = 2\lambda^2 - 6\lambda$. Hence, solve the following problem:

Minimize

$$2\lambda^2 - 6\lambda$$

subject to

$$0 \leq \lambda \leq 1$$

The optimal solution is $\lambda_1 = 1$ so that $\vec{x}_2 = \vec{x}_1 + \lambda_1\vec{d}_1 = (0,1,1,0)^t$. This completes the first iteration.

Table 1 **Summary of Computations for the Convex Simplex Method of Zangwill**

Iteration			Search Direction		Line Search	
k	$\vec{x}_k$	$f(\vec{x}_k)$	$\vec{r}$	$\vec{d}$	λ_k	$\vec{x}_{k+1}$
1	$(0, 0, 2, 5)$	0.0	$(-4, -6, 0, 0)$	$(0, 1, -1, -5)$	1	$(0, 1, 1, 0)$
2	$(0, 1, 1, 0)$	−4.0	$(-\frac{28}{5}, 0, 0, \frac{2}{5})$	$(1, -\frac{1}{5}, -\frac{4}{5}, 0)$	$\frac{35}{31}$	$(\frac{35}{31}, \frac{24}{31}, \frac{3}{31}, 0)$
3	$(\frac{35}{31}, \frac{24}{31}, \frac{3}{31}, 0)$	−7.16	$(0, 0, 0, 1)$			

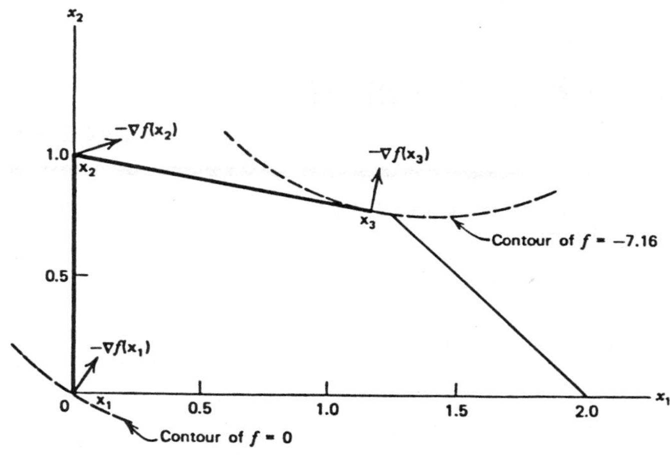

Illustration of the convex simplex method of Zangwill.

Fig. 1

At the third iteration, α = maximum $\{-r_1, -r_2, -r_3\} = 0$ and β = maximum $\{x_1r_1, x_2r_2, x_3r_3, x_4r_4\} = 0$. Hence, the point $\vec{x}_3 = (\frac{35}{31}, \frac{24}{31}, \frac{3}{31}, 0)^t$ is optimal. The summary of the computations is given in Table 1. The progress of the algorithm is depicted in Figure 1.

CHAPTER 11

QUADRATIC, GEOMETRIC, FRACTIONAL AND SEPARABLE PROGRAMMING

QUADRATIC PROGRAMMING

• PROBLEM 11-1

In each of the following cases write the objective function in the form

$$y = \vec{x}^T \vec{H}\vec{x} + \vec{q}^T\vec{x}:$$

(a) $y = x_1^2 + 2x_1x_2 + 4x_1x_3 + 3x_2^2 + 2x_2x_3 + 5x_3^2 + 4x_1 - 2x_2 + 3x_3.$

(b) $y = 5x_1^2 + 12x_1x_2 - 16x_1x_3 + 10x_2^2 - 26x_2x_3 + 17x_3^2 - 2x_1 - 4x_2 - 6x_3.$

(c) $y = x_1^2 - 4x_1x_2 + 6x_1x_3 + 5x_2^2 - 10_2x_3 + 8x_3^2.$

Solution:

(a) $\vec{H} = \begin{bmatrix} 1 & 1 & 2 \\ 1 & 3 & 1 \\ 2 & 1 & 5 \end{bmatrix}, \quad \vec{q} = \begin{bmatrix} 4 \\ -2 \\ 3 \end{bmatrix}.$

(b) $\vec{H} = \begin{bmatrix} 5 & 6 & -8 \\ 6 & 10 & -13 \\ -8 & -13 & 17 \end{bmatrix}, \quad \vec{q} = \begin{bmatrix} -2 \\ -4 \\ -6 \end{bmatrix}.$

(c) $\vec{H} = \begin{bmatrix} 1 & -2 & 3 \\ -2 & 5 & -5 \\ 3 & -5 & 8 \end{bmatrix}, \quad \vec{q} = \begin{bmatrix} 0 \\ 0 \\ 0 \end{bmatrix}.$

• PROBLEM 11-2

Consider the quadratic function in two variables

$$f(x_1,x_2) = k + dx_1 + ex_2 + cx_2^2 + bx_1x_2 + ax_1^2,$$

where a, b, d, e, and k are constant real numbers. Find the conditions under which $f(x_1,x_2)$ is positive definite, and determine the shape of its level curves.

Solution: Rewrite the problem in vector-matrix notation.

$$f(\vec{x}) = k + \ d,e \begin{bmatrix} x_1 \\ \\ x_2 \end{bmatrix} + \frac{1}{2}\begin{bmatrix} x_1, x_2 \end{bmatrix} \begin{bmatrix} 2a & b \\ \\ b & 2c \end{bmatrix} \begin{bmatrix} x_1 \\ \\ x_2 \end{bmatrix} . \quad (1)$$

Here the matrix $\vec{A}$ is given by

$$\vec{A} = \begin{bmatrix} 2a & b \\ \\ b & 2c \end{bmatrix}$$

Now if

$$a > 0,$$

$$c > 0,$$

and

$$4ac - b^2 > 0,$$

then $\vec{A}$ is positive definite. Hence by definition,

$$f(x_1,x_2)$$

is also positive definite. Now by definition, $4ac - b^2$ is the discriminant of the quadratic equation given by the problem. If the discriminant is positive, then the graph in E^2 of $f(x_1,x_2) = k$ (a constant) is an ellipse. Thus the level curves of $f(x_1,x_2)$ are concentric ellipses.

• PROBLEM 11-3

Consider the quadratic function given by

$$f(x_1,x_2) = k + dx_1 + ex_2 + cx_2^2 + bx_1x_2 + ax_1^2$$

where

$$a = d = k=1,$$

$$e = -1,$$

$$b = 0,$$

and

$$c = 2.$$

Draw its level curves.

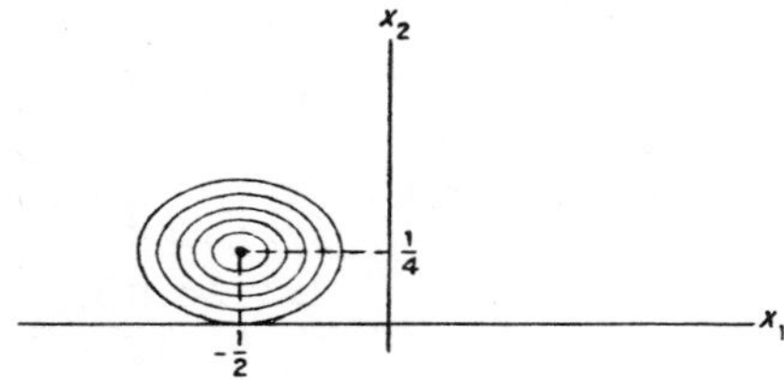

Fig. 1

Solution: Write

$$f(x_1,x_2) = 1 + x_1 - x_2 + x_1^2 + 2x_2^2$$

$$= \frac{5}{8} + \left(x_1 + \frac{1}{2}\right)^2 + 2\left(x_2 - \frac{1}{4}\right)^2$$

by completing the square. From the above equation

$$f(x_1,x_2) = k$$

(a constant) is an ellipse with center at

$$x_1 = -\frac{1}{2}$$

and

$$x_2 = \frac{1}{4},$$

as shown in the Fig. 1. Also note that

$$f(x_1,x_2) \geq \frac{5}{8}$$

and

$$f\left(-\frac{1}{2}, \frac{1}{4}\right) = \frac{5}{8},$$

i.e.,

$$f(x_1,x_2)$$

attains a minimum at the center of the set of concentric ellipses.

• PROBLEM 11-4

Apply Wolfe's algorithm to the following problem:

$$\text{Max } z = 3x_1 + 4x_2 - x_1^2 + 2x_1x_2 - 2x_2^2$$

subject to

$$x_1 + 2x_2 \leqq 7,$$

$$-x_1 + 2x_2 \leqq 4,$$

and

$$x_1,\ x_2 \geqq 0.$$

Solution: Observe that the quadratic form

$$-x_1^2 + 2x_1x_2 - 2x_2^2 = -(x_1 - x_2)^2 - x_2^2$$

is negative definite. The constraints may be converted to the standard form

$$\text{Max } \vec{z} = \vec{c}^T\vec{x} + \vec{x}^T\vec{D}\vec{x}$$

subject to

$$A\vec{x} = \vec{b}$$

and

$$\vec{x} \geq 0$$

by the addition of slack variables:

$$x_1 + 2x_2 + x_3 \qquad = 7$$

$$-x_1 + 2x_2 \qquad + x_4 = 4,$$

and

$$x_1, x_2, x_3, x_4 \geqq 0.$$

$$\vec{A} = \begin{bmatrix} 1 & 2 & 1 & 0 \\ -1 & 2 & 0 & 1 \end{bmatrix}$$

and

$$\vec{D} = \begin{bmatrix} -1 & 1 & 0 & 0 \\ 1 & -2 & 0 & 0 \\ 0 & 0 & 0 & 0 \\ 0 & 0 & 0 & 0 \end{bmatrix},$$

and the system of constraint equations

$$\vec{A}\vec{x} = \vec{b}$$

$$2\vec{D}x - \vec{A}^T\vec{\lambda} + \vec{A}^T 1\lambda_0 + \vec{V} = -\vec{C}$$

$$\vec{x},\ \vec{\lambda},\ \lambda_0,\ \vec{V} \geq 0$$

$$x_i v_i = 0,$$

$$j = 1,\ldots,n$$

is written as follows:

$$\begin{aligned}
x_1 + 2x_2 + x_3 &= 7, \\
-x_1 + 2x_2 + x_4 &= 4, \\
-2x_1 + 2x_2 - \lambda_1 + \lambda_2 + v_1 &= -3, \\
2x_1 - 4x_2 - 2\lambda_1 - 2\lambda_2 + 4\lambda_0 + v_2 &= -4, \\
-\lambda_1 + \lambda_0 + v_3 &= 0, \\
-\lambda_2 + \lambda_0 + v_4 &= 0,
\end{aligned}$$

with

$$\vec{x},\ \vec{\lambda},\ \lambda_0,\ \vec{v} \geqq \vec{0}$$

and

$$x_j v_j = 0,$$

$$j = 1,\ldots,4.$$

It is convenient to use as a starting point the origin

$$x_1 = x_2 = 0,$$

the associated basic solution to

$$\vec{A}\vec{x} = \vec{b}$$

is then

$$\vec{x}_B = (x_3, x_4) = (7,4).$$

Now compute

$$\vec{\hat{u}} = -\vec{c} - 2\vec{D}_B\vec{x}_B = (-3,\ -4,\ 0,\ 0)$$

and add artificial variables to the constraints above in accordance with

$$\Delta_j = \begin{cases} +1 & \text{if } \hat{u}_j \geq 0 \\ -1 & \text{if } \hat{u}_j < 0 \end{cases}$$

$$\begin{aligned}
x_1+2x_2+x_3 & & & & &= 7,\\
-x_1+2x_2 \quad +x_4 & & & & &= 4,\\
-2x_1+2x_2 & -\lambda_1+\lambda_2 & +v_1 & & -u_1 &= -3,\\
2x_1-4x_2 & -2\lambda_1-2\lambda_2+4\lambda_0 & +v_2 & & -u_2 &= -4,\\
& -\lambda_1 \quad +\lambda_0 & +v_3 & & +u_3 &= 0,\\
& \quad -\lambda_2+\lambda_0 & +v_4 & & +u_4 &= 0,
\end{aligned} \tag{1}$$

with

$$\vec{x},\ \vec{\lambda},\ \lambda_0,\ \vec{v},\ \vec{u} \geqq \vec{0}.$$

The initial basic solution to this set of constraints is then

$$\begin{bmatrix} x_3 \\ x_4 \\ u_1 \\ u_2 \\ u_3 \\ u_4 \end{bmatrix} = \begin{bmatrix} 7 \\ 4 \\ 3 \\ 4 \\ 0 \\ 0 \end{bmatrix}, \quad \text{with basis matrix} \begin{bmatrix} 1 & 0 & 0 & 0 & 0 & 0 \\ 0 & 1 & 0 & 0 & 0 & 0 \\ 0 & 0 & -1 & 0 & 0 & 0 \\ 0 & 0 & 0 & -1 & 0 & 0 \\ 0 & 0 & 0 & 0 & 1 & 0 \\ 0 & 0 & 0 & 0 & 0 & 1 \end{bmatrix},$$

and the task now is to use the simplex method with restricted basis entry to maximize

$$z' = -u_1 - u_2 - u_3 - u_4$$

subject to the constraints (1) and to the complementary slackness conditions

$$x_j v_j = 0,$$

$$j = 1,\ldots,4.$$

Before beginning the computations, however, note that two of the artificial basic variables, u_3 and u_4 , have zero values. Therefore attempt to simplify matters somewhat by dropping them from the problem entirely and replacing them in the basis with v_3 and v_4, whose columns of constraint coefficients in (1) are, respectively, identical. This maneuver is permissible in that it does not violate the conditions

$$x_j v_j = 0.$$

However, it does have the disadvantage of introducing two complementary pairs of variables into the basis simultaneously, which means that in subsequent pivots we shall have to keep an eye on the values of all basic variables in order to be sure that complementary slackness is preserved.

Now proceed with the computations. The problem will be solved by the revised simplex method. The initial basic variables are

$$\vec{x}_B = (x_3, x_4, u_1, u_2, v_3, v_4) = (7,4,3,4,0,0),$$

with the cost coefficients

$$c_B = (0,0,-1,-1,0,0),$$

and the basis matrix $\vec{B}$ is as given above.

$$\vec{B}^{-1} = \vec{B},$$

so the auxiliary vector for computing reduced costs is

$$\vec{C}_B^T\vec{B}^{-1} = [0,0,1,1,0,0],$$

and the augmented matrix inverse used by the revised simplex method is

$$(\vec{B}^*)^{-1} = \begin{bmatrix} \vec{B}^{-1} & 0 \\ \vec{C}_B^T\vec{B}^{-1} & 1 \end{bmatrix} = \begin{bmatrix} 1 & 0 & 0 & 0 & 0 & 0 & 0 \\ 0 & 1 & 0 & 0 & 0 & 0 & 0 \\ 0 & 0 & -1 & 0 & 0 & 0 & 0 \\ 0 & 0 & 0 & -1 & 0 & 0 & 0 \\ 0 & 0 & 0 & 0 & 1 & 0 & 0 \\ 0 & 0 & 0 & 0 & 0 & 1 & 0 \\ 0 & 0 & 1 & 1 & 0 & 0 & 1 \end{bmatrix}$$

In general, the reduced cost of any nonbasic variable x_j is obtained by multiplying the last row of $(\vec{B}^*)^{-1}$ by the augmented "activity column"

$$\vec{a}_j^* \equiv (\vec{a}_j, -c_j),$$

where $\vec{a}_j$ is the column of constraint coefficients associated with x_j. In the case of x_1, for example, the reduced cost is

$$z_1 - c_1 = [\vec{c}_B^T\vec{B}^{-1}, 1] \cdot (\vec{a}_1, -c_1)$$

$$= [0,0,1,1,0,0,1] \cdot (1, -1, -2,2,0,0,0) = 0$$

and find that the reduced costs for the other nonbasic variables x_2 λ_1, λ_2, λ_0, v_1, and v_2 are, respectively, -2, - 3, -1, 4, 1, and 1. Because this is a maximization problem, choose the variable having the most negative reduced cost, in this case λ_1, to enter the basis; note, however, that this choice must be rejected if it leads to a violation of complementary slackness. To determine which basic variable will be replaced, compute

$$\vec{y}_5^* = (\vec{B}^*)^{-1}\vec{a}_5^* = \begin{bmatrix} 1 & 0 & 0 & 0 & 0 & 0 & 0 \\ 0 & 1 & 0 & 0 & 0 & 0 & 0 \\ 0 & 0 & -1 & 0 & 0 & 0 & 0 \\ 0 & 0 & 0 & -1 & 0 & 0 & 0 \\ 0 & 0 & 0 & 0 & 1 & 0 & 0 \\ 0 & 0 & 0 & 0 & 0 & 1 & 0 \\ 0 & 0 & 1 & 1 & 0 & 0 & 1 \end{bmatrix} \begin{bmatrix} 0 \\ 0 \\ -1 \\ -2 \\ -1 \\ 0 \\ 0 \end{bmatrix}$$

$$= \begin{bmatrix} 0 \\ 0 \\ 1 \\ 2 \\ -1 \\ 0 \\ -3 \end{bmatrix} = \begin{bmatrix} \left.\begin{matrix} \\ \\ \\ \\ \\ \end{matrix}\right\} y_5 \\ z_5 - c_5 \end{bmatrix},$$

where the subscript 5 is used because λ_1 is the fifth variable, reading from left to right, in the constraint set (1). Applying the simplex exit criterion, one finds that

$$\min_i \left(\frac{x_{Bi}}{y_{i5}}, \; y_{i5} > 0 \right) = \min \left(\frac{3}{1}, \frac{4}{2} \right) = \frac{4}{2} = \frac{x_{B4}}{y_{45}}$$

so $x_{B4} = u_2 = 4$ leaves the basis. The columns of $(\vec{B}^*)^{-1}$ and the vector of values

$$\vec{x}_B^* = (\vec{x}_B, z')$$

are updated in exactly the same way as the columns of the simplex tableau in a standard simplex pivot. In the present case the computational vector is

$$\vec{\phi} = \left(\frac{-y_{15}}{y_{45}}, \frac{-y_{25}}{y_{45}}, \frac{-y_{35}}{y_{45}}, \frac{1}{y_{45}} - 1, \frac{-y_{55}}{y_{45}}, \frac{-y_{65}}{y_{45}}, \frac{-(z_5 - c_5)}{y_{45}} \right)$$

$$= (0,0,-.5,-.5,.5,0,1.5),$$

and the new values of the basic variables turn out to be

$$\vec{x}_B^* = (x_3, x_4, u_1, \lambda_1, v_3, v_4, z') = (7,4,1,2,2,0,-1). \qquad (2)$$

But observe that

$$x_3 v_3 \neq 0$$

in this solution. Complementary slackness has been violated, and one concludes that some variable other than λ_1 must be chosen to enter the basis. Return to the initial basic solution and select x_2, which has the second most favorable reduced cost, to be the entering variable. Now find that

$$\vec{y}^* = (2,2,-2,4,0,0,-2),$$

the exiting variable is

$$x_{B4} = u_2 = 4,$$

the computational vector

$$\vec{\Phi} = (-.5,-.5,.5,-.75,0,0,.5),$$

and the new values are

$$(\vec{B}^*)^{-1} = \begin{bmatrix} 1 & 0 & 0 & .5 & 0 & 0 & 0 \\ 0 & 1 & 0 & .5 & 0 & 0 & 0 \\ 0 & 0 & -1 & -.5 & 0 & 0 & 0 \\ 0 & 0 & 0 & -.25 & 0 & 0 & 0 \\ 0 & 0 & 0 & 0 & 1 & 0 & 0 \\ 0 & 0 & 0 & 0 & 0 & 1 & 0 \\ 0 & 0 & 1 & .5 & 0 & 0 & 1 \end{bmatrix} \quad \text{and} \quad \begin{bmatrix} x_3 \\ x_4 \\ u_1 \\ x_2 \\ v_3 \\ v_4 \\ z' \end{bmatrix} = \begin{bmatrix} 5 \\ 2 \\ 5 \\ 1 \\ 0 \\ 0 \\ -5 \end{bmatrix}.$$

Complementary slackness has been preserved, and the pivot is accepted.

Moving on to the next iteration, it is determined that the reduced costs of the nonbasic variables $x_1,\lambda_1,\lambda_2,\lambda_0,v_1$, and v_2 are $-1,-2,0,2,1$, and $.5$. The first choice for basis entry is therefore the fifth variable λ_1. However, one finds that

$$\vec{y}^*_5 = (-1,-1,2,0.5,-1,0,-2)$$

and

$$\min_i \left(\frac{x_{Bi}}{y_{i5}}, \; y_{i5} > 0 \right) = \min \left(\frac{5}{2}, \; \frac{1}{.5} \right) = \frac{1}{.5} = \frac{x_{B4}}{y_{45}},$$

so that if λ_1 were to enter the basis the variable ejected would be

$$x_{B4} = x_2 = 1.$$

This would again produce the basic solution (2), which is already known to be unacceptable. Therefore pass on to the second choice and try to bring x_1 into the basis. The computations proceed as follows:

$$\vec{y}_1^* = (2,0,1,-0.5,0,0,-1),$$

$$\min_i\left(\frac{x_{Bi}}{y_{i_1}},\ y_{i_1} > 0\right) = \min\left(\frac{5}{2},\ \frac{5}{1}\right) = \frac{5}{2} = \frac{x_{B_1}}{y_{11}},$$

$$\vec{\Phi} = (-.5,0,-.5,.25,0,0,.5)$$

and

$$(\vec{B}^*)^{-1} = \begin{bmatrix} .5 & 0 & 0 & .25 & 0 & 0 & 0 \\ 0 & 1 & 0 & .5 & 0 & 0 & 0 \\ -.5 & 0 & -1 & -.75 & 0 & 0 & 0 \\ .25 & 0 & 0 & -.125 & 0 & 0 & 0 \\ 0 & 0 & 0 & 0 & 1 & 0 & 0 \\ 0 & 0 & 0 & 0 & 0 & 1 & 0 \\ .5 & 0 & 1 & .75 & 0 & 0 & 1 \end{bmatrix} \text{ and } \begin{bmatrix} x_1 \\ x_4 \\ u_1 \\ x_2 \\ v_3 \\ v_4 \\ z' \end{bmatrix} = \begin{bmatrix} 2.5 \\ 2 \\ 2.5 \\ 2.25 \\ 0 \\ 0 \\ -2.5 \end{bmatrix}.$$

The complementary slackness conditions are satisfied, and the new solution is accepted.

In recomputing the reduced costs for the third iteration it is again found that λ_1 is the preferred candidate for basis entry. This time, however, the pivot is successful:

$$\vec{y}_5^* = (-.5,-1,2.5,.25,-1,0,-2.5),$$

$$\min_i\left(\frac{x_{Bi}}{y_{i5}},\ y_{i5} > 0\right) = \min\left(\frac{2.5}{2.5},\ \frac{2.25}{.25}\right) = \frac{2.5}{2.5} = \frac{x_{B3}}{y_{35}},$$

$$\vec{\Phi} = (.2,.4,-.6,-.1,.4,0,1),$$

and

$$\vec{x}_B^* = (x_1,x_4,\lambda_1,x_2,v_3,v_4,z')$$

$$= (3,3,1,2,1,0,0).$$

Complementary slackness remains satisfied, and the last artificial variable has been driven out of the basis. The current basic solution is therefore optimal, which means that

$$(x_1,x_2,x_3,x_4) = (3,2,0,3)$$

constitutes an optimal solution to the original quadratic program. The value of the objective at this point is

$$z = 12.$$

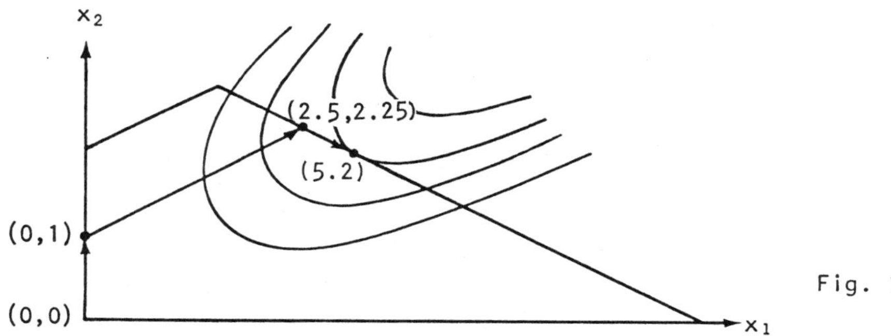

Fig. 1

The feasible region of the original problem and the sequence of solution points generated by Wolfe's algorithm are plotted in Fig. 1. Several indifference curves of the objective function are also shown. Notice that the solutions generated at the various stages do not always coincide with extreme points. In fact, in the general case they need not even be boundary points.

• PROBLEM 11-5

Consider the problem

maximize

$$x_1 + x_2 - (1/2)x_1^2 + x_1x_2 - x_2^2$$

subject to

$$x_1 + x_2 \le 3$$

$$2x_1 + 3x_2 \ge 6$$

$$x_1,\quad x_2 \ge 0$$

Use Wolfe's algorithm to solve this quadratic program.

Solution: Here

$$\vec{D} = \begin{bmatrix} -1/2 & 1/2 \\ 1/2 & -1 \end{bmatrix}$$

$$\vec{c} = \begin{bmatrix} 1 \\ 1 \end{bmatrix}$$

$$\vec{b} = \begin{bmatrix} 3 \\ -6 \end{bmatrix}$$

$$\vec{A} = \begin{bmatrix} 1 & 1 \\ -2 & -3 \end{bmatrix}$$

D is negative definite since all principal minor determinants of -D are positive; i.e.,

$$|1/2| = 1/2$$

and

$$\begin{vmatrix} 1/2 & -1/2 \\ -1/2 & 1 \end{vmatrix} = 1/2 - 1/4 = 1/4$$

The equation

$$\begin{bmatrix} 2\vec{D} & \vec{0}_{n\times m} & -\vec{A}^1 & \vec{I}_n \\ \vec{A} & \vec{I}_m & \vec{0}_{m\times m} & \vec{0}_{m\times n} \end{bmatrix} \begin{bmatrix} \vec{X} \\ \vec{X}_s \\ \vec{Y} \\ \vec{V} \end{bmatrix} = \begin{bmatrix} -\vec{c} \\ \\ \vec{b} \end{bmatrix}$$

implies that the initial tableau is

Tableau 1

$\vec{c}_B$	Basis	P_0	P_1	P_2	P_3	P_4	P_5	P_6	P_7	P_8	A_1	A_2	A_3	θ
-1	A_1	1	1	-1	0	0	1	-2	-1	0	1	0	0	-1
-1	A_2	1	-1	[2]	0	0	1	-3	0	-1	0	1	0	1/2
0	P_3	3	1	1	1	0	0	0	0	0	0	0	0	3
-1	A_3	6	2	3	0	-1	0	0	0	0	0	0	1	2
	$\vec{z} - \vec{c}$	-8	-2	-4	0	1	-2	5	1	1	0	0	0	

Before introducing appropriate artificial variables to establish an initial solution,one must multiply each row by -1 if its right-hand component is negative since the simplex algorithm requires that the constraint vector be greater than or equal to zero. Also, in Tableau 1 only three artificial variables are introduced since the vector P_3 is in the initial basic solution; the three artificial variables can be assigned any arbitrary negative cost, for convenience say -1.

Now introduce any vector with a corresponding negative

$$z_j - c_j$$

to enter the solution. Choosing P_2 to enter, one sees that A_2 leaves the basis since

$$\theta_2 = 1/2 = \min_i \{\theta_i | \theta_i \geq 0\}.$$

This results in Tableau 2. Now one can delete A_2 from the tableau since it will never be considered as a candidate for re-entry into the basis.

Tableau 2

$\vec{c}_B$	Basis	P_0	P_1	P_2	P_3	P_4	P_5	P_6	P_7	P_8	A_1	A_2	A_3	θ
-1	A_1	3/2	1/2	0	0	0	3/2	-7/2	-1	-1/2	1	1/2	0	3
0	P_2	1/2	-1/2	1	0	0	1/2	-3/2	0	-1/2	0	1/2	0	-1
0	P_3	5/2	3/2	0	1	0	-1/2	3/2	0	1/2	0	-1/2	0	5/3
-1	A_3	9/2	[7/2]	0	0	-1	-3/2	9/2	0	3/2	0	-3/2	1	9/7
	$\vec{z} - \vec{c}$	-6	-4	0	0	1	0	1	1	-1	0	2	0	

The vector P_1 can enter the basis without violating rules

(1). If a variable x_j (or v_j) is currently in the basis at a positive level, do not consider v_j (or x_j) as a candidate for entry into the basis. If x_j (or v_j) is currently in the basis at a zero level, then v_j (or x_j) may enter the basis only if x_j (or v_j) remains at a zero level.

or

(2). If a variable y_i (or x_{s_i}) is currently in the basis at a positive level, do not consider x_{s_i} (or y_i) as a candidate for entry into the basis. If y_i (or x_{s_i}) is in the basis at a zero level, x_{s_i} (or y_i) may enter the basis only if y_i (or x_{s_i}) remains at a zero level; hence when P_1 enters the basis then A_3 will leave the basis. Thus the following tableau is obtained.

Tableau 3

$\vec{c}_B$	Basis	P_0	P_1	P_2	P_3	P_4	P_5	P_6	P_7	P_8	A_1	A_2	A_3	θ
-1	A_1	6/7	0	0	0	1/7	12/7	-29/7	-1	-5/7	1	5/7	-1/7	6
0	P_2	8/7	0	1	0	-1/7	2/7	-6/7	0	-2/7	0	2/7	1/7	
0	P_3	4/7	0	0	1	[3/7]	1/7	-3/7	0	-1/7	0	1/7	-3/7	4/3
0	P_1	9/7	1	0	0	-2/7	-3/7	9/7	0	3/7	0	-3/7	2/7	
	$\vec{z}-\vec{c}$	-6/7	0	0	0	-1/7	-12/7	29/7	1	5/7	0	2/7	8/7	

The vectors P_4 and P_5 are candidates for entry into the basis; however if P_5 enters, rule (2) will be violated. Therefore, let P_4 enter the basis and P_3 leave the basis. The corresponding tableau follows

Tableau 4

$\vec{c}_B$	Basis	P_0	P_1	P_2	P_3	P_4	P_5	P_6	P_7	P_8	A_1	A_2	A_3	θ
-1	A_1	2/3	0	0	-1/3	0	[5/3]	-4	-1	-2/3	1	2/3	0	2/5
0	P_2	4/3	0	1	1/3	0	1/3	-1	0	-1/3	0	1/3	0	4
0	P_4	4/3	0	0	7/3	1	1/3	-1	0	-1/3	0	1/3	-1	4
0	P_1	5/3	1	0	2/3	0	-1/3	1	0	1/3	0	-1/3	0	
	$\vec{z}-\vec{c}$	-2/3	0	0	1/3	0	-5/3	4	1	2/3	0	1/3	1	

Now P_5 is eligible to enter the basis without violating rule (2), and A_1 will leave the basis. The next tableau yields an optimal solution

$$\begin{bmatrix} x_1^0 \\ \\ x_2^0 \end{bmatrix} = \begin{bmatrix} 9/5 \\ \\ 6/5 \end{bmatrix}$$

since all the components $z_j - c_j$ are nonnegative.

Tableau 5

$\vec{c}_B$	Basis	P_0	P_1	P_2	P_3	P_4	P_5	P_6	P_7	P_8
0	P_5	2/5	0	0	-1/5	0	1	-12/5	-3/5	-2/5
0	P_2	6/5	0	1	2/5	0	0	-1/5	1/5	-1/5
0	P_4	6/5	0	0	12/5	1	0	-1/5	1/5	-1/5
0	P_1	9/5	1	0	3/5	0	0	1/5	-1/5	1/5
	$\vec{z}-\vec{c}$	0	0	0	0	0	0	0	0	0

• PROBLEM 11-6

$$C = 6 - 6x_1 + 2x_1^2 - 2x_1x_2 + 2x_2^2$$

is to be minimized, subject to the constraints

$$x_1 \geq 0,\ x_2 \geq 0,\ x_1 + x_2 \leq 2$$

Solve by Beale's method making use of the simplex algorithm.

Solution: The simplex method can be applied to Beale quadratic programming. Since the constraints are all linear, one can select basic variables and solve for these in terms of the remaining, non-basic, variables in the usual way. Leaving the objective function aside for the moment, the constraints can then be expressed in tableau form as follows--

$$X_i = \bar{a}_{i0} + \sum_j \bar{a}_{ij}(-z_j)$$

where the X_i represents m of the variables x_j. In this equation the symbol z_j is used for a typical non-basic variable, rather than x_j, because introduction of additional non-basic variables that are not original variables of the problem will be considered later on.

One may assume that the $\bar{a}_{i0}$ are all non-negative-otherwise the trial solution (obtained by putting all the non-basic variables equal to zero) is infeasible. The problem of finding a basic feasible trial solution is the same in linear and quadratic programming, since the ultimate objective function is irrelevant at this stage.

One can now use the equations for the basic variables to express the objective function C, which is being minimized, in terms of the non-basic variables. One can then consider the partial derivative of C with respect to any one of them, say z_q, assuming that the other non-basic variables remain fixed and equal to zero.

If now

$$\partial C/\partial z_q > 0,$$

then a small increase in z_q, with the other non-basic variables held equal to zero, will not reduce C; but if

$$\partial C/\partial z_q < 0,$$

then a small increase in z_q will reduce C. If C is any linear or non-linear function with continuous derivatives, then it will be profitable to go on increasing z_q until either

(a) one has to stop to avoid making some basic variable, say X_p, negative, or

(b) $\partial C/\partial z_q$ vanishes and is about to become positive.

In case (a), which is the only possible case when C is linear, change the basis by making X_p non-basic instead of z_q, using the equation

$$X_p = \bar{a}_{po} + \sum \bar{a}_{pj}(-z_j)$$

to substitute for z_q in terms of X_p and the remaining non-basic variables throughout the constraints and also the expression for C.

In case (b) one is in trouble if C is an arbitrary function; but if C is a quadratic function, then $\partial C/\partial z_p$ is a linear function of the non-basic variables.

The theoretically simplest way to express C is as a symmetric matrix $(\bar{c}_{jk})$ for j,k = 0,1,..., such that

$$C = \sum \sum \bar{c}_{jk} z_j z_k$$

where

$$z_0 = 1$$

and

$$z_1, \ldots$$

denote the non-basic variables. Then

$$\frac{1}{2} \frac{\partial C}{\partial z_q} = \bar{c}_{q0} + \sum \bar{c}_{qk} z_k$$

and if this quantity becomes positive as z_q is increased (keeping the other non-basic variables equal to zero) before any basic variable goes negative, then define a new variable

$$u_t = \bar{c}_{q0} + \sum \bar{c}_{qk} z_k$$

(where the subscript t simply indicates that this is the t-th such variable introduced into the problem). Then make u_t non-basic, using the above equation to substitute for z_q in terms of u_t and the other non-basic variables throughout the constraints and the expression for C. Note that if z_q is an x-variable, then there will be one more basic x-variable after this iteration than there was before.

Note that u_t is not restricted to non-negative values. It is therefore called a free variable, to contrast it with the original x-variables which are called restricted variables. But there is no objection to having a free non-basic variable. One simply has to remember that if

$$\partial C/\partial u_t > 0,$$

then C can be reduced by making u_t negative (or alternatively by replacing u_t by the variable

$$v_t = -u_t$$

and increasing v_t in the usual way). In fact $\partial C/\partial u_t$ will remain equal to zero until another x-variable becomes non-basic. At this stage all previously defined non-basic free variables are made basic in turn, being either increased or decreased so as not to increase C. When a free variable is removed from the set of non-basic variables it can be forgotten. There are only two reasons for keeping track of the expressions for the basic variables: one is to know their values in the final solution, but the more important reason is to prevent such a variable from surreptitiously becoming negative. Neither reason applies to these free variables.

There remains the problem of justifying this particular choice of free variable to be made non-basic. It is obviously convenient to have a set of non-basic variables that all vanish at the trial solution, since the values of the basic variables are then simply given as the constant terms in the tableau, but many other expressions would achieve this.

The mathematically correct way to express this justification is to say that the new variable is chosen so that the direction defined by increasing it and keeping the other non-basic variables constant is conjugate (with respect to the quadratic objective function) to any direction defined by changing some other non-basic variable and keeping the new variable constant. In other words one tries to choose the new variable u_t so that it will not be profitable to change its value when the values of any other non-basic variables are changed.

One succeeds in this objective until some other x-variable becomes non-basic. Also, the method terminates in a finite number of steps.

Up-dating the tableau from one iteration to the next requires special methods.

The essential problem can be formulated algebraically as follows. Given the expression

$$C = \sum \sum \bar{c}_{jk} z_j z_k$$

and given the transformed pivotal row, in the form

$$z_q = e_0 + e_q N + \sum_{k \neq p} e_k z_k$$

substitute for z_q in terms of N (the new non-basic variable, which is not present in the given expression for C) and the other non-basic variables.

The new expression can be written as

$$C = \sum \sum \bar{c}'_{jk} z_j z_k$$

where

$$\bar{c}'_{qq}$$

denotes the coefficient of N^2, and

$$\bar{c}'_{qj} = \bar{c}'_{jq} ,$$

the coefficient of $2Nz_j$, so that the variable N has replaced z_q. One then finds that the $\bar{c}'_{jk}$ are given in terms of the $\bar{c}_{jk}$ and the e_k by the formulae

$$\bar{c}'_{qq} = \bar{c}_{qq} e_q^2$$

$$\bar{c}'_{jq} = \bar{c}'_{qj} = \bar{c}_{jq} e_q + \bar{c}_{qq} e_q e_j$$

$$\bar{c}'_{jk} = \bar{c}_{jk} + \bar{c}_{jq} e_k + \bar{c}_{qk} e_j + \bar{c}_{qq} e_j e_k$$

where

$$j,k \neq q.$$

These formulae simplify if one writes

$$c^*_q = \frac{1}{2}\bar{c}_{qq}e_q$$

$$c^*_j = \bar{c}_{jq} + \frac{1}{2}\bar{c}_{qq}e_j \qquad (j \neq q)$$

for one then has

$$\bar{c}'_{qq} = 2c^*_q e_q$$

$$\bar{c}'_{jq} = \bar{c}'_{qj} = c^*_j e_q + c^*_q e_j$$

$$\bar{c}'_{jk} = \bar{c}_{jk} + c^*_j e_k + c^*_k e_j$$

For this problem, introducing x_3 as a slack variable, and making it basic in the initial tableau one can write the problem in the form

$$x_3 = 2 + 1(-x_1) + 1(-x_2)$$

$$\begin{aligned} C = \; & 6 - 3x_1 \\ & + (-3 + 2x_1 - x_2)x_1 \\ & + (- x_1 + 2x_2)x_2 \end{aligned}$$

This method of displaying the objective function shows the coefficients $\bar{c}_{jk}$, and can also be read as an intelligible equation.

$$\frac{1}{2}\,\partial C/\partial x_1 = -3,$$

so increase x_1. This remains possible as far as the only basic variable x_3 is concerned until

$$x_1 = 2,$$

and at this stage

$$\frac{1}{2}\,\partial C/\partial x_1 = -3 + 2 \times 2 = +1,$$

so the first new non-basic variable is a free variable u_1, defined by

$$u_1 = -3 + 2x_1 - x_2$$

i.e.

$$x_1 = \frac{3}{2} + \frac{1}{2}u_1 + \frac{1}{2}x_2$$

Hence

$$q = 1, \qquad e_0 = \frac{3}{2}, \qquad e_1 = \frac{1}{2}, \qquad e_2 = +\frac{1}{2},$$

$$\frac{1}{2}\bar{c}_{qq} = 1, \qquad c^*_0 = -\frac{3}{2}, \qquad c^*_1 = \frac{1}{2},$$

$$c^*_2 = -\frac{1}{2}$$

and the new tableau reads

$$x_1 = \frac{3}{2} - \frac{1}{2}\ (-u_1)\ - \frac{1}{2}\ (-x_2)$$

$$x_3 = \frac{1}{2} + \frac{1}{2}\ (-u_1)\ + \frac{3}{2}\ (-x_2)$$

$$C = \left(\frac{3}{2} \qquad - \qquad \frac{3}{2}\, x_2\right)$$

$$+ \left(\qquad \frac{1}{2}\, u_1 \qquad \right) u_1$$

$$+ \left(- \frac{3}{2} \qquad + \frac{3}{2}\, x_2\right) x_2$$

Now

$$\frac{1}{2}\ \partial C/\partial x_2 = -\ \frac{3}{2}\ ,$$

so increase x_2. This remains possible until

$$x_2 = \frac{1}{3}\ ,$$

and at this stage

$$\frac{1}{2}\ \partial C/\partial x_2 = -\ \frac{3}{2} + \frac{3}{2} \times \frac{1}{3} = -1$$

so next non-basic variable is x_3.

The transformed pivotal row then reads

$$x_2 = \frac{1}{3} - \frac{1}{3}\ u_1 - \frac{2}{3}\ x_3$$

Hence

$$q = 2, \qquad e_0 = \frac{1}{3}\ , \qquad e_1 = -\ \frac{1}{3}\ , \qquad e_2 = -\ \frac{2}{3}\ ,$$

$$\frac{1}{2}\ \bar{c}_{qq} = \frac{3}{4}\ , \qquad c^*_0 = -\ \frac{5}{4}\ , \qquad c^*_1 = -\ \frac{1}{4}\ ,$$

$$c^*_2 = -\ \frac{1}{2}$$

and the new tableau reads

$$x_1 = \frac{5}{3} - \frac{1}{3}\ (-u_1)\ + \frac{1}{3}\ (-x_3)$$

$$x_2 = \frac{1}{3} + \frac{1}{3}\ (-u_1)\ + \frac{2}{3}\ (-x_3)$$

$$C = \frac{2}{3} + \frac{1}{3}\ u_1 + \frac{2}{3}\ x_3$$

$$+ \left(+ \frac{1}{3} + \frac{2}{3}\ u_1 + \frac{1}{3}\ x_3\right) u_1$$

$$+ \left(+ \frac{2}{3} + \frac{1}{3}\ u_1 + \frac{2}{3}\ x_3\right) x_3$$

Since an x-variable is made non-basic, u_1 must be made basic. Since

$$\partial C/\partial u_1 > 0$$

decrease u_1. This is possible until

$$u_1 = -5,$$

when

$$\frac{1}{2}\,\partial C/\partial u_1 = \frac{1}{3} - 10/3 = -3,$$

so the next non-basic variable is a free variable u_2, defined by

$$u_2 = \frac{1}{3} + \frac{2}{3}\,u_1 + \frac{1}{3}\,x_3$$

i.e.

$$u_1 = -\frac{1}{2} + \frac{3}{2}\,u_2 - \frac{1}{2}\,x_3$$

Hence

$$q = 1, \qquad e_0 = -\frac{1}{2}, \qquad e_1 = \frac{3}{2}, \qquad e_2 = -\frac{1}{2}$$

$$\frac{1}{2}\,\bar{c}_{qq} = \frac{1}{3}, \qquad c^*_0 = \frac{1}{6}, \qquad c^*_1 = \frac{1}{2}, \qquad c^*_2 = \frac{1}{6}$$

and the new tableau reads

$$x_1 = \frac{3}{2} - \frac{1}{2}\,(-u_2) + \frac{1}{2}\,(-x_3)$$

$$x_2 = \frac{1}{2} + \frac{1}{2}\,(-u_2) + \frac{1}{2}\,(-x_3)$$

$$\begin{aligned} C = &\left(\frac{1}{2} + \frac{1}{2}\,x_3\right) \\ &+ \left(+\frac{3}{2}\,u_2\right)u_2 \\ &+ \left(+\frac{1}{2} + \frac{1}{2}\,x_3\right)x_3 \end{aligned}$$

This is the final tableau. The solution is

$$x_1 = \frac{3}{2},$$

$$x_2 = \frac{1}{2},$$

$$C = \frac{1}{2}$$

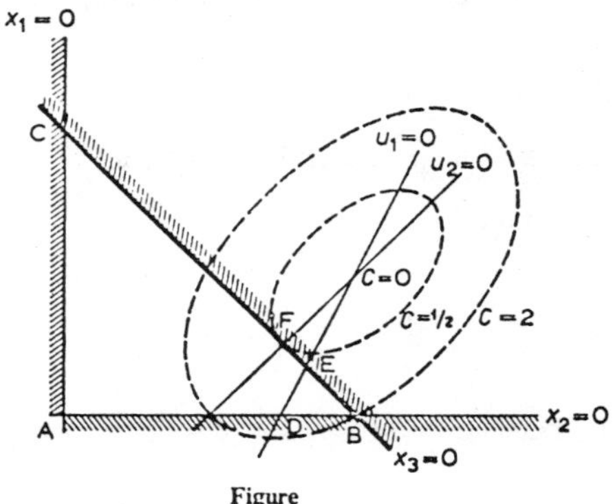

Figure

The steps towards the solution are illustrated in the figure. The feasible region consists of the triangle ABC. The contours of constant value of the objective function are ellipses centered at the point

$$x_1 = 2,$$

$$x_2 = 1$$

- two such ellipses are shown as broken lines. The first trial solution was at the point A, with x_1 and x_2 as non-basic variables. It is found profitable to increase x_1, moving towards B, but it was not profitable to proceed all the way to B. Therefore stop at D which is where C is minimized conditional on x_2 taking some prescribed value - geometrically

$$u_1 = 0$$

is the set of points at which the contours of constant values of C have horizontal tangents. It is next found expedient to increase x_2 keeping

$$u_1 = 0,$$

and if it had not been for the constraint that

$$x_3 \geq 0$$

one would have reached the final solution at the center of the system of ellipses at this iteration. In fact one is stopped at the point E by the basic variable x_3 becoming zero. At this stage the free variable u_1 must be removed from the set of basic variables- we are no longer interested in horizontal tangents. One finds one can reduce C by decreasing u_1, moving to the point F where C is minimized conditional on x_3 being equal to zero, and one introduces the new non-basic variable u_2 that is equal to zero at all points where C is minimized conditional on x_3 taking some prescribed value. This is the final solution.

• PROBLEM 11-7

Solve using Beale's algorithm

$$\text{Max } z = -12x_2 + x_1^2 + x_2^2$$

subject to

$$x_1 + x_2 + x_3 = 12,$$

$$-x_1 + x_2 + x_4 = 6,$$

and

$$x_j \geqq 0,$$

$$j = 1,\ldots,4.$$

Solution: The objective is to maximize the distance from the point (0,6). Assume one begins at

$$x_1 = 0,$$

$$x_2 = 6,$$

which is a local minimum; the corresponding basic solution is then

$$x_2 = 6,\ x_3 = 6,$$

with basic matrix and inverse

$$\vec{B} = \begin{bmatrix} 1 & 1 \\ 1 & 0 \end{bmatrix}$$

and

$$\vec{B}^{-1} = \begin{bmatrix} 0 & 1 \\ 1 & -1 \end{bmatrix}$$

and the initial tableau is as follows:

	x_1	x_2	x_3	x_4
$x_{B1} = x_2 = 6$	-1	1	0	1
$x_{B2} = x_3 = 6$	2	0	1	-1

Partitioning the problem

$$\vec{x} = (\vec{x}_B, \vec{x}_R) = (x_2, x_3 \,\vdots\, x_1, x_4),$$

$$\vec{c}^T = \vec{c}_B^T, \vec{c}_R^T = [-12, 0 \,\vdots\, 0, 0],$$

$$\vec{A} = [\vec{B}\ \vec{R}] = \left[\begin{array}{cc|cc} 1 & 1 & 1 & 0 \\ 1 & 0 & -1 & 1 \end{array}\right],$$

and

$$\vec{D} = \begin{bmatrix} \vec{D}_{11} & \vec{D}_{12} \\ \vec{D}_{21} & \vec{D}_{22} \end{bmatrix} = \left[\begin{array}{cc|cc} 1 & 0 & 0 & 0 \\ 0 & 0 & 0 & 0 \\ \hline 0 & 0 & 1 & 0 \\ 0 & 0 & 0 & 0 \end{array}\right],$$

and one finds that

$$z_0 = 36, \ \vec{p} = [0,0],$$

and

$$\vec{Q} = \begin{bmatrix} 2 & -1 \\ -1 & 1 \end{bmatrix}.$$

The components of $\vec{p}$ are both zero, so the initial solution immediately satisfies the termination criterion

$$\frac{\delta z}{\delta x_{R_j}} \begin{cases} \leq 0 & \text{(a)} \\ = 0 & \text{(b)} \end{cases}$$

(a) if x_{R_j} is a restricted (i.e., nonnegative) variable,

(b) if x_{R_j} is a free variable.

This nonoptimal termination resulted solely from the choice of a starting point at which the partial derivatives

$$\delta z/\delta x_{R_j}$$

happened to vanish. Fortunately, when Beale's algorithm is being used there is a very simple way of recovering from a false optimum in such cases as this: It is only necessary to examine the second partial derivatives

$$\delta^2 z/\delta x_{Rj}^2.$$

If the second derivative is positive for some x_{Rh}, then the current solution must be a minimum, not a maximum, with respect to displacement in the X_{Rh}-direction (in nonbasic space), and the value of the objective function can be increased by bringing x_{Rh} into the basis. In this problem, both q_{11} and q_{22} are positive, with

$$q_{11} > q_{22};$$

accordingly, $x_{R_1} = x_1$ should be chosen to enter the basis. The new basic solution will be

$$x_1 = 3, \; x_2 = 9,$$

with an improved objective value of $z = -18$.

• PROBLEM 11-8

Consider the problem

minimize $\quad -x_1 - 2x_2 + (1/2)x_1^2 + (1/2)x_2^2$

subject to

$$2x_1 + 3x_2 \leq 6$$

$$x_1 + 4x_2 \leq 5$$

$$x_1, \quad x_2 \geq 0$$

Use Hildreth's algorithm to solve.

Solution: Therefore

$$\vec{A} = \begin{bmatrix} 2 & 3 \\ 1 & 4 \\ -1 & 0 \\ 0 & -1 \end{bmatrix} \quad \vec{b} = \begin{bmatrix} 6 \\ 5 \\ 0 \\ 0 \end{bmatrix} \quad \vec{c} = \begin{bmatrix} 1 \\ 2 \end{bmatrix}$$

$$\vec{D} = \begin{bmatrix} -1/2 & 0 \\ 0 & -1/2 \end{bmatrix} \quad \vec{D}^{-1} = \begin{bmatrix} -2 & 0 \\ 0 & -2 \end{bmatrix}$$

To solve the dual problem one must determine the vector

$$\vec{h} = (1/2)AD^{-1}\vec{c} + \vec{b} = \begin{bmatrix} -2 \\ -4 \\ 1 \\ 2 \end{bmatrix}$$

and the matrix

$$G = -(1/4)AD^{-1}A' = \begin{bmatrix} 13/2 & 7 & -1 & -3/2 \\ 7 & 17/2 & -1/2 & -2 \\ -1 & -1/2 & 1/2 & 0 \\ -3/2 & -2 & 0 & 1/2 \end{bmatrix}$$

By plugging into the equation

$$y_i^{\ell+1} = \max \{0, (-1/g_{ii})[h_i/2 + \sum_{j<i} g_{ij} y_j^{\ell+1} + \sum_{j \geq i} g_{ij} y_j^{\ell}]\}$$

$$i = 1,2,\ldots,m \qquad \ell = 0,1,2,\ldots$$

the four linear programming problems yield the following four iterative equations

$$y_1^\ell = \max\{0, (-2/13)[-2/2 + 7y_2^{\ell-1} - y_3^{\ell-1} - (3/2)y_4^{\ell-1}]\}$$

$$y_2^\ell = \max\{0, -(2/17)[7y_1^\ell - 4/2 - (1/2)y_3^{\ell-1} - 2y_4^{\ell-1}]\}$$

$$y_3^\ell = \max\{0, -2[-y_1^\ell - (1/2)y_2^\ell + 1/2 + 0]\}$$

$$y_4^\ell = \max\{0, -2[-(3/2)Y_1^\ell - 2y_2^\ell + 0 + 2/2]\}$$

Since $\vec{\bar{y}} = 0$ is a feasible solution, start the iterative procedure with this vector. At the end of the first iteration

$$y_1^1 = 2/13 \qquad y_2^1 = 24/221 \qquad y_3^1 = 0 \qquad y_4^1 = 0$$

TABLE 1

Iteration	y_1	y_2	y_3	y_4
1	2/13	24/221	0	0
2	106/2.873	10.008/48.841	0	0
3	0	4/17	0	0
4	0	4/17	0	0

Proceeding in this manner an iteration log is developed in Table 1 which, at the end of the fourth iteration, yields the optimal solution. Thus the solution to the original problem is

$$x_1^0 = 12/17, \; x_2^0 = 18/17.$$

• PROBLEM 11-9

Consider the problem,

Maximize

$$f(x) = 6x_1 - 2x_1^2 + 2x_1x_2 - 2x_2^2$$

subject to

$$x_1 + x_2 \leq 2$$

and

$$x_1, x_2 \geq 0.$$

Solve by Van-de-Panne and Whinston method for a quadratic programming problem.

Solution: Most quadratic programming methods solve the problem by

(i) trying to satisfy the Kuhn-Tucker optimality conditions:

$$\begin{aligned} p - Qx - v'A + u &= 0 \\ Ax + Iy &= b \\ v'(Ax - b) = v'y &= 0 \\ u'x &= 0 \\ u, v, x, y &\geq 0, \end{aligned} \tag{1}$$

(y: a slack vector of m non-negative components corresponding to m inequalities.

v: a vector of m unknowns for the m inequality constraints

u: a vector of n unknowns for the nonnegativity constraints on x variables), for the Lagrangian

$$F(x,v,u) = p'x - \frac{1}{2}x'Qx - v'(Ax-b) + u'x.$$

when (1) holds one can define a variable u_0:

$$u_0 = 2f(x) = \sum_{j=1}^{m} p_j x_j + \sum_{k=1}^{m} v_k b_k$$

$$u_i = p_i + \sum_{j=1}^{n} q_{ij} x_j + \sum_{k=1}^{m} a_{ki} v_k \qquad i = 1,2,\ldots,n$$

$$y_i = b_i - \sum_{j=1}^{n} a_{ij} x_j, \qquad i = 1,2,\ldots,m$$

and display in the following Tableau, 1.

TABLEAU 1

	$-x_0$	$-x_1$	$-x_2$	$-x_n$	$-v_1$	$-v_2$	$-v_m$
$2f(x) = u_0$	0	$-p_1$	$-p_2$	$-p_n$	$-b_1$	$-b_2$	$-b_m$
u_1	$-p_1$	$-q_{11}$	$-q_{12}$	$-q_{1n}$	$-a_{11}$	$-a_{21}$	$-a_{m1}$
u_2	$-p_2$	$-q_{21}$	$-q_{22}$	$-q_{2n}$	$-a_{12}$	$-a_{22}$	$-a_{m2}$
		$-Q$				$-A'$	
u_n	$-p_n$	$-q_{n1}$	$-q_{n2}$	$-q_{nn}$	$-a_{1n}$	$-a_{2n}$	$-a_{mn}$
y_1	b_1	a_{11}	a_{12}	a_{1n}			
y_2	b_2	a_{21}	a_{22}	a_{2n}			
		A				0	
y_m	b_m	a_{m1}	a_{m2}	a_{mn}			

The algorithm due to Van-de-Panne and Whinston is as follows:

To start with, the following need to be defined.

1. Standard tableau

If for each x or y (i.e., primal variable) in the basis its corresponding u or v (dual variable) is non-basic and vice-versa, then such a tableau possesses a symmetry/skew-symmetry property and is called a "Standard Tableau".

2. Non-standard tableau

A tableau in which one pair of x, u or y, v variable together appear in the basis is called a "Non-standard Tableau" (or a "Nearly Complementary Tableau").

The pivot choice rules for transforming the tableau may now be stated as follows.

Rule 1: Choice of variable to enter the basis.

In the case that the tableau is in standard form, select as the new basic variable the y or x-variable having the largest negative corresponding basic u or v variable solution value. In the case that the tableau is not in standard form introduce as the new basic variable the u or v variable of the non-basic pair from the list of the non-basic variables.

Rule 2: Choice of the variable to leave the basis.

Select as the variable to leave the basis, from the set of basic x, y variables and u_s or v_s the variable which first becomes zero upon introducing the new basic variable by a positive amount. Here u_s or v_s is the dual variable corresponding to the x or y variable in the standard tableau, and in a non-standard tableau it is the dual variable of the basic pair.

If I denotes the set of indices of the rows in which the x or y variables are pivoted and the variable $u_s (v_s)$ is pivoted, then the pivot choice rule may be expressed as:

Choose as the pivot row r such that,

$$\min_{i \in I} \left\{ \frac{\alpha_{io}}{\alpha_{ij}} \,\middle|\, \frac{\alpha_{io}}{\alpha_{ij}} \geq 0 \,,\right.$$

and

$$\left. \alpha_{ij} \neq 0 \right\} = \frac{\alpha_{ro}}{\alpha_{rj}} \,,$$

where α_{ij} denotes the (i,j)th element of any intermediate tableau and j is the column corresponding to the variable chosen to enter the basis.
Having chosen the pivot element of course, the tableau is transformed by transformation rules identical to those used in the simplex method of linear programming.

This may be expressed in vector notation as

$$f(x) = \overset{p'}{[6,0]} \overset{x}{\begin{bmatrix} x_1 \\ x_2 \end{bmatrix}} - \frac{1}{2}\overset{x'}{[x_1 \ , x_2]} \begin{bmatrix} 4 & -2 \\ & Q & \\ -2 & 4 \end{bmatrix} \overset{x}{\begin{bmatrix} x_1 \\ x_2 \end{bmatrix}}$$

$$\overset{A}{[1,1]} \overset{x}{\begin{bmatrix} x_1 \\ x_2 \end{bmatrix}} \leq \overset{b}{2} \qquad x_1, x_2 \geq 0.$$

	$-x_0$	$-x_1\downarrow$	$-x_2$	$-v_1$
u_0	0	-6	0	-2
u_1	-6	$-\underline{4}$	2	-1
u_2	0	2	-4	-1
y_1	2	1	1	0

Standard Tableau 2

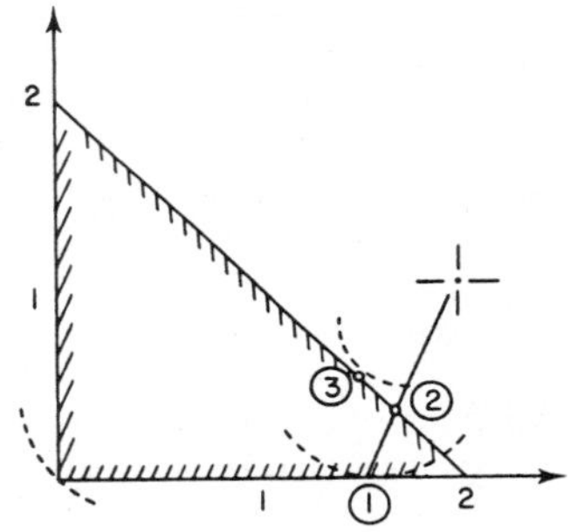

Fig. 1

The problem is set up in Tableau 2 which is a standard tableau and the accompanying diagram illustrates the unconstrained and constrained maximum of f(x) which defines a system of ellipses.

At the point (0,0) Tableau 2 the value of $u_1 = -6$ and hence x_1 is chosen to come into the basis. The rationale for such a step may be expressed from the first principles as follows. Setting all the other variables to zero

$$f(x) = 6x_1 - \frac{1}{2} \cdot 4 \cdot (x_1)^2$$

and

$$\frac{\partial f}{\partial x_1} = 6 - 4x_1$$

hence the function value increases with x_1.

From

$$y_1 = 2 - x_1 - x_2$$

it follows that x_1 can go up to

$$\frac{2}{1} = 2$$

and from

$$\partial f/\partial x_1 = 0 = 6 - 4x_1$$

the maximum of f(x) is obtained for

$$x_1 = \frac{6}{4} = \frac{3}{2}$$

(look at row 2). Therefore the min of the ratios

$$\left\{\frac{3}{2}, \frac{2}{1}\right\}$$

is taken and the element -4 in Tableau 2 is chosen for pivoting and Tableau 3 is obtained after transformation. After a sequence of pivot choices and transformations the optimum solution is obtained and this is contained in Tableau 5.

	$-x_0$	$-u_1$	$-x_2\downarrow$	$-v_1$
u_0	9	$-\frac{3}{2}$	-3	$-\frac{1}{2}$
x_1	$\frac{3}{2}$	$-\frac{1}{4}$	$-\frac{1}{2}$	$\frac{1}{4}$
u_2	-3	$\frac{1}{2}$	-3	$-\frac{3}{2}$
y_1	$\frac{1}{2}$	$\frac{1}{4}$	$\frac{3}{2}$	$-\frac{1}{4}$

STANDARD TABLEAU 3

	$-x_0$	$-u_1$	$-y_1$	$-v_1\downarrow$
u_0	10	-1	2	-1
x_1	$\frac{5}{3}$	$-\frac{1}{6}$	$\frac{1}{3}$	$\frac{1}{6}$
u_2	-2	1	2	-2
x_2	$\frac{1}{3}$	$\frac{1}{6}$	$\frac{2}{3}$	$-\frac{1}{6}$

NON-STANDARD TABLEAU 4
True function value in Tableau 4
is $2f(x) = 10 - u_2x_2 = 10\frac{2}{3}$

	$-x_0$	$-u_1$	$-y_1$	$-u_2$
u_0	11	$-\frac{3}{2}$	1	$-\frac{1}{2}$
x_1	$\frac{3}{2}$	$-\frac{1}{12}$	$\frac{1}{2}$	$\frac{1}{12}$
v_1	1	$-\frac{1}{2}$	-1	$-\frac{1}{2}$
x_2	$\frac{1}{2}$	$\frac{1}{12}$	$\frac{1}{2}$	$-\frac{1}{12}$

Optimal

STANDARD TABLEAU 5

• PROBLEM 11-10

Maximize

$$4x_1 + 3x_2 + 2x_3 - x_1^2 - x_2^2 - \frac{1}{2}x_3^2 - x_1x_2 - x_1x_3,$$

subject to

$$x_1 + x_2 + 2x_3 \leq 3, \quad x_1 \geq 0, \quad x_2 \geq 0, \quad x_3 \geq 0.$$

Solve the above quadratic programming model by applying Dantzig's method.

Solution: For the quadratic programming problem

$$\text{Max } \{p^T x - \frac{1}{2} x^T C x \mid Ax \leq b, \; x \geq 0\} \qquad (1)$$

the optimality conditions are

$$p - Cx = A^T u - v \;, \; u \geq 0, \; v \geq 0 \qquad (2)$$

$$u^T y = 0, \qquad v^T x = 0 \qquad (3)$$

with

$$y = b - Ax, \qquad x \geq 0, \qquad y \geq 0. \qquad (4)$$

The tableau used for solving (1) is constructed as follows

		x	u
v	$-p$	$-C$	$-A^T$
y	b	A	0

and it corresponds to the relations (2) and (4). The matrix $\begin{pmatrix} -C & -A^T \\ A & 0 \end{pmatrix}$ is negative semi-definite as

$$(s_1^T, s_2^T) \begin{pmatrix} -C & -A^T \\ A & 0 \end{pmatrix} \begin{pmatrix} s_1 \\ s_2 \end{pmatrix} \begin{aligned} &= -s_1^T C s_1 - s_1^T A^T s_2 + s_2^T A s_1 \\ &= -s_1^T C s_1 \leqq 0. \end{aligned}$$

Let

$$w = \begin{pmatrix} x \\ u \end{pmatrix}, \quad z = \begin{pmatrix} u \\ y \end{pmatrix}, \quad Q = \begin{pmatrix} -C & -A^T \\ A & 0 \end{pmatrix}, \quad q = \begin{pmatrix} -p \\ b \end{pmatrix}.$$

so that

$$Qw + z = q, \; w \geqq 0, \; z \geqq 0, \; w^T z = 0,$$

then the rules for complementary pivoting are:

(1) Choose

$z^*_\rho < 0$

(usually the most negative z^*_i; if

$\forall i (z^*_i \geqq 0)$,

then it is completed); let $k = \rho$.

(2) Increase w^*_k until

(a) either $z^*_\rho = 0$,

(b) or one of the variables in the basis, which was $\geqq 0$, becomes $= 0$, say $z_i{}^*$.

(3) In case (2a), interchange z^*_ρ and w^*_k and go to (1); in case (2b), interchange $z_i{}^*$ and w^*_k; choose $k = i$ and go to (2).

For this problem:

$$g = \begin{pmatrix} 4 - 2x_1 - x_2 - x_3 \\ 3 - x_1 - 2x_2 \\ 2 - x_1 \qquad - x_3 \end{pmatrix},$$

$$C = \begin{pmatrix} 2 & 1 & 1 \\ 1 & 2 & 0 \\ 1 & 0 & 1 \end{pmatrix}.$$

The tableaux are:

		x_1	x_2	x_3	u
v_1	-4	$\boxed{-2}$	-1	-1	-1
v_2	-3	-1	-2		-1
v_3	-2	-1		-1	-2
y	3	1	1	2	

$z^*_\rho = v_1$, $w^*_k = x_1$, case (2a) →

		v_1	x_2	x_3	u
x_1	2	$-\frac{1}{2}$	$\frac{1}{2}$	$\frac{1}{2}$	$\frac{1}{2}$
v_2	-1	$-\frac{1}{2}$	$-\frac{3}{2}$	$\frac{1}{2}$	$-\frac{1}{2}$
v_3	0	$-\frac{1}{2}$	$\boxed{\frac{1}{2}}$	$-\frac{1}{2}$	$-\frac{3}{2}$
y	1	$\frac{1}{2}$	$\frac{1}{2}$	$\frac{3}{2}$	$-\frac{1}{2}$

$z^*_\rho = v_3$, $w^*_k = x_2$, $i = 3$ →

		v_1	v_3	x_3	u
x_1	2		-1	1	2
v_2	-1	-2	3	-1	-5
x_2	0	-1	2	-1	-3
y	1	1	-1	$\boxed{2}$	1

$z^*_\circ = v_2$, $w^*_k = x_3$, $i = 4$ →

		v_1	v_3	y	u
x_1	$\frac{3}{2}$	$-\frac{1}{2}$	$-\frac{1}{2}$	$-\frac{1}{2}$	$\frac{3}{2}$
v_2	$-\frac{1}{2}$	$-\frac{3}{2}$	$\frac{5}{2}$	$\frac{1}{2}$	$\boxed{-\frac{9}{2}}$
x_2	$\frac{1}{2}$	$-\frac{1}{2}$	$\frac{3}{2}$	$\frac{1}{2}$	$-\frac{5}{2}$
x_3	$\frac{1}{2}$	$\frac{1}{2}$	$-\frac{1}{2}$	$\frac{1}{2}$	$\frac{1}{2}$

$z^*_i = v_2$, $w^*_k = u$, case (2a) →

		v_1	v_3	y	v_2
x_1	$\frac{4}{3}$	-1	$\frac{1}{3}$	$-\frac{1}{3}$	$\frac{1}{3}$
u	$\frac{1}{9}$	$\frac{1}{3}$	$-\frac{5}{9}$	$-\frac{1}{9}$	$-\frac{2}{9}$
x_2	$\frac{7}{9}$	$\frac{1}{3}$	$\frac{1}{9}$	$\frac{2}{9}$	$-\frac{5}{9}$
x_3	$\frac{4}{9}$	$\frac{1}{3}$	$-\frac{2}{9}$	$\frac{5}{9}$	$\frac{1}{9}$

Optimal solution:

$$x_1 = \frac{4}{3}, \quad x_2 = \frac{7}{9}, \quad x_3 = \frac{4}{9}.$$

The way of pivoting has caused that the rows and columns are no longer in their "natural" order but this can be easily restored, if necessary. Equalities (unrestricted) and unrestricted variables x_j (require $v_j = 0$) do not present any problem.

GEOMETRIC PROGRAMMING

• PROBLEM 11-11

Each month 1000 m^3 of a chemical have to be shipped by N.F.B. Company in rectangular containers of length z_1, width z_2 and height z_3.

The sides and bottom of the container will be made of scrap material in limited supply: only 10 m^2 is available per container per month. Material for both ends will cost \$20 per m^2 while material for the top will cost \$30 per m^2. The shipping cost will be \$2 per container. It is asked to minimize total cost.

Set up the Geometric Programming model for this problem.

Solution: Geometric programming is developed by R. Duffin and C. Zener. It finds the solution by considering an associated dual problem. The advantage here is that it is usually much simpler computationally to work with the dual.

Geometric programming deals with problems in which the objective and the constraint functions are of the following type.

$$x_0 = f(X) = \sum_{j=1}^{N} U_j$$

where

$$U_j = c_j \prod_{i=1}^{n} x_i^{a_{ij}}, \quad j = 1,2,\ldots,N$$

It is assumed that $c_j > 0$ and N is finite. The exponents a_{ij} are unrestricted in sign. The function f(X) takes the form of a polynomial except that the exponents a_{ij}

may be negative. For this reason, and because all $c_j > 0$, Duffin and Zener give $f(X)$ the name posynomial.

The equation that describes N.F.B. Company's problem is:

$$\text{Min}\ \{2 \cdot \frac{1000}{z_1 z_2 z_3} + 40 z_2 z_3 \frac{1000}{z_1 z_2 z_3} + 30 z_1 z_2 \frac{1000}{z_1 z_2 z_3} \mid 2z_1 z_3 + z_1 z_2 \leqq 10,\ z_1 > 0,\ z_2 > 0,\ z_3 > 0\}.$$

• PROBLEM 11-12

A chemical company must send 1000 cubic meters of chlorine gas to its research laboratory in another state. Because the gas is dangerous, a special hermetically sealed rectangular railroad car must be built for transporting it. The material from which the top and bottom must be constructed costs \$200 per square meter, while the siding material costs half as much; however, only 50 square meters of siding can be obtained. Moreover, the maximum height of the car permitted by tunnels and other overhead clearances is 3 meters. Regardless of the car's dimensions, each round trip to the laboratory and back will cost \$800. Assuming no time limit on the overall procedure, set up a mathematical programming problem to determine what dimensions would minimize the total cost of constructing the car and delivering the gas.

Solution: Let d, w, and h be the car's length, width, and height. The objective is to minimize overall cost; that is,

$$\text{Min}\ 800 \left(\frac{1000}{dwh}\right) + 2dw(200) + (2dh + 2wh)(100),$$

where the three terms are contributed by transportation cost, top-and-bottom material, and siding, respectively. The constraints mentioned in the problem are

$$2dh + 2wh \leqq 50 \quad \text{and} \quad h \leqq 3.$$

Finally, eliminate the possibility of negative dimensions:

$$d,\ w,\ h \geqq 0.$$

• PROBLEM 11-13

Minimize the posynomial

$$g_0(\vec{t}) = 40 t_1^{-1} t_2^{-\frac{1}{2}} t_3^{-1} + 20 t_1 t_3 + 20 t_1 t_2 t_3 \qquad (1)$$

subject to the constraint

$$g_1(\vec{t}) = \frac{1}{3} t_1^{-2} t_2^{-2} + \frac{4}{3} t_2^{\frac{1}{2}} t_3^{-1} \leq 1, \qquad (2)$$

by applying Geometric Programming.

Solution: The dual program associated with this problem consists of maximizing the dual function

$$v(\vec{\delta}) = \left(\frac{40}{\delta_1}\right)^{\delta_1}\left(\frac{20}{\delta_2}\right)^{\delta_2}\left(\frac{20}{\delta_3}\right)^{\delta_3}\left(\frac{1/3}{\delta_4}\right)^{\delta_4}\left(\frac{4/3}{\delta_5}\right)^{\delta_5}(\delta_4 + \delta_5)^{(\delta_4+\delta_5)} \quad (3)$$

subject to the dual constraints

$$\delta_1 \geq 0,\ \delta_2 \geq 0,\ \delta_3 \geq 0,\ \delta_4 \geq 0,\ \delta_5 \geq 0, \quad (4)$$

$$\delta_1 + \delta_2 + \delta_3 = 1 \quad (5)$$

and

$$\begin{aligned} -\delta_1 + \delta_2 + \delta_3 - 2\delta_4 \qquad\qquad &= 0 \\ -\frac{1}{2}\delta_1 \qquad + \delta_3 - 2\delta_4 + \frac{1}{2}\delta_5 &= 0 \\ -\delta_1 + \delta_2 + \delta_3 \qquad\qquad - \delta_5 &= 0. \end{aligned} \quad (6)$$

One obtains basis vectors for the dual space by a standard procedure of linear algebra. The first step in this procedure is to use elementary column operations on the exponent matrix to obtain a "diagonalized matrix"; for example

$$\begin{bmatrix} -1 & -\frac{1}{2} & -1 \\ 1 & 0 & 1 \\ 1 & 1 & 1 \\ -2 & -2 & 0 \\ 0 & \frac{1}{2} & -1 \end{bmatrix} \rightarrow \begin{bmatrix} 1 & 0 & 0 \\ -1 & -\frac{1}{2} & 0 \\ -1 & \frac{1}{2} & 0 \\ 2 & -1 & 2 \\ 0 & \frac{1}{2} & -1 \end{bmatrix} . \rightarrow \begin{bmatrix} 1 & 0 & 0 \\ 0 & 1 & 0 \\ -2 & -1 & 0 \\ 4 & 2 & 2 \\ -1 & -1 & -1 \end{bmatrix}$$

$$\rightarrow \begin{bmatrix} 1 & 0 & 0 \\ 0 & 1 & 0 \\ -2 & -1 & 0 \\ 2 & 0 & -2 \\ 0 & 0 & 1 \end{bmatrix}. \quad (7)$$

The resulting "diagonalized matrix" can be written more conveniently as

$$\left[\begin{array}{ccc} 1 & 0 & 0 \\ 0 & 1 & 0 \\ 0 & 0 & 1 \\ \hline 2 & 0 & -2 \\ -2 & -1 & 0 \end{array}\right], \quad (8)$$

where the third and fifth rows of (7) have been interchanged so that the 3 × 3 unit matrix appears in the top position as shown. Next, take the negative transpose of the submatrix lying below the 3 × 3 unit matrix and on the bottom append to it the 2 × 2 unit matrix to obtain

$$\left[\begin{array}{cc} -2 & 2 \\ 0 & 1 \\ 2 & 0 \\ \hline 1 & 0 \\ 0 & 1 \end{array}\right]. \quad (9)$$

It is clear from construction that each column vector of this matrix is orthogonal to each column vector of matrix

(8). However, the ordering of the components of these column vectors is not consistent with the ordering in (7) because the rows three and five were interchanged in passing from (7) to (8). Therefore interchange the third and fifth rows of both (8) and (9) to obtain

$$\begin{bmatrix} 1 & 0 & 0 \\ 0 & 1 & 0 \\ -2 & -1 & 0 \\ 2 & 0 & -2 \\ 0 & 0 & 1 \end{bmatrix} \qquad (10)$$

and

$$\begin{bmatrix} -2 & 2 \\ 0 & 1 \\ 0 & 1 \\ 1 & 0 \\ 2 & 0 \end{bmatrix}, \qquad (11)$$

respectively. The column vectors of (11) are of necessity orthogonal to the column vectors of (10). Since (10) is the same as (7) and since (7) is obtained from the exponent matrix by elementary column operations, one concludes that the column vectors of (11) are orthogonal to the column vectors of the exponent matrix. Moreover, it is clear that the column vectors of (11) are linearly independent. It then follows from linear algebra theory that they form a basis for the space of solutions to the orthogonality condition, that is, the dual space.

Dividing the first column vector of (11) by the sum of its first three components, one obtains a vector

$$\vec{b}^{(0)} = \begin{bmatrix} 1 \\ 0 \\ 0 \\ -\frac{1}{2} \\ -1 \end{bmatrix}, \qquad (12)$$

which satisfies both the orthogonality condition and the normality condition. Thus

$$\vec{b}^{(0)}$$

is a normality vector for the problem.

Since matrix (11) has only two columns, there is only one nullity vector

$$\vec{b}^{(1)}$$

for the problem. To obtain $\vec{b}^{(1)}$ add the first three components of the remaining column vector of (11) and subtract from this vector the product of this sum with the normality vector

$$b^{(0)},$$

giving

$$\vec{b}^{(1)} = \begin{bmatrix} -2 \\ 1 \\ 1 \\ 2 \\ 4 \end{bmatrix}. \qquad (13)$$

The general solution to the normality and orthogonality conditions is

$$\vec{\delta} = \vec{b}^{(0)} + r\vec{b}^{(1)}$$

or, in component form,

$$\begin{aligned} \delta_1 &= 1 - 2r, \\ \delta_2 &= r \\ \delta_3 &= r, \\ \delta_4 &= -\frac{1}{2} + 2r, \\ \delta_5 &= -1 + 4r. \end{aligned} \qquad (14)$$

It is clear from these equations that $\vec{\delta}$ satisfies the positivity condition only when r is restricted so that

$$\frac{1}{4} \leq r \leq \frac{1}{2} . \qquad (15)$$

The existence of a vector $\vec{\delta}^*$ with positive components that satisfies the dual constraints is guaranteed by letting r be $\frac{3}{8}$ in (14). Moreover, the problem is superconsistent, hence consistent, because

$$g_1(2,1,2) = \frac{3}{4} < 1.$$

It then follows from the second duality theorem of geometric programming that

$$g_0(\vec{t})$$

attains its constrained minimum value at a point $\vec{t}'$ which satisfies the primal constraints. Thus the hypotheses of the first duality theorem are satisfied; hence its conclusions are applicable to the problem.

Substituting values of $\frac{1}{4}$, $\frac{3}{10}$, and $\frac{7}{20}$ for r into (14) and computing the corresponding values of the dual function, one obtains

$$v\left(\frac{1}{2}, \frac{1}{4}, \frac{1}{4}, 0, 0\right) = 80$$

$$v\left(\frac{2}{5}, \frac{3}{10}, \frac{3}{10}, \frac{1}{10}, \frac{1}{5}\right) = 90.9 \qquad (16)$$

$$v\left(-\frac{3}{10}, \frac{7}{20}, \frac{7}{20}, \frac{1}{5}, \frac{2}{5}\right) = 97.14.$$

Evaluating $g_0(\vec{t})$ for trial values of t_1, t_2, and t_3 which satisfy the primal constraints gives

$$g_0(1,1,4) = 170$$

$$g_0(1,1,3) = 133.3 \qquad (17)$$

$$g_0\left(1,1, \frac{5}{2}\right) = 116$$

$$g_0\left(1,1, \frac{17}{8}\right) = 103.82.$$

According to the duality theorem,

$$g_0(\vec{t}) \geq g_0(\vec{t}') \geq v(\vec{\delta}),$$

where $\vec{t}'$ is a minimizing vector for the problem and $\vec{t}$ and $\vec{\delta}$ are arbitrary vectors satsifying the primal and dual constraints, respectively. It follows that (16) provides lower bounds for $g_0(\vec{t}')$, whereas (17) gives upper bounds for $g_0(\vec{t}')$. In particular it can be seen that

$$103.82 \geq g_0(\vec{t}') \geq 97.14.$$

Hence the constrained minimum value for g_0 is 100 with an error of less than 4%.

• PROBLEM 11-14

Minimize the posynomial

$$g_0(\vec{t}) = 40t_1t_2 + 20t_2t_3$$

subject to the constraint

$$g_1(\vec{t}) = \frac{1}{5} t_1^{-1} t_2^{-\frac{1}{2}} + \frac{3}{5} t_2^{-1} t_3^{-2/3} \leq 1, \qquad (1)$$

by applying Geometric Programming.

Solution: Notice that there are four terms but only three variables.

The dual function for this problem is

$$v(\vec{\delta}) = \left(\frac{40}{\delta_1}\right)^{\delta_1}\left(\frac{20}{\delta_2}\right)^{\delta_2}\left(\frac{1/5}{\delta_3}\right)^{\delta_3}\left(\frac{3/5}{\delta_4}\right)^{\delta_4} (\delta_3 + \delta_4)^{(\delta_3+\delta_4)} .$$

The normalization condition is

$$\delta_1 + \delta_2 = 1,$$

and the orthogonality condition is

$$\begin{aligned} \delta_1 \qquad\quad - \delta_3 \qquad\quad &= 0 \\ \delta_1 + \delta_2 - \frac{1}{2}\delta_3 - \delta_4 &= 0 \\ \delta_2 \qquad\quad - \frac{2}{3}\delta_4 &= 0. \end{aligned}$$

These conditions constitute a system of four linear equations in four variables and have a unique solution $(\delta_1', \delta_2', \delta_3', \delta_4')$ in which

$$\delta_1' = \frac{1}{2}, \qquad \delta_2' = \frac{1}{2}, \qquad \delta_3' = \frac{1}{2}, \qquad \delta_4' = \frac{3}{4}.$$

It is then clear from the formula for $g(\vec{t})$ that the hypotheses for both the first and second duality theorems of geometric programming are satisfied; hence their conclusions are applicable.

The value of the dual function at $\vec{\delta}'$ is

$$v\left(\frac{1}{2}, \frac{1}{2}, \frac{1}{2}, \frac{3}{4}\right) = 40.$$

Since $\vec{\delta}'$ is the only point in the domain of $v(\vec{\delta})$, one concludes from the duality theorem that the constrained minimum value of $g_0(\vec{t})$ is

$$g_0(t_1', t_2', t_3') = 40.$$

It is worth noting that the constrained minimum value of $g_0(\vec{t})$ has been determined without first obtaining the minimizing vector (t_1', t_2', t_3'). However, the maximizing vector $(\delta_1', \delta_2', \delta_3', \delta_4')$ for the dual function has been determined, and it turns out that this vector has important significance. According to the fourth conclusion of the first duality theorem the numbers δ_1' and δ_2', when multiplied by $g_0(\vec{t}')$, give the first and second terms, respectively, of $g_0(\vec{t}')$; that is

$$40t_1't_2' = \frac{1}{2} \cdot 40 \tag{2}$$

and

$$20t_2't_3' = \frac{1}{2} \cdot 40. \qquad (3)$$

According to the third conclusion of the first duality theorem, the fact that δ_3' and δ_4' are not zero implies that forced constraint (1) is active; that is,

$$g_1(\vec{t}') = 1.$$

It then follows from conclusion 4 that the first and second terms of $g_1(\vec{t}')$ are given by

$$\delta_3'/(\delta_3' + \delta_4')$$

and

$$\delta_4'/(\delta_3' + \delta_4'),$$

respectively; that is,

$$\frac{1}{5} t_1'^{-1} t_2'^{-\frac{1}{2}} = \frac{2}{5} \qquad (4)$$

and

$$\frac{3}{5} t_2'^{-1} t_3'^{-2/3} = \frac{3}{5}. \qquad (5)$$

To obtain the values of t_1', t_2', and t_3', take the lograrithm of both sides of (2), (3), (4), and (5). This shows that (t_1', t_2', t_3') satisfies the system

$$\begin{aligned}
\log t_1 + \log t_2 &= -\log 2 \\
\log t_2 + \log t_3 &= 0 \\
-\log t_1 - \frac{1}{2}\log t_2 &= \log 2 \\
-\log t_2 - \frac{2}{3}\log t_3 &= 0,
\end{aligned}$$

which is linear in the variables $\log t_1$, $\log t_2$ and $\log t_3$. This system has a unique solution $(-\log 2,0,0)$, which means that $g_0(\vec{t})$ attains its constrained minimum value at the point

$$(\frac{1}{2}, 1,1).$$

FRACTIONAL PROGRAMMING

• PROBLEM 11-15

Minimize

$$\frac{4x_{11} + 2x_{12} + 7x_{21} + 9x_{22}}{5x_{11} + 3x_{12} + 6x_{21} + 2x_{22}} = \frac{P}{Q},$$

subject to

$$x_{11} + x_{12} = 3, \qquad x_{11} + x_{21} = 6$$

$$x_{21} + x_{22} = 5, \qquad x_{12} + x_{22} = 2$$

$$x_{ij} \geq 0 \qquad (i,j = 1,2).$$

Solve by Fractional Programming Method.

Solution: If the objective function to be minimized is of the form

$$\sum_i \sum_j c_{ij}x_{ij} / \sum_i \sum_j d_{ij}x_{ij}$$

and the constraints are those of a transportation problem, namely

$$\sum_j x_{ij} = a_i \text{ (for all i)},$$

and

$$\sum_i x_{ij} = b_j \text{ (for all j)},$$

then use an algorithm reminiscent of that of the transportation problem.

Write

	6	2
3	4,5	2,3
5	7,6	9,2

and start with some basic feasible solution, say

	6	2
3	3	
5	3	2

Then P = 51, Q = 37.
Compute two sets of shadow costs, u_i', v_j' and u_i'', v_j'', referring respectively to c_{ij} and d_{ij}:

			u'	u"
	4,5		0	0
	7,6	9,2	3	1
v'	4	6		
v"	5	1		

Compute, for all empty cells,

$$\bar{c}_{ij} = c_{ij} - u_i' - v_j'$$

and

$$\bar{d}_{ij} = d_{ij} - u_i'' - v_j''.$$

If $\bar{c}_{ij}Q - \bar{d}_{ij}P$ is negative, then it is worthwhile to enter that cell, and this leads to modifications in filled-in cells, as in the algorithm of the transportation problem.

In this case one gets

$$\bar{c}_{ij} = 2 - 0 - 6 = -4$$

and

$$\bar{d}_{ij} = 3 - 0 - 1 = 2, \qquad \bar{c}_{12}Q - \bar{d}_{12}P = -250$$

so enter cell (1,2)

	6	2
3	1	2
5	5	

and have shadow costs

			u'	u"
	4,5	2,3	0	0
	7,6		3	1
v'	4	2		
v"	5	3		

Now P = 43, Q = 41, $\bar{c}_{22} = 4$, $\bar{d}_{22} = -2$, $\bar{c}_{22}Q - \bar{d}_{22}P =$

$$250 > 0,$$

and the final answer is reached:

$$x_{11} = 1,\ x_{12} = 2,\ x_{21} = 5,\ x_{22} = 0.$$

• PROBLEM 11-16

maximize

$$\frac{-x_1 + 2x_2 + 4}{x_1 + x_2 + 2},$$

subject to

$$2x_1 + x_2 \leq 2, \qquad x_1, x_2 \geq 0.$$

Solve by Fractional Programming Method.

Solution: Introduce two non-negative variables

$$t = (x_1 + x_2 + 2)^{-1}$$

and

$$s = (-x_1 - x_2 - 2)^{-1}.$$

Also write $x_j t = y_j$ and $x_j s = z_j$ and multiply the numerator and denominator of the objective function by t for the first problem, and by s for the second. Then one has:

maximize $-y_1 + 2y_2 + 4t,$

subject to $y_1 + y_2 + 2t = 1$

$2y_1 + y_2 - 2t \leq 0$

maximize $z_1 - 2z_2 - 4s,$

subject to $-z_1 - z_2 - 2s = 1$

$2z_1 + z_2 - 2s \leq 0$

The solution of the first problem is

	y_1	y_3	
t	$-\frac{1}{4}$	$-\frac{1}{4}$	$\frac{1}{4}$
y_2	$\frac{3}{2}$	$\frac{1}{2}$	$\frac{1}{2}$
	3	0	2

i.e., $x_2 = 2$, $x_1 = 0$ or, alternatively, $x_1 = x_2 = 0$,

objective function 2.

The second problem has contradictory constraints. If one computes s from the equation and substitutes into the inequality, one gets

$$3z_1 + 2z_2 + 1 \leq 0,$$

which is impossible with non-negative z_1, z_2.

If a finite optimum is at a point where the denominator is positive, then the problem with t produces the answer, while the problem with s is contradictory. The opposite holds if the optimum is reached at a point where the denominator is negative. Thus one of two problems will always produce the answer.

Actually, in this problem, it was obvious, to begin with, that the denominator was positive in the whole feasible region. In such a case it is unnecessary to formulate both problems.

Maximize

$$(x_1 + 2x_2)/(4x_1 + 3x_2 + 3),$$

subject to

$$x_1 + x_2 \leq 2, \quad -x_1 + x_2 \leq 1,$$

$$x_1, x_2 \geq 0.$$

Solve by Fractional Programming Method.

Solution: The denominator remains positive in the feasible region.

$4x_1 + 3x_2 + 3 = t^{-1}$, $y_1 = tx_1$, $y_2 = tx_2$.

Maximize

$$y_1 + 2y_2,$$

subject to

$$y_1 + y_2 - 2t + y_3 = 0$$

$$-y_1 + y_2 - t + y_4 = 0$$

$$4y_1 + 3y_2 + 3t = 0,$$

$$y_i \geq 0.$$

Final tableau:

	y_3	y_4	
y_1	$\frac{6}{19}$	$-\frac{9}{19}$	$\frac{1}{19}$
y_2	$-\frac{1}{19}$	$\frac{11}{19}$	$\frac{3}{19}$
t	$-\frac{7}{19}$	$\frac{1}{19}$	$\frac{2}{19}$
	$\frac{4}{19}$	$\frac{13}{19}$	$\frac{7}{19}$

Interpretation: $x_1 = \frac{1}{2}$, $x_2 = \frac{3}{2}$

Objective function: $\frac{7}{19}$.

Maximize

$$(3x_1 + 5x_2 - 3x_3)/(x_1 - 4x_2 + 2x_3 + 3),$$

subject to

$$2x_1 + x_2 + 6x_3 \le 3$$

$$-5x_1 + 4x_2 - x_3 \ge 5$$

$$x_1, x_2, x_3 \ge 0.$$

Solve by Fractional Programming Method.

Solution: Write $y_j = tx_j$.

$$t^{-1} = x_1 - 4x_2 + 2x_3 + 3,$$

or

$$t^{-1} = -x_1 + 4x_2 - 2x_3 - 3.$$

Maximize

$3y_1 + 5y_2 - 3y_3,$	$-3y_1 - 5y_2 + 3y_3,$

subject to

$2y_1 + y_2 + 6y_3 - 3t \le 0$	$2y_1 + y_2 + 6y_3 - 3t \le 0$
$-5y_1 + 4y_3 - y_3 - 5t \le 0$	$-5y_1 + 4y_2 - y_3 - 5t \le 0$
$y_1 - 4y_2 + 2y_3 + 3t = 1,$	$-y_1 + 4y_2 - 2y_3 - 3t = 1,$
$y_j, t \ge 0.$	

Slack variables z_1, z_2.

y_2 unbounded, answer infinite, not relevant.

Final tableau:

	z_1	y_3	z_2	
y_2	$-\frac{5}{27}$	$-\frac{101}{54}$	$-\frac{1}{6}$	$\frac{25}{54}$
t	$-\frac{56}{27}$	$-\frac{1}{2}$	$-\frac{1}{6}$	$\frac{13}{54}$
y_1	$\frac{4}{27}$	$\frac{43}{54}$	$-\frac{1}{6}$	$\frac{7}{54}$
	$\frac{13}{27}$	$\frac{107}{27}$	$\frac{4}{3}$	$-\frac{73}{27}$

Interpretation: $x_1 = \frac{7}{13}$, $x_2 = \frac{25}{13}$.

Objective function: $-\frac{73}{27}$.

Minimize

$$\frac{2x_{11} + 8x_{12} + 2x_{13} + 9x_{21} + x_{22} + 6x_{23}}{x_{11} + 10x_{12} + 5x_{13} + 4x_{21} + 6x_{22} + 5x_{23}} = \frac{P(x)}{Q(x)},$$

subject to

$$x_{11} + x_{12} + x_{13} = 5, \qquad x_{21} + x_{22} + x_{23} = 5$$

$$x_{11} + x_{21} = 3, \qquad x_{12} + x_{22} = 3,$$

$$x_{13} + x_{23} = 4$$

$$x_{ij} \geq 0 \text{ (all ij)}.$$

Solve by Fractional Programming Method.

Solution:

	3	3	4
5	2,1	8,10	2,5
5	9,4	1,6	6,5

				u	u'
	3	2	.	0	0
	.	1	4	-7	-4
v	2	8	13		
v'	1	10	9		

$\bar{c}_{13} = c_{13} - u_1 - v_3 = -11$, $P(x) = 47$

$\bar{d}_{13} = d_{13} - u_1' - v_3' = -4$, $Q(x) = 49$

$\bar{c}_{13}Q(x) - \bar{d}_{13}P(x)$ negative

3	.	2	0	0
1	3	2	4	0
2	-3	2		
1	6	5		

$$\bar{c}_{21} = c_{21} - u_2 - v_1 = 3, \quad P(x) = 25$$

$$\bar{d}_{21} = d_{21} - u_2' - v_1' = 3, \quad Q(x) = 41$$

$$\bar{c}_{21}Q(x) - \bar{d}_{21}P(x) \text{ positive.}$$

Optimal.

SEPARABLE PROGRAMMING

• PROBLEM 11-20

Which one(s) of the functions are separable?

$$x_1^2 + 2x_2 + e^{x_3},$$

$$x_1x_2 + \frac{x_2}{1 + x_1} + x_3$$

Solution: A separable function is a function which can be expressed as the sum of functions of a single variable.

The function

$$x_1^2 + 2x_2 + e^{x_3}$$

is separable since each of terms x_1^2, $2x_2$, e^{x_3} is a function of a single variable. On the other hand the function

$$x_1x_2 + \frac{x_2}{1 + x_1} + x_3$$

is not separable since the terms x_1x_2 and $x_2/(1 + x_1)$ are functions of more than one variable.

• PROBLEM 11-21

Consider the nonlinear programming problem

Minimize

$$x_1^2 - 4x_1 - 2x_2$$

subject to

$$x_1 + x_2 \leq 4$$

$$2x_1 + x_2 \leq 5$$

$$-x_1 + 4x_2 \geq 2$$

$$x_1, x_2 \geq 0$$

Is the objective function convex? Give a graphical presentation of the problem. Derive a piecewise linear approximation (with three straight line portions) to the nonlinear term(s) occurring in the problem and set up a model which would allow the problem to be treated with separable programming techniques.

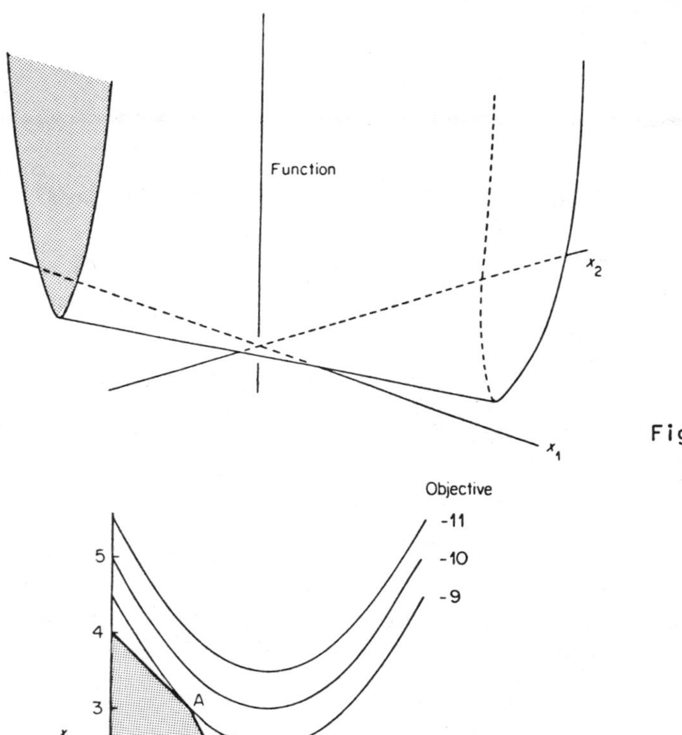

Fig. 1

Fig. 2

Solution: The function

$$x_1^2 - 4x_1 - 2x_2$$

is represented in Figure 1 and easily seen to be convex.

This model is represented graphically in Figure 2 with different objective values represented by the curved lines which arise from contours of the surface in Figure 1. Clearly the optimal solution is represented by point A.

The only non-linear term occurring in the model is x_1^2. A piecewise linear approximation to this function is illustrated in Figure 3.

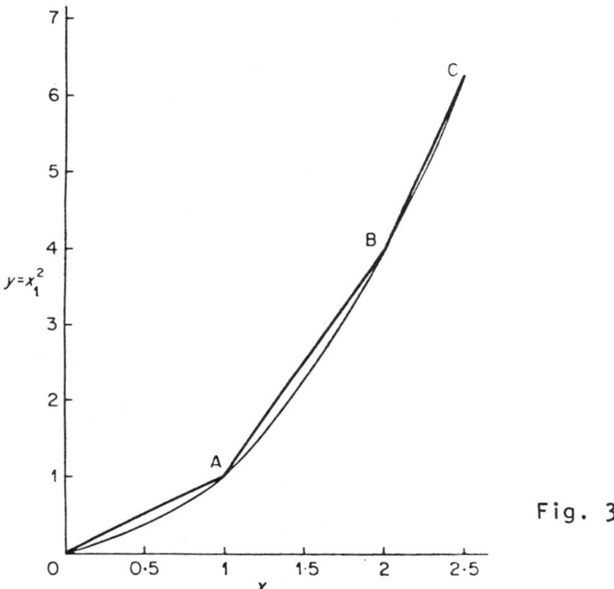

Fig. 3

It is easy to see that x_1 can never exceed 2.5 from the second constraint of the problem. The piecewise linear approximation to x_1^2 need, therefore, only be considered for values of x_1 between 0 and 2.5. The curve between O and C is divided into three straight line portions. This inevitably introduces some inaccuracy into the problem. For example, when x_1 is 1.5 the transformed model will regard x_1^2 as 2.5 instead of 2.25. Such inaccuracy can obviously be reduced by a more refined grid involving more straight line portions. For our purpose, however, the grid indicated in Figure 3 will be accurate. If such inaccuracy is considered serious one approach would be to take the value of x, obtained from the optimal solution, refine the grid in the neighborhood of this value, and re-optimize.

The aim is to eliminate the non-linear term x_1^2 from the model. This can be done by replacing it by the single (linear) term y. It is now possible to relate y to x_1 by the following relationships:

$$x_1 = 0\lambda_1 + 1\lambda_2 + 2\lambda_3 + 2.5\lambda_4 \quad (1)$$

$$y = 0\lambda_1 + 1\lambda_2 + 4\lambda_3 + 6.25\lambda_4 \quad (2)$$

$$\lambda_1 + \lambda_2 + \lambda_3 + \lambda_4 = 1 \quad (3)$$

The λ_i are new variables introduced into the model. They can be interpreted as 'weights' to be attached to the vertices O, A, B, and C. It is, however, necessary to add another stipulation regarding the λ_i:

At most, two adjacent λ_i can be non-zero (4)

The stipulation (4) guarantees that corresponding values of x_1 and y lie on one of the straight line segments OA, AB, or BC. For example if

$$\lambda_2 = 0.5 \qquad \text{and} \qquad \lambda_3 = 0.5$$

(other λ_i being zero) one could get $x_1 = 1.5$ and $y = 2.5$. Clearly ignoring stipulation (4) would incorrectly allow the possibility of values x_1 and y off the piecewise straight line OABC.

(1), (2), and (3) give rise to constraints which can be added to the original model. The term x_1^2 is replaced by y. This results in the model:

$$\begin{array}{lrcl}
\text{Minimize} & & y - 4x_1 - 2x_2 & \\
\text{subject to} & x_1 + x_2 & & \leqslant 4 \\
& 2x_1 + x_2 & & \leqslant 5 \\
& -x_1 + 4x_2 & & \geqslant 2 \\
& -x_1 & + \lambda_2 + 2\lambda_3 + 2{\cdot}5\lambda_4 & = 0 \\
& -y & + \lambda_2 + 4\lambda_3 + 6{\cdot}25\lambda_4 & = 0 \\
& & \lambda_1 + \lambda_2 + \lambda_3 + \lambda_4 & = 1 \\
& & y, x_1, x_2, \lambda_1, \lambda_2, \lambda_3, \lambda_4 \geqslant 0 &
\end{array}$$

It is important to remember that stipulation (4) must apply to the set of variables λ_i. A solution in which for example one has

$$\lambda_1 = \frac{1}{3} \qquad \text{and} \qquad \lambda_3 = \frac{2}{3}$$

would not be acceptable since this results in the wrong relationship between x_1 and $y(x_1^2)$. In general, stipulation (4) cannot be modelled using linear programming constraints. It can, however, be regarded as a 'logical condition' on the variables λ_i and be modelled using integer programming. Fortunately in the above case no difficulty arises over stipulation (4). This is because the original model was convex. Take, for example, the set of values

$\lambda_1 = 0.5$, $\lambda_2 = 0.25$, $\lambda_3 = 0.25$, and $\lambda_4 = 0$.

This clearly breaks stipulation (4). From the relations (1) and (2) it clearly leads to the point

$$x_1 = 0.75$$

and

$$y = 1.25$$

on Figure 3. This is above the piecewise straight line. Since the objective involves minimizing $y\,(x_1^2)$ one would expect to get a better solution by taking $x_1 = 0.75$ and $y = 0.75$ when one drops onto the piecewise straight line. In view of the (convex) shape of the graph values for λ_i cannot be obtained, which give points below the piecewise straight line. Therefore one must always obtain corresponding values of x_1 and y which lie on one of the line segments by virtue of optimality. Stipulation (4) is therefore guaranteed in this case. Therefore solve the transformed model by linear programming and obtain a satisfactory optimal solution. It is not even necessary to resort to the separable extension of the simplex algorithm in this case.

CHAPTER 12

PRODUCTION PLANNING AND INVENTORY CONTROL

SINGLE - ITEM MODELS WITH DETERMINISTIC - STATIC DEMAND

• PROBLEM 12-1

In this problem where shortages are not permitted, the appropriate parameters are

K(= 12,000): fixed cost of a replenishment order,

h(= 0.30): inventory carrying cost per unit per period,

a(= 8,000): demand rate in units per period,

what is the optimum production level and cycle time?

Solution: $Q^* = \sqrt{\dfrac{(2)(8,000)(12,000)}{0.30}} = 25,298$

and $t^* = \dfrac{25,298}{8,000} = 3.2$ months.

Hence the production line is to be set up every 3.2 months and produce 25,298 units. The cost curve is rather flat near this optimal value, so that any production between 20,000 and 30,000 units is acceptable.

• PROBLEM 12-2

In a central grain store, in the town of Memed, it takes about 15 days to get the stock after placing the order, and daily 500 tons are despatched to neighboring markets. On an adhoc basis buffer stock is assumed to be 10 days' stock. Calculate the reorder point P.

Solution: From the formula

$$P = B + S_o L$$

where

B = buffer stock

S_o = quantity used up per period

L = delivery lag,

one has

$$P = 500 \times 10 + 500 \times 15$$

$$= 12{,}500$$

• PROBLEM 12-3

A company purchases valves that are used at the rate of 200 per year. The cost of each valve is \$50 and the cost of placing each order is \$5. The inventory carrying-cost rate is assumed to be 0.10. Shortage losses are a fixed cost of 20 cents per unit and a variable cost of \$10 per unit per year. The lead time is six months. Find the optimal order quantity and reorder point.

Solution: $D = 200$, $i = 0.10$, $\pi = 0.20$, $\hat{\pi} = 10$, $C = 50$, $A = 5$, and $\tau = 0.5$. Using Equations 1 and 2,

$$Q^* = \sqrt{\frac{2AD}{iC} - \frac{(\pi D)^2}{iC(iC + \hat{\pi})}}\sqrt{\frac{iC + \hat{\pi}}{\hat{\pi}}} \qquad (1)$$

$$b^* = \frac{(iCQ^* - \pi D)}{(iC + \hat{\pi})}, \qquad (2)$$

one obtains $Q^* = 23.8 \cong 24$ and $b^* = 5.28 \cong 5$. The cycle length is $T = 24/200 = 0.12$ year. Thus the reorder point is

$$r^* = \tau D - mQ^* - b^* = (0.5)(200) - \left[\frac{0.5}{0.12}\right](24) - 5$$

$$= 100 - 4(24) - 5 = -1$$

The reorder point is negative, indicating that an order for 24 units should be placed when the backorder level reaches one valve.

• PROBLEM 12-4

A manufacturer has to supply his customer with 24,000 units of his product per year. This demand is fixed and known. Since the unit is used by the customer in an assembly-line operation, and the customer has no storage space for the units, the manufacturer must ship a day's supply each day. If the manufacturer fails to supply the required units, he will lose the account and probably his business. Hence, the cost of a shortage is assumed to be infinite, and, consequently, none will be tolerated. The inventory holding cost amounts to $0.10 per unit per month, and the setup cost per run is $350.

The problem is to find the optimum run size q_0, the corresponding optimum scheduling period t_{s0}, and the minimum total expected relevant yearly cost TEC_0. In this case, then,

$$T = 12 \text{ months}$$

$$R = 24{,}000 \text{ units}$$

$$C_1 = \$0.10 \text{ per month}$$

$$C_s = \$350 \text{ per production run}$$

Solution: Substituting in eqs.

$$q_0 = \sqrt{2\frac{R}{T}\frac{C_s}{C_1}} \ ,$$

$$t_{s0} = \sqrt{2\frac{T}{R}\frac{C_s}{C_1}} \ , \quad \text{and}$$

$$TEC_0 = \sqrt{2RTC_1C_s}$$

the following solution is obtained.

$$q_0 = \sqrt{2\frac{24{,}000}{12}\cdot\frac{350}{0.10}} = 3740 \text{ units per run}$$

$$t_{s0} = \sqrt{2\frac{12}{24{,}000}\cdot\frac{350}{0.10}} = 1.87 \text{ months} = 8.1 \text{ weeks between runs}$$

$$TEC_0 = \sqrt{2(24{,}000)(12)(0.10)(350)} = \$4490 \text{ per year}$$

• **PROBLEM 12-5**

Assume the demand for number 2 pine 2 by 4's is 10,000 board feet per year and the purchase price from suppliers is \$0.05 per board foot. If it costs \$0.01 to hold one board foot in inventory for one year and if it costs \$10 to place an order, then find the optimal order quantity and the total cost when ordering the optimal quantity.

Solution: The optimal order quantity is found using the equation

$$Q^* = \sqrt{\frac{2Dk_2}{k_1}}$$

where D is the demand per period, k_1 is the cost rate per year for holding an average of one board foot in inventory for a year, and k_2 is the cost per order.

$$Q^* = \sqrt{\frac{2(10,000)(10)}{0.01}} = 4472 \text{ board feet}$$

is the optimal order quantity.

The total cost when ordering the optimal quantity will be

$$C_T(Q^*) = k_1 \frac{Q^*}{2} + k_2 \frac{D}{Q^*} + k_3 D$$

where k_3 is a constant,

$$= \frac{k_1}{2} \sqrt{\frac{2Dk_2}{k_1}} + k_2 \frac{D}{\sqrt{\frac{2Dk_2}{k_1}}} + k_3 D$$

$$= 1/2 \sqrt{2Dk_1k_2} + 1/2 \sqrt{2Dk_1k_2} + k_3 D$$

$$= \$23.86 + \$23.86 + \$500$$

$$= \$547.72$$

• **PROBLEM 12-6**

Find the total inventory carrying costs and the total ordering cost using the economic order quantity inventory model.

C: unit variable cost of production, I: inventory carrying cost rate per period, R: demand rate in units per period, S: fixed cost of a replacement order.

C = \$1, I = 20 percent, R = 8,000 units, and S = \$12.50.

Solution: Q: Economic order quantity

$$Q = \sqrt{\frac{2(8{,}000)(\$12.50)}{\$1 \cdot (20\%)}}$$

$$= \sqrt{\frac{(16{,}000)(12.50)}{0.20}}$$

$$= \sqrt{\frac{200{,}000}{0.20}}$$

$$= \sqrt{1{,}000{,}000}$$

$$= 1{,}000 \text{ units}$$

Substituting the value for Q in the original terms of the model, total inventory carrying costs = (Q/2)CI or (1,000/2)($1) x 20% = $100, and total ordering costs = (R/Q)S or (8,000/1,000)($12.50) = $100. The adding of the two costs equals the lowest minimum cost per year of $200 for the economic ordering quantity.

• PROBLEM 12-7

Varan Bus Co., is a city-owned transit company which operates a fleet of 400 buses. Varan Bus Co. is interested in establishing an inventory policy for bus tires which minimizes the sum of annual ordering and carrying costs. All buses use the same type of tire and the annual requirements are estimated at 5,000 tires. Ordering cost per order is $125 and the cost of carrying a tire in inventory for one year is estimated at $20. For practical purposes lead time is zero, as the supplier will deliver on the day an order is placed. Note that the basic unit of measurement for a time period is one year. What is the order quantity that minimizes inventory costs, the optimal number of orders per year and the length of the inventory cycle?

Solution: The order quantity which minimizes total inventory cost per year is

$$Q^* = \sqrt{2DC_0/C_h}$$

$$= \sqrt{2(5{,}000)(125)/20}$$

$$= \sqrt{62{,}500}$$

$$= 250.$$

The optimal number of orders each year is

$$N^* = \frac{D}{Q^*}$$

$$= \frac{5,000}{250}$$

$$= 20.$$

The length of the inventory cycle is 0.05 year; that is,

$$t_c^* = \frac{Q^*}{D}$$

$$= \frac{250}{5,000}$$

$$= 0.05$$

or

$$t_c^* = 1/N^*$$

$$= 1/20.$$

This means that the time between any two successive order arrivals (or order placements) is approximately 2.5 weeks.

• PROBLEM 12-8

The demand per unit time of a product is found to be 55 units. There is a fixed cost of $132 associated with each order, and a holding cost per unit time per unit inventory, of $0.3. It takes 7 units of time for an order to be fulfilled. It is required to find the economic lot size and reorder point.

Solution: The formula for economic lot size for this case is

$$Q^* = \sqrt{\frac{2DA}{h}} = \sqrt{\frac{2 \times 55 \times 132}{.3}} = 220 \text{ units}$$

The cycle length is 4 time units and lead time 7 time units. Therefore, reordering should occur when the level of inventory is just sufficient to satisfy the demand for 7 - 4 = 3 days. Q* is ordered when the inventory comes down to 165 units.

• PROBLEM 12-9

Consider the following make or buy decision problem facing the XYZ Company. The demand for a given product can be met by either purchasing from outside or manufacturing from within the plant. The demand rate of the item is 2,000 units per year and the inventory holding cost, C_h, is $0.20 per unit per year. No shortages are allowed.

The remaining parameter values are given in the table.

Decide which choice is better and calculate Economic Lot Size.

	Purchase	*Manufacture*
Item cost (C_u)	\$7.50	\$7.35
Replenishment Cost (C_r)	\$8.00	\$40.00
Replenishment Rate (P)	(instantaneous)	3000 units per year

Solution: The minimum total system cost for the purchase alternative, TC^*_p, can be found by using the equation

$$TC^* = DC_u + \sqrt{2DC_rC_h} \qquad (1),$$

(C_u: item cost, d: demand rate, C_r: replenishment cost per order) as

$$TC^*_p = \$7.50\ (2{,}000) + \sqrt{2(2{,}000)(8)(0.20)}$$

$$= \$15{,}080.00 \text{ per year}$$

Similarly, the minimum total system cost for the manufacturing alternative, TC^*_m may be computed from the equation

$$TC^* = DC_u + \sqrt{\frac{2DC_hC_r(P-D)}{P}} \qquad (2),$$

(P: production rate) as

$$TC^*_m = \$7.35(2{,}000) + \sqrt{\frac{2(2{,}000)(40)(0.20)(3{,}000 - 2{,}000)}{3{,}000}}$$

$$= \$14{,}603.44 \text{ per year}$$

Therefore, the total system cost is minimum for the manufacturing alternative. The analysis suggests that the XYZ Company should decide to manufacture the item under consideration, themselves instead of purchasing it from the outside source. Having made this decision, now determine the economic lot size and the time interval between successive production runs. Use of the equation

$$q^* = \sqrt{\frac{2DPC_r}{(P-D)C_h}} \qquad (3)$$

gives the ELS as

$$ELS = q^* = \sqrt{\frac{2(2{,}000)(3{,}000)(40)}{(3{,}000 - 2{,}000)(0.20)}} = 1{,}566 \text{ units/run}$$

The time interval between successive runs, t*, is obtained by dividing ELS by annual demand; that is,

$$t^* = \frac{1566}{2000} = 0.783 \text{ years} = 9.396 \text{ months}$$

Rounding off the cycle time to three-quarters of a year, the ELS to be adopted would be 1,500 units, and total system cost would be \$14,803.33 per year.

• PROBLEM 12-10

The manager of an inventory system must make the decision whether to purchase or manufacture an item. Suppose that an item may be purchased for \$25 per unit and manufactured at the rate of 10,000 units per year for \$22 each. However, if purchased the ordering cost is only \$5 compared to a setup cost of \$50 if it is manufactured. The yearly demand for this item is 2500 units and the inventory holding cost rate is 10 percent. Find which option should be preferred.

Solution: Assume one decides to purchase. The minimum average annual cost from (1) (letting $P \to \infty$ and $\hat{\pi} \to \infty$),

$$K^* \equiv K(Q^*) = CD + \sqrt{\frac{2ADiC(1 - D/P)\hat{\pi}}{(iC + \hat{\pi})}} \quad (1)$$

K: average annual cost

C: unit variable cost of production (purchase)

A: fixed cost of a replenishment order

i: annual inventory carrying cost rate

D: demand rate in units per year

P: production rate in units per year

$\hat{\pi}$: shortage cost per unit short per year

is,

$$K^* = CD + \sqrt{2ADiC} = (25)(2500) + \sqrt{2(5)(2500)(0.10)(25)}$$

$$= \$62,750$$

If the item is manufactured, then from (1)

$$K^* = CD + \sqrt{1 - D/P}\,\sqrt{2ADiC} = (22)(2500) + \sqrt{1 - 2500/10,000}\,\sqrt{2(50)(2500)(0.10)(22)}$$

$$= \$55,642$$

and it can be seen that the item should be produced.

• PROBLEM 12-11

A wholesale distribution company buys large lots of products and sells to many small retail outlets. One of their products is a beverage they sell at a predictable constant rate of 600 cases/month. They hold an inventory based upon costs of \$60/order and a \$0.20/case/month holding cost for this product. The unconstrained problem is to find the distributor's optimum order quantity, the associated inventory cost per month for the product, and the time between orders. The manufacturer, concerned with product age, sets a new condition that the distributor must not hold the product in inventory for more than

3 weeks. Find the distributor's inventory policy subject to this new constraint. What is the distributor's additional cost per month due to this constraint?

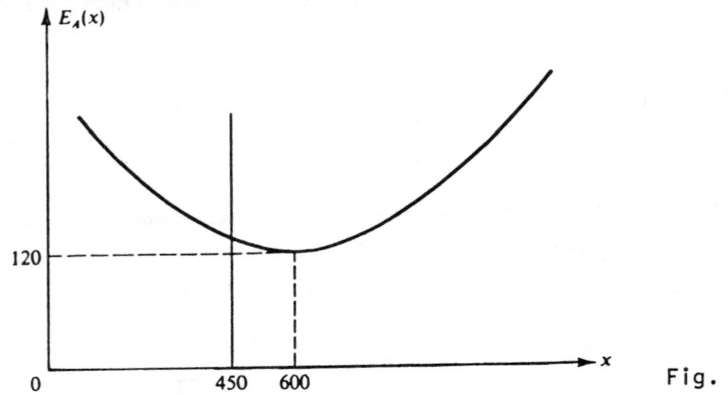

Fig. 1

Solution: The unconstrained problem is clearly an inventory problem with the parameters

Demand: D = 600 cases/month (constant)

Order cost: c_s = \$60/order

Holding cost: c_h = \$0.20/case/month

The order quantity that minimizes the inventory cost rate is

$$x^* = \sqrt{\frac{2c_sD}{c_h}} = \sqrt{\frac{2 \times 60 \times 600}{.2}} = 600 \text{ cases}$$

The total inventory cost per month is

$$E_A(x) = \frac{c_sD}{x} + \frac{c_hx}{2}$$

$$E_A(600) = 60 + 60 = \$120/\text{month}$$

The cycle length is

$$T(x^*) = \frac{x^*}{D} = \frac{600}{600} = 1 \text{ month}$$

The graph in Fig. 1 shows the objective function as a function of the decision variable. It also shows the point that exactly satisfies T(x) = .75 month. It is the point satisfying x/600 = .75 or x = 3/4(600) = 450. The constrained problem requires that the solution have the property that $T \leq .75$ month. This implies the restriction $x \leq 450$ upon the decision variable. The points to the left of the line x = 450 obey this constraint and are feasible; those to the right are infeasible.

The solution to the constrained problem in this case is easily seen from the graph. The x within (0,450) that gives the minimum value of the objective function is x = 450 because the function $E_A(x)$ is decreasing in that interval. The best value of the objective function is

$$E_A(450) = 80 + 45 = \$125/\text{month}$$

The constraint has the effect of reducing the cycle length and increasing the total cost. The distributor's additional cost due to the constraint is 125 - 120 = \$5/month. This is \$5/600 = \$5/6 x .01 = 5/6 cent/case.

• PROBLEM 12-12

Consider the Bach Manufacturing Company that wishes to meet a demand of 100 units per month by purchasing the items from a vendor with a lead time of three-quarters of a month. The item cost is \$2.50 per unit, replenishment cost is \$3.50 per order, and the holding cost is \$0.50 per unit per month. The company estimates the shortage cost to be \$0.20 per unit per month. By letting the period be one month, one has $D = 100$, $C_u = 2.5$, $C_h = 0.50$, $C_r = 3.50$, $C_s = 0.20$, and $L = 0.75$. What is the optimal inventory policy and the total cost of the system under the optimal policy?

Solution: The EOQ (= q*) = economic order quantity is given by equation (1). Substituting the values of parameters in equation (1)

$$q^* = \sqrt{\frac{2DC_r(C_h + C_s)}{C_h C_s}} \tag{1}$$

one gets,

$$EOQ = q^* = \sqrt{\frac{2(100)(3.50)(0.50 + 0.20)}{(0.50)(0.20)}}$$

$$= 70 \text{ units per order}$$

The minimum total system cost per month , TC*, is obtained by using the equation

$$TC^* = DC_u + \sqrt{\frac{2DC_r C_h C_s}{(C_h + C_s)}} \tag{2}$$

and is

$$TC^* = 100(2.50) + \sqrt{\frac{2(100)(3.5)(0.50)(0.20)}{(0.50 + 0.20)}}$$

$$= \$260.00 \text{ per month}$$

The reorder level, R, is calculated by substituting the parameter values in the equation

$$R = \min\left[DL - \sqrt{\frac{2DC_r C_h}{C_s(C_h+C_s)}} \; ; \; \sqrt{\frac{2DC_r C_s}{C_h(C_h+C_s)}}\right] \tag{3}$$

to yield

$$R = \min \left[100(0.75) - \sqrt{\frac{2(100)(3.5)(0.5)}{(0.50 + 0.20)}}; \sqrt{\frac{2(100)(3.5)(0.20)}{(0.50)(0.50+0.20)}} \right]$$

$$= \min [25,20] = 20 \text{ units}$$

Therefore, for the conditions of the problem, the optimal inventory policy calls for ordering 70 units whenever the inventory level falls to 20 units. The total cost of the system under the optimal inventory policy will be \$260.00 per month.

• PROBLEM 12-13

A subcontractor undertakes to supply Diesel engines to a truck manufacturer at the rate of 25 per day. There is a clause in the contract penalizing him \$10 per engine per day late for missing the scheduled delivery date. He finds that the cost of holding a completed engine in stock is \$16 per month. His production process is such that each month (30 days) he starts a batch of engines through the shops, and all these engines are available for delivery any time after the end of the month. What should his inventory level be at the beginning of each month (i.e., immediately after taking into stock the engines made in the previous month, and then shipping engines to fill unsatisfied demand from the previous month)?

Solution: In this case the problem is balancing the costs of holding inventory against the costs of delayed deliveries to customers. Since the subcontractor has already decided to produce a batch of engines every month, he has fixed the size of each batch at 750 engines, and one may assume that he is no longer concerned with economies in run size.

The following notation shall be used:

C_1 = cost per day of holding an engine in inventory

C_2 = penalty cost per day of failing to deliver one engine on schedule

R = contracted number of engines per day

z = planned inventory level at beginning of a month

The problem is to find the value of z that minimizes costs.

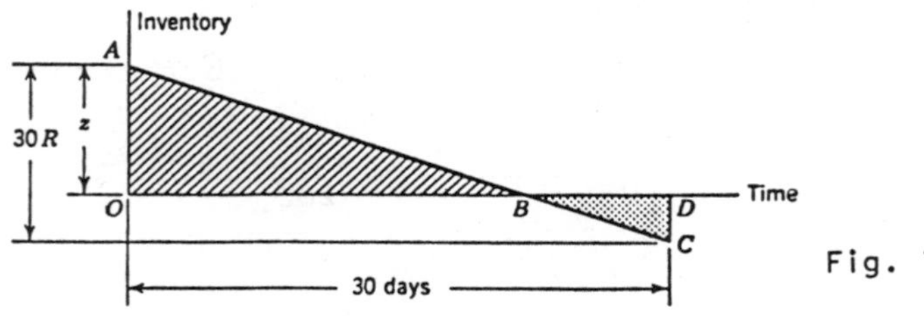

Fig. 1

The inventory situation during each month is represented approximately by Figure 1. The cross-hatched area represents inventory, and the dotted area represents failure to meet delivery. (Although delivery actually takes place in batches of R engines per day, approximate to the actual situation by assuming continuous delivery at the rate of R per day.) With this approximation, the number of "engine-days" of inventory is given by the area of triangle OAB, and the cost of holding inventory is C_1 times this area. By similar triangles OB/30 = z/30R, and OB = z/R. Therefore the area of triangle OAB is $z^2/2R$, and the cost of holding inventory is $c_1 z^2/2R$.

The number of "engine-days" by which the delivery schedule is missed is given by the area of triangle BDC, easily computed to be

$$(30R - z)^2/(2R)$$

Hence the cost of shortages is $(C_2/2R)(30R - z)^2$.

The total cost F(z) is found by adding these two costs. Therefore

$$F(z) = \frac{C_1 z^2}{2R} + \frac{C_2(30R - z)^2}{2R}$$

For the minimum cost dF/dz = 0, and it is obtained

$$z = 30R \frac{C_2}{C_1 + C_2}$$

It will be observed that, since $C_2/(C_1 + C_2) < 1$, the optimum inventory level is less than the number of engines to be delivered each month, and one would deliberately plan for a shortage. Here R = 25, $C_1 = 16/30$, $C_2 = 10$, so that the best starting inventory is

$$30 \times 25 \times \frac{10}{10 + 16/30} = 712 \text{ engines}$$

• PROBLEM 12-14

A contractor undertakes to supply Diesel engines to a truck manufacturer at a rate of 25 per day. He finds that the cost of holding a completed engine in stock is $16 per month, and there is a clause in the contract penalizing him $10 per engine per day late for missing the scheduled delivery data. Production of engines is in batches, and each time a new batch is started there are setup costs of $10,000. How frequently should batches be started, and what should be the initial inventory level at the time each batch is completed?

Solution: In these circumstances economies in production costs per engine can be achieved by increasing the batch size. Such economies will be offset by the resulting increase in inventory cost; so it is necessary to consider simultaneously the inventory level and the batch size.

The following notation shall be used:

C_1 = cost per day of holding an engine in inventory

C_2 = penalty cost per day of failing to deliver one engine on schedule

C_3 = setup cost

R = contracted number of engines per day

z = planned inventory level at beginning of a month

t = interval between starting batches

The number of "engine-days" by which the delivery schedule is missed is computed to be

$$(30R - z)^2/(2R)$$

Hence the cost of shortages is

$(C_2/2R)(30R - z)^2$. Then, the costs of holding inventory together with the penalty costs of missed deliveries will total

$$\frac{C_1 z^2}{2R} + \frac{C_2(tR - z)^2}{2R}$$

over the interval t between batches.

In addition, there is now a setup cost C_3, so that the average cost over time F(t, z) is given by

$$F(t,z) = \frac{1}{t}\left[\frac{C_1 z^2}{2R} + \frac{C_2(tR - z)^2}{2R}\right] + \frac{C_3}{t}$$

(It is necessary to consider average cost, in order to make comparisons between different values of t.) For minimum cost, $\partial F/\partial z = 0$, and $\partial F/\partial t = 0$.

$$\frac{\partial F}{\partial z} = \frac{1}{t}\left[\frac{C_1 z}{R} - \frac{C_2(tR - z)}{R}\right] = 0 \qquad \text{or}$$

$$z = \frac{tRC_2}{C_1 + C_2}$$

$$\frac{\partial F}{\partial t} = -\frac{1}{t^2}\left[\frac{C_1 z^2}{2R} + \frac{C_2(tR - z)^2}{2R} + C_3\right] + \frac{C_2(tR - z)}{t} = 0$$

Substituting for z in the second equation yields, with some rearrangement,

$$t = \sqrt{\frac{2C_3(C_1 + C_2)}{C_1 C_2 R}} \qquad (1)$$

and hence

$$z = \sqrt{\frac{2C_2 C_3 R}{C_1(C_1 + C_2)}} \qquad (2)$$

Substitute the numerical values into Eq. (1) and (2)

C_1 = \$16/30 per day per engine

C_2 = \$10 per day per engine

C_3 = \$10,000

R = 25 engines per day

One obtains t = 40 days, and z = 943 engines.

Thus it would be better to start a new batch approximately every 6 weeks, rather than every month.

The average cost per day is

$$F(t,z) = \frac{1}{t}\left[\frac{C_1 z^2}{2R} + \frac{C_2(Rt - z)^2}{2R} + C_3\right] = \$503$$

with t = 40 and z = 943.

MULTIPLE - ITEM MODELS WITH DETERMINISTIC - STATIC DEMAND

• PROBLEM 12-15

Company management has decided that because of limitations on available capital, the average stock level must not exceed 750 items of all types. The company makes three products, and the following are given. What are the optimal production quantities?

Product	1	2	3
C_1 (storage cost)	0.05	0.02	0.04
C_3 (setup cost)	50	40	60
r (demand)	100	120	75

Solution: This inventory control problem is of the form

$$\text{Min } K = K(q_1^0, q_2^0, \ldots, q_n^0)$$

$$\text{subject to } g(q_1^0, q_2^0, \ldots, q_n^0) = d$$

where d (=750 in this case) is the overall constraint, q_i^0 is the optimal lot size for product i.

The procedure to solve this problem is as follows. First, solve the problem ignoring the constraint, that is, choose minimum cost q_i^0 for each item separately. If these q_i^0 satisfy the constraint, then they are the optimal parameters for the multiitem system. On the other hand, if they do not satisfy the constraint, then form the function

$$L = K(q_1^0, q_2^0, \ldots, q_n^0) + \lambda[g(q_1^0, q_2^0, \ldots, q_n^0) - d]$$

where λ is a Lagrange multiplier. The optimal q_i^0 can be determined by solving the 2n + 1 equations in 2n + 1 unknowns given by

$$\frac{\partial L}{\partial \lambda} = 0; \qquad \frac{\partial L}{\partial q_i^0} = 0.$$

Use the economic lot-size formula

$$q_i{}^0 = \sqrt{\frac{2r_iC_{3i}}{C_{1i}}}$$

to obtain

$$\text{Product 1:} \quad q_1{}^0 = \sqrt{\frac{2 \times 100 \times 50}{0.05}} = 100\sqrt{20} = 447$$

$$\text{Product 2:} \quad q_2{}^0 = \sqrt{\frac{2 \times 120 \times 40}{0.02}} = 100\sqrt{48} = 693$$

$$\text{Product 3:} \quad q_3{}^0 = \sqrt{\frac{2 \times 75 \times 60}{0.04}} = 100\sqrt{21.5} = 464.$$

The average inventory will be one-half the sum of these quantities, which is 1604 ÷ 2 = 802 and exceeds the 750 allowed. Therefore use the equation

$$q_i{}^0 = \sqrt{\frac{2C_{3i}r_i}{C_{1i} + \lambda 2}}\ .$$

where λ is the Lagrange multiplier which can be obtained from

$$\sum_{i=1}^{3} \sqrt{\frac{2C_{3i}r_iC_{1i}}{\frac{C_{3i}}{C_{1i}} + 2\lambda^*}}\ .$$

First try $\lambda = 0.005$ and obtain

$$\text{Product 1:} \quad q_1{}^0 = \sqrt{\frac{2 \times 100 \times 50}{0.06}} = 100\sqrt{16.67} = 409$$

$$\text{Product 2:} \quad q_2{}^0 = \sqrt{\frac{2 \times 120 \times 40}{0.03}} = 100\sqrt{32} = 566$$

$$\text{Product 3:} \quad q_3{}^0 = \sqrt{\frac{2 \times 75 \times 60}{0.05}} = 100\sqrt{18} = 424.$$

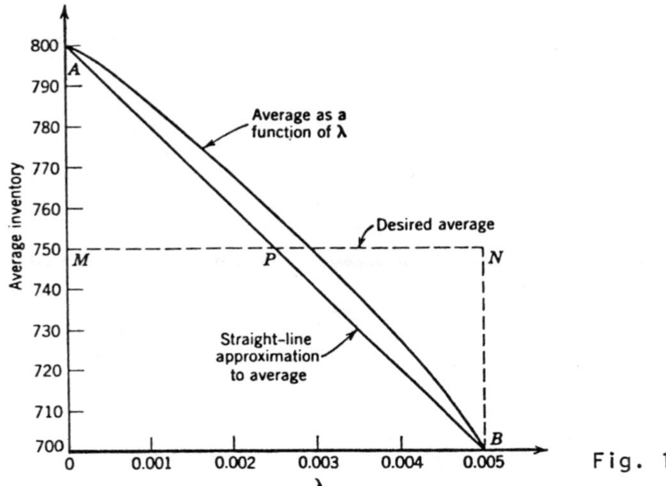

Fig. 1

The average inventory will now be 1/2(409 + 566 + 424) ≅ 700. Because this is too low, a smaller value of λ is required, and the best way of finding it is by interpolation. Suppose that average inventory had been computed as a function of λ and obtained as in Figure 1. The two points A and B corresponding to λ = 0 and λ = 0.005 are known, and one can argue that between A and B the unknown curve can be approximated by a straight line. In this case the point P where average inventories are 750 can be found from the similar triangles AMP and BNP. One gets

$$\frac{MP}{AM} = \frac{NP}{NB} \quad \text{or} \quad MP = \left(\frac{MN - MP}{NB}\right) AM$$

$$= \left(\frac{0.005 - MP}{50}\right) 52$$

or

$$MP = \lambda \cong 0.0025.$$

One can either use this value of λ to recompute the production quantities or interpolate on the quantities found. Because the new value of λ is midway between the earlier values, one argues that the lot sizes will be approximately midway between those found previously. That is,

$$q_1{}^0 = 1/2(447 + 409) = 428$$

$$q_2{}^0 = 1/2(693 + 566) = 628$$

$$q_3{}^0 = 1/2(464 + 424) = 444.$$

The average inventory is now 750, so that the problem is solved.

• PROBLEM 12-16

A small electronics company purchases three types of subcomponents. The management desires never to have an investment in these items in excess of $15,000. No backorders are allowed and the inventory carrying-cost rate for each item is 20 percent. The pertinent data for each item is shown in Table 1. Determine the optimal lot size for each item.

TABLE 1

	ITEM 1	ITEM 2	ITEM 3
Demand rate, D_j	1000	1000	2000
Item cost, C_j	50	20	80
Setup cost, A_j	50	50	50

Solution: The optimal lot sizes, ignoring the constraint, are obtained by using

$$Q^* = \sqrt{\frac{2AD}{iC}}$$

Q^*: optimal lot size

i: inventory carrying cost rate

are found as follows,

$$Q_1 = \sqrt{\frac{2(50)(1000)}{(0.2)(50)}} = 100,$$

$$Q_2 = \sqrt{\frac{2(50)(1000)}{(0.2)(20)}} = 158,$$

$$Q_3 = \sqrt{\frac{2(50)(2000)}{(0.2)(80)}} = 112.$$

If these lot sizes are used, the maximum investment in inventory would be

$$(50)(100) + (20)(158) + (80)(112) = \$17,120.$$

Since this is greater than the maximum allowable investment in inventory, the constraint is active and the Lagrange multiplier method must be used. The problem becomes

$$\text{minimize } K = \sum_{j=1}^{3} \left[C_j D_j + \frac{A_j D_j}{Q_j} + iC_j \frac{Q_j}{2} \right]$$

subject to

$$\sum_{j=1}^{3} C_j Q_j = d$$

where d is the maximum inventory investment allowed. Now construct the Lagrangian function,

$$L = \sum_{j=1}^{3}\left[C_jD_j + \frac{A_jD_j}{Q_j} + iC_j\frac{Q_j}{2}\right] + \lambda\left[\sum_{j=1}^{3} C_jQ_j - d\right]$$

and

$$\frac{\partial L}{\partial Q_j} = -\frac{A_jD_j}{Q_j^{\,2}} + \frac{iC_j}{2} + \lambda C_j = 0; \qquad j = 1,2,3$$

$$\frac{\partial L}{\partial \lambda} = \sum_{j=1}^{3} C_jQ_j - d = 0.$$

These have the unique, optimal solution

$$Q_j^* = \sqrt{\frac{2A_jD_j}{C_j(i + 2\lambda^*)}} \qquad j = 1,2,3$$

where λ^* is the solution of the equation

$$\sum_{j=1}^{3} C_j\sqrt{\frac{2A_jD_j}{C_j(i + 2\lambda^*)}} = d$$

or

$$\sum_{j=1}^{3}\sqrt{\frac{2A_jD_jC_j}{i + 2\lambda^*}} = d.$$

Substituting into this last equation, obtain

$$\sqrt{\frac{(2)(50)(1000)(50)}{0.20 + 2\lambda^*}} + \sqrt{\frac{(2)(50)(1000)(20)}{0.20 + 2\lambda^*}} + \sqrt{\frac{(2)(50)(2000)(80)}{0.20 + 2\lambda^*}} = 15,000$$

whose solution is

$$\lambda^* = 0.03.$$

Therefore, the optimal $\{Q_j^*\}$ are

$$Q_1^* = \sqrt{\frac{(2)(50)(1000)}{(50)(0.30)}} = 88$$

$$Q_2^* = \sqrt{\frac{(2)(50)(1000)}{(20)(0.30)}} = 139,$$

$$Q_3^* = \sqrt{\frac{(2)(50)(2000)}{(80)(0.30)}} = 98.$$

Substitution of these $\{Q_j^*\}$ values into the constraint will show that it does hold as a strict equality.

• PROBLEM 12-17

Consider the following situation, which involves three items made from a common raw material. Assume that the raw material has an ordering cost (setup) of $1000 and that storage costs 1¢ per unit per day. Deliveries of raw material take 7 days. For the finished items the data are shown in Table 1. Shortages of finished items are back-ordered at the costs shown. Shortages of raw materials do not in themselves result in costs, but may cause production delays which, in turn, may cause shortages of finished items. How much should be ordered each month?

TABLE 1

	Items		
	A	*B*	*C*
Mean daily demand, r	43	78	25
Standard deviation, σ	20	14	5
Holding cost per day, C_1	1	0.5	1.2
Shortage cost per day, C_2	20	10	30
Setup cost, C_3	800	1000	3000
Setup time, days	0.5	1.0	1.0
Production rate per day, k	192	385	90
Amount of raw material per unit	3	2	5

Solution: The first items to notice in Table 1 are the setup times and production rates. For example, it is impossible to set up all three items every day, because it takes either a half day or a full day to make the setup. It should also be noted that only the mean daily demand and standard deviations are given, not the distribution functions. However, if it is assumed that the distribution functions are independent, then with any reasonably symmetric demand function , the law of large numbers assures us that the total demand over several days (perhaps 10 or more) will be approximately normally distributed.

Start by computing the mean daily demand for raw material and its standard deviation. Because the three items require 3, 2, and 5 units of raw material respectively, the total daily demand for raw material averages

$$3 \times 43 + 2 \times 78 + 5 \times 25 = 410,$$

using the equation

$$\bar{z} = a\bar{x} + b\bar{y} + c\bar{w}$$

where bars denote averages, the variance is

$$9 \times 20^2 + 4 \times 14^2 + 25 \times 5^2 = 5009,$$

using the equation

$$V = a^2V(x) + b^2V(y) + c^2V(w).$$

The standard deviation is about 71.

Now, the economic lot-size equation gives the optimal order quantity as

$$q^0 = \sqrt{\frac{2C_3r}{C_1}} = \sqrt{\frac{2 \times 1000 \times 410}{0.01}} \cong 9000,$$

which is 22 days' supply. In practice, if the plant works seven days a week, one would probably order every three weeks. If the plant works a five-day week, one would order every month. To continue the problem, assume a seven-day week.

Because the amount ordered plus the amount on hand must last until the next delivery, which will occur after an order interval plus a lead time, that is, 22 + 7 = 29 days, a total quantity of 29 days' demand plus a buffer stock are needed to take care of the variance. Assume that three standard deviations will be a sufficient buffer. The daily standard deviation is 71. Therefore, for 29 days one shall require a buffer of

$$3 \times \sqrt{29} \times 71 = 1130.$$

Consequently, to cover all contingencies over 29 days, a quantity of

$$1130 + (29 \times 410) = 13,020$$

is needed. The ordering rule would be:

> Every 22 days order enough to make the stock on hand together with that on order total 13,020.

Therefore, if the stock on hand is 3000, one would order 13,020 - 3000 = 10,020.

An alternative policy would be to order an economic lot-size quantity (9000) every time the stock is just sufficient to last over the lead time (7 days). Thus orders would be placed whenever stocks drop to

$$7 \times 410 + 3\sqrt{7} \times 71 = 3431.$$

Such a policy would result in slightly lower stocks, but might involve the increased costs of a "continuous" review as contrasted with a regular review every 22 days.

QUANTITY DISCOUNTS

• PROBLEM 12-18

Assume that the supplier of tires to Metro Bus Co. has made an offer in which a discount of 2 percent off the normal cost of $100 per tire will be applied if Metro Bus Co. purchases in quantities of 1,000 or more. Analysts have decided to compare total costs under the current EOQ policy with those which would exist under the discount situation.

$D = 5{,}000$ tires per year, $Q^* = 250$ tires, $C_o = \$125$ per order, and $C_h = \$20$ per tire per year. Find the annual costs under the present policy and that of the discount and then compare.

Solution:

$$TC(Q^*, P) = (D/Q^*)C_o + (Q^*/2)(C_h) + D \times P$$

$$TC(250, 100) = (5{,}000/250)(125) + (250/2)(20) + (5{,}000)(100)$$

$$= 505{,}000.$$

This means that an EOQ ordering policy with no discount incurs a cost of $505,000 per year.

Under the discount policy, P = 98 and Q is set to the minimium lot size which qualifies for a discount (Q = 1000). This reduces the ordering cost, increases the carrying cost, and reduces the purchasing cost:

$$TC(1{,}000, 98) = (5{,}000/1{,}000)(125) + (1{,}000/2)(20) + (5{,}000)(98)$$

$$+ 500{,}625.$$

If total annual cost is the primary criterion, then there is an apparent savings of $4,375 per year.

• PROBLEM 12-19

Consider the inventory model with the following information:

Setup cost K = 10, holding cost per unit inventory per unit time h = 1, the demand rate per unit time $\beta = 5$, cost per unit $c_1 = 2$ for $y < q$ (=15) and $c_2 = 1$ for $y \geq q$, where q is the quantity at which the price break occurs, y is the actual quantity to be ordered. y_m is the quantity that would be ordered, without considering the price breaks. The relationship between these variables are as shown in Figure 1.

$TCU_1(y)$ stands for total cost per unit time $y < q$ and $TCU_2(y)$ stands for total cost per unit time for $y \geq q$. Find $TCU(y^*)$.

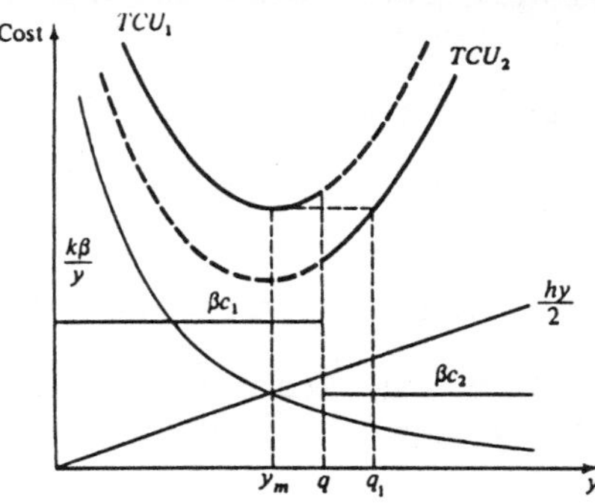

Fig. 1

Solution: First compute y_m; thus,

$$y_m = \sqrt{\frac{2K\beta}{h}} = \sqrt{\frac{2 \times 10 \times 5}{1}} = 10.$$

Since $y_m < q$, it is necessary to check whether q is less than q_1. The value of q_1 is computed from

$$TCU_1(y_m) = TCU_2(q_1)$$

or

$$c_1\beta + \frac{K\beta}{y_m} + \frac{hy_m}{2} = c_2\beta + \frac{K\beta}{q_1} + \frac{hq_1}{2} .$$

Substitution yields

$$2 \times 5 + \frac{10 \times 5}{10} + \frac{1 \times 10}{2} = 1 \times 5 + \frac{10 \times 5}{q_1} + \frac{1 \times q_1}{2}$$

or

$$q_1^2 - 30q_1 + 100 = 0.$$

This yields $q_1 = 26.18$, or $q_1 = 3.82$. By definition, q_1 is selected as the larger value. Since $q_1 > q$, it follows that $y^* = q = 15$ and

$$TCU(y^*) = TCU_2(15) = c_2\beta + \frac{K\beta}{15} + \frac{h \times 15}{2}$$

$$= 1 \times 5 + \frac{10 \times 5}{15} + \frac{1 \times 15}{2}$$

$$= 15.83.$$

A manufacturer uses large quantities of a purchased part in his assembly operations. He wants to use a constant purchase lot size, and he specifies that no shortages be planned. The following data are relevant to the problem of determining the optimal lot size:

a. Annual requirements -- 300,000 units, uniformly required over the year.

b. Manufacturer's fixed cost of placing an order -- $80.

c. Annual cost of interest, insurance, and taxes on average inventory investment -- 20 percent of the value of average inventory.

d. Cost of storage -- 10 cents per month, based on average quantity stored.

e. Vendor's price schedule -- a fixed charge of $20 per order, plus a charge per unit determined according to the following schedule:

ORDER SIZE	UNIT VARIABLE COST
$0 < Q < 10{,}000$	$1.00
$10{,}000 \leq Q < 30{,}000$	0.98
$30{,}000 \leq Q < 50{,}000$	0.96
$50{,}000 \leq Q$	0.94

Find the optimal lot size.

Suppose the price schedule above had been of the incremental discount type. Calculate the optimal lot size, for this case.

Solution: For the All Units Discounts schedule, suppose that the procurement cost for a lot size Q is $A + C_jQ$. if $N_{j-1} \leq Q < N_j$, $j = 1,2,\dots,J$, where $C_j < C_{j-1}$. N_0 is the minimum quantity that can be ordered and N_J is the maximum order size, usually unlimited.
Let

$$K_j(Q) = \frac{AD}{Q} + C_jD + iC_j\frac{Q}{2} . \qquad (1)$$

K is a mathematical function of Q, which over the range $N_{j-1} \leq Q < N_j$ gives the average annual cost of an order of size Q. The average annual cost function is then written as

$$K(Q) = K_j(Q), \text{ if } N_{j-1} \leq Q < N_j, \quad (j = 1,2,\dots,J)$$

To find the optimal value of Q, find the minimum cost point on each segment of K and compare the costs at these points to determine the global minimum. This procedure can be stated more precisely as follows: Let Q_j^* be the value of Q that minimizes $K_j(Q)$ in the range $N_{j-1} \leq Q_j < N_j$, and define Q^* as the overall optimal lot size. Then $K(Q^*) = \min_j K_j(Q_j^*)$.

To find the minimum cost value, $K_j(Q_j^*)$, in each segment, first find Q_j^*. Let Q_j^0 be the minimum point of the mathematical function $K_j(Q)$,

$$Q_j^0 = \sqrt{\frac{2AD}{iC_j}} . \tag{2}$$

Then if Q_j^0 is in the range $[N_{j-1}, N_j)$, $Q_j^* = Q_j^0$. If

$$Q_j^0 < N_{j-1}, \quad Q_j^* = N_{j-1};$$

and if

$$Q_j^0 \geq N_j, \; Q_j^* = N_{\bar{j}}.$$

In the latter case of $Q_j^0 \geq N_j$, the overall optimal lot size cannot lie in the region $Q < N_j$. This follows from the facts that

$$Q_j^0 < Q_{j+1}^0$$

and

$$K_j(Q_j^*) > K_{j+1}(Q_j^*).$$

Thus, begin with the K_J segment and proceed to find Q_J^*, $Q_{J-1}^*, \ldots,$ until reaching an interval, say k, where $Q_k^* = Q_k^0$. The optimal solution must be one of the values $Q_k^0, Q_{k+1}^*, \ldots, Q_J^*$.

To solve this problem, first write the total annual cost function, noting that the fixed cost per order is $100, the sum of the manufacturer's internal cost and the vendor's fixed charge, and that there is a storage cost charge of $1.20 per year per unit of average inventory. For $N_{j-1} \leq Q < N_j$, the price is C_j and the average annual cost is (from (1))

$$K_j(Q) = \frac{(80 + 20)(300{,}000)}{Q} + (300{,}000)C_j$$

$$+ [(0.20)C_j + 1.20]\frac{Q}{2} ; \qquad j = 1,2,3,4.$$

The values of C_j, N_{j-1}, and N_j are given in the price schedule. The minimum point on the entire K_j curve is at

$$Q_j^0 = 1000\sqrt{\frac{60}{1.20 + 0.2C_j}}$$

from (2).

For $j = 4$, $C_4 = \$0.94$ and $Q_4^0 = 6580 < N_3 = 50{,}000$, so the minimum cost point on the K_4 segment occurs at $Q_4^* = 50{,}000$.

For $j = 3$, $C_3 = \$0.96$ and $Q_3^0 = 6570 < N_2 = 30{,}000$, so $Q_3^* = 30{,}000$. (Obvious, actually, since $Q_3^0 < Q_4^0$.)

For $j = 2$, $C_2 = \$0.98$ and $Q_2^0 = 6560 < N_1 = 10{,}000$, so $Q_2^* = 10{,}000$. (Again obvious from knowledge that Q_2^0 will be less than Q_4^0.)

For $j = 1$, $C_1 = \$1$ and $Q_1^0 = 6550$. This value is in the range for which C_1 applies; therefore $Q_1^* = 6550$.

The costs must be calculated for Q_1^*, Q_2^*, Q_3^*, and Q_4^*:

$K(6550) = \$309{,}155$

$K(10{,}000) = \$303{,}980$ -- minimum

$K(30{,}000) = \$309{,}880$

$K(50{,}000) = \$317{,}500$.

The optimal lot size is $Q^* = 10{,}000$ units. The average time between orders is 0.033 year. The total cost curve is shown in Figure 1.

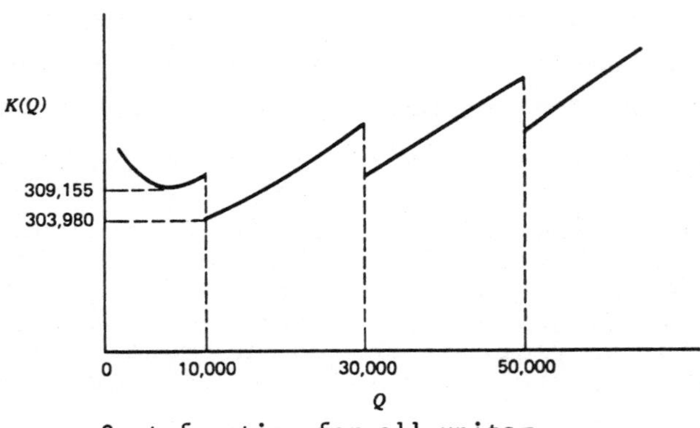

Cost function for all-units-discounts schedule. Fig. 1

In the Incremental Discount Schedule, the price associated with an interval applies only to the units within that interval. Assuming $N_0 = 0$, the first N_1 units would cost C_1 each, the next $(N_2 - N_1)$ units, C_2 each; the next $(N_3 - N_2)$ units, C_3 each, and so on.

The procurement cost of Q units would be $A + V(Q)$, where $V(Q)$ is the total variable cost of the lot and is given by

$$V(Q) = \sum_{k=1}^{j-1} C_k(N_k - N_{k-1}) + C_j(Q - N_{j-1}),$$

$$N_{j-1} \le Q < N_j$$

$$= V(N_{j-1}) + C_j(Q - N_{j-1}), \quad N_{j-1} \le Q < N_j. \qquad (3)$$

The average annual cost is

$$K(Q) = K_j(Q), \text{ if } N_{j-1} \le Q < N_j$$

where

$$K_j(Q) = [A + V(Q)]\frac{D}{Q} + i\left(\frac{V(Q)}{Q}\right)\frac{Q}{2}$$

$$= [A + V(N_{j-1}) + C_j(Q - N_{j-1})]\frac{D}{Q} + \frac{i}{2}[V(N_{j-1})$$

$$+ C_j(Q - N_{j-1})]. \qquad (4)$$

The term $V(Q)/Q$ in Equation 4 represents the average price per unit and is used to find the dollar value of average inventory. Optimal lot size will never equal the quantity defining a price break.

To find the optimal lot size, compute for $j = 1,2,\ldots,J$,

$$Q_j^0 = \sqrt{\frac{2D[A + V(N_{j-1}) - C_jN_{j-1}]}{iC_j}}\ . \qquad (5)$$

If $N_{j-1} \le Q_j^0 < N_j$, compute $K_j(Q_j^0)$. Choose lot size Q^* as the value of Q_j^0 yielding the minimum $K_j(Q_j^0)$.

Thus from (4)

$$K_j(Q) = [100 + V(N_{j-1}) + C_j(Q - N_{j-1})]\frac{300{,}000}{Q}$$

$$+ \frac{(0.20)}{2}[V(N_{j-1}) + C_j(Q - N_{j-1})] + (1.20)\frac{Q}{2}$$

j	C_j	N_j	$V(N_j)$	$V(Q) = V(N_{j-1}) + C_j(Q - N_{j-1})$
1	\$1.00	10,000	\$10,000	Q
2	0.98	30,000	29,600	$200 + 0.98Q$
3	0.96	50,000	48,800	$800 + 0.96Q$
4	0.94	—	—	$1800 + 0.94Q$

from Equation 3.

Using the values given,

$$K(Q) = \begin{cases} K_1(Q) = \dfrac{30 \times 10^6}{Q} + 300{,}000 + 0.70Q, & 0 < Q < 10{,}000 \\ K_2(Q) = \dfrac{90 \times 10^6}{Q} + 294{,}020 + 0.698Q, & 10{,}000 \leq Q < 30{,}000 \\ K_3(Q) = \dfrac{270 \times 10^6}{Q} + 288{,}080 + 0.696Q, & 30{,}000 \leq Q < 50{,}000 \\ K_4(Q) = \dfrac{570 \times 10^6}{Q} + 282{,}180 + 0.694Q, & 50{,}000 \leq Q. \end{cases}$$

The minimum points on curves K_1, K_2, K_3, and K_4 are obtained using Equation 5 , with the denominator including the storage cost component, 1.20.

$$Q_1{}^0 = 6550$$

$$Q_2{}^0 = 11{,}360$$

$$Q_3{}^0 = 19{,}660$$

$$Q_4{}^0 = 28{,}700.$$

The values $Q_3{}^0$ and $Q_4{}^0$ are not in the range where K_3 and K_4 apply, respectively; therefore they are not considered further. The optimal lot size is either $Q_1{}^0$ or $Q_2{}^0$. To determine which, one must calculate average annual costs. It turns out that K(6550) = \$309,360 and K(11,360) = \$309,860, so the optimal lot size is 6550 units. The optimal time between orders is 0.022 year. This is illustrated in Figure 2.

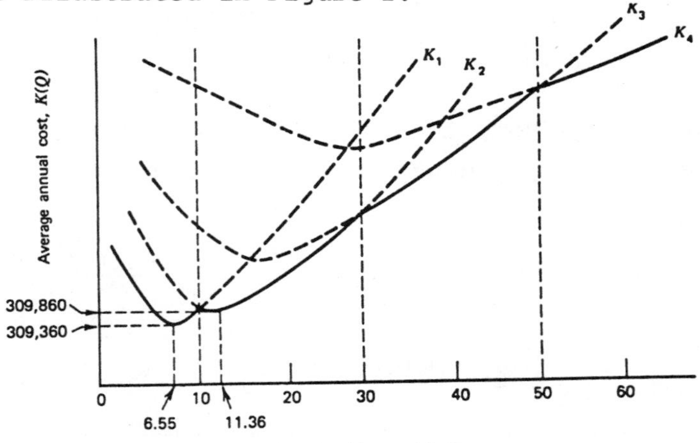

Cost function for incremental discount schedule. Fig. 2

Comparing the solution with that of the previous, where the price schedule was interpreted as an all units discount, note that the optimal lot size is 6550 here versus 10,000 there. This reduction in lot size is to be expected because with the incremental discount where the price discount does not apply to all units, there is less incentive to order to large lots.

SINGLE - ITEM MODELS WITH STOCHASTIC - STATIC DEMAND

• PROBLEM 12-21

A baking company sells one of its types of cake by weight. If the product is not sold on the day it is baked, it can only be sold at a loss of 15¢ per pound. But there is an unlimited market for 1-day-old cake. The cost of holding a pound of cake in stock for one day, then, is 15¢. On the other hand, the company makes a profit of 95¢ on every pound of cake sold on the day it is baked. Thus the cost of a shortage is 95¢ per pound. Past daily orders form a triangular distribution as shown in Fig. 1.

In this case, the probability density function of r is

$$f(r) = 0.02 - 0.0002r$$

Determine how many pounds of cake the company should take daily.

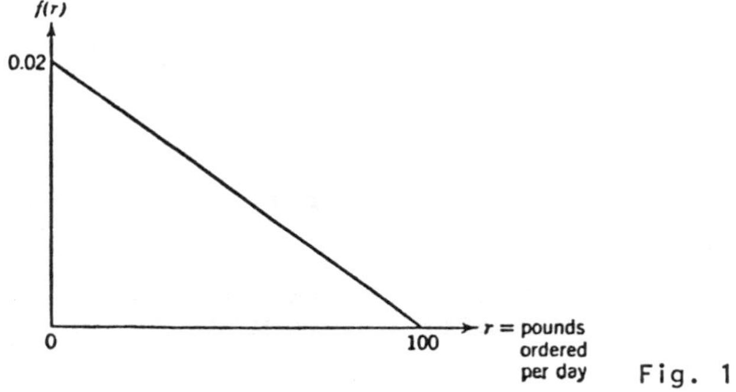

Fig. 1

Solution: In this case $C_1 = 15¢$ and $C_2 = 95¢$. Then

$$\frac{C_2}{C_1 + C_2} = \frac{95}{15 + 95} = 0.8636$$

To find the optimum order quantity q_0, find a stock level S which satisfies the condition

$$F(S) = \frac{C_2}{C_1 + C_2} = 0.8636; \text{ i.e., } \int_0^S f(r)\, dr = 0.8636$$

This can be done as follows

$$\int_0^S f(r)\, dr = \int_0^S (0.02 - 0.0002r)\, dr$$

$$= 0.02r - \left(\frac{0.0002r^2}{2}\right)\Bigg|_0^S = 0.8636$$

$$0.02S - 0.0001S^2 = 0.8636$$

Therefore

$$S = 100 \pm 36.93$$

Consequently, there are two solutions:

1. $q_1 = 100 + 36.93 = 136.93$ pounds

2. $q_2 = 100 - 36.93 = 63.07$ pounds

The first solution is not applicable since the given probability distribution for r is not applicable over 100 pounds. Therefore, the second solution is used.

• PROBLEM 12-22

A daily newspaper sells for 7¢ per copy and costs the printer 2¢ per copy to print. The publisher estimates that the demand each period is appxoimately exponentially distributed according to the following formula:

$$P[D \leq x] = (1 - e^{-x/1000}) = F_D(x) \qquad (x \geq 0)$$

with density

$$f_D(x) = e^{-x/1000} \frac{1}{1000} .$$

The graph of the demand distribution function is given in Figure 1.

The publisher must decide on the number, I, to print each day. His net profit per period is, from

$$N = pS - C(I) \tag{1}$$

where p: selling price

C(x): cost of producing x units in one period

S: number of units sold per period

one gets

$$N = (.07)S - (.02)I.$$

The publisher's question is how to determine I, the number of papers to be published. Obviously, if too many copies are printed, some will be left over and money will be lost. On the other hand, if too few copies are available, sales will be lost. Some compromise must be sought. Thus, he wishes to set the level, I, so as to maximize his "expected net profit" per period.

Solution: Proceed by determining expected net profit as a function of I. Then select that value of I maximizing the expected net profit.

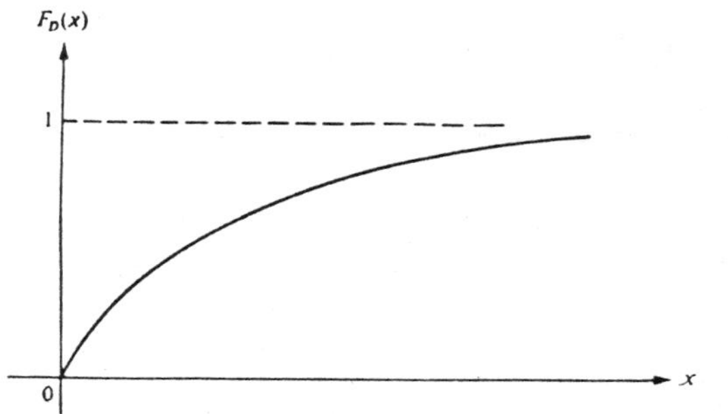

Fig. 1

Using the representation

$$S = \begin{cases} D & \text{if } D < I \\ I & \text{if } I < D \end{cases},$$

where D is the random demand, for sales as a function of demand, and (1), for profit as a function of sales, the one-period profit can be expressed as a function of that period's demand:

$$N(D) = \begin{cases} pD - cI & \text{if } D < I \\ pI - cI & \text{if } D \geq I \end{cases} \tag{2}$$

In other words, the profit is a random variable that is a function of the random variable D. Letting $N = g(D)$:

$$g(x) = \begin{cases} px - cI & \text{if } x < I \\ pI - cI & \text{if } x \geq I \end{cases},$$

find the expected profit by

$$E[N(D)] = \int_0^\infty g(x) f_D(x)\, dx,$$

$$= p\left[\int_0^I x f_D(x)\, dx + \int_I^\infty I f_D(x)\, dx\right] - cI, \tag{3}$$

$$= p\int_0^I x f_D(x)\, dx + pI[1 - F_D(I)] - cI.$$

Now the last expression may be maximized with respect to I. Differentiate (3) with respect to I and set the result equal to zero. Remembering that the derivative of an integral with respect to its upper limit is just the integrand

$$\frac{d}{dI}\int_0^I g(x)\, dx = g(I)$$

and that the derivative of a continuous distribution is the density, obtain

$$\frac{dE[N(D)]}{dI} = pIf_D(I) + p[1 - F_D(I)] - pIf_D(I) - c = 0.$$

After cancellation, one finds the equation

$$p[1 - F_D(I)] = c,$$

or

$$F_D(I) = 1 - \frac{c}{p} . \tag{4}$$

Since the distribution function $F_D(I)$ is always positive, the equation above has a solution if, and only if $p > c$. This value of I, denoted by $\bar{I}$, is the optimum inventory level. Now, it must be shown that $\bar{I}$ represents a maximum. A second differentiation gives

$$\frac{d^2E[N(D)]}{dI^2} = \frac{d}{dI}\{p[1 - F_D(I)] - c\} = -pf_D(I) < 0,$$

and since f_D, being a density, is always nonnegative, it follows that the solution of (4) is indeed the optimum inventory, provided $p > c$. If $p < c$, then it can be seen intuitively that the newspaper business is unprofitable, and I should be zero.

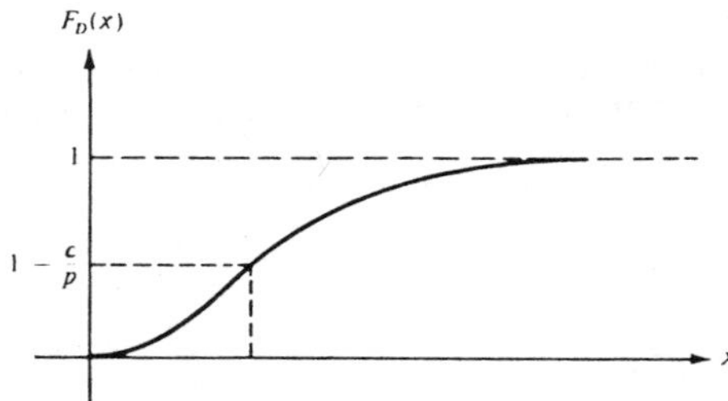

Fig. 2

The solution of (4) may be represented graphically, as shown in Figure 2. To summarize, the optimum inventory level $\bar{I}$ satisfies

$$F_D(\bar{I}) = 1 - \frac{c}{p} \quad \text{if} \quad p > c,$$

$$= 0 \qquad \text{if} \quad p < c,$$

where the net profit function is given by (2).

• PROBLEM 12-23

At a particular shop the price of Christmas trees is \$5.00 and the unit cost is \$2.00. Demand is (approximately) exponentially distributed. It can be represented by

$$F(x) = 1 - e^{-x/m} \quad \text{if} \quad x \geq 0$$
$$= 0 \qquad \text{if} \quad x < 0, \tag{1}$$

m being the expected number of trees.

The best estimate available for the expected number of trees to be demanded is

$$E[D] = m = 100,$$

but there is a possibility that the expectation may be 10% higher—that is, 110. Determine how much profit will be lost, on the average, if the inventory stocked is based on the estimated mean demand of 100 if, in fact, mean demand turns out to be 110. The magnitude of the answer would indicate how much it might be worth spending to improve the quality of the demand estimation in use.

Solution: Note that the optimum inventory level $\bar{I}$ satisfies

$$F_D(\bar{I}) = 1 - \frac{c}{p} \quad \text{if} \quad p > c, \tag{2}$$

where p and c are unit price and cost of commodity. The one-period profit as a function of that period's demand is

$$N(D) = \begin{cases} pD - cI & \text{if} \quad D < I \\ pI - cI & \text{if} \quad D \geq I \end{cases}$$

and the expected profit

$$E[N(D)] = \int_0^\infty g(x) f_D(x) dx,$$

($g(x) = N$ and $f_D(x)$ is the probability density function) from which one can derive

$$E[N(D)] = p \int_0^I x f_D(x) dx + pI[1 - F_D(I)] - cI \tag{3}$$

When (3) is differentiated with respect to I, one finally gets

$$p[1 - F_D(I)] = c \tag{4}$$

Following (1) and (2),

$$1 - e^{-\bar{I}/m} = 1 - \frac{c}{p} .$$

so

$$e^{-\bar{I}/m} = \frac{c}{p} ,$$

and taking logarithms, one finds

$$\bar{I} = m \log_e\left(\frac{p}{c}\right) \quad \text{for } p > c.$$

Now this inventory level may be substituted back into the cost function (3) to obtain the lowest possible inventory cost. First, however, since (4) is the derivative of (3), one can integrate to obtain

$$E[N|I] = \int_0^I \frac{dE[N|I']}{dI'} dI',$$

$$= \int_0^I \{p[1 - F(I')] - c\} dI', \qquad (5)$$

$$= p \int_0^I [1 - F(I')] dI' - cI.$$

Substituting the exponential demand distribution into (5), find that

$$E[N|I] = p \int_0^I e^{-I'/m} dI' - cI = pm[1 - e^{-I/m}] - cI. \qquad (6)$$

Finally, substitute in the expression for $\bar{I}$, the optimal inventory level, to find the value of the optimal policy, which turns out to be

$$E[N|\bar{I}] = pm\left[1 - \frac{c}{p}\right] - cm \log\left(\frac{p}{c}\right)$$

$$= m\left\{p - c\left[1 + \log\left(\frac{p}{c}\right)\right]\right\}. \qquad (7)$$

If a nonoptimal inventory level is suggested, one can substitute it into (6) and compare to (7) in order to find the advantage of $\bar{I}$.

The calculation proceeds as follows. If mean demand is actually 110, then the optimal inventory level is

$$\bar{I}_{110} = 110 \log\left(\frac{5}{2}\right),$$

$$= (110)(0.916),$$

$$= 100.76,$$

and, from (7), the resulting maximum expected profit is

$$E[N|\bar{I}_{110}] = 110\{5 - 2[1 + 0.916]\} = \$128.48.$$

Now if it is believed that the mean demand is 100, then one would stock

$$\bar{I}_{100} = 100 \log\left(\frac{5}{2}\right).$$

$$= 91.6.$$

(Actually, both $\bar{I}_{110}$ and $\bar{I}_{100}$ should be rounded off to integer values.) However, to discover the profit resulting from following the policy $\bar{I}_{100}$ when m = 110, one must utilize the actual profit function, expression (6) with m = 110. Substituting, find

$$E[N|\bar{I}_{100}] = 5 \times 110 \times [1 - e^{-\bar{I}_{100}/110}) - 2 \times \bar{I}_{100},$$

$$= 550[1 - e^{-0.83}] - 183.2,$$

$$= 550 \times 0.564 - 183.2,$$

$$= \$127.00.$$

It is plain to see that a 10% error in the mean demand reduces the expected profit hardly at all; hence one would not wish to spend much to improve the estimate in this case. Although such insensitivity is rather common, it does not always occur, and sensitivity analyses are worth making.

• PROBLEM 12-24

Suppose the demand in gallons for a soft drink syrup during a week is exponentially distributed with a mean of 100, that is

$$f(D) = 0.01e^{-0.01D}, \quad D > 0$$

The syrup is produced in batches, one each week. If not used within a week following production, it spoils. The production cost is \$1 a gallon. Any unused syrup must be disposed of at the end of the week at a cost of 10 cents per gallon for handling and waste treatment. A shortage of syrup results in lost sales. A gallon of syrup normally yields \$2 in sales revenue, net of remaining manufacturing and distribution costs. What should be the optimal batch size?

Solution: Items are produced (or purchased) for a single period of demand at a cost of C dollars per item. There is no fixed procurement cost. Each unit brings a price of V dollars when it is sold. Units left at the end of the period are charged a holding cost H. Denote by I the number of units on hand before the ordering decision at the start of the period, and let D be a random variable that represents the demand during the period. D is continuous, with density function f(D). The problem is to determine the optimum inventory level, say R*, that should be on hand at the start of the period so that the expected cost is minimized. Once the optimal stock level is known, the amount to be procured at the start of the season can be computed as max (0, R* - I).

This model describes the inventory process of an item whose demand occurs during a relatively short interval, after which it becomes obsolete (for example, newspapers and certain apparel), spoils (such as produce and Christmas trees), or else is not in demand for a long period, say until next season (such as Christmas cards and antifreeze). It can also describe that of an item that can be obtained only once, such as a spare part that must be bought at the time of initial production. The distinguishing characteristic of this model is that there is only one opportunity for procuring the item and that is at the start of the period.

The amount sold during the period if R units are on hand at the beginning of the period is

$$\left.\begin{array}{ll} D, & \text{if } D < R \\ R, & \text{if } D \geq R \end{array}\right\} = \min\ (D,\ R)$$

The amount of excess inventory at the end of the period is

$$\xi(R,\ D) = \begin{cases} R - D, & \text{if } D < R \\ 0, & \text{if } D \geq R \end{cases}$$

and the shortage condition at the end of the period is

$$\psi(R,\ D) = \begin{cases} 0, & \text{if } D \leq R \\ D - r, & \text{if } D > R \end{cases}$$

The expected costs for the period consist of the sum of the expected costs of ordering, holding inventory, and shortage. Denoting the expected costs by $E\{K(R)\}$, and assuming the initial on-hand inventory, I, to be zero, write

$$E\{K(R)\} = CR + H\int_0^\infty \xi(R,\ D)f(D)\ dD + V\int_0^\infty \psi(R,\ D)f(D)dD$$

$$= CR + H\int_0^R (R - D)f(D)dD + V\int_R^\infty (D - R)f(D)dD$$

The optimum R, say R*, is the solution to

$$\frac{dE\{K(R)\}}{dR} = 0$$

or

$$C + H\int_0^R f(D)dD - V\int_R^\infty f(D)dD = 0 \tag{1}$$

Equation (1) can be written as

$$C + HF(R) - V[1 - F(R)] = 0$$

where F is the cumulative distribution function of demand. This implies that

$$F(R^*) = \frac{V - C}{V + H} \tag{2}$$

It can be seen that R* is defined only if $V \geq C$. If $V < C$ one would not operate the inventory system.

R* being the optimal batch size, one has from (2):

$$F(R^*) = \int_0^{R^*} 0.01e^{-0.01t}\,dt = \frac{2.00 - 1.00}{2.00 + 0.10}$$

$$1 - e^{-0.01R^*} = 0.476$$

$$R^* = 64.6 \text{ gallons}$$

• PROBLEM 12-25

At a certain large bakery there are on the average 1000 inidividual demands for bread a day. More precisely, the number of demands for bread on a day, N(1), has the Poisson distribution with mean or expectation 1000. Two-thirds of these demands are for one loaf; one-third are for six loaves; that is, with independent probability 2/3, a customer requests one loaf of bread, while with probability 1/3, six are requested. The selling price per loaf is p = \$0.35, and the production cost is c = \$0.10. Determine the optimum number of loaves of bread to be baked in anticipation of daily demand; it is convenient to use the normal distribution approximation.

What would the optimum number be, if demand was doubled? Imagine two separate bakeries, each confronted with independent demands averaging 1,000 per day. Compare this case with one where the two bakeries are consolidated, in terms of optimum inventory level.

Solution: When the total number of demands over a time period, N(t), is Poisson distributed and the sizes of the individual demands, S_i, i = 1, 2, . . ., N(t), are independently distributed according to F(x), $x \geq 0$, then the total demand over a fixed time period (0, t), expressed as

$$D(t) = S_1 + S_2 + \ldots + S_{N(t)},$$

has the compound Poisson distribution. The random process $\{D(t), t \geq 0\}$ is a compound Poisson process with demand rate $\bar{\lambda}$.

For the compound Poisson process the expected value and variance of the total demand over a period of length t are, respectively,

$$E[D(t)] = \lambda t \int_0^{\infty} x\, dF(x) = \lambda t E[S], \qquad (1)$$

$$Var[D(t)] = \lambda t \int_0^{\infty} x^2\, dF(x) = \lambda t E[S^2]. \qquad (2)$$

As the period length becomes large or, equivalently, as the demand rate, λ, increases (in such a way that $\lambda t \to \infty$), the distribution of D(t) becomes approximately normally distributed:

$$\lim_{\lambda t \to \infty} P\{D(t) > \lambda t E[S] + x\sqrt{\lambda t E[S^2]}\} = \frac{1}{\sqrt{2\pi}} \int_x^\infty e^{-(1/2)z^2} dz. \qquad (3)$$

Also recall that, for an inventory model, if F(x) represents the distribution of total demand over a time period, then an optimal initial stocking quantity is obtained by stocking $\bar{I}$ items, where

$$F(\bar{I}) = 1 - \frac{c}{p} \quad (c < p); \qquad (4)$$

p is the selling price and c is the unit cost of production. First, the expected or mean daily demand is, from (1),

$$E[D(1)] = \lambda E[S] = (1,000)\left[\left(\frac{2}{3}\right)(1) + \left(\frac{1}{3}\right)(6)\right],$$

$$= \frac{8,000}{3} = 0.67 \times 10^3,$$

and the variance of daily demand is, from (2),

$$Var[D(1)] = \lambda E[S^2] = (1,000)\left[\left(\frac{2}{3}\right)(1^2) + \left(\frac{1}{3}\right)(6^2)\right],$$

$$= \frac{38,000}{3} = 12.67 \times 10^3.$$

Next, it is apparent from (3) that if

$$F(x) = P\{D(t) \leq x\},$$

then the normal approximation provides

$$F(I) = \frac{1}{\sqrt{2\pi}} \int_{-\infty}^{(I-E[D(t)]/\sqrt{Var[D(t)]}} e^{-(1/2)z^2} dz$$

$$= \frac{1}{\sqrt{2\pi}} \int_{-\infty}^{(I-2.67\times10^3)/116} e^{-(1/2)z^2} dz. \qquad (5)$$

Now $\bar{I}$, the optimum production (initial inventory), is found by solving (4). To carry this out, use the approximation (5),

$$\frac{1}{\sqrt{2\pi}} \int_{-\infty}^{(I-E[D(t)]/\sqrt{Var[D(t)]}} e^{-(1/2)z^2} dz$$

$$= 1 - \frac{c}{p} \quad \left(\frac{c}{p} < 1\right), \qquad (6)$$

$$= 1 - \frac{0.10}{0.35} = 0.715,$$

and solve for $\bar{I}$.

To solve, let U_α represent the $\alpha(100)$ percent point for the normal distribution with mean zero and unit variance; that is, U_α satisfies

$$\frac{1}{\sqrt{2\pi}} \int_{-\infty}^{U_\alpha} e^{-(1/2)z^2} dz = \alpha \qquad (0 < \alpha < 1).$$

Reference to a table of the standard normal distribution shows that if $\alpha = 0.715$ as in (6), then $U_\alpha = 0.57$. Hence, the normal approximation gives, for the optimum number of loaves of bread with which to start the day,

$$\bar{I} = E[D(t)] + U_\alpha \sqrt{Var[D(t)]}, \qquad \alpha = 1 - \frac{c}{p}, \tag{7}$$

$$= \frac{8,000}{3} + (0.57)\frac{\sqrt{38,000}}{3},$$

$$= 2,667 + 64 = 2,731 \text{ loaves.}$$

Observe the U_α depends only on the cost-profit ratio, c/p, and that if the latter decreases, inventory should be increased. Inventory should also be increased if the variance of demand increases.

If the demand rate is doubled to become $2\lambda = 2,000$, then (7) gives

$$\bar{I} = \frac{16,000}{3} + (0.57)\sqrt{\frac{76,000}{3}},$$

$$= 5,333 + 91 = 5,424,$$

or 38 loaves less than twice the optimum inventory when demand rate is 1,000. An intuitive explanation for the economy associated with pooling or combining stock in one location is easily furnished. Clearly the stocking of inventory in excess of expected demand (64 loaves when demand rate is 1,000, as in (7)) is for protection against lost sales caused by unusually large total daily demand. Consider the two separate bakeries, each confronted with independent demands averaging 1,000 per day. If each carries the appropriate inventory, as given by (7), then examination of (5) and (6) shows that the chance of a stockout at just one of the two bakeries is 2(0.715)(0.285), or about 0.41. On these occasions bread is left over at one bakery that could have been sold at the other. If the two bakeries were consolidated (actually moved together physically) and the extra stock shared, some of the resulting lost sales could have been avoided. Hence an optimum inventory for the two bakeries acting cooperatively may be made somewhat smaller than the sum of the two optimum inventories when the bakeries are acting independently.

PERIODIC AND CONTINUOUS REVIEW MODELS WITH STOCHASTIC - STATIC DEMAND

• PROBLEM 12-26

The demand rate for fuel oil at a certain remote refueling station (an island in the Atlantic) is

λ = 1 demand per week.

The magnitude of an individual demand is an exponentially distributed random variable with mean

$\xi = E[S] = 500$ gallons.

Oil is stored in a tank having 1500 gallon capacity. At irregular time intervals a tanker appears to replenish the inventory of fuel oil at the station. The time intervals are long, so the station's policy is to refuel whenever the tanker appears, or, equivalently, to reorder as soon as replenishment has occurred and the tanker departs. Thus the time between two successive tanker appearances is the lead time. Assume that the lead time is an exponentially distributed random variable L, with mean

$E[L] = v^{-1} = 10$ weeks

or rate $v = 0.1$ (weeks).

What is the probability of emptiness? What can be suggested to improve the situation?

Solution: Under the assumptions above, the total demand (in gallons of oil) during a random lead time, which is denoted by D(L), has the distribution

$$P\{D(L) \le x\} = \begin{cases} 0 & \text{for } x < 0 \\ \dfrac{v}{v+\lambda} & \text{for } x = 0 \\ 1 - \dfrac{\lambda}{\lambda + v} e^{-x/[(1+\lambda/v)\xi]} & \text{for } x > 0 \end{cases}$$

$$P\{D(L) > x\} = \frac{\lambda}{\lambda + v} e^{-x/[(1+\lambda/v)\xi]} \qquad \text{for } x > 0.$$

Since the tank is always full after each visit, the probability of emptiness, or stockout, is,

$$P\{D(L) > 1500\} = (0.9091)e^{-1500/5500} = 0.69.$$

That is, there is nearly a 70% chance that the tank is empty when replenishment occurs. Apparently, a larger tank or more frequent replensihment visits are required in order to guarantee satisfactory refueling service at the station.

• PROBLEM 12-27

Consider a situation in which the planning horizon consists of N periods. Assume that a review is made at the start of each period, the delivery lead time is zero, shortages are backlogged (except at the end of period N, when they are lost), and that demands in each of the N periods are independent and identically distributed continuous random variables with probability density f(D). The purchase cost, C, is independent of the number of units ordered, the holding cost per unit is H, and the shortage cost per unit short is π. Finally, define a cost discounting factor α, $0 < \alpha \leq 1$, such that $\alpha = (1 + k)^{-1}$, where k is the interest rate per period.

The demand for an item in each of two periods is uniformly distributed from 0-10, i.e., $f(D) = 0.10$, $0 \leq D \leq 10$. The cost of purchasing is $2 per item. If excess inventory remains at the end of a period, it is charged at $6 per item. The shortage cost is $10 per item. Find the optimum two-period policy for $\alpha = 1$.

Assume that an order up to R policy is to be followed. That is, if I_j is the net inventory at the start of period j, then the policy implies

$$\begin{cases} \text{Order } R_j - I_j, & \text{if } R_j > I_j \\ \text{Do not order}, & \text{if } R_j \leq I_j \end{cases}$$

in the absence of a fixed ordering cost, the order up to R policy is an optimal policy. Use recursive relationships to determine R_j^* for jth period.

Solution: The cost in period j is

$$\begin{cases} C(R_j - I_j) + G(R_j), & \text{if } R_j > I_j \\ G(I_j), & \text{if } R_j \leq I_j \end{cases}$$

where G is the single-period expected sum of holding and shortage costs,

$$G(R_j) = H\int_0^{R_j}(R_j - D)f(D)dD + \pi\int_{R_j}^{\infty}(D - R_j)f(D)dD$$

The optimization problem involves finding an order quantity R_j^* for each period $j = 1, 2, \ldots, N$ such that the expected discounted cost

$$K = E\left\{\sum_{j=1}^{N}\alpha^{j-1}[C(R_j - I_j) + G(R_j)]\right\} \tag{1}$$

is minimized.

Dynamic programming may be used to minimize Equation (1). The appropriate recursive relationship is

$$K_j(I_j) = \min_{R_j \geq I_j} \{C(R_j - I_j) + G(R_j) + \alpha E[K_{j+1}(R_j - D)]\},$$

$$j = 1, 2, \ldots, N \tag{2}$$

where $K_{N+1}(I_{N+1}) = 0$, and

$$E[K_{j+1}(R_j - D)] = \int_0^\infty K_{j+1}(R_j - D) f(D)\,dD$$

In (2), $K_j(I_j)$ is the minimum expected discounted cost over the periods $j, j + 1, \ldots, N$, when the net inventory at the start of period j is I_j. Note that $C(R_j - I_j) + G(R_j)$ is the expected cost in period j and $K_{j+1}(R_j - D)$ is the minimum attainable cost over the last $N - j$ periods as a function of the decision in period j and the demand that occurs in period j. Averaging over D and discounting to the start of period j yields the last term in Equation (2).

A backwards solution procedure for (2) is used. That is, for period N compute $K_N(I_N)$ given $K_{N+1}(I_{N+1})$, then compute $K_{N-1}(I_{N-1})$ given $K_N(I_N)$, etc., until $K_1(I_1)$ is determined.

Consider period 2. Equation (2) becomes

$$K_2(I_2) = \min_{R_2 \geq I_2} \{2(R_2 - I_2) + G(R_2) + 0\}$$

and since the shortage and holding costs are linear, the R_2^* that minimizes the quantity in braces is

$$F(R_2^*) = \frac{\pi - C}{\pi + H} = \frac{10 - 2}{10 + 6} = 0.5$$

Thus the optimal $R_2^* = 5$. Now in general,

$$G(R) = 6\int_0^R (R - D)(0.1)\,dD + 10\int_R^{10} (D - R)(0.1)\,dD$$

$$= 0.8R^2 - 10R + 50$$

Therefore

$$E[K_2(R_1 - D)] = \int_0^{10} K_2(R_1 - D)(0.1)\,dD$$

$$= \int_0^{R_1 - R_2^*} G(R_1 - D)(0.1)\,dD$$

$$+\int_{R_1-R_2^*}^{10} [C(R_2^* - R_1 + D) + G(R_2^*)](0.1)dD$$

$$= \int_0^{R_1-5} \{0.8(R_1 - D)^2 - 10(R_1 - D) + 50\}(0.1)dD$$

$$+\int_{R_1-5}^{10} \{2(5-R_1+D) + 50 - 10(5) + 0.8(5)^2\}(0.1)dD$$

$$= \frac{8}{300}R_1^3 - \frac{4}{10}R_1^2 - \frac{1100}{30}$$

Now consider period 1. The recursion (2) becomes

$$K_1(I_1) = \min_{R_1 \geq I_1} \{2(R_1 - I_1) + 0.8R_1^2 - 10R_1 + 50 + \frac{8}{300}R_1^3 - \frac{4}{10}R_1^2 - \frac{1100}{30}\}$$

$$= \min_{R_1 \geq I_1} \{-2I_1 + \frac{40}{3} - 8R_1 + \frac{4}{10}R_1^2 + \frac{8}{300}R_1^3\}.$$

Differentiating $K_1(I_1)$ with respect to R_1 and equating to zero yields

$$-8 + \frac{8}{10}R_1 + \frac{24}{300}R_1^2 = 0$$

whose positive solution is $R_1 = 6.18$. Therefore, the optimal policy is to order up to 6.18 units if the initial stock on hand does not exceed 6.18 units. At the start of period 2, if the amount on hand does not exceed five units, order up to five units.

• PROBLEM 12-28

The demand distribution for a commodity for each of eleven periods is uniform between 0 and 20, that is, $f(D) = 0.20$, $0 \leq D \leq 20$. The shortage cost (π) is \$12 per unit, the holding cost (H) is \$8 per item and the purchase cost is \$15. The cost discount factor α, $0 < \alpha, 1$, such that $\alpha = (1 + k)^{-1}$, where k is the interest rate per period, is 0.6. What is the optimum inventory level? Note that planning horizon is long enough to make the unbounded horizon assumption.

Solution: If the number of periods in the planning horizon is greater than three or four, then an approximate solution, obtained by assuming the number of periods to be infinite, will generally be satisfactory. This solution is obtained from the cumulative distribution equation

$$F(R^*) = \frac{\pi - C(1 - \alpha)}{\pi + H} \tag{1}$$

From Equation 1, compute

$$F(R^*) = \frac{12 - 15(1 - 0.6)}{12 + 8} = \frac{6}{20}$$

and since

$$F(R^*) = \frac{R^*}{20},$$

$R^* = 6$ units.

• PROBLEM 12-29

A large supplier of electronic components has decided to control the inventory of a certain item by a periodic review, order up to R policy. The mean demand rate for this item is 500 units per year. The lead time τ is nearly constant at three months. The demand in the time $\tau + T$ can be represented by a normal distribution with mean $500(\tau + T)$ and variance $800(\tau + T)$. The cost of each unit is \$10, the inventory carrying charge is computed using $i = 0.10$, the cost of making a review and placing an order is \$15, and the cost of a backorder is estimated to be \$30. It is desired to find the optimal R and T. Hint: Find average annual cost $K(R,T)$ as a function of R and T and evaluate $K(R^*,T)$, R^* for $T = 0.20, 0.25, 0.30$.

Solution: If T is specified, R^* can be found easily. For example, suppose the inventory level is to be reviewed every three months. Then $\tau + T = 0.5$, and the expected demand in $\tau + T$ is $500(0.5) = 250$, and the variance of demand in this time is $800(0.5) = 400$. Thus R^* is the solution to

$$\Phi'\left(\frac{R - 250}{20}\right) = \frac{(0.1)(10)(0.25)}{30} = 0.0083$$

where

$$\Phi'(u) = \int_u^\infty (2\pi)^{-1/2} e^{-z^2/2} dz$$

is the complementary cumulative distribution of the standard normal random variable. From the normal tables,

$$\frac{R - 250}{20} = 2.40$$

Thus

$$R^* = 250 + 20(2.40) = 298$$

If T is not specified, then the average annual cost becomes

$$K(R,T) = \frac{15}{T} + (0.1)(10)[R - 125 - 250T] + \frac{30}{T}\int_R^\infty (x - R) f(x;T)\,dx$$

where the density f(x;T) is normal with mean 500(0.25 + T) and variance 800(0.25 + T). It can be shown that for a normal random variable x, having mean μ and variance σ^2,

$$\int_a^\infty (x - a)\,n(x;\mu,\sigma^2)\,dx = \sigma\phi\left(\frac{a - \mu}{\sigma}\right) + (\mu - a)\Phi\left(\frac{a - \mu}{\sigma}\right)$$

where

$$\phi(z) = (2\pi)^{-1/2} e^{-z^2/2}$$

and

$$n(x;\ \mu,\ \sigma^2) = \frac{1}{\sigma}\phi\left(\frac{x - \mu}{\sigma}\right)$$

Using this result, write the cost K(R,T) as

$$K(R,T) = \frac{15}{T} + (0.1)(10)[R - 125 - 250T] + \frac{30}{T}\left\{\sqrt{800(0.25 + T)}\,\phi\left(\frac{R - 500(0.25 + T)}{\sqrt{800(0.25 + T)}}\right) + [500(0.25 + T) - R]\,\Phi'\left(\frac{R - 500(0.25 + T)}{\sqrt{800(0.25 + T)}}\right)\right\}$$

Using this expression, now tabulate K(R*,T) as a function of T, where the optimum R* depends on the particular T chosen. Such a tabulation is shown below. T* = 0.25 would be chosen as the optimum review period and R* = 298 as the optimum target inventory, as these parameters result in a minimum cost. In computing the optimal T, an increment of 0.05 years was used, and hence the optimum T* is only accurate to within 0.025 years. Smaller increments could be used if more accurate results are required.

T(YEARS)	*R**(UNITS)	*K*(*R**, *T*) (DOLLARS)
0.20	272	178
0.25	298	177
0.30	324	181

Assume mean demand m = 1000 (items per week) standard deviation σ = 100 and the "smoothing constant" $\alpha = \frac{1}{3}$, for a production smoothing problem. Assume further, that the production level for a given week is determined as a linear combination of the actual demand and the production level of the previous week. What are the standard deviations of inventory and production, and the value of production-change measure?

Given that carrying cost c_C = \$0.10, and backorder cost c_B = \$1000 (management considers it very serious to be out of stock) what is the optimum inventory level and the probability of being out of stock?

Assume that successive demands arise independently, from a normal distribution.

Solution: Under the above assumptions, the following facts can be established:

The inventory level at week n is normally distributed with variance

$$\mathrm{Var}[I_n] = \sigma^2\left\{\frac{1 - (1 - \alpha)^{2n}}{\alpha(2 - \alpha)}\right\}.$$

In the long run, that is, as $n \to \infty$, the variance tends to

$$\sigma_I{}^2 = \mathrm{Var}[I] = \frac{\sigma^2}{\alpha(2 - \alpha)} . \qquad (1)$$

The production level of week n is normally distributed with variance

$$\mathrm{Var}[P_n] = \sigma^2\alpha\left\{\frac{1 - (1 - \alpha)^{2n-2}}{2 - \alpha}\right\}.$$

In the long run the variance tends to

$$\sigma_P{}^2 = \mathrm{Var}[P] = \frac{\sigma^2\alpha}{2 - \alpha}.$$

A measure of the amount of production-level change between two successive periods is

$$K = E[(P_n - P_{n-1}{}^2].$$

In the long run, it can be shown that $E[P_n - P_{n-1}] = 0$, so

$$K = \mathrm{Var}[P_n - P_{n-1}] = 2\frac{\sigma^2\alpha^2}{2 - \alpha} .$$

The last expression allows one to understand that effect of choosing a value of the smoothing constant, α. From (1) it is clear that the variance of the inventory level, σ_I^2, increases as α is made small, and so it follows that the probability of a backorder situation existing also increases. To compensate for this effect, however, σ_P^2, the variance in production level, and K, the measure of production change, both diminish.

The production rule for this problem is

$$P_{n+1} = \frac{1}{3}X_n + \frac{2}{3}P_n.$$

From the formulas one finds that

$$\sigma_I^2 = \frac{\sigma^2}{\alpha(2 - \alpha)} = (10,000)\left(\frac{9}{5}\right) = 18,000,$$

so the standard deviation of inventory variation is

$$\sigma_I = 134,$$

while the variance of production is

$$\sigma_P^2 = \sigma^2 \frac{\alpha}{2 - \alpha} = (10,000)\left(\frac{1}{5}\right) = 2,000,$$

giving the approximate production standard deviation

$$\sigma_P = 45$$

and the value of the production-change measure

$$K = 2\frac{\sigma^2\alpha^2}{2 - \alpha} = 2(10,000)\left(\frac{1}{15}\right) = 1,333.$$

Assuming that there is no cost due to production change, the total average cost associated with the inventory policy will be expressed as

$$C(B,\alpha) = c_c B + c_B \int_{-\infty}^{0}\left(\frac{e^{-(1/2)[z-m_I)/\sigma_I]^2}}{\sqrt{2\pi}}\right)\frac{dz}{\sigma_I} + k\sqrt{K},$$

where the dependence on the smoothing parameter α occurs in the expressions for σ_1 and K.

To optimize $C(B,\alpha)$, first let α be fixed and differentiate with respect to B:

$$\frac{\partial C}{\partial B} = c_c - \frac{c_B}{\sqrt{2\pi}\sigma_I}e^{-(1/2)(B/\sigma_I)^2}.$$

A necessary condition that a minimum occur for given B is that the derivative be zero; since $e^{-t} \leq 1$ for $t \geq 0$, it follows that (i) the derivative is always positive, and hence the optimum inventory level $B_{opt} = 0$ if

$$\frac{c_c}{c_B} > \frac{1}{\sqrt{2\pi}\,\sigma_I};$$

otherwise (ii) the optimum inventory level is

$$B_{opt} = \sigma_I \sqrt{2 \log \left(\frac{c_B}{\sqrt{2\pi}\; c_c \sigma_I}\right)}.$$

Substituting,

$$B_{opt} = 212 \sqrt{2 \log \left(\frac{1000}{2.50 \times 0.1 \times 134}\right)} = 350.$$

The probability of being out of stock is computed as follows:

$$\int_{-\infty}^{0} \frac{1}{\sqrt{2\pi}} e^{-(1/2)[(z-m_1)/\sigma_I]^2} \frac{dz}{\sigma_I} = \int_{-\infty}^{-m_1/\sigma_1} \frac{e^{-(1/2)v^2}}{\sqrt{2\pi}} dv$$

$$= \int_{-\infty}^{-2.62} \frac{e^{-(1/2)v^2}}{\sqrt{2\pi}} dv,$$

$$= 0.0044$$

• PROBLEM 12-31

A microcomputer dealer orders a similar computer, whenever he sells one; customers wait for delivery whenever he is out of stock. This model microcomputer costs about \$1000 and is sold for an average of \$1200, when the cash value of any trade-in is considered (which is immediately sold wholesale to a used-computer dealer). After a thorough analysis the demand is found out to be Poisson distributed with a mean of 7.5 per week and lead times are exponentially distributed with a mean of 2 weeks. 20 percent annual inventory carrying cost rate is used for calculations. He can earn a 10 percent annual return on his capital and there is no fixed backorder cost.

What is the appropriate base stock level for this base stock system? Assume that the only effect of a backorder is to postpone the receipt of the \$200 profit on the sale. What will be his average inventory, average backorder position and what percent of the time will he be out of stock?

Solution: To find the appropriate base stock level, utilize the average cost per unit time as function of base stock level R:

$$K(R) = h\bar{I} + \hat{\pi}\bar{B} + \pi\lambda\gamma$$

$$= (h + \hat{\pi})[RP(R - 1; \rho) - \rho\, p(R - 2; \rho)] - \hat{\pi}(R - \rho) + \pi\lambda[1 - p(R - 1;\rho)] \quad (1)$$

where

h: inventory carrying cost per unit per year,

$\overline{I}$: average on hand inventory,

$\hat{\pi}$: shortage cost per unit short per year,

$\overline{B}$: average backorder level,

π: shortage cost per unit short, independent of the duration of the shortage,

λ: parameter of Poisson distribution,

γ: the expected number of backorders in a unit of time,

$\rho = \lambda/\nu$,

ν = parameter of exponentially distributed lead times.

The first difference of K is

$$\Delta K(R) = K(R + 1) - K(R) = (h + \hat{\pi})P(R;\rho) - \pi\lambda P(R;\rho) - \hat{\pi} \quad (2)$$

The optimal base stock level is the smallest integer value of R for which $\Delta K(R) \geq 0$.

In this case $\lambda = 7.5$, $\nu = .50$, $\rho = \lambda/\nu = 1.5$ and h = (.20)(1000) = 200. There is no fixed backorder cost ($\pi = 0$). The cost of backorder for a year is $\hat{\pi}$ = (0.10)(200) = 20, since the dealer can earn 10 percent annual return on his capital.

Therefore

$$K(R) = (200 + 20)[RP(R - 1;\ 15) - 15P(R - 2;\ 15)] - 20(R - 2)$$

and R* is the smallest integer for which

$$(200 + 20)P(R;\ 15) - 15 > 0$$

$$p(R;\ 15) > \frac{15}{220} \cong 0.06818$$

From Poisson Distribution Function table find P(8;15) = 0.0374 and P(9;15) = 0.0699; therefore, R* = 9.
From

$$\overline{I} = RP(R - 1;\rho) - \rho P(R - 2;\rho)$$

$$\overline{B} = \overline{I} - (R - \rho)$$

$$\gamma = 1 - P(R - 1;\rho)$$

with a base stock level of microcomputers, the dealer will have an average inventory of 0.07 computers, an average back-order position of 6.07 computers and will be out of stock 96 percent of the time.

LOT - SIZE PROBLEMS WITH DYNAMIC DEMAND AND SINGLE FACILITY

• PROBLEM 12-32

During the next year, the demand rate for a product is expected to vary according to $\delta(t) = 1000 - 400t$, $0 \leq t \leq 1$, where t is in years. The item is purchased for $20 per unit, and the fixed procurement cost is $200 per order. The inventory carrying cost rate is 20 percent annually. No shortages are permitted. The initial inventory is 192 units. No final inventory is required. Determine when and in what quantities to order during the next year.

Solution: Let

n = number of lots to be procured during (0,T).

Q_j = size of the lot added to inventory at time t_j

A = fixed cost associated with procurement of a lot

C = unit variable procurement cost

h = inventory carrying cost per unit per unit time

D(t) = cumulative demand in the interval (0,t)

I(t) = inventory level at time t

The problem is to choose n lots of sizes $Q_1, Q_2, \ldots, Q_n$, to be added to inventory at times $t_1, t_2, \ldots, t_n$, respectively, to minimize

$$K_n = nA + CD(T) + H_n \tag{1}$$

where nA is the total fixed procurement cost, CD(T) is the total variable procurement cost, and H_n is the total inventory carrying cost during the planning horizon. Note that n is a decision variable as well as the $\{t_j\}$ and $\{Q_j\}$. Since CD(T) is a constant, omit it in the following solution.

Suppose only one order is to be placed. This should be done when the initial inventory is exhausted. Since $D(t) = 1000t - 200t^2$, the cumulative requirements will equal 192 at $t_1 = 0.20$. Given

$$Q_j = \int_{t_j}^{t_{j+1}} \delta(t)\ dt = D(t_{j+1}) - D(t_j);$$

$$j = 1, 2, \ldots, n \tag{2}$$

and

$$D(t_1) = I(0), \tag{3}$$

order

$$Q_1 = D(T) - I(0) = 800 - 192 = 608$$

units at that time.

The total inventory carrying costs are given by

$$H_n = h \sum_{j=0}^{n} \int_{t_j}^{t_{j+1}} I(t)\ dt \tag{4}$$

The inventory level at time t is given by

$$I(t) = \begin{cases} I(0) - D(t), & \text{for } 0 \le t \le t_1 \\ D(t_{j+1}) - D(t), & \text{for } t_j \le t \le t_{j+1} \end{cases} \tag{5}$$

$$(j = 1, 2, \ldots, n)$$

Substituting for $I(t)$,

$$H_n = h \sum_{j=0}^{n} (t_{j+1} - t_j) D(t_{j+1}) - h \int_0^T D(t)\ dt \tag{6}$$

By Equation (6), $H_1 = \$980$, with $h \equiv iC = 4$, and thus $K_1^* = A + H_1 = \$1180$.

If exactly two orders are to be placed, the first should be placed at $t_1 = 0.20$ and the second at a time t_2, satisfying Equation (7) for $j = 2$;

$$D(t_{j+1}) = D(t_j) + (t_j - t_{j-1})\delta(t_j), \quad (j = 2, 3, \ldots, n) \tag{7}$$

$$D(t_3) = D(t_2) + (t_2 - t_1)\delta(t_2)$$

Using Equation (8)

$$D(t_{n+1}) = D(T) \tag{8}$$

$$D(t_3) = D(T) = 800,$$

and one gets

$$800 = 1000t_2 - 200t_2^2 + (t_2 - 0.20)(1000 - 400t_2)$$

Solving, obtain $t_2 = 0.626$, so that

$$Q_1 = D(0.626) - D(0.200) = 548 - 192 = 356$$

$$Q_2 = D(1) - D(0.626) = 800 - 548 = 252$$

Using three results, one finds H_2 = \$551 and $K_2^* = 2A + H_2$ = \$951. The optimal two-lot policy is better than the optimal one-lot policy, since $K_2^* < K_1^*$.

Now consider n = 3. Again $t_1 = 0.20$. The values for t_2 and t_3 must satisfy

$$D(t_3) = D(t_2) + (t_2 - 0.2)(1000 - 400t_2)$$

$$D(t_4) = D(t_3) + (t_3 - t_2)(1000 - 400t_3) \equiv D(T) = 800$$

The solution is $t_2^* = 0.383$ and $t_3^* = 0.577$, for which

$$Q_1 = D(0.383) - D(0.200) = 354 - 192 = 162$$

$$Q_2 = D(0.577) - D(0.383) = 511 - 354 = 157$$

$$Q_3 = D(1) - D(0.577) = 800 - 511 = 289$$

This policy gives H_3 = \$428 and K_3^* = \$1028. Since $K_3^* > K_2^*$, decide to terminate the analysis and use a two-lot policy.

The solution is to order 356 units for delivery at time 0.20 and 252 units for delivery at time 0.626.

• PROBLEM 12-33

Four products are manufactured on the same facility. Relevant data are given in the Table shown. The inventory carrying-cost rate is 20 percent annually. No shortages are to be permitted.

Find the optimal rotation cycle, determine when and how much of each product to produce. Plot inventory behavior of the four products, assuming they are produced in the order A-B-C-D, omitting set up times for convenience.

TABLE

PRODUCT j	ANNUAL DEMAND D_j	PRODUCTION RATE (UNITS/YEAR) P_j	SETUP COST A_j	SETUP TIME (YEARS) s_j	VARIABLE COST/UNIT c_j
A	3000	10,000	\$50	0.001	\$10
B	2000	5,000	70	0.002	15
C	5000	50,000	120	0.005	5
D	1000	10,000	80	0.003	20

Solution: By using a rotation cycle policy, one can conveniently arrive at lot sizes that are easily scheduled to avoid shortages. In a rotation cycle, all products have the same cycle time, T, and during an interval of length T, a lot of each product is produced on the facility. The products are run in a fixed sequence ("rotation"), which is repeated from cycle to cycle. Since no shortages are permitted, the lot size for product j must equal the demand during the cycle; that is,

$$X_j = TD_j \tag{1}$$

The expression for the average cost per unit time is

$$K(T) = \sum_{j=1}^{n} \left[\frac{A_j}{T} + c_j D_j + icj \cdot \frac{TD_j}{2} \left(1 - \frac{D_j}{P_j}\right) \right]. \tag{2}$$

K(T), average cost per unit time, is minimized by

$$T^* = \sqrt{\frac{2 \sum_{j=1}^{n} A_j}{i \sum_{j=1}^{n} c_j D_j (1 - D_j/P_j)}} \tag{3}$$

However, before one can adopt T* as the cycle length, one must consider the time required for setups during the cycle. Suppose the setup time for product j is s_j. Since the total setup time per cycle plus the total production time per cycle must be no more than the cycle length, one has the following constraint on T:

$$\sum_{j=1}^{n} \left(s_j + \frac{X_j}{P_j} \right) \leq T$$

or, using $X_j = TD_j$,

$$T \geq \frac{\sum_{j=1}^{n} s_j}{1 - \sum_{j=1}^{n} (D_j/P_j)} \equiv T_{min} \tag{4}$$

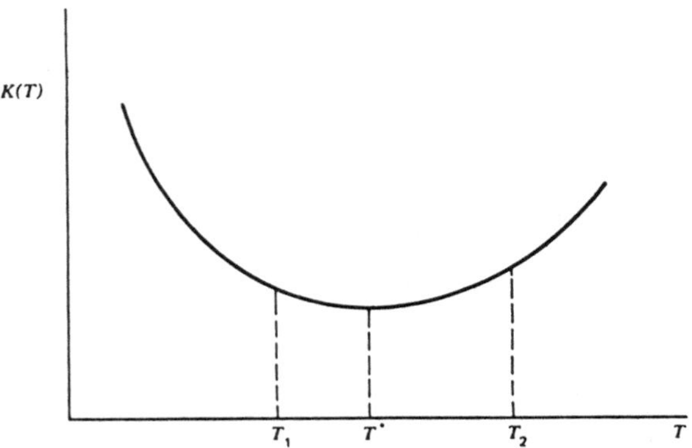

Optimal rotation cycle determination. Fig. 1

Notice that the denominator of (4) is the fraction of time the facility will not be producing. Since K(T) is convex in T, one should use a cycle time equal to the maximum of T* and T_{min}. To see this, observe from Figure 1, that if T_{min} is at a point $T_1 < T^*$, T^* is feasible and hence the solution; however, if T_{min} is at $T_2 > T^*$, T^* is not feasible and T_{min} gives the lowest cost of all feasible T.

Before finding the optimal rotation cycle, verify that it is possible to meet the demand by computing $\sum (D_j/P_j) = 0.90$. This means that the facility must run 90 percent of the time, with the remaining 10 percent available for setups, maintenance, etc. Since the sum of the setup times is $\sum s_j = 0.0011$, the minimum cycle length is $T_{min} = 0.011/0.10 = 0.11$ year.

Using Equation (3), obtain

$$T^* = \sqrt{\frac{(2)(320)}{15,900}} = 0.20$$

Because $T^* > T_{min}$, choose the cycle length to be 0.20 year. The associated lot sizes are, from (1), $X_1^* = 600$, $X_2^* = 400$, $X_3^* = 1000$, and $X_4^* = 200$. Using (2), find that the average annual cost using the optimal rotation cycle is K(0.20) = $108,190.

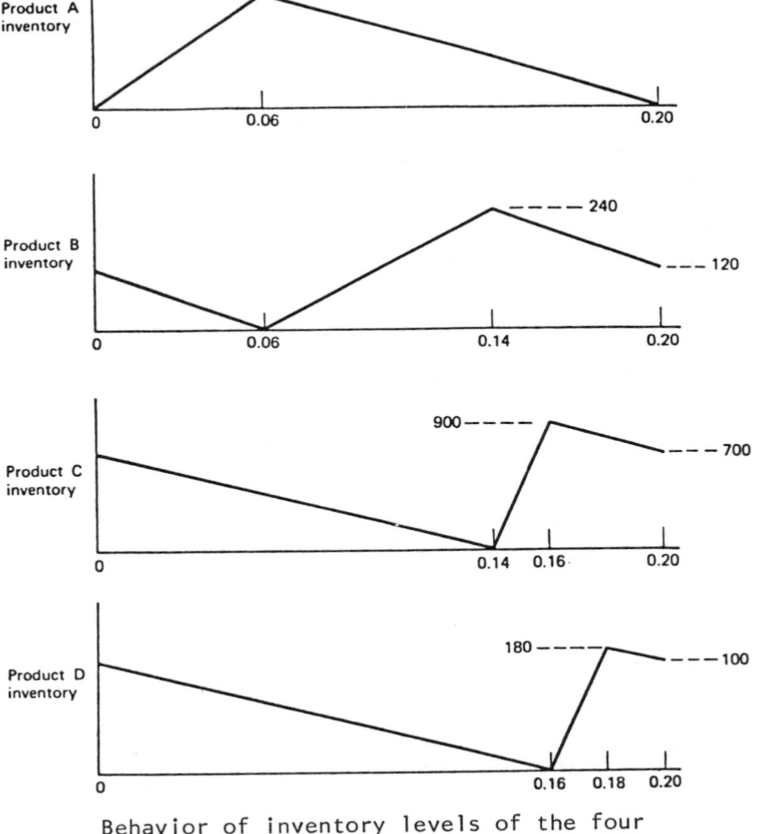

Behavior of inventory levels of the four products (Setup times not shown.)

Fig. 2

The ease of scheduling a rotation cycle can be observed by studying Figure 2, where the inventory behavior of the four products during a cycle have been plotted, assuming that they are produced in the order A-B-C-D. From the start of the cycle (time zero) to 0.06, the facility is producing A; from 0.06 to 0.14, B; from 0.14 to 0.16, C; from 0.16 to 0.18, D; and from 0.18 to 0.20, the facility is idle. (For convenience, setup times are not shown in Figure 2 or included in the immediately preceding description of the utilization of the facility. Note that the effect of setup times on Figure 2 is to shift the start of production to the right for each product.)

MULTIPERIOD MODELS

• PROBLEM 12-34

It is required to plan production for three periods, with demands by period 9, 13 and 12 units, respectively. Inventory holding costs are of the form $h_t I_t$ (h_t: inventory holding cost per unit, in period t; I_t: inventory at the end of period t) with $h_1 = 2$, $h_2 = 1$ and $h_3 = 1$. No shortages are allowed , the initial net inventory is zero and the final inventory is required to be zero. The production costs are given in Table 1. They are the marginal production costs, assumed to be constant for a given range of production.

Find the optimum production levels for every range and for every period.

TABLE 1 Marginal Production Costs

range of production	Period of Production 1	2	3
$1 \le x_t \le 5$	2	1	3
$6 \le x_t \le 12$	3	6	4
$13 < x_t \le 15$	4	7	5

Solution: Put the problem into a form that can be handled by the transportation tableau. Assume that the given ranges of production as different sources of production having given capacities and proportional costs. Table 2 is thus, constructed. Numbers in upper right-hand corners of cells are the incremental production costs plus incremental inventory costs.

Assignments to the cells are made starting with period 1. Demand in this period is satisfied by allocating as much to the cheapest and then- if there still is demand- to the next cheapest and so on. Once the whole demand is satisfied, pass to period 2 and consider the whole column under it. Review all periods in this manner. The optimal production plan obtained is $x_1^* = 10$, $x_2^* = 12$, $x_3^* =$

14. Note that $I_1 = 1$, $I_2 = I_3 = 0$ and minimum total cost is 113.

Table 2

Period	source of production	demand 1	2	3	unused capacity	capacity
1	$1 \leq x_1 \leq 5$	5 [2]	- [4]	- [5]	0	5
	$6 \leq x_1 \leq 12$	4 [3]	1 [5]	[6]	2	7
	$13 \leq x_1 \leq 15$	[4]	[6]	[7]	3	3
2	$1 \leq x_2 \leq 5$		5 [1]	- [2]	0	5
	$6 \leq x_2 \leq 12$		7 [4]	- [5]	0	7
	$13 \leq x_2 \leq 15$		[7]	[8]	3	3
3	$1 \leq x_3 \leq 5$			5 [3]	0	5
	$6 \leq x_3 \leq 12$			7 [4]	0	7
	$13 \leq x_3 \leq 15$			2 [5]	1	3
	demand	9	13	14	9	45

• PROBLEM 12-35

Production is to be planned for a four-period horizon. There is no initial inventory and the final inventory level is to be zero. No shortages are allowed. Production and inventory costs have the following forms:

$$C_t(X_t) = \begin{cases} 0, & \text{if } X_t = 0 \\ A_t + c_t X_t, & \text{if } X_t > 0 \end{cases}$$

$$H_t(I_t) = h_t I_t$$

Estimates of cost parameters and demand are given in Table 1. Determine a production plan to give optimal production and inventory levels for each period.

TABLE 1

PERIOD t	PREDICTED DEMAND D_t	SETUP COST A_t	UNIT VARIABLE COST c_t	UNIT HOLDING COST PER PERIOD h_t
1	20	\$30	\$3	\$2
2	30	40	3	2
3	40	30	4	1
4	30	50	4	1

Solution: A forward recursive algorithm for solving the problem is as follows:

Let M_{jk} denote the cost of producing in period j + 1 to satisfy demands in periods j + 1, j + 2, . . ., k(j = 0, 1, . . ., T − 1; k = j + 1, j + 2, . . ., T). M_{jk} includes inventory costs as well as production costs. Note that it is assumed that the end of period j and the end of period k are regeneration points (points in time where the inventory level is zero are called regeneration points and for every time period where production is scheduled, the start of the period is a regeneration point); that is, $I_j = 0$ and $I_k = 0$. Then

$$X_{j+1} = D_{j+1} + D_{j+2} + \cdots + D_k$$

and

$$I_t = X_{j+1} - \sum_{r=j+1}^{t} D_r = \sum_{r=t+1}^{k} D_r,$$

$$(t = j + 1, j + 2, \ldots, k - 1)$$

Therefore,

$$M_{jk} = C_{j+1}(X_{j+1}) + \sum_{t=j+1}^{k-1} H_t(I_t)$$

$$= C_{j+1}\left(\sum_{r=j+1}^{k} D_r\right) + \sum_{t=j+1}^{k-1} H_t\left(\sum_{r=t+1}^{k} D_r\right)$$

Let F_k denote the optimal policy costs for periods 1, 2, . . ., k, given $I_k = 0$. Then

$$F_k = \min_{0 \leq j \leq k-1} [F_j + M_{jk}], \quad (k = 1, 2, \ldots, T)$$

and $F_0 \equiv 0$.

To organize computations, define α_{jk} to be the optimal cost for periods 1, 2, . . ., k (a k-period horizon), when $I_k = 0$ and j + 1 is the period of last production; that is, when $X_{j+1} > 0$ and $X_{j+2} = X_{j+3} = \cdots = X_k = 0$. Then

$$\alpha_{jk} = F_j + M_{jk}$$

and

$$F_k = \min_{0 \leq j \leq k-1} [\alpha_{jk}]$$

Next construct a table. For a k-period horizon, the optimal last regeneration point is j*(k), defined by

$$\alpha_{j^*(k),k} = \min_{0 \leq j \leq k-1} \alpha_{jk}$$

Given any regeneration point k, one can find the optimal last time point prior to k, j*(k), when the inventory is to be zero. This means that production last takes place in period $j^*(k) + 1$. By starting with $k = T$ and working backwards, one can identify the regeneration points in the optimal solution.

For the above problem, first consider the one-period problem ($k = 1$):

$$M_{01} = A_1 + c_1 D_1 = 30 + (3)(20) = 90$$

$$F_1 = \alpha_{01} = F_0 + M_{01} = 0 + 90 = 90$$

Solution: $j^*(1) = 0$ and $X_1^* = 20$

Next consider the two-period problem ($k = 2$):

$$M_{02} = A_1 + c_1(D_1 + D_2) + h_1 D_2 = 30 + (3)(20 + 30) + (2)(30) = 240$$

$$M_{12} = A_2 + c_2 D_2 = 40 + (3)(30) = 130$$

$$F_2 = \min \begin{cases} \alpha_{02} = F_0 + M_{02} = 0 + 240 = 240 \\ \alpha_{12} = F_1 + M_{12} = 90 + 130 = 220 \end{cases}$$

Solution: $F_2 = 200$, $j^*(2) = 1$, and $X_1^* = 20$, $X_2^* = 30$

For the three-period problem ($k = 3$):

$$M_{03} = A_1 + c_1(D_1 + D_2 + D_3) + h_1(D_2 + D_3) + h_2 D_3 = 520$$

$$M_{13} = A_2 + c_2(D_2 + D_3) + h_2 D_3 = 330$$

$$M_{23} = A_3 + c_3 D_3 = 190$$

$$F_3 = \min \begin{cases} \alpha_{03} = F_0 + M_{03} = 0 + 520 = 520 \\ \alpha_{13} = F_1 + M_{13} = 90 + 330 = 420 \\ \alpha_{23} = F_2 + M_{23} = 220 + 190 = 410 \end{cases}$$

Solution: $F_3 = 410$, $j^*(3) = 2$, and $X_1^* = 20$, $X_2^* = 30$, $X_3^* = 40$

Finally, for the four-period problem ($k = 4$):

$$M_{04} = A_1 + c_1(D_1 + D_2 + D_3 + D_4) + h_1(D_2 + D_3 + D_4) + h_2(D_3 + D_4) + h_3 D_4 = 760$$

$$M_{14} = A_2 + c_2(D_2 + D_3 + D_4) + h_2(D_3 + D_4) + h_3 D_4 = 510$$

$$M_{24} = A_3 + c_3(D_3 + D_4) + h_3 D_4 = 340$$

$$M_{34} = A_4 + c_4 D_4 = 170$$

$$F_4 = \min \begin{cases} \alpha_{04} = F_0 + M_{04} = 0 + 760 = 760 \\ \alpha_{14} = F_1 + M_{14} = 90 + 510 = 600 \\ \alpha_{24} = F_2 + M_{24} = 220 + 340 = 560 \\ \alpha_{34} = F_3 + M_{34} = 410 + 170 = 580 \end{cases}$$

Solution: $F_4 = 560$, $j^*(4) = 2$, and $X_1^* = 20$, $X_2^* = 30$, $X_3^* = 70$, and $X_4^* = 0$

These computations are summarized in Table 2.

TABLE 2 Determination of F_k and $j^*(k)$ from Values of α_{jk}

j \ k	1	2	3	4
0	90•	240	520	760
1		220•	420	600
2			410•	560•
3				580
F_k	90	220	410	560
$j^*(k)$	0	1	2	2

Note that problems having one-, two-, three-, and four-period horizons have been successively solved. To understand how the optimal production program is determined for the four-period problem, consider the information in Table 2. For k = 4, the optimal last regeneration point is 2. This means $I_2^* = 0$, $X_3^* = D_3 + D_4 = 70$, $I_3^* = D_4 = 30$, and $X_4^* = 0$. Since the inventory at the end of period 2 is zero, let k = 2, and find that the optimal last regeneration point is 1. Thus $I_1^* = 0$ and $X_2^* = D_2 = 30$. For k = 1, $j^*(1) = 0$, so $X_1^* = D_1 = 20$.

CHAPTER 13

PROBABILISTIC METHODS: QUEUING THEORY, GAME THEORY AND MARKOV CHAINS

QUEUING MODELS

• PROBLEM 13-1

The mean arrival rate (λ) at Bo's gas station is one customer every 4 minutes and the mean service time (μ) is $2\frac{1}{2}$ minutes. The calculations for arrival and service times in minutes and, on the basis of an hour, are as follows:

$$\lambda = \frac{1}{4} = 0.25 \text{ arrivals per minute or 15 arrivals per hour}$$

$$\mu = \frac{1}{2.5} = 0.4 \text{ service time per minute or 24 service times per hour}$$

What is the average number of customers in the system, the average queue length, the average time a customer spends in the system, and the average time a customer waits in line to be served?

Solution: 1. The average number of customers in the system is:

$$E(n) = \frac{\lambda}{\mu - \lambda} = \frac{0.25}{0.4 - 0.25} = \frac{0.25}{0.15} = 1.66 \text{ customers}$$

$$\frac{15}{24 - 15} = \frac{15}{9} = 1.66 \text{ customers}$$

2. The average number of customers waiting to be served, or average queue length is:

$$E(w) = \frac{\lambda^2}{\mu(\mu - \lambda)} = \frac{(0.25)^2}{0.4(0.4 - 0.25)} = \frac{0.0625}{0.06} =$$

1.04 customers

$$\frac{(15)^2}{24(24 - 15)} = \frac{225}{216} = 1.04 \text{ customers}$$

Calculation for the average number being served:

1.66 (average number in system) - 1.04 (average queue length) = 0.62 (average number being served)

3. The average time a customer spends in the system is:

$$E(v) = \frac{1}{\mu - \lambda} = \frac{1}{0.4 - 0.25} = \frac{1}{0.15} = 6.66 \text{ minutes}$$

$$\frac{1}{24 - 15} = \frac{1}{9} = 0.111 \text{ hour}$$

4. The average time a customer waits before being served is:

$$E(y) = \frac{\lambda}{\mu(\mu - \lambda)} = \frac{0.25}{0.4(0.4 - 0.25)} = 4.16 \text{ minutes}$$

$$\frac{15}{24(24 - 15)} = \frac{15}{216} = 0.07 \text{ hour}$$

• PROBLEM 13-2

For a simple queue, what is the average number of customers in the system for a traffic intensity (ρ) of 0.5, 0.8, 0.9 and 0.95?

Solution:

ρ	$1 - \rho$	$\rho/(1 - \rho)$ = Average number of customers in the system
0.5	0.5	1
0.8	0.2	4
0.9	0.1	9
0.95	0.05	19

• PROBLEM 13-3

If the mean service rate is 10 per hour, what is the average time a customer is in the queue for the traffic intensities of 0.5, 0.8, 0.9, and 0.95?

Solution:

ρ	$\frac{\rho}{1 - \rho}$	$\frac{\rho}{1 - \rho} \times \frac{1}{\mu}$ = Average time a customer is in the queue
0.5	1	0.1 hours
0.8	4	0.4
0.9	9	0.9
0.95	19	1.9

Thus when the traffic intensity is as high as 0.95, customers will have to wait in the queue for 114 minutes (on average) before being served in 6 minutes (on average).

• PROBLEM 13-4

Find the probability that there are no customers in the system, given that:

(i) number of channels in parallel = 3

(ii) mean arrival rate = 24 per hour

(iii) mean service rate of each channel = 10 per hour

Solution: The traffic intensity, $\rho = \frac{\lambda}{c\mu} = \frac{24}{3 \times 10} = 0.8$

The number of channels, c = 3

Hence, substituting these values into the equation for P_0,

$$P_0 = \frac{c!\ (1 - \rho)}{(\rho c)^c + c!(1 - \rho)\left\{\sum_{x=0}^{c-1} 1/n!(\rho c)^n\right\}}$$

$$P_0 = \frac{3 \times 2 \times 1 \times (1 - 0.8)}{(0.8 \times 3)^3 + 3 \times 2 \times 1}$$

$$\times (1 - 0.8)\{1 + (0.8 \times 3) + (0.8 \times 3)^2/2\}$$

$$= \frac{6(0.2)}{(2.4)^3 + 6(0.2)(1 + 2.4 + (2.4)^2/2)}$$

$$= \frac{1.2}{13.82 + 1.2(6.3)} = 0.056$$

Thus, with a traffic intensity of 0.8, the system will be completely idle for about 6% of the time.

• PROBLEM 13-5

Assume that a telephone switchboard, with $\lambda = 10$ calls per minute, has a large number of channels. The calls are of random and independent length, but average 4 minutes each. Approximate the probability that, after the switchboard has been in service for a long time, there will be no busy channels at some specified time t_0.

Solution: Use the formula

$$\int_0^\infty [1 - F(s)]ds = E(Y).$$ Thus, for a large value t_0,

$$E[X(t_0)] = \lambda \int_0^{t_0} [1 - F(s)]ds$$

$$= \lambda E(Y)$$

$$= 10(4) = 40.$$

Since $X(t)$ has a Poisson distribution,

$$P[X(t_0) = 0] = \exp\{- \lambda \int_0^{t_0} [1 - F(s)]ds\}$$

$$= \exp(-40).$$

• PROBLEM 13-6

An insurance company has three claims adjusters in its branch office. People with claims against the company are found to arrive in a Poisson fashion, at an average rate of 20 per 8-hour day. The amount of time that an adjuster spends with a claimant is found to have an exponential distribution, with mean service time 40 minutes. Claimants are processed in the order of their appearance.

(a) How many hours a week can an adjuster expect to spend with claimants?

(b) How much time, on the average, does a claimant spend in the branch office?

Solution:

(a) Here $\lambda = \frac{5}{2}$ arrivals per hour

$\mu = \frac{3}{2}$ services per hour for each adjuster

$$P_0 = \frac{1}{1 + \frac{5}{3} + \frac{1}{2}\left(\frac{5}{3}\right)^2 + \frac{1}{6}\left(\frac{5}{3}\right)^3 \frac{\frac{9}{2}}{\frac{4}{2}}} = \frac{24}{139}$$

The expected number of idle adjusters, at any specified instant, is

$$3P_0 + 2P_1 + 1P_2 = 3\left(\frac{24}{139}\right) + 2\left(\frac{40}{139}\right) + 1\left(\frac{100}{3 \text{ x } 139}\right) = \frac{4}{3} \text{ adjusters}$$

Then the probability that any one adjuster will be idle at any specified time is 4/9; and the expected weekly time an adjuster spends with claimants is (5/9)40 = 22.2 hours.

(b) The average time an arrival spends in the system is found from the equation

$$E(v) = \frac{M(\lambda/M)^k}{(k-1)!(kM-\lambda)^2} P_0 + \frac{1}{M}$$

to be 49.0 minutes.

• PROBLEM 13-7

Arrivals at a telephone booth are considered to be Poisson, with an average time of 10 minutes between one arrival and the next. The length of a phone call is assumed to be distributed exponentially, with mean 3 minutes.

(a) What is the probability that a person arriving at the booth will have to wait?

(b) What is the average length of the queues that form from time to time?

(c) The telephone company will install a second booth when convinced that an arrival would expect to have to wait at least three minutes for the phone. By how much must the flow of arrivals be increased in order to justify a second booth?

Solution:

Here $\lambda = 0.1$ arrival per minute

$\mu = 0.33$ service per minute

(a) $P\langle\text{an arrival has to wait}\rangle = 1 - P_0$

$$= \lambda/\mu, \text{ by } P_n = \left(1 - \frac{\lambda}{\mu}\right)\left(\frac{\lambda}{\mu}\right)^n$$

$$= 0.1/0.33 = 0.3$$

(b) $$E(m/m > 0) = \frac{\mu}{\mu - \lambda}$$

$$= \frac{0.33}{0.23} = 1.43 \text{ persons}$$

(c) $$E(\text{waiting}) = \frac{\lambda}{\mu(\mu - \lambda)}$$

$$= \frac{\lambda}{0.33(0.33 - \lambda)} \text{ if } \mu \text{ is fixed at } 0.33$$

Seek the new value λ' for which E(waiting) = 3 minutes.

Solving the equation

$$3 = \frac{\lambda'}{0.33(0.33 - \lambda')}$$

obtains an answer of $\lambda' = 0.16$ arrival per minute. So one must increase the flow of arrivals from 6 per hour, the present figure, to 10 per hour.

• PROBLEM 13-8

The Hadjet Hospital emergency room Management Engineer has concluded that the emergency cases arrive pretty much at random (a Poisson input process) and that the time spent by a doctor treating the cases approximately follows an exponential distribution. Therefore he has chosen this basic model for a preliminary study of this queueing system.

By projecting the available data for the early evening shift into next year, it appears that patients will arrive at an average rate of one every half-hour. A doctor requires an average of 20 minutes to treat each patient. Thus, using an hour as the unit of time,

$$\frac{1}{\lambda} = \frac{1}{2} \text{ hours per customer}$$

$$\frac{1}{\mu} = \frac{1}{3} \text{ hours per customer,}$$

so

$$\lambda = 2 \text{ customers per hour}$$

$$\mu = 3 \text{ customers per hour}$$

The two alternatives being considered are to continue having just one doctor during this shift (s = 1) or to add a second doctor (s = 2). In both cases, traffic density is

$$\rho = \frac{\lambda}{s\mu} < 1,$$

so that the system should approach a steady-state condition. Calculate operating characteristics for both of the queuing models. Can you make a tentative suggestion as to which model is preferable.

Solution: Actually, since λ is somewhat different during other shifts, the system will never truly reach a steady-state condition, but it feels that steady-state results will provide a good approximation. Thus the above equations are used to obtain the results shown in Table 1.

On the basis of these results, it was tentatively concluded that a single doctor would be inadequate next year for providing the relatively prompt treatment needed in a hospital emergency room.

Table 1

	$s = 1$	$s = 2$	
ρ	$\frac{2}{3}$	$\frac{1}{3}$	traffic density
P_0	$\frac{1}{3}$	$\frac{1}{2}$	probability of exactly 0 customers in the system
P_1	$\frac{2}{9}$	$\frac{1}{3}$	probability of exactly 1 customer in the system
P_n for $n \geq 2$	$\frac{1}{3}\left(\frac{2}{3}\right)^n$	$\left(\frac{1}{3}\right)^n$	probability of exactly n customers in the system
L_q	$\frac{4}{3}$	$\frac{1}{12}$	expected number of customers in the queue
L	2	$\frac{3}{4}$	expected number of customers in the system
W_q	$\frac{2}{3}$	$\frac{1}{24}$ (in hours)	expected waiting time per customer in the queue
W	1	$\frac{3}{8}$ (in hours)	expected waiting time per customer in the system
$P\{\mathscr{W}_q > 0\}$	0.667	0.167	probability that W_q be greater than 0 time units
$P\left\{\mathscr{W}_q > \frac{1}{2}\right\}$	0.404	0.022	
$P\{\mathscr{W}_q > 1\}$	0.245	0.003	
$P\{\mathscr{W}_q > t\}$	$\frac{2}{3}e^{-t}$	$\frac{1}{6}e^{-4t}$	
$P\{\mathscr{W} > t\}$	e^{-t}	$\frac{1}{2}e^{-3t}(3 - e^{-t})$	

• **PROBLEM** 13-9

Analysis of arrivals to a single pump gas station has shown that the times between arrivals can be depicted by negative exponential distribution with a mean of 10 minutes. Service times were observed to be distributed negative exponentially, as well, with a mean time of 6 minutes. What is the steady-state mean number of customers at the station and the steady-state mean number that are waiting?

Solution: λ (arrival rate) is 1/10 per minute, and μ (service rate) 1/6 per minute. These give a traffic intensity (ρ) of λ/μ. When the system reaches steady state, the mean number of customers at the station will be

$$\pi_i = (0.4)(0.6)^i.$$

So,

$$\pi_0 = 0.4.$$

This means that 40% of the time there are no cars at the station. 60% of the time there is one or more cars. This information can be interpreted as the probability that a car will have to wait (or, as the utilization of the server):

P(Delay) = Utilization = ρ = 0.6

The steady-state mean number of customers at the station will be

$$L_c = \frac{\rho}{1 - \rho} = 1.5$$

and the steady-state mean number waiting will be

$$L_q = \frac{\rho^2}{1 - \rho} = 0.9$$

• PROBLEM 13-10

Consider a service booth where the arrival rate of customers is 12 per hour. If the customer is being served he incurs a waiting cost of $5.00 per hour. The cost of service is $2.00 per customer. It is desired to find the service rate that will minimize total system cost.

Solution: By letting one hour be the unit of time, one gets A = 12 customers/hour, C_W = $5.00 per customer per hour, C_f = $2.00 per customer, and S* = ?

The minimum cost service rate, S*, is given by the equation

$$S^* = \sqrt{\frac{AC_w}{C_f}}$$

as:

$$S^* = \sqrt{\frac{(12)(5.00)}{(2.00)}} \approx 5.5 \text{ customers/hour}$$

and the minimum total system cost is obtained from the equation

$$TC^* = \sqrt{2\ AC_wC_f}$$

as

$$TC^* = 2\ \sqrt{(12)(2.00)(5.00)} \text{ or } \$22.00 \text{ per hour}$$

Therefore, the management should select a service facility that will service 11 customers every two hours and will cost (2) (5.50) = $11.00 per hour for its operation.

GAME THEORY

• PROBLEM 13-11

A new soda company, Super-Cola, recently entered the market. This company has three choices of advertising campaigns. Their major competitor, Cola-Cola, also has three counter campaigns of advertising to choose from in order to minimize the number of people switching from their soda to the new one. It has been found that their choices of campaign results in the following pay-off matrix:

Number, in 10,000's, of people switching from Cola-Cola to Super-Cola.			
	Cola-Cola		
Super-Cola	Counter-Compaign 1	Counter-Compaign 2	Counter-Compaign 3
Campaign 1	2	3	7
Campaign 2	1	4	6
Campaign 3	9	5	8

Find the best strategies for Super-Cola and Cola-Cola.

Solution: Each company wishes the strategy that is best for them. Super-Cola wishes to get the maximum amount of people from Cola-Cola, and Cola-Cola wishes to minimize their losses to Super-Cola. To do this, use the minimax procedure. Super-Cola realizes that Cola-Cola will always look for the minimum losses, thus Super-Cola considers the minimum of what will happen for each choice of campaign. Super-Cola notices that the minimum gain for campaign 1 is 20,000 people, the minimum gain for campaign 2 is 10,000 people, but the minimum gain for campaign 3 is 50,000 people. Thus, Super-Cola will choose campaign 3 - the maximum of the minimums. Similarly Cola-Cola realizes that Super-Cola will want to choose the maximum for each of Cola-Cola's counter-campaigns. Thus; Cola-Cola only looks at the maximums. For counter-camapgin 1 the maximum loss is 90,000 people, for counter-campaign 2 the maximum loss is 50,000 people, and for counter-campaign 3 the maximum loss is 80,000 people. Thus, Cola-Cola will choose counter-campaign 2 which is the minimum of the maximums. In this way they will minimize the losses. The point on the payoff matrix which they both choose is called the "saddle point". At this point neither company will change it's strategy for they are doing the best that they can. This type of a "game" is called a two-player zero-sum game, because whatever one player wins, the other player loses. Thus, the algebraic sum of the two is zero. Another way of looking at this problem is "pure-strategy". Super-Cola will look at the matrix and note that campaign 3 contains the largest numbers in each column. Thus, campaign 3 is the best choice regardless of which counter-campaign Cola-Cola chooses. Cola-Cola will notice this also. They will choose counter-campaign 2, for that one contains the minimum of all their choices, given Super-Cola will choose campaign 3.

• PROBLEM 13-12

Two land agents are interested in puchasing land for their competing companies. Company A has three options on how to buy its land, and Company B has four options on how to buy its land. They found that depending on how each company chooses the way they purchase their land, they will take some of the other company's business. They found the amounts to be as in the following payoff matrix. Find the best strategy for the two companies.

		Company B Options			
		B_1	B_2	B_3	B_4
Company A options	A_1	-2	3	-3	2
	A_2	-1	-3	-5	12
	A_3	9	5	8	10

Percent of business going from Company B to Company A (Note: A negative percent goes from Company A to Company B).

Solution: Each land agent realizes that the other land agent will choose the best strategy for his company. Company A will want the highest number it can get from the matrix, while company B will try to get the smallest number from the matrix (recall that a negative number means that percent goes to company B). Since each land agent will not underestimate their opponent, they will assume that their opponent will make the best choices. Using "pure strategy", the agent for Company B will never choose plan B_4, because independent of Company A's choice, B_1's entries are smaller than B_4's.

Similarly, Company A will never choose plan A_1, because independent of Company B's choice, A_3 has larger entries than A_1. Thus, in reality the matrix is reduced to:

	B_1	B_2	B_3
A_2	-1	-3	-5
A_3	9	5	8

By looking at the above matrix, Company A will surely choose plan A_3 because independent of Company B's choice, the entries in A_3 are larger than those in A_2. Noting that, Company B will choose plan B_2 which is the minimum of the choices left to it. Thus, Company A will take 5% of the Company B's business. This point (A_3, B_2) is called the "saddle-point". It is the point where both companies must operate, otherwise they will lose more in the long run, for the other company will choose a better strategy. This type of "game" is called a two person zero-sum game, because whatever one "person" loses the other "person" gains. Thus, if the gains and losses are added, one gets zero. Another way of determining the best move is called the "minimax" procedure. In this procedure, Company A's agent realizes that Company B will always pick the minimum number, thus they will look at the minimum of each choice. The minimum for choice A_1 is -3, the minimum for choice A_2 is -5, and the minimum for choice A_3 is 5. Now Company A will choose plan A_3 which is the maximum of the minimums, guaranteeing a gain of at least 5% of Company B's business. Similarly, Company B realizes that Company A will take the maximum of their choice. Thus, they will consider only the maximum for each plan. If they choose plan B_1 the maximum is 9, B_2 the maximum is 5, B_3 the maximum is 8, B_4 the maximum is 12. Thus, they will choose the minimum of those maximums, namely B_2 and only lose 5% of their business. Note that either procedure will result in the same play for each agent.

• PROBLEM 13-13

Country A is a member of OPEC, the cartel which fixes the price of oil. Country A's economists realized that if they cheat on the cartel, they could make more money. Meanwhile the head of OPEC was warned by his informants that country A has intentions of cheating. OPEC now wishes to lower their prices to induce country A not to cheat, but they still wish to make profit. It has been found that the following payoff matrix comes about as a result of their choices.

Profit to Country A (in billions of dollars) Country A			
OPEC price per barrel	cheats slightly	cheats moderately	cheats heavily
\$20	4	15	35
\$15	5	10	12
\$13	4	5	-5

Find the best strategy, for OPEC and for Country A.

Solution: Country A wants to make the most profit that they can. OPEC on the other hand wants to minimize Country A's profits in order to increase their own. Country A realizes that OPEC wants to minimize Country A's profits; when they consider their plan of action they look at the minimum amounts for each choice. The minimum for cheating a little is \$4 billion, for cheating moderately it is \$5 billion, and a \$5 billion loss for cheating heavily. Therefore, Country A chooses the maximum of the minimums, so they will cheat moderately. OPEC meanwhile knows that Country A wants the maximum amount, so they will look at the maximum amounts for each of their choices. For a \$20 price the maximum profit to Country A is \$35 billion, for a \$15 price it is \$12 billion, and for a \$13 price it is \$5 billion.

Thus, OPEC will choose the minimum of the maximums, namely they will have a \$13 per barrel price so that Country A will get a \$5 billion profit. This point is called the "saddle point". Both OPEC and Country A have an interest in remaining at this point.

• PROBLEM 13-14

Two competing ice cream chains, Kool Ice and Ice Kold, want to hold ice cream sales in order to capture some extra business from each other.

They each have the option of having a sale either on their most popular flavors or on all their ice cream. They found the following payoff matrix to show which way the business is turning for each of their choices.

Number of customers of Kool Ice switching to Ice Kold (in hundreds of people). Note that a negative number means they are switching from Ice Kold to Kool Ice.

Find the best strategy for each of them.

	Kool Ice	
Ice Kold	Sale on All	Sale on Popular
Sale on All	4	-3
Sale on Popular	-3	2

Solution: Kool Ice wants to sell to the most people, thus they want the smallest number (negative means consumers switching to Kool Ice). Ice Kold also wants the most people, thus they want the largest number. If the minimax procedure is used, one will end up with two different points. Kool Ice will want -3 and Ice Kold will want 2. Thus, there is no saddle point in this problem. The best strategy to get the best results is to choose one appraoch with a certain probability. Assuming Ice Kold has a sale on all the ice cream with probability p, then it has a sale on the popular ice cream with probability 1-p. To find p, find the expected values of the two columns. Expected value is the value of the box times its probability, summed up. So one has

		C_1	C_2
Ice Kold	p	4	-3
	1 - p	-3	2

Thus, the expected value of column C_1 is

$$4p + (-3)(1-p) = 7p - 3.$$

The expected value against a sale of popular flavors by Kool Ice is

$$(\text{Column } C_2)\ (-3)\,p + 2\,(1-p) = 5p + 2.$$

To solve for p set the two equations equal to each other:

$$7p - 3 = -5p + 2 \quad \text{or} \quad 12p - 3 = 2 \quad \text{or}$$

$$12p = 5 \quad \text{or} \quad p = 5/12$$

The reason for this is that the same result is wanted to occur independently of the other company's choice. Hence set the expected values of each column equal to each other. Therefore, Ice Kold should have a sale on their most popular ice cream 7/12 of the time and a sale on all of their ice cream 5/12 of the time. This gives an expected value of

$$-5\ (5/12) + 2 = -1/12,$$

or Kool Ice acquires an expected 8 people (1/12 x 100) of Ice Kold's clientele. Similarly, the probabilities for Ice Kold are the same. So they should have a sale on all of their ice cream 5/12 of the time and the rest of the time a sale on their popular ice cream. This also yields an expected loss of 8 people to Kool Ice.

• PROBLEM 13-15

Two players, A and B, each call out one of the numbers 1 and 2 simultaneously. If they both call 1, no payment is made. If they both call 2, B pays A $3.00. If A calls 1 and B calls 2, B pays A $1.00. If A calls 2 and B calls 1, A pays B $1.00.

What is the payoff matrix for this game? Is the game fair to both players?

Solution: This is a two person zero-sum game. It is zero-sum since whatever one player wins, the other must lose. Thus cooperation is impossible.

Construct the payoff matrix by listing A's strategies as rows and B's strategies as columns. The convention is to tabulate the payoffs to the row player.

A \ B	call 1	call 2
call 1	0	1
call 2	-1	3

The game is said to be fair if the value of the game is the same to both players. To find the value of the game to A assume he behaves rationally and see what conclusion he is forced to. A reasons that if he calls 1 his worst payoff is 0. If he calls 2, his worst payoff if $-1. Thus, he will always call 1, so as not to lose anything.

B thinks that: If he calls 1 he can at worst draw with A, if he calls 2 the worst payoff if $3.00. Thus he should call 1. Since the value of the game is the same to both A and B it is a fair game.

• PROBLEM 13-16

Players A and B simultaneously call out either of the numbers 1 and 2. If their sum is even, B pays A that number of dollars, if odd, A pays B. What kind of strategy should both players adopt?

Solution: Games may be classified according to the following criteria:

1) Number of players

2) Number of moves

3) Whether or not they are zero-sum

4) Whether or not they are of full information

Here the number of players is two. There are two moves to the game, A's move and B's move. The game is zero-sum since A's gain is B's loss and vice-versa. Finally, a game is said to be of full-information if, at each stage of the game, all previous moves are known to both players. The given game is not of full-information since both players play simultaneously.

The analysis of a game is simplified by constructing its payoff matrix. For the given game

	B:	1	2	Row Min.
A:				
	1	2	-3	-3
	2	-3	4	-3
col. max		2	4	

The optimal strategy for a is the maximum value of the game,i.e., the maximum of the row minima. By calling out either 1 or 2 his maximum value is -3. For B's optimum strategy the minimax value of the game is +2 (from calling 1). Thus A expects to lose 3 while B expects to lose 2 (recall that positive entries in the payoff matrix are payments by B to A). But since this is a zero-sum game, the above conclusion cannot be true. The paradox arises because the game has no saddle point. When there is one element that will clearly be chosen by both players, it is called a saddle point. Thus, there is no predictable solution to a single game. Over many games, both players play their strategies to mixed strategies in a random manner, the frequencies being chosen to give them their best payoffs over many games. It can be said that the players have moved from pure strategies to mixed strategies. Note that if either player chose a pure strategy he would be bound to lose over many games. Thus if B persists in calling 1, A will continue to call 1.

• PROBLEM 13-17

Solve the following game:

A: \ B:	B_1	B_2	B_3
A_1	1	2	3
A_2	0	3	-1
A_3	-1	-2	4

Solution: From A's point of view, none of the strategies dominate each other. Similarly from B's point each strategy has some reward that cannot be exceeded by the other strategies. Thus, this is an irreducible 3 x 3 payoff matrix.

A knows that if he adopts strategy A_1 the worst that can happen is that he will receive 1 (if B plays B_1). Similarly the minimum returns from A_2 and A_3 are -1 and -2 respectively. Since A wants to maximize his payoff, he chooses the strategy that will yield him the maximum payoff amongst the minimum returns. Thus, he will play strategy A, where maximin = 1.

B, on the other hand wants to minimize the amount that he must pay A. If he plays B_1 the most he must pay A is 1 (if A plays A_1). Similarly, the maximum payments from playing B_2 and B_3 are 3 and 4 respectively (negative entries represent payments by A to B). B chooses the strategy that will yield him the minimum penalty amongst the maximum payments. Thus, he will play B_1 since minimax = 1.

The maximin and the minimax represent the values of the game to A and B, respectively. When they are equal, as in this case, the common value is the value of the game and is called a saddlepoint.

Every two-person zero-sum game with full information (i.e., each player knows the strategies of his opponent) has a saddlepoint. But if maximin $\neq$ minimax, the value of a single game is uncertain. By introducing the expected value of a game (i.e., the average value of the game when many games are played) even games without full information can be shown to have a unique value.

• PROBLEM 13-18

Consider the following payoff matrix:

	C_1	C_2	C_3	C_4
R_1	2	3	-3	2
R_2	1	3	5	2
R_3	9	5	8	10

Find the value of this game.

Solution: The game is in matrix form. Since there are two players, (R the row player and C the column player) and four choices for C with three choices for R, the matrix is of order 3 x 4. Each entry is considered as a payment by C to R if C pursues action C_j while R pursues action R_i. The value of the game is the choice that R and C make, provided this choice is common.

Assuming R and C behave rationally, one would observe the following behaviour. R, the row player reasons as follows: If I pick row 1, the worst that can happen is that I collect -$3 (this means R pays C, the column player, $3), if I choose row 2 the minimum I receive is $1.00 and if I select row 3 my minimum payoff will be $5.00. Thus, considering my three possible choices, selecting row 3 guarantees that I will receive $5.00 from C. This is the maximum of the minimum payoffs.

C, on the other hand, will reason as follows: If I pick column 1, it is possible that I may have to pay R $9.00. If I choose column 2, I may have to pay R $5.00, while choosing column 3 means the maximum I have to pay R is $8.00. Finally, if I decide to play column 4, my maximum payoff to R will be $10.00. Thus, to minimize the maximum payoff to R, I must choose column 2.

Hence R chooses row 3, C chooses column 2 and R receives a $5.00 payoff from C. The value of the game is 5.

• PROBLEM 13-19

Simplify the following payoff matrix

A's strategies \ B's strategies	B_1	B_2	B_3	B_4
A_1	0	-1	2	-4
A_2	1	3	3	6
A_3	2	-4	5	1

Solution: It is usual to try to reduce the size of a game in order to solve it more easily. There are two basic ways in which this may be accomplished. Eliminate:

1) Duplicate strategies

2) Dominated strategies

Use 2) in the given problem to reduce the size of the payoff matrix. The strategy A_i is said to be dominated by A_j if the payoffs to A in A_i are less than or equal to the payoffs to A in A_j. It is strictly dominated if the inequality is a strict inequality. It can be seen that if A_j dominates A_i, then A will never play A_j, assuming rational behaviour.

Examining the given payoff matrix, A_1 is strictly dominated by A_2 since every element in A_1 is less than the corresponding element in A_2. Hence A_1 may be eliminated from contention.

Similarly, from B the column player's point of view, a strategy B_i is dominated by B_j if the payoffs to B in B_i are less than or equal to the payoffs to B in B_j. In the given payoff matrix B_2 dominates B_3 since the payoffs to B from playing B_2 are always greater or equal to the payoffs to B from playing B_3(recall that a negative entry represents a payment by A to B and that positive elements are payments by B to A; hence from B's point of view, smaller numbers are preferable to larger numbers). Thus obtain the reduced payoff matrix.

A: \ B:	B_1	B_2	B_4
A_2	1	3	6
A_3	2	-4	1

But now, since A_1 was eliminated, B_2 strictly dominates B_4 and further reduction is possible:

A: \ B:	B_1	B_2
A_2	1	3
A_3	2	-4

Thus the matrix has been reduced from one of order 3 x 4 to a payoff matrix of order 2 x 2.

• PROBLEM 13-20

Consider the game with the payoff matrix shown in Table 1. The payoff matrix has no saddle point; therefore in this case A and B do not have single best plans as their best strategies. Consequently, each player has to devise some mixed strategy in order to maximize his gain or minimize his loss.

What is the best mixed strategy for the players? Can A insure some minimum gain and what is this gain? Similarly, can B insure that he will not lose more than some maximum amount?

Solution: Let A play P with the frequency x, and Q with a frequency (1 - x). Then, if B plays S all the time, A's gain will be

$$g(A, S) = x(-3) + (1 - x)6 = 6 - 9x$$

If B plays T all the time, A's gain will be

$$g(A, T) = x(7) + (1 - x)1 = 1 + 6x$$

Table 1

		B	
	Plan	*S*	*T*
A	*P*	−3	7
	Q	6	1

It can be shown mathematically that if A chooses x, so that g (A, S) = g(A, T), then this will lead to the best strategy for him. Thus

$$6 - 9x = 1 + 6x$$

$$5 = 15x$$

i.e.

$$x = \frac{1}{3}$$

One gets the result

$$g(A) = \frac{1}{3}(-3) + \frac{2}{3}(6) = \$3.00$$

Thus, regardless of the frequency with which B plays either S or T, A's gain will be $3.00.

Therefore, by choice of frequencies $\frac{1}{3}$ and $\frac{2}{3}$, A can assure himself a gain of $3.00.

The same method can be applied by player B. Let frequency of choice of S be denoted by y and that of T be denoted by (1 - y). For best strategy one has

$$g(B, P) = y(-3) + (1 - y)7 = y(6) + (1 - y)1 = g(B, Q)$$

$$7 - 10y = 1 + 5y$$

$$6 = 15y$$

$$y = \frac{2}{5}$$

$$1 - y = \frac{3}{5}$$

$$g(B) = \frac{2}{5}(-3) + \frac{3}{5}(7) = \$3.00$$

Note that g(A) = g(B), as expected for a zero-sum game. A complete solution of the given game is:

1. A should play P and Q with frequencies $\frac{1}{3}$ and $\frac{2}{3}$ respectively.
2. B should play S and T with frequencies $\frac{2}{5}$ and $\frac{3}{5}$ respectively.
3. The value of the game is $3.00.

• PROBLEM 13-21

Show how a game with the payoff matrix below can be converted to a linear programming problem.

B's strategies

A's strategies

2	4
6	1

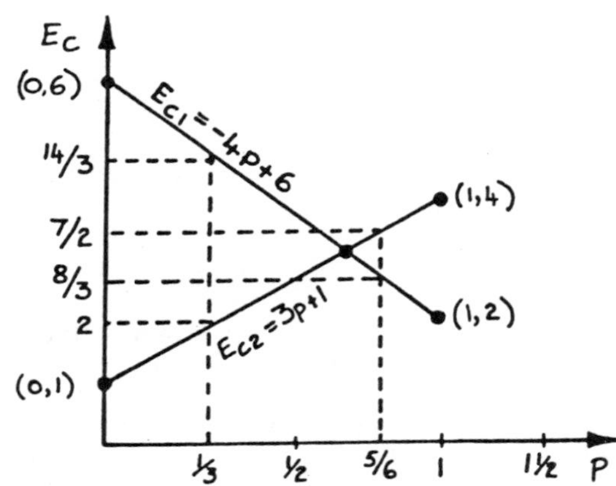

Solution: Since A's maximin strategy is to play row 1 while B's minimax strategy is to play column 2, see that maximin ≠ minimax, i.e., no saddle point exists. However, if A chooses row 1 with probability p and row 2 with probability 1-p then one can compute the expected value of the game to A. Now A has an expected value E_{c_1} against the column player playing column 1 of

$$E_{c_1} = 2p + 6(1-p) = -4p + 6.$$

Similarly, $E_{c_2} = 4p + (1)(1-p) = 3p + 1$. Graph E_{c_i} versus p:

(See fig.)

For any choice of p, $0 \leq p \leq 1$, E_{C_1}, $E_{C_2} > 0$. Let M denote the minimum expected value to the row player corresponding to his choosing row 1 with probability p and row 2 with probability 1-p. For example, if $p = 1/3$, $M = E_{C_2}$ since $E_{C_2} = 2$ is smaller than $E_{C_1} = 14/3$. Conversely, if $p = 5/6$, $M = E_{C_1}$ since $E_{C_1} = 10/3$ is smaller than $E_{C_2} = 7/2$. Define s and t as follows:

$$s = p/M \qquad t = \frac{1-p}{M} . \tag{1}$$

Then, $s+t = \frac{p}{M} + \frac{1-p}{M} = 1/M$. Thus, the maximization of M is equivalent to the minimization of s+t where s and t are both non-negative. Further restrictions on s and t are obtained by noting that for any p, E_{C_1} and $E_{C_2} \geq M$, i.e.,

$$2p + 6(1 - p) \geq M \tag{2}$$

$$4p + (1)(1 - p) \geq M.$$

But, from (1), $p = sM$ and $1 - p = tM$. Hence, the inequalities (2) become

$$2sM + 6tM \geq M$$

$$4sM + tM \geq M .$$

Dividing through by M,

$$2s + 6t \geq 1$$

$$4s + t \geq 1 .$$

Thus, A's problem is:

Minimize $s + t$

subject to

$$2s + 6t \geq 1$$

$$4s + t \geq 1 \tag{3}$$

$$s \geq 0, \ t \geq 0.$$

By analogous logic, B's problem is:

Maximize $x + y$

subject to

$$2x + 4y \leq 1$$

$$6x + y \leq 1 \tag{4}$$

$$x \geq 0, \ y \geq 0.$$

Note that (4) is the dual of (3). From the theory of duality it is known that if they exist, the optimal values of (3) and (4) are the same. From game theory one knows that the value of a game computed from either player's point of view must coincide.

George Dantzig, (the inventor of the simplex method), has shown that any game can be converted to a linar program and, conversely, any linear program can be converted to a game.

• PROBLEM 13-22

In a game of matching coins with two players, suppose A wins one unit of value when there are two heads, wins nothing when there are two tails, and loses ½ unit of value when there are one head and one tail. Determine the payoff matrix, the best strategies for each player, and the value of the game to A.

Solution: The payoff matrix (for A) is seen to be:

		B: H	B: T
A	H	+1	-½
	T	-½	0

Since there is no saddle point, it is known that the optimal strategies will be mixed strategies. The solution is obtained most easily by use of the formulas

$$\frac{x_1}{x_2} = \frac{a_{22} - a_{21}}{a_{11} - a_{12}}, \quad \frac{y_1}{y_2} = \frac{a_{22} - a_{12}}{a_{11} - a_{21}},$$

and

$$v = \frac{a_{11}a_{22} - a_{12}a_{21}}{a_{11} + a_{22} - (a_{12} + a_{21})};$$

where a_{ij}s refer to values in the payoff matrix for A as such:

$$\begin{bmatrix} a_{11} & a_{12} \\ a_{21} & a_{22} \end{bmatrix}$$

and x_1: probability of A choosing row 1, x_2: probability of A choosing row 2, y_1: probability of B choosing column 1, y_2: probability of B choosing column 2, v: units of value that A will gain each time the game is played.

Thus

$$\frac{x_1}{x_2} = \frac{1}{3}$$

So

$$x_1 = \frac{1}{4}, \quad x_2 = \frac{3}{4}$$

$$\frac{y_1}{y_2} = \frac{1}{3}, \quad y_1 = \frac{1}{4}, \quad y_2 = \frac{3}{4}$$

$$v = \frac{0 - \frac{1}{4}}{1 + 1} = -\frac{1}{8}$$

Thus each player should show heads 1/4 of the time and tails 3/4 of the time. The game is unfair to A, as he will lose on average 1/8 unit each time the game is played.

• PROBLEM 13-23

Consider a game with the following payoff matrix:

	B:	B_1	B_2	min
A:	A_1:	2	-3	-3
	A_2:	-3	4	-3
max		2	4	

Find the value of the game when both players use mixed strategies.

Solution: The game has no saddle point since maximin = 2 ≠ minimax = -3. Thus for a single game, there is no predictable value. Now a fundamental result in the theory of games is that by using mixed strategies every finite two-person zero-sum game has a solution, this solution being at the same time the best for both players. To find the common value of the game reason as follows: Let

$$S_A^* = \begin{Bmatrix} A_1 & A_2 \\ p & 1-p \end{Bmatrix} \qquad S_B^* = \begin{Bmatrix} B_1 & B_2 \\ q & 1-q \end{Bmatrix} \tag{1}$$

S_A^* in (1) is to be interpreted as saying that the strategy of A is to play A_1 with probability p and A_2 the remaining proportion of the time. S_B^* is the strategy of B. If S_A^* is optimal then V(A) does not depend on the frequencies with which B_1, B_2 are used, where V(A) denotes the value of the game to A. Hence,

$$V = p(2) + (1 - p)(-3) \quad \text{(if B uses } B_1 \text{ only)}$$

$$V = p(-3) + (1 - p)(4) \quad \text{(if B uses } B_2 \text{ only)}.$$

Equating these, one gets

$$p = 7/12, \ (1 - p) = 5/12 \quad \text{and} \quad V = -1/12.$$

Similarly, if B keeps to S_B^*, then

$$V = 2(2) + (1 - q)(-3) \quad \text{(A uses } A_1\text{)}$$

$$V = q(-3) + (1 - q)(4) \quad \text{(A uses } A_2\text{)}$$

giving $q = 7/12$, $(1 - q) = 5/12$ and $V = -1/12$. Hence

$$S_A^* = \begin{Bmatrix} A_1 & A_2 \\ 7/12 & 5/12 \end{Bmatrix} \qquad S_B^* = \begin{Bmatrix} B_1 & B_2 \\ 7/12 & 5/12 \end{Bmatrix}$$

and the value of the game is -1/12 to A, i.e., B will win 1/12.

• PROBLEM 13-24

Consider the payoff table in which player I has only two pure strategies:

			II		
		Probability	y_1	y_2	y_3
Probability		Pure strategy	1	2	3
I	x_1	1	0	-2	2
	$1-x_1$	2	5	4	-3

Maximize the minimum expected payoffs of both players.

<u>Solution</u>: Since his mixed strategies are (x_1, x_2) and $x_2 = 1 - x_1$, it is only necessary for him to solve for the optimal value of x_1. However, it is straightforward to plot the expected payoff as a function of x_1 for each of his opponent's pure strategies. This graph can then be used to identify the point that maximizes the minimum expected payoff. The opponent's minimax mixed strategy can also be identified from the graph.

For each of the pure strategies available to player II the expected payoff for player I would be

(y_1, y_2, y_3)	Expected payoff
(1, 0, 0)	$0x_1 + 5(1 - x_1) = 5 - 5x_1$
(0, 1, 0)	$-2x_1 + 4(1 - x_1) = 4 - 6x_1$
(0, 0, 1)	$2x_1 - 3(1 - x_1) = -3 + 5x_1$

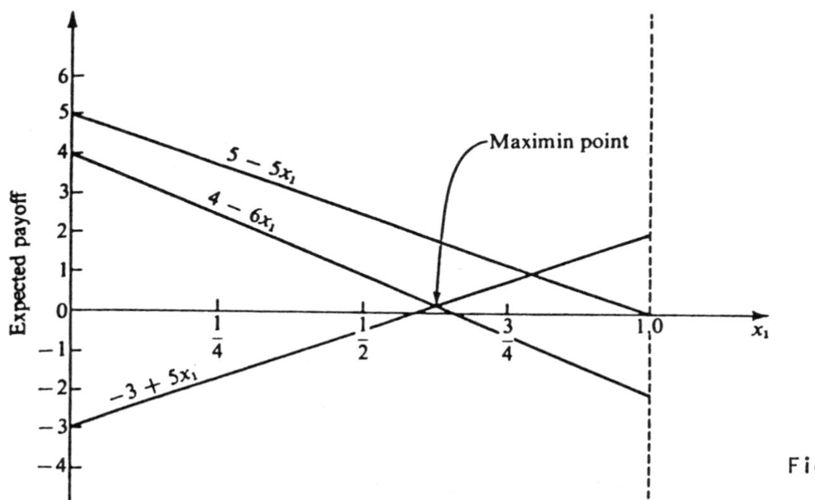

Fig. 1

Now plot these expected payoff lines on a graph, as shown in Fig. 1. For any given value of x_1 and of (y_1, y_2, y_3), the expected payoff will be the appropriate weighted average of the corresponding points on these three lines. In particular

$$\text{Expected payoff} = y_1(5 - 5x_1) + y_2(4 - 6x_1) + y_3(-3 + 5x_1).$$

Thus, given x_1, the minimum expected payoff is given by the corresponding point on the "bottom" line. According to the minimax (or maximin) criterion, player I should select the value of x_1 given the largest minimum expected payoff, so that

$$\underline{v} = v = \max_{0 \leq x_1 \leq 1} \{\min(-3 + 5x_1, 4 - 6x_1)\}.$$

Therefore the optimal value of x_1 is the one at the intersection of the two lines $(-3 + 5x_1, 4 - 6x_1)$. Solving algebraically,

$$-3 + 5x_1 = 4 - 6x_1,$$

so that $x_1 = 7/11$; thus $(x_1, x_2) = (7/11, 4/11)$ is the optimal mixed strategy for player I, and

$$\underline{v} = v = -3 + 5\left(\frac{7}{11}\right) = \frac{2}{11}$$

is the value of the game.

To find the corresponding optimal mixed strategy for player II, one would now reason as follows. According to the definition of upper value and the minimax theorem, the expected payoff resulting from this strategy $(y_1, y_2, y_3) = (y_1^*, y_2^*, y_3^*)$ will satisfy the condition,

$$y_1^*(5 - 5x_1) + y_2^*(4 - 6x_1) + y_3^*(-3 + 5x_1) \leq \overline{v} = v = \frac{2}{11}$$

for all values of $x_1 (0 \leq x_1 \leq 1)$; furthermore, when player I is playing optimally (that is, $x_1 = 7/11$), this inequality will be an equality, so that

$$\frac{20}{11}y_1^* + \frac{2}{11}y_2^* + \frac{2}{11}y_3^* = v = \frac{2}{11}\ .$$

Since (y_1, y_2, y_3) is a probability distribution, it is also known that

$$y_1^* + y_2^* + y_3^* = 1.$$

Therefore $y_1^* = 0$ because $y_1^* > 0$ would violate the next-to-last equation, i.e., the expected payoff on the graph at $x_1 = 7/11$ would be above the maximin point. (In general, any line that does not pass through the maximin must be given a zero weight to avoid increasing the expected payoff above this point.) Hence,

$$y_2^*(4 - 6x_1) + y_3^*(-3 + 5x_1)\begin{cases} \leq \frac{2}{11}, & \text{for } 0 \leq x_1 \leq 1 \\ = \frac{2}{11}, & \text{for } x_1 = \frac{7}{11}\ . \end{cases}$$

But y_2^* and y_3^* are numbers, so the left-hand side is the equation of a straight line, which is a fixed weighted average of the two "bottom" lines on the graph. Since the ordinate of this line must equal 2/11 at $x_1 = 7/11$, and it must never exceed 2/11, the line necessarily is horizontal. (This conclusion is always true, unless the optimal value of x_1 is either zero or 1, in which case player II also should use a single pure strategy.) Therefore

$$y_2^*\ (4 - 6x_1) + y_3^*\ (-3 + 5x_1) = \frac{2}{11},\ \text{for } 0 \leq x\ \ \leq 1.$$

Hence, to solve for y_2^* and y_3^*, select two values of x_1 (say, zero and 1), and solve the resulting two simultaneous equations. Thus

$$4y_2^* - 3y_3^* = \frac{2}{11},$$

$$-2y_2^* + 2y_3^* = \frac{2}{11},$$

so that $y_3^* = 6/11$ and $y_2^* = 5/11$. Therefore the optimal mixed strategy for player II is $(y_1, y_2, y_3) = (0, 5/11, 6/11)$.

Consider the following game. Two players A and B must each select a number out of 1, 2, or 3. If both have chosen the same number, A will pay B the amount of the chosen number. Otherwise A receives the amount of his own number from B. The payoff table for this game is shown in Table 1. What are the best strategies for A and B? Use LInear Programming to solve.

Table 1

		B	
A	1	2	3
1	-1^B	1	1
2	2	-2^B	2^A
3	3^A	3^A	-3^B

Solution: The linear program for A's best random strategy, x_1, x_2, x_3 (fractions of time during which row 1, 2, and 3 will be chosen so as to maximize A's gains) is

$$\max v$$

subject to

$$-x_1 + 2x_2 + 3x_3 \geq v$$

$$x_1 - 2x_2 + 3x_3 \geq v$$

$$x_1 + 2x_2 - 3x_3 \geq v$$

$$x_1 + x_2 + x_3 = 1$$

and

$$x_1, x_2, x_3 \geq 0$$

The optimal v could be negative because the payoff table does contain negative payoffs. However, if the number 3 is added to all a_{ij}'s, then all will be nonnegative. Then define $v' = v + 3$ or $v = v' - 3$. The problem can be rewritten with all non-negative variables as

$$\max v' - 3$$

subject to

$$2x_1 + 5x_2 + 6x_3 \geq v'$$

$$4x_1 + x_2 + 6x_3 \geq v'$$

$$4x_1 + 5x_2 \geq v'$$

$$x_1 + x_2 + x_3 = 1$$

$$x_1, x_2, x_3, v' \geq 0$$

It is best with hand calculation to eliminate the equality constraint by substituting

$$x_3 = 1 - x_1 + x_2$$

and replacing the nonnegativity condition $x_3 \geq 0$ by

$$x_1 + x_2 \leq 1$$

The resulting problem is

$$\max v' - 3$$

subject to

$$4x_1 + x_2 + v' \leq 6$$

$$2x_1 + 5x_2 + v' \leq 6$$

$$4x_1 + 5x_2 - v' \geq 0$$

$$x_1 + x_2 \leq 1$$

and

$$x_1, x_2, v' \geq 0$$

Slack variables are then used to convert the four inequality constraints to equalities. The problem becomes

$$\max v' - 3$$

subject to

$$4x_1 + x_2 + v' + s_1 = 6$$

$$2x_1 + 5x_2 + v' + s_2 = 6$$

$$4x_1 + 5x_2 - v' - s_3 = 0$$

$$x_1 + x_2 + s_4 = 1$$

The initial BFS will have basic variables s_1, s_2, s_3, s_4 and zero variables x_1, x_2, v'. This corner point is degenerate because the third constraint passes through the origin. However, the degeneracy gives no trouble. The first tableau of the simplex method is

	Const.	x_1	x_2	v' (Pivot)	Ratio	
E	−3	0	0	1		
s_1	6	−4	−1	−1	−6	
s_2	6	−2	−5	−1	−6	
s_3	0	4	5	−1	−0	Pivot
s_4	1	−1	−1	0	∞	

The next tableau shows no gain in objective because of the degeneracy:

Pivot

	Const.	x_1	x_2	s_3	Ratio	
E	-3	$+4$	5	-1		
s_1	6	-8	-6	$+1$	-1	
s_2	6	-6	-10	$+1$	$-\frac{6}{10}$	Pivot
v'	0	$+4$	$+5$	-1	0	
s_4	1	-1	-1	0	-1	

The next tableau is

Pivot

	Const.	x_1	s_2	s_3	Ratio	
E	0	1	$-\frac{1}{2}$	$-\frac{1}{2}$		
s_1	$\frac{24}{10}$	$-\frac{44}{10}$	$+\frac{6}{10}$	$+\frac{4}{10}$	$-\frac{24}{44}$	Pivot
x_2	$\frac{6}{10}$	$-\frac{6}{10}$	$-\frac{1}{10}$	$+\frac{1}{10}$	-1	
v'	3	1	$-\frac{1}{2}$	$-\frac{1}{2}$	$+3$	
s_4	$+\frac{4}{10}$	$-\frac{4}{10}$	$+\frac{1}{10}$	$-\frac{1}{10}$	-1	

The next tableau gives the optimal solution:

	Const.	s_1	s_2	s_3	Ratio
E	$\frac{6}{11}$	$-\frac{10}{44}$	$-\frac{4}{11}$	$-\frac{9}{22}$	
x_1	$\frac{6}{11}$	$-\frac{10}{44}$	$\frac{6}{44}$	$\frac{1}{11}$	
x_2	$\frac{3}{11}$	$+\frac{6}{44}$	$-\frac{2}{11}$	$\frac{1}{22}$	
v'	$\frac{39}{11}$	$-\frac{10}{44}$	$-\frac{4}{11}$	$-\frac{9}{22}$	
s_4	$\frac{2}{11}$	$+\frac{4}{44}$	$+\frac{1}{22}$	$-\frac{7}{110}$	

The result is

$$x_1 = \frac{6}{11}$$

$$x_2 = \frac{3}{11}$$

$$x_3 = \frac{2}{11}$$

and

$$v = \frac{6}{11}$$

The first three constraints hold as equalities in the optimal solution. Therefore it is known that B uses all three of his courses of action. The best random strategy for B can be found from these results by solving three simultaneous equations in three unknowns. The ith equation represents the expected loss to B if A uses A_i. All these must equal the expected gain to A that is known. The equations are

$$-y_1 + y_2 + y_3 = \frac{6}{11}$$

$$2y_1 - 2y_2 + 2y_3 = \frac{6}{11}$$

$$3y_1 + 3y_2 - 3y_3 = \frac{6}{11}$$

The solution is

$$y_1 = \frac{5}{22}$$

$$y_2 = \frac{4}{11}$$

$$y_3 = \frac{9}{22}$$

This completes the solution to the game problem.

• PROBLEM 13-26

1) Two stores, R and C, are planning to locate in one of two towns. Town 1 has 60 percent of the population while town 2 has 40 percent. If both stores locate in the same town they will split the total business of both towns equally, but if they locate in different towns each will get the business of that town. Where should each store locate?

2) Consider an extension of the above problem. Stores R and C are trying to locate in one of three towns. The matrix game is:

		Store C locates in		
		1	2	3
Store R	1	50	50	80
locates in	2	50	50	80
	3	20	20	80

The entries in the matrix above represent the percentages of business that store R gets in each case. Where should each store locate?

Solution: 1) By the information given, it is known that the payoff matrix is:

		Store C locates in	
		1	2
Store R	1	50	60
locates in	2	40	50

The entries of the matrix represent the percentages of business that store R gets in each case.

Definition: A game defined by a matrix is said to be strictly determined if and only if there is an entry of the matrix that is the smallest element in its row and also the largest element in its column. This entry is then called a saddle point and is the value of the game.

Therefore, find the maxima of the columns and the minima of the rows.

		Store C		
		1	2	Row Minima
Store R	1	50	60	50
	2	40	50	40
Column Maxima		50	60	

Entry $a_{11} = 50$ is a saddle point. Hence it is the best strategy for both stores to locate in Town 1.

2) Examine the matrix game for column maxima and row minima.

		Store C locates in			
		1	2	3	Row Minima:
Store R	1	50	50	80	50
locates in	2	50	50	80	50
	3	20	20	50	20
Column Maxima:		50	50	80	

(1)

Note that each of the four 50 entries in the 2 x 2 matrix in the upper left-hand corner of (1) above is a saddle value of the matrix, since each is simultaneously the minimum of its row and maximum of its column. Note the 50 entry in the lower right-hand corner is not a saddle value. The game is strictly determined with optimal strategies:

For store R: "Locate in either town 1 or town 2"

For store C: "Locate in either town 1 or town 2".

• PROBLEM 13-27

Suppose that two costume companies each make clown, skeleton, and space costumes. They all sell for the same amount and use the same machinery and workmanship. Furthermore, the market for costumes is fixed; a certain given number of total costumes will be sold this Halloween. But each company has its own individual styles which affect how the costumes sell. On the basis of past experience, the following matrix has been inferred. It indicates, for example, that if both make clown outfits, then for every 20 that are sold, company I will lose 2 sales to company II. Similarly, if company I makes clown outfits and company II makes space suits, then for each 20 sold, company I will sell 4 more than company II.

		Company II		
		Clown	Skeleton	Space
Company I	Clown	-2	0	4
	Skeleton	0	2	1
	Space	-1	-4	0

How should each company plan its manufacturing?

Solution: Company I can quickly decide not to make space outfits, because it will do better with skeleton costumes, no matter what company II does. Similarly, company II should not make space outfits, because it can always be better off by making clown outfits, no matter what the choice of company I. Thus the matrix has been reduced as follows:

$$\begin{bmatrix} -2 & 0 & 4 \\ 0 & 2 & 1 \\ -1 & 1 & 0 \end{bmatrix}$$

With the remaining 2 by 2 matrix, it is clear that company I will profit most from playing the second row, and that company II should always play the first column. Thus this game also has a saddle point. It is $a_{21} = 0$.

The value of the game is 0; company I should always make skeleton outfits and company II should always make clown costumes.

• PROBLEM 13-28

Consider a buyer who at the beginning of each month decides whether to buy brand 1 or brand 2 that month. Each month the buyer will select either brand 1 or 2. The selection he makes at the beginning of any one month depends at most on the selection he made in the immediately preceding month and not on any other previous selections. Let P_{ij} denote the probability that at the beginning of any month the buyer selects brand j given that he bought brand i the preceding month. Suppose it is known that $p_{11} = 3/4$, $p_{12} = 1/4$, $p_{21} = 1/2$ and $p_{22} = 1/2$.

1) First draw the transition diagram.

2) Assuming that the first month under consideration is January, determine the distribution of probabilities for April.

Solution: 1) The transition diagram is:

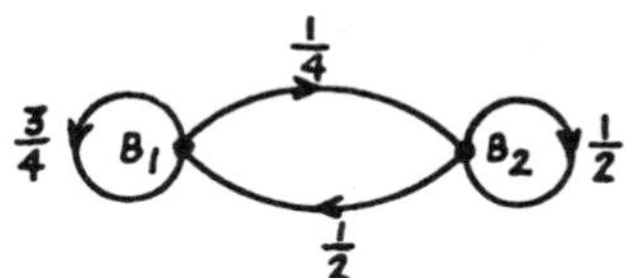

(Note: B_1 and B_2 represent brand 1 and brand 2, respectively.)

2) Since $p_{11} = 3/4$, $p_{12} = 1/4$, $p_{21} = 1/2$ and $p_{22} = 1/2$ then the transition matrix is:

$$P = \begin{bmatrix} 3/4 & 1/4 \\ 1/2 & 1/2 \end{bmatrix}$$

If $p^{(0)} = [p_1^{(0)} \quad p_2^{(0)}]$ denotes the probability vector for January, then the probability vector for February is $p^{(0)}P$, the probability vector for March is $p^{(0)}P^2$, etc. Since April is in the third step of the process, its probability vector is $p^{(0)}P^3$. Calculate that

$$P^3 = \begin{bmatrix} 3/4 \\ 1/2 \end{bmatrix} \begin{bmatrix} 1/4 \\ 1/2 \end{bmatrix} \begin{bmatrix} 3/4 & 1/4 \\ 1/2 & 1/2 \end{bmatrix} \begin{bmatrix} 3/4 & 1/4 \\ 1/2 & 1/2 \end{bmatrix}$$

$$= \begin{bmatrix} 43/64 & 21/64 \\ 21/32 & 11/32 \end{bmatrix},$$

so

$$p^{(3)} = p^{(0)} \begin{bmatrix} 43/64 & 21/64 \\ 21/32 & 11/32 \end{bmatrix}$$

$$= \begin{bmatrix} p_1^{(0)} & p_2^{(0)} \end{bmatrix} \begin{bmatrix} 43/64 & 21/64 \\ 21/32 & 11/32 \end{bmatrix}$$

$$= \begin{bmatrix} 43/64\, p_1^{(0)} + 21/32\, p_2^{(0)} & 21/64 p_1^{(0)} + 11/32 p_2^{(0)} \end{bmatrix}$$

• PROBLEM 13-29

Consider a market that is controlled by two brands B_1 and B_2. Suppose it is known that 10% of the buyers of each brand switch to the other brand during any given month. At the beginning of a given month 500 buyers are divided so that 300 purchase B_1 and 200 purchase B_2. What will be the number of buyers who will purchase B_1 and B_2 during the given month?

Solution: The movement of buyers in the market during the month can be described by the product of a buyer vector, B_1 and a transition matrix, T. Let $B = [b_1, b_2]$ where for i = 1, 2, b_i represents the number of buyers who purchase brand B_i at the beginning of the month. The transition matrix, T, on the other hand, is

$$T = [p_{ij}] = \begin{bmatrix} p_{11} & p_{12} \\ p_{21} & p_{22} \end{bmatrix},$$

where for i = 1,2 and j = 1,2, p_{ij} is the probability that a current buyer of brand B_i will buy brand B_j during the month in question. In this problem one then has: $B = [300 \quad 200]$ and

$$T = \begin{bmatrix} .9 & .1 \\ .1 & .9 \end{bmatrix}.$$

$$\text{Therefore, } BT = [300 \quad 200] \begin{bmatrix} .9 & .1 \\ .1 & .9 \end{bmatrix}$$

$$= [270 + 20 \quad 30 + 180]$$

$$= [290 \quad 210].$$

The entries in the product matrix therefore represent the number of buyers who will purchase B_1 and B_2 in the given month. Therefore 290 will buy product B_1 and 210 will buy product B_2.

• PROBLEM 13-30

P_1 and P_2 each extend either one, two, or three fingers, and the difference in the amounts put forth is computed. If this difference is 0, the payoff is 0; if the difference is 1, the player putting forth the smaller amount wins 1; and if the difference is 2, the player putting forth the larger amount wins 2.

Each player has three pure strategies. Let s_i denote P_1's pure strategy of extending i fingers, $1 \le i \le 3$, and similarly define t_j, $1 \le j \le 3$, for P_2. The payoff tableau is then

	t_1	t_2	t_3
s_1	0	1	−2
s_2	−1	0	1
s_3	2	−1	0

Formulate an equivalent linear programming model for determining an optimal strategy and security level for P_2. Solve by using the simplex method.

Solution: The simplex method is not directly applicable if the value of the game is not positive. For such a game a constant must first be chosen such that when this constant is added to each entry of the original payoff matrix, the game corresponding to this new matrix has a positive value. Then the simplex method can be applied to this new game, with the value of the original game equal to the value of the new game less the constant. Note that it may not be necessary to make all the entries in the modified payoff matrix positive; for example, if the matrix has at least one row with all positive entries, the value of the corresponding game is positive (the possibility of P_1 using the pure strategy of playing that particular row shows that his security level is positive).

By symmetry it is reasonable to expect the value of this game to be 0. To verify this and compute optimal strategies, first add 2 to each entry of the above matrix, giving the following matrix, which corresponds to a game with value at least 1 as all the entries in the last two rows are greater than or equal to 1.

$$\begin{pmatrix} 2 & 3 & 0 \\ 1 & 2 & 3 \\ 4 & 1 & 2 \end{pmatrix}$$

The associated linear programming problem corresponding to P_2's determination of an optimal strategy and security level is to

$$\text{Maximize} \quad y'_1 + y'_2 + y'_3$$

subject to

$$\begin{aligned} 2y'_1 + 3y'_2 \qquad\qquad &\le 1 \\ y'_1 + 2y'_2 + 3y'_3 &\le 1 \\ 4y'_1 + y'_2 + 2y'_3 &\le 1 \\ y'_1,\ y'_2,\ y'_3 &\ge 0 \end{aligned}$$

Adding three slack variables and solving leads to the tableaux of Table 1:

Table 1

	y'_1	y'_2	y'_3	y'_4	y'_5	y'_6	
y'_4	2	3	0	1	0	0	1
y'_5	1	2	(3)	0	1	0	1
y'_6	4	1	2	0	0	1	1
	-1	-1	-1	0	0	0	0
y'_4	2	(3)	0	1	0	0	1
y'_3	$\frac{1}{3}$	$\frac{2}{3}$	1	0	$\frac{1}{3}$	0	$\frac{1}{3}$
y'_6	$\frac{10}{3}$	$-\frac{1}{3}$	0	0	$-\frac{2}{3}$	1	$\frac{1}{3}$
	$-\frac{2}{3}$	$-\frac{1}{3}$	0	0	$\frac{1}{3}$	0	$\frac{1}{3}$
y'_2	$\frac{2}{3}$	1	0	$\frac{1}{3}$	0	0	$\frac{1}{3}$
y'_3	$-\frac{1}{9}$	0	1	$-\frac{2}{9}$	$\frac{1}{3}$	0	$\frac{1}{9}$
y'_6	($\frac{32}{9}$)	0	0	$\frac{1}{9}$	$-\frac{2}{3}$	1	$\frac{4}{9}$
	$-\frac{4}{9}$	0	0	$\frac{1}{9}$	$\frac{1}{3}$	0	$\frac{4}{9}$
y'_2	0	1	0	$\frac{5}{16}$	$\frac{1}{8}$	$-\frac{3}{16}$	$\frac{1}{4}$
y'_3	0	0	1	$-\frac{7}{32}$	$\frac{5}{16}$	$\frac{1}{32}$	$\frac{1}{8}$
y'_1	1	0	0	$\frac{1}{32}$	$-\frac{3}{16}$	$\frac{9}{32}$	$\frac{1}{8}$
	0	0	0	$\frac{1}{8}$	$\frac{1}{4}$	$\frac{1}{8}$	$\frac{1}{2}$

The value of the modified game is 2, and so the value of the original game is 0, as suggested. Since the optimal value of the above problem is attaned by $(y'_1, y'_2, y'_3) = \left(\frac{1}{8}, \frac{1}{4}, \frac{1}{8}\right)$, an optimal strategy for P_2 is $2\left(\frac{1}{8}, \frac{1}{4}, \frac{1}{8}\right) = \left(\frac{1}{4}, \frac{1}{2}, \frac{1}{4}\right)$. Similarly, the solution to the dual problem, found in the bottom row in the slack variable columns, is $(x_1, x_2, x_3) = \left(\frac{1}{8}, \frac{1}{4}, \frac{1}{8}\right)$, and so an optimal strategy for P_1 is also $2\left(\frac{1}{8}, \frac{1}{4}, \frac{1}{8}\right) = \left(\frac{1}{4}, \frac{1}{2}, \frac{1}{4}\right)$.

• PROBLEM 13-31

Consider the game matrix

$$\vec{A} = \begin{bmatrix} -6 & -1 & 2 \\ 8 & -2 & -4 \\ 10 & -3 & 3 \end{bmatrix}$$

Find the optimal strategies for the two players involved, by transforming the game into a Linear program and solving by the simplex method.

Solution: Reduction of a Game to a Linear Program:

(a) Calculate a^0 or a_0 as below:

$$\begin{aligned} &\text{If } m \leq n, \text{ let } a_{k\ell} = a^0 = \min_j \max_i a_{ij}, \\ &\text{If } m > n, \text{ let } a_{k\ell} = a_0 = \max_i \min_j a_{ij}, \end{aligned} \qquad (1)$$

where m, n, a_{ij} are numbers of rows, numbers of columns and i_j-th entries of the game matrix $\vec{A}$. If a^0 is the smallest in its row or a_0 the largest in its column, it is a saddle point (optimal pure strategies for the game can be obtained right away); stop. If a^0 or $a_0 = 0$, calculate the other for use as the first pivot $a_{k\ell}$.

(b) If there is no saddle point, form a tableau by adjoining the following to the game matrix $\vec{A}$: a first row of labels 1, $\vec{y}$, -z and a first column 1, $\vec{x}$, 1 (these follow the usual convention except that -z and the non-basic 1 have changed places); a value d = 0 in the lower right corner; all $b_i = 1$ in the remainder of the last column and all $c_j = -1$ in the remainder of the last row. (In a conventional tableau all these b_i and c_j would be described as infeasible; obviously they go with the given labels.)

(c) Pivot first on the selected $a_{k\ell}$ and then on the entry (1 over the denominator $a_{k\ell}$) in the lower right corner. The result is a conventional tableau that is primal feasible if $a_{k\ell} = a^0$ and dual feasible if $a_{k\ell} = a_0$.

(d) One or more additional pivot steps are required to optimize this conventional tableau, unless a saddle point was overlooked in step (a). Player J's probability vector is $\vec{y}^*$ and Player I's probability vector is $\vec{u}^*$, the dual counterpart of $\vec{x}$.

Applying this procedure to the game

$$\vec{A} = \begin{bmatrix} -6 & -1 & 2 \\ 8 & -2 & -4 \\ 10 & -3 & 3 \end{bmatrix}$$

$$\max_i a_{ij} = \underbrace{10 \quad -1 \quad 3}_{\min = a^0 = -1}$$

Since the matrix is square, there is no "shorter" direction (one prefers to optimize the a_{ij} in the "short direction" first; by choosing the less effective direction for the more effective optimization (the first of the two), one may hope to obtain that one of a^0 and a_0 that is closer to a*). But (1) calls for optimizing vertically first by finding the larges a_{ij} in each column. The following tableaus result from the initial pivot $a_{k\ell} = a^0 = a_{12} =$

-1; this is not a saddle point because it is not the smallest in its row.

I

1	y_1	y_2	y_3	$-z$
x_1	−6	−1*	2	1
x_2	8	−2	−4	1
x_3	10	−3	3	1
1	−1	−1	−1	0

II

−1	y_1	x_1	y_3	$-z$
y_2	−6	1	2	1
x_2	−20	2	8	1
x_3	−28	3	3	2
1	−5	1	3	1*

III

1	y_1	x_1	y_3	1
y_2	1	0	1	−1
x_2	15*	−1	−5	−1
x_3	18	−1	3	−2
$-z$	−5	1	3	−1

IV

15	x_2	x_1	y_3	1
y_2	−1	1	20	−14
y_1	1	−1	−5	−1
x_3	−18	3	135	−12
$-z$	5	10	20	−20

The primal simplex rules give the last pivot 15.

The last tableau gives z* = a* = -20/15. The column equations with u_j in place of x_j give $\vec{u}^*$ = (10,5,0)/15, and the row equations give $\vec{y}^*$ = (1, 14, 0)/15.

• PROBLEM 13-32

Solve the game given for optimal strategies of the two players, by applying the simplex method.

$$\begin{matrix} 3 & 1 & -5 \\ -1 & -2 & 2 \\ 1 & 3 & -1 \end{matrix}$$

Solution: The result is as follows: The optimal strategies are

$\vec{u}^*$ = (0,.4,.6)

$\vec{y}^*$ = (.6,0,.4),

with optimal value

a* = .2

and pivot locations $k\ell$ = 23 or 33.

• PROBLEM 13-33

Solve the game below for optimal strategies of the two players, by applying the simplex method.

$$\begin{matrix} 1 & 0 & 2 \\ 0 & 2 & 0 \\ 2 & 0 & -1 \end{matrix}$$

Solution: The result is as follows: The optimal strategies are

$$\vec{u}^* = \vec{y}^* = (6,5,2)/13.$$

The optimal value of the program is

$$a^* = 10/13,$$

and the pivot locations $k\ell$ = 13, 22 or 31.

• PROBLEM 13-34

You are involved in a game of chess with Bobby Fischer. There are three possible outcomes, you win(?), event A, you draw, event B, or you lose, event C. Setting u(A) = 1 and u(C) = -1, what should u(B) be? Because of abilities of your opponent, much satisfaction would be gained from a draw, and so clearly u(B) should be positive. More precisely, suppose you feel equally disposed to a draw and a lottery in which you have a probability of $\frac{19}{20}$ of being accorded a victory over Fischer and a probability of $\frac{1}{20}$ of being accorded a loss.

Solution: The desirability of B lies somewhere between the desirability of C and of A. It is reasonable to assume that there exists a particular r, $0 < r < 1$, such that you are indifferent to the events B and the lottery with outcomes A and C, A occurring with probability r and C with probability $1 - r$. Denote this particular lottery by the symbol $rA + (1 - r)C$.

Since you are indifferent to these two events, the utility of B, u(B), should equal the utility of the lottery, denoted by $u(rA + (1 - r)C)$. Analogous to the definition of expected value in probability theory, the desirability of the lottery $rA + (1 - r)C$ can be given by $ru(A) + (1 - r)u(C)$, since this can be considered to be the "expected utility value" of the lottery. Thus, to determine u(B), all you need to determine is u(A), u(C), and the above r, and then set

$$u(B) = ru(A) + (1 - r)u(C).$$

Since $r = \frac{19}{20}$ in this question,

$$u(B) = u\left[\frac{19}{20}A + \frac{1}{20}C\right]$$

$$= \frac{19}{20}u(A) + \frac{1}{20}u(C)$$

$$= \frac{19}{20} - \frac{1}{20} = \frac{9}{10}$$

• **PROBLEM 13-35**

Find for a Markov chain with transition probabilities indicated in Figure 1, the probability of being at the various possible states after three steps, assuming that the process starts at state a_1.

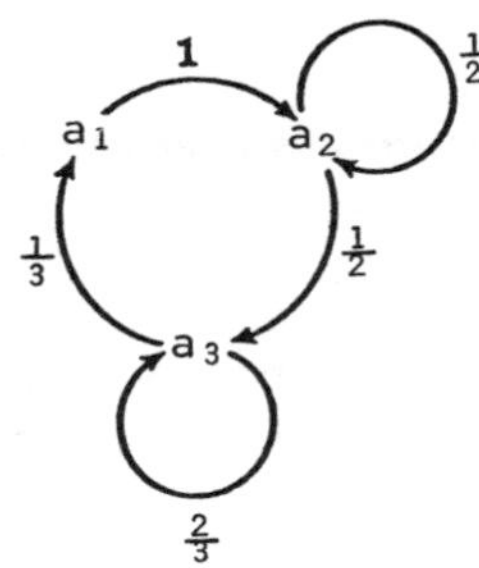

Fig. 1

Solution: These probabilities are found by constructing a tree and a tree measure as in Figure 2.

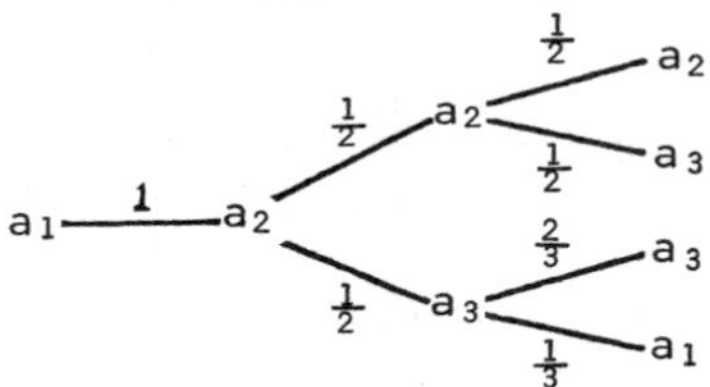

Fig. 2

The probability $p_{13}^{(3)}$, for example, is the sum of the weights assigned by the tree measure to all paths through the tree which end at state a_3. That is,

$$1 \cdot \frac{1}{2} \cdot \frac{1}{2} + 1 \cdot \frac{1}{2} \cdot \frac{2}{3} = \frac{7}{12} .$$

Similarly $\quad p_{12}^{(3)} = 1 \cdot \frac{1}{2} \cdot \frac{1}{2} = \frac{1}{4}$

and $\quad p_{11}^{(3)} = 1 \cdot \frac{1}{2} \cdot \frac{1}{3} = \frac{1}{6}$.

By constructing a similar tree measure, assuming that one starts at state a_2, one could find $p_{21}^{(3)}$, $p_{22}^{(3)}$, and $p_{23}^{(3)}$. The same is true for $p_{31}^{(3)}$, $p_{32}^{(3)}$, and $p_{33}^{(3)}$. If this is carried out the results can be written in matrix form as follows:

$$P^{(3)} = \begin{array}{c} \\ a_1 \\ a_2 \\ a_3 \end{array} \begin{array}{c} \begin{array}{ccc} a_1 & a_2 & a_3 \end{array} \\ \begin{pmatrix} \frac{1}{6} & \frac{1}{4} & \frac{7}{12} \\ \frac{7}{36} & \frac{7}{24} & \frac{37}{72} \\ \frac{4}{27} & \frac{7}{18} & \frac{25}{54} \end{pmatrix} \end{array} .$$

Again the rows add up to 1, corresponding to the fact that if one starts at a given state one must reach some state after three steps. Notice now that all the elements of this matrix are positive, showing that it is possible to reach any state from any state in three steps.

• PROBLEM 13-36

A fire extinguisher service company works under contract to service all fire extinguishers in large factories and office buildings. Each extinguisher has a required pressure level that must be maintained for proper operation. The service company sends its men periodically to each customer to inspect and recharge all extinguishers in the building. The service company has a pricing problem: For each new potential customer, it must propose a contract that will specify both the inspection period and the service charge, given the type of extinguishers and the number present. The pricing decision is based upon the estimates that the worth to the customer is \$0.20 per day for every extinguisher that is up to required pressure, but it is equivalent to a \$0.80 loss per day for every extinguisher below required pressure. The pressure loss process is a Markov process. Each extinguisher is either above (state A) or below (state B) its required pressure. An extinguisher which is in state A at the start of a week has probability .05 of falling below pressure during 1 week. Once it drops below pressure it will remain below. All extinguishers are in state A at the completion of one periodic inspection. Consider a large office building having 100 extinguishers. The total charge for one inspection and service would be \$100. What inspection period (in weeks) would maximize the net worth to the customer?

Solution: The Markov process has two states: A and B. The starting condition is that $P(A_0) = 1$. The matrix of conditional probabilities is

	A_n	B_n
A_{n-1}	.95	.05
B_{n-1}	0	1

The equation relating $P(A_n)$ to $P(A_{n-1})$ is

$$P(A_n) = .95P(A_{n-1})$$

This, together with the initial condition, gives the probability that the extinguisher will still be in state A at time n weeks after the last inspection, as shown in Table 1.

The expected worth of the first week is

$$W(1) = +\ (100)(7)[.20(.95) - .80(.05)] = \$105$$

This takes into account the expected worth produced by 100 extinguishers during 7 days a week: \$105. The benefit from the second week is

$$W(2) = 700 \cdot [.20(.9025) - .80(.0975)] = \$71.75$$

Table 1

n	$P(A_n)$	$P(B_n)$
0	1	0
1	.95	.05
2	.9025	.0975
3	.8574	.1426
4	.8145	.1855
5	.7738	.2262
6	.7351	.2649

A criterion for selecting the inspection period is to maximize the expected net worth per week. The calculations are shown in Table 2.

Table 2

n	Expected Worth of Week n	Cumulative Expected Worth	Net Worth of First n Weeks	Average over n Weeks
1	105.00	105.00	5.00	5.00
2	71.75	176.75	76.75	38.37
3	40.18	216.93	116.93	38.98
4	10.15	227.08	127.08	31.77

The net benefit per week to the customer is maximized by an inspection period of 3 weeks. The customer's expected worth is \$216.93 less the cost of \$100 for the inspection. This pricing policy enables the service company to offer the best value for the estimated cost of service.

• PROBLEM 13-37

Markov chains may be applied to genetics. According to the Mendelian theory of genetics, many traits of an offspring are determined by the genes of the parents.

Suppose the genotype of one parent is unknown and the genotype of the other parent is hybrid (heterozygous). Their offspring is mated with a person whose genotype is hybrid. This mating procedure is continued. In the long run, what is the genotype of the offspring?

Solution: A given individual is either dominant, with genotype AA, hybrid with genotype Aa or recessive with genotype aa.

An offspring inherits one gene from each parent in its own genotype. For example if both parents are dominant, the offspring will also be dominant

```
      Parents AA          AA
                ↘        ↙
   Offspring  A          A
```

It is known that one parent is hybrid, i.e., Aa. Hence the various possibilities are

Aa × AA	Aa × Aa	Aa × aa
$P(A) = \frac{1}{2}$, $P(a) = \frac{1}{2}$; A	$P(A) = \frac{1}{2}$, $P(a) = \frac{1}{2}$; $P(A) = \frac{1}{2}$, $P(a) = \frac{1}{2}$	$P(A) = \frac{1}{2}$, $P(a) = \frac{1}{2}$; a.
$P(AA) = \frac{1}{2}$	$P(AA) = P(aa) = \frac{1}{4}$	$P(Aa) = \frac{1}{2}$
$P(Aa) = \frac{1}{2}$	$P(Aa) = \frac{1}{2}$	$P(aa) = \frac{1}{2}$

Thus if the unknown parent is dominant, the probability of the offspring being dominant or hybrid is 1/2 respectively. If the unknown parent is recessive, the offspring will be either recessive or hybrid with probability 1/2. Finally, if the parent is hybrid the offspring will be dominant or recessive with probability 1/4 respectively or hybrid with probability 1/2. The transition matrix is therefore

$$P = \begin{array}{c|ccc} & D & H & R \\ \hline D & \frac{1}{2} & \frac{1}{2} & 0 \\ H & \frac{1}{4} & \frac{1}{2} & \frac{1}{4} \\ R & 0 & \frac{1}{2} & \frac{1}{2} \end{array}$$

Since

$$P^2 = \begin{bmatrix} \frac{3}{8} & \frac{1}{2} & \frac{1}{8} \\ \frac{1}{4} & \frac{1}{2} & \frac{1}{4} \\ \frac{1}{8} & \frac{1}{2} & \frac{3}{8} \end{bmatrix}$$

the transition matrix P is regular. Thus, there exists a fixed probability vector t which all the rows of P^n approach as n increases.

Thus

$$[t_1 \ t_2 \ t_3] \begin{bmatrix} \frac{3}{8} & \frac{1}{2} & \frac{1}{8} \\ \frac{1}{4} & \frac{1}{2} & \frac{1}{4} \\ \frac{1}{8} & \frac{1}{2} & \frac{3}{8} \end{bmatrix} = [t_1 \ t_2 \ t_3]$$

Solving this system yields

$$t = \begin{bmatrix} \frac{1}{4} & \frac{1}{2} & \frac{1}{4} \end{bmatrix}.$$

In the long run, no matter what the genotype of the unknown parent, the probabilities for the genotype of the offspring to be dominant is 1/4, to be hybrid is 1/2 and to be recessive is 1/4.

• PROBLEM 13-38

There are three dairies in a community which supply all the milk consumed: Abbot's Dairy, Branch Dairy Products Company, and Mark's Milk Products, Inc. For simplicity, refer to them hereafter as A, B, and C. Each of the dairies knows that consumers switch from dairy-to-dairy over time because of advertising, dissatisfaction with service, and other reasons. To further simplify the mathematics necessary, assume that no new customers enter and no old customers leave the market during this period.

Consider now the following data on the flow of customers for each of the dairy companies as determined by their respective Operations Research Departments:

Flow of Customers

	June 1	Gains			Losses			July 1
		From	From	From	To	To	To	
Dairy	Customers	A	B	C	A	B	C	Customers
A	200	0	35	25	0	20	20	220
B	500	20	0	20	35	0	15	490
C	300	20	15	0	25	20	0	290

Given the above data as well as all the assumptions made, determine

a) The one-step transition probabilities

b) Interpret the rows and the columns of the matrix of transition probabilities

Solution: This is an illustration of the use of Markov chain methods in broad-switching analysis. The first step would involve the computation of transition probabilities for all three of the dairies which are nothing more than the probabilities that a certain seller C, a dairy, in this case, will retain, gain, and lose customers. In other words, dairy B observes from the above table that it loses 50 customers this month; this is the same as saying that it has a probability of .9 of retaining customers; similarly, dairy A has a probability of .8 of retaining its customers; dairy C has a probability of .85 of retaining its customers. These transition probabilities for the retention of customers are calculated in the following table.

Transition Probabilities for Retention of Customers

Dairy	June 1 customers	Number lost	Number retained	Probability of retention
A	200	40	160	160/200 = .8
B	500	50	450	450/500 = .9
C	300	45	255	255/300 = .85

In the matrix of transition probabilities in this problem, include for each dairy the retention probability and the probability of its loss of customers to its two competitors. The rows in this matrix show the retention of customers and the loss of customers; the columns represent the retention of customers and the gain of customers. These probabilities have been calculated to three decimal places.

Retention and Loss →

Retention and Gain ↓

$$\begin{array}{c} \\ A \\ B \\ C \end{array} \begin{array}{c} \begin{array}{ccc} A & B & C \end{array} \\ \begin{bmatrix} .800 & .100 & .100 \\ .070 & .900 & .030 \\ .083 & .067 & .850 \end{bmatrix} \end{array}$$

Below is a matrix of the same dimensions as the one above illustrating exactly how each probability was determined:

$$\begin{array}{c} \\ A \\ B \\ C \end{array} \begin{array}{c} \begin{array}{ccc} A & B & C \end{array} \\ \begin{bmatrix} 160/200 = .800 & 20/200 = .100 & 20/200 = .100 \\ 35/500 = .070 & 450/500 = .900 & 15/500 = .030 \\ 25/300 = .083 & 20/300 = .067 & 255/300 = .850 \end{bmatrix} \end{array}$$

The rows of the matrix of transition probabilities can be read as follows:

Row 1 indicates that dairy A retains .8 of its customers (160), loses .1 of its customers (20) to dairy B, and loses .1 of its customers (20) to dairy C.

Row 2 indicates that dairy B retains .9 of its customers (450), loses .07 of its customers (35) to dairy A, and loses .03 of its customers (15) to dairy C.

Row 3 indicates that diary C retains .85 of its customers (255), loses .083 of its customers (25) to dairy A, and loses .067 of its customers (20) to dairy B.

Reading the columns yields the following interpretation:

Column 1 indicates that dairy A retains .8 of its customers (160), gains .07 of B's customers (35), and gains .083 of C's customers (25).

Column 2 indicates that dairy B retains .9 of its customers (450), gains .1 of A's customers (20), and gains .067 of C's customers (20).

Column 3 indicates that diary C retains .85 of its customers (255), gains .1 of A's customers (20), and gains .03 of B's customers (15).

• PROBLEM 13-39

Consider again the following original matrix of transition probabilities in the three-dairy problem:

	A	B	C
A	.800	.100	.100
B	.070	.900	.030
C	.083	.067	.850

a) Find out what the final or equilibrium shares of the market will be

b) Prove that an equilibrium has actually been reached in part (a).

Solution: a) First of all, an equilibrium has been defined as a position that a Markov process reaches in the long run after which no further net change occurs. This condition can only be reached if no dairy takes action which alters the matrix of transition probabilities. From a marketing point of view, one would want the answer to the question: "What would the three final or equilibrium shares of the market be?"

To determine A's share of the market in the equilibrium period (labelling this unspecified future period the eq. period), use the following relationship:

.800 times the share A had in the (eq. - 1) period (i.e., the period immediately preceding equilibrium)

\+ .070 times the share B had in the (eq. - 1) period

\+ .083 times the share C had in the (eq. - 1) period.

Writing this relationship as an equation, one has

$$A_{eq} = .800\ A_{eq-1} + .070\ B_{eq-1} + .083\ C_{eq-1}$$

The following two equations are B's and C's shares of the equilibrium market.

$$B_{eq} = .100\ A_{eq-1} + .900\ B_{eq-1} + .067\ C_{eq-1}$$

$$C_{eq} = .100\ A_{eq-1} + .030\ B_{eq-1} + .850\ C_{eq-1}$$

Rewrite the three equations as follows:

$$A = .800\ A + .070\ B + .083\ C$$

$$B = .100\ A + .900\ B + .067\ C$$

$$C = .100\ A + .030\ B + .850\ C$$

since at equilibrium it can be assumed shares of dairies are stabilized.

Because the sum of the three market shares equals 1.0, add another equation

$$1.0 = A + B + C.$$

Solving the equations simultaneously for the equilibrium market shares, yields

$A = .273$

$B = .454$

$C = .273$

b) To prove that an equilibrium has been reached, multiply the equilibrium market share (A, .273; B, .454; c, .273) by the matrix of transition probabilities:

$$(.273 \quad .454 \quad .273) \times \begin{bmatrix} .800 & .100 & .100 \\ .070 & .900 & .030 \\ .083 & .067 & .850 \end{bmatrix}$$

$$= (\ .272 \quad .454 \quad .273)$$

Therefore, an equilibrium market condition has been reached.

To recapitulate on the equilibrium market shares calculated, it is important to bear in mind that they are based upon the assumption that the matrix of transition probabilities remains fixed, and the propensities of all three dairies to retain, gain, and lose customers do not change over time.

In many circumstances, those assumptions may be somewhat invalid, but the general method remains the same. For the period during which the transition probabilities are stable, one can calculate the equilibrium which will result. However, if there is good reason to believe that the transition probabilities are indeed changing because of some action by management, use the new transition probabilities and calculate the equilibrium market shares which will result. In that manner, Markov analysis is used essentially as a short-or-intermediate-run tool.

• PROBLEM 13-40

There are three types of grocery stores in a given community. Within this community (with a fixed population) there always exists a shift of customers from one grocery store to another. On January 1,1/4 shopped at store I, 1/3 at store II and 5/12 at store III. Each month store I retains 90% of its customers and loses 10% of them to store II. Store II retains 5% of its customers and loses 85% of them to store I and 10% of them to store III. Store III retains 40% of its customers and loses 50% of them to store I and 10% to store II.

a) Find the transition matrix.

b) What proportion of customers will each store retain by Feb. 1 and Mar. 1?

c) Assuming the same pattern continues, what will be the long-run distribution of customers among the three stores?

Solution: a) The transition matrix will represent the probabilities of customers changing stores or remaining at the same store. Thus,

$$P = \begin{array}{c|ccc} & I & II & III \\ \hline I & .90 & .10 & 0 \\ II & .85 & .05 & .10 \\ III & .50 & .10 & .40 \end{array}$$

b) The initial distribution is $A^{(0)} = [.25, .33, .42]$. Thus, by Feb. 1, the percentage of customers shopping at the three stores will be

$$A^{(0)}P = [.25 \quad .33 \quad .42] \begin{bmatrix} .90 & .10 & 0 \\ .85 & .05 & .10 \\ .50 & .10 & .40 \end{bmatrix}$$

$$= [.7166 \quad .0832 \quad .1999]$$

To find the probability distribution after two months, note that $A^{(2)} = A^{(0)}P^2$

$$P^2 = \begin{bmatrix} .90 & .10 & 0 \\ .85 & .05 & .10 \\ .50 & .10 & .40 \end{bmatrix} \begin{bmatrix} .90 & .10 & 0 \\ .85 & .05 & .10 \\ .50 & .10 & .40 \end{bmatrix}$$

$$= \begin{bmatrix} .895 & .095 & .010 \\ .857 & .098 & .045 \\ .735 & .095 & .170 \end{bmatrix}.$$

Interpret p^2 as follows. The first element is composed of the sum (.90)(.90) + (.10)(.85) + 0(.50). (.90)(.90) is the probability of people who shop at store I continuing to shop at shop I. (.10)(.85) represents the probability of people switching from store I to store II and then back to store I. (0)(.50) is the probability of people switching from store I to store III and then back to store I. The sum is therefore the probability of people who were shopping at store I winding up shopping there after two months.

$$A^{(2)} = A^{(0)}p^2 = [.25 \quad .33 \quad .42] \begin{bmatrix} .895 & .095 & .010 \\ .857 & .098 & .045 \\ .735 & .095 & .170 \end{bmatrix}$$

$$= [.8155 \quad .0956 \quad .0882].$$

c) To determine the long-run shopping behaviour of this community the following facts are needed:

A transition matrix, P, is regular if for some power of p, all the entries are positive. If P is a regular matrix, then all the rows of p^n will be identically equal to some probability vector t for all $m \geq n$.

In the given problem, p^2 contains positive elements only. Hence p is regular, i.e., there exists a fixed probability vector $[t_1 \ t_2 \ t_3]$ where $t_1 + t_2 + t_3 = 1$ such that

$$[t_1 \ t_2 \ t_3] \begin{bmatrix} .9 & .10 & .00 \\ .85 & .05 & .10 \\ .50 & .10 & .40 \end{bmatrix} = [t_1 \ t_2 \ t_3].$$

Obtain the set of linear equations

$$.9t_1 + .85t_2 + .50t_3 = t_1$$
$$.10t_1 + .05t_2 + .10t_3 = t_2$$
$$.00t_1 + .10t_2 + .40t_3 = t_3$$

The solution vector is

$$[t_1 \ t_2 \ t_3] = [.8888 \quad .0952 \quad .0158]$$

In the long run store I will have about 89% of all customers, store II 9.5% and store III 1.5%.

• PROBLEM 13-41

Union Industries, a manufacturer of ladies' sleepwear classifies its sewing operators into four categories depending upon their productivity during the preceding month; the lowest category is 1 and the highest is 4. Historically, the sewing work force has been distributed across the four categories as follows:

1 = 30%

2 = 35%

3 = 25%

4 = 10%

A year ago, Union has introduced a new organizational system into its Idaho plant, one of its largest units, with 450 operators. The new system in effect groups the operators into voluntary work units which not only elect their own supervisors but also determine their own work schedules. Production records compiled since the new plan was adopted have enabled Mr. John Hayward, Plant Manager, to construct the following matrix of transition probabilities illustrating month-to-month changes in employee productivity:

		Lowest 1	2	3	Highest 4
Lowest	1	.5	.3	.2	0
	2	.3	.4	.3	0
	3	.1	.2	.2	.5
Highest	4	.1	.1	.1	.7

It is also known that operators earn an average of \$700 a month and that productivity losses for the four categories of employee are 40 percent, 25 percent, 15 percent, and 5 percent for categories 1, 2, 3, and 4 respectively.

Suppose you were hired by the management of Union Industries to evaluate the effectiveness as well as efficiency of the new system, what will be your conclusion insofar as savings in productivity losses in its Idaho plant are concerned.

Solution: This problem is an application of Markov Analysis in employee productivity. First, determine the equilibrium probabilities of Mr. Hayward's matrix by solving the following equations simultaneously.

$$x_1 = .5x_1 + .3x_2 + .1x_3 + .1x_4$$

$$x_2 = .3x_1 + .4x_2 + .2x_3 + .1x_4$$

$$x_3 = .2x_1 + .3x_2 + .2x_3 + .1x_4$$

$$x_4 = .5x_3 + .7x_4$$

$$1 = x_1 + x_2 + x_3 + x_4$$

where $x_1 = 1$ (the highest) $x_4 = 4$ (the lowest)

The equilibrium probabilities are as follows:

Highest	1	.247
	2	.241
	3	.192
Lowest	4	.320
		1.000

Then set up the cost comparison of the old and new organization system

	Employee category	Percent of employees		Productivity loss	
Old organizational system	1	30	x	40%	= 12.00%
	2	35	x	25	= 8.75
	3	25	x	15	= 3.75
	4	10	x	5	= .50
					25.00%

25% x $700/mo. x 450 employees = $78,750

	Employee category	Percent of employees		Productivity loss	
New organizational system	1	24.7	x	40%	= 9.88%
	2	24.1	x	25	= 6.03
	3	19.2	x	15	= 2.88
	4	32.0	x	5	= 1.60
					20.39%

20.39% x $700/mo. x 450 employees = $64,229

Therefore, in the above cost comparison of the old and new organization system, it appears that the new organization system has the potential to save Union over $14,000 per month in productivity losses in its Idaho plant.

• PROBLEM 13-42

Randolph Raleigh is the Coca-Cola dealer in Pittsburgh, Pennsylvania. His warehouse manager inspects his soft drink crates (these are the wooden crates that hold 24 bottles) each week and classifies them as "just rebuilt this week," "in good working condition," "in fair condition," or "damaged beyond use." If a crate is damaged beyond use, it is sent to the repair area, where it is usually out of use for a week. Randolph's warehouse records indicate that this is the appropriate matrix of transition probabilities for his soft drink crates:

	Rebuilt	Good	Fair	Damaged
Rebuilt	0	.8	.2	0
Good	0	.6	.4	0
Fair	0	0	.5	.5
Damaged	1.0	0	0	0

Randolph's accountant informs him that it costs $2.50 to rebuild a crate, and the company incurs a loss of $1.85 in production efficiency each time a crate is found to be damaged beyond use. This efficiency is lost because broken crates slow down the truckloading process.

a) Given the above information calculate the expected weekly cost of both rebuilding and loss of production efficiency.

b) Assuming that Randolph wants to consider rebuilding crates whenever they are inspected and found to be in fair shape, determine the new matrix of transition probabilities and the average weekly cost of rebuilding and loss of production efficiency under these circumstances.

Solution: This is an illustration of Markov analysis to equipment repair. To calculate the expected weekly cost of both rebuilding and loss of production efficiency, the equilibrium probabilities of Randolph's matrix are needed. Here are 5 equations with 4 unknowns as shown below.

$$\begin{aligned} x_1 &= 0x_1 + 0x_2 + 0x_3 + x_4 \\ x_2 &= .8x_1 + .6x_2 + 0x_3 + 0x_4 \\ x_3 &= .2x_1 + .4x_2 + .5x_3 + 0x_4 \\ x_4 &= 0x_1 + 0x_2 + .5x_3 + 0x_4 \\ 1.0 &= x_1 + x_2 + x_3 + x_4 \end{aligned}$$

or

$$\begin{aligned} x_1 &= x_4 \\ x_2 &= .8x_1 + .6x_2 \\ x_3 &= .2x_1 + .4x_2 + .5x_3 \\ x_4 &= .5x_3 \\ 1.0 &= x_1 + x_2 + x_3 + x_4 \end{aligned}$$

where x_1 = Rebuilt
x_2 = Good
x_3 = Fair
x_4 = Damaged

Solving simultaneously the above equations, the following transition probabilities are arrived at.

Rebuilt	$\frac{1}{6} = .167$
Good	$\frac{1}{3} = .333$
Fair	$\frac{1}{3} = .333$
Damaged	$\frac{1}{6} = .167$
	1.000

The average weekly cost of rebuilding and loss of production efficiency is then:

Rebuilding cost + Damage (out of use) loss

$\frac{1}{6}$ x \$2.50 + $\frac{1}{6}$ x \$1.85 = \$ .725 per crate per week

b) Suppose now that Randolph wants to consider rebuilding crates whenever they are inspected and found to be in fair shape. This eliminates the possibility of a crate being damaged. In this instance, the new matrix of transition probabilities would be:

	Rebuilt	Good	Fair
Rebuilt	0	.8	.2
Good	0	.6	.4
Fair	1.0	0	0

The equilibrium probabilities for this matrix are found to be

x_1 = Rebuilt $\frac{1}{4}$ = .25

x_2 = Good $\frac{1}{2}$ = .50

x_3 = Fair $\frac{1}{4}$ = .25

1.00

The average weekly cost of rebuilding and loss of production efficiency under these circumstances is:

Rebuilding Cost + Damage (out of use) loss

$\frac{1}{4}$ x \$2.50 + 0 = \$.625 per crate per week

Therefore, rebuilding crates as soon as they are found to be in "fair" shape will save Randolph a little over 10 cents per week. Since Randolph owns over six thousand crates, this is a substantial saving for him.

• PROBLEM 13-43

A camera store stocks a particular model camera that can be ordered weekly. Let D_1, D_2, ..., represent the demand for this camera during the first week, second week, ..., respectively. It is assumed that D_i are independent and identically distributed random variables having a known probability distribution. Let X_0 represent the number of cameras on hand at the outset, X_1 the number of cameras on hand at the end of week one, X_2 the number of cameras on hand at the end of week two, and so on. Assume that $X_0 = 3$. On Saturday night, the store places an order that is delivered in time for the opening of the store on Monday. The store uses the following (s,S) ordering policy. If the number of cameras on hand at the end of the week is less than s = 1 (no cameras in stock), the store orders (up to) S = 3. Otherwise, the store does not order (if there are any cameras in stock, no order is placed). It is assumed that sales are lost when demand exceeds the inventory on hand. Assuming further that X_t is the number of cameras in stock at the end of the tth week (before an order is received), and that each D_t has a Poisson distribution with parameter $\lambda = 1$, determine:

a) the one-step transition probabilities.

b) Given that there are two cameras left in stock at the end of a week, what is the probability that there will be three cameras in stock two weeks and four weeks later.

c) Compute the expected time until the cameras are out of stock, assuming the process is started when there are three cameras available; i.e., the expected first passage time, μ_{30}, is to be obtained.

d) Determine the long-run steady-state probabilities.

Solution: This is an application of Markov Chains to the problem of having an optimal inventory policy. The principle of (s,S) ordering policy as given in the above problem refers to the periodic review policy that calls for ordering up to S units whenever the inventory level dips below s ($S \geq s$). If the inventory level is s or greater, then no order is placed.

(a) to obtain the one-step transition probabilities, the following elements of the transition matrix would be utilized.

$$P = \begin{bmatrix} p_{00} & p_{01} & p_{02} & p_{03} \\ p_{10} & p_{11} & p_{12} & p_{13} \\ p_{20} & p_{21} & p_{22} & p_{23} \\ p_{30} & p_{31} & p_{32} & p_{33} \end{bmatrix}$$

To determine p_{00}, which is the conditional probability of having 0 cameras at the end of the week given that one has 0 cameras on hand, it is necessary to evaluate $P\{X_t = 0 \mid x_{t-1} = 0\}$.

Summation of Terms of the Poisson Distribution 1,000 P {Poisson with parameter $\lambda \leq c$}

c \ λ	0.01	0.02	0.03	0.04	0.05	0.06	0.07	0.08	0.09	
0	990	980	970	961	951	942	932	923	914	
1	1000	1000	1000	999	999	998	998	997	996	
2				1000	1000	1000	1000	1000	1000	
c \ λ	**0.10**	**0.15**	**0.20**	**0.25**	**0.30**	**0.35**	**0.40**	**0.45**	**0.50**	
0	905	861	819	779	741	705	670	638	607	
1	995	990	982	974	963	951	938	925	910	
2	1000	999	999	998	996	994	992	989	986	
3		1000	1000	1000	1000	1000	999	999	998	
4							1000	1000	1000	
c \ λ	**0.55**	**0.60**	**0.65**	**0.70**	**0.75**	**0.80**	**0.85**	**0.90**	**0.95**	**1.00**
0	577	549	522	497	472	449	427	407	387	368
1	894	878	861	844	827	809	791	772	754	736
2	982	977	972	966	959	953	945	937	929	920
3	998	997	996	994	993	991	989	987	984	981
4	1000	1000	999	999	999	999	998	998	997	996
5			1000	1000	1000	1000	1000	1000	1000	999
6										1000
c \ λ	**1.05**	**1.10**	**1.15**	**1.20**	**1.25**	**1.30**	**1.35**	**1.40**	**1.45**	**1.50**
0	350	333	317	301	287	273	259	247	235	223
1	717	699	681	663	645	627	609	592	575	558
2	910	900	890	879	868	857	845	833	821	809
3	978	974	970	966	962	957	952	946	940	934
4	996	995	993	992	991	989	988	986	984	981
5	999	999	999	998	998	998	997	997	996	996
6	1000	1000	1000	1000	1000	1000	999	999	999	999
7							1000	1000	1000	1000
c \ λ	**1.55**	**1.60**	**1.65**	**1.70**	**1.75**	**1.80**	**1.85**	**1.90**	**1.95**	**2.00**
0	212	202	192	183	174	165	157	150	142	135
1	541	525	509	493	478	463	448	434	420	406
2	796	783	770	757	744	731	717	704	690	677
3	928	921	914	907	899	891	883	875	866	857
4	979	976	973	970	967	964	960	956	952	947
5	995	994	993	992	991	990	988	987	985	983
6	999	999	998	998	998	997	997	997	996	995
7	1000	1000	1000	1000	1000	999	999	999	999	999
8						1000	1000	1000	1000	1000

Therefore if $X_t = 0$, then the demand during the week has to be 3 or more since if we don't have cameras, we order up to 3. Hence $p_{00} = P\{D_t \geq 3\}$. This is just the probability that a Poisson random variable with parameter $\lambda = 1$ takes on a value of 3 or more, which is obtained from a table on the Summation of Terms of the Poisson Distribution, so that $p_{00} = 0.08$. $p_{10} = P\{X_t = 0 | X_t - 1 = 1\}$ can be obtained in a similar way. To have $X_t = 0$, the demand during the week has to be 1 or more. Hence $p_{10} = P\{D_t \geq 1\} = 0.632$. To find $p_{21} = P\{X_t = 1 | X_{t-1} = 2\}$, then the demand during the week has to be exactly 1. Hence $p_{21} = P\{D_t = 1\} = 0.368$. The remaining entries are obtained in a similar manner, which yields the following (one step) transition matrix:

$$P = \begin{array}{c} \\ 0 \\ 1 \\ 2 \\ 3 \end{array} \begin{array}{c} \begin{array}{cccc} 0 & 1 & 2 & 3 \end{array} \\ \begin{bmatrix} 0.080 & 0.184 & 0.368 & 0.368 \\ 0.632 & 0.368 & 0 & 0 \\ 0.264 & 0.368 & 0.368 & 0 \\ 0.080 & 0.184 & 0.368 & 0.368 \end{bmatrix} \end{array}$$

(b) The probabilities that there will be three cameras in stock two weeks and four weeks later given that there are two cameras left in stock at the end of a week are obtained by using the Chapman-Kolmogorov difference equations which provide a method for computing the n-step transition probabilities i.e., 2 and 4 weeks.

The two-step transition matrix is given by

$$P^{(2)} = P^2 =$$

$$\begin{bmatrix} 0.080 & 0.184 & 0.368 & 0.368 \\ 0.632 & 0.368 & 0 & 0 \\ 0.264 & 0.368 & 0.368 & 0 \\ 0.080 & 0.184 & 0.368 & 0.368 \end{bmatrix} \begin{bmatrix} 0.080 & 0.184 & 0.368 & 0.368 \\ 0.632 & 0.368 & 0 & 0 \\ 0.264 & 0.368 & 0.368 & 0 \\ 0.080 & 0.184 & 0.368 & 0.368 \end{bmatrix}$$

$$= \begin{array}{c} \\ 0 \\ 1 \\ 2 \\ 3 \end{array} \begin{array}{c} \begin{array}{cccc} 0 & 1 & 2 & 3 \end{array} \\ \begin{bmatrix} 0.249 & 0.286 & 0.300 & 0.165 \\ 0.283 & 0.252 & 0.233 & 0.233 \\ 0.351 & 0.319 & 0.233 & 0.097 \\ 0.249 & 0.286 & 0.300 & 0.165 \end{bmatrix} \end{array}$$

Thus, given that there are two cameras left in stock at the end of a week, the probability is 0.097 that there will be three cameras in stock 2 weeks later;

that is, $p_{23}^{(2)} = 0.097$.

The four-step transition matrix can also be obtained as follows:

$$p^{(4)} = p^4 = p^{(2)} \cdot p^{(2)}$$

$$= \begin{bmatrix} 0.249 & 0.286 & 0.300 & 0.165 \\ 0.283 & 0.252 & 0.233 & 0.233 \\ 0.351 & 0.319 & 0.233 & 0.097 \\ 0.249 & 0.286 & 0.300 & 0.165 \end{bmatrix} \begin{bmatrix} 0.249 & 0.286 & 0.300 & 0.165 \\ 0.283 & 0.252 & 0.233 & 0.233 \\ 0.351 & 0.319 & 0.233 & 0.097 \\ 0.249 & 0.286 & 0.300 & 0.165 \end{bmatrix}$$

$$= \begin{bmatrix} 0.289 & 0.286 & 0.261 & 0.164 \\ 0.282 & 0.285 & 0.268 & 0.166 \\ 0.284 & 0.283 & 0.263 & 0.171 \\ 0.289 & 0.286 & 0.261 & 0.164 \end{bmatrix}$$

Therefore, given that there will be two cameras in stock at the end of a week, the probability is 0.171 that there will be three cameras in stock 4 weeks later; that is, $p_{23}^{(4)} = 0.171$.

(c) The first passage time refers to the length of time it will take the process in going from state i to state j for the first time. When j = 1, this first passage time is just the number of transitions until the process returns to the initial state i. In this case, the first passage time is called the recurrence time for state i which has to be assumed in this particular problem. Given the equation

$$\mu_{ij} = 1 + \sum_{k \neq j} p_{ik}\,\mu_{kj}, \text{ yields}$$

$$\mu_{30} = 1 + p_{31}\mu_{10} + p_{32}\,\mu_{20} + p_{33}\,\mu_{30},$$
$$\mu_{20} = 1 + p_{21}\mu_{10} + p_{22}\,\mu_{20} + p_{23}\,\mu_{30},$$
$$\mu_{10} = 1 + p_{11}\mu_{10} + p_{12}\,\mu_{20} + p_{13}\,\mu_{30},$$

or

$$\mu_{30} = 1 + 0.184\,\mu_{10} + 0.368\,\mu_{20} + 0.368\,\mu_{30}$$
$$\mu_{20} = 1 + 0.368\,\mu_{10} + 0.368\,\mu_{20}$$
$$\mu_{10} = 1 + 0.368\,\mu_{10}$$

The simultaneous solution to this system of equations is

$$\mu_{10} = 1.58 \text{ weeks},$$
$$\mu_{20} = 2.51 \text{ weeks},$$
$$\mu_{30} = 3.50 \text{ weeks}$$

so that the expected time until the cameras are out of stock is 3.50 weeks given that there are 3 stocks of cameras on hand.

(d) The long-run steady-state probabilities can be obtained by using the following steady-state equations as follows:

$$\pi_0 = \pi_0 p_{00} + \pi_1 p_{10} + \pi_2 p_{20} + \pi_3 p_{30}$$
$$\pi_1 = \pi_0 p_{01} + \pi_1 p_{11} + \pi_2 p_{21} + \pi_3 p_{31}$$
$$\pi_2 = \pi_0 p_{02} + \pi_1 p_{12} + \pi_2 p_{22} + \pi_3 p_{32}$$
$$\pi_3 = \pi_0 p_{03} + \pi_1 p_{13} + \pi_2 p_{23} + \pi_3 p_{33}$$
$$1 = \pi_0 + \pi_1 + \pi_2 + \pi_3$$

Substituting values for p_{ij} into these equations leads to the equations

$$\pi_0 = (0.080)\pi_0 + (0.632)\pi_1 + (0.264)\pi_2 + (0.080)\pi_3,$$

$$\pi_1 = (0.184)\pi_0 + (0.368)\pi_1 + (0.368)\pi_2 + (0.184)\pi_3,$$
$$\pi_2 = (0.368)\pi_0 + (0.368)\pi_2 + (0.368)\pi_3,$$
$$\pi_3 = (0.368)\pi_0 + (0.368)\pi_3,$$
$$1 = \pi_0 + \pi_1 + \pi_2 + \pi_3$$

Solving the last four equations provides the simultaneous solutions

$$\pi_0 = 0.285$$
$$\pi_1 = 0.285$$
$$\pi_2 = 0.264$$
$$\pi_3 = 0.166$$

Thus, after many weeks, the probability of finding zero, one, two, and three cameras in stock tends to 0.285, 0.285, 0.264, and 0.166 respectively. The corresponding expected recurrence times are

$$\mu_{00} = \frac{1}{\pi_0} = 3.51 \text{ weeks},$$
$$\mu_{11} = \frac{1}{\pi_1} = 3.51 \text{ weeks},$$
$$\mu_{22} = \frac{1}{\pi_2} = 3.79 \text{ weeks},$$
$$\mu_{33} = \frac{1}{\pi_3} = 6.02 \text{ weeks}.$$

• PROBLEM 13-44

A supermarket stocks three brands of coffee, A, B, and C, and it has been observed that customers switch from brand to brand according to the transition matrix

$$P = \begin{bmatrix} 3/4 & 1/4 & 0 \\ 0 & 2/3 & 1/3 \\ 1/4 & 1/4 & 1/2 \end{bmatrix},$$

where S_1 corresponds to a purchase of A, S_2 to B, and S_3 to C. That is, 3/4 of the customers buying A also buy A the next time they purchase coffee, whereas 1/4 of these customers switch to brand B.

(a) Find the probability that a customer who buys brand A today will again purchase A 2 weeks from today, assuming that she purchases coffee once a week.

(b) In the long run, what fraction of customers purchase the respective brands?

Solution: (a) Assuming that the customer is chosen at random, her transition probabilities are given by P. The given information indicates that

$$p^{(0)} = (1,0,0);$$

that is, we are starting with a purchase of brand A. Then

$$p^{(1)} = p^{(0)}P = (3/4,1/4,0)$$

gives the probabilities for next week's purchase. The probabilities for 2 weeks from now are given by

$$p^{(2)} = p^{(1)}P = (9/16,17/48,1/12).$$

That is, the chance of purchasing A 2 weeks from now is only 9/16. (b) The answer to the long-run frequency ratio is given by π, the stationary distribution. The equation

$$\pi = \pi P$$

yields the system

$$\pi_1 = (3/4)\pi_1 + (1/4)\pi_3$$

$$\pi_2 = (1/4)\pi_1 + (2/3)\pi_2 + (1/4)\pi_3$$

$$\pi_3 = (1/3)\pi_2 + (1/2)\pi_3.$$

Combining these equations with the fact that $\pi_1 + \pi_2 + \pi_3 = 1$ yields

$$\pi = (2/7,3/7,2/7).$$

Thus the store should stock more brand B coffee than either A or C.

• PROBLEM 13-45

A particle moves on a line; each time it moves one unit to the right with probability ½, or one unit to the left. Introduce barriers so that if it ever reaches one of these barriers it stays there. Let the states be 0, 1, 2, 3, 4. States 0 and 4 are absorbing states. The transition matrix is then

$$P = \begin{array}{c} \\ 0 \\ 1 \\ 2 \\ 3 \\ 4 \end{array} \begin{array}{c} \begin{array}{ccccc} 0 & 1 & 2 & 3 & 4 \end{array} \\ \begin{pmatrix} 1 & 0 & 0 & 0 & 0 \\ \frac{1}{2} & 0 & \frac{1}{2} & 0 & 0 \\ 0 & \frac{1}{2} & 0 & \frac{1}{2} & 0 \\ 0 & 0 & \frac{1}{2} & 0 & \frac{1}{2} \\ 0 & 0 & 0 & 0 & 1 \end{pmatrix} \end{array}$$

The states 1, 2, 3 are all nonabsorbing states, and from any of these it is prossible to reach the absorbing states 0 and 4. Hence the chain is an absorbing chain. Such a process is usually called a random walk.

(a) On the average, how many times will the process be in each nonabsorbing state?

(b) On the average, how long will it take for the process to be absorbed?

(c) What is the probability that the process will end up in a given absorbing state?

Solution: (a) Consider then an arbitrary absorbing Markov chain. Renumber the states so that the absorbing states come first. If there are r absorbing states and s nonabsorbing states, the transition matrix will have the following canonical (or standard) form.

$$P = \begin{array}{c} \\ r \\ s \end{array} \begin{array}{c} \begin{array}{cc} r \text{ states} & s \text{ states} \end{array} \\ \left(\begin{array}{c|c} I & O \\ \hline R & Q \end{array}\right) \end{array}$$

Here I is an r-by-r identity matrix, O is an r-by-s zero matrix, R is an s-by-r matrix, and Q is an s-by-s matrix. The first r states are absorbing and the last s states are nonabsorbing.

The transition matrix in canonical form is

$$\begin{array}{c} \\ 0 \\ 4 \\ 1 \\ 2 \\ 3 \end{array} \begin{array}{c} \begin{array}{ccccc} 0 & 4 & 1 & 2 & 3 \end{array} \\ \left(\begin{array}{cc|ccc} 1 & 0 & 0 & 0 & 0 \\ 0 & 1 & 0 & 0 & 0 \\ \hline \frac{1}{2} & 0 & 0 & \frac{1}{2} & 0 \\ 0 & 0 & \frac{1}{2} & 0 & \frac{1}{2} \\ 0 & \frac{1}{2} & 0 & \frac{1}{2} & 0 \end{array}\right) \end{array}$$

From this it can be seen that the matrix Q is

$$Q = \begin{pmatrix} 0 & \frac{1}{2} & 0 \\ \frac{1}{2} & 0 & \frac{1}{2} \\ 0 & \frac{1}{2} & 0 \end{pmatrix}$$

and

$$I - Q = \begin{pmatrix} 1 & -\frac{1}{2} & 0 \\ -\frac{1}{2} & 1 & -\frac{1}{2} \\ 0 & -\frac{1}{2} & 1 \end{pmatrix}$$

Computing $(I - Q)^{-1}$, one finds

$$N = (I - Q)^{-1} = \begin{array}{c} \\ 1 \\ 2 \\ 3 \end{array} \begin{array}{c} \begin{array}{ccc} 1 & 2 & 3 \end{array} \\ \begin{pmatrix} \frac{3}{2} & 1 & \frac{1}{2} \\ 1 & 2 & 1 \\ \frac{1}{2} & 1 & \frac{3}{2} \end{pmatrix} \end{array}$$

Thus, starting at state 2, the mean number of times in state 1 before absorption is 1, in state 2 it is 2, and in state 3 it is 1.

(b) If all the entries in a row are added, we will have the mean number of times in any of the nonabsorbing states for a given starting state, that is, the mean time required before being absorbed. That is, considering a Markov chain with s nonabsorbing states and letting c be an s-component column vector with all entries 1, one gets the vector $t = Nc$ having as components, the mean number of steps before being absorbed for each possible nonabsorbing starting state.

In this problem

$$t = Nc = \begin{matrix} \\ 1 \\ 2 \\ 3 \end{matrix} \begin{matrix} 1 & 2 & 3 \\ \end{matrix} \begin{pmatrix} \frac{3}{2} & 1 & \frac{1}{2} \\ 1 & 2 & 1 \\ \frac{1}{2} & 1 & \frac{3}{2} \end{pmatrix} \begin{pmatrix} 1 \\ 1 \\ 1 \end{pmatrix}$$

$$= \begin{matrix} 1 \\ 2 \\ 3 \end{matrix} \begin{pmatrix} 3 \\ 4 \\ 3 \end{pmatrix} .$$

Thus the mean number of steps to absorption starting at state 1 is 3, starting at state 2 is 4, and starting at state 3 is again 3. Since the process necessarily moves to 1 or 3 from 2 it requires one more step starting from 2 than from 1 or 3.

Now consider question (c). That is, what is the probability that an absorbing chain will end up in a particular absorbing state? This probability will depend upon the starting state and be interesting only for the case of a nonabsorbing starting state. Write the matrix in the canonical form

$$P = \left(\begin{array}{c|c} I & 0 \\ \hline R & Q \end{array}\right) .$$

Letting b_i be the probability that an absorbing chain will be absorbed in state a_j, if it starts in the nonabsorbing state a_i; and B being the matrix with entries b_{ij}, one gets $\quad B = NR$

where N is the fundamental matrix and R is as in the canonical form.

$$N = \begin{pmatrix} \frac{3}{2} & 1 & \frac{1}{2} \\ 1 & 2 & 1 \\ \frac{1}{2} & 1 & \frac{3}{2} \end{pmatrix} .$$

From the canonical form it is found that

$$R = \begin{pmatrix} \frac{1}{2} & 0 \\ 0 & 0 \\ 0 & \frac{1}{2} \end{pmatrix} .$$

Hence

$$B = NR = \begin{pmatrix} \frac{3}{2} & 1 & \frac{1}{2} \\ 1 & 2 & 1 \\ \frac{1}{2} & 1 & \frac{3}{2} \end{pmatrix} \begin{pmatrix} \frac{1}{2} & 0 \\ 0 & 0 \\ 0 & \frac{1}{2} \end{pmatrix}$$

$$= \begin{matrix} 1 \\ 2 \\ 3 \end{matrix} \begin{pmatrix} \frac{3}{4} & \frac{1}{4} \\ \frac{1}{2} & \frac{1}{2} \\ \frac{1}{4} & \frac{3}{4} \end{pmatrix} .$$

Thus, for instance, starting from a_1, there is probability $\frac{3}{4}$ of absorption in a_0 and $\frac{1}{4}$ for absorption in a_4.

• PROBLEM 13-46

A manager of one section of a plant has employees working at level I and level II. New employees may enter his section at either level. At the end of each year the performances of employees are evaluated; they can either be reassigned to level I or II jobs, terminated, or promoted to level III, in which case they never come back to I or II. The manager can then keep track of employee movement as a Markov chain. The absorbing states are termination (S_1) and employment at level III (S_2), whereas the nonabsorbing states are employment at level I (S_3) and level II (S_4). Records over a long period of time indicate that the following is a reasonable assignment of probabilities;

$$P = \begin{bmatrix} 1 & 0 & 0 & 0 \\ 0 & 1 & 0 & 0 \\ .2 & .1 & .2 & .5 \\ .1 & .3 & .1 & .5 \end{bmatrix}$$

Thus, if an employee enters at a level I job, the probability is .5 that he will jump to level II work at the end of the year, but he has a probability equal to .2 of being terminated. Find (a) the expected number of evaluations an employee must go through in this section, and (b) the probabilities of being terminated or promoted to level III eventually.

Solution: For the P matrix,

$$P = \begin{bmatrix} 1 & 0 & 0 & 0 & 0 \\ 0 & 1 & 0 & 0 & 0 \\ p_{31} & p_{32} & p_{33} & p_{34} & p_{35} \\ p_{41} & p_{42} & p_{43} & p_{44} & p_{45} \\ p_{51} & p_{52} & p_{53} & p_{54} & p_{55} \end{bmatrix} = \begin{bmatrix} I & 0 \\ R & Q \end{bmatrix}$$

$$R = \begin{bmatrix} .2 & .1 \\ .1 & .3 \end{bmatrix}$$

and

$$Q = \begin{bmatrix} .2 & .5 \\ .1 & .5 \end{bmatrix} .$$

Thus

$$I - Q = \begin{bmatrix} .8 & .5 \\ -.1 & .5 \end{bmatrix}$$

and

$$M = (I - Q)^{-1} = \begin{bmatrix} 10/7 & 10/7 \\ 2/7 & 16/7 \end{bmatrix} .$$

It follows that

$$m_1 = 20/7, \; m_2 = 18/7,$$

or, a new employee in this section can expect to remain there through 20/7 evaluation periods if he enters at level I. Also,

$$A = MR = \begin{bmatrix} 3/7 & 4/7 \\ 2/7 & 5/7 \end{bmatrix} ,$$

which implies that an employee entering at level I has a probability of 4/7 of reaching level III, whereas entering at level II raises this probability to 5/7.

Hamilton's Clothing Cupboard is a clothing-store catering to college students. Mr. Hamilton divides his accounts receivable into two classifications: 0-60 days old and 61-180 days old. He has currently $6,500 in accounts receivable and from analysis of his past records, he has been able to provide the following matrix of transition probabilities (the matrix can be thought of in terms of what happens to one dollar of accounts receivable):

	Paid	Bad debt	0-60 days	61-180 days
Paid	1	0	0	0
Bad debt	0	1	0	0
0-60 days	.5	0	.3	.2
61-180 days	.4	.3	.2	.1

a) Determine the probability that a dollar of 0-60 day or 61-180 day receivables would eventually find its way into either paid bills or bad debts.

b) Forecast the future of Mr. Hamilton's $6,500 of accounts receivable given that $4,500 is in the 0-60 day category and $2,000 is in the 61-180 day category.

Solution: a) This is an application of the Markov chain analysis in the area of accounts receivable specifically to the estimation of that portion of the accounts receivable which will eventually become uncollectible (bad debts).

First determine the four probabilities of interest to Mr. Hamilton which is done in four steps:

Step 1 - First, partition Hamilton's original matrix of transition probabilities into four matrices, each identified by a letter:

$$\left[\begin{array}{cc|cc} 1 & 0 & 0 & 0 \\ 0 & 1 & 0 & 0 \\ \hline .5 & 0 & .3 & .2 \\ .4 & .3 & .2 & .1 \end{array}\right]$$

$$I = \begin{bmatrix} 1 & 0 \\ 0 & 1 \end{bmatrix} \qquad o = \begin{bmatrix} 0 & 0 \\ 0 & 0 \end{bmatrix}$$

$$K = \begin{bmatrix} .5 & 0 \\ .4 & .3 \end{bmatrix} \qquad M = \begin{bmatrix} .3 & .2 \\ .2 & .1 \end{bmatrix}$$

Step 2 - Subtract matrix M from matrix I to get a new matrix which is called R.

$$\overset{I}{\begin{bmatrix} 1 & 0 \\ 0 & 1 \end{bmatrix}} - \overset{M}{\begin{bmatrix} .3 & .2 \\ .2 & .1 \end{bmatrix}} = \overset{R}{\begin{bmatrix} .7 & -.2 \\ -.2 & .9 \end{bmatrix}}$$

Step 3 - Find the inverse of matrix R which is found to be

$$\begin{bmatrix} 1.5254 & .3390 \\ .3390 & 1.1864 \end{bmatrix}$$

Step 4 - Multiply this inverse by matrix K from Step 1. This multiplication is

$$\begin{bmatrix} 1.5254 & .3390 \\ .3390 & 1.1864 \end{bmatrix} \begin{bmatrix} .5 & 0 \\ .4 & .3 \end{bmatrix} = \begin{bmatrix} .8983 & .1017 \\ .6441 & .3559 \end{bmatrix}$$

Interpreting the answer for Mr. Hamilton, one has as follows:

The top row in the answer is the probability that $1 of his accounts receivable in the 0-60 day category will end up in the "paid" and "bad debt" categories. Specifically, there is a .8983 probability that $1 currently in the 0-60 day category will be paid and a .1017 probability that it will eventually become a bad debt. Consider the second row. These two entries represent the probability that $1 now in the 61-180 day category will end up in the "paid" and the "bad debt" categories.

He observes from this row that there is a .6441 probability that $1 currently in the 61-180 day category will be paid and a .3559 probability that it will eventually become a bad debt.

b) If Mr. Hamilton would want to know the future of his $6,500 of accounts receivable given that his accountant tells him that $4,500 is in the 0-60 day category and $2,000 is in the 61-180 day category, the following matrix multiplication has to be performed:

$$(\$4,500 \quad \$2,000) \begin{bmatrix} .8983 & .1017 \\ .6441 & .3559 \end{bmatrix}$$

$$(\$5,330.55 \quad \$1,169.45)$$

The above computation would indicate that $5,330.55 of his current accounts receivable is likely to wind up being paid and $1,169.45 is likely to become bad debts. Therefore, if he follows the standard practice of setting up a reserve for "doubtful" accounts, his accountant would set up $1,169.45 as the best estimate for this category.

INDEX

Numbers on this page refer to PROBLEM NUMBERS, not page numbers

Numbers on this page refer to PROBLEM NUMBERS, not page numbers

Numbers on this page refer to PROBLEM NUMBERS, not page numbers

Numbers on this page refer to **PROBLEM NUMBERS**, not page numbers

Numbers on this page refer to <u>PROBLEM NUMBERS</u>, not page numbers

Numbers on this page refer to PROBLEM NUMBERS, not page numbers

Numbers on this page refer to <u>PROBLEM NUMBERS</u>, not page numbers

Numbers on this page refer to PROBLEM NUMBERS, not page numbers

Numbers on this page refer to PROBLEM NUMBERS, not page numbers

Numbers on this page refer to **PROBLEM NUMBERS**, not page numbers